THE EDINBURGH ENCYCLOPEDIA OF CONTINENTAL PHILOSOPHY

THE EDINBURGH ENCYCLOPEDIA OF CONTINENTAL PHILOSOPHY

General Editor
Simon Glendinning

FITZROY DEARBORN PUBLISHERS
CHICAGO • LONDON

© Edinburgh University Press, 1999

Published in the United Kingdom by
Edinburgh University Press
22 George Square, Edinburgh

Published in the United States of America by
Fitzroy Dearborn Publishers,
919 North Michigan Avenue,
Chicago, Illinois 60611

Typeset in Goudy
by Hewer Text Ltd, Edinburgh, and
printed and bound in Great Britain
by the Bath Press
A CIP record for this book is available from
the British Library
A cataloging-in-publication record for this
book is available from the Library of Congress

ISBN 1-57958-152-8 Fitzroy Dearborn

CONTENTS

CONTENTS

PREFACE

Since the Second World War, a particular species of philosophy, usually called analytical philosophy, has dominated academic philosophy in English-speaking universities. Rightly or wrongly, analytical philosophy is generally accepted as contrasting sharply with the prevailing philosophies of the countries of Continental Europe; that is, with Continental philosophy. The nature, extent and even coherence of this contrast are all live issues, but, on the whole, analytical philosophy has tended to conceive Continental philosophy as a tradition with which it has, and would like to continue to have, very few ties. In recent years, however, interest in the Continental tradition has grown markedly in the English-speaking world. Even philosophers who consider the analytical tradition to be far superior to its supposed rival are likely to acknowledge that there is a place for Continental philosophy in a comprehensive course in philosophy. Part of the reason for this change is the increasingly intense interest in Continental thought developing in university departments other than philosophy, and in language and literature departments in particular. However, this interest has not been oriented towards or specially concerned with the *philosophical* context of the ideas being explored. And there has been little guidance on this context, particularly for the beginner. This *Encyclopedia* aims to rectify this situation by offering a comprehensive and in-depth overview of the central movements, authors and themes that comprise what has become known as the Continental tradition of philosophy.

In compiling this book I have been very fortunate to work with an excellent team of specialist Section Editors. Among these, I owe a special debt to John Protevi who came very late to the project following the tragic death of Honi Harber. It was a difficult time and John took on a formidable task with tremendous enthusiasm and dedication. I should also like to take this opportunity to thank the editorial staff at Edinburgh University Press. I am particularly grateful to Jonathan Price, who conceived the project in the first place, to Jane Feore, who oversaw it, and to Sarah Carty, who, when the deadlines were looming, worked tirelessly and efficiently as my unofficial assistant.

Simon Glendinning
London, 1998

NOTES ON CONTRIBUTORS

Linda A. Bell is Professor of Philosophy at Georgia State University. She is the author of *Sartre's Ethics of Authenticity* (Alabama University Press) and *Rethinking Ethics in the Midst of Violence* (Rowman and Littlefield) and is the editor of *Overcoming Racism* (Rowman and Littlefield).

Michal Ben-Naftali is Lecturer in Comparative Literature at the Hebrew University of Jerusalem. A graduate of the Hebrew University and Oxford University, she has written a number of articles dealing with various philosophical approaches to the Holocaust.

Christian Berner specialises in hermeneutics and German philosophy. He is *Maître de Conférences* in the Department of Philosophy at the University of Bourgogne, and editor of the *Revue de Métaphysique et de Morale*. He is the author of *La Philosophie de Schleiermacher* (Paris, Editions du Cerf, 1995).

James Bohman is Danforth Professor of Philosophy at Saint Louis University. His books include: *Public Deliberation: Democracy Pluralism and Complexity* (MIT Press, 1996) and *New Philosophy of Social Science: Problems of Indeterminacy* (MIT/Polity Press, 1991). His current research interests include democratic theory and the epistemology of interpretative social science.

Thomas W. Busch is Professor of Philosophy at Villanova University. He is the author of *The Power of Consciousness and the Force of Circumstances in Sartre's Philosophy* (Indiana University Press, 1990) and teaches phenomenology, hermeneutics and existentialism.

Peter Caws is University Professor of Philosophy at the George Washington University. He is the author of *Sartre* (Routledge) and *Structuralism: The Art of the Intelligible* (Humanities Press). He also edited *Current French Philosophy* (a special issue of *Social Research*, Summer 1982) and *The Causes of Quarrel* (Beacon Press).

Howard Caygill is Professor of Cultural History at Goldsmith College, University of London. He is the author of *Act of Judgement* (1989), *A Kant Dictionary* (1995) and *Walter Benjamin: The Colour of Experience* (1997).

Daniel Cefaï is *Maître de Conférences* at the University of Paris, Nanterre. He is the author of *Phénoménologie et Science Sociales* (Droz, 1997). He has written a number of articles on political philosophy and the methodology of the social sciences. He is currently working on a book on the epistemology of social science and a book on the concept of political culture.

Tina Chanter teaches feminist theory and recent French and German philosophy at the University of Memphis. Her books include *Ethics of Eros: Irigaray's Rewriting the Philosophers* (Routledge), *Rethinking Sex and Gender* (Cambridge University Press, forthcoming) and *Feminist Interpretations of Emmanuel Levinas* (Penn State Press, forthcoming).

Andrew Collier is Reader in Philosophy at Southampton University, and author of *R. D. Laing* (1977), *Scientific Realism and Socialist Thought* (1989), *Socialist Reasoning* (1990) and *Critical Realism* (1994). He has recently completed a book on Marxism and Christianity, and is currently working on realism in ethics.

Steven Galt Crowell is Associate Professor of Philosophy and Humanities at Rice University. His research interests include the phenomenologies of Husserl and Heidegger, and the project of transcendental philosophy and aesthetics. He has written numerous articles on these and other subjects in the Continental tradition. He is editor of *The Prism of the Self: Philosophical Essays in Honor of Maurice Natanson* (Kluwer, 1995).

Simon Dentith is Reader in English at Cheltenham and Gloucester College of Higher Education. His books include: *George Eliot, A Rhetoric of the Real, Bakhtinian Thought: An Introductory Reader* and *Society and Cultural Forms in Nineteenth-Century England*.

Andrew Edgar studied sociology at undergraduate and postgraduate levels, completing a doctorate on Adorno's sociology of culture in 1988. He is Lecturer in Philosophy at the University of Wales, Cardiff. His research interests are in Continental philosophy, aesthetics and the philosophy of medicine.

Gregory Elliott is a Senior Lecturer in Politics at the University of Brighton. An editor of *Radical History*, his publications include: *Althusser: The Detour of Theory* (1987) and *The Merciless Laboratory of History: Aspects of Perry Anderson* (1998). He is currently researching for an intellectual biography of Louis Althusser.

Peter Fettner is a doctoral student in the graduate programme in Philosophy at George Washington University.

Simon Glendinning is Lecturer in Philosophy at the University of Reading. He is the author of *On Being With Others* (Routledge, 1998) and has published articles on Heidegger, Derrida, Austin and Wittgenstein. He is currently engaged in research for a book on philosophy and ordinary language.

Lewis R. Gordon is Professor of African Studies and Contemporary Religious Thought at Brown University. He is the author and editor of a number of books on the study of race and philosophy of existence including *Bad Faith and Anti-black Racism* (Humanities Press), *Fanon and the Crisis of European Man* (Routledge) and *Existence in Black: An Anthology of Black Existential Philosophy* (Routledge).

Iain Hamilton Grant is Lecturer in Philosophy, Science and Culture at the University of the West of England. He is currently researching the materialist roots of Romantic *Naturphilosophie* in relation to idealism in the contemporary sciences. He is the author of numerous essays in critical and post-critical European philosophy and is the translator of works by Lyotard and Baudrillard.

Jean Grondin is Professor of Philosophy at the University of Montreal. His books include: *Hermeneutische Wahrheit? Zum Wahrheitsbegriff Hans-Georg Gadamer* (1982), *Introduction to Philosophical Hermeneutics* (Yale University Press, 1994), and *Sources of Hermeneutics* (SUNY Press, 1995).

Jim Hopkins is Reader in Philosophy at King's College, London. His main interests are the philosophy of Wittgenstein, the philosophy of mind and the philosophy of psychology. His current research is concerned principally with interpretation, particularly as this figures in commonsense and psychoanalytic understandings of the mind.

Gillian Howie is Lecturer in Philosophy at the University of Liverpool. She has published articles on feminist philosophy, gender roles, and on de Beauvoir, Marx and Cixous. She is currently working on a book on Deleuze and Spinoza (Macmillan, forthcoming).

Fiona Hughes studied at Edinburgh, Tübingen and Oxford and is Lecturer in Philosophy at the University of Essex. She has published on Kant and Nietzsche, and is currently working on a book on the links between Kant's epistemology and his aesthetics. Her work also examines the relationship of Kant and Nietzsche's thought to phenomenology.

Simon Jarvis is a Fellow of Robinson College, Cambridge. He is the author of *Adorno: A Critical Introduction* (Polity, 1998) and *Scholars and Gentlemen* (Oxford University Press, 1995). He has published several articles on the idea of the gift and is currently writing a study of Wordsworth.

Jeremy Jennings is Professor of History of Political Thought at the University of Birmingham. He is the author of a number of books and articles on modern French thought and history. He will shortly publish an edition of George Sorel's *Reflections on Violence* with Cambridge University Press, and is currently working on a history of political thought in France since 1789 for Oxford University Press.

Galen A. Johnson is Professor of Philosophy and Director of the University Honors Program at the University of Rhode Island. He is the author of *Earth and Sky: History and Philosophy* (1989) and a number of articles on Merleau-Ponty, Husserl, Nietzsche and Piaget. He is the editor of the *Merleau-Ponty Aesthetics Reader: Philosophy and Painting* (1993) and the co-editor of *Ontology and Alterity in Merleau-Ponty* (1990).

John E. Joseph is Professor and Head of Applied Linguistics at the University of Edinburgh. His research focuses on language standardisation, language and identity, and the history of language theory from ancient times to the present. He has written extensively on the life and ideas of Ferdinand de Saussure.

Susan F. Krantz is Associate Professor of Philosophy at St Anselm College, Manchester, NH, USA. She earned her doctorate in philosophy in 1980 at Brown University, with a dissertation on Brentano's theodicy, written under the direction of Roderick Chisholm. She has published several articles on Brentano's thought.

Guy Lafrance is Professor of Political Philosophy and Philosophy of Law at the University of Ottawa, Canada. He has published many articles and books in these areas and has also published on French philosophy and philosophy of the Enlightenment. He is the author of *La Philosophie Sociale de Bergson* (1974) and *Philosophie, Sciences et Valeurs* (1994), and editor of *Ethics and Basic Rights* (1989). He is the co-author, with Lorraine Clark, of *Rousseau and Criticism* (1995), and, with Pierre Laberge, of *Kant, Essai sur la Paix* (1997).

C. Scott Littleton is Professor of Anthropology at Occidental College, California. He is the author of

The New Comparative Mythology: An Anthropological Assessment of the Theories of Georges Dumézil (University of California Press, 1982) and the co-author, with Linda A. Malcor, of *From Scythia to Camelot* (Garland, 1994).

W. J. Mander was educated at University College London and Corpus Christi College, Oxford. He is currently Tutor in Philosophy at Harris Manchester College, Oxford. He is the author of *An Introduction to Bradley's Metaphysics* (Oxford University Press, 1994).

James L. Marsh is Professor of Philosophy at Fordham University. He is the author of *Post-Cartesian Meditations* (Fordham University Press) and *Critique, Action and Liberation* (SUNY Press).

Martin J. Beck Matuštík is Associate Professor of Philosophy at Purdue University. He is the author of *Postnational Identity: Critical Theory and Existential Philosophy in Habermas, Kierkegaard and Havel* (Guilford Press, 1993) and *Specters of Liberation* (SUNY Press, 1998), and is the co-editor, with Merold Westphal, of *Kierkegaard in Post/Modernity* (Indiana University Press, 1995).

Drew Milne is the Judith E. Wilson Lecturer in Modern Drama and Poetry, Trinity Hall, Cambridge. He is the editor of *Parataxis: Modernism and Modern Writing*, co-editor, with Terry Eagleton, of *Marxist Literary Theory: A Reader* and is currently completing studies on philosophy and theatre, and on Marxism and critical theory.

Michael Moriarty is Professor of French Literature and Thought at Queen Mary and Westfield College, London. He has published *Taste and Ideology in Seventeenth-Century France* (Cambridge, 1988) and *Roland Barthes* (Cambridge, 1991), and researches in seventeenth- and eighteenth-century French thought and critical theory.

Véronique Munoz-Dardé is Lecturer in Political Philosophy at University College London. She has published articles on social justice, and on the family and justice. She is the author of *La Justice sociale* (Nathan Université) and *La Fraternité, un concept politique?* (Presses Universitaires de France).

Thomas Nenon is Professor of Philosophy and former Director of the Center for the Humanities at the University of Memphis. His major publications include *Objektivität und Endliche Erkenntnis* and numerous articles on German philosophy.

Christopher Norris is Distinguished Research Professor of Philosophy at the University of Wales, Cardiff. He is the author of sixteen books on various aspects of philosophy and critical theory, among them (most recently) *Reclaiming Truth, Resources of Realism, New Idols of the Cave* and *Against Relativism*. His main research interests are in critical theory, epistemology and philosophy of science.

Dorothea E. Olkowski is Chair and Associate Professor in the Department of Philosophy at the University of Colorado, where she founded and directed the programme in Women's Studies until 1995. She is the co-editor, with Constantin V. Boundas, of *Gilles Deleuze and the Theatre of Philosophy*. She is author of a book on feminism and French philosophy entitled *The Ruin of Representation*.

David Owen is Lecturer in Politics and Assistant Director of the Centre for Post-Analytic Philosophy at the University of Southampton. He is the author of *Maturity and Modernity* (1995) and *Nietzsche, Politics and Modernity* (1996) as well as numerous articles on Continental philosophy. He is currently editor of the *Journal of Nietzsche Studies* and is writing a book on philosophical perspectives on enlightenment.

Jacob Owensby is an Anglican Priest and is currently Assistant Rector for Christian Formation at St Mark's Episcopal Church, Florida. He is the author of *Dilthey and the Narrative of History* (Cornell University Press). He has published a number of articles on Continental philosophy and the history of philosophy.

Diane Perpich is Assistant Professor of Philosophy at Duquesne University. She undertook her doctoral dissertation on Levinas's thought at the University of Chicago, and is co-editor of a special issue of the Graduate Faculty Philosophy Journal devoted to Levinas's contribution to contemporary philosophy.

Terry Pinkard is Professor of Philosophy at Georgetown University. He has also been a Visiting Professor at Tübingen. He has published articles on the philosophy of social science, German Idealism and bioethics, and is the author/editor of five books. His most recent book is *Hegel as Phenomenology: The Sociality of Reason* (Cambridge University Press, 1994). He is currently working on an intellectual biography of Hegel to be published by Cambridge University Press.

William A. Preston is the author of *Nietzsche as Anti-Socialist* (Humanities Press). He received his Ph.D. from Yale University and has taught at Johns Hopkins University.

John Protevi is Research Associate in the Center for French and Francophone Studies, Louisiana State University. His *Time and Exteriority* was published in 1994 by Bucknell University Press. In addition to his continuing work on the history of philosophy, he is now working on the philosophical significance of so-called chaos or complexity theory.

Robert Aaron Rethy is Professor of Philosophy and Chair of the Philosophy Department at Xavier University. He has published widely in the history of philosophy, from Heraclitus to Nietzsche. His current research interests include the connection between Nietzsche's moral critique and the rise of political anti-Semitism in Germany in the 1880s.

Tom Rockmore is Professor of Philosophy at Duquesne University and is the author of many books on Continental philosophy, his most recent being *Cognition: An Introduction to Hegel's Phenomenology of Spirit* (University of California Press, 1997).

Gary Roth is the Associate Dean of the Graduate School at Rutgers University. He received his doctorate in Sociology from the Freie Universität, Berlin. He is also the co-author, with Anne Lopes, of *Men's Feminism: August Bebel and the German Socialist Movement* (Humanities Press).

Katherine Rudolph received her Ph.D. from Johns Hopkins University and currently teaches philosophy at De Paul University. As a post-doctoral fellow at Brown University, she completed a book which examines contemporary linguistic and social constructivist models of identity in relation to the theories of language that enable them.

Lawrence S. Stepelevich edited the journal of the Hegel Society of America, *The Owl of Minerva*, from 1977 to 1996. He is currently President of that Society. In addition to his publications on Hegel's philosophy, he has written numerous articles focusing on the nature and history of Young Hegelianism.

Philip Stratton-Lake is Lecturer in Philosophy at Keele University. He has published articles on Kant, ethical intuitionism and the philosophy of Gabriel Marcel. He is Secretary of the UK Kant Society and Assistant Editor of *The Kantian Review*.

Chris Thornhill is Lecturer in German at King's College, London. He is a specialist in critical theory and twentieth-century German political theory.

J. E. Tiles is Professor of Philosophy at the University of Hawai'i at Manoa. He is the author of *Things that Happen* (1981), *Dewey* (1988) and, with Mary Tiles, *An Introduction to Historical Epistemology* (1993). He has also edited a four-volume set of 'Critical Assessments' of John Dewey. In addition to work on the classical pragmatists (Peirce, James and Dewey), he has published articles on ancient philosophy and philosophy of science.

Nicholas Walker is a Research Fellow at Magdalene College, Cambridge. His recent work has been on Hölderlin and the origins of German Idealism. His other central interests include critical theory, existential phenomenology and the relations between post-analytical philosophy and contemporary thought. He has published articles on Hölderlin, Hegel and German Idealism, and translated a number of essays and books by Adorno, Habermas and Gadamer. He recently co-translated Heidegger's *Fundamental Concepts of Metaphysics*.

Gail Weiss is Associate Professor of Philosophy at the George Washington University. Her research interests and published work focus on the intersections between phenomenology and existentialism, feminist theory and philosophy of literature. She has two books forthcoming with Routledge: *Body Images: Embodiment as Intercorporeality*, and an edited volume *Perspectives on Embodiment: The Intersection between Nature and Culture*.

Alistair Welchman is a Research Council Scholar studying Evolutionary and Adaptive Systems at Sussex University. He was educated at the Universities of Oxford, Madison-Wisconsin and Warwick. He has published articles on Deleuze, Sade, Kant, contemporary science and recent art theory.

Alan White is Professor of Philosophy at Williams College. He has published three books: *Absolute Knowledge: Hegel and the Problem of Metaphysics*, *Schelling: An Introduction to the System of Freedom* and *Within Nietzsche's Labyrinth*.

Caroline Williams is Lecturer in Political Theory at Queen Mary and Westfield College, London. Her research interests focus on the problematic of the subject in European philosophy and in political thought. She has published a number of essays on Lacanian psychoanalysis and on selfhood and subjectivity, including a contribution to *Knowing the Difference: Feminist Perspectives in Epistemology* (Routledge, 1994).

Elizabeth Wright is a Fellow of Girton College, Cambridge. Her main publications are: *Psychoanalytic Criticism* (1984), *Postmodern Brecht* (1989); as editor: *Feminism and Psychoanalysis: A Critical Dictionary*, (1993); as co-editor: *Coming out of Feminism?* (Basil Blackwell, 1996). Her new edition of *Psychoanalytic Criticism*, and a new book *Passion in the Text*, are forthcoming (Polity Press, 1998 and 1999 respectively).

INTRODUCTION

WHAT IS CONTINENTAL PHILOSOPHY?

Simon Glendinning

Continental currents: surveying the waters

Most people familiar with contemporary philosophy, particularly philosophy as it is taught at universities in the English-speaking world, will also be familiar with the category of 'Continental philosophy'. However, such familiarity typically extends no further than being able to say whether or not a given author is typically *called* a 'Continental philosopher'. Situations of this type normally reflect the shortcomings of a beginner or non-specialist, but in this case it seems to be more like a normal feature of the use of this label. Indeed, as I hope to show in this Introduction, as a term of classification, the category of 'Continental philosophy' somewhat *lives* on being vague and free-floating. This may seem a rather sorry state of affairs for a book going by the title of an 'Encyclopedia of Continental philosophy', but the title does give the most accurate indication of its contents. The category 'Continental philosophy', ill-defined as it may be, is one that students of philosophy are bound to come across in their studies and it is widely recognised and used. For example, it regularly appears in university prospectus descriptions of what is (or, indeed, is not) covered by a philosophy degree programme; it commonly appears in or as the title of a philosophy degree course or option; it might be included in a job specification for a philosophy post, and so on. And, as a consequence of this institutional use, bookshops, libraries, journals and publishers all acknowledge the category too.

It is with this use in mind that the *Encyclopedia* has been compiled. Essentially this means that those authors who are most regularly classified as 'Continental philosophers' have all been included in it. It does not mean, however, that the *Encyclopedia* is simply a survey of a (strange) grouping of authors. Even if the category itself is problematic and troubling, there are levels of classification *below* that of 'Continental philosophy' which are far more certain and reliable. Indeed, it is probably most helpful to think of Continental philosophy as comprising a number of smaller, relatively interrelated, schools or movements of thought. It is this family of movements which is the focus of examination in the *Encyclopedia*. Prefaced by special introductions by the Section Editors, each section presents the authors, theories and preoccupations centrally associated with particular movements. This 'movement-based' approach ensures that the content of the *Encyclopedia* has the greatest possible unity and coherence without imposing order where there is none.

No strategy for the selection and presentation of material as wide-ranging as that covered in the *Encyclopedia* could be problem-free. The method followed here has at least one obvious difficulty; namely, that since it makes use of distinguishing groupings it may give the misleading impression that authors in the same grouping *must* have more in common than authors in different groupings. Thus, for example, the strategy may suggest that the relationship between, for example, Heidegger and Sartre must be more real or more significant or deeper than the relationship between, for example, Heidegger and Derrida. But if they are misleading, such impressions are also readily correctable, and, indeed, will be corrected in the articles on the authors in question. The degree of unity within a section will be explored and assessed in the introduction to each section, and the articles on individual authors take the reader through their ideas, as it were, *on their own terms.*

'On their own terms' – but not necessarily *in* their own terms. The central difficulty that students typically find with the authors covered in the *Encyclopedia* is the complexity of their language and style. For that reason, we have striven to make the articles as accessible as possible. Terms of art are carefully introduced, and if the philosopher featured has a peculiar style this is explained and not mimicked.

The very issue of style takes us into a minefield – the possession of a less-than-plain style is often taken to be precisely what distinguishes 'Continental philosophy' from its supposedly distinctive 'analytical' (or 'analytic') rival. Indeed, for many analytical philosophers, 'Continental philosophy' just is that species of philosophy characterised by a (too) literary, rather than plain, style; a species which thereby makes (regrettable) recourse to rhetoric rather than reason and argument.

Even if this kind of view is inept and prejudiced, it might be agreed that there is a basic distinction to be drawn between Continental philosophy and analytical philosophy, a distinction which, though perhaps seen by analytical philosophy through a glass darkly, is somehow focused on the distinction of styles. That may well be so. However, what is rarely considered is the extent to which what is to be seen here may be more revealing about that species of philosophising that calls itself 'analytical' than what that same species calls 'Continental'.

What I am suggesting here is well illustrated by P. F. Strawson's assumption that 'more or less systematic reflection on the human condition' belongs to a 'species of philosophy' other than that of 'analytical philosophy' (Strawson, 1992, p. 2). The 'aim' of the latter is, he states, 'something quite different' (ibid.). But is that right? Of course, one must take care not to erase differences, but it is surely questionable whether analytical philosophical reflection in general, and the 'descriptive metaphysics'

which Strawson has elaborated on in particular, can be thought of as anything else *but* a more or less systematic reflection on the human condition (see, for example, Strawson, 1959, p. 9). How else can we understand Strawson's arguments for the 'primitiveness of the concept of a person' (ibid., 101) and against the idea that this concept is 'to be analyzed as that of an animated body or of an embodied anima' (ibid., p. 103)? What is, therefore, most striking is not an obvious difference of styles or subject matter but a tendency on the part of analytical philosophy to *conceive itself* as having ambitions which are other than (and perhaps less grandly ambitious than) other movements in Western philosophy.

None of this is intended to deny differences in conceptions of philosophy or in philosophising. In an essay on this issue, David Cooper rightly refers to analytical philosophy's 'sanguine acceptance of a reduced role for philosophy' (Cooper, 1994, p. 10), but I would like to emphasise that even in view of this self-conception analytical philosophy still remains a kind of enquiry whose questions are characterised by what is classically called *depth*. Of course, what being 'deep' is is more or less the same question as what philosophy and philosophising is, and I suspect that analytical philosophers are likely to lie at the conservative and cautious end of the spectrum of views on the human, cultural or 'spiritual' importance of the subject. Ultimately, however, the point is this: in whatever way one conceives of depth, or the importance and role of reflections on deep questions, the range of responses to such questions does not divide neatly into two. What we do have, however, is a movement in modern philosophy, the analytical movement, which tends to conceive itself as having a 'reduced scope', and which, for that reason, tends to conceive itself as distinctively different to other movements in modern philosophy, *movements which it has come to collect under the title 'Continental philosophy'.*

Thus, the difficulty is not to grasp what 'Continental philosophy' is, but to see that what is non-arbitrary about this particular collection of texts is not something that can be unearthed solely through *their* reading. As the name itself should indicate, Continental philosophy was not named from the inside. Indeed, what we shall see is that the idea of a distinctive 'Continental' tradition in philosophy is a peculiarly Anglo-Saxon assumption. Or, more precisely, what we shall see is that 'Continental philosophy' emerges as a fruitfully distinguishable philosophical category from *within* the movement that calls itself 'analytical philosophy'.

Without further qualification, this claim does not confer any problematic status upon the category of 'Continental philosophy'. However, in what follows I will argue that what is at issue here is not, and has not been, the identification by analytical philosophers, *en passant* as it were, of a distinctive philosophical approach, but exclusions of a strictly non-logical and at times thoroughly indefensible character. 'Continental philosophy', as a category, is, I will suggest, part of analytical philosophy in a strong sense: it is, as it were, the defining 'not-part' of analytical philosophy. In psychoanalysis this would be called 'incorporation'; where something is constructed and retained 'within' but *as* an excluded outside, *as* a foreign body which is impossible to assimilate and which must be rejected. This Introduction thus comprises a sketch for an investigation of Continental philosophy as the incorporated other of analytical philosophy.

Towards the end of the Introduction I will suggest that, in significant respects, the English-speaking philosophical culture is becoming less concerned with, and less shaped by, the idea of a philosophical division or rift between analytical and Continental philosophy. Nevertheless, even today, labelling an author as a 'Continental philosopher' can never be a wholly value-free gesture or merely geographical determination. On the contrary, the current use of this label carries with it the burden of an evaluative accent which has suggested that the author is doing work not only of a supposedly distinctive kind but also of an *inferior* quality. Thus, while analytical philosophy has conceived itself in terms of its logical rigour and clarity, it has castigated what it calls 'Continental philosophy' for its dependency on rhetoric and its metaphysical pretensions. For many analytical philosophers, 'Continental philosophy' represents all that is 'arbitrary, pretentious and soul-destroying' in modern philosophy, wherever it is written (Passmore, 1968, p. 497).

This profoundly negative evaluation is, I think,

now (or, for the moment, still) a feature of the grammar of 'Continental philosophy'. That is, *in so far as* one affirms that 'what one does' is analytical philosophy, then Continental philosophy will be not only *What one (qua* analytical philosopher) *does not do*, but *What ought not to be done* if one wants to think seriously within the central channels of the Western philosophical tradition. In what follows, I will explain how this evaluation developed along with the emergence of the analytical movement in English-language philosophy.

For starters: Continental breakfast

By the middle of the seventeenth century, the English word 'continent' had taken on its current geographical sense of 'a vast landmass not broken by seas'. But when preceded by a definite article (and often written with a capital 'C') it had also developed a specific British use as the name for 'the mainland of Europe, as distinguished from the British Isles' (*Oxford English Dictionary*). The Continent, in this sense, is 'over there'. So, as the name of a place, its origins are 'over here'. It is from this specific, and specifically British, use of the term 'continent' that the category of 'Continental philosophy' takes its title. As we shall see, it develops its modern evaluative accent during the middle of the twentieth century when British academic philosophers, especially those working at the older English universities, sustained a vigorous attack on what they conceived as dangerous and disreputable 'foreign' ideas.

It is perhaps worth noting that this attack contrasted starkly with the cosmopolitan openness of the literary intelligentsia in London. Jonathan Rée has calculated that during the 1950s, at the height of English academic antipathy to 'Continental' ideas, '[of] all the philosophical books reviewed in the *Times Literary Supplement*, only twenty-two a year, or 6 per cent, represented the Oxfordian ["analytic"] line, whereas four times that number came from their "Continental" rivals' (Rée, 1993, p. 16). This kind of division over the merits of association with what can, broadly speaking, be called 'Continental culture' has long been a feature of British life, going back, at least, to the debate over the educational worth of 'The Grand Tour' during the seventeenth and eighteenth centuries. The Grand Tour marked the first major development in modern European tourism. In Britain the Tour involved the adolescent sons and daughters of the wealthy classes being sent off to visit the cultural centres of 'the Continent', often with a tutor, ostensibly to 'finish' their education. But the value of having the cream of British youth mixing with and acquiring foreign mores and tastes was hotly disputed. (French food and Italian opera were supposed to be especially pernicious by those who attacked the Tour. See Black, 1992, Ch. 13; and Hilbert, 1974, Epilogue.) One cannot help but see this British (or, more accurately, English) division between hostile and cosmopolitan attitudes to 'Continental culture' at work in both the terms and the tone of the English-language reception of 'Continental philosophy' in the second half of the twentieth century.

It needs to be emphasised that it is difficult even to articulate these issues in a language other than English. (It is notable that the Collins-Robert (1992) dictionary details the capitalised use of 'continental' in the English/French section but not in the French/English section.) In this respect the current use of the term 'Continental philosophy' can be compared to that of a 'Continental breakfast'. It would be ridiculous to think of anyone living in mainland Europe calling their morning meal a 'Continental breakfast'. Indeed, no one in those countries can, without the 'assistance' of the British, think of themselves as 'Continentals' at all. But now there is not only a kind of breakfast which can be called a 'Continental breakfast', it is possible to eat one anywhere. It is a truly intercontinental phenomenon. One can even order it as such, to some local puzzlement, on the Continent.

A similar point can be made about Continental philosophy. It is not simply that Continental philosophy, as it is understood today, can be 'done' elsewhere or anywhere, but it takes on its modern, generic sense only when it *can* be done anywhere. Of course, even to say this assumes that, like a Continental breakfast, there *is* something which has an identity sufficient to be detachable from wherever 'it' was initially located. But there is good reason to think that what analytical philosophy assumes to be 'Continental philosophy' does not quite exist. Hes-

itancy is unavoidable here. To take the culinary example again, the point would be that British diners did not simply invent the idea of a Continental breakfast; it was (more or less literally) given to them. However, that it was 'given *to them*' inflects the identity of the gift. A Continental breakfast, while not a pure invention, does not arise from pure reception either. It is what, as it were, British tourists were able to take home with them. And what they took home was, perhaps even in their own eyes, a fairly obvious simplification. Perhaps no one supposed, still less now supposes that the morning eating habits of the peoples of mainland Europe can be identified with any rigour with the taking of 'a light breakfast of rolls and coffee' (*Oxford English Dictionary*).

The situation is similar, if more complex and problematic, in the case of Continental philosophy. The point is that Continental philosophy is 'given' to analytical philosophy as beyond the pale. Specifically, it is thought to involve a kind of failure of inheritance, an abandonment of the 'accepted standards of clarity and rigour' which should characterise properly philosophical inquiry (see Smith et al., 1992). Thus, it is not as if Continental philosophy has been conceived as representing a genuine alternative to the central interests and concerns of analytical philosophy. On the contrary, for many adherents of analytical philosophy the 'central interests and concerns' of Continental philosophy (whatever they are is precisely what is free-floating) simply do 'not merit serious attention, or [are] deserving even of *argued* dissent' (Warnock, 1976, p. 48, p. 50. It should be noted that Warnock's judgement here is directed at the Idealist tradition which briefly dominated British philosophy at the turn of the nineteenth century. That the context bears more than just a passing comparison to the present issue is spelt out in the final section of this Introduction.)

We must take this kind of judgement *au pied de la lettre*. There really have been very few serious attempts by analytical philosophers to attend to, or argue with, the work called 'Continental'. No doubt this partly explains why the idea of Continental philosophy is so vague, but it also gives reason to suspect that this category, at least in part, *lives on* being free-floating. It survives only as long as the thinkers and themes which are placed within it are not only supposed not worth reading but, in fact, *are not seriously read*. Such, in any case, is the suspicion I want to explore. In order to do so I want to examine the arguments of some analytical philosophers on the subject of the division in the philosophical culture. None of the writers I will examine would claim to speak for all, but either by notoriety or desert they have made the most significant impact on this issue. I will begin with two examples of what I will call 'gulf-seekers': philosophers who have attempted to establish an identity for analytical philosophy by way of a radical contrast with a 'Continental' 'not-part'. I will then turn to two recent attempts at giving a *philosophical* explanation of the division. Finally, a new way of conceiving the history and field described by this division will be presented. This may, I hope, enable the reader of this book to receive the articles that follow in the right spirit and, for newcomers who know 'Continental philosophy' only as a term of contempt, with goodwill.

Weather reports: Continental storms

A certain *doxa*, or opinion, informs the English-language weather reports concerning what is currently 'happening' in philosophy. Philosophy, it is said, has divided into two fronts, two broad traditions: analytical and Continental philosophy. For many analytical philosophers the existence of this division is treated as a fact, a given for and in the contemporary philosophical culture.

As we have seen, however, what is given here is not a symmetrical or balanced description. The so-called Continental philosophers are charged with a failure, if not of rationality, then at least of inheritance. To cite an example I will return to in the next section, L. J. Cohen has argued that what today is called 'analytical philosophy . . . may be regarded as a continuous strand in the development of Western philosophy from its beginnings in Socratic dialogue' (Cohen, 1986, p. 57). So analytical philosophy is really just going on doing 'philosophy', but Continental philosophy, by contrast, although in a very broad sense part of the history of the subject, is not part of that central strand (ibid., p. 5).

What is in question, then, is a matter of inheritance, and one's fidelity to the history of a long-standing tradition of inquiry. And, so the *doxa* goes, Continental philosophers, or some of them, or all of them sometimes, have lost faith with that tradition. They have either given up or just do not like the dominant, argumentative modes of Western philosophy (ibid., p. 146).

If, then, the analytical and the Continental traditions are typically identified by their different ways of going on, this must be taken as referring, in the first instance, not to typical tenets or methods but to their different ways of *going on*, of continuing doing philosophy, by their possession or neglect of a past. Describing the appearance of this division of inheritance, Bernard Williams notes that 'it is a feature of our time that the resources of philosophical writing typically available to analytical philosophy . . . present themselves so strongly as the responsible way of going on, the most convincing expression of a philosopher's claim on people's attention' (Williams, 1996, p. 27). As before, we must not be misled by avowals of reception. Williams's point here is not that being an heir to philosophy can be reduced to the (pure) reception of something available, of a given which presents itself strongly. On the contrary, he is faithfully giving voice to a position for which the division of inheritance has already been drawn: 'the resources available to analytical philosophy' just are what it typically cites as its resources. The novel 'feature of our time' is that, *in view of a larger stock*, analytical philosophy evinces little or no anxiety about its limits. In question, then, is not the passive acquisition of a forceful fragment of what is available, but relatively confident acts of endorsement, what one might call the countersigning of a particular way of going on. And the analytical philosopher is confident, Williams is suggesting, that Continental philosophers are signing up the wrong tree.

But is the supposition of philosophical division really justified? Is there a philosophical rift in the contemporary philosophical culture? For many this question will sound absurd. For there is, surely, no doubt that there is a rift. But I am not disputing the fact of division. The question is not whether there is a rift in philosophy but whether the rift is philosophical. Is the difference *of philosophy?* Through looking at what I see as telling texts, texts in which analytical philosophy has told of its other, I will suggest that in crucial respects it is not. I will not argue, however, that the division in the contemporary philosophical culture is without classically philosophical significance. To the question 'What is Continental philosophy?' I will answer: 'It is the false personification, by analytical philosophy, of a possibility which is internal to, and which threatens, all philosophising; the possibility of being empty'. Now, as a *false* personification, I take it that the history of its emergence betrays injustice and misunderstanding. In what follows I want to explore some of that history, and expose some of that injustice. What I hope to show is that writers of analytical philosophy capable of genuinely sophisticated and powerful work seem ready and willing, at defining moments, to abandon the standards of scholarship which otherwise characterise them. So while (rightly) it will be deemed essential to reconstruct the positions and arguments of others ('others' supposedly in general) accurately, judiciously, and in modes which are open to correction or refutation, suddenly, when what is at stake is the identification of the 'not-part' of analytical philosophy, we will see that these principles are allowed to give way.

An 'exemplary' case of this tendency is Gilbert Ryle's address to the conference 'La Philosophie Analytique' held at Royaumont, France, in 1958. The conference had been organised by French philosophers who, while clearly not unfamiliar with the published work of their Anglophone contemporaries, sought discussion with, among others, the already notoriously insular 'Oxford School' of 'philosophical analysis'. While the French title of the conference nicely anticipates the distinction between analytical and Continental philosophy, these terms had not yet become the dominant currency of English-language metaphilosophy. The dominant vocabulary was, in fact, national, and for Ryle and his fellow Oxford analysts Continental philosophy still meant, basically, 'philosophical work on the Continent'.

Nevertheless, the modern metaphilosophical evaluative contrast was definitely being prepared for. The very title of Ryle's contribution 'Phenomenol-

ogy versus *The Concept of Mind*' reflected and encouraged the English contingent's assumption of, and perhaps desire for, confrontation and division. And the contents of Ryle's talk (mis)treated the participants to some of the most extraordinary and inflammatory remarks ever (publicly) voiced on the superiority of 'Anglo-Saxon' or 'English-speaking' philosophy over its 'Continental' cousin.

Ryle began with what appeared to be a brief summary of Husserl's conception of phenomenology. The sentence which concludes that summary, however, gave it an unexpected but important spin: 'This caricature of Husserl's phenomenology is intended to show up by contrast some of the predominant features of recent philosophy and in particular of the philosophy of mind in the English-speaking world' (Ryle, 1971, p. 181). In this single sentence we see the signals of the two most abiding features of what I am calling 'gulf-seeking' presentations of analytical philosophy. First, that it is drawn through a contrast to some other style of philosophy; and second, and more seriously, that this other is presented without the kind of critical care which analytical philosophers would (quite rightly) expect if someone were presenting *their* work. Ryle's case is developed by contrast not with Husserl's philosophy (although he sometimes puts it that way) but with a 'caricature' of Husserl's philosophy. Ryle seems to have been happily unconcerned by the threat this posed to his analysis. Indeed, when, in discussion, he was politely reproached by Husserl's translator Herman van Breda for 'not having sufficiently read his Husserl' (Merleau-Ponty, 1992, p. 59), Ryle bluntly declared that he 'care[d] little' whether the caricature resembled Husserl and hoped that the debate would not 'degenerate' into a 'colloquium on Husserl' (ibid., p. 61).

Apparently content with caricature, Ryle's address makes use of it to 'show up' by contrast the distinctive Anglo-Saxon alternative. Of course, the trouble now is that we cannot be confident that this represents a genuine contrast to a 'bad' philosophical road that was actually being followed. Still, Ryle's two basic claims are worth quoting in full, if only to acquaint newcomers with the mode of his philosophical gulf-seeking:

(1) Apart from one or two brief flirtations, British thinkers have showed no inclination to assimilate philosophical to scientific enquiries; and *a fortiori* no inclination to puff philosophy up into the Science of sciences. Conceptual enquiries differ from scientific enquiries not in hierarchical rank but in type. They are not higher or lower, since they are not on the same ladder. I guess that our thinkers have been immunised against the idea of philosophy as the Mistress Science by the fact that their daily lives in Cambridge and Oxford Colleges have kept them in personal contact with real scientists. Claims to *Führership* vanish when postprandial joking begins. Husserl wrote as if he had never met a scientist – or a joke.

(2) Even inside philosophy, no privileged position has with us been accorded to the philosophy of mind. Certainly, with us as elsewhere, and in this century as in other centuries, many philosophers have been primarily interested in problems of epistemology, of ethics, of politics, and of jurisprudence. But many others have been primarily interested in the philosophy of mathematics, of physics, and of biology. We have not worried our heads over the question Which philosopher ought to be *Führer*? If we did ask ourselves this question, we should mostly be inclined to say that it is logical theory that does or should control other conceptual enquiries, though even this control would be advisory rather than dictatorial. At least the main lines of our philosophical thinking during this century can be fully understood only by someone who has studied the massive developments of our logical theory. This fact is partly responsible for the wide gulf that has existed for three-quarters of a century between Anglo-Saxon and Continental philosophy. For, on the Continent during this century, logical studies have, unfortunately, been left unfathered by most philosophy departments and cared for, if at all, only in a few departments of mathematics. (Ryle, 1971, pp. 181–2)

All the above is, because outrageous, arrogant and complacent, crazily funny. But what would Ryle, acknowledged 'King' if not *Führer* of British philosophy at the time (Dummett and Pataut, 1996, p. 10), have thought had his own work, or, say, that of G. E. Moore or Bertrand Russell, been mistreated in this way. Would he have enjoyed the 'joke'?

Joke or no joke, the use of caricature here is bad scholarship and inferior philosophy. At a time when memories of the Second World War were still vivid, Ryle chides Husserl (a Jew) for claiming *Führership* for philosophy. But in discussion afterwards he showed no interest in the point made from the floor that many philosophers, including Aristotle and Kant, had 'defended a certain priority for philosophy'. And he (Ryle) would not consider 'ridiculing *them*' (Merleau-Ponty, 1992, p. 60).

Biographer of both Russell and Wittgenstein, Ray Monk raises a further complaint against Ryle's argument, concerning the viability of its appeal to a national distinction to underwrite the reference to 'the massive developments of *our* logical theory'.

> *Our* logical theory? But didn't Russell learn his logic from an Italian (Peano), and a whole lot of Germans (Cantor, Weierstrass, Dedekind and Frege)? In the following section of Ryle's paper, it transpires that what he means by 'the massive developments of our logical theory' is the progression from Russell's theory of descriptions to Wittgenstein's theories of meaning in, first, *Tractatus Logico-Philosophicus* and then *Philosophical Investigations*. These developments he characterizes as 'The *Cambridge* Transformation of the Theory of Concepts' [R. M.'s italics], thus bypassing the slightly awkward fact that Wittgenstein was more Germanic than Anglo-Saxon. Wittgenstein, for all that he wrote in German and felt like an alien in England, was, it seems, a Cambridge man through and through, and not really a 'Continental' at all. (Monk, 1996, p. 3)

Ryle, however, is (or, for some reason, needs to be) blind to the extent to which his intellectual world had Continental debts and is determined to affirm what he calls a 'wide gulf' between 'Anglo-Saxon and Continental philosophy'. Yet, and this is crucial, it is not simply the terms of Ryle's distinction which are inadequate or distorting. One of the participants at the conference was Maurice Merleau-Ponty, a critic as well as an indebted reader of Husserlian phenomenology. In discussion he raised a series of points seeking clarification from Ryle. The points were varied, but they were all posed in order, not to exhibit differences or show up contrasts, but to 'make precise how far our agreement goes'. For, like other participants, he was not convinced by Ryle's talk of a 'gulf' between 'British' analysis and 'Continental' phenomenology:

> I have also had the impression, while listening to Mr Ryle, that what he was saying was not so strange to us, and that the distance, if there is a distance, is one that he puts between us rather than one I find there. (Merleau-Ponty, 1992, p. 65)

As we shall see, this is a recurrent response from the 'Continental philosophers' to the supposition of a 'wide gulf' in the inheritance and practice of philosophy. For reasons I will return to, L. J. Cohen later described the conference at Royaumont as 'the sort of set piece affair . . . where the participants meet once, as it were, and rather sterilely agree to differ' (Cohen, 1986, p. 5). The truth seems rather more to be that the British analysts had *already decided* that communication was or should be impossible and that it was, in any case, worthless.

The putative impossibility of serious philosophical communication between Britain and the Continent was also the theme of another early gulf-seeking text: R. M. Hare's lecture on British philosophy 'given at a number of German centres in the summer of 1957'. Like Ryle, Hare does not think of the philosophical landscape in terms of a distinction between analytical and Continental philosophy. But, again like Ryle, he definitely thinks of it as *philosophically* divided. In his lecture, the 'two different ways' in which 'the same subject' is studied, ways concerning which 'one might be forgiven for thinking . . . are really two quite different subjects' (Hare, 1960, p. 107), are primarily labelled nationally, as 'British' and 'German' philosophy. This lexicon may have the virtue of avoiding the 'strange cross-classification' of analytical and Continental philosophy

(Williams, 1996, p. 25), but Hare's distinction is not without at least two major complications of its own. First, he virtually identifies British philosophy with work being done at 'the older British universities' and especially Oxford; and second, he can hardly be said to identify 'German philosophy' with anything at all. He does speak of 'a typical German philosopher' and refers to 'huge volumes' and 'long obscure books' which nobody in Oxford will read, and which, as E. W. F. Tomlin noted in a rejoinder, 'seems to be tilting at German productions' (Tomlin, 1960, p. 5). But not one example or sample of such work is cited or even referred to in the lecture. As we shall see, Hare's argument is seriously compromised by this vagueness. Indeed, Hare is even more willing than Ryle to make use of, and recourse to, caricature.

Hare's lecture begins with a brief presentation of the benefits to philosophy of the Oxford tutorial system. In such a system, he stresses, a student of philosophy will be taught 'how to think more clearly and to the point' (Hare, 1960, p. 108); taught, that is, 'to express his thought clearly to himself and to others; to make distinctions where there are distinctions to be made, and thus avoid unnecessary confusion – and not to use long words (or short ones) without being able to explain what they mean' (ibid., p. 108). These points are intended to introduce us to the basic characteristics of Oxford, and by implication British, philosophy generally. For British philosophy, Hare insists, is guided by the intellectual virtues it teaches; namely, 'clarity, relevance and brevity' (ibid., p. 112). Such virtues will then ensure that arguments between 'British philosophers' can circulate and develop through the defence and refutation of work with what he calls 'an unambiguously stated thesis' (ibid.). This, according to Hare, is the central characteristic and great strength of British philosophical analysis.

The unambiguously stated thesis of Hare's paper is that 'British' and 'German' philosophy is 'the same subject studied in two different ways'. The unstated, less clear, but certainly no less unambiguous thesis is that the 'German' philosophical way is the *wrong* philosophical way. Supposing, as is in fact constantly invited, the contrast to the 'British' way is, even when unstated as such, the 'German' way, then the latter enjoys the 'delights of erecting, in solitary thought, imposing edifices – of writing huge volumes which only a handful of people will ever understand' (ibid., p. 110); and the typical author of such 'long or difficult books' (ibid., p. 113) or 'monstrous philosophical edifices' (ibid., p. 115) likes, Hare suggests, to 'collect a private coterie to listen to him' (ibid., p. 111); and he will not be averse to 'the turning of philosophy into *mystique*' (ibid., p. 110) or to producing 'verbiage' disguised as 'serious metaphysical inquiry' (ibid., p. 115). In short, according to Hare, the 'typical German philosopher' thrives on, and finds 'uplifting', approaches and styles of thought characterised by 'ambiguities and evasions and rhetoric', that is, precisely those characteristics which 'British philosophers' regard 'as the mark of a philosopher who has not learnt his craft' (ibid., pp. 112–13).

A grave nod. But who are these German philosophers who 'have chosen to ignore [the] important developments [made by Vienna Circle positivism] and carry on in their old ways as if nothing had happened' (ibid., p. 117)? The trouble is not merely that we are not told (there are, as we know, usual suspects in this game), but that not one example of the 'German way' is presented as an illustration. Thus, the idea of philosophical division remains a kind of air-castle or, lest we forget certain Viennese developments, at least unverified. Some striking home truths are revealed on this point in a passage where Hare discusses the 'British' philosopher's (pre-Research Assessment Exercise) conception of his duty as a philosopher:

We do not think it is a *duty* to write books; still less do we think it a duty to *read* more than a few of the books which others write – for we know that, given our heavy load of teaching, to read more than the essential books would take us away from more important things. Our duty is to discuss philosophy with our colleagues and to teach our pupils to do the same – books and articles are an unconsidered by-product of this process; their content is generally quite familiar from verbal discussion years before they get published. We find out which 'the essential books' are by each reading a very few and telling the others about them. The result is that, if one wants a book to be

read by one's colleagues it will have to be short, clear and to the point . . . The certain way to obscurity, on the other hand, is to write long obscure books. Nobody will ever read them. (ibid., p. 114)

He later adds that 'British' philosophers 'find it hard to discuss philosophy with, *or to read the books of*, people who do not even seem worried about convincing the sceptic that their philosophical propositions mean something' (ibid., p. 115, my emphasis). Thus, what Hare calls the 'essential books', books, that is, which will in fact be read by 'British' (Oxford) philosophers with any seriousness whatsoever, will prove, in practice, to be their own alone. So much for avoiding 'coteries'. What can one conclude here but that the very idea of a *philosophical* division within the European philosophical culture must, at least in part, *live* on being free-floating? Again, one cannot help but wonder whether the supposition of a distinctive 'Continental' tradition in philosophy survives only as long as the thinkers and themes which are placed within it are, in fact, not seriously read.

Since Hare's account is developed in ways which force him to slip from the standards of 'rigour and honesty and clarity' which, rightly, he upholds for philosophy generally (ibid., p. 120), he cannot have properly or satisfactorily demonstrated his unambiguously stated thesis that there are two ways in which the subject is currently studied. However, perhaps he has succeeded in showing something else; namely, that 'the rise of the analytical movement' has at times relied on its self-authorised defenders failing to be 'an example of the virtues' which, officially at least, they were 'seeking to inculcate' (ibid., p. 116). I will return to this in the next section where I explore two more recent, and in certain ways more rigorous, attempts to give content to the distinction between analytical and Continental philosophy.

Mapping the Continent: tour guides

The two examples of philosophical 'gulf-seeking' just reviewed might be thought more frivolous than serious, but the impact of this kind of aggressive arrogance has been profound. The aim may have been below the belt, but they succeeded in their aim. For even if many, if not most, contemporary philosophers who think of themselves as in some sense 'analytical' would now accept that Ryle and Hare, in these two texts, approached their subject with cavalier indifference to the usual canons of exegetical accuracy and fairness, this may not be thought to diminish the adequacy of their basic thesis; namely, that there is a rift, *a philosophical rift*, in contemporary philosophy. So much is, surely, obvious.

But is it? Of course, there is no question that the development of twentieth-century thought has seen the rise of a movement calling itself 'analytical philosophy' which, for the most part, has had very few dealings with what it calls 'Continental philosophy'. But are the roots of this division *philosophical*? Michael Dummett and L. J. Cohen have both recently argued that they are, and so have attempted to give greater academic respectability to the rhetoric of the gulf-seekers. In this section I will look at these attempts.

Dummett's claim to provide a wholly philosophical characterisation of 'what distinguishes analytical philosophy' is an interesting one in that it requires that we completely reject the philosophical nationalism and Anglocentrism that characterises Ryle and Hare's polemics. 'Analytical philosophy' cannot be contrasted with 'Continental philosophy', Dummett insists, because the roots of the former are 'principally or exclusively' located in the intellectual soil of the latter. Indeed, he suggests that 'the *only* grandfather of analytical philosophy' is the German mathematical logician Gottlob Frege (Dummett, 1993, p. 171, my emphasis). This is a controversial thesis, and it would seem wrong both ideologically and historically not to include, at least, G. E. Moore and Bertrand Russell in any account of the emergence of the self-distinguishing 'analytical tradition'. Dummett's apparently 'Continental' emphasis is not naive, however, and can be readily understood against the background of his two central theses: that, while not usefully conceived by the analytical/Continental distinction, there *is* a genuine and deep *philosophical* rift in twentieth-century philosophical culture; and that the roots of this rift lie in the different routes taken by Frege and Husserl from a common inheritance which both derived from Bolzano and Brentano (see Lowe, 1994, p. 246). Thus,

as Dummett conceives it, 'the roots of analytical philosophy are the same roots as those of the phenomenological school' (cited in Monk, 1996, p. 4). The two traditions, he says, 'may be compared with the Rhine and the Danube, which rise quite close to one another and for a time pursue roughly parallel courses, only to diverge in utterly different directions and flow into different seas'.

While Dummett's approach seeks to locate analytical philosophy within the overall development of philosophy in Europe in the nineteenth and twentieth centuries, he is not, he emphasises, only engaged in a historical exercise concerning sources and influences, and the only non-analytic philosopher whose views are confronted is, again, Husserl. Nevertheless, unlike the gulf-seekers, Dummett does explore Husserl's work in some depth. And while Husserl specialists may not agree with his interpretation, this is so in just the sense that other Frege specialists dispute Dummett's interpretation of Frege. The effect of this approach on Dummett's account is striking; namely, that he arrives (as it were from the home side) at exactly the same kind of conclusion as that of Merleau-Ponty listening to Ryle: this supposedly alien work (in this case Husserl's) is not so unfamiliar, and is, in fact, not so very different to Frege's. This raises new questions for analytical philosophy's self-conception:

> At the very beginning of the century, say at the time Husserl published the *Logical Investigations*, there wasn't yet phenomenology as a school. There wasn't yet analytic philosophy as a school. There were lots of currents there and you would have to put Frege and Husserl quite close together, and yet their progeny diverged so widely. It's a very interesting question from which it seems to me that much understanding must come. Why did they diverge so widely? . . . [T]he question of determining what is essential to analytic philosophy . . . [cannot be understood] unless you go back to its origins. What distinguishes this kind of philosophy from others? Where exactly does the divergence come in? (Dummett and Patant, 1996, p. 14)

Dummett's answer lies in his view of Frege's and Husserl's respective accounts of grasping a meaning:

while the former holds that meaning is essentially capable of being fully expressed in language, the latter holds that there remains an essentially inexpressible layer (Dummett, 1993, p. 97). This answer, so Dummett holds, explains why post-Fregean but *not* post-Husserlian philosophy was able to make a decisive 'linguistic turn' and thus, in time, separate into their 'widely diverging' rivers.

Now, both the Fregean and the Husserlian aspects of Dummett's answer are highly questionable. (For short statements of rival interpretations see the series of articles on Frege and Husserl in *The Journal of Philosophy* Vol. LXXXIV, No. 10, 1987. See also J. N. Mohanty, 'Dummett, Frege and Phenomenology', *Journal of the British Society for Phenomenology*, Vol. 15, No. 1, 1984.) However, they are jointly essential to his attempt to offer an explanation of the subsequent events in the history of philosophy (the divergence of their progeny) in exclusively philosophical terms. For they underpin the cogency of his metaphilosophical thesis concerning 'what is essential to analytic philosophy'; namely, 'the belief, first, that a philosophical account of thought can be attained through a philosophical account of language, and, secondly, that a comprehensive account can only be so attained' (Dummett, 1993, p. 4).

The problem with this philosophical answer to the question of the roots of the contemporary division is that while the idea of the 'linguistic turn' probably fits the kind of work pursued by many of the Oxford analysts of the post-War generation, it has been convincingly argued that it cannot be taken to capture the work of Bertrand Russell or G. E. Moore (see Monk, 1996), Carnap (see Kemp, 1995), or even Donald Davidson and W. V. O. Quine (see Engel, 1995). And Gareth Evans, John McDowell and Christopher Peacocke have all more or less explicitly repudiated Dummett's thesis of the primacy of language over thought as object of philosophical investigation (see Glock, 1989). Yet without doubt, all of those listed above are counted, or even count themselves, as analytical philosophers. Moreover, if Dummett's notion of the linguistic turn is broadly conceived, it *does* fit the work of Jacques Lacan and Jacques Derrida, and they are definitely not counted as analytical philosophers by analytical philosophers (see Monk, 1993).

If Dummett's proposal does not provide the right sort of borderlines to establish the division in strictly philosophical terms, one response to this failure would be to search for a better one that does. This is the approach taken by L. J. Cohen in *The Dialogue of Reason*. Cohen's proposal is to conceive of analytical philosophy as 'a relatively well-bounded dialogue' (Cohen, 1986, p. 5) which 'may be regarded as a continuous strand in the development of Western philosophy from its [ancient Greek] beginnings' (ibid., p. 57). In terms of this dialogue it is not difficult, Cohen suggests, to distinguish analytical philosophy from 'other modern movements'; for 'few if any . . . serious discussions or exchanges of criticism' have taken place between them (ibid., p. 5). These other modern movements are not part of the central dialogue. However, and in my view quite rightly, Cohen does not see the actual composition of this dialogue as of itself sufficient to answering the question as to 'what holds [analytical philosophy] together' as a distinctive philosophical movement (ibid., p. 5). For, like Dummett, Cohen does not seek an explanation of analytical philosophy in developmental or historical terms but in exclusively philosophical and conceptual terms. Thus, he concludes that there is

a characteristically philosophical question to be asked about the analytical movement, in abstraction from any consideration of its personal composition, of its temporal ordering, or of external influences that have affected it. What counts here is the content of what has been said, not the date or author of its utterance. Specifically, we may ask: on what assumptions about the nature of philosophical problems, methods, or doctrines can all, or very nearly all, the relevant strands of the dialogue be regarded as sharing a distinctive philosophical objective. (ibid., pp. 6–7)

In short, like Dummett, Cohen seeks to explain what holds analytical philosophy together (and apart from other movements) not through a history of a 'dialogue of thinkers' but through an idealised history: a 'dialogue of thoughts'. So, Cohen seeks to offer a 'philosophical analysis of philosophical analysis' (ibid., p. 10). Such an analysis will reinforce analytical philosophy 'from within' by providing a wholly conceptual articulation of 'what they are doing or have done' (ibid., p. 9). By revealing its preoccupations, this analysis will thus give real content to 'the contrast that is commonly, and rightly, drawn today . . . between analytical philosophy on the one side, and, on the other, philosophies preoccupied with God, with dread, with consciousness, with personal belief, with deconstruction, or with politico-economic class struggle' (ibid., p. 11). A list of the latter type are later summarised as including the 'Thomist, Kantian, Hegelian, Marxist, phenomenologist, [and] existentialist' schools of thought (ibid., p. 114). Unlike Dummett, however, Cohen does not attend to the work of any of these movements in any detail. Taking the existence of a gulf for granted ('the contrast that is commonly, and rightly, drawn today') his primary concern is to identify the preoccupations, the 'pervasive features of the problems', of 'analytical philosophy' (ibid., p. 11), those features which characterise the supposedly distinctive 'analytical' dialogue of thoughts.

However, with respect to such a concern, it should now be stressed, as Cohen in fact does not, that the historical absence of 'any serious discussions or exchanges of criticism' between certain *thinkers* in the development of analytical philosophy cannot be taken as *decisive* as to whether certain 'thoughts' are relevantly related to the dialogue (to find that out one must, for example, *read a thinker's books*). Hence the significance to Cohen that the conference at Royaumont was supposed to be an occasion where the participants 'rather sterilely agree to differ'. For if that were true it would be the kind of *prima facie* evidence one would need for the assumption that certain thoughts *do* lie 'outside' the dialogue (ibid., p. 5). However, as I have indicated, this was not the unanimous view of the Royaumont exchanges.

Holding that point in suspense for a moment, let us consider Cohen's proposed 'philosophical analysis of philosophical analysis'. Taking the fact of philosophical division as a given, Cohen suggests, not at all implausibly, the following thesis:

Analytical philosophy is occupied, at an appropriately general level, and in a great variety of ways, with the reasoned discussion of what can be a reason for what. As such it is a strand in the total history of Western philosophy from Socrates onwards rather than just a modern movement. (ibid., p. 49)

The idea is that analytical philosophy consists of reasoning about the rationality of anything; of judgements, of attitudes, of scientific procedures, of actions, and, of course, of rationality itself. Thus, Cohen's own account, while structurally 'metaphilosophical', is itself a piece of philosophy: it raises the question 'How is the reasoned study of rationality possible?' (ibid., p. 64). And Cohen's basic answer to that is: by arguments of appropriate kinds, by sound reasoning.

Clearly that basic answer cannot be the end of the matter since, like debates over the question of what 'depth' is in philosophy, there can be (and are) real and important divergences over what constitutes 'sound reasoning'. But Cohen's point is that these simply need to be explored, and 'since no tenets are sacrosanct' (ibid., p. 61), they can be explored only through disputes characterised by 'argument and counter-argument, rather than in the use or threat of violence' (ibid., p. 61).

I think this is a reasonable, if suitably vague, description of analytical philosophy. But of analytical philosophy alone? My own view is that Cohen's definition is simply a broad definition of philosophy. That, in any case, it is too wide for his purposes is suggested by the fact that in order to secure the limits he wishes for his definition, Cohen too, as we shall see, has to betray the philosophical virtues which he rightly seeks to reveal and defend.

At the close of his investigation of the (internal) relationship between analytical philosophy and reasoned argument, Cohen concludes that such philosophy cannot 'proceed satisfactorily without the backing of either deductive or inductive reasoning' and that 'the possibility of arguing for or against [philosophical statements] in these ways' is what 'guarantees' their distinctive meaningfulness (ibid., pp. 146–7). At this point Cohen attempts to draw a boundary. For the other kinds of philosophy he has mentioned proceed, he suggests, without such argument. And in doing so they commit philosophy to becoming nothing but 'a form of poetic monologue or obscurantist mystery-mongering' (ibid., p. 147).

At this crucial juncture Cohen purports to support his view with a reference to (but not a quotation from) Jacques Derrida apparently confessing himself to 'detest discussion, subtleties, and ratiocinations' (ibid., p. 146). Unfortunately, an examination of the passage to which we are referred seems not to support Cohen's imputation. The passage in question is drawn from a (more or less parenthetical) discussion in which Derrida is explaining the source of the title of a section of his essay 'Signature Event Context'. The section in question addresses the topic of those phenomena of language which the Oxford philosopher J. L. Austin had called 'parasitic' or 'non-serious' (uses of language including stage recitation, quotation, jokes and soliloquy). In the parenthetical discussion, Derrida points out that his section title 'Parasites. Iter, Of Writing: That It Perhaps Does Not Exist' is itself a kind of parasite, being a cryptic citation of the title of Descartes's Fifth Meditation 'On the Essence of Material Things; And Likewise of God [*et iterum de Deo*], That He Exists'. Derrida then poses the following more or less anonymous objection to himself for doing such a thing:

> In view of this parasitism, effected *in* and *by* a discourse on parasitism, are we not justified in considering the entire chapter, the entire discussion of Austin, as only an exercise in parody designed to cause serious philosophical discourse to skid towards literary play? Unless, that is, this seriousness were already the parasite of such play, a situation which could have the most serious consequences for the serious. But – one may enjoin – if he has discussed Austin solely in order to play games with Descartes' titles, it's not serious and there is no theoretical issue worthy of discussion: he is evading the discussion. This might be true: I detest discussions, their subtleties and ratiocinations. But I still have to ask myself how it can be explained that such a frivolous game, doing its best to avoid discussion, could have involved and fascinated other 'philosophers' (from the very first day on), responsible theoreticians aware of being very serious and assuming their discourse? (Derrida, 1988, p. 84)

I assume that none of this is unproblematically presentable as 'Derrida's view'. Indeed, it should be clear that the first hypothesis proposed in this passage belongs precisely to the gulf-seeker; one who wants to condemn Derrida as one of those philosophically irresponsible authors who 'play games' and seek merely literary effects: it is not worthy of discussion and does not deserve of even argued dissent. And, of course, if Derrida himself entertained that suggestion what could explain it better than the possibility or hypothesis ('this might be true') that he 'detests discussions, their subtleties and ratiocinations'? But it does not seem plausible to suppose that the suggestion is being seriously proposed. (Had Derrida said: 'This is true: I detest . . .', one might have had to read this passage differently.) So, we are thrown back to explain why supposedly 'responsible theoreticians' who *do* think that Derrida's work is just 'a frivolous game' which 'avoids all discussion' are moved (as many have been) to oppose it, apparently 'so seriously'. 'Who', Derrida asks (seriously or non-seriously?) 'is responsible here?' The one who claims to be involved with a subtle and serious citation of Descartes and who asks questions about philosophical seriousness, or the one who seriously involves himself with work he considers to be a frivolous game?

While this passage cannot be supposed to support Cohen's reference, neither will Derrida's complex use of irony find adherents everywhere. Nevertheless, I challenge anyone to find in this passage Cohen's Derrida; someone who opposes 'the possibility of arguing for or against' philosophical statements. What I find, by contrast, is someone who is tired of being tarred with just such a brush. A gesture which Cohen repeats, ironically with Derrida's own ironic words.

The essay on Austin discussed in this passage is of particular significance for the present discussion, for it is part of one of those supposedly 'sterile' occasions in which the two sides of the supposedly philosophically divided philosophical community 'exchange criticisms' – but that view of the debate is far from compulsory. That is, one is neither forced or obliged to think of the names 'Austin' and 'Derrida' as representing two prominent philosophical traditions engaged (at last) in a warring (or sterile) exchange. Significantly, Derrida says as much himself:

Among the many reasons that make me unqualified to represent a 'prominent philosophical tradition', there is this one: I consider myself to be in many respects quite close to Austin, both interested in and indebted to his problematic. This is said in ['Signature Event Context'] very clearly. (ibid., p. 38; see also pp. 13, 14, 19 and 85)

Thus, like Merleau-Ponty, Derrida neither seeks nor claims to find a great distance between his work and Austin's. Teasing the reader bent on finding such a gulf, when and where Derrida *does* contest and take issue with Austin's theoretical presuppositions he explicitly identifies them with what he calls 'the most central presuppositions of the *Continental* metaphysical tradition . . . from Kant to Husserl' (ibid., p. 38). In so far as this suggestion acknowledges the presence of the contemporary division it does so only to resituate it – or, rather, to indicate its essential non-pertinence to his philosophical dispute with Austin. Indeed, Derrida goes so far as to suggest that, at bottom, 'what these "fronts" [namely, "Austin" and "Derrida"] represent, what weighs upon them both . . . are forces of a *non-philosophical* nature' (ibid., p. 38).

Everything that has been reviewed thus far speaks in favour of this suggestion. What holds the current analytical and Continental 'fronts' apart are not diverging philosophical presuppositions or commitments but, for example, the deeply unphilosophical polemics of 'gulf-seekers', polemics in which the fact of division is urged and insisted upon rather than argued for or demonstrated. Like Merleau-Ponty in his response to Ryle, Derrida suggests that it is Austin's 'analytical' defender John Searle who 'produces' and 'initiates' the scene of confrontation, not one which he (Derrida) finds there: 'if there is a confrontation, is it not provoked by [Searle's] "Reply"?' (ibid., p. 35).

The suggestion is, then, that the (undeniable) division in the contemporary philosophical culture is not an essentially *philosophical* rift. If that is right, as I think it is, then what needs explaining is not what is distinguishingly different about 'Continental philosophy', but rather how there came to be heirs of philosophy who call themselves 'analytical philoso-

phers' and who cut themselves off, supposing themselves to be a world apart from the rest of the Western philosophical community. In my view, to understand this we need to turn away from Dummett and Cohen's *idealised* history of thoughts and towards an account of 'what has been said' by self-naming 'analytical philosophers' which sees their work of words as riven by 'complicated patterns of source and influence' which can never be wholly abstracted away. This 'real' analysis of analytical philosophy is not the story of 'external influences' on 'what has been said' but of what English philosophers hailed as the 'revolution in philosophy' in the 1950s, a revolution which, though it called itself 'linguistic', was never a purely linguistic event. It is to this that I will now turn.

The end of the tour: revolution in England

Both Dummett and Cohen suppose that an account of what distinguishes analytical from Continental philosophy can be given in exclusively philosophical and conceptual terms. While I am sympathetic to the idea that it is thoughts and not thinkers that we need to focus on, it seems clear that neither Dummett nor Cohen establishes their views satisfactorily. In my view, the reason for this lies, at least in part, in their questionable assumption that propositional content ('what has been said') can be determined independently of the historico-cultural context of actual speech-acts. Can we really achieve an adequate grasp of Ryle's discussion of Husserl's philosophy if we do not co-ordinate his utterances with, say, British cultural responses to the War against Germany? How else are we to read remarks about 'claims to Führership' with any rigour?

Having said this, however, I do not want to imply that the modern category of Continental philosophy can, or should, be understood in wholly non-philosophical or non-conceptual terms either. Indeed, as I have suggested, I think that it has a classically philosophical significance. And this is because I see the post-War articulation in Britain of the idea of the 'Continental philosopher' as tied to a distinctively philosophical figuration, a figure which has, since ancient Greek times, permeated and haunted the philosophical imagination; namely, that of the

Sophist. In what follows I will offer a sketch of this philosophically figured history.

After the Second World War, the development and professionalisation of philosophy at English universities had become so pronounced that the (now predominantly young) personnel began to talk of a 'revolution in philosophy'. A history of this revolution was also emerging, and it told of the emphatic rejection of distinctively *foreign* ideas. Why this was so finds its classic 'insider' articulation in Geoffrey Warnock's *English Philosophy Since 1900*. Published in 1958, Warnock's book appeared at a time when those who adhered to the name of analytical philosophy had become *the* dominant figures in academic philosophy in English universities. Warnock's argument gives a lively and vigorous historical expression to, and justification of, that hegemony. At the heart of that argument is an image of English philosophy which would not have been recognised only a quarter of a century earlier, but which is, to this day, a central part of analytical philosophy's self-conception. According to Warnock, 'most philosophy written in English [in the twentieth century] has been, for better or worse, and I shall not here say which, something vastly unlike most philosophy in other languages' (Warnock, 1958, p. 14). This idea of a 'vast' difference, is, of course, the putative philosophical rift with which we are now familiar. That Warnock's apparent judiciousness concerning the division ('for better or worse') is disingenuous is evident from the tone of his brief discussion of the supposed exception to this state of affairs; the pre-revolutionary, *fin-de-siècle* movement of British Idealism, the British philosophical movement which uniquely was *not* 'vastly unlike most philosophy in other languages', the British philosophical movement with which the new historical narrative begins and against which the revolution is launched.

In marked contrast to his treatment of the British philosophers who he considers 'most important', Warnock does not regard it as necessary to actually present or discuss any of the Idealists' writings. Instead, he considers it 'enough' to characterise them simply as advancing 'highly and ambitiously metaphysical' claims about 'Reality' (ibid., p. 6). For a reading of their thoughts Warnock substitutes an attack on what he calls their 'characteristic manner of writing', confidently castigating their 'highly coloured rhetorical dress' (ibid.). In what is, rhetorically speaking, a rather thin veneer of objectivity, we are informed that a reader 'attached to the presently prevailing mode, and with the courage of his convictions . . . might well find the style of the Idealists almost unbearable' (ibid., p. 6). Bosanquet, for example, 'wrote sometimes with an air of vague high seriousness, in which the serious intent was almost completely muffled by the vagueness. And in the writings of the lesser men solemnity and unclarity seem to rise not seldom to the pitch of actual fraud' (ibid.). Similarly, Bradley's 'opinions' depended for their 'persuasive force' not on 'the relatively unimportant trappings of argument' but the 'artifice of their presentation' (ibid., p. 7).

What is so striking about this kind of dubious, and frankly indefensible, form of unsupported criticism is that it is precisely characteristic of the 'gulf-seeking' attacks on 'Continental philosophy' examined earlier. And this, I suggest, is no accident. For the fate of British Idealism is precisely what precipitated the focus on 'Continental philosophy' which we can still see today. The coming-into-view of this focus is nicely captured by a crucial aspect of Warnock's account; namely, that behind the 'ambitiously metaphysical' claims and 'vivid, violent, and lofty imprecision' of this species of 'British philosophy' lay 'German influences'. And these influences were, he states, 'very much an alien import' (ibid., p. 9).

The 'alien' status here is finely balanced between a national and a philosophical moment. And it will stay that way. In this irreducibly polysemic voice, Warnock declares that the philosophical movement of Idealism in Britain was never *really* 'British' anyway. Indeed, British philosophy was, he suggests, not long occupied with such 'strange things' before it freed itself from what the Idealists had called 'the main stream of *European* thought' and returned to what Warnock called 'the main stream of *British* thought' (ibid., p. 9).

At home, Warnock later revealingly reflected, the 'real campaign' (the expulsion/exclusion of Idealism) was already over' by 1948 (Warnock, 1976, p. 51). Henceforth, what English philosophy had for some time designated as 'Continental philosophy' begins to take on the role of that hated species of philosophy which is 'not deserving even of argued dissent'. 'Continental philosophy' in its current sense was thus born. Figured as 'exotic', 'alien', 'strange', 'vague', 'rhetorical' and 'literary', this was the supposed mainstream of thought in 'mainland Europe as distinguished from the British Isles'. In short, this was distinctively 'Continental' thought. As 'British' philosophy came to its healthy analytical senses, 'Continental' influences were expelled and were supposed, where at all possible, to be avoided.

Were they avoided, through? As we have seen, it cannot be denied that some of the most powerful and pervasive influences on English-language philosophy in the twentieth century were precisely 'Continental' in origin. The picture of British philosophy coming home is thus never going to be, cannot be, convincing. Moreover, even its self-imposed insularity has never completely stopped analytically trained philosophers from engaging with writers in the supposedly 'Continental' camp. In fact, recent developments in the teaching of philosophy at British universities (particularly outside 'the older universities') suggests that the gulf-seeking rhetoric of the post-War period is now on the decline. This is nicely illustrated by the Warwick University philosophy department. Today, Warwick has one of the most wide-ranging and adventurous syllabuses in Britain, but as recently as 1972 it was otherwise. In its prospectus of that year it made the following statement:

> The courses at Warwick are those which would be recognised in universities throughout the English-speaking world, and we would expect our graduates to be equipped to deal with the kinds of discussions going on in the graduate schools of Oxford, Harvard or Canberra. They would, however, be in some difficulty in the Sorbonne, the University of Moscow, or a Zen Buddhist monastery. You should apply to the latter institutions, rather than to ourselves, if you have no desire to study within the broad tradition represented by such writers as Russell, Wittgenstein, Carnap, Popper, Quine, Ryle, Ayer, Austin and Strawson. (Cited in Sayers, 1985, p. 185)

The selection of unthinkables, the Sorbonne, Moscow and Zen, is of course a (by now familiar) caricature, but nevertheless it accurately reflects the kind of work which was – which it was thought, *must* – be excluded by professional philosophy. It should now be clearer why 'Continental philosophy' became the tag for that which must be excluded. But what perhaps remains unclear is analytical philosophy's *emphasis* on it. As I have indicated, I think that this can be explained. Derrida was, I think, quite right to say, in the context of his sometimes acrimonious exchange with Searle, that 'no one will be astonished when I observe that [the Sophists] haunt our present debate' (Derrida, 1988, p. 42). For this is the very image of that 'incorporation' which is philosophy's own, the very image of that which is *philosophically foreign to philosophy*, that which threatens philosophy from within, and so *must* be excluded. In virtue of the particular circumstances of its emergence, English-language philosophy in the post-War decades situated that philosophically 'foreign' thinking as that mode of nationally 'foreign' philosophy which had, by the 1950s, been almost completely 'expelled' by the 'revolution'. Thus, 'Continental philosophy' became the insider's own outsider, and was represented in a convincing but free-floating story of a philosophical rift in contemporary philosophy. However, as we have seen, this has not been a well-told tale. This is not *simply* because work identified as 'Continental philosophy' is not so very different to, and possesses qualities supposedly definitive of, its 'analytical' relation (although I would strongly suggest that, as Dummett found in his reading of Husserl, this is normally the case) but, more importantly, because the very process, or becoming, of the designation and distinction involved a *false personification* of philosophy's own *interminable possibility* – the possibility of failure most famously figured as Sophistry. Sadly its effect occasioned the realisation of just that possibility: at defining moments analytical philosophy has been able to fail as philosophy. This, I believe, is what happens when analytical philosophers condemn thinkers as irrational and obscurantist without taking the trouble to read and argue with them.

The personification of an internal possibility as an 'expelled' (and literally) foreign body gave analytical philosophy the false assurance that it was, essentially, 'healthy' philosophy. Ironically then, its very sense of health, the sanguine confidence in its certain possession of 'rigour and honesty and clarity', lives off an essentially non-logical exclusion. Perhaps the assumption of a radical gulf will not survive for too much longer. Perhaps what is needed is a more open mind. A more open *Mind*. Now there's a thought. (In an article in the centenary number of *Mind* J. N. Findlay complained that the journal had simply become 'the organ of [the analytic] school' (Findlay, 1976, p. 60). He hoped that it would gradually revert to 'the catholicity of coverage' which had characterised it in earlier decades, but saw no sign of this (ibid.). The current editor of *Mind*, Mark Sainsbury, has suggested to me in a private communication that the journal 'has been said to be getting narrower rather than broader' in recent years. He states, however, that he 'would bend over backwards to try to discern the value of a submission emerging from a different tradition rather than dogmatically dismiss what is strange'.)

I do not believe that the appeal to the idea of 'analytical philosophy' either has been or is a uniformly bad thing. It is somewhat like the classical, theological idea of the immortal soul: it may, ultimately, be deemed unsatisfactory, but there is no doubt that it has inspired, and continues to inspire, some great, enriching and beautiful cultural achievements. Nevertheless, I do hope for a future in which it is not so widely assumed that the highest standards of rigour in argument, precision in analysis, and rationality in debate, are the distinctive preserve of the analytical philosopher alone.

In this Introduction I have tried to explain why there may be something suspect about the very idea of Continental philosophy, and so something suspect about the title of this book. To conclude, let me add a further word of warning, the discussion of which is reserved until the very last article; namely, that the very idea that this book (or any other for that matter) is (or might have been) an 'encyclopedia', strictly so called, is just as suspect. As Michal Ben-Naftali notes in the final paragraph of the final article, and thus in the final paragraph of the *Encyclopedia* 'as a whole', the very idea of covering or grasping a 'whole' in this kind of context is an illusion. Here, as elsewhere, 'There will always be, there has always already been, a space left untouched, untouchable, the recognition of which may be even more intensely felt during the very rare graceful moments of encounter'.

I hereby leave and commend this encounter to you.

Bibliography

References and further reading

Black, J. (1992), *The British Abroad: The Grand Tour in the Eighteenth Century*, Bath: Ian Sutton Publishing.

Cohen, L. J. (1986), *The Dialogue of Reason: An Analysis of Analytical Philosophy*, Oxford: Clarendon Press.

Cooper, D. E. (1994), 'Analytical and Continental philosophy', *Proceedings of the Aristotelian Society*, XCIV.

Derrida, J. (1988), *Limited Inc.*, Evanston: North Western University Press.

Dummett, M. (1993), *Origins of Analytical Philosophy*, London: Duckworth.

— (1996), with Fabrice Pataut, *Philosophical Investigations*, 19:1.

Engel, P. (1995), Review of M. Dummett, *Origins of Analytical Philosophy*, *Philosophical Quarterly*, 45:179.

Findlay, J. N. (1976), 'Mind under the Editorship of David Hamlyn', *Mind*, LXXXV.

Glock, H. J. (1989), Dummett on the Roots of Analytical Philosophy; review of Michael Dummett, *Ursprung der Sprachanalytischen Philosophie*, *Mind* 98, 646–9.

Hare, R. M. (1960), 'A School for Philosophers', *Ratio*, II.2.

Hilbert, C. (1974), *The Grand Tour*, London: Hamlyn.

Kemp, G. (1995), Review of M. Dummett, *Origins of Analytical Philosophy*', *Journal of the History of Philosophy*, 33:4.

Lowe, E. J. (1994), Review of M. Dummett, *Origins of Analytical Philosophy*, *Philosophy*, 69.

Merleau-Ponty, M. (1992), *Texts and Dialogues*, eds H. Silverman and J. Barry, New York: Humanities Press.

Mohanty, J. N. (1984), 'Dummett, Frege and Phenomenology', *Journal of the British Society for Phenomenology*, 15:1.

Monk, R. (1993), Review of M. Dummett, *Origins of Analytical Philosophy*, *The Independent*, 7 August 1993.

— (1996), 'Bertrand Russell's Brainchild', *Radical Philosophy*, 78.

Passmore, J. (1968), *A Hundred Years of Philosophy* (second edition), London: Penguin.

Rée, J. (1993), 'English Philosophy in the Fifties', *Radical Philosophy*, 65.

Ryle, G. (1971), 'Phenomenology versus *The Concept of Mind*', *Collected Papers*, London: Hutchinson.

Sayers, S. (1985), *Reality and Reason*, Oxford: Blackwell.

Smith, B. et al. (1992), 'Derrida Degree: A Question of

Honour', from a letter to *The Times*, Saturday, 9 May, London.

Strawson, P. F. (1959), *Individuals: An Essay in Descriptive Metaphysics*, London: Methuen.

— (1992), *Analysis and Metaphysics: An Introduction to Philosophy*, Oxford: Oxford University Press.

Tomlin, E. W. F. (1960), 'Mr Hare's Paper: A Rejoinder', *Ratio*, III:1.

Warnock, G. (1958), *English Philosophy Since 1900*, Oxford: Oxford University Press.

— (1976), '*Mind* under Gilbert Ryle's Editorship', *Mind*, LXXXV.

Williams, B. (1996), 'Contemporary Philosophy: A Second Look', in N. Bunnin and E. P. Tsui-James (eds), *The Blackwell Companion to Philosophy*, Oxford: Blackwell.

Section One
CLASSICAL IDEALISM

INTRODUCTION

Philip Stratton-Lake

The term idealism has been defined in very different ways. For some, it is identified with Berkeley's thesis that all that exists is minds and ideas. For others, it is defined as the doctrine according to which spiritual values determine the order of the universe. If we accept the first of these definitions we will find that there are very few idealist philosophers in the history of philosophy. Certainly, many philosophers who regarded themselves, and are generally regarded as idealists – for example, Schelling, Hegel and Bradley – will turn out not to be. If we accept the second definition we will find ourselves with the opposite problem, for the view that the world is ordered by spiritual values is one which cuts across the idealist/realist divide. But despite the difficulties of providing a satisfactory definition of idealism, idealists can be characterised as adhering to the view that the knowable world is in some sense mind-dependent; although they do not think that it is dependent upon any individual mind.

The first modern idealist is Berkeley. I have not, however, included Berkeley in this section as his influence on Continental philosophy is negligible. It was Kant, rather than Berkeley, who was the immediate inspiration for the idealist systems of the late eighteenth and nineteenth century. However, although Kant seemed to be familiar with Berkeley, he thought that Berkeley still held on to some basic realist assumptions and hence saw him as a sceptic. I will begin, therefore, with Kant rather than Berkeley.

Kant and Continental philosophy

Kant is often said to be the last point of contact between analytic and Continental philosophy. He is a common point of reference and influence for both traditions, but this cannot be said for his immediate successors, Fichte, Schelling, Hegel and Schopenhauer. Analytic philosophers regard post-Kantian German Idealists as, at best, unimportant, whereas these figures remain pertinent in the Continental tradition. Even where they do not directly influence later Continental philosophers, one can detect strong affinities between them and philosophers such as Heidegger (Schelling), Sartre (Fichte and Hegel), Adorno (Schelling and Hegel) and, to a lesser extent, Habermas (Hegel). Although there is an element of truth in the claim that Kant represents a parting of the ways between the two traditions, there is also at least as much falsehood. It is true that most analytic philosophers today have much more time for Kant than they do for Fichte, Schelling or Hegel, whereas these figures are still seen as important points of reference on the Continent. It would, however, be a great mistake either to exaggerate this claim or to understand it chronologically. The contrast should not be exaggerated as there are many Continental philosophers (Nietzsche, Husserl and Derrida, to mention just three) who are as hostile to the German Idealists as any analytical philosopher. Furthermore, it would be a great mistake to think that up until Kant there was a happy marriage between analytic and Continental philosophy which was ruined in the late 1790s by Fichte. Analytic philosophy did not begin as a distinctive tradition until the beginning of the twentieth century, with the work of Moore and Russell; and even then, they did not regard themselves as working in a very different tradition from what was later to be called the Continental tradition. On the contrary, both Moore and Russell were familiar with and to a certain extent sympathetic to, the work of philosophers such as Brentano and Meinong who were key figures in the development of the Continental tradition. The philosophical movement they saw themselves as opposed to was British Idealism. So although they were not familiar with the work of Fichte and Schelling, they were at least indirectly familiar with Hegel, for analytic philosophy grew out of their rejection of the neo-Hegelianism which was dominant in Britain at the time.

It is sometimes said that what leads analytic philosophers to reject post-Kantian German Idealists is their abandonment of Kant's epistemological standpoint and adoption of traditional metaphysics, or something approaching this, but this claim is also far too simple. For although early analytic philosophers such as Moore and Russell rejected the speculative metaphysics of Hegel and neo-Hegelianism, they were by no means hostile to metaphysics as such. It was not really until the Logical Positivists that a certain hostility to all metaphysics emerged in this tradition, but this view represents merely one position within the analytic tradition. There is nothing distinctive about the analytic tradition as such which makes it hostile to metaphysics. Furthermore, there are many philosophers within the Continental tradition (Kierkegaard, Nietzsche, Heidegger, Derrida) who share the Logical Positivists' hostility to metaphysics, albeit for very different reasons, so we should not try to explain the different ways in which the different traditions regard post-Kantian German Idealism simply with reference to metaphysics. It is true that the Logical Positivists regarded the philosophy of Heidegger as well as of the German Idealists as metaphysical, but this was because they had a different, and rather narrow, conception of what it is for a view to be metaphysical.

However, if there is not a sharp parting of the ways between analytic and Continental philosophy with Kant, why is it that analytic philosophers have far more time for Kant than they tend to have for Fichte, Schelling, Hegel or Schopenhauer? The reason for this is, I think, that the German Idealists' rejection of the epistemological standpoint survived in the Continental tradition in a way it did not in analytical

philosophy. Kierkegaard thought that epistemological questions were wholly inappropriate to the most important issues, Nietzsche was simply not interested in these sorts of questions, Husserl suspended such questions in his phenomenological bracketing and Heidegger thought that it was a scandal that the most basic epistemological questions were ever asked in the first place. It is the epistemological slant to Kant's philosophy which is the source of his appeal to analytic philosophers but which is seen in a negative light by many post-Idealist Continental philosophers. Although the existential phenomenologists followed Kant in the respect that they felt that philosophical reflection should constrain itself to appearances, they followed the German Idealists in so far as they abandoned the Kantian notion of the thing in itself conceived of as some ineffable thing behind appearances, and in the respect that they wanted to subordinate epistemology to ontology. In this sense their antipathy to metaphysics took a different form to the Logical Positivists. The Logical Positivists took the methodology of the empirical sciences as their model, whereas classical phenomenologists aimed to found the scientific understanding of the world in a pre-theoretical, everyday understanding of the world which could only be accessed by the phenomenological method. This is most apparent in Heidegger's early work which, despite its many differences from the project of German Idealism, shared the aim of showing how the basic concepts and dichotomies of empirical science and epistemology are founded in something to which these concepts and distinctions are inapplicable. For the German Idealists this something is the Absolute: for Heidegger it is Being-in-the-world.

Kant's transcendental idealism

Given the importance of the move away from epistemology to metaphysics in German Idealism we need to see how this transition occurred. Indeed, since the German Idealists saw themselves as developing, if not completing, Kant's philosophy, how this move took place may seem rather puzzling. How did Kant's thoroughly epistemological orientation become transformed into speculative metaphysics in the course of its development?

The fundamental thesis of Kant's epistemology is that our knowledge can only ever be of appearances, never of things regarded as they are in themselves. Things in themselves are things thought of as completely mind-independent in the sense that they are thought of in complete abstraction from our knowledge of them, and of the necessary conditions of our knowledge. Appearances, on the other hand, are objects considered as constituted by the ways in which our knowledge of them is constrained. The mistake all earlier philosophers had made, according to Kant, was that they thought of the object of knowledge as completely independent of any knowledge we might have of it. For this reason he described them as transcendent or transcendental realists. But if the object of knowledge, or rather, the *aim* of knowledge is thought of in accordance with transcendent realism, then this aim will be unachievable, for we cannot know anything about objects which are so alien from our cognition. We could only know the world as it is in itself with the aid of something like God, but how do we know that God, another transcendent entity, or thing in itself, exists? This was the problem which confronted Descartes. He held that knowledge aims at things as they are in themselves, and so needed God to guarantee that his representations of the world corresponded with an utterly mind-independent reality. However, his attempts to prove that God exists are generally regarded as a failure, and with this the attempt to hold on to the view that we can have knowledge of a completely mind-independent reality fails also.

Thus, Kant held, there are only two options for the transcendental realist: he can either dogmatically assert knowledge claims, or become a sceptic. The dogmatist simply asserts knowledge claims about the world without any warrant, for any warrant he could possibly have would only justify knowledge of appearances, not of things in themselves. The sceptic still holds on to the view that the aim of knowledge is, or should be, the thing in itself, but has come to realise that this aim is unattainable. The sceptic does not, therefore, break with the basic assumption of transcendent realism, but is simply a transcendent realist who has come to acknowledge the sceptical implications of this assumption. Transcendent realism, therefore, leads either to dogmatism or scepticism.

Kant's radical suggestion was to abandon the basic assumption of transcendent realism. Instead of conceiving of knowledge as oriented towards radically mind-independent entities, we should, he suggested, see how we get on on the assumption that the object of knowledge is determined by our knowledge of it. This is his famous philosophical Copernican Turn; but what does it mean to say that the object of knowledge is determined by our knowledge of it? To think of the object in this way is to think of it as determined by the ways in which it *must* be represented by beings for whom the content of knowledge must be empirically given. The content of knowledge is 'given' for any mind which does not create this content merely by thinking it. For us, at least, therefore, the content of knowledge must be given. Although I could choose to look in one direction or another, I cannot choose what it is I will see when I do this. In this respect, then, our knowledge is passive, but although there is an element of passivity in our knowledge, our knowledge is not merely passive, as the empiricists thought, for knowledge involves judgement. We must order the manifold of given representations by subsuming them under the relevant concepts; and in this respect, the mind is active in knowledge. What then are the ways in which we must represent the object of knowledge, that is, empirical objects?

Kant calls these necessary conditions of knowledge the forms of intuition, and the categories of the understanding. There are only two forms of intuition: space and time. We can only individuate objects in the external world spatially, and can only represent anything as temporally ordered. Once we abandon transcendent realism this means that the objects of knowledge must be either spatio-temporal objects, if this is knowledge of the external world, or merely temporal, if this is self-knowledge (knowledge about one's beliefs, imaginings, etc.).

There are four types of categories: quality, quantity, relation and modality. Each of these types contains in turn three categories, the most important of which are the categories of causality, unity, reality and existence. The categories are ways in which a manifold of given representations must be synthesised if we are to have knowledge. Since we must think of the object of knowledge in these ways, it follows from Kant's transcendental idealism that objects to which these categories apply must have these qualities; for example, the quality of being causally related to each other. However, they only have these qualities in so far as they are regarded as possible objects of knowledge, that is, as appearances.

The forms of intuitions and the categories of the understanding do not exhaust the necessary conditions of knowledge. There is one further precondition, which Kant calls the transcendental unity of apperception. This notion does not signify self-knowledge, but the ability to self-ascribe any of our mental states to a numerically identical individual. This ability must be assumed if there is to be any sort of knowledge whatsoever, for it is the transcendental unity of apperception which is the condition of the possibility of any sort of synthesis (judgement) of a manifold, and hence, any sort of empirical knowledge.

This then is Kant's transcendental idealism. It is the view that we can know nothing whatsoever about things in themselves, but only things as they appear to us. Appearances are understood as objects determined by the ways in which we must represent and think about them. These necessary conditions are the forms and categories, which are, in turn ultimately grounded in the unity of apperception.

German Idealism

Kant's immediate followers were dissatisfied with two aspects of his idealism. The first is the notion of the thing in itself. The second is the lack of systematicity. The thing in itself was regarded as a dogmatic remnant from transcendent realism which was incompatible with the general idealist thrust of Kant's thought. Kant's idealism was regarded as lacking systematicity in the sense that it did not begin with a self-evident first principle and derive everything from this. It is true that Kant arrived at an ultimate condition of knowledge in the transcendental unity of apperception, but what was required by his followers was that philosophy *begin* with something like this principle. Otherwise, concepts and distinctions will be introduced before they have been accounted for.

Reinhold was the first to attempt to systematise Kant by treating what he called the 'proposition of consciousness' as basic – that is, the claim that in consciousness the subject distinguishes the representation both from the subject and from the object, but at the same time, relates it to both.

Although Fichte was critical of this attempt to systematise Kant, he was sympathetic to the aim. In place of the proposition of consciousness Fichte proposed that the basic principle is what he called the absolute ego. Consciousness is always consciousness of something by a subject. We can, however, separate out the constitutive elements of consciousness in reflection. This gives rise to two possible ultimate principles; we can either explain consciousness in terms of the activity of the objective world upon it, or explain the objective world in terms of the activity of consciousness. Spinoza took the first option but Fichte felt this to be incompatible with our consciousness of freedom. Only the second option fits with this. The ultimate principle in terms of which all things are explained is thus consciousness. But the ego, or consciousness which constitutes the fundamental principle of philosophy, is not some individual consciousness (the emergence of individual consciousnesses is part of what will be explained with reference to this principle). Rather, it is consciousness in general, or the absolute ego, which, for Fichte, was pure activity. This consciousness in general is not self-conscious. None the less it is a striving to become self-conscious, and in particular, a striving to become conscious of its own freedom through moral self-realisation, but in order to become self-conscious it must limit itself by positing something which is not conscious, a not-I. This not-I constitutes Fichte's second principle but a third is needed to resolve the tension which arises between the first and the second, between the absolute ego and the world which is not consciousness. This third principle is that of reciprocal limitation. The first principle is only consistent with the second if we think of the activity of the absolute ego as limited by something which is other than itself, and as limiting this not-I. In this way Fichte aimed to ground the very distinctions between the finite (individual) ego and the objective world; the very terms presupposed by Reinhold's principle of consciousness.

Fichte also aimed to ground the distinction between theoretical and practical philosophy in this way. It is a conception of the ego as limited – that is, as acted upon – by the world which forms the basis of theoretical philosophy, and from which Fichte goes on to deduce the categories and the forms of space and time. It is a conception of the ego as limiting – that is, as acting upon – the world which is basic to practical philosophy, and from which he deduces the principles of right and of ethics. His practical philosophy, however, leads to an infinite striving after an unattainable ideal, for the ego's striving presupposes obstacles against which the ego strives, and gradually overcomes, in its struggle for complete self-transparency. It can, however, never completely succeed in this, as the object-I, the self of whom we are aware in self-consciousness, can never completely be eliminated. This final dichotomy is, in Fichte's view, unsurpassable.

We can see quite clearly in Fichte that the abandonment of the thing in itself and the desire for a kind of foundationalist systematicity led him quickly away from Kant's epistemological standpoint to a form of speculative metaphysics. If Kant is understood as claiming that it is the activity of consciousness which creates, or determines, the world of appearances, and one abandons the idea that there is anything apart from appearances, that is, no thing in itself, one will be committed to the view that the activity of consciousness is the origin of everything. And if one insists on a fundamental principle from which to begin, then one will begin with this activity and derive everything from it, including the individual consciousness. Fichte does not, however, completely ignore the epistemological question of how we know of the existence of this absolute activity. He claimed that, in reflection, we can become conscious of it through intellectual intuition – that is, by means of an immediate, non-empirical knowledge. Kant denied the possibility of intellectual intuition for finite rational beings like us; but, Fichte maintained, his view was consistent with Kant's in this respect. He saw Kant's denial of intellectual intuition as a denial of the view that we can know the external world as it is in itself, and he was not denying this. All Fichte claimed is that consciousness can become aware of its own activity, not of some transcendent world, by means of intellectual intuition.

Schelling was the next significant figure in the development of German Idealism. In his early work (which he wrote when he was only nineteen) he was heavily influenced by Fichte. None the less, Schelling was critical of Fichte right from the start. He felt that, just as Spinoza had illegitimately absolutised the object of knowledge, so Fichte had illegitimately absolutised the subject. Consequently, both systems of philosophy were one-sided and in that respect inadequate. Schelling was, however, convinced that the system had to be idealist, as it would otherwise fail to acknowledge Kant's insights, but if it was to avoid Fichte's one-sidedness, it must not be a subjective idealist system. So, instead of treating the absolute ego as basic, Schelling used the bare notion of the absolute, or absolute indifference. The absolute is still regarded as a teleological system orientated towards self-knowledge, but nature is not regarded as a mere means or instrument to the ego's end of achieving self-consciousness. Rather, the conscious individual is regarded as the evolutionary end of nature. The absolute, however, cannot be regarded as the absolute subject or as the absolute object, but as the absolute indifference of subjectivity and objectivity. The absolute, for Schelling is logically prior to the subject-object dichotomy, or any other distinction for that matter. These distinctions arise only in reflection, that is, for conceptual thought. None the less, Schelling held that we are, in some sense, aware of the absolute. But, following Fichte, he also held that the absolute can only be apprehended in an intellectual intuition. Only in this way can the absolute indifference of subjectivity and objectivity be apprehended.

Schelling's early philosophy forms the essential link from Fichte to Hegel. It would, however, be a mistake to think of him as important solely as an intermediary between Kant and Fichte, on the one hand, and Hegel, on the other. In his later philosophy, what is often referred to as his positive philosophy, he raised important criticisms of Hegel's system. None the less, it is clear that Hegel stands to Schelling as Schelling's early work stood to Fichte. Indeed, up until the publication of his monumental *Phenomenology of Spirit* in 1807 Hegel was regarded simply as a disciple of Schelling.

Like Schelling, Hegel thought Fichte was right to attempt to find a unifying principle for the Kantian system, but criticised him for conceiving of this as an isolated foundation which was left behind as his system moved into the set of Kantian oppositions. He believed that this model implied that these dichotomies could not be reconciled. In this respect, he saw Schelling as an advance on Fichte, for he attempted to hold on to the absolute unity of thought and the system. None the less, Hegel could not follow Schelling in conceiving of the absolute as absolute indifference, or as a kind of mystical night in which all cows are black, as he put it in his *Phenomenology of Spirit*. Furthermore, he felt that, despite his advances over Fichte, Schelling still conceived of the absolute as a kind of impenetrable reality behind its determinate manifestations, and hence still failed to reconcile the infinite (the absolute) and the finite (its determinate manifestations).

Hegel did not treat the relation between the absolute and its manifestations as Schelling did – in analogy to the relation between a disease and its symptoms, that is, as distinct phenomena or entities. Rather, for him, the absolute *is* both its self-manifestation and the process of self-manifesting. Like Schelling, Hegel saw this process as oriented towards the absolute's grasping itself both as substance and as subject – that is, as spirit. Unlike Schelling, however, this absolute knowledge is nothing other than knowledge of the process of the absolute's self-unfolding. The understanding is an inadequate tool for attaining this knowledge, for it tends inevitably to fix concepts into oppositions, and hence fails to see how these supposed opposites pass into each other. What is needed, therefore, is a type of dialectical thinking which can only be attained by reason that is able to see the internal relations of concepts – that is, how one passes into the other, and vice versa. It is only by means of reason that the identity in difference of these concepts can be grasped, and by means of which the absolute can attain knowledge of itself.

The moving force for such thinking is contradiction. It is contradiction which forces us to move on to higher and higher levels of understanding until all oppositions are overcome and the identity in difference is grasped. Thus, for example, in his *Phenomenology* we see how, at each stage of its development (consciousness, self-consciousness and reason), the mind is compelled to move on to the next stage. The concrete particularity which is sought in sense certainty is lost as soon as we attempt to articulate this in language. This pushes consciousness on to the level of perception, where the thing is regarded as the bearer of its properties, but the fact that no unity can be found at the level of sense forces consciousness on to the level of the understanding, where sensory phenomena are regarded as the manifestation of hidden forces. It then turns out that the transphenomenal world is really the world of the understanding, so that consciousness is forced to turn back on itself. This is the stage of self-consciousness. This stage first takes the form of desire which utilises objects but it breaks down with the attempt to utilise another subject in Hegel's famous master-slave dialectic. This breakdown forces consciousness on to retreat to the inner realm; a stage Hegel calls Stoic Consciousness but this form is unstable because it ignores concrete relations and merely adopts a negative attitude to everything external. It thus passes into Sceptical Consciousness, and then to Unhappy Consciousness, in which the master-slave relation is internalised.

The oppositions within Unhappy Consciousness are resolved only in the move from self-consciousness to spirit. Hegel's dialectic then sets off again on its final stage through moral consciousness, religious consciousness and finally to reason, which is the synthesis of consciousness and self-consciousness. From this standpoint, Nature, the finite, is seen as the objectification of infinite spirit, and the identity in difference is grasped. This is already grasped in Religious Consciousness, but in an inadequate, representational form. In Absolute knowledge this identity is grasped in its appropriate, philosophical form.

British Idealism

Hegel's influence after the publication of the *Phenomenology* was enormous. He quickly shed his reputation as a mere disciple of Schelling and went on to completely dwarf Schelling and his reputation.

During his lifetime Hegel's philosophy dominated in German universities; and critics such as Schelling had little effect, but after his death in 1831 his influence began to wane. Although, at first, his followers developed different strands of his thought, internal conflict soon developed, leading gradually to the demise of Hegelian philosophy in Germany. There was, however a rebirth of interest in him in Britain in the 1770s. During the first half of the nineteenth century there was little interest or knowledge of what was happening in Germany. This changed, however, when T. H. Green and E. Caird discovered and embraced the philosophy of Kant and German Idealism, especially that of Hegel.

T. H. Green held that empiricism lead inevitably to the scepticism of Hume, and hence reached a dead-end which British philosophers had simply failed to realise. Consequently, rather than move on to the sort of idealism of Kant and his successors, British philosophers had become bogged down in their empiricist tradition. In order to regenerate philosophy, therefore, we need to move beyond empiricism to German Idealism. Green drew on both Kant and Hegel in constructing his idealistic view of the world. For him the world is mind-dependent in the sense that material entities need to be related to each other in various ways, and this is only conceivable as the work of the intellect. The world was not, however, regarded as dependent upon any individual mind, but upon an infinite intellect in which particular minds participate. This infinite intellect is God. Caird, like Green, held that the ultimate reality is God, but conceived of the world in more dynamic, dialectical terms. For him reality is an evolutionary, dialectical process in which reality moves to higher and higher levels through a process of contradiction and synthesis.

Although both Green and Caird generated an interest in German Idealist philosophy, it was F. H. Bradley who was the most important and influential figure among the British Idealists of the late nineteenth century. Bradley thought that reality could not be understood either as intellect or as God. It cannot be understood as intellect as this would be to absolutise one side of the opposition between the real and the ideal. It could not be God, because God is a being to whom we can stand in a relation, but

reality is not characterised by the diversity which is presupposed by any relation. He also disagreed with Caird that reality evolves. For Bradley, all change is mere appearance. The absolute, or real, is unchanging and simple. What makes us think that the real involves plurality and change is conceptual thought. Like Kant, Bradley held that the mind imposes its conceptual structure upon reality as it appears. Unlike Kant, however, he conceived of such appearances in the ordinary sense of the word, that is, as mere semblance, and of the noumenal world, what ultimately underpins all experience, as the real world. Reflection reveals, however, that the world as it appears is contradictory. For example, it appears as involving various relations, but reflection reveals that these are impossible because they lead to a vicious infinite regress. Since relations are essential to any pluralist view of the world, if they are illusory, then so is the apparent plurality. All experience is, for Bradley, a mere semblance of a reality which is simple and unchanging. We can, however, by a process of abstraction, encounter the absolute in experience. In reflection we can abstract away the various structures the mind imposes on the real and acquire a glimpse of absolute reality.

One figure who did not have anywhere near the influence Bradley had, but who none the less represents an important position within idealist thought, is J. M. McTaggart. Like Bradley, he argued for the unreality of time and space. He disagreed with Bradley, however, in the respect that he thought that reality is not simple, but involves a plurality of immaterial, atemporal selves who do nothing but perceive one another and themselves. The perceptual relations in which the plurality of selves stand to each other are, at the same time, relations of love. He then goes on to focus on love as the binding force of the universe. His metaphysic strikes one initially as a deeply Christian theory but McTaggart had no place for God in his metaphysics. Indeed, he was unusual amongst the British Idealists in that he was a convinced atheist.

This burst of enthusiasm for speculative idealism in late nineteenth-century Britain was largely exhausted by the turn of the century, and quickly lost ground to a more common-sensical realism, and the analytical techniques introduced by Moore and

Russell. In British Idealism the confidence in speculative metaphysics inspired by German Idealism found its last expression. With its demise the confidence died also. Although an interest in metaphysical questions continued (and still continues) to flourish, speculative metaphysics has never re-emerged as a serious philosophical force.

Schopenhauer's idealism

One figure I have not yet mentioned as he does not fit into the neat chronological narrative I have offered, is Arthur Schopenhauer. Unlike many of the other philosophers I have mentioned, Schopenhauer's thought did not bring him instant recognition. On the contrary, the dominance of his contemporary, Hegel, meant that it was only very late in life that his work attracted the serious attention it deserved. Like the German Idealists, Schopenhauer abandoned Kant's epistemological viewpoint, and adopted a more metaphysical view of his idealism but unlike the German Idealists he wanted to hold on to the thing in itself. Indeed, it is the peculiar twist he gives to this notion which is distinctive of his philosophy and his conception of the world as will and representation.

Following Kant, Schopenhauer maintained that our knowledge of the world can only be of appearances, or as he puts it, only of the world as representation. The world of representation is constituted by the forms imposed upon it by the mind. In general we can know nothing of the underlying reality, or noumenal world. We do, however, have knowledge of this in the case of one representation; the representation of our own body for we are aware of an inner mechanism which moves our body. This inner mechanism Schopenhauer calls will. This will is perpetually striving after what it does not possess but it never comes to rest because, once it has satisfied one desire, it strives after some other object. Dissatisfaction of one sort or another thus characterises human life from beginning to end. There is, however, one exception to this general rule. In aesthetic experience the will's driving force is momentarily quelled. For in aesthetic contemplation we become mere will-less subjects of knowledge.

The will is the noumenal body, or body in-itself.

However, Schopenhauer maintains there cannot be plurality in the noumenal realm, as plurality is the result of the mind's imposing its forms upon the noumenal realm. There is, therefore, plurality only in the world as representation. Yet if the will of which I am aware is *my* will, the will of this individual body, it seems that there are as many things in themselves as there are wills, and hence plurality in the noumenal world after all. The only option, it seems, is to admit solipsism, and maintain that my body is the only body which is also will. Schopenhauer avoids this conclusion by maintaining that the will of my body is one and the same will which is objectified in every other body, indeed, every other thing. Behind every representation stands a single will of which the particular representation is a particular manifestation. He does not, however, go so far as to ascribe consciousness to every representational object. Although will underlies all events in the phenomenal world, it operates differently in different types of entities. In animals it operates as conscious motives, whereas in inanimate objects it operates as an unconscious force.

Although Schopenhauer's philosophy failed to make an immediate impact on the philosophical world, it was later to influence such thinkers as Camus, Freud, Nietzsche and Wittgenstein. None the less, he remains a neglected figure who continues to stand in the shade of his great contemporaries.

Summary

Kant's transcendental idealism was clearly crucial for the various idealistic systems mentioned, but the philosophy of Bradley, Hegel and Schelling is as alien to Kant as it is to many who reject Kant's basic assumptions and starting points. The aim of developing and completing Kant's philosophy led with astonishing speed to a kind of speculative metaphysics which Kant could never endorse. There are, however, certain general affinities amongst the post-Kantian idealists we have discussed. They all held the view that the empirical world is a distorted appearance of some non-empirical reality which in some sense underpins it. This is generally referred to as the absolute, although Fichte calls it the ego, Schopenhauer calls it will, for Hill and Caird it is God, and for McTaggart it is a plurality of perceived and perceiving selves. With the exclusion of McTaggart, the absolute was regarded monistically, as allowing no distinctions, or at least, no absolute distinctions. Furthermore, with a couple of notable exceptions (Green and Bradley) the absolute was regarded as a dynamic force. For Fichte and Schopenhauer, its striving is regarded as never ending, whereas for others it was regarded as having come to an end with the absolute's knowledge of itself; although this end is thought of as achieved in different ways by different idealists. Finally, all the post-Kantian idealists considered here share a faith in the capacity of philosophical reflection to reveal the underlying reality, a faith which has not been repeated since, and which seems unlikely to be repeated. This is not, however, to say that the idealist philosophers considered here are only of historical interest. One need not buy into a complete speculative system in order to find some philosophical insight, or something of philosophical interest; and idealism remains a rich source for even the most metaphysically cautious of philosophers.

Bibliography

References and further reading

Full bibliographical details for the authors discussed in this article can be found listed at the end of the relevant articles.

Behler, E. (ed.) (1987), *The Philosophy of German Idealism: Fichte, Jacobi and Schelling*, New York: Continuum.
Beiser, F. C. (1987), *The Fate of Reason: German Philosophy from Kant to Fichte*, Cambridge, Massachusetts: Harvard University Press.
Copleston, S. J. (1965), *A History of Philosophy*, vols. 6 and 7, New York: Image Books.
Ewing, A. C. (ed.) (1957), *The Idealist Tradition*. Illinois: The Free Press.
Hartmann, N. (1960), *Die Philosophie des Deutschen Idealismus*, Walter de Gruyter: Berlin.
Kroner, R. (1961), *Von Kant bis Hegel* (two volumes), Tübingen: Mohr.
Nauen, F. G. (1971), *Revolution Idealism and Human Freedom: Schelling, Hölderlin and Hegel and the Crisis of Early German Idealism*, The Hague: Nijhoff.
Reill, P. H. (1975), *The German Enlightenment and the Rise of Historicism*, Berkeley: University of California Press.
Russell, B. (1946), *History of Western Philosophy and its Connection with Political and Social Circumstances from the Earliest Times to the Present Day*, London: George Allen and Unwin.
Vesey, G. (ed.) (1982), *Idealism Past and Present*, Cambridge: Cambridge University Press.

1.1

KANT'S TRANSCENDENTAL IDEALISM

Philip Stratton-Lake

It is difficult to imagine what modern philosophy would have been like without Kant. Few accept the unrevised form of his transcendental idealism as it appears in the *Critique of Pure Reason* (hereafter referred to simply as the *Critique*), but his view that the way in which we know objects determines the nature of those objects has had an influence in both the Continental and analytical traditions of philosophy which is difficult to exaggerate. None the less, the central thesis of his transcendental idealism is often misunderstood. Sometimes it is misunderstood in philosophically productive ways, as I think it was with his immediate successors (Fichte, Schelling and Hegel), but this misunderstanding has given rise to a number of unjust criticisms of Kant, many of which vanish once his transcendental idealism is properly understood. What I want to do here is offer a sympathetic interpretation of his transcendental idealism which presents it as a plausible philosophical position, and then show how Kant uses this to resolve some persistent metaphysical problems. Along the way I shall offer reasons for rejecting the traditional interpretation of Kant.

Empirical and transcendental appearances

Kant's transcendental idealism is characterised by the thesis that the object of knowledge is not the thing in itself, but appearances. Things in themselves are objects regarded in complete abstraction from our subjectivity – that is, the way in which we represent them as being, and the conditions of our representing them as being this way. They are, therefore, unknowable by us, for we can only know them by subsuming them under concepts and categories which are alien to them.

Given that things in themselves are understood merely negatively, in contrast to things as appearances, we will not have a clear idea of what a thing in itself is until we have a clear understanding of appearances in Kant. What is a thing as appearance? Kant distinguishes between transcendental and empirical appearances and identifies his own use of the term with the transcendental notion (Kant, 1929 [1781], A45–6). The concept of empirical appearances corresponds to our ordinary use of the term appearance, where this is understood to mean semblance. Thus, one might ordinarily say of a rainbow that it is a mere appearance caused by the refraction of light through rain. The rainbow would then be understood simply as the way in which rain appears, or seems to us under certain conditions. Accordingly, this distinction between appearances and things in themselves is understood as one between different things. Empirically, things in themselves are real, physical objects, while appearances are the mental sensations caused in us by these objects. Kant describes this distinction as empirical because both the raindrops and the rainbow are possible objects of experience. The former is an experience of an outer (physical) object, whereas the latter is the experience of an inner, that is, mental, object.

Kant contrasts his own transcendental distinction between appearances and things in themselves to this empirical distinction. The transcendental distinction is neither one between what seems to be the case and what is the case, nor one between different types of objects. It is, rather, a distinction between objects of possible experience and things which can never be such objects. In the technical sense in which Kant uses the term, appearances are not distorted images of things in themselves, but are simply things regarded as subject to the necessary conditions of our knowledge of them. Things in themselves are understood merely negatively, as things regarded in abstraction from these conditions. The transcendental distinction is not, therefore, one between different objects, but between different ways of regarding one and the same object. To conceive of this distinction as one between different types of objects is to conflate the transcendental with the empirical distinction with which Kant explicitly contrasts it. The empirical distinction between mere sensations in us and the physical causes of these sensations are both appearances for Kant – that is, possible objects of experience. The former is an inner appearance, and the latter an outer appearance. The physical things to which the empirical appearances correspond are spatial objects, and as we shall see, Kant maintains that space is applicable only to certain transcendental appearances.

This distinctive way in which Kant understands the distinction between appearances and things in themselves is obscured by the fact that he uses the terms 'representation' and 'appearance' interchangeably, but just as he uses the notion of an appearance in a technical, transcendental sense, so his use of the notion of a representation must be understood transcendentally. It should not, therefore, be assumed that whenever Kant uses the term 'representation' he is referring to mental states because this concept refers to anything which is a possible object of perception, and not all such objects are in the head.

The distinction between transcendental and empirical appearances allows Kant to distinguish between two different types of idealism and realism (Kant, 1929 [1781], A369ff.). Transcendental realism is the view that the immediate object of knowledge is the (transcendental) thing in itself – that is, an object held to be completely independent of our sensibility and its conditions. Empirical realism is the view that we are immediately acquainted with an external, spatio-temporal world. According to this view the real world is not conceived of as completely mind-independent in the way in which the transcendental realist conceives of it. Rather, the real world is the world of (transcendental) appearances.

Empirical realism is one and the same doctrine as transcendental idealism. Transcendental idealism is the view that we can never know things in abstraction from the conditions of our experience; we can only ever know transcendental appearances and never things as they are in themselves, but the appearances which we know are not simply representations in us. They include outer appearances, that is, spatio-temporal objects. Empirical idealism, however, maintains that we can only know our own mental states, that is, empirical appearances, and can have no immediate knowledge of the things in the physical world to which they may or may not correspond. Kant believes this position to be the inevitable outcome of transcendental realism (ibid., A369). If one maintains that objects exist which are absolutely mind-independent, then one will be driven inexorably to the conclusion that we cannot know them, but can only infer their existence from the representations they cause in us.

These distinctions present the traditional interpretation of Kant, usually referred to as the two-world interpretation, with a serious difficulty. According to this interpretation appearances and things in themselves are understood to be different types of objects. Appearances are mental states; representations, ideas impressions, sensations, sense-data, etc., while things in themselves are something like physical, real or extra-mental objects. Kant is then understood as claiming that unknowable things in themselves (real, physical objects) cause mental representations in us (appearances), and that the physical world – what these representations represent – is constructed by the mind from the sense data available to it. Thus, Kant's claim that we can only ever know appearances, and never things as they are in themselves, is understood as the claim that we can only ever know our mental representations of physical objects, and never the physical objects themselves. Kant is then interpreted as claiming that we should relinquish the aim of knowing the real world and console ourselves with knowledge of our representations of this world.

This interpretation seems simply to conflate Kant's transcendental idealism with the empirical idealism he so clearly rejects. The transcendental realist, according to Kant, aims at knowledge of things as they are in themselves, but inevitably comes to realise that he can never attain such knowledge. He then becomes an empirical idealist, maintaining that we can only ever have knowledge of mental representations caused in us by things in themselves, but without knowing the cause of these representations. Kant thinks that we can only ever know representations, or appearances, but, as we have noted, understands 'appearance' in a technical sense which enables him to maintain that external, physical objects are appearances. The empirical idealist holds that we can only ever know inner appearances, while Kant's transcendental idealism is the doctrine that we can know both inner and outer appearances.

The fact that Kant clearly distinguishes between empirical and transcendental idealism and rejects the former should lead us to reject the traditional interpretation of Kant's idealism. There are further serious objections to this interpretation, of which I list only four. First of all, if what we mean by a physical object is a spatio-temporal object, the identification of things in themselves with physical objects is deeply implausible as an interpretation of Kant. It is a central tenet of his transcendental idealism that space and time are properties only of appearances; and this supports the view that, for Kant, physical objects are not things in themselves, but appearances. Secondly, once it is recognised that Kant does not equate physical objects with things in themselves, the view that appearances are representations of things in themselves loses any credibility. What inner appearances represent are physical, that is, spatio-temporal, objects, and these are not things in themselves, but (outer) appear-

ances. Thirdly, Kant's view that outer appearances are physical objects means that he can only be interpreted as identifying the realm of appearances with the mental realm at the cost of ascribing to him the implausible view that mental representations are spatially extended. Fourthly, according to the two-world interpretation of Kant, things in themselves cause corresponding appearances in us but causality, for Kant, is a category, and hence is only applicable to appearances. In any case, even if things in themselves did cause appearances in us, they could not, according to Kant, be known to do so for we cannot know anything whatsoever about things as they are in themselves, and hence cannot know whether they have causal powers, or, if they do, we cannot know what these are. It is true that there are a number of passages in the *Critique* which seem to support the two-world interpretation – it would be difficult to explain the persistence of this view if there were not – but there is an alternative to the two-world interpretation which can accommodate at least some of these passages. This alternative is usually referred to as the two-standpoint interpretation.

According to this general understanding of transcendental idealism, an object regarded as an appearance, a chair for example, is not held to be a different object from the chair as it is in itself, with the latter conceived of as causing the former in us. Rather, the chair as appearance is understood as being one and the same object as the chair in itself. The chair *qua* appearance is conceived of as the object regarded as subject to the conditions of sensible intuition, space, time, etc., whereas the chair in itself is *one and the same* object regarded in abstraction from these conditions. So understood, transcendental idealism does not commit one to a belief in two ontologically distinct worlds, but to one world which may be regarded from two very different standpoints, rather like the way in which a drawing may be regarded both as a duck and as a rabbit.

In order to achieve a better understanding of Kant's transcendental idealism we need to specify those necessary conditions of experience which are constitutive of objects as appearances. These fall into two groups: the conditions under which an empirical manifold can be given to us, and the conditions under which this manifold can be thought. The former are the forms of space and time, and are described as pure, or *a priori*, intuitions. The latter are the categories of the understanding and transcendental self-consciousness, and are pure, or *a priori* concepts.

Empirical and *a priori* intuitions

Sensibility is the faculty through which empirical intuitions are given. An intuition is described by Kant as an *immediate* relation of knowledge to the object of knowledge (Kant, 1929 [1781], A19). Immediacy here means that this form of knowledge is direct – that is, its relation to the object is not mediated by *judgement*. Kant also describes intuitions as particular. By this he means that the object to which an intuition relates immediately is not a general concept of an object or property, but some particular object or property instance.

We tend to think of intuition as sensible, that is, as an empirical perception, but this way of understanding intuition was not necessarily how it was understood in the rationalist tradition within which Kant was writing. Within this tradition, intuition simply meant immediate knowledge. Thus, intuition could be either sensible or intellectual. The object of a sensible intuition is given empirically. The object of an intellectual intuition, however, is not given but is the result of the spontaneous activity of the understanding. Intellectual intuition is impossible for us, according to Kant. Moreover, we cannot comprehend what it would be like to apprehend the world by means of intellectual intuition. This apprehension would be equivalent to knowing the world as it is in itself. Thus we can add to our understanding of the transcendental distinction between appearance and thing in itself one between the object of sensible intuition, and of intellectual intuition. The conditions of our intuition of outer appearances which Kant gives in the *Critique* are only valid as conditions of *sensible* intuition.

Although intuitions are given from without, Kant wants to claim that there are certain pure, or *a priori*, intuitions. These intuitions are not given empirically, but 'lie ready for the sensations *a priori* in the mind' (Kant, 1929 [1781], A20). As such, these intuitions can be considered apart from all empirical sensation. The claim that intuitions are *a priori* should not be understood as the claim that they can be known prior to any experience. Rather, this claim should be understood simply as stating that these intuitions are necessary and universal conditions for sensible intuition, and hence can be known necessarily to obtain. Kant claims there are only two such intuitions: space and time.

Kant provides two arguments for the *a priority* of space. His first argument involves two distinct claims.

1. Space is a necessary presupposition of the reference of my sensations to something outside *of me*.
2. Space is a necessary presupposition of the representation objects as outside of *one another*.

These claims may appear tautologous – the 'outside' of the 'outside of me' and 'outside of one another' is a spatial term, so all Kant seems to be saying is that space is a necessary condition of spatial relations. This is certainly how it looks at first sight. However, as Henry Allison points out, what Kant means by 'outside of me' is 'distinct from me and my mental states' (Allison, 1983, p. 83). The first claim is therefore better rephrased as: 'Space is a necessary presupposition of the reference of my sensations to an origin *other* than myself'. A similar reconstruction of Kant's meaning can be given for his second claim, that space is the necessary presupposition for our representation of objects as outside one another. This is not the tautological claim that we must presuppose space in order to represent objects as occupying different spaces. Rather, it is the claim that space is a necessary condition of the representation of objects as numerically distinct from each other.

Thus, Kant's *first* argument for the *a priority* of space can be summarised as follows: as the condition of the representation of the reference of my sensations to an origin *other* than myself, and of the representation of objects as numerically distinct from each other, space is prior to these empirical representations. Space is prior not in the temporal sense that it exists prior to any representation of objects, but in the transcendental sense that it is the necessary condition of the possibility of the representation of any objects.

His second argument is fairly straightforward. Here he argues that space is a necessary condition of our intuition of objects on the ground that 'we can never represent to ourselves the absence of space, though we can quite well think it as empty of objects' (Kant, 1929 [1781], A24). Because we cannot represent objects without simultaneously representing them as situated in space, space is a necessary condition of the possibility of experience. In so far as objects are regarded as appearances, space is not only regarded as a necessary condition of experience, but also of the objects experienced.

Whereas space is the form of outer sense, time is the form of inner sense. Kant provides two arguments which closely parallel those for space as a necessary condition of outer sense. In experience objects are represented as existing simultaneously and/or successively. Only on the presupposition of time is this simultaneity and succession possible (ibid., A30). Without time, succession would not be experienced as such, but would be experienced as a contradiction. Imagine a light being turned on. At one moment the light bulb is represented as dull and grey; the next moment it is represented as bright and illuminated. These two different states are temporally separate. However, if it is possible to imagine this scene without time, we would have to attempt to imagine the light bulb as dull and grey *and* as bright and white, but these are exclusive ways of representing the same object. Thus, without the presupposition of time we could not coherently represent change or motion. As Kant puts it; 'only in time can two contradictorily opposed predicates meet in one and the same object, namely, *one after the other*' (ibid., A32).

This shows how time must be prior to inner representations of alteration or motion as the condition of their possibility, but what of our representations of objects which are neither changing nor moving? Do these also presuppose time as their *a priori* condition, or is space sufficient to explain their possibility? Kant maintains that even if no change or motion takes place our representations presuppose time, since these representations must be thought of first as existing at the same time, and second as

existing as unchanging and unmoving during some period of time. Thus, whether or not the representations of inner sense are represented as changing, moving, or simply as existing in an unchanging unmoving state, the form of time is presupposed as their necessary condition. As the necessary condition of representations of inner sense, time is their *a priori* condition.

It seems odd, however, that Kant should limit time to inner sense, that is, to inner appearances, and hence separate it from the external, spatial objects which are simultaneous, changing, moving, etc. We can see why he should say that inner sense is not spatial, and therefore that space is the form of outer sense only. The inner appearance of, for example, a chair, does not literally take up space in our mind in the way in which the real chair occupies a space, but why Kant felt that time is the form only of inner appearance is not clear. One would have expected him to say that time is the form of both inner and outer appearances, whereas space is the form only of the latter.

H. J. Paton suggests that a solution to this puzzle can be found in §6 of the Aesthetic (Paton, 1936, p. 149). Here Kant writes:

> Time is the formal *a priori* condition of all appearances whatsoever. Space, as the pure form of all *outer* intuition, is so far limited; it serves as the *a priori* condition only of outer appearances. But since all representations, whether they have for their objects outer things or not, belong, in themselves, as determinations of the mind, to our inner state; and since this inner state stands under the formal condition of inner intuition, and so belongs to time, time is an *a priori* condition of all appearance whatsoever. It is the immediate condition of inner appearances (of our souls), and thereby the mediate condition of outer appearances. (Kant, 1929 [1781], A34)

Here Kant seems to understand time to be related to objects of outer sense, but only *mediately*. All that is given immediately are our inner states – that is, the temporal stream of our ideas. These temporal relations are then *ascribed* to spatial objects outside of us by means of the categories of the understanding. Thus, Kant can be understood as maintaining not that time only applies to inner representations, but that it applies only immediately to these. He can then be presented with the more plausible view that external objects are not only spatial but also temporal.

However, although this makes sense of how outer objects are conceived of as *both* spatial *and* temporal, it does not seem to fit with his view that the objects of outer and inner sense are *both* immediate objects of perception (Kant, 1929 [1781], A38, A371). This explanation of how time can be predicated of external objects implies that our knowledge of outer appearances is mediated by an apprehension of inner ones. Perhaps his view is that, although time is primarily predicated of inner appearances and only to outer appearances by means of the application of the categories, we are not aware of this first stage, but only of the temporal relations amongst objects once the categories have been applied to the manifold.

Empirical and *a priori* concepts

Space and time are the two necessary conditions of sensibility, but intuitions and their necessary conditions are not sufficient for empirical knowledge. The concepts of the understanding are also necessary. In a famous passage in §1 of the Transcendental Logic, Kant states:

> our nature is so constituted that our *intuition* can never be other than sensible; that is, it contains only the mode in which we are affected by objects. The faculty, on the other hand, which enables us to *think* the object of sensible intuition is the understanding. To neither of these powers may a preference be given over the other. Without sensibility no object would be given to us, without understanding no object would be thought. Thoughts without content are empty, intuitions without concepts are blind. (Kant, 1929 [1781], A51)

Intuitions without concepts would be a mere blind cacophony. By subsuming intuitions under concepts these intuitions are ordered by understanding. Concepts, like intuitions, can be either empirical or *a priori*. *A priori* concepts are called categories. I shall

come to these in a moment. First, I shall explain empirical concepts.

A concept is a rule for synthesising a manifold of intuitions. Concepts relate to their object mediately by means of intuitions. Their relation to their object is mediated by judgement of intuitions in two ways. First, concepts are *formed* by means of judging intuitions through a process of comparison, reflexion and abstraction. For example, the concept of a tree is formed by abstracting the common feature from different trees. Second, concepts are used as a criterion for the recognition of individual things of the same type. This process of recognition is that of judging the manifold of intuitions as falling under a specific concept. Thus, both the formation and the application of a concept is mediated by a judgement of intuitions. For this reason Kant claims that all acts of understanding can be understood as judgements, and understanding itself may be represented as the faculty of judgements (ibid., A69).

However, although empirical concepts are always involved in experience, they are not sufficient for it. In order to distinguish mere sensations in me from objective experience I must be able to apply concepts such as 'reality' and 'cause' which do not have an empirical origin. Kant makes this point in the *Prolegomena* by distinguishing between judgements of perception and judgements of experience (Kant, 1902 [1783], pp. 56–7). Judgements of perception are those which are only subjectively valid. When, for example, I judge that the room is warm I do not expect everyone to agree with my judgement. Nothing is predicated of the object (the room); rather, all that is expressed is that 'it seems warm to me'. Judgements of experience, on the other hand, refer the sensation to the object, and are thus objectively valid. Such judgements do not express the way something seems to me, but the way something is, and hence involve the assumption that everyone should necessarily connect the same perceptions under the same circumstances. Empirical concepts cannot explain the possibility of such universality and necessity. This can be explained only by presupposing *a priori* concepts. Kant calls these *a priori* concepts categories. The categories are thus the condition of the possibility of our experience of (real) objects, for without these we would only be able to say how things seem to us, and never how they are. Given that objects are conceived of as appearances only, that is, as possible objects of experience, the necessary conditions under which we can experience objects are at the same time the condition of the possibility of those objects.

In the chapter Kant refers to as 'the metaphysical deduction' he attempts to discover what categories there are by deriving them from the different types, or forms, of judgement. To subsume a manifold of intuitions under a concept is to synthesise or unite them, but the manifold can be united in different ways, and the forms of judgement as stated by formal logic specify the different ways in which representations can be synthesised. These forms fall under four headings: quantity, quality, relation and modality. Three forms of judgement are listed under each heading to give the following table of judgements:

Quantity
Universal
Particular
Singular

Quality
Affirmative
Negative
Infinite

Relation
Categorical
Hypothetical
Disjunctive

Modality
Problematic
Assertoric
Apodeictic

Kant thought that these forms of judgement constituted a complete list of the ways in which the understanding can unify a manifold. Thus, by attempting to derive the categories from these forms he claimed his list (unlike Aristotle's) will be systematic, and hence exhaustive.

He attempts to derive the categories from the forms of judgement by arguing that each form presupposes a certain category as the condition of its application to a manifold. Thus, for example, he claims that the category of cause and effect is presupposed by hypothetical judgements, because in order to make such judgements we must distinguish between the ground and the consequent, and this assumes a rule (concept) in accordance with

which this distinction is made. In this way, Kant arrives at the following table of categories:

Quantity
Unity
Plurality
Totality

Quality
Reality
Negation
Limitation

Relation
Inherence and subsistence
Causality and dependence
Community

Modality
Problematic
Assertoric
Apodeictic

The Transcendental Deduction

Having derived his list of categories from what he takes to be a complete list of functions of judgement, Kant attempts to provide a transcendental deduction of the categories – that is, to show their objective validity. To show that the categories are objectively valid consists in showing that they are necessary for our experience of any object whatsoever. Despite the fact that the transcendental deduction is in many respects the most important chapter of the *Critique*, it is also the most opaque. There is debate not only over the structure of the argument, but also about what Kant is arguing for. These issues are complicated by the fact that Kant completely rewrote the deduction for the second edition of the *Critique* (this is known as the 'B' deduction, and the first edition version as the 'A' deduction). These different versions are not obviously different presentations of the same argument, but seem to offer different arguments. Consequently, there is some debate over whether the A or B deduction best captures Kant's thought. I shall simply gloss over these debates and present what I take to be a coherent account of the deduction, without arguing that it is the best account, and without pretending that it is the only coherent account.

The A deduction begins by describing the three syntheses which are necessary for empirical knowledge, or experience. These are the syntheses of apprehension, reproduction and recognition.

Although Kant describes these in a way which sometimes suggests that these syntheses take place one after the other, he should not be understood in this way. They should be understood as inseparable and simultaneous aspects of perception, rather than as successive acts.

All the representations which are given to the mind must be brought into a relation to each other. In order for a manifold of representations to be experienced as such they must be 'run through, and held together' (Kant, 1929 [1781], A99). This act of running through and holding together the manifold of representations is what Kant calls the synthesis of apprehension, but in order for me to have experience, as opposed to a disconnected sequence of manifolds, each of which suddenly appears before the mind only to become instantly forgotten, the manifolds of representations given immediately prior to the present one must not only be retained, or remembered, but also brought into an ordered connection with my present manifold. This act of retaining and holding together the manifold of manifolds, as it were, is the synthesis of reproduction, and is carried out by the imagination. The reproductive synthesis is always a synthesis of representations sequent upon one another; 'But in the imagination this sequence is not in any way determined in its order, as to what must precede and what must follow' (ibid., A201). This order is determined by the synthesis of recognition. This is carried out by the understanding and involves subsuming the manifold of representations under both empirical and a priori concepts. Empirical concepts are simply concepts of empirical objects, such as cats, dogs, chairs, tables, etc. To subsume a manifold under an empirical concept, therefore, is to recognise the representation as a representation of, for example, a cat. A priori concepts, on the other hand are not concepts of empirical objects, but are the categories. To subsume a manifold under a category is to refer it to objective relations. Thus, two successive representations may be referred to the objective relation of cause and effect, or may be synthesised as subject and predicate.

Experience thus presupposes the syntheses of apprehension, reproduction and recognition, but these syntheses do not constitute the most basic presupposition of experience and knowledge. Kant states that, 'the concept of combination includes, besides the concept of the manifold and its synthesis, also the concept of the unity of the manifold' (Kant, 1929 [1787], B130). Since Kant uses the notions of synthesis and combination interchangeably, this means that all synthesis presupposes a unity in the manifold. Without this unity, the manifold would not be a manifold at all but would be a plurality of disconnected, isolated intuitions. Unity cannot be *given* with the manifold of intuitions since this unity is the condition of the possibility of these intuitions being represented as a manifold. Hence, the condition of unity must precede the givenness of the manifold as the condition of its possibility. Unity cannot stem from one of the categories, for the category of unity has to be applied to a manifold of intuitions which already possess a unity *as a single* manifold. Thus, the category already presupposes the unity of the given intuitions and cannot be its source. This unity can be grounded only in the identity of the subject in which the manifold is found (ibid., B132). This identical subject is the 'I think' which must necessarily be able to accompany all my representations, which Kant refers to as transcendental self-consciousness, transcendental apperception, or the transcendental unity of apperception.

Every thought of a single complex object presupposes, according to Kant, the thought of the identity of the subject which can think each of the representations contained in this single complex thought. Thus, it is claimed, consciousness of objects presupposes transcendental self-consciousness as its ground of unity; and this self-consciousness constitutes the ultimate condition of the possibility of knowledge. Transcendental self-consciousness is not self-knowledge, because I can only know myself as I appear to myself, and transcendental self-consciousness is not consciousness of the self as it appears, but is purely formal – that is, empty of content. It is, as Kant puts it, not consciousness of what I am, but merely consciousness that I am. It is this purely formal self-consciousness which constitutes the ground of unity amongst the manifold of representations.

What Kant has to do now is show that this necessary condition of knowledge implies the categories. This part of Kant's deduction is probably the most obscure aspect of it, but I think a clue to the connection between the unity of apperception and the categories is given in the chapter on the refutation of idealism. Here he writes:

> I am conscious of my own existence as determined in time. All determination of time presupposes something *permanent* in perception. The permanent cannot, however, be something in me, since it is only through this permanent that my existence in time can itself be determined. Thus perception of this permanent is possible only through a *thing* outside me and not through the mere *representation* of a thing outside me. (ibid., B275)

The transcendental unity of apperception is mere consciousness of my existence. More precisely, it is consciousness of the identity of the existent 'I' which can accompany all my representations. Here Kant claims that this consciousness of my numerical identity through time is only possible on the condition of something permanent in perception. This cannot be the permanence of a mere representation in me, as the permanence of the representation presupposes the identity of the subject in whom it persists. The permanent must, therefore, be a real object of experience, that is, an outer appearance. The categories are the condition of the possibility of consciousness of objects, as opposed to mere inner sensations, for it is only by means of these that representations are referred to objective relations. Thus, the categories are presupposed by consciousness of the numerical identity of the 'I think' which must be able to accompany all of my representations.

This may seem to contradict Kant's claim that the transcendental unity of apperception is the ultimate condition of the possibility of experience. He now seems to be saying that transcendental apperception presupposes the categories, which, presumably, must be the ultimate condition of the possibility of experience. Furthermore, it may be asked how transcendental apperception can explain the possibility of the application of the categories if the categories in turn ground transcendental apperception. I think the answer to this must be that Kant held that transcendental apperception and the categories reciprocally imply each other. It is not the case that transcendental apperception exists first, and this makes possible the application of the categories, or vice versa. Rather, these must be conceived of as being, to use a Heideggerian term, equiprimordial (*Gleichursprünglich*).

In the second half of the transcendental deduction (§§22–7) Kant proceeds to argue that the categories are valid only for objects of possible experience, that is, in relation to empirical knowledge. This has to be shown, for the concepts of mathematics seem to be subject to the categories but do not have empirical objects corresponding to them. Kant's response is to say that these concepts only constitute knowledge in so far as there are things given in intuition which conform to these pure formal concepts.

> Consequently, the pure concepts of the understanding, even when they are applied to *a priori* intuitions, as in mathematics, yield knowledge only in so far as these intuitions – and therefore indirectly by their means the pure concepts also – can be applied to empirical intuitions. (ibid., B147)

The second problem is that it may be objected that a non-sensible intuition could be given which can be associated with certain predicates, namely, negative ones such as, being non-spatial, having no duration in time, etc. but such negative knowledge is no knowledge at all unless it is possible to specify positively the content of the intuition. Otherwise, not a single one of all the categories could be applied (ibid., B149).

Finally, it may be maintained that transcendental self-consciousness constitutes a form of knowledge which, as the ultimate condition of all empirical knowledge, must be non-empirical. However, as we have already noted, Kant's view is that transcendental self-consciousness is not self-knowledge; it has no content, but is purely formal, a thought, not an intuition (ibid., B157). Since there is no content for the categories to work on, they do not apply to such self-consciousness. I can know myself as I appear, and it is to this knowledge that the categories are applicable. Transcendental self-consciousness, on the other hand, can be thought, but not known.

The schematism

In the schematism Kant addresses the issue of how the subsumption of intuitions under pure concepts is possible (Kant, 1929 [1781], A138). Empirical concepts can be applied to instances given in perception in virtue of some corresponding intuition which allows the latter to be subsumed by the former. The problem with the categories is that there is no intuition corresponding to the concept, by means of which they can be applied to empirical objects. We do not literally see the property something has of being a cause of something else, or that of being an effect of some event. Kant's solution to this problem is to seek out a third thing which can bridge the gap between sensibility and understanding (ibid.). This third thing is time, which has something in common with both the categories and the manifold of intuitions. Time is homogeneous with the categories in so far as it is universal and necessary, that is, *a priori*. It is homogeneous with the manifold of intuitions in so far as it is contained in every empirical representation. As the bridge between the categories and the manifold of intuitions, time is described as the schema of the concepts of the understanding. It is a transcendental schema in the sense that it makes possible the application of pure concepts to intuitions. Thus, the different ways in which a manifold of appearances can be synthesised in time provides the exemplar of the more abstract concept of synthesis which constitutes each category. Consequently, the relevant category can be applied to a manifold on the basis of this temporal order. Since all sensible objects must be related within one time, the different ways in which they are so related can be used as a mark determining which categories be applied to which manifolds. Thus, for example, the category of causality can be applied to a manifold on the basis of *succession* in the manifold (ibid., A144). Of course, in so far as all experience is temporal, all representations succeed one another. What is distinctive about the schema of the category of cause and effect is that the succession is rule-governed. We can apprehend a house by first perceiving the ground floor, then the first floor then the roof. Alternatively, we could start with the roof and work our way down to the ground

floor. The series of representations can be synthesised either backwards or forwards. However, if we apprehend a ship floating downstream, the series of representations can be synthesised in only one way, that is the earlier representations necessarily precede the latter (ibid., A201). It is this rule of synthesis which distinguishes the schema of the category of causality from others.

The illusions of speculative metaphysics

The final important sections of the *Critique* which I shall consider are those containing the paralogisms and the antinomies. In these chapters Kant uses his transcendental idealism to resolve what he describes as the illusions of speculative psychology and cosmology. Speculative psychology and cosmology err in failing to make the transcendental distinction between appearances and things in themselves, and thus think that the unconditioned is something knowable.

Speculative, or rational, psychology makes the primary mistake of hypostatising the transcendental ego, the 'I think' which must be able to accompany all my representations, and treats this merely formal conception of the self as some sort of substantive thing. In so doing it makes the mistake of applying the category of substance to the self regarded as it is in itself. This is a mistake because the category of substance, like all the categories, is applicable only to objects regarded as appearances, not to things considered as they are in themselves. Once this primary error is diagnosed, the associated errors – that it is a simple substance (second paralogism), that it is a substance which remains numerically identical through time (third paralogism), and that it is the only object of which we have immediate knowledge (fourth paralogism) – can be dissolved also. If the transcendental ego is not a substance, it cannot be a simple, numerically identical substance. This 'I' is not the only thing of which we have immediate knowledge, for we do not know ourselves as we are in ourselves – that is, the transcendental ego is not an object of a possible knowledge for us. We only know ourselves as we appear but if the object of all knowledge is appearances (where appearances constitute empirical reality and are contrasted with unknowable things in themselves), then we will not only have immediate knowledge of inner objects, but of outer objects also (Kant, 1929 [1781], A371).

Kant's critique of speculative cosmology takes the form of showing the contradictions into which reason falls if we fail to distinguish objects as things in themselves from the same objects regarded as appearances; for without this distinction, opposing views relating to the issues of the spatio-temporal origin of the world, the existence of simple substances, the existence of freedom, and the existence of a necessary being will appear equally warranted. These issues constitute respectively the four antinomies. The first two are called mathematical, and the third and fourth, dynamical antinomies. Each antinomy consists of a thesis, an antithesis which simply negates whatever is stated in the thesis, and an argument supporting these opposing views. Kant wants to say that both the thesis and antithesis in the mathematical antinomies are false, and that both the thesis and antithesis of the dynamical antinomies are true.

He can maintain that both the thesis and the antithesis of the mathematical antinomies are false because he maintains they rest on a self-contradictory concept. The debate is analogous to one over whether a square circle is round or rectangular. One may argue that it cannot be round because it is rectangular, or that it cannot be square because it is circular, but the point is that it is neither square nor circular because the very concept is self-contradictory. Kant maintains that the opposing claims of the mathematical antinomies are claims about self-contradictory concepts, and hence are all false. Claims about the world as a whole are self-contradictory because we can only know possible objects of experience, and the world as a whole, be it finite or infinite, is not such an object.

The thesis of the first antinomy is false, Kant maintains, because in the empirical regress of experience we can have no experience of an unconditioned condition. All appearances are in space and time and are hence conditioned by these. The antithesis is false because an infinite series is not a possible object of experience.

All beginning is in time and all limits of the extended are in space. But space and time belong only to the world of sense. Accordingly, while appearances *in the world* are conditionally limited, *the world itself* is neither conditionally nor unconditionally limited. (ibid., A522)

The notion of the infinite series (the unconditioned) is a mere idea of reason. This means that it is a rule, or regulative principle, which can guide our empirical enquiries, but which does not correspond to any possible object which could be given in experience. This idea must guide our empirical investigation if this is to aim at systematic knowledge, but it can never be attained in the progress of experience.

The thesis of the second antinomy is false because every object of experience is a spatial object and no matter how much a space is divided we will still be left with a space which is as such further divisible. But although space, and thus spatially extended empirical objects, are infinitely divisible, we cannot say that every part of an organised whole is itself an organised whole, and so on *ad infinitum*, for such an infinite series is not a possible object of experience (ibid., A526). It is merely a regulative idea of our reason.

The third antinomy is the most important in relation to Kant's ethics, for with this he aims to reconcile universal determinism with freedom unconstrained by causal laws of nature, and such freedom is, he maintains, necessary for ethics. His strategy is simple. In so far as we consider the world as appearance we regard it as governed by the universal law of natural causality. There is, therefore, no place for freedom in so far as we regard the world in this way, for the concept of freedom is the concept of an uncaused cause, and this does not fit with universal determinism; but once we make the transcendental distinction between the world regarded as appearance, and the same world regarded in itself, we can find a place for a causality of freedom, that is, an uncaused cause. For, in so far as the world is considered in itself, it is considered in abstraction from the law of natural causality, and this makes possible a ground of an event which is not preceded by any further cause. All events in the world are governed by the law of natural causality in so far as it is regarded as appearance, but these same events can be regarded as having their cause in the world considered in abstraction from this law, that is, as it is in itself. But since freedom is only possible in the world regarded as it is in itself, and we cannot know anything about the world so regarded, we cannot know that there is freedom. Freedom is thus an idea of reason. Kant attempts to hold on to the truth of the thesis and antithesis of the fourth antinomy in a similar way. He maintains that there is no necessary being, or cause within the phenomenal world, but that the idea of such a being is possible within the world regarded as it is in itself. Consequently, we can neither know that there is such a being, nor that there is not. We may, however, assume the existence of such a being in order to satisfy reason's demand for system, so long as we remember that this assumption does not constitute knowledge.

I have tried to present an account of Kant's transcendental idealism which does not lumber him with an incoherent or implausible view. The fundamental aspect of this two-aspect interpretation is an understanding of the distinction between things in themselves and appearances, not as one between different types of objects, but between different ways of regarding one and the same object. Once we understand this distinction in this way, we will no longer be tempted to think of Kant as claiming that unknowable things in themselves cause appearances in our minds, and that the mind reconstructs the cause of these representations by means of the forms of sensibility and the categories. What mental representations represent is not things in themselves, but outer appearances or representations. These appearances, however, do not represent anything. Rather, they are real, spatio-temporal objects. Kant calls them representations, or appearances simply in order to remind us that they are not absolutely mind-independent, that is, things in themselves.

Bibliography

Writings

Kant, I. (1902) (first edn, 1783), *Prolegomena to any Future Metaphysics that can Qualify as a Science*, trans. P. Carus, La Salle: Open Court.
— (1929) (first edn, 1781; second edn, 1787), *Critique of Pure Reason*, trans. N. Kemp-Smith, Basingstoke: Macmillan.

References and further reading

Allison, H. (1983), *Kant's Transcendental Idealism: An Interpretation and Defense*, New Haven: Yale University Press.
Aquila, R. (1983), *Representational Mind: A Study of Kant's Theory of Knowledge*, Bloomington: Indiana University Press.
Bird, G. (1962), *Kant's Theory of Knowledge: An Outline of One Central Argument in the Critique of Pure Reason*, London: Routledge and Kegan Paul.

Guyer, P. (1987), *Kant and the Claims of Knowledge*, Cambridge: Cambridge University Press.
Henrich, D. (1969), 'The Proof-structure of Kant's Transcendental Deduction', *The Review of Metaphysics*, 22, 640–59.
Hintikka, J. (1969), 'On Kant's Notion of Intuition (Anschauung)', in T. Penelhum and J. MacIntosh (eds), *The First Critique: Reflections on Kant's Critique of Pure Reason*, Belmont: Wadsworth, pp. 38–53.
Höffe, O. (1994), *Immanuel Kant*, trans. M. Farrier, New York: State University of New York Press.
Mathews, H. (1969), 'Strawson on Transcendental Idealism', *Philosophical Quarterly*, 19, 204–20.
Neiman, S. (1994), *The Unity of Reason: Rereading Kant*, Oxford: Oxford University Press.
Paton, H. J. (1936), *Kant's Metaphysic of Experience*, 2 vols, London: George Allen and Unwin.
Pippin, R. (1982), *Kant's Theory of Form: An Essay on the Critique of Pure Reason*, New Haven: Yale University Press.
Strawson, P. (1966), *The Bounds of Sense*, London: Methuen.

1.2

FICHTE'S IDEALISM

Tom Rockmore

The German philosopher Fichte belongs to the post-Kantian movement in German Idealism, which, with classical Greek philosophy, is often regarded as one of the two richest moments in the philosophical tradition. In virtue of the quality and the influence of his writings, Fichte can be justifiably considered a major philosopher. This chapter presents some of the main elements of Fichte's position, including problems in addressing his theory; the origins, nature and later evolution of his theory; and its influence on the later philosophical discussion.

Problems in interpreting Fichte

Important philosophers are important because they innovate with respect to contemporary philosophical discussion. The more original they are, the more difficult it is to find ways to understand their views and, in some cases, lengthy periods are necessary to assimilate new ideas. Fichte's important, but highly original theory is, like other original theories, difficult to interpret. It is additionally difficult to interpret for at least four other reasons specific to it.

One obvious enough problem is the relative dearth of adequate translations into English, which places obstacles in the way of any reader who cannot read Fichte in the original German. Fortunately, this problem has been addressed in recent years through a series of mainly good translations that have made Fichte's thought increasingly available in English.

A second problem is stylistic in nature. His hermetic style, partly due to the extreme rapidity with which he worked – his main work was produced between 1794 and 1807, an extremely short period for a major philosopher – is difficult even for native Germans. This is partly due to the fact that Fichte (who originally intended to join the clergy and possessed unusual speaking abilities) used the model of oral presentations for his writings. Indeed, most of his work in print, including the celebrated Jena *Wissenschaftslehre* (1796/99), are merely versions of his lecture courses. He also frequently modified his terminology from work to work, which only makes it more difficult to discern the continuity in the evolution of his basic theory. It is, then, not surprising that Fichte has frequently been misunderstood, even by important philosophers; J. H. Jacobi, for instance, a distinguished contemporary whom Fichte valued highly but who accused him of nihilism.

A third problem is Fichte's misleading claim to be a seamlessly perfect Kantian, which suggests that his theory is only Kant's theory expressed in his own terms. In the wake of the publication of Kant's *Critique of Pure Reason* (1781, 1787), a number of his contemporaries, including Reinhold, Beck, Maimon and Fichte each claimed to be the only one to understand, or to understand fully, Kant's critical philosophy. Fichte routinely made variations of this claim, even going to the extreme of alleging that he understood Kant better than he (Kant) understood himself. The excessive immodesty of this remark is perhaps moderated if we recall that Kant made a similar comment about his relation to Plato. There seems to have been some confusion in Fichte's mind concerning the relation between Kant and himself.

In a 1 March 1794 letter to Reinhold (see Breazeale, 1988, p. 376), he even suggests that the critical philosophy follows in fact from his own premises.

This claim received mixed reactions. Not surprisingly, Kant rejected Fichte's general claim when he accused Fichte of trying to deduce a real object from pure logic. On the contrary, Fichte's claim to be the only legitimate successor to Kant was given special weight by his contemporaries, and was accepted by both the young Schelling and the young Hegel. Yet although Fichte is clearly inspired by Kant, and just as clearly intended to bring Kant's philosophical revolution to a successful conclusion, it is misleading to make a stronger claim, such as the claim that Fichte's views are identical to Kant's.

The fourth, perhaps most difficult, problem in understanding Fichte is due to Hegel's misleading interpretation of his philosophical contemporaries. Hegel, who invented the history of philosophy as we understand it today, presented a tendentious, but very influential, reading of the views of Fichte and Schelling. For although he regarded them as the only contemporaries worthy of the name philosopher, he also saw them as significant only in so far as their views led up to his own view. This reading, which is widely, indeed routinely, reproduced in discussions of German Idealism, features a progression leading from Kant's critical idealism, ascending through Fichte's subjective idealism and then Schelling's objective idealism, to Hegel's absolute idealism, which is depicted as the peak of the idealist movement. From this perspective, Fichte and Schelling are not important in themselves, but as intermediaries between Kant and Hegel. However, although Fichte and Schelling did in fact mediate between Kant and Hegel, they are also major philosophers whose views deserve consideration on their own merits and not simply because of their considerable influence on either the evolution of later German Idealism or on later philosophy. Recent scholarship, which has done much to rescue Hegel's great contemporaries from his presentation of German Idealism, presents a very different image of both Fichte and Schelling.

Fichte's view of representation

The origins of important philosophical positions are often difficult to discern, since they are usually overdetermined by numerous factors, hence not explicable in terms of a single or even a small series of influences. It is not easy, but easier, to discern the origins of Fichte's position in his distinctive theory of representation that provided the conceptual basis of his theory. There is widespread agreement that his position was the result of a single occasion, in the course of his preparation of his extremely sober and thoughtful review of Schulze's polemical attack on Reinhold's elementary philosophy. G. E. Schulze (1761–1833) was Professor of Philosophy at Helmstedt. Schulze's book, which appeared in 1792 under the awkward title *Aenesidemus, or concerning the Foundations of the Elementary Philosophy Propounded in Jena by Professor Reinhold, including a Defense of Skepticism against the Pretensions of the Critique of Reason*, offered a detailed critique of K. L. Reinhold's pioneer effort to systematise Kant's critical philosophy. At the time, Fichte, who had been a student with Schulze and who admired Reinhold as an early Kantian and his predecessor in Jena, had already become a Kantian. In his review, Fichte modified his previous Kantianism in a way leading to his own original theory.

The interaction between Reinhold, Schulze, and Fichte is complex and technical. It is useful here to introduce a fourfold distinction between Kant's theory, Reinhold's version of it, Schulze's criticism of both, and Fichte's response to Schulze. The four philosophers can be understood as proposing four different views of representation. In his critical philosophy, Kant typically claimed to have found a third way between dogmatism, or a theory asserted without proof, or at least without sufficient proof, and skepticism, or the claim that nothing can be known. According to Kant, philosophy must not only be scientific, but must in fact be a science, and science requires system. Kant's theory is intended by him to elucidate the conditions of the possibility of knowledge of objects and experience. In Kant's theory, the object given in experience is taken as an appearance of what stands outside experience and appears in it.

Kant typically uses the word *Vorstellung*, which should be translated as representation, to refer to the object of experience, which can be said to represent or to stand for another, further object. In an important letter, written to his friend Markus Herz (letter of 21 February 1772) when he was working out his critical philosophy, Kant describes his concern through the idea of representation: 'What is the ground of the relation of that in us which we call "representation" to the object?' (Kant, 1967–71). In an important passage of the *Critique of Pure Reason* Kant insists that all knowledge is representational, hence based on a distinction between an appearance and what appears. Without this distinction, he argues, we should be landed in the absurd conclusion that there can be appearance without anything that appears (Kant, 1961 [1787], B xxvii).

Kant's enthusiastic followers, including Reinhold, accepted Kant's view that philosophy must be a scientific system, while disagreeing that the latter offered the system in question in the critical philosophy. Reinhold made the initial attempt to restate Kant's critical philosophy in systematic form by returning to a rationalist form of system, or an initial principle known to be true and from which the remainder of the system could be rigorously deduced. It is well known that Descartes invoked the *cogito*, or 'I think' (from *cogitare*, to think) as such a principle. Since he referred to the *cogito* as a foundation (French *fondement*, Latin *fundamentum*), Descartes's strategy for knowledge is now frequently known as foundationalism because of the obvious analogy between a building that rests on a foundation and the first principle of a philosophical theory that can be said to found, or to ground, the theory deduced from it. Distantly following Descartes, Reinhold proposed a capacity of representation (*Vorstellungsvermögen*, from *Vorstellung* or representation, and *Vermögen* or capacity) as the first principle of his *Elementary Philosophy*, which he intended as a systematic reconstruction of Kant's critical philosophy. In an important passage, Reinhold writes 'In consciousness the representation is distinguished by the subject from subject and object, and related to both' (Reinhold, 1790, Vol. I, p. 18).

Aenesidemus, the name that Schulze took as his pseudonym, belonged to an important sceptic of Greek antiquity who flourished in the first century BC. As a sceptic, Schulze was committed to the idea that no strategy for knowledge could be successful. In response to Reinhold, he attempted to show that the effort to ground the principles of the critical philosophy in a proposition of consciousness (*Satz des Bewusstseins*) is unsuccessful. Schulze offers three main criticisms of the proposition of consciousness: First, it is not a basic proposition. Second, it is not self-contained. Third, it expresses neither a generally valid proposition nor a fact. He properly objected to Reinhold's proposition on the grounds that Reinhold had failed to observe the asymmetry in the relation of representation to the subject and object of experience.

Although Fichte partially endorses Schulze's criticisms of Reinhold, in his review he rejects the sceptical conclusions that Schulze draws. For Fichte, Schulze is wrong to deny Reinhold's capacity of representation, yet he concedes that Reinhold's idea is inadequately formulated. Fichte's twofold response consists in an effort to find an adequate formulation for Reinhold's idea and to rethink it further with respect to the problem of knowledge. The link between his reaction to Schulze and the latter's reaction to both Reinhold and to Kant is clear. Like Reinhold, Fichte accepts Kant's results and rejects the manner in which they are formulated, although he further rejects Reinhold's attempted restatement of them.

With Schulze's objection in mind, Fichte reformulates Reinhold's idea, in his own language, as the claim that the 'representation is related to the object as the effect is related to its cause and to the subject as the accident is related to the substance ('Review of Aenesidemus', in ibid., 1988, p. 72). In the space of a single sentence, this statement provides the outlines of a theory of consciousness in terms of three elements, including the subject, the object, and their interrelation through the object's representation.

Fichte's theory draws on Kant, Aristotle and Spinoza. Kant famously distinguished in the critical philosophy between the object as actually given in experience and the object considered as a mere object of thought, as what he called a thing-in-itself, apart from any possible experience. Kant understands the difference between the thing taken as an object of thought and as an object of experience on a causal model. According to Kant, the thing-in-itself can, without contradiction, be considered as the cause of the object given in experience that can, without contradiction, be considered as the effect. In writing that the representation is related to the object as the effect is related to the cause, Fichte presents a closely Kantian view of the relation between the object that must be assumed to act upon, or to affect, the subject as a condition of experience, and what is given in experience. For Fichte, as for Kant, the object of experience is an effect representing an external cause. According to Aristotle, an accident is a merely incidental predicate, or quality that does not belong to the essence of a thing. Furthermore, according to Spinoza, there is only one substance and individual human beings are only modes of it. Similarly, for Fichte the subject, or finite human being, is a subject that is modified by the action of the object upon it. According to Fichte, consciousness results from an interaction between a subject and an external object that, in acting on the subject, causes a representation of itself within consciousness.

Concerning the concept of the *Wissenschaftslehre* or of so-called 'Philosophy'

Fichte's novel analysis of consciousness became the basis of his own distinctive theory, whose outlines are only dimly apparent in the review of *Aenesidemus*. Fichte, who accepted Schulze's criticism of Reinhold, remained committed to the latter's rationalist reconstruction of Kant's critical philosophy in the form of a system generated from a single first principle, yet Schulze's critique convinced him that the first principle required to ground the system he had in mind had not yet been discovered. When he submitted his review of Aenesidemus for publication, Fichte believed he had found the required principle. This principle, which is not explicitly developed in his review, is central to the new theory he rapidly worked out after his arrival in Jena in his *Foundations of the Entire Teaching of Science* (*Grundlage der gesamten Wissenschaftslehre*, 1794).

The title of his treatise indicates Fichte's predilection for a scientific approach to philosophy. Throughout his career he followed Kant and many others in insisting that philosophy is literally science. Fichte's term for his theory in general, which is not easily translated into English, is *Wissenschaftslehre*, combining terms meaning teaching (*Lehre*) and science (*Wissenschaft*), or, literally, teaching of science. To avoid confusion, I shall use the term *Wissenschaftslehre* to refer, not to any version of the theory, but to the theory that Fichte repeatedly expounded and that he applied to specific problems in other texts.

In discussing Fichte's position, it is useful to distinguish between its central insight, or insights, and its development in various versions of the *Wissenschaftslehre*. Certainly, one central insight is the idea of system. This idea dominates the post-Kantian movement in German philosophy, and can be depicted as an effort to supply the system felt to be lacking in Kant's critical philosophy. In a long article, 'Concerning the Concept of the *Wissenschaftslehre* or, of So-called "Philosophy"' (1794), where the term appeared for the first time in his writings, Fichte undertook to explain his conception of system in clear, non-technical language. This text, which merely comments on the system, provides in a compressed form a highly useful anticipation of some key doctrines he later elaborates in other texts.

Fichte claims here to be engaged in merely clarifying Kant's theory. He describes his discussion as critique lying beyond metaphysics, whose purpose is to clarify metaphysics, which itself lies beyond, and clarifies, natural thinking. Fichte thus presupposes an analysis on three levels, the highest of which is contained in his study of the nature and conditions of the *Wissenschaftslehre* as first philosophy.

Fichte's view of philosophy is specifically influenced by Kant and Reinhold. Following Kant, he maintains that philosophy is a science, that a science possesses systematic form, and (now going beyond Kant, but following Reinhold) that all the propositions of a science are joined together in a single first principle. Philosophy is, then, a unified science, whose certainty derives from the absolutely certain status of its initial proposition, which is preserved in other propositions rigorously derived from it. There can be only one initial proposition, since otherwise there would be more than one science. The *Wissenschaftslehre* is, thus, the science on which the other, special, sciences are based. Obviously, philosophy is a certain science deriving from a first principle; everything depends upon the first principle, which is said to be exhausted when a complete system, with no explanatory gaps, has been derived from it.

Another central insight, perhaps the single most important idea in Fichte's theory, is his conception of the subject as a finite human being. Here we see the immediate fruits of the view of consciousness Fichte presented in the review of *Aenesidemus*. In the critical philosophy, Kant, who takes the subject as the highest concept of the critical philosophy, insisted on the relation between the subject and experience, since there is no experience without a subject of experience. It follows that experience is composed of a subject, object or representation, and, by implication, something that is represented. An example might be the snow I see when looking out of my window. That can be said to be the representation within experience of the snow that, as independent of me, stands outside my experience, but appears within it through its representation.

In his text, Fichte develops Kant's analysis of experience from the perspective of the subject. Following Kant, he suggests that the highest concept is the I, or subject of experience, and that everything else is the not-I, or what is not the subject. He introduces the concept of positing (*setzen*) to indicate that, in experience, the subject and the object interact through the representation of the object that is given within the subject's consciousness. To return to my example, the snow that I perceive within consciousness, the object of experience, can be considered as the result of an interaction between the I, or subject, a finite human being, and an objective external world independent of the subject. Striving (*streben*), a further concept introduced by Fichte, is the contrary activity in which the subject overcomes the resistance, opposed to its activity, of the real external world.

In Kant's critical theory, the subject is wholly reduced to its function within his view of knowledge. Although Fichte's theory is based on Kant's, he understands the subject of knowledge as a finite human being that is capable of knowledge but is not reducible to its cogntive capacity. His theory features an interaction between subject and object, or, in Fichte's language, the I and the not-I. We can derive three basic principles, which Fichte quickly, perhaps too quickly and hence very obscurely, sketches in an account of the hypothetical division of the *Wissenschaftslehre*: first, there is the I, or subject, an absolute subject posited as acting absolutely, or without limitations of any kind. What Fichte has in mind is a wholly free, rational being, which, unlimited by anything else, obeys only its own laws, and which functions as the first principle of human knowledge from the subject's perspective. This is a merely 'theoretical' view of a real human being comprehended abstractly, as in the Kantian theory, a person who has abstracted himself from the interaction between people and the external world in order to think in a wholly unconstrained manner. Then, secondly, there is an opposition of the real external world to the human subject, which is opposed by reality, against which it strives; for when we act, we always act in the context of the real external world. Thirdly, there is the interaction between subject and object, between the finite human subject and real external world.

Ideally, the subject acts freely, limited only in its actions by its own laws. Then there is the realm of practice, which is for Fichte much more important than mere theory, serving as its foundation. According to Fichte, who here refers to Kant, no philosophical theory goes beyond these three absolutes, which include: the absolute I, or view of the subject understood purely theoretically in abstraction from the real world, hence as ideally fully free; the not-I that is all that the I, or real, finite human being is not; and the I, or real finite human being that is the real subject of experience.

Fichte's Jena *Wissenschaftslehre* [1794]

Fichte's early article on the Concept of the *Wissenschaftslehre* suggests two central tasks: to provide the foundations of the *Wissenschaftslehre* and, on that basis, to provide a systematic elaboration of the system; that is, to apply the basic insights constituting the foundations of the theory to a series of problems in various domains. Like Kant, who revised the form in which he expressed his theory whose content he held to be unrevisable, Fichte laboured long and hard to find a way to express his basic ideas, whose truth he never doubted. The extent of Fichte's concentration on this task is unusual, even amazing. The basic statement of his theory as a *Wissenschaftslehre* exists in no less than sixteen separate versions, many of which are completely different in form and content from other versions. The first, and best-known, version is the *Foundation of the Entire Wissenschaftslehre* that Fichte composed with extraordinary speed in the spring of 1794 as an aid to his students.

This text is centrally important for several reasons: it is the initial, and perhaps most adequate, statement of his theory; it is the text that presented the original theory that was not yet formulated when Fichte burst on to the intellectual stage through the anonymous publication of his early work on religion; and it is this version of his theory which decisively influenced the evolution of post-Kantian German Idealism that had already largely occurred before other, later, versions appeared. In view of its importance, it is unfortunate that the published text is written in an extremely abstract, often forbiddingly technical style, with few direct references to other philosophical theories, and without any aids to Fichte's students, who, like his colleagues who readily misunderstood his views, must have found his thoughts almost inacessible.

In the preface to the first edition of his Jena *Wissenschaftslehre*, Fichte suggested in a typical burst of enthusiasm that, together with another work which appeared soon after, 'Outline of the Distinctive Character of the *Wissenschaftslehre* with Respect to the Theoretical Faculty' ('Grundriss des Eigenthümlichen der Wisenschaftslehre in Rücksicht auf das theoretische Vermögen', 1795) he had already carried his work to the point where any intelligent reader could comprehend not only the foundations of the system but the system as whole. Yet as early as the appearance of the second edition of the Jena *Wissenschaftslehre* in 1801, Fichte acknowledged the defects of the initial statement of his theory, for which he never ceased to search for an adequate expression, while maintaining that the original version of his theory could not be fully replaced by another. He further complained that most members of the philosophical public, in which he had earlier expressed his confidence, were still not ready to grasp his new perspective, and were certainly not ready to do so in two rather different forms.

The main ideas of the Jena *Wissenschaftslehre*, which Fichte so quickly composed for his students' usage, had already been worked out in an unpublished sketch of the theory written in 1793 in Zurich and then adumbrated in his article 'Concerning the Concept of the *Wissenschaftslehre*' on arriving in Jena. In the preface to the first edition of the Jena *Wissenschaftslehre*, Fichte expressed the belief, guiding his original research throughout his career, that he had 'discovered the way in which philosophy must raise itself to the level of a manifest science' (Fichte, 1980 [1794], p. 89).

As in the previous version, in the Jena *Wissenschaftslehre* Fichte presents a theory of experience from the perspective of the subject, or finite human being, through the expansion and transformation of the Kantian view of subjectivity. His theory is based on the analysis of the mutual interaction between the subject and object, or individual human being and the external world. Fichte analyses this basic proposition from two vantage points: theoretically, as the determination of the subject by a surrounding real world; and practically, as the ideal determination by the subject of the surrounding world.

The discussion is unequally divided into three parts, including a short account of the 'Fundamental Principles of the Entire *Wissenschaftslehre*' followed by accounts of the 'Foundation of Theoretical Knowledge' and of the 'Foundation of the Science of the Practical'. With numerous additions, and elaborations, the Jena *Wissenschaftslehre* follows the hypothetical division of the position already sketched in briefest fashion in Fichte's article. In his article, Fichte several times remarks that claims to know are hypothetical. He now expands on the meaning of this claim in a passage at the very beginning of his account of the fundamental principles of his new science in writing: 'Our task is to *discover* the primordial, absolutely unconditioned first principle of all human knowledge. This can be neither *proved* nor *defined*, it is to be an absolutely primary principle' (Fichte, 1980, p. 93; Fichte's emphases).

In writing that human knowledge must base itself upon a first principle from which everything else follows but which itself cannot be proven, Fichte is clearly breaking with the very idea that philosophy can justify itself. Unlike Descartes, a great geometer who seems to go beyond the geometrical model in his view of a theory of knowledge in which the first principle is demonstrably true, Fichte takes the geometrical model very seriously. Like geometry, whose proofs depend upon the prior assumption of the truths of certain indemonstrable axioms or postulates, Fichte is suggesting that human knowledge rests upon at least one theoretically indemonstrable assumption, in his theory, the assumption of the finite human being as the real subject of human experience and knowledge. It follows that, if philosophy requires a theoretical demonstration, then it can be said to come to an end in Fichte; but if, on the contrary, philosophy can be understood as a science founded on a theoretically-indemonstrable, but practical, principle, namely the assumption of the finite human being as basically active, not passive, then Fichte's contribution is to reformulate philosophy as a science on a practical basis.

Fichte's account of the three fundamental principles of the *Wissenschaftslehre* elaborates ideas more rapidly sketched in his article. According to Fichte, the first two principles are derived from a fact of consciousness independently of each other, and the third principle is derived by reason alone. The first, absolutely unconditioned principle, which Fichte also refers to as the principle of identity, concerns an act that is not given in consciousness but rather makes consciousness possible. Fichte formulates it in various ways to reflect the fact that 'The I begins by an absolute positing of its own existence' (ibid., p. 98; translation modified). This is his way of expressing Kant's claim that the experience of anything presupposes a subject; according to Fichte, a finite human being. Fichte himself draws attention to the continuity between this claim and the theories of Kant, Descartes and Reinhold.

What Fichte calls the second principle, or the principle of opposition, conditioned as to content, expresses the fact that consciousness depends on a factual opposition, or an opposition between a subject that is conscious and an object of which it is conscious. Fichte expresses this as the claim that in empirical consciousness there is 'a not-I opposed absolutely to the I' (ibid., p. 104; translation modified).

What Fichte calls the third principle, or grounding principle, which is conditioned as to form, concerns the interaction between the subject, posited in the first principle, and the opposition between subject and object referred to in the second principle; namely, the relation between the subject from which the analysis begins, and the object which opposes it as a condition of consciousness. We recall that all experience contains both a subject and an object in interaction. Fichte expresses the interaction between the subject and object of experience and the consciousness caused by this interaction in writing that 'in the I, I oppose a divisible not-I to the the divisible I' (ibid., p. 110). For Fichte, then, subject and object each limit, or exert an influence on, the other, and the interaction between them produces the subject's consciousness.

The three fundamental principles of Fichte's theory provide a systematic elaboration of the Kantian theory of experience and knowledge from the perspective of the subject. This corresponds to his desire to systematise Kant's critical philosophy. The basis of Fichte's theory is an interaction between the finite human being and an independent external world that is known through representations in consciousness. Fichte repeatedly insists on the compatibility of his own theory and Kant's. Like Kant, who regards his concept of the subject as the transcendental unity of apperception as the highest principle of the critical philosophy, Fichte regards the absolute self, which is arrived at through abstraction from the real self, or finite human being, as the highest theoretical principle of his own transcendental philosophy. The difference is that Fichte, unlike Kant, claims to derive his theory from the principle in question.

Now the essence of the critical philosophy consists in this, that an absolute self is postulated as wholly unconditioned and incapable of determination by any higher thing; and if this philosophy is derived in due order from the above principle, it becomes a *Wissenschaftslehre*. (ibid., p. 117; translation modified)

Parts II and III of the Jena *Wissenschaftslehre* are devoted to accounts of theory, or theoretical knowledge, and practice, or practical knowledge. A main difference between the accounts of theory and practice is that the theoretical subject is passive, or acted upon, whereas the practical subject acts freely. At the level of theory, we are concerned with the postulated action of the real external world upon the subject, a result of which it is known through consciousness: 'The I posits itself as limited by the not-I' (ibid., p. 122; translation modified).

Fichte's discussion clearly reflects Spinoza's influence. In *The Ethics*, Spinoza attempts to deduce his analysis in geometrical form. Here, and elsewhere in his work, Fichte too makes a great show of deducing his theory in an analysis that is often appallingly obscure. The obscurity of the discussion is relieved by insights of great importance. One such insight concerns idealism and realism, which are frequently taken as basically opposing, and consequently mutally exclusive, doctrines. Fichte avoids the apparent opposition by suggesting that both are correct, so one need not choose between them.

> Hence the real question at issue between realism and idealism is as to which road is to be taken in explaining representation . . . Both roads are correct; under a certain condition we are obliged to take the one, and under the opposite condition we must take the other. (ibid., p. 147; translation modified)

Consistent with his emphasis on system, Fichte is persistently concerned with deductions of various types. His account of theoretical knowledge reaches its peak, and its end, in a very important 'Deduction of Representation' that concludes the theoretical part of his treatise. Here he presents a view of the subject as basically active. According to Fichte, we become conscious of, and know, the external world when our activity encounters an obstacle, such as a real object outside us, which resists our activity that,

in his words, is 'reflected' back toward the subject. Knowledge of the outside world is given in consciousness as a series of representations of external objects produced through the imagination. Fichte is often misunderstood to hold that the subject literally produces the real external world through its own activity. This would, indeed, be an absurd view. What he is suggesting is that the result of the interaction between a subject and an object, a person and the real external world, is a representation of external reality produced through the imagination.

The preceding account of theory was necessary in order to comprehend practice. From the beginning of his career, Fichte was primarily interested in practice. In his analysis of practical knowledge, or practice, Fichte analyses the proposition that 'the I posits iself as determining the not-I' (ibid., p. 218; translation modified). He presents a view of the subject as acting upon and determining everything else. This is not the passive, theoretical subject but rather the active, practical subject, such as the person who interacts with others, especially in the framework of moral or ethical actions.

In his analysis of practice, Fichte presents a view of human beings as constantly striving to overcome the resistance of real external objects in order to realise intentions and purposes. Such striving is limitless, or infinite. As human beings, we are always engaged in the attempt, constitutive of what it means to be a person, to become infinite through activity that surpasses obstacles of all kinds. 'The result of our inquiry so far is therefore as follows: *in relation to a possible object*, the pure . . . activity of the self is a *striving*; and as shown earlier, *an infinite striving* at that' (ibid., p. 231; translation modified). Following what Kant calls practical reason, Fichte conceives striving as the individual's demand that everything conform to his wishes or desires. Fichte further distinguishes two kinds of striving. Finite striving concerns a real object in the real external world. Infinite striving concerns a merely imaginary object, such as a wish or a desire. The condition of striving is that the subject must encounter a resistance or check to its activity that must, accordingly, be overcome. In other words, what ought to be arises in virtue of the fact that what the individual tries to do is restricted in some way. The human subject as described by Fichte is an intrinsically practical, or moral, being.

Fichte ends the book with a sustained discussion of feeling, understood as the way in which the real external object, which stands over against and opposes our activity, is brought to consciousness. Feeling becomes possible when a person's wishes or desires are not satisfied. A typical example is the individual's feeling of limitation. Fichte develops his idea of feeling in various ways; in discussions of drives and, finally, harmony, for example.

Later versions of the *Wissenschaftslehre*

The Jena *Wissenschaftslehre* is merely the first and most influential form of a theory that Fichte somewhat obsessively continued to reformulate in numerous later texts. We can summarise the theory as a rigorously systematic analysis of experience and knowledge from the perspective of the subject, or finite human being, which cannot be deduced but from which we must begin.

Fichte was conscious of the difficulties in presenting a finished version of his system. As early as 1794, the same year in which he worked out his theory, in his article 'Concerning the Concept of the *Wissenschaftslehre*' he correctly foresaw that it would take years to provide an adequate version of the system (see Fichte, 1988 [1794], p. 95). In a letter to Reinhold he correctly indicated that it would take an entire lifetime (letter to Reinhold, 2 July 1795, in ibid., p. 401).

Fichte attempted to improve on his initial exposition of his theory in numerous later texts. His career can be divided into a series of periods with respect to the Jena *Wissenschaftslehre*. These include the very early writings, prior to the move to Jena in 1794, which concern mainly political and religious topics; then the writings of the Jena period, including the various versions of the *Wissenschaftslehre* composed before he resigned his position in 1799; and finally a later period, ending only with his death in 1814, during which he composed still further versions of his basic theory, especially the versions of 1801 and 1804.

While still in Jena, Fichte wrote two introductions

to his position and gave a series of lectures that are collectively known as the *Wissenschaftslehre nova methodo* (1796/99). The two introductions are very different. The 'First Introduction to the *Wissenschaftslehre*' (1797) is an extremely simple statement of Fichte's basic position, perhaps the clearest and most accessible of all his writings. Fichte states here that, since Kant has not been understood, he has decided to devote his life to explaining the critical philosophy in independence of Kant. He presents his theory as a theory of experience defined as those contents of consciousness, or representations, which are accompanied by a feeling of necessity, and hence are not merely a product of our imagination. For Fichte, the task of philosophy is to explain experience. He further distinguishes between idealism and realism, or dogmatism, roughly explained as accounts of experience made from the perspective of the subject or from that of the object. In this context, he made his famous remark that 'What sort of philosophy one chooses depends . . . on what sort of man one is' (Fichte, 1980, p. 16).

The *Second Introduction to the Wissenschaftslehre* (1797) is a very different kind of text, written on a more technical level. It was intended by Fichte for readers who already possessed a philosophical system, and who, for that reason, may have been prejudiced against his view; and in it he presents his theory in a more rigorous fashion. Particularly notable is the explicit discussion of the concept of intellectual intuition, or intuiting by the subject of itself. This concept, which Fichte introduces here as the only basis for philosophy, since it is only through abstraction that we reach the subject that is posited in the first of the three fundamental principles of his theory, is not more than implicit in the Jena *Wissenschaftslehre*.

In a series of lecture courses given in 1796–9 before he left Jena, Fichte devised a second presentation of his basic principles that was rewritten 'as if I had never worked it out at all, and as if I knew nothing about the old presentation' (Letter to Reinhold, March 1797, in Breazeale, ed. 1988, p. 417). Fichte was unsuccessful in his plans to revise his manuscripts for publication and eventually abandoned the project. The original manuscript was lost but what survived are two different, but detailed, student transcripts of the lectures that almost certainly provide an accurate idea of the content of Fichte's lectures. In the Jena *Wissenschaftslehre*, he stressed that consciousness is founded in laws of thought. Here, he further argues that the intelligible world is the substrate for the empirical world. This version of the *Wissenschaftslehre* is also notable for the short but very clear 'Deduction of the subdivisions of the *Wissenschaftslehre*'.

After he left Jena, Fichte continued his efforts to arrive at a satisfactory presentation of his theory. Although Fichte himself may have regarded the different versions of the *Wissenschaftslehre* he produced between 1794 and 1814 (the year of his death) as so many different presentations of the same basic theory, the theory obviously changed over time. Not surprisingly, his *Exposition of the Wissenschaftslehre* (*Darstellung der Wissenschaftslehre*, 1801), the first after his expulsion from Jena because of his presumed atheism, shows traces of that controversy as well as of his dispute with Schelling, his former disciple. Especially interesting here is a transformation of the idea of the absolute, which in the Jena *Wissenschaftslehre* emerged in consideration of the finite human subject as wholly independent through abstraction from the interrelation of subject and object. Here Fichte reinterprets the absolute as an ontological principle that is neither knowledge, being, nor identity, nor, in a dig at Schelling who emphasised a view of the absolute as a so-called indifference point in his *System of Transcendental Idealism* [1800], the indifference of both, but simply the absolute. Yet by the end of the second part of the manuscript, Fichte is already invoking what he calls absolute being as the final ground of all concrete, objectively existing entities, such as tables and chairs.

The *Wissenschaftslehre* of 1804, like that of 1801, belongs to writings left unpublished at Fichte's death. Here he continues a return to religion, his earliest philosophical concern, in the wake of the controversy over his supposed atheism. The discussion further develops the idea, which is the basis of his ontological reinterpretation of the absolute, that everything in the world can be regarded as a manifestation of the absolute to human beings. In this text, Fichte again claims that his theory of transcendental philosophy merely develops the basic ideas of Kant's critical philosophy. He maintains that the essence of philosophy consists in explaining multiplicity through unity, or the exposition of the absolute, as a result of which the difference between thought and being allegedly disappears. The link between his later view of philosophy and theology is made clear, for example in the assertion that if one interprets the self-manifesting unity of being as God, then real existence is nothing more than the intuition of God.

Some applications of the *Wissenschaftslehre*

Fichte's theoretical writings about the *Wissenschaftslehre* are meant to ground his strong interest in more practical matters. Throughout his life, he was distinguished by his concern with the wider realm of practice. His publications on rights, ethics and political economy, written while he was struggling with the basic elements of his theory, are properly regarded as belonging to his many efforts to articulate further aspects of his overall philosophical system. *The Foundations of Natural Right According to the Principles of the Wissenschaftslehre* (1796) is influenced by Fichte's desire, writing in the wake of the French Revolution, to deny that the nobility could effectively guarantee the rights of the people. The same concerns are evident in his reading of Montesquieu's *Spirit of the Laws*. Fichte's influences include Rousseau as well as Kant.

The ancient idea of natural right presupposes that certain rights belong to human beings by nature, hence in independence of custom or convention. We recall that Fichte proposed a view of the finite human subject as freely acting in Part III of the Jena *Wissenschaftslehre*. Here, Fichte develops a view of society as possible only as a contract among free beings, or human beings considered as free. A rational being can only act as an individual within a social context. The concept of rights, which concerns the necessary relations between free beings, suggests a society composed of free beings as such. The rule of law suggests that each must limit his freedom through the freedom of others. In his text, Fichte deduces the concept of right as the limitation of self-consciousness together with its object, including its realisation in the real world. He defines the concept of right as something a person can avail himself of as following directly from the law of reason.

Fichte rapidly followed this analysis with *The Theory of Ethics According to the Principles of the Wissenschaftslehre* (1798). This book can be understood as a sharp criticism of the formalism of Kant's view of morality. Once again he is concerned with the realisation of the free activity of finite human beings. With respect to practical action, Kant is mainly concerned with the intention motivating the act, whereas Fichte is mainly concerned with the consequences of the act. It is often noted that Kant's analysis of morality, what he calls practical reason, as merely following formal rules – for example, act in the following way – leads to a split between moral commands (for example, love thy neighbour) and their realisation in the real concrete world. To a greater extent than Kant, Fichte is directly concerned with the understanding of consequences following directly from the free self-limitation of the finite subject. Unlike Kant, who starts his analysis of morality from abstract reason, Fichte starts from freedom understood as the identity including both acting and being. Fichte insists on what he calls the causality of pure concepts on objects. In opposition to Kant's view of freedom as a capacity to determine oneself to act according to an abstract principle, Fichte thinks of real human freedom as rooted in a social setting that makes possible interactions between human beings and nature. Fichte's transposition of the analysis of practical activity to the social world supposes, as Hegel clearly saw in his own theory, a transition from morality to ethics.

Fichte further proposed the outlines of a theory of political economy in his study of *The Closed Commercial State* (1800). Following up on his study of natural law, Fichte examines here the idea of a juridical state considered as a self-enclosed commercial entity. Fichte's pure theory of the legal state presupposes that all individuals are subjected to similar legal relations. This in turn presupposes an analysis of the relations of trade which are founded in property that must be protected. Fichte typically understands the right to property with respect to actions, not things. He regards property as the result of the sphere of free actions, which are regulated through a contract. He envisages the rational state as self-enclosed realm of individuals and laws, where laws regulate access to means to achieve specific goals.

On Fichte's influence

Like Kant, Fichte analysed experience and knowledge from the perspective of the subject. By substituting the finite human being for Kant's abstract view of the subject, Fichte changed the level of the discussion from an ultimately abstract, Kantian account to an analysis of what human beings really do and know. In this specific sense, and despite his reiterated claim to be a Kantian, Fichte is a post-Kantian. Later post-Kantian German Idealism, including the work of Schelling and Hegel, builds on Fichte's concern to develop the spirit of Kant's critical philosophy. Fichte's influence on later philosophy is profound and far-reaching. Although space does not permit a detailed defence of this claim, a short list of those with important debts to Fichte would include Marx, Husserl, Heidegger, Sartre; German Romantic thinkers such as Novalis and Friedrich von Schlegel; French Socialists such as Jaurès; and Marxists such as Max Adler and Georg Lukács.

Bibliography

Writings

Fichte, Johann Gottlieb, *The Vocation of Man* (1956), ed. with an Introduction by Roderick M. Chisholm, Indianapolis and New York: LLA.

— (1968), *Addresses to the German Nation*, ed. with an Introduction by George A. Kelly, New York and Evanston: Harper and Row.

— *The Science of Knowledge with the First and Second Introductions* (1980), trans. and ed. Peter Heath and John Lachs, New York: Cambridge University Press.

— (1988), *Early Philosophical Writings*, trans. and ed. Daniel Breazeale, Ithaca and London: Cornell University Press.

— (1992), *Foundations of Transcendental Philosophy (Wissenschaftslehre nova methodo (1796/99)*, trans and ed. Daniel Breazeale, Ithaca and London: Cornell University Press.

— (1994), *Introductions to the Wissenschaftslehre and Other*

Writings, trans. and ed. Daniel Breazeale, Indianapolis and Cambridge: Hackett.

References and further reading

Hegel, G. W. F. (1977), *The Difference Between Fichte's and Schelling's System of Philosophy*, trans. H. S. Harris and Walter Cerf, Albany: State University of New York.

— (1977), *Phenomenology of Spirit*, trans. Arnold V. Miller, New York: Oxford University Press.

Hohler, Thomas (1982), *Imagination and Reflection: Intersubjectivity. Fichte's Grundlage of 1794*, The Hague: Martinus Nijhoff.

Jalloh, Chernor (1988), *Fichte's Kant-Interpretation and the Doctrine of Science*, Washington, DC: Center for Advanced Research in Phenomenology and the University Press of America.

Kant, Immanuel (1961) (first edn 1787), *Critique of Pure Reason*, trans. N. Kemp-Smith, London: Macmillan/St Martin's.

— (1967), *Philosophical Correspondence, 1759–99*, trans. and ed. Arnulf Zweig, Chicago: University of Chicago Press.

Neuhouser, Frederick (1990), *Fichte's Theory of Subjectivity*, Cambridge: Cambridge University Press.

Reinhold, Karl Leonhard (1790), *Beyträge zur Berichtigung bisheriger Missverständnisse der Philosophie*, 2 vols, Jena: Mahnke.

Rockmore, Tom (1980), *Fichte, Marx and the German Philosophical Tradition*, Carbondale, IL: Southern Illinois University Press.

Schelling, F. W. J. (1978) (first edn 1800), *System of Transcendental Idealism*, trans. Peter Heath with an Introduction by Michael Vater, Charlottesville: University of Virginia Press.

Williams, Robert R. (1992), *Recognition: Fichte and Hegel on the Other*, Albany: State University of New York Press.

HISTORY AND PHILOSOPHY: HEGEL'S *PHENOMENOLOGY OF SPIRIT*

Terry Pinkard

Hegel's interest in history spanned his entire philosophical career. His early essays – which remained unpublished in his own lifetime and have since become known under the rubric of 'Hegel's early theological writings' – were often historical in nature, and it is well known that he was an avid reader of history, of Gibbon among others, in his youth. In the 1807 work that carved out what came to be universally recognised as the Hegelian approach, the *Phenomenology of Spirit*, historical considerations played an obviously central role. However, in the *Science of Logic* of 1812 and the Heidelberg *Encyclopaedia of the Philosophical Sciences* of 1817 (the basis of what came to be known simply as the 'system'), history seemed not to be quite as obviously present. After moving to Berlin in 1818, however, Hegel consistently returned to historical themes in his lectures on art, religion and philosophy, and his book *Philosophy of Right* (1821) ended with a short section on world history, which was itself elaborated in lectures that were edited and published after his death under the title of *The Philosophy of History*. Almost all Hegel scholars have since recognised that, for Hegel, historical considerations were integral to his philosophical concerns and were not items tacked on to some non-historically conceived approach to philosophy. The problem has been to determine exactly what that role is and how it fits into Hegel's less obviously historical approaches (such as the *Logic* and the 'system').

The project of the Phenomenology of Spirit

The problem is made particularly acute by the fact that Hegel himself remained ambivalent about the status of his 1807 *Phenomenology*. According to his student Karl Ludwig Michelet, Hegel always referred to the *Phenomenology* as his 'voyage of discovery'. His use of the cliché was apt. In that work, Hegel came to terms with what for him had been an abiding concern since his days in the Protestant Seminary at Tübingen – the problems involved in determining what would count as a *modern* form of life. He had originally been interested in this in terms of how it would be possible for a religion to serve as the basis of the kind of moral and spiritual renewal of life that he and his friends hoped would come out of the French Revolution. Subscribing to his friend, Schelling's, aphorism, that 'the beginning and end of all philosophy is – *freedom*!', Hegel came to see that the problems of modern life were in fact the problems associated with freedom and what it entailed.

Indeed, he came to think that the problems with modern life went deeper than he or others had originally supposed. The old props that European culture had used to support its institutional, social and religious arrangements had undermined themselves; modern life thus found that it had no fixed place from which to derive any of judgements or justifications. The 'higher criticism' had undermined the immediate authority of scripture; scripture's authority had come to be dependent on theological interpretations. Beliefs about the beneficence of nature had been effectively undermined both by natural science and by the contested accounts of what nature supposedly required of us. Likewise, in the unsettled times of the French Revolution and the equally unsettling economic doctrines coming out of Britain and France at the time, the hold of tradition on people's minds could no longer be taken for granted – that our ancestors had done things in a particular way simply no longer counted as an authoritative reason for belief or action. Finally, even the idea of the voice of God or of divine commands had lost its immediate hold on people; the Reformation had undermined the idea that Christianity spoke with one authoritative voice that simply had to be accepted, and the resulting claims for freedom of conscience further undermined the idea that God's word could be the immediate, taken-for-granted basis for modern life.

It was thus not surprising that many intellectuals had taken to calling for a return to a reliance on a taken-for-granted authority, such as the sacredness of tradition, the givens of so-called common sense, the unrestricted authority of the Church, and so on. The task of philosophy in such a situation, Hegel came to think, had to be to show whether the modern reliance on freedom was indeed capable of providing any viable alternative to such discarded norms or to the appeals for a new form of dogma. In effect, he thought, Kant's claim for Enlightenment – think for yourself – had become the central norm for modern life. The only viable normative constraints on what we were to judge as true, as right, as being art, or as being worthy of worship had therefore to be *self-imposed* constraints. The issue thus naturally came to be how such constraints could be imposed without assuming some such normative constraint from the outset.

Hegel's response to this was to propose that we begin with the position in which we find ourselves and try to see what is viable within that position. To do that, he proposed in the 'Introduction' to the

Phenomenology that we treat all claims to knowledge (or moral rightness, aesthetic quality or divine status) as appearances, as simply one more historically shaped 'form of life' (to use the phrase popularised much later by Wittgenstein) in which certain typical claims about the world and ourselves take shape. The issue then is whether those types of claims can be satisfactory *in their own terms*, can live up to the promises they set for themselves and the standards that they employ to judge their own success, and not whether they live up to claims that we or others happen to have. In particular, they must *not* be judged in terms of how well they fit into *our* plans, *our* conceptions and *our* standards for what counts as success. Indeed, we cannot at the outset even presuppose that there is one shared standard as to what counts as *rational* for all these different appearances. We must approach all these different appearances in terms of scepticism about whether they succeed in their own terms.

Each of the different appearances is taken as a particular Gestalt of consciousness, a basic way in which a form of life understands itself and its relations to the world. In particular, any distinctive Gestalt of consciousness is differentiated from another by virtue of the core *norms* that each takes as *authoritative* for itself and the accounts that they give as to the binding, non-optional quality of what they take as authoritative for themselves. The *Phenomenology* shows that each Gestalt of consciousness has within itself what Hegel called its own negativity, its capacity to generate out of its accounts of itself a kind of self-undermining scepticism about its core norms and therefore about *itself*, a generating of internal paradoxes or displays of unfulfillable promises that gradually lead to the self-unravelling of what had been taken to be necessary for such forms of life.

The developmental path of the *Phenomenology* was thus laid out as being thoroughly sceptical and at the same time thoroughly historical. Indeed, in an intended pun in the German text, Hegel said it must be seen 'as the path of doubt (*Zweifel*), or, more authentically, as the path of despair (*Verzweiflung*)'. That is, it might seem to hold out no more than the possibility of a series of self-undermining points of view that lead to nothing. However, there is inherently a teleology at work in such efforts. We are trying to 'get it right', so Hegel thinks, and this breathes some life into what would otherwise be a succession of self-undermining Gestalts of consciousness since it shows that each succeeding form of life must understand what is non-optional for itself in terms of what it takes to be the necessary failures of its predecessors.

Consciousness and self-consciousness

The *Phenomenology* begins with a section entitled, 'Consciousness'. Hegel realised he had to begin in a place where many of his readers already were, namely, with the kind of post-empiricist, post-Enlightenment idea that there were certain 'givens' in consciousness that put normative constraints on what we could be said to know – namely, that there was a kind of sense-certainty that could neither be doubted nor undermined by conscious reflection and which guided our more refined attempts to make claims about the world. The alleged normative constraints of sense-certainty, however, loosen up quite a bit when we begin to try to explain just how they constrain what we can know. Once we begin to try to articulate what it is which we are supposedly aware of in sense-certainty, we find that our *articulations* of those items quickly begin to contradict themselves. Therefore, the deliverances of sense-certainty actually cannot offer us any reasons for belief one way or the other, since they offer equally good reasons for holding contradictory beliefs.

Hegel follows up the chapter on 'Sense-Certainty' with chapters on 'Perception' and 'The Understanding'. In the chapter on 'Perception', he tries to show how a putative direct awareness of individual things instantiating universal properties itself turns out to involve more than it originally claimed; namely, an awareness of the nexus of connection between individual and universal, which is not itself a matter of direct perception. Thus, the claim that we are directly perceiving things turns out to prove something else: namely, that we are actually *seeing them as* such and such, *taking* them to be this or that; that is, evaluating our experience in the light of certain norms.

Those who wish to say that our ordinary consciousness of objects puts normative constraints on what we can be said to know are led to take a last stand in the idea that we possess a certain mental faculty, a kind of 'mind's eye' – which at that point in the *Phenomenology* Hegel calls 'the understanding' – which somehow takes us behind the curtain of appearance to the supersensible substrate of things. Once again, Hegel shows that the deliverances of the understanding (when so construed) result in a level of abstraction that also licenses a variety of mutually incompatible conclusions.

The chapter on 'Consciousness' thus shows that there can be no direct *normative* constraints that arise from any so-called direct awareness of objects, and that our consciousness of things is always a *self-consciousness* of them in the sense that we are always *taking* things to be such and such and are implicitly aware of ourselves as doing this. In the section titled 'Self-Consciousness', he then turns to what he takes to be an equally one-sided notion, namely, the idea that if the so-called objects of direct awareness are not imposing any normative constraints on how we take them, then we must be imposing those normative constraints ourselves, independently of whatever the objects of the world are. At first it would seem that the only normative constraints would be those given by life itself, that agents impose an order on the world that helps them to satisfy their desires, but the problem of deciding which of our desires is more important is rendered particularly acute when the object of awareness is another desiring agent. Both agents would take themselves to be the independent member of the subject/object relation, imposing an order on the world in terms of getting what they want. For the agents, therefore, there would be no difference between their subjective points of view and a more objective point of view on the world. Yet as each encounters the other, they both find that the immediate identification of their own, subjective point of view with that of the 'objective' point of view (with being the way the world effectively is) is challenged as both understand themselves in exactly the same way. Each therefore demands of the other *recognition* as being the kind of entity whose point of view is the 'true' point of view. (The term for recognition is *Anerkennung*; it carries the sense of bestowing a kind of normative status on someone, as when one awards a medal to someone in recognition of some feat performed.)

Recognition emerges in Hegel's argument as *the* basic desire for such agents, not because it is natural to human beings but because it is required by the logic of their coming to take themselves as self-conscious entities. Moreover, since it is so basic, it is potentially more important than life itself, and one or both of the agents can therefore quite rationally decide to wager everything, even his own life, on realising this desire and making the realisation effective. If, for contingent reasons, one of the agents comes to fear the loss of his life more than he fears denial of recognition, then he becomes the vassal to the other, who in turn becomes his master. The master secures dominion over the vassal by getting the vassal to come to take his (the master's) *subjective* own point of view as counting for the vassal as an *objective* point of view and the vassal's own desires as worthy of satisfaction only to the extent that they fit into the master's scheme of desires.

However, such social relations of domination and servitude are no more epistemically and dialectically stable than are the more abstract considerations in 'Consciousness'. As the vassal comes to reflect on his status, he comes to realise that his status as a vassal is just as much dependent on his continuing to confer a certain normative status on the master as it is on the master's continuing to regard him as a vassal. The vassal, in fact, comes to realise the brute contingency of his position; for him, everything he had taken as fixed has been shaken, and he has been forced because of his fear to cede what he had taken to be true, but once the vassal sees that that there is no deeper metaphysical or natural fact that makes him a vassal, and that his servitude is in part constituted by his own continuing recognition of the master's authority over him, he implicitly recognises that he has a capacity to withdraw such recognition and therefore to resist such domination. The master's own point of view, which was seen as the 'fixed', determinate part of the relation becomes 'unfixed', as much in need for its authority of recognition by the vassal as the vassal requires the point of view of the master to maintain a critical distance towards his own beliefs and desires. The only normatively 'fixed'

thing is the vassal's (and the master's) own freedom, the ability to revise and assess those judgements that they make about the world and themselves.

Stoicism, scepticism and the unhappy consciousness

Indeed, so Hegel argues, it was at that point in antiquity where the old orders were losing their hold on people that realisation of the lack of fixity of social and epistemic relations led to the beginning of history in the proper sense. To have a history – as opposed to a mere sequence of events following each other in time – requires that one have some way of narrating the events, of establishing a connection between the events themselves. Establishing a narrative connection therefore requires that we bring something to the events which is none the less not something we simply impose on them but is something that is immanent to them. Since what characterises human action is its normative character, the attempt by agents at 'getting it right' in their epistemic, aesthetic, religious and practical lives, this normative character of action inherently gives us an internal standard of adequacy: what counts as adequate is that which we can come to understand as succeeding in its own terms, as making good on the criteria that it itself counts as success. Historical narration is thus fundamentally in terms of how people's actions, collectively and individually, fit into a scheme that understands the importance of events in terms of the role they play in establishing or undermining key norms.

The development of the *Phenomenology* begins with rather abstract arguments showing that there are no normative constraints imposed on us by the objects of awareness and that even 'life' itself does not impose any higher-order constraints on us in our practical dealings (that, instead, it was the desire for recognition which functioned as the kind of basic normative constraint on practical life). At the conclusion of those arguments, it suddenly shifts into a discussion of ancient stoicism and scepticism. Hegel's rationale for doing so is that he thinks that at the point where the authoritative norms of the slave-owning societies of the ancient world lost their hold on the minds of the people, it opened up a way of regarding the past that saw it not merely as being past but as being a *predecessor* whose attempts at 'getting it right' had internally miscarried in such a way as to require their successors to come to have the authoritative norms they did. Ancient stoicism was thus required by the internal failures of the dialectic of master and vassal; the stoic came to see that it is his power to bestow and withhold significance on things that counts as authoritative for him, that nothing can exercise normative dominion over his thought unless he grants it such dominion, and that all else is merely contingent. The sceptic radicalises the stoic's point: If nothing is really to be held fixed except for the free activity of thought, then we cannot even presume at the outset that free thought itself has the powers that the stoic claims for it; it too must be thrown into doubt.

Ancient stoicism and scepticism were expressions of how people in the ancient world began to sense that everything in their world had been undermined, that nothing could be held as authoritative and that they were left with an unconsoled way of living. On the one hand, they had certain norms in terms of which they lived and in which they could not help but believe; but on the other hand, they came to see that they could not justify or redeem their basic claims. They thus believed and did not believe, held fast to something that no longer gripped them but for which there did not seem to be much alternative. Hegel calls this mixture of belief and detachment the unhappy consciousness and he takes it to characterise not only the denouement of the ancient world but also the early medieval world of the early Christians, for whom the idea of Jesus's imminent return was becoming less and less plausible. Those despairing Christians instead came to develop practices to prepare themselves for the Second Coming, to make themselves worthy of grace, and in doing so came to understand themselves as participating in a practice that shaped humanity so that it was capable of receiving the divine 'truth'. They put their faith in priests, who, unlike the slave-owning 'masters' of the ancient world, were not people who simply imposed their own point of view as authoritative, but were instead people who attempted to mediate between the authoritative, 'God's eye' point of view and that of limited, finite individuals such as themselves. The

ascetic practices of devotion (*Andacht*), of inserting oneself into a social discipline that brings one closer to the 'truth' about the world thus came to be a type of thought (*Denken*), and in that way medieval religious asceticism transformed itself into modern science, establishing disciplined activities that let the world itself mediate our observations of it. That is, the medieval practices of Christian devotion created a form of life and a type of discipline that people came to understand as a self-imposed discipline that allowed the world to manifest itself to them in the way that it really was, and thus modern science with its reliance on the unlimited power of reason was born.

Reason, individualism and modern life

Hegel thus switches the *Phenomenology* away from discussions of the unhappy consciousness and begins a new, much longer, section titled 'Reason', which concerns itself with the way in which modern life has attempted to certify itself by reliance on reason instead of power or Church dogma. He begins the section with a discussion of how the successes of Baconian science helped to underwrite the faith in the capacity of reason to discover the nature of world. Baconian science's mastery of nature in the service of human needs – through its devotion to the idea of there being a rigorous method by which nature could be interrogated – thus shifted European life away from the figure of the priest as its authoritative figure and towards the more modern figure of the 'man of reason'.

Faith in reason rather than Church dogma, however, generated its own problems. Baconian methods did not easily carry over to the study of human affairs. Such methods establish correlations between independently identifiable types of events, whereas human life is a normative matter, with people responding to situations in terms of what they think they ought to do or believe, not merely in terms of some set of correlations. Hegel amuses himself in the *Phenomenology* with the leading pseudo-sciences of his time – phrenology, the determination of character by correlations with bumps on the skull, and physiognomy, the determination of character by appeal to anatomy – showing how they are misapplications of an otherwise successful method for studying nature, since they presume that character is something fixed, determinate and 'inner' that can be correlated with something fixed, determinate and 'outer'. Likewise, the various attempts at studying the mind by studying the psychological laws of association are based on a misunderstanding of what is at stake – which is, first, that thoughts themselves are only identifiable in terms of the normative roles they play in chains of theoretical and practical inference, and, second, that our basic concern must therefore be not with how we *in fact* think but with how we *ought* to think.

But the failures of misapplications of scientific method only sharpened the issue at hand. If reason really was to supplant Church authority as the basis of modern life, then it had to show not merely that it was successful in *theory* but also in *practice*, that it could actually *orient* people in their practical lives. In the *Phenomenology*, Hegel sketches out several alternative versions of these attempts in early modern European life. Taking Goethe's drama *Faust* as his starting point, Hegel attempted to show how the application of reason to practical life led early modern agents to adopt an experimentalist attitude to life and thus to use their rational powers to get what they want; such agents instead ended up subject to a 'necessity' that they had imposed on themselves and which contradicted the sort of the freedom they had imagined for themselves. (Faust wanted Gretchen, got her, but then found it impossible to save her from the fate in which his actions had then cast her.) In their quest for self-realisation, the Faustians found that more was needed to be said about the very *self* that was supposedly to be realised in the rational pursuit of satisfying our desires.

The failures of Faustian attempts at self-realisation required a later generation to generate a more determinate conception of what they therefore *truly* wanted. The result was an appeal to one's *own* feelings and emotions, an appeal articulated in Pascal's well-known aphorism about how we can only know the truth of certain first principles through our 'heart' and how reason recognises its limitations in the laws of the heart. But, of course, people's individual 'hearts' differed in the norms they dictated, and even where they coincided, no indi-

vidual could take the declarations of another's 'heart' to be authoritative for himself, since authoritativeness could only reside in his own 'heart'. Moreover, such a conception put a premium on hypocrisy since it gave individuals a positive motivation to feign certain feelings where they had none. What had promised to be a reign of reason in the service of sweet affectivity thus turned into something more nearly resembling Hobbes's war of all against all, a result which was all the more galling for those early modern sentimentalists who had taken themselves to be endorsing something completely at odds with what the wicked Mr Hobbes had affirmed.

The paradoxes inherent in the idea that gracious sentiment might lead us to distasteful Hobbesian conclusions therefore required that the appeal to sentiment be reworked and made more palatable. In this context, sentimentalism was joined to a celebration of the rebirth of classical virtue by uniting it with a doctrine of moral beauty or 'beauty of soul'. The most successful writer to attempt this was the third Earl of Shaftesbury, who used the idea of the 'beautiful soul' to provide an account of how reason could be made efficacious in our practical lives. The sheer *beauty* of self-sacrificing virtue (which Shaftesbury, like many others at the time, identified with ancient virtue) would be enough to motivate a well-brought-up person into identifying his own personal interest with the altruistic requirements of impersonal duty. In moral beauty, reason becomes practical, and the common good coalesces with personal interest by virtue of reason's attraction to the *natural* 'beauty of soul' contained in the notion of self-sacrificing virtue.

This conception of the congruence of personal interest and common good was quickly challenged by another group, the most well-known of which came to be represented by Bernard Mandeville's *The Fable of the Bees: Private Vices, Public Benefits*. Mandeville created an allegory by which a formerly prosperous hive of bees suddenly falls apart and sinks into ruin by acquiring the kinds of virtues recommended by people such as Shaftesbury. When they were narrowly self-interested and not altruistic, they prospered; when they became virtuous, they collapsed. The moral of the story was clear: the common good depends less on virtue than it does on the co-ordination of otherwise self-seeking, non-altruistic behaviours; reason can become efficacious only by being tied into something decidedly non-beautiful; namely, the chaotic give-and-take of modern economic life (what, to the followers of the aristocratically-minded Shaftesbury, could only appear as the wicked 'way of the world'). The debate between the followers of Shaftesbury and the followers of Mandeville turned on what was most natural to human action – on what really was in our 'self-interest' and would thereby actually motivate us, make reason efficacious in practical life. But what, in fact, decided the issue were the developing social practices and institutions of the emerging market economies of Europe, to which the Mandevillean account was much more attuned.

In fact, the development of modern life's attempt to make reason practical had been to undermine gradually all the traditional props of practical life that had held the old order together. As the so-called fixed points of social life each began to get unstuck, individuals found that they had nothing authoritative on which to rely except themselves. The unintended consequence of modern life's attempt at making reason efficacious in social life was thus the creation of an individualist model of social life. Once that became fully explicit in early modern European life, what came to count as authoritative reasons were related to what was taken to *express* the individuality of each agent, and what counted would be how well an individual expressed his already formed self and his sincerity in doing it, not with how those expressions were taken by others. (This invokes Rousseau's complaints about how the goodness of his heart was always misunderstood by others because of the way in which he failed adequately to express his 'true' self and the way in which others failed to see the goodness of heart behind his actions.) But this conception of expressive individuality also destabilises itself. For the agent to be taking himself as meaning such-and-such by his actions, he must appeal to like-minded others. Both aspects – what the individual takes himself to mean and what others take him to mean – are thus essential for the constitution of the meanings of one's acts and works.

Modern individualism, that is, is, on its own, self-defeating as an account of what it is doing; it requires a more fully social account of what is entailed in the process of coming to be 'like-minded'. But that was easier said than done. Kant attempted to show how each person would necessarily come to understand himself as self-authorising and would thereby also be led to understand that self-authorisation requires him to impose a norm on himself, which, if such self-imposition is to be genuinely *autonomous*, requires him to abstract himself away from all the contingent, merely 'given' conditions of his own life (including his own personal inclinations). The fully autonomous individual would thereby act only on those principles he could see as holding for *all* such individuals who had gone through that process of abstracting themselves away from all contingencies. Rational 'like-mindedness' would thus arise out of a series of individuals reflecting on themselves and coming to impose the same rational laws on each other. However, as Hegel argued, Kant's own solution ran aground on the sheer formalism of his doctrine; at that level of abstraction, nothing definite could be willed, and thus his account of our coming to be rationally like-minded failed. The application of reason to human affairs had thus paradoxically led to a great crisis of faith in reason itself. The self-undermining nature of modern, Enlightenment 'reason' thus required an account of how such 'reason' had come to be essential to the structure of modern European life and why that form of social life was not simply a way that the moderns just 'happened' to do things, but was itself something required by the historical insufficiencies of earlier forms of social life. The requirement for a more historical account of how we would come to be like-minded, therefore, led Hegel to follow his long section on 'Reason' in the *Phenomenology* with an even longer section bearing the title, *Geist*, 'Spirit'; that is, mindedness and like-mindedness.

Greece, Rome and Europe

Geist is one of the most obviously historical of the divisions of the *Phenomenology*, beginning as it does with ancient Greece and culminating in Hegel's own day. The purpose of the section is to explore the authoritativeness of modern life itself, especially in light of the growing dissatisfaction with it in Hegel's own day and the cacophony of putative alternatives that were springing up (ranging from calls for social revolution to nostalgia for medieval Christianity). Hegel attempts to show that modern life is not some merely contingent affair or some decline from a more glorious past but is in fact that which has come to be normatively required by virtue of the insufficiencies of the past.

Hegel begins the section of *Geist* with an account of an idealised version of Greek life that showed how reason was unreflectively efficacious within its habitual ways of doing things. The *Sitte* of a form of life are its customs and mores, things that people 'just know' without any intervening reflection (how far to stand from another in conversation, when to scratch, how to hold oneself, and so on). For the (idealised) Greeks, *ethical* norms formed part of those habitual, unreflectively known customs and mores; by virtue of the roles they played in society, they 'just knew' what they were ethically required to do. Thus, Greek life, according to Hegel embodied a form of *Sittlichkeit*, a way in which certain ethical norms were directly translated into action by virtue of their taken-for-granted status. The efficaciousness of *Sittlichkeit* itself, of course, presupposed that the social whole was harmonious, something that the tragedians of ancient Greece began to show was not the case. As the tragedians began to expose the hidden stresses and strains of Greek life, the immediate identification with their social roles lost its hold on the Greeks. They became, as it were, Socratic and philosophical. Greek life, with its spontaneous sense of duty and enjoyment, could not survive that kind of alienation, and thus what had been authoritative for them – their *Sittlichkeit*, their implicit belief that the social whole was harmonious and in order – began gradually to seem like a mere matter of historical contingency, and Greek life began its inevitable slide into historical oblivion.

Roman life, which took the Greeks as its teachers, simply embodied the alienation that had come to take hold of Greek life in its decline. Sensing that there was nothing to hold the people together that was immediate to them, Rome relied instead on law and the threat of coercion to compel obedience to its dictates. In Roman life, what was authoritative was

not anything like *Sittlichkeit* but something more like individuals constructing their inner lives for themselves, all the while obeying (out of fear and self-interest) the legal dictates of the Empire. Thus, once the Empire began to totter and people no longer feared its legions, there was nothing left to prop it up. What had counted as authoritative for Roman life – the uneasy balance between legal association as the third-person point of view and the stoical, sceptical and Epicurean cultivation of private interiority as the first-person point of view – had also undermined itself.

The result of the self-undermining nature of both Greek and Roman life had been the creation of Europe, with its characteristic 'society of orders' and its tripartite structure of estates: the aristocracy, the clergy and everyone else (the commoners). (The division into three estates was supposedly based on the functionalist principle 'I fight for you, I pray for you, I work for you'.) Hegel calls this a world of self-formation and self-cultivation – the German term is *Bildung* – in which people try to shape their own personal lives in terms of these alien social models (for example, the noble who cultivates his tastes and demeanour in light of certain aristocratic ideals). Political power rests in the hands of the aristocracy, since, as the estate of those people who are willing to risk all for glory, they have the interest of the whole (represented by the king, to whom they pledge fealty) at heart and not their own personal interest. The commoner, who pursues his own self-interest by seeking profit, is deemed unfit for such political office. In a lengthy and historically rich section, Hegel traces out how the growing power of the merchant class supplanted that of the aristocracy, and how finally, under the spell of Louis XIV, the French aristocracy, always proud of its desire for 'glory' and its military past, devolved into a set of fawning courtiers at Versailles. The aristocratic self sought 'honour' above all else – Lovelace's famous lines 'I could not love thee, Deare, so much/Lov'd I not honour more' nicely captured that conviction – but this 'honour' could only come from recognition from other nobles. The logic of that situation led to the idea of absolute monarchy, to there being a highest point in the scale of recognition from which all honour flows. Thus, as Louis XIV crushed the independent power of the nobility by making them dependent on his whims for the recognition they required, the military nobility of medieval life came to be the fawning courtiers of the early modern courts, and the distinction between the aristocratic noble and the base merchant was erased. Both were seeking to satisfy self-interest, and the merchant was increasingly showing he was better at it.

Enlightenment and revolution

The collapse of the authority of the aristocratic ideal, however, was devastating for modern European life. With its collapse came the disintegration of the distinction between the 'higher' sentiments and the 'lower' passions and the basis on which power had been distributed in social life. Indeed, with the increasing cynicism of the court at Versailles and its ethos that 'all is vanity', it seemed that modern life had lost its mooring entirely, that everything was 'groundless'. The failures of the aristocratic ideals, and thereby of the whole society of orders, thus required modern life to find its resources within itself, to become *self-grounding*. There were necessarily several attempts at this: both the Enlightenment and modern emotionalist religions attempted in their own ways to provide an alternative basis for a modern life free of all reliance on accepted tradition and authority; the former by basing life on what unbiased, detached individuals would believe and do and the latter in terms of what individuals listening only to God's voice within their own hearts would believe and do. (Hegel argues that the antipathy between the Enlightenment and these emotionalist religions blinded them to how much of a common position they shared.) The Enlightenment, however, partially won the day and advanced a series of abstract notions of how a more rational ordering of society could come about. That was famously put to the test in the explosiveness of the French Revolution, which was followed by the Terror, during which the guillotine's blade ruled. This showed how the abstractness of the doctrine of self-grounding as 'absolute freedom' combined with Enlightenment utilitarianism led to the wholesale sacrifice of many lives for the good of the Nation.

The individualism of the Enlightenment thus led strangely to a doctrine that denied the moral distinctiveness of individuals.

The Revolution contingently stabilised itself in the figure of Napoleon, who managed to institutionalise the gains of the Revolution. It fell, however, to German philosophy to think through the implications of what it meant for modern life to become fully self-authorising and self-directing. The first attempt at this was something which Hegel describes as the 'moral worldview', and the first and most basic expression of this was, of course, Kant's philosophy and his argument that behind the acceptance of any norm – epistemic, moral or aesthetic – was an element of spontaneity, of the completely free self-imposition of that norm. Self-direction – autonomy, as Kant called it – would be possible only if people determined themselves independently of all alien and contingent conditions, which a *priori* required them to abstract themselves out of their personal, particular conditions and act according to principles that are therefore valid for all rational agents. Kant's own heroic attempt at working this out, however, had foundered on the high level of abstractness and formalism to which his theory had led him. On the one hand, he wished to say that one should do duty for duty's sake; yet his various postulates of practical reason showed that he also tried to supply additional motivation in the form of promises in the next life and so on. Even Kant showed that he found it difficult to account within his own terms for any incentive for moral action, for a way in which an individual might see *himself* reflected in his moral actions.

Modern morality and beautiful souls

The failures of Kantian (and Fichtean) morality therefore required some account of how genuine *self-direction* was possible. The movement of German Romanticism that followed articulated that difficulty in its stress on the *individuality* of the self that was directing itself. For the Romantics, an agent could be said to be self-directing only to the extent that he was following out his own personal projects and plans, that his self was sovereign and above all laws, responsible only to its own conscience. Hegel characterizes such Romantics as 'beautiful souls', agents whose inner life is supposedly characterised by a kind of aesthetic perfection that is identical with morality and virtue itself, whose inner beauty projects an outward goodness. The problem with such 'beautiful souls' is that they must act and therefore sully their 'beautiful souls', since action in the world can never be as pure and exquisite as the supposed inner beauty they possess. Thus, 'beautiful souls' either never act and metaphorically just fade away like dying embers, or they must act but distance themselves from such action so as to maintain their inner purity and beauty. Thus, they either become Romantic ironists, who hold that, because the context of action is always so complex, their reasons for action must always be particular to them; or they become hard-hearted moralists, who direct their actions completely in terms of what they take to be required by the abstract moral law. Each appears to the other as a hypocrite: the Romantic ironist appears as someone who, behind the facade of morality, acts on his own particularist reasons for action; and the hard-hearted moralist appears as someone who invokes the abstract moral law but incorporates his own prejudices into it as he applies it to the particular case. The two 'beautiful souls' reconcile themselves with each other when each comes to see that in fact the charges are true on both sides, that each claims a universal validity for what they are doing and that each imports a particularist understanding of what the moral norms require into their own actions; in seeing their common identity, they forgive each other, and each comes to see that they have come to share a certain like-mindedness, that they are participants in *Geist*, and that at the core of their personal, subjective points of view, they have come to accept the claims of a type of universalistic reason. Each is doing what he takes to be necessary to realise his freedom, and such freedom has come to require a unity of the 'particularist' (Romantic) and the 'universalist' (Kantian) points of view.

At this point, they come to realise that such forgiveness and reconciliation in modern life is possible only in terms of a shared *religious* point of view about what is ultimately at stake in such like-mindedness: the conception of what is ultimately

and inherently of value is necessary to human life and gives it an orientation which structures the particularism of the human heart with the universal demands of reason.

He thus concludes his chapter on 'Spirit' and proceeds to another lengthy chapter on 'Religion' in which he develops the idea of religious consciousness in the historical manner in which he had developed the earlier chapters on 'Reason' and 'Spirit'. Religious consciousness of the divine – of that which is of ultimate and inherent value and which orients us – is shown to develop according the ways in which various religious reflections undermine themselves and in which later forms of religious reflection necessarily take their form because of the way in which past religions had, on their own terms, come to seem inadequate and to require just that type of resolution.

Religion and humanity

Hegel thus traces out how primitive, 'natural religion' begins by conceiving of the divine as radically other than the human; such religion remains, however, too abstract and indeterminate to provide any real orientation. The crucial turning-point is that of Greek religion, which sees the divine as similar, yet different from, the human; the divine is understood as the beautiful idealisation of the human without sharing in human mortality. Out of the Greek religion of beauty, art develops as a reflection on the same ends, on what orients us not by means of rite and ritual but by the creation of sensuous, beautiful form. Hegel thus attributes the creation of epic, tragedy and comedy to Greek life, with comedy evolving as that form of life plunges into a deeper crisis about its own inadequacies, the comic character creating a form of individual self-distancing from his own despair.

Only in Christianity are these problems resolved. The divine comes to be taken as identical with the human, not in the Feuerbachian sense that 'man is god' but in the sense that we come to see that the concerns of the divine and humanity are not radically separate, and we come to worship what is divine within our lives; namely, self-renewing, rational, self-conscious communal life. (Hegel's radical reinterpreation of Christianity as teaching that the full nature of the divine has thus been made wholly manifest in the life and death of Jesus of Nazareth has remained, naturally enough, one of his most controversial legacies and has led to charges of both atheism and excessive theism.) But even Christianity cannot adequately comprehend this about itself. Religion is a form of 'absolute spirit', or set of practices in which we reflect on humanity's highest interests by reflecting on what constitutes our like-mindedness via its expression in texts, symbols and artefacts; thoughts embodied in works of art; rites and rituals of religion; and works of philosophy. Like art, which offers a reflection on humanity's highest interests by producing objects of beautiful form, religion offers a similar reflection on humanity's orientation through its rites, rituals and symbolic devotions about the divine; but only philosophy, at least in modern life, can articulate what it is that is at stake in all of these 'absolute' practices, what the conceptual truth contained in them is. Modern life is neither fully beautiful nor capable of being exhaustively understood by rite and ritual. Philosophical 'absolute knowing', however, is fully self-mediating; it does not need to conduct experiments (as do the natural sciences), nor need it accept anything on faith (as does, ultimately, all religion). Only such absolute, conceptual reflection is capable of understanding that what counts as necessary for us has to do with its being required for us by virtue of the inadequacies of past attempts at articulating authoritative norms. Neither art nor religion can articulate authoritative norms for modern life that can, on their own, be convincing; in a modern, reflective culture they must always have an air of contingency and happenstance about them; only philosophy is capable of demonstrating their necessity, and it can do this only by virtue of the kind of self-reflexive historical account given by the *Phenomenology*.

Absolute knowledge

The 'absolute knowledge' at the end of the *Phenomenology* is thus the realisation by modern life itself that the traditional props that have supported its practices – tradition, divine commands, the 'voice of nature' and sacred texts – have fallen away, and it has found that it must rely only on its own self-critical and self-renewing resources to give itself any orientation. That is, modern life finds that it has come to require of itself that it be self-orienting because of the failures of past attempts at taking itself to be oriented by something transcendent to itself. It also finds that the resources it finds within itself are enough to enable it to avoid the nihilism, scepticism and despair that might seem to follow from such a rejection of all the traditional props; that by taking its own freedom as a norm, by accepting no normative constraints that it does not impose on itself, it has come to have a shape of like-mindedness that has room for great diversity within itself while still maintaining a rational structure for that diversity. Modern life becomes self-authorising by becoming reflexively aware of itself as having been rationally required and justified by the development of its own history.

The conclusion of the *Phenomenology* thus sets the stage for the rest of Hegel's system. If the basic norm of modern life is to be 'freedom', then the goal of the rest of the system must be to work out the realisations of that freedom. That is, it must show how free, self-certifying thought is possible (thus, the *Science of Logic*). It must show how the findings and practices of modern science do not implicitly undermine this kind of faith in our ability to be self-certifying nor are they incompatible with our more experiential encounter with nature (thus, the 'Philosophy of Nature'). It must show how our 'like-mindedness' grows out of our individual, subjective 'mindedness' (thus, the philosophy of 'subjective spirit'), and how our like-mindedness realises freedom as practical reason in the practices embedded in the familial, social, economic and political institutions of the modern world (thus, the philosophy of 'objective spirit'). Finally, it must show how a free, self-determining form of art, religion and philosophy is itself possible (thus, the philosophy of 'absolute spirit'). However, all these projects for the so-called *system* must seem merely arbitrary, the result of some particular philosophy professor's contingent view of the world unless the results of the *Phenomenology* are taken seriously; and so the *Phenomenology* remained, despite Hegel's own ambivalence towards it, the presupposition for the rest of his system.

Bibliography

Writings

Hegel, G. W. F. (1977), *Phenomenology of Spirit*, trans. A. V. Miller, Oxford: Oxford University Press.
— (1988), *Phänomenologie des Geistes*, eds Hans Friedrich Wessels and Heinrich Clairmont, Hamburg: Felix Meiner Verlag.

References and further reading

Becker, Werner (1971), *Hegel's Phänomenologie des Geistes*, Stuttgart: Kohlhammer.
Findlay, John (1958), *Hegel: A Re-examination*, London: Allen and Unwin.
Flay, Joseph (1984), *Hegel's Quest for Certainty*, Albany: State University of New York Press.
Harris, H. S. (1995), *Hegel: Phenomenology and System*, Indianapolis: Hackett Publishing.
— (1997), *Hegel's Ladder*, Indianapolis: Hackett Publishing.
Heidegger, Martin (1994) *Hegel's Phenomenology of Spirit*, trans. Parvis Emad and Kenneth Maly, Bloomington: Indiana University Press.
Heinrichs, Johannes (1974), *Die Logik der 'Phänomenologie des Geistes'*, Bonn: Bouvier Verlag.
Horstmann, Rolf-Peter (1991), *Die Grenzen der Vernunft: Eine Untersuchung zu Zielen und Motiven des Deutschen Idealismus*, Frankfurt a.M.: Anton Hain.
Houlgate, Stephen (1991) *Freedom, Truth and History: An Introduction to Hegel's Philosophy*, London: Routledge.
Hyppolite, Jean (1974), *Genesis and Structure of the Phenomenology of Hegel*, trans. S. Cherniak and John Heckman, Evanston: Northwestern University Press.

Kainz, Howard (1983, 1988), *Hegel's Phenomenology* (2 vols), Athens: Ohio University Press.
Kojève, Alexandre (1980), *Introduction to the Reading of Hegel*, trans. James H. Nichols, Jr, Ithaca: Cornell University Press.
Labarrière, P.-J. (1968), *Structures et Mouvement Dialectique dans la Phénoménologie de l'Esprit de Hegel*, Paris: Aubier-Montaigne.
Lauer, Quentin (1976), *A Reading of Hegel's Phenomenology of Spirit*, New York: Fordham University Press.
Pinkard, Terry (1994), *Hegel's Phenomenology: The Sociality of Reason*, Cambridge: Cambridge University Press.
Pippin, Robert (1989), *Hegel's Idealism: The Satisfactions of Self-Consciousness*, Cambridge: Cambridge University Press.
Pippin, Robert (1996), *Modernism as a Philosophical Problem: On the Dissatisfactions of European High Culture*, Cambridge: Basil Blackwell.
Pippin, Robert (1996), *Idealism as Modernism: Hegelian Variations*, Cambridge: Cambridge University Press.
Redding, Paul (1996), *Hegel's Hermeneutics*, Ithaca: Cornell University Press.
Rockmore, Tom (1993), *Before and After Hegel: A Historical Introduction to Hegel's Thought*, Berkeley: University of California Press.
Siep, Ludwig (1992), *Praktische Philosophie im Deutschen Idealismus*, Frankfurt a.M.: Suhrkamp Verlag.
Taylor, Charles (1975), *Hegel*, Cambridge: Cambridge University Press.
Westphal, Kenneth (1989), *Hegel's Epistemological Realism: A Study of the Aim and Method of Hegel's Phenomenology of Spirit*, Dordrecht: Kluwer Academic Publishers.
Westphal, Merold (1979), *History and Truth in Hegel's Phenomenology*, New Jersey: Humanities Press.

1.4

SCHELLING'S IDEALISM

Alan White

Friedrich Wilhelm Joseph Schelling, born in 1775 in south-western Germany, was a classmate of Hegel and Hölderlin at the university in Tübingen. He published his first philosophical essay in 1794, aged nineteen, and produced over twenty books and essays in the next fifteen years. After 1809 he virtually ceased to publish, but continued to lecture, developing new material, until the late 1840s. He died in 1854.

In the course of his fifty-year philosophical career, Schelling published such a variety of works that he has been referred to as 'the Proteus of German Idealism', derided for so often changing his form. Yet this tag is countered by Heidegger, who asserts that 'seldom has a thinker fought so passionately, from the beginning, for his one sole position' (Heidegger, 1985, p. 7). Schelling first identifies that position – better understood as a project than as a standpoint – in his second publication, which appeared when he was twenty years old; seeking 'the antithesis to Spinoza's *Ethics*' (Schelling, 1980a, p. 159). In the same year, he characterises the antithesis in positive terms as the 'system of freedom' (Schelling, 1980b, p. 315). Thirty-two years later, as Schelling developed his final system, his goal had not changed: 'A system of freedom – as great in scope and at the same time as simple as Spinoza's, its complete antithesis – that would really be the highest' (Schelling, 1994, p. 66). Throughout his career, Schelling sought an equilibrium between the demand for a system, which ties him to the rationalist metaphysicians of the eighteenth century, and the demand for freedom, through which he anticipates the emergence of twentieth-century existentialism.

From project to system

Starting with his earliest works, Schelling agrees with Spinoza on three basic points: that what the philosopher should seek is a comprehensive system grounded in the absolute; that the absolute must be self-determined, because if it were determined by another, it would be dependent upon that other, and hence no longer absolute; and that the absolute must be unique. But here he diverges from Spinoza by insisting that the absolute can, and indeed must, despite its uniqueness, share certain properties with at least one of the entities grounded in it, that is the human subject.

Schelling has two chief reasons for asserting a homogeneity between the absolute and the human subject, both of which he inherited from Kant. The first concerns freedom: if none of the absolute's characteristics can be shared by any of the entities grounded in it, then none of those entities can be self-determined, so none can be free. This, however, contradicts the important Kantian conclusion that, in Schelling's words, even the 'lowest degree of spontaneity in theoretical philosophy', the spontaneity we exhibit through our ability to reflect or to direct our attention, presupposes the independence of the subject from the object and thus manifests human freedom as fully as does 'the highest [degree of spontaneity] in practical philosophy' (Schelling, 1980a, p. 205), that is, the spontaneity exhibited in free choice and moral resolution. Freedom is thus, Schelling concludes, as necessary to human being as it is to the being of the absolute.

Schelling's second reason for connecting the human subject with the absolute derives from Kant's objections to rationalist metaphysics. Although Kant, in the *Critique of Pure Reason*, attempts to establish that the limits of human experience are also the limits of human knowledge, experience itself does not provide him with his knowledge of those limits. That knowledge develops instead from reflection on human subjectivity. From this the young Schelling concludes that although Kant proves that metaphysics cannot be grounded in an absolute that would be alien to the human subject, he thereby opens the way for a comprehensive system grounded in reflection on the subject.

To succeed in completing the Spinozist project while avoiding the Kantian critique, then, Schelling must ground his system in an absolute immanent to the human ego rather than opposed to it, an absolute that can ground an account of human beings as free and conscious subjects. To see how this might be done, Schelling looked to the work of Fichte.

Like Schelling, Fichte seeks to ground a system in the human ego. In his earliest works, in 1794, Fichte reaches four conclusions that were particularly important to the young Schelling: the subject as fully infinite would be beyond all consciousness and determinate content; full infinitude is the only state in which all the subject's desires would be satisfied; such satisfaction can be approached, but never attained; the philosophising subject in some sense transcends its own finitude through the self-reflective act of intellectual intuition. Taken together, the four suggested to Schelling that the goal of Fichte's philosophy is a form of mysticism: Fichtean satisfaction is to be found neither in action in the world nor in reflection upon it, but rather only beyond it, in the empty and ineffable realm of the absolute. Thus, although Schelling looks to Fichte for a path to the fulfilment of human being, he concludes that Fichte's path would end only with the annihilation of human being. If Schelling follows this path, he cannot develop his system of freedom.

Having sketched a path that proves to be, in his view, a dead-end, Schelling reacts in 1796 as he does throughout his career. He looks back to where the path begins. His Fichtean path begins with the determination of the absolute as subjective rather than objective, but that path leads him towards the obliteration of human subjectivity. Reconsidering the determination of the absolute, he concludes that it is, in principle, impossible. To determine the absolute is to limit it, and thus to destroy its absoluteness. Instead of saying what the absolute is, then, the philosopher must begin by interpreting the experience of absoluteness, the intellectual intuition within which all determinate content disappears. This task of interpretation, Schelling believes, presented Spinoza with a choice:

> Either he had become identical with the absolute, or it had become identical with him. In the latter case, the intellectual intuition would be of himself – in the former, intuition of an absolute *object*. Spinoza preferred the former. He believed himself to be identical with the absolute object, and lost in its infinitude. (Schelling, 1980b, p. 319)

Confronted with the experience of intellectual intuition, Spinoza first had to answer a *theoretical* question. Had he found himself, or had he lost himself? Was the experience one of self-realisation, or of self-negation? Theory alone cannot establish the superiority of either interpretation, because, given the emptiness of the experience, either interpretation fits. The two differ drastically, however, in their *practical* consequences. For 'dogmatists' like Spinoza, who view intellectual intuition as self-negation, the resultant practical demand is to 'strive to become identical with the infinite, to drown in the infinity of the absolute object'. In theory, this option is wholly defensible; in practice, however, it is viable only 'for one who is able to realize it . . . in himself, one for whom it is bearable to work for his own annihilation, to remove from himself all free causality, to be the modification of an object in whose infinitude he will, sooner or later, find his (moral) downfall (ibid., p. 339).

For those who interpret intellectual intuition as an experience of self-realisation – thereby embracing 'criticism' rather than 'dogmatism' – a different practical project emerges:

> If I thus *posit* everything in the *subject*, I thereby *negate* everything of the *object*. Absolute causality

in me would be the overcoming, for me, of all objective causality as *objective*. In expanding the limits of *my* world, I restrict those of the objective. . . .

My *determination* in criticism is, namely: *Strive toward intransient selfhood, unconditioned freedom, unlimited activity.* (ibid., p. 335)

Although Schelling does not clarify just what one should do in 'striving toward intransient selfhood', he soon concludes that the critical project, which has this goal, is not an essential improvement on the dogmatic, Spinozist alternative. Both aim toward the absolute, and thus toward emptiness. Once again, Schelling's path has led to a form of mysticism.

His path ends in mysticism, Schelling next concludes, because it ends with the absolute. This prevents it from leading to a system, and thus from being truly philosophical: philosophy must seek to *explain* everything, not to *escape* everything. But it can explain everything, Schelling now reasons, only if it *starts from* the absolute, not if it *ends with* the absolute. The philosopher must see how all is grounded in the absolute, not how all is swallowed up by it. In other words, whereas the mystic seeks the absolute as absolute, the philosopher seeks the absolute as ground. This search, however, seems to be undermined, before it can even begin, by a fundamental paradox. The philosopher demands an absolute that is the unconditioned condition, the groundless ground of all that is, yet the absolute is unconditioned and groundless only if it is indeterminate, and if it is indeterminate, then it can be determined neither as condition nor as ground. The systematic beginning requires, paradoxically, the determination of the indeterminate; the successful beginning must overcome the conflict between absolute as absolute and absolute as ground.

In 1797 Schelling avoids the paradox of the absolute's determination by means of a teaching he will return to again and again throughout his career. The absolute must be initially undetermined, and it cannot be determined by anything outside itself, but this leaves open the possibility that it can become self-determined. We can think of the absolute as beginning to determine itself through a primal act of self-reflection, its attempt to know itself.

Moreover, through the act of intellectual intuition, we can attain a standpoint that, because it is without content, resembles the primal standpoint of the absolute. The challenge becomes that of showing how the primal act of self-reflection initiates a process that leads to the world as we know it, and to us ourselves as knowers.

Schelling does not claim to prove that the absolute must have engaged in a primal act of self-reflection. Instead, the argument is that, unless the absolute is conceived in terms of a tendency to posit itself, it cannot be conceived as spiritual, it cannot function as a source of content, and the system of freedom is finally indistinguishable from the system of necessity: there is no antithesis to Spinoza. If the subjective absolute is to *exist* as absolute – if it is to function as ground – then it must intuit itself and, in intuiting itself, it must not cease to be absolute. At the same time, a system can result only if both nature and finite spirit can be derived from the primal self-intuition.

The task of Schelling's antithesis to Spinoza, as envisioned in 1797, is thus that of a derivation of content from the absolute; only through such a derivation – not, as Schelling earlier believed, simply through presentation of an absolute that is essentially one with the human ego – could the system of freedom be completed. Nevertheless, an affinity between the human subject and the absolute remains a crucial condition for the possibility of the completion of the system. Only if the human subject can replicate the primal self-reflection and the process that follows from it can the antithesis to Spinoza be developed.

The system of identity

The works written by Schelling between 1794 and 1796 are short and programmatic: all are less than one hundred pages long, and all concentrate on the principles and form of Schelling's projected system rather than on its concrete development. In the next seven years, Schelling moves from the programmatic to the systematic and from the general to the specific. Schelling's systematic constructions begin with nature, chiefly because this had been ignored by Fichte: between 1797 and 1799 he produces three lengthy works – between 250 and 350 pages long – developing his philosophy of nature. Beginning from the dualism of light and matter, Schelling attempts to demonstrate that nature develops through a series of increasingly complex polarities – from the magnetic, through the electrical, to animalian sensation and irritation [*Sensibilität, Irritibilität*] – all of which are best understood as resulting from the absolute's primal self-reflection.

With his philosophy of nature, Schelling attempts to convince the Fichtean that nature *can* be treated philosophically, albeit only within the larger context of a philosophy of spirit; he also attempts to convince the natural scientist that nature *must* be treated philosophically, that even the empirical scientist who depends solely on experiments for results must rely on theories for indications of what sorts of experiments will be valuable. Finally, and most importantly, Schelling attempts to show both scientists and philosophers that the mechanistic conception of the universe is fundamentally mistaken. In the Romantic tradition, Schelling objects to the notion that the universe is a grand machine within which plants, animals and humans can be nothing other, and nothing more, than complicated parts. To the view that matter in motion is reality and that life and freedom are mere appearance, Schelling opposes the view that even matter only appears to be dead, that it too is encompassed within what he now calls the 'world soul'.

By developing his philosophy of nature, Schelling attempts to establish his independence from Fichte; to establish his superiority, however, he must complete his system by adding a philosophy of spirit. He first attempts to do so in his *System of Transcendental Idealism* (1800), a work more ambitious and more comprehensive, but also more precarious, than any other he ever published. Here Schelling attempts to show how one attains the level of the absolute and how one then reproduces or reconstructs the process leading to the development of nature; he describes the origin of human beings and identifies the traces of absoluteness visible in the realm of ordinary experience. In only three hundred pages, Schelling attempts to cover all of what philosophy must cover: he gives an account of the whole, moving quickly from finite to infinite and then, more slowly, back

again to the starting point. The absolute, posited at the beginning through an act of intellectual abstraction, is discovered at the end through aesthetic appreciation:

> Only the work of art reflects for me that which is reflected through nothing else, that absolute identical that has already divided itself in the ego; that which the philosopher allows to divide itself already in the first act of consciousness; that which is inaccessible to any other form of intuition: it shines forth out of its own products through the work of art. (Schelling, 1800, p. 230)

Writing the 1800 *System*, Schelling believes that he has discovered the land beyond the 'land of pure understanding', to which Kant believes we are limited; he is convinced that he had found the land of rational intelligibility Spinoza had sought in vain. Confident of his success, Schelling moves through that land with the eagerness and haste of the conqueror, not with the patience and care of the explorer. It is not surprising, considering both the immensity of Schelling's subject matter and the relative brevity of his treatment of it, that the 1800 *System* does not solve – or even clearly recognise – all the problems that arise within it. The unsolved problems are what make the *System* precarious, so precarious indeed that Schelling abandons it within a year.

Of the problems resulting from the 1800 *System*, three are particularly important for Schelling's later development. First, there is a difficulty with the system's principle: although the principle from which the system begins is self-consciousness, described as 'the source of light for the entire system' and a light that 'shines only forward, not backward' (ibid., p. 18), the light ultimately does shine backwards, because the principle to which the system returns, as it comes full circle, is 'absolute identity', which becomes ego by dividing itself in the primal act of self-reflection. Whereas the absolute as ground appears to be self-consciousness, then, the absolute as absolute is pure identity – and in the 1800 *System*, the two are not smoothly reconciled.

A second problem with the 1800 *System* is that it presents the derivation of concrete, individual, subjectivity – my reconstruction of *my own* individual life, *my own* individual perspective – as both necessary and impossible. It is necessary, because the system must be complete, but it is impossible because the system must be the same for all.

Likewise, the third major problem with the 1800 'System' involves a criterion Schelling introduces but fails to satisfy. The successful system must 'solve all the problems that philosophers have always attempted to solve' (ibid., p. 19), but Schelling's system dodges some of the most important of those problems including, ironically, the one most stressed by the younger Schelling himself, that is, the problem of freedom:

> How the original limitedness – according to which, for example, it is impossible that a man attain during his life a certain degree of excellence, or that he outgrow the guardianship of another – how this limitedness can be brought into harmony with freedom in the case of moral actions, that is a matter with which transcendental philosophy need not be concerned, for it must, in general merely deduce phenomena, and freedom is for it nothing other than a necessary phenomenon. (ibid., p. 170)

The second and third of the 1800 'System' basic problems – individuality and freedom – derive from the unavoidable conflict between the conditions for the possibility of Schellingian construction and the conditions for the possibility of human freedom. The conflict is present in the 1800 'System', but it is far beneath the surface. It comes to the surface for the first time in his works of 1804 and is directly confronted only in the 'Freedom' essay of 1809. Immediately after 1800 Schelling concentrates on the first of the 'System's' serious flaws, namely, the conflict between absolute as absolute and absolute as ground.

The *System of Transcendental Idealism* is superseded within a year by the 'system of identity', which Schelling works and reworks between 1801 and 1804. In *Exhibition of My System of Philosophy* (1801) and *Further Exhibitions from the System of Philosophy* (1804), he returns to the part of the system in which he has the most confidence: the development from the absolute's primal self-reflec-

tive act to the fundamental forces of nature, including light, magnetism, and electricity. Only in the 1804 *System of Philosophy in General and of the Philosophy of Nature in Particular* does Schelling sketch the system in its entirety, thereby encountering again the 1800 *System's* problems of freedom and individuality. However, unusually for Schelling at that time, he decides not to publish this complete system.

From system to project

The non-publication of the 1804 system suggests that Schelling may have concluded that its problems are insoluble. A second indication of growing doubts about the system of identity is provided by a series of non-systematic works beginning with the dialogue *Bruno* (1802), continuing with the essay 'Philosophy and Religion' (1804), and culminating with 'Philosophical Investigations Concerning the Essence of Human Freedom and Related Subjects' (1809), Schelling's last major publication.

It is clear enough that Schelling abandoned the system of identity; less obvious is why he abandons it. One factor might be the 1807 appearance of Hegel's *Phenomenology of Spirit*, whose Preface contains passages that appear to be strongly critical of Schelling without actually mentioning him by name. Yet Schelling never acknowledges the relevance of Hegel's objections, and his final system, worked on from around 1815 into the 1850s, does nothing to avoid them. It seems more likely, therefore, that problems internal to the system of identity – most importantly, problems of individuation, and the tension between absolute as absolute and absolute as ground – lead Schelling to seek an alternative.

This seems clear from the 1809 essay translated under the title *Of Human Freedom*. Although presented as the culmination of the system of identity (Schelling, 1809, pp. 3–5), it is also introduced as the treatment of a problem that that system cannot recognise, that is, the opposition between freedom and necessity. He now insists that if freedom becomes merely a form of necessity – as it does in his own 1804 *System* – then philosophy becomes 'wholly worthless' (ibid., p. 9).

Schelling begins his attempted resurrection of

human freedom by arguing that the thesis that all is grounded in the absolute not only does not preclude human freedom, it *requires* human freedom: 'the emergence of things from God is a self-manifestation of God. God can however be manifest only in what is similar to himself, in free beings that can act on their own: beings for whose being there is no ground save God, but that are, just as God is' (ibid., p. 19). Thus, 'the concept of a derived absoluteness or divinity is so little contradictory that it is in fact the central concept of all philosophy' (ibid., p. 20). And because freedom rather than subjectivity is now seen as essential, the link between the divine and the human now appears as will:

> There is, in the last and highest instance, simply no being other than will. Will is primordial being, and only to it do all the predicates of the latter apply: groundlessness, eternity, independence from time, self-affirmation. The entirety of philosophy strives only to find will's highest expression. (ibid., p. 24)

The divine will begins to 'express itself' in a manner familiar to readers of Schelling's earlier works: an initial self-reflection leads to increased articulation. The process, however, develops along different lines. In the earlier dialectic, the content comes from the reflecting moment (the absolute as knower) not from the moment that is reflected upon (the absolute as known); at each intermediate phase, the absolute as knower is frustrated by the inadequacy of its knowledge, so seeks to know more. In the *Freedom* essay, however, content arises from the attempts of the absolute as known (now termed the absolute as ground, or the will to exist) to avoid being encompassed by the absolute as knower (or the absolute as understanding). As Schelling puts his new teaching in a lecture from 1810, 'Were there not something entirely opposed to the light and to thought, something not to be grasped, then there would be no creation at all, everything would be unravelled in mere thought' (Schelling, 1994, p. 217).

The primal act, then, liberates the ground moment (the will to exist) but the divine ground can never escape the moment of understanding (the will to know), it can only reveal itself to divine understanding. The process of self-revelation leads to the development of the natural world – wherein, at every stage, there is a temporary balance or harmony between ground and understanding – and then to its culmination with human beings. Human beings complete the process in that we mirror the absolute. Each of us, like the absolute, has the capacity to release the moment of ground from the moment of understanding. Indeed, true individuation seems to require not merely release of the dark or grounding moment, but identification with this moment, because whereas the will to understanding, in human beings, aims at comprehension and harmony, the will to existence strives for independence and separation. The tension between the two determines the human condition:

> Man is placed on a peak: he has within himself the capacity for spontaneous movement toward good or toward evil; the bond holding these principles in him is not necessary, it is free. He stands at the point of divergence: whatever he chooses, it will be his deed, but he cannot remain undecided. . . . The essence of man is essentially *his own deed*. (Schelling, 1936, pp. 50, 63)

With this assertion – which by over a century anticipates Sartre's teachings that human existence precedes human essence and that human existence is grounded in a 'primordial choice' by over a century – Schelling raises himself to a philosophical peak, he places himself at the point of divergence between two paths. Either he can focus on human beings as radically free agents confronted throughout their lives with the necessity of making decisions and choosing courses of action, or he can continue to cast his gaze beyond the human level, he could persevere in his attempts to uncover the supersensible source that gives rise both to humans and to the good and evil between which they must choose. A step along the former path would have been a step into the twentieth century, the beginning of the existential attempt to explain the world in human terms. Schelling does not take that step. Instead, he retains his affinity to Spinoza and to the eighteenth century; his insistence upon freedom cannot overpower his desire for a system.

The freedom of the *Freedom* essay is, for the most part, transcendent rather than existential: it is a freedom that cannot be experienced. Yet Schelling does not hold with complete consistency to the teaching that the primordial choice for good or evil is absolutely determinative. Instead, he at least suggests – but no more than suggests – the possibility of primordial decisions that, although tending toward the good or the evil, do not exclude the alternative. Individuals making such decisions can be led, by God or by other individuals, to change or strengthen their commitments (ibid., 67), although Schelling does not explain how such developments can occur.

Schelling's examination of human freedom is suggestive and provocative, but far from exhaustive. Instead of pursuing it, he turns back, in the second half of his essay, to that one of the 'Related Subjects' that has most concerned him from the beginning: the absolute. He returns to the problem of the derivation of content, now couching his account in terms appropriated from the mystic Jakob Böhme. Yet he merely suggests the teaching that will be the basis for his final system, developed after he ceases to publish. This teaching requires the application of a conclusion about human being to the being of the absolute: just as I can know who I am – most importantly, whether I am good or evil – only by examining what I do, we can know what the absolute is – most importantly, whether or not it is God – only by examining what it has done. The *Freedom* essay suggests this teaching, but neither in it, nor in any other work Schelling published, is this teaching developed.

Positive philosophy

For most of the first decade of the nineteenth century, Schelling was the brightest star in the heavens of German philosophy. In the two succeeding decades, his star was eclipsed by the brilliance of Hegel. From Berlin, the capital city of Prussia, Hegel ruled academic Germany; Schelling, banished to the provincial universities of Erlangen and Munich, was all but forgotten. According to Hegel, Schelling had played his role in the history of philosophy: he took the step past Fichte but was then left behind when Hegel himself took a further step and attained absolute knowledge. During the 1820s, in particu-

lar, Hegel was remarkably successful in convincing others of his absolute knowledge; no philosopher had any public success in opposing his teachings until after his death in 1831. And even afterwards, no rival appeared immediately. His power began to dissipate not so much because of external attacks as because of internal dissension among those who regarded themselves as his true followers: the implications of Hegelian 'absolute knowledge' are so ambiguous that some 'Hegelians' can be Christian monarchists while others are atheistic revolutionaries. Understandably, the Prussian king was more concerned by the revolutionaries, and seriously worried by the right-wing Hegelians' inability to silence their left-wing adversaries. The Prussian state, then, needed a critique of Hegel – particularly, of what appears to be leftist in Hegel – presented by one who would command academic respect. Consequently, in 1841 the king summoned Schelling to the University of Berlin to save the state from the 'legions sprung from the teeth of Hegel's pantheistic dragon' (White, 1983b, p. 146).

Not surprisingly, those of the Hegelian left were not inclined to be sympathetic to teachings supported – some would say commissioned – by the Prussian king. Arnold Ruge expressed his reaction in a letter to Feuerbach: 'Schelling is called to Berlin, Schelling after *Hegel*! . . . how irresponsible it would be if this challenge from the reactionaries were not greeted with bombs and grape-shot' (ibid., p. 147). But Schelling was not greeted in this way, and was even welcomed by some. Kierkegaard was so impressed by the first two Berlin lectures that he recorded in his journal: 'I have set all of my hopes on Schelling' (ibid.). Those hopes were set on Schelling's 'positive philosophy'.

Kierkegaard's hopes for Schelling were unfulfilled. Although Schelling promised to speak of life, what he spoke of, instead, was once again the absolute, continuing his quest for a metaphysical theology. By 1809, his own investigations should perhaps have forced him to conclude that his quest was hopeless, yet neither earlier nor later failures ever forced him to that conclusion. He continued to strive to produced a comprehensive system grounded in God, not out of perversity or obstinacy, but rather because he was convinced that nothing else could satisfy the demands of philosophy. He could not turn from theology to philosophical anthropology – from concentration on the absolute to a focus on human life – because he was convinced that anthropology not grounded in theology cannot possibly be philosophical:

> Philosophy means love of, striving for, wisdom. Thus, not just any sort of knowledge will satisfy the philosopher, but only the knowledge that is wisdom.
>
> If man demands a knowledge that is wisdom, he must presuppose that there is wisdom in the object of this knowledge. . . . There is no wisdom for man if there is none in the objective course of things. The first presupposition of philosophy as the striving for wisdom is thus that there is wisdom in . . . being, in the world itself. (Schelling, 1856–61, Vol. 13, pp. 201–3)

This conviction concerning the nature of philosophy ties Schelling decisively and irrevocably to the metaphysical project; it prevents him from embracing Fichte's 'highest maxim', which requires that the philosopher 'seek only the truth, however it may be', so that 'even the truth that there is no truth would be welcome to him, if that were indeed the truth' (White, 1983b, p. 150). For Schelling, the only welcome truth would be wisdom.

Schelling continues, then, to strive for the system of freedom, and thus confronts once again his fundamental problem: if everything follows necessarily from the absolute, then there can be no freedom, but if nothing follows necessarily from the absolute, there can be no system. Schelling's problem continues to be that of finding the proper balance between all and nothing; he seeks it, now, by distinguishing between negative and positive philosophy. He develops this distinction in two series of lecture courses, *Philosophy of Mythology* and *Philosophy of Revelation*, published only after his death.

Negative philosophy, for Schelling, is purely rational or logical philosophy. (Spinoza's is such a philosophy, for it unfolds wholly on the basis of deductive logic.) His own system of identity, and in its wake Hegel's encyclopedic system, rely on dialectic rather than deduction, but the difference in logic fails to address the fundamental flaw: 'We

can produce everything that comes forth in our experience in pure thought, but then it is *only* in thought. If we wanted to transform this into an objective claim – to say that everything is, in itself, merely in thought – then we would have to return to the standpoint of a Fichtean idealism' (Schelling, 1856–61, Vol. 13, p. 164).

Negative philosophy is trapped in thought because it cannot make the move from thinking to being; a positive philosophy must therefore begin somehow with being – otherwise, it will not be positive – and then move to thinking – otherwise, it will not be philosophy. What is required, Schelling concludes, is best characterised by what appears to be an oxymoron: what is required is a metaphysical empiricism. The move to the absolute is now considered not as a move away from experience, but as one that goes more deeply into experience:

> It is a mistake to limit empiricism to the sensibly apparent [*Sinnenfällige*], as though that were its only object, in that, for example, a freely willing and acting intelligence, such as each of us is, does not *as such*, as intelligence, encounter the senses, and yet each is knowable empirically, indeed *only* empirically; for no one knows what is in a man if he does not express himself; with respect to his intellectual and moral character, he is knowable only *a posteriori*, through his expressions and acts. Assuming we were concerned with an acting, freely willing intelligence that was a presupposition for the existence of the world, that intelligence also would not be knowable a *priori*, but rather only through its deeds, deeds that would be visible in the realm of experience; it would thus, although supersensible, be knowable only through experience. Empiricism as such thus by no means excludes all knowledge of the supersensible. (ibid., Vol. 13, p. 113)

Are we concerned with 'an acting, freely willing intelligence that is a presupposition for the existence of the world'? We must be, if we are philosophers in Schelling's sense, because only if the world is grounded in such an intelligence can we possibly become wise. Can thought alone tell us whether or not the world is grounded in such an intelligence? No, Schelling insists, it cannot. Yet pure thought –

thus, negative philosophy – continues to play an essential role in Schelling's systematic thinking, for it can reveal certain features that he will be able to discover in the world if, but only if, the world is grounded in God.

The shape of Schelling's final system can thus be expressed in terms of a syllogism. The first premise, to be established by negative or logical philosophising, is that the finite world can have the specifiable characteristics *x*, *y* and *z* only if it is grounded in God. The second premise, to be investigated through positive or empirical philosophising, is that *x*, *y* and *z* are present in the world as experienced. The conclusion that follows, if the premises are accepted, is that the world is grounded in God.

Superficially, Schelling's syllogism resembles what Kant calls the 'physicotheological' proof of God's existence, that is, that the world is too coherent to have resulted from chance alone. Schelling's argumentative strategy, however, does not begin with a naive description of the world – it does not reason simply from consequent to ground. Instead, it begins purely rationally or constructively. Positive philosophy is, with respect to the world, an *a priori* science, starting from the very beginning – the absolute *prius* (the *prius* that is presupposed by the endeavour of philosophy) – and deriving determinations from it in the original order; with respect to the complete absolute spirit, though, it is an *a posteriori* science, 'in that it proves the existence of that spirit, it explains or is the science of that spirit, only by examining what is posterior to it' (ibid., Vol. 13 p. 249).

The negative philosophy that shows Schelling what would follow if the absolute were God is, not surprisingly, closely related to the dialectic of powers developed in the system of identity and modified in the *Freedom* essay: we can, he argues, identify basic features of the development, but because content emerges from the dark or irrational power – the moment of existence or ground, not the moment of understanding – there will also be contingent features we cannot reconstruct. As in the *Freedom* essay, Schelling argues also that the powers, initially released by God, are harmonised again in humanity. In our primordial form, we are like God in that we are above the powers, we contain them; but

we are different from God in that we do not yet rule over the powers, because they have not yet, for us, become actualised as distinct. And we – again, in our primordial form – do not realise that the difference indicated by this 'not yet' is crucial: we can release the powers, but we cannot control them.

From our negative or purely rational consideration of God and creation we learn, according to Schelling, (1) that if the absolute ground is God, then we were created in God's image; that is, as unity of the three powers; (2) given that – as we cannot deny – there is a finite world, if the absolute is God then the world has resulted from our attempts to retain mastery over the powers while allowing them to develop individually, that is, from our attempts to become fully like God; and (3) if the finite world has originated in this manner, then we have failed, at least temporarily, to rule the powers in their independence from each other, and the first and second powers will be fully reconciled into a third only following a temporal process. The next question is, which features of the constructed world would, if correspondent to the existent world, provide evidence that the latter really does have its origin in our attempt to become fully like God.

If the real creation is grounded in our wilful fall – as it is if the absolute is God – then the fundamental human desire within the finite realm must be to master the powers by positing them as God, as the primal spiritual unity in and through which all would be made rational; the fundamental human desire must be to regain the paradise that was lost when the powers were freed. Yet the regaining of paradise through the positing of God is not a simply intellectual or purely rational matter: human beings must posit the powers as they are in the world process, not as they are in God, for the latter would be no real mastery or reconciliation of them. This means, however, that the powers must be posited differently in different historical epochs, because the human act that resulted in the fall and in the real creation has involved the powers themselves in the temporal process. God himself is not involved in that process, and the relation of powers in him does not change; yet the powers freed by human action are cosmic rather than divine, and they govern the development of the finite world. The first power, now termed the objective principle, attempts to retain its autonomy; it resists the efforts of the subjective principle to know it. Thus, throughout the first part of the historical process, the ruling principle of the world is none other than the dark, irrational power, and early attempts to posit it as such – attempts reflected in myths – result from accurate insight into the state of the world as it is, and not from any philosophical, scientific, or religious naivety.

Until the second power begins to articulate the first clearly, human beings will see the world, if they see it as it truly is, as governed by a single, unintelligible god. As the conflict between powers develops, the original unity of the dark principle is fragmented. The new powers that arise will appear to human consciousness as gods that are related to the first god: they will appear as its offspring, and human accounts of them will develop into systems of theogonic myths. Finally, with the development in which the principle of understanding comes to have real ascendancy over the principle of ground, such that the two are united while remaining distinct, it will become possible for humans to posit the true trinitarian monotheism of the Christian religion. At this point, the cosmic powers will relate to each other just as the divine powers do; the positing of the Christian godhead is thus the positing of the one true, eternal God.

The central contention of Schelling's philosophy of mythology is, then, that the gods of myth are in fact the cosmic powers. His positive argument for this contention takes the from suggested by his fundamental syllogism. Before presenting the positive argument, however, Schelling attempts to give his contention negative support in the presystematic 'historical-critical' introduction to the philosophy of mythology (ibid., Vol. 11, pp. 3–252). There, he purports to demonstrate that traditional theories – some of which claim that myth is grounded in poetry, others that it is best understood as a primitive form either of natural science or of rational philosophy – fail to explain the phenomenon. Summarising the conclusions of that argument in the *Philosophy of Revelation* lectures, he insists that

> these representations – the mythological ones – cannot be explained in any other way [save my

own], as the results of all previous hypotheses have clearly shown; they cannot be explained as invented [*erfundene*], nor as imagined [*erdichtete*], nor as resulting either from a merely contingent confusion or from a prior revelation; they are, rather, thinkable only as necessary products of the fallen human consciousness that is under the domination of the powers, which themselves, in their separation, have lost their divine significance, and have become merely cosmic. (ibid., 61, Vol. 13, p. 378)

Negative philosophy's understanding of the dialectic powers makes possible the distinction of essential gods – ones corresponding to moments of the dialectic – from inessential ones; but with the assertion that some gods are inessential, the danger of question-begging arises for the endeavour as a whole. Positive philosophers are to examine the structures of myths hoping to find certain relations, but they will recognise as essential to those structures only the relations they know to seek. Given such a procedure, success might appear to be guaranteed, but of minimal importance. There are enough myths in the world, it might seem, that it would be difficult to imagine any structure not somehow reflected in at least some of them.

This objection is only partially applicable to Schelling's procedure. Schelling does not introduce contingency into his account in order to allow himself to explain away insignificant gods, those unrelated to the powers; rather, as he argues as early as the *Freedom* essay, since the ground principle is a principle, irrational and contingent features *must* be present in the factical world. And although one consequence of this is that the correspondence of gods and powers cannot be complete, Schelling's project does not require that it be complete. Schelling acknowledges that he cannot definitively prove that the world process is theogonic; he therefore need not explain the origins of all mythic gods, but need only reveal enough correspondence between powers and gods to establish his account as superior to the alternatives.

In his treatment of historical myths, Schelling reveals that he has not lost either the attention to detail nor the insight into analogous structures that he first exhibited in his philosophy of nature; he presents his investigations of polytheistic myth in twenty-three lectures comprising 540 pages. But the philosophy of mythology does not exhaust positive philosophy. Rather it gives way to the philosophy of revelation.

The status of 'revelation' as a source of knowledge distinct from reason is established, according to Schelling, by the prior demonstration that mythic consciousness has accurate but non-rational access to the cosmic powers themselves: 'A real relation of the human essence of God is verified by the philosophy of mythology prior to all revelation, and grounded on so broad a base that I may assume it as firmly and unshakably established' (ibid., Vol. 14, 296). The fact that pre-Christian mythmakers accurately reflected the relations of the powers in their myths proves that our relation to the divine is real rather than merely ideal: we have access to God, but it is not primarily through reason. The truth can be revealed at the historical point where the powers themselves have achieved a state of balance correspondent to their balance in the divine unity; at that point, it becomes possible in principle for human beings to grasp the highest truth. At first, it is grasped only by a privileged few. Because access to the principles and to God is at this point through revelation rather than through reason, intelligence is not a factor in determining who the few will be.

The 'truth' of revelation is, according to Schelling, the truth of the world, the truth that reveals that there is 'wisdom in the world'. Schelling devotes fourteen lectures to developing this truth and to relating it to the person of Jesus Christ, but he denies that either Christ or revelation can mark the completion of the world process. He insists instead that revelation must be followed – in what remains the future – by a 'philosophical religion', a teaching grounded not in a knowledge or truth revealed only to a few apostles and communicated by them to others who have faith in them, but rather in a knowledge 'that would be possible for and accessible to human beings under all circumstances, at all times and in all places, that is, universally human knowledge, as free, scientific knowledge' (ibid., Vol. 14, p. 296). Schelling's positive philosophy purports to provide the theoretical ground for this 'truly spiritual house of God . . .

in which all human striving, willing, thinking, and knowing would be brought into complete unity' (ibid., Vol. 14, p. 296).

Schelling's legacy

The rhetoric of the opening lectures encouraged those in Schelling's audience to believe that even his metaphysical doctrines would have important and immediately obvious practical implications. His emphasis on reality and existence was welcome to leftists and rightists alike. The former longed for evaluations of existing governments rather than Hegelian descriptions of abstract political forms, the latter for a presentation of God as a personal force acting in the world rather than as Hegel's 'absolute idea'. Kierkegaard reports that Schelling's second lecture brought him 'indescribable' joy, that his spirits soared when Schelling used 'the word "reality" ' and spoke 'of the relation of philosophy to reality' (White, 1983b, p. 187).

Despite their profound philosophical and ideological differences, those who attended Schelling's lectures agreed with near unanimity that what he promised was extremely valuable; they also agreed that what he delivered as his own teaching was utterly worthless. Expecting to hear discussions bearing on the problems raised either by the failure of the French Revolution to do away with monarchy or by the success of the Enlightenment in doing away with religion, Schelling's audience was subjected instead first to descriptions, presented by the self-professed philosopher of life, of obscure powers and their even more obscure interrelations, and then to examinations of archaic myths and the historical Jesus. Kierkegaard concluded, within three months, that Schelling surpassed other philosophers not in profundity but in shamelessness and that 'the whole of the doctrine of powers betrays the greatest impotence' (ibid., p. 188).

The apparent failure of positive philosophy led many to conclude that metaphysics is impossible as theology; that is, as the science of the highest being, the science that would explain finite entities in terms of their relation to an infinite entity. The abandonment of metaphysical theology is the first part of Schelling's philosophical legacy; the second part of that legacy developed from Schelling's critique of Hegel. Through the apparent cogency of that critique, Schelling has established, to the satisfaction of most who have been exposed to it (including Kierkegaard, Feuerbach, Engels, Marx and Bakunin) that metaphysics is also impossible as ontology, that is, as the science of the categories of being, the science that would explain finite entities in terms of the ideas or concepts that make them intelligible. Schelling convinced his philosophical successors that metaphysics, the fundamental rational science that would ground all other sciences, is impossible as ontology and as theology; he thereby convinced them to abandon the metaphysical quest for rationality altogether.

Schelling struggled for over fifty years to develop a rational system that would account, and leave room, for contingency and freedom. He devoted his career to successive attempts to produce the one system – the antithesis to Spinoza – that would have satisfied his longing for freedom. And even if he never succeeded, the obstinacy with which he held to his project reveals the intensity of his philosophical eros. Schelling demands our admiration because he, like his great rival, 'risked everything, desiring either the whole truth, in its entire magnitude, or no truth at all' (Schelling, 1980a, p. 152).

Bibliography

Writings

All page references are to the German editions, as indicated in the margins of the English translations.

Schelling, F. W. J. (1980a) (first edn, 1795a), 'Of the I as Principle of Philosophy', in Fritz Marti (ed.), *The Unconditional in Human Knowledge*, Lewisburg: Bucknell University Press.
— (1980b) (first edn, 1795b), 'Philosophical Letters on Dogmatism and Criticism', in Fritz Marti (ed.), *The Unconditional in Human Knowledge*, Lewisburg: Bucknell University Press.
— (1994) (first edn, 1797a), 'Treatise Explicating the Idealism of the *Science of Knowledge*', in Thomas Pfau (ed.), *Idealism and the Endgame of Theory*, Albany: State University of New York Press.
— (1978) (first edn, 1800), *System of Transcendental Idealism*, trans. Peter Heath, Charlottesville: University of Virginia Press.
— (1984) (first edn, 1802), *Bruno, or On the Nature and the Divine Principle of Things*, trans. Michael Vater, Albany: State University of New York Press.
— (1988) (first edn, 1803), *Ideas For a Philosophy of Nature as Introduction to the Study of this Science*, trans. Errol. E. Harris and Peter Heath, Cambridge/New York: Cambridge University Press.
— (1994) (first edn, 1804); 'System of Philosophy in General and of the Philosophy of Nature in Particular', in Thomas Pfau (ed.), *Idealism and the Endgame of Theory*, Albany: State University of New York Press.
— (1936) (first edn, 1809), *Of Human Freedom*, trans. James Gutmann. La Salle, IL: Open Court.
— (1994) (first edn, 1810), 'Stuttgart Lectures', in Thomas Pfau (ed.), *Idealism and the Endgame of Theory*, Albany: State University of New York Press.
— (1994) (first edn, 1827), *On the History of Modern Philosophy*, trans. Andrew Bowie, Cambridge/New York: Cambridge University Press.
— (1974–6) (first edn, 1856–61); *Sämmtliche Werke (Collected Works)*, 14 Vols, Stuttgart and Augsburg: J. G. Cotta'scher Verlag. Reprint edition of selected works, Darmstadt: Wissenschaftliche Buchgesellschaft.

References and further reading

Beach, Edward (1994), *The Potencies of God(s): Schelling's Philosophy of Mythology*, Albany: State University of New York Press.
Bowie, Andrew (1993), *Schelling and Modern European Philosophy: An Introduction*, London/New York, Routledge.
Brown, Robert F. (1977), *The Later Philosophy of Schelling: The Influence of Boehme on the Works of 1809–15*, Lewisburg: Bucknell University Press.
Esposito, Joseph L. (1977), *Schelling's Idealism and Philosophy of Nature*, Lewisburg: Bucknell University Press.
Heidegger, Martin (1985), *Schelling's Treatise on the Essence of Human Freedom*, trans. Joan Stambaugh, Athens, OH: Ohio University Press.
Marx, Werner (1984), *The Philosophy of F. W. J. Schelling: History, System, and Freedom*, trans. Thomas Nenon, Bloomington: Indiana University Press.
Snow, Dale E. (1996), *Schelling and the End of Idealism*, Albany: SUNY Press.
Tillich, Paul (1974a), *Mysticism and Guilt-Consciousness in Schelling's Philosophical Development*, trans. Victor Nuovo, Lewisburg: Bucknell University Press.
— (1974b), *The Construction of Historical Religion in Schelling's Positive Philosophy*, trans. Victor Nuovo, Lewisburg: Bucknell University Press.
White, Alan (1983a), *Absolute Knowledge: Hegel and the Problem of Metaphysics*, Athens, OH: Ohio University Press.
— (1983b), *Schelling: An Introduction to the System of Freedom*. New Haven: Yale University Press.

1.5

THE WORLD AS WILL: SCHOPENHAUER

Robert Aaron Rethy

Life and writings

Arthur Schopenhauer (born 1788 in Danzig, died 1860 in Frankfurt am Main), was the son of Heinrich Floris Schopenhauer, a wealthy merchant and Johanna Trosiener, who was later to become a well known member of Goethe's circle in Weimar and, subsequently, a popular novelist whose collected works, published in 1831, filled twenty-four volumes. The death of his father (a probable suicide) in 1805 led to the future philosopher's ultimate abandonment of the plan that he enter business. After further study, he attended the University of Göttingen in 1809 where he studied with G. E. Schulze, whose *Aenisidimus* (1796), with its critique of Kant's conception of the thing-in-itself, had played a crucial role in the early development of Fichte's *Wissenschaftslehre*. It was through Schulze that he became acquainted not only with Kant, but also with Plato and Schelling. The connection between Plato and Kant, a crucial thesis of his philosophy as a whole, is the subject of some of his earliest and most penetrating notebook entries (Schopenhauer, 1988, vol. I, nos 17, 228, 442). Schopenhauer left Göttingen for Berlin to attend Fichte's lectures; but, despite apparently serious attempts, testified by his voluminous notebooks (preserved in Schopenhauer, 1988, vol. II), he found himself deeply out of sympathy with the Fichtean philosophy of reflection, and his distaste for German idealism, which only increased with the years, dates from this encounter. Following Napoleon's invasion of Berlin, Schopenhauer retired to a small town, outside of Weimar, where he wrote his dissertation *On the Fourfold Root of the Principle of Sufficient Reason*, whose simplification and transformation of the Kantian doctrine of the concepts of the understanding into a third form of intuition next to space and time forms the basis of his distinctive epistemology and its difference from Kant's.

The ideality of sensation is the theme of *On Vision and Colours*, written in 1815 under the influence of his encounter with Goethe's *Farbenlehre* (an enthusiasm not reciprocated by Goethe for the younger man's contribution). At this time, Schopenhauer moved to Dresden where, for four years, he worked out *The World as Will and Representation* in intellectual isolation. In addition to the dual influence of Plato and Kant, he had also been introduced to doctrines of Eastern religion by F. Meyer in Weimar (1813), and is often said to be the first Western philosopher seriously to incorporate Eastern thought into his system. The work is announced in a note from 1813, which begins:

> Beneath my hands and rather within my mind a work is growing, a philosophy, which is going to be ethics and metaphysics *in one* [*in Einem*], though they have previously been so falsely separated, like soul and body. (Schopenhauer, 1988, vol. I, no. 92)

After the completion of his major work at the age of thirty, Schopenhauer hoped to teach at the

University of Berlin, where Hegel had only recently been installed. Although unimpeded in his appointment by Hegel, Schopenhauer chose to lecture at the same time as the more senior philosopher and at first attracted few, and then no, students. His deep antipathy for Hegel can be dated from this event, thus post-dating the publication of *The World as Will and Representation*. All references to him in that work or the earlier dissertation were added to later editions. Schopenhauer published nothing further until *On the Will in Nature*, seventeen years after the publication of *The World as Will and Representation*.

In 1837 he encouraged the separate publication of the first edition of Kant's *Critique of Pure Reason*, establishing himself as the first to recognise publicly the importance of the divergence between the first and second editions, a commonplace of Kantian scholarship today. The two writings devoted to ethics, *On the Freedom of the Will* (1839), and *On the Foundation of Morality* (1840) were both submitted as responses to public competitions. The former was awarded first prize, the latter, although the only entry, was pointedly refused any award. Schopenhauer had them published together, in 1841, as *The Two Fundamental Problems of Ethics* and characterised them (in the Preface) as a 'supplement to the Fourth Book of my main work as my writing *On the Will in Nature* is a very essential and important supplement to its Second Book'. In 1844 the second edition of *The World as Will and Representation* appeared at his own insistence. The first edition had gone out of print and had also aroused little interest among reviewers and the academy. The second edition comprised additions (there were no substantive corrections) to what was now Volume I, and a second volume whose chapters were keyed to sections of the first. Schopenhauer's fortunes with the public slowly began to change at this point, Schelling's famous lectures in 1842 perhaps marking the beginning of the decline of Hegelianism in the German academy (see Hübscher, 1989 p. 352). However, it was the disillusionment that followed upon the failure of the left-Hegelian-inspired Revolutions of 1848 – in which he had been a willing, if minor, participant on the side of the Government forces – along with the publication in 1851 of the popular essays contained in *Parerga and Paralipomena*

whose title indicates their frankly secondary philosophical importance, that led to the phenomenal growth of Schopenhauer's fame in the last decade of his life. Characteristically, it was a discussion of this work in the English *Westminster Review*, Oxenford's 'Iconoclasm in German Philosophy', which was then translated into German, that paved the way for his recognition. Schopenhauer himself announces this ultimate vindication ('their Caspar Hauser has escaped') in his Preface to the Second Edition (1854) of *On the Will in Nature*. In 1859 he published a Third Edition of his major work, and died one year later.

Overview and epistemological basis: the world as representation

Schopenhauer emphasised the unitary nature of his philosophy in his earliest Preface to *The World as Will and Representation*, as in the early note already quoted: 'What is supposed to be communicated by [this book] is a single thought' which, 'viewed from different sides, shows itself as what people have called metaphysics, what they have called ethics, and what they have called aesthetics' (Schopenhauer, 1969, vol. I, p. xii). However, to call it a single thought is not to imply that it is singular. Its formal unity of purpose is matched by a thoroughgoing material duplicity. The Kantian insight, said to be both his greatest discovery and the core of his philosophy, is precisely the discovery of the *duality* of appearance and thing-in-itself, a duality mirrored in the fundamental dualism of Schopenhauer's 'system', that of world as representation and world as will. Of these two aspects of the world, neither is itself a unit. Due to its essential division within itself the will, the 'single' thing-in-itself, is not itself a unit. And knowledge, forming the other structural axis of the system, is divided between knowledge 'in accordance with the principle of sufficient reason' in its first two books (knowledge of appearance and the will) and knowledge independent of this principle in its last two books (the intuitive knowledge that constitutes art in Book III and the insight that leads to morality and saintliness in Book IV). This duplicity is connected with the duplicity of our essence which does not rest in an absolute unity and thus makes unitary self-consciousness, the Holy Grail or Philosopher's Stone of German Idealism, impossible in one sense, the miracle κατ' ἐξοχήν (par excellence) in another.

These various dualities of consciousness seem to go back to one that pervades the early notebook entries, and whose presence, despite the terminological changes, is felt throughout Schopenhauer's writings: the opposition of the better consciousness and empirical consciousness. The former is a timeless, transcendent state of awareness in direct and fierce opposition to empirical awareness and its objects. It is the obvious source of the impersonal, contemplative vision common to the artist of Book III and the philosopher-saint of Book IV. In 1813, prior to the publication of any of his books, Schopenhauer wrote:

> The source of all true happiness, of all comfort that is secure and not built upon shifting sand but rather on an unshakable foundation (the better consciousness) is, for our empirical consciousness, total destruction, death, and annihilation. No wonder, then, that we can gain no comfort from it as long as we remain on the standpoint of the empirical consciousness . . . Hence, in order to be true to that better consciousness, we must renounce this empirical consciousness and separate ourselves from it. Self-mortification [Selbstertö-tung]. (Schopenhauer, 1988, no. 128; see Zint, 1954)

Schopenhauer, then, begins his philosophy from this characteristically modern experience of self-division, an experience designated by Hegel, in his 1800 Differenz-Schrift as that which gives rise to the need for philosophy and which is particularly characteristic of the post-Kantian epoch. Schopenhauer, however, certainly did not place himself in such systematic proximity to any of these near-contemporaries whom he mercilessly pilloried throughout his works. Rather he urges his readers to view him as a follower of Kant, alone among the moderns, correcting and completing the latter's grand work. He marks himself as a critical philosopher in his epistemological beginning: 'The world is my representation' is the assertion with which The World as Will and Representation begins. This statement signifies, according to the first section of the book, that everything that belongs to the world is conditioned by the subject of knowledge, without which there could be no object. Schopenhauer identifies three forms of intuition – space, time and causality – that constitute the world of representation as a world of interrelated individual objects. By including causality as one of the sensuous forms of intuition, Schopenhauer makes a fundamental revision in Kant's epistemology, which separated a priori sensuous forms of intuition (space and time) from categories of the understanding (causality being one of the twelve). Through their transcendental deduction, the categories guarantee the objectivity of knowledge for Kant. For Schopenhauer, on the other hand, causation is a form of intuition that proceeds from the body and is present equally in humans and animals. These forms constitute a screen, a 'Veil of Maja' that is placed between 'the world inside my head and the world outside my head' (Schopenhauer, 1969, vol. II, p. 3). The world of representation thus lacks true objectivity ('the world is my representation'): 'if it [causality] is a priori given, as Kant has more correctly taught us, then it is of subjective origin, and then it is clear that we always remain in the subjective' (ibid., vol. II, p. 11). Due to this focus on non-discursive, receptive intuition, Schopenhauer views Kant on a continuum with the English empiricists. The elevation of intuition is also co-ordinate with the subsidiary role that both understanding and reason play for Schopenhauer, both in experience and philosophy. Schopenhauer summarises this in Chapter Seven of Volume II of The World as Will and Representation:

> To intuit, to let the things themselves speak to us, apprehend new relationships among them, only afterward to deposit and store this all in concepts in order to possess it securely: this yields new knowledge . . . The innermost core of every genuine and actual knowledge is an intuition, every new truth is also the product of one. All originary thinking happens in images. (ibid., vol. II, p. 72)

This last sentence, added in the third edition, and repeated, significantly, in the chapter on artistic genius shows clearly the way in which this view of the relation of thought, intuition and knowledge leads to the apotheosis of art as objective knowledge in Book III. Its denial of the spontaneity of reason and understanding will clearly entail the impotence of reason as a force against the passions or as a source of goals for action.

The will as thing in itself

According to Chapter 17 of the Second Volume of *The World as Will and Representation*, 'On the Metaphysical Need of Human Beings', in a passage echoed by Nietzsche: 'only to thoughtless beasts do the world and existence seem to be self-understood. For human beings, on the other hand, they are a problem' (Schopenhauer, 1969, vol. II, p. 171). This problem leads beyond investigations that follow the principle of sufficient reason, beyond the knowledge we share with animals, to metaphysics, which attempts to solve the 'riddle of existence' by discovering 'the correct, universal understanding [*Verständnis*] of experience itself, the true interpretation of its sense and content. This is the metaphysical' (ibid., vol. II, p. 183).

The image of experience as a riddle or cipher whose meaning must be interpreted, and whose solution is the thing-in-itself, indicates Schopenhauer's attempt to construct an immanent metaphysics that does not violate the Kantian strictures against transcendent speculation. It also indicates the anthropological turn characteristic of Schopenhauer. He may lay claim to be the originator of the metaphysics of meaning – foremost protagonist of which is Heidegger – since, according to him, the concern for the metaphysical is neither for the being of beings nor for the indubitable foundation of knowledge, but for the meaning of an otherwise phantom-like existence. Schopenhauer claims that he has discovered the answer to this riddle by avoiding two traditional errors, the rationalist's error of identifying being and thinking and the dogmatist's error of identifying an (external) appearance with the thing-in-itself. Contra rationalism, Schopenhauer offers an inverse proportionality of knowability and genuine reality:

> The more necessity that knowledge bears along with it . . . the clearer and more sufficient it is, the less pure objective content it has or the less genuine reality is given to it. And on the other hand, the more that must be grasped in it as purely contingent, the more that impresses itself upon us as merely empirically given, the more genuinely objective and true reality there is in such knowledge. (ibid., vol. I, p. 122)

In asserting the primacy of will over self-consciousness and denying the hegemony of consciousness, Schopenhauer believes he is reversing millennia of philosophical presumption that set knowledge, a mere tool of the will, over the will. He does not mention such characterisations, of which Hume's is only the clearest, that reason is only to be the slave of the passions. As for the metaphysical elevation of the will, it is certainly anticipated, if not independently articulated, in Schelling.

In contrast to the dogmatist, Schopenhauer claims to have taken a pathway from the inside in which we are able to become immediately acquainted with our will as that groundless thing-in-itself, the animating essence first, of my body which is its immediate objecthood [*Objektität*], and then the essence of all representations. (Schopenhauer explains the distinction between *objecthood* [*Objektität*] – as inherent in the objects themselves – and objectivity [*Objektivität*] – as a matter of judgement – in Schopenhauer, 1988, vol. I, p. 286). The immediacy of my acquaintance with my will allows me to identify it as thing-in-itself without fear of the deception inherent in other such (dogmatic) assertions. Just as the will as thing-in-itself is not subject to the principle of sufficient reason and is thus groundless and unfathomable, so is it independent of the forms of space and time, which are now, in the discussion of the will (Book Two), characterised by Schopenhauer as the *principium individuationis* (principle of individuation). The two negative characteristics, groundlessness and independence of the *principium individuationis*, permit Schopenhauer to assert two crucial elements of the will as thing-in-itself: its unity and purposelessness. Not subject to the *principium individuationis* the will is one, something like the metaphysical One of Parmenides, Plato, and the neo-Platonists. Secondly, Schopenhauer interprets the groundlessness of the will as entailing its inaccessibility to any purpose: no answer can be given to the question why we will, so that absence of any goal, of any limits belongs to the essence of the will in itself. It is only at this point that the stage is set for Schopenhauer's pessimism, a term today inextricably associated with his philosophy and which becomes central in his works only with the *Parerga* of 1851 and the third edition (1859) of *The World as Will and Representation* (see Hübscher 1989: 257ff.). The will as that which initiates and impels action in living beings, as that which resists penetration in inorganic nature and which maintains itself in motion and life in all beings, is goalless and purposeless. From the infinite and goalless motion of the heavens to the plant and animal and human world, the will is a 'blind pressure [*Drang*], a dark, dull driving force [*Treiben*] . . . striving deprived of knowledge [*erkenntnisloses Streben*]' (Schopenhauer, 1969, vol. I, p. 149) and as such cannot reach satisfaction: having no goal, it has no end, and without either, it has no purpose. But that such restless activity is an evil is only clear once the unitary essence of the will is recalled. The striving of the manifold of living things to maintain and augment themselves in life, the will to life, is then seen not merely as purposeless, but as self-defeating, since it is the one will that is at odds with itself, attempting to take its satisfaction by doing violence to itself. In a passage added to the third edition, Schopenhauer writes that 'the will must consume itself because nothing exists other than it and it is a hungry will'. It is only a short step from the dual assertion of the will as an endless striving and the will as a self-divided and self-consuming entity to the final assertion, echoed by Freud in *Beyond the Pleasure Principle*, that death is the genuine result and to that degree the purpose of life (Schopenhauer, 1969, vol. II, p. 223).

Ambiguous aesthetic transcendence

In turning from knowledge and will in their empirical manifestations to a second consideration of each, independent of the principle of sufficient reason, or in turning from the empirical consciousness to the better consciousness, Schopenhauer had also to turn away from Kant, for whom knowledge that was independent of these *a priori* conditions of the possibility of experience was impossible. It is thus not surprising that at the beginning of Book III of *The World as Will and Representation* Schopenhauer speaks of the fundamental identity of Kant and Plato. In one of his early marginalia to Kant, Schopenhauer had observed that 'it is perhaps the best expression of Kant's inadequacy if one says that he was unacquainted with contemplation' and he notes the complementarity of the negative insight of Kant and the positive, intuitive knowledge of Plato (Schopenhauer, 1988, vol. I, no. 17). Having given content to the necessarily formal Kantian conception of the thing-in-itself, Schopenhauer proceeds to fill in the chasm that separates it and its appearances with what he somewhat ambivalently calls the (Platonic) idea, the 'immediate and hence adequate objecthood of the thing-in-itself' that is independent of the conditions of space, time and causality and is determined as an object merely by the presence of a subject of knowledge opposed to it (Schopenhauer, 1969, vol. I, p. 175). The Schopenhauerian system thus takes on a decidedly neo-Platonic structure, with its ineffable One thing-in-itself, its many (Platonic) ideas, and its indefinite individual appearances.

Correlative to the object released from its empirical conditions is the subject of such knowledge, the better consciousness of Schopenhauer's notebooks, a pure subject no longer determined by the will and its search for causes that will be useful for the satisfaction of its needs. Once one discards concepts of reason and gives 'the whole power of one's spirit over to intuition' one's 'whole consciousness is filled by the calm contemplation of the natural object present'. Having 'totally lost oneself in this object', that is, having forgotten one's will, the subject remains 'only as pure subject, as clear mirror of the object', the 'pure, will-less, painless, timeless *subject of knowledge*' (ibid., vol. I, p. 179), the eternal world-eye (ibid., vol. II, p. 371). The object of contemplation that was veiled by the forms of intuition in science is liberated in such artistic intuition. It is thus the artistic genius, that human being capable of such contemplation, rather than the scientist who merely pursues the relations constituted by the subjective forms of intuition in the pragmatic service of the will, who is the one able to apprehend and present the world in its true objectivity. 'Art repeats the eternal ideas apprehended in pure contemplation, what is essential and enduring in all the appearances of the world . . . Its sole origin is knowledge of the ideas; its sole goal the communication of this knowledge (ibid., vol. I, pp. 184f.).

Such contemplation involves a twofold paradox, both epistemological and metaphysical. In the first place, it is a knowledge that is devoid of all forms of intuition (and a fortiori, concepts, for Schopenhauer). Given Schopenhauer's sympathy for the English empiricists, one might hazard that it is the Schopenhauerian equivalent of knowledge by acquaintance. Metaphysically, the pure subject is willless, and yet the will is the thing-in-itself. The genius, then, is at odds with the very ground of being. This has several significant consequences. First, because the self-consuming will is the ground of suffering, the genial moment, in the artist as well as the audience, is a moment of unmixed and supreme pleasure, which is fundamentally negative for Schopenhauer, a release from pain. (This analysis of pleasure is also, significantly, a Platonic one, and the images he uses, for example, the sieve of the Danaids, are Platonic as well.) Released from the will, we experience the 'state of the gods. For that moment we are released from the harsh pressure of the will, we celebrate the Sabbath of the penal servitude of willing' (ibid., vol. I, p. 196). Second, since the aesthetic intuition involves a turn away from the shared reality of appearance and its spatio-temporal, causal relations as well as from the insistent reality of the will, genius is akin to madness. Finally, the aesthetic pleasure is of necessity temporary, since alienation from the ground of being, or knowledge turning against will, cannot be sustained without a turn against life itself; that is, without the artist becoming a saint. And it is just for that reason that art, particularly in its highest (discursive) form, tragedy, functions as a quietive of the will that leads to resignation and the renunciation not merely of life, but of the whole will to life introducing us to the problematic that forms the climax of Schopenhauer's philosophy: the affirmation or negation of the will to life itself.

Ethics and the negation of the will to life

In a note written at the age of twenty (1808/9), Schopenhauer asks: 'If we take the few moments of religion, art and pure love from life, what remains but a series of trivial thoughts?' (Schopenhauer, 1988, vol. I, no. 12). Art as the contemplation of the ideas, the pure love that is pity and the human good, and the godless religion of renunciation are the subjects of the last two books of *The World as Will and Representation*, relieved as they both are of the trivial concerns of the empirical consciousness in favour of those of the better consciousness. The intermittency of the contemplative state and the insubstantiality of Schopenhauer's Platonic Ideas lead us from art to the Fourth Book's twin themes of love and renunciation. At this climax, the various threads of his philosophy are brought together, animated by fundamentally ethical concerns. Here he answers both the particular ethical question of what constitutes goodness in human action and behaviour, and the larger and most properly religious question of 'the worth or worthlessness of . . . existence' (Schopenhauer, 1969, vol. I, p. 271). Goodness is the love that is pity [*Mitleid*], the negation of the will's egoism determined by an understanding of, and involvement in, the suffering of all creatures. This leads to the ultimate question of the value of the will to life. Since essentially *all life is suffering* [*Leiden*], and since the only way to diminish this suffering is to renounce one's own particular will to life by renouncing one's attachment to one's own self (love as pity), then life itself, and its metaphysical principle, the will to life, must also be valueless, and ought not to be. (The logic of this argument shows the hedonistic basis of Schopenhauer's ethics.) Such a renunciation of the will to life does not entail suicide of the individual, which is in fact the affirmation of life and the will, since here it is the individual will that exercises itself on a disappointing existence. It rather involves an ascetic withdrawal from active participation in, and appreciation of the pleasures of, life, as exemplified by sexual desire, or physiologically the genitals, according to Schopenhauer the focus of the will. Such asceticism ultimately leads to a withdrawal from life itself. The final stage of human goodness is thus saintliness or holiness and 'the inner essence of saintliness, self-denial, mortification of willfulness [*Eigenwille*], askesis . . . [is] negation of the will to life' (ibid., 1969, p. 383).

> The greatest, most important and significant appearance which the world can display is not he who has conquered the world, but he who has overcome the world, thus in fact nothing other than the quiet and unnoticed way of life of such a man in whom that knowledge [of the unity of the will] has dawned. (ibid., vol. I, p. 386)

Finally, and despite Schopenhauer's express atheism and his characterisation of traditional philosophy as a mere cover for theological speculation (in, for example, the Preface to *On the Will in Nature*), philosophy must nevertheless give way to religion if its ultimately self-contradictory and negative teaching is to have any content. As the epistemic emptiness of sensuous reason must be supplemented by the so-called Platonic ideas of art, so the inevitable formalism of reason must be supplemented by the visions of the mystics of Christianity and the Eastern religions, whose intuitions function as evidence for the truth of Schopenhauer's teaching. This mystical apprehension at the peak of godless reflection is one of the most striking points of contact between Schopenhauer, Nietzsche, Wittgenstein (see Clegg, 1978, p. 45) and perhaps Heidegger as well.

But if the interconnection of the various strands of Schopenhauer's analysis is clear, the mechanism of the negation of the will to life is less so. The subtitle of the Fourth Book, the 'Second Consideration of the World as Will' is instructive in this regard: 'Upon Attaining Self-Knowledge, Affirmation And Negation Of The Will To Life'. Since, as we have noted, the will, through violence (suicide) cannot negate itself, the negation of the will to life must come about through something else: namely, knowledge. The will comes to know its own nullity, either through the insight into the subjective source of individuation, or through the experience of suffering. Yet, due to the essential weakness of the intellect and its subordination to the will, it is only the very few whose intellect can see through the will. For the

majority, then, it is the second case, the experience of suffering, that may lead to insight into the will's nullity. For them,

> the final mystery of life has been revealed in the excess of pain, that woe and evil, suffering and hatred, the tormented and the tormentor, however different they appear to the knowledge that follows the principle of sufficient reason, are in themselves *one*, appearances of the one will to life that objectifies its conflict with itself by means of the *principium individuationis*. (ibid., vol. I, p. 394)

It is only when the will, through such knowledge of itself, however attained, sees its own self-contradiction and turns away from itself, that the true self-negation of the will and the destruction of the will to life itself, as manifested in that individual, can be said to occur. This self-negation of the will involves Schopenhauer in affirming two events that deeply contradict his general teaching: the identity of the subject of knowing and the subject of willing, and the advent of freedom of the will, the choice of self-renunciation, in the strictly deterministic realm of appearances. Knowledge in its empirical state cannot escape from the duality of subject-object. This is the grounds of the criticism of Fichte's philosophy (see Weimer, 1982, pp. 37 ff.); the will, considered according to the principle of sufficient reason, or in its phenomenality, is totally determined. At its peak, however, Schopenhauer's philosophy must accept precisely these two miracles, cornerstones of the post-Kantians he rejected so harshly, shadowed forth in the *First Critique*'s third antinomies, paralogism and transcendental analytic: the binding miracle of the unity of the self grasped in self-consciousness, and the dissolving miracle of the advent of freedom in the realm of necessity, the two transcendent characteristics of the notebooks' better consciousness. Beyond the determined and determinate realm of objects and its complement of subjects, the newly unified, transparent and self-determining self floats free, into a nothingness that is merely its invisibility to the dull eyes of embodied, impulsive human beings.

We freely admit it. What remains after complete destruction [*Aufhebung*] of the will is, for all those who are still full of the will, certainly nothing. But on the contrary for those in whom the will has turned and negated itself, this our so very real world with all its suns and galaxies, is-nothing. (Schopenhauer, 1969, vol. I, pp. 411f.)

Influence

There is no philosopher for whom the disparity between popularity, influence and academic reputation is as great as it is for Schopenhauer. Even today, Schopenhauer is the most popular philosopher in Germany. It is possible that the almost proverbial contradictoriness of Schopenhauer's philosophy has something to do with its easy academic dismissal, as does the harshness of his polemic against 'academic philosophy'. Today, too, his undeniable misogyny (memorialised in another infamous essay of the *Parerga* I, 'On Women'), and the anti-Semitism for which his name became a byword in the nineteenth century, are certainly unappealing elements as well. It is nevertheless striking that such disparate artists of the *fin de siècle*, from Hardy to Tolstoy, as well as many of the founders of the culture of the twentieth century, from Wagner in music and Mann and Proust in literature, to Nietzsche and Wittgenstein in philosophy, to Freud in psychiatry, owe such deep intellectual debts to Schopenhauer or, in Freud's case, found themselves uncannily anticipated by him. The connection with Wagner is indisputable (see Magee, 1983, pp. 326–78). In fact, the themes of the last two books of *The World as Will and Representation*: art, love and renunciation, read almost as subtitles to Wagner's last three operas. Wagner's attraction to Schopenhauer, and especially his epoch-making theory of music which elevates it above all other arts, as imaging, not the formal ideas but the formless thing-in-itself, the will, is not difficult to understand, and Schopenhauer's theory of music had an important influence, not merely on other composers, but on Nietzsche, Mann and Proust. It is not surprising that so many, and such significant, artists should have found themselves influenced by Schopenhauer. The artist is not necessarily bothered by the glaring inconsistency in Schopenhauer's theory

of music, is honoured by the Schopenhauerian elevation of the artist over the scientist and of intuition over reason, and is stimulated by the vigour, passion and surface clarity of Schopenhauer's presentation.

More striking is the fact that three of the great intellectual revolutionaries who helped shape twentieth century thought were more deeply influenced, or anticipated, by Schopenhauer than by any other philosopher. Although at one time the relation of Wittgenstein and Schopenhauer had forcibly to be brought to the attention of his rather incredulous disciples, for whom the history of philosophy, and certainly German metaphysics, held nothing positive, today the fact of Schopenhauer's influence on Wittgenstein, particularly the latter portions of the *Notebooks* and the *Tractatus Logico-Philosophicus* is beyond dispute, although its extent and significance is still a matter of controversy (see Janaway, 1989, pp. 317–42).

The case of Nietzsche is rather more complex. The influence of Schopenhauer upon Nietzsche is too wide-ranging and all-encompassing to be treated with any adequacy in the space we have here. An ardent disciple in his early works, despite specific differences in, for example, *The Birth of Tragedy*, he wrote a homage to Schopenhauer as 'the philosopher', *Schopenhauer as Educator* (1874), and if his later works are sharply critical of Schopenhauer as exemplification of the nihilism of Western philosophy, his own philosophical coinages, for example, the will to power, the eternal return of the same as the supreme affirmation, bear the unmistakeable stamp of a constant regard for the Schopenhauerian terms, as does the whole problematic of *Toward the Genealogy of Morality*, culminating as it does in the question of the meaning of ascetic ideals, that is of the Schopenhauerian ideal of saintliness, of not willing or, alternatively, willing nothing. It is fair to say that it is impossible to understand Nietzsche correctly without an understanding of Schopenhauer, the only philosopher whose complete writings he read, and to whom he is indebted for his whole conception of the history of philosophy. The fact that relatively little attention has been paid in recent years to Schopenhauer's continuing influ ence on Nietzsche is probably due to Heidegger's comments in his Nietzsche book – originally published in 1961 but based on lectures delivered in 1936 – which turn attention away from Schopenhauer to Schelling and Hegel as the true sources of the conception of the will to which Nietzsche (misled, according to Heidegger, by Schopenhauer's perfidy) is truly indebted. It may be that this has led many to reject Nietzsche's true – if in their minds humble – philosophical predecessor in favour of grander, if false, relations.

Perhaps the strangest case is that of Freud. Although Freud claims not to have read Schopenhauer's main work, nor even to have realised its congruence with his own until it was pointed out to him by Otto Rank in 1911, the parallels between the two are striking, and were noted by Freud himself (see Freud, 1955a and 1957). The Schopenhauerian anticipation of the unconscious and the Freudian id in the will, of the ubiquity (and unconsciousness) of the sexual motive in human action, as well as the conception of the weak, yet not powerless, ego or intellect, along with the similarity in their (negative) conceptions of pleasure, and hence their agreement about the connection of happiness and death (Freud's death instinct, Schopenhauer's negation of the will to life), as well as Schopenhauer's own anticipation of the Freudian theory of repression, point to their agreement. And yet no monograph has been written on this generally known, but highly underestimated, relation.

Completeness would demand that mention, at least, be made not only of other philosophers, such as Bergson, but also of historians and social philosophers like Jacob Burckhardt and Max Horkheimer. Horkheimer's conversion from left-wing activist to conservative Schopenhauerian pessimist (see Horkheimer's essay of 1960) might be said to have heralded the decline of European Marxism, a function performed by Schopenhauer a second time, more than one hundred years after his recognition coincided with the failure of the Revolutions of 1848. Horkheimer's position is even more relevant today. Our current social and political, as well as intellectual condition can only be clearly comprehended if the often unmentioned, but ever-present, role of Schopenhauer is understood. It may be said that an account of the character, contradictions and impasses of our age and its revolutionary pretensions can best be undertaken through an examination of the attractions, contradictions and impasses of Schopenhauer's thought.

Bibliography

Writings

Schopenhauer, A. (1969) *The World as Will and Representation* trans. E. F. J. Payne, 2 vols, New York: Dover. [All translations in the text are the author's, but references are to the pagination of this translator's editions.]
— (1965), *On the Basis of Morality* trans. E. F. J. Payne, New York: Macmillan.
— (1974a), *On the Fourfold Root of the Principle of Sufficient Reason*, trans. E. F. Payne, La Salle, IL: Open Court Press.
— (1960), *On the Freedom of the Will*, trans. Konstantin Kolenda, Indianapolis-New York: Bobbs Merrill.
— (1974b) (first edn 1851) *Parerga and Paralipomena*, trans. E. F. J. Payne, 2 vols. Oxford: Clarendon Press.
— (1988), *Manuscript Remains in Four Volumes*, trans. E. F. J. Payne, London-New York-Hamburg: Berg Publishers. Vol. I: *Early Manuscripts (1804–18)*. [References to Vol. I are by note number.] Vol. II: *Critical Debates, 1809–18*.
— (1994), *Philosophical Writings*, ed. Wolfgang Schirmacher, New York: Continuum.

References and further reading

Beckett, Samuel (1958), *Proust*, New York: Grove Press.
Blondel, Eric (1991), *Nietzsche: Philosophy as a Philological Genealogy*, trans. Seán Hand, London: Athlone Press.
Brandell, Gunnar (1979), *Freud: A Man of his Century*, trans. Iain White, Sussex: Harvester Press/Atlantic Highlands, New Jersey: Humanities Press.
Clegg, J. S. (1978), 'Logical Mysticism and the Cultural Setting of Wittgenstein's *Tractatus*', *Schopenhauer Jahrbuch*, 59, 29–47.
Freud, Sigmund, *The Complete Psychological Works of Sigmund Freud*, London: The Hogarth Press. (1955a) Volume XVII, *A Difficulty in the Path of Psychoanalysis*. (1955b) Volume XVIII *Beyond the Pleasure Principle*. (1957) Volume XIV *History of the Psychoanalytical Movement*. (1964) Volume XXII *New Introductory Lectures on Psychoanalysis*.
Heidegger, Martin (1991), *Nietzsche, Volumes One and Two*, trans. David Farrell Krell, San Francisco: Harper and Row.

Horkheimer, Max (1980), 'Schopenhauer Today', in Michael Fox (ed.), *Schopenhauer: His Philosophical Achievement*, Sussex: Harvester Press/New Jersey: Barnes and Noble Books.

Hübscher, Arthur (1989), *The Philosophy of Schopenhauer in its Intellectual Context: Thinker Against the Tide*, trans. Joachim Baer and David E. Cartwright, Lewston, New York: Edwin Mellon Press.

Hume, David (1967), *A Treatise of Human Nature*, ed. L. A. Selby-Bigge, Oxford: Clarendon Press.

Janaway, Christopher (1989), *Self and World in Schopenhauer's Philosophy*, Oxford: Clarendon Press.

— (1994), *Schopenhauer*, New York: Oxford University Press.

Magee, Brian (1983), *The Philosophy of Schopenhauer*, Oxford: Clarendon Press.

Rethy, Robert (1986/7), 'The Metaphysics of Nullity', *Philosophy Research Archives*, vol. XII, 367–86.

Safranski, Rüdiger (1990), *Schopenhauer and the Wild Years of Philosophy*, trans. Ewald Osers, Cambridge, MA: Harvard University Press.

Weimer, Wolfgang (1982), *Schopenhauer*, Darmstadt: Wissenschaftliche Buchgesellschaft.

Zint, Hans (1954), 'Schopenhauer's Philosophie des doppelten Bewusstseins', in *Schopenhauer als Erlebnis*, Munich-Basel: Ernst Reinhardt Verlag.

1.6

BRITISH IDEALISM

W. J. Mander

Introduction

If great ideas have a power to influence people in times and places far removed from those of their original conception, then the ideas of classical German Idealism must be counted among the greatest. Of their many and varied influences, one of the most substantial and interesting was that which took place in Britain towards the end of the nineteenth century. At a time when its influence in its native Germany was beginning to wane, in Britain Idealism's ideas were taken up and developed in new directions with such enthusiasm that it quickly became the country's dominant philosophical school.

That the British were so slow to discover these new ideas may be put down to the general intellectual isolation that characterised British universities in the early nineteenth century, but as the century progressed, and the discipline became increasingly professionalised, philosophical ideas from the continent began to appear more and more frequently. There were several reasons why these ideas, quite alien to the British tradition, once encountered were so rapidly adopted. Of great importance was the growing sense of conflict between the findings of natural science (especially evolutionary theory) and the claims of religion. Equally crucial was the desire for a political theory that, by giving a more significant role to the notion of state itself, might serve to combat the predominantly individualistic approach to social questions which had prevailed hitherto, and which had, by the mid-nineteenth century, so clearly failed the greater part of society. These contextual

factors are significant for they determined just which aspects of the idealist tradition attracted its new champions and in which directions it was subsequently developed. Generally, although not exclusively, the focus of attention was metaphysical and hence it is principally with metaphysics that I shall be concerned here.

Since the idealistic movement was never slavishly adherent to its originating sources, preferring instead to follow the more general sweep of their ideas, there has been some debate as to whether it was primarily Kantian or Hegelian in inspiration. In this connection it needs to be remembered that, in so far as the British idealists were influenced by Kant, this was Kant read through Hegelian eyes. In the end, although Kant had more impact than has generally been recognised, Hegel must be accepted as the movement's principal influence.

The two philosophers chiefly responsible for spreading the new idealism were Thomas Hill Green (1836–82) and Edward Caird (1835–1908). Although known today for little other than his ethical and political views, the sphere of Green's influence in his own day was much wider. Of great importance was his interpretation of the history of modern philosophy which, although now out of fashion, was very popular for a long time. According to that interpretation the development of British empiricism from Locke to Hume had resulted in an inevitable progression up a sceptical blind alley, but while the significance of this outcome had been recognised by Kant, who had in consequence attempted a new philosophical approach, brought in

91

turn to its fruition by Hegel, the British themselves, in continuing to mine the long-exhausted seam of empiricism, had simply failed to observe the eclipse of their own thought. In support of this historical interpretation championing idealism over empiricism Green offers a wealth of detailed arguments, but his basic point is the Kantian one that empiricism cannot avoid making *a priori* presuppositions of the very ideas which it is attempting to explain empirically, the problem tending to get masked by an uncritical use of ordinary language. While he never produced a detailed idealist system, Green did set out the metaphysical framework for one based on the facts that reality is inconceivable without relations and that relations are inconceivable without mind. But if mind-dependent, the world certainly does not depend upon the individual mind. Thus, Green suggests that we need to think of reality as given to an eternal, all-inclusive, consciousness in which finite minds somehow participate, and which he tentatively identifies with God.

The idealism of Caird differs from that of Green in emphasis only. He is for example, more explicit in his endorsement of both Kant and Hegel, presenting the latter's position as simply a natural continuation of the former's. It is also notable that in Caird's hands dialectic, whereby opposites are synthesised in a higher unity, becomes not just a method of knowledge, but an evolutionary pattern to be displayed within reality itself. Caird's thought is much concerned with the all reconciling concept of Absolute Spirit, which could, he thought, be elucidated in terms of self-consciousness. But where Green is somewhat tentative, Caird enthusiastically and explicitly draws the religious conclusions to be had from this, claiming, for example, that it can be seen to capture the essence of Christianity.

If Green and Caird may be thought of as relatively orthodox, it should be noted that there was dissent right from the start about the direction in which the new idealism should proceed. Andrew Seth (1856–1931) was the first to raise two worries which, in one form or another, continued to be raised against the movement. He challenged the seeming dissolution of individual personality into the Absolute, insisting that selves be regarded as real and separate from each other. God, too, he argued must be viewed as just such a self and not pantheistically. Seth also criticised the attempt to construct the world out of abstract thought, urging that this ignores the individual datum of experience and cannot account for contingency; but he was, nevertheless, an idealist, and instead of an Absolutist system, he attempted to construct a theistic idealism that could do justice to the diversity of individual selves.

Once idealism took hold in the country, it began to produce new and original metaphysical theories, but, as can be seen by looking at those of Bradley and McTaggart, the dichotomy between Absolutist and personalist systems continued.

Bradley

We see in the orthodox idealism of Green and Caird the belief that ultimate reality is rational thought and the view that it thereby displays the same continual process of conflict and resolution thought by many to exist among our concepts and known as dialectic. Bradley (1846–1924) found himself unable to accept either of these views; to him it was as clear that reality was far more than mere thinking as it was that contradiction is a mark of error and not truth. In his words, 'the notion that existence could be the same as understanding strikes as cold and ghost-like as the dreariest materialism' ([1883] 1922 p. 591), while it may be accepted as a basic principle that 'Ultimate reality is such that it does not contradict itself' ([1893] 1897 p. 120). These two denials are of crucial importance to an understanding of his system, and may be thought of as the twin springs from which most of his central metaphysical claims flow. Looked at together, their messages seem to reinforce each other and to suggest a criterion of reality, thus producing a distinction between what merely seems to be, and what truly is, the case, with all that is in thought or subject to contradiction falling on the side of appearance, and that which is beyond thought and free from contradiction on the side of reality. But does this not amount to complete abandonment of, and an attack on, the new idealist programme as set out by its founding fathers? The answer to this is that it would do were it not for two further features of Bradley's philosophy – his holism and his idealism. We shall look at each of these in turn.

For philosophers like Caird, the continual process whereby contradictions emerge at one level to be solved at a higher one was as much an evolution of reality itself as of our thought. Bradley, on the other hand, takes it as axiomatic that reality itself is something consistent and complete, something harmonious and unchanging, so that any contradiction or evolution encountered must be taken to lie simply in our more or less inadequate thought about it. Indeed, Bradley argues that thought is not only the locus of contradiction but the very source and explanation of it as well. The problem as he sees it lies in the fact that while reality is something concrete and unified, it belongs to the very essence of thought to abstract and divide, to take a part or aspect of reality and consider it out of its context, and it is precisely this that renders it contradictory and false. The pluralistic way of thought is thus riddled with contradiction. Naturally, the way to heal this is to bring in more and more of this context, but there are limits to this holistic cure. While the divisive tendencies of thought can be counteracted they can never be wholly eradicated, and thus no thought can ever be truly adequate. For example, the basic distinction between thought and reality is clearly essential to thought, and could only be overcome at the expense of thought itself. Yet overcome it must be, insists Bradley, and it is in this sense that he believes that reality lies beyond thought – none of the abstractions we use in thought can be taken as ultimately real, not even thought itself for that too is something abstracted from reality as a whole. Isolation from a wider context is the cause of contradiction, making contradiction itself a sign of a wider, more unified, whole. Crucially for Bradley, it is only a sign of something beyond thought and thus merely points to it rather than asserts its being; in this way he believes himself to have avoided the standard anti-realist charge of thinking of that which is beyond thought.

The most famous part of Bradley's critique of pluralistic thought is his attack on relations. It is clear that relations, even if only of similarity and difference, are crucial to any pluralistic world view. But asks Bradley, what exactly are relations? In an initial mood of ontological parsimony we might think of relations as a mere *façon de parler*, and

suppose that there is nothing more to a relational complex than the related objects and their natures. What more, for example, do we need than A and its height and B and its height to account for the fact that A is taller than B? Yet, on further thought, it is clear that this is not enough. If we admit as real nothing more than individual objects, our account of the world would be incomplete, for it can hardly be denied that the same objects may be arranged in many different ways. However, since these are changes solely in the relations holding between a fixed stock of objects, such variability is a fact that our ontology would be unable to explain. This tends to get overlooked because many of an object's qualities are already implicitly relational; for instance, in calling something a 'finch' we fix it at a determinate location in the natural classificatory order, while to call something else a 'pencil' fixes it in relation to a set of social and cultural practices. Even something as simple as calling an object 'blue' places it in relation to light, space and the phenomenon of sight. Perhaps, then, we need to take relations more seriously, and introduce them into our ontology as an additional connecting element between related objects. But would this really help? Bradley objects that this would simply give us three elements, which, on the face of it, could still exist in many different arrangements, so that now we would seem to need a new relation to say how our first relation is in fact related to its terms. To bring in new entities is thus simply to launch on a regress. In reply to this it might be said we are being obtuse, and that a relation is not to be found either 'inside' its terms or 'outside' them, but straddling both. Bradley was unimpressed. For what does this mean? If it means half-in and half-out, then a gap (itself producing a new relation) opens up between the part of the term affected and the part of the term unaffected by the relation. At this point a note of exasperation may be sounded, and it might be urged that relations are too basic to explain. They simply have to be accepted. In part this is Bradley's own conclusion – relations are indeed unintelligible in that there is simply no conceptual 'room' for them to do what they claim to do – but rather than accept a mysterious entity that somehow does the unintelligible, Bradley denies that such a thing could ever be real. This is not, of course, to deny that the world appears to contain relations, but rather to urge that ultimate reality is, as he likes to put it, supra-relational.

There can be few notions more central than that of relations and if they are dismissed as ultimately unreal, a host of other categories must share the same fate. Hence also rejected by Bradley as ultimately unreal are space, time, motion, change, causation, activity and the self. Dismissed too is the very idea of a many-propertied thing, on the grounds that whether we treat the properties as a unified bundle or as the possessions of some common substratum, it will be a relational complex that holds them all together as one thing. This last critique is of particular importance in that it is paralleled by a corresponding logical critique of subject-predicate thought, which Bradley sees as both supporting, and supported by, the metaphysics of pluralism.

The inevitable result of the attack on pluralism is, of course, monism. Although it does not exclude diversity like the homogeneous One of the Eleatics, Bradley concluded that ultimate reality, or the Absolute, is fundamentally one. And hence we see that although, in contrast to Hegelian orthodoxy, reality does not contradict itself, the apparent significance of this deviation is turned around by Bradley and used to support, rather than undermine, one part of the traditional Hegelian picture.

Unity provides us with the form or structure of the Absolute, but what is its content or nature? Philosophers such as Green and Caird identified it with rational thought, but nothing could be further from Bradley's own view. We have already seen that, for him, thought was precisely the unreal, that which is abstracted, or separated out, from reality, which in itself was something far more than just concepts and ideas; but what exactly?

How can we find out what ultimate reality is made of? It is at this point that we encounter one of the most surprising twists in our story – Bradley is an empiricist. He believes that reality is precisely that which is given in experience, and thus that the only way to discover its nature is through experience. Though it could hardly be thought unbefitting to the inheritor of a long British empirical tradition, this fact about Bradley's thought has all too often been ignored and it is simply assumed that he shared the rationalism of other metaphysicians. The probable explanation of this fact is that, although Bradley is clear that experience is our only certain contact with reality, he is at the same time all too familiar with the Kantian and post-Kantian critique of knowledge to think that we experience reality exactly as it is in itself. He argues that all experience is filtered through a framework of conceptual interpretation. Moreover, and as we have just seen, since it belongs to the essence of thought to distort and falsify, the picture of reality that we consequently get in experience cannot be taken at face value and needs to be corrected. Were we to remove these distortions, which for Bradley means to remove all thought and interpretation whatsoever, what we would be left with is, he argues, a wholly non-conceptual kind of experience, mere feeling. Idealism, then, is our result. Although there is a world beyond thought, it is not beyond sentience. Rather it is sentience or experience itself, in all its colours and shades, but without its divisions and oppositions.

The final structure of Bradley's idealist metaphysics is more complicated than this initial picture might suggest. It is possible to distinguish three separate levels or stages in his system. At the start there is feeling or immediate experience, the basic state in which reality is given. Bradley thinks of it as wider than mere sense experience, including, for instance, both will and emotion. He also thinks of it as a state prior to all thought and as such prior to all discrimination, including both that between concept and object and that between knower and known. The originating model for this conception of experience is to be found in Hegel's 1807 *Phenomenology of Spirit* but Bradley certainly felt it to be confirmed by the empirical and introspective psychology of his day almost a century later. He was not alone in this view, and it is interesting to note that close relatives of his conception may be found in the philosophies of contemporaries such as James, Bergson and Whitehead. Bradley further argues that immediate experience is filtered through what he calls finite centres, which although not selves, act as the foundations out of which individual selves may be constructed.

It is the fact of its being filtered through these finite centres, argues Bradley, that leads immediate experience to break down and evolve into the second stage of his tripartite system, relational experience. At this stage distinctions break out – between subject and object, for example, or between thought and feeling, between thought and its objects, as well as space, time, thing, event and so on. As we have seen, this stage, which is, of course, the stage in which our own lives are played out, is riddled with contradictions meaning that, for all its familiarity, and even, Bradley is prepared to admit, for creatures like us, its inevitability, the relational way of thought cannot provide a true way of looking at the world.

Since, for Bradley, contradiction is the result of abstraction, he urges that the failings of relational experience must be taken as pointing beyond themselves to their own solution in a higher more inclusive state. This is the Absolute. The Absolute is a form of experience that recaptures the lost unity and immediacy of our first stage of feeling. It is thus something beyond those distinctions which emerged in the second stage, such as that between concept and object or between knower and known, but it is more than simply a return home. It transcends even the finite and limiting perspective of the experiencing centre, and may thus be thought of as wholly consistent and real. Beyond thought yet governing thought, it constitutes the absolute standard to which everything points and against which everything else is measured and stands condemned as merely one of its appearances. It is the limit towards which all our thoughts tend.

Those features of the world designated as its appearances fall short of the Absolute with respect to their harmony and inclusiveness. They are neither as complete nor as integrated as it but features such as these, it must be noted, are a matter of degree, and hence not all appearances need be judged as bad as each other. This fact opens up room, which Bradley exploits, for a theory of degrees of truth and reality. He suggests that every category of finite thought may be assigned a place in a hierarchy of appearances based on their degree of harmony and inclusiveness. At one end would be the Absolute itself, while everything else would be assigned a determinate level based on how far it fell short of that ideal, or as Bradley alternatively puts it, since all appearances are the result of distortion due to some degree

or other of abstraction from the Absolute, based on the amount of context that would have to be added to turn it back into the Absolute.

This provides Bradley with a mechanism by which to relate metaphysics to the other disciplines. He argues that, in general, its results stand to theirs as higher to lower truths. However, with respect to natural science at least, he suggests that this should not be seen as any defect, arguing that the aim of science is not to uncover ultimate reality but rather to accurately describe and forecast the vicissitudes of this world of appearances, for which instrumentalist task a lower degree of truth is more than sufficient.

While admitting that religion is an important appearance of the Absolute, Bradley refuses to follow the likes of Caird or Green in calling it God. To do so, he thinks, is simply to contribute towards an already unhelpful linguistic muddle. For one thing, God must of necessity be something to which we stand in certain kinds of a relation (among other things, it protects us and we worship it), but the Absolute is beyond all relations and certainly is not related to its appearances. For another thing, Bradley considers, and ultimately rejects as unreal, the notion of an individual person, with the result that, as well as not containing persons, the Absolute cannot itself be regarded as personal. And that, at least to an ordinary conception, means that it cannot be divine. However, Bradley's metaphysical system is not altogether without spiritual significance, for he is prepared to admit that the Absolute is perfect. His argument for this position is not one of his strongest. He urges that because Reality is fully harmonious in logical or metaphysical terms, it must be similarly harmonious in evaluative terms. Specifically he argues that pain is caused by conflict, but that unresolved conflict or discord are precisely what it has been shown that the Absolute in being a unified whole cannot contain. Thus he concludes that there can be no pain that is not ultimately overcome and reconciled within the Absolute, which he takes as equivalent to saying that it is perfect.

McTaggart

Bradley's system was highly original. It was also very well regarded and influential, and he was widely regarded in his day as the greatest British philosopher alive. The other truly original and individual thinker of the British idealist tradition made far less impact on the philosophical world. This was McTaggart (1866–1925). An initial impression of McTaggart's philosophy may be gained by making some comparisons. Like Bradley and the other British idealists his emphasis is on metaphysics. Indeed, perhaps more than with any other philosopher of this school, questions of epistemology and logic simply drop out of the picture for McTaggart. Moreover, like Bradley, the metaphysical stance he takes is conditioned largely by what he rejects as contradictory and unreal. The two principal victims of this attack are time and the material world, which were found by Bradley to be equally unreal. And, like Bradley, he is led by these denials to an idealist conclusion. However, quite unlike Bradley, McTaggart was a pluralist and a firm believer in the ultimate significance of personhood. His relation to Hegel is also interesting. His first published works were largely devoted to the exposition of Hegel's philosophy, and in so far as they presented his own independent metaphysical system, did so in a strictly Hegelian manner. But by the time he came to put forward a full account and defence of this position, he chose to abandon the dialectical method of presentation altogether, favouring instead a more neutral style of *a priori* argument. In this regard he may serve as a good example of how adaptable many of the later idealists became faced with an increasingly hostile philosophical climate. Yet in a strange way, for all his professed allegiance to, and Bradley's professed distance from, Hegel, McTaggart's ultimate system is less Hegelian than Bradley's. In fact, the philosophical system that springs most often to mind in reading McTaggart is that of Leibniz.

McTaggart's argument to prove the unreality of time has become very famous and is well known by many who know nothing of the rest of his system. Indeed, this argument now forms the starting point for nearly all modern discussions of nature of time. For this reason it may be dealt with here quite quickly. McTaggart begins by making a basic observation. Temporal language, he urges, is divided into two kinds, the tensed and the tenseless. Because they can arrange the same events he rather confus-

ingly calls them the A and the B series. The B series orders events by the dyadic relations of before, after and simultaneous with each other, while the A series determinations pick them out by the determinations past, present and future. The crucial difference between the two is that the B series statements are timelessly true or false (it was, is and always will be true to say that Hegel lived after Kant), while the A series statements change their truth-value according to the time at which they are uttered (though it was once false, it is now true to say that Kant and Hegel's lives are past).

The argument McTaggart offers has two parts. First, he argues that the A series is essential to time. Without tense, he thinks, there would be no change at all, and this is of the very essence of time. Not everyone has agreed with this, suggesting that no more is needed to secure change than the possession of different properties at different times, something that can be perfectly well accounted for using the B series alone. But that, McTaggart responds, is just temporal variation, which is no more to be thought of as genuine change than spatial variation.

The second part of the argument is that, despite being essential, the A series is none the less contradictory. It is, he argues, impossible and hence time itself must be pronounced unreal. The problem that he claims to find is as simple to put as it is difficult to solve. He objects that past, present and future are all incompatible, but that every event must none the less have them all. The natural response to this challenge is to say that no event need have more than one of these determinations at a time. For instance, it might be that an event was future, is present and will be past, but, anticipating this reply, McTaggart urges that this means no more than that the event's futurity is past, its presence present, and its pastness future. However, he objects that this is simply to court the problem at a higher level, since each of these predications must, but cannot, be joined by the other two. Despite its intuitive strangeness McTaggart's argument has won allies, particularly among those who would reject the A series in favour of the B series, but far from everyone has found themselves in agreement with it.

It is a great shame that McTaggart's work is not

better known, for besides his celebrated attack on time he has an equally interesting, but much less well-known, attack on matter, which at the same time works as his principal argument for idealism. It starts with two principles which he urges us to accept. The principle of sufficient description says that every object has a unique and wholly general description. This must be so, thinks McTaggart, for otherwise it would not be a separate thing since surely if it exists it must have some character or other. The principle of infinite divisibility says that every substance is divisible into substances which are themselves further divisible into substances. McTaggart argues for it on the grounds that everything may be divided into temporal parts. This might seem surprising in view of his attack on time, but he reasons that even if time is unreal, it appears to be real, and its appearance must be based on something (which he terms the C series), so that objects found to be divisible in time may at least be taken as divisible in whatever feature it is that grounds the appearance of time.

Together these two principles require that there must be an infinite sequence of sufficient descriptions. How is this possible? McTaggart finds himself unable to accept that the required descriptions might just happen to be available, thinking instead that it must be possible somehow to derive them one from another. But how? The most obvious way to attempt this would be in an upwards fashion by constructing sufficient descriptions of wholes out of those of their parts, but if substance is infinitely divisible this would be impossible and we should be unable to distinguish any substance until we had distinguished each of its infinite parts. The only alternative, argues McTaggart, is that we attempt to construct the required descriptions in a downwards fashion by implication from those above, and he therefore concludes that all substance must be structured in such a way as to permit this derivation of sufficient descriptions of each of its infinite parts.

He then presents us with an ontology that he considers able to meet this requirement according to which there exists nothing but a system of atemporal and immaterial selves who do nothing but perceive each other and themselves. If A and B are two such individuals, A will consist of A's perception of B (or,

in McTaggart's symbolism, $A!B$) and A's perception of himself ($A!A$). At the next level A's perception of B will consist in A's perception of B's perception of A ($A!B!A$), and A's perception of B's perception of himself ($A!B!B$), while A's perception of himself will consist of his perception of his perception of B ($A!A!B$) and his perception of his perception of himself ($A!A!A$). This system meets McTaggart's requirement since, starting with sufficient description of A and B, we can derive sufficient descriptions of each of their infinite parts.

Finding this story coherent requires one to concede a number of things, for example, that perceptions may be parts of the self or that selves might be directly perceived by one other, but to begin with McTaggart asks no more than that we accept the scenario as possible. He then goes on to argue that nothing else, especially not the existence of matter, is able to satisfy the demands set out for infinitely divisible reality, inviting us to conclude that, since the system sketched out is the only one found to be possible, it must, despite its implausibility, be the way things really are. Crucial to McTaggart's dismissal of the possibility of matter is an insistence that we stick to the non-spatial qualities of things. Using spatial qualities we could identify the parts of a repeatedly bisected line as, say, the longest part, the shortest part of the longest part, the shortest part of the shortest part of the longest part, and so on. But McTaggart argues, in Leibnizian fashion, that all spatial differences require a non-spatial basis, and he fails to see how one could construct any comparable system of endless implication using only non-spatial qualities, such as colours and smells.

McTaggart therefore concludes that, despite appearances to the contrary, ultimate reality in fact consists in a timeless realm of mutually perceiving immaterial selves. It cannot be denied that, at times, the path to this conclusion can seem rather abstract and contrived, but those who follow McTaggart this far are rewarded with a discussion that brings his whole system to life. This is his account of love and its role in ultimate reality, something which he considered to be the most important of all his doctrines. He argues that the mutual perceptions linking the community of finite spirits that make up ultimate reality are at the same time relationships of love, and thus, that all spirits are bound together in an interlocking system of loving perception. The association of love and perception via the common idea of union is weak, but despite that, McTaggart has much of independent value to contribute to the theory of love – indeed, his is one of the most significant contributions on that subject written in the twentieth century. He makes a sharp distinction between its object and its cause, arguing that love for the individual, while it may be caused by certain characteristics, is not necessarily held in respect of them – a great passion may be inspired by a very minor cause. Indeed, he suggests that genuine love for individuals is not held in respect of any characteristics; we may love one person but perhaps not love another identical one, nor are we obliged to cease loving that person even if the characteristics we most admire change. In this sense, thinks McTaggart, we love others as we love ourselves, as whole subjects and not in virtue of any particular characteristics.

McTaggart's universe is an individualistic one with a central place given to personal love and timeless immortality. It is thus McTaggart, of all the British Idealists, who comes closest to presenting a Christian metaphysic. But here is the great irony, for it was McTaggart of all the British Idealists and unlike all the other personal idealists, who was the most committed atheist. For fairly standard, but deeply committed, reasons he felt quite unable to accept the idea of God and spent much of his effort arguing against the theism of his day. McTaggart never commanded the same importance as Bradley – indeed he does not seem to have had a single disciple – but it would be wrong to take this as a reflection on the value of his thought, for by the time he was writing Idealism as a philosophical force was on the decline.

Conclusion

There were a great many other neo-Hegelians, such as Bosanquet, Muirhead, Sorley, Ward and Mackenzie, who, although not such original thinkers as Bradley or McTaggart, did much to popularise Idealism. There was also a parallel, if smaller, idealist movement in the USA, centring around the philosophy of Josiah Royce. But despite this dominance of the philosophical scene, during the first quarter of the twentieth century Idealism went into rapid decline.

The factors that lead to the disappearance of any philosophical school are as complex as those governing its emergence. The early years of the century saw the birth of new schools of realism and pragmatism which quickly came to challenge and then supplant Idealism, but although these ways of thinking were able to offer important alternatives to the current orthodoxy, it would be a mistake to believe that they ever actually presented any decisive refutations of Idealism. Indeed, modern research has shown that many of the objections offered simply failed to engage with their intended targets. In view of this we need to bring in other factors to explain Idealism's rapid, and almost complete, fall from grace. Here we might mention the idealist's lack of interest in science and logic, their love of bold and nebulous metaphysical systems, and their overall cosmic optimism which contrasted sharply with the general mood of disillusionment that prevailed after the First World War.

The indirect influence of the idealistic movement was considerable. Since realist and pragmatic philosophy arose and developed itself in opposition to Idealism (Bertrand Russell and William James both entered into extended exchanges with Bradley in their correspondence as well as in published articles), there is no chance of truly understanding these movements which have so influenced modern philosophy without appeal to their origins. Several recent studies have successfully probed this connection. On the other hand, however, the direct influence of the British Idealists to date has not been great. Widely criticised and caricatured by the new philosophies, it came to be believed that idealist thought contained little or nothing of any value, and in consequence it has been simply ignored for much of the twentieth century. Indeed, it is only in very recent years that philosophers have begun to look again at these thinkers and to attempt to make a more balanced assessment of their contribution to philosophy.

The British idealist episode is an important one in the history of philosophy since it represents a genuine fusion between the otherwise separated traditions of British and Continental philosophy. Once we learn to see past unhelpful historical labels it is possible to recognise that British Idealism was able to take both traditions of thought and to develop and weave them together in ways that were quite untraditional for either. Though not perhaps a synthesis that we could live with today, it does give the lie to those who think the two schools of thought must remain separate.

Bibliography

Writings

Bradley, F. H. (1897) (first edn 1893), *Appearance and Reality*, Oxford: Clarendon Press.

— (1922) (first edn 1883), *The Principles of Logic*, Oxford: Clarendon Press.

Caird, E. (1877), *The Critical Philosophy of Kant*, Glasgow: James Maclehose.

— (1883), *Hegel*, Edinburgh and London: William Blackwood and Sons.

Green, T. H. [1883] (1907), *Prolegomena to Ethics*, Oxford: Clarendon Press.

McTaggart, J. M. E. (1921–7), *The Nature of Existence*, Cambridge: Cambridge University Press.

Seth, A. (1887), *Hegelianism and Personality*, Edinburgh: William Blackwood and Sons.

References and further reading

Geach, P. T. (1979), *Truth, Love and Immortality, An Introduction to McTaggart's Philosophy*, London: Hutchinson and Co.

Hylton, P. (1990) *Russell, Idealism and the Emergence of Analytic Philosophy*, Oxford: Clarendon Press.

Lewis, H. D. (1985), 'The British Idealists', in *Nineteenth Century Religious Thought in the West, Volume II*, eds Ninian Smart, John Clayton, Patrick Sherry and Steven T. Katz, Cambridge: Cambridge University Press, pp. 271–314.

Mander, W. J. (1993), *An Introduction to Bradley's Metaphysics*, Oxford: Clarendon Press.

Quinton, A. (1971), 'Absolute Idealism', *Proceedings of the British Academy*, 57: 303–29.

Sprigge, T. L. S. (1993), *James and Bradley, American Truth and British Reality*, Chicago and LaSalle, IL: Open Court.

Section Two
PHILOSOPHY OF EXISTENCE

INTRODUCTION

Lewis R. Gordon

Varieties of existentialism

Philosophy, in its many Western manifestations at least, has been marked by concern for the perennial and the universal. Existence, on the other hand, is notorious for its elusiveness, its concreteness and its paradoxical universal particularity. Philosophy of existence is thus marked at the outset by irony. Nearly all its chief advocates have harboured a deep suspicion of philosophy, where philosophy is understood as the systematic study of the universal and perennial features of reality itself.

One of the most influential and striking practioners of such suspicion was Kierkegaard, whose ruminations on existence, rooted in a profound devotion to individuality, faith and good writing, emerged, primarily through resistance to Hegel's grandiose efforts at absolute thought. Where, paraphrasing Kierkegaard, is there room for the living individual in this scheme of things? Kierkegaard accuses Hegel of building a great mansion without doors, in which the human being is left to live in the outhouse. In the literary efforts of Leo Tolstoy (1828–1910) and Fyodor Dostoevsky (1821–81), we find similar concerns. Tolstoy is troubled by problems of moral responsibility under the overwhelming weight of history. Dostoevsky is concerned by our ability to live, as he says, 'in spite of logic'. It is in the realisation of the human being's living beyond logical and systematic impositions on existence that a wide array of existential critiques of philosophy has been advanced. Much philosophy of existence is philosophy, then, by virtue of its critical

view and, at times, hostile rejection of philosophy. It is a philosophy that is critical of philosophical institutionalisation. Existential irony is evident here, where its place in an encyclopedia of continental philosophy is indubitable.

Philosophy of existence is divided into several historical movements. That is because, as almost all philosophers of existence have attested, existence in-itself is conceptually empty and demands context through which to manifest its problems. The European roots of this position are in the eighteenth century, where the argument of existence's resistance to predication emerged in Kant's *Critique of Pure Reason*. Kant (1724–1804) pointed out that the *concept* of an object remains the same whether we conceptualise it as existing or not existing. Existence, in other words, adds conceptually nothing to a thing, and in that regard, it is not properly a predicate. For philosophers of existence, this observation has meant that existence must be *situated or contextualised*. Existence in itself transcends phenomenalisation, a point that Sartre (1905–80) stressed repeatedly in *Being and Nothingness* as 'transphenomenality'.

Although we tend in English to refer to existence as separate from the life of a living individual, in other languages, particularly French, the term for existence usually has a dual reference. *Exister*, for example, means both to exist and to live. And in Latin, from which emerge both the French and English cognates, the term is derived from *ex sistere*, which means to stand apart or to emerge. Many philosophies of existence, whether in the European,

American, African or Asian variations, begin with the primal realisation of the human being's consciousness of standing apart from, or being other-than, while being submerged in his or her surroundings. In that regard, the focus emerges on the lived-reality of human individuals. The lived-reality of individuals is usually what philosophers of existence mean by existence, and in that regard, philosophy of existence can also be considered philosophy of lived-reality. In philosophical thought, the *study* of existence has thus been predicated upon varieties of philosophical movements with regards to methodological problems of 'study'.

Nineteenth-century philosophy of existence

The European strain of this period of existential philosophy is motivated primarily by a critical response to the thought of Immanuel Kant (1724–1804) and G. W. F. Hegel (1770–1831). The chief European spokespersons of this moment are Søren Kierkegaard (1813–55) and Friedrich Nietzsche (1844–1900). The chief proponent of religious existential thought, Kierkegaard laid the groundwork for nearly every issue in philosophy of existence. Nietzsche stands as the fountainhead of atheistic existential thought. Both thinkers converged on their critique of forces that militate against individual fulfilment and their rejection of philosophy as a paramount vehicle through which to examine problems of existence. They diverged, however, on their diagnosis of Christianity and the religious sentiment. Kierkegaard saw in Christianity a passionate past from which there is a challenge to the banality of the present age. Nietzsche saw Christianity as a rotten manifestation of ressentiment, wherein a herd mentality militated against excellence and individual achievement.

Although there were American (pragmatic) revolts against Hegelianism, the American *existential* version emerges from the thought of black abolitionists, especially those who were former slaves like Frederick Douglass (1817–95). This strain was not influenced by Kant and Hegel but was, instead, animated by a critique of the dehumanising significance of slavery. That modern slavery was linked to a dehumanising rationalisation in the form of racism

placed the question of the human being and humanisation at the heart of these thinkers' theoretical work.

Existential phenomenology

This strain of existential philosophy emerges from groundwork laid by Edmund Husserl (1859–1938) and Wilhelm Dilthey (1833–1911). It has four major offshoots. The first is Heideggerian fundamental ontology, which centres questions of Being and reformulates both existence and phenomenological reflection in terms of Dasein, 'being-there'. This existential philosophy culminates in an analysis of authenticity through the boundary-constituting impact of death and the emergence of 'care'. This philosophy of existence has been influential in the academy, although one can find its impact in some existential thinkers from North East Asia, Africa and the Caribbean; for example, Katsuki Sekida, Léopold Senghor, Tsenay Serequeberhan and Wilson Harris.

The second is Sartrian phenomenology of ontology, sometimes referred to as existential phenomenology. This offshoot focuses on the transphenomenality of existence, the anthropological significance of *bad faith* (an effort to hide from freedom and responsibility), and the problematisation of self-other relations. Its starting point of standing-apart, what Sartre calls *nihilation*, uses much of the Husserlian language of intentionality, *epoché*, *eidos* and intersubjectivity, roughly referring respectively to consciousness, reduction, essence and sociality. The credo of this branch of existential philosophy is the philosophical anthropological thesis that in human modes of existence, essence cannot be a prior reality. When the notion of a human essence is lived as preceding human existence, this phenomenon is described as bad faith. It is a lived lie in which a free being denies its own freedom. A hallmark of this branch of existential philosophy is that it also is peculiarly systematic: it pushes the boundaries of reason to conclusions in which *reductio ad absurda* emerge. Unlike classical systematic philosophers, however, existential phenomenologists use contradictions and push them further to the level of paradox.

Existential phenomenologists include Maurice Merleau-Ponty (who argued in the preface to his *Phenomenology of Perception* that we should not lose existence for the sake of validity), Simone de Beauvoir (who attempted to link existential conversion with phenomenological reduction), Paul Ricoeur (who developed what he calls an existential hermeneutical or interpretive phenomenology), and, in the USA, Maurice Natanson (who explored the possibility of an existential interpretive sociology of anonymity), Hazel Barnes (who sought an existential ethics of freedom), Calvin O. Schrag (who developed an existential phenomenology of communicative praxis and human science), William R. Jones (who recognised the methodological significance of existential phenomenology in the study of oppression), Hwa Yol Jung (who explores a convergence of Schutzean and Merleau-Pontian phenomenology in theories of identity formation). In Asia, Nishida Kitārō's development of a juxtaposition of Husserlian phenomenology with Zen Buddhism is rich with existential phenomenological insight, and, perhaps the most creative recent example of existential phenomenology, the thought of Nishitani Keiji, who, in his critique of Heidegger and Sartre and his creative use of Zen Buddhism, has developed a unique existential phenomenology. Beyond the academy, Frantz Fanon, the Martinican psychiatrist, philosopher and revolutionary, is perhaps the most famous representative. Noel Chabani Manganyi, the South African psychiatrist, has developed a novel discussion of 'being black in the world' through an existential phenomenological analysis of the body and sociality. Paulo Freire, the Brazilian philosopher of education, is another influential figure. His theory of conscientisation and his criticism of the subject-object dichotomy stand as contributions to existential philosophy.

The third offshoot emerges from the philosophy of Emmanuel Levinas, who developed what he called an 'ethical transcendental' philosophy on the basis of Husserlian phenomenology, focusing on the ethical dimensions of intersubjective relations. It differs from the Sartrian model, in spite of the shared concern for problematised intersubjectivity, by suspending the ontological in the name of the ethical. Here, it is not the being of the good that is questioned but the good of being. That the ethical are not raised in ontological terms militates against the ascription of a prior essence. Like all the other existential phenomenologies, then, Levinasian philosophy places the human predicament ahead of systematic conceptualisation. Its philosophical anthropology is characterised by the thought that ethical obligation precedes ontological essentialisation. The influence of this offshoot is primarily among post-structuralists, particularly deconstructionists – for example, Jacques Derrida and Drucilla Cornell – although the liberation philosopher and theologian Enrique Dussel builds much of his philosophy on Levinasian ethical transcendentalism.

Finally, by way of Dilthey, there is the thought of Karl Jaspers (1883–1973), whose *Existenz*-philosophy is a phenomenological approach that focuses on the question of the human being as a potential that calls for an analysis of the relation between Dasein and *Existenz*, sign and symbol, immanence and transcendence.

Religious existential philosophy

The Western roots of this form of existential philosophy are in the Jewish and Christian experience; they are motivated by the morals that emerge from the lives of such biblical figures as Abraham and Job, but in philosophical thought, the primary influence is the most influential response to Hegel in nineteenth-century existential philosophy: Søren Kierkegaard. Major twentieth-century figures who stand out in this regard are Martin Buber (1878–1965), Karl Jaspers, Gabriel Marcel (1889–1973), Paul Tillich (1886–1965) and Paul Ricoeur. Many of the atheistic existential philosophers stand out in this regard as well, since even atheism has a religious element to it. Here, Sartre, de Beauvoir, Camus and Frantz Fanon come to mind.

In Africana (African, African-American and Afro-Caribbean) religious existential reflection, major influences are the traditional African religions' conception of struggling against predestiny. Concerns with anguish, dread and despair abound here. In the New World context, these concerns focus primarily upon Christological reflections in Black and Latin-American theologies. Here, the problematics are similar to Kierkegaard's depiction of Abraham at Mount Moria: how could Abraham have faith that God is not evil and will maintain the covenant for Abraham to become a father of a nation when God has asked Abraham to kill Isaac, his promised son? In Black and Latin-American religious thought and theologies, this theodicean question takes the form of faith in God beyond the evil manifested by his creation. It is not accidental that the writings of these theologians tend to make detailed use of the writings of European philosophers of existence, in addition to indigenous thinkers. Representative figures here would be James Cone, Enrique Dussel, Jacquelyn Grant, Gustavo Guttierrez, Dwight Hopkins, William R. Jones, Juan Luis Segundo, Deotis Roberts, Theosophus Smith, Cornel West and Josiah Young. In Asia, several influential contributors to religious existential philosophy have developed a synthesis of Western philosophy and indigenous Asian religions. Most influential in this regard are Nishida Kitāro, Katsuki Sekida and Nishitani Keiji. A central feature of Asian religious existential philosophy is its focus on the Zen Buddhist notion of Absolute nothingness and meditative articulations of authenticity.

A tension exists between religious existential thought and existential theology. The former, from Kierkegaard to Buber and Jaspers, is critical of the notion of a rational, systematic articulation of God. For its proponents, God is an absolute that transcends universal categorisation. The theologians, on the other hand, regard God as accessible to systematic articulation in a paradoxical way: the systematic articulation reveals God's transcendence of such articulation. In the end, then, the disagreement is more over the nature of the project than its subject matter.

Finally, as Maurice Friedman has argued in his introduction to *Worlds of Existentialism* (1991), for religious existentialists, it is considered redundant to ascribe the adjective 'religious' to existential thought since existential thought often demands a form of conversion from inauthentic existence into an authentic mode of existence. This conversion, even in its supposedly secular manifestation, is religious in that it demands the recognition of the ultimate or transcendent features of existence.

Existential philosophies of liberation

It can be said that existential philosophy has been a philosophy of liberation from the beginning. Kierkegaard argued, after all, for the Liberation of the individual from the yoke of systematisation and the self-imposed shackle of despair. In the African-American experience, systematisation took concrete form in the notion of legalised slavery. Frederick Douglass's writings are the most well known here. Then there are the anticolonial writings of Aimé Césaire, Frantz Fanon and Edouard Glissant. Sartre's discussion of bad faith in *Being and Nothingness* was undoubtedly unsettling for an almost comfortably occupied France, and Sartre's persistent identification with liberation struggles afterward – the Algerian people, the Jewish people, the Vietnamese people, the Cuban people, African-Americans and Francophone Africans – continued this theme. Simone de Beauvoir's *Le deuxième sexe* and *Pour une morale de ambiguïté* offer arguments for female liberation from the premise of existentially becoming: a woman's essence (womanness), as it were, succeeds her existence. In liberatory philosophies of education, the most influential voice is Paulo Freire, whose dialogical theory of rejecting subject-object dichotomies and pedagogical goal of *conscientisation* (consciousness of one's humanity) pose the human possibility of radical conversion through a distantiation from being. In critical theory, an active contemporary spokesperson is Martin J. Beck Matuštík, who has also argued that the liberatory writings of Herbert Marcuse (1898–1979) reveal an existential philosophy beyond the Heideggerianism of Marcuse's early literary excursions. This existential critical theory, in conjunction with Kierkegaardian criticisms of false identity and Habermas's theory of communicative action, also calls for existential commitments and political acts of solidarity with peripheral or marginalised communities.

Returning to African-American liberation thought, a pragmatic existential philosophy emerges in the prophetic pragmatism of Cornel West. West explores the debilitating impact of nihilism, dread and despair on human beings under conditions of injustice and exploitation. In his early work, he argues that this philosophy emerges from a conjunction of Deweyan pragmatism, Marxism and Christianity, but from those texts through to the present, his existential categories have been Kierkegaardian, with Nietzschean genealogical influences.

In Latin America, Enrique Dussel's philosophy of liberation, which juxtaposes the thought of Levinasian phenomenology, Marxism and dependency theory, has gained considerable influence.

The guiding motif of existential philosophies of liberation is that oppression is a condition of unfreedom that militates against the humanity of oppressed peoples. Unfreedom is presented as a 'determined' or 'natural' condition to oppressed peoples. The transition from unfreedom to freedom is a transition from inhumanity to humanisation. This transition involves a radical conversion of consciousness of the condition of unfreedom to an undetermined and unnatural condition.

Existential philosophies of history

Philosophers of existence's concerns with liberation and human potential (personal and social) have led many of them to explore the dimensions of agency in history and history itself as a philosophical concern. In terms of the former, the discussion emerges primarily as a dialogue with Marxism. Among the most comprehensive efforts is Sartre's *Critique of Dialectical Reason*, but concerns of this kind also emerge in the work of Merleau-Ponty. The latter concern is most dominated by Nietzsche, Husserl and Martin Heidegger (1884–1976), but Sartre, too, is a major contributor.

Existential approaches to Marxism usually focus on the relation between agents (individuals) and agencies (institutions). How is it possible that agents embody agencies, especially when agents emerge, often through the agencies they embody? This question relates, as well, to the problem of individuals' relation to groups. How are group formations *formed* and how do they assume an air of necessity in the midst of their contingency? The contingency factor, most deeply explored by Sartre but later also by Hans Blumenburg, raises a problem for the second concern with history. The intervention of the contingency narrative raises the question of whether history, in its classical Christian and Marxist senses

as culminating in a redemptive conclusion or conclusive resolution of social contradictions, could any longer be 'believed' or substantiated as an organising theme of social life. The Nietzschean response was to unmask the peculiarly Christological dimensions of this conception of history. For Nietzsche, the question of which history we should make or assert as the story of humankind required a collapse of Christological hegemony. Heidegger picks up on this insight and reconfigures history in terms of an ontological 'fall', where the centrality of ontological questions – questions of Being – have fallen to the wayside. At the heart of this collapse and fall is a critique of what may be called the Western notion of progress. A familiar version of this critique emerges in the work of Karl Löwith (1897–1973), who argued that modern philosophies of history are ultimately secularised eschatological narratives. Two responses, however, mark the uniqueness of the existential position. Although Heidegger, the most post-modern of the thinkers associated with philosophy of existence, would agree with the critique of secularisation and the thesis of theological reassertion, the significance of the secular and the persistence of theological themes have a different impact on the work of Sartre and Blumenberg. Sartre is less concerned with secularisation but more concerned with totalisation (the historical variation of the bad faith advancement of essence preceding existence). For Sartre, the problem with narratives of progress is that they often call for an overarching teleology that precedes human agency, but he adds that the concern with agency requires the possibility of social change. This concern for agency and social change also requires an understanding of what human needs are in concrete historical moments.

Although not often studied as an existentialist, there is remarkable similarity between Blumenberg and Sartre's views. Blumenberg regards the modern age as not marked by secularisation of theological concepts but by an assertion of the human being in the face of concrete problems that speak to human needs. He rejects the secularisation thesis primarily because modern notions of progress and history do not advance the notion of an intervening transcendent force. Change, for better or worse, is expected to emerge out of human resources of curiosity and deed. In Blumenberg, we see both the anti-essentialist and the human-centrism that mark nearly all existential philosophies. Even where many existentialists believe in God, their theodicy entails a conscientious objector's role for the deity.

Philosophy of the absurd

The chief spokesperson of this branch of existential thought is Albert Camus, and the primary text is his collection of essays 'The Myth of Sisyphus' and Other Essays. This branch of existential philosophy makes no pretence of philosophical appeals; it focuses, instead, on the problem of nihilism. Here, the concern is on how individuals bring meaning to a meaningless world. In 'The Myth of Sisyphus', Sisyphus is condemned by Zeus to push a boulder up a mountain, whereupon it will roll down to repeat the process infinitely. Camus argues that, without positing Sisyphus' freedom, and consequently his decision to go down the hill to push the rock back up the hill, in spite of its going to roll right back down again, Sisyphus' fate bears no meaning for us, nor for Sisyphus. His existence is absurd from a third-person perspective. In the first person, however, his freedom offers no external assurances; its weight, that is, is his responsibility to bear.

Absurdity and alienation are found particularly in existential aesthetic productions. Fyodor Dostoevsky explored the dynamics of living in a godless world, a world in which one lives, as he characterised it, 'in spite of logic'. Franz Kafka (1883–1924) explored similar themes in his many short stories and novels. Working from Kierkegaardian dread, Richard Wright (1908–60) explored dynamics of alienation, death and despair in a racially stratified environment, where even the criminal's worst guilt, as his character Damon Cross observed at the end of The Outsider, is his dying with a sense of innocence. Similar themes are explored by Ralph Ellison (1914–94), in his portrait of African-American invisibility and alienation. In sculpting, Alberto Giacometti (1901–66) evoked a sense of the human being's extreme spiritual isolation through a series of elongated, skeletal human figures. In film, there is perhaps no equal to Ingmar Bergman, whose films explore almost every dimension of the human being's confrontation with absurdity and despair. And in music, although existential themes were explored among European avant-garde musicians, philosophy of existence has had a close relationship with jazz or African-American classical music. The music form appears in many existential novels from the 1930s onward. The blues and improvisation lend themselves to a philosophy against despair and essentialism.

Existential psychology

Although existentialists are critical of the neo-positivism and biologism that undergird much of modern psychology, nearly every existentialist has offered competing forms of existential psychology. Kierkegaard offered a complex psychology premised upon three types of personality: the faithful, the ethical and the aesthetic, for which there are correlate concerns with the Absolute, the Universal and the Interesting. Nietzsche offered a psychology of life-fulfillment, wherein one could be freed from ressentiment, the life-denying attitude of envy and fear. Similarly, José Ortega y Gasset (1883–1955) developed a life-affirming philosophical psychology. For Ortega y Gasset, psychological health rested in human existence guided by 'vital reason' (life-affirming reason). Like all existential psychologists, Ortega y Gasset's position is guided by a rejection of the view that human beings have a nature. For him, the human being has possibilities, which, when realised, mean that the human being could have a history. In the evasion of one's possibilities, one's life is less real and is therefore inauthentic. In pursuing such self-formation, one increases the possibility of finding one's true vocation and achieving authenticity. The theme of achieving one's potential in relation to history and the world of culture is also taken up by Karl Jaspers in his Existenz-philosophy, which defends a form of authenticity that transcends the mundane world of Dasein. Sartre, although antipathetic to the psychoanalytical notion of an 'unconscious', defended the hermeneutical significance of psychoanalysis premised upon the dynamics between bad faith and existential conversion. The underlying basis of this psychology is the recognition of the human desire to escape from freedom. The motif of 'escape' was also taken up by Erich Fromm (1900–80), who centred loneliness instead of freedom as the motivating factor behind dynamics of existential flight. He ultimately saw this flight as leading to five types of personalities: receptive, hoarding, exploitative, marketing and productive. He regarded the productive type, rooted in social and supportive environments, as the best. The others are reactionary and conformist. And finally, although not exclusively, there was Fanon, who, like Sartre, argued that psychoanalysis had limited application to the human condition. Unlike Sartre, however, Fanon's critique also extended to the mythopoetics of psychoanalysis. He argued that the Oedipus complex, for instance, was culturally specific, and that psychoanalysis encountered its limitations on matters of race and racism because people of colour emerge as material realities instead of symbolic and significative realities in Western psychodynamics of culture. The ontogenic or individual conditions supported by psychoanalysis always fell to the wayside in the face of social-cultural influences. Instead, sociogenic diagnoses were called for, which meant, in the end, that one could at best hope to develop a social psychology. But even there, the existential demand of humanisation requires radical demands of agency on the level of systemic resistance. Fanonian existential psychology calls for a co-operative struggle towards developing a world of positive human relations that are strikingly similar to Fromm's view of love and social productivity.

The list of psychologists and psychiatrists who theorise and practise therapy from an existential perspective include Ludwig Binswanger, Medard Boss, Hussein Bulhan, Leslie H. Farber, Viktor Frankl, Rollo May, Noel Manganyi and Carl R. Rogers.

Analytical existentialism

This final strain will not be elaborated on since this volume exemplifies *Continental* philosophies of existence. I will leave aside here the question of whether philosophy of existence *could be* anything other than Continental philosophy. Let it be said simply that there are analytical philosophers who consider themselves to be existentialists. Influential thinkers of this strain are primarily influenced by Wittgenstein and Sartre, although the Cambridge collection on Kierkegaard offers some other possibilities. In the 1950s, William Barrett was a chief spokesperson of this branch of existential thought. His work explored the meaning of existence and ontological problems of existential quantification. In effect, analytical philosophy of existence is concerned with the meaning of existential terms, the possibility of an epistemological rendering of existential problems, and relations between philosophy of existence and philosophy of language. Subsequent work of influence emerged from the writings of Robert C. Solomon (who has written considerably on Frege, Husserl and Sartre), Phyllis Morris (1931–97) and Ron Santoni (in their analytical discussions of Sartre on the body and bad faith), and Naomi Zack (in her critique of race and racial authenticity).

Central themes

One difficulty in developing the central themes of the philosophy of existence rests in the diverse complex of thinkers that comprise its history. As we have already seen, existential philosophers are animated by a set of valuative concerns by which they may, at first, seem at odds with one another. That there are theistic existentialists and atheistic existentialists is but one instance. This seeming contradiction of membership is easily explained, however, by the earlier consideration of transphenomenality. That existence is not a predicate enables the conceptual connections to be wide-ranging and at times contradictory. Along their way, however, there are points of convergence that are recognisable as earmarks of existential philosophy. Among these convergences is the dialectic of being and history through the lived-reality of the human being (often demarcated without the definite article, the result of which is simply *human being*). This convergence is marked by anti-essentialism and the centring of the human condition. We can, however, provide a chart of these dual concerns, which, for existentialists, do not represent a dualism but an active interplay of the human being's resistance to closure. For all existentialists, that is, the human is always a possibility, and as such poses a challenge to ontological determination. For the existentialist, the 'what' is thus always imbedded in the 'whether'.

An extension of the 'what' is identity. 'What' calls for definition, which requires boundaries, contours and limitations, for the sake of meaning. Identity, in other words, calls for an essence. 'Whether' refers to the active dimension of calling meaning into question. It emerges from the possibility of contradicting a chosen identity formation. In phenomenology, this problem is familiar. It is called the problem of constitution, where the act of constituting or determining meaning leads to an encounter with meaning as already constituted, meant, determined or encountered. We could call this the interplay between the passive and the active. We actively seek, and often develop, what in the end is already meant. In Kierkegaardian thought, this active epistemic project encounters the Hegelian system of essential relations that collapse the rational into the real and the real into the rational. In Sartrean thought, this active project resists the precluding forces of a Husserlian transcendental ego. Put differently, for the existentialist, pure, descriptive meaning is performatively contradicted by the human effort to ascribe meaning. Meaning, in other words, is a value.

Although Kierkegaard and Sartre defend the active element of meaning constitution, their trajectories diverge on theistic concerns. Here we find irony as a self-referential dimension of existential philosophy. The story could be told through Nietzsche, who is regarded as the father of atheistic existential thought. Whereas Kierkegaard saw the systemic predilections of Hegelianism as an obstacle towards human fulfilment – no individual human being could 'live' in such a system – and passionate devotion to God, Nietzsche saw the Hegelian system as but another manifestation of false gods or idols. For Nietzsche, God, too, was an idol to be broken. This collapse of God into idol signalled the end of a consciousness that received value instead of making it. Heidegger and Sartre are most noted for their appropriation of this shift. For Heidegger, the death of God signalled the death of metaphysics, the death of mediating bridges to real being (as we find in theology). In his words, from 'Nietzsche's Statement "God is Dead" ', in *The Question of Technology and Other Essays*:

In order to pay heed to it and to learn to pay heed, it can be enough for us simply to ponder for once what the madman says about the death of God and how he says it. Perhaps we will no longer pass by so quickly without hearing what is said at the beginning of the passage that has been elucidated: that the madman 'cried incessantly: I seek God! I seek God!' . . . Has a thinking man perhaps here really cried out *de profundis*? And the ear of our thinking, does it still not hear the cry? It will refuse to hear it so long as it does not begin to think. Thinking begins only when we have come to know that reason, glorified for centuries, is the most stiff-necked adversary of thought. (Heidegger, 1977, pp. 111–12)

For Sartre, however, this death took the form of an ontology, where a being-for-itself (*ex sistere/pour-soi*) is simultaneously a being-in-itself (*in sistere/en-soi*), which would be a being prior to its being. Constructed in *Being and Nothingness* as the being-in-itself-for-itself, God is dismissed by Sartre as a contradiction. God is, that is, *conceptually* contradictory. As a rational intervention, then, God is incomplete, although God is supposed to be complete. The same applies to the human being, whose only form of completeness is a history that could never be lived through the first-person but only through third-person assessments of the deceased.

The elegance of Sartre's argument could be appreciated through a comparison to the formal work of Kurt Gödel. In his discussion of systems sophisticated enough to be self-referential, Gödel demonstrated that such systems yield paradoxes and contradictory statements and are therefore incomplete. Similarly, Sartre has shown that the desire to be complete is incomplete, and he extends this conclusion to the level of human reality: the human being is an incompleteness in search of its completeness. Among the many formulations of bad faith in Sartre's corpus is completeness's achievement in human reality only as self-delusion. To live as complete is achievable only through denial of one's incompleteness, a denial achievable only through one's incompleteness since the absence that calls for such presence is a necessary condition of the act. Phenomenologists would recognise this form of argument as appresentation, where a phenomenon is made present by virtue of its absence. In Sartrean existential phenomenology, this phenomenon is given a name. It is Pierre, for whom Sartre is searching, from his early treatises on imagination through to interviews near the end of his life.

Returning to God, who functions like Pierre, the in-itself-for-itself's failure to achieve conceptual consistency brings the hegemony of reason into question. If God were reason, then by its own premises reason has been contradicted. In other words, if it is complete, then it is incomplete. That is because dismissing reason's contradictory formulation of God would have to be done on reasonable grounds. But those reasonable grounds are that the contradictory conclusion contradicts reason. Contradiction would here be rejected in the name of a contradiction. We are reminded here of the classical problem of theodicy: how do we account for God's goodness, omnipotence and omniscience in a world inhabited by evil? The classical response by St Augustine is that evil is a function of man's responsibility, not God's, and in fact St Augustine's theodicean excursions often compelled him to defend the thesis of radical freedom – a position erroneously attributed to Sartre. (In later sections of *Being and Nothingness*, Sartre argues that radical freedom is a form of bad faith: the reduction of the human being to pure transcendence.) Sartre's argument raises the limit of reason, that there is a point at which the human being brings value to reason, not the other way around. A similar view is held by Karl Jaspers in his conclusion of *Existenz* bringing value to reason.

Now, the existential position that reason does not precede the act of valuing reason has been criticised by some commentators (pro and con) as a form of irrationalism. For example, William Barrett's *Irrational Man*, a text produced by a staunch supporter of existential philosophy. Existentialists from Kierkegaard through Sartre to the present would argue, however, that irrationalism suffers from the same existential critique as rationalism and reason: both are premised upon the notion of a value that precedes the human constitution of value. Existence, in or by itself, is neither rational nor irrational. It is properly *nonrational*. We see here how philosophy of existence sets the basis for poststructural advance-

ments of meaning: one neither means nor values anything outside of a value-rendering system, all of which are fundamentally incomplete with regard to self-assessments of their values.

The existential thematics that emerge here are problems of responsibility over values. Notice that responsibility is itself a value, which leads to the problem of valuing values. All existential thinkers take this problem a step further and link it to the constitution of the self. For existential thinkers, the self is a constellation of meanings animated by values wrought with anguish. By anguish is nearly always meant the Kierkegaardian formulation of facing decisions whose consequence is the constitution of the self. In anguish, we face whom we could become. That no one could make these decisions for us forces us into a confrontation with the self; we stand out, that is, we exist.

Kierkegaard's conception of anguish has influenced the work of nearly every twentieth-century existential philosopher. Heidegger drew upon this theme in his analysis of *Sorge* ('care'), where *Angst* over the finitude born from realisation and acceptance of one's death throws renewed significance to one's existence as an existence of conscience. We see here another version of the death of God motif: an unbound being has not only no reason to care, but no possibility of doing so since possibility could only emerge through boundaries or horizons. Such a being would have no idea of the 'beyond' since there would be an isomorphic relation between what that being thinks and what there is. Sartre, on the other hand, drew upon anguish in a different way. For him, anguish provided the impetus for a chosen flight from anguish. It is a necessary condition for the possibility of bad faith. Bad faith is an anguish-laden flight from anguish.

Returning to the problem of value, we also find in anguish the basis for what Nietzsche called the spirit of seriousness. The spirit of seriousness emerges from an ossification of values into objective or law-like determinations over our existence. Sartre connected this attitude to Manichæism, where good and evil are treated as material conditions of the world. Most existential philosophers, especially Sartre, de Beauvoir and Linda Bell, regard play as a basis of overcoming the spirit of seriousness. In play, we take exigency out of our attitude towards the world and place the constructivity of our rules into focus. In other words, in play we assume our responsibility for the way values and rules are advanced or denied.

Anguish, bad faith and seriousness raise the theme of authenticity. Although not all existential philosophers use the term, authenticity emerges as a major concern in the thought of many existentialists. In confronting one's anguish, critically facing bad faith, and not taking one's values too seriously, one lays claim to one's existence. The formulations of this assumption vary. For Kierkegaard and Nietzsche it means becoming an 'individual'. For Jaspers, it means achieving *Existenz*. For Heidegger, it is called authenticity. Sartre is critical of the notion in *Being and Nothingness*, but in *Notebooks for an Ethics*, he uses the term to represent the achievement of a human mode of existence. In the end, then, authenticity is about the ongoing project of humanisation. It is about living as a human being, where a human being is articulated as an anguish-confronting emergence.

At this point, many of the central themes of philosophy of existence have been touched on. Many of them pertain to two basic twentieth-century theoretical concerns. We could call them the ontological concern and the teleological concern. Although the ontological–teleological divide is not appealing to most existentialists, the influence of this divide is evinced by the theoretical energy that has been put into analysing their correlates: identity and liberation; essence and humanity; necessity and contingency; past and future; totalisation and history; sign and symbol. Existential philosophy stands firmly with the second conjunct of each conjunction. To that end, its critical role has been to demonstrate that in the world of existence, the first conjuncts are already-failed projects. Their failure is rooted in the incompleteness of the subject they are designed to render complete: the human being. That is why, as should be evident by now, philosophical anthropology underlies the humanism of existential philosophy. Existential philosophical anthropology is an anthropology without a human nature, where nature is defined as a determined mode of being. Without a nature, studying the human being calls for a hermeneutic, or an interpretation rather than a science. But now there is the problem of meaning itself. If the human being is responsible for values and meaning, what do we make of the human being who no longer believes in values or meaning?

Perhaps no three thinkers have addressed this problem better than Kierkegaard, Camus and Nishitani. Kierkegaard called it despair, the sickness unto death. The theme of death is central. Camus later took it up as the problem of suicide, which he linked to the problem of nihilism. Simply formulated: 'Why go on?' or 'Why bother?', a nihilist proper does not take any pro-active steps in his or her existence. It is improper even to say that a nihilist 'lives'. Such versions are, as Camus rightly pointed out, performative contradictions. Nihilism is best characterised by death since an effort to live negates it. This is not to say that nihilism could not haunt one's existence. Dostoevsky's Underground Man announced that if God is dead, then all is permitted. The 'Catch 22', however, is that if all is permitted, there is no framework or context in which 'being permitted' could make sense. Permission makes sense where there is possibility of prohibition.

So we find, finally, a taste of irony in existential thought. At first, existential philosophers are antipathetic to systems and rationalisations, but the actual arguments used to dismiss nihilism or various inauthentic modes of existence are *transcendental* arguments. They are transcendental not only because they show the necessary and universal conditions for an idea, but they also make the move of pointing out the contradiction in acting otherwise. The argument against nihilism ultimately appeals to the condition of being able to argue against, if not *through*, nihilism. That act is blatantly *not* nihilist. In a similar vein, many of the arguments against relativism and reductionism appeal to the same transcendental move: the act defended or denied would not make sense without its limitation. Claims to pure subjectivity would make no sense without objectivity; claims to pure objectivity would render the ability to make such claims impossible. At the heart of existential philosophy, then, is that the meaning of life rests in the meaning of meaning, and the clue to that meaning rests in our understanding of the being that can realise such a possibility. The existential focus on the human being is not, then, mere human-centrism. It is the situated precondition for the existential project addressing the relation between lived reality and posited reality.

Bibliography

References and further reading

Augustine, St (1950), *The City of God*, trans. Marcus Doas with an Introduction by Thomas Merton, New York: Modern Library.

Barnes, Hazel (1967), *An Existentialist Ethics*, New York: Vintage Books.

Barrett, William (1962), *Irrational Man: A Study in Existential Philosophy*, Garden City, New York: Doubleday/Anchor Books.

Beauvoir, Simone de (1947), *Pour une morale de l'ambiguïté*, Paris: Gallimard.

— (1949), *Le deuxième sexe*, Paris: Gallimard.

Bell, Linda (1993), *Rethinking Ethics in the Midst of Violence*, Boston: Rowman and Littlefield.

Buber, Martin (1958), *I and Thou*, trans. Ronald Gregor Smith, New York: Scribner's Sons, Collier Books.

Butler, Judith (1993), *Bodies that Matter: On the Discursive Limits of 'Sex'*, New York: Routledge.

Camus, Albert (1955), *'The Myth of Sisyphus' and Other Essays*, New York: Vintage Books.

— (1956), *The Rebel: An Essay on Man in Revolt*, trans. Anthony Bower with a Foreword by Sir Herbert Read, New York: Vintage.

— (1960), *Resistance, Rebellion, and Death*, trans. with an Introduction by Justin O'Brien, New York: Vintage Books.

Dostoevsky, Fyodor (1968), *Great Short Works of Fyodor Dostoevsky*, ed. with an Introduction by Ronald Hingley, New York: Perennial Classic, Harper & Row.

Fanon, Frantz (1963) *The Wretched of the Earth*, Preface by Jean-Paul Sartre, trans. Constance Farrington, New York: Grove Press.

— (1967), *Black Skin, White Masks*, trans. Charles Lam Markmann, New York: Grove Press.

Freire, Paulo, (1990), *Pedagogy of the Oppressed*, New York: Continuum.

Friedman, Maurice (ed.) (1991), *The Worlds of Existentialism: A Critical Reader*, Atlantic Highlands, NJ: Humanities Press.

Fromm, Erich (1969), *Escape from Freedom*, New York: Avon Books.

Gordon, Lewis R. (1995a), *Bad Faith and Antiblack Racism*, Atlantic Highlands, New Jersey: Humanities Press.

— (1995b), *Fanon and the Crisis of European Man: An Essay on Philosophy and the Human Sciences*, New York and London: Routledge.

— (ed.) (1997), *Existence in Black: An Anthology of Black Existential Philosophy*, New York and London: Routledge.

Heidegger, Martin (1962), *Being and Time*, trans. John Macquarrie and Edward Robinson, New York, Hagerstown, San Francisco and London: Harper & Row.

— (1977), *'The Question Concerning Technology' and Other Essays* trans. William Lovitt, New York: Harper and Row.

Jaspers, Karl (1955), *Reason and Existenz: Five Lectures*, trans. with an Introduction by William Earle, New York: Noonday Press.

— (1969–71), *Philosophy*, trans. by E. B. Ashton, Chicago: University of Chicago Press.

Jones, William R. (1973), *Is God a White Racist?: A Preamble to Black Theology*, New York: Anchor Press/Doubleday.

Kierkegaard, Søren (1983), *Kierkegaard's Writings, VIII, 'Fear and Trembling' and 'Repetition'*, trans. with an Introduction and notes by Howard and Edna Hong (eds), Princeton: Princeton University Press.

Löwith, Karl (1949), *Meaning in History: The theological implications of the Philosophy of History*, Chicago: University of Chicago Press.

— (1966), *Nature, History, and Existentialism, and Other Essays in the Philosophy of History*, with a critical Introduction by Arnold Levinson (ed.) Evanston, IL: Northwestern University Press.

Manganyi, Noel Chabani (1973), *Being-Black-in-the-World*, Johannesburg: Ravan Press.

— (1977), *Alienation and the Body in Racist Society: A Study of the Society that Invented Soweto*. New York, London, and Lagos: NOK Publishers.

Matuštík, Martin (1993), *Postnational Identity: Critical Theory and Existential Philosophy in Habermas, Kierkegaard, and Havel*, New York and London: The Guilford Press.

Merleau-Ponty, Maurice (1962), *Phenomenology of Perception*, trans. Colin Smith, Atlantic Highlands, NJ: Humanities Press; New York and London: Routledge.

Natanson, Maurice (1970), *The Journeying Self: A Study in Philosophy and Social Role*, Reading, MA: Addison-Wesley Publishing Company.

— (1986), *Anonymity: A Study in the Philosophy of Alfred Schutz*, Bloomington: Indiana University Press.

Nietzsche, Friedrich (1968), *Will to Power*, trans Walter Kaufmann and R. J. Hollingdale, New York: Vintage Books.

— (1974), *The Gay Science*, trans. Walter Kaufmann, New York: Vintage Books.

Nishida Kitārō (1987), *Last Writings: Nothingness and the Religious Worldview*, trans. with an Introduction by David A. Dilworth, Honolulu: University of Hawaii Press.

Nishitani Keiji (1982), *Religion and Nothingness*, trans. Jan Van Bragt with a Foreword by Winston L. King, Berkeley: University of California Press.

Sartre, Jean-Paul (1956), *Being and Nothingness: A Phenomenological Essay on Ontology*, trans. with an Introduction by Hazel Barnes, New York: Washington Square Press.

— (1964), *The Words: The Autobiography of Jean-Paul Sartre*, trans. Bernard Frechtman, New York: George Braziller.

— (1968), *Search for a Method*, trans. with an Introduction by Hazel Barnes, New York: Vintage Books.

— (1988), 'What Is Literature?', trans. Bernard Frechtman, in *'What Is Literature?' and Other Essays*, with an introduction by Steven Ungar (ed.), Cambridge, MA: Harvard University Press, pp. 21–245.

Schrag, Calvin O. (1980), *Radical Reflection and the Origin of the Human Sciences*, West Lafayette, Indiana: Purdue University Press.

Sekida, Katsuki (1975), *Zen Training: Methods and Philosophy*, with an introduction by A. V. Grimsoned, New York: Weatherhill.

Senghor, Léopold Sédar, (1948), *Anthologie de la nouvelle poésie Nègre et malgache*, Paris: Pésence Africaine.

Serequeberhan, Tsenay, (1994), *The Hermeneutics of African Philosophy: Horizon and Discourse*, New York and London: Routledge.

Solomon, Robert C. (1987), *From Hegel to Existentialism* New York and Oxford: Oxford University Press.

Twiss, Sumner B. and Walter H. Conser, J. (eds) (1992 *Experience of the Sacred: Readings in the Phenomenolog of Religion*. Hanover and London: Brown Universi Press.

West, Cornel, (1982), *Prophesy, Deliverance!: An Afr American Revolutionary Christianity*, Philadelphia: Wes minster Press.

— (1993), *Keeping Faith: Philosophy and Race in America* New York: Routledge.

Wild, John (1963), *Existence and the World of Freedom* Eaglewood Cliffs, NJ: Prentice-Hall.

Wright, Richard (1953), *The Outsider*, New York: Harpe and Row.

Zack, Naomi (1993), *Race and Mixed Race*, Philadelphia Temple University Press.

114

KIERKEGAARD'S EXISTENTIAL PHILOSOPHY AND PRAXIS AS THE REVOLT AGAINST SYSTEMS

Martin J. Beck Matuštík

My dear reader, thou dost see that this does not promptly lead to profit. That will be the case only after my death, when the sworn teachers and tradesmen will appropriate my life too for salting down in the brine tubs.

Thou plain man! I have not separated my life from thine; thou knowest it, I have lived in the street, am known to all; moreover I have not attained to any importance, do not belong to any class egoism, so if I belong anywhere, I must belong to thee, thou plain man . . .

Kierkegaard, 'My Task' (1944, pp. 286–7)

Introduction

Søren Kierkegaard (1813–55) is best known as a religious rebel against systems of speculative thought. Along with Nietzsche he is considered one of the fathers of European existential philosophy. Many commentaries describe him as a staunch defender of the singular individual. To expand this received view, in Continental and Anglo-American thought, of Kierkegaard, I shall focus on his contribution to debates in contemporary philosophy in general and to moral and socio-political theory in particular. In doing so, I hope to show that his work is surprisingly relevant for interdisciplinary research in communications studies as well as in critical gender and race theory.

I will begin by addressing an existential situation of a Kierkegaardian reader concerned with issues of the present age. In what follows, I explain how Kierkegaard's philosophy and practice, aimed in revolt against abstract thinkers of his and all times, contributes to three contemporary philosophical topics. The discussion aims to establish three co-ordinate claims. First, that Kierkegaard employs communicative reason not only to expose the stiffness of abstract rationality and society, but also to fashion existential drama as an innovative teaching (and writing) style. Second, that his category of the individual relies on a positive evaluation of free and egalitarian social relations, thereby inaugurating the possibility of existential ethics and pedagogy as forms of liberation praxis. And third, that his authorship opens to a future possibility of a critical theory and practice of existential democracy.

An existential situation of a Kierkegaard reader

As a reader of Kierkegaard's authorship, I face a difficulty of beginnings: to enter into a dialogue with his multiple authoring masks, I must begin as a self-authoring reader in the present age. This is my difficulty: I may not (should not wish to) read off Kierkegaard's point of view (see Kierkegaard, 1939) directly from what the 'author' and authored masks say between the book covers. Since Kierkegaard's beginnings in the present age (see Kierkegaard, 1978, Part III) are not temporally equal to other beginnings, my historical difficulty cannot replicate his. Another path into this difficulty is Kierkegaard's active authoring which contravenes dogmatic, doctrinal and didactic reading of his completed authorship. The form and content of his works spearhead the revolt against that system-building which waters down the difficulty of beginnings. The difficulty marks existential situations and pathos of self-authoring readers (see Kierkegaard, 1992).

An existential situation proffers an ongoing challenge and task to everyone in every generation (see Kierkegaard, 1985): what is and how shall I be myself? How shall I choose to be this or that self which I have always-already become in so far as I am born and exist within a given society? The philosophical text which, in its content and form, intensifies the question of existential situation may be broadly called a philosophy of existence. The twentieth-century existentialists are but an instantiation of existential authoring. Kierkegaard is a philosopher of existence, though he or numerous others before and after him today cannot be easily grouped with the existentialists. The Kierkegaardian question of beginnings contributes to Sartre's twentieth-century insight into human situations, namely, that human existence precedes essential definitions of humanity, and not *vice versa* (see Sartre, 1974). Kierkegaard can contribute further to the debates on performativity in critical gender and race studies: should some essence define me before I begin in life, I could never be responsible for choosing myself, for example, face a gender trouble (Butler, 1990) or anti-black racism as a form of bad faith (Gordon, 1995a). For one radical self-choice transpires always already in a mid-stream of my historical situation, this precludes identifying existential performativity with unsituated voluntarist constructivism. Beginnings that matter (see Butler, 1993) are not those of a Robinson Crusoe or a Cartesian talking head: they are embodied in history, language and socio-political contexts of my era (Matuštík, 1993).

How can a reader become contemporary with Kierkegaard (cf. 1991, p. 9, p. 40, pp. 133f., p. 137, pp. 141ff.) – his era and his concerns – yet as a contemporary of *this* present age? Kierkegaard wrote in the nineteenth century, procuring as his immediate audience the manifestly Christian citizens of a provincial Eurocentric town: this most theocentric of all centuries has also been the most spiritless. Human beings have forgotten what it means to exist as a self. That 'God is dead' could be as much Kierkegaard's claim about Christian practices in Danish Christendom as it was Nietzsche's aphorism about the European will to truth and the good. Europeans built an exquisite set of businesses, slave trade, conquest, and power-politics out of the Crucifixion. They smuggled genuine humanity out of the professed religiousness and morality of the nation-states, and they placed will to power by the established order over and above existential self-choice of ordinary citizens (ibid., p. 36, p. 47, pp. 88–94, pp. 106f., p. 144, pp. 216–32, p. 253; and 1944).

Kierkegaard is concerned with wanting to become a Christian, while his present age celebrates having Christian virtues. The card-carrying members of Christendom profess the religious point of view and morality. He limits himself to becoming first of all human and only thus in any sense also religious. While the point of view of his signed and pseudonymous pen names, *en tout*, has been religious – Kierkegaard tells us directly (see Kierkegaard, 1939) – becoming religious has never been a settled matter. Towards and of his life, Kierkegaard became a street agitator against the established state Church, calling for the general boycott of churches. He died refusing to receive the sacrament from the servant of the church whom he considered a mere emissary of the state (Kirmmse, 1990, p. 521, n. 15). The religious sphere of existence – whether in his point of view or in his present age – marks what one is to become, what is therefore absent from concrete history. That the author's task is to prompt readers to become religious in no sense grants the authorship an *imprimatur* (Kierkegaard, 1992, p. 619) or defines religiousness doctrinally (Westphal in Connell and Evans, 1992, pp. 110–29). The existential and ethico-political axes of Kierkegaard's authorship thus fall outside his collected volumes or his proper name.

Crucial for becoming contemporary with Kierkegaard is his concern for becoming genuinely that which the age failed to have become – that is, concretely human. This need not require that the reader disregard Kierkegaard's historical and existential situation as a religious writer in Christendom. Such disregard would indicate as poor a scholarship as if one ignored Kierkegaard's wish that we do not identify him with his pseudonyms. Yet, as an existential and philosophical reader, one is not compelled to replicate his particular concerns in an antiquarian manner. If Kierkegaard's authorship invites me to become contemporary with it, and thus him through making it my own in active authoring, then becoming more than a scholar of his collected works, I must not simply replicate his concerns for his present age. The vanishing point of the existential and ethico-political axes for reading Kierkegaard aims beyond his era and his concerns for it. This reading is subjectively and philosophically true: it satisfies the extent of Kierkegaard's authorial authority over his pseudonymous masks as well as over his writings.

In this sense Sartre faced his twentieth-century existential and historical situation with a dialectical counterpoint to Kierkegaard. Sartre set his critical concerns for this pluralistic age as 'becoming-an-atheist' and a concrete democrat (1974, p. 168). I call this a contemporaneity in counterpoint since, notably in the early texts of the Frankfurt School of Social Criticism, dialectical atheism marks a deliberate social transformation of Kierkegaard's revolt. The existential-political axis of the present age invokes the negating, dangerous memory of the damaged forms of life, namely, Auschwitz (Adorno, 1973); hope for the sake of those without hope (Marcuse, 1991, p. 257); and the desire for the wholly other than this unjust world (Matuštík, 1993, pp. 263f; cf. Derrida, 1995, pp. 53–81).

Existential pedagogy as drama

Kierkegaard's influence on shaping philosophical hermeneutics (a theory of interpretation) has been long known (cf. Evans, 1992, p. 180). Gadamer (1975) shows that truth pertaining to human and social sciences is communicated to us through modes of appropriation. The truth of traditions and texts is not available by impersonal methods; it cannot be recovered from, or deposited to, a store of givens (for example, protocol sentences). Truth is an ongoing historical and existential drama of establishing and rupturing continuities: continuities represent a historical event manifest through evolving languages, and they represent one's existential and ethical task of making traditions and texts living at this time and place.

That truth is subjectivity (Kierkegaard, 1992, pp. 189–251) need not reduce the validity of truth-claims (including the one cited) to a status of asocial, irrational, acosmic, subjectivist whims. Kierkegaard's authorship embodies a broad notion of communicative reason. It is not, therefore, the fact (what) but the mode (how) that is at issue in existential communication. There are propositions communicated in direct speech; existential communication on the other hand calls attention indirectly to the mode of appropriating communicated propositional contents. What any validity claim means can be discerned both in one's first and second reflection on claims, both by elaborating the direct truth-contents and engaging one's subjective mode of their acceptance. The latter can be verified only when one witnesses the claim, for example, that truth is subjectivity, in one's self-activity.

Kierkegaard's subjective thinker moves within contexts of discovery, creative insight, and innovative thinking. These contexts anticipate the post-empiricist revisions of positivist philosophies of science. Kierkegaard's critique of instrumental rationality contributes to contemporary rationality debates in human, social and even natural sciences: he restores human pathos (second reflection) to the objective (first reflection) delimitation of justification in scientism (see Kierkegaard, 1992). The rationality debate has led to a breakdown of objectivist prejudice against subjective dimensions of evidential rationality. Yet besides employing communicative reason to expose the stiffness of abstract thinkers, systems and social levelling, Kierkegaard performs existential drama. I will now approach an existential mode of communicative rationality from within his dramatic theory and practice of education.

Consider Kierkegaard as a performer fashioning his pseudonyms in a manner similar to the playwright creating dramatic masks. Consider that Kierkegaard's dramatic genre is an existential drama, at times bordering on the theatre of the absurd (see Kierkegaard, 1983, pp. 34–7, p. 40f., pp. 46–59, p. 69, p. 99, p. 101, p. 115, p. 119, and p. 185). In this situation, the classical unity of time and space need not be respected. Nor must the author honour the binary division between the stage and the audience, authorship and discipleship, etc. Not only do texts become living stages, but each reader-individual is now the primary actor drawn into a drama in search of an author (cf. Kierkegaard, 1967). The proper name of 'Kierkegaard' refers to that individual dramaturge who makes himself vanish, who is the absent one (see Kierkegaard, 1939). To live this existential situation, one must enter the theatre stage as a whole, and literally become it in one's self-transformation. Perhaps critics can psychoanalyse a playwright or dramaturge for holding this or that position of masks. I find it wise to become contemporary with Kierkegaard in his dramatic staging, leaving the latter gripes to antiquarians.

In *Either/Or*, for example, Victor Eremita, an editor-mask, introduces two other masks, A and B who portray two forms of life, that of the Seducer and that of the married man. It is true that internal to each portrait, there are certain recommendations – for example, to seek the erotic escapades of the Seducer or to choose the bliss of married life. Yet the text as a whole leaves the choice between the two to the reader. Indeed, Copenhagen admirers of this text have been affected by insights into the joys of the seductive erotica as much as, if not more than, by the marital conventions celebrated by Judge William. The dramaturge can mask the authorial choice so well that the opposite can exercise an equal, if not stronger, attraction. (In Dostoyevsky's *Brothers Karamazov*, the atheistic Ivan tends to overshadow the saintly brother Alyosha, in spite of what we know of the author's religious point of view, making Dostoevsky's last book one of the greatest existential dramas of the present age.)

Kierkegaard fashions author-masks who are given just as little final authority on the stage as Kierkegaard claims for himself behind the curtain or in the position of a director, choreographer or playwright who left some instructions for staging. This is clear from the Appendix to Chapter II and the last Appendix by Climacus in *Concluding Unscientific Postscript* as well as from 'A First and Last Explanation' by Kierkegaard. In his review of Kierkegaard's

pseudonymous works, Climacus (also a pseudonym) jests that he is merely 'a reader' and a tragic-comic interested witness of texts, (Kierkegaard, 1992, p. 252). He praises the author-masks for not taking doctrinaire positions on their own production, for example, in writing a Hegelian Preface pushing for one systematic, namely, absolute knowing. Radical self-choice presents an either/or whose truth is gained via inward or subjective action, not by following an authorial command ethic. Existential drama ironises didacticism, it teaches by withholding answers and conclusions (ibid., p. 300). Frustrating the audiences and classrooms alike, an absent (pseudonymous) authority may liberate spaces for self-transformation (ibid., p. 253). Climacus might quite possibly agree with Pink Floyd and ridicule fundamentalists or traditionalists: the classroom does not need another brick in the systematic wall, dogmatic teachers should leave the kids alone.

Following the suit of other pseudonyms, and his own insistence that truth is subjectivity, Climacus appends to the concluded book 'An Understanding with the Reader'. He humours the readership and the audience by deliberately distancing himself even further from any authority. He does not publish in order not to perish in the academic, political, and financial markets; his book might as well remain unread. (Kierkegaard used his inheritance to pay for having his books published without calculating income or profit; he completed his works and died when his funds were almost exhausted [see Kierkegaard, 1992, p. 268; 1944, p. 286].) Instead of moral and religious approval (namely, an *imprimatur* from a bishop), Climacus revokes his completed book (Kierkegaard, 1992, pp. 617–19). His ideal public sphere would be an open society with authors without authority (Kierkegaard, 1985, pp. 11f.), with singular readers liberated from manipulation by the mass communication media, such as the press. 'In a well-ordered state' bereft of such a public sphere, the pseudonym projects 'an imagined reader' no longer in a hurry to read in order to get good marks, win a contest or to parrot the author (Kierkegaard, 1992, pp. 620–1).

Kierkegaard assumes under his name the burden of 'legal' and 'literary' responsibility for authoring the pseudonyms and their works (ibid., p 627). Ye existentially, he calls himself their self-authoring reader along with other readers. He is a stage prompter. One must not focus on Kierkegaard but rather on reading one's self-authoring (ibid., p. 626, p. 629). Thus, Kierkegaard begins all his religious, signed (non-pseudonymous) works with short Prefaces addressing his texts to a singular 'dear reader' (see Kierkegaard, 1940, 1990b, cf. 1990a, 1993a, 1993b). This singular one – hoped for and imagined – is an ideal friend, lover, partner or public. An existential axis of this production and an authorial point of view are performatives in search of earnest authors and readers alike. This education and drama cannot lie within any canonical text or between book covers.

Perhaps one may wonder whether or not Kierkegaard's production remains hopelessly solipsist and utterly monological: who but a person lacking lover, friends and active public life would need to invent an audience (see Adorno, 1940)? And must not an autoerotic partner or imagined community be but an acoustical illusion or a narcissistic echo of this author's male ego? (cf. Kierkegaard, 1985, pp. 49–54) A biographical psychoanalysis can be historically illuminating as it offers half of the reasons for inventing alternative forms of life. How is psychoanalysing Kierkegaard's melancholy personality helpful to the reader here and now? Are these the lessons (even though they could disclose some truth about the author) on which a 'dear reader' should waste time?

The socio-political aspects of Kierkegaard's authorship have been one-sidedly played down. Yet it is also revolutionaries, not just melancholy people, who invent forms of life and bring them into existence (Fanon, 1967, p. 229; Evans, 1983, p. 162f.). Because they suffer as individuals, we do not hold psychoanalytic motives against them. When enfleshed in active existence, the personal can become the political, and vice versa. Materially and historically, concrete existence begs for social transformation. Thus, the author's loneliness is not the most interesting motive for others who dare to imagine existential communication with earnest readers in a liberated public sphere. Kierkegaard's standpoint can be harnessed from its activist axis – as an attack on the established order and on the legitimation of this order by churches, media, markets, and nationalist or pseudo-democratic politics. His masks and inventions dramatically unmask both systematically deployed amoral reason and dehumanising social forms of life (cf. Adorno, 1940, p. 423).

Existential ethics as education for liberation

Parallel to developments in philosophical hermeneutics (Gadamer, 1975), pragmatism (Mead, 1934), and post-Kuhnian philosophy of science, Anglo-American analytic philosophers elaborated the linguistic turn. Habermas (1984, 1987) is recognised as integrating all four strands of thought into a methodology of communications theory. Given these contemporary trends, a new challenge to existential thought after Kierkegaard can be stated as follows: if one is individualised only in so far as one is socialised, then self-relation must be coterminous with relations to others. One is never born with a private language with which one may utter 'I' prior to being addressed as a 'You'. Expressing the meaning of the personal pronoun 'I' is learned within a language game. Granted the intersubjective origins of human communicative competencies, how can one meaningfully consider inwardness as incommensurable with, or critical of, sociality? If language, in its grammar, is that system in which humans live just as immediately as fish swim in water, what credence can one assign to a Kierkegaardian revolt against this system? Kierkegaard's revolt antedates post-modern and post-structuralist critiques of modern rationality; yet in significant regards, it differs from them (see Evans, 1992, p. x, p. 178f., p. 181; Emmanuel, 1992; Derrida, 1995).

A Kierkegaardian answer to the challenge of the linguistic-communications turn in philosophical methodology is supplied by existential authoring and dramatic performatives. Inwardness that matters is neither a locus of an originary essential definition of self, nor of arbitrary social constructions out of nowhere. Kierkegaard satisfies the Wittgensteinian proscription against privately-generated languages because he satisfies the Hegelian, pragmatic and hermeneutical insights into individualisation through socialisation: existential dissent problematises lives of already well-socialised individuals. Self-choice is not a private affair of atomistic, disencumbered selves. How is one to become a self, given that one has become already one in individualisation through socialisation (for example, as a member of the English-speaking world)? In questioning self-relation, one questions self-relation to tradition – hence to culture, gender, race, politics, society, economy. Inwardness that matters spearheads the personal revolt always-already as an ethico-political act, and vice versa.

This questioning is radical – going to the roots – and open-ended. One meets here that ethics which alone befits Kierkegaard. If care for existing did not reveal a chasm, self-choice could be settled by tradition, conventions, formal procedures or a defined utopia. Choices can be supplied by previous socialisation, advertising or other indoctrination. Disclosing an abyss – bankruptcy – of such offers, Kierkegaard launches existential ethics (Kierkegaard, 1992, p. 409; cf. 1980).

The risky kinesis of repetition differs from the home run to a metaphysical base of recollection (see Caputo, 1987). The latter movement could rely on a pre-existing affinity between the human social and the intelligible universe (on Platonic *anamnesis*, see Kierkegaard, 1985, pp. 9–15). One could recollect natural moral law (on *eudaimonistic* ethics, see Kierkegaard, 1992, pp. 423–6). One could adopt a religious doctrine or wear a uniform, but existence is not a matter of doctrine (ibid., p. 326f., p. 371, pp. 379–83, p. 579, pp. 607–10), and dress code need not correspond to inwardness (ibid., pp. 401–7, pp. 414–17). When one can be supported no longer by authority or uphold a dogmatic discipleship, one could attempt to move with the aid of nationalist idols or exclusionary togetherness or elitist consensus (see 1944, 1955, 1978 and 1991).

Kierkegaard's ethics begins with an attack on this safe kinesis; it begins through unlearning a flawed tradition though movements of existential repetition. His existential ethics provides an education for liberation. Because liberation practice inaugurates repetition in a given society (for example, in conservative Christendom or in a liberal-nationalist democracy), performing revolt makes use of ongoing symbolic and material practices. Revolt can proceed by subversive appropriations (for example, becoming human among the card-carrying Christians) or in revolting refusals (for example, by boycotting the established nationalist-religious order).

I noted before that, from an existential point of view, it does not get the reader very far to ascribe existential individualism to Kierkegaard's melancholy personality. And it would now seem too easy to conclude from Kierkegaard's generally conservative bent, or from his earlier sympathy with preserving monarchical rule, to a negatively disjunctive relation between existential inwardness and the socio-political engagement (see Kierkegaard, 1992, p. 620f., 'The Individual' in 1939, pp. 107–38; 1978, and 1967–78, entries from 1948). Yet it would be a mistake to locate him among the twentieth century's conservative revolutionaries, whether the German political existentialists of the 1930s (see Kellner, 1984, pp. 96–104, p. 408f.) or the religious-political right in the late twentieth century (see Connell and Evans, 1992; Kirmmse, 1990; Matuštík, 1994; Westphal, 1987; Matuštík and Westphal, 1995; Perkins, 1990). All this would ignore an egalitarian nature of Kierkegaard's ethics (see Kierkegaard, 1962; 1985; 1992) — of his liberation theory and practice in conservative and liberal Christendom, conservative and liberal nation-state alike (Kierkegaard, 1978; 1982; 1990c; 1991; and 'An Open Letter' in 1968).

Human teachers can serve merely as occasions, not grounds for another's learning. This is because one's temporal existence – Climacus locates the ethical in temporality – cannot be communicated directly (see Kierkegaard, 1985, p. 9, p. 12, p. 14, p. 23f.; see also 1988). Not only teachers, but likewise communities and prevailing social mores are dethroned: they are at best occasions for self-transformation, and at worst gods with clay feet. The true, the good, and the beautiful pivot as objective uncertainties just as much as faith does (see Kierkegaard, 1992, p. 204f., p. 209f.). To demand positive values – namely, Meno's question to Socrates whether virtue can be taught – is to kill both any living truth and ethics (see Kierkegaard, 1985, pp. 9–13), but this is the slaughter that a conservative revolutionary commits, in turn fuelling the disdain by a relativist or a nihilist, none of whom seems to care any longer. Climacus ridicules the divine command theory of ethics as a confusion of inwardness with an outward symbolic of piety and status (Kierkegaard, 1992, pp. 401–9, pp. 414–16). In irony and humour, Climacus's existential ethics out wardly resembles irresponsibility: for example, one could be 'playing cards at the club' instead of wearing a monastic robe to display spiritual inwardness (ibid., p. 401).

That 'truth is subjectivity' (ibid., pp. 189–251) need not mean that self-relation stands apart from social relations, that inwardness can live safely apart from the political. The above claim about truth may not legitimate Ivan Karamazov or a contemporary adolescent to hold that without an ability to secure truth and values once and for all, anything goes. A pathos of existence at risk – intensifying an ethical task of responsible living – brings much needed correctives to falsely responsible technocratic, authoritarian, fundamentalist trends in the present age (ibid., pp. 387–561).

Kierkegaard's existential ethics proffers not only drama but also a unique communication theory and practice. Existential communication imparts the ethical indirectly, maieutically (Kierkegaard, 1985, p. 10, p. 231f.), via education seeped in responsible, yet anti-doctrinaire, irony and humour. This ethics is imbued with the pathos for a radical liberation in the recipient. Remember that Kierkegaard's individual is a well-socialised Copenhagen citizen living an embodied, historical, linguistic and social existence. The recipient of radical liberation must thus be the present age. This radical ideality of liberation projects the opposite of monological individualists, each confined as a monad in a solitary cell. Any pseudo-existentialist or possessive individualism would be caricatured along with the crowd as untruth (see Kierkegaard, 1939 and 1962). Truth as subjectivity cannot be, however, delivered by a conservative agenda for restoring family values or a nation's soul. Kierkegaard revolts against conservatives who despair of living at risk (Kierkegaard, 1980), he would dissent from postmoderns celebrating 'levelling reciprocity' (Kierkegaard, 1978, p. 63). Existential ethics is more earnest and humorous than either: its unbearable lightness of existing, paraphrasing Kundera (1984), nurtures relational individuals for ventures in open communities (Kierkegaard, 1962, pp. 153–70).

Existential democracy

If it is plausible that Kierkegaard anticipates both the hermeneutical (or dialogical) and the linguistic-communications turns in philosophical methodology, then it makes even better sense to enquire into his relevance for critical social theory. Similar to the above two rejoinders, this move marks a departure from the received view of existential philosophy.

Kierkegaard's category of the individual is often portrayed as antithetical to socio-political analysis. His presumed acosmic and anti-social stance is a common opinion. This view is repeated over and over in college texts on existentialism: usually selections from Johannes de Silentio's *Fear and Trembling*, Climacus's *Postscript* and Kierkegaard's 'The Individual' accompany a commentary on Kierkegaard's apolitical and individualistic irrationalism. To wit, most critical social theorists working out of the mainstream Continental, Euro-American provenance, with notable exceptions (see Matuštík and Westphal, 1995), have found existential concerns to be an anathema to democratic theory and liberation struggle (Lukács, 1974).

At the margins of this Euro-American, mainstream reception of Kierkegaard, one finds a significantly different situation. To give three less than exhaustive examples: in East Central Europe, a rich tradition of existential phenomenology informs political dissent from the 1960s to the revolutions of 1989 to the present (see works by Havel; Kosík; Kundera; Matuštík, 1993, 1998; Patočka, 1990). Within African-American experience, black existential thought nurtures anti-slavery and Civil Rights struggles (Douglass, 1968; King, Jr, 1986; Fanon, 1963, 1967); most importantly, it opens recent developments in critical race and liberation theory (West, 1993; Gordon, 1995a, 1995b, 1997). And among the post-Beauvoirean critical gender theorists, many are developing methodologies which are not entirely alien to existential subject-positions originated by Kierkegaard's revolt against systems (for example, Butler 1993; Cornell 1991, 1995; hooks, 1991; Huntington, 1998). Given that all these trends are inspired also by Kierkegaard, can one dismiss the existential turn in philosophy on account of Heidegger's practical, perhaps theoretical, involvement with National Socialism, lest one is satisfied with writing a Eurocentric, mostly white and masculinist intellectual history?

Let us say that a philosopher need not shun Kierkegaard as, at best, merely a religious thinker (see Heidegger's self-distancing in 1962, p. 235, n. vi). And one need not view him as, at worst, a precursor to the Nazi *Führer principle* or to the politics of exceptional authority (Lukács, 1974, p. 219, p. 264). It is nevertheless a chore to show whether or not Kierkegaard's individual could become an anti-democratic exception: a secular or religious fanatic, a decisionistic political sovereign or a proto-fascistic *Übermensch*.

Perhaps no other pseudonymous text contributes more to this burden than Johannes de Silentio's *Fear and Trembling*. It is the college undergraduate who shrinks in horror from the prospect that Abraham's willingness to sacrifice his son Isaac for God seems indiscernible from a crazy attacker on the streets of New York or London, or from a Middle Eastern suicide bomber. If de Silentio's text offers nothing to block a sophomoric interpretation, then it is possible that, for example, the assassin of Yitzhak Rabin (the late Israeli Prime Minister) could be a latter day Abraham. This murderer claims to have been obeying God and furthering the Abrahamic promise to Israel. Or it could be that the White Supremacist militias represent the contemporary teleological suspension of ethical and political orders for the sake of a higher religious command. Abraham is the father of three religious faiths, yet he seems either to exhibit poor family, patriotic, and Church values or is unable to stop others from imitating him in increasingly frightening ways. Today's religious and political fundamentalist might appear indiscernible from him.

De Silentio leaves compelling clues for an anti-fundamentalist reading, and these stare the reader in the face: formally, his story of Abraham breaks down into multiple perspectival narratives only to conclude with three unresolvable problemata. Substantively, fear and trembling are the opposite of security and certainty, the latter being the markers of fanatics for any cause in every generation (cf. Havel, 1990a, 1990b; Mooney, 1991). Abraham cannot speak; de Silentio who can poetise him remains silent where a more apodictic answer would be forthcoming from a religious fanatic or arrogant fascist. Kierkegaard's Abraham could become just such a fanatic – hearing an echo of his own desire – and both he and de Silentio know this. Ultimately, de Silentio's poetic sketch of Abrahamic faith must be considered within a Kierkegaardian dramatic axis. De Silentio's unsafe guidance is apparent in dialogue with masks who strip his one-sidedness.

In his later work, *Practice in Christianity*, Kierkegaard situates fear and trembling socio-politically in the present age, thereby offering his contribution to a critical social theory. (This work was originally written by Anti-Climacus (1850) as a corrective defence of Christian life. It functions at that time as a doubly-reflected communication: it could be a praise or a critique. But, given the continued silence of Bishop Mynster on the confusion between the official Church and earnest faith, this book becomes part of a direct attack on Christendom. Kierkegaard revokes the pseudonym and signs his own name under the second edition (30 April 1855). This date marks, the beginning of Kierkegaard's open attack on the established religious-political order.) Kierkegaard suspects of symbolic and material integrations that they use family, moral, national, even religious, values to entrench totalitarian systems of thought and society. He moves from suspension to suspicion of ethical, political, and religious conventions. The teleological suspension and the hermeneutical suspicion of cultural conventions become a revolt against the established secular and religious orders (Westphal in Connell and Evans 1992, pp. 110–29).

Kierkegaard revolts for the sake of the responsible individual, who, like Abraham, is placed higher than the levelling universal. Abraham suspends conventional ethics (Kierkegaard, 1983, pp. 54f.), but not responsibility as such – otherwise he could replace fear and trembling with a fundamentalist political plank. Yet, note now that a dissident in Christendom is not a sovereign political exception from all sociality either. Against the fanaticism of a traditionalist, nationalist, fundamentalist polity, this dissident projects another sociality, a concrete universal (Kierkegaard, 1962, p. 153; see also Sartre, 1974). From the point of view of existential dissent, the anti-racist and anti-patriarchal individual stands higher than the racist and sexist society – their 'levelling reciprocity' (Kierkegaard, 1978, p. 63). Civil and human rights struggles hermeneutically suspect, telelogically suspend and politically subvert oppressive universals. Only bigots and tyrants charge as fanatics the rebels rising against the established facts of inferior Blackness (Fanon, 1967, pp. 109–40), or abject Femininity (Bartky, 1990), or a superior economic class. The blackmail of these charges by dominant powers is evident; it cannot rob political dissent of its inward authenticity and publicly manifest legitimacy.

With Climacus, we laugh at inane traditionalists who are proud to own positive values or name the proper name of the ethico-political ideality as their God (see Kierkegaard, 1985, p. 10, p. 21, p. 23). Climacus's irony and humour go hand in hand with de Silentio's fear and trembling. The pathos of interested existence ruptures the metaphysical desire for a recollective movement within a closed totality (see Kierkegaard, 1983, p. 43f., p. 149). The bracketing of traditionalist, convention authoritarian or fundamentalist claims in ethics and politics culminates when the doors of hidden inwardness open (Kierkegaard, 1992, p. 475, pp. 498–501): inwardness becomes manifest in the public sphere (Kierkegaard, 1991, pp. 214–20, p. 253, p. 283; 1944, p. 41f.). The lonesome Abrahamic fear and trembling on a secluded Mt Moriah becomes a shared struggle against powers that be:

> Every human being is to live in fear and trembling, and likewise no established order is to be exempted from fear and trembling. Fear and trembling signify that we are in the process of becoming; and every single individual, likewise the generation, is and should be aware of being in the process of becoming. (Kierkegaard, 1991, p. 88)

One is a Kristevan subject-in-process, a stranger to oneself: thus one's inwardness, too, can be experienced as the wholly other yet not apart from but in the face-to-face encounter with others. In Derrida's Judaic, Lévinasian view of Kierkegaard's ethics and politics, Abraham's plight occurs for everyone in relation to others and 'every day':

> If God is completely other, the figure or name of the wholly other, then every other (one) is every (bit) other . . . This formula disturbs Kierkegaard's discourse on one level while at the same time reinforcing its most extreme ramifications. It implies that God, as the wholly other, is to be found everywhere there is something of the wholly other. (Derrida, 1995, pp. 77f.)

This is a plausible Kierkegaardian position: none of us is a god (Camus, 1956, p. 306), and is none of us owns the proper messianic name (Derrida, 1994). And none of us can approach the religious apart from responsibility to the ethico-political (Buber, 1965), that is, fear and trembling does not happen apart from the human sphere. Thus, hope, fear, and trembling raise certain socio-political spectres of a world wholly other than this unjust one (Derrida, 1994). These spectres radically democratise the individual exception (see Derrida, 1995, p. 79). They bring the self-identified conservative Kierkegaard at the end of his life closer to Marx's proletarian (Kierkegaard, 1944, pp. 286–7; cf. Kirmmse, 1990; Westphal, 1987; Marsh, 1990). This Kierkegaard is hardly akin to Nietzsche's sovereign or Schmitt's exception or the latter day right or left fascist revolutionary. What Havel (1990b) projects as an existential revolution by the powerless, and what West (1993) hopes for in a post-colonial existential democracy, offers a shorthand for Kierkegaard's timely contribution to critical social theory and practice.

Conclusions: Hope given for the sake of those without hope

Nicolaus Notabene's authorial praxis marks Kierkegaard's totalisation without a totaliser. Notabene foresees no telos of world history since he cannot even finish a book. When his wife frustrates his drive to totality – she burns each of his manuscripts before its completion – Notabene resorts to writing multiple prefaces to a never finished *oeuvre*. This fellow would be a poor vanguard spouting a dogmatic revolutionary theory, and he could hardly lead the ultimate victorious revolution. As a revolutionary of sorts, he escapes pressures to be done with loving his wife, to publish or perish, to see his collected works bear profit and fame, to catechise and indoctrinate, to finish before he has begun in the difficulty of beginnings (Kierkegaard, 1989b).

Concrete democracy and politicians could benefit from such self-irony (see Havel, 1990a). One may quibble over Kierkegaard as an individual and author who seems to write in an objectless inward comfort of financial inheritance or who may exhibit patriarchal, typically male anxieties. Kierkegaard's concerns and setting may even strike non-Europeans or non-Christians as rather parochial. Yet, if de Silentio's, Notabene's or Climacus's writing experiences are performatively convincing, then the axis of Kierkegaard's own authoring disrupts the intent of its author. For better or worse Kierkegaard may be saved from his own insights, oversights, and follies. The question remains for the present reader: what is to be done?

The feminine fire burning Notabene's masculinist gaze becomes even more aggravated in the twentieth-century *écriture*; our sense of world history – religious or secular – has made our age even less monocultural. If Kierkegaard's view is religious but not 'philistine-bourgeois' (Kierkegaard, 1980, p. 41f.), as he claims (1939), then it must refuse a patriarchal, anti-black, and colonising theodicy. God the liberator cannot be a white racist (Gordon, 1995a, pp. 140–57), a male supremacist or an oppressor of the poor (Marsh in Matuštík and Westphal, 1995, pp. 199–215).

Maybe this is too much perfection to be satisfied by any one author, past or present, although, perhaps, not too much by authors in an existentially receptive dialogue. It is safe to hold that no matter what the limits of author's texts and era are, Kierkegaard's attack on the established order projects hope for existential sociality of an open, polycentric sort (cf. Adorno, 1940, pp. 424–7; Kierkegaard, 1962, p. 153). After all, 'Christianity is no doctrine' . . . (Kierkegaard, 1991, p. 106), is no food for a homogeneous crowd. The religious, too, must belong to a medium of 'an existence-communication' (Kierkegaard, 1992, p. 380). And communicating temporal existence, one together with others cannot but break down crowds – their monogenealogy of individuals, communities, cultures, races, ethnicities, genders, and creeds. A polycentric secular polity would thus resemble neither real existing socialism nor established liberal democracies, in so far as they exhibit what Kierkegaard hated about Christendom. Neither did he harbour a nostalgic hope for an elitist golden age (Kirmmse, 1990). Refusing to prophesy in the first place (Kierkegaard, 1978, p. 109f.), nationalism or the neo-liberal New World Order is not the theodicy that Kierkegaard could accept as a way out from our levelling age.

Still, Kierkegaard does not celebrate the end of humanity, history, and liberating narratives. We should not confuse his attack on speculative Hegelian history with a carnival of *posthistoire* bereft of all emancipatory pathos. He is quite aware that an individual yet socially deployed motivated deception continues to be an obstacle to any genuine liberation (see Kierkegaard, 1980). Formal liberty is not yet embodied freedom; the present age is not yet at that beginning of history which is also the end of ideology.

What seems too narrow a Kierkegaardian concern to be deemed socio-politically and philosophically relevant – becoming a Christian in nineteenth-century Denmark – can command a more universal appeal. Kierkegaard does not imagine human equality in a poetic or spiritual distance from, but still within, material history, 'here in Copenhagen, in the market on Amagertorv, in the middle of the daily bustle of weekday life! (Kierkegaard, 1991, p. 59f.). He lets the Messiah 'completely give up his difference and in earnest seek the company of, completely live with, the poor and lowly of the people, the workers, the manual laborers, the cement mixers, etc!' (ibid., p. 58). That the Messiah has been '*quite literally one with the most wretched* . . . this is "too much" for people . . .' (ibid., p. 59, emphasis in the original; cf. Fanon, 1963).

Indeed, Kierkegaard's existential philosophy could be read as a theory of liberation with practical intent (cf. Adorno, 1940, pp. 423). This is what defines that critical social theory which can form a coalition and solidarity with existential philosophy: one is not merely to contemplate one's inward spiritual possibilities but also manifest interior self-transformation in the necessity of embodied and finite existence. One ought to liberate human existence radically and in its entirety, namely, both in actual personal and material history of one's relations with others (see Kierkegaard, 1991, p. 65).

Existential thinkers have often been rebels against totalitarian systems of thought and social organisation. Yet these same rebels have also integrated their personal dissent against such systems into a socio-political vision of a more just world. At decisive moments, existential protest becomes more than a European middle-class despair (cf., Fanon, 1967, pp. 224–9; Marcuse, 1969, p. 6). Textual revolts become invigorated by the refusals of persons with a human face (Kierkegaard, 1944), by the powerless (Havel, 1990b), by the wretched of the earth (cf. Sartre's Preface in Fanon, 1963, pp. 7–31). And today, if hope for radical personal and social liberation could become possible, then it might be given for the sake of those without hope (Marcuse, 1991, p. 257). One meets these people increasingly on our street corners.

Bibliography

Writings

Kierkegaard, Søren (1968), *Armed Neutrality* and *An Open Letter*, trans. Howard V. Hong and Edna H. Hong, Bloomington and London: Indiana University Press.
— (1940), *Christian Discourses*, including *The Lilies of the Field and the Birds of the Air* and *Three Discourses at the Communion on Fridays*, trans. Walter Lowrie, London and New York: Oxford University Press.
— (1980), *The Concept of Anxiety*, trans. Reidar Thomte in collaboration with Albert B. Anderson, Princeton: Princeton University Press.
— (1989), *The Concept of Irony* together with 'Notes on Schelling's Berlin Lectures', trans. Howard V. Hong and Edna H. Hong, Princeton: Princeton University Press.
— (1992), *Concluding Unscientific Postscript*, two vols, trans. Howard V. Hong and Edna H. Hong, Princeton: Princeton University Press.
— (1982), *The Corsair Affair*, trans. Howard V. Hong and Edna H. Hong, Princeton: Princeton University Press.
— (1967), *The Crisis [and a Crisis] in the Life of an Actress*, trans. Stephen Crites, New York: Harper and Row.
— (1990a), *Early Polemical Writings*, trans. Julia Watkin. Princeton: Princeton University Press.
— (1993a), *Edifying Discourses in Various Spirits*, trans. Howard V. Hong and Edna H. Hong, Princeton: Princeton University Press.
— (1990b), *Eighteen Edifying Discourses*, trans. Howard V. Hong and Edna H. Hong, Princeton: Princeton University Press.
— (1987), *Either/Or*, two vols, trans. Howard V. Hong and Edna H. Hong, Princeton: Princeton University Press.
— (1983), *Fear and Trembling* and *Repetition*, trans. Howard V. Hong and Edna H. Hong, Princeton: Princeton University Press.
— (1990c), *For Self-Examination* and *Judge for Yourselves*, trans. Howard V. Hong and Edna H. Hong, Princeton: Princeton University Press.
— (1944), *Kierkegaard's Attack upon Christendom*, trans. Walter Lowrie, Princeton: Princeton University Press.
— (1965), *The Last Years*, trans. Ronald C. Smith, New York: Harper and Row.
— (1978), *Letters and Documents*, trans. Hendrik Rosenmeier, Princeton: Princeton University Press.
— (1955), *On Authority and Revelation, The Book on Adler*, trans. Walter Lowrie, Princeton: Princeton University Press.
— (1985), *Philosophical Fragments* and *Johannes Climacus*, trans. Howard V. Hong and Edna H. Hong, Princeton: Princeton University Press.
— (1939), *The Point of View for My Work as an Author*, including the appendix ' "The Single Individual", Two "Notes" Concerning My Work as an Author', and *On My Work as an Author*, trans. Walter Lowrie, London and New York: Oxford University Press.
— (1991), *Practice in Christianity*, trans. Howard V. Hong and Edna H. Hong, Princeton: Princeton University Press.
— (1989b), *Prefaces: Light Reading for Certain Classes as the Occasion May Require*, trans. with Introduction William McDonald, Foreword Marc C. Taylor, Tallahassee: The Florida State University Press.
— (1980), *The Sickness unto Death*, trans. Howard V. Hong and Edna H. Hong, Princeton: Princeton University Press.
— (1967–78), *Søren Kierkegaard's Journal and Papers*, eds and trans. Howard V. Hong and Edna H. Hong, assisted by Gregor Malantschuk, Bloomington and London: Indiana University Press.
— (1988), *Stages on Life's Way*, trans. Howard V. Hong and Edna H. Hong, Princeton: Princeton University Press.
— (1993b), *Three Discourses on Imagined Occasions*, trans. Howard V. Hong and Edna H. Hong, Princeton: Princeton University Press.
— (1978), *Two Ages: the Age of Revolution and the Present Age. A Literary Review*, trans. Howard V. Hong and Edna H. Hong, Princeton: Princeton University Press.
— (1962), *Works of Love*, trans. Howard V. Hong and Edna H, Hong, New York: Harper and Row.

References and further reading

Adorno, Theodor W. (1989), *Kierkegaard: Construction of the Aesthetic*, trans. Robert Hullot-Kentor, Minneapolis: University of Minnesota Press.
— (1940), 'On Kierkegaard's Doctrine of Love', *Studies in Philosophy and Social Science* 8, 413–29.
Bartky, Sandra Lee (1990), *Femininity and Domination: Studies in the Phenomenology of Oppression*, New York: Routledge.
— (1973), *Negative Dialectics*, New York: Seabury Press.
Buber, Martin (1965), 'The Question to the Single One', *Between Man and Man*, New York: MacMillan Press.
Butler, Judith (1993), *Bodies that Matter: On the Discursive Limits of 'Sex'*, New York: Routledge.
— (1990), *Gender Trouble: Feminism and the Subversion of Identity*. New York: Routledge.

Caputo, John D. (1987), *Radical Hermeneutics: Repetition, Deconstruction, and the Hermeneutic Project*, Bloomington: Indiana UP.

Connell, George B. and C. Stephen Evans (eds) (1992), *Foundations of Kierkegaard's Vision of Community: Religion, Ethics, and Politics in Kierkegaard*, Atlantic Highlands, NJ: Humanities Press.

Cornell, Drucilla (1991), *Beyond Accommodation: Ethical Feminism, Deconstruction, and the Law*, New York: Routledge.

— (1995), 'What is Ethical Feminism?', in Seyla Benhabib et al., *Feminist Contentions: A Philosophical Exchange*, Introduction by Linda Nicholson, New York: Routledge, 75–106.

Derrida, Jacques (1995), *The Gift of Death*, trans. David Wills, Chicago and London: University of Chicago Press.

— (1994), *Specter of Marx: The State of Debt, the Work of Mourning, and the New International*, trans. Peggy Kamuf, New York: Routledge.

Douglass, Frederick (1968) (first edn, 1845), *Narrative of the Life of Frederick Douglass an American Slave, Written by Himself*, New York: Signe.

Emmanuel, Steve M. (1992), 'Reading Kierkegaard', *Philosophy Today* 36: 3–4, 240–55.

Evans, C. Stephen (1983), *Kierkegaard's 'Fragments' and 'Postscript': The Religious Significance of Johannes Climacus*, Atlantic Highlands, NJ: Humanities Press.

— (1992), *Passionate Reason: Making Sense of Kierkegaard's Philosophical Fragments*, Bloomington: Indiana UP.

Fanon, Frantz (1967), *Black Skin, White Masks*, New York: Grove Press.

— (1963), *The Wretched of the Earth*, trans. Constance Farrington, New York: Grove Press.

Gadamer, Hans-Georg (1975), *Truth and Method*, trans. G. Barden and J. Cumming, New York: Seabury Press.

Gordon, Lewis R. (1995a), *Bad Faith and Antiblack Racism*, Atlantic Highlands, NJ: Humanities Press.

— (1995b), *Fanon and the Crisis of European Man: An Essay On Philosophy and the Human Sciences*, New York: Routledge.

— (ed.) (1997), *Existence in Black: An Anthology of Black Existential Philosophy*, New York: Routledge.

Habermas, Jürgen (1984, 1987), *The Theory of Communicative Action*, two vols, trans. Thomas McCarthy, Boston: Beacon Press. Vol. 1: *Reason and the Rationalization of Society*, 1984; Vol. 2: *Lifeworld and System: A Critique of Functionalist Reason*, 1987.

Hannay, Alastair and Gordon D. Marino (eds) (1998), *The Cambridge Companion to Kierkegaard*, Cambridge UP.

Havel, Václav (1990a), 'Kafka and My Presidency'. Hebrew University speech, 26 April 1990.

— (1990b), 'The Power of the Powerless', trans. P. Wilson, in Jan Ladislav (ed.), *Living in Truth: Twenty-Two Essays Published On the Occasion of the Award of the Erasmus Prize to Václav Havel*, London: Faber and Faber, 36–122.

— (1993), 'The Post-Communist Nightmare', *The New York Review of Books*, 27 May 1993, 8, 10.

Heidegger, Martin (1962), *Being and Time*, trans. John Macquarie and Edward Robinson, New York: Harper and Row.

hooks, bell (1991), *Yearning: Race, Gender and Cultural Politics*, Boston: South End Press.

Huntington, Patricia J. (1998), *Ecstatic Subjects, Utopia, and Recognition: Kristeva, Heidegger, Irigaray*, Albany, NY: The SUNY Press.

Kellner, Doug (1984), *Herbert Marcuse and the Crisis of Marxism*, London and Berkeley: MacMillan and University of California Press.

King, Jr, Martin Luther (1986), 'Letter from Birmingham Jail', in James Melvin Washington (ed.), *A Testament of Hope: The Essential Writings of Martin Luther King, Jr.*, New York: Harper and Row.

Kirmmse, Bruce H. (1990), *Kierkegaard in Golden Age Denmark*, Bloomington: Indiana UP.

Kosík, Karel (1976), *Dialectics of the Concrete: A Study on Problems of Man and World*, trans. Karel Kovanda with James Schmidt, Dordrecht, Boston: D. Reidel Publishing Co.

Kundera, Milan (1984), *The Unbearable Lightness of Being*, trans. Michael Henry Heim, New York: Harper and Row.

Lukács, György (1974), *Die Zerstörung der Vernunft. Werke* 9, Darmstadt: Luchterhand.

— (1948), *Existentialisme ou marxisme?*, Paris: Nagel.

Mackey, Louis (1971), *Kierkegaard: A Kind of Poet*, Philadelphia: University of Pennsylvania Press.

Marcuse, Herbert (1969), *An Essay on Liberation*, Boston: Beacon Press.

— (1991), *One-Dimensional Man: Studies in the Ideology of Advanced Industrial Society*, with a new Introduction, Douglas Kellner, Boston: Beacon Press.

Marsh, James L. (1995), *Critique, Action, and Liberation*, Albany, NY: the SUNY Press.

— (1990), 'Marx and Kierkegaard on Alienation', in Robert L. Perkins (ed.), *International Kierkegaard Commentary: The Present Age*, 155–74.

Matuštík, Martin J. (1994), 'Kierkegaard as Socio-Political Thinker and Activist', *Man and World*, 27:2, 6 April 1994, 211–24.

— (1993), *Postnational Identity: Critical Theory and Existential Philosophy in Habermas, Kierkegaard, and Havel*, New York and London: Guilford Press.

—, Martin J. Beck (1998), *Specters of Liberation: Great Refusals in the New World Order*, Albany, NY: The SUNY Press.

— and Merold Westphal (eds) (1995), *Kierkegaard in Post/Modernity*, Bloomington and Indianapolis: Indiana UP.

Mead, Georg Herbert (1934), *Mind, Self, and Society: From the Standpoint of a Social Behaviorist*, Chicago: The University of Chicago Press.

Mooney, Edward F. (1991), *Knights of Faith and Resignation: Reading Kierkegaard's 'Fear and Trembling'*, Albany, NY: The SUNY Press.

Patočka, Jan (1990), *Kacířské eseje o filosofii dějin* (Heretical Essays about the Philosophy of History), with an Introduction by Ivan Dubský, Prague: Academia.

Perkins, Robert L. (ed.) (1990), *International Kierkegaard Commentary: The Corsair Affair*, Vol. 13, Macon, GA: Mercer UP.

Sartre, Jean-Paul (1974), 'Kierkegaard: The Singular Universal', *Between Existentialism and Marxism*, New York: New Left Books.

Westphal, Merold (1987), *Kierkegaard's Critique of Reason and Society*, Macon, GA: Mercer UP, reprinted by Penn State UP, 1991.

— (1993), *Suspicion and Faith: The Religious Uses of Modern Atheism*, Grand Rapids, MI: William B. Eerdmans Publishing Co.

West, Cornel (1993), *Keeping Faith: Philosophy and Race in America*, New York: Routledge.

NIETZSCHE AND THE WILL TO POWER

William A. Preston

Zarathustra and overcoming

Friedrich Nietzsche was born in 1844 in Röcken, Saxony, the son of a Lutheran pastor. He studied theology and classical philology at Bonn and Leipzig. At the age of 24, he became professor of classics at the University of Basel, where he taught for ten years and then retired to devote himself fully to his writing. Nietzsche experienced a permanent mental collapse in 1889 and died in 1900.

It is common to think of philosophy as a purely 'academic' exercise, something for the professors and beyond serious consideration by the practical, worldly and wise. If any philosopher in human history has ever successfully proven this common view to be false, surely it is Nietzsche. And yet Friedrich Nietzsche's central preoccupation with justifying life might appear to the casual eye to be remote from the bloody worldwide struggles over human fate in modern times.

Tragic myth, Nietzsche writes in his first book, *The Birth of Tragedy*, justifies 'the existence of even the "worst world"' (Nietzsche, 1967a, p. 143). The worst world, from Nietzsche's first to his last books, is the socialist world: under socialism, art is trampled underfoot by that 'class of barbaric slaves', the modern proletariat. Yet life is worth living none the less, in spite of all such horrors, because it is justified aesthetically.

The need to justify life, as a response to the nausea induced by its ugly, indeed horrible, aspects, is a recurring concern of Nietzsche's writings from *The Birth of Tragedy* on. *The Birth of Tragedy* finds this justification by looking backward in time, to the pre-Socratic, tragic culture of the Greeks. The object of scrutiny is, for this reason, distinctly national: one people, the ancient Greeks, are said to possess in their hands the reins of every subsequent attempt at superior culture. The perspective from which Nietzsche contemplates the return to Hellenic anti-quity is also national: the return to Greek tragic culture would signify for Germans a return to their true 'home' as a people (ibid., pp. 135–9). Later writings inaugurate a quite different approach to life-justification. With *Human, All-Too-Human* Nietzsche replaces this national spiritedness with the supra-national ideal of the free-spirited 'good European' (Nietzsche, 1984, pp. 228–9). And in Nietzsche's mature writings, the writings I want to discuss in this article, life-justification assumes a form that is not only supra-national but also sometimes super-human.

Thus Spoke Zarathustra narrates the spiritual pilgrimage of Zarathustra, the prophet *par excellence* of this superhuman mode of justifying life. The book's core message proclaims a desire to overcome humanity through the creation of a superhuman species.

A nauseous realisation motivates Zarathustra's call to overcome humanity. It is the fact that the greatest man is still too small (Nietzsche, 1969, p. 117). When Zarathustra compares the greatest men in human history to the most wretched, he finds the two types of men disgustingly similar. And so he arrives at the conclusion that the human race must be overcome.

The overman, embodiment of this superhuman overcoming of man, incarnates all Zarathustra's aspirations for affirmative, life-justifying power. The overman would affirm life specifically through his creation of a goal for mankind and his endowment of the earth with a meaning and a future.

Zarathustra finds that life-affirmation is unavoidable for him, but he is sorely tested. In particular, he is tested by the 'abysmal thought' that in order to affirm life, he also has to affirm all that is wretched and human-all-too-human in life. And in this test Zarathustra confronts, and must resist, the seductions of pessimism. Pessimism tempts humans to declare that everything is in vain. Zarathustra is choked by pessimism when he realises that human wickedness is too small.

In order to affirm life, one must test the pessimism that tempts one's soul to woefulness. This lesson goes to the heart of Zarathustra's teaching on revenge and redemption. The pessimist who concludes that all is in vain affirms not life but only his own powerlessness before fate. When the pessimist surveys his past, he is like 'an angry spectator' looking backwards in time. Life has not met his expectations. Evidently, he feels it should have respected his hopes. He nurses a grudge, and is vengeful in temperament. He desires to exact revenge on time. Time, or, to be more exact, his experience of the passage of time, keeps reminding him that what happened in the past cannot be changed. But he wishes that things could have been otherwise. Nietzsche gives this wish the name of 'time's desire', suggesting that the desire that things could have been otherwise is a non-contingent feature of the human experience of time's passage. Nietzsche, moreover, specifically defines revenge as a hatred of time.

The temperament Nietzsche counterposes to the vengeful outlook is the redemptive temperament. One who approached matters redemptively would affirm, in relation to the past, that he desired things to turn out as they had. Although redemption reconciles one to the past, it cannot be understood solely in terms of this reconciliation.

Doing so would reduce redemption to a fatalism that inclines toward pessimism. Nietzsche instead conceives redemption as a complicit relation to the past: one wills this past and becomes, as it were, its creator.

The notion that one can in effect create the past receives its comprehensive explanation in the doctrine of eternal recurrence proclaimed for the first time in *Thus Spoke Zarathustra*:

> Must not all things that *can* happen *have* already happened, been done, run past? . . . And are not all things bound fast together in such a way that this moment draws after it all future things? *Therefore* – draws itself too? For all things that *can* run *must* also run once again forward along this long lane . . . Must we not all have been here before? – and must we not return and run down that other lane out before us, down that long, terrible lane – must we not return eternally? (ibid., pp. 178–9)

That will to power recurs eternally is due, as Stanley Rosen correctly notes, in *The Question of Being*, to the 'finitude' of 'world-producing evaluations' (Rosen, 1993, p. 179).

The vision of eternal recurrence does not free Zarathustra from pessimism. Indeed, it accentuates the temptation. For if everything recurs eternally, by implication the absurd and terrible in existence recur eternally as well. Zarathustra's disgust threatens to drown him upon his realisation that the little man – who, like the great man with whom he shares much in common, must be overcome – recurs eternally. The little man recurs eternally, and, Zarathustra would say to higher men and the overman (since they recur eternally as well), higher men and the overman always suffer the presence of the little man.

The eternally-recurring little man brings along with him his religion and his politics: the God of the little man, and socialism too, though they may die a thousand deaths, come back again and again. Lukács asserts, in *The Destruction of Reason* (1980, p. 380), that, for Nietzsche, the stakes for the masters in their struggle against the slaves include 'obtaining and establishing *ultimate* control' (my emphasis). However, eternal recurrence, it should be clear, precludes any 'ultimate control' by the masters.

The Jewish God of the Roman slaves and His late-modern descendant the communist devil keep coming back, again and again.

As the wanderer and shadow tells Zarathustra, the death of god is 'always' a mere 'prejudice' (Nietzsche, 1969, p. 323). Certainly, the life of God is no less a mere prejudice, but that fact offers no consolation to a higher man confronting the little man's eternal recurrence.

If, as Zarathustra states, life equals suffering (including, naturally, the suffering that comes with the realisation that the little man recurs eternally), it does indeed take much courage to affirm all of life; that is, to love fate. But that kind of *amor fati* precisely characterises the overman. He does not deny, but is rather too well-acquainted with, his fears. His knowledge does not overwhelm him with nausea. He masters his fears. He peers into the abyss – that is, into the abysmal thought of the eternal recurrence of the most absurd and horrible aspects of existence – and looks at it with life-affirmative pride.

An interesting affirmation of the eternal recurrence of 'whatever was and is' occurs in a later work, *Beyond Good and Evil*. There, Nietzsche praises what I would call a fanatic of eternal recurrence – the one who is 'shouting insatiably *da capo*' – calling him the most life-affirmative human being (Nietzsche, 1968a, p. 258). Perhaps this life-affirmative human described by Nietzsche harbours suppressed doubts about whether he wants 'what was and is' to recur eternally. That may be why he 'shouts insatiably'. It would certainly explain why Nietzsche calls him human, and not superhuman.

Zarathustra's visions of the overman and eternal recurrence address the ownmost needs of higher men in the present age but do not claim for themselves the status of a belief. The unbelieving man disgusted with the conformism of his contemporaries in these modern times, to whom Nietzsche directs his concerns, is challenged to overcome not his lack of belief but rather his humanity. Zarathustra urges men to become his equals and, indeed, to surpass him in the race to superhumanity. Laurence Lampert (1986) accurately observes that instead of seeking imitators after the fashion of Christian discipleship, Zarathustra wants emulators after the noble 'model' of the Greek contest. It is not 'imitation' that Zarathustra

desires, but rather 'outdoing'. Nevertheless, those Zarathustra commands to 'outdo' him 'are not to be disloyal to his goal of the superman'.

In order to outdo Zarathustra, men must first give themselves their own will and renounce all submission. In his call to shatter the law-tables, Zarathustra declares that 'he who obeys *does not listen to himself!*' (Nietzsche, 1969, p. 218). Not a tragic culture's embrace of limits and boundaries to human action, but what I would call a 'culture of overcoming' now nourishes hopes for redemption. 'Overcoming' best describes this prophesied culture, since it would sanctify the transgression of all limits and boundaries for the sake of creating the overman. Where the tragic culture of *The Birth of Tragedy* would encourage men to respect limits and not dare to correct existence, Zarathustra tempts us to transgress existing limits.

Transgression's *raison d'être*, though, is not to correct existence. Transgression as called for by Zarathustra has nothing in common with the meliorist agenda of Socratism. The crucial distinction here is between existence-correction and existence-redemption. The point is not to change the world by making it better but to redeem the world by creating it, that is, by wilfully sculpting reality. Zarathustra's call for creators who would treat millennia as 'wax' pressed by hand is a far cry indeed from the counsels of deference to the Greek example in *The Birth of Tragedy* (ibid., p. 231).

Overcoming, as conceived by Nietzsche in *Thus Spoke Zarathustra*, does not, however, entail the demolition of all standards of judging conduct. God is dethroned, certainly, but his place is taken by the overman, the new divine standard whereby man measures himself. Unlike previous divinities, however, this new authority is to be – explicitly, without discretion – of man's own conception. Some idea of how supremely elevated the overman will be could be gleaned from Zarathustra's comment that the overman will be as far above humanity as humanity is above animality. In order to envision the distances imagined here, consider how an enlightened man sees the difference between himself and the ordinary man. The former, according to Zarathustra, sees the latter as on the level of animals. The overman, though, will look down on modern enlightened men as animals. For their part, the wise and enlightened men of today, were they ever to confront the overman, would react like parochial villagers and call him a devil.

Against what passes for wisdom among the enlightened men he encounters, Zarathustra propounds a set of notions about truth and nobility that accord with the practice of the overman. Nobility, on Zarathustra's understanding, is defined as value-creation. And values express what Nietesche calls a will to power. This understanding of what values express presupposes a view of the will to truth, and in reality of all aspects of life, as expressions of will to power. The breakthrough represented by Nietzsche's notion of will to truth as will to power can perhaps best be described by opposing will to power to the idea that truth is unsullied by power. Zarathustra calls this idea the doctrine of immaculate perception. Believers in immaculate perception see desire in perception as indecent. They want a decent perception, which they think is innocent of desire. They understand that desire-in-perception is egotistical and, as they ground their findings in an implicit or explicit morality of accountability, judge indecent, egotistical perception as guilty of something spiritually repugnant. Believers in truth so understood, desire (if that indeed is the word for it) knowledge in the manner of mirrors reflecting reality. Zarathustra, on the contrary, states that one should learn only in order to create. The analysis of truth presented in *Thus Spoke Zarathustra* initiates a revolution in morality whose further political implications in modernity are drawn in the *Genealogy of Morals* and in *The Anti-Christ*, which I will shortly discuss. The realisation that will to truth is will to power, far from condemning the former for failing to distinguish itself from the latter, concludes in exposing the innocent nature of creative desire in perception.

The revolution described in *Thus Spoke Zarathustra* affects not only the analysis of truth but, true to Nietzsche's concept of what it means to do philosophy, it also affects the way higher men should live. Simply put, the incorporation of the overman becomes the goal of higher men.

Zarathustra also issues an appeal for a league of value-creators. This appeal should not be confused with a call for political action. Value creators are not public men. They are solitaries. Echoing the *Apology* of Socrates to the effect that truly just men are ill-suited for public, political life, Zarathustra asserts that men hailed in the public sphere are merely acting the part of greatness. Furthermore, Zarathustra asserts, only those types of men succeed in drawing the crowd around them. Zarathustra likens his solitaries to a chosen people from whose midst the overman will one day emerge.

That the members of the new chosen people would be solitaries does not entail the absence of public, indeed world-shattering, consequences to the solitary practices of higher men. Firstly, Zarathustra himself feels compelled to the task of self-perfection, an obligation he owes to his children and to his childrens' children. This responsibility, to self-perfection and to all the overcoming that that requires, also falls to the higher men whom Zarathustra addresses with all manner of appeals to overcome themselves.

Yet quite drastic changes in culture must naturally occur in the course of creating the overman. For example, the purpose of marriage between higher men and women undergoes a radical innovation. No longer is marriage's function to breed the next generation of higher men. Marriage's purpose is instead the creation of the overman. And the women of higher men, according to Zarathustra, should acquire as their specific hope the desire to bear the overman. But in order to bear the overman, a woman of the higher men should be of sound mind as well as sound body. Peter Berkowitz makes the very good point that the 'nongifted man' is lower than woman in Zarathustra's scheme because he 'lacks an essential function' (in the case of woman that function is to breed ever higher forms of humanity) and is therefore 'expendable' (Berkowitz, 1995, p. 170). The drastic changes Zarathustra intends pertain not to the political status of women, as nothing in *Thus Spoke Zarathustra* suggests that that should be rendered equal with men, but to the ends of human culture. Those ends are no less divine now that God has been removed from the centre of man's preoccupations. It is simply that culture's *raison d'être* and main task is the human creation of the superhuman overman.

In sum, cultures which abide by limits to human action are to be replaced by a culture affirming the transgression of all that blocks the emergence in the world of the overman. But this entails a commensurate shift in how modern higher men view the conservatism which traditionally serves as the bulwark of privilege and greatness's possibility against the socialist rabble. Perhaps nothing captures the violence of *Thus Spoke Zarathustra*'s antipathy to the conservative sensibility more than Zarathustra's comment that '[t]hat which is falling should also be pushed' (Nietzsche, 1969, p. 226).

Zarathustra's various appeals to higher men shape an intention to set these men on the proper course to the creation of the overman. By reconciling themselves to the failure of conservative strategies seeking to recreate the past, higher men gird themselves, to use the words of The Doors, to 'break on through to the other side'. The 'other side' in this case is a zone of moral possibility in which the privileged are freed from the guilt feelings plaguing their selfishness, deployed with revolutionary intent by culture-destroying socialism. *Thus Spoke Zarathustra* instructs modern higher men in overcoming and in value-creation. Overcoming requires of them a certain purge: Socratism, slave morality and democracy have to be exposed, isolated and expelled from the instincts of higher men because they sustain the socialist threat to higher culture's very existence. The crisis must be faced in all its enormity, however. This purge, after all, demands a frontal assault on values which have hitherto defined the Occident. In order to summon the strength needed to shatter these reigning tablets of good and evil, higher men must first learn to esteem their own power to create values. Only through the creation of entirely novel, non-Socratic, non-slave-morality, non-democratic values can the world and all of its culture-creative inequalities be redeemed.

Nietzsche contra slave morality

Willing the eternal recurrence makes the temporal, in a certain sense, sacred. But the world-calumniators recur eternally as well, profaning time. One of the ways they defile existence is by trying to impose upon it the clumsy construction of historical optimism.

The scientific optimism Nietzsche attacks in *The Birth of Tragedy* for giving the go-ahead to workers' hopes for a better world co-exists in the modern age with another, in many ways more daunting, spiritual roadblock facing resurgent elites.

Nietzsche had discerned in Socratic, scientific optimism the positive programme of the rationalistic rabble's attempts to overturn the domination of the aristocrats. In modern Europe, an additional poisonous ingredient had been mixed into the brew responsible for intoxicating the rabble bent on revenge: the slave's *moral* condemnation of the master. If language was initiated by the masters, as Nietzsche claims, with morality the slaves had seized language; now, it must be taken back from them. The slaves must be deprived of the power to wield morality as a weapon against their masters. This goal frames Nietzsche's argument in *On the Genealogy of Morals*.

As its title indicates, *On the Genealogy of Morals* relates an attempt to trace the origins of morals. Nietzsche conceives his own project as a break with the customary practice of philosophers to analyse morality unhistorically (Nietzsche, 1989, p. 25).

That 'good' originally meant noble or aristocratic and 'bad' base and plebeian constitutes for Nietzsche a 'fundamental insight' of a genealogy of morals. Recovery of this original meaning, Nietzsche argues, takes place with him only because the 'democratic prejudice' previously obstructed this recovery by others. The recuperation of the original meaning of good and bad, together with further analysis of the origins of morals, provide new weapons for the struggle against democratic prejudices. Judith Shklar (1972) exaggerated when she stated that Nietzsche had no 'use for historical facts'. Rather, it is closer to the truth to say that Nietzsche used facts as he saw fit. Shklar is right to surmise, though, that it would have been 'unthinkable' for Nietzsche to have composed a detailed, empirical history of 'European moral development' (Nietzsche, 1972, p. 142).

Nietzsche understands the modern democratic prejudices initially as expressions of the struggle by the base and plebeian against the higher orders. He clearly understands that it will require more than a feat of etymological skill to beat back the democratic attack. The genealogy of morals, however, plays a crucial role in de-moralising the lower classes, in depriving them of the moral certainties they rely on in condemning the higher classes and social inequality. The democratic attackers, too, beginning with the socialists, will have to be de-moralised: the interpretation of the world they ground their actions in, a worldview in which they themselves are good and the higher classes are evil, must be de-valued. Recovering the original meaning of 'good' is simply the first act in unearthing the genealogy of morals, a genealogy that, as Nietzsche conducts it, lends itself naturally to this struggle. The next act involves an examination of the moral world which the lower classes inhabit.

The base and plebeian people marked as 'bad' by the naming power of the noble and the aristocratic seethe with resentment towards their social betters. Too weak to confront the higher orders in an open challenge to their rule, the 'slaves' (as Nietzsche calls this type of socially ignoble people) 'compensate themselves with an imaginary revenge' (Nietzsche, 1989, p. 37). The 'slave revolt in morality' thereby begins.

A year before, in *Beyond Good and Evil* (1886), Nietzsche announced that the prophetic Jewish value-inversion whereby 'poor' was equated with 'holy' and 'rich' with 'evil' commenced the slave revolt in morals (1968a, p. 298). This radical inversion, whereby the noble Roman world is turned upside down, constitutes the 'world-historic' significance of the Jewish people. Indeed, the whole countermovement against noble morality, *The Anti-Christ* claims, was an invention out of the most desperate need of the Jews, who, with a *ressentiment* shrewd to the point of genius, became the spiritual and sometimes even practical leaders of all the various life-denying and 'world-calumniating' tendencies (Nietzsche, 1990a, pp. 146–7).

At first, the slave revolt only succeeds in making the slave more wretched. Unable to fight the master, the slave scrutinises him from below. He concentrates his glare on the master who profits from the suffering that is his wretched existence, and he develops in his mind a 'real caricature and monster' (Nietzsche, 1989, p. 37). The slave broods about the master, while the master, when he casts a glance in the direction of the slave, does so carelessly and with the impatience of contempt. The slave is thus doubly tormented: by his already existing condition of slavery, and by the supplement he adds to this condition in the form of his image of his master. Unable to overcome his torments through action – in other words, through open revolt against the master – the slave's vengefulness at first festers in his own impotent rage.

The slave is literally poisoned by his own resentment, which can find no discharge, on account of the *de facto* prohibition on an open struggle against the master. But while the slave cannot yet struggle to overthrow the master, he is condemned to remember all the master's perceived insults and humiliations to his person. The slave's memory becomes a stimulant to his unforgetting resentment. Into the slave's memory of the master go the raw materials of his wretched existence that are then worked up into his concept of 'evil' (ibid., p. 39).

With the creation of the concept of 'evil', the slave has forged his one basic idea. With the idea of 'evil' in hand, the slave sets out to re-label the master, who still takes himself as 'good' and who regards the slave, when he bothers to do so, as 'bad' (ibid., p. 110). The slave re-labels the master 'evil' by attempting to impose on him an idea of the master's own moral *accountability*. By this concept of accountability, the slave also excuses his own inability to tyrannise others, a special case of which is his inability to conquer the master anywhere on the fields of manly battle. Nietzsche explains this through the allegory of the lambs and the birds of prey. Slaves who wield a concept of evil with which they label the master, Nietzsche suggests, are akin to sheep who would reproach eagles for seizing and eating their young. It is absurd, Nietzsche asserts, to insist that strength does not express itself in the structuring of relations of domination and subordination. This is especially true if all life itself is essentially injury and exploitation, as Nietzsche had claimed in *Beyond Good and Evil*.

However, the demand that the strong ought not abuse and kill the weak is in fact the core proposition of slave morality. This pretence of the weak should, he argues, be exposed for the despicable fraud that it is.

By invoking what is for Nietzsche the fraudulent pretence of moral accountability, the oppressed and downtrodden declare that those who refrain from 'evil' deeds are good. They are only fooling themselves, though. The actual explanation for why they are 'good' (in their slavish sense of refraining from evil), Nietzsche holds, is that they are too weak to be 'evil'. They have no choice in the matter of not expressing strength through mastery over and injury to others. They simply have little or no strength to speak of.

Shattering the subject

A specific error that has become 'petrified' in language needs to be overcome. This is the error that separates cause from effect when creating a distinction in thought between 'strength' on the one hand and 'expressions of strength' on the other. Popular morality, Nietzsche suggests, separates the strong man from his actions, from the expressions of his strength. The popular morality upheld by the value-table of 'good and evil' implies that behind the strong man and the weak man there exist 'neutral substrata' free to display strength or not. Nietzsche goes so far as to suggest that the strong man and the weak man do not even exist as distinct from the deeds through which strength and weakness are displayed: ' "the doer" is merely a fiction added to the deed – the deed is everything' (Nietzsche, 1989, p. 45). There is no such thing as a strong man who decides not to oppress and dominate the weak, or a weak man whose weakness is fundamentally the result of a decision to abide by his oppression and domination and not to strike back in rage. (This proposition of the *Genealogy* finds an earlier, negative confirmation in Zarathustra's suggestion that a slave reveals some nobility only by rebelling against his master.) But with this fiction of a doer as distinct from his deed, the subject is born, morally accountable for alleged decisions to be evil or not.

The subject must die. Strength must be ethically liberated from the moralistic frame-up that, Nietzsche contends, is the belief that the strong man is at liberty to refrain from injuring others. Weakness must be isolated from the moral presuppositions with which the weak man would clothe his miserable essence in the garb of a rational decision to not do harm. The book Nietzsche published just prior to the *Genealogy*, *Beyond Good and Evil*, had already sketched how this

liberation of the strong would demolish existin practices in the moral judgement of men and the actions. Therein, he had written about master mo ality that it does not judge a man by his actions: judges the man (Nietzsche, 1968a, p. 395). That is, judges who he essentially is.

Nothing in this essential judgement of who a ma is presumes that the actions whereby his essenc reveals itself are caused by the agency of an ego That the predicate is not conditioned by a subject an argument advanced in *Beyond Good and Ev* against 'the prejudices of philosophers'. The infer ence from the evidence of action to the existence c agency, Nietzsche claims, is not so much a logica cognition of a material reality as it is a mere inter pretation. Given Nietzsche's premises, it is no sur prise that the notion of a morally accountable soul ridiculed as bad fiction. In place of slave-morality morally accountable soul, Nietzsche would put th idea of a mortal and divisible soul. *Beyond Good an Evil* suggests that the soul be seen as a 'multiplicit' and even as a 'social structure of the drives an affects' (Nietzsche, 1968a, pp. 210–11). This 'socia perspective on souls clears the way for a hierarchica judgement modelled after social and political dis tinctions: the anarchy disordering and renderin uncreative the souls of the base can be contraste to the kingly self-command displayed by more crea tive, and hence nobler, types. The agency of the eg equal (and equally accountable for its actions) to a others of its kind by the value-tables of good and ev does not so readily accord with such judgements c who people essentially are.

The 'critique of the subject' is thus, for Nietzsche an integral component of any overcoming of th value-tables of slave morality. This overcoming wil as a matter of course, entail a reconstruction of th self-understanding of science, which currently relie on a language whose grammar posits the existence c a subject as factually distinct from its actions. But an criticism of existing grammar, however necessary will be insufficient unless the instinctive make-u of the dominators is altered accordingly. The 'cri tique of the subject' will not have succeeded until th lords of the earth, the dominators and oppressor thoroughly assimilate a critique of the subject. Fo this assimilation to occur, the dominators will hav to realise, instinctively, that they have no choice but to express their strength through acts of domination.

Once the dominators are instinctively reconciled to dominating others with no sense of guilt or moral accountability, the conscious expression of a 'critique of the subject' will no longer be so important. The objectionable character of the notion of a morally accountable subject would be a self-evident presupposition of ruling-class existence. But there is a long way to go, Nietzsche thinks, before this becomes the case. An entire epoch of history lies ahead in which this struggle against the slave morality will unfold. This is the epoch of 'the next two centuries in Europe', during which the presently dominant morality, which is really the slave morality that has assumed the form of Christianity, will die (Nietzsche, 1989, p. 161). This death agony of morality is coterminous with 'the will to truth' becoming 'self-conscious', meaning that the will to truth comes to recognise itself, as *Thus Spoke Zarathustra* argues, as will to power. The self-recognition of will to truth marks a final release from the bonds of slave morality: truth-claims in morality are to be seen not as discoveries of facts but as 'aggressive' (albeit perhaps creative) interpretations that express a 'form-giving' will to power (ibid., p. 79). The will to truth acquiring self-consciousness should kill slave morality because all moral assertion will be seen as the operation and enhancement of a power-will.

Henceforth, it will be socially illegitimate to advance extravagant (or for that matter, any) truth-claims on behalf of morality. Any man who remains a moralist will be dismissed as dishonest. Higher men will look at him as one who denies, evades, or otherwise underestimates the will to power manifest in his own practices. The man rightly seen as far more honest would be the dominator who admits that everything he does is motivated by will to power.

The end of metaphysics and the death of God

The fact that men can reason at all stems from the fact that their ancestors erroneously assumed that, when they gave names to things, they were not just engaged in labelling acts but were demonstrating their knowledge of things. The enormous pride our ancestors derived from their belief that they pos-sessed objective knowledge enabled them to tyrannise the other animals and become, in their own eyes at least, better-than-animal. The metaphysical ideas were thus historically and psychologically – but not philosophically – justified as necessary for the achievement of this and other victories. The lies of morality, sanctified with the aid of its 'postulates' grounded in language's metaphysical presuppositions, were needed for our ancestors to impose expectations on themselves in accordance with – and in order to incorporate, and thereby 'prove' – the prejudice that they really were better than the other animals (Nietzsche, 1984, p. 45). Only on an apparently durable 'foundation of ignorance' could human knowledge ascend to its present heights (Nietzsche, 1968a, 24).

The realisation that language does not allow humans access to an objective cognition of things as they really are is 'only now' beginning to occur, according to Nietzsche. The crisis this is generating is not really a crisis of reason, in the sense that reasoning abilities may wither and die as a result of the collapse of the metaphysical presuppositions of language: '[f]ortunately, it is too late to be able to revoke the development of reason, which rests on that [erroneous] belief [in language]' (Nietzsche, 1984, p. 19). The crisis pertains, however, to the source from which strength in the future is going to be derived, now that strength can no longer be mined in the discredited presuppositions of language.

The construction of any kind of new society is now impossible because metaphysical ideas lack the powers of compulsion they once had: nothing can truly bolt men down to one place or idea anymore. In *Daybreak*, Nietzsche writes that men are now unable to 'believe in a future' outlined for and imposed on them because moderns have lost faith in 'omens, oracles, soothsayers or the stars' (Nietzsche, 1982, p. 98). The kind of confidence that would be required for the sons and daughters to carry on and realise over a long duration the projects of their parents who initially committed a society to build socialism no longer exists. And it no longer exists because what no longer exists are the supernatural positings and determinations needed to support that type of commitment on the part of descendants who have not decided for themselves the project to which they are devoting their lives.

Metaphysical ideas, and especially the idea of eternal salvation or damnation as rewards and punishments for behaviour in 'this world', would authorise a multi-generational commitment to endure the sacrifices needed for the completion of a new society. But precisely this sanction is disowned by the socialists themselves. Even in the event that they claimed this authorisation, though, socialists would probably do their cause little good. 'For there is no "ought" anymore', writes Nietzsche, referring to the destruction of effective binding moral imperatives by 'our way of reflection' (Nietzsche, 1984 p. 371). Modern man and woman may, for example, continue to obey Sabbath formalities, but in the matters that concern how and to what they devote their lives, and why, they act very much as if they were atheists. Here, in *Human, All Too Human*, aphorism 22, we have an outline of the crisis indicated by the message that 'God is dead', which is enunciated for the first time later in *The Gay Science*.

The crisis of metaphysics is global. The death of God may be an occurrence that takes place in Europe, but that does not mean on Nietzsche's account that the God once killed on that continent will be anymore alive elsewhere. The death of God is a worldwide event that just happens to have taken place in Europe.

God's death is an overwhelming *fact* in the lives of the common people, Nietzsche contends. The madman in the famous parable in *The Gay Science* went looking for God in the souls of his own contemporaries, and found Him murdered. Nietzsche knows very well the danger inherent in publishing the truth about God, but thinks the consequences of not acknowledging His death to be far more calamitous. The old, Christian moral order in the souls of men, upon which the present political order in the city is based, is disintegrating anyway. Conflict with the rabble, with men and women whose souls are radically disordered and who desire to impose on the city a new, egalitarian world order, cannot be avoided.

Nietzsche's influence

In the philosophy of existence, Nietzsche's analyses of the death of God, his philological challenge to the hegemony of science and philosophy, his critique of the subject and his transvaluation of values have been most influential. But his influence has been all pervasive, especially in Germany. As Karl Jaspers declared in *Reason and Existenz* '[Nietzsche's] effect in Germany was like that of no other philosopher . . . it seems as though every attitude, every world-view, every conviction claims him as authority. It might be that none of us really knows what this thought includes and does' (Jaspers, 1955, p. 46).

Most controversial is Nietzsche's relation to National Socialism. The most profound commentators on Nietzsche – Georg Lukács, Leo Strauss, Eric Voegelin and Thomas Mann – have known that Nietzsche intoxicates the rabble to fascist crime. Lesser heads, eagerly scavenging for *reconditus* in the hope of appearing nuanced and attuned to the complexity of things, tend to miss or downplay this dimension of Nietzschean reception.

The deliberate refusal to countenance what Nietzsche was saying extended even to some of the most renowned critics of Nietzsche's own time. An example is Georg Brandes. Brandes wrote one of the earliest scholarly treatments of Nietzsche, 'An Essay on Aristocratic Radicalism' in 1889. Brandes had corresponded with Nietzsche, and was the first to apply the term 'aristocratic radicalism' to Nietzsche's philosophy (Nietzsche wrote back that it was 'the cleverest thing I have yet read about myself'). Brandes was also the first to lecture on Nietzsche's ideas (at Copenhagen). In a letter to Nietzsche, dated 17 December 1887, Brandes reproaches Nietzsche for not being 'nuanced' enough in his treatment of socialism. In his answer to Brandes, dated 8 January 1888, Nietzsche cautions against excessive nuance. Obsession with nuance, Nietzsche writes, leads to ignorant views, views that ignore 'all events below the surface'. The French, Nietzsche jokes, are too nuanced to see in his *Beyond Good and Evil* anything more than 'a medley of a hundred promiscuous paradoxes and heterodoxies'. Nietzsche's analogy between nuance and surface should be taken into account when considering the strivingly nuanced readings of Nietzsche produced by such commentators as Derrida.

Strivingly nuanced 'left-wing' or (like Derrida) liberal disciples of Nietzsche do not so much ignore the obvious, as they as well as anyone will acknowledge the empirical fact that there have always been more believers in Nietzsche who misunderstood him. (Did he not after all, like Zarathustra, disdain all believers?) But they ignore the significance of the obvious. Nietzsche apologists act very much in the manner of those disciples of Marx who try to deny their own master's directly inspirational role in the history of the Soviet Union. Like politically naive Marxists, naive Nietzscheans neglect the question: what kind of a philosophy is it which, unlike the philosophy of Aristotle, sets the minds of the many on fire with dreams of glorious violence? But then, as Stanley Rosen correctly observes (Rosen, 1989, p. 199, n. 32), courage is the lowest-ranking of Aristotelian virtues, while it is the highest Nietzschean virtue. Courage is one thing in a man who really deserves to rule, a noble man, and a different matter among people governed by envy and desires for revenge, as both Aristotle and Nietzsche knew.

Nazism would, however, be too lowly for Nietzsche. Take, for example, the most famous philosophy professor to lend his prestige to the Nazi party: Heidegger. When the 1953 (German) edition of *An Introduction to Metaphysics* (delivered as a series of lectures in 1935) came out, Heidegger decided, against advice to the contrary, to leave in the acclaim for Nazism. Long after the War, Heidegger continued to insist that Nazism had 'taken the road' to 'a satisfying relationship with technology'. Inherent in Nietzsche's way of thinking is a deeper objection to Heidegger and Hitler's politics. Fascism, and especially its National Socialist variant, would be for Nietzsche *too egalitarian*. Did not the Nazis claim that Germans, *qua* Germans, were superior to Jews? But this nonsense is egalitarian nonsense, presuming as it does the equality of all German Gentiles. The essential division for Nietzsche is not between Jews and Germans but between the spiritually gifted few and the mediocre many. His fervent hope for Germany is for the unity of the most noble Jews and the most noble Gentiles, *a unity of the few in struggle against the many*.

Certainly, spiritually higher men would never be *engagé*, fascistically or otherwise, as political commitment by definition entails one's voluntary servitude to an idea or a leader. The spiritually higher man's

responsibility, though, is not social. Social responsibility is alien to the specific responsibility proper to a philosopher of the future.

Attempts to combine Nietzsche with individualistic self-assertion reflect other elements of Nietzsche reception. Two waves of this brand of Nietzsche scholarship after the Second World War indicate the highly circuitous and rather furtive recovery of Nietzsche's real outlook. There was, in the beginning, the Nietzsche scholarship symbolised by Walter Kaufmann's efforts. Kaufmann is mostly to be credited with habilitating Nietzsche as a great philosopher and psychologist in the eyes of a liberal-democratic audience. But what Kaufmann's Nietzsche lacked was that frenzied, Dionysian dimension that explodes politically as an ecstatic outburst of violence against the poor and the weak.

The second wave of Nietzsche scholarship, which looks to France and to Heidegger for direction, reflects an abortive attempt to tap into that energy. There have always been new Nietzscheans but the balance sheet of the latest crop is decidedly mixed. Unlike Kaufmann, the new Nietzscheans turn to Heidegger for instruction. By so doing, they keep alive the possibility that Nietzsche scholarship will reconnect with, and be animated by, an illiberal political cause. As yet, though, that illiberal hope remains only a possibility. The 1960s generation of new Nietzscheans, however much it may reject liberalism as a philosophy, generally prefered the liberal political order to any of the historical alternatives. Though reconciled to modern liberalism, post-modernist Nietzscheans nevertheless yearn for something nobler than the further intensification of the regime of the Last Man.

Even after his death, Michel Foucault retained a role he acquired when French Marxism's star was fading: the leading man of the Nietzschean Left. Foucault played different roles within the Nietzschean-left repertoire, depending on what his will to power at the moment inspired him to embody. Whatever the costume, though, the political objective was the same, and in complete accord with Nietzsche on one key point: the public denigration of liberalism's claims of truth. Here was a political thrust Kaufmann utterly lacked. Foucault was even shrewd enough to declare that he was distorting Nietzsche to suit his own contingent ends, implying, quite correctly, the inherently paradoxical nature of an attempt to practise a politics that has a built-in contempt for its own would-be consistent practitioners.

Foucault employs strategies at will and appropriates for his own purposes the kind of master's freedom Nietzsche celebrates. But he also claims to side with the slaves, 'the masses' (Foucault, 1977, p. 207). The analogy between Foucault and the truly free-spirited 'masters of the earth' thus remains formal and superficial. Foucault is, after all, the critic of normalisation, of modern disciplinary systems of comparing, differentiating, hierarchising, homogenising and excluding people. But the destruction of normalising reason might also herald the overman – in so far as disciplinary normalisation privileges the normal, average human being over the abnormal, superior human being.

The overman, however, is not what Foucault affirmed in his prison support work and in his criticism of psychiatry. He supported groups that sought to let prisoners, among other beneficiaries of modern discipline, speak for themselves about their demands (in the case of prisoners, quite understandably, for the abolition of the prison system). Furthermore, Foucault's attack on modern discipline in *Discipline and Punish* does not target the normalisation of men who are superior human beings being aggressed by resentful normal people (ibid., p. 183). He rejects normalisation *tout court*. He affirms his will to power by protesting the normalisation of all people including, obviously, those who are not superior but inferior. By doing so, Nietzsche would argue, Foucault lumps the beautifully formed and the lucky strikes of men with cripples and gruesome accidents among humans. Precisely this, though, would, to Nietzsche, be normalising in the most revolting, because egalitarian, sense. The superior, because integral, man who exhibits a unity of style, would be treated as if he were equal to the inferior, because fragmented, person who lacks a unity of style and is in fact a chaotic hodgepodge of styles.

Foucault, of course, does not endorse the aggression of the noble ones but instead expresses sympathy for the 'plebeian quality' in things. The grounds for endorsing a revolt of the plebeian quality, Nietzsche would argue, could only be said to exist in so far as the plebeian quality embodies a value to life itself, substantial enough to warrant for its sake the accommodation or even sacrifice of other, non-plebeian, qualities. Such grounds, of course, are lacking in Nietzsche's view. Plebeians have value only in so far as their existence as plebeians realises – through their labour and their envy – the provisioning of those above with certain material necessities and the nourishment of their most spiritual feelings of distinction. Plebeians have value to life only through their subordinate but most necessary integration into the pathos of distance. Their revolt may bring out what little nobility they have, and one can appreciate this, like Zarathustra, from above, as a discerning judge of nobility in the unlikeliest places. But such appreciation, at bottom aesthetic and not moral, is certainly no cause for solidarity with those who revolt. With Foucault, the disciplined are affirmed in their victimhood, and the punisher is scorned. Prisoners, for example, lose the shame that is properly their own. Foucault's solidarity with the punished and with the disciplined in general heralds the Last Man, who, like the higher man, esteems himself and feels no need to justify his pride with reason but, unlike the higher man, is incapable of shame.

Yet the new Nietzscheans, even Foucault, are modern university professors and not revolutionaries or radical anti-revolutionaries. Were Nietzsche alive to comment on his academic admirers, he might find Zarathustra's discourse, 'Of Scholars', relevant. In *Thus Spoke Zarathustra* (p. 147), the grazing sheep who come upon the sleeping Zarathustra exclaim in disgust that he is no longer a scholar. The new Nietzscheans, in spite of their rhetorical excesses, are not really in the business of 'shattering the good and the just'. They have demonstrated no willingness and certainly no ability to replace liberal democracy and modern malaise with an ecstatically aggressive political regime of the kind I think Nietzsche favours. Many of the new Nietzscheans no doubt sincerely believe in a version of the Left's traditional egalitarianism, but precisely that, I contend, renders a disservice to the Left whose heritage they would like to uphold. For, like Kaufmann, the new Nietzscheans, especially those self-designated Left Nietzscheans, rehabilitate a thought which, were its profoundest hopes embodied, would have little place for them.

Bibliography

Writings

Nietzsche, Friedrich (1980), *Sämtliche Werke: Kritische Studienausgabe in 15 Bänden*, Giorgio Colli and Mazzino Montinari (eds), Berlin: Walter de Gruyter.

— (1986), *Sämtliche Briefe: Kritische Studienausgabe in 8 Bänden*, Giorgio Colli and Mazzino Montinari (eds), Berlin: Walter de Gruyter.

In translation:

— (1990a), *The Anti-Christ*, trans. R. J. Hollingdale with an Introduction by Michael Tanner, New York: Penguin Books.

— (1968a), *Beyond Good and Evil*, trans. with a Preface by Walter Kaufmann, in *Basic Writings of Nietzsche*, New York: Random House.

— (1967a), *The Birth of Tragedy*, trans. with an Introduction by Walter Kaufmann, New York: Vintage Books.

— (1967b), *The Case of Wagner*, trans. with an Introduction by Walter Kaufmann, New York: Vintage Books.

— (1982), *Daybreak*, trans. R. J. Hollingdale with an Introduction by Michael Tanner, Cambridge: Cambridge University Press.

— (1989), *Ecce Homo*, trans. with an Introduction by Walter Kaufmann, New York: Vintage Books.

— (1974), *The Gay Science*, trans. with an Introduction by Walter Kaufmann, New York: Vintage Books.

— (1989), *On the Genealogy of Morals*, trans. Walter Kaufmann and R. J. Hollingdale with an Introduction by Walter Kaufmann, New York: Vintage Books.

— (1954), *Homer's Contest*, trans by Walter Kaufmann, in *The Portable Nietzsche*, New York: The Viking Press.

— (1984), *Human, All Too Human*, trans. Marion Faber with Stephen Lehmann and an Introduction by Marion Faber, Lincoln: University of Nebraska Press.

— (1986), *Human, All Too Human*, vol. 2, *Assorted Opinions and Maxims* and *The Wanderer and His Shadow*, trans R. J. Hollingdale with an Introduction by Erich Heller, Cambridge: Cambridge University Press.

— (1954), *Nietzsche contra Wagner*, trans. Walter Kaufmann, in *The Portable Nietzsche*, New York: The Viking Press.

— (1979), *Philosophy and Truth: Selections from Nietzsche's Notebooks of the Early 1870s*, trans. and ed. Daniel Breazeale, Atlantic Highlands, NJ: Humanities Press.

— (1962), *Philosophy in the Tragic Age of the Greeks*, trans. with an Introduction by Marianne Cowan, Washington: Regnery Gateway.

— (1969), *Thus Spoke Zarathustra* trans. with an Introduction by R. J. Hollingdale, New York: Penguin Books.

— (1990b), *Twilight of the Idols*, trans. R. J. Hollingdale with an Introduction by Michael Tanner, New York: Penguin Books.

— (1983), *Untimely Meditations*, includes *David Strauss, the Confessor and the Writer, On the Uses and Disadvantages of History for Life, Schopenhauer as Educator* and *Richard Wagner in Bayreuth*, trans. R. J. Hollingdale with an Introduction by J. P. Stern, New York: Cambridge University Press.

— (1968b), *The Will to Power*, trans. Walter Kaufmann and R. J. Hollingdale, ed. with an Introduction by Walter Kaufmann, New York: Vintage Books.

References and further reading

Ackermann, Robert (1990), *Nietzsche: A Frenzied Look*, Amherst: The University of Massachusetts Press.

Allison, David B. (ed.) (1985), *The New Nietzsche: Contemporary styles of Interpretation*, Cambridge: The MIT Press.

Ansell-Pearson, Keith (1994), *An Introduction to Nietzsche as Political Thinker: The Perfect Nihilist*, New York: Cambridge University Press.

— (1993), and Howard Caygill (eds) (1993), *The Fate of the New Nietzsche*, Aldershot: Avebury Press.

Aschheim, Steven E. (1992), *The Nietzsche Legacy in Germany: 1890–1990*, Berkeley: University of California Press.

Bataille, Georges (1994), *On Nietzsche*, trans. Bruce Boone with an Introduction by Sylvere Lotringer, New York: Paragon House.

Berkowitz, Peter (1995), *Nietzsche: The Ethics of an Immoralist*, Cambridge, MA: Harvard University Press.

Bloom, Harold (ed.) (1987), *Friedrich Nietzsche*, New York: Chelsea House Publishers.

Brandes, George (1972), 'An Essay on Aristocratic Radicalism' and other writings, including Brandes-Nietzsche correspondence, in *Friedrich Nietzsche*, New York: Haskell House Publishers.

Clark, Maudemarie (1990), *Nietzsche on Truth and Philosophy*, Cambridge: Cambridge University Press.

Danto, Arthur C. (1965), *Nietzsche as Philosopher*, New York: The Macmillan Company.

Deleuze, Gilles (1983), *Nietzsche and Philosophy*, trans. Hugh Tomlinson, New York: Columbia University Press.

Derrida, Jacques (1979), *Spurs: Nietzsche's Styles*, trans. Barbara Harlow with an Introduction by Stefano Agosti, Chicago: The University of Chicago Press.

— (1985), *The Ear of the Other: Otobiography, Transference, Translation: Texts and Discussions with Jacques Derrida*, trans. Peggy Kamuf and Avital Ronell, ed. Christie V. McDonald, New York: Schocken Books.

Foot, Philippa (1991), 'Nietzsche's Immoralism', *The New York Review of Books*, 13 June: 18–22.

Foucault, Michel (1977), 'Nietzsche, Genealogy, History,' in *Language, Counter-Memory, Practice: Selected Essays and Interviews*, trans. Donald F. Bouchard and Sherry

Simon, ed. Donald F. Bouchard, Ithaca: Cornell University Press.

— (1977), *Discipline and Punish*, trans. A. Sheridan, Harmondsworth: Penguin.

— (1977), *Selected Essays and Interviews*, trans. Donald F. Bouchard and Sherry Simon, ed. Donald F. Bouchard, Ithaca: Cornell University Press.

— (1980), *Power/Knowledge: Selected Interviews and Other Writings, 1972–1977*, trans. Colin Gordon, Leo Marshall, John Mepham, Kate Soper, ed. Colin Gordon, New York: Pantheon Books.

Heidegger, Martin (1959), *An Introduction to Metaphysics*, trans. R. Manheim, New Haven: Yale University Press.

— (1977), 'The Word of Nietzsche: "God is Dead" ', in *The Question Concerning Technology and Other Essays*, trans. William Lovitt, New York: Harper and Row.

— (1979), *Nietzsche*, Vol. 1: *The Will to Power as Art*, trans. David Farrell Krell, New York: Harper and Row.

— (1984), *Nietzsche*, Vol. 2: *The Eternal Recurrence of the Same*, trans. David Farrell Krell, San Francisco: Harper and Row.

— (1986), *Nietzsche*, Vol. 3: *Will to Power as Knowledge and as Metaphysics*, trans. Joan Stambaugh and Frank A. Capuzzi, ed. David Farrell Krell, San Francisco: Harper and Row.

— (1992), *Nietzsche*, Vol. 4: *Nihilism*, trans. Frank A. Capuzzi, ed. David Farrell Krell, San Francisco: Harper and Row

Higgins, Kathleen Marie (1987), *Nietzsche's 'Zarathustra'*, Philadelphia: Temple University Press.

Jaspers, Karl (1955), *Reason and Existenz*, trans. with an Introduction by William Earle, New York: Noonday.

Kaufmann, Walter (1974), *Nietzsche: Philosopher, Psychologist, Antichrist*, 4th edn, Princeton: Princeton University Press.

Lampert, Laurence (1986), *Nietzsche's Teaching: An Interpretation of Thus Spoke Zarathustra*, New Haven: Yale University Press.

Lukács, Georg (1980), *The Destruction of Reason*, trans. Peter Palmer, London: The Merlin Press.

Mann, Thomas (1947), *Nietzsche's Philosophy in the Light of Contemporary Events*, Washington: The us Library of Congress.

Nehamas, Alexander (1985), *Nietzsche: Life as Literature*, Cambridge, MA: Harvard University Press.

Preston, William A. (1997), 'Nietzsche on Blacks', in Lewis R. Gordon (ed.), *Existence in Black: An Anthology of Black Existential Philosophy*, New York: Routledge.

— (1998 forthcoming), *Nietzsche as Anti-Socialist*, Atlantic Highlands, NJ: Humanities Press.

Rosen, Stanley (1989), *The Ancients and the Moderns: Rethinking Modernity*, New Haven: Yale University Press.

— (1993), *The Question of Being: A Reversal of Heidegger*, New Haven: Yale University Press.

— (1995), *The Mask of Enlightenment: Nietzsche's 'Zarathustra'*, New York: Cambridge University Press.

Shklar, Judith N. (1972), 'Subversive Genealogies', *Daedalus*, Winter 1972, 129–54.

Solomon, Robert C. and Kathleen M. Higgins (eds) (1988), *Reading Nietzsche*, New York: Oxford University Press.

Staten, Henry (1990), *Nietzsche's Voice*, Ithaca: Cornell University Press.

— (1968), *Liberalism Ancient and Modern*, New York: Basic Books.

Strauss, Leo (1959), *What Is Political Philosophy? And Other Studies*, Glencoe, IL: The Free Press.

Voegelin, Eric (1987), *The New Science of Politics: An Introduction*, with a Foreword by Dante Germino, Chicago: The University of Chicago Press.

FAITH AND EXISTENCE

Lewis R. Gordon and James L. Marsh

Philosophy of existence, whether in its atheistic or theistic forms, is no longer the main topic of the day the way it was, or approached being, in the 1940s and 1950s. Like Marxism, it is treated at the end of the twentieth century as a philosophical movement condemned to a past, and often more passionate, age. Nevertheless, it is important to resist premature thoughts of closure. Both philosophy of existence and Marxism have important things to say that illuminate our contemporary situation. The difference between the two is that Marxism aims at illuminating the historical specificity of dynamics of exploitation, suffering and social change. The concern is on its relevance *today*. Philosophy of existence, on the other hand, is concerned with the disclosed dynamics of human modes of being. In that regard, although the historical specificity of human modes of being may change, the constant calling into question of that being stands at the heart of humanity's concerns from the problematic of disobedience in Genesis 2 to contemporary struggles between authority and freedom. Whereas the critical theorist or the Marxist may seek a world in which social contradictions have been resolved, the existentialist explores the dynamics of why such resolution would not entail utopia. Why is it, the existentialist asks, that there is always something more at the heart of human self-realisation?

The aim of this article is to articulate the set of issues that emerge from the convergence of philosophy of existence with philosophy of religion. Central figures in this regard include Søren kierkegaard, Martin Buber, Gabriel Marcel and Karl Jaspers.

The atheistic thinkers could also be included in this category by virtue of the contributions they have made to the discussion of religion and theology. Friedrich Nietzsche, Martin Heidegger and Jean-Paul Sartre are the most noteworthy in this regard. Since independent articles are devoted to Kierkegaard and Nietzsche, and since Heidegger and Sartre receive much individual attention in this section of the *Encyclopedia*, this article will be devoted to Buber, Jaspers and Marcel. The reader is encouraged to consult the other articles for discussion of the others.

Theology is the systematic study of God, the project of bridging a gap between thought or science or understanding and God. In this sense, there is no existential theology proper, since no existentialist believes that any *logos* could bridge such a gap. This conclusion of the folly in any attempt to conceptualise God and religious experience is a motif of nearly all religious philosophies of existence. Such conceptualisation, according to the criticisms, requires the subordination of God and religious experience to universal categories of thought. That is because language, conceptualisation and communication are within the realm of universal, though not absolute, reality. In the Kierkegaardian version of this argument, formulated as early as *Fear and Trembling*, God, as the Absolute, transcends all universal limitations. A conceptual formulation of God refers, in the end, to an idol, a figure that stands for God but is not God, a figure that is a false god or, at most, a *representation of* God. A concern raised by this argument is whether God is communicable. As existential writers frequently discuss God, it would seem that their communication is the performative contradiction of their argument against communicability. For Kierkegaard, this problem was surmounted by the turn to indirect communication. What this turn signifies is that God does not communicate to us, nor do we to and about God, in an isomorphic language of concept and thing conceptualised. God is communicated through the limitations of communication. This access to the unlimited by virtue of the limited is an existential paradox: the limitation of communication is a communication. It is in that-which-is-not-directly communicated that the absolute is indirectly communicated to us. Although popularly known as a 'leap of faith', where there are no mediating bridges between our cognitions and trust in God, the claim emerges in various forms: the face (Levinas), absolute Thou (Buber), the face, symbol and transcendence (Jaspers), Mystery (Marcel), Ultimate Concern and the God above God (Tillich). For existentialists, the gap between the human being and God could only be bridged through the human being's willingness to bind her or his existence or life project with that God or ultimate concern.

Religion emerges from the Latin *religare* (to bind fast). One can easily see how philosophy of existence lends itself more readily to a religious incarnation than a theological one. All existential philosophies call upon the human being to recognise her or his role in the act of binding the self to her or his ultimate concern(s). Whether toward God, the self, or the absence of both God and the self, authenticity has peculiarly *religious* significance.

God as personal and eternal thou

Martin Buber (1878–1965) is the most iconographic of the twentieth-century existential philosophers of religion. His influence transcends the academy in the world of ideas. (The most influential systematic academic religious existentialist is undoubtedly Paul Tillich.) A professor first of religion (University of Frankfurt am Main, 1923–33) and then a professor of philosophy (Hebrew University, 1938 onward), he was often characterised as a Jewish philosopher and mystic. His work fused the thought of Kierkegaard

with the mysticism of the Hasidim, the result of which is a powerful, indirect calling-into-question of the self–Other relation that dominates much existential, phenomenological and social thought. Buber asks us to consider our relations to each other, the world and God. To each other, he is critical of the notion of a self–Other relation, although he appreciates its importance for rational discourse. For him, the self–Other relation is on the level of an I–it relation. One could think of Descartes's third-person account of why others could simply be hollow physiological analogues of the self. A genuine human-to-human relation does not call for the other, her, him or them. It calls for first and second-person relations: I and thou; we and thou. A similar relation is called for when we refer to God. God (as a third-person reference) is a misguided reference, for God is made manifest even through the communicated point to which the third-person reference was meant to be informative. In attempting to communicate *about* God, one communicates *to* and *through* God. God is always Thou. God's oblique reference is paradoxically direct, and God's direct reference is paradoxically oblique. To speak *to* God (Thou) is to recognise also God's presence in the 'it' by which God is supposedly absent. God's relation to the world (our 'it') is always Thou.

Now, an error in many interpretations of Buber's thought is to reduce it to a rejection of I–it relations between human beings. Here, the misrepresentation of Buber's thought is shared by many other existentialists, where it is believed that existential thinkers are antipathetic to the material and social world. Buber recognises the importance of I–it relations for the theoretical attitude, where science prevails. The scientific foe of Buber's position is positivism, where the world is reduced to the scientifically designated and the tautological, as one finds in works by A. J. Ayer, such as *Language, Truth, and Logic*. For the positivist, the world consists *only* of it–it relations, and what stands for the 'I' is at best an emotional attachment explainable on physiological grounds. Existentialists do not regard it–it as a relation proper. For them, such a notion is a world without consciousness and a world without either God or the human being. Such a world is the conclusion of objectivism – a view from everywhere, which constitutes a view from nowhere, a view that is not a view. Buber, like all other existentialists, offers a properly I–it relation for science, which requires, then, that all sciences have, if but a hint of, an element of subjectivity and, hence, perspectivity. In Buber's thought, this dimension shares much with the artistic attitude.

Both the scientific and artistic attitude could be regarded respectively as the standpoints of *observer* and *onlooker*. The former analyses (breaks down) the universally translatable features of the human being and nature in a realm of repeatability and predictability. The latter takes hold of the impressions for the purposes of synthesis. In both versions, the human being is ultimately usable. Moreover, both are located in the objective third-person reality. The scientist and the artist need not enter into an 'inside' relation with that which is observed or created. For Buber, then, the aesthetic attitude does not by itself afford a level of indirect calling into question of the other human being as Thou. The status of Buber's own work is, therefore, in spite of its poetic flavour, called into question: is it a manifestation of I–Thou or I–it? An immediate response is that it is an I–it that calls upon us to be cognisant of an I–Thou. A more complex response is that the evocative force of Buber's work could place one in an I–Thou relation with it. Think, for instance, of the internal relation that emerges in artistic productions like plays, films, and hymns: they have to suspend the *aesthetic* attitude enough to draw us into a world of I and Thou.

Returning to his philosophy of religion, then, Buber's position emerges out of his philosophical anthropology, which is a philosophy founded on dialogue. This anthropology, like Kierkegaard's, requires a distinction between direct, universal discourse (I–it) and indirect, absolute discourses of faith (I–Thou). The I–Thou relation need not be between one human being and another. The I–Thou relation could also be between a human being and an artistic production or a living piece of nature. An example is his famous (and much criticised) discussion in *I and Thou* of an I–Thou relation between a human being and a tree:

It can, however, also come about, if I have both will and grace, that in considering the tree I

become bound up in relation to it. The tree is no longer *it*. I have been seized by the power of exclusiveness. . . . The tree is no impression, no play of my imagination, no value depending on my mood; but it is bodied over-against me and has to do with me, as I with it–only in a different way. (Buber, 1958, pp. 7–8)

We see here that a dialogical relation is not necessarily a relation of mutual communication in Buber's thought. The relation is the establishment of value and recognition from the standpoint of the 'I'. A comparison is Kierkegaard's famous discussion of loving the dead in his *Works of Love*: how is it possible that one could love and be in communion with the dead? There, there is no 'answer' from the dead beyond the established relation of loving them. No external guarantee is available. One must simply take the risk of establishing such a relation, of living it on the level of faith. (Note that even 'on the level of faith' is a form of stepping out of that relationship since 'faith' is a third-person designation of that relationship. The relationship is not even as a 'relationship'. There simply 'is' Thou.) Without external, mediating factors of assessment, the status of Thou is ontological and normative. It excludes all other possibilities and is the sum total of being because it *is* all possibilities – including possibilities of *ought*. Thus, Thou also stands as teleological and, consequently, value incarnate. It is this dimension that brings forth his understanding of the religious and the theistic.

In *Israel and the World*, Buber argues that 'Even though I must of necessity use theological concepts when I speak of . . . faith, I must not for a moment lose sight of the nontheological material from which I draw these concepts' (Buber, 1948b, p. 13). Here, Buber is speaking of the I–it implications of the effort to establish a *logos* of God. God is the Thou that signifies the 'nontheological material' from which the concept of God is drawn for the theologian. This means, in effect, that the theologian is attempting to conceptualise that which is not a concept. In *I and Thou*, this nonconceptualisable notion is the eternal Thou. This eternal Thou is that which 'by its nature cannot become *It*. . . . which cannot be limited by another *Thou* . . . the being that is directly, most nearly and lastingly over-against us, that may properly only be addressed not expressed' (Buber, 1958, pp. 75–6 and 80–1). We see here the basis of an emergence of a Thou relation between a human being and a Tree: it is an instance of our relation with the eternal Thou.

We may here wonder whether Buber's position commits him to pantheism. If so, difficulties of solipsism and individuation emerge, for if everything is ultimately a manifestation of the eternal Thou, how is an I–Thou relation possible? Is it not a Thou–Thou relation?

Buber faces two seemingly competing claims. First, God, as Thou, is individuated, personal. Think of Abraham's El, who introduces himself to Abraham in Genesis 17: 1 as El Shaddai (God of the Mountain). That being so, how, then, could God be the second incarnation – God as an eternal, underlying Thou? In scholastic language, Buber faces God's sufficiency and necessity. God is sufficiently present in dialogue but necessarily hidden as infinite and eternal. The notion of 'knowing' the true nature of God is thus misguided since such knowledge would require God's finitude. Buber's position is unapologetic: one does not know God; one encounters God.

A paradox emerges from Buber's discussion. Malcolm Diamond expresses it thus: 'Is it not a severe limitation of the divine to insist that it does not truly disclose itself in the structure of human thought?' (Diamond, 1967, p. 247). In other words, God resists human thought because God is unlimited, but that resistance poses a limit to God.

We see here a vexing dimension of existential thought. Unlike science and systematic philosophy, existential thought *welcomes* paradoxes. For Buber, the limit posed by dialogue is not its weakness. It is its strength.

The symbolic and the transcendent

Karl Jaspers (1883–1973) is among the most widely read but ironically underrepresented existential philosophers. There are currently no seminars outside of German institutions devoted to his thought, which leaves knowledge of his importance primarily in the hands of references through other texts. He is seconded only by Heidegger in twentieth-century German intellectual history, and that status may be based on the occlusion of his work in Germany during the reign of National Socialism and the subsequent prominence of Heidegger's influence by way of the ascent of French post-structuralism – especially the thought of Jacques Derrida.

Like most twentieth-century existential thinkers, he denied being an existentialist. His doctorate was in medicine, and the first six years of his career were devoted to psychiatric work. He became Professor of Philosophy in Heidelberg in 1921, lost the position in 1937 and was reinstated in 1945. He subsequently became Professor of Philosophy at Basel in 1948.

His writing was prodigious, and their remarkable prescience pertains not only to diagnoses of the political predicament of his times, as in *Man and the Modern World* (1931), but also his understanding of the human being as a philosophical problem of our times, an understanding that emerges in all of his work, but most notably in his *Philosophy* (1932, 3 volumes) and his widely read *Reason and Existenz* (1933), *The Question of Guilt* (1946), and (with Rudolf Bultmann) *Myth and Christianity* (1954).

Jaspers's writings focus on the humanistic dimensions of existential thought. He is concerned with the human potential for humanity. This potential is characterised by him as 'authenticity' and *Existenz*.

Like Buber, Jaspers recognised a dimension of human being in what phenomenologists called the natural attitude – the world of causality and everyday experience. For Jaspers, the human being is there designated as *Dasein*, the 'being there' of time and space, of facts. The human being is also consciousness and *Geist* or 'spirit' (ideal totalities and history). These dimensions of human reality do not signify the achievement of human possibility. At this stage, should the human being settle for these modes of being, her or his humanity would not be made manifest. The human being could treat these dimensions of her or his sum totals, as her or his 'essence'. Such treatment would be remiss, however, because it is in the human ability to accept them that also rests the human ability to transcend them. It is through the achievement of self-awareness, of standing before each of these dimensions with realisation and acceptance of freedom and responsibility, that the human being makes the transition into *Existenz*.

This achievement is usually stimulated by the human confrontation with forces that facilitate self reflection: death, suffering, struggle and guilt. In effect, *Existenz* is the normative reality of standing out as a human being. In Jaspers's philosophy, then, *Dasein* is an inauthentic mode of being.

Although Jaspers recognises the world of empirical knowledge, he locates truth in the dialogical reality of communication. He regards reason and truth as fundamentally public modes of existence. These public realms are realms of 'signs', where there is shared understanding of how to negotiate one's way through the empirical world. Without reason and truth, *Existenz* collapses into a private, solipsistic world, wherein even its claims for awareness would make no sense. Like Wittgenstein, then, Jaspers rejects the notion of a private language, and he roots truth and meaning in the social practices of communication. The openness of *Existenz*, however, is such that it will always transcend reason's effort to bound it in the universal. *Existenz* raises the question of transcendence.

The question of transcendence leads to consciousness of 'encompassing'. What this means is that in each human formulation of its limitation is a boundary or horizon to be surpassed. Thus, every effort to subsume the human being under complete rationalisation is itself incomplete. The most complete achievable attitude for a human being thus becomes her or his recognition of incompleteness, which, if comfortably accepted, paradoxically collapses into completeness, which is inauthentic. This ongoing struggle with incompleteness is the human confrontation with the truth of Being and transcendence. In this struggle, there is the limitation of conceptual analysis. The transcendent emerge from direct existential engagement. Think here of Kierkegaard's understanding of the Absolute and Buber's understanding of Thou: they are not translatable into universal concepts, yet they can be understood through experiences of giving up mediation. Jaspers calls the activity of 'reading' these transcendent dimensions of reality, which he calls 'ciphers', metaphysics. Ciphers are symbols; they are that which do not point to signs but point beyond them to the transcendent. Although they function like signs – that is, they point toward something – unlike signs,

their designations are always deferred; they transcend isomorphic relations of signifier and signified. Communication of ciphers is, then, at best, *indirect* communication, although the experience of ciphers is direct, as in the case of existential communion with the face of another human being. Ciphers can be read through myth. Here, it is important to bear in mind that for Jaspers myth is not identical with fiction. Myth is here properly understood through its communion with ritual: in myth, a form of being emerges, which makes the internal relation to myths far from mythical (in the fictive sense). The influence of Kierkegaard is unmistakable here.

Jaspers's views on transcendence and myth raise the limitations of *Dasein*, or what Kierkegaard would call the universal and Buber would call I–it relations. The religious experience, properly understood, is one in which the transcendent *sufficiently* appear. In *From Text to Action*, Paul Ricoeur shows an affinity with Jaspers in his existential hermeneutics with the observation that in biblical hermeneutics, God appears. To read the Bible without the appearance of God is, in effect, not to *read* the Bible. The proper relation, then, is biblical interpretation's relation to other biblical interpretations. In similar spirit, Jaspers has argued, in *Myth and Christianity*, that myth is properly related only to myth:

> Mythical thinking is not a thing of the past, but characterizes man in any epoch. It is true that the term 'myth' is by no means unequivocal. It contains the following elements;
>
> 1. The myth tells a story and expresses intuitive insights, rather than universal concepts. The myth is historical, both in the form of its thinking and in its content. It is not a cloak or disguised put over a general idea, which can be better and more directly grasped intellectually. It explains in terms of historical origin rather than in terms of a necessity conceive as universal law.
> 2. The myth deals with sacred stories and visions, with stories about gods rather than with empirical realities.
> 3. The myth is a carrier of meanings which can be experienced only in the language of myth. The mythical figures are symbols which, by

their very nature, are untranslatable into other language. They are accessible only in the mythical element, they are irreplaceable, unique. They cannot be interpreted rationally; they are interpreted only by new myths, by being transformed. Myths interpret each other. (Jaspers, 1958, pp. 15–16)

In Jaspers's thought, religion is not treated as a vestige of the human being's historical adolescence. Religion is the symbolic instantiation of the human encounter with transcendence. Religion reminds the human being of the incompleteness at the heart of human existence, an incompleteness that enables human beings always to transcend the predicament of mundane existence. All religions remind human beings that we are not gods, but that reminder enables the human being to live in the realm of possibility. Every human being faces the project, as Sartre would formulate it, of what he or she is to become.

Although not often discussed in post-structural and semiotic analyses of culture, it should be clear that Jaspers's theory of symbols and signs are highly relevant for such treatments of religion. A major point of divergence, however, would be the discussion of authenticity and *Existenz*. The question of the human being's humanity is at the centre of Jaspers's thought, whereas in post-structuralism and semiotics, the human being is subordinated to, and often by, the sign.

LRG

The mysterious

In general, 'being' in Gabriel Marcel (1889–1973) refers to the incarnate, receptive presence of the human being to her- or himself and to her or his other, whether that be nature, other human beings or God. 'Having' refers to the stance of manipulation and control directed toward us ('me') or the other possessed as a thing or object. The fundamental and immediate level on which Marcel's discussion of being and having takes place is in his phenomenology of embodiment. Here, the fundamental distinction is between the body as something had or possessed like an instrument, and the body as something that one is. The main thrust of the argument is

to deny that the most fundamental experience of one's body is the experience of it as an instrument. Indeed, any use of an instrument presupposes a deeper experience of embodiment. Using anything – a knife, fork, pen – presupposes a prior incarnate presence of oneself to the world such that one is capable of using anything as an instrument. If one's body were an instrument, therefore, one would run the risk of infinite regress of instruments. The body as an instrument would have to be wielded by a second body; if this were an instrument, one would need a third body and so on. What stops and prevents the infinite regress is to affirm the body not as an instrument but as one's incarnate presence in the world. As Marcel formulates this conclusion in *Creative Fidelity*: 'I am my body' (Marcel, 1964, pp. 18–19).

One's body is not initially, and most primordially, that which one has or possesses, but that which one *is*. To make this claim, however, is not to affirm a materialism. To claim that one is one's body does not imply total, but rather partial, identity with one's body. The body as one's presence in the world manifests a subjectivity that also has spiritual aspects, aspects of transcendence. These are 'founded' on embodiment, we might say, but not reducible to it.

One of the ways that this foundedness is revealed is that there is a receptivity even on very high spiritual levels, which Marcel describes as manifesting 'disposability' or 'creative fidelity', that is similar to and founded on the receptivity of bodily perception. It is a mistake, Marcel argues, to conceive of sensation on the model of physical transmission or telegraphy. Is the receiving organism, he asks, like a radio set that translates into sensation a message passively received from a transmitter? Transmission implies two sets of data, one of which is not available to us. Nor do we possess any interpretative code whereby we can translate one set of data into another. 'Sensation', he writes in *Creative Fidelity*, 'is immediate, the basis of all interpretation and communication, hence not itself an interpretation and communication' (ibid., pp. 24–6).

Nonetheless, sensation or perception is not purely passive but rather actively receptive; to see something as 'red' is to see it as something, and our attention can shift to something else, for example, the blue chair next to our window. Marcel here affirms a fundamental receptivity that 'has a wide range of meanings extending from suffering or undergoing to the gift of the self; for hospitality is a gift of what is one's own, of oneself' (ibid., p. 28).

Feeling, therefore, is not, and cannot be, mere passivity because it implies activity. Feeling is not an undergoing, like a piece of wax receiving an imprint; and because even feeling is not totally passive, there is continuity between the fact of feeling and creativity on very high artistic, intellectual and religious levels. As Picasso's Cubist painting of Wilhelm Uhde, in which we can recognise an individual person with a distinctive kind of personality, shows, even on the highest levels of artistic creativity there is a receptive element, and even on the lowest levels of sensation and feeling there is an active element. The human being is an active, lived, incarnate presence in the world, receptive to it and open to it but also actively engaged and involved with it.

Such incarnate presence, as it develops and emerges on higher levels of the human being, is an affair of freedom. Such a freedom comes into play in so far as our thinking about ourselves in relation to the world moves from an analytic, primary reflection concerned with problems, with data external to the self, to secondary reflection on experience as mystery, an experience in which and with which the self is involved. Freedom operates in such reflection in so far as there is refusal to think about the self as a thing and there is a choice to think about the self as a subject, as mystery.

Philosophy as a chosen openness to the mystery becomes a form of disciplined wonder, and such wonder becomes another, higher form of active receptivity or receptive activity. Marcel, in *Creative Fidelity*, write:

> Whoever philosophizes *hic* and *nunc*, is, it may be said, a prey to reality; he will never become accustomed to the fact of existing; existence is inseparable from a certain astonishment. . . . Personally I am inclined to deny that any work is philosophical if we cannot discern in it what we may call the string of reality. (ibid., pp. 63–4)

For this reason, no one in whom there is not a reverence for experience giving rise to reflection can be a philosopher; mere historians, mere specialists need not apply. To be a philosopher requires a kind of second innocence, an intellectual virginity that is inseparable from a certain asceticism. Such asceticism, of course, implies and requires freedom, a chosen, disciplined openness to the mystery of metaproblematic.

For all of these reasons it is a mistake to think of philosophy as something one possesses or has. Because the philosopher is in too deep, and open to mystery, because such mystery implies an inseparable link between self and world, self and other, he or she does not possess her or his philosophy. To think this way is to risk getting into competition with other philosophers, all of whom has their own system, which they think is better than, say, 'my' system. Thus philosophical conversation and dialogue and reflection degenerate into conceptual wrangling and contending and arguing. In *Man against Mass Society*, Marcel confesses: 'The truth is that there is nothing less patentable than philosophy, nothing more difficult to appropriate' (Marcel, 1978, p. 14).

The genuine philosopher, then, is characterised by an openness to experience in its depth and mystery and variety; as Marcel observes in *Tragic Wisdom and Beyond*, this involves being characterised by a certain 'ear for experience' analogous to somebody who has an ear for music, 'a wonder which tends to take the form of disquiet . . . in not taking reality for granted' (Marcel, 1973, p. 6), not even something as apparently obvious as an ordered succession of temporal moments. Such openness is an openness to otherness in several senses: to other experiences, other points of view, other persons. Marcel's philosophy in this sense is inherently dialogical; a patient, reverent, dialogical interrogating of experience.

The other person, therefore, is a central theme of reflection in Marcel's philosophy, and we notice here a crucial distinction, like those between being and having, secondary reflection and primary reflection, mystery and problem, I–thou or I–you and I–it. I can treat the other as a thing, an 'it', as something to be catalogued, or I can treat the other as a mysterious centre to which I respond creatively and receptively. To the extent that I respond to the other in such a way, I become 'disposable' to the other. He or she is somebody to whom I relate actively and receptively, creatively and respectfully, and disposability is this active receptivity.

Such disposability avoids two extremes – that of belonging to the other to the point of being her or his slave and that of the other belonging to me as a thing. Rather what occurs is a mysterious sharing between persons in which walls break down; I discover myself and he or she discovers her- or himself. 'I communicate effectively with myself only in so far as I communicate with the other person, that is, when he becomes thought for me', declares Marcel in *Creative Fidelity* (Marcel, 1964, p. 34). I can meet someone on a subway who initially appears as a 'her' or 'him', we begin to converse, common ground is discovered, our defences break down, and a relationship is established. For a brief time at least, we have ceased being isolated atoms indifferent to one another, competing for space on the subway, and we have begun to matter to one another.

Marcel then notes, in the same volume, a connection between indisposability and having:

> I tend to treat myself as indisposable just so far as I construe my life or being as having which is somehow quantifiable, hence as something capable of being wasted, exhausted, or dissipated. Indeed where having is concerned I find that I am in the state of chronic anxiety of the man hanging over the void, who has a small sum of money which must last as long as possible since when it is spent he will have nothing left. (ibid., p. 54)

To the extent that we are indisposable, we are not able to distinguish between coercion of a person, on the model of physical causality, and appeal to his freedom, or tend to submerge the latter in the former. Moreover, because we see the other competitively, we are unable to admire the other:

> To affirm: admiration is a humiliating state, is the same as to treat the subject as a power existing for itself and taking itself as center. To proclaim, on the other hand, that it is an exalted state is to start from the inverse notion that the proper function of the subject is to emerge from itself and realize itself primarily in the gift of oneself and in the various forms of creativity. (ibid., p. 54)

Philosophical wonder, admiration and respect become impossible in a world dominated by having, by the thing, by the commodity. Liberation from such a world is only possible, first of all and in its deepest aspect, as an appeal to God as ultimately mysterious, metaproblematic and free: God as the ultimate Thou who helps me liberate my freedom in thrall to a reified world of having. Marcel's very insightful point here again is that we do not belong to God nor S/He to us as a prop:

> Indeed, who am I to pretend that I do not belong to You? The point really is that if I belong to you, this does not mean: I am Your possession; this relation does not exist on the level of having as would be the case if You were an infinite power. Not only are You freedom but You also will me, You arouse me to freedom, you invite me to create myself, you are this very invitation. And if I reject it, that is, Thou, if I persist in maintaining that I belong only to myself, it is as though I walled myself up; as though I strove to strangle with my own hands that reality in whose name I believed I was resisting You. (ibid., p. 100)

Conservative forms of Christianity, which use religion as an escape from freedom, need not apply.

To know that I belong to God in this sense is to know that I belong to myself only on this condition, that this belonging is the only complete, authentic freedom to which I can lay claim, and that this freedom is a gift that I am called to accept. Here again is the idea of an active receptivity; indeed, belief in God and commitment to God are the final flowering of disposability and wonder and admiration. To the extent that such commitment is lived out over a lifetime, it becomes a form of creative fidelity which is very much like repetition in Heidegger's sense – an active taking over of my past, reinterpreting it in the light of a lived present and emerging future. Creative fidelity is again a form of active receptivity. Prayer, we might say, is the highest form of such receptivity: contemplative reverent awe before the Mystery.

Marcel is not without ideas on the links between his philosophy as laid out above and politics; indeed he has written whole books, the most important of which is *Man Against Mass Society*, on this relation ship. In this work he insists on an 'unbreakable link' between his philosophy and his political reflections. Indeed, any other approach would be guilty of a spirit of abstraction against which it has been the whole point of his work to contest.

Mass society is seen by Marcel as rooted in a world of technique that he defines as 'a grasp of procedures, methodically elaborated, and consequently capable of being taught and reproduced, and when these procedures are put into operation they assure the achievement of some definite concrete purpose' (ibid., p. 1). While technique by itself is not to be despised, indeed it is or can be good, in modern societies it functions to degrade the human being. In so far as technique is something that can be acquired, it may be compared to a possession, to something had. And such dominance functions as an expression of an unjust, manipulative, dominating society, whether that be capitalist or state socialist.

As technical progress occurs in modernity, a development of communication happens that implies a growing uniformity, homogeneity and loss of individuality. A mass society emerges in which the lowest common denominator is money or cash, and such money, by a vicious dialectical process, loses all substantial reality and becomes a fiction. Men and women are ruled by abstractions that have become ends and not means; and techniques of communication such as advertising and propaganda help to bring this about. A person's value tends to be interpreted economically in terms of her or his output, and he or she is more encouraged to model herself or himself on the machine and to think of herself or himself as a machine: 'Everything tends to show that, in what is pretentiously called present-day civilization, it is the man whose output can be objectively calculated ... who is taken as the archetype: that is to say (and let us note this carefully) directly comparable to a kind of machine' (ibid., p. 129). The affinities of this thinking with Marx and neo-Marxism, which also have things to say about the human being as the appendage of the machine, about the role of money as a least common denominator, about the dominance of inhumane abstractions, and about the loss of individuality in bourgeois society, should be obvious.

Just as a person can become a slave of her or his habits, so also he or she can be a slave of her or his techniques, and this is what has happened in modern societies. One example is a motorist who, instead of seeing a car as a means of travel, acquires a passion for the car, spends time swapping one for another, and thus becomes less and less capable of considering the car as a means for getting about. A kind of inverted world emerges here in which end becomes means and means becomes end. I derive my worth from what I possess. Such an account has great affinities with Marx. Marcel, we are tempted to say, in his social analysis up to a point is Marxist or crypto-Marxist, but in an undeveloped way. And we mean that point as a compliment to Marcel.

So-called 'progress' then, is more and more oriented to a world of amusement, conveniences and reliance on gadgets. Such a technical world, for Marcel, can lead only to despair if it is taken as the whole story. In such a busy world, in which the business of First World nations is business or busyness, the fundamental response can only be contemplative and religious. As he declares in *Mystery of Being*:

> But I do affirm that it is through ingatheredness only, through recollection in the highest sense of that word, through a concentrated recalling of ourselves to ourselves, that these powers of love and humility can be born and be grouped in strength, which alone, in the long run, can form an adequate counterpoise to the blind, and blinding, pride of the technician, closed in by his techniques. (Marcel, 1960, pp. 100–1)

Marcelian, theistic humanism demands and requires radical social critique and transformation. If one wishes that being flourish over having, then such a stance is always going to be at odds with a society such as capitalism that systematically subordinates being to having and that now rules worldwide in an increasingly virulent manner. The claim is analytic. Otherwise such humanism is self-contradictory, inconsistent, incomplete, merely ideal and, true as it may be in its fundamental claims, runs the risk of functioning as a kind of consolation and bourgeois ideology. We go to a class or lecture that extols being over having, subjectivity over objectivity, and I–Thou over I–it, and then leave the classroom or lecture hall and ignore the real, day-in and day-out negation of being by having, subjectivity by objectivity, and I–Thou by I–it in the real competitive world. The lecture functions as bourgeois consolation, the jargon of being subjectivity or authenticity.

Marcel gives us rich existential analyses of the unique individual (level one) linked to general accounts of human society and ontological generality (levels five and seven). For Marcel's level seven, of course, 'nature is included in and related to' as Bertell Ollman observes 'a broader context of being and God' (Ollman, 1993, pp. 53–7).

Religious belief all too often functions as a prop and consolation and ideology of ruling groups. All too often religion justifies a division between the religious Sunday, in which we prayerfully express a love for God and human beings, and a secular working week, in which we cheerfully exploit human beings, participating in, or allowing or remaining silent about such exploitation. One example of this kind of Christianity is the individualistic Pro-life Christian, as fanatically concerned about life within the womb as he or she is indifferent to life outside of it exploited by institutionalised racism, sexism, heterosexism and classism. Here we distinguish between 'Pro-life' as an ethical stance on abortion and pro-life as a conservative political movement. As Merold Westphal has argued (Westphal, 1993, pp. 123–216), the first does not imply the second, and the first can be, and is, linked to progressive political stances and movements that are not indifferent to life outside the womb.

JLM

Bibliography

References and further reading

Augustine, St (1950), *The City of God*, trans. Marcus Doas, with an Introduction by Thomas Merton, New York: Modern Library.

Buber, Martin (1948a), *Das Problem des Menschen*, Heidelberg: Verlag Lambert Schneider.

— (1948b), *Israel and the World: Essays in a time of Crisis*, New York: Schocken Books.

— (1958), *I and Thou*, trans. Ronald Gregor Smith, New York: Scribner's Sons, Collier Books.

— (1965), *Between Man and Man*, trans. Ronald Gregor Smith with an Introduction by Maurice Friedman, New York: Collier Books.

— (1967), *The Philosophy of Martin Buber*, in Paul Arthur Schilpp and Maurice Friedman (eds), Library of Living Philosophers XII, La Salle, Illinois: Open Court.

Diamond, Malcolm L. (1967), 'Dialogue and Theology', in *The Philosophy of Martin Buber*, 235–47.

Friedman, Maurice (ed.) (1991), *The Worlds of Existentialism: A Critical Reader*, with Introduction and Conclusion by Maurice Friedman, Atlantic Highlands, NJ: Humanities Press.

Jaspers, Karl (1955), *Reason and Existenz: Five Lectures*, trans. with an Introduction by William Earle, New York: Noonday Press.

— with Rudolf Bultmann (1958), *Myth and Christianity: An Inquiry into the Possibility of Religion without Myth*, trans. Sorbet Guterman, New York: Noonday.

— (1969–71), *Philosophy*, trans. E. B. Ashton, Chicago: University of Chicago Press.

Jones, William (1973), *Is God a White Racist?: A Preamble to Black Theology*, New York: Anchor Press/Doubleday.

Kierkegaard, Søren (1962), *Works of Love: Some Christian Reflections in the Form of Discourses*, trans. Howard and Edna Hong, New York: Harper and Row.

— (1983), *Kierkegaard's Writings*, VIII, 'Fear and Trembling' and 'Repetitions', trans. with Introduction and Notes by Howard and Edna Hong (eds), Princeton: Princeton University Press.

[See also the bibliography on Kierkegaard in article 2.1 of this volume.]

Marcel, Gabriel (1964), *Creative Fidelity*, trans. Robert Tosthal, New York: Noonday Press.

— (1960), *Mystery of Being*, I and II, trans. R. Hague. Chicago: Henry Regnery.

— (1973), *Tragic Wisdom and Beyond*, trans. Stephen Jolin and Peter McCormick, Evanston, Illinois: Northwestern University Press.

— (1978), *Man Against Mass Society*, trans. G. S. Fraser, South Bend, Indiana: Gateway Editions.

Nietzsche, Friedrich (1968), *Will to Power*, trans. Walter Kaufmann and R. J. Hollingdale, New York: Vintage Books.

— (1974), *The Gay Science*, trans. Walter Kaufmann, New York: Vintage.

Ollman, Bertell (1993), *Dialectical Investigations*, New York: Routledge.

Ricoeur, Paul (1981), *From Text to Action*, Cambridge: Cambridge University Press.

Tillich, Paul (1951), *Systematic Theology*, I, Chicago: University of Chicago Press.

— (1958), *Dynamics of Faith*, San Francisco: Harper Collins.

— 1952), *The Courage to Be*, New York and London: Yale University Press.

Twiss, Sumner B. and Walter H. Conser, Jr (eds) (1992)

Experience of the Sacred: Readings in the Phenomenology of Religion, Hanover and London: Brown University Press.

Westphal, Merold (1993), *Suspicion and Faith: The Religious Uses of Modern Atheism*, Grand Rapids, Michigan: William B. Eerdmans Publishing Company.

— (1984), *God, Guilt, and Death: An Existential Phenomenology of Religion*, Bloomington: Indiana University Press.

West, Cornel (1983), *Prophecy, Deliverance!: An Afro-American Revolutionary Christianity*, Philadelphia: Westminster Press.

2.4

PHILOSOPHY OF EXISTENCE AND PHILOSOPHICAL ANTHROPOLOGY: SARTRE AND HEIDEGGER

Peter Caws and Peter Fettner

Martin Heidegger (1889–1976) and Jean-Paul Sartre (1905–80) are the two major figures associated with the important movement in mid-twentieth-century philosophy broadly known as existentialism. The emergence of this movement can be seen as the culmination of a trend of thought going back to the beginning of modern science but sharpened by a series of profound crises experienced by European society in the nineteenth and twentieth centuries: the carnage of the First World War, the mechanisation and bureaucratisation of daily life, a decrease of religious faith, the weakening of accepted traditions. The associated strains on belief were in part provoked by a decentring of the place of the human being in the universe, effected by the work of Copernicus, Darwin and Freud, which deprived men and women of their sense of security and belonging to an established order, and left those who were sensitive to such matters in a state of alienation, dread and anxiety.

The main concerns of existentialism manifested themselves in diverse ways – in popular culture, literature and religious enquiry. In the nineteenth century, philosophers like Kierkegaard and Nietzsche produced texts of great dramatic and rhetorical power in which these ideas had a central place, texts which called into question the Western tradition in philosophy and its reliance upon reason and logic. However, with Sartre and Heidegger the technical resources of philosophy are applied to the very problems of existence and philosophical anthropology which had been expressively explored by Nietzsche and Kierkegaard. We deal below with some of the ways in which the more technical writings of Heidegger and Sartre intersect with the popular movement, but turn first to some preliminary definitions.

By 'philosophy of existence' we shall understand *the questioning of the fact and conditions of being*; by 'philosophical anthropology' we shall understand *the questioning of the nature of the human*. (To avoid misunderstanding, we note at once that philosophical anthropology is distinct from, and largely independent of, the discipline of anthropology as a social science, especially as practised in the English-speaking world. In the latter, the concept of the human tends to be taken as given, and the activity of the discipline consists of recording and theorising human differences; in the former the concept of the human is itself the central problematic.) The root question of philosophical anthropology is of great antiquity, going back at least to the Psalms of David – 'What is man, that thou art mindful of him?' (In what follows because of the language of the philosophers under consideration, it will, unfortunately, be impossible to avoid the dominance of the masculine form as generic, otherwise we face a text of painful and repeated circumlocution; we therefore offer a blanket apology in advance.) The question recurs throughout the history of Western philosophy. The root question of the philosophy of existence is implicit since Parmenides, but its modern formulation goes back to Gottfried Leibniz (1636–1716) and is echoed by Heidegger in 'What is metaphysics?' (in Heidegger, 1977). 'Why should there be anything at all, why not much rather nothing?'

The two domains are linked in an obvious and fundamental way at the beginning of modern Western philosophy by René Descartes (1596–1650), who poses the anthropological question in the personal form: 'What am I?', and gives an existential answer. I, who suppose myself a man, am the only being of whose existence I can be certain. 'I am, I exist, is necessarily true each time that I pronounce it, or that I mentally conceive it' – that is, I exist just to the extent that I problematise my own existence; if the question of existence is to be raised at all, there must be at least this one existing thing, this supposed man who raises the question. It was exactly this reliance upon the subject that Heidegger opposed. His dislike of Descartes's subjectivist ontology was to structure his critique of modern philosophy throughout his career. Although his 1957 lecture course on Leibniz's principle of sufficient reason is part of a later, 'post-existentialist' period which is beyond the scope of this article, it is useful to us because of the consistency of Heidegger's position.

In the vocabulary of Leibniz, the question 'why is there something rather than nothing' must be asked because the principle of sufficient reason demands it. Heidegger interprets that principle as claiming that everything has a reason for existing, a reason which is, in principle, accessible to the cognising powers of the subject. For Heidegger, the notion that even Being itself can have an understandable reason for existing is merely an intensification of the subjectivism invented by Descartes. The principle of sufficient reason amounts to an aggressive demand that Being conform to human reason; that is, conform to the subject. Leibniz's question is thus an important episode in the history of the forgetting of Being.

In short, for Heidegger the subject-object scheme misses what is essential because it fails to address the question of Being. We can see that the ideas in the later *Principle of Reason* lectures are merely developments of an anti-Cartesian position already well developed in *Being and Time*:

> [Descartes] investigates the '*cogitare*' of the '*ego*' . . . on the other hand, he leaves the '*sum*' completely undiscussed, even though it is regarded as no less primordial than the *cogito*. Our analytic raises the ontological question of the being of the '*sum*'. Not until the nature of this being has been determined can we grasp the kind of being which belongs to *cogitationes*. (Heidegger, 1962, p. 72)

Heidegger is interested in the being of the subject, rather than in the subject itself. He correctly sees himself as departing from the course taken by modern philosophy, which has the subject as its focus. One of his main contributions is therefore to develop an ontology of the subject, to understand '*that* and *how* being and being's structure can be clarified in terms of the Dasein itself' (Heidegger, 1982, p. 123). One of Heidegger's central criticisms of modern philosophy is that the subject has been thought of in the same terms as the object – as a kind of objectively present *thing*. However, we should also notice that Sartre, Cartesian though he may be, is just as insistent that the self is not an object, a point to which we shall return.

The concept of existence (as opposed to being) has its origin in theology. There is no *existentia* in classical Latin; the verb *exsisto*, subsequently simplified to *existo*, meant 'to stand forth', 'to appear', but not in a technical sense (Lucretius uses it in describing how worms come from dung). The root is *sto* 'to stand', and there is an intermediate form *sisto* 'to cause to stand, to place'. In its intransitive form *sisto* already sounds existential in the Sartrian sense – it means to place oneself, to take a stand, to stand firm. (The root leaves traces in the English terms 'insist', 'resist', 'obstinate'.) But when *existentia* enters the language of scholasticism it is as a derivative form of being: 'the mode of being of a being that receives its being from another being than itself'. The other being in question is God.

This early usage contrasts sharply with the meaning of the term 'existence' in Heidegger and Sartre. The idea of standing-forth is still present, but the emphasis falls on the condition of what immediately experiences itself as standing-forth rather than on the dependent relation to that from which it stands forth. At the same time, that relation serves to bring out a fundamental difference between Sartre and Heidegger. We might say that, in Heidegger, the existent stands forth from Being, while in Sartre it stands forth from Nothing. (This marks a contrast in philosophical temperament, no doubt traceable to the contrast between the presence of Heidegger's father, the good pastor of Messkirch, and the absence of Sartre's, the late naval officer of Cherbourg.) This existential standing-forth is, however, to be distinguished from the standing-out from itself that Heidegger attributes to temporality under the name of *ecstasis*. The root here is Greek and roughly means 'displacement'; the three *ecstases* of temporality are past, present and future. In his later writings, Heidegger fuses the Greek and Latin derivations in his concept of 'ek-sistence', a 'way of Being', as he says, '. . . proper only to man' (Heidegger, 1977, p. 204). We shall return to this point. Although Sartre uses the term *ekstasis* for his own purposes (as will be seen below), there is a further contrast with Heidegger on the issue of temporality. In *Being and Time*, Heidegger shows Dasein to be mired in an everyday world, speaking an everyday discourse rooted in history and tradition. In addition, every instance of Dasein carries its own history. Therefore, freedom for the early Heidegger consists in an authentic retrieval of Dasein's history, a recovery and acceptance of the past which allows Dasein to project itself into the future freely and resolutely.

In spite of the association between what we have called the existential question and the anthropological question in Descartes, the relation between the two remains problematic. Heidegger and Sartre stand in contrast to one another on this point also. In Sartre, the philosophy of existence is the philosophy of *human* existence. The lapidary formula 'Existence precedes essence' introduced in the brief 1944 article 'About Existentialism: A Clarification' and taken up again in the more popular *Existentialism is a Humanism* (1946), applies to human being and not to peas

or paper-knives. 'Essence' is defined in the earlier text as 'a constant ensemble of properties,' 'existence' as 'a certain effective presence in the world' (Contat and Rybalka, 1970, pp. 654–5). Human being is the kind of being that finds itself effectively present in the world – standing forth into the world in ways that have consequences – before it comes to know the ensemble of its properties. (It is worth nothing that this conclusion is anticipated almost textually by Descartes in the second of his *Meditations*: 'but I do not yet know clearly enough what I am, I who am certain that I am'.)

For Sartre, then, the philosophy of existence is the necessary foundation of, and prologue to, philosophical anthropology. As early as 1938, in the *Outline of a Theory of the Emotions*, he speaks of a 'hermeneutic of existence' that is to found an anthropology on which all the psychological disciplines will then have to draw. By 1944 this hermeneutic has become a full-fledged existentialism, defined as 'a certain way of envisaging human questions while refusing to give to man a nature fixed for ever' (Contat and Rybalka, 1970, p. 655). Here the anthropology is implicit; for a brief time, during what we think of as the heroic period of existentialism, the positive doctrine of human freedom overwhelms the more reflective categories of our title, but the philosophy of existence is never conceived of by Sartre as independent of an eventual anthropology. This stands in sharp contrast to the place of philosophical anthropology in Heidegger's *Being and Time*, where it must be overcome in order to begin posing the real question of Dasein's being. Heidegger takes care to distinguish his analytic of Dasein from anthropology, psychology and biology. He declares that all these disciplines have missed the real philosophical question (the question of Being), and that 'the scientific structure of the above mentioned disciplines . . . is today thoroughly questionable and needs to be attacked in new ways which must have their source in ontological problematics' (Heidegger, 1962, p. 71). Heidegger puts this criticism in terms of the ontology of personhood, making a strong association between Cartesian subjectivism and anthropology. Finally, philosophical anthropology makes of human being an objective presence – the same type of being which characterises objects. However, we may question whether this criticism rings true in the case of Sartre.

For reasons indicated in our opening paragraphs the term 'existentialism' does not occur in our title, but because of the vogue of the existentialist movement it does deserve some further notice before we proceed. Sartre's bibliographers, Contat and Rybalka, say that the word was introduced by Gabriel Marcel in 1943, but a photomontage of Sartre by a student at the Lycée Pasteur at Neuilly in 1939 (published in the Pléiade *Album Sartre*) is entitled 'Lycée plus triste . . . à l'existentialisme' (Cohen-Solal, 1991, p. 56), so Sartre must already have been using the term in his teaching at that time. However, it does not occur in the major work from his early period, *Being and Nothingness*, nor, for that matter, in Heidegger's major work at that time, *Being and Time*, even though Sartre explicitly acknowledges Heidegger's influence on existentialism in his 'Clarification' of 1944. The present article, to repeat, is not an introduction to the existentialist movement, whose historical manifestation *under that name* was short-lived and essentially French. It foregrounded certain variants on the general themes mentioned earlier, variants that surfaced in the moral chaos and uprootedness of the period immediately following World War II: abandonment in a meaningless universe, radical freedom of choice and the responsibility (and anxiety) consequent upon it, the contingency of the situation.

Heidegger was never an existentialist in this sense. (In some late interviews Sartre suggests that he was not either, but he was certainly the spokesman for the movement in its critical years.) In the 1930s there was an independent German 'philosophy of Existenz' or *Existenzerhellung*, associated mainly with the name of Karl Jaspers – Sartre alludes to it in *Search for a Method* as the 'existentialist movement which refused all collusion with Hitlerism' (Sartre, 1963, p. 38) – but the German term *Existenzialismus* seems to come into use only after the War and to be a straight translation from the French.

The German context, and Sartre's reference to 'collusion', suggests that this is an appropriate point at which to deal with another parenthetical issue, the more notorious 'Heidegger question'. Heidegger was a member of the National Socialist party, and during a brief term as Rector of the University of Freiburg under the Nazis was a vocal supporter of Hitler. This issue is explicitly raised by Sartre in the context of his acknowledgement of his debt to Heidegger, well before the end of the War. In view of the amount of ink that has since been spilled on Heidegger's politics what Sartre says about it seems as trenchant now as then. The 'Clarification' appeared in the Communist journal *Action* as a response to its running critique of existentialism, and in it Sartre says:

> What do you reproach us with? First of all for taking our inspiration from Heidegger, a German philosopher and a Nazi . . . Heidegger was a philosopher well before being a Nazi. His attachment to Hitlerism is to be explained by fear, opportunism perhaps, certainly conformism: it is not pretty, I agree. Only this is enough to refute your fine reasoning: 'Heidegger', you say, 'is a member of the National Socialist party, therefore his philosophy must be Nazi.' It isn't that: Heidegger has no spine, there's the truth; do you dare conclude that his philosophy is an apology for cowardice? Don't you know that it sometimes befalls people not to be up to the level of their works? And will you condemn the *Social Contract* because Rousseau abandoned his children? (Contat and Rybalka, 1970, p. 654)

After the euphoria of the liberation, reality set in for Sartre in the form of his coming to terms with Marxism. Philosophical anthropology came to be conceived as structural and historical, in its Marxist form building on and transcending existentialism. 'From the day that Marxist thought will have taken on the human dimension (that is, the existential project) as the foundation of anthropological Knowledge, existentialism will no longer have any reason for being', says Sartre in *Search for a Method* (Sartre, 1963, p. 181). That day would seem to have been indefinitely postponed, given the current status of Marxist theory and praxis. Not that existentialism has fared much better – the whole issue under discussion here has the flavour of an earlier epoch.

However, epochs in philosophy have a way of confounding chronology. Sartre's Marxist turn did not attract a numerous following, and in spite of his continuing to produce powerful theoretical works, notably the *Critique of Dialectical Reason* and the philosophically definitive third volume of his monumental study of Flaubert (*The Family Idiot*), his influence on more recent philosophy in France and elsewhere has been disproportionately slight. (Time, of course, may yet redress this situation.) Heidegger, on the other hand, with only a few late texts and the publication for the first time of his early lecture courses, has enjoyed a resurgence of popularity.

The reasons for this are not unrelated to our topic. Sartre's philosophy of human existence is uncompromisingly atheistic. Also, he writes very long-winded texts, which are at the same time – and partly indeed because of his tendency to repeat, elaborate and illustrate – relatively open and lucid; reading them requires time, attention and concentration, but rarely hermeneutic ingenuity. They are, to use a distinction due to Roland Barthes, *lisible* rather than *scriptible*, offering understanding but not inviting participation – modernist texts *par excellence*. Heidegger on the other hand, who was recognised by his contemporaries as a philosopher of religion, lends himself to mysticism: his works can be read as leaving room, if not actually calling, for God – 'only a God can save us', as his last *Der Spiegel* interview proclaims. They are also dense and elliptical, offering a serious challenge to interpretation – texts, in short, of powerful post-modern appeal. Influential figures on the post-modern scene find Heidegger and not Sartre to be worth their effort. It would not be wholly unfair to say that Heidegger feeds both their professional narcissism and their yearning for the transcendent, while Sartre is disdainful of these weaknesses; his texts cannot help conveying this disdain, which may be why such thinkers avoid them even though they can do so, by his criteria, only in bad faith. But there is more to it than that. Part of Heidegger's project is to save the philosophy of existence from metaphysics; if his critique of metaphysics is justified, then this undercuts Sartre's project altogether, and the latter's lucidity becomes nothing more than the reworking of an idle and outmoded discourse.

We have seen that, for Sartre, the philosophy of (human) existence is the foundation for philosophical anthropology, which is implicit in that philosophy from the start. For Heidegger, however, while philosophical anthropology is *almost* as important as the philosophy of existence, and requires the latter as a precondition, the two are essentially independent. 'In the existential analytic of Dasein,' he says,

> we also make headway with a task which is hardly less pressing than that of the question of Being itself – the task of laying bare that *a priori* basis which must be visible before the question of 'what man is' can be discussed philosophically. The existential analytic of Dasein comes *before* any psychology or anthropology. (Heidegger, 1962, p. 71)

Even though the question of Being is indissolubly linked to the question of *our* being, it would be begging that question to assume that we are anything recognisably belonging to familiar categories such as

> the subject, the soul, the consciousness, the spirit, the person. All these terms refer to definite phenomenal domains which can be 'given form': but they are never used without a notable failure to see the need for inquiring about the Being of the entities thus designated. So we are not being terminologically arbitrary when we avoid these terms – or such expressions as 'life' and 'man' – in designating those entities which we are ourselves. (ibid., p. 72)

This disclaimer is repeated more than once in *Being and Time*: for example, 'the analytic of Dasein is not aimed at laying an ontological basis for anthropology; its purpose is one of fundamental ontology' (ibid., p. 244).

Both Heidegger and Sartre begin their existential analyses from the point of view of 'an entity which I am myself': in Heidegger's case *Dasein*, in Sartre's the *pour-soi*, or 'for-itself'. These terminological choices signal a profound difference of emphasis, between the stasis of presence-to-Being in Heidegger and the dynamics of the existential project in Sartre.

Dasein is customarily rendered in English simply as 'Dasein', although a case could be made for 'dasein' instead, since the upper-case D is only an accident of German orthography, while in English it lends unnecessary portent to the term. Dasein is at first positional; the German term means 'presence' as well as 'existence', and Heidegger sometimes – especially in his later works – hyphenates it, Da-sein, to underline its literal meaning as 'being-there' (perhaps even better would be 'being-here'). *Da*, it is true, also has a temporal sense, so Dasein might also be rendered 'being-here-and-now'. The temporality of Dasein turns out, for Heidegger, to be the key to understanding it. (Here, however, it seems that anthropology creeps back into the philosophy of existence, in spite of the distinction Heidegger is at pains to maintain between them. For, as we shall see, one of the chief forms of the temporality of Dasein is its being-towards-death, and death would seem to be definitive of the human, and not of the existential, condition – there is nothing inconsistent in eternal presence to self or world, indeed this is a familiar theological concept.) From its position here and now Dasein stands forth existentially; one of the ways it stands forth is into Nothing, which, as Heidegger points out in 'What is Metaphysics?' is experienced as anxiety.

> The constitutive move on the part of Dasein is the raising of the question of its own being: Dasein always understands itself in terms of its existence – in terms of a possibility of itself: to be itself or not itself. Dasein has either chosen these possibilities itself, or got itself into them, or grown up in them already. Only the particular Dasein decides its existence, whether it does so by taking hold or neglecting. The question of existence never gets straightened out except through existing itself. (Heidegger, 1962, p. 33)

We may compare Heidegger's insistence on the engagement of Dasein with the insistence on praxis with which Sartre closes *Being and Nothingness* – but in sharp contrast to the primacy of ethical life that Sartre emphasises: 'All these questions [about freedom, responsibility and situation] can find their reply only on an ethical plane' (Sartre, 1966, p. 798). For Heidegger, however, there are two philosophical approaches to existence. He distinguishes existenti*ell* questions, which arise 'through existing itself', from existenti*al* ones which arise through reflection on existence. The latter do not 'straighten out' the question of existence but rather analyse its structure; their concern is ontological rather than ontic, 'ontic'

meaning the immediacy of Being as opposed to its mediation by discursive or theoretical understanding. Our existentiell self-awareness does not yet imply existential self-knowledge, for the essence of Being is obscured by the everydayness in which Dasein is ensnared: 'Ontically, of course, Dasein is not only close to us – even that which is closest: we *are* it, each of us, we ourselves. In spite of this, or rather for just this reason, it is ontologically that which is farthest' (Heidegger, 1962, p. 36).

For Heidegger, human being is essentially and immediately open to Being: '. . . we must presuppose that precisely what we are seeking in this inquiry (the meaning of Being as such) is something that we have found already and with which we are quite familiar' (ibid., p. 48). However, human being is self-alienated, for Dasein is itself the location of the ontological difference between beings and Being. Heidegger seeks what he has already found, for Being is always already 'here' but we as human are alienated from Being by our engagement with the everyday, an alienation which Heidegger calls 'inauthenticity'.

In Sartre the relation of the (human) existent to its own being involves a distinction similar to Heidegger's ontic/ontological scheme, though he does not use the language of the ontic and the ontological: for him there is a pre-reflexive and a reflected level of self-awareness, but both are tied to the Cartesian *cogito*, which Heidegger is at pains to deconstruct. Sartre accounts for his existential position in more developmental terms: an object is first encountered as 'for-me' (*pour-moi*); its constancy over time, and in spite of absence, suggests that it has being 'in-itself' (*en-soi*). These two aspects are clearly separable, in that an object can be in itself but not for me (it may be lost or hidden, I may never have encountered or heard of it) and can equally well be for me but not in itself (it may be remembered or imaginary).

To the question of how it comes about that there is anything at all, Sartre answers in terms of pure contigency, the 'upsurge' of being from nothingness: in his early work he makes occasional reference to being 'by-itself' (*par-soi*), which seems to us to avoid the metaphysical burden of the traditional *ens causa sui* and to lay a basis, if worked out (which Sartre never does), for a possible answer to the Heideggerian critique. Finally, the being that we are ourselves is arrived at by the consideration that I clearly qualify as 'for me' but cannot, precisely because of my temporality, assign to myself a status as 'in itself'. I am therefore constitutively 'for myself' and the kind of being that I am is properly called the 'for-itself' (*pour-soi*). At every moment, in Sartre's terms, the for-itself is what it is not and is not what it is, an oracular remark that can be construed as meaning that *in the same moment* (a) it is what it is about to be (but is not yet), and (b) it is no longer what it has (just) been; it is not *object* but *project*. Sartre would say – but the expression is too odd in English to be used without warning – 'it is no longer what is 'is been' (*est été*), he introduces this non-standard locution to exploit the reflexive connotations of the auxiliary verb 'to be' in French.

The standing-out of the for-itself from itself in temporality takes three forms, called by Sartre, borrowing from Heidegger, its *ekstases*. Two of them are implicit in 'it is what it is not and is not what it is' namely the for-itself as the negation of its own past, and the for-itself as the lack of its own future; the third is the dynamic interplay of the first two, in which the for-itself perpetually flees and pursues itself in what Sartre calls a 'game of mirrors'. This formulation does seem to catch some characteristics of human existence in the modern era – restlessness, multiplicity, vertigo, speed – and to provide a philosophical counterpart to movements (such as Futurism and Cubism) that stressed those characteristics in the arts. By contrast, Heidegger's Dasein, in spite of its temporal structure (never fully worked out, since it was put off for the second volume of *Being and Time*, which did not appear), is more contemplative and serene. It dwells poetically on the earth, according to a late formula of Heidegger's, and belongs to the mountain peaks (poetry and philosophy, for Heidegger, occupy neighbouring but separated peaks).

To be accurate, Heidegger's late formula is that *man* dwells poetically on the earth; and this brings us back to the links and the tension between philosophy of existence and philosophical anthropology. Sartre is wary of elevating human concerns to a transcendent level; the nearest he comes to Being

in the Heideggerian sense is perhaps in the conclusion to *Being and Nothingess*, where he uncharacteristically (and briefly) capitalises Being In-itself (*En-soi*) and For-itself (*Pour-soi*) and then (relapsing into lower case) says '*everything takes place as if* the in-itself in a project to found itself gave itself the modification of the for-itself' (Sartre, 1966, pp. 789–90). Elsewhere it is clear that the human is the foundation of the existential: 'Fundamentally man is *the desire to be*' (ibid., p. 722). Being in its fullest sense would be at once in-itself and for-itself; realising such a condition, says Sartre, is the fundamental value that presides over the human project. That is, man's basic desire is to achieve what Sartre calls 'the ideal of a consciousness which would be the foundation of its own being-in-itself by the pure consciousness which it would have of itself' (ibid., p. 723). But this desire is doomed to frustration. For, as Sartre continues:

> It is this ideal which can be called God. Thus the best way to conceive of the fundamental project of human reality is to say that man is the being whose project is to be God . . . To be a man means to reach toward being God. Or if you prefer, man fundamentally is the desire to be God. (ibid., pp. 723–4)

Thus, whereas for Heidegger Being is a constantly receding origin from which we are estranged, for Sartre Being is an impossible goal which forms a self-estrangement that is part of the human condition.

In Sartre's world, then, as in Marx's, 'there are only men and real relations between men' (1963, p. 76). He cannot countenance a philosophical approach that begins with some transcendent Other. In such a case,

> man would become what Walter Biemel, in his commentary on Heidegger, calls 'the bearer of the Opening of Being.' . . . But any philosophy which subordinates the human to what is Other than man, whether it be an existentialist or a Marxist idealism, has hatred of man as both its basis and its consequence. (Sartre, 1976, p. 181)

But Heidegger's claim is that man *needs* what is other than man in order to become fully human. In his 'Letter on Humanism', an indirect response to

Sartre's *Existentialism and Humanism* (*L'Existentialisme est un humanisme*), he acknowledges that, to some extent, the thinking in *Being and Time* is against humanism. However, this opposition does not mean that such thinking aligns itself against the humane or promotes the inhuman and deprecates the dignity of man. Humanism is opposed because it does not set the *humanitas* of man 'high enough' (Heidegger, 1977, p. 210). In this text Heidegger seeks to make more explicit just what is the relation of man to Dasein. He distinguishes 'ek-sistence' both from *ecstasis* and from *existentia*. *Existentia* for him stands to *essentia* as actuality to possibility, while *ecstasis* is the standing-out of Dasein towards its past and future, but 'ek-sistence' means 'standing in the lighting of Being' (ibid., p. 204) or 'standing out into the truth of Being' (ibid., p. 206). Ek-sistence is not a merely human condition, but 'as far as our experience shows, only man is admitted to the destiny of ek-sistence' (ibid., p. 204).

The 'ownness' of death, the solitude in the face of one's own constant possibility of dying, is what structures freedom as conceived by Heidegger. He makes a clear distinction between the end of Dasein and the 'going-out-of-the-world of what is only alive [which] we formulate as "perishing"' (Heidegger, 1962, p. 47). The death of Dasein terminates a whole set of existential possibilities. In terms of temporality, the possibility which is essential to human being is oriented toward the future: '*Dasein*, as itself, has to become, that is, be what it is not yet. . . . The not-yet is already included in its own being, by no means as an arbitrary determination but as a constituent. Correspondingly, *Da-sein* . . . is always already its not yet as long as it is' (ibid., p. 48). It is this being constantly projected beyond the present as care which makes us free, and this vision of freedom, a rather dark and anxious freedom given the way in which we are structurally, is one of the themes in Heidegger which led to him being labelled (albeit incorrectly perhaps) an existialist.

The account of Dasein as unwhole in constantly 'being-ahead-of-itself' sounds very much like Sartre's account of consciousness as that being which is what it is not, and is not what it is. And yet, Heidegger would like to distance himself from consciousness

and from the subject in general in favour of the deeper ontological structures which underlie the subject. Again, Heidegger claims that the Cartesian idea of subject is determined by 'objective presence'. How, then, can Sartre's consciousness, the nature of which is to flicker between being and nothingness, be a Cartesian idea of the subject? For Heidegger, Dasein is essentially being towards its own possibility of not being: 'The ending that we have in view when we speak of death does not signify a being-at-an-end of Dasein, but rather a being-towards-the-end of this being' (ibid., p. 48). For Sartre, too, human presence is a radical incompleteness – consciousness brings absence into the world; for the subject, the world is riddled with half-being. This is not exactly the existence of a solid, objectively present object as Heidegger's criticism of Descartes (and, by extension, Sartre) would have it.

Existentialism is not a bad name, Heidegger thinks, for a philosophy that opposes *essentia* to *existentia*, an opposition he attributes, anachronistically enough, to Plato, whose stand on the question is reversed by Sartre. But this, he insists, has nothing to do with his own position in *Being and Time*. Both Plato and Sartre are trapped in metaphysics, while Heidegger is trying to work out – clumsily enough, he admits – something 'precursory'. Perhaps, he conjectures, his work will be able to guide

> the essence of man to the point where it thoughtfully attends to that dimension of the truth of Being which thoroughly governs it. But even this could take place only to the honor of Being and for the benefit of Da-sein which man eksistingly sustains; not, however, for the sake of man so that civilization and culture through man's doings might be vindicated. (Heidegger, 1977, p. 209)

So much, then, for philosophical anthropology in the Sartrian mode. The human is thoroughly and essentially subordinate to the transcendent – to Being, which in Heidegger's words is 'the *transcendens* pure and simple'.

However, this is not quite the last word on Heidegger's anthropology. Ek-sistence belongs to the essence of man, and 'as ek-sisting, man sustains Dasein in that he takes the *Da*, the lighting of Being, into "care"' (Heidegger, 1977, p. 207). Care (*Sorge*) is one of the key concepts of *Being and Time*; it is a looking-forward full of concern and, as such, brings temporality to Being through Dasein. We remarked earlier that Dasein's existentiell Being-towards-Death looked suspiciously empirical and humanistic; the same might be said for the other mode of manifestation of care, the equally existentiell encounter with conscience. Thinking the totality of Dasein evokes its limitation toward death; thinking its authenticity evokes its need for a conscience (Heidegger, 1962, p. 277), but these evocations do not seem to spring from the inner nature of just any being that raises the question of Being. Either they are arbitrary designations or they arise from Dasein's prior knowledge that it is indeed a human form of being, with its moral sentiments and its anxiety about eventual extinction. Some translators were unfortunate enough to render 'Dasein' as 'human being', and were roundly rebuked by Heideggerian critics for this misunderstanding; but they may have been closer to the mark than these critics thought.

There is one further aspect of Heidegger's early thought that lends itself to anthropological, or even sociological, reflection – his concepts of 'the "they"' (*das Man*), of 'idle talk', and of 'everydayness'. These constitute the unreflective situation of Dasein, and have to be brought out or 'disclosed' as part of the analytic of Dasein's Being-in-the-world. Here again, though, Heidegger blocks the anthropological move: 'our own Interpretation is purely ontological in its aims, and is far removed from any moralizing critique of everyday Dasein, and from the aspirations of a "philosophy of culture"' (ibid., p. 211) – though a lot of what he says about these concepts does in fact sound like moralising. It is tempting, but would require a longer treatment than is possible here, to contrast this with Sartre's very different move toward common ground with the everyday preoccupations of ordinary people in his concept of the 'just-anyone' (*n'importe qui*). One of the differences – to which we will return briefly in closing – is that Sartre takes his place among the 'just anyones', whereas Heidegger seems to remain poised well above the 'they' and the everyday.

In the end it must be said for Heidegger that he is at least faithful to his original *project* of keeping fundamental ontology clear of anthropology and at the same time of metaphysics. In the later works he leaves all of them behind in favour of an almost mystical naturalism of the supernatural, if we may so put it: the 'fourfold', earth, sky, gods and mortals, enshrines the nearness of Being in a thinking that is more and more ontic, less and less ontological and closer to the nameless. 'Mortals': not quite an acknowledgement that Dasein is human after all, but a shift of attention from the old struggle against metaphysics. In *Being and Time* Heidegger distances himself from the historical and metaphysical identifications of man as rational animal, man as made in the image of God. Yet his more and more explicit commitment to transcendence means that he has not escaped metaphysics; transcendence does *not* follow from fundamental ontology but seems to have been brought in as a metaphysical assumption from an independent and almost certainly religious source in Heidegger's own development.

Sartre is said to have misunderstood Heidegger altogether; his existentialism had its roots in that misunderstanding, a fruitful one indeed in view of what he made of it. Sartre's later ventures into the theory of the human take him in the direction of the Marxist theory of group formations, elaborated and enriched beyond recognition in the *Critique of Dialectical Reason*, and eventually he arrives at an answer to his own challenge – 'Do we have today the means to constitute a structural, historical anthropology?' (Sartre, 1963, p. xxxiv) – in his working out of the being-in-the-world of one monumental figure, Gustave Flaubert. In these developments he remains faithful to his own formulation of what he calls the existentialist 'motto for man' in the 'Clarification' of 1944: 'to make and in making to make himself and to be nothing but what he has made himself' (Contat and Rybalka, 1970, p. 655). He is thus committed to immanence, as Heidegger is committed to transcendence – and on similarly unphilosophical grounds.

The positions of these two thinkers on the philosophy of existence are not, misunderstandings to the contrary notwithstanding, as far apart as they are sometimes thought, but their positions on philosophical anthropology are diametrically opposed. One of the most striking differences – although here we are straying from the philosophical to the personal – is the way in which each deals with his own insertion into his own thought. Sartre is plunged into his own thinking, he stakes himself on it, he brings us in without a hint of distance and with his familiar scorn of academic authority; at the end of his autobiographical essay 'Les mots' (The Words) he democratically characterises himself as 'a whole man, made of all men and equal to them all and to whom anyone is equal' (Sartre, 1964, p. 214). Heidegger, however, is almost wholly absent from his thinking, and the one place in which he seems to admit, implicitly at least, to a self-conception is at the moment of his having assumed the highest academic authority, in the notorious Rectoral Address at Freiburg. He is conscious of his exalted calling to leadership, Führung; the University is to be the leader of the nation, the leader of the University the leader of the leader of the nation, the Führer of the Führer himself – this seems to have been Heidegger's self-image at the time. Contrast this with Sartre's hatred of the very idea of the leader, the quintessential embodiment of bad faith and what he calls the 'spirit of seriousness':

> Many men, in fact, know that the goal of their pursuit is being . . . But to the extent that this attempt still shares in the spirit of seriousness and that these men can still believe that their mission of effecting the existence of the in-itself-for-itself

is written in things, they are condemned to despair; for they discover at the same time that all human activities are equivalent (for they all tend to sacrifice man in order that the self-cause may arise) and that all are on principle doomed to failure. Thus it amounts to the same thing whether one gets drunk alone or is a leader of nations. If one of these activities takes precedence over the other, this will not be because of its real goal but because of the degree of consciousness which it possesses of its ideal goal; and in this case it will be the quietism of the solitary drunkard which will take precedence over the vain agitation of the leader of nations. (Sartre, 1966, p. 797)

'To sacrifice man in order that the self-cause may arise': this, for Sartre, is the betrayal implicit in every appeal to transcendence.

The ancient contrast between the transcendent and the immanent serves to summarise the root difference between Heidegger and Sartre. It goes back to the contrast between Plato and Aristotle on the question of universals. And it must be said once again, in spite of Heidegger's protestations to the contrary, that it is a thoroughly metaphysical difference. Heidegger's desire, and the desire of the post-moderns that has kept his desire alive, to move the philosophical debate beyond metaphysics cannot yet be said to have been satisfied.

Bibliography

References and further reading

Anderson, Thomas C. (1993), *Sartre's Two Ethics: From Authenticity to Integral Humanity*, Chicago and LaSalle: Open Court.

Cohen-Solal, Annie (1991), *Album Jean-Paul Sartre*, Paris: Gallimard.

Contat, Michel and Michel Rybalka (1970), *Les Ecrits de Sartre*, Paris: Gallimard. [Translations from this work by Peter Caws]

Heidegger, Martin (1982), *The Basic Problems of Phenomenology*, trans. Albert Hofstadter, Bloomington: Indiana University Press.

— (1962), *Being and Time*, trans. John Macquarrie and Edward Robinson, London: SCM Press.

— (1977), 'Letter on Humanism', trans. Frank A. Capuzzi in collaboration with Glenn Gray, in *Martin Heidegger: Basic Writings*, ed. David Farrell Krell, New York: Harper and Row.

— (1941), *Existentialism and Humanism*, trans. P. Mairet, London: Methuen.

Fell, Joseph P. (1979), *Heidegger and Sartre: An Essay on Being and Place*, New York: Columbia University Press.

Olafson, Frederick A. (1995), *What is a Human Being?: A Heideggerian View*, New York: Cambridge University Press.

Rockmore, Tom (1995), *Heidegger and French Philosophy: Humanism, Antihumanism*, New York: Routledge.

Santoni, Ronald E. (1995), *Bad Faith, Good Faith, and Authenticity in Sartre's Early Philosophy*, Philadelphia: Temple University Press.

Sartre, Jean-Paul (1966), *Being and Nothingness*, trans. Hazel E. Barnes, New York: Washington Square Press.

— (1976), *Critique of Dialectical Reason*, trans. Alan Sheridan-Smith, London: New Left Books.

— (1964), *Les Mots*, Paris: Gallimard. [Translation from this work by Peter Caws]

— (1963), *Search for a Method*, trans. Hazel E. Barnes, New York: Alfred E. Knopf.

Zimmerman, Michael E. (1986), *Eclipse of the Self: The Development of Heidegger's Concept of Authenticity*, revised edition, Athens and London: Ohio University Press.

2.5

EXISTENTIAL ETHICS

Linda A. Bell

Introduction

Søren Kierkegaard, generally regarded as the founder of European philosophy of existence, offered little in the way of a uniquely existentialist ethics. For him, the ethical was a 'stage on life's way', to be left behind by one who moves into the higher religious stage – the highest stage – and becomes the knight of faith. Moreover, when discussing the ethical, Kierkegaard seems unable to think of any ethical system other than the Kantian with its central criterion of universalisability, which clearly looks in the wrong direction for one whose central concern was the individual.

It fell, then, to others, like Albert Camus, Simone de Beauvoir and Jean-Paul Sartre, to develop this concern for the individual in ethical rather than religious directions. This they did, initially in a France occupied by the Nazis during the Second World War, a context that made their ideas seem particularly poignant and significant to the generations that followed.

By placing freedom and ambiguity at the heart of their philosophical analyses, and subsequently their ethics, these thinkers placed themselves in the centre of philosophical controversy, raising questions of ethical relativism that many had rejected. Worse, Camus had suggested in *The Myth of Sisyphus* that one could be an absurd 'hero' in many different ways, including by being a conqueror and running roughshod over others. He had even presented Caligula, in a play of the same name, although not exactly as a hero but still somewhat closer to being one than

most would accept. Sartre, in *Being and Nothingness*, had characterised human existence in such a way that inauthenticity seems inevitable, both individually and in relationships, with the latter doomed to a frustrating conflict based ultimately on the objectification of 'the look'.

Even though Sartre later characterised that work as an analysis of consciousness in bad faith (Sartre, 1992, p. 201), critics tended to discount his famous footnote reference to 'the possibility of an ethics of deliverance and salvation', an ethics which, he suggested, could be achieved 'only after a radical conversion which we can not discuss here (Sartre, 1956, p. 412n). Instead, they paid special attention to the book's conclusion, particularly to the notorious affirmation that since 'all are on principle doomed to failure . . . it amounts to the same thing whether one gets drunk alone or is a leader of nations' (Sartre, 1956, p. 627), and to the earlier bleak depiction of human relationships in which love seems nothing more than 'a battle between two hypnotists in a closed room' (Murdoch, 1953, p. 65). Moreover, Sartre's well-known *Existentialism is a Humanism*, in which he developed the seeming rudiments of an ethics, was dismissed by many, including Sartre himself (apparently because of his disappointment with its reception and the many misinterpretations it had received).

Although de Beauvoir wrote an existential ethics, it was frequently ignored by other philosophers, many of whom viewed her merely as Sartre's mistress. In the 1967 edition of *The Encyclopedia of Philosophy* she is not included in the index and is mentioned only as one of the founders of *Les Temps Modernes*, In fact, her writings generally have not received the care they deserve, with no translations of some of her work and inadequate translations of others, particularly *The Second Sex*. So strong has been many critics' *a priori* conviction of the impossibility of an existential ethics that little serious study of Sartre's later published work, let alone of de Beauvoir's *Ethics of Ambiguity*, seems to have been deemed necessary.

However not all have been so dismissive. Much of the more optimistic analysis has focused on Sartre's later work, a portion of which was never published by Sartre himself. Some has resulted from feminist philosophers' re-examination of the work of de Beauvoir, taking her seriously as the philosopher that much of the philosophical tradition, her society, and, unfortunately, even she herself, refused to acknowledge she was. The former is the careful work mainly of Sartre scholars who continue to be intrigued by the possibility of existential ethics. This work begins with Francis Jeanson's 1947 *Le problème moral et la pensée de Sartre* (with a letter-forward by Sartre and translated by Robert V. Stone as *Sartre and the Problem of Morality*) and continued in 1967 with *An Existentialist Ethics*, written by Hazel E. Barnes, the translator of *Being and Nothingness*. More recently, this analysis has been fuelled by the discovery after Sartre's death of several treatments of morality, in various stages of completion – in particular, *Cahiers pour une morale*, published in 1983 and translated by David Pellauer in 1992 as *Notebooks for an Ethics*, and Sartre's *Notes for the 1964 Rome Lecture*, still unpublished but discussed in several articles by Elizabeth A. Bowman and Robert V. Stone.

Willing freedom – one's own and that of others

The ethics that emerges from a study of Sartre's and de Beauvoir's writings is an ethics independent of religion and theology. It has neither a loving nor an authoritarian deity as its support, and does not even play anything other than a symbolic role in its actual development. It is an ethics that recognises freedom, not the absolute freedom often ascribed to Sartre (and to de Beauvoir, when she is mentioned), but a situated freedom, circumscribed and affected by the actions of others over whom the individual may have no control.

While there are no grounds justifying any particular values or warranting their imposition on others, Sartre and de Beauvoir none the less propose limits for morally acceptable choices. Any choice denying freedom is morally unacceptable. Whatever values we choose individually we must will our own freedom, since our freedom is a necessary precondition for any choice and consequent action. This is very like the hypothetical imperative disparaged, but recognised as analytic, by Immanuel Kant: 'whoever wills the end wills the means' (Kant, [1785] 1963, p. 86). Existentially, though, freedom is recognised as a precondition to *any* ends individuals may choose rather than as a means to a specific end. As a precondition of all value, freedom underlies all choice and thus itself acquires value through any choice of value. Kant himself recognises something like this when he challenges suicide by maintaining that 'it annuls the condition of all other duties; it goes beyond the limits of the use of free will, for this use is possible only through the existence of the Subject' (ibid., p. 149).

A similar recognition holds with respect to the freedom of others. In as much as human existence is an ambiguous, embodied existence, human beings are always vulnerable to others; and to the extent that their activities take place in a world of others, the success of their projects depends at least on the non-interference of others and often on active assistance. To recognise being-for-others is to acknowledge the extent to which one's acts are not totally within one's own power. As de Beauvoir says:

> [B]y taking the world away from me, others also give it to me, since a thing is given to me only by the movement which snatches it from me. To will that there be being is also to will that there be men by and for whom the world is endowed with human significations. One can reveal the world only on a basis revealed by other men. No project can be defined except by its interference with other projects. (de Beauvoir, 1964, p. 71)

Thus, in willing one's own ends, one must will not just the non-interference of others but also their active aid, hence their freedom as precondition of that aid.

Here, de Beauvoir and Sartre are not judging means by the ends they accomplish, as utilitarians would do, but rather, once again in the analytic spirit of 'whoever wills the end wills the means', affirming something about what it means to will any end. Whatever one wills, one implicates all others and thereby wills for everyone. Though the authentic individual does not, as Hazel Barnes observes, 'insist that everyone must go where he goes', authenticity does require that the individual hold as absolute 'the possibility of choice' (Barnes, 1967, p. 109).

Thus, the authentic individual is one who wills her or his own freedom and the freedom of others. Whatever values are chosen, those values inevitably implicate others. This affirms universalisability in moral judgements without either adopting a Kantian view of human reason or importing an unsupported and insupportable 'absolute' value (such as consistency) into ethics.

Overcoming alienation

This ethics affirms a way of avoiding or overcoming certain alienation. Although some alienation is fundamental to the human condition and cannot be overcome, the alienation resulting from bad faith or self-deception – self-alienation – is not fundamental and is avoidable. Such avoidable alienation can, and should, be overcome. Moreover, on the level of societies, two similar forms of alienation exist, one being fundamental and inescapable, such as the seriality Sartre describes in The Critique of Dialectical Reason, the other not fundamental, an alienation which can, and should, be eliminated. Given these forms of alienation, oppressive societies are criticised for the alienation(s) they impose, in a similar way to individuals who act in ways that fail to recognise and affirm their own freedom and that of others.

Oppression is a complex network of individual and institutional relations. The situation of the oppressed varies greatly from one type of oppression to the next. As Sartre became increasingly aware of oppressions, he recognised that the freedom of many is so seriously curtailed as to be little more than the

freedom 'to choose the sauce with which it will be devoured' (Sartre, 1965, p. 58). It was de Beauvoir, though, who saw that oppression may be so severe that its victims never become aware even minimally of themselves and their options and, as a result, have no freedom, a recognition of concrete possibilities and divergent 'situations' that, she tells us, she had 'upheld' against Sartre in their discussions (de Beauvoir, 1964, pp. 37–8; 1992, p. 434).

An ethics of freedom can and does maintain intentions and consequences in tension, refusing to negate the significance of either or to try to reduce without remainder one to the other. Sartre maintains this tension in large part by undercutting the foundation on which the distinction between utilitarianism and Kantian ethics rests – the clear separation of act and intention. Separating choice from action leads to an 'abstract ethics . . . that of the good conscience' – 'the idea that one can be good without changing the situation' – a morality Sartre clearly rejects (Sartre, 1992, p. 17).

Sartre objects to those who, like his character Garcin in the play No Exit, think they can divorce choice from action: 'A man', Garcin declares, 'is what he wills to be', to which Inez mercilessly responds that a man is what he does (Sartre, 1955, p. 44). For Sartre, an individual's intentions and even potentiality are manifest in, though not reducible to, actions. Even Garcin is unable to distinguish his intention from his act. He tries to convince himself he fled his country to further the revolution; yet his death left his action standing alone and uninterpreted. Since no actions followed it, this lone action is ambiguous. He cannot be sure whether his choice was the pragmatic choice of a dedicated revolutionary or the skin-saving choice of a coward.

For Sartre, act and intention are inseparable, just as being-for-others and being-for-oneself are too. Action requires embodiment and embeddedness in the world. Since an action is an effort to do something, it can be blocked or impeded, either by one's own temporary or permanent disabilities or by the resistance of things or others. To act requires, if not the assistance of others, at least their non-interference.

Thus, moral beings must will and act to further the

freedom of all. To be moral, one must will the freedom of others; and this requires, in appropriate circumstances, working against oppression. If one has the potential to do something to prevent or oppose the oppression but chooses not to, then to that extent one is actively involved in, and supportive of, the oppression.

Moreover, to act against oppression is not, in turn, to oppress those who are prevented from oppressing. To the extent that oppressive action denies the freedom of others, it is unacceptable and should be stopped. By rejecting the acceptability of oppression, action against it affirms rather than denies freedom, even that of would-be oppressors: it says, in effect, that no one, not even former oppressors, should be oppressed. Admittedly, action against oppression will limit and constrain the freedom of those who would oppress, perhaps even doing them bodily harm. To use constraint and bodily harm in order to object to constraint and bodily harm is indeed problematic for those who will and try to further the freedom of all. Yet the only other option in such cases – to allow and thereby endorse violence and oppression – is clearly unacceptable since it, too, involves the violation of freedom. This means that violence is sometimes unavoidable. In such cases, those who recognise the immorality of violence must violate the freedom of oppressors in order to deny that the violation of freedom is acceptable.

Thus, violence against oppressors does not create new oppression. Would-be oppressors are simply not allowed to oppress; however they may feel, they are not thereby subordinated to anyone else. Simply to be denied opportunity to subordinate others is not to be subordinated in turn.

The necessity and impossibility of violence

As Sartre considers resistance to oppression, he wrestles with issues such as what means are permissible in pursuit of a goal and whether violence can ever be condoned. He notes that some means undermine the ends to be realised by them. In particular, since it contradicts that end, violence is to be rejected as a means of establishing a society where each individual respects and treats every other as an end and not merely as a means.

A similar means/end problem renders problematic any utilitarian ethics. To will whatever means is necessary to achieve an end is 'the maxim of violence', where violence is understood quite literally as violation, as treating the other merely as means. 'A lie', for example, 'places the other's freedom in parentheses' (Sartre, 1992, p. 199, p. 202). Sartre challenges precisely this openness to any means necessary as insidious to the utopian goal of treating all human beings as ends in themselves.

The use of violence as a means is thus problematic. Ideologically, it supports the prevalent understanding and use of power. Moreover, by treating others in the way forces of oppression urge as necessary and warranted, those who fight for a better society make such a society more, rather than less, remote. Both they and the recipients of their violence are affected in negative ways by the violence, becoming less like the type of people who would and could live in a better world.

Consequently, Sartre proposed a different way of treating means and ends: the goal must be viewed, not as exterior and indifferent to the means, but rather as in the means, as 'the organic unity of the means'. In other words, such a goal 'is not the last link in the causal series A. B. C. D. E. F (which, in effect, would allow us to assert that the end is indifferent to the means), instead it is the organic totality of the operation'. If the end is seen in the means and not as totally separate from them, each means will be a 'prefiguration of the city of ends'. (ibid., p. 172, p. 435, p. 167). Instead of working to achieve some distant or even unactualisable utopia with whatever means are necessary, each and every means will be chosen because it partially embodies the ideal. Each means is thus in some sense an achievement of the ideal; the dangerous and destructive conflict of means with end is thereby avoided.

Despite his rejection of the maxim of violence, Sartre was quite aware that absolutely non-violent resistance to oppression may do little to bring into existence a kingdom of ends and, in fact, often reinforces systems of oppression in which some are treated merely as means for the pleasure or profit of others. Thus, in his 'Preface' to Frantz Fanon's *The Wretched of the Earth*, Sartre condemns believers in nonviolence, disputing their claim to be neither

ecutioners nor victims: 'Very well then; if you're
ot victims when the government which you've
oted for, when the army in which your younger
others are serving without hesitation or remorse
ave undertaken race murder, you are, without a
adow of doubt, executioners' (Sartre, 1968, p. 25).
nly in a situation without previously existing
olence would claims in support of such passivity
e at all plausible. Since violence is morally unac-
eptable, Sartre concludes, 'ethics is not possible
iless everyone is ethical' (Sartre, 1992, p. 9).

In saying this, Sartre does not intend to sanction an
nything goes' attitude. Rather, he is attempting to
eal with a problem of dirty hands. His point is that in
ertain situations of violence there are no unambigu-
isly good alternatives. Whatever one wills will be
olent: one must either sanction the previous vio-
nce or exercise a different violence against it. Thus,
Fanon observes, 'everybody will have to be com-
omised in the fight for the common good. No one
is clean hands; there are no innocents and no
ilookers. We all have dirty hands; we are all soiling
em in the swamps of our country and in the
rrifying emptiness of our brains. Every onlooker is
ther a coward or a traitor' (Fanon, 1968, p. 199).
his does not, however, mean that no one is guilty.
Neither does it mean that violence against oppres-
on and pre-existing violence is moral or that
olence is an acceptable means when used toward
good end. To see it as moral (or justified) is to slip
to a complacency vis-à-vis violence that changes
e end we seek. Our goal would then change from
ing the total eradication of violence to the eradi-
tion of only the violence that does not lead to a
od end.

Thus, violence can be neither avoided nor justi-
d. Rather, it must be condemned, not only by the
orality of right (a morality that supports the *status*
to against which the condemned action revolts) but
so, and far more importantly, by the morality of the
ty of ends, toward which the revolt may indeed be
ogress. Sartre says:

[I]f the goal is concrete and finite, if it is part of a
future available to man, it has to exclude violence
(at least in that it should not itself be violence or
evil), and if one is obliged to make use of violence

to attain this goal, at least it [the violence] will
appear as unjustified and *limited*. This will be the
failure at the heart of the success. (Sartre, 1992,
p. 406; cf. p. 172, p. 207)

Surely this dilemma is what Sartre has in mind when
he later says, in *Saint Genet*, 'any ethic is both
impossible and necessary' (Sartre, 1964, p. 247).

This affirmation of dirty hands is thus more than
acknowledgement of conflicting values and moral
obligations. It is rather a very conscious way to keep
the end in view in a series of actions where there is no
way that the goal can be seen as the organic unity of
the means. Sartre's struggle with violence resembles,
though his resolution of the dilemma greatly differs
from, that of Camus. In the play *The Just Assassins*,
Camus has one of the characters, Kaliayev, argue that
he must give his life to demonstrate that all murder,
including the assassination of which he is guilty, is
unacceptable, even when the victim is pivotal in
maintaining a society where children starve. The
assassin's proposal manifests an unacceptable desire
for moral purity, given Sartre's analysis of violence, an
analysis ultimately more sympathetic to that of the
assassin's fellow terrorist Dora: 'It's easy, ever so much
easier, to die of one's inner conflicts than to live with
them'. Yet Sartre's analysis allows an appreciation of
the assassin's dominant concern that he does not 'add
to the living injustice all around me for the sake of a
dead justice'. In the play, the Chief of Police, Skur-
atov, cynically acknowledges how difficult that is to
do: 'One begins by wanting justice – and one ends by
setting up a police force' (Camus, 1958, pp. 233–302;
cf. p. 260, p. 297, p. 281); and he clearly knows from
experience how far one has then strayed from the goal.

Both Sartre and Camus's assassins are trying to
allow violence under certain circumstances without
condoning the maxim of violence. This also seems to
be de Beauvoir's concern when she states: 'violence
is justified only if it opens concrete possibilities to the
freedom which I am trying to save . . .' (de Beauvoir,
1964, p. 137).

Replacing seriousness with play

Sartre, de Beauvoir and Camus all reject seriousness.
In its place, Sartre clearly proposes play as an alter-

native. Individuals who refuse to recognise freedom and who pretend that values exist prior to and independently of their creation by human beings are serious. Cognisant of freedom and of responsibility for values, the authentic individual is playful rather than serious, acting out of freedom rather than an alleged determinism. Given the recognition of choice as the origin of values, relativism and futility present special problems; but these are resolved by play.

The resolution of the problem of futility centrally involves play. After all, particularly in a culture where winning is virtually everything, the recognition of futility would seem particularly demoralising. Why should we keep trying to win when we know we either cannot do so, or are unlikely to do so? Camus presents Sisyphus as an 'absurd hero', somehow happy and surely admirable in his moment of wisdom as he descends to his stone for one more attempt in what he clearly realises is a futile task (Camus, 1955, pp. 88–91). Why does Sisyphus keep trying when he knows the stone will not stay at the top of the hill? Camus cannot answer by appealing to the determinism in the older myth he is retelling since Sisyphus can be seen as a hero only if he is free. If he returns to the stone because he must, then he is simply performing his task in a robot-like manner, and that is that. Only if he somehow voluntarily returns for yet another try to accomplish what he knows to be impossible is he even interesting to Camus or to us. Only then does he rise above his fate and assert human values – or his values – in the face of insurmountable odds. Only then does his return indicate that there is something unacceptable, humanly speaking or perhaps just Sisyphusly speaking, about the way things are.

Friedrich Nietzsche describes an endeavour like that of Sisyphus's as 'remain[ing] faithful to the earth, ... giv[ing] ... the earth a meaning, a human meaning' (Nietzsche, 1954, p. 188). Unfortunately, unlike Camus, Nietzsche affirms the natural as the source of all legitimate values, thus returning to a seriousness about values and thereby giving human choice too little recognition for its role in creating them. His characterisation of the creator of new values as a child, innocent and forgetful, is a part of this naturalism and not at all useful to those who wish to build an ethics on freedom.

However, he does emphasise the lightness and playfulness required in one who remains faithful to the earth while acknowledging eternal recurrence, Nietzsche's symbol (and doctrine) of ultimate futility. Zarathustra demonstrates how difficult accepting and living with futility can be, as he 'chokes' on the knowledge that 'All is the same, nothing is worth while' and particularly on his 'great disgust with man', on the painful recognition that 'Alas, man recurs eternally! The small man recurs eternally'! Thinking of the 'smallness', the pettiness, of human beings, and its eternal recurrence leads Zarathustra to despair and inertia: 'Man's earth turned into a cave for me, its chest sunken; all that is living became human mold and bones and musty past to me. My sighing sat on all human tombs and could no longer get up. . . .' Only when he can look into this 'abyss' and accept eternal recurrence, is he able, having killed the 'spirit of gravity' (with laughter), to return with lightness to the world to dance, sail 'uncharted seas' and generally 'live dangerously' (Nietzsche, 1954, p. 97, p. 153, p. 304, p. 331).

Games indicate how play enables an individual to live with futility and relativism. A player participates in a game as if the rules or values of the game have some sort of necessary and objective reality and validity. At the same time, as long as players are playing and not so caught up in winning that they mistake the game for something else, they recognise these rules and values as having no such necessity or objectivity. In other words, one who plays avoids the seriousness of those who no longer play.

Even inescapable futility is not an insurmountable problem for those who play. In play, not only may we spend time and energy in trying to unbalance well-balanced objects without much likelihood of success, but we may also exert great effort in attempting to balance unbalanceable objects and to fill sieves with water without any likelihood of success. A playful spirit of engagement makes possible full and frequently joyful concentration on the activity itself even while the players recognise the futility of their endeavours.

If existentialists are correct, the value of freedom itself emerges in the context of willing other values and those values in turn set the parameters for the valuing of freedom and of the life of which it is a part for example, the freedom willed by the lucid dare-devil may be part of a short life, but one lived intensely. The values created and sustained in play are not frivolous in comparison with those of the players' lives; rather, no values, including the value of those lives, exist apart from individuals' choices. Certainly there is no hierarchy of values independent of such choices. Serious human beings try to convince themselves (and others) otherwise, but their consternation over the irrationality of those who play 'for keeps' cannot count as a legitimate objection to the non-serious play of those who are authentic.

Impossible ideals treated as regulative

Although impossible ideals are viewed by many as an insurmountable problem for ethics, such ideals are integral to the ethics of Camus, de Beauvoir and Sartre. Impossible ideals are an inescapable ingredient in the human situation. They become morally problematic only when they are pursued in a particular way. Those who are serious take ideals as 'given', as somehow pre-existing all choices and actions, perhaps as unreachable, and are unlikely to gauge correctly how far from the mark their own behaviour falls.

However, even those who are not serious inevitably set standards that cannot be reached. Authentic individuals and groups turn, to some extent, from impossible goals to what is within their control; but impossible goals are not abandoned. Rather, such goals, according to Sartre, must be taken as 'regulative ideals' and pursued playfully. This means taking them as guiding behaviour but not as depicting goals actually to be realised. While the harmony and unity represented by such ideals as God and organism are unachievable, they may none the less guide behaviour.

Concretely, this would mean that, instead of trying to be, for example, an identity of being-for-others and being-for-self, individuals would strive to be (for themselves) what they appear (to others) and to appear to be (to others) what they are (to themselves). The authentic individual assumes responsibility for, and attempts to harmonise as far as possible, those disparate aspects of herself or himself

while the individual in bad faith tries to unify, to reduce them without remainder to one another, and, failing to unify, then uses the impossibility of such unity as a justification for any and all behaviour.

As long as the city of ends is taken as a non-regulative ideal, that is, as a goal actually to be realised, ethics confronts a dilemma. Either this utopian goal is unrealisable, or it is only realisable in some distant future. On the one hand, if the goal is not in fact realisable, if it is merely ideal, then, as Sartre says, 'hope disappears'. On the other hand, if the city of ends is regarded as realisable but only by projecting this possible actualisation into some far-distant future, then the end remains beyond and outside the means and potentially able to justify any and all means. It would then lead to 'the maxim of violence': 'the end justifies the means'. Neither will it do to abolish all infinite ends, such as the city of ends: 'As soon as a goal is assigned to the human species and this goal is finite, as soon as one pictures it as reality, . . . the human species become ants' (Sartre, 1992, p. 167). But the goal must be both infinite and finite: 'This signifies that each person has to realize it and yet it is still to be realized. A *finite* enterprise for each person within humanity's infinite enterprise' (ibid., p. 448).

Because Sartre's resolution of his dilemma requires us to see the end in the means and not as totally separate from them, the means will truly be a 'prefiguration of the city of ends':

> The solution of this antinomy is not to distinguish the end from the means, but to treat man as an end to the same measure that I consider him a means, that is, to help him think of himself and freely want to be a means in the moment when and to the extent that I treat him as an end, as well as to make manifest to him that he is the absolute end in that very decision by which he treats himself as a means. (ibid., p. 207)

Far from being a cause of despair, the human failure to coincide with self is the very basis of ethics for Sartre and de Beauvoir. As the latter recognised:

> [T]he most optimistic ethics have all begun by emphasizing the element of failure involved in the condition of man; without failure, no ethics;

for a being who, from the very start, would be an exact coincidence with himself, in a perfect plenitude, the notion of having-to-be would have no meaning. One does not offer an ethics to a God. (de Beauvoir, 1964, p. 10)

Realising the nonidentity of facticity and transcendence and the inescapability of both, authentic individuals will affirm their facticity as subject to their freedom and their freedom as inevitably situated in their facticity. Thus, they harmonise and co-ordinate these aspects of themselves to the extent such aspects can be harmonised and co-ordinated.

Authentic human relationships

Sartre's early work led many critics of existentialism to conclude that all human relationships had been exhaustively delineated in the appropriative sorts of love and desire depicted so memorably in *Being and Nothingness*. This conclusion ignores not only his later characterisation of that book as a depiction of consciousness in bad faith but also much of his other work, including various fictional characters who exemplify possibilities of a non-appropriative love, a love that approaches the other with confidence in freedom and with trust and generosity.

In *Notebooks for an Ethics*, Sartre discusses how, in helping another, one not only comprehends the other's end but makes it one's own. 'The other's end', he says, 'can appear to me as an end only in and through the indication of my adopting that end'. In choosing to help someone, I engage myself but none the less recognize the end as not mine. To will this end authentically, I must will the end to be realized by the other – To want a value to be realized not because it is mine, not because it is a value, but because it is a value for someone on earth (Sartre, 1992, pp. 277–80).

Sartre's example of the 'human relation of helping' illuminates both the appeal and the help and offers further insight into the ideal society for which we are to strive. His example concerns a man helped by another on to a moving bus: 'A runs toward the bus, B, on the platform, extends his hand. . . . In grasping it as an instrument, [A] contributes to realizing his own project'. But A becomes an instrument for B,

since A serves as a means to realising B's end (in this case, that of himself serving as an instrument). A's hand is grasped and pulled; and A becomes an object seen, appraised, and pulled, a passivity. Yet A does not become an object against his own freedom since he becomes an instrument precisely in pursuing his own end. He discovers the other's freedom, not as opposed to and threatening his freedom, but *in* his own freedom: 'he unveils it at the heart of his own freedom as a free movement accompanying him toward his ends. . . . Each freedom is wholly in the other one' (ibid., pp. 287–8).

In the relation of appeal/help, the one who assists adopts the other's end in such a way that it none the less remains the end of the other, to be realised by the other. This is quite different from having a common project or fighting the same enemy. One who helps responds to the appeal not because the helper happens to share the other's end but rather just because the other has this end.

This means that there is gratuity in the appeal; and gratuity, according to Sartre, is at the heart of morality: 'But at the start, I recognize that my end has to be conditional for the other as it is for me. That is, that it must always be possible for the other to refuse to help if the means used in such help alter his own ends'. In appealing to others, one adheres to the others' ends: 'I uphold them in their concrete content through my approbation'. This is why the appeal is a 'promise of reciprocity' and why one does not demand help from those whose ends one cannot approve, from those whom one would not oneself aid (ibid., pp. 283–4).

In the relation appeal/help, each discovers and wills the other's freedom and each is totally in the other. This is why Sartre sees in the appeal a sketch of a utopian world ('where each person treats the other as an end – that is, takes the other person's undertaking as end') – 'a world where each person can call upon all the others' (ibid., p. 49). It is why Sartre sees an authentic appeal as necessarily 'conscious of being a surpassing of every inequality of condition toward a human world where any appeal of anyone to anyone will always be possible' (ibid., p. 285).

These analyses indicate the possibility of a love that recognises and affirms the freedom of the beloved as well as one's own. However much social structures render problematic or impossible the expression or realisation of such love, the authentic individual must affirm and actively support the freedom of others. To love authentically is to move beyond the sadomasochistic dialectic of enslaving freedoms to a 'deeper recognition and reciprocal comprehension of freedoms'. For this love, 'tension is necessary: to maintain the two faces of ambiguity, to hold them within the unity of one and the same project' (ibid., p. 415). It is 'something wholly other than the desire to appropriate' (ibid., p. 507).

Authentic relationships, like other authentic activity, maintain a tension between what is sought and what is achieved, between coincidence and inevitable alienation and separateness, between treating the other as an end and treating her or him as a means. An authentic individual can approach another with a confidence concerning human freedom, both the individual's own and the other's.

The authentic individual has lost any illusions of being justified and made essential by another. This individual recognises her or his own freedom and thereby, if Sartre's analysis in *What Is Literature?* is correct, experiences a kind of joy. Like the writer, one who loves authentically can approach the other with confidence in freedom and with a trust and generosity (Sartre, 1965b, p. 49). Aesthetic joy and the joy of love may be momentary, but none the less they are intimations of the harmony sought in each case. As momentary, they may bring sorrow and negate the aspirations of those who sought therein to be justified and essential and to escape their freedom and responsibility. But for the authentic, such intimations may be taken in stride as temporal, albeit fleeting and ambiguous, embodiments of the ultimate but impossible goals towards which they strive.

Such love is not part of a morality attempting to fuse individuals into a single consciousness. The attempt to fuse two individuals into one is the goal of bad faith and thereby rejected as the basis of authentic relationships. Moreover, Sartre warns against a morality of fusion as well as against a kingdom of ends that recognises each consciousness only in its Kantian universality. Rather, the morality

he develops would take each individual in her or his 'concrete singularity' (Sartre, 1992, p. 89). Thus, Sartre can affirm once again an aspect of Kantian ethics – the kingdom of ends – without at the same time affirming the Kantian view of human reason.

Several of Sartre's fictional characters evince a love that affirms freedom and respects the other as an end. Such love can be seen in Hilda's love of Goetz (in *The Devil and the Good Lord*) and is unlike the love depicted by Goetz as having the same enemy, although Sartre continues to recognise, as he did in that play, the ways the injustices of the age will inevitably intervene and vitiate 'at the roots' the good one strives to accomplish. This means 'it is quite impossible to treat concrete men as ends in contemporary society' (Sartre, 1965b, p. 269), a recognition to which Eve and Pierre (in *The Chips Are Down*) are slowly drawn even as they affirm the attempt to love one another with perfect coincidence and confidence in spite of their different enemies and their opposing class and other loyalties.

Thus, Sartre envisions authentic human relationships and a utopian future in which they would be possible with no qualifications and with no interference from oppressive structures in society. This ideal of reciprocity and genuine co-operation provides a basis for a new understanding of autonomy, one premised on interrelationship and interdependence, not on complete independence. Sartre's notion of a city of ends and of the relation of appeal/help denies the independent, self-sufficient individual of liberalism without postulating fusion in a community as the social ideal.

Conclusion

Existential ethics's recognition of embodiment is an acceptance of multiple ambiguities, one of the most important of which is the ambiguity of agents who act in oppressive situations not of their own making. While freedom can be curtailed in any number of ways, those whose freedom is curtailed are not responsible for limitations imposed upon them that they cannot prevent or change. At the same time, if there are any options available to them, those individuals are responsible for whatever choices they make among these. While oppressors are responsible for the limitations they impose on the range of options available to the oppressed, the latter are responsible for what they do, and thereby make of themselves, within those limited opportunities. This understanding of freedom thus encourages heightened awareness of the choices available to those whose freedom has been curtailed, thereby supporting revolutionary thinking in the oppressed and encouraging victims to avoid defeatism and the sense of powerlessness that comes from seeing themselves merely in terms of their victimisation.

Thus, for Sartre as for de Beauvoir, actions are always seen in a rather intricate context. The will is embodied and acting. Both embodiment and acting develop in social situations. Unlike Kant's autono-mous self, such contextualised freedom enables this ethics to avoid the dreamy but harmful idealism of those who invoke the kingdom of ends with inadequate recognition of the oppression and violence involved in the *status quo*, with insufficient allowance for acts that would resist and overthrow this oppression and violence, and with little or no awareness of the extent to which their ethics perpetuates the oppression and violence. Existential ethics allows for the development of a standard beyond the pleasures, needs, and values constructed by oppressions, a standard by which societies, institutions, and individual actions can be critiqued and in terms of which strategies for overthrowing systems of oppression can be evaluated and supported.

Bibliography

References and further reading

Anderson, Thomas C. (1979), *The Foundation and Structure of Sartrean Ethics*. Lawrence: The Regents Press of Kansas.
— (1993), *Sartre's Two Ethics: From Authenticity to Integral Humanity*, Peru, IL: Open Court Publishing Company.
Barnes, Hazel E. (1967), *An Existentialist Ethics*, New York: Vintage Books.
Beauvoir, Simone de (1964), *The Ethics of Ambiguity*, trans. Bernard Frechtman, New York: The Citadel Press.
— (1992), *The Prime of Life*, trans. Peter Green, ed. Toril Moi, New York: Paragon House.
— (1974), *The Second Sex*, trans. H. M. Parshley, New York: Vintage Books.
Bell, Linda A. (1993), *Rethinking Ethics in the Midst of Violence: A Feminist Approach to Freedom*, Lanham, MD: Rowman and Littlefield Publishers, Inc.
— (1989), *Sartre's Ethics of Authenticity*, Tuscaloosa: The University of Alabama Press.
Bowman, Elizabeth A. and Robert V. Stone (1991), ' "Making the Human" in Sartre's Unpublished Dialectical Ethics', in Hugh J. Silverman (ed.), *Writing the Politics of Difference*, Albany: The SUNY press, 111–22.
Camus, Albert (1955), *The Myth of Sisyphus and Other Essays*, trans. Justin O'Brien, New York: Vintage Books.
— (1958), *Caligula*, trans. Stuart Gilbert, *Caligula & Three Other Plays*, New York: Vintage Books, 1–74.
— (1958), *The Just Assassins*, trans. Stuart Gilbert, *Caligula & Three Other Plays*, 233–302.
Catalano, Joseph S. (1995), *Good Faith and Other Essays: Perspective on a Sartrean Ethics*, Lanham, MD: Rowman and Littlefield Publishers.

Fanon, Frantz (1968), *The Wretched of the Earth*, trans. Constance Farrington, New York: Grove Weidenfeld.
Jeanson, Francis (1980), *Sartre and the Problem of Morality*, trans. Robert V. Stone, Bloomington: Indiana University Press.
Kant, Immanuel (1963), *The Moral Law*, trans. H. J. Paton, New York: Barnes and Noble.
Murdoch, Iris (1953), *Sartre, Romantic Rationalist*, New Haven: Yale University Press.
Nietzsche, Friedrich (1954), 'From *The Gay Science* [1882]', trans. Walter Kaufmann in Walter Kaufmann (ed.), *The Portable Nietzsche*, New York: Viking Press, 93–102.
— (1954), *Thus Spoke Zarathustra*, trans. Walter Kaufmann, in *The Portable Nietzsche*, 103–439.
Sartre, Jean-Paul (1948), *The Chips Are Down*, trans. Louise Varèse, New York: Lear.
— (1949), *Men Without Shadows*, trans. Kitty Black, London: Hamish Hamilton.
— (1955a), *Dirty Hands*, trans. Lionel Abel, *No Exit and Three Other Plays by Jean-Paul Sartre*. New York: Vintage Books, 129–248.
— (1955b), *No Exit*, trans. Stuart Gilbert, *No Exit and Three Other Plays by Jean-Paul Sartre*, New York: Vintage Books 1–47.
— (1956), *Being and Nothingness*, trans. Hazel E. Barnes, New York: The Philosophical Library.
— (1960a), *The Devil and the Good Lord*, trans. Kitty Black, *The Devil and the Good Lord and Two Other Plays*, New York: Vintage Books, 1–149.
— (1960b), *Kean*, trans. Kitty Black, *The Devil and the Good Lord and Two Other Plays*, New York: Vintage Books, 151–279.
— (1963), *Existentialism is a Humanism*, trans. Philip Mairet, in Walter Kaufmann (ed.), *Existentialism from*

Dostoevsky to Sartre, New York: World Publishing Company, 287–311.

— (1964), *Saint Genet*, trans. Bernard Frechtman, New York: The New American Library.

— (1965a), *Anti-Semite and Jew*, trans. George J. Becker, New York: Schocken Books.

— (1965b), *What Is Literature?*, trans. Bernard Frechtman, New York: Harper and Row.

— (1968), 'Preface', *The Wretched of the Earth*, 7–26; see Fanon, 1968.

— (1976), *Critique of Dialectical Reason*, trans. Alan Sheridan-Smith, Atlantic Highlands, NJ: Humanities Press.

— (1992), *Notebooks for an Ethics*, trans. David Pellauer, Chicago: The University of Chicago Press.

Simons, Margaret A. (ed.) (1995), *Feminist Interpretations of Simone de Beauvoir*, University Park: The Pennsylvania State University Press.

Stone, Robert V. in collaboration with Elizabeth A. Bowman (1986), 'Dialectical Ethics: A First Look at Sartre's Unpublished 1964 Rome Lecture Notes', *Social Text*, Vols 13–14 (Winter/Spring) 1986), 195–215.

EXISTENTIAL PHILOSOPHY AND LITERATURE: SARTRE'S *NAUSEA*

Katherine Rudolph

This article will address existential philosophy of literature. It will be concerned both with philosophy *in* literature and the philosophy *of* literature. Let me note at the outset, however, that this distinction may itself be in question for a certain existential philosophy of literature. For example, the shift from traditional ontology to existential or fundamental ontology made by Heidegger involves a concomitant shift to literature, philosophically significant in that literary works are no longer conceived as merely popular expositions of an autonomous field called philosophy. For Sartre too, the existential predicament cannot be treated merely abstractly by philosophical reflection. A problem may be capable of abstract treatment, but it also has to be lived and, according to Sartre in *What Is Literature?*, requires exemplification and support from those 'fictional and concrete experiences which are novels' (Sartre, 1949, p. 217). Nevertheless, the distinction between the abstract and the concrete does not preclude an interplay of philosophy and literature. The point is rather that philosophy not only has to live with the living personality of the philosopher, but self-consciousness as such is, for Sartre, always of the particular, contingent individual. Sartre's commitment to writing literature is thus not an extraneous addition to his philosophy, but is actually essential to it. Moreover, there is a sense in which Sartre's philosophical commitments developed after coming to terms with ostensibly philosophical topics in his literary writings. Thus, he explains that he wrote

Nausea as a novel, because he did not have a 'solid enough idea of it to make a philosophical work out of it' (Sartre, 1976, p. 180). This explanation seems to suggest that literature does not operate with the clear and distinct ideas which are still seen as the prerogative of philosophical abstraction. However, we should not forget Sartre's commitment to the concrete as essential to his philosophy. For him, literature is not merely another version of his philosophy, nor do his philosophical writings constitute an autonomous philosophy. Sartre's philosophy is *essentially* affiliated with literature.

A similar argument could be made about the affiliation of Merleau-Ponty's philosophy with landscape painting, and of Heidegger's affiliation of philosophy with poetry. However, the argument for an essential affiliation is most compelling in Sartre's case, since he is himself the author of the affiliated works and considered himself primarily a writer of literature and only secondarily a philosopher. This is a unique case where the question of the relation between existential philosophy and literature is constantly at work in both the literary and philosophical productions of the same author. Sartre will thus be the focus of examination in the following analysis.

I propose to examine this relation between literature and existential philosophy by turning first to one of Sartre's major literary works, *Nausea*, which was published in 1938. (I do this partly because this novel already complicates the relation between literature and existential philosophy in that it is itself a literary rendering of a visual rendering of melancholia by Dürer. Thus, the original title of *Nausea* was in fact *Melancholia*, which in turn is an explicit reference to Dürer's engraving by the same title. However, the publisher replaced Sartre's original title with the title *Nausea*. (See Cumming, 1992, p. 158.) Of course, the interplay between art and philosophy takes many different forms in existential philosophy, and I do not intend to obscure this heterogeneity by emphasising Sartre in particular, but there are enough common themes in the existential philosophy of literature to warrant such a move. Almost all the major figures in this movement are indebted in one way or another to Dostoevsky, Kierkegaard and Nietzsche, and in some instances the latter writers also owe a debt to each other. Thus, Nietzsche, famously considered Dostoevsky one of the few psychologists from whom he could still learn something (Dostoevsky was the only psychologist from whom I had anything to learn: he belongs to the happiest windfalls of my life . . .). Moreover, there are common themes that link the existential philosophy of literature, such as the concept of the absurdity of existence, the concern to justify man's resolve to live meaningfully in an indifferent universe (a consequence of the death of God), the search for the ground of human solidarity, the refusal to accept the category of absolute good and evil, the concomitant search for the grounds of authentic existence as opposed to bad faith, the value of the individual understood in terms of her/his freedom, and the attendant category of responsibility in relation to the individual's situatedness (being-in-the world). These themes are particularly and variously instantiated by those we call existential philosophers. For the purposes of this essay, however, we will focus, as I have indicated, on Sartre.

The basis for Sartre's aesthetic theory is laid out in his phenomenological study *Imagination*. For Sartre, the act of perception implies the possibility of imagining more than can be assimilated by the senses. This transcendence of the imagination provides the key to his concept of freedom and is, indeed, its correlate. It is the connection between the freedom of human consciousness and the imagination that explains his interest in art. Aesthetic experience, whose condition of possibility resides in the imagination, transcends life or the immediacy of the factic here and now, and in so transcending life reveals freedom and the possibility of purposive action. The consequence of this revelation, for Sartre, is his concern with art as a forum for human liberty and social commitment.

The crucial point here is that images are potential rather than actual, and cannot be evoked simultaneously with the perception itself. It is precisely because imagination negates the real or perceptual world, is 'irreal,' that it is capable of going beyond it. The object of perception is both real and present, whereas the object of the image is absent: the image is unreal and depends on the spontaneity (freedom) of the person imagining. Images cannot be caused. They can only be motivated. Sartre's theory of the imagination is clearly indebted to Hussrel's phenomenological method for whom imagination and perception are also two distinct modes of consciousness.

According to Husserl, consciousness of something remains 'empty' so long as the 'something' is referred to merely by a word. Similarly for Sartre, words as signs point beyond themselves to another reality. Reading involves the transcendence of signs towards meanings. An 'empty' consciousness becomes intuitively 'fulfilled' when 'evidence' is 'immediately given' – that is, when something is actually perceived or imagined, and thereby receives 'illustrative exemplification' (*Veranschaulichung*). Could this methodological emphasis on the moment of 'fulfilment' prepare the way for Sartre's reliance on the novel as an illustrative exemplification of phenomenological philosophy, as well as his reliance in the novel on works of art as illustrative examples of the essential structure of a work of art? Engravings are only one of the examples in *Nausea*; there are the paintings which Sartre's protagonist looks at in the museum, the statues and the jazz lyric, 'Some of These Days'. This variety, in fact, respects a methodological requirement of Husserl's eidetic reduction, whereby examples are to be varied in order to eliminate the contingent features of a particular example and arrive at the essential structure, which is exhibited as remaining invariant by the multiplication of examples.

However, if we can detect a phenomenological

criterion being carried over here from Husserl's eidetic reduction, Sartre's use also betrays a different conception of the relation between particular experiences and their essential structure. Whereas Husserl sharply distinguishes between the transcendental ego, as the impersonal agency conducting an analysis and what is personal to himself as a particular individual, Sartre's use of examples betrays considerable tampering with the relation between particular and essential. Sartre thus repudiates Husserl's transcendental ego. Moreover, just as the particular individual is no longer transcended in Sartre by a transcendental ego, as he is in Husserl, so a particular work of art does not simply serve to illustrate the essential structure of an act of imagination. Unlike Husserl, Sartre thus regularly writes reviews of particular works of visual and literary art, as well as analyses of particular writers – of Baudelaire, Genet and Flaubert, and of himself in *The Words* (1965). Husserl in contrast, who in fact also offers an analysis of another Dürer engraving in *Ideas*, does so only to display the essential structure of an act of imagination in general when it is carried out with reference to a visual work of art. Whatever is particular to the example of this engraving is disregarded in *Ideas* in a fashion that is implicit in the offhanded manner with which Husserl, apparently by chance, produces the example of the Dürer engraving, *The Knight*, 'taking it out of a folder' (see Cumming, 1992, pp. 4–5, p. 113, p. 171). Husserl is interested in the move from what was previously perceived of as merely 'black lines' to a knight of 'flesh and blood' (*leibhaftig*). He is thus interested in the way an 'empty' consciousness becomes intuitively 'fulfilled' when something is actually imagined and thereby receives 'illustrative exemplification' (*Veranschaulichung*). Again, he is interested in the essential structure of an act of imagination. For, traditionally at least, the most important function of the imagination has been to contribute to the transition from the particulars delivered by visual perception to pure thought's grasp of what is general and essential.

For Husserl, what the illustrative example of Dürer's engraving illustrates is an essential structure, which, as soon as it is exhibited, eliminates the particularity of the example, whereas for Sartre, the relation between particular and essential is complicated by his attention to particular examples. (For an alternative interpretation see Cumming, 1992, p. 165.) He is interested precisely in the relation of an act of imagination to its physical basis.

Thus, if Husserl's *Ideas* serves in some sense as the starting point for Sartre's own theory of the imagination, as it is presented, for example, in *Imagination*, it does so by revising Husserl's phenomenological method, by transforming it into a dialectical method. The point can be illustrated with an example. *Melancholia*, the engraving, is in some sense a self-portrait, but if it is Dürer's self-portrait, he has created an external object, a work of art, which portrays him as unable to create a work of art. For Sartre, the potential for imposing significance is an essential part of human reality, and yet the fact that meaning is never essentially given but always particular reveals the contingency of the human situation and thereby the limits of freedom. Freedom exists only in situation, and *Melancholia* could thus commend itself to Sartre, given his dialectical method, by virtue of its contradictory self-reference.

Simone de Beauvoir addresses such limits to freedom beautifully in *The Blood of Others* (1957), where she shows that while the physical world may offer resistance to activity and creation, it is human beings who determine the significance of this limitation. Thus her character, Bloment, cherishes the illusion that is possible to avoid making decisions and to remain guiltless by remaining a pacifist in the face of war. The point is that all freedom involves choice, and hence limitation, for a freedom without limits would be a meaningless concept. The dialectic between inaction and action in the face of freedom is then a central theme of the existential philosophy of literature. Thus *Nausea* is similarly a work about the work which his protagonist, Roquentin, was unable to write. What emerges instead is Roquentin's posthumously published diary in which he abandons the biographical work he was writing about a historical figure, the Marquis de Rollebon, whom he once identified with, in favour of a novel about his own life.

In *Nausea*, Sartre's protagonist lives in Bouville, which can be translated literally as 'mucktown'. This is significant in that it illustrates quite literally how the physical world offers resistance to activity. Again, freedom exists only in situation. In other words, the total living individual is both the subject and the object of philosophy and the principles of existence can only be expressed in a concrete setting. Of course, the question here becomes, how can literature qualify as lived experience? For Sartre, it can do so because the imagination at the basis for all fiction is the living element of existential philosophy. It is what enables the transcendence of the muck of the here and now, and leaves open the possibility of producing a novel out of the experience of contingency.

The first occurrence of the mood of nausea in the novel happens when Roquentin picks up a stone covered with mud – earth. This physical basis for melancholia is transposed by Sartre into the mood of nausea whose primary function in Sartre is that of revealing my body to my consciousness. No longer upheld by a transcendental ego, consciousness in effect succumbs to its relation to the body as providing a physical basis for it.

Nausea is an existential novel in that it is the story of his protagonist's attempts to exercise his freedom in order to achieve some external realisation of himself. Consciousness is not a thing, but a Nothingness. Man is the being who has at his heart a nothingness, a power to nihilate Being. Hence Sartre's famous distinction in *Being and Nothingness* between Being-in-itself and Being-for-itself. Being-in-itself is all of nonconscious reality. Being-for-itself, which is the being of man, is not actually a separate kind of being, it is rather a consciousness of something, and 'is', in fact, nothingness. Human being is thus a project, a finite process of becoming, which is always in some sense doomed to failure since no human being as a for-itself can strictly speaking ever *be*. *Nausea* is an existential novel in that it mediates between the human condition and the specific situation in which each person is writing her or his own history. But it is also a phenomenological novel in that it is the story of Roquentin's attempts to become conscious of something as his own work. However, consciousness here encounters an obstacle which cannot be eliminated as it is in Husserl – the contingent and nausea itself as the

individual's sense of contingency, and ultimately of his own contingency as an individual. This sense of sloppy superfluity is aroused in Roquentin, not only by the solidity of the stone to which the wet muck clings, but also by a work of art that is not his own but has been made by someone else. The first encounter with a work of art actually occurs earlier than with Roquentin's picking up the stone. Although it is not recalled until later, it is to be compared with the other episode, since it is an encounter with something made of stone and is recognised in retrospect to have been a bout of nausea which inhibited Roquentin from exercising his freedom and achieving self-realisation by doing what he thought he wanted to do – to go to Bengal. When the opportunity came, however: 'Well, I was paralyzed, I could not say a word. I was staring at a little Khmer statuette. . . . I seemed to be full of lymph or warm milk. . . . The statue seemed to me unpleasant and stupid and I felt terribly, deeply bored' (Sartre, 1964, p. 5).

This nauseous experience of his own superfluity paralyses Roquentin in the traditional fashion that melancholia and its romantic affiliate, *ennui*, had done. But there is also a striking departure from this tradition in that nausea overcomes him dialectically: he feels his own contingency in the presence of a work of art made out of stone. The experience of solidity is at the same time the visceral experience of his own lack of solidity, of the shapelessness of his own life, of his own superfluity. There is no structure available for his realisation as a self. Clearly, the Dürer engraving is no longer, as it was for Husserl, simply a work of art that has its own unity. Indeed, whatever Sartre saw in the engraving as a model for his novel, may have had more to do with the solidity of the metal plate, its physical basis, through which he could feel his nausea, than its explicit theme of melancholia.

In *Nausea*, the individual's self-realisation is analogised to the shaping of a work of art: the individual makes something of himself by making something. However, consistent with Sartre's repudiation of an ego transcending the individual, this effort fails in the face of his own contingency. This is not an evasion on Sartre's part, but must be the acceptance of an existential tension: the individual must make her or his decisions alone, with no certainty of being right and no possibility of knowing the total effects of her or his acts or of passing an absolute judgement upon them. Within whatever situation one finds oneself, one must choose among the limitations offered. There is no escape from choice and responsibility. The work of art cannot offer a means of escape from the absurdity of the human condition. Thus, while Sartre certainly considers aesthetic creation as capable of making life more significant, the essential thing for the existentialist or absurd writer is to never forget that her or his work is contingent and is not capable of a higher or essential meaning. For the existentialist this indicates humanity's anguish and weights down the burden of freedom.

Thus, Roquentin discovers in *Nausea* that the appropriate therapy may not be something solid, but another genre, music. He reflects after having been listening to a jazz record in a café, 'some of these days, you'll miss me honey . . . What has just happened is that the nausea has disappeared . . . My glass of beer has shrunk, it seems heaped up on the table. It looks dense and indispensable' (ibid., p. 22). The analogy to music is significant in that, according to Sartre, the meaning of a melody does not refer beyond itself and is not beyond the melody itself. At this early stage in his career, he therefore considers music, as well as poetry and painting, non-signifiying art. They are vague and inseparable from the sensory qualities producing them. Poets use words, Sartre suggests, in much the same way as painters use colours and musicians use sounds: to create objects. The consequence of this state of affairs for Sartre is that these 'pure' arts cannot be committed or political. His conception of committed literature applies to prose alone for only prose is instrumental in relation to meaning and thus serves the function of communication. In other words, literature conveys conceptual meaning, whereas the poet communicates through the material, rather than the conceptual, aspect of the word. Thus, Roquentin's musical therapy proves only temporally efficacious when the analogy to the statue is revived to the extent that the disappearance of nausea is associated with the shaping up of the glass of beer. The glass becomes almost essential in its structure.

However, as Cumming notes (1992, p. 206), by the end of the novel the jazz lyric reinstates a dialectical opposition between its 'arid purity' and the wet dirtiness of Roquentin's life, and his self-disgust returns:

> All the things around me were made of the same material as I, a sort of messy suffering. The world was so ugly, outside of me, these dirty glasses on the table were so ugly, and the brown stains on the mirror. . . . Now there is this song on the saxophone. And I am ashamed. A glorious little suffering has just been born, an exemplary suffering. Four notes on the saxophone . . . they seem to say: you must suffer like us, suffer in rhythm (*en mesure*). Naturally, I'd like to suffer that way, *en mesure*, without complacence, without self-pity, with an arid purity. But is it my fault if the beer at the bottom of my glass is warm, if there are brown stains on the mirror? (Sartre, 1964, p. 174)

Husserl's distinction between the essential and the contingent, which Husserl regarded as itself essential, is again being tampered with by Sartre. Initially the beer glass has somehow been ennobled by the melody as if it were as essential in its structure as the development of the musical theme Roquentin has been listening to. But lack of proportion soon returns, and the *en mesure* of the music is finally, in an ironic deployment of Husserl's own description of music, redescribed as 'not existing'.

En mesure carries a reference at once to measurement and to music – to a world where circles and melodies keep their pure and rigid lines. Sartre presumably has in mind the traditional affiliation of music with geometry. A 'measure' is a bar of music, but the implication of measurement is extended, so that measure becomes the proportion that is respected by something that has shape, as opposed to the lack of proportion that is felt when 'suffering' is sloppy. Thus 'en mesure' becomes a sort of impossible moral imperative here, one that does not jeopardise its necessity by tolerating any compromise with the sloppy contingency of human suffering, the sort of indulgence, for example, that Roquentin's Aunt sought: 'Chopin's *Preludes* were such a help to me when your poor uncle died' (ibid.). Such an attitude is an illustration of bad faith, which consists in this case in letting oneself believe that one can be saved by art. Any such compromise is resisted by the autonomous circularity of the pure and rigid line of the melody, which is reproduced by its physical basis: 'no, they certainly cannot tell me it is compassionate'. For the needle, which turns in a circle above the record, 'spins gaily, completely self-absorbed' (ibid.). (These geometrical allusions suggest that we have not entirely left Husserl behind, for it was Husserl who took geometry as a model for his phenomenological philosophy as a science of essential structures.)

Reflecting on the record to which he has been listening, Roquentin cherishes the aspiration: what if my own life were to make the matter of the melody? He recognises that his interest in the composer's life, 'to find out the type of troubles he had, if he had a woman or if he lived alone', is prompted by the reflection, 'that that man made it' (ibid., p. 177). And Roquentin thus visualises the physical act of production: 'The moist hand seizes the pencil on the piano: "some of these days, you'll miss me honey." ' (ibid., p 176). But then an eidetic reduction in effect threatens to interrupt, for the autonomy of the work of art has no regard, no need for the contingencies of the physical act that produced it:

> That's the way it happened. That way or another way, it makes little difference. That is how it was born. It is the worn-out body of this Jew . . . which it chose to create it. He held the pencil limply and the drops of sweat fell from his ringed fingers onto the paper. And why not I? Why should it need precisely this fat fool full of stale beer and whisky for the miracle to be accomplished? (ibid., p. 176)

Once again Husserl's distinction between the essential and the contingent, on which the effectiveness of the eidetic reduction depends is being tampered with. Having ostensibly disposed of contingency – 'that way or another' – Sartre continues his description of the particular contingency of the work's physical basis ('the worn-out body of this Jew') and of its physical production in a fashion that elicits a nauseous sense of revulsion: the 'body' is 'fat', the 'hand' is 'moist', and the beer is 'stale' like the beer in front of Roquentin in the café.

At least the elimination of the Jew as superfluous permits the conviction 'why not I?' to take over. The interest Roquentin has temporarily taken in the Jew's life is novelistic, and he recognises that in the case of his own life a melody could not be in question but another genre: that 'it would have to be a book'. This turn to the novel as the appropriate genre illustrates Sartre's commitment to prose and to literature as engaged art (ibid., p. 178).

Existential literature is concerned with the fundamental situations in which freedom asserts itself. A literature of characters or an interest in purely psychological characterisations is inadequate, because it fails to see that human attitudes change in the face of the most typical situations. Similarly, according to Sartre, the realistic writer has too little respect for a character's ability as a free individual. Sartre does not necessarily reject psychological exploration in literature, but he insists that it must integrate life. For Sartre, the writer is *engagé*, whether or not he or she likes it, in the political historical situation of the day.

Thus, *Nausea* as a work in which we would expect Roquentin to describe his own troubles is not a psychological explanation of these troubles. Rather, just as the record anticipates 'some of these days', so Roquentin anticipates the time 'when the book would be written. . . . Then, perhaps, because of it, I could remember my life without repugnance (ibid., p. 178). To this extent he would have overcome his nausea and its sense of contingency, for he would have vindicated the notion that a 'situation' need not remain a merely contingent event, but can be privileged as literature.

The first entry of *Nausea* starts with the decision to keep a diary in order to see clearly, and since this diary composes the novel that has been written, the decision corresponds to the decision at the end to write a novel. The rest of the first entry illustrates with examples Roquentin's effort at clarity and why it is needed, notably by recalling the nauseous reaction to the stone that has wet muck clinging to it. In the second entry a temporary cure for this nauseous feeling is provided by the regularities of a world that is spatially and temporally oriented (in effect, the everyday world as described by Heidegger in *Being and Time*). As Roquentin reflects:

My odd feeling of the other week seems to me quite ridiculous today. . . . I am quite at ease this evening, quite solidly *terre à terre* in the world. Here is my room facing northeast. Below the Rue des Mutelés and the construction-yard of the new station. . . . The Paris train has just come in. (Sartre, 1964, p. 2)

Roquentin accordingly anticipates the arrival of the travelling salesman in room number 2 on the second floor of the hotel. He does indeed arrive, and his arrival is echoed in the penultimate sentence of the novel: 'On the second floor of the Hotel Printania two windows have just lightened up' (ibid, p. 178).

This scheduling of the novel between the arrival of the train from Paris and the departure of a train for Paris is art not life, as Roquentin warns us by telling a story within his story:

For the most banal even to become an adventure, you must (and this is enough) begin to recount it . . . Nothing happens while you live [*il n'arrive rien*] . . . But everything changes when you tell about life. . . . You seem to start at the beginning 'It was a fine autumn evening in 1922. I was a notary's clerk in Marommes.' And in reality you have started at the end. It was there, invisible and present; it is the one which gives to words the pomp and value of a beginning. (ibid., pp. 39–40)

Nausea, is itself visibly present from its start, and with everything in place and on schedule, Roquentin repudiates his decision to keep a diary: 'I am going to bed. I am cured. I'll give up writing my daily impressions, like a little girl in her nice new notebook' (ibid., p. 3).

This decision corresponds to Sartre's repudiation of literature as the psychological exploration of the inner life of the character. But the 'undated pages' then break off: 'In one case only it might be interesting to keep a diary: it would be if. . . .' (ibid.). It would be interesting to keep a diary, we can infer, if something were to happen. What happens is the coming on of the illness that will eventually be diagnosed as nausea. Here we confront a paradox which renders the novel as ambiguous as it was when it bore the title *Melancholia*, which carried a reference to the work of art that Dürer created as a

portrayal of himself as an artist who was unable to create.

Roquentin's discovery that there are no adventures is the discovery that there are only adventure stories. To believe in adventure, that something is happening to me, is to confuse art with life. Art is to be distinguished, as imposing an essential structure, from life as a sloppy succession of contingent events. However, *Nausea* does not succeed in the attempt to catch time by the tail: *Nausea* does not come full circle and achieve the autonomy Roquentin credited to the jazz lyric as a model for the novel he decides to write. The scheduling of the novel between an arrival and a departure exploits the reader's own recollections of those arrivals and departures which have come to be accepted as marking starting points and life changes.

There is a further ambiguity. In spite of his anticipation of it, Roquentin has no future. We are not allowed to forget that the future was not yet there, in spite of his premonitions. He exists only in the past with respect to which he anticipates that in the future he will be able to accept himself via the novel. This open-endedness of the novel serves Sartre's sense that the function of the writer is to reveal to humankind its own possibilities. Indeed, there is the explanation, ostensibly from the publisher, that the diary was 'found among the papers of Antoine Roquentin' (ibid., p. 1) so that we can draw the conclusion that he is dead, even though we are not told this explicitly.

If Roquentin will be able to accept himself via the novel, *Nausea*, without the revulsion of nausea, it can only be because he has produced a work of art, with its necessary and autonomous structure, but then there will be no self to accept, because Roquentin can be eliminated as contingent, along with nausea as a sense of contingency, just as the Jew could be eliminated in favour of the jazz lyric which he produced and which Roquentin takes as a model for his novel as a work of art.

In any case, *Nausea* remains ambiguous, not only as a novel which is anti-novel, as a work of art that melancholia precludes the creation of, as an adventure story where there are no adventures, but also as a phenomenological novel, which is anti-phenomenological . . . It is phenomenological in that the objective of the diary Roquentin decides to keep is 'clarity of vision', Further, Roquentin's method for achieving this objective has been from the start descriptive of what he is conscious of. Yet, this phenomenological novel is also anti-phenomenological, not just in the sense that only 'a little . . . clarity' (ibid., p. 178) can be anticipated as achievable by the novel, but also in the sense that the novel subverts Husserl's method for achieving clarity, the eidetic reduction, by subverting the distinction on which its effectiveness depends – the distinction between an essential structure and the contingent which is finally to be eliminated by the reduction in favour of the essential structure. This distinction is, of course, essential to philosophy itself. It should thus come as no surprise that Sartre has to find an affiliate in literature to deconstruct this distinction for philosophy.

Bibliography

References and further reading

Beauvoir, Simone de (1957), *The Blood of Others*, trans. Y. Moyse and R. Senhouse, Cleveland: World Publishing.

Cumming, Robert D. (1992), *Phenomenology and Deconstruction*, Vol. II., Chicago: Chicago University Press.

Heidegger, Martin (1962), *Being and Time*, trans. J. Macquarrie and E. Robinson, New York: Harper and Row.

— (1971), 'The Origin of the Work of Art', in *Poetry, Language, Thought*, trans. A. Hofstadter, New York: Harper and Row.

Husserl, Edmund (1978), *The Origin of Geometry*, with an Introduction by J. Derrida, trans. J. Leavey, Brighton: Harvester.

— (1982), *Ideas Pertaining to a Pure Phenomenology*, trans. F. Kersten, The Hague: Martinus Nijhoff.

Nietzsche, Friedrich (1990), *Twilight of the Idols*, trans. R. J. Hollingdale, New York: Penguin Books.

Panofsky, J. (1971), *The Life and Art of Albrecht Dürer*, Princeton: Princeton University Press.

Sartre, Jean-Paul (1949) *What is Literature?*, trans B. Frechtman, New York: Philosophical Library.

— (1962), *Imagination: A Psychological Critique*, trans. F. Williams, Ann Arbor: University of Michigan.

— (1964), *Nausea*, trans. L. Alexander, New York: New Directions.

— (1965), *The Words*, trans. B. Frechtman, New York: Braziller.

— (1976), *Situations*, Vol. 10, Paris: Gallimard.

Section Three
PHILOSOPHIES OF LIFE AND UNDERSTANDING

INTRODUCTION

Fiona Hughes

A way of reading these articles

One might think that the combination of herme-neutic philosophers – Schleiermacher, Dilthey, Ga-damer, Ricoeur – with the vitalist Bergson and, of all things, American pragmatism is a difficult one to sustain. There are, however, strong connections, even though they must be seen as a family resem-blance, in Wittgenstein's sense, rather than a cen-trally-structured unity. What unites all these authors horizontally, rather than vertically in relation to one overarching principle, is their concern to rearticulate the account of the relation between human beings and the world they inhabit in order to show the limits of theoretical reason and insist on a new form of reflective activity, which some of them call 'understanding'. The aim is to find a way of framing mental activity in such a way that humans are no longer seen primarily as theoretical beings face-to-face with an external world, but rather as reflective beings engaged in an ongoing relation with a world which they construct and interpret linguistically and historically. Reflection is brought closer to experi-ence (or life) through this new articulation of mental activity. The selected authors' various ways of fram-ing this project are opened up for us by the seven writers who have contributed to this Section.

Having introduced the terms 'life' and 'experience' we must immediately stop short and register some caution. Both terms are so general as to risk being misleading. 'Life' sometimes suggests a biological organisation, that is, the identity of an individual organic being or class at whatever level of biological complexity. It can also be used qualitatively, and with reference to human beings in relation to cultural, evaluative and even moral considerations. 'Experience' carries with it similar problems as it can amount to a very low level of consciousness, but can also be equivalent to 'knowledge'. (This is how Kant uses the term.) All the authors in this Section think of 'life' as human life and 'experience' as broader than knowledge. Beyond that there are many varia-tions in their usage. Should such general terms not be excluded from any properly philosophical discussion? The argument might be that examples of particular lives and experiences will be admitted as useful for testing the validity of a philosophical theory, but that introduction of general terms would entail a category mistake. However, extreme intellectual caution can be as dangerous as lack of restraint. The dangers in this case would be of excluding all indeterminate notions because they pose problems for rigorous technical debates. Were the relation between philosophy and life deemed inadmissible, a long-standing philosophical preoccupation, dating back at least to Socrates, would be ruled out.

In fact, one of the recurrent features of the writings examined in this Section is the thought that philosophy has often lost sight of the living context within which any possible reflection arises. This stress on the concrete is allied to a notion of life as not reducible to an aggregate of particular instances, but, equally, encourages scepticism to-wards theoretical systematicity, particularly that of German Idealism. In place of abstract systems of human experience, obsessed with the theoretical intellectual faculty of reason, the attempt has been made, in various ways, to rearticulate the independence of experience in the face of theory. However, this has not entailed giving up all pretension to approaching experience systematically, that is, as a whole. While each of the philosophers examined believes that the notion of a whole life or experience – and the systematicity that goes with it – is inherently problematic, all of them seek to articulate it. Thus, the abstract system becomes a *concrete whole*, albeit in a variety of different ways. The whole may be a body of knowledge (Schleiermacher and Pierce), a cultural unity (Schleiermacher, Dilthey, Gadamer, Ricoeur, Dewey, Rorty) a movement of pure experience (Bergson and James) or an individual person (Bergson). These may be seen as the establishment of a concrete universal in Hegel's sense. He used this expression specifically to express how the state can come to embody or express the spirit or rationality of a people within reality. I am using it more broadly to signify how a universal becomes embodied within experience.

The choice of 'understanding' to replace 'reason' is in part a conventional one, but the new linguistic convention marks out a different world-view, one which situates human intellect within this world and undercuts any tendency to see it as 'transcendent' or as an expression of another world. Within the Western philosophical tradition an equation has often been made between human reason and an ability to detach ourselves from the here and now in the interests of a higher religious, ethical or speculative destiny. While it is not simply the case that German Idealism was guilty of situating human reason beyond the world, a resistance to any such tendency is apparent in all the authors in this Section. This does not preclude there being a transcendental element in their conception of understanding. For while the 'transcendent', as Kant had already established, relates human intellect to a world beyond, the transcendental approach which he adopted concentrated rather on the limitations of our cognitive ability, which he, following Locke and Hume, called 'understanding'. The transcendental focus on human finitude allows the old notion of the transcendent to be partially rehabilitated as that which goes beyond any mechanical or purely natural description of our experience. I will call this 'transcendence', signalling the inclusion of human purposes and values within a finite or immanent account of experience or life. For Kant 'immanent' principles apply strictly within the limits of possible experience and are opposed to transcendent principles. While he established a transcendental philosophy fitted for inhabiting an immanent space, the authors discussed in this Section begin with immanence, allowing transcendence to emerge within it, to a greater or lesser degree.

Another way of approaching all of this is by turning to the classical question of the relation between the universal and the individual. The 'universal' is what belongs to either everything in the universe or every member of a class. It can often be replaced by 'essence', 'principle' or 'ground'. The 'individual' is the member of the class. It is important to differentiate 'generality' from 'universality', the former being comparative and the latter absolute. The term 'particular' is often used as equivalent to 'individual'.

The philosophical concern with the relation between universal and individual instance coincides with the history of the tradition of Western philosophy. Plato's theory of forms sought to establish universal principles as the foundation of human experience, thus, of all individual instances arising within it. While it would be rash to interpret Plato as having claimed that there is a world beyond this in some simply material fashion, the ideas or universals are ontologically independent of the everyday world, while the objects and events we experience are founded on universals. At the highest level of the complex hierarchy of universals are the ideas of the true, the good and the beautiful. Aristotle insisted, against Plato, that the universal should be understood as being ontologically inseparable from its instantiation within an individual substance. Thus began the debate, which continues even now, about the relation between universal and individual. Given this long historical heritage, it would be culpably naive for modern-day thinkers to suggest that there was one, and only one, account of the relation between universal and individual instance within the Western tradition. Philosophers did not always simply subsume the individual instance under the universal rule; instead, there was a constant re-articulation of the relation. Sometimes this led to the meaning of subsumption being reinterpreted, while at other times the autonomy of the universal was questioned. This undermined the claim that the individual instance should be subsumed under the universal rule. For instance, in British Empiricism universality was seen as a general pattern emerging from individual instances and not as autonomous or formal, as in the Platonic or Aristotelian versions of Universalism. This potted history may serve to alert us to the complexity of the relation between universal and individual. It will also prepare us for the new balance between transcendence and immanence discussed in the articles in this Section.

All the authors treated in this Section share the view that an abstract *a priori* system cannot grasp the particularity of the individual instance, whether it is an object, an event, a person or a culture. They see the systematically oriented philosophies of German Idealism as presenting a subsumptive model of the relation between universal and individual, although the case was, in fact, more complex than this would suggest. For some of the authors, culture or tradition is not only one of the things which might be misconstrued or even missed by a universalist pro-cedure: it also becomes part of the alternative procedure which will seek to reassert the balance between universal and individual in the direction of the latter within an immanentist perspective. Thus, universals, patterns and rules should be investigated as to their historical, linguistic and cultural forma-tion rather than seen as absolute, autonomous and *a priori*. What I am calling 'concrete universals' are considered to be more effective for grasping indivi-dual instances within experience. Understanding will be the faculty appropriate to these immanently constructed universals, which are true of a class or culture rather than of the universe *per se*.

The pressing question which arises from this move to situate intellect closer to the world of experience is the following: if intellect becomes too attuned to the particular and to the culturally-constructed forms of experience, does this eliminate all ways in which the universal might serve as a foundation for truth, morality and beauty as Plato had intended? Even if we might happily give up 'foundationalism' as

being too mechanistic an abstraction, can we really do without some standards for value that go beyond the particularly constituted preferences of individual people and the cultures they inhabit? Is there not, in other words, a need for transcendence even if ontological foundationalism has been found want-ing? Some of the authors try to resituate transcen-dence through a Kantian regulative principle, as I discuss in the next Section. Clearly for Gadamer (and perhaps for Dilthey), culture provides a differ-ent form of transcendence within immanence, while Bergson and James look to pre-theoretical *sense-data* as the non-abstract source of experience. Dewey and Rorty, who prescribe a return to everyday experi-ence, stand somewhat apart from all of these ap-proaches. It is important to be aware that none of these authors is wholly particularist, in that none of them suggest that the whole should be given up in favour of the particular alone. All are, nevertheless, immanent thinkers in Kant's sense, limiting their thought to the range of possible experience.

The horizons and presuppositions of this introduction

I now want to backtrack and say something about my relation to the articles in this Section and the authors they discuss. While I have been interested in many of the central questions raised by these authors for some time, I am not a specialist in hermeneutics, nor in philosophies of life. My own philosophical commitments have primarily been to Kant, Hegel and Nietzsche, and to topics in epistemology, phi-losophical aesthetics and political philosophy. I am also extremely interested in the phenomenological movement. So what brings someone of my interests to this Section? In short, it is because a number of issues which I have found important in my own work are directly taken up by these authors. I approach this section with some already existing interests which predispose me towards wanting to generate and learn from a dialogue with the writers of the six articles and, through them, with the authors they discuss. Firstly, I am interested in the relation between the structures and the particularity of experience – or 'life as it is lived' to use a Diltheyan turn of phrase. Secondly, focusing on interpretation allows knowledge to be seen as an ongoing activity or project and not an automatic matter. I therefore come to these discussions of hermeneutics and philosophies of life with a pre-existing sense of their importance. With the help of my specialist writers, my relative ignorance may lead to a number of discoveries, not least about my own 'specialisations'.

In the first book of the *Critique of Judgement*, Kant introduces two forms of human awareness: 'aesthetic apprehension' and 'aesthetic judgement'. These introduce a new relation between mind and world highlighting the role of synthesis – a prototype for interpretation – within experience. In fact, they are best understood as two extremes of one complex experience. Whereas 'aesthetic apprehension' captures the attention we pay to something given to us and which we find beautiful, 'reflective judgement' is the reflection appropriate to this attention. We seek out an idea or universal in order to try to disclose the meaning of what we are apprehending. However, what actually matters is the search for an ordering principle and not its discovery. The combination of these two sorts of awareness counts as a form of cognition for Kant, but is distinct from both epistemic and moral judgements which determine an individual instance by a universal principle. We cannot apprehend a thing aesthetically if we do not reflectively explore it, and reflective judgement would not be truly reflective if it did not work with, and in some sense limit itself by, the sort of attention which counts as apprehension. Thus, this sort of reflection is not a metajudgement, but part of the process of responding aesthetically. While I have simply given a sketch of what is a highly complex and problematic set of arguments, I want to suggest why my engagement with the *Critique of Judgement* leads me to be interested in accounts of understanding as a form of reflection combining a receptive and an interpretative dimension. What I call the receptive dimension is one which reveals the finite nature of human intellect and its necessary dependence on a world which is already given and constituted naturally and, even, culturally. The interpretive dimension combines this attention to what is prior to human intervention with the contribution made by the judging subject, not only as an individual but also as a member of a tradition, culture or interest group. While the cultural specification of the combination of receptivity and interpretation is post-Kantian, the fundamental model of a subject interpreting a world is already to be found in his critical system.

Additionally, there are certain hermeneutic methodological insights that I have found extremely valuable: for instance, the ideas of presupposition, horizon and the so-called 'hermeneutic circle'. For hermeneutists, beginning with Schleiermacher, we always bring certain 'presuppositions' to our reading of a text, a dialogue with another, an argument or an experience. While some of these count as prejudices in a pejorative sense and may be eliminable, there are others of which we cannot so easily dispose. This suggests that transparency and a total objectivity of reason is a myth. Indeed, that we have presuppositions at all is not only a limitation – which it surely is, as it means that we do not have total control over what and how we know – but also a curious strength. It is only from the perspective of projecting a god's eye, omniscient view of the world that the necessity of presuppositions counts as a failing or lack. When the myth of transparency is abandoned, it is possible for us to recognise that the background and even the ignorance, out of which our projects of achieving knowledge and truth arise, can be conducive to the project of understanding. The hermeneutic notion of a 'horizon', already used by Nietzsche, but developed most systematically by Gadamer following Heidegger, is closely allied with this. What it expresses is the necessity of contexts within which all attempts to know develop: the contexts belong to the individual, the group, the society and the historical period. These various horizons overlap, complement and sometimes compete with one another. Next, the 'hermeneutic circle' introduced by Schleiermacher – claiming that there is a reciprocal relation between part and whole – articulates the way in which individual statements and persons relate to the wider contexts within which they appear. The hermeneutic circle is not a vicious circle because it is not closed; that is, the dynamic relation between part and whole arises within an interpretative context in which neither side is always dominant; the relation is a changing one. Using these notions it is easier to develop an account of understanding as a form of intellect which relates a judging subject to an already existing world. Finally, the 'principle of charity' encourages us to find the most plausible reading of a text – or even of an experience – and is a good counterbalance to the reductionist tendency within explanation.

This is, perhaps, the point at which I should introduce those of my presuppositions which are in some tension with the discussions in this Section. I bring with me some worries, critical in a Kantian sense. One of these is: can a place can be found for transcendence within an immanent world-view? For, while Kant denies that it is meaningful for us to talk about a transcendent objective sphere of things-in-themselves, he does insist that we must establish the transcendental structure which makes experience possible. In this way, objectivity becomes not foundational in the sense most often associated with Plato, but, rather, critical in the sense that it is concerned with the necessary limits of our experience. System is reinterpreted in conjunction with this. It ceases to be a closed unity and becomes identical with the establishment of the principles which are necessary but not sufficient for our cognition and action. Further, although Kant develops a pluralist account of the role of reason and establishes specific modes in which it is attuned to empirical experience ('understanding') and to moral practice ('practical reason'), a necessary place is conserved for unapplied ('speculative') reason. These features make for a position that is more transcendentally oriented than any author discussed in this Section.

One way in which some of the authors discussed here try to negotiate this problem is by rehabilitating a methodological strategy which Kant introduced in the *Critique of Pure Reason* (1781) and developed in the third Critique. This is the notion of a regulative use of reason aiming at an idea of systematicity which is never wholly realised. Using this paradigm, the foundations of value and truth can be reintroduced as goals at which we aim, rather than as already existing standards. The advantage of this way of seeing things is that our relationship to values and truths can be understood as exploratory, thus congenial to our paying attention to the specificities of life and not just to some rules which might be considered to determine the latter. This introduces an interpretative element into experience. However it is not a question of 'anything goes' or a counsel of laziness, but is, instead, quite the reverse. Objectivity has become problematic, but it is still a necessary organising idea for experience and as such must be constantly rearticulated and investigated rather than taken as given. Schleiermacher, Ricoeur and Peirce all use versions of the regulative principle.

Hermeneutic insights are often assumed to be either so commonsensical as to be hardly worthy of rigorous philosophical attention or, at the other extreme, spurious. I want to suggest that we cannot afford to ignore what allows us to develop more dexterous ways of understanding not only texts but also experience in general. This is not to claim that all philosophy should be hermeneutic and life-oriented, but these options should be included within the range of philosophical sensibilities and concerns. There is not one sole proper method of philosophising and often we need to work at several different levels at the same time. This insight itself has important hermeneutic resonances.

A particular reading of the articles in this section

The ideas I have developed above have arisen out of my dialogue with the writers of the six articles in this Section. I am greatly indebted to their particular interpretations, some aspects of which I will now discuss.

Christian Berner's interpretation of Schleiermacher reveals how the latter's hermeneutics functions within a broader philosophical framework. This is in contrast to those readings which present Schleiermacher as either insisting on the pervasiveness of interpretation in experience and those which see him as supplying only a narrow technical method for reading texts. Dialectics and ethics are, according to Schleiermacher (read with the help of Berner), properly philosophical pursuits concerned, respectively, with the systematicity of philosophical principles and the application of this systematic rationality within the world or 'nature'. While hermeneutics is primarily understood as a technique rather than being of direct philosophical relevance, it is necessary for the development of a coherent philosophical position by making contradictions identifiable, preparing for their solution in dialectics. The former does this by interpreting discourses in such a way as to make them publicly accessible. Not all forms of understanding count as objects for hermeneutic attention as this would require their displaying a level of complexity. And while we are capable of understanding by means of our feelings or sentiments, our responses to works of art and our use of symbols, none of these is as yet sufficiently articulated to count as appropriate objects for methodical interpretation. Moreover, the sort of discourse that merely repeats the ideas of others also falls below the threshold of hermeneutic attention because it has not yet attained the authenticity characteristic of an individual's attempt to understand her or his own point of view. Berner insists that while Schleiermacher's hermeneutics aim to develop a technique, it is also 'an activity of reflecting judgement', consciously echoing Kant in the sense that there are no general rules for interpretation. The rules generated by hermeneutics are only relevant within the philosophical context of dialectics and ethics, and thus cannot count as apodeictic. What does ethics add to the story? Ethics is the source of the will to understand and be understood, necessary for the dialectical aim of resolving conflicts and approaching the truth. Without an interest in the fit between our ideas and the reality they represent, even dialectical activity would be merely technical. Only within the context of a concern for truth, which must count as a regulative idea rather than a foundation for experience, do dialectics and hermeneutics become relevant, both philosophically and experientially. Regarding the relation between universal and individual discussed above, we find a series of intricate moves within which this relation develops. At the most superficial level, hermeneutic interpretation allows an individual point of view to become articulated so that it can be discussed in the public sphere of dialectics, with a view to judging its contribution to the ethical project of constructing a universal account of truth. Truth is a task arising for a plurality of subjects who enter into argument with the intention of reaching agreement: the standard for truth is the regulative ideal of an ethical community where such agreement would be achieved. Thus, hermeneutics is given a very specific identity and yet a general relevance. This is a very attractive way of accepting the generalisation of interpretation while insisting that a plurality of philosophical devices and methods are necessary. Berner's presentation of Schleiermacher not only answers many of Gadamer's objections, it also combines an attention to interpretation with an insistence on its relation to an extra-textual reality, avoiding the grosser excesses of some twentieth-century enthusiasm for the 'world as text'. While the latter can be a useful notion, especially when used with the attention to reality which we find in the discussion of Ricoeur's writings, it can be dangerous when its own metaphorical status becomes invisible.

Jacob Owensby's interpretation of Dilthey clarifies many of the central themes that I have mentioned. Dilthey's commitment to an understanding oriented towards life leads him to insist on the historical dimension of the latter. Life is to be understood as an 'I–World relation', not reducible to an internal or subjective experience: it is the 'dynamic continuum' of the interaction between the individual and the historical and cultural contexts he or she inhabits. The individual is thus shaped by a whole which is not to be conflated with a set of abstractly universal principles because it is specific, though complex. There is no ultimate opposition between inner and outer – a view also held by Nietzsche – and thus no primary opposition between subject and object. In a move which prefigures Heidegger, Dilthey holds that a primary whole of experience predates any such separation. The notion of the whole of experience arises as 'life nexus' and as 'world-view' (Weltbild). These are contexts arising out of the ongoing relation between 'I' and world, within which arise our values and particular ways of understanding. Dilthey talks of the 'human environment' and, while later Gadamer comes to insist on a distinction between the 'environment' of animals and the 'horizon' of humans, it is clear that what is at issue here is the notion of a horizon as the field of possibility for our experience. The reflexive awareness which Dilthey outlines is one adequate to his critique of the inner–outer relation. This form of understanding is not exterior to life, but is 'a pre-cognitive felt sense of the mineness of both the acts and the objects of consciousness'. In his later writings Dilthey develops a hermeneutics of historical understanding, allied with a narrative account of our self-understanding of life. These, along with an interest in the way in which art serves as a symbol for the nexus which is life, make for parallels with the hermeneutists in this Section.

Guy Lafrance's discussion of Bergson reveals that, for the latter, life counts as essentially temporal and mobile. Whereas mathematical models of time use the metaphor of points on a line and thus present time as essentially a succession of atomic static instants, Bergson prefers to use biological metaphors to express what he sees as the 'flow' or 'becoming' of life. This is similar to Nietzsche's 'will to power'. Seeing life as 'flow' also prefigures phenomenological notions of 'the lived' as flux, which gains form when it is taken up by a conscious subject. Importantly, Lafrance says that Bergson distinguishes between the superficial self which adapts to society and the fundamental self which is closer to pure temporality and is characterised by a specific conception of freedom. The free self is a whole and is capable of a degree of innovation and choice analogous to artistic creation. Bergson intends to move beyond oppositional forms of thought towards a more organic understanding. The use of biological metaphors, allied with the stress on the body and the brain, are anti-idealist but not materially reductionist, for the emphasis is on life as a qualitative developmental process and not as a measurable quantity. These themes ally Bergson not only to Nietzsche but also to Merleau-Ponty. While Dilthey and Bergson share a mistrust of oppositional thinking, the latter aims to go beyond everyday and culturally-determined thinking towards an integrated relation of the individual or self as an experiential whole, whereas the former insists that the individual cannot be detached from the cultural nexus. One way in which we can see how biology and consciousness are intertwined is in Bergson's insistence that even perception requires memory. He distinguishes two forms of memory: one more passive which resembles an archive of associations and one more active which creates links between past and present through the formation of a habit, that is, a creative repetition. Both forms of memory are necessary and complementary. Our freedom arises as the embodied activity of beings able to remember both passively and innovatively. This conception of freedom and life leads Bergson to develop a specific account of understanding and knowledge. Intellect is, he says, particularly well adapted to dealing with material objects and social objects like language. However, it has often been mistakenly thought capable of transcending the experience within which it emerges and thus, of standing outside of life. In contrast, instinct, which also belongs to animals, is closely bound up with the process of life and involves little freedom or creativity. What is needed is a combination of these two, or the introduction of a third thing, which will make it possible to combine these different but complementary capacities. The intermediate faculty called 'intuition' 'would not have the rigidity or the narrowness of instinct nor the formal abstractness of intelligence'. By means of this faculty we do not *think* real time: we *live* it. Intuition integrates feelings into the knowing process – as Dilthey also wished – and allows instinct to become disinterested, self-conscious and capable of reflecting on objects. Expressions of it can be found in 'direct vision, contact, coincidence, sympathy and immediate consciousness'. This conception of intuition as the third thing is analogous to, but broader than, the Kantian and Husserlian one of intuition as an immediate relation to an external object in space and time.

Jean Grondin shows how Gadamer follows in the path established by Heidegger, who combined phenomenological insights with a hermeneutics of being-in-the-world. Gadamer is suspicious of what he sees as an excessively technical conception of hermeneutics in Schleiermacher and Dilthey and insists on a dimension of 'incapacity' which is a necessary part of a language user's capacity to understand. This combination is especially apparent in the encounter with an artwork, which serves Gadamer as a paradigm in his account of understanding. For Gadamer, the individual subject emerges in relation to a cultural tradition which, as a framework or horizon for experience, is particular and not abstractly universal. (This echoes the perspective we have already found in Dilthey.) Grondin insists that this concern for tradition is not to be understood as a celebration of traditionalism. 'Pointing to tradition as a source of understanding does not mean that one favours tradition over critical or argumentative inquiry, but simply that one can never fully account for the sources and grounds of one's beliefs'. Taking Aristotle as representative of a similar view on the relationship between moral knowledge and tradition, Grondin explains that the 'concernedness' of ethical knowledge does not hamper its claims to validity, but is, rather, a condition for the possibility of such claims. Thus, ethics based on abstract universality misconstrues the relation between the concrete situation, its cultural context and the knowledge that can arise from these. Truth arises out of a relation between individual instances and the tradition which is their context, not from a move to a level of analysis over and beyond experience. Hermeneutics has universal relevance because of the essentially dialogical nature of our understanding. This begins with an acceptance of one's ignorance and the attempt to reveal the truth through a dialogical exchange with another. Language is the 'horizon' of our understanding or 'being-in-the-world'. The theme of dialogue echoes that already found in Schleiermacher, but here the generalisation of hermeneutics arises from the linguistic and interpretative nature of *all* understanding.

Paul Ricoeur is a philosopher with a huge range of commitments, some of the most important of which are discussed in the essay written jointly by Daniel Cefaï and Véronique Munoz-Dardé. While Cefaï concentrates on the way in which Ricoeur's threefold theory of mimesis has informed the social sciences, Dardé discusses the ethical and political implications of his work. Ricoeur combines phenomenological and hermeneutic insights with an openness to works in the analytical mode. His notion of understanding is one which links knowledge to practical questions of morality and cultural self-interpretation. He sees consciousness as arising in a cultural context in response to an objectively-existing external world, but the latter has to be interpreted or taken up in order to become our world. He sees this as the temporal and narrative structure of our experience. In order to express the complexity of the relation between individual and world, he develops a tripartite theory of mimesis or figuration which shows how our constructive processes contribute to experience without ever being simply creative of it. Utter creativity is ruled out by the commitment (which Ricoeur shares with other authors in this Section) to the view that human experience is finite and thus, in part, dependent on forces and objects external to us. We implicitly arrange our experience in a narrative in our everyday lives and this is then taken up and detached from the particularity of experience by historians. At the third level of mimesis, the imagination of the reader allows for a new understanding of the original experiences in such a way as to open up a dialogue between the original agents and the readers or observers. The particularity of the original viewpoint is productively placed in dialogue with the more universalising perspective of the historians. The different levels of understanding are intertwined with one another and only thus is the third and most creative level of mimesis able to 'open up a fictitious world' which is nevertheless a world. Linking understanding to imagination does not lead Ricoeur to eliminate the more objectivising tendency of explanation, but rather to insist that both are necessary for our attempts to understand the social world. In Dardé's discussion of Ricoeur's ethical work, she shows how he again makes use of a narrative strategy. He develops an account of personal identity as both interior and publicly discernible, thus allowing for an understanding of 'oneself as another' and the 'other as oneself'. Ethics cease to be abstract when the mediation between individuals is facilitated by the establishment of concrete institutions which ensure justice. These are based on a contract which he presents as 'fictitious' but facilitating real effects in the world. Ricoeur is no complacent liberal: he insists on the value of utopian thought as a source of social critique. The real is not necessarily rational, but it can become so, as Hegel also put it, in what must count as a rather Kantian thought.

Jim Tiles's essay on the American Pragmatists carefully details the continuities and discontinuities between these thinkers and some of their approximate contemporaries in France and Germany. Tiles shows how Peirce, who was greatly interested in

Kant, defends the reality of universals within human experience and not in some sphere of things-in-themselves, where they would be the unexperienced cause of our perceptual experiences. This is an idea very close to Kant's own claim that things-in-themselves are transcendent and thus excluded from the transcendental analysis of experience. Those who try to explain experience in terms of sensory causes count as nominalists for Peirce in the specific sense that they render reality inaccessible. For him, universals may be regarded as real just because they arise in the experience of the community of enquirers. Again, the universal is made more concrete through its being situated within, and not beyond experience. Meaning is to be sought in terms of practical consequences – that is, in the establishment of habits – which he understands as general patterns of responding to experience. However, he takes a long-term view on this process, seeing agreement as a regulative ideal rather than as a present and actual fact. The universals, which Peirce considers to be necessary for, and constitutive of, experience, are expressed in a reworking of Kant's theory of the categories. Tiles shows how Peirce shares Dilthey's emphasis on knowledge emerging within a community, while focusing on the natural rather than on the human sciences. He also shows how Peirce develops a notion that is very close to a phenomenological one of intentionality; that is, that all thought is object-directed. James, like Bergson and Husserl – despite their differences of approach – saw the goal of his 'radical empiricism' as a return to 'pure pre-theoretical experience'. James is a nominalist in Peirce's terms, looking for short-term agreement about the pure given in experience and sidestepping concerns about reality. His view of the self is a case in point, as he holds that it amounts to continuity within experience rather than anything more substantive. While James and Bergson turn towards a pure given, Dewey is more inclined to stress everyday experience. He considers Bergson's understanding of perception too passive, it being rather 'a process of determining the indeterminate'. Thus, creativity is restored to everyday life. Rorty comes closest to developing a purely immanent account, immediately linking meaning to the culture one finds oneself within. Rorty readily labels himself 'nominalist' in Peirce's sense. However, as Tiles explains, he does not do so in order to enter into a debate on the reality or otherwise of universals. Instead, he intends to resist any notion that there may be constraints on action 'which might be given an abstract articulation'. Here the rejection of abstraction is equivalent to an epistemological and ethical immanentism which has long since given up considering that the question of transcendence is important.

I hope that my hobby-horses have served as a way into engaging with these articles and the authors they discuss. Certainly other readers will discover different aspects of them. Read on!

3.1

UNDERSTANDING UNDERSTANDING: SCHLEIERMACHER

Christian Berner (Translated by Robert Vallier)

Introduction

F. D. E. Schleiermacher (1768–1834), first known as a Protestant theologian, was a distinguished philologist, the illustrious German translator of Plato, a philosopher and the contemporary of the great German Idealists Fichte, Schelling and Hegel. Like them, he taught at the University of Berlin, elaborated a philosophy or a science of spirit in its appearance, which he called 'ethics', and conceived a theory of science which he named neither a 'doctrine of science' (Fichte), nor a 'science of logic' (Hegel), but rather, recalling Plato, a 'dialectic'. It is, however, due to his reflections on hermeneutics, preoccupations which he did not consider philosophical, that he is remembered. His reflections were inherited by Dilthey, leading him to develop a critique of historical reason and also to reconstitute the moral sciences of spirit; and were later revived by Gadamer.

Schleiermacher was a Romantic thinker. His hermeneutics were founded on 'intropathy', that is, they were concerned only with the pure phenomena of expression in texts, independent of all pretention to truth. One normally attributes to Schleiermacher the merit of having formulated the necessity of a *general* hermeneutics defined as the 'art of understanding', and so of having removed the art of interpreting from the more specialised fields of ancient philology or biblical exegesis. In the perspective of such a project of generalisation, one can see Schleiermacher as the initiator of a philosophy in which human being or the fulfilment of its existence comes about as understanding, no longer simply conceived as an act of knowing, but as an authentic mode of being. One must, however, be prudent and remain wary of unwarranted assimilation: in order to grasp how Schleiermacher understands understanding, one must begin by respecting the rules of interpretation that he himself established, starting from the famous hermeneutic circle, which seeks to clarify the whole by the part, and vice versa. This means that Schleiermacher's hermeneutics will have philosophical significance only when clarified by the two elements which constitute his philosophy in his own eyes: *ethics*, which is the science of the unity of reason and of nature, and *dialectics*, which is the science of the principles of all philosophising.

The art of understanding

Hermeneutics is defined by Schleiermacher as the 'art of understanding'. Art is to be taken here in a double sense: on the one hand, it designates a technique for formulating rules which any methodical interpretation must respect; on the other hand, it is to be understood in a wider sense, referring to the activity of reflective judgement. To understand is thus an art to the extent that the rules enunciated by hermeneutics cannot be led back to other rules – that is, to the extent that there are not general rules for the application of rules. As such, hermeneutics, like all art, appeals in the last resort to the faculty of judgement. How then, in the absence of general rules, can Schleiermacher proceed to a generalisation of hermeneutics? If understanding, of which the special hermeneutic techniques speak, is always determined by the particularity of its objects, what will be the object of a general hermeneutics, and what will be the methods adapted to grasping it? For Schleiermacher, the object of hermeneutics is foreign discourse (*Rede*), be it oral or written. The latter is not only the discourse of the foreign or the strange, but all discourse which carries in it something foreign or strange. Hermeneutics does not cover all types of understanding for Schleiermacher; for example, those of the sentiments, of works of art, or even of signs in general. Discourse, or thinking oriented towards exposition, is for Schleiermacher, the exclusive object of hermeneutics. It is here that is found the ground of the philosophical aspect of his hermeneutics: the art of understanding is concerned only with those discourses that convey a content or communicate thoughts.

According to Schleiermacher, it is necessary to establish a hierarchy within the discourses as not every discourse is an object of interpretation to an equal degree: certain objects have no value for this art, while others have an extreme value, the majority of them being situated between the two. For example, propositions reporting the weather do not have value: they only maintain the existence of the language via the continuity of repetition without determining thinking in any way. Authentic interpretation is enacted only when confronted by sophisticated thinking; that is, by a discourse which has a content, the understanding of which entails the development of one's understanding. Accordingly, the art of understanding will focus on the communication and diffusion of knowledge in general – that is, it will develop the conformity of spirit to reality. For Schleiermacher, hermeneutics thus responds to the moral imperative of making knowledge public; which is familiar to us in its Kantian version. (By contrast, simple repetition, which does not require

the art of understanding, is neither ethical nor philosophical, for it in no way develops spirit.)

However, the affirmation of the necessity of a general hermeneutics runs into an immediate objection. In effect, what is its necessity if people understand before possessing this theory of hermeneutics? From childhood, simple daily understanding seems able to do without such a theory. To what then does its necessity and generality belong? Namely, to the fact that we can unexpectedly find ourselves caught up in hermeneutic operations, even before the existence of a theory which aims to capture them. For example, I may seek to discover the manner in which the passage from one idea to another came about for my interlocutor, instead of being satisfied with the ordinary degree of understanding. Hermeneutics is thus not called for in all conversations, but only in that cultivated exchange of ideas where discussions and conversations have a content that provokes contemplation.

How then to proceed concretely in hermeneutics? The object of interpretation is discourse as the objectivation of thinking and of knowing in a particular language. This process can be seen as relating two poles, depending on whether it refers to the general structure of language or to the contribution of the individual. As a result, it is a matter both of 'understanding the language' and of 'understanding the one who speaks' (Schleiermacher, 1996, p. 88). In this way, one penetrates the heart of the problem of hermeneutics, which is to understand thinking's pretention to generality, even when its origin is in the heart of an individual subject. In order to understand thinking, I must begin by understanding its medium, its condition of possibility and of achievement; that is, language. It is there that is realised what Schleiermacher calls 'grammatical interpretation', which determines the semantic objectivity and syntactic structure of language. Grammar affords knowledge of language as system: it establishes the general rules and the structures proper to a language in a given historical context. As such, it establishes a relative universality in the framework of which individuals will be able to find the possibility of understanding each other. This study of linguistic rules in general is, however, neither easy nor sufficient. Language itself is in effect historical, constantly shaped by people who participate in it while speaking it. Authentic thinking, in its very activity, which is an individual's usage of her or his own understanding, acts inevitably on language. Understanding, then, requires perceiving how the universal carries the mark of the singular, how the individual is inscribed in language and subverts the existing rules.

Understanding a discourse also has a second orientation, which seeks not to reconstruct language in general, but rather to grasp the thoughts proper to the one who discourses and her or his particular way of combining them. Schleiermacher calls this second aspect of interpretation 'technical' or 'psychological'. In taking discourse as starting from the individual who constructs it – that is, the person who speaks – technical interpretation does not seek to grasp how humans receive a language that they inherit, but rather how they transform it; that is, how discourse becomes the instrument which affirms individuality. To discover individuality in the particularity of the exposition is to discover *style*. This type of interpretation also pushes the interpreter, on the one hand, to be clearly aware of what was the origin of a writer's thoughts and motivation, and, on the other hand, depends on the former's capacity for reconstruction: the interpreter must be equal to the task of identically reconstructing the discursive construction of the author of the discourse. This aspect of interpretation takes into account that every authentic discourse brings with it something new which one must evaluate.

In both grammatical and technical interpretation, the task of the art of understanding is thus the reconstruction of the necessary structure of a 'given' discourse. Hermeneutics can thus be defined as a logic of individual discourse, since it investigates the art of thinking inflected by the subject who discourses. (This is not the place to retrace in detail the methods deployed in order to achieve this understanding. These rest on philological imperatives and are founded on the circle of understanding, the so-called hermeneutic circle. The latter affirms that one can understand the universal only by starting from the singular and vice versa, that the whole is intelligible only starting from the detail and vice versa, and requires a continuous work of correction and critical adjustment.)

To these two aspects, grammatical and technical, of interpretation, are added two principle methods: the *comparative* and the *divinatory*. The first aims at raising itself to generality by the comparison of constitutive elements; the second seeks to divine the singular and is more intuitive. Its concern is that which seems to escape every discursive approach represented by the comparative method which subordinates the particular to the general in order to achieve understanding. The two methods are put to work in each of the aspects of interpretation, and are necessarily complementary for the development of spirit. All comparison must in effect lay out fixed elements which serve as terms of comparison; yet these stable elements must, from the beginning, have been fixed in an immediate fashion, without which an infinite regression would prevent us from conceiving of any comparison whatsoever. Inversely, the comparative method must come to confirm what has been obtained by the intuition of divination. Schleiermacher's positive definition of hermeneutical work is thus as follows: 'To reconstruct the given discourse in such a way that is at once historical and divinatory, objective and subjective' (Schleiermacher, 1996, p. 328). The complementarity of methods finally enables the interpreter to understand the author better than he had understood himself (ibid., p. 288). As such, it is necessary to be conscious not only of the unconscious of the author, that is, the psychological and historico-geographical determinations of every type, but also of the unconscious of the discourse itself. Interpretation completes the work because it contributes to the determination of its meaning. To understand the text better than its author did is then an ethical imperative in that it is the appeal to the development of spirit, and this at the same time underlines the essentially dialogic dimension of thinking which links the author to the listener or reader.

The impulse to understand

As we have seen, hermeneutics has thinking for both an object and a model, and this is what grounds its generality. This generality does not mean that it is applied to a large number of objects, but only to that universal object which is thinking-in-itself present in the discourse. The individual thinking is always clarified in the light of the universal. Thus, Schleiermacher's hermeneutics finds a natural place in a philosophical perspective: understanding thoughts not only concerns the impetus (*Trieb*) of reason, but, as the development of the thinking by the interpreter, it is inscribed in the process of philosophical ethics, defined as the realisation of reason in nature, of which humans are a part.

Concretely, however, where will we find the origin of hermeneutics? Following Schleiermacher, the art of understanding in the rigorous sense begins from the fact of non-understanding. This fact is not the contingent appearance of nonsense, something that one encounters or a difficulty with which one is suddenly faced. The fact of non-understanding must be methodically constructed in accordance with the hermeneutical maxim which leads to it being posited as initial in a methodological perspective. This is for two reasons. First, the will to understand is not aroused by error or non-understanding. On the contrary, these make sense only on the assumption of a *will to understand*. The incomprehensible can appear only if I *want* to understand. The will to understand is thus at the origin of the awareness of error or of non-understanding and, as a result, this will must rule method. Second, to posit an initial non-understanding responds to a technical imperative: awareness of error or non-understanding never permits locating their origin or cause, and therefore prevents correcting them. Error or non-understanding often in effect arises from carelessness of which we are only aware much later. Therefore, in hermeneutics, non-understanding must be methodical: to want to understand a discourse is at first to act as if I did not understand it. The task of hermeneutics is the reconstruction of the necessity and the totality of the combination of thoughts. There is thus no immediate understanding in hermeneutics. At the same time, Schleiermacher recognises elsewhere that we are not always engaged in hermeneutical operations, thus ruling out calling understanding existential in Heidegger's sense. If it is thus undeniable that there is an immediate understanding in everyday life, it remains useless for resolving difficulties since it is characterised by the fact that we pay no attention to it. Understanding has a hermeneutical status for Schleiermacher only from the moment when it is reflected on and when the subject is aware of its operations. Even so, it is necessary sometimes to cultivate an immediate understanding, leafing through a work, for example, or reading its summary, and this immediate understanding takes the place of the necessary pre-understanding of all understanding. But such a pre-understanding will not be a simple prejudice, for if its immediateness is reflected on, it is found to be marked by a hypothetical indication, and, in its methodological necessity, its provisional character is something of which we are conscious. This is why, despite the reality of ordinary understanding, it is necessary to say that there are certain things that one *wants* to understand with precision.

From what, then, is derived this will to understand, which gives hermeneutics its philosophical import? For Schleiermacher, this will concerns a need of reason: if thinking is inseparable from language, it is because thinking tends to exteriorise itself, and reason is the impulse (*Trieb*) towards communication. There is no discourse without a will to communicate, and thus none without a will to be understood, without a will for exchange and for the transmission of meaning. Just like understanding, entering into discourse is the ethical movement in which, starting from oneself, one turns towards the other. In communication one presupposes the possibility of an ethical community which has the status of a regulative ideal, such that it is true that goal-oriented understanding is only rarely effective. One must always understand, then, that philosophical ethics, in the sense given to it by Schleiermacher, is the framework for the generalisation of hermeneutics. In effect, the hermeneutical work is identified with the genesis of spirit itself. Speaking of the 'affair of understanding and of interpretation', Schleiermacher writes of a 'permanent whole, being developed progressively . . . It is thinking spirit which is progressively discovering itself' (ibid., p. 446). Spirit grasps itself in understanding its own objectification in discourse. The hermeneutics of thinking is thus a privileged form of self-knowledge. This is what explains the singular limitation of hermeneutics at the very moment when, in the philosophical perspective, it raises itself to a general method. But there is also a modern sense of the 'ethics' of interpretation, which expresses the fact that all understanding is an understanding *of others*, and that others can never be dissolved entirely in the one who understands. One can never understand without respect or consideration for the alterity of the other, for only the respect of this alterity prevents me from believing that I have understood before I undertake the effort of the hermeneutic work. Prejudice is non-respect or unwarranted assimilation. Certainly, there is, following Schleiermacher, an immoral kind of understanding, which abases the other, transforming their thoughts into simple means to the end of mine – but then the other is not understood. Truly understanding implies a recognition of the other as other: this recognition is meaningful, however, only when joined to the possibility of being in a community with the other. In recognising the other as able to be understood or as worthy of being understood, I recognise a rational being with whom I can exchange ideas and with the help of whom I can come to understand myself.

Truth and dialectic

Hermeneutics thus assures the understanding of discourses; but understanding the meaning of a discourse tells us nothing of its truth, which is what philosophy seeks above all else. Is understanding a discourse not simply knowing what it says, rather than knowing whether what it says is true? Certainly, hermeneutics pretends to truth, but the 'truth' at which it aims is simply that of meaning, which can only be the first stage of any search for the truth: before knowing if a discourse reveals the truth, one must know what it means and what it 'truly' says. The subject must in this way become transparent to itself in the constitution of its discourse, and only when the meaning of the discourse is established in a univocal manner can one judge its effective truth by comparing it with reality. If discourse is the accomplishment of thinking in its communicative dimension, then the essence of thinking is the power of being communicated, that is, of being understood by others. Language thus becomes the central and unique place of the appearance of spirit. Thus it is here that we find the synthesis of reason and nature sought by the majority of post-Kantian systems.

However, the idea of communication would not be able to provide the hypothesis of an identical structure of thinking in people without the effectiveness of this being measured by the test of intersubjective communication. The latter then becomes one of the criteria of the scientific advance which is the object of what Schleiermacher calls the 'dialectic', and which consists in 'continually comparing singular acts of knowing to the means of the discourse until an identical [adequate] knowing comes forth' (Schleiermacher, 1981a, p. 88). However, even if the dialectic seeks the production of knowledge, this is initially inscribed in a historical perspective, for understanding a discourse is also understanding a language in its becoming, as the meaning of words are never definitively fixed. Knowing, itself linked to the relativity of linguistic reason, is thus also historical. It is irremediably linked to sedimentations which mark language in its evolution and bears the trace of the traditions within which it emerges.

Because Absolute Knowing is not human, we are, following Schleiermacher, condemned to confine ourselves to the intersubjective verification of our thoughts. The result is that knowing and philosophy are formed in a community where thoughts are exchanged: to form concepts aimed at the truth is to form them with others, and here the idea of community finds a theoretical ground. As a result, the necessity of dialogue on the one hand, and that of conflict on the other, are justified for the individual: one must suppose initial differences between my representations and those of the other in order to engage in a dialogue that aims at overcoming them.

We find here a new definition of philosophy by Schleiermacher: it is dialectical and aims at the construction of knowledge; that is, the constitution of a discourse about reality. In order to achieve this, hermeneutics as the art of understanding is necessary. In effect, thinking can become knowledge only because it is communicable, and this linguistic necessity at the same time limits the pretension of thinking to universality. All discourse is a process of individuation in language at several levels, from the particularity of the historical language to the specificity of the individual. However, since it must be understood, all discourse implies a process of mutual understanding and dialogue. Consequently, hermeneutics as the art of understanding is once again required since the individual reconstitutes the thinking of an other only in interpreting her or him. Even the author constitutes her or his discourse in interpreting herself or himself, in giving body to the meaning (*vouloir-dire*) and the will to signify, which is equivalent to the will to be understood. Making oneself understood is thus initially rendering oneself comprehensible, and the discourse is helped by the other's initial interpretation founded on the same will to understand and be understood.

Dialectic, as a dialogical art of thinking, thus finds, according to Schleiermacher, its natural complement in hermeneutics. Hermeneutics must allow for the overcoming of the relativity of thinking without succumbing to the illusion of universality, since it takes account of the irreducibility of the individuality of every discourse. However, at the same time, it presupposes an identity of reason in everyone, as the condition of the possibility of being understood. In this, it guards itself just as much against a radical scepticism as against a pure relativism. If hermeneutics moves in the domain of relativity, linked to the individuality of discourses, then it is at the heart of language itself that it forges the means for surpassing relativity. Hermeneutics takes account of individuality and historicity by distinguishing the general from the particular, and, in this way, participates in the constitution of the two. This complementarity of the perception of the general and the particular is only the expression of the necessity of the critical moment, which makes it possible to extract the difference or the irrationality which inhabits thinking, in making it an object of knowledge. This does not signify that knowledge of the difference by itself suppresses the difference and renders the critique irrelevant; historicity and the individual of knowledge remain inevitable for the person seeking to think truthfully and seriously.

Conflict and argument

Hermeneutics is of significance to philosophy because, as humanity is rational and finite, understanding becomes a constitutive moment of cognition and knowledge 'de la connaissance et du savoir'. Hermeneutics and the theory of knowledge are thus intimately linked. Only on this ground does dialectics, which is this theory of knowledge, develop one of its fundamental categories: conflict (*Streit*). Conflict is the absolute starting point of the dialogue which must allow for the construction of true thinking. Moreover, 'conflict is the proper form in which to conduct dialogue in the domain of pure thinking, and is the presupposition of all dialectic' (1988, p. 136). And if it is not a matter of establishing knowledge as a system, it is at least necessary to develop the method which aims at this knowledge, in the form of a technique of the mastery of conflicts. Hermeneutics is a fundamental premise in this process. Conflict, in effect, presupposes understanding in order to establish the identity of the object to which representations or thoughts will be compared; such conflict is, moreover, inevitable, due to the relativity of thinking linked to both language and the individuality of the thinking subject. This is why one must begin by knowing how to recognise conflicts, and in this the role of hermeneutics is confirmed as essential for eliminating false conflicts. Not all conflicts are, in effect, dialectical, and non-understanding by itself does not signal the necessary existence of a dialectical conflict leading into a true dialogue.

Dialogue will be authentic for Schleiermacher from the moment when the interlocutors understand each other, and when the advance of thinking is made 'across the *logos*', that is, by the exchange of *arguments* contributing to the production of true thinking. Dialogue is authentic, therefore, to the extent that the *logos* is exercised purely in the theoretical field of knowledge, and not aimed at either the aesthetic satisfaction of a discourse that pleases, nor at the practical determinate effect that it produces in the audience. The obstacle met in the work of thinking arises from the fact that the arguments may be contradictory and so must be given up in the interest of the construction of true knowledge.

What slows down thinking is thus not the non understanding of opposed arguments, but, first and principally, their very existence. Two potentially compatible thoughts are in opposition as far as one and the same object is concerned: it is this contradiction which inhibits thinking and is thus constitutive of conflict, but contradiction by itself is not sufficient for engendering conflict or for putting thinking to work. In conflict, the two subjects seek to affirm contradictory determinations pertaining to the *same* object. Conflict is thus engendered by a contradiction between the representations of different cognising subjects. Understanding extends its impetus into a subjective logic showing how individuals participate in the formation of concepts and judgements which constitute thinking. In Schleiermacher, we have principally to deal with a dialectic of reflection in which his particular view of being depends on the being belonging to the subject, to its situation, or to what Schleiermacher calls its 'has-become' (*être-devenu*) and its 'being-determined-by-something-other-than-itself'.

The dialectic which strives for understanding thus aims at knowledge without sinking into a sceptical indifference in view of the diversity of representations. It does so even if the effective agreement aimed at by its work remains improbable. Dialectic is 'in truth the art of the exchange of thoughts, arising from a difference in thought without which there would be no exchange, proceeding to an agreement, without which there would be no end' (ibid., p. 8). The orienting idea is that of truth: only in its name is it possible to transcend the simple juxtaposition of thoughts which, pretending only to meaning, would amount to infinitely multipliable interpretations.

The effort of thinking is thus guided by the idea of truth, which rules rational argumentative communication and finds richness not in the number of arguments, but rather in their pertinence and commitment to the assumption that one can be superior to another. (This does not mean that Schleiermacher challenges all diversity of thought. On the contrary, he affirms its necessity in, for example, opposing the idea of a universal language and in affirming the richness of the conceptions of the world, of nature and of history that each historical language builds.) And so one captures the essence of understanding in the will to dissolve the conflict of representations – that is, in the will to establish knowledge despite its inherent linguistic limitations and the part played by already-formed individuals. The hope for agreement is thus constitutive of the will to know, even if the agreement or the end of all conflict is only hypothetical.

Conclusion

Schleiermacher strikingly summarises this philosophy in the following formula: 'ethical reason in the will to communicate even when the success is uncertain' (Schleiermacher, 1981b, p. 323). One finds here the whole problem of the relation between ethics, hermeneutics and dialectic. If dialectics, is presented as a reflection on the process of mastering conflicts 'with the assurance of success' (Schleiermacher, 1988, p. 8), hermeneutics must, on the other hand and in the light of the irreducibility of the individual, accompany the whole process of knowledge; it must, with the diversity of its methods, participate in a reconstruction that could never completely absorb the singular which it also partially constitutes. The two sides of hermeneutics are found in this movement towards the truth: the *ethical pole* facilitates the formation of the individual which becomes more transparent to itself, and the *dialectical pole* aims at the establishment of intersubjective agreement. At the beginning of the hermeneutical task, the dialectical task becomes infinite and success uncertain. What Schleiermacher calls 'philosophical ethics' is brought about at this moment, as a movement towards knowledge and towards the accomplishment of spirit in nature: to want to communicate, and thus to want to be understood and to work at it despite the infinity of the task and the uncertainty of the result.

Hermeneutics thus insists that, even if the general structure of language can be mastered, what makes for individuality – that is, the difference that Schleiermacher calls style – always remains. All communication, at the same time that it aims at being shared by others, is also self-communication or self-attestation. As such, the originality of the singular is saved in the very heart of the movement towards the absolute. In this regard, and in contrast to the systems of German Idealism, the philosophy of Schleiermacher renounces a speculative reason too assured of itself, yet without succumbing to the opposite in a simple denial of reason. Schleiermacher poses, in general and in new terms, the problem of a concept of reason which is not speculative, and he discovers it as dialogical and hermeneutical reason. In other words, Schleiermacher seeks to think the structure of reality in such a way that autonomous individualities may exist as elements of the totality rather than as simple moments of the universal. What Schleiermacher's hermeneutica philosophy testifies to is thus a reason restored to its human proportion. That is, it testifies to a reason whose path is destined to take a necessary detour via the other.

Bibliography

References and further reading

As with most of his philosophical works, *Hermeneutics* was never actually published by Schleiermacher, but was constantly reworked. The most recent complete edition is Marassi's Italian bilingual version from which translations from *Hermeneutics* in the article have been made. Marassi's version includes a full bibliography of writings and secondary works. The two partial translations of *Hermeneutics* in English (listed below) also contain useful bibliographical material.

Schleiermacher, F. D. E. (1977a), *Hermeneutics: The Handwritten Manuscripts*, trans. J. Duke and J. Forstman, Missoula, Atlanta: Scholars' Press.

— (1977b), 'The Aphorisms on Hermeneutics from 1805 and 1809–10', trans R. Haas and J. Wojcik, in *Cultura Hermeneutics*, Vol. 4, pp. 367–90.

— (1981a), *Brouillon zur Ethik* [1805–6], ed. H.-J. Birkner Hamburg: Felix Meiner.

— (1981b), *Ethik (1812–13)*, ed. H.-J. Birkner, Hamburg Felix Meiner.

— (1988), *Dialektik (1814–15). Einleitung zur Dialektik (1833)*, ed. A. Arendt, Hamburg: Felix Meiner.

— (1996), *Ermeneutica: Testo tedesco a fronte*, ed. M Marassi, Milan: Rusconi.

3.2

PHILOSOPHY OF LIFE AND HISTORICAL UNDERSTANDING: DILTHEY

Jacob Owensby

Wilhelm Dilthey (1833–1911) did not narrowly restrict his writing to what we think of today as the field of academic philosophy. On the contrary, he was a historian, biographer and literary critic. Psychology, anthropology and sociology each occupied him at one time or another, but at the centre of this diverse work lay a single, enduring project. He sought to provide what is often called a 'Critique of Historical Reason'. That is, he worked steadily towards securing an epistemological foundation for those disciplines concerned with exploring the meaning, value and purpose of human life. Dilthey called these disciplines the human sciences. There is no definitive list of the disciplines to be included but he variously mentions history, aesthetics, moral philosophy, psychology, anthropology, economics, religion, literary criticism and linguistics. Dilthey's work bore fruit in a theory of historical understanding rooted in the very structures of human life itself.

The project of a critique of historical reason

Although he never gave any of his writings the title, Dilthey, who saw himself as heir to Kant's critical philosophy, thought of his life's work as a Critique of Historical Reason. Kant's *Critique of Pure Reason* contained an epistemological foundation for the natural sciences, especially for Newtonian physics, as empirical sciences and his approach was to

demonstrate that the *a priori* conditions for experience are found in the knowing subject. Dilthey agreed with Kant that all knowledge is empirical, and so he too sought to provide the conditions for experience in order to show how historical understanding is possible; but while Kant insisted that experience is grounded in pure, autonomous reason, Dilthey argued that experience is rooted in life as it is lived. Accordingly, historical understanding rests on life as it is lived.

Life is an I–World relationship, or what Dilthey calls a life-nexus. In other words, life includes human consciousness, but is not reducible to the inner life of individual humans. Human consciousness always finds itself within a variety of larger and smaller social, historical systems. We are always already a member of such and such family, born into one or another economic class, citizens of this or that nation at a particular time in history, and so on. As a result, a Critique of Historical Reason must demonstrate how historical understanding is made possible by both the volitional, emotional, cognitive structures of humans as practical agents and the social and political systems within which these agents operate.

Dilthey's critical philosophy is designed from the start to provide a knower with real blood in her or his veins. In his view, the epistemologies of Locke, Hume, and even Kant, suffered from a one-dimensional model of the knower. While these earlier epistemologies dealt only with the intellectual and perceptual dimensions of the knower Dilthey saw that our intellectual and perceptual processes are always internally related to the will, the emotions and the instincts, and that these very processes arise in the service of practical human existence. The knower is social and historical, and this social and historical particularity makes knowledge possible. We need not strip it away in hopes of arriving at something ahistorical or *a priori*. Human life itself is thus the foundation of all knowing, and the transcendental task becomes an explication of those life-structures which make knowledge possible.

Scholars differ about the degree of continuity in Dilthey's work over the years. Still, there is consensus that his approach to the Critique of Historical Reason changed after the turn of the twentieth century. Before 1900 Dilthey used a descriptive psychology to articulate the conditions of knowledge, which he believed to be immediately given in lived experience; after 1900 he came to see the limits of description. He realised that many of the conditions of experience transcend the present lived experience. For example, our own past experiences and the social systems in which we live effect experience without being always present in experience. Dilthey came to believe that such conditions of experience could only be arrived at indirectly through the interpretation of written works. Accordingly, hermeneutics displaced psychology at the foundation of the human sciences. Let us look in more detail at these two phases of Dilthey's thought.

The earlier, descriptive approach to the Critique was announced in 1883, with the publication of the first of a projected two volumes of the *Introduction to the Human Sciences* (*Einleitung in die Geisteswissenschaften*). In this first volume Dilthey delineated the human sciences from the natural sciences and provided a brief history of the human sciences. He promised to take up the epistemological work in the second volume, which was never published but did exist in the form of two drafts. These can be found in Volume 19 of the *Gesammelte Schriften*. (Both volumes of the *Introduction* can be found together in Volume One of the *Selected Works*.) In 1894 he wrote his *Ideas Concerning a Descriptive and Analytic Psychology*. Though not necessarily intended for inclusion in the drafts of the second volume of the *Introduction*, the *Descriptive Psychology* was clearly meant to address the task of the required descriptive, psychological base of the human sciences.

Descriptive psychology differs from what Dilthey called explanatory psychology. Explanatory psychology attempts to explain experience by using hypotheses. The British empiricists, for example, assumed that experience could be reduced to simple elements. The task of psychology was thus to analyse experience into these atomic building blocks and then the psychologist would seek to explain the original connections between these elements with psychological laws such as association. By contrast, descriptive psychology begins with lived experience as a given whole. The connections between the various components of experience are always already given. Indeed, these connections are just as real as the components of experience that they join together. Psychology is thus charged with describing experience as it is given, not with explaining why experience is given the way that it is.

In the twentieth century Dilthey came to use the term 'lived experience' in a technical way to refer to experience as it is given, but in the nineteenth century he had used the term in a non-technical way. In fact, he often used the term 'inner experience' interchangeably with 'lived experience'. His point is that descriptive psychology begins with a kind of total lived experience. Experience as it is really lived is much broader than the positivists maintain. Experience certainly includes the five senses, but it also includes our feelings, values, purposes, acts of will, imagination and instincts. Indeed, the inner–outer distinction of subject's experience and transcendent world is derived from a more primordial experience. Lived experience encompasses our perceptual, intellectual, volitional and emotional acts and their correlative objects in a given, already connected whole.

At its most basic level, consciousness is self-given in what Dilthey calls reflexive awareness (*Innewerden*). Reflexive awareness is different from reflective awareness. Reflective awareness presupposes a conscious subject on one hand and an object on the other. In reflective awareness there is a distance between consciousness and its object. In reflexive awareness, however, consciousness becomes aware of itself without taking this kind of distance on itself. In other words, consciousness grasps itself without making itself into an object. One must not, however, assume that reflexive awareness is some sort of intellectual intuition. On the contrary, it more closely resembles an appropriation of one's own life. It is a pre-cognitive, felt sense of the mineness of both the acts and the objects of consciousness.

The first step in descriptive psychology is to see that not only the acts of my own consciousness (for example, seeing, hearing, thinking), but also objects, other persons and even social and historical systems are in a certain sense facts of consciousness. This is not to say that we are locked in our own experience and must find a bridge to the world beyond our minds. That was Descartes's dilemma, not Dilthey's. Instead, Dilthey means that the people and objects we encounter in our everyday experience are related to us perceptually, intellectually, emotionally and volitionally. Other people, things, social systems and the like exist independently of me, but I cannot speak of them apart from my consciousness of them.

Description of lived experience yields what Dilthey calls life-categories (*Lebenskategorien*). These life-categories are the fundamental categories for the human sciences. They are not imposed upon experience by reason, as are Kant's purely rational categories, but are immanent in life itself. They are the very structure of what Dilthey calls the life-nexus (*Lebenszusammenhang*). This unified 'I–World' relation prefigures Heidegger's notion of human existence as Being-in-the-World. Dilthey explicitly distances his notion of life-categories from Kant's purely formal categories which are the purely intellectual conditions of experience. They impose order on the otherwise disorderly contents of experience. By contrast, the life-categories articulate the order implicit in life itself. The relations which bind experience together are not only intellectual. They are also emotional, volitional and instinctual. The life-categories make explicit these representational-emotional-volitional structures. Life-categories like meaning, purpose and value articulate the human practical engagement with the world.

Description yields not only the synchronic struc-

tures of consciousness. It also clarifies the diachronic or temporal dimension of consciousness. Time is the structure of pre-reflective consciousness, the constant advance of the present. The present is neither simple nor static. It is the dynamic crossing-point of both the past and the future. Contents are constantly emerging in the present from the future and constantly draining out of the present into the past.

In addition to this pre-reflective connection of the past and the future in the present, consciousness produces reflective connections between past, present and future. According to Dilthey, we gradually develop a pre-conscious world-view on the basis of accumulated experience. He calls this the acquired psychic nexus (*psychischer erworbener Zusammenhang*). As we interact with the social, historical and natural world around us, we form concepts about the principles by which the world works and their relation to our highest values and our sense of ultimate purpose. This acquired world-view or psychic nexus provides a context within which present experiences become meaningful. By virtue of the acquired psychic nexus, we can interpret phenomena as parts of larger processes or instances of natural law. The value system and the overall sense of life's purpose contained within the acquired psychic nexus thus grants richer significance to choices made in day-to-day existence. In this way, the past and the future shape the meaning of the present.

In 1900 Dilthey began to reformulate his approach to the Critique with the essay 'The Rise of Hermeneutics'. Scholars disagree about the role that Dilthey allowed for psychological descriptions of lived experience in this later phase of his work, but it is quite clear that he came to see the limits of description. After 1900, he came increasingly to insist that the depth and breadth of lived experience emerged only in expressions (and especially written expressions) arising from lived experience. Accordingly, only the interpretation of such expressions could disclose the richness of lived experience. He thus resumed the task of a Critique of Historical Reason from this hermeneutical perspective, publishing *The Formation of the Historical World in the Human Sciences* (*Aufbau der geschichtlichen Welt in den Geisteswissenschaften*) in 1910.

There are at least two ways in which description fails to do justice to the breadth and depth of lived experience. First, description takes the present as its object but the present is itself shaped by the past and the future. The very temporality of lived experience itself means that descriptions cannot adequately grasp lived experience, because the present is constituted by the past and the future in a way which is not merely given in the present. Second, our lived experience is shaped by our participation in social, historical systems, which Dilthey calls systems of influence. These social, historical influences on our lived experience are only implicit in lived experience as it is given in day-to-day experience. They can be made explicit only by interpretation. I will discuss interpretive hermeneutics in further detail in the section on historical understanding below.

What Dilthey means by 'life'

Dilthey's critical philosophy of history is accurately called a philosophy of life precisely because life is, for him, the foundation of all knowing. But just as his approach to the Critique of Historical Reason changed with time, so too did his concept of life. It is safe to say that Dilthey always thought of life as relational, that is, as a relation between a perceiving, thinking, feeling, willing agent and the world within which that agent is immersed. This is why life is properly thought of as a life-nexus. Life is a practical relationship between agent and world. Agent and world always refer to one another.

Before 1900, Dilthey's concept of life drew largely on psychological categories. He used the language of an organism and its environment to describe the dynamic relationship between the inner life of will, instinct, feeling and perception to its correlative world. After 1900 he placed greater emphasis on the social, political, and cultural conditions for understanding.

In his earlier, psychological approach to life, Dilthey claims that life exhibits a subjective-immanent purposiveness. That is to say, the agent's inner life of feelings, will, perception and cognition stands in an adaptive, reciprocal relationship with an environment of ends, means and obstacles. Life is

purposive because adaptation occurs for the purpose of enhancing the agent's life. This purposiveness is subjective and immanent because it is given in lived experience itself. The environment contains both the means and the limits of the agent's self-preservation and gratification. Agents cognitively process stimuli received from the environment and emotionally assess them as either injurious or life-enhancing. Our emotional response to stimuli gives rise to acts of will whose intention is either to change the environment or the agent for the sake of self-preservation and gratification.

Even though Dilthey makes liberal use of the terms adaptation and reciprocity, he did not mean that life is best understood biologically. Biologists can draw data only from the five senses. Any analysis of inner life is merely hypothetical in biology. Descriptive psychology, by contrast, has immediate access to the inner life of feelings and will as facts of consciousness, because psychology begins with lived experience. The agent's inner response to the environment is given in lived experience.

This psychological analysis emphasises two basic principles of life. First, life is a dynamic continuum between inner and outer, agent and environment. Life cannot be reduced to either one or the other. Second, in the agent, perception, cognition, feeling, will and instinct are always internally related. Accordingly, the knowing subject can never be construed as a purely intellectual being. The knowing subject is at once cognitive, emotional, and volitional. In other words, thought serves life.

After 1900, Dilthey further developed the insight that thought serves life by exploring the social, communicative function of human thought and action. He came to see more clearly that the human environment consists of diverse social, historical, political and cultural systems. These systems in large part shape the meaning of life. Dilthey makes use of Hegel's term 'objective spirit' to refer to the human world of social, historical systems. For Hegel, objective spirit was a stage in the rational evolution from subjective to absolute spirit, but Dilthey appropriates the term without accepting Hegel's speculative philosophy of history. For Dilthey, objective spirit is the plurality of human products, expressions and systems of interaction. It includes family, state, language, customs, art, religion and philosophy; it has been built up by human praxis through history, but it also shapes human praxis and experience. Praxis always occurs within the meaning-granting context of objective spirit.

Objective spirit is not, however, a single, monolithic context. It is a general term used to refer to the plurality of objective, social, historical systems which shape the meaning of our words and deeds. Dilthey calls these systems (for example, language, religious institutions, artistic schools or movements) systems of influences (*Wirkungszusammenhänge*). Systems of influences shape meaning, produce values and realise goals. They provide a context within which human communication can occur by providing a set of rules delimiting the range of meaningful communicative action. We can interact with each other only by following one or another set of rules provided by a system of influences.

Historical understanding

The heart of Dilthey's Critique of Historical Reason was his theory of historical understanding. In the 1880s and 1890s, Dilthey gave a psychological account of understanding. In his twentieth-century writings, he adopted a hermeneutic approach that focused on the relationship between lived experience, the expressions that emerge from and articulate lived experience, and understanding. Let us examine these two phases of Dilthey's thought in turn.

In the 1880s and 1890s, Dilthey sought to provide a foundation for understanding by describing the psychological processes involved in it. At this stage of his writing, he held that understanding other people begins with the inner perception of our own psychological states along with the outer, or sensory, perception of our own gestures, facial expressions and so on. We understand other people through a process of analogy. Having recognised in ourselves the connections between certain gestures, facial expressions and so on, and certain psychological states, we infer the psychological states of other people by observing their behaviour. It is important to remember that Dilthey begins with lived experience. That is, he begins with experience as it is given. Experience is given as an internally-related

whole. It is organic. There are no isolated psychological elements like John Locke's simple ideas. When we are stricken with grief, for example, the tears we shed and the wrenching sense of loss and sadness that we feel are different aspects of a unified, total experience. We can differentiate the act of crying, which others can perceive, from the emotional pain, which only the grieving individual can feel but they are given to us as internally related, and this relation is as much a fact of our lived experience as the crying and the pain. Accordingly, we can quite justifiably (although not infallibly) infer that someone is sad when we see them cry. This psychological process of analogy may be more or less certain. The more we know about the larger context of the other person's life and present circumstances, the more certain we may be about the other person's psychological state.

This model of understanding is obviously devoted to our everyday understanding of contemporaries. Historians, however, rarely deal with contemporary subjects. Instead, the historian's subject matter stands at a greater or lesser historical distance. Still, Dilthey insisted that historical understanding is rooted in the everyday processes of life. However, this is not to say that he considered bodily gestures and facial expressions to be the fundamental data of historiography. Instead, he argued that historians formalise the everyday process of understanding, raising it to an analogical method for historical study.

Dilthey's own historical work centred on great figures, particularly great literary figures. Accordingly, he worked out the foundation of the analogical method of historical understanding by focusing on the psychological processes of poetic creation in *The Imagination of the Poet: Elements for a Poetics* (usually called the *Poetics*). The concept of an acquired psychic nexus is particularly important in his explanation of the poetic creative process.

The acquired psychic nexus is acquired as we accumulate experience over time. But we do more than merely store away our past experiences. Our past and ongoing experience forms within us, in a more or less pre-conscious way, a kind of world-view. The acquired psychic nexus contains within it our concepts of how the world works, our basic value system and our sense of the overall purpose of our lives. It develops gradually and changes with ongoing experience. In a manner of speaking, it is the continuing influence of the past on our present lived experience, because the significance of any present experience is derived from the larger context of our acquired psychic nexus. It is a nexus in as much as it is not merely a heap of accumulated experiences. It is, instead, a psychological whole whose cognitive, emotional and volitional parts are internally related. The relations between feelings, perceptions, concepts, goals and values are just as real as the actual feelings, perceptions and so on. In other words, we do not merely heap one past experience upon another but begin to discern typical patterns of experience. Emotions, volitions, perceptions and concepts relate to one another in recurring ways (comparable to the example of sadness and tears above). We then appropriate our ongoing experiences in the larger context of our acquired psychic nexus.

It is important to note that in a way the acquired psychic nexus is more than merely psychological. After all, it arises in the individual's practical engagement with the social, historical world. As a result, the acquired psychic nexus reflects the historical world of the individual, appropriated by that individual. So, even in this psychological phase of his writings, Dilthey held that the historical world provides our conceptual, evaluative and purposive context. Nevertheless, these historical considerations were seen through what Dilthey took to be the more fundamental categories of psychology.

The acquired psychic nexus is at work in the poet's formation of images, particularly in the imaginative process that Dilthey calls completion. Poets can do more than merely rearrange images stored in their memory. They can transform images by showing their internal relations to the inner life of feelings and will, beginning with a given image and enlivening it by filling in its emotional and volitional dimensions, or they can find images that embody given moods and feelings. When Dickens portrays life in London he uses the former strategy. Goethe takes the latter approach in *Faust*. In both cases, the poet makes explicit previously implicit relations between feelings, volition and images within their own acquired psychic nexus. Something new can be

created precisely because images are not atomic, self enclosed, unchanging particles. They are internally related to the rest of the acquired psychic nexus, and their meaning is a function of how they fit within this organic whole. Accordingly, poets can do more than simply rearrange static images. They can transform images by bringing to the fore how they are connected to the whole of the acquired psychic nexus. One can think of the poet's image as a sort of crossing-point where the many and various strands of the acquired psychic nexus meet. The poet's creative act pulls these implicit connections into a sharp focus, thus bringing her or his inner life to a clearer unity than ever before.

This theory of the creative process forms the basis for Dilthey's analogical method of historical understanding. To understand the poetic image we must let the image arouse in us the same processes that were at work in the poet in the process of creation. We can, as it were, imaginatively approximate the poet's acquired psychic nexus within ourselves, because the basic structures of the human psyche are universal. We can thus come to understand not only a historically-distant person, but also that person's social, historical context, because the acquired psychic nexus is itself psycho-historical.

The publication of 'The Rise of Hermeneutics' (1900) marked Dilthey's move away from the psychological, analogical approach to historical understanding. Dilthey continued to seek a way to understand life as lived by individuals, and he still maintained that gestures, actions, etc. embody inner psychological states. However, the process of understanding no longer starts with the interpreter's own inner life. Instead, it begins with the objectification or expressions of life, especially the written expressions of life. From 1900 to the time of his death in 1911, Dilthey came to focus increasingly on the objective conditions for understanding human expressions. His basic view was that gestures, actions and writings derive their meaning from the context within which they occur.

Expressions of lived experience

In *The Formation of the Historical World in the Human Sciences* (1910), Dilthey worked out his hermeneutics in greater detail. There he holds that the human sciences are based on the internal relation between lived experience, expression and understanding. Although he had never thought of lived experience as only the psychological processes of the individual, he had previously left his usage of the term technically imprecise. Now, he gave the term 'lived experience' a technical precision it had previously lacked. Lived experience is a matrix of relationships between a practical agent and her or his social, historical context. It is also a dynamic relationship between past, present and future. These relations *constitute* lived experience, but they are by no means all clearly *given* in lived experience. In everyday existence we matter-of-factly, but quite unreflectively, participate in a host of social, historical contexts. Furthermore, our pasts influence our interpretations of, and interactions with, other people in ways that often remain obscure to us in the moment. In short, the relations that form lived experience remain largely implicit in the present. These relations become explicit, however, in expressions.

Expressions are sensible objects but they convey a human meaning. However, this is not to say that they embody only a person's private psychological states. On the contrary, expressions also convey an impersonal meaning as a function of the social, historical contexts within which they reside. There are three kinds of expressions, and each yield a different kind of understanding.

Mathematical formulae and technical scientific propositions belong to the first class of expressions. These expressions convey a purely conceptual content which tell the interpreter nothing about the concrete lived experience of the person who uttered the expression. For example, it is unnecessary to know the life context of a person to understand what he or she means by $e=mc^2$. Two very different people from very different social, cultural and historical contexts can utter such an expression with no shift in the meaning of the expression. Since these intellectual expressions convey only a conceptual content irrespective of the speaker's concrete context, their meaning is very stable. The understanding we gain is complete, but for this very same reason our understanding is also impoverished. We learn nothing of the human condition of the speaker.

Actions – swinging a hammer, throwing a ball or opening a door – belong to the second class of expressions. Some actions, like waving good-bye or raising one's hand in class, are intended by the agent to communicate something but the actions which form this second class of expressions are not intended to communicate a meaning. Instead, they are performed to achieve a purpose. For the most part, actions of this kind are performed in a context that at least some others would recognise and with tools common to that context. For example, when we see someone standing behind the base-line of a tennis court, holding a racket, and throwing a ball in the air, we see that the purpose is to serve and presumably to win the point. The action itself embodies its purposiveness because it is embedded in a specific context. Actions thus mean something to us. We understand actions by placing them within the proper context. We also understand something about the agent, albeit something limited to a very specific context. We do not necessarily know anything about the larger circumstances of someone's life from the actions we understand within a limited context. Returning to our tennis example, we know only that the player is more or less talented and (probably) wishes to win. We know nothing of her or his religious, political, cultural or family life. Actions express only one dimension of our existence.

Works of literary genius belong to the third and final class of expression, which Dilthey calls expression of lived experience (*Erlebnisausdruck*). Expressions of lived experience make explicit the social, historical depth and temporal breadth of lived experience. Dilthey works out this third notion of expression most clearly in his later aesthetics. In the 1908 'Fragments for a Poetics' (see Volume Five of the *Selected Works*), Dilthey continues to adhere to his earlier position that poetry articulates life, but now has in mind the articulation of lived experience instead of the inner life of the individual. This leads to a change in his conception of this articulation process and his theory of understanding.

In the later aesthetics Dilthey abandons psychological explanations of the creative process and replaces them with analyses of the value and meaning relations found in literary expressions. Expressions are not the external representation of an individual's private psychological economy. They are the self-articulation of lived experience. Life tends to make explicit its implicit connectedness. Expressions are, as it were, a continuation of the very same life process of which lived experience is a part. Life includes the inner, private lives of individuals and their relationships with the surrounding world, but it also includes social, historical systems or systems of influences (*Wirkungszusammenhänge*). Lived experience is thus a function of larger contexts of life.

Furthermore, lived experience is temporal. The present is not a static now, but a dynamic crossing-point of the past and the future. There is an implicit unity between past, present and future. For example, walking down the hall from one room to the next involves a rudimentary sense of the temporality of lived experience. To be en route to somewhere from somewhere else requires that we hold the future and the past in tension within the present, however unreflectively. However, we seek to make more reflectively explicit the relations between our past, present and future. We seek to discern a pattern in the myriad lived experiences of the past, a pattern that accounts for how we have come to this juncture now. Lived experience is thus characterised by two impulses: the impulse to expand the variety of experiences and the impulse to unify these experiences into recurring themes. Expressions of lived experience find unity in the diversity of lived experience while retaining its richness and variety. The poet's expression draws the past into the present, as it were, using images in the present to make the temporal connectedness of life more explicit.

In his 1910 essay on Goethe (see Volume Five of the *Selected Works*), Dilthey clarified this relationship between lived experience and expression. Lived experience is a network of life-relations (*Lebensbezüge*). The individual life is a crossing-point of a multitude of purposive and evaluative relations between I and world, and lived experience is the pre-reflective and reflective awareness of these relations. Lived experience is our appropriation of these life-relations, not merely a copy of them in our consciousness.

We are all linked by life-relations to a wide range of objective, more or less encompassing, social, historical contexts. An expression of lived experi-

ence makes explicit the relationships between these systems in the life of the writer. These systems can be narrow, like the family of origin, or they can be quite broad, like social, economic class. Expressions of lived experience do not harmonise the various forces at work in a person's life. Rather, they make explicit the ways in which systems influence the individual, even if those influences stand in tension. For example, one may be caught in a conflict of duties to the State on the one hand and the Church on the other, or torn between family and career. In any event, poets, playwrights and novelists draw together the diverse threads of lived experience in expressions of lived experience. We already exist in a world of lived relations. The creative act brings this world to a level of greater determinacy in language. Expressions of lived experience do not externalise something internal. They make explicit the implicit web of lived relations within which the poet, playwright, etc., already resides.

In *The Formation of the Historical World in the Human Sciences* Dilthey continued to insist that historical understanding formalises the processes at work in our everyday social interactions. Our everyday understanding of those around us is driven by practical considerations for the most part, and we can understand each other because we share social, historical contexts. In historical understanding, we must make use of historically and culturally-distant contexts to determine the meaning of expressions but this move from common to historically-distant contexts is again only a more reflective and formalised version of everyday understanding. This becomes clearer with Dilthey's distinction between elementary and higher understanding.

Elementary understanding is at work in the mostly unproblematic communication of day-to-day life. As we navigate through our daily routines we almost automatically understand simple expressions (facial expressions, gestures etc.) and actions (swinging a hammer, for example). There is no gap between the physical sign that bears meaning and the meaning that it bears. We simply see someone waving 'hello' for instance. We are not typically puzzled by a gesture, only inferring its meaning on reflection. However, this meaning tells us nothing about the individuality of the other person or her or h concrete social, historical circumstances. At the level of elementary understanding we simply take an expression to be an instance of a regularly recurring type that occurs in contexts common to both the person who used the expression and the person who interpreted it.

Elementary understanding is as automatic as it is because the meaning of simple expressions is not derived primarily from subjective intentions. On the contrary, expressions derive their meaning from the common, practical contexts within which they occur. As infants we are placed within an already existing network of communicative contexts. We come to understand simple expressions precisely because they occur repeatedly and for the most part bear the same meaning. We are gradually oriented within a world of communicative relations.

Elementary understanding first gives way to higher understanding when communication breaks down. A gap opens up between the sensory expression and its meaning that requires reflection. We commonly encounter others who, perhaps because they are from a different region or belong to a different generation, use words and gestures in a way that is unfamiliar to us. We may find that someone's words do not match her or his facial expressions or deeds. In cases like this we grow uncertain of the expression's meaning. We recognise that the contexts we used for understanding the other person were inadequate, and we search for alternative or larger contexts by which to determine the expression's meaning.

Life involves more than passing relationships with others. In our practical existence we often need to know something of another person's character, perhaps as a function of friendship, occupational co-operation, or enmity. In any event, we need to know if others are trustworthy, competent and reliable. Such judgements involve reflection on larger contexts of life: for instance, a person's family life, religious affiliation and political leanings. This kind of understanding is never complete, and it is never certain. Like this practical higher understanding, historical understanding involves situating another person within the social, historical contexts in which he or she participates. However, in historical understanding we seek to understand someone whose contexts are historically distant from our own. In

addition, we understand our contemporaries because it is in our interest to do so – our own interests can bias our interpretations of our contemporaries. Therefore, Dilthey seeks to find a way to provide historical understanding with a kind of disinterestedness.

The highest level of understanding, and the model for historical understanding, is achieved when we take expressions of lived experience as our object. With expressions of lived experience, our understanding can become a re-experiencing (*Nacherleben*). Consider how we understand a play. We trace connections between characters, action and setting in the unfolding plot. Whereas the elementary understanding of simple expressions occurs with only an implicit reference to a whole to which they belong, 're-experiencing' can occur only by virtue of an imaginative reproduction of the temporal whole in which meanings develop. In *Nacherleben* we animate characters and setting. We recreate meanings and values in their living dynamism.

Nacherleben is the correlate of the process by which expressions of lived experience emerge. Expressions of lived experience embody the social, historical relations within which the poet or author lived. Remember that these relations are implicit in lived experience. The expression of lived experience makes these relations explicit. The poet or playwright can draw upon the life-relations within which he or she resides and transform them imaginatively into structures of life that are not merely personal. The lyric poem, for example, is more than an autobiographical portrait. It brings to focus a way of living in a certain age by articulating recurring patterns of human interaction in the concrete existence of an individual.

Nacherleben is an active but disinterested production of an aesthetic object. It can also be the disinterested recreation of a historically-distant person within her or his social, historical context. We can use another's poems, letters, official documents, second-hand reports, diaries, and so forth, as artifacts to understand her or him as a function of her or his concrete social, historical relations. Historical understanding works backwards then forwards. That is, we start with the termination of a series of actions and we trace them backwards to their beginning. We understand human life by forming it into a story, and individual expressions become significant as a function of the way the story unfolds before and after them. We must know the end of the story in order to put together the elements of the narrative. With *Nacherleben* we move in the forward direction of life as it was lived. We recreate the social, historical context and retrace the person's life as it unfolded in this context.

In *Nacherleben* we use an individual life as a sort of focal point in order to reanimate a historically-distant matrix of life-relations. We come to understand the development and interaction of various social, historical contexts by forming the life of a historical figure into a narrative. Historians, like poets, imaginatively transform their own life circumstances in order to construct a narrative world. Unlike poets, however, historians are constrained in their production of a narrative world by the expressions they seek to understand. Dilthey believed that historical imagination is disinterested because historians are not practically engaged in the historical world that they reconstruct.

Historical consciousness and world-views

Historical consciousness emerges with the philosophical use of historical understanding. Dilthey arrives at his philosophy of philosophy and formulates his final criticisms of metaphysics through the use of historical consciousness (see his 'Die Typen der Weltanschauung und ihre Ausbildung in den metaphysischen Systemen' ['The Types of World-view and their Development in Metaphysical Systems'] in Volume Eight of the *Gesammelte Schriften*). Historical consciousness shows us that metaphysical systems are not scientific systems but a kind of world-view. Metaphysical systems seek to grasp the world and human existence in a single theoretical scheme, but at bottom they are actually interpretations of life. Metaphysical world-views belong to one of three types. Each type of metaphysical world-view is derived from one of three limited perspectives on life.

Naturalism is the first world-view type. From this materialist perspective, humans are part of nature. Knowledge is derived from the five senses, and we seek knowledge to gain control of nature in order to satisfy our desires. The second type of world-view is subjective idealism. In this view, humans are moral agents. We confront the forces of nature with our free will, and we try to shape the world in accordance with moral ideals. Objective idealism is the third type. Here, reality is construed holistically. Humans are situated harmoniously in a whole that embodies the highest ideals and values. In addition to the onesidedly intellectual metaphysical world-views, there are world-views in art and religion.

All world-views share a common structure. Permeating any world-view is what Dilthey calls moods of life or *Lebensstimmungen*, the broadest categories of which are pessimism and optimism. These life-moods are not so much subjective states of mind as they are precognitive, intentional relations to the world. A *Weltbild*, or image of the world, forms the bottommost layer of all world-views. It is a representation of the world derived from experience. Theoretical models like quantum mechanics are highly sophisticated examples. Our value systems and the meanings we assign to people and things in the world form a second layer in the world-view, and it arises from the first layer. The third and final layer is the sense of life's overall purpose, which is rooted in life's system of values and meaning. (In his later essay 'Historical Consciousness and Worldviews' (see Volume Eight of the *Gesammelte Schriften*), Dilthey differentiates the metaphysical, religious and artistic world-views, and in the process shows that the representational foundation of the world-view is itself influenced by the higher layers of value and purpose.)

The representational contents of consciousness (sense data, perceptions, concepts) are always internally related to emotions and volitions, values and purposes. Metaphysical world-views lose sight of the connections between the representational, emotive and conative dimensions of consciousness, precisely because metaphysics is devoted to finding a fixed and final conceptual representation. Religious and artistic world-views exhibit greater conceptual fluidity because they emphasise a closer connection between the representational, emotional and volitional components of life.

In the religious world-view, the world image, the value system and the purpose of life are all informed b a central focus on the relation of the individual to the unseen. Fidelity to the unseen shapes one's values and purposes. The visible things becomes signs of the unseen – for example, bread and wine become the visible signs of invisible grace for Christians. The highest values and purposes of life are derived from the unseen. Accordingly, in the religious world-view, emotions and volitions, values and purposes, shape and even transform the image of the world.

Artists, and particularly poets, have the most dynamic world-view. The poetic medium is language and, as a result, poets can take as their subject matter everything that can come into human consciousness. Lyric poetry especially can show us the typical life-relations between setting, motives, actions, consequences and responses. Poets can offer insights into the inner dynamics of characters and plot unavailable to the senses. These insights into life can then change our view of the world. The poetic world-view, like the religious world-view, retains the dynamic, internal relation between our conceptual image of the world and the rest of consciousness but the poet's linguistic medium provides a more all-sided approach than that found among either religious or metaphysical geniuses. The poet's multi-dimensional approach to life works against the development of a fixed world image and a stable world-view.

Bibliography

Writings

Dilthey, Wilhelm (1914–90), *Gesammelte Schriften*, 20 vols, Vols. 1–12, Stuttgart: B. G. Teubner and Göttingen: Vandenhoeck and Ruprecht; Vols. 13–20, Göttingen: Vandenhoeck and Ruprecht.
— (1954), *The Essence of Philosophy*, trans. Stephen A. Emery and William T. Emery, New York: AMS Press, Inc. (Reprinted with permission of The University of North Carolina Press).
— (1970), *Das Erlebnis und die Dichtung: Lessing, Goethe, Novalis, Hölderlin*, 15th edn, Stuttgart: B. G. Teubner; Göttingen: Vandenhoeck and Ruprecht.
— (1977), *Descriptive Psychology and Historical Understanding*, trans. R. M. Zaner and K. L. Heiges with an Introduction by R. A. Makkreel, The Hague: Martinus Nijhoff.
— (1985–), *Selected Works*, 6 vols, eds Rudolf A. Makkreel and Frithjof Rodi, Princeton: Princeton University Press.

References and further reading

Bulhof, Ilse (1980), *Wilhelm Dilthey. A Hermeneutic Approach to the Study of History and Culture*, The Hague: Martinus Nijhoff.

Ermarth, Michael (1978). *Wilhelm Dilthey: The Critique of Historical Reason*, Chicago: The University of Chicago Press.
Hodges, H. A. (1952), *The Philosophy of Wilhelm Dilthey*, London: Routledge and Kegan Paul.
Ineichen, Hans (1975), *Erkenntnistheorie und geschichtlich-gesellschaftliche Welt*, Frankfurt-am-Main: Vittorio Klostermann.
Johach, Helmut (1974), *Handelnder Mensch und objektiver Geist. Zur Theorie der Geistes- und Sozialwissenschaften bei Wilhelm Dilthey*, Meisenheim am Glan: Verlag Anton Hain K G.
Makkreel, Rudolf A. (1975), *Dilthey, Philosopher of the Human Studies*, Princeton: Princeton University Press.
Müller-Vollmer, Kurt. (1963), *Towards a Phenomenological Theory of Literature. A Study of Wilhelm Dilthey's 'Poetik'*, The Hague: Mouton and Co.
Owensby, Jacob (1994), *Dilthey and the Narrative of History*, Ithaca, New York: Cornell University Press.
Rickman, H. P. (1979), *Dilthey: Pioneer of the Human Studies*. Berkeley: University of California Press.
Rodi, Frithjof (1969), *Morphologie und Hermeneutik. Zur Methode von Diltheys Aesthetik*, Stuttgart: W. Kohlhammer Verlag.

3.3

BERGSONIAN VITALISM

Guy Lafrance

Henri Bergson was born in Paris on 18 October 1859 and died on 4 January 1941. A professor at the Collège de France and an elected member of the French Academy, he was awarded the Nobel Prize for literature in 1927. Bergson's philosophy is contained in four major books: *Time and Free Will* (1889), *Matter and Memory* (1897), *Creative Evolution* (1907), *The Two Sources of Morality and Religion* (1932); and two smaller books: *Laughter* (1990) and *Duration and Simultaneity* (1922). He also published two other books containing a series of articles and lectures: *Mind Energy* (1919) and *An Introduction to Metaphysics: The Creative Mind* (1934).

Bergson's thought was inspired by classical ancient philosophers such as Plato, Aristotle and Plotinus; and modern philosophers such as Spinoza and Berkeley. Like many young philosophers of his time, he was fascinated by Herbert Spencer's *First Principles* (1862). However, he was soon disappointed by the weakness of these principles and reacted, against this type of mechanistic philosophy which appeared to him to be unable to grasp the significance of the 'latest ideas' of mechanics, and, more specifically, to deal properly with the notion of time. From his contact with Spencer's approach to time and movement, Bergson was very much struck at how real time 'eludes mathematical treatment'. This first intuition became the cornerstone of his entire philosophy.

Time, life and freedom

Bergson's philosophy was guided by his conception of real, concrete duration, which is opposed to abstract concepts commonly used in the sciences of physics and mathematics, and also in ordinary language. Real concrete duration expresses the movement and creativity of life more adequately, and gives a better account of the intensity of conscious states and freedom in particular. Real time or duration, for Bergson, cannot be measured in space like several separate moments on a line. That way of measuring time is not true duration since the line is complete, already made, and its different moments are immobile. Real time or duration is mobility; it is 'what is happening, and more than that, it is what causes everything to happen' (Bergson, 1970, p. 12).

When we consider a living being, we find that its deep reality is connected with time, so that time seems to be the very essence of life. Like duration, life is a flow, a change that is a continuous undivided movement, a true becoming. For Bergson, life is duration and time is life. Thus, wherever life exists, there is a kind of a register to inscribe time in it. To live means changing unceasingly in a continuous and creative movement and not in a succession of separate states succeeding one another like different points on a line drawn in space. Time so understood within duration is the stuff of which things are made; it constitutes the essence of things, the essence of life at all levels of its manifestation.

Bergson's philosophical work could be considered an attempt to demonstrate how reality is best understood when it is perceived through duration. The reality which Bergson studied through duration goes from the self, consciousness, freedom and free will, to the mind, memory, evolution of life, morality and religion. But the reality which Bergson considers to be the best manifestation of life and duration is freedom as the expression of the mind and the whole self. The link established between life and freedom represents the first step of Bergson's philosophy of time. It is the topic of his first book, as well as his doctoral thesis, devoted to the study of the immediate data of consciousness. This basic theme of Bergson's philosophy is maintained in all his subsequent works.

What, then, is the nature of this relation between life as the expression of duration and freedom in the Bergsonian perspective? As Bergson says in *The Creative Mind*, 'in the labyrinth of acts, states and faculties of mind, the thread which one must never lose is the one furnished by biology' (Bergson, 1970, p. 53). This biological thread must be understood in its broader sense, including the various aspects or dimensions of life on its higher levels of realisation or manifestation. In the first description of free acts provided by Bergson in *Time and Free Will*, his preoccupation is to present free will as the expression of the real meaning of life; that is to say, life seen as an organic whole with a deep unity. Thus, we may better understand Bergson's argument against the associationist approach which he regarded as a theory which reduced the self 'to an aggregate of conscious states' (Bergson, 1960, p. 165), leading to a complete misunderstanding of free will. To properly understand what free acts are, according to Bergson, we must be able to reach the fundamental self. Here alone can we discover the real meaning of life, for only a free act expresses the whole self and is produced by the self alone. Although freedom admits some degrees, it does not admit a partial expression of the self and it cannot be the expression of the superficial self alone. Bergson claims that 'It is the whole soul, in fact, which gives rise to the free decision, and the act will be so much the freer the more the dynamic series with which it is connected tends to be the fundamental self' (Bergson, 1960, p. 167). This Bergsonian distinction between the superficial self and the fundamental self aims at expressing more adequately the different levels of life and freedom. The superficial and external self does not really belong to us; it belongs as much, if not more so, to society as to ourselves. This explains its static and conformist character, which is adapted to practical social life, language and communication; whereas the fundamental self is directly connected with freedom, life and pure duration. With this distinction we can understand the importance given by Bergson to the necessary reflective effort to reach within oneself to the fundamental self associated with the birth and growth of free will. True freedom, for Bergson, must be the expression of the whole self in so far as it reaches the depth of conscious life and creative duration. As a consequence of this, free acts are exceptional, and many live and die, according to Bergson, 'without having known true freedom' (ibid., p. 166).

This holistic conception of freedom is based on a Platonist vision of the soul, with Plato's notion of the 'whole soul', becoming 'the entire self' in Bergson's analysis. Free acts must be the expression of our 'whole personality' and should not be distinct from it, having the kind of resemblance which one sometimes finds between 'the artist and his work' (ibid., p. 172). The unity of the self, or the entire self, makes possible the autonomy of the self. Consequently, freedom is the result of the unity and autonomy of the self. So understood, every free act which springs from the entire self and from the self alone, in expressing our personality, is truly free, since, as Bergson says, 'our self alone will lay claim to its paternity' (ibid., p. 173).

In order to express more adequately the real meaning of freedom as deriving from the organic unity of the self, Bergson repeatedly uses biological metaphors in his arguments against those believers in free will who define it as the equal possibility of two contrary actions (something which could be represented by the spatial image of the forking of a road). That way of defining freedom reveals, according to Bergson, a geometrical symbolism of a mechanical kind and a self that perceives itself only through space. Such a mechanical conception of freedom leads naturally to determinism. Real freedom is something else; it must be sought in a certain quality of action itself and not in relation to possible choices already defined in advance. This is why freedom is more adequately expressed by images and metaphors than by intellectual concepts and mechanical definitions. For Bergson, biological images, in particular, are the most useful, and most frequently used, to express the true meaning of freedom. As an example of this, upon arriving at a first conclusion from his argument against the geometrical representation of free acts, Bergson makes the comparison between free will and an over-ripe fruit. This comparison aims at excluding all forms of dualism to represent free acts. For Bergson, freedom is a whole and unique movement like the unity of the self 'which lives and develops by means of its hesitations, until the free action drops from it like an over-ripe fruit' (ibid., p. 176).

This kind of biological metaphor is also used repeatedly by Bergson in his analysis of laughter. Bergson's thesis on laughter and the comic is that laughter is fundamentally a social gesture and the consequence of a misadaptation to social life. The misadaptation or maladjustment in another is commonly perceived by us through the other's mechanical movements or gestures, stiffness of the body, automatism, and any kind of behaviour that express a certain rupture from social life, a distraction from life. Again, we are dealing with mechanism superimposed on life; something mechanical grafted on to something living, a movement without life. Laughter is a reaction of society to this situation; it is a reproof from society which highlights the absentmindedness of the movement of life. Actual life, including social life, for Bergson, is everchanging continuity, irreversible progress, undivided unity. This is why it is serious, as is freedom. What makes the seriousness of life is precisely our freedom. It comes from 'the feelings we have matured' and 'the passions we have brooded over', to use again Bergson's biological metaphors. Since these feelings, actions and passions come from us and are our very own, they give life its serious, and sometimes dramatic, aspect. But all this could be transformed into a comedy when 'our seeming freedom conceals the strings of a dancing-jack' (Bergson, 1937, p. 79). It is no longer life, but automatism imitating life, which belongs to the comic.

In order to specify his conception of freedom in its relation to life and duration, Bergson gives it a sense which lies somewhere between freedom and free will. On the one hand, since freedom consists in being entirely oneself, in acting in conformity with oneself,

this would be then, to a certain extent, the moral freedom discussed by philosophers; the freedom of the wise person who obeys only herself or himself, the independence of the person towards all that is not herself or himself. Bergson does not completely deny this conception of freedom because, for him, freedom consists in obeying only oneself. He could not, however, fully accept this definition of freedom. For even though obeying only oneself means to be independent, this type of independence is not exclusively moral. Moreover, the freedom of the wise person could lead to slavery, it could mean dependence upon dead reason. Such moral freedom could be an obedience to fixed ideas, and in this case, to obey only oneself does not mean to obey the whole self. Accordingly, Bergson could not fully accept this conception of freedom, although he keeps one dimension of it. His main hesitation about the moral freedom of the wise person concerns the fact that it is not sufficiently alive. This type of freedom could easily lead to auto-repetition and does not necessarily follow the continuous and creative movement of life.

Hence, Bergson considers his conception of freedom to be closer to the definition of free will. Free will is the freedom of a person who is able to choose equally between two opposites. This type of freedom implies a certain innovation with the idea of choice, but the kind of innovation involved is not wholly creative, because a choice is made between possibilities which are defined in advance. These possibilities are conceived according to the pattern of previous situations; they are possibilities which are conceived according to a general type, making them the equivalent of essences. This type of definition is too abstract, too intellectual and too rational. It is seriously mistaken about the nature of time, and not fully in accordance with living reality. It is an artificial reconstruction which does not fully express the whole person. Free will, as it is usually defined, also reveals a kind of rupture between the future and the past. A rupture which destroys the profound dependence of the becoming-self upon the past self. This is why Bergson situates his conception of freedom at an intermediate position between moral freedom and free will, but an intermediate position which is closer to free will than to moral freedom.

For Bergson, true freedom is like life and duration. It is unforeseeable innovation and continuity at the same time. The Bergsonian conception of freedom is, first of all, an affirmation of the plenitude of the self; it is the in-depth expression of the person. So understood, freedom reaches down to the dimension of life itself, of duration and creativity: 'to act freely', as Bergson says, 'is to recover possession of oneself, and to get back into pure duration' (Bergson, 1960, pp. 231–2). This is why 'man is all freedom', and free acts proceed from this living totality in the same manner as a ripening in the biological sense of the term. Consequently, a free act cannot display a division between two selves since it fully integrates being and action into deep personality as a kind of organic relation.

However, true freedom, as Bergson sees it, is much more than a simple identification with the whole self and an expression of the autonomy of the person. It is action and creation, like artistic activity and life in its most advanced developments. Therefore, freedom should express the different movements and levels of life. With this in mind, Bergson's two books on *Matter and Memory* and *Creative Evolution* may be read as a history of life and freedom.

Mind and body

In *Matter and Memory*, the studies concerning the function and the meaning of the body in the phenomena of memory and perception are quite revealing of Bergson's conception of freedom and its connection with life and duration. Although the dualism of mind and body is clearly stated at the beginning of the study, it becomes progressively evident that what Bergson is interested in is the interrelation and the unity of body and mind, that is, precisely those functions which best express freedom in its involvement in life. The body, in particular, is considered an instrument of choice, actively participating in the unity of the self and real freedom so that freedom is neither a pure creation nor a mechanical composition. It is something in between, involving at the same time continuity and innovation, and revealing the double dimension of the human being. This is why the free act, in this sense, may be termed a 'synthesis of feelings and

ideas' (Bergson, 1962, p. 243). Moreover, freedom, or free will in the sense that Bergson gives to this expression, is closely related to the functions of the body according to the particular function that Bergson assigned to the brain and nervous system. Through the phenomena of memory and perception, the brain acts as an instrument of choice in selecting images and actions. The brain, according to Bergson, makes free actions possible by establishing the connection between matter and spirit, between the past and the future, and between continuity and creation. Thus, free actions are neither totally undetermined, nor do they amount to pure creativity *ex nihilo*. They are deeply rooted in life, biological life, which has different levels of indeterminacy according to the different relations between spirit and matter. The degree of freedom is directly related to the level of indeterminacy. Consequently, the level of freedom of actions is linked to the greater or lesser tension of their duration which expresses their 'intensity of life' (ibid., p. 279). In using the word 'tension' Bergson aims to express the creative action of Spirit on matter. But instead of matter being merely passive, the combination of both poles, that is, matter and Spirit, gives use to a two-sided relation which counts as a 'tension'. Freedom aimes within and not either in contrast to or on one side of this tension.

Bergson's thesis on freedom thus seems to be perfectly in tune with his conception of duration and life. In those three aspects of reality – life, duration and freedom – there is a continuous movement going from pure matter to pure spirit. Real duration, as real life and real freedom, is a mixture of matter and spirit. The degrees of life and freedom are located between these two extreme points. The highest levels of life and freedom are reached in the direction of spirit, and it is the more complex organisation of the nervous system that makes this possible. Therefore, there is, according to Bergson, a direct relation between the degree of freedom and the close relation that spirit has with matter: 'between brute matter and the mind most capable of reflexion', says Bergson, 'there are all possible intensities of memory or, what comes to the same thing, all the degrees of freedom' (ibid., p. 296).

The studies presented by Bergson on the phenomena

of perception and memory reveal a particular conception of the mind–body relationship. The body is presented as a centre of action as it is organised for action. In perception, the nervous system and the brain, in particular, perform this function of action and selection. The body is the actual present contact with the world of objects, but it is incapable of real continuity in perception without the help of memory. For Bergson, then, there is no real perception without memory. A pure perception would be an instantaneous perception, wholly in the present, as a pure memory would be wholly in the past. Real perception takes place in time and duration which includes the present and the past. 'It is indisputable', Bergson says, 'that the basis of real, and so to speak instantaneous, intuition, on which our perception of the external world is developed, is a small matter compared with all that memory adds to it' (Bergson, 1960, p. 70). Since memory plays an essential role in perception, Bergson suggests an interesting distinction between two forms of memory. One is simple or passive memory, keeping the images of the past; the other is more active in establishing the connection between the present and the past, like the development of a habit. When we learn a lesson by heart after reading it and repeating it a certain number of times, there is progress culminating in the words making a continuous whole. At that moment the lesson is said to be known by heart. It is fixed and imprinted in our memory.

But let us look more closely at the distinction between reading to learn the lesson and the lesson itself when it has been learnt. The memory we have of the lesson is different from the memory of the reading, although we are referring to the same words and images. Specifically, the former 'has all the marks of a habit' (ibid., p. 89). This is so because, like a habit, it is acquired by effort and repetition. This type of memory is what Bergson calls habit-memory. In contrast, the memory of each reading necessary to learn the lesson 'has none of the marks of a habit' (ibid., p. 90). Each reading is complete by itself, it is unique and like an image occupying its own place in time with all the details. It is an immediate representation of a reality grasped instantaneously as a whole. This kind of memory Bergson calls memory-image. The distinction between these

two kinds of memory is fundamental, according to Bergson, since the memory-images store up the past and make possible the recognition of a perception already experienced and is relatively passive; the habit-memory is 'always bent upon action', it makes the connection between the past and the present and looks for the future. It is (with the support of memory-images) what makes true perception in time really possible. 'In truth', Bergson says, 'it no longer *represents* our past to us, it *acts* it; and if it still deserves the name of memory, it is not because it conserves bygone images, but because it prolongs their useful effect into the present moment' (ibid., p. 93).

As significant as the distinction between these two forms of memory is their relation to one another. Indeed, they are not wholly separate things, being essentially complementary and mutually supportive. The memory-images offer the elements of the past which need to be connected with present action in order to make them alive; just as the habit-memory which is directly connected to action needs the support of the past images to give action its living dimension in time. The quality of human perception relies on the precision with which these two memories are connected. This is where, Bergson says, 'we recognize a "well-balanced" mind, that is to say, in fact, a man nicely adapted to life' (ibid., p. 198).

The conclusion of *Matter and Memory* gives a kind of synthesis of the dialogue between mind and matter, (of which Bergson saw a particularly intense co-operation in the phenomena of perception and memory). Again, the basic thought is that freedom follows the movement of life which adopts all the various forms of organisation between spirit and matter, starting from the highest degree of creativity (in the direction of spirit) and ending at the doors of necessity (in the direction of matter). In the case of a human being, in particular, the greater complication of the nervous system makes it possible acts whose indetermination will pass more easily through 'the meshes of necessity' (ibid., p. 332). As a consequence of this, the human being has a more developed conscious life and a greater power of choice and decision than other animals but human freedom still needs to proceed in conjunction with the brain and memory. It is this necessary co-operation to which Bergson refers in claiming that

> whether we consider it in time or in space, freedom always seems to have its roots deep in necessity and to be intimately organized with it. Spirit borrows from matter the perceptions on which it feeds, and restores them to matter in the form of movements which it has stamped with its own freedom. (ibid., p. 332)

Freedom, as Bergson sees it at work in the phenomena of memory and perception, is always a freedom operating in space and in time, and this freedom thus expresses organic life, at least as long as life means to choose and to create without forgetting the accumulated past. For Bergson, then, freedom appears with life, so much so that it is considered to be an essential character of the living being who must choose and even create. So understood, the history of life is thus linked with the movement of freedom, or with what Bergson calls the current of spirit, passing through matter and pulling it away from pure determinism. The levels of indetermination of matter correspond to the different tensions of life and so to the several degrees of liberty.

The evolution of life

Creative Evolution is probably the best expression of Bergsonian vitalism, not only for the theory of evolution based on the *élan vital* or vital impetus developed in the book, but also for the theory of knowledge which is inseparable from that theory. For a good understanding of these two key theories, it is useful to keep in mind Bergson's criticism of Spencer's mechanistic position expressed in his conception of time and movement. This criticism aims at a particular theory of knowledge and leads Bergson to develop an alternative based on a distinctive theory of intuition and theory of evolution of life.

Bergson's theory of knowledge is couched in terms of a distinction between intelligence and instinct, and it is deeply rooted in biology. Before considering the whole problem of the evolution of life Bergson raises the reflexive question concerning the capacity of human intellect to do so: since human intellect is itself a product of the evolution of life, how can it

adequately embrace life 'of which it is only an emanation or an aspect' (Bergson, 1983, p. x)? Intellect, for Bergson, is a dimension of life, which has been created and 'deposited' by life in the evolutionary movement; how, then, could intellect pretend to embrace its own creator? 'As well contend that the part is equal to the whole, that the effect can reabsorb its cause, or that the pebble left on the beach displays the form of the wave that brought it there' (ibid.).

Through the examination of the genesis of human intellect, Bergson questions the function of knowledge, the practical function and the speculative function of human intellect. It is clear, for Bergson, that human intellect is first of all a practical function. It is the practical function of *Homo faber* who deals with the necessities of life and practical action. Consequently, the intellect feels most at home when dealing with solids and inanimate objects. Its proper tools are concepts and logic which 'have been formed on the model of solids' (ibid., p. ix). This explains why intellect is at home when it operates with matter and those sciences related to matter, such as geometry, physics and mathematics. In being required by practical action the intellect is also defined by it. It is essentially a tool for action and that also explains why it aims at fabrication, not only of material things, but also of social life (for example language).

However, human intellect is also speculative and analytical. This makes it, in a sense, quite different from instinct which is determined and almost invariable. By contrast, human intellect is variable in the sense that it does not have any definite proper object. Moreover, it is capable of producing ideas and reflection or speculation, made possible by words and language. This is what Bergson calls the 'supplementary' and 'disinterested' work of intelligence, which becomes a 'faculty of representation' and a 'creator of ideas' (Bergson, 1983, p. 159); it is the birth of *Homo sapiens*. The difficulty begins, according to Bergson, not when the intellect 'troubles itself about theory', but when 'its theory would fain embrace everything, not only inanimate matter, over which it has a natural hold, but even life and thought' (ibid., p. 160). Bergson's verdict on the capacity of intellect to comprehend life is rather negative: 'The intellect', he says, 'is characterized by a natural inability to comprehend life' (ibid., p. 165). In order to really understand life, we would need a better instrument of knowledge than the human intellect.

The alternative, then, seems to be instinct. In his analysis of instinct, Bergson presents it as a function closer to life than to the intellect. It is, as he says, 'molded on the very form of life' and it proceeds 'organically' (ibid., p. 165). Like intellect, instinct is a product of life evolution, but it is more common to living beings than intellect. In that sense, it is a faculty of knowledge which is more natural and more innate in living beings than intellect. Moreover, it is a knowledge which bears on things in a very specific and immediate way. Indeed, according to Bergson, instinct provides an 'intimate and full' knowledge of particular things. Intellect, by contrast, is the knowledge of a form, and consequently, it is an 'external and empty knowledge' (ibid., pp. 149–50).

This comparison between intellect and instinct may give the impression that Bergson despises human intellect and admires instinct. In fact, he claims that these two forms of knowledge are complementary, but that each alone is insufficient to comprehend life. The best instrument of knowledge should be a mixing of instinct and intellect. While the human being is not a purely instinctive creature (like other animals) it has nevertheless kept some instinctive capacities, capacities which can be developed and made reflective with the help of intelligence. The result would be an intermediate faculty or capacity of knowledge which Bergson calls 'intuition'. Intuition would have neither the rigidity or the narrowness of instinct nor the formal abstractness of intelligence. Bergson formulates the hypothesis that this more extensive power of knowledge actually exists somewhere in an 'indistinct fringe' formed around the intellectual concept (ibid., p. 46). The existence of this power is known to us by the fact that 'we do not *think* real time. But we *live* it, because life transcends intellect' (ibid.).

The Bergsonian theory of intuition has been much discussed and very often misunderstood. For an adequate understanding of it we have to keep in mind that Bergson wanted to make us aware of the possible errors arising from the too-rigid concepts of intellect; while wanting to maintain belief in the human capacity for acquiring genuine knowledge of the meaning of life and evolution through intuition. What, then, is Bergson's definition of intuition? 'By intuition I mean instinct that has become disinterested'. Bergson says, 'self-conscious, capable of reflecting upon its objects and of enlarging it indefinitely' (ibid., p. 176). The expressions used by him to define intuition are 'direct vision', 'contact', 'coincidence', 'sympathy' and 'immediate consciousness' (ibid., p. 32, p. 161). As an example of intuitive knowledge, Bergson refers to the experience of the self: 'There is at least one reality which we all seize from within, by intuition and not by simple analysis', he says, it is our own person in its flowing through time, the self which endures' (ibid., p. 162). It is clear from this quotation that intuition bears upon internal duration. It is also much more in the direction of spirit than in the direction of matter, but it does not exclude matter as long as matter could be grasped by spirit. 'Intuition is what attains the spirit, duration, pure change', says Bergson, 'its real domain being the spirit, it would seek to grasp in things, even material things, their participation in spirituality' (ibid., p. 33). Therefore, intuition is distinguished from intellect by its object, and it is in virtue of this that it is the proper 'tool of knowledge' for comprehending life and duration. Intuition is, for Bergson, the proper tool to build a metaphysics of life which is the first objective of *Creative Evolution*. This objective is summarised by Bergson in the following question: 'If every living thing is born, develops and dies, if life is an evolution and if duration is in this case a reality, is there not also an intuition of the vital, and consequently a metaphysics of life?' (ibid.).

Bergson presents his metaphysics of life as an alternative point of view to the Lamarckian theory of evolution – in particular to its radical finalism and mechanism. Without rejecting finalism entirely, Bergson suggests that it should be modified in such a way as to include real duration in life, which means true creativity and true evolution. The fundamental modification proposed by Bergson is that finalism should exclude all fixed ends or targets to be reached by life. If there is any finality to be kept, is should be an initiating finality, like a *vis a tergo* or an original impulse given to life at the beginning without any precise predefined or fixed plan. Although keeping the idea of an harmonious world, Bergsonian finalism considers the harmony 'rather behind us than before' since the harmony resides in the complementarity of diverse tendencies. Harmony, then, relies on an 'identity of impulsion' given at the start by the vital impetus and not on a 'common aspiration' (ibid., p. 51). This kind of harmony admits of considerable discord since it does not assign to life a pre-existing plan which is supply to be realised, but instead leaves to life its creative movement which really progresses and endures in time. The Bergsonian theory of evolution and vitalism must be seen essentially as a divergent evolutionism; that is to say, a conception of life as a creation renewed unceasingly and constantly producing new forms of life.

Bergson's theory of evolution presents life as a unique vital impetus given at the outset, but immediately meeting the resistance of innert matter which serves as an obstacle to be overcome. In meeting matter, the impetus is split in several divergent tendencies or directions developed 'in the form of a sheaf' (ibid., p. 99), and representing the different forms of organic life from vegetative life,

to animal and human life. However, the evolution of life, according to Bergson, is not pure creative activity since life is not pure consciousness. Nor is it only 'a movement forward', because it is confronted with the resistance of matter; 'in many cases', Bergson says, 'we observe a marking-time, and still more often a deviation or turning back' (ibid., p. 104). But the vital impetus is not stopped by matter, it seizes upon it and 'strives' to introduce into it the largest possible amount of indetermination and liberty' (ibid., p. 251).

Even though life movement is slowed down and stopped in many divergent ways, the vital impetus follows its path and succeeds in two main directions which are represented by instinct and intelligence; but the difference between these is radical. Bergson says, since animal instinct is routine and automatic while human intelligence is conscious and free. Instinct for the animal is like a chain which can be pulled and stretched but can never be broken. With man, by contrast, 'consciousness breaks the chain. In man, and in man alone, it sets itself free' (ibid., p. 264). Humanity, in this sense, continues the vital movement for which Bergson foresees no end; a possible victory of humankind over every resistance, perhaps even over death.

Bibliography

Writings

— Bergson, Henri (1920), *Mind Energy*, trans. H. Wildon Carr, New York: Holt.
— (1932), *The Two Sources of Morality and Religion*, trans. R. Ashley Audra and Cloudesley Brereton, with the assistance of W. Horsfall Carter. Garden City, NY: Doubleday and Company, Inc.
— (1937), *Laughter*, trans. Cloudesley Brereton and Fred Rothwell, New York: The MacMillan Company.
— (1960), *Time and Free Will, An Essay on the Immediate Data of Consciousness*, trans. F. L. Pogson, Harper and Brothers, New York.
— (1965), *Duration and Simultaneity*, trans. Leon Jacobson, Indianapolis, Indiana: Bobbs-Merrill.
— (1967), *Matter and Memory*, trans. Nancy Margaret Paul and W. Scott Palmer, London: George Allen and Unwin, Ltd.
— (1970), *The Creative Mind*, trans. Mabelle L. Andison, Totowa, NJ: Littlefield, Adams and Co.
— (1983), *Creative Evolution*, trans. Arthur Mitchell, University Press of America.

3.4

UNDERSTANDING AS DIALOGUE: GADAMER

Jean Grondin

Introduction

If one were asked to put in a nutshell Hans-Georg Gadamer's contribution to philosophy, one would have to say that it lies in the development of a philosophical hermeneutics. But this would only invite the further question: what is hermeneutics? Following Gadamer's own practice, the answer to this question would have to draw on the long history of hermeneutics. Hermeneutics used to be – and for some still is or should be – a discipline that offered guidelines (rules, canons, precepts) for the correct interpretation of texts. As long as texts, or discourse in general, presented no challenge to interpretation, there was really no need for such an auxiliary discipline. The immediate context and meaning of the texts were evident in themselves and did not require the interplay or 'mediation' of any hermeneutic reflection. It is only when difficulties, ambiguities or inconsistencies arise, or a temporal distance needs to be bridged, that one requires a hermeneutical mediation. In ancient times, this mediating function of hermeneutics was etymologically associated with the mediator-god Hermes – although the etymological link between the name Hermes and the Greek word *hermeneuein* (mediation, interpretation, explanation, understanding, translation) has been cast into doubt by recent research, but this new discovery perhaps only casts doubt on the reliability of etymological insights themselves. Nevertheless, the 'hermetic' element in hermeneutics is worth pondering, for that which we seek to understand is always something that also resists understanding, that retains an intriguing, incomprehensible element.

Traditional hermeneutics, then, understood itself as a mediating tool that could help sort out the meaning of texts or traditions which were no longer self-evident. It is therefore unsurprising that traditional hermeneutics was mostly preoccupied with religious or sacred texts whose meaning was, or had become, uncertain and ambiguous. How could it be otherwise since they used a corporal, physical language to express spiritual realities? This distinction between body and spirit consequently became one of the favourite metaphors of the hermeneutic tradition. To understand the meaning of a text was to understand its spirit, to leap from the bodily, literal sense to the spirit or thought behind it. Such a practice equated hermeneutics with the deciphering of allegorical meaning and interpretation. For allegorical interpretation, a literal text actually aims at something different from what it is openly stating (*allo agoreuein*); through a physical language, it points to something higher, something spiritual.

The most basic definition of hermeneutics offered by the entire tradition was that it consisted in the 'art of understanding'. It is in this sense that Friedrich Schleiermacher spoke of hermeneutics as a '*Kunstlehre des Verstehens*' an art of understanding but he was only summing up the main purpose of the hermeneutic discipline from its inception as an *ars interpretandi*. The German term *Kunstlehre* used by the tradition in which Schleiermacher stands is, however, a tricky one and probably has no equivalent in any other language. It is clearly the German translation of the Latin word *ars* as in 'art of comprehending', but *Kunst* would itself suffice to translate *ars*. *Kunstlehre* adds a theoretical, doctrinal, but also more technical, element to the mere notion of *Kunst* or art. Literally, *Kunstlehre* would be the doctrine of an art. This sounds cumbersome, since it seems to imply that there is no art (in this case no artful understanding) without a doctrine of this art. But is this really the case? Can one only practice an art if one also has a doctrine of how this art functions? Therein lies Gadamer's modest question – and challenge – to the hermeneutical tradition of modernity.

Let us see how this applies to the case in point, the art of understanding that is hermeneutics. Is there such a thing as a *Kunstlehre*, say, a 'methodology' of understanding? That would be a useful tool indeed and would certainly respond to a widespread desideratum in this disoriented world of ours into which we are thrown without being given a fully secure grasp on things. The question: how are we to understand? is universal enough and is certainly not restricted to sacred texts. As Hans Blumenberg argued in his 1981 book on *The Readability of the World*, in modern times the entire universe came to be seen as a text with some meaning (the 'book of nature'), but this also became true of our own lives. Indeed, the question of the meaning of life presupposes that life has been 'hermeneuticised'; that it can be interpreted, deciphered, acquire deeper meaning, and so on. The answer to the question 'how are we to understand ourselves?' would certainly provide much-needed orientation. This also explains why so many techniques of understanding are offered by so many 'specialists' of understanding in all walks of life, but also on the more general issue of 'the meaning of it all'. This leads to the proliferation of what one could call the 'how-to' books: how to become rich, how to write a philosophical dissertation, how to talk in public, how to become a good teacher, how to be a good lover, etc. The how-to literature is immense and probably boundless. One could say that all these techniques of understanding

profess to offer a hermeneutical *Kunstlehre*, the doctrine of an art.

The basic, simple question of Gadamer is whether hermeneutics can be such a technical discipline, whether this very idea of a *Kunstlehre* in the case of understanding is not a delusion after all. He asks, in other words, if this idea of an understanding-technique is not a distortion of what understanding (and its art) is all about. But what is understanding? one must ask. There is now a natural tendency to construe understanding as something that has to do with knowledge, that is theoretical, epistemological. For this theoretical, epistemological behaviour there would be a science or doctrine that could produce rules, guidelines, principles, etc. Certainly, many of these guidelines are quite useful and, indeed, fundamental (avoid contradiction, seek clarity, make sure what you assert corresponds to the text or to the author's intentions, etc.), but the fundamental question is whether understanding is properly understood when it is perceived in such a theoretical, epistemological mood.

The finitude of human understanding

How then is understanding to be understood? In his major work *Truth and Method* (1960), Gadamer answers somewhat enigmatically that he follows his teacher Heidegger when he takes understanding to be the 'basic motion' of our existence, of what we are as '*Da-sein*', that is, as beings who are thrown into existence without any certainty, other than death. This means that understanding is not some theoretical posture we can adopt when we try to grasp something; it is something we 'are' and 'do' all the time. In Heideggerian terms, it is already an essential aspect of the 'there' in the being-there of 'da'-sein. That is, we are 'there' precisely in the motion or mould of understanding. We always have an understanding of this 'there', of our capacities and incapacities, of our possibilities and impossibilities of being in this world. Moreover, this understanding is always a troubled or concerned one. It suffers namely from a basic insecurity: itself. This is why this understanding is always a 'projective' affair. Whether we are fully aware of it or not, we project, that is, we anticipate events in the light of certain possibilities of existence which make up our 'understanding'.

Heidegger stressed the pre-theoretical dimension of this understanding by relying on the idiomatic German expression 'sich auf etwas verstehen' which means as much as to 'know how', to be able to cope with something, to be 'up to it'. For instance, a skilful writer is not someone who understands the rules of writing, but someone who is 'up to it', who can do it. The same holds for a good cook, an apt lover or a devoted teacher, but perhaps also for a good doctor or a good friend. Understanding is here less a matter of knowing this or that but of being able to do or to be. The English verb 'to cope' is often used in this context, but one has to see that it perhaps also misses an important point. Understanding is not only a possibility, an ability, but at the same time an impossibility, an inability. This can already be heard in the expression 'to be up to it': taken literally, it also means that we have to rise up to something that is taller than us, beyond us. To be up to it, to be capable of it, thus implies, in a paradoxical way, that one is at the same time *not* up to it. The ability of understanding – which we 'are' – masks a sheer inability, that of understanding itself. If one is asked, for example, can you write an encyclopedia article on philosophical hermeneutics? (or a term paper on a similarly narrow subject), one might tentatively answer 'Well, yes, I can', but this also entails: basically, I cannot, this is too much for me, and I can only offer to do my best, and that can never be enough. Understanding can never be fully sure of the understanding it is risking. We strive to understand because, at a basic level, we do not fully understand at all. This is the predicament of human finitude. Understanding is the paradoxical art of being able to do something of which we are basically incapable: understanding. The understanding that 'nevertheless' happens, and on which we thrive, should not, for that matter, necessarily be viewed as treachery or deceit, but rather as a surprise, like the joy, but also the eerie feeling that shines on the face of a child who suddenly finds out he or she can ride a bicycle, despite swinging perilously to and fro.

Human understanding, therefore, always implies an element of self-understanding. It is always a possibility of our own self that is played out when something is understood. But this notion should not be confused with the idealistic and sovereign notion of self-consciousness. It is crucial to note that Gadamer does not borrow this notion of self-understanding from Hegel's idea of a transparent self-consciousness, but rather from the dialectical theology of Rudolf Bultmann. (See Gadamer, 1985–95, II, p. 75, p. 121, p. 406.) Theological self-understanding, according to Bultmann, marks less the achievement than the failure at understanding one's self. But this inability to understand turns out to be the way in which adequate understanding begins. The self-understanding implied in every understanding is the very opposite of a self-possession.

The philosophical hermeneutics of Gadamer can be seen, to a large extent, as the philosophical unfolding of this basic insight into the finitude of human understanding. As a hermeneutics, it is also an art of understanding, but its critical point lies in the proper understanding of the notion of 'art' that is involved here. This art is anything but a *Kunstlehre*, a doctrine for which there would be secure rules, guidelines, canons, etc. There are indeed such guidelines, as we have seen, and some of the best minds of the hermeneutical tradition have devoted their acumen to these canons, but the exclusive focus on absolutely secure guidelines might also hide a misunderstanding, a delusion of what understanding is. Gadamer's hermeneutics is thus a permanent transcendence of the simple 'how-to', 'technical' approach to understanding, that is prevalent in so many spheres of life, even in politics and in ethics. The wisdom of this approach is that understanding is more a matter of a practical *know-how* than a theoretical *know-that*, but mere technical rules often arrive too late in the event of understanding. They have a desperation written on them that signals their origin in the ideal of a science consisting of methods.

Gadamer's basic idea is therefore rather simple: a *Kunstlehre*, or mere technique of understanding, is a misunderstanding of what happens in understanding as the basic motion of our existence. The art of understanding is not a matter of method, it is, rather, an 'art', yet an art in which we encounter truth. Gadamer's philosophical hermeneutics is an effort to sort out this hermeneutical experience of truth which is rooted in our finitude and to free it from the exclusive claim that the idea of method makes on the notion of truth. According to this methodical dream, truth results from the proper following of a transparent set of rules; is wholly independent of the observer; can be objectively verified by some criteria; and can be stated in formulae or laws, and, in the best of cases, mathematical phraseology. The restriction of truth to what obeys these criteria was perhaps an understanding necessary at the outset of modernity, in the works of Bacon and Descartes, in order to free scientific and philosophical knowledge from the straitjacket of tradition. Furthermore, these criteria may very well account for the success and mastery of the knowledge of nature, but now that we stand at the other end of modernity, it could also be the case that these truth-securing criteria tend to cover up the basic experience of truth which can be described as an event of understanding that presupposes an essential impossibility of understanding. Heidegger drew on the Greek word for truth, *aletheia*, to think of this experience of truth as an 'unconcealedness' (reading the 'a' in *aletheia* as negating, a lifting of the veil of forgetfulness, *lethè*), but this concealment still carries the mark of the basic concealment that is the lot of our finitude in time. Gadamer asks: is not the quest for methodic security actually a fleeing away from this finitude? Does not true wisdom emerge from the acknowledgement of one's own finitude, as demonstrated by the example of Socrates' knowing ignorance?

Art and truth

In the three major parts of his 1960 *magnum opus*, *Truth and Method*, Gadamer strives to reconquer this understanding of truth and save it from the deformation which the notion of method, with its obsession with security, inflicts upon it. The three sections are devoted to art, history and language. That the *starting point* of Gadamer's work is the domain of art should not be surprising, since, as we have seen, hermeneutics can be characterised as the art of understanding. But what is art? And can one speak of an identical meaning in both cases: the art of understanding and the broad field of 'the arts' that provide material for our art centres, art museums and arts section in the newspaper? There is, perhaps, more similarity to the basic notion of 'art' hinted at here than meets the

eye, for the art involved is, in both cases, a matter of ability, to some extent of 'knowledge', but in any event an instance of truth which cannot be accounted for by the idea of method. But, is it not the case that art relinquishes any claim to truth by establishing its autonomy independently of the requirements of science, even to the extent of defining itself in opposition to the reign of science (arts – even the 'liberal arts' – as opposed to science)? This alleged autonomy of art above any truth claim will be the first victim of Gadamer's attack on the dominion exerted by the modern idea of method. Surely art prospered as it became autonomous, but only at the expense of its truth claim. The splendid isolation of the aesthetic, Gadamer will argue, was in effect, imposed upon it by the presuppositions of methodical science in the nineteenth century. Since science and method were responsible for the entire domain of truth, art could only defend its legitimacy by concentrating on purely aesthetic features that had little or nothing to do with knowledge or truth. At best, truth was a form of 'expression', and the expression of some genius, of some creator of beauty and aesthetic feelings. For Gadamer, this amounts to a tacitly scientistic distortion of the aesthetic experience which is, at its core, an encounter with truth. It can also be called a hermeneutical truth, because the truth which addresses us in the experience of art can never be fully grasped. What Gadamer describes here is a truth which is experienced like an event of meaning that takes us into its play, as it were, and in which we are only participants. In the experience of art we are not independent subjects standing in front of 'aesthetic' objects (only as tourists can we come to feel this to be the case). Art, true art, involves our entire being, leads us to rethink our world, rediscover it, not through some aesthetic colouration, but as it stands and as it can only be revealed by an experience of art. When confronted with a work of art, something overcomes us, strikes us, discloses some truth about the world, yet we cannot perfectly say what it is. However, it is convincing, and much more so, in fact, than a mere truth statement that could be objectively verified and isolated.

Why is it, then, that an artwork can be more convincing than a philosophical or scientific argument? A novel, an opera, a poem, a film, leave an imprint on us and remain in our memory in a way that no arguments can equal. The names of Proust, Rimbaud, Beethoven, Goya, even Plato or Augustine will immediately awaken something in us, they will speak to us, unfolding a world of experience. This also means, of course, that we learn something from them, but what it is cannot be reduced to a specific message, expression or argument. It is even enough to evoke their names to know what I am talking about. Why is this? The work of art does not really argue, but it makes sense, it opens our eyes. Everyone understands the sublimity that is meant when one evokes, for example, the name of Mozart or hums one of his arias. But then again, who can explain it? At best, one should play it, and some do attempt to. The most appropriate thing one can say is, perhaps, that some failures are not as bad as others. But the only point is this: art *speaks* (which could be one way to translate the title of Gadamer's 1993 volume on aesthetics in his Collected Works edition: *Kunst als Aussage*); it addresses us and makes us see in a way no other medium can even hope to approximate.

What is experienced in a work of art – and which can be called truth since it reveals something that is there, in a way that is astoundingly adequate – is, according to Gadamer, also a self-encounter, at root an encounter with oneself. This is a precious indicative of the truth experience which art can help us rediscover. We are always intimately concerned by the truth which occurs in a piece of art. An artwork with no truth is one that does not speak to us, and many clearly do not, for whatever reasons. This hint is important because it runs counter to the prevailing model of truth heralded by science for which truth is something that is independent of the observer, where our subjectivity does not come into play. While this type of truth might be applicable in realms where apodeictic certainty is construable, in mathematics, for instance, or in the knowledge of mathematicised nature (whether there is such a thing is unimportant here; what counts is that it can be constructed), it is clearly out of place in the realm of art and in questions that pertain to meaning and understanding, where our own questioning selves are at stake. Gadamer's enterprise, however, is not just to

safeguard the truth experience of art from the trivialisation imposed upon it by the dominion of methodical knowledge. It is far more ambitious than that and, indeed, quite subversive. In effect, one could say that he draws on the aesthetic experience in order to rethink the entire experience of truth in such a way that it will force any reader to even reconsider the epistemological model that allegedly obtains in science. Indeed, recent developments in the theory of science (in the wake of Thomas S. Kuhn's groundbreaking work) that tend to highlight the rhetorical and aesthetic elements in science can be seen as corroborating the universality of the hermeneutic experience but Gadamer is far too prudent, too modest, to address the domain of exact science directly, claiming it is foreign to his experience. This is why he focuses, in the central part of his work, on the sciences that are most familiar to him, the *Geisteswissenschaften*, or the human sciences as one might call them, before attempting to establish the universality of hermeneutic experience on the common ground of understanding, the element of linguisticality. But since he raises a universality claim for the insights of hermeneutics, it is hard to escape the conclusion that the harder sciences must themselves be understood more hermeneutically. However, this has to be seen as a *consequence* of *Truth and Method*, one that belongs not so much to its stated theses as to its impact, the productive work of its historical reception (or *Wirkungsgeschichte*). In *Truth and Method*, Gadamer is, at the beginning, only concerned with the deformation exerted by the model of methodic science on the aesthetic experience and the truth claim of the humanities.

The human sciences and ethics

The transition from the aesthetic to the humanities is also quite natural for Gadamer's argument because the humanities themselves tend to be seen as a mere aesthetic pursuit if measured by the standards of knowledge in the sciences. This is the tacit presupposition behind the general view of the humanities as soft sciences. This entails that 'real' knowledge can only be obtained through methodical enquiry. According to this leading prejudice, it can, perhaps, be a useful distraction to read poetry, listen to music, learn foreign languages, study theology, or become acquainted with history, women's studies, etc., but in these fields, one can say almost anything one wants. There are hardly any cogent means of verification as in the hard sciences. In short, these pursuits are at best 'aesthetic', and must relinquish the serious matter of truth to the real sciences. In this situation, if the humanities want to avoid the aesthetic trivialisation of their truth claim, their only alternative would be to 'get real'; that is, to adopt the norms of methodical science, to seek, for instance, general laws and regularities, 'statistics', as it were, of the historical world. According to Gadamer, this has been the constant temptation of the humanities for the last two centuries as they sought a methodology – a *Kunstlehre* – that would enable them to share equal footing, if not equal funding, with the exact sciences. According to a conception Gadamer associates with Wilhelm Dilthey, who transformed the impetus he received from his long-time study of Schleiermacher into a philosophical programme, hermeneutics could be understood as the *Kunstlehre* or methodical foundation that would set out rules to assure the scientific status of the humanities or *Geisteswissenschaften*. The knowledge attained through these methodical means would be independent from the observer, tradition and the prejudices of the time and would yield secure, definitive knowledge. A positivistic, but mostly pathetic ideal, Gadamer would argue, because it fails to do justice to the way in which truth actually takes place in the humanities.

Truth, Gadamer counters, has perhaps much more to do with the belongingness to tradition than the methodical ideal and its dream of a zero-point of knowledge would allow us to believe. He subtly turns the tables on the methodical ideal by arguing that this ideal, if applied uncritically, itself suffers from an unacknowledged prejudice: the prejudice against prejudices. As concerned, questioning and self-questioning beings, we always understand out of some anticipations, as Heidegger contended, but these anticipations continuously change as they apply to ever new situations and challenges. Our understanding feeds on two sources: first, the tradition that bequeaths us the anticipations through which we try to come to grips with our world and ourselves, but also the present situation that requires a response, an

adaptation of our understanding. Understanding, as a means of orienting oneself in a world, is rooted in the constant tension between the work of tradition and the demands of the present situation.

This is an insight Aristotle deemed fundamental for the very constitution of the field of ethics. Moral knowledge comes to us from tradition, but has to be applied in a given situation that always concerns us directly; thus, it can never be the affair of some mathematical-cosmological knowledge that one could pursue (and apply) regardless of one's concrete concerns and situation. To claim that this 'concernedness' of ethical knowledge hampers the stringency of its truth claim would be to miss the point of what ethical knowledge is, and has to be, in the first place. Besides the limited realm of mathematical cognition, which has to do with what always remains the same and can thus be taught (the term 'mathematics' comes from the Greek *mathemata*, that which is 'learnable'), there is, according to Aristotle, 'another mode of knowledge' which is less a matter of theoretical knowledge than of 'experience'. 'Experience' here does not allude to the type of experiment a scientist can create (and therefore recreate) in a laboratory (this is yet another seduction of modern science), but to the insight that belongs to the very 'practice' of our temporal and situated lives. For this inescapably temporal existence, there are no rules, but the experience and truths that belongs to it, and can be shared, need to be safegarded against the scientistic illusion that there could be a methodical mastery of this experience, some type of firm knowledge and know-how that only science could secure. This kind of human knowledge Aristotle called 'practical' because it belongs to the very praxis and experience of our lives. He linked it to the 'ethical' dimension in the widest possible sense. Gadamer seizes on this idea and recommends it to the hermeneutics of the humanities, hoping to rekindle a more adequate conception of what understanding is. To measure the achievements of understanding according to the criteria of methodical science would be to miss entirely what truth is about in this field.

It is also important that this insistance on the weight of tradition should not be seen as a form of 'traditionalism', although this misunderstanding is perhaps unavoidable in a world which is so prone to quick labels, name-tags and isms. Pointing to tradition as a source of understanding does not mean that one favours tradition over critical or argumentative inquiry, but simply that one can never fully account for the sources and grounds of one's beliefs. The tradition (or *Wirkungsgeschichte*) which Gadamer refers to is not a specific tradition (for example, a conservative one), but the hidden or unnoticed tradition that supports us. It is first and foremost an acknowledgement of the finitude, and therefore of the modesty and necessary openness, of our knowledge. It is certainly a noble task to reflect on and examine critically all the grounds of our knowledge, but in an age governed and blinded by the quick-fixes of technology and the constant availability of information it is also important to remind ourselves that this reflection can never be total, nor totally self-transparent. The illusion of complete self-transparency through reflection can be a very uncritical and naive ideal indeed. Gadamer does not want to question the merits of methodical science. That would indeed be reactionary. Rather he wants only to correct a self-misunderstanding of understanding which is predicated on methodical science alone. This is why, as he asserts in his important 'self-presentation' (ibid., II, p. 498) the hermeneutics of understanding had perhaps 'less to learn from the theory of modern science than from older, now forgotten traditions' like the traditions of practical philosophy and rhetoric. 'Less to learn' entails that there is also plenty to be gained from the methodology of modern science, and that its critical insights should not be lost or neglected, but that one should not be blinded by the mystification it induces in its universal claim on truth. It is this universalism that Gadamer calls into question because it rests on premisses he deems incompatible with the finitude, situatedness and concernedness of human knowledge.

Gadamer's insistence on the situatedness of understanding, then, is not a defence of tradition, but a philosophical recognition of human finitude, one that is destined to sharpen a critical awareness of the limits of one's understanding. This acknowledgement of finitude, as an act of modesty on the part of our self-understanding, leads to an openness to refutation and other perspectives. An understanding atuned to its own shortcomings will necessarily be dialogical. In his later writings, Gadamer often repeated the phrase that 'the soul of hermeneutics lies in the recognition that the other might be right'. It is only if one accepts this that one can hope to learn anything. Gadamer's hermeneutics is thus a philosophical justification for the inescapable frailty of our own understanding. To argue that one's truth claim is valid because it rests on a stringent method could also be a way to close oneself off from the truth that emerges in dialogue, in the encounter with others and with other traditions.

The dialogical understanding of language

This dialogical dimension of our understanding forms the focus of the last section of *Truth and Method*, the general theory of the latent linguisticality of our understanding that will establish the universality of philosophical hermeneutics. The transition from the hermeneutics of the humanities to the broader theme of language will be provided by the dialectic of question and answer. Its fundamental insight is that no statement can be understood unless it is understood as an answer to a question. Every statement emerges out of a motivation, a situation, an urgency that one needs to understand if one wants to uncover the truth of what is said. In other words, for philosophical hermeneutics, there is no such thing as a first word, for every word is itself an answer to a situation, a question or a preceding set of questions; but there is also nothing like a last word either. Any utterance invites a reception, an understanding response. This dialectics of question and answer makes up the fundamental 'linguisticality' of our understanding. To seek to understand is to seek for words than can be heard as answers to questions we can also ask. The failure to find such words is not a refutation, but a confirmation, of a hermeneutics that recognises in the failure to understand the very beginning of understanding.

The paradigm for this dialogical understanding of language can be seen this time in the Socratic-Platonic tradition. True wisdom begins with the insight that one knows that one knows nothing. The philosophy derived from this basic insight could only be expressed in dialogical form, in the Platonic dialogues. Gadamer, who was a Plato-scholar all his life (from the time of his habilitation thesis on *Plato's Dialectical Ethics* published in 1931 and his unpublished doctoral thesis of 1922 on *The Essence of Pleasure in Plato's Dialogues*, to the Seventh Volume of his Collected Works Edition under the title *Plato in Dialogue*, published in 1991) will draw far-reaching hermeneutical consequences from this dialogical nature of human understanding. Without needing to state it quite so explicitly, it is with this insight that he parts with Heidegger. Certainly, he basically followed in the footsteps of his mentor in the first two sections of his work when he stressed the truth-event of art and the rootedness of understanding in situated and open anticipations. But in the third section, he tacitly breaks with Heidegger's understanding of Plato as a foundationalist thinker who subjugated the totality of being to the authority of the idea or the concept and thus inaugurated the era of metaphysics and its forgetfulness of the temporality of being. What Heidegger himself 'forgot', according to Gadamer, was that Plato wrote in dialogues and that he was a pupil of Socrates. It is the history of metaphysics that made Plato into a metaphysician, but Heidegger, of all people, ought to have known that the history of metaphysics mastered the art of covering up its own origins. Gadamer fully developed this opposition to Heidegger's negative reading of Plato in later works, but the opposition had been simmering for some time.

The conception of language defended in *Truth and Method* still sounds very Heideggerian. In 1959, as Gadamer was finishing his *magnum opus*, Heidegger had just published his book, *Unterwegs zur Sprache* (On the Road to Language), in which he sought in language, and more specifically in the language of poetry, the privileged manifestation of the dwelling of Being. This is a conception which could rightly be seen as the *terminus ad quem* of his entire philosophy, driven by a quest for Being. Gadamer also spoke in this mould about the 'ontological turn of hermeneutics following the lead of language', but the Heideggerian overtones may hide more important dissimilarities. Gadamer's emphasis is less on the revelation of Being that occurs in language than on the dialogical nature of our understanding: to

speak is to seek understanding, and to understand is to seek words. Language lives in this dialogical interplay, in the dialectics of question and answer, as one can express it if one wants to follow the still somewhat epistemological model suggested by the hermeneutics of the human sciences. Again, this understanding of language is directed against the seduction of methodical science, which conceives of language as a theoretical set of statements on matters of facts that are independently verifiable from the utterer, tradition and history. This technical construction of language conceives of language as a tool or an instrument that would enable us to master the world. It finds its fulfillment in the dream of an ideal language that could be constructed from scratch and which would be thoroughly logical (and lives on today in the research on artificial intelligence, which, in effect, seeks to understand or, worse still, replace intelligence through a *Kunstlehre*). But, Gadamer asks, is this still language, a language we can share and understand, or just another technical dream? Language, Gadamer will argue, is less a tool or an instrument which stands at the disposal of our constructing minds than the true element, horizon and mode of realisation (*Vollzug*) of our understanding and our being-in-this-world. Gadamer also followed the lead of Heidegger when he appeared to sum up his thesis on the hermeneutical nature of language by coining the much-cited, much-maligned and often misunderstood: '*Sein, das verstanden werden kann, ist Sprache*' – 'Being that can be understood is language'. Gadamer does not mean by this that the entirety of Being can be reduced to language, nor does he mean that there is no non-linguistic understanding. He means that being that is understood is, as long as it is understood, one that seeks language, that it is on the way to language. But this language is not something that can be stated once and for all, it is especially not the language of propositions that so galvanises contemporary thinking on language, it is the search for language that one can hear in any utterance, a quest that is never fully satisfied.

This dialogical understanding of language which breaks with the focus on propositional language and propositional logic could even find some support in the Augustinian notion of the 'process' character of language, which understands language (albeit in an originally theological, Christological context) as the exterior proffering of an inner word which one can always hear and strive to understand, but which, for humans, can never be fully uttered. In more down-to-earth terms, the intention of what is said always exceeds what is, and can be, said. What is uttered is, as it were, the tip of the iceberg, the part of language that one *hears*, but not all that one *listens* to or all the words that resound in one's inner ear. The finitude of our understanding is also the finitude of the words we use. They are able to convey our intentions, our situation, our distress, but at the very same time, they reveal their failure to do so. The capacity of language and understanding goes hand-in-hand with their incapacity. Words are never adequate for their purpose, to say what words ought to say (their *vouloir-dire*). This eloquent inability is perhaps their finest ability. For a hermeneutics rooted in this dialogical intelligence of language, there is no such thing as a last word.

Bibliography

Between 1985 and 1995, Hans-Georg Gadamer published a ten-volume edition of his 'Collected Works' (*Gesammelte Werke*) in the J. C. B. Mohr Verlag in Tübingen. It is the standard edition, but as an *Ausgabe letzter Hand*, the final edition overseen by Gadamer himself, it leaves out publications the author deemed less important and incorporates additions and corrections to earlier published texts. For an extensive bibliography of Gadamer's writing, see Etsuro Makita, *Gadamer-Bibliographie (1922–1994)*, Frankfurt-am-Main: Peter Lang, 1995.

Writings

Gadamer, Hans-Georg (1976), *Philosophical Hermenéutics*, Berkeley LA, London: University of California Press.
— (1976), *Reason in the Age of Science*, Cambridge: MIT Press.
— (1976), *Hegel's Dialectic*, New Haven: Yale University Press.
— (1980), *Dialogue and Dialectic*, Eight Hermeneutical Studies on Plato, New Haven: Yale University Press.
— (1985), *Philosophical Apprenticeships*, Cambridge: MIT Press.
— (1986), *The Relevance of the Beautiful and Other Essays*, Boston: Cambridge University Press.
— (1989), *Truth and Method*, 2nd edn, New York: Crossroad.
— (1991), *Plato's Dialectical Ethics: Phenomenological Interpretations Relating to the Philebus*, New Haven/London: Yale University Press.
— (1992), *Applied Hermeneutics: Hans-Georg Gadamer on Education, Poetry, and History*, Albany: SUNY Press.
— (1994), *Heidegger's Ways*, Albany: SUNY Press.
— (1994), *Literature and Philosophy in Dialogue*, Albany: SUNY Press.
— (1996), *The Enigma of Health*, Cambridge: Polity Press.

References and further reading

Grondin, Jean (1994), *Introduction to Philosophical Hermeneutics*, New Haven: Yale University Press.
— (1995), *Sources of Hermeneutics*, Albany: SUNY Press.
Hahn, Lewis E. (ed.) (1997), *The Philosophy of Hans-Georg Gadamer*, The Library of Living Philosophers, LaSalle, II.: Open Court Publishing.
Hollinger, Robert (1985) *Hermeneutics and Praxis*, University of Notre Dame Press.
Palmer, Richard E. (1969), *Hermeneutics: Interpretation Theory in Schleiermacher, Dilthey, Heidegger, and Gadamer*, Evanston: Northwestern University Press.
Palmer, Richard E. and Diane Michelfelder (eds) (1989), *Dialogue and Deconstruction. The Gadamer–Derrida Encounter*, Albany: SUNY Press.
Ricoeur, Paul (1981), *Hermeneutics and Human Sciences*, New York: Cambridge University Press.
Schmidt, Lawrence K. (ed.) (1995), *The Specter of Relativism. Truth, Dialogue, and Phronesis in Philosophical Hermeneutics*, Evanston: Northwestern University Press.
Silverman, Hugh J. (ed.) (1991), *Gadamer and Hermeneutics*, New York: Routledge.
Wachterhauser, Brice (ed.) (1994), *Hermeneutics and Truth* Chicago: Northwestern University Press.
Warnke, Georgia (1987), *Gadamer: Hermeneutics, Tradition and Reason*, Stanford: Stanford University Press.
Weinsheimer, Joel (1985), *Gadamer's Hermeneutics: A Reading of Truth and Method*, New Haven: Yale University Press.
Wright, Kathleen (ed.) (1990), *Festivals of Interpretation: Essays on Hans-Georg Gadamer's Work*, Albany: SUNY Press.

3.5

SOCIAL AND MORAL UNDERSTANDING: RICOEUR

Daniel Cefaï and Véronique Munoz-Dardé

Introduction

Born in 1913, Paul Ricoeur occupies a unique place in twentieth-century philosophy in virtue of the diversity of areas in which his contribution has been crucial; from phenomenology to hermeneutics, philosophy of language to philosophy of psychoanalysis, social theory, moral, political and legal philosophy, and his recent groundbreaking exploration of the relationship between memory, history and truth. He is unequalled in his eagerness to break down the provincial boundaries between different philosophical traditions.

Even to list the problems he has looked into throughout his life would require much space. A systematic exposition of his work is thus well beyond the scope of this article, which will concentrate instead on one of the common themes of his work, namely, the challenge to relativism and scepticism, combined with a scrutiny of whether abstract universalism can grasp the existential specificity of human life. It is this theme that we will explore here: first, from the perspective of his reassessment of explanation and understanding in the human sciences, and then through his more recent exploration of the ongoing debate between Kantian universalism and theories of the good life in moral and political philosophy.

Explanation and understanding in the human sciences

Paul Ricoeur began his dialogue with the human sciences in the 1960s. As early as 1963, he engaged in a debate with Claude Lévi-Strauss's structuralism. This debate took the form of a series of articles in the journal *Esprit*, edited by a group of left-wing Christians, many of whom were his friends. Ricoeur had already attracted a great deal of attention, particularly for his writings on Karl Jaspers and Gabriel Marcel, his translation of Husserl (*Ideen I*), the two volumes of his *Philosophy of the Will*, and his books *Fallible Man* and *The Symbolism of Evil*. He was also well respected for actively protesting against French policy during the war in Algeria.

In the articles published in *Esprit*, critics aimed to show that Lévi-Strauss's understanding of symbolic systems of kinship or mythology overlooked the meaning of these structures from the perspective of the subjects themselves. They therefore described his theory as a 'transcendentalism without a subject', and argued that it produced the effect of detemporalising and decontextualising action and discourse. In the course of this debate, Ricoeur, who was critical of the Cartesian and Husserlian conceptions of self-transparency and direct knowledge of the self, undertook a project analysing the cultural mediations of consciousness. This point of departure is worth considering, as it contains some of the themes which Ricoeur explores in his later works.

Freud and Philosophy: An Essay on Interpretation was published in 1965. In it, Ricoeur confronts the notion of a philosophical understanding of Freud's psychoanalytical approach. In sharp contrast with Lacan's deconstruction – which he claims to find (variously) incomprehensible and incoherent – Ricoeur is concerned with trying to understand the specificity of Freud's interpretation of meaning and symbolic language. Ricoeur's explicit aim is to propose a non-partisan philosophical reading of Freud whom he places alongside Marx and Nietzsche ('the masters of suspicion'), claiming that all three show there to be no such thing as a transparent consciousness separated from the external or social world, and available through introspection. What attracts him towards Freudian theory is the possibility of a philosophy that is aware of human nature. He recasts concepts such as regression, identification, sublimation, representation, and idealisation, in order to question the dichotomy between the *cogito* and anti-Cartesian thought. According to Ricoeur, the discovery of the Unconscious-conscious or of the Id-Ego-Superego dynamic should not lead to radical doubt concerning the capacity of deliberation and individual conscience. However, he also considers that the phenomenological tradition has not been conscious enough of an aspect of human nature put in evidence by psychoanalysis, that is, the existence of the 'absolutely involuntary': that part of human beings which resists conscious control and analysis. In his customary dialectical mode, Ricoeur proposes the 'conflict of interpretations' between psychoanalysis and phenomenology, in terms of a dual archaeology of reflective consciousness. He advocates the respect of the peculiarity of both orders of analysis, arguing for their equal right to validity. Anticipating his later understanding of 'meaningful actions' as 'cultural texts', he deepens and amplifies the aperture of 'phenomenological hermeneutics' towards a more general art of deciphering symbols. Thus, the subject does not know itself directly, but only through cultural signs and symbols. His encounter with Freud's theory allows him to develop the idea that because thought does not manifest itself in the transparency of the *cogito*, it can only be apprehended through the task of interpretation carried out by hermeneutics. The reading of Freud thus does not lead to radical doubt regarding rationality and morality, but rather to a better understanding of their 'conditions of possibility'.

The next step of this exploration is Ricoeur's confrontation with rhetoric, semiotics and narratology. The problem now is to take into account the phenomenon of 'semantic innovation' – the invention of meaning through the use of metaphors and storytelling. Ricoeur refuses merely to denounce objectivism. He assumes the linguistic perspective, and carefully studies literature, figures of discourse and genres of narrative. In *The Rule of Metaphor* (a series of semi-autonomous articles which together constitute a reappraisal of Anglo-American and French theories of metaphor), he attempts to show that the 'abuses' or 'deviances' of language that we call metaphoric, have a 'picturing function'. The innovating force of metaphors comes from the fact that they violate the codes of semantic relevance which rule the ascription of predicates in ordinary use. They disturb the usual associations of meaning between words – and also, as Benveniste and Jakobson had acknowledged, the order of sentences (predication) and of texts (emplotment). As in poetry, they open 'metaphoric references' which change our sense of being-in-the-world. Ricoeur builds on Kant to analyse metaphors as new ways of looking at things, as new configurations of poetic worlds through new compositions of language. In congruence with Goodman, he holds an iconic, fictive and affective dimension to the cognitive process, and rejects the claimed opposition between the faculties of intellect and intuition. The importance of the faculty of imagination is thus restated. One of the important conclusions of the book is the relation of metaphor to truth and the discovery of reality: through metaphors, invention and discovery are allowed to concur. Ricoeur later applies this analysis to the study of fictive and historical narratives, and to the understanding of political utopias and ideologies. (See his *Lectures on Ideology and Utopia*.)

The main argument of *Time and Narrative* (1984) is an extension of this perspective on creativity in language. The point of departure is an exegesis of the experience of time in Augustine's *Confessions* and of the emplotment of narrative in Aristotle's *Poetics*. Through this dialogue, Ricoeur attempts to illuminate the dynamic relation between temporality and narrativity, and to identify their respective aporias. In particular, he wants to test the extent to which history can remain a science (explain past events) while retaining its link with our capacity to follow a story (our understanding). To account for the relation between temporality and narrativity, he coins new concepts, in particular what he calls the threefold conception of the 'mimesis' or the imitation of action in narrative. A comparison can be made between, on the one hand, the act of attention in the lived experience, underlined by the passive dynamic of temporal rememoration and expectation, and, on the other hand, the poetic act in the tragic experience, affected by the dispersive effects of the reversals and peripeteia of the drama.

The tensions within the *animus* (spirit) accord with the tension of the *mythos* (fiction): 'Time becomes human to the extent that it is articulated through a narrative mode, and narrative attains its full meaning when it becomes a condition of temporal existence' (Ricoeur, 1984, p. 51). The missing link between time and narrative is action. We come into contact with different figures of time, grounded in actions before they are expressed. These are then configured through the unfolding of narratives, calling for new (post-reception) actions and expressions. The narrative structure is 'prefigured' in experience before it is 'configured' in narrative by the historian, and 'refigured' by the reader: 'We are therefore following the destiny of a pre-figured time (mimesis 1) that becomes a re-figured time (mimesis 3) through the mediation of a configured time (mimesis 2)' (ibid., p. 54).

The first 'mimesis' starts with the pre-intelligibility of the practical world. The specificity of actions, in contrast to events, comes from their insertion in a 'semantic network' of intentions and purposes, reasons and motives, strategies and projects, obstacles and occasions, circumstances and interactions, wills and responsibilities, success and failure, happiness and misfortune. Actions cannot be explained only in terms of cause and effect, they have to be understood through lists of descriptive and analytical, evaluative and prescriptive words. Moreover, they are pre-ordered through 'symbolic mediations', like the sets of conventions which make us able to interpret a gesture as a salutation, a benediction or a supplication, or to judge that this promise is reliable and that justification reasonable. Actions are pre-understandable, in the first mimesis, because they are compre-

hensible to the actors and the interpreters, who can grasp them under perceptive and linguistic categories. Further to these two conditions, drawn from Anscombe and Geertz, Ricoeur adds a third, inherited from Husserl and Heidegger. The composition of the plots which express actions, is embedded in the 'temporal structures' of the practical field: I can, I do, I suffer. Temporalities of action and narrative are intertwined with one another. We can apprehend and appreciate actions, because we experience the threefold dimension of what has been but is no longer, what is to be but is not yet, and what is being at the moment. We master the uses of verbal tenses, temporal adverbs, and of commonsense existential expressions, such as 'to take', 'to waste', 'to gain', or 'to kill' time. And we feel nostalgia, hope, surprise, boredom, deception, anxiety and patience, before we code them into language.

Through mimesis 2, narratives are emplotted, and acquire a kind of autonomy. They are no longer dependent on the context of their enunciation, or on the intention of the author; they can be reiterated in other socio-cultural conditions for other addressees. One could talk of the 'objectivity of the text', whose public meaning owes nothing to the private intentions of the speaker and the listener, or of the writer and the reader. A coherent and intelligible story is drawn from the multiplicity of practical incidents and contingencies. These hang together and make sense, and are ordered in an intelligible whole. Who did what, when and where, why and what for, with and against whom? These questions are answered if one follows the thread of the plot and then 're-enacts the configurational act'. In correlation with these definitions of characters and motives, the narrative embodies ethical and political predicates of good and evil, hatred and love, justice and fairness, authority and legitimacy, right and violence. This synthetic operation, of knowledge and judgement at one and the same time, produces its own temporal order. It displays a very singular series of events and actions which structures the course of episodes and shapes the rhythm of dramatic effects, leading to its own issues and conclusions.

Yet, however objective it may be, the narrative never puts absolute constraints on the reader or listener. The work of figuration is to be completed, through mimesis 3. The acts of reception, as Jauss or Iser say, or the acts of application, according to Gadamer, take part in the constitution of the meaning of the narrative. The configured text is a sketch for the reader's and the listener's imagination: it is a mediation between the worlds opened by the text, and the worlds lived in by the 'receptor'. In *The Rule of Metaphor*, the opposition between real and imaginary had been reapprehended. The same theme reappears in *Time and Narrative*, with the 'interweaving reference' of fictional and historical narratives. The fiction opens a fictitious world, but nevertheless, a world. It is not a mere reproduction of a pre-given reality, rather an activity which shapes and reshapes reality. Narratives, as modes of expression, are not decorative or repetitive devices. They act as a creative mimesis. They configure new contexts of meaning, both dense and polysemic – from the most (poetry) to the least (science). They require diverse strategies of appropriation and reformulation to make sense, raising up new constellations of times and actions. The loop returns to practical experience. In a wider sense, ethical and political experiences could equally be thought of in terms of a 'creative mimesis', with their own temporal and narrative structures.

The most immediate application of this new conception of acting, imagining and narrating, are located in the theory of knowledge, with particular regard to the topics of explanation and understanding. First, understanding is related to the hermeneutic capacity of deciphering meanings, externalised and objectified in texts, whether literary texts, preserved in books, or 'cultural texts', readable in the human world. The conclusions of the analysis of history and narrative are extended to the whole universe of the human sciences. Second, this implies a rehabilitation of common sense. Artificial languages are haunted by the ideal of a *mathesis universalis*, an instrumental language used as a set of logical rules and univocal concepts, making possible an exact picture of facts. But we live in 'lifeworlds' where the semantic relevance is one of practical reasoning and ordinary language: describing a human situation or evaluating a moral action require other ways of thinking and speaking than physics or biology.

Finally, far from opposing explanation and understanding, Ricoeur tries to reconcile them. He shows that the logic of discovery and justification, commonly put forward by Popper, does not fit the process of interpretation in history and the social sciences. Interpretation is concerned with another logic of verisimilitude or plausibility – the one Ricoeur has displayed with the configuration of narratives. However, Ricoeur also holds that this logic is compatible with some aspects of scientific explanation.

Focusing on the special problem posed by history, Ricoeur connects what he calls the 'eclipse of narrative' with the success of the French historiography of the *Annales* School, and of the epistemological matrix of neo-positivism. On the one hand, Hempel's law models relied on a homology between history and the natural sciences. Official chronicles, eyewitness testimonies and personal memories therefore had no scientific status. What is important is the subsumption of a statement about an individual event under a universal hypothesis. The occurrence of the event is explained when logically deduced from initial conditions (prior events, prevailing conditions) according to some cause-effect schemes. The event is intelligible as long as it is a particular case of general laws. On the other hand, the event had to be thought of in a long-term span (*longue durée*). This meant the privileging of mathematical models, of durable equilibriums in a tendency inspired by the Durkheimian School of sociology as read by Braudel, for example. The choice of structure against conjuncture was not only a characteristic of economic and demographic history, but also of social history. Commenting on theorists as diverse as Dray and von Wright, Danto and Veyne, Ricoeur shows how the classical opposition between nomological and idiographic, or rationalist and hermeneutic approaches, can be challenged: the 'threefold mimesis' establishes an 'art' of interpretation which embraces both the logic of understanding and explanation.

D.C.

Moral and political philosophy

A second dimension of Ricoeur's work is his moral philosophy, which led him to make frequent incursions in political and legal philosophy. Ricoeur took an early interest in politics and social justice. The anarchists Sacco and Vanzetti were executed when he was in his early teens and, in his intellectual autobiography, he remembers his indignation: 'It seems to me that my political conscience was born that day.' This precocious political conscience was constantly nourished by an acute awareness and rejection of social injustices, encouraged by his Protestantism. An early friendship with the Christian Socialist Emmanuel Mounier, founder of the journal *Esprit*, strengthened Ricoeur's own liberal egalitarian orientation, and his commitment to political institutions based on an equal concern for persons and a concrete realisation of distributive justice. It is against this moral and political background, this resolute commitment to individual liberty and social justice, that Ricoeur's contribution to normative thought takes place.

'I never ceased to be a post-Kantian of sorts', says Ricoeur (1995, p. 128). The Kantian orientation of his work can be seen in the way he links two questions, with their corresponding answers, namely, 'What can I know?', and 'What ought I to do?'. Following a similar trajectory to that of the German neo-Kantian Jürgen Habermas, Ricoeur moves from an analysis of the validity of description in the social sciences, to a reflection on the validity of norms and moral deliberation, from the rational requirements for thought to rational requirements for moral action. The similarity between the two authors goes further than this in the respect that both want to challenge the opposition between abstract universalism and particularism in ethics, and are both impelled by a recognition of the need to ground politics on a sound ethical basis. This explains why both authors have found themselves in a fruitful dialogue with John Rawls's *Theory of Justice*.

One way in which this dialogue takes place is through Ricoeur's critical appraisal of the Kantian heritage, an appraisal which is Aristotelian in inspiration. This was not fully articulated until *Oneself as Another* (1992), but was prepared by a series of earlier reflections. During the late 1980s, Ricoeur published the three volumes of *Time and Narrative*, as well as a series of articles in which he proposed an innovative reading of Rawls and of some of his critics. The last volume of *Time and Narrative* closes with a sketch of the notion of 'narrative identity', which would be fundamental in the next phase of Ricoeur's work for the formulation of what he calls – with some irony – his 'small ethics'. To this is added a close reading of A *Theory of Justice* and the participants in the ongoing debate on the just and the good society. (See the articles gathered in *Lectures I. Autour du politique*, parts 2 and 3, and in *Le juste*.) These writings could be seen to prepare the ground for Ricoeur's own synthetic conception of individuals' desire to live the good life with and for others, not only in close interpersonal relationships, but also through just institutions.

A fundamental element of Ricoeur's work appears through his analysis of Kantian contractualism. Ricoeur describes the specificity of this tradition of contractual thought as follows. (See 'Le cercle de la démonstration' in *Lectures I*.) The contractual device intervenes in the context of reflection on norms that could be agreed on by members of a political community, but who do not ever meet, and are deprived of face-to-face dialogue. The heuristic device of the contract therefore provides a conceptual means to envisage norms, such that they allow each member to take part in political institutions that will in turn guarantee each of them a fair distribution of burdens and benefits, and of rights and obligations. According to Ricoeur, the fact that contractualism takes as its starting point the conditions under which individuals can live together and be partners in society makes it immune to accusations of abstract formalism. He sees the just institutions defined by contractualist thought as situated *between* the deontological level of morals and legal norms, and the intimate level of close interpersonal relationships. Ricoeur thus agrees with Rawls that social justice is a co-operative endeavour, whilst stressing an aspect less emphasised by Rawls; namely, that just institutions are the necessary link between the concrete other of intimate relations and the completely impersonal other. Through contractual reflection on just institutions we are led to take into consideration the distinctiveness of each member of society. In other words, the impersonal mass of others becomes a series of distinct persons, thus allowing the mutuality of interpersonal ethics to be transposed into just political institutions.

Thus, through the theoretical device of the contract, the Aristotelian demands of deliberation and a good life, lived with and for others, are made compatible with the necessity of impartial norms. However, the contract is a theoretical *fiction*. Within such a framework, how is the individuality of each person as an end in herself or himself *concretely* respected? How is the gap between theoretical just agreement and institutional practices bridged? Ricoeur's answer is given in two moves.

The first move takes the form of a return to the idea of deliberation. The hypothetical contract is *concretely* used by each of us to submit our inner convictions to the test of their consistency with different personal positions in society. Through this device, I am invited to find a rational application for each concrete moral dilemma, of the fundamental but abstract moral impulse which dictates that I respect humanity in the person of each 'other' as well as in myself. Hence the epistemological status that Ricoeur assigns to the veil of ignorance in Rawls is as an effort to provide coherent expression and clarification of our most fundamental moral beliefs, as a 'constructive interpretation' of otherwise well-established moral norms. Moral philosophy does not progress, says Ricoeur, by introducing entirely new principles, but by proposing a more coherent interpretation and formulation of familiar values, resulting in their practical articulation. According to this reading, the veil of ignorance does not lead to an *ex nihilo* discovery of original principles, but constitutes a remarkable device that enables us to justify and clarify our common moral convictions. It thus allows us to better understand under which conditions institutions in which principles are grounded are legitimate.

The second move takes place in *Oneself as Another* (1992) which constitutes Ricoeur's main contribution to moral philosophy. In this book the notion of personal identity is deepened and used in order to further bridge the gap between abstract respect for the law and concrete respect for persons. To be able to operate this move, Ricoeur returns to some of the conclusions he reached in earlier works. The endeavour begins with one of the aspects which already appeared in his analysis of the pitfalls of Cartesian foundationalism within the context of *Freud and Philosophy* (1970), an analysis which led him to criticise Husserlian idealism without accepting Nietzschean scepticism. Ricoeur believes there is a partial insight in both positions, but neither gives a completely successful account. We saw the effects of this position on his understanding of the individual conscience. Human self-knowledge is acquired through the mediation of human creations, the interpretation of ideas, institutions and cultural forms, through which consciousness objectifies itself.

The correlative problem examined in *Oneself as Another* is how to preserve a firm notion of the person, and that person's autonomy, if one accepts the contra-idealistic insights of the 'masters of suspicion' (to recall: Marx, Nietzsche and Freud). Here is where the notion of narrative identity, only briefly sketched in the third volume of *Time and Narrative*, intervenes, and finds its full elaboration. The role this notion plays here is as an intermediary between the descriptive level, which responds to the question: 'Who am I?' and the prescriptive level, which responds to the question 'What ought I to do?'. Ricoeur begins by distinguishing between two notions of personal identity, a distinction which springs from two Latin terms: *idem* (same) and *ipse* (self). Both notions of identity refer to permanence through time.

In the first sense, that of *sameness*, for me to be identified as the *same person* at two different periods of time is to refer to me as the person who has a particular genetic code, fingerprints, etc. These distinctive features of my person allow my reidentification as being the same human being; they constitute the set of lasting traits and dispositions by which I am recognised.

The second sense, that of *selfhood*, refers, by contrast, to what has to remain, even if I change, even if I am not the same. Ricoeur considers that the paradigm of this second sense of personal identity is the notion of keeping a promise. When I commit myself to keeping a promise, I say that I will maintain it even if I change, whether physically or spiritually. It is an identity willed, a form of permanence which does not depend on absolute sameness, but on being faithful to oneself.

Ricoeur's thesis is that narrative identity is constituted in the dialectic between both forms of identity. More precisely, narrative identity constitutes a link between the different events of my life, in the dialectic between identity-sameness (the constancy of what allows me to be identified as the same person at different moments of time), and identity-selfhood (the constancy of the word given which makes me accountable). This narrative link gives the person I am a unity and singularity. Additionally, the distinction between two forms of identity enables the isolation of the type of actions which are linked to identity-selfhood, which constitute the basis for a robust conception of responsibility and autonomy. The type of fidelity to myself that allows me to make promises and prompts me to act in such a way that others can count on me constitutes a basis on which I am accountable for my actions. This can be separated from any other circumstance or disposition constitutive of identity-sameness, and from actions that are the result of these variables. Thus, the work on personal identity helps to provide an answer to radical doubts concerning normative thought.

With this exploration of personal identity, Ricoeur is equipped to propose how one can understand the other from the perspective of identity-selfhood, and evaluate the answers accordingly. Thus, being able to account for the unity and singularity of one's life allows each person to understand the other as herself or himself. (Hence one of the meanings of 'oneself as another'.) Ricoeur believes this explains the fundamental ethical aim of an accomplished or good life with and for others, in just institutions.

Let us conclude this Section with this formulation of 'a good life with and for others in just institutions'. What it suggests is the need to combine an Aristotelian 'teleological ethics' of the good life, including reciprocity with, and solicitude for, others, with a Kantian deontological concern with universal moral norms. But it also suggests the primacy of the ethical goal over the moral claims of obligation.

This is where Ricoeur converges with critics of theories that relegate the role of the state to the mere protection of antecedent individual rights. His objections here are similar to those which Bernard Williams has been pressing against Kantians: always wanting to privilege antecedent impartial values and individual rights leads to a society in which people are encouraged to act towards everyone out of duty, thus impoverishing and diminishing fundamentally humane feelings such as compassion or solicitude. However, Ricoeur still wants to state this objection in Kantian terms (if unfaithfully so). In his phrasing, when respect for the law and respect for persons conflict, the latter has the primacy, for it represents the fundamental ethical orientation.

Justice thus appears as an extension of interpersonal relationships through an institutionalised solicitude for persons, in their insubstitutable singularity.

Conclusion

Ricoeur's work is immense, and only a small part of it has been considered in this presentation. (Even the works considered in some detail here have only been partially analysed.) A primary omission is that, with the exception of Freud, we have said nothing of Ricoeur's constant rereading and interpretation of major classics as varied as Weber, Husserl, Jaspers, Eric Weil, Marx, Heidegger, Augustine and Hannah Arendt, emphasising instead his own particular contributions. But this should not obscure the fact that one of Ricoeur's most distinctive bequests to philosophy lies in his patient, fair and generous engagement with other authors' arguments.

Other aspects have been left unexplored for more fundamental reasons, as is the case of his incursions into the hermeneutics of religious texts. Ricoeur has often expressed his desire to keep philosophy proper separate from his Protestant faith and, more generally, from what he terms the 'non-philosophical sources of his convictions'. He therefore presents his incursions in the interpretation of religious language as a peripheral theme, at least as far as his philosophical work is concerned. Religion might have been one of the reasons for his becoming a philosopher, but it is not one of his central *themes*. He writes:

> There is no doubt that the religious experience expressed in stories, symbols, and figures is a major *source* of my taste for philosophy. Acknowledging

this is not a source of embarrassment for me, inasmuch as I do not believe that a philosophy can be stripped of presuppositions. One always philosophizes from somewhere. This affirmation does not concern simply the fact of belonging to a religious tradition, but involves the entire network of cultural references of a thinker, including the economic, social and political conditions for his or her intellectual commitment. (Ricoeur, 1995, p. 443)

But Ricoeur repeatedly claims that the autonomy of philosophical method and thought should be preserved, and no confusion of genres allowed.

There is, finally, a third important omission here, namely, his work in progress. Any current overview of the philosophy of Paul Ricoeur is bound to be incomplete, for he is constantly approaching new questions. Even at time of writing the conclusion of this article, Ricoeur has immersed himself in a new problem, namely, the relation between the notions of memory, forgetting and history. In the course of this enquiry, he examines how, if at all, it is possible to make sense of the notion of 'collective memory', other than by mere superficial analogy with the personal non-transferable memory of individuals. This leads to an account of the relation between memory and identity, both personal and collective. In turn, this induces an analysis of the different claims to truth, on the one hand of memory, as fidelity to the past; and, on the other hand, of history, with its distinct requirements of evidence, and coherence.

V.M.–D.

Bibliography

Writings

For a complete list of writings, see the exhaustive compilation by Frans D. Vansina and Paul Ricoeur, 'Bibliography of Paul Ricoeur: a primary and secondary systematic bibliography', in Lewis H. Hahn (ed.) (1995), *The Philosophy of Paul Ricoeur. The Library of Living Philosophers*, vol. xxii, Chicago and LaSalle: Open Court, pp. 604–815.

Ricoeur, Paul (1970), *Freud and Philosophy: An Essay on Interpretation*, trans. D. Savage, New Haven: Yale University Press.
— (1971), 'The model of the text: meaningful action considered as a text', *Social Research* 38, 529–62.
— (1974), *The Conflict of Interpretations: Essays in Hermeneutics*, trans. D. Ihde, Evanston: Northwestern University Press.
— (1976), *Interpretation Theory: Discourse and the Surplus of Meaning*, Fort Worth: Texas Christian University Press.
— (1977), *The Rule of Metaphor*, trans. R. Czerny with K. MacLaughlin and J. Costello, Toronto: Toronto University Press.
— (1980), 'La grammaire narrative de A. Greimas', in *Actes sémiotiques. Documents*, II, 15., Paris: EHESS-CNRS, 5–35.
— (1981), *Hermeneutics and the Human Sciences*, trans. and ed. J. B. Thompson, Cambridge: Cambridge University Press.
— (1984–8), *Time and Narrative*, 3 vols, trans. D. Pellauer, K. McLaughlin and K. Blamey. Chicago: Chicago University Press.
— (1986), *Lectures on Ideology and Utopia*, New York: Columbia University Press.
— (1991), *Lectures I. Autour du politique* (On the Political), Paris: Seuil.
— (1992), *Oneself as Another*, trans. Kathleen Blamey, Chicago: University of Chicago Press.
— (1995), *La critique et la conviction* (Critique and Conviction), Paris: Calmann-Lévy.
— (1995), *Le Juste* (The Just), Paris: Editions Esprit.

References and further reading

Hahn, Lewis H. (ed.) (1995), *The Philosophy of Paul Ricoeur. The Library of Living Philosophers*, vol. xxii, Chicago and LaSalle: Open Court.

3.6

AMERICAN PRAGMATISM:
PEIRCE TO RORTY

J. E. Tiles

Trajectory of a tradition

Pragmatism was launched by William James at the University of California at Berkeley in August 1898. In a lecture entitled 'Philosophical Conceptions and Practical Results', James advanced the thesis 'that the effective meaning of any philosophic proposition can always be brought down to some particular consequence, in our future practical experience, whether active or passive' (James, 1920, p. 412). With characteristic generosity James declared the source of his thesis to be his long-time friend, Charles S. Peirce, and he adopted the name Peirce had given it, 'pragmatism' (although James allowed it might be more appropriate to name it 'practicalism'). James's lecture was published the following year. It quickly attracted the attention of academic critics and placed James at the centre of a lively controversy, particularly over the application of the doctrine to the concept of truth.

At the time of James's Berkeley lecture Peirce was living in obscure and impoverished retirement. His response to the publicity James gave to his work was decidedly ambivalent. The increased attention he received, and the new opportunities to expound his own doctrines, were offset by his disagreeing with some of James's versions of his ideas. Furthermore, James's new allies, including F. C. S. Schiller at Oxford and John Dewey at Chicago, were often people whose views Peirce regarded with some distaste. Peirce moved to distance himself from what

was passing as 'pragmatism' and adopted another label, 'pragmaticism', for his own position (Peirce, Vol. 5, p. 414).

Following the death of James in 1910, Dewey, now at Columbia University, participated in disputes conducted in leading American academic journals, doggedly defending what was perceived by the academic public to be the trend James had started. Prior to the First World War Dewey attracted a following outside of university circles for the application he had made of his views to educational issues, and after the War he increased his public profile as an activist and political pundit. As the part played in the early days by such Europeans as Schiller and Giovanni Papini had been forgotten, the memory of James and Dewey's prominence gave currency to the idea of pragmatism as a philosophic tradition peculiar to the United States – originating from an obscure genius, Peirce, brought to light by the charming communicator, James, and sustained by the homespun intellectual, Dewey.

These three are taken to constitute the core of the tradition. A younger colleague and close friend, whom Dewey had left at Chicago, George Herbert Mead, is commonly accepted to be the fourth of the prominent pragmatists. Clarence Irving Lewis, an undergraduate at Harvard prior to James's retirement from there, is sometimes counted as the fifth because he labelled his position 'conceptual pragmatism', but the development of his thought tended to be confined by the terms of disputes (in this case idealism versus realism), which other pragmatists hoped to transcend.

Pragmatism failed to shift the prevailing problematic in academic philosophy and never held a dominant position within American universities. There were other fashions: in the wake of the demise of nineteenth-century idealism, varieties of realism attracted a greater following, and between the wars pragmatism became increasingly marginalised. Events leading up to the Second World War brought academic refugees from Europe to teaching posts in American universities. Alongside the representatives of Logical Positivism, phenomenology and the Frankfurt school, pragmatism appeared unsophisticated. Following Dewey's death in 1952 it lost the status of even a marginalised movement and sympathisers increasingly had to accept the status of scholars whose role was to specialise in the recent history of American philosophy. As a movement, pragmatism appeared dead.

Early in the 1980s, however, Richard Rorty came to the fore and acquired a following for something he called 'pragmatism' (or 'neo-pragmatism', when scholars still familiar with classical pragmatist texts were present). Pragmatist sympathizers found themselves greeting Rorty's efforts with the same mixed emotions Peirce had experienced when James first brought 'pragmatism' to public attention. The attention was welcome, but the gap between the old pragmatism and the new meant that it was difficult to draw and hold people's attention to what — according to those who studied the tradition — had been undeservedly neglected.

Where classical pragmatism had appeared critical of philosophic tradition, Rorty's 'neo-pragmatism' was aggressively iconoclastic — not merely towards the way philosophy traditionally framed the issues over which it conducted its disputes, but towards the pragmatist tradition itself. Rorty dismissed Peirce's philosophy as a mistake and held up a highly revisionist version of Dewey — along with Heidegger and the later Wittgenstein — as examples of how philosophy should conduct itself. Several prominent analytic philosophers — Wilfrid Sellars, Willard Quine and Donald Davidson, none of whom could be said to share Rorty's enthusiasm for either Dewey

or, especially, Heidegger — were co-opted into the pragmatist tradition.

Whatever the merits of Rorty's treatment of tradition, he challenged prevailing ideological maps. The territories occupied by the great (analytic and continental) powers in relation to the small, seemingly unallied, tradition of pragmatism have yet to be carefully determined.

Doubtful parentage

Pragmatism spoke English, but analytic philosophy treated it as a cuckoo in its nest. The strangeness encountered reading Dewey was put down to his having begun his career in the 1880s as a neo-Hegelian idealist but while he cheerfully admitted this had left a 'permanent [Hegelian] deposit' in his thought (Dewey, LW Vol. 5, p. 154), Hegelian scholars found it difficult to recognise. The reluctance to embrace Dewey's thought was not new; realists, who dominated English and American universities before analytic philosophy became fashionable, claimed that whatever conversion Dewey may have experienced on reading James's *Principles of Psychology* (1890) it had not taken his philosophy beyond idealism.

James's hostility to idealism was indisputable but even his version of pragmatism was thought to have made too many concessions to it — Bertrand Russell argued trenchantly against James's account of truth (see Russell, 1910). Just as F. C. S. Schiller's role in the early days of pragmatism was overlooked, so was the role of James's *Principles of Psychology* in the formation of Husserl's phenomenology — although not by Husserl's disciples. Alfred Schutz nominated James as one of the three thinkers who, along with Husserl and Bergson, had done most 'to remodel the contemporary style of philosophizing' and Schutz contributed to the founding of what became in the 1960s and 1970s a flourishing cottage industry interpreting James in the light of Husserl's phenomenology. (See Schutz, Vol. 3, p. 1; see also Edie, 1987, pp. 86–7.)

Those who read James as a proto-phenomenologist, however, acknowledged that James himself would probably not have approved. James expressed genuine admiration for the 'English spirit of philosophy' and distaste for the German style of philosophy, for example, the 'ponderous artificialities of Kant' (James, 1920, p. 436). In the absence of deeper differences these sentiments alone would have been enough to alienate Peirce. Peirce had begun his career by grappling intensely with Kant's first *Critique*, and he defined his own position in opposition to important elements of the British empiricist tradition. The first published expression of Peirce's hostility to what he called 'nominalism' appeared in 1871 in a long article ostensibly reviewing a new edition of the works of George Berkeley. The 'Berkeley Review' (Peirce, Vol. 8, pp. 7–38) is an important document not only for understanding Peirce but for identifying the tensions between the first two pragmatists.

Two views of the real

Peirce professed to be a realist in the medieval sense: that is, he was committed to the reality of universals. To render this position plausible he first offered what he saw as a definition of reality that would be acceptable to all parties: 'the real is that which is not whatever we happen to think it [is], but is [what is] unaffected by what we may think of it', that is to say, 'the thing independent of how we think it' (Peirce, Vol. 8, p. 15). He then distinguished two possible ways of regarding reality thus defined. One, which he held to underwrite nominalism, took reality to be things outside the mind which cause sensations and, through sensations, constrain our thoughts; 'because it is out of mind, [it] is independent of how we think of it, and is, in short, the real' (ibid.). The other, which Peirce held to underwrite realism, regarded all thought and opinion as containing 'an arbitrary accidental element, dependent on limitations in circumstances, power and bent of the individual; an element of error, in short' (ibid., p. 16). The real is what would be represented in thought purged of all limitations of perspective; it is not 'the unknowable cause of sensation but . . . the last products of the mental action set in motion by sensation' (ibid., p. 17).

To those who regard reality in the first way, the route to knowledge lies in individual efforts to trace the constraints of sensation as carefully as possible. The problem of knowledge is how well things in themselves are represented by their causal effects in sensation. And the basis for claiming that two things have anything real in common is that we use 'one mental term or thought sign' to stand 'indifferently for either of the sensible objects caused by the two external realities' – but as 'not even the two sensations have in themselves anything in common . . . far less is it to be inferred that the external realities have' (ibid., p. 16).

To those who regard reality in the second way, the route to knowledge lies in communal efforts to eliminate the limitations in perspective which condition thought – that is, to purge thought of error. There is no place for the notion of thing-in-itself (ibid., p. 17); reality is represented rather in the ideal thought from which no further limitations need to be purged. Universals may be regarded as real, as there is no reason to think that generality as such represents an error or limitation in thought which needs to be, or can be, purged.

The tension between Peirce and James arose from the nominalist slant that the latter attached to his formulations of pragmatism. While both agreed that meaning was to be sought in terms of practical consequences, James spoke of such consequences in terms of particular sensory experiences whereas Peirce looked to differences in habits, that is, general patterns of responding to experience. For James the meaning of a belief was its contribution to foretelling particular turns in our sensory experience; belief for Peirce was to be analysed in terms of habits and he was prepared to reject as a candidate for meaning anything which had no reference to how we act. Peirce's pragmatic principle had arisen as a natural expression of this outlook: what did not make a difference to our conduct should not be counted as distinct. To find this harnessed to a nominalist wagon was a source of irritation, for nominalism was not an isolated metaphysical doctrine; its 'daughters' were sensationalism, phenomenalism, individualism and materialism (ibid., p. 37).

The importance of the choice Peirce offered between the two views of reality also went beyond the issue of the status of universals. By adopting the second view Peirce was led to articulate a doctrine of truth as the ideal end of enquiry. To claim that a belief or other representation is true is to claim we will have no reason to modify it in any way, to see it as a product of our conditions or limitations, so long as we enquire. As there is no way to assure ourselves in advance of enquiring that any of our beliefs will not prove to be infected by limitations of perspective, Peirce embraced the mild form of scepticism, which he called fallibilism, that declines to seek apodeictic certainty for any of our beliefs. Although confident of a number of his beliefs, Peirce insisted that none of them could be held to be absolutely certain.

Peirce's conception of truth as a limit concept, or *Grenzbegriff*, the weight this conception placed on the community of enquirers and his repudiation of absolute certainty all resemble in noteworthy ways the epistemological posture adopted by his German contemporary Wilhelm Dilthey. But where Dilthey was assessing the prospects for the sciences of man (the *Geisteswissenschaften*), Peirce thought largely in terms of the natural sciences. He was by profession a physical scientist (employed for most of his working life by the US Coast and Geodetic Survey) and able to speak from first-hand experience both of laboratory practice and of scientific collaboration.

In general, the pragmatists confronted mechanistic, materialist and reductionist views of man ('scientism') not by seeking a foundation for the studies of man apart from natural science but by rejecting the scientistic view of science. They regarded human thought as thoroughly purposive and science as a teleologically structured enterprise, conducted from within the lived experience of human beings, affording no superior perspective incompatible with that experience. Dewey followed James in treating scientific conceptions as instruments to be judged by their success in furthering the practical objectives of those enquiring into aspects of the natural world. Peirce was as concerned to repudiate the view that natural science supported nominalism (and its daughters, including materialism) as he was to counter the view of science generated by nominalism (ibid., pp. 37–8).

Phenomenology

One of the fruits of Peirce's early critical study of Kant was a thorough revamping of Kant's doctrine of

categories. Peirce replaced Kant's twelve categories with three (Firstness or quality, Secondness or action, actuality, and Thirdness or law, general fact) which were not only universal in the sense of being necessary for experience but elementary in that they were constituents of all experience (see Rosensohn, 1974, p. 45). At later points in his life Peirce refined and developed this doctrine, which first appeared in print in 1867. Just after the turn of the century he elaborated an architectonic of philosophy in which there appears, as one of three main divisions, 'Phenomenology, or the Doctrine of Categories, whose business it is to unravel the tangled skein [of] all that in any sense appears and wind it into distinct forms' (Peirce, Vol.1 p. 280). (Peirce soon abandoned 'phenomenon' and 'phenomenology', terms which had established uses in the natural sciences, in favour of neologisms, 'phaneron' and 'phaneroscopy' (ibid., p. 284).)

Although 'phenomenology' appears in Peirce's writings a year after Husserl first announced the project of '*Phänomenologie*', Peirce appears to have been unaware of Husserl's work. More interesting than the question of influence is the question of whether in seeking in phenomenology a way of underwriting his doctrine of categories Peirce was undermining another of the doctrines he had advanced early in his career (see Apel, 1981, pp. 109–19). In 1868 he had published a comprehensive repudiation of Cartesian principles which included denying that humans had a faculty of intuition, meaning by this a capacity for cognition which had not been determined by previous cognitions (Peirce, Vol. 5, p. 213). It appears, however, that Peirce's phenomenology was Cartesian only to the extent of seeking a standpoint without presuppositions. Given Peirce's broad conception of the notion of inference, the process of suspending presuppositions which this involved would not have required 'cognitions undetermined by previous cognitions' or (Peirce's alternative formulation) 'premises not themselves conclusions'.

Another of the faculties which Cartesians assumed was that of introspection. Peirce insisted that neither our knowledge of our sensations nor our knowledge of our emotions is derived by direct perception of an internal world but in each case involves complex inferences from our experiences of external objects (ibid., pp. 244–7). This, together with the claim that all thought must necessarily be in signs (ibid., p. 251) and an analysis of the concept of sign which entails the necessity of its standing for an object (Peirce, Vol. 2, p. 228), virtually commits Peirce to the phenomenological theory of intentionality: all thought is object-directed. But the commitment remained virtual; intentionality is there but is not given pride of place in Peirce's phenomenology.

The superficial similarities between the phenomenologies of Peirce and Husserl are striking. From closely comparable conceptions of thought, both call for a suspension of the question of whether phenomena correspond to anything real (Husserl's 'phenomenological reduction' or *epoché*) in order to embark on transcendental investigations – in order, that is, to enquire what must be the structure of thought if our experience has the character it does. The different outcomes are equally striking. Instead of discovering the subjective constitution of meaning as did Husserl, Peirce professed to find the three categories on which he had lovingly meditated for over thirty years.

Radical empiricism

Pragmatism was by no means the only theme James developed in the last decade of his life. In applying the pragmatic principle to the concept of truth, he acknowledged that 'truth' was, as Peirce had suggested, the name of an ideal to be approached over the long term, but his interest gravitated toward the immediate and the short term. Consequently he emphasised verification – to the point of inviting confusion between 'true' and 'currently accepted as verified' – insisting that verification must take place in terms of concrete experience. What is true (that is, what may be accepted as verified for the time being) is what helps us to get into satisfactory relations with other parts of our experience. This sounds like the logical empiricism of the Vienna Circle in the 1930s, but harnessed to James's conception of experience the doctrine took a very different turn.

James criticised classical empiricism for being insufficiently empirical. A 'radical empiricist', as he styled himself, did not impose pre-conceptions on experience such as the assumption found in Hume that experience consists of disconnected elements, or the assumption found in Locke that experiences ('ideas') arrive marked as derived from sensation or reflection. Radical empiricists take experience as they find it and what James claimed to find in experience were relations and connections, indifferents and undecideds, 'flights and perchings'. Left to itself, what is given in experience is not either the effect of something outside the mind or of the mind itself. One may adopt a pragmatist attitude, in particular with regard to truth, without a critical examination of how one thinks about experience, but what we need in order to avoid misconstruing the process of verification, according to James, is a disciplined return to pure (pre-theoretical) experience.

On being sent an off-print outlining James's project, Peirce immediately identified what James proposed with his own phenomenology (see Perry, 1935, p. 431). Scholars, who were later to see James's *Principles of Psychology* as moving along a path parallel to that taken by Husserl, read the posthumous *Essays in Radical Empiricism* as James's version of a long-standing phenomenological impulse made self-conscious. Husserl himself credited James with showing him how descriptive psychology could be done without lapsing into the error of 'psychologism' (see Husserl, 1970, p. 420, n. 1) – of treating the data of consciousness as subjective facts to be studied in the manner of the empirical sciences. This is testimony to a striking reversal that James made in the process of writing the *Principles*.

James began by conceiving the task of a natural science of the mind as ascertaining empirical correlations between, on the one hand, thoughts and feelings and on the other, definite conditions of the brain. To go further than this 'thoroughgoing dualism' was to 'become metaphysical' (James, 1890, Vol. 1, p. vi, p. 218) but James found it difficult to stick to this, even as a mere methodological constraint. He continually found that he had to go beyond enquiring into the causal conditions of cognition and address what were, for Husserl and his followers, logical conditions. There is, he appreciated, no access to, no way of specifying, a mental act except via its object, 'a close attention to the matter shows that *there is no proof that the same sensation is ever got by us twice. What is got twice is the same* OBJECT' (ibid., p. 231).

The *Principles* contained many references to current European literature, including the work of Brentano. James did not follow Brentano in adopting intentionality *simpliciter* as his criterion of mentality; for him 'the mark and criterion of the presence of mentality' was 'the pursuance of future ends and the choice of means for their attainment' (ibid., p. 8). This is a less general concept of intentionality, but one more firmly tied to a natural perspective. James did not turn the concept of intentionality into the basis of a technical vocabulary, but the framework that this concept provides is more obvious in James's writing than in Peirce's. 'The thing we mean to point at may change from top to bottom and we are ignorant of the fact. But in our meaning itself we are not deceived; our intention is to think of the same' (ibid., p. 460). Of James's own terms, 'conception' is the closest to the technical use of 'intention' in phenomenology: '["conception"] properly denotes neither the mental state nor what the mental state signifies, but the relation between the two, namely the *function* of the mental state in signifying just that particular thing' (ibid., p. 461).

One consequence of James's increasing preoccupation with questions of meaning is that one of the categories he originally sought to correlate, the physical world in time and space, becomes a specific mode of the other category, thoughts and feelings. The way in which the former acquires a claim to be privileged is explored in a chapter of the *Principles* dealing with the concept of reality. Reality is what we attribute to an object when we acquiesce or believe in it. This is a natural response of the mind to any object and it is only when something interferes with this response that we suspend belief and cease to attribute reality: 'Any relation to our mind at all, in the absence of a stronger relation suffices to make an object real' (James, 1890, Vol. II, p. 299).

In order to cope with important parts of experience that would otherwise interfere with one another, we distinguish the worlds represented in science, mythology and fiction as well as in our everyday actions and sense perceptions. Our assessments of what is real and which things are more real than others is a function of our interests, 'whatever excites and stimulates our interest is real' (ibid., p. 295). For the physicist, molecular vibrations are more real than felt warmth 'because [they are] so intimately related to all those other facts of motion in the world which he has made his special study' (ibid., pp. 300–1). However, for James, the answer to the question 'Where do our true interests lie?' was obviously in the world we experience every day. *'Sensible objects are thus either our realities or the tests of our realities. Conceived objects must show sensible effects or else be disbelieved'* (ibid., p. 301).

Although James accepted Spinoza's claim that belief, the attribution of reality, was a natural response to experience, he also explicitly accepted Brentano's doctrine that conceiving and believing are distinct psychic phenomena and 'the mere thought of the object may exist as something quite distinct from the belief in its reality' (ibid., p. 286). The project of radical empiricism thus called, as did the phenomenologies of Peirce and Husserl, for questions of reality to be suspended and a level of pure experience, pure given, to be sought.

The ego

What James emphatically did not find given in experience was the distinction between a subject-entity and (representations of external) object-entities. What happens as our purposive activities come to impose structure over pure experience is that a functional polarisation takes place around certain objects, the most important of which are our bodies, helping us to form conceptions of our selves. As a straightforward treatment of the self as simply a special object encountered in experience does not do justice to the complexities of our sense of the self, James distinguishes the empirical self (the 'Me') and a pure ego (the 'I') (James, 1890, Vol. 1, pp. 292–342).

The former is further analysed into 'the material self', including our bodies, possessions, families and products of our labour; 'the social self' consisting of our roles and relationships; 'the spiritual self' which James treats as based on more intimate experiences of our bodies, such as breathing, intracephalic muscular adjustments, etc. The 'I' or pure ego answers the question 'Who experiences the empirical self?' Given that all experience is of objects, and it does not seem possible to treat the *empirical* self as experiencing itself, the 'I' in turn appears to be something not able to be experienced, yet necessary to our concept of experience. James resisted any attempt to posit a substantial entity or even a bare and empty Kantian transcendental unity to account for the continuity of experience. He offered instead an account in which a fleeting ownership of experience is passed from one experience to the next by a process of successive objectification: 'Each thought is thus born an owner, and dies owned, transmitting whatever it realised as its Self to its own later proprietor' (ibid., p. 339).

Scholars familiar with the work of Husserl have noted the parallels between James's distinction between the empirical self and the pure ego on the one hand, and Husserl's distinction between the human ego and the pure phenomenological ego on the other. In each case the second term is interpreted in terms of function, although the tendency in Husserl appears to be to assign more permanence and a greater degree of self-awareness to the pure ego than does James. (See Stevens, 1974, pp. 83–4.) This may well be the consequence of a Kantian impulse in Husserl to seek for necessary laws by which the pure ego constitutes meaning and the structure of experience. James is inclined to stress choice (via the capacity for selective attention) in the way the pure passing ego draws the past into itself and constitutes an object for the next act of appropriation. The more this process appears to the self to be constrained in some uniform way (by some aspect of its own nature), the greater will be its sense of its own permanence and substantiality.

James would very likely have found Husserl's treatment of these issues distasteful on grounds of style and motivation as well as on such matters of doctrinal tendency. It is difficult to imagine James reading Husserl and not reacting as he did to Kant's style ('ponderous artificialities', etc.), and there is evidence that James had no sympathy for the project of establishing philosophy as some kind of rigorous science. (See Edie, 1987, p. 85, p. 23.) James was far more ready to recognise Bergson as his ally. He saw Bergson's invitation to suspend our practical preoccupations and return to the flowing world of perceptual experience as identical to his own call for an investigation of the neutral data of pure experience. (See Stevens, 1974, p. 21.)

Creatures of habit

Dewey claimed that James's *Principles of Psychology* had marked a turning point in his career and he repeatedly cited from the *Principles* with approval. Dewey's enthusiasm for Bergson, however, was much more qualified than was James's, and his assessment of Bergson's philosophy reveals a very different attitude to the conceptual encrustations that arise from the interests we take in what we experience.

Bergson, like James, saw an intimate connection between our everyday experience and our purposive actions. By reaching beneath any experience that might be infected by its involvement in our active lives, Bergson suggested, we would somehow achieve a more intimate 'touched, penetrated, lived' experience of reality. Not to suspend conceptual thought and exercise what Bergson called 'intuitive' thought was to accept reality distorted by the fictions and illusions that we fashion in order to satisfy our bodily needs. 'And are our actions, the uses we make of things to satisfy our organic needs, not functions of "reality"?' asked the pragmatist Dewey. We should by all means try to understand the contribution made to our perceptions by our interests, but on what basis can we say that reality is other than what we engage with by acting, planning, choosing, contriving?

The idea of another route to reality, that favoured by Bergson, arose, according to Dewey, from a flawed account of perception. Like the pragmatists, Bergson emphasised that perception was a process of selection and elimination, but at the same time he denied that it had an ampliative or creative office. It thus makes sense to think of restoring full contact with reality by suspending practical concerns and removing our selectively imposed blocks. But if we conceive of perceived objects as representing possible ways of acting on the environment, Dewey asked, does this not amount to introducing complication, qualitative alteration, into the world? Indeed, we select in order to identify material upon which we may act, but we also seek in perception the consequences of acting in various ways. 'Perception is not an instantaneous act of carving out a field through suppressing its real influences . . . but a process of determining the indeterminate' (Dewey, MW Vol. 7, p. 13).

Dewey brings to bear at this point his critical analysis of the basic concept used in the physiology of perception, the reflex arc (Dewey, EW Vol. 5, pp. 96–109). He insists that – and this even at a very low level of organic complexity, any level at which it is possible for an organism to form habitual responses – perception is not a stimulus to action but an act of constituting influences present in an indeterminate situation into a determinate stimulus (Dewey, MW Vol. 7, p. 20), that is, into a stimulus to determinate action. There is no perception that is not an act of constituting on the part of the organism. A determinate reality waiting to be experienced when our active life has been suspended and our active interests have been disengaged is yet another of the fictions created by importing unwarranted presupposition into the project of understanding experience.

Dewey was otherwise sympathetic to the claims of radical empiricism. We do experience indeterminacies – they are the stimuli to perception – as well as connections. There are indeed myriad qualities of experience and the error of traditional philosophy has been to treat them as objects. These qualities are not, at least in the first instance, encountered cognitively, but rather are the felt qualities of our organic interactions with the environment (Dewey, LW Vol. 1, pp. 69–99; and pp. 191–225). Experience modifies those interactions; the required capacity here is precisely the ability to form and modify habits in response to events we undergo. As our habits change, so do the qualities of our experience. Habits, moreover, are formed as our interests (in the first instance our biological needs) motivate, and the environment constrains, our activities. There is no pure experience in the sense of experience free of the sediment of interest.

From a phenomenological perspective Dewey fails to suspend the natural standpoint; from Dewey's perspective there is no need, once a presupposition has been called into question, not to reinstate that presupposition if it is required to understand experience. In particular, Dewey insisted on the importance of a framework based on general features of what it is for a moderately complex living creature (that is, sentient and capable of learning) to main-

tain itself in its normal habitat. In this he saw himself as following the example set by James in the *Principles*; James's abandonment of dualism and of attempts at inappropriate causal explanations did not entail the need to abandon altogether a naturalistic perspective, merely to avoid an over-restrictive conception of nature.

Dewey's treatment of cognition and reflection is carried out in his functionalist natural teleology. Creatures such as ourselves often need to represent the conditions and consequence of certain of the qualities of our experience; that is, of the organic events constituting that experience. This is done by objectifying, and by this use of our cognitive capacities we acquire control over, and freedom within, experience. Cognitive functions not only serve to modify habits so as to overcome problems and achieve ends, they are themselves constituted by habits which introduce new (felt) qualities into experience.

Scholars examing Dewey's philosophy with the benefit of hindsight and knowledge of later developments in the phenomenological movement see him as offering an account of the source of the structures of pre-reflective experience (or pre-objective intentionality) remarkably similar to that found in Merleau-Ponty. Both repudiated dualism, mistaken views of science and the kind of intellectualism that treats all experience as a form of knowing; both pointed to habit as the foundation of meaning. (See Kestenbaum, 1977, pp. 7–8. See also Rosenthal and Bourgeois, *passim*, on Merleau-Ponty as the best vantage point in the phenomenological movement from which to view pragmatism.)

(Re)making history

Dewey, like Peirce, found it helpful to explain his views by situating them in opposition to certain historical trends. As Peirce worked to combat a syndrome he called 'nominalism', Dewey read the history of philosophy as expressing a deep-seated insecurity and declared the time had come to give up, as the title of his Gifford Lectures called it, the *Quest for Certainty* (Dewey, LW Vol. 3). Rorty recommends – as his understanding of what Hegel meant when he defined philosophy as 'holding you time in thought' – 'finding a description of all the things characteristic of your time of which you most approve, with which you unflinchingly identify, a description which will serve as a description of the end toward which the historical developments which led up to your time were means' (Rorty, 1989, p. 55).

Rorty's treatment of the pragmatist tradition is itself an expression of this understanding of philosophy. His version of pragmatism has made 'the linguistic turn' similar to that of analytic philosophy. Although none of the classical pragmatists failed to emphasise the importance of language and the use of signs, attention in Rorty's pragmatism shifts decidedly from experience and teleologically-structured organic habits to language and sentential attitudes. The world appears as images projected by language, no one of which is more representative of the world (or of human beings) than any other. Meaning is what is produced by using words in familiar ways. The non-substantialist self emerges as a complex of sentential attitudes, 'a centerless web of beliefs and desires' (see Hall, 1994, pp. 83, 90, 97).

Rorty not only dismisses Peirce from the tradition and discards significant portions of Dewey's philosophy – especially those according a special dignity (cultural privilege) to the methods and practices of natural science – he adopts as his banner the term Peirce applied to his arch adversary, 'nominalism'. Rorty's view of the real is a version of that which Peirce saw as giving rise to nominalism. The only non-linguistic constraints on language are pain and causality ('quasi-natural kinds', Hall, 1994, p. 90, p. 101); there is no final opinion towards which our enquiries tend in the long run. Rorty is clearly at home with two of what Peirce identified as the daughters of nominalism, namely, materialism and individualism: he is comfortable with the prospect of a physicalist description of the mind; he holds self-assertion to be the primary value.

But the point of professing to be a 'nominalist' for Rorty is not to signal the metaphysical repudiation of universals but the rejection of any constraints that might be given an abstract articulation. Coupled with another self-description, 'historicist', Rorty is claiming the freedom to construct narratives about history that are alternatives to argument, neither doxography nor intellectual history, neither rational nor historical reconstructions. Philosophy is not a natural kind; as an exercise of 'holding one's time in thought', philosophy appears in Rorty's hands as a vehicle for self-assertion. Pragmatism is not a natural kind either. Small wonder those loyal to what they took to be the pragmatist tradition are uncertain of how to react to a cuckoo in their nest that has the face to announce himself as such.

Bibliography

Writings

Dewey, John (1969–90), *Works* (in three series – *Early Works*, EW, Middle Works, MW and *Later Works*, LW – thirty-seven vols, ed. Jo Ann Boydston, Carbondale, IL: Southern Illinois University Press.

James, William (1920), *Collected Essays and Reviews*, ed. Ralph Barton Perry, New York: Longmans, Green.

— (1950) (first edn 1890), *The Principles of Psychology*, New York: Dove.

— (1977–89), *The Works of William James*, sixteen vols, ed. F. Burkhardt, F. Bowers and I. K. Skrupskelis, Cambridge, MA: Harvard University Press.

Peirce, Charles Sanders (1931–58), *Collected Papers of Charles Sanders Peirce*, eight vols, eds (vols 1–6) Charles Hartshorne and Paul Weiss and (vols 7–8) Arthur W. Burks, Cambridge MA: Harvard University Press, (Vols 1–6) 1931–5, (Vols 7–8) 1958.

Rorty, Richard (1979), *Philosophy and the Mirror of Nature*, Princeton, NJ: Princeton University Press.

— (1982), *Consequences of Pragmatism*, Minneapolis, MN: University of Minnesota Press.

— (1989), *Contingency, Irony and Solidarity*, Cambridge: Cambridge University Press.

— (1991), *Philosophical Papers*, two vols, Cambridge: Cambridge University Press.

References and further reading

Apel, Karl-Otto (1981), *Charles S. Peirce: From Pragmatism to Pragmaticism*, trans. John Michael Krois, Amherst, MA: University of Massachusetts Press.

Edie, James M. (1987), *William James and Phenomenology*, Bloomington, IN: Indiana University Press.

Hall, David (1994), *Richard Rorty: Prophet and Poet of the New Pragmatism*, Albany, NY: State University of New York Press.

Husserl, Edmund (1970), *Logical Investigations*, trans. J. N. Findlay, London: RKP.

Kersten, Fred (1969), 'Franz Brentano and William James', *Journal of the History of Philosophy*, 7, 177–91.

Kestenbaum, Victor (1977), *The Phenomenological Sense of John Dewey*, Atlantic Highlands, NJ: Humanities Press.

Perry, R. B. (1935), *The Thought and Character of William James*, Vol. II, Boston: Little, Brown and Co.

Rosensohn, William L. (1974), *The Phenomenology of Charles S. Peirce*, Amsterdam: B. R. Grüner BV.

Rosenthal, Sandra B. and Patrick L. Bourgeois (1980), *Pragmatism and Phenomenology: A Philosophic Encounter*, Amsterdam: B. R. Grüner BV.

Schutz, Alfred (1966), 'On Multiple Realities' and 'William James's Concept of the Stream of Thought Phenomenologically Interpreted', *Collected Papers*, The Hague: Martinus Nijhoff. Vol. I, Maurice Natanson (ed.), 207–59; Vol III, I. Schutz (ed.), 1–14.

Spiegelberg, Herbert (1956), 'Husserl's and Peirce's phenomenologies: coincidence or interaction?', *Philosophy and Phenomenological Research*, 2, 164–85.

Stevens, Richard (1974), *James and Husserl: The Foundations of Meaning*, The Hague: Martinus Nijhoff.

Russell, Bertrand (1910), 'Pragmatism' and 'William James's Conception of Truth', *Philosophical Essays*, London: Allen and Unwin, 87–149.

Wilshire, Bruce (1968), *William James and Phenomenology: a Study of the 'Principles of Psychology'*, Bloomington, IN: Indiana University Press.

Section Four
PHENOMENOLOGY

INTRODUCTION

Gail Weiss

'What is phenomenology?' Merleau-Ponty asks in the preface to his 1945 *Phenomenology of Perception*. Despite Husserl's groundbreaking work in explicating and defining the method and scope of phenomenological investigation, Merleau-Ponty claims that the question has still not been definitively answered. And, despite Merleau-Ponty's own substantive contributions to phenomenology, as well as the contributions made by the other authors discussed in this Section, it seems that the deceptively simple question 'What is phenomenology?' continues to plague Continental philosophy. Rather than viewing this as failure, however, the possibility of repeatedly returning to this question with fresh responses, reflects a renewed and deepening commitment to phenomenology on the part of its well-known adherents and has also served as an inspiration for those who are coming to this particular way of 'doing' philosophy for the first time. That is, it is precisely because the question has not yet been answered satisfactorily, that there is more work to be done; work whose promise lies in the future, but which is indebted to the past and present authors discussed in the pages that follow. As Merleau-Ponty says at the end of his 1964 essay, 'Eye and Mind':

> If no painting completes painting, if no work is itself ever absolutely completed, still, each creation changes, alters, clarifies, deepens, confirms, exalts, re-creates, or creates by anticipation of all the others. If creations are not permanent acquisitions, it is not just that, like all things, they pass away: it is also that they have almost their entire lives before them. (Merleau-Ponty, 1993, p. 149)

Phenomenology, like painting, draws on its rich historical tradition and, also like painting, has an inexhaustible future. The future is inexhaustible precisely because the phenomena that comprise the life-world are themselves unlimited; not only are new phenomena constantly emerging but those previously encountered and described are capable of showing themselves in different ways against horizons that are also continually shifting. As Merleau-Ponty notes in *Phenomenology of Perception*, there are an infinite number of perspectives which can be take up in reference to any given figure, and therefore, the impossibility of achieving an aperspectival vantage point does not mean being locked into any given perspective. Further, as Husserl maintained, each phenomenon has its own internal, as well as external, horizon, both of which offer themselves as points of departure for new ways of interrogating and grasping the significance of the phenomenon in question.

Before addressing the possibilities that belong to phenomenology's own future, let us begin by examining the tradition out of which it developed; in particular, specific themes that emerge from the work of neo-Kantians such as Hermann Cohen, Paul Natorp, Heinrich Rickert, Ernst Cassirer, Max Scheler, and other contemporaries of Husserl such as Nicolai Hartmann, Karl Jaspers and Roman Ingarden.

The neo-Kantian underpinnings of phenomenology

Contemporary students of phenomenology often think of the three famous 'H's' – Hegel, Husserl and Heidegger – as the founders of the phenomenological movement. However, careful historical scrutiny reveals that Kant's influence on phenomenology was just as substantial (if not more so) than Hegel's. Although Kant, unlike Hegel, never actually used the word 'phenomenology' in the title of any of his works, his emphasis on the unifying and schematising function of consciousness, as exemplified in transcendental apperception, set the stage for Brentano's discussion of the intentionality of consciousness; and Kant's ongoing concern about possible connections between the phenomenal and noumenal realms provided a critical framework for subsequent phenomenological discussions of the relationship between the phenomenon that appears to consciousness and the transcendent status of the object that is revealed in and through its appearances. Moreover, the Kantian project of articulating the conditions for the possibility of experience as such, rather than focusing on experiences themselves, lent philosophical credibility to the Husserlian claim that phenomenology seeks merely to describe, rather than to explain or prescribe anything about the nature or existence of the phenomena it investigates.

Kant's influence on phenomenology can also be demonstrated, albeit more indirectly, through the work of his neo-Kantian successors. Not only did Cohen, Natorp, Rickert, Cassirer and Scheler serve as links between Kant and the phenomenological tradition, but their work also helped to further the association of phenomenology with Germany, and more particularly, with the Universities of Marburg, Freiburg, and Heidelberg (an association that continues to this present day). Hermann Cohen, in arguing that 'real' metaphysics must think the origin, presaged Heidegger's own preoccupation with the origin in *Being and Time* (1927) and in 'The Origin of the Work of Art' (1960). A concern for avoiding unquestioned starting points by interrogating them as to their originary status is also expressed by Husserl in his claim that phenomenology is a search for true or veritable essences. The search for these essences, Husserl maintained, could only occur once we bracketed or suspended our customary presuppositions about the world and how it functions.

Cohen's colleague at Marburg, Paul Natorp, argued for a non-materialistic, transcendental analysis of the subjective act and also maintained that consciousness itself should be understood as a unity supporting both subjective and objective approaches in the domains of art, science and morality. Natorp's call for philosophical investigation into individual personality as a phenomenon in its own right anticipated Husserl's claim in *The Crisis of European Sciences and Transcendental Phenomenology* (1954) that psychology and transcendental philosophy are inseparably allied and that psychology is the truly decisive field in so far as it takes universal subjectivity as its subject matter (Husserl, 1970, p. 208).

Heinrich Rickert, like Natorp, was interested in demonstrating the connections between the natural and human sciences while at the same time acknowledging the crucial methodological differences between them. Adopting a Kantian critical approach, Rickert interrogated the epistemological presumptions of the various sciences in order to show that they are as firmly grounded in historical reality as are the human sciences. While acknowledging that phenomenology offered a viable method for describing the contents of consciousness, Rickert was critical of phenomenology for its lack of attention to the intelligibility of these contents of consciousness as well as their relation to objective reality. Despite this alleged limitation of phenomenology, Rickert also rejected Hegel's strong identification of the real with the rational because, according to Rickert, it could not properly account for the pluralistic nature of reality. One of Rickert's key contributions to post-Husserlian phenomenological thought was his focus on the historical development of a given phenomenon over time, a point which could later be used to rethink the very concept of a phenomenological 'essence'; a project that began with Heidegger (Rickert's student) and which was also taken up by Merleau-Ponty in a manner that worked against the static, a-historical conception of essence associated with the Platonic tradition.

Cassirer and Scheler are well-known philosophers whose contributions to phenomenology have been noted much more frequently than those of Cohen, Natorp and Rickert. None the less, Cassirer and

Scheler were themselves strongly influenced by these neo-Kantians as well as by Kant, Hegel and Husserl. Cassirer, a student of Cohen's, claimed that he was providing a phenomenology of consciousness, a phenomenology that centres on the power of human symbolisation and symbolising activity. It is our collective ability to symbolise our experience, Cassirer maintained, that has led to the development of a symbolic world of human culture. Being concerned, like many of his neo-Kantian predecessors, with demonstrating the organic unity of the natural and human sciences, Cassirer understood this unity in terms of the power of symbolic representation which, he argued, was as operative in the realm of science as it was in religion, art, or language itself.

Scheler, who met and was influenced by Brentano and Husserlian scholars early on in his career, has been credited with spreading the influence of phenomenology outside of Germany into France and Spanish-speaking countries. Admired by José Ortega y Gasset and impacting sociologists, psychologists and religious thinkers as well as philosophers, Scheler argued that phenomenology is capable of effecting a fundamental transformation in our manner of understanding ourselves and the world. Like Natorp, Scheler understood personality as the crucial subjective phenomenon to be investigated philosophically, and this led directly to his view, which has come to be associated more closely with Heidegger, that philosophy must take as its foundation and point of departure, the Being of human beings.

Scheler's focus on the transformative potential of phenomenology is developed much more fully in Karl Jaspers' work and this can be seen most readily in his substitution of the term 'philosophy' (which suggests an existing body of doctrine) with the term 'philosophising' (which highlights the activity of doing philosophy). Philosophy, according to Jaspers, must be practised not preached, and must begin with the personal experience of a concretely existing individual. Personal experience, however, is already interpersonal experience; for Jaspers, my own existence is confirmed and reflected in the existence of others. In a manner that prefigures Sartre's famous claim that 'man is a useless passion' Jaspers argued that human existence is condemned to endless striving; a striving toward infinity that is doomed to failure in so far as it continually comes up against the limits of finitude. This tension between the constraints of a finite existence and the desire for infinity, however, achieves a resolution in Jaspers that Sartre remains much more suspicious of: namely, the salvation offered by a recognition of the eternal within each of us that Jaspers identifies with transcendence.

Nicolai Hartmann, a realist philosopher who was a neo-Kantian in the earlier part of his career and an anti-Kantian later on, also concentrated on transcendence but focused on the transcendence of the object to consciousness and on the paradox this created for consciousness in so far as this same object could only be grasped as one of consciousness's immanent contents, a paradox that was taken up and addressed by Husserl in *Ideas I*. Like Hartmann, Husserl's response to this paradox was to adopt a transcendental realist position regarding the existence of the intentional object (*noema*). Influenced by Heidegger's *Being and Time*, Hartmann was persistently concerned with the nature of the relation between subject and object rather than the fact that such a relationship exists. In his three-volume work on ethics ([1936], 1962), Hartmann developed a phenomenology of morality where he sought to describe the moral phenomenon in its own right rather than focusing on the ethical theories that presuppose it.

Yet another philosopher who embraced both realism and the phenomenological method was Roman Ingarden, a Polish phenomenologist who was a student of Husserl's at both Göttingen and Freiburg. Influenced by Scheler and Brentano, as well as by Polish analytical philosophy, Ingarden's work addresses some of the same issues regarding existence that are addressed by Hartmann. According to Ingarden, existence designates not what exists but what makes something exist and he was opposed to any form of transcendental idealism (which he felt was still prevalent in Husserl, despite the latter's transcendental realism regarding the actual existence of the objects of consciousness). Ingarden's emphasis on ontology, which he defined as a science of pure possibilities, ties his work to that of Heidegger who explicitly identified phenomenology with the project of fundamental ontology in *Being and Time*.

Like Heidegger, Ingarden saw his own work as both indebted to, but also departing from, a Husserlian approach to phenomenology.

Central phenomenological themes

As can be seen through the brief survey offered above, there are some recurring concerns linking the work of early and later phenomenologists. The transcendent existence of the contents of consciousness, the unity of conscious experience, the connection(s) between the human sciences and the natural sciences, the relation between ontology and phenomenology, how to grasp and affirm subjective experience in a manner that does not lead to a rejection of objectivity, are all ongoing preoccupations of the thinkers that have been mentioned. In this Section, I would like to trace the development and refinement of some of these themes in the work of Brentano, Husserl, Heidegger, Sartre, Merleau-Ponty and contemporary feminist phenomenologists.

Perhaps the dominant theme in phenomenology, associated most often with Husserl but actually articulated first in Brentano's work, concerns the intentionality of consciousness. The idea that to be conscious is always to be conscious *of* something or other may, at first glance, appear to be a rather simple statement. However, once one begins to examine the subtle implications of this seemingly straightforward claim, the nature of the relationship between the intentional activity that constitutes consciousness and its intentional object becomes much less clear and also much more exciting. Indeed, before one even turns to consider the nature of the relationship between *noesis* (intentional activity) and *noema* (intentional object), one may find oneself captivated by the numerous modes of intentional activity itself. Some of these modes, which Husserl identified and discussed, are: willing, believing, imagining, daydreaming, judging, perceiving and hallucinating. They all represent different ways of being conscious of an intentional object and, once this is acknowledged, we are compelled to recognise that one and the same object will appear differently according to the manner in which it is grasped. It is at this point that the existential status of the intentional object becomes a serious issue. Is there

a single object that shows itself in different ways or does the object have a purely phenomenal status such that it cannot be said to exist except in and through a given appearance?

Though Husserl's famous phenomenological battle-cry, 'to the things themselves', is often invoked by contemporary phenomenologists, Husserl's own transcendental realism regarding the existence of the intentional object is often forgotten or, at the very least, superseded by Heidegger's discussion of this issue in the introduction to *Being and Time*. Here, Heidegger traces the etymology of the word 'phenomenology' to its Greek roots and reminds us that, taking its two components together, phenomenon and logos, phenomenology itself signifies: 'to let that which shows itself be seen from itself in the very way in which it shows itself from itself' (Heidegger, 1962, p. 58). For Heidegger, then, it is important to recognise that: there is indeed some being that shows itself; that this showing is itself an active process that is, at the same time, a way of being in the world; and that what shows itself must be unconcealed or freed from distortions that would make it appear in ways that do not reflect how it is 'in itself'. In so far as the object can only be said to appear to consciousness through the intentional activity of consciousness, the question becomes: in what intentional mode can the object best be grasped as it is 'in itself'? For Heidegger, this question is complicated by his belief that there is no such thing as 'neutral' intentional activity; Dasein (human being-in-the-world) is always already directed *concernfully* towards the world, through some mood or other.

With respect to Dasein's own disclosure, Heidegger ends up privileging certain moods as more revelatory of the phenomenon of being-in-the-world than others (though moods themselves are all ways of being-in-the-world) and these include anxiety as well as joy. For Heidegger as well as Sartre, anxiety reveals something fundamental about our existence; namely, that it is contingent, grounded in nothingness and lacking any absolute origin or transcendental source of justification. Although the concepts of anxiety and nothingness are developed quite differently in Heidegger and in Sartre, what both philosophers emphasise through them is that the intentional activity that leads us to objects is also what detaches us from them. That is to say, no one intentional object can 'fill' consciousness once and for all since it will in turn be superseded by another one; moreover, as noted above, the different modes that characterise the intentional activity of consciousness themselves guarantee that our manner of accessing any given intentional object will change over time (for example, we may get sleepy or distracted and lose our concentration).

Rather than view our inability to maintain a fixed grasp on any one intentional object as a deficiency in consciousness or in phenomenological description more generally, Husserl saw this as a source of richness that he articulated in Gestaltist terms. Specifically, Husserl claimed, following the Gestalt psychologists, that just as all perception of a discrete object occurs by isolating it as a determinate figure against a more indeterminate ground, so too, does all of our intentional experience occur by isolating a given intentional object against a horizon comprised of other possible intentional objects as well as our past, present and future intentional activity. According to Husserl, then, the determinateness of the figure is always inversely proportionate to the indeterminacy of the ground; thus, the clarity and distinctness of the table in front of me depends directly on the lack of clarity and distinctness of what is behind, beneath, to the sides and above the table as well as the invisibility of the contribution that previous memories of the table, present perceptions of the table and anticipatory expectations regarding the table are playing in the present experience. For Husserl, the figure cannot be seen independently of this ground, but the point is that in order for it to appear over and against the ground, the ground must recede to reveal the figure. (See Husserl, 1962.)

Merleau-Ponty, especially, was fascinated by this Gestaltist relationship between figure and ground, and by the way it served to structure and illuminate the nature of our relationship to the world. While Husserl acknowledged that there is a 'zone of indeterminacy' that surrounds each of our experiences in the life-world, the existence of this zone also seemed to be a threat to his understanding of phenomenology as a search for essences that could be undertaken with the same rigour characterised by the natural sciences. Merleau-Ponty, however, was captivated by this zone of indeterminacy and the incredibly powerful role it played in all of our experience, most notably in the phenomenon of visibility itself. In Merleau-Ponty's own phenomenological inquiry into painting, for example, he argued that the painter must become aware of that which is ordinarily invisible to the perceiver including the effect of lighting and shadow, perspective and the 'empty space' against which objects stand out and actively incorporate this knowlege into the painting in a manner that, like perception itself, preserves and draws upon its invisible power to render visible the subject matter of the painting.

The interdependency between figure and ground, or even visibility and invisibility, has been productively utilised by several feminist phenomenologists in ways that neither Husserl nor Merleau-Ponty would ever have considered. Beginning with Simone de Beauvoir's phenomenological description of how women appear to themselves and to men within a patriarchal society in *The Second Sex* (1952), a text that makes visible the background role that women play in maintaining and perpetuating a male-dominated power structure, feminist phenomenologists have continually called our attention to the ways in which what comes to be taken as the figure and what comes to be taken as the ground are themselves influenced by sex, gender, race, class, age and other aspects of the individual that, historically, have been regarded as irrelevant to philosophy, much less to our understanding of the intentional object or even intentional activity itself. Feminist philosophers have also questioned the status of phenomenology itself as a purely descriptive method in which the phenomenologist tries to free herself or himself from all of her or his presuppositions about a given subject. This Husserlian characterisation of 'pure' phenomenology, feminists have argued, implies that phenomenology is itself an apolitical enterprise, one unaffected by reigning ideologies regarding societally accepted sex roles and their implicit heterosexist assumptions.

And yet, numerous examples abound in the work of phenomenologists such as Sartre and Merleau-Ponty that challenge this alleged neutrality of phenomenological description. These examples are especially prevalent in the descriptions of women's sexual conduct and motives that occur in the context of broader discussions of being-for-others for Sartre and of the body's sexual being for Merleau-Ponty. In these examples, both Sartre and Merleau-Ponty tend to radically oversimplify, and thereby distort, the complexity of women's own behaviour and attitudes in a manner that draws directly from stereotypical masculinist explanations of how women think, act and view themselves and others. More specifically, both philosophers evince what Luce Irigaray has identified as a specular, voyeuristic approach to women's sexuality and sexual experience, in so far as they acknowledge any form of sexual differentiation to begin with. Usually sexual differentiation and corresponding variations in the experience of men and women that may be tied to it are not even addressed in their work, nor are these issues raised by their fellow phenomenologists such as Heidegger or Husserl.

Feminist phenomenologists have therefore faced a double challenge: first, to offer critiques of accepted phenomenological descriptions of human experience that seem to presuppose that this experience is more homogeneous than it in fact is; and, second, to offer new descriptions of these same experiences that do justice to the ways in which sex, race, age, class, education and ability affect the nature of the experience or phenomenon in question. For, as Husserl has pointed out, we can never grasp a given phenomenon without sustaining some sort of intentional relationship to it and, as feminists have pointed out, the danger of seeing intentional activities such as willing, judging, daydreaming, perceiving and imagining as general faculties that function in the same way for all people, is that it obscures the fact that these faculties themselves develop (or fail to develop) within environments that may be more or less conducive to their full expression.

Recognition of the heterogeneity of human experience within what Husserl called 'the natural attitude', has led to a rethinking of central topics of phenomenological enquiry such as being-for-others, the body image and even the concept of intentional activity itself. One of the ways in which Hegel has influenced phenomenology has been through his depiction of the master-slave dialectic as a paradigm for the experience of being-with-others. Sartre works explicitly from this antagonistic model of intersubjective relationships in *Being and Nothingness* (1956). The limitations of this model are evident even to newcomers to phenomenology who read Sartre's famous chapter on 'The Look' and wonder if this battle of subjectivities is all that human relationships are capable of achieving. The fact that Sartre's discussion of the inevitable tensions that arise between being-for-itself and being-for-others is presented in the language of pure phenomenological description makes it even more difficult to see how it can be critiqued. And yet, to raise questions about the reductive nature of such a combatative picture of human relationships does not require that one abandon phenomenology or phenomenological description altogether. What it does require is that one attend more closely to the ground or horizon which situates a given figure in order to discover how the former helps to construct the significance of the latter and to discover alternative perspectives from which a given phenomenon can be presented and described.

Iris Young's 1980 essay, 'Throwing Like a Girl', offers a wonderful illustration of how it is possible both to point out the limitations of existing phenomenological descriptions of a particular subject (in this case the body image), and to offer a richer account that does more justice to the nature of the phenomenon in question. Taking Merleau-Ponty to task for failing to acknowledge how body image itself is gendered, and Erwin Straus, who does acknowledge gendered differences in the body image but attributes them to mysterious biological forces, Young shows that the body images of men and women can be radically different from each other and, moreover, that these differences cannot be explained through an appeal to physiological differences between men's and women's bodies. Young's poignant description of the contradictory bodily modalities that serve as a framework for many women's experience of their bodily abilities is a phenomenological account of how sexist patterns of socialisation lead to distinctive body images in boys and girls; body images that, in the case of girls in particular, tend to be inhibiting and constraining and whose contradictions are amplified rather than diminished as boys and girls move on into adulthood. Through this account, Young offers a useful model of how to pursue a phenomenological inquiry in a manner that refuses to oversimplify or universalise a given experience but which none the less seeks to provide an essential description of it.

The future of phenomenology

One of the virtues of phenomenological investigation (or one of its curses if one is antagonistic to its basic project) is that there is literally no aspect of human experience that lies outside of its range. That is to say, it is possible to systematically investigate something as seemingly insignificant as the difference between a blink and a wink, or as monumental as Husserl's phenomenology of consciousness or even Heidegger's phenomenological enquiry into the relationship between Being and time. Taking as its point of departure the life-world itself, which Husserl defined as the horizon of all actual as well as possible experience, it is clear that there will always be new phenomena to describe, as well as existing phenomena to redescribe as they appear in new guises against changing horizons of significance. Phenomenology's claims to describe rather than explain or prescribe can also appear retrograde, however, when viewed against the backdrop of contemporary Western society's increasingly vociferous demands that individuals who pursue expertise in a given field demonstrate that expertise in the form of concrete recommendations or predictions. So, an important question that will affect phenomenology's own future becomes, what is the role of 'pure' description in an increasingly technological society that is more focused upon quantifiable results than in uncovering and describing the presuppositions that ground the demand for them?

While the very project of a phenomenology of technology is itself viable, timely and increasingly pursued since Heidegger first asked the famous question, 'What is technology?' it has become rather déclassé to depict oneself as merely concerned with describing this (or any other) complex phenomenon rather than in supplying judgements about how it could or should be dealt with. Moreover, post-structuralist concerns about the status of the subject who does phenomenology have also chipped away at the solid respectability associated with this philosophical enterprise since Husserl's day. Hence, it is not a trivial question to ask whether there is, indeed, a future for phenomenology within Continental philosophy, or even a future for Continental philosophy within an increasingly analytically-oriented society. To answer affirmatively to both questions is to acknowledge rather than deny the political implications of one's commitment to a certain way of doing philosophy, and to be willing to serve as an advocate for it without distorting the very meaning of the philosophical project one is engaged in. For, as Husserl reminds us, phenomenology, like science, is one activity among others that one can participate in within the life-world and, as such, it is as amenable as any other to reflection and careful scrutiny.

To the extent that phenomenology calls upon us to identify and interrogate our own presuppositions about any given phenomenon, and to make that interrogation a central component of the description we offer of it, it is an ideal method not only for philosophers, but for all those who wish to make more reflective decisions about how to conduct themselves in their everyday affairs. Hence, not only should we encourage an increasing use of the phenomenological method in domains where a non-partisan description of a given experience may be helpful (for example, a phenomenology of politics is long overdue), but we should also encourage individuals to take a more phenomenological and less results-oriented approach to their everyday experiences since this can shed light on the significance those experiences have acquired through time. Husserl referred to this process as the sedimentation of meaning, and the crucial role that temporality plays in the constitution of meaningful experience has itself been an ongoing phenomenological theme.

While phenomenology itself, as first conceived by Husserl, may stop at the level of description, these descriptions offer invaluable information about individual and societal priorities which can in turn lead to a discussion of how to reorder those priorities by rethinking the underlying presuppositions. So, while phenomenology does not and should not claim to be a recipe for social change, it can and should be an essential ingredient in any such endeavour. It is only by letting a given phenomenon 'show itself as it is in itself' without trying to grasp it through a specific pre-established agenda, that we can come to understand how best to grapple with it and to maximise the potentialities it offers.

Today, the idea of a 'presuppositionless philosophy' as Husserl conceived of phenomenology, seems so idealistic and unachievable that many people with only a superficial acquaintance with phenomenology find it hard to take seriously. And yet, Husserl himself was well aware that this goal ought best to be conceived as a regulative ideal, and that even if one could never be sure that one had recognised and uncovered all the hidden presuppositions that affected one's description of a given phenomenon, the attempt to do so in as systematic and rigorous a manner as possible was none the less itself a practically achievable goal.

It is in this spirit of an ongoing endeavour to come to terms with what is most fundamental to a given phenomenon by critically examining notions that have been superimposed upon it and which may cause its significance and relation to other phenomena to be obscured, that phenomenology's life has only just begun. Even if the project of phenomenological description defies completion, this does not mean that progress cannot be made. Tracing the discussion of the phenomenon of intentionality itself, through Brentano, Husserl, Heidegger, Sartre, Merleau-Ponty and feminist phenomenology, leads to the recognition that phenomenology is best conceived not as an individual project, but as a joint enterprise that leads to a greater understanding of the life-world and our place within it. The fact that so many phenomenologists are themselves associated with the existentialist tradition, supports an understanding of phenomenology as not only a way of doing philosophy but also as a way of life.

To identify oneself as a phenomenologist today is to associate oneself with a relatively small number of philosophers who have taken up the mantle of the strong figures discussed in this Section by extending the domain of phenomenological enquiry to include horizons that Brentano, Husserl, Heidegger, Sartre and Merleau-Ponty had never considered or encountered. Alternatively, it is always possible to go back to a phenomenon they had addressed and to describe it from a fresh perspective. And yet, whether rereading their work or coming upon it for the first time, one is struck by how timeless so many of their insights are. From Heidegger's proclamation that the meaning of Being is temporality to Merleau-Ponty's provocative and enigmatic discussion of the 'flesh of the world' one can see that every description of experience offered only opens up, rather than closes off, other possible descriptions of human being-in-the-world. It is perhaps for this reason that the phenomenological method has been increasingly employed in the human sciences, in fields other than philosophy such as sociology and psychology, and even in various specialisations within philosophy such as aesthetics, language and perception.

Perhaps the domain in which phenomenology has had least influence is in the natural sciences, despite the recognised importance of the work of phenomenologists such as Alfred Schutz in the social sciences. The neo-Kantian concern with discovering a way of linking the natural and the human sciences, which achieved its heyday in Dilthey's work, but which has fallen into disrepute through the association of this project with Romanticism (an accusation made by one of Heidegger's own students, Hans-Georg Gadamer), has still not been satisfactorily achieved. While phenomenology may not be able to offer a solution to this goal, the Husserlian understanding of phenomenology as capable of serving as the foundation for all of the natural as well as human sciences, cannot yet be discredited. Although most of the aspects of experience that have been investigated by phenomenologists so far have tended to fall within the range of the human sciences (for example, consciousness, language, the body, perception, aesthetic experience, etc.), there is much work to be done in uncovering the presuppositions that are operative in the natural sciences and in bracketing or suspending them to redescribe the phenomena that are the subjects of these sciences in a manner that will be useful to the sciences themselves. Only then can we concentrate on the connections that link the human and the natural sciences with one another in order to assess the viability of the project of thinking their unity.

One consequence of taking phenomenology seriously is to recognise that the dominant analytical paradigm is not the only way of articulating philosophical problems or of grappling with their solutions. The lack of dialogue that continues to exist between phenomenologists (and Continental philosophers more generally) and analytic philosophers has been unfortunate and has served to marginalise phenomenology even further within the philosophical tradition. Analytic philosophers often find phenomenological terminology to be dense and obscure and the tendency of so many phenomenologists to imitate the idiosyncratic styles of Husserl and Heidegger has often added fuel to the fire. Another goal for phenomenology must therefore consist of finding ways not of justifying its methodology to outsiders but of demonstrating its own efficacy through clear and thought-provoking descriptions that seek not to simplify the phenomena in question but to do justice to all of their richness and complexity. In so doing, it should become clear that there need not be an unproductive tension between analytic philosophy and phenomenology but that they are two different ways of grasping the fundamental features of human existence, ways that can and should complement, rather than stand opposed to, one another.

To say that any subject can become the theme of a phenomenological investigation is not to say that any description we provide of our experience is a phenomenological one. What makes phenomenology philosophical is precisely its commitment to providing as thorough and rigorous a description of a given phenomenon as possible. Moreover, phenomenology, as with philosophy more generally, seeks not so much to interrogate the unfamiliar as to look at that which is most familiar and to render the ordinary extraordinary by doing justice to its unsuspected depth and corresponding layers of significance.

By forcing us to think carefully about what it means to be conscious, about how human consciousness as both temporal and temporalising differs from other forms of consciousness, about how the ways in which we are conscious affect, and are affected by, the objects of which we are conscious, as well as about the dangers of favouring consciousness over other aspects of human agency such as the body and the unconscious, phenomenology engages in a reflexive task of self-interrogation. A crucial project for phenomenology today is to move definitively beyond the infamous 'problem of the other' by providing more adequate descriptions of the continual interplay between self-interrogation and social interrogation; in so doing, we can take up our respective positions within the 'natural attitude' better informed about its limits as well as its untapped possibilities.

Bibliography

References and further reading

Beauvoir, Simone de (1952), *The Second Sex*, trans. H. M. Parshley, New York: Vintage Books. (*Le Deuxième Sexe: I. Les Faits et Les Mythes, II. L'Expérience Vécue* [1949], Paris: Librairie Gallimard.)

Brentano, Franz (1973), *Psychology from an Empirical Standpoint*, trans. Linda L. McAlister, London: Routledge. (*Psychologie vom empirischen Standpunkt* [1874], Leipzig: Duncker and Humblot.)

Cassirer, Ernst (1953, 1955, 1957), *Philosophy of Symbolic Forms*, 3 vols, trans. Ralph Manheim, New Haven: Yale University Press. (*Philosophie der Symbolischen Formen* [1923, 1925, 1929], Berlin.)

Cohen, Hermann (1902), *Die Logik der reinen Erkenntnis*, Berlin: Walter de Gruyter.

Dilthey, Wilhelm (1976) *Selected Writings*, ed. H. P. Rickman, Cambridge: Cambridge University Press.

Hartmann, Nicolai (1932), *Ethics*, trans. Stanton Coit, London: G. Allen and Unwin Ltd. (*Ethik* [1926], Berlin)

Heidegger, Martin (1962), *Being and Time*, trans. John Macquarrie and Edward Robinson, New York: Harper and Row. (*Sein und Zeit* [1927], Tübingen: Neomarius Verlag.)

— (1971), 'The Origin of the Work of Art', in *Poetry Language, Thought*, trans. Albert Hofstadter, New York: Harper and Row. (*Der Ursprung des Kunstwerkes* [1960])

Husserl, Edmund (1962), *Ideas: General Introduction to Pure Phenomenology*, trans. W. R. Boyce Gibson, New York: Collier Books. (*Ideen aus einer reinen Phänomenologie und phänomenologischen Philosophie* [1913], Freiburg: Max Niemeyer, Halle a. d. S.)

— (1970), *The Crisis of European Sciences and Transcendental Phenomenology: An Introduction to Phenomenologi-*

cal Philosophy, trans. David Carr, Evanston: Northwestern University Press. (*Die Krise der europäischen Wissenschaften und die transzendentale Phänomenologie: Eine Einleitung in die phänomenologische Philosophie* [1954], ed. Walter Biemel, The Hague: Martinus Nijhoff.)

Ingarden, Roman (1964), *Time and Modes of Being*, trans. Helen Michejda, Springfield (*Spór O Istnienie Swiata*, 2 vols [1947–8], Cracow).

Jaspers, Karl (1971), *Philosophy of Existence*, trans. Richard Grabau, Philadelphia: University of Pennsylvania Press. (*Existenzphilosophie* [1938], Berlin: Walter de Gruyter and Co.)

Merleau-Ponty, Maurice (1962), *Phenomenology of Perception*, trans. Colin Smith, London: Routledge and Kegan Paul. (*Phénoménologie de la Perception* [1945], Paris: Editions Gallimard.)

— (1993), 'Eye and Mind', in Galen Johnson (ed.), *The Merleau-Ponty Aesthetics Reader*, trans. Michael Smith, Evanston: Northwestern University Press, 121–49. (*L'Oeil et l'Esprit* [1964], Paris: Editions Gallimard.)

Natorp, Paul (1925), *Vorlesungen über praktische Philosophie*, Erlangen: Verlag der Philosophischen Akademie.

Rickert, Heinrich (1928), *Der Gegenstand der Erkenntnis: Einführung in die Tranzendentalphilosophie*, Tübingen: Mohr.

Sartre, Jean-Paul (1956), *Being and Nothingness*, trans. Hazel Barnes, New York: Washington Square Press. (*L'être et le néant* [1943], Paris: Editions Gallimard.)

Scheler, Max (1966), *Der Formalismus in der Ethik und die materiale Wertethik: Neuer Versuch der Grundlegung eines ethischen Personalismus*, Bern: Francke.

Young, Iris (1990), 'Throwing Like a Girl', in *Throwing Like a Girl and Other Essays in Feminist Philosophy and Social Theory*, Bloomington: Indiana University Press, 141–59.

4.1

INTENTIONALITY AND CONSCIOUSNESS: BRENTANO

Susan F. Krantz

Franz Brentano (1838–1917) is most famous for his so-called 'intentionality thesis' but he contributed widely to the entire field of philosophy of mind (what he called descriptive psychology) as well as to metaphysics and ethics. Most of his work was not prepared for publication during his lifetime, but has since become available in German editions as well as in an increasing number of English translations.

Life and influence

Brentano was born in Marienberg, Germany on 16 January 1838, to a prominent Italian-German family. Franz, the second child and oldest son of Christian Brentano and Emilie Genger, was encouraged by his mother to enter the Catholic priesthood and did so in 1864. However, he left the Church in 1879, due to inconsistencies he perceived in Church teaching, specifically the firm assent required in faith to doctrines that cannot be known with certainty by the human intellect to be true. Because he had been teaching at the University of Würzburg as a priest, his position there was terminated and he moved on to a position at the University of Vienna where he was a professor for some years. However, when he married Ida Lieben in 1880 he was relegated to the low rank of *Privatdozent* because the marriage of former priests was considered to be illegal in Austria at the time. Nevertheless, he had students and exerted influence in Vienna for some twenty years. For this reason he is usually referred to as having been an Austrian philosopher. Austrian philosophy of the time was more analytical and empirical and more closely tied to medieval traditions than was philosophy elsewhere in the German-speaking world, where Kantian and Hegelian idealism reigned. In this respect, too, Brentano is appropriately classed with the Austrians. Students who studied with him in Vienna, and who later became well-known, included Sigmund Freud, Edmund Husserl and Alexius von Meinong. In 1895 Brentano moved to Italy, and lived mainly in Florence until 1915. He then moved to Zürich in Switzerland, where he died on 17 March 1917. In his later years, Brentano lost his eyesight, but he continued to write philosophy by means of dictation. Many of these dictations are included in the posthumous editions of his works. His influence during his lifetime extended to Britain, where both Bertrand Russell and G. E. Moore paid attention to his work. In recent decades, interest in Brentano's philosophy has been renewed, both in Europe and in the USA, largely due to the work of Professor Roderick M. Chisholm of Brown University. The Brentano Institute [*Brentano Forschung*] at the University of Würzburg, under the leadership of Professor Wilhelm Baumgartner, is working steadily on critical text editions of Brentano's works, and also produces the annual journal, *Brentano Studien*. The journal, *Grazer Philosophische Studien*, published by the University of Graz in Austria, also pays significant attention to the work of Brentano and his students. The Brentano archive is currently housed at Graz.

The primacy of consciousness

Brentano's emphasis on consciousness as fundamental to philosophy significantly influenced such subsequent philosophers as Husserl and Heidegger, but this concern was not original with Brentano. The philosopher to whom he looked for inspiration, and whom he most respected and studied more assiduously than any other, was Aristotle. Brentano's doctoral thesis, *On the Several Senses of Being in Aristotle* (which had a profound effect on Heidegger), was a study of Aristotle's ontology via the various uses of the term 'being' in Aristotle's works. Later work focused on Aristotle's psychology in the *De Anima*, inspired by Aristotle's claim that, in knowing, the mind becomes the things it knows. In fact, there is a close connection between the mind's being what it knows and Brentano's concept of 'intentional inexistence' (see below). Another famous Aristotelian, the medieval philosopher Thomas Aquinas (for whom the young Brentano had a great enthusiasm, and whose complete works remained in his personal library), pointed out in commenting on the *De Anima* that psychology is the most certain of the sciences, since one knows from within that the soul gives life. Thus, Brentano's insistence on the primacy of consciousness has its roots in his work on Greek and medieval philosophy.

In modern times, Descartes is the philosopher most famous for having based his philosophy on the fact of consciousness – 'I think, therefore I am'. Brentano applied a Cartesian outlook to the philosophies of Aristotle and Thomas Aquinas, and it was this combination that led to his distinctive brand of consciousness-based philosophy, and to later developments in phenomenology. However, neither its antecedents nor its descendants have quite the Brentanian blend of classical thinking with modern, scientific commitment. The flavour of Brentano's philosophy is unique.

Nowhere is his distinctive style of philosophising more apparent than in his later metaphysical theses, many of which are collected in the volume entitled *The Theory of Categories*. For example, Aristotle had said that matter individuates; identical twins, for instance, are separate individuals in virtue of being materially distinct (even if their features are indistinguishable). Brentano took this idea one step further, saying that place is the principle of individuation of material things. Thus, he concluded, a body in motion is in fact a series of bodies because it occupies a series of places.

The intentionality thesis

The primacy of consciousness involves the concept of intentionality, which may be traced to medieval philosophers who used it to distinguish between objects in the world and objects of thought. In particular, they noted the unique kind of existence that objects of thought have, and called this 'intentional inexistence' (see Brentano, [1874] 1973). In this context, 'intentional' means intended by the mind (referred to, entertained, imagined, posited by the mind). 'Inexistence', though it may seem to indicate non-existence, actually means mental existence, existence within the mind, as opposed to extramental existence, existence outside the mind. If one thinks of a horse, then the thought-of horse has intentional inexistence. Likewise, if one thinks of a unicorn, the thought-of unicorn has intentional inexistence. But horses also exist outside the mind, whereas unicorns do not, although pictures of them and stories about them do.

Brentano's intentionality thesis, then, is a statement about existence, and also a statement about the human mind. The thesis is that, 'Every mental phenomenon is characterized by what the Scholastics of the Middle Ages called the intentional (or mental) inexistence of an object . . .' (Brentano, [1874] 1973, p. 88). This means that every thought, perception, judgement, desire and emotion is directed toward some object. One thinks of something, perceives something, judges about something, desires something, and feels in a certain way with respect to something. An object is therefore always included within any mental phenomenon but this need not be an object that exists in the outside world. It may be an object that exists only in the mind. In either case however, in so far as the object is referred to by the mind, it has intentional inexistence.

In proposing his intentionality thesis, Brentano intended to provide a definition of 'mental phenomenon'. His definition in terms of intentional inexistence is a systematic definition; that is, it purports to show the essential nature of mental phenomena. If one were simply to list the kinds of things that count as mental phenomena for Brentano, the list would include all thoughts, sense perceptions, plans, emotions and desires. According to the intentionality thesis, it is true of all these phenomena that they include objects, and that the objects they include have intentional inexistence. This is precisely what distinguishes mental phenomena from physical phenomena, according to Brentano. Physical phenomena – the colours, sounds, tastes, smells, temperatures and textures with which we are familiar – are not directed upon objects and do not include objects within them. Rather, it is the act of perceiving, thinking or feeling in various ways which may include presentations of physical phenomena as objects.

Another way to understand the distinction between mental phenomena (which exhibit intentionality) and physical phenomena (which do not exhibit intentionality) is to consider certain implications of the way language is used. A child may be said to hope for a horse, whether there are any horses to be had or not, and whether or not she ever gets one. But she may not be said to ride a horse except when she actually sits on a real horse. The hoping in this case is intentional; it is a mental phenomenon. But the riding is not intentional, not a mental phenomenon; rather, it could be said to involve a complicated set of physical phenomena. Thus, intentionality provides a unique kind of independence from extramental reality.

Brentano's intentionality thesis is a starting point for his whole philosophy in that it determines his approach to understanding reality. Roughly speaking, he saw reality as composed of mental phenomena and physical phenomena. The term 'phenomenon' is derived from a Greek word meaning 'appearance'. This is not the sense of the term in which appearance is contrasted with reality; rather it points to the fact that things appear to us, and their appearing provides us with a way of accessing them. Thus, for example, a crime would be solved on the basis of evidence that appears, or comes to light. Brentano's mental and physical phenomena are realities that are brought to light in our experience, that make an appearance in our mental life. It is in this sense that his philosophy may be called phenomenology, or a precursor to phenomenology: phenomenology is the study of what appears in human experience. Brentano himself preferred to avoid using the term 'phenomenology' to refer to his own work. Disagreements arose between him and his student Husserl concerning the charge of 'subjectivism', from which Brentano thought his own system to be immune, and to which he thought Husserl's phenomenology vulnerable.

Descriptive psychology

By isolating the intentional inexistence of their objects as the defining feature of mental phenomena, Brentano opened his enquiries to a careful analysis of those objects. This analysis of the objects of mental phenomena is his descriptive psychology. The first step in the analysis distinguishes three categories: presentations, judgements and emotive phenomena.

Presentations are those mental phenomena that are merely presented; that is to say, they are not true or false, loved or hated. Descartes and Locke had called them 'ideas'. Brentano uses the term 'presentation' to indicate what is unique about their content, namely that it is simply entertained or presented. It is easier to see that presentations constitute a distinct class of mental phenomena when we consider the other classes.

Judgements have traditionally been defined in terms of always being either true or false. According to Brentano, judgements are those mental phenomena in which something is accepted or rejected. Acceptance and rejection (affirmation and denial) must be of something which is also before the mind. For example, I cannot reject the existence of unicorns without thinking of unicorns. Or, when I judge that horses were brought to the Americas from Europe, I must be thinking of horses (among other things). Thus, judgement always includes presentation.

Emotive phenomena constitute the third class of mental phenomena. Where Descartes spoke of 'volitions' Brentano isolates what he calls phenomena of love and hate (the basic emotions) and desire. Emotive phenomena include judgements in the same way judgements include presentations. Thus, for example, if I love horses, I am also judging that horses are good (worthy to be loved), and in order to make that judgement I am thinking of horses (I have a horse-presentation). Emotive phenomena are the most complicated mental phenomena. (For further clarification, see the section on ethics below.)

According to Brentano, desire is to be understood in terms of the phenomena of love and hate. This is because desire for something is really a preference for that thing, and preference means loving a thing more (or, perhaps, hating it less) than some other thing. On this view, acts of will are fundamentally desires, desires are preferences, and preferences are at root relative degrees of love or hate.

Brentano considered each of the three categories of mental phenomena to be a distinct class, neither overlapping with, nor reducible to, any of the others. In adopting this categorial system, he was inspired by Descartes, who had distinguished 'ideas', 'judgements' and 'volitions'. Brentano's categories are not, however, quite identical to these.

The objects of mental phenomena are distinguished by Brentano in various ways. The object of the judgement that horses exist, for instance, is neither the being of horses, nor a proposition to the effect that there are horses; rather, the object is simply *horse*, and the affirmative act of judging, in this case, is to accept a horse or horses. (More precisely, the object of a judgement about horses is a horse-acceptor or horse-rejector; see below, the section on metaphysical reism.) Any judgement about horses has a horse-presentation as a proper part. Likewise, any emotive phenomenon includes the presentation of its loved or hated object, as well as the relevant judgement concerning it, as proper parts.

Brentano further distinguished primary and secondary objects. The primary object of a presentation would be, for example, a horse, while its secondary object would be the act or mental phenomenon itself, the presentation. This accounts for the fact that when I am (directly) aware of a horse, I am also aware (indirectly) of my awareness of a horse.

(Brentano's views about our awareness of our own conscious acts constitute an important and subtly complicated topic, which cannot be fully developed here.)

Because mental phenomena are distinct from physical phenomena, and because only a mental phenomenon (and not a physical phenomenon) can be a part of a mental phenomenon, Brentano also distinguished between external perception and inner perception. The objects of external perception are physical phenomena; the objects of inner perception are mental phenomena. Thus, I am aware of a horse through external perception, but I am aware of my awareness through inner perception.

This distinction between external perception and inner perception is a distinction that holds for consciousness generally. Sciences such as physics and chemistry are the projects of external consciousness. Psychology is a project of inner consciousness, because only inner consciousness can have mental phenomena as its objects. Consciousness itself was originally construed by Brentano as an activity involving mental phenomena; later he came to view it as a relation between a substance (a thinker) and an accident (presentation, judgement or emotive phenomenon). The later view, known as Brentano's reism (from Latin *res*, thing) is explained below, following the discussion of his ethical views.

Ethics

The primacy of consciousness is apparent in Brentano's treatment of ethics, which he bases on descriptive psychology. The origin of our concept of the good, he says, is to be found in our emotive phenomena. Any love, as noted above, includes within it the judgement that the loved object is worthy to be loved. What is worthy to be loved is, precisely, the good. But, he adds, not every love is correct. Sometimes, accepting a mistaken judgement, we perversely love things that are actually worthy to be hated. So love alone does not justify; it must be correct love. Correct love and correct preference are the standard by which all intuitions, utilities, actions and duties must be judged. Human nature as a provider of moral standards is satisfactory only in so far as it may be construed as the disposition to love correctly what is worthy to be loved. Certain loves, according to Brentano, are indeed 'experienced as being correct' (Brentano, [1889] 1969, p. 24). Among these are the love of knowledge, of beauty, of joy and of life. The reason such loves are experienced as being correct is that we can understand immediately that knowledge, beauty, joy and life are good in themselves.

Brentano's fundamental ethical principle is that one ought to act in such a way as to produce as much good as possible within one's sphere of influence. One is obliged to maximise the (correctly characterised) good in the world, but only so far as possible. (As he points out, if there are people on Mars, we should wish them well, but we cannot be expected to make their concerns our own.) He called this 'the principle of summation'. Other things being equal, two goods are better than one; in other words, given the choice between producing one good, and producing another good in addition to that one, the correct preference is for the latter option. This preference, too, is experienced as being correct. The force of the principle of summation is to promote a theory of preference in which the various goods (life, knowledge, health, beauty, joy, friendship) are not hierarchically ordered, but given more or less equal weight. With this, Brentano anticipated recent developments in natural law ethics. At the same time, his approach includes an element of utilitarianism, in that the results of our actions are important criteria of their rightness. Yet the deontologist's insistence on certain inviolable goods is also maintained, because Brentano insists it is universally correct to prefer knowledge to ignorance, existence to non-existence, and a greater to a lesser good. The influence of Aristotle is obvious in Brentano's moral philosophy; but he also injects his own peculiar note with the theory of correct preference and correct love, and with his insistence that ethics (as indeed all of philosophy) is based on the science of descriptive psychology.

Brentano held an interesting view on freedom of the will; namely, that unless determinism is true, responsibility cannot be assigned. This is not to deny that we are free, but rather to insist that on an indeterministic model there is no reason for praise or blame, the causality of the agent having been rendered ineffectual. Brentano is thus a compatibilist regarding free will and determinism.

Metaphysical reism

Brentano's idiosyncratic development of classic philosophical concepts is plain in what has come to be called his reism. Its underlying intuition is, again, one that comes from Aristotle: everything that really exists is an individual. In Aristotle this represented an empirical approach, distinct from the idealism of Plato. In Brentano, Aristotle's proposition is subordinated to the primacy of consciousness and becomes a theory of the individuation of minds.

The original reason why Brentano insisted that every existing thing is an individual is that he questioned the reality of such abstractions as 'humanity', 'horseness' and 'existence'. It seemed to him incorrect to hold that when one judges that a horse exists, one is attributing existence to a horse, or horseness to an animal. In fact, he concluded, one is, in this case, simply accepting a horse, and the real individual who exists is the horse-acceptor. Abstract nouns, like 'horseness' or 'humanity', are better understood, Brentano believed, as adjectives modifying individuals. But the individual whose existence is evident to me, when I judge that a horse exists, is the thinker or perceiver, that is, myself. 'Horseness' and 'existence' are *entia fictiva*, fictitious entities.

Among *entia fictiva* are likewise to be included: numbers, sensible qualities such as colour and sound, mental activities, relations, truth, falsehood and being itself. The real entities, respectively, are: one who thinks of a number, a perceiver, a thinker, one who compares, a correct judger, an incorrect judger, a thing. In each case the reality is an individual thing, or substance, with its accidents, if any.

The substance/accident relation had been fundamental in Aristotle's ontology, and it was fundamental for Brentano, too, but in an entirely different way. For Aristotle, the notion of substance (a being or thing capable of acquiring attributes, as distinct from those attributes themselves) was arrived at through a biological consideration of what constitutes an individual man or ox. It was, for Aristotle, a given fact that such individuals exist. For Brentano, on the other hand, the primacy of consciousness was a given fact, such that the individual 'man or ox' has to be understood in terms either of a set of presentations, or of one who has presentations, that is, a thinker. Since a presentation without a thinker is impossible (presentations considered in isolation from thinkers are mere *entia fictiva*), it follows in Brentano's ontology that the substance is the thinker and the presentation is an accident (attribute) of a thinker. Once he had adopted his reistic outlook, he preferred to avoid reference to accidents except as including their substances as parts. (See below.)

It is important to note in this connection that Brentano held strict views about the relations of wholes to their parts. Specifically, he adhered to the principle of mereological essentialism, according to which, parts are necessary to their wholes, such that a whole which lost or gained any part would thereby become a different whole. The ancient Greek puzzle about the ship of Theseus had asked, when would it no longer be the same ship because too many of its parts had been removed for repairs? According to Brentano, the mereological essentialist, a ship whose parts are replaced plank by plank (perhaps while a second ship is assembled out of the removed planks, one by one) loses its self-identity with the removal of the first plank. Aristotle, on the other hand, was not a mereological essentialist; that is, he would not have thought an individual thing is necessarily incapable of losing or aquiring parts while maintaining its identity. Organisms do this all the time, of course, and Aristotle was, among other things, a biologist; but Brentano, with his consciousness-based philosophy, was disposed to view the matter differently.

In considering wholes and their parts from the viewpoint of consciousness, one immediately notices the phenomenon of comparative perception. The one who now hears may be the same one who now sees, or the one who now remembers having heard may be the one who now sees, and so forth. In fact, it is evident to us in inner perception that this is possible; but it would not be thus evident if, say, the one who now sees and the one who now hears were distinct individuals. (A similar situation arises if several persons each read one word of a sentence; perhaps each word is read by somebody, but nobody

reads the whole sentence, so although the sentence may be said to have been read, nobody could be said to have read it.) In Brentanian terms, one and the same thinker is the one-sidedly separable proper part of each of the several accidents (one who now hears, one who now sees, etc.) whenever the several accidents are compared in, or joined by, inner consciousness. The comparison is possible due to the unity of consciousness. Mereological essentialism is preserved for thinkers even as they think a variety of thoughts, because what is really happening is that a single substance is being enriched by a variety of accidents. Strictly speaking, neither the thinker, nor any of its accidents, loses or assumes different parts during this process. In this way, Brentano's reism may be said to recall Plato's theory of participation. A substance, then, can be enriched by a variety of accidents, as when a thinker becomes one who thinks of a horse, or one who accepts horses (that is, judges that they exist), or one who loves horses.

But what is a horse, for Brentano? If I were a horse, I could perhaps say that a horse is a thinker, enriched by a variety of accidents. From the human point of view, however, a horse is something perceived or thought-of. Now, I know that I cannot ride a merely thought-of horse. To go riding, I need a 'real' horse – but what is the assurance that a given horse is real? Like Descartes, Brentano believed that the only individual of whose existence I can be absolutely certain is myself (at the present time, he would add, to accommodate the unreliability of memory). In judging that a presented horse is rideable and real, I am accepting (affirming that there exists) a correct rideable-horse acceptor, (that is, myself). In other words, I am one who accepts a correct rideable-horse acceptor. Thus, the real individual that exists whenever a horse is perceived, is the perceiver (or thinker) of a horse. A presented horse is an object of external perception, and external perception is not infallible. So, to be precise, what I am certain of when I judge that a horse is real, is that I am indeed one who accepts a correct horse acceptor. This type of locution is considerably more unwieldy in English than in Brentano's German; he is notorious for having coined a variety of expressions to serve his philosophical ideas.

The relation between substance and accident is

fundamental to Brentano's reism, but he construed it in a peculiar way. As in the classical conception, 'substance' designates a thing with properties, while 'accident' designates a property, quality or characteristic. But as we have seen, Brentano considered it impossible for accidents to exist on their own. In his view, an accident is actually a whole that has a substance as a proper part. That is to say, the accident includes the substance. We can illustrate this by considering the three categories of mental phenomena: presentation, judgement and emotive phenomena of love or hate. Even on a non-Brentanian view, love can be considered an accident or property that a person may have. Suppose I love music; then I have the property of being a music lover. The Brentanian analysis would be somewhat as follows: the music lover is an accident containing as a proper part one who judges that music is worthy to be loved. This in turn is an accident that contains as a proper part one who hears (or remembers having heard) music. (In fact, the music hearer is also an accident which contains as a proper part one who hears sound, and, given the descriptive complexity of the experience of hearing sounds over time, there will be a variety of accidents involving memory as well, to say nothing about the complexities introduced by hearing several sounds at once, as in a chord.) Finally, the hearer is an accident which contains as a proper part, simply, a thinker (or perceiver). The reason for this is that the thinker (or perceiver) can continue to exist even if it ceases to hear (it may continue to see, taste, dream, etc.); but the hearer cannot continue to exist without the thinker (or perceiver). Why? Because the hearer (hearing) is an accident that enriches a substance (a thinking or perceiving subject), and not the other way around. Likewise, ascending from the hearer to the music hearer, we see that the hearer can continue to exist without the hearer of music (it may hear ambient sounds of another sort); but the music hearer cannot likewise continue to exist without the hearer. Again, the music hearer can continue to exist without the judger (that music is worthy to be loved), because it is possible to dislike what one hears, or to withhold judgement altogether; but the judger-that-music-is-worthy-to-be-loved cannot likewise continue to exist without the hearer (who hears, or has heard, music). Finally, the judger that music is worthy to be loved can continue to exist without the actual music lover – perhaps by simply taking the judgement on authority, without feeling anything – yet the music lover cannot likewise continue to exist without the judger. In each case, we have in Brentanian terms an accident, which includes a substance as a proper part. The substance is the bearer of properties or accidents, as in traditional Aristotelian metaphysics; Brentano's addition to the theory is to insist that any real accident is a whole that comprises a substance which is a thinker.

Natural theology

Remarkably, Brentano made use of his conclusions regarding comparative perception and the unity of consciousness even in his lectures on the existence of God. Throughout his career, despite his break with the Catholic Church and his not having affiliated with any other religious denomination, he maintained his interest in, and defence of, theistic positions. In particular, the existence of God and the triumph of good over evil were topics he lectured on at length. His approach was empirical, and he claimed very high probability rather than strict certainty for his conclusions. He thus rejected the ontological argument for God's existence (as well as arguments purporting to show that God's existence cannot be proven), and defended versions of the teleological argument, the argument from motion and the cosmological argument.

In addition, he devised a unique argument of his own, which he called the 'psychological proof' (Brentano, [1929] 1987, pp. 290ff.). Based on the fact that inner perception shows us it can be the same subject that sees and hears, etc., Brentano concludes that the thinking subject cannot be physical but must be a mental substance. He thus rejects neurophysiological reductions of mental activity, and insists instead that if different areas of the brain are associated with different mental functions, this only proves that the brain is used by a thinker that is not confined to a single place. But if the thinker is not confined to a single place, then it is not a material, but rather a spiritual, thing. It thus follows, according to Brentano, that this spiritual thing must have a spiritual creator, since it would be contrary to reason to assume that something having consciousness could be produced by something incapable of consciousness. The spiritual creator is God, of course, and Brentano goes on to demonstrate the infinite perfection and unity of the intelligent first principle of all things (Brentano, [1929] 1987, pp. 302–7). Interestingly, Brentano rejects one of the traditional perfections of God; namely, immunity to change. As he points out, if God did not undergo a steady, infinitesimal change due to the passage of time, then omniscience would be jeopardised due to the fact that what is true at one time may not be true at another. (The judgement that there *are* dinosaurs, although true in the Jurassic, became false in later geological epochs, when it became true, rather, that there *had been* dinosaurs.)

The passage of time was also an important consideration in Brentano's theodicy, his defence of God's goodness despite the obvious evils that exist. Because the world is in the process of becoming at all times, and never achieves a state of complete realisation (which would contradict God's infinite power to create), there is always a steady unfolding of further goods. In other words, perfection, although never achieved, is never decisively ruled out either, because further and further perfections are coming into being.

The other component of Brentano's theodicy is the ingenious ploy of asking, with respect to any entity you like, whether its non-existence would be preferable to its existence. The first point to bear in mind when evaluating answers to this question, is that existence, thought, perception and knowledge are good in themselves. Every natural evil involves existence, and every moral evil involves thought, perception and knowledge; so it always turns out that there is an irreducible element which is such that its existence is correctly to be preferred to its non-existence. The second point is that for anything which exists, it must be such that God prefers its existence to its non-existence, for whatever unknown (but not, in principle, unknowable) reason. This should give us pause, at least, when we are tempted to suggest improvements to the divine plan.

Other contributions

Besides philosophy of mind, ethics, metaphysics and natural theology, Brentano also contributed to epistemology, logic, history of philosophy and aesthetics.

His epistemology is notable for a novel approach to evidence and truth. The criterion of evidence, for Brentano, is the evident nature of certain claims of inner perception. That is to say, I understand what it is for a claim to be evident because I can know with evidence that I now see, or hear, or think. Although I do not have detailed knowledge *a priori* of my conscious self, I am able to know certain facts about myself as a thinking thing; for instance, that I now see a colour or hear a sound. Understood in the sense of knowing that I seem, at least, to see a colour or hear a sound, this knowledge is certain and thus functions as a standard for all knowledge.

Brentano rejected the traditional correspondence theory of truth, on the grounds that there is no meaningful way a proposition can bear a relation of correspondence to any individual or set of individuals in the world. Propositions may be related to other propositions, though, and he proposed a theory of truth relating all propositions ultimately to evident propositions.

Brentano's distinctive approach to logic is characterised by fidelity to the results he had obtained from the science of descriptive psychology, in particular, concerning the nature of judgement. In his view, the rules of elementary syllogistic logic need complete revision (for instance, he rejects the old rule that no conclusion follows from two negative premises); but he concedes that traditional errors about both form and content in syllogistic logic have fortunately cancelled each other out in the main.

Brentano was at pains to point out that the history of philosophy is replete with surprisingly obvious errors, both because he thought it a bad thing that the errors should go unnoticed, and because in many cases he believed he could correct them. He viewed the history of philosophy as a repetition through time of four basic phases, two each of flourishing and decline. The beginning of a four-phase sequence is the stage of wonder and natural philosophy (for example, the Presocratics). This is followed by the maturing of metaphysics, epistemology, logic and philosophical psychology (for example, Plato and Aristotle). Thereafter, the decline begins with an overemphasis on practical philosophy (for example, the Stoics and Epicureans), and ends with a degeneration into mysticism (for example, neo-Platonism and Plotinus). In modern times, Leibniz represents the height of philosophical development, Kant and Hegel the depths of its decline.

One topic Brentano attempted to rescue from decadent philosophy was aesthetics (translation forthcoming) which had been born in the eighteenth century as a formulaic account of the elements of beauty. Brentano derided this as a 'top-down' approach, dictating to artists what they ought to prefer, rather than learning from them what art actually is. Brentano's own 'bottom-up' approach was typically empirical and involved studying artworks and artists' own experience. From this, prin-ciples of art could be derived which could then be used and developed in the future for the production of beautiful works and the development of correct taste. (As in ethics, so in aesthetics; a thing is not loved correctly simply in virtue of the fact that it is loved.)

There is, in all Brentano's thought, an element of nineteenth-century optimism – the belief in scientific progress and in the human ability to make a better world – but his optimism was never a blind or uncritical habit of positive thinking. Rather, it involved a deep personal dedication to clarity of thought, and a contemplative attitude toward the wonders of all reality. Brentano died during the First World War, surrounded by barbarism like Augustine at Hippo, but leaving behind him an inspiring example of the love for truth.

Bibliography

Writings

Brentano, Franz (1966), *The True and the Evident*, trans. Roderick M. Chisholm, Ilse Politzer and Kurt R. Fischer, New York: Humanities Press.
— (1969), *The Origin of Our Knowledge of Right and Wrong*, trans. Roderick M. Chisholm and Elizabeth H. Schneewind, London: Routledge.
— (1973a), *Psychology From an Empirical Standpoint*, trans. Linda L. McAlister, Antos C. Rancurello and D. B. Terrell, London: Routledge.
— (1973b), *The Foundation and Construction of Ethics*, trans. Elizabeth H. Schneewind, New York: Humanities Press.
— (1975), *On the Several Senses of Being in Aristotle*, trans. Rolf George, Berkeley: University of California Press.
— (1977), *The Psychology of Aristotle*, trans. Rolf George, Berkeley: University of California Press.
— (1978), *Aristotle and His World View*, trans. Roderick M. Chisholm and Rolf George, Berkeley: University of California Press.
— (1981a), *The Theory of Categories*, trans. Roderick M. Chisholm and Norbert Guterman, The Hague: Martinus Nijhoff.
— (1981b), *Sensory and Noetic Consciousness*, trans. Linda L. McAlister, London: Routledge.
— (1987), *On the Existence of God: Lectures Delivered at the Universities of Würzburg and Vienna, 1868–1891*, trans. Susan F. Krantz, The Hague: Martinus Nijhoff.
— (1988), *Philosophical Investigations on Space, Time and the Continuum*, trans. Barry Smith, London: Croom Helm.
— (1995), *Descriptive Psychology*, trans. B. Muller, London: Routledge.

References and further reading

Brentano Studien, International Journal of the Franz Brentano Institute.
Chisholm, Roderick (1960), *Realism and the Background of Phenomenology*, Atascadero, California: Ridgeview.
— (1966), 'Brentano's theory of correct and incorrect emotion', *Revue internationale de philosophie* 78: 4, 395–415.
— (1978), 'Brentano's conception of substance and accident', *Grazer Philosophische Studien*, 5, 197–210.
— (1982), *Brentano and Meinong Studies*, Amsterdam: Rodopi.
— (1986), *Brentano and Intrinsic Value*, Cambridge: Cambridge University Press.
McAlister, Linda L. (1976), *The Philosophy of Brentano*, London: Duckworth.
— (1982), *The Development of Franz Brentano's Ethics*, Amsterdam: Rodopi.
Smith, Barry (1994), *Austrian Philosophy: The Legacy of Franz Brentano*, Chicago: Open Court.

4.2

TRANSCENDENTAL PHENOMENOLOGY: HUSSERL

Thomas Nenon

Edmund Husserl was not, and never claimed to be, the inventor of the philosophical term 'phenomenology' nor even the sole initiator of phenomenology as one the most important movements in twentieth-century philosophy. None the less, it is no exaggeration to say that, during the first few decades of the twentieth century, the term 'phenomenology', as designating a philosophical method and direction of research, became so closely associated with the thinking and the works of Edmund Husserl that it now generally accepted as being the kind of philosophising associated with his name, his philosophical allies, including Max Scheler and Alexander Pfänder, and his successors, including Martin Heidegger and Maurice Merleau-Ponty.

Early works

Husserl, born in 1859 of Jewish descent in the town of Proßnitz (Prostějov) in the district of Maehren, now part of the Czech Republic and then part of the Austro-Hungarian empire, was educated at the universities of Leipzig, Berlin and Vienna. He came to philosophy through investigations into the foundations of mathematics and logic. Karl Weierstraß and Leopold Kronecker had been his principal teachers in mathematics in Berlin before his transfer to Vienna, where he completed his doctoral degree in mathematics under Leo Königsberger with a dissertation on *Contributions to a Theory of Variable Calculus* in 1882. It was also in Vienna that Husserl began to work

under Franz Brentano, who then recommended Husserl to his former student Carl Stumpf in Halle, under whose supervision Husserl enjoyed his first regular academic appointment in philosophy and completed his first major work *Concerning the Concept of Number*. During this period Husserl also came to know and be influenced by George Cantor and his work in set theory. In his early studies, Husserl took up the question of the foundation of mathematics as an enquiry into its origins. He attempted to show how the science of arithmetic and the concept of number upon which it is founded, are dependent upon certain elementary operations. For example, to form the concept of 'one' a person must abstract from the specific character of what one experiences and form the notion of 'something in general' as the basis for the idea of 'unit'. Forming the notion 'multiplicity' involves the operation of collectively conjoining such abstract units. By tracing back the origin of arithmetic as a discipline to such elementary operations as abstraction and conjunction, this grounding takes place through what Husserl, at this stage, called 'psychological' analyses or investigations (Husserl, 1951, Vol XII). He also argued that symbolic representation is a necessary element in arithmetic since the development of a system of integers for a finite discursive intellect necessarily involves the ability of consciousness to conceive of numbers that it cannot intuitively represent to itself. Hence symbolic representations such as numerals are required to conceive of larger numbers.

Husserl's general approach at this stage was closely tied to Brentano's notion of 'intentionality' which posits a directedness to objects as an essential feature of all mental states and thereby also sets the stage for an approach that analyses objectivity as it presents itself to consciousness in certain mental acts. Thus, the promising approach to questions concerning the foundation of mathematics and logic appears to be through an analysis of certain kinds of acts that must be presupposed if certain kinds of conceptions and entities are to be present for consciousness. However, both in substance and in the description of such investigations as 'psychological analyses', there is a danger of confusing questions concerning the origin and status of mathematical entities with the question concerning the origin and status of the possible representation of those entities. It is easy to gain the impression that Husserl is trying to suggest that the objects of mathematics and logic are psychological or subjective rather than genuinely objective, ideal entities.

Gottlob Frege was one critic who read Husserl's early work in this vein and voiced his objections in a well-known review of Husserl's *The Philosophy of Arithmetic* (see Mohanty, 1977, pp. 6–21). He accuses Husserl of mixing logic and psychology so as to distort the status of the mathematical entities that he purports to analyse, including 'number', which is not a mental representation. Thus, in 1900, when Husserl opened his next major published work, *The Logical Investigations*, with a 'Prolegomena' dedicated to the refutation of 'Psychologism' as the confusion of mathematical and logical principles with statements about psychological necessities or mental states, he is commonly understood as having adopted as his own Frege's criticisms of his earlier work and to have achieved a significant breakthrough towards a new approach that does not reduce ideal entities, such as meanings or logical principles, to mental acts. In fact, it is now apparent from letters and minor publications, such as book reviews, written during the period 1891–1900 that Husserl himself had become aware of the ambiguities and possible confusions involved in his earlier work, and that the *Logical Investigations* are more an extension and clarification of the general approach taken in earlier work than a repudiation of it.

Logical investigations

The *Logical Investigations* was published in two volumes – the 'Prolegomena to a Pure Logic' as Volume I in 1900, followed by six specific investigations into topics pertaining to the foundation of such a pure logic in Volume II a year later. This was Husserl's first work to reach a broad philosophical audience. Husserl describes the pure logic it purports to found as a '*mathesis universalis*' for all individual sciences, as a universal and formal theory of theories in general that could ground a universal system of all knowledge. The investigations thus centre around such concepts as meaning, object, truth and evidence; concepts whose clarification are essential for any theory of science.

Given Frege's criticisms of Husserl's earlier position as 'psychologistic', it is ironic that it was the extended and devastating criticism of psychologism in Volume I of the *Logical Investigations* that initially attracted the most attention. Here Husserl defines psychologism as the view that pure logic can ultimately be reduced to psychology; that is, that logical principles are essentially nothing more than assertions about the predominant patterns of human cognition. Husserl's refutation points to the differences in character between *a priori* logical principles and empirical generalisations about actual human thinking. Empirical laws are necessary vague (that is, they always include *ceteris paribus* conditions), merely probable and, as supposed causal principles governing existing things, also have implicit existential import. Logical laws, by contrast, hold unconditionally. They are exact (that is, they are not restricted by *ceteris paribus* conditions), certain and do not presuppose actually existing entities. The reality of logical principles is therefore of a fundamentally different kind than that of material or psychological objects. Husserl refers to them as 'ideal objects' and insists that their ideality does not make them any less genuine than physical objects or mental states. It is fair to say, however, that Husserl does not explicitly turn to ontological questions in the 'Prolegomena' in order to clarify how such non-physical and non-mental objectivity might be possible.

His later investigations, however, do begin to

address such questions. In the 'First Logical Investigation', for instance, Husserl turns to the question of meaning. Again he distinguishes the meaning of an expression from the mental state of the person uttering the expression, and he does so on the grounds that the same expression may mean the same thing when uttered by the same speaker on different occasions, by different speakers, or even by an unknown speaker. Thus, the function of expressions as bearers of meaning is different from the function that they may play as indicators of a speaker's beliefs or emotions. Husserl tries to show that the meaning of an expression must also be distinguished from the object that the expression refers to, since different expressions with different meanings may point to different aspects of the same object (for example, the victor at Jena and the vanquished at Waterloo), and the same meaning (for example, horse) can be used to refer to different objects. Nor are meanings and expressions identical either, since there may be different expressions within a language, or across languages, for the same meaning, or different meanings for the same expression. Meanings are an abstract, ideal stratum of expressions which have both a material and an ideal side, and can be viewed in terms of their function of expressing meaning or of indicating the mental state of the speaker.

Meanings and logical principles are not the only kinds of ideal entities for Husserl in the *Logical Investigations*. In the 'Second Logical Investigation', he also defends the position that meanings may refer not only to individual physical objects, but also to ideal objects he call 'species' or classes of things. 'Red', for instance, is the object referred to by the general concept 'red' and is neither itself a red object nor a mental operation. It emerges for a knower through the process of abstraction, but is not itself a mental process, as some empiricist theories might suggest. The 'Third Logical Investigation' makes clear, however, that Husserl does not view species and other abstract objects as existing independently, but as non-independent 'moments' of concrete wholes in which they actually occur. Moreover, he asserts that there are essential laws governing which kinds of meanings (and their corresponding objects) are independent and which

kinds are dependent, and he asserts that there are essential laws that even state which specific kinds of independent or concrete meanings and objects provide the foundation for specific kinds of dependent or abstract objects and meanings. The project of a pure phenomenological ontology, then, would be to investigate systematically and lay out these essential relationships. Closely related to this is the project of a pure grammar, described in the 'Fourth Logical Investigation'. A pure grammar would reflect upon essential relationships governing those meanings that are compatible with each other and those which are not, and which kinds of simpler meanings must be combined in which ways to result in more complex meanings such as those expressed in sentences.

The 'Fifth Logical Investigation' is particularly significant since it is here that Husserl introduces the notion of intentionality with explicit reference to Brentano and grants it a significant role in explicating the notion of meaning that has been functioning in the previous four investigations. Meanings become connected to intentionality since it is through meanings that a specific mode of directedness towards an object is established. Brentano had reintroduced the Scholastic notion of intentionality in his attempt to distinguish the realm of the mental from that of the nonmental. It is the unique property of mental acts to be about some object towards which they are directed, and Husserl adopts this view when he defines consciousness as intentional experiencing. In the 'Sixth Logical Investigation' he complements this insight with the assertion that all objects for knowledge are at the same time intentional objects, that is, mediated through some meaning that governs the specific way in which they are intended.

Already in the 'Fifth Logical Investigation', however, Husserl further distinguishes between the content or material and the quality of an intentional act, whereby the material names the particular object and the meaning through which consciousness is directed to it (for example, an ice-cream cone) and the quality of the act concerns the way that consciousness is directed to the object (imaging, desiring or perceiving the ice-cream cone). He is also careful to distinguish the material as the intentional object from the material of sense perception that may serve as the basis for the intention of that object, since, from the phenomenological perspective, those aspects of a sensibly perceptible object that are given through the senses (such as its specific colour or taste) occur for consciousness only as aspects of the object as a whole (in this case, the ice-cream cone) and not as independent objects. Thus, by 'material' Husserl does not mean something like sense data, but rather intended objects that may include sensibly perceptible moments as part of their complete intention, but these sensibly perceptible moments are not separately intended objects.

Among the various kinds of intentions, Husserl identifies 'representations' as the most basic units which are presupposed by others. He follows Brentano's analysis that it is indeed conceivable that one may represent, for instance, an ice-cream cone to oneself without desiring it, but that one cannot desire it without implicitly representing it to oneself, so that there is a one-sided foundational relationship, in which representations found all other sorts of intentions.

In the 'Sixth Logical Investigation', Husserl turns explicitly to the relationship between intentions and intended objects. He begins by focusing on the so-called 'objectifying intentions', that is, those intentions that can be verified or falsified through appropriate intuitions. Thus, the traditional question about the relationship between subject and object, knowing and the known object, is approached in terms of the question of intentions and their fulfilment. An objectifying intention establishes a relationship to the object such that certain kinds of intuitions count as fulfilling the intention and thus presenting the intended object not merely as intended, but as actually known. The object of knowledge is exactly what is given in a fulfilled intention. Hence, corresponding to every intention is an intended object, but in the case of an empty intending, that is, an intending not based upon actual sense intuitions, there may or may not be an actual object which corresponds to the intention. In the case of a fulfilled intention, intuition confirms that there is an existent object that does indeed correspond to the intention and that the object is just as it has been intended, so that there is an identity between

intending and the actual intended object itself. The ideal of a completely fulfilled intention is captured in the notion *Evidenz*, the experience of an object being evidently given just as it has been intended, so that it is apparent that the actual object coincides precisely with the intention of it. In Husserl's view, the experience of the evidentness of the object for us as it is in itself lies at the basis of the notion of truth in all its various manifestations, which all proceed from this notion of evidentness. Taken as a property of the intending or of a judgement expressing a specific intention, truth refers to the ability of an intention to be fulfilled by such an evidential experience. Truth can also be taken to be a property of the intended object or state of affairs, in the sense that something is indeed a true object or a true state of affairs if it can be evidentially experienced in the appropriate manner. Moreover, one can further distinguish between truth as the actual experience of the identity between the intention and the intended object by an observer and the claim that such an experience could be had by an ideal observer. However, the claim that a proposition or a state of affairs is a true one must ultimately bear some relationship to this experience of evidentness that is the fundamental phenomenon to which any truth claim must be referred.

The 'Sixth Logical Investigation' makes clear that the objects of legitimate intention are not limited to sensible individuals, but may also be states of affairs or other kinds of objectivities that may be founded in, but are not necessarily reducible to, that which may be directly perceived through the senses. Having articulated the general relationship between intention, fulfilment and the objects of the intentions that are presented through the fulfilment of an intention in the first half of the 'Sixth Logical Investigation', Husserl then turns to what he calls 'categorial objects' such as states of affairs and the corresponding 'categorial intuitions' that fulfil them. Not only does Husserl recognise as legitimate objects those states of affairs which are intended through complex meaningful expressions such as sentences, he also maintains that there are other meaningful expressions, such as those referring to universals (or 'species' as he called them in the Second Investigation), that each have their own appropriate and unique form of fulfilment. Thus, in addition to sense intuition, Husserl proposes that there are other forms of intuition, among them, for instance, categorial intuition (for example, seeing that *a* is *b*) as the fulfilment of the intention of categorial objects (*a*'s being *b*), each with its own unique structure that is an appropriate topic for phenomenological investigation. Particularly important in this regard is his assertion that there may be kinds of intuitions parallel to categorial intuitions that could fulfil the intention of ideal objects, so that the fulfilment of intentions with regard to mathematical or logical truths would be possible, although not reducible to sense intuitions. Husserl asserts that there is an essential sameness in character in the function that fulfilment plays in all these forms of intuition in its ability to confirm or disappoint an intention, and that the parallel relations between intention, fulfilment and objectivity make it necessary to recognise each fulfilling act of the confirming self-presentation of an object (even a complex object such as a state of affairs or an ideal object such as a logical principle) as a perception, each fulfilling act in general as an intuition and its intentional object as an object (*Gegenstand*). Thus the realm of perception extends beyond the realm of sense perception and the range of possible objects extends beyond that of mere individual physical objects.

This opens the way for a whole range of investigations into the nature of these various realms or 'regions' of objects, into the nature of the kinds of intentions and fulfilments appropriate to them, and into the relationship between the various kinds of objects, intentions and fulfilments that belong to each of these realms to see how they are essentially related. The sensually perceivable or 'real' objects are characterised as objects of the lowest stage of possible intuition, the categorial or ideal objects that are founded upon them are, by contrast, higher-order objectivities. The project of spelling out just how they are related, what the essential structures of each of these regions are and what essential relations obtain between the intentions, fulfilments and objects of the various regions is not carried out in the *Logical Investigations*, but the possibility of such a project is outlined and the necessity for it as part of an overall grounding for all of the particular sciences is asserted.

This project remains at the heart of phenomenology as a systematic field of study throughout all Husserl's later work. However, a decisive question which remained at this stage of his thinking was the proper method for the execution of the project. What guarantees the necessary correlation between intention and object? How is reflection upon such essential states of affairs possible, and how is it different from the kind of internal observation of one's own mental states that would amount to nothing other than a new version of psychologism? What is the proper method for studying such essential correlations? Husserl's turn to transcendental phenomenology during the decade that followed the *Logical Investigations* intended to answer such questions.

The turn to transcendental phenomenology

Shortly after the appearance of the *Logical Investigations*, Husserl received a professorship in Göttingen, where he would remain until 1916. During this period, he developed phenomenology as an explicit methodology and field of research, coming to be regarded as the leading figure in phenomenology, now also an intellectual movement centred around a group of sympathetic scholars in Munich (some of whom were already well-established on their own and who were introduced to Husserl's work by an independent scholar by the name of Johannes Daubert). These included, among others, Theodor Lipps, Alexander Pfänder and Max Scheler; and later a circle of students in Göttingen that included Adolf Reinach (originally from Munich) and Edith Stein. In his discussions with these circles, as well as in critical yet friendly debates with leading representatives of neo-Kantianism (such as Paul Natorp) and the philosophy of life, Husserl came to see phenomenology as the study of pure transcendental consciousness, its intentional acts and the correlative forms of objectivity constituted through these acts. The process of 'transcendental phenomenological reduction', through which all forms of objectivity are traced back to the processes in subjectivity through which they are constituted, was recognised as the key mode of access to the realm of pure phenomenology. This was now seen not as a reflec tion upon the individual mental life of existing subjects within the world, but as the analysis of the realm of 'pure transcendental subjectivity'. I will explain this contrast.

From the outset of his work, one of Husserl's problems had been distinguishing his own analysis of the essential processes through which various forms of objectivity become apparent to consciousness from a study of the mental processes which actually take place in individual subjects. In a polemical essay written in 1911 for the journal *Logos*, Husserl described the need for a philosophical method that could make philosophy into a rigorous, indeed the most rigorous, science, since it would presuppose no other. In order to fulfil this task, phenomenological philosophy must avoid the twin dangers of 'naturalism', that is, approaching consciousness only from the standpoint of other natural, ultimately material phenomena, and 'historicism', that is, reducing philosophical issues to matters of historical world-views. As opposed to either of these ultimately empirical approaches, phenomenological philosophy, if it is to fulfil the task of philosophy as a rigorous science, must be a 'pure', *a priori*, and hence certain, discipline. If it is to study invariant, essential structures and not merely psychological patterns, then phenomenology must find a way to exclude all merely empirical elements from its analyses. First in working manuscripts composed in 1905, then in lectures presented in 1907 and published posthumously under the title *The Idea of Phenomenology*, Husserl proposed the procedure of phenomenological reduction as the means of accomplishing this goal. The first step is to exclude, bracket out or put out of play as fallible and thus not the source of genuine evidence, those elements in any claim to knowledge that refer not to the processes through which the objects of knowledge are given to consciousness, but to the objects themselves. The technical term Husserl employs to such suspension of belief is the Greek term *epoché*, which arose in ancient Stoicism. Accordingly, it is not a phenomenological, but rather an empirical, question whether there actually is a tree outside my window, whether there are such things as magnetic force fields (or phlogiston, for that matter) or whether any particular physical object at all exists. The first step, it seems, is thus to concentrate not on the tree that is seen or the magnetic force field that is proposed as an explanation for certain phenomena, but upon the seeing of the tree or the explaining of the phenomena through the proposal of something like a force field, since – following a motif familiar to philosophers since Descartes – it seems that the seeing or explaining, at least at the moment they are happening, are indubitable occurrences for the subject that is performing the seeing or explaining. But, even here, it turns out that a further kind of reduction or bracketing is necessary to exclude all empirical, and thus non-apodeictic, elements, since mental processes themselves are empirical facts about which one can be mistaken. It is not just possible to be mistaken about whether the tree is such as I perceive it, or even whether there is even a tree there at all. It is also, at least in principle, equally open to doubt whether it is me, the empirical person with this or that specific identity and history, that is doing the perceiving as it is whether or not the tree is actually such as I perceive it. So, in addition to bracketing out all commitments to the truth of the statement about whether the object is such as I perceive it, the phenomenologist must also bracket all empirical psychological claims about the perceiver. What is indubitable is the nature of the purported perceiving itself, including any beliefs that the perceiver holds about her or his own identity and empirical character. The phenomenologist can reflect upon those claims without any commitment to their empirical truth at all. Moreover, the phenomenologist can even reflect upon what would count as good empirical evidence for those claims and the necessary limitations of such evidence. There can be doubt about whether there is anything that corresponds to these contents of consciousness, and even about the identity of the consciousness that is aware of them, but whenever these contents are present for consciousness, there can be no doubt of their presence for the consciousness that is aware of them. Thus, if phenomenology limits itself to an analysis of these 'pure' contents, that is, the contents apart from all of the empirically dubitable claims attached to them, it has available to it a sphere which is beyond doubt, a realm of apodeictic certainty for its analyses.

Within this realm of pure self-givenness, Husserl's

interest is, and remains, the analysis of essential structures and connections within cognition, of its various forms and correlative objectivities. Thus, transcendental phenomenological reduction involves a third moment, which one might term eidetic reduction. Phenomenology's interest pertains to the eidetic, that is, the invariant, and thus essential, elements that present themselves to pure consciousness. In the 'Sixth Logical Investigation', Husserl had maintained that such invariant structures or essences can be just as much an object for pure intuitions as an empirical physical object can be given to sense perception. With this reduction to the sphere of pure universal self-givenness, Husserl now believes he can distinguish phenomenology from descriptive psychology, since the investigation no longer concerns the immanent sphere of empirical consciousness, but rather the realm of the purely self-given contents that can be made apodeictically evident to phenomenological reflection. Phenomenological reduction thus builds upon and presupposes the procedure of imaginative variation through which those things that can conceivably be otherwise than they are, may be separated from those that cannot conceivably change. This procedure, known as 'eidetic variation', is a kind of thought experiment employed by the phenomenologist to distinguish empirical associations and contingent conjunctions from essential structures that cannot conceivably be different from the way they are. Phenomenology is thus a science of 'pure possibilities' whose interest is directed to the necessities that underly any such possibilities and consequently also hold for any conceivable actuality, so that they apply to all possible and actual relationships without implying any commitment to which actual relationships and objects genuinely exist.

Husserl introduced the phenomenological reductions for the first time to a wider audience during his lifetime in his major programmatic work, *Ideas Pertaining to a Pure Phenomenology and Phenomenological Philosophy. First Book*, which he described as a general introduction to pure phenomenology (commonly referred to simply as *Ideas I*). It was published in 1913 as the first volume of the *Yearbook for Philosophy and Phenomenological Research*, which he co-founded and co-edited with Alexander Pfänder,

Moritz Geiger, Max Scheler and Adolf Reinach, and which was to remain the leading venue for phenomenological research until its final volume in 1930. In the General Introduction, Husserl describes the sphere of phenomenological research as the 'region of pure consciousness', as the 'region of all regions', since it is within and for that sphere that all other regions are constituted. Transcendental phenomenology is said to be a kind of transcendental idealism, within which the pure or invariant structure of an act of consciousness (the 'noesis'), its corresponding intentional object (the 'noema'), and the necessary correlation between the two are investigated. It does not purport to supplant the individual sciences that operate in the natural attitude and concern themselves with empirical facts, but rather to ground them all as well as formal disciplines such as logic and mathematics by showing how each of them presupposes certain essential structures or essences, whose description and explication can be properly executed only by transcendental phenomenology, which brackets out or neutralises the assumptions made within the natural attitude. The term Husserl now introduces to describe the process by which subjects come to intend objects is 'constitution', through which he seeks to avoid causal terms that would imply a dependency relationship between two existing things such as consciousness and objects, but at the same time stresses the necessary role of specific cognitive operations (*noeses*) if various kinds of objects are to become present for consciousness (*noemata*).

In the final section of *Ideas I*, Husserl turns to the questions of reason and actuality. How does phenomenology fit in with the traditional philosophical project of securing a rational foundation for knowledge and action, and what is the relationship between the eidetic analyses undertaken in phenomenology and actual existence? Husserl describes the two problems as interrelated, for to speak 'reasonably' or rationally about objects involves a claim to justification or possible confirmation through evidence. Thus, under 'reason' in this context Husserl understands the inherent directedness of intentions towards fulfilment. There is not only a corresponding *noema* for each *noesis*, but also the inherent directedness of objective consciousness towards the confirmation or fulfilment that would establish the relationship towards an actually existent object that would be identical to that *noema*. However, since there can be different kinds of objectivities, there will also be correspondingly different kinds of confirming intuitions that fulfil them. Thus, the philosophical project of reason is to lay out what these would be and to systematically delineate the various kinds of essential relationships that hold between them. Again, which of them is actually fulfilled is a non-philosophical question, but that does not mean that phenomenology as the science of reason does not address questions of actual existence or actual objects, but that it addresses them only in terms of their 'meaning' and their structure. It analyses the kinds of fulfilment that would be appropriate to these intentions and their corresponding objects, but does not claim to be able to take a stance as a pure science upon which of them actually has been or will be fulfilled or not.

It is during this period that, in addition to intentionality, temporality emerges for Husserl as the second significant essential structure of all consciousness. He demonstrates how consciousness occurs as a flow so that each event in conscious life has a temporal location with regard to all others. The appearance of any object can necessarily be characterised in terms of a 'now', a 'before' or an 'after'. Moreover, his rate analyses reveal these distinct modes of past, present and future as not only mutually related to each other, but also that each temporal modes of presentation should not be conceived as discrete moments, each separated sharply from the other. Rather, the now appears always with a temporal fringe or horizon. The now taken as a moment around which past and future gather is never strictly an isolated point. Indeed, the very idea of the now as a point is merely a limit concept that is never experienced in itself, since in conscious life every now also involves the consciousness of a having-been that has immediately preceded it and a not-yet that is about to become now. Thus, the 'now' for consciousness is always an extended living presence that, as the originary temporal field, also includes the no-longer and the 'not-yet' (Husserl, 1991, pp. 66ff. and pp. 379ff.).

One of Husserl's original contributions to the discussion of temporality, which he had taken up from Brentano, is his distinction between 'retention' as that form of the no-longer which is part of the immediate horizon of the now, from 'memory' which involves making present again to consciousness what was no longer immediately present for consciousness. Retention, along with 'protention', its corresponding form of the not-yet, is a mode of what Husserl calls 'impressional consciousness'. Memory, by contrast, is a form of 'representational consciousness' (ibid., pp. 378–9). For example, when one hears a melody, a note runs off into the retentional past as it comes to be replaced by a new one, but without disappearing from consciousness, since it would otherwise be impossible to hear a melody as such. Similarly, there arises at each moment a new anticipation of a coming note (its 'protention') emanating from the present, which Husserl calls the 'primal' impression in order to distinguish the way that it is present for retentive and protentive consciousness. All of these modes of temporal awareness of objects are ultimately grounded for Husserl in the temporality of consciousness itself; that is, in the self-constitution of its own identity throughout its different moments in the flow of consciousness. Another name for transcendental subjectivity is therefore 'absolute primordially constituting consciousness' or 'absolute primordial temporality', that has a specific structure that can be the object of phenomenological analysis and forms the horizon against which the constitution of the empirical consciousness of the individual and the objects of consciousness takes place. However, in *Ideas I* and other works from this period, Husserl does not trace back the constitution of specific kinds of objects to their ultimate temporal foundations, even though it is during this period that the framework for such a project was laid.

The Freiburg years (1916–38)

A few years after the appearance of *Ideas I*, Husserl was named Chair of Philosophy at the University of Freiburg, the successor to Heinrich Rickert, who had accepted an appointment in Heidelberg and recommended Husserl to follow him. Husserl remained there beyond his retirement from academic life in

1928, until his death in 1938. During this time, he concentrated upon the completion of phenomenology not just as a methodology, but as a concrete and comprehensive research project. This involved, on the one hand, pursuing a wide range of specific phenomenological constitutional analyses into the relationship between nature and spirit, or the naturalistic and personalistic attitudes, as well as into the structure of the everyday life-world out of which science emerges; into intersubjectivity and into nature as the correlate of intersubjective intentionality; into the constitution of ideal objects such as numbers or geometrical shapes; into the foundations of sense experience and formal logic; and into the phenomenological foundation for normative sciences such as ethics and value theory. On the other hand, it also involved a deepened understanding of what phenomenological analysis must entail if it is indeed supposed to trace back the constitution of various kinds of objects to their ultimate origins. Instead of being a static description of various kinds of essential structures and the necessary relationships that obtain between them, if phenomenology is to be a genuine science of absolute origins, it would ultimately have to trace back all forms of objectivity to the structures of consciousness and its basic forms of intentionality and temporality. Constitutive phenomenology thus explicitly evolves into genetic phenomenology, which traces higher-order forms of objectivity back to lower-order forms, and these in turn to the most elementary structures of intentional consciousness that in turn have their ultimate basis in modes of temporality. Accordingly, phenomenology must not only provide a description of the essential relationships governing all reality, but must also provide an account of the necessary origins of these relationships in and for consciousness in accordance with its most elementary structures. It must describe not only the constitution of the predicative realm and the operations most directly and easily accessible to reflection, but also trace these back to activities at the pre-predicative level that are generally thought of rather as passivities, the passive syntheses that take place at the most basic levels of consciousness as it organises sense experience into the experience of individual material objects, on the basis of which higher-order objects are constituted.

One guiding theme throughout this period of Husserl's work and beyond is his opposition to philosophy's recent attempt to model itself after the natural sciences and to reductionistic tendencies in many other sciences that have also falsely attempted to pattern themselves after that model. This is already a familiar theme developed in Husserl's earlier refutation of psychologism, where he argued against the attempt to reduce mathematics and logic to natural phenomena in the *Logical Investigations*, and then later again in his critique of naturalism, where he refutes the attempt to reduce all mental phenomena to externally observable physical entities in 'Philosophy as a Rigorous Science'. Already during his middle period, he had discovered commonalities in this regard with the philosophy of life as represented by Wilhelm Dilthey, and with philosophers such as Wilhelm Windelband and Heinrich Rickert, neo-Kantians of the South-west German school who stressed the independence of the cultural sciences from the natural sciences. Whereas the critique of naturalism in the 'Logos' essay clearly demonstrated Husserl's common ground with them, the polemical tone of the critique of historicism offered in the second part of that essay (which exhibits Husserl's concern with the topic of history and the relationship between philosophy and the cultural sciences) stresses Husserl's differences from, instead of commonalities with, Dilthey and related thinkers. Indeed, not until the very last major published work by Husserl, *The Crisis of the European Sciences and Transcendental Phenomenology* in 1936, does it become apparent that he shares with the philosophers of life and of culture an appreciation of the cultural and historical dimensions that are constitutive of everyday human existence, dimensions that provide the background against which abstract disciplines like the modern natural sciences arise. However, posthumously published writings such as the Second Book of Husserl's *Ideas* reveal that he had gained an appreciation for the non-naturalistic attitude that constitutes everyday life much earlier and that he had been decisively influenced in this regard by Dilthey, Windelband and Rickert.

In *Ideas II*, Husserl constrasts the naturalistic and the personalistic attitudes. Each attitude may be described as a noetic stance, within which specifi kinds of entities appear for consciousness. In the naturalistic attitude, everything appears as nature in the sense of modern natural science: what exists is spatially and temporally located, causally determined, and measurable. Husserl analyses the fundamental concepts or categories governing this region and shows how anything which does not fit into these categories is dismissed as non-existent by these standards. However, Husserl makes clear that the naturalistic attitude is only one possible stance towards objects, and that other equally legitimate attitudes can reveal other kinds of equally genuine objects. For instance, in the personalistic attitude, governed by the category not of causality but of motivation, other human beings are encountered as subjects of intentional states who behave in the way they do not because of material causes, but on the basis of motivating mental states such as beliefs and desires. Moreover, even the everyday non-human objects which surround us are organised not in terms of the predicates of natural science, but rather in terms of their serviceability to our needs. In contrast to the world of 'nature' and its seemingly objective properties, the everyday world in which we live as persons is filled with cultural objects like tables and chairs and with other human beings that are also persons with beliefs, needs and desires of their own. In *Ideas II*, Husserl also examines the essential relationships that hold between the two different regions that emerge in the two different, that is, the naturalistic and the personalistic, attitudes, and concludes not only that the personalistic realm is every bit as much a realm of genuine objects as the naturalistic realm, but also that the latter, that is, the scientific realm, is grounded in the former, the realm of everyday life, and not the other way around. Although it is true that the higher-order objects such as cultural objects or persons are founded on natural objects in the sense that each of these more complex, higher-order objects necessarily contains a stratum that can be described simply in naturalistic terms (its weight, spatial location, etc.), Husserl demonstrates that the realm of nature as such arises only through abstraction from the predicates that present themselves to us as genuine predicates of the objects in our everyday, concrete lived existence. The realm of nature of science is an abstraction derived from,

and therefore dependent upon, the realm of concrete everyday existence that we encounter in the personalistic attitude. Moreover, in the personalistic world, which Husserl calls the *Umwelt* ('environment' or literally 'surrounding world') in contrast to nature, it is apparent that objectivities emerge for us in the way they do (show up as tables or chairs) in view of certain subjective acts (see Husserl, 1989, pp. 194ff.). This realm makes the subjective role in the constitution of objects more readily apparent than an approach through the realm of nature, since the latter, in its search for universal and reliable structures of the objects, constitutes an idea of 'objectivity' that is seemingly independent of any subjective acts or attitudes. Phenomenological investigation reveals, however, that this very notion of 'objectivity' is itself a subjective construct that can be traced back to certain motivations and interests of persons. As such it is also subject to critical examination. If it is clear that the everyday surrounding world shows up the way it does partly as a result of the activity of a subject or a community of subjects, then critical reflection upon its origins and justification is also possible. Whereas the world of science can tend to forget or hide its subjective origins and thus seem to remove itself from the necessity for critical scrutiny, the personalistic attitude is much closer to the truths which phenomenology reveals, namely, that all supposed objectivities are correlates of subjective activities and attitudes which are amenable to reflective analysis and criticism.

In his final works, Husserl returned to these themes and developed them further. In a 1935 essay entitled 'Philosophy and the Crisis of European Humanity' he expanded his critique of naturalism into a sweeping indictment of recent developments in Western culture in general under the heading of 'objectivism', which, according to Husserl, is the belief that all genuine knowledge is objective knowledge and that objective knowledge is to be gained only by science after the model of modern natural science as it has developed since Galileo. Questions not accessible to the modern mathematical sciences are taken to be outside the realm of the rational; entities that cannot be captured in, or reduced to, these terms are taken to be non-existent. Husserl, by contrast, claims that phenomenology realises the true telos of Western science that was initiated by the Greeks and reawakened at the beginning of the modern age through its quest for absolute rational grounding of the subject and its activities by means of radical self-reflection. Rather than grounding all other sciences, modern mathematically-oriented natural science must itself be grounded in a more radical and basic science: that of pure phenomenology.

In his final major published work, *The Crisis of the European Sciences and Transcendental Phenomenology*, Husserl presents an extended and detailed study of precisely how Galilean science emerged against the backdrop of a much broader attempt to capture nature in an all-encompassing rational framework. Husserl traces how this ideal mathematisation arose out of the everyday practice of measuring, then ultimately took on a dynamic of its own so that it came to appear as if nature as the construction of modern natural science bears no inherent relationship at all to human motivations and practices. Modern science involves a kind of subjective self-forgottenness in which the subjects have come to take for granted certain tenets about the nature of reality and knowledge that now seem to be exempt from, or even nullify, the possibility of critical reflection upon them. For instance, the assumption that all real knowledge can be, or must be, empirically verified is not itself an empirical tenet, nor is the modern assumption that all real entities are natural entities. These basic philosophical assumptions arise out of and express a specific world-view that cannot be justified or falsified through the procedures of modern natural science. The name for the ultimate sphere out of which science and all other human practices arises is now termed the 'life-world'. Since it is the source for all other spheres of human activity and cognition, its investigation is the proper object of transcendental phenomenology.

The reference to Galileo and the mathematisation of nature in modern science points to another central theme in Husserl's later work; namely, the origin of ideal entities such as logical principles and mathematical entities out of the most basic tendencies in human cognitive life. This topic, the foundation and origin of mathematics and logic, had, of course, been one of Husserl's guiding concerns since his earliest work. In the other major published work from

Husserl's later period, *The Formal and Transcendental Logic* (1929), he once again returned to this problem, now not just in regard to arithmetic and its basic operations, or even just to certain questions related to the general nature of formal logic as he had in the first volume of the *Logical Investigations*. Rather, he now tried to show in a very detailed way how the formalisation of reason and its operations can result in the discipline of formal logic and its various divisions along with a pure science of manifolds or quantities. He also tried to show how even formal logic, since it necessarily aims at truth, still implicitly refers back to, and depends upon its roots in, the life-world out of which it arises. In this work, Husserl also introduces a distinction between apodeicticity and adequacy that has far-reaching implications for his own phenomenological project. In his original formulations of the phenomenological method, Husserl had contrasted the apodeicticity, or certainty, of phenomenological analysis under the presupposition of the transcendental reduction with the inherent inadequacy of empirical knowledge about external objects, suggesting that the difference between the two removed any source of uncertainty or error from phenomenological research. If, however, even non-empirical research, phenomenological investigations, for example, always has absolute universality as part of its very intention and the attainment of such apodeictic knowledge must at least in principle be reconfirmed over and over by the same researcher at different times and by other members of the community of researchers in order to test its adequacy, this makes phenomenology not only an endless project that must be continually renewed, but also an inherently intersubjective enterprise to be carried out by individuals working in concert with one another and guided by the ideals of truth and self-responsibility.

There is one other final, predominant theme in Husserl's later work worthy of mention here. If, on the one hand, phenomenology proceeds through pure reflection on the part of individual subjects, but on the other hand, as a genuine science, lays claim to intersubjective validity, then the problem of intersubjectivity and the idea of intersubjective validity will be especially pressing for it. Husserl's most extended and best-known treatment of the problem can be found in the fifth of his *Cartesian Meditations*, based on a series of lectures he gave at the Sorbonne in 1929 and published only in French translation during his lifetime. The intention of the this meditation is to show that phenomenology is not a solipsistic enterprise. Consistent with his general project of showing how higher-level, more complicated, intentions arise from simpler lower-order intentions, he traces out the constitution of intersubjectivity for subjective consciousness. He begins by isolating that stratum of consciousness that is conceivable without any reference to other subjects. By abstracting from everything that involves a commitment to the existence of other subjects and any elements of consciousness that depend upon others, Husserl identifies that stratum of conscious life he terms the 'sphere of ownness' (see Husserl, 1960, pp. 92ff.). Within this primordial sphere, however, he notes there is still a stratum of the world as the correlate of my isolated but ongoing experience, a stratum he calls 'nature within ownnness' that is different from the full notion of intersubjectively constituted nature that we intend in our everyday experience. Within this sphere there is also one unique object, namely one's own lived body (*Leib*) that is the organ of sense impressions and of movement and activity. Even as an isolated individual, one would thus be capable of recognising objects within the world, of constituting oneself as a unity of body and soul, and of organising the world in terms of use and value predicates. However, a subject that had constituted the notion of a lived body as a unity of mental and physical nature in her or his own case would also be capable of recognising other perceivable entities that resemble her or his body in their appearance and behaviour. The apprehension of these entities as lived bodies involves seeing them and their behaviour as an expression (*Ausdruck*) of mental states. He calls this apprehension 'empathy' (*Einfühlung*) – although he does admit that this term is easily misleading. He also describes it as an 'appresentation', since the specifically subjective side of the other, the other's first-person awareness as such, is still never given to one directly. One can indeed have genuine and reliable awareness of at least some of another person's mental states, but only on the basis of some externally observable deed or statement. The experience of the other is therefore said to be founded on, but not reducible to, the physically observable states of her or his body as a material object in the world. In imputing to the other a subjectivity like mine, I also constitute the idea of a world that is the same for us all in spite of different perspectives, an intersubjective nature, and I can envisage myself as an object for others, as part of that intersubjective world. Moreover, it is also possible to constitute on this basis a world of shared values, a cultural world that could ultimately serve as the norm against which all individual beliefs and actions can be measured. Phenomenology as the realisation of the inherent striving of all agents for rationality in the form of beliefs and norms that can be universally justified is thus necessarily an intersubjective enterprise towards which Husserl viewed his own work as an important, but merely initial contribution.

From its beginnings as a theory in the foundations of logic and mathematics and as a method of reflection upon the pure contents of the mental life of individual subjects, Husserl's phenomenology evolves into an all-encompassing research programme that reveals the historical and intersubjective origins of the world in which we live and the objects within them. Husserl himself never rejects the centrality of the method of transcendental reduction nor does he overlook the important foundational role of the simplest elements of conscious life; for example, sense perception and an individual's direct first-person awareness of her or his own mental states. But Husserl's analyses demonstrate at the same time that the concrete world – the world in which we all live and which provides the basis from which any specialised scientific research occurs, the world from which even phenomenology itself must proceed – is constituted historically and intersubjectively. Later successors to Husserl's phenonomenological project, notably Martin Heidegger, Eugen Fink, Maurice Merleau-Ponty, Jacques Derrida and Emanuel Levinas attempt to go beyond Husserl by purging his approach and his results of what they perceive as undue Cartesian residues in the emphasis upon logic, science, perception, theory and subjective reflection. They consciously acknowledge their debt to the phenomenological method as developed by Edmund Husserl, but attempt to take his insights and develop them into a new way of doing philosophy that moves from the sphere of modern philosophy, in which he still located himself, into a new kind of philosophy that overcomes the modern scientifically-orientated philosophy of subjective reflection. On this reading, Husserl represents an important transitional figure in the history of Continental philosophy, since he stands as a leading, and perhaps the last, great representative of classical modern philosophy and a key figure in the transition to a philosophy that goes beyond it.

Bibliography

Writings

Husserl, Edmund (1951–), *Husserliana*, vols I–xxx, Dordrecht: Kluwer Academic Publishers. The definitive and ongoing critical edition of Husserl's writings (in German).
— (1960), *Cartesian Meditations*, trans. Dorion Cairns, The Hague: Martinus Nijhoff.
— (1965), *Phenomenology and the Crisis of Philosophy*, trans. Quentin Lauer, New York: Harper and Row.
— (1969), *Formal and Transcendental Logic*, trans. Dorion Cairns, The Hague: Martinus Nijhoff.
— (1970a), *Logical Investigations*, trans. J. N. Findlay, two vols, New York: Humanities Press.
— (1970b), *The Crisis of European Sciences and Transcendental Phenomenology*, trans. David Carr, Evanston: Northwestern University Press.
— (1982), *Ideas Pertaining to a Pure Phenomenology and to a Phenomenological Philosophy*, First Book, trans. F. Kersten, The Hague: Martinus Nijhoff.
— (1989), *Ideas Pertaining to a Pure Phenomenology and to a Phenomenological Philosophy*, Second Book, trans. Richard Rojcewicz and André Schuwer, Dordrecht: Kluwer Academic Publishers.
— (1991), *Lectures on the Phenomenology of Inner Time Consciousness*, trans. John Brough, Dordrecht: Kluwer.

References and further reading

Bernet, Rudolf, Iso Kern and Eduard Marbach (1993), *An Introduction to Edmund Husserl's Phenomenology*, Evanston: Northwestern University Press.
Boer, Theodor de (1978), *The Development of Husserl's Thought*, The Hague: Martinus Nijhoff.
Elliston, Frederick and Peter McCormick (eds) (1977), *Husserl, Expositions and Appraisals*, Notre Dame: Notre Dame University Press.
Gurwitsch, Aron (1966), *Studies in Phenomenology and Psychology*, Evanston: Northwestern University Press.
Lapointe, François (1980), *Edmund Husserl and His Critics. An International Bibliography (1899–1979)*, Bowling Green, OH: Philosophy Documentation Center.
Mohanty, J. N. (ed.) (1977), *Readings on Edmund Husserl's Logical Investigations*, The Hague: Martinus Nijhoff.
Mohanty, J. N. and William R. McKenna (eds) (1989), *Husserl's Phenomenology: A Textbook*, Lanham, MD: University Press of America.
Schuhmann, K. (1977), *Husserl-Chronik. Denk- und Lebensweg Edmund Husserls*, The Hague: Martinus Nijhoff.
Sepp, H. R. (ed.) (1988), *Edmund Husserl und die phänomenologische Bewegung*, Freiburg: Alber Verlag.
Sokolowski, R. (1964), 'The Formation of Husserl's Concept of Constitution', *Phaenomenologica* 18, The Hague: Martinus Nijhoff.

4.3

PHENOMENOLOGY AND THE QUESTION OF BEING: HEIDEGGER

Steven Galt Crowell

As a motto for the first edition of his collected writings Heidegger proposed the phrase, 'Ways, not works', thus expressing his conviction that philosophical thinking does not aim at fixed results and systems but rather in ever-renewed impulses of questioning, seeks to open up previously unsuspected paths into what, hidden within the familiar, requires thinking. Thus, while Heidegger himself claimed that the topic of his thinking from first to last was the 'question of being', it is impossible to grasp what this means without also identifying the moment in his career when some specific version of the question was first posed. The matter of thinking and the way to it (method) are, in Heidegger's writings, inseparable. But if a certain periodisation thus becomes necessary to understand Heidegger, any such identification of stages or phases is controversial, since it presumes substantive decisions concerning what his philosophy is about. Following Heidegger's own, not unambiguous, lead, it is customary to distinguish between works done before and after the 'turn' (*Kehre*) – that is, between those works written primarily before 1930, focused on the human being's 'understanding of being', and those written after the 1930 'turn' to being itself – but this is by no means sufficient to capture even the most important interrelations among the ways traversed during a career that spanned seven decades, from the dissertation of 1914 to the last addresses of the 1970s. Since no alternative periodisation commands consensus among scholars, however, the present article will

resolve the issue by tracing the concept of meaning (*Sinn*) in Heidegger's thought – both because thematisation of meaning distinguishes phenomenological philosophy from traditional epistemology and metaphysics, and because it frames Heidegger's first formulation of the question of being as the question of the 'meaning of being' (*Sinn von Sein*).

From this perspective, Heidegger's thought appears to develop in four stages. Drawn to the question of the 'meaning of "meaning"' through his earliest reflections on logic (1912–17), Heidegger spent the next decade (1917–27) refining and reworking Husserl's phenomenology, Dilthey's hermeneutics and Aristotle's metaphysics into the question of the 'meaning of being', to which his first major work, *Being and Time* (1927), was devoted. That volume solidified Heidegger's reputation as Germany's leading philosopher and became, against his own intentions, a sourcebook for subsequent existentialism. Although Heidegger continued to cultivate the phenomenological ontology established in *Being and Time* until 1930, already in 1929 a shift in orientation is noticeable. For the next fifteen years, as Heidegger explored the relation between his thought and traditional metaphysics, the phenomenological question of the 'meaning' of being was increasingly posed as a question of the 'truth' of being – a transformation prefigured in Heidegger's own novel interpretation of truth as 'disclosedness' or 'clearing'. After 1945 he pursued the task of 'overcoming' metaphysical thinking, the hitherto exclusive form taken by the 'history of being' (*Seinsgeschichte*), until, finally, even the enquiry into the truth of being was displaced by an attempt to think about the primordial 'event' (*Ereignis*) granting or giving both being and truth. The present article tries to clarify something of what is at stake in each of these stages, with primary attention given to the first two, since it is there that Heidegger most clearly belongs to that phenomenological tradition committed to carrying on the 'Kantian' impulse of autonomous philosophising. At no stage does Heidegger truly abandon that impulse, but his later thought contains strong elements of post-phenomenological or 'post-modern' suspicion regarding both the matter and the method of philosophical enquiry.

From meaning to being: ontological phenomenology

Fundamental to Heidegger's thought is his claim that the metaphysical tradition fails to do justice to the 'ontological difference', to the difference between entities (or beings) and the being *of* entities. Aristotle, for example, registers this difference in his observation that the term 'being' is equivocal, that it does not exhibit the unity of a highest genus of entities; yet he subsequently confounds the difference in his thesis that 'substance' (*ousia*) is the primary meaning of being. Aristotle does not explain why *ousia* plays this paradigmatic role in defining being, but by 1923 Heidegger had his breakthrough answer: it is because the Greeks think of being within the unreflected horizon of time. *Ousia* – what is present – appears primary because being is already understood in terms of presence, a modality of time. The modern period alters nothing in this regard since its own 'primary' being – the self-certain knowing subject – is conceived as that which is permanently present to itself. *Being and Time*, then, seeks to recover the difference between being and beings by reflecting upon the hidden presupposition of both ancient and modern philosophy; namely, the structuring of all understanding (including the understanding of being) by time. The philosophy that uncovers time as the horizon of understanding will be 'critical' in that it simultaneously uncovers the

conditions of its own possibility as a mode of understanding. Here the importance of phenomenology for the early Heidegger becomes apparent, for phenomenology provided a way to raise the ancient metaphysical question of being without ignoring the claims of modern critical or transcendental philosophy.

In his *Logical Investigations* (1900), Husserl had rejected the idea that logical laws and concepts express psychological realities; instead, they designate ideal or necessary structural connections between meanings, given through (linguistically expressable) acts of thinking but not reducible to them. In his 1913 dissertation, written under the direction of the neo-Scholastic philosopher Arthur Schneider, Heidegger applied Husserl's critical insights to five 'psychologistic' theories of judgement, showing how each fell into self-contradiction by failing to acknowledge the proper object of logic, 'valid meaning' (*geltender Sinn*). Heidegger concludes by asking 'What is the meaning of meaning?' Neither psychically subjective nor physically objective, meaning is irreducible and underivable; yet it can be 'pointed out' phenomenologically. Traditional categories seem unable to capture it, but, since logical validity pertains precisely to this domain of meaning, the very existence of logic seems to call into question the adequacy of traditional ontological dichotomies such as realism and idealism.

Heidegger's *Habilitation* thesis of 1915, written under the direction of the neo-Kantian Heinrich Rickert, deepens the enquiry into the meaning of meaning. In the context of examining 'Duns Scotus's' (really Thomas of Erfurt's) theory of significations – a logical grammar or truth-functional theory of language – Heidegger employs the concept of 'intentionality' to distinguish the realm of meaning from the metaphysically real and the epistemologically ideal. Drawing upon Husserl's description of consciousness as a field of evidence (the intentional correlation, consciousness-of-something), Heidegger identifies the origin of logical categories in the projective and constitutive character of the knowing subject. Neither the empirical psyche nor a formal epistemological construct, the 'being' of this 'phenomenological' subject became Heidegger's lifelong theme. Already, in the conclusion to his thesis,

Heidegger was insisting that reflection on the intentionality of the knowing subject is not enough; the phenomenon of valid meaning will remain philosophically unclear until one goes beyond transcendental logic and, by means of philosophy's genuine 'optics', metaphysics, recognises the full being of what Heidegger, borrowing from Dilthey and life-philosophy, calls the 'living historical spirit'. The future trajectory of Heidegger's move from meaning to being is adumbrated here: collapsing the distinction between historical and systematic enquiry, the logical (categorial) theory of meaning must be grounded in the concrete life of the historical subject, or spirit, while avoiding both uncritical metaphysics and non-philosophical empiricism.

Between 1916 and 1923 Heidegger explored this requirement in a series of reflections that culminated in a 'hermeneutics of facticity'. These years saw two significant developments of the earlier work: first, Husserl's phenomenology was revised in the direction of hermeneutic theory, and second, the connection between meaning and being that Husserl had established at the level of logic was made at the level of everyday practical life.

In the Emergency War Semester of 1919 Heidegger posed the question to which *Being and Time* provided the answer: How is philosophy, as the 'primordial science' (*Urwissenschaft*), possible? In 1911 Husserl had argued that only as phenomenology could philosophy become rigorous science; Heidegger pushed the question of a scientific philosophy to the point where the whole idea of 'scientificity', of philosophical knowledge and method, must be transformed. This is because the 'theoretical' sciences with their 'object-constituting' categories prove incapable of illuminating philosophy's genuine theme, the origin of meaning, which must be sought instead in the 'pre-theoretical' movement of 'factic life'. Reflecting on the problem of authentic religious life in St Paul, Augustine and Luther, Heidegger came to believe that philosophy seeks what 'is' prior to its diffraction into the objects that form the correlates of intentional consciousness. Because it seeks the 'there is' (*es gibt*) before the 'there is something', philosophy cannot take place as an objectifying reflection on experience but must instead engage in the indirect interpretive strategy

Heidegger calls 'formal indication'. Following Dilthey, Heidegger attempts to understand life's primordial movement by tracing the 'formal' (initially empty) directions 'indicated' in the very terms life uses to interpret itself ('concern', 'significance', 'ruinance', 'torment', etc.) back to their evidential sources in pre-theoretical experience. These 'categories of factic life' thus serve as formal indications of that primal something (*Uretwas*) which sustains all scientific and pre-scientific grasp of objects.

The hermeneutics of facticity remains phenomenological in its conviction that this primal something is *meaningful*. In the early Freiburg lectures Heidegger generally does not distinguish rigorously between being and meaning: to ask after being is to ask after the 'being-meaning of a being' (*Seinsinn eines Seienden*). To grasp the being of an entity is to grasp the 'full meaning in which it is what it is. Full meaning = phenomenon' (Heidegger, 1985, p. 53). Here Heidegger introduces the idea of an 'ontological phenomenology' (ibid., p. 60) that will define his project through 1929: rejecting traditional metaphysics, being can only be approached phenomenologically – with reference to how being is evidentially given – thus, by deepening the transcendental turn towards 'the way such "being" is understandable: the *meaning* of being' (ibid., p. 58). Heidegger holds that the 'full phenomenon' of meaning/being does not have an intentional structure; it is rather, as intensive preoccupation with Aristotle in his Marburg years will reveal, an 'opening' or temporal-horizonal framework that 'situates' constituting subject and constituted object in Husserl's sense.

The attempt to grasp the phenomenon of meaning more originally than is possible in the theory of intentional consciousness led to crucial modifications in the understanding of philosophy's starting point. As early as 1921 Heidegger introduced the key that would allow *Being and Time* to break with the Cartesian conception of human being without altogether abandoning the transcendental point of departure. Instead of starting with a being who doubts, knows, and thus 'posits', the world, Heidegger identified the philosophically more primary sense in which the beginning philosopher is a *questioner*. To ask about the meaning of being is thus first to ask about the being of the one who raises the question, and consequently, about the conditions for the possibility of raising questions at all. The systematic heart of *Being and Time* lies in the idea of a 'pre-ontological' understanding of being (*Seinsverständnis*) as the first such condition which any entity capable of raising the question of being must fulfil. For this reason, Heidegger introduces 'Dasein' as a *terminus technicus* to indicate that being for whom 'in its very being that being is an *issue* for it', namely, a being for whom questioning is possible (Heidegger, 1962, p. 32).

Heidegger's project of 'fundamental ontology', then, can be understood as one in which the philosopher tries to clarify her or his own being in so far as that being makes it possible to raise the question of being in a fully 'ontological' way; that is, to bring the pre-ontological understanding of being into explicit philosophical comprehension. The 'analytic of Dasein' (whose title, echoing Kant's 'Analytic of Concepts', announces itself as the successor to transcendental logic) is an attempt to articulate those categories (which Heidegger calls 'existentials') that make possible not objects but meaning. On that basis, then, and mindful of the ontological difference between being and beings, one is in a position to raise the question of the meaning of *being* in an explicit, phenomenologically grounded, way.

Being and Time is thus conceived as a propaedeutic. That this propaedeutic can already be ontological knowledge, prior to answering the ontological question, is due to its phenomenological character as Heidegger understands it. For him, phenomenology is neither a school nor a method defined by arcane techniques but is the very way we come to understand ourselves in the course of our lives. This does not mean, however, that our ordinary ways of seeing things are to be taken at face value, or that the handed-down conceptions of being are simply to be patched together into a new theory. Rather, Heidegger, like Husserl, sees the task of phenomenology as one of bringing to light, making explicit, that which, for the most part, does not show itself – not because it is an inaccessible thing-in-itself, but because it is concealed by misinterpretation and by the very commonplaces of the tradition which it supports. The process of phenomenology is thus 'hermeneutic'; it interrogates our everyday understandings so as to reveal their experiential sources, 'interprets' them so as to expose what they conceal and brings them into the fluidity of living thought.

Hence, in an historico-hermeneutic move that has little parallel in the more positivistic phenomenology of Husserl, the phenomenological method in *Being and Time* requires reflection on the history of philosophy, not in order to find precursors but to 'deconstruct' the categories which, in the present, serve to veil the phenomena to which an enquiry into the meaning of being must attend. This 'destruction of the history of ontology' – which was scheduled to appear as Part II of *Being and Time* – thus has a positive aim; namely, to recover a sense for what was really at stake in traditional ontological inquiry and to reinvest its vocabulary (truth, being, *logos*, reason) with something of the evidential 'force' it had in its original existential setting. Although this part of *Being and Time* was never published, some germs of the project do exist piecemeal within the published pages, and, beginning with *Kant and the Problem of Metaphysics* (1929), Heidegger fulfilled its spirit in a series of critical reflections on figures in the history of metaphysics. The attempt to recover a concealed, but more authentic, impulse behind the official history of philosophy became increasingly important in Heidegger's thinking during the 1930s.

Being and Time offers a phenomenological reinterpretation of the being of human being (Dasein) such that both the ancient metaphysical concept of a 'rational animal' and the modern epistemological concept of a 'subject' of representations are displaced. Against the view that holds reason to be the distinguishing mark of human being, Heidegger argues that human rationality is itself dependent on what he calls 'care' (*Sorge*), a certain sort of self-relatedness irreducible to the metaphysical tradition's idea of self-consciousness. Care is reflected in the fact that my own being is an issue for me, that it matters to me. This cannot be explained in terms of my rational faculties alone, yet without such 'care' those rational faculties would not find motive for their exercise. Both animality and rationality as traditionally understood can be clarified, as elements of Dasein, only by being derived phenomenologically from the structure of care.

The idea of structure here points to a crucial aspect of Heidegger's approach to Dasein; for care is not a property (even an essential property) of a substance, human being, but rather a complex, articulated whole which makes possible those properties we can be said to have. Thus, *Being and Time* conceives care – the being (*Sein*) of human being – as a dynamic structure of 'ways to be' (*Zu-sein*). Against the modern concept of subjectivity – which only repeats, on the level of reflection, the ancient tendency to think of being as what is present as an object – Heidegger argues that Dasein's mode of being is not that of a thing (whether object or subject), but 'existence' (*Existenz*). Existence here is not the opposite of essence – the 'that' as opposed to 'what' – but signifies rather that Dasein 'has its own being *to be*'. In having it, it 'has to be' it, has no choice but to adopt its existing in one way or another precisely not as something given, whose meaning is determined once and for all, but as a 'to be', as something that is always at issue (Heidegger, 1962, p. 32, p. 67).

To say that Dasein 'exists' is to say that it is primordially a 'being possible'. This does not mean that there is an ideal set of (logical or physical) possibilities that are consistent with Dasein as an actual being. Rather, it means that I always understand myself in terms of normative alternatives of success or failure. Socially, for example, I can be a citizen or a brother simply by fulfilling some institutional criteria; existentially, however, I can be these things only by continually succeeding (or failing) to live up to what being a brother or a citizen means. Existental possibility characterises the very way existence is 'mine' what it means to be oneself. As a function of *Existenz*, selfhood cannot be the simple identity or perdurance of a subject but is, instead, poised between the modalised alternatives (possibilities) of finding and holding oneself (which Heidegger calls 'authenticity') or fleeing and losing oneself (which he calls 'inauthenticity'). Authenticity and inauthenticity are definitive of selfhood as such, and although they obviously involve a normative component, the evaluation they express is strictly speaking neither moral (which phrases evaluations in terms of the good or the right) nor aesthetic (which phrases evaluations in terms of

the beautiful). To be authentic is to maintain oneself in a certain transparency with regard to the nature of one's own being – to understand that selfhood has the character of a charge or responsibility and not a fixed ground – while to be inauthentic is to conceal the 'ungrounded' quality of one's existence. Such existential concealment has complicated relations to moral, political and other sorts of evaluation, but Heidegger says little about these in *Being and Time*.

The concept of authenticity has methodological significance and is intimately connected to those analyses of anxiety, death, conscience and guilt that so impressed Heidegger's first readers. Because he begins by describing Dasein in its 'everyday' way of being – in which it is to a certain extent 'lost' to itself, absorbed in the practical negotiation of its everyday affairs – it becomes necessary to show how it is possible for Dasein to come to an explicit understanding of its own being. To do this, Heidegger explores those moments in which Dasein's everyday self-understanding is most radically challenged, its complacency most disturbed. In anxiety (*Angst*) this dislocation is accomplished in such a way that authentic self-understanding can be made explicit as an existential possibility (although it need not be). Only if it is, however, can the philosopher carry out the task of fundamental ontology, achieve the 'transparency' necessary for making explicit the ontological structure of that being who is capable of raising the question of the meaning of being. Authenticity, a clear grasp of one's own being, is a condition of philosophy's possibility.

Authentic self-understanding grasps the 'finitude' and 'situatedness' of my being. To be situated is to see that the familiar and stable world that provides the unquestioned normative context of my everyday life is essentially contingent ('factic'), a historical, sociocultural milieu; while to be finite is to see that my own identity finally lies in the 'resoluteness' (*Entschlossenheit*) with which I take responsibility for the choices I make in the clear-sighted acknowledgement of my 'being toward death'. With this, the ultimate 'horizon', the ultimate clarificatory framework for understanding the care-structure of *Existenz*, comes into view. For what holds these possibilities together, makes them intelligible as a whole, is what

Heidegger calls 'temporality' (*Zeitlichkeit*). Dasein is radically 'temporal' – not merely in time, as are all things, but rather 'temporalising' already in a world but always ahead of itself, pressing into possibilities. In temporalising Dasein clears a historically particular space in which things can show up, 'present' themselves as meaningful. At the limit of Heidegger's ontological phenomenology of the human being, then, is a kind of transcendental historicism: historicality belongs to Dasein – hence to the very constitution. of meaning – and selfhood itself has a narrative structure. Heidegger does not think that this sort of historicism implies thoroughgoing historical relativism, for if transcendental historicism recognises relativity of meaning at the 'ontic' level of particular historical and cultural traditions, as a phenomenological philosophy it also uncovers ontological structures that condition or account for such ontic relativisation. The ultimate cogency of this distinction has been disputed, and Heidegger later seems to distance himself somewhat from it, tending towards a more radical historicising of philosophy.

Brief mention should be made of some principal features of Heidegger's description of Dasein in which his departure from traditional philosophical ideas becomes most evident. This departure is already clear when, in opposition to the Cartesian tradition and Husserlian phenomenology's presumed appeal to a 'worldless' transcendental consciousness, Heidegger describes Dasein as 'being-in-the-world'. *Being and Time* analyses three mutually-implicating aspects of this structure, that is, worldhood, being-with and being-in.

In one of his most celebrated contributions Heidegger asks us to consider the being (worldhood) of the world. His analyses show that world cannot be understood as the collection of existing entities; it is not something pieced together out of independently-existing things, but rather that in which, and in terms of which, these things show themselves as existing in one way or another. Thus (in his famous example) the 'world' is adumbrated in the workshop, which is itself no mere collection of tools but an organised context, or 'referential totality', that remains a taken for granted background until such time as a tool in use (a hammer, for example) breaks

down. When the hammer becomes unusable, its references to other items in the workspace, oriented around the work to be done (but now in danger of not being done), become perspicuous to varying degrees. Even then I do not attain a 'theoretical' grasp of the workspace as a well-defined object; its very mode of being – holistic and horizonal – precludes that.

While the workshop is a local context of meaning linked to specific practices of building, the world is the ultimate context or horizon in which the practice or project of existing as such takes on significance. Thus, world is prior to subject and object; these can emerge only as items 'in' the world. Nor can the world be a system of 'representations' grounded in a subject; representations arise only against the background of the world. As the workshop example makes plain, the worldhood of the world is not equivalent to the epistemological notion of an implicit 'theory' (set of propositions) or categorial framework; it is rather linked to the practices in which human beings are engaged in everyday life. Thus, the world belongs to a 'form of life' in Wittgenstein's sense – a culturally and historically specific, normative and finite horizon of meaning, the logically ungrounded space of intelligibility in which beings, entities, take on significance, show themselves as the things they are.

What Heidegger calls 'being with' (*Mitsein*) follows from the nature of the world of being-in-the-world. The world is shared 'with' others. Against the solipsism and mentalism of the modern tradition, Heidegger insists that the 'who' of Dasein, the self, is hopelessly misunderstood if one begins with an isolated subject whose mental life would be radically private. Heidegger argues that, since all understanding takes place within the horizon of shared norms, practices, rules and conventions that belong to the world, so too does any self-understanding. Thus, my identity is formed in terms of the roles I assume within a specific community, roles which, as social possibilities, are anonymous and typical. Practically, I understand myself not in terms of how I differ from others but in terms of how I do not differ from them: I do what one ordinarily does in specific circumstances. This is not an accident that somehow befalls a self that would otherwise have a pre-social identity; rather, to speak of a self at all is to speak of a socialised self, which Heidegger calls 'the they' or 'one' (*das Man*). Because features of Dasein's being – including selfhood as being-with-others – are existential possibilities, however, a Kierkegaardian reversal of the traditional solipsistic problem emerges: the question is not how an individual subject transcends its solipsistic condition towards genuine encounter with the other; rather, it is how an initially undifferentiated anonymous 'they-self' can become individuated. At this point, Heidegger's phenomenology of the self connects with the previous remarks on authenticity: individuation begins with the collapse, in anxiety, of the 'they-self' and the intelligibility of its taken-for-granted way of doing things.

With Dasein described as being-in-the-world, some have found it strange that Heidegger does not offer a phenomenology of embodiment in *Being and Time*. The primary reason for this is that he is trying to conceptualise the being of human being prior to the traditional distinction between mind and body. Thus, just as Dasein is not 'consciousness' but cannot for that reason be said to be 'unconscious' so too, though Dasein does not 'have' a body it cannot be said to be 'disembodied'. Heidegger holds that what it means to talk either of consciousness or of the body as aspects of human being cannot be properly determined without first explicating the essential categorial features of that being who questions (Dasein). What is ordinarily referred to with the term 'body' is, of course, everywhere present in Heidegger's analyses (as in the famous example of wielding a hammer), but to explain Dasein by appeal to some category of embodiment is to put the cart before the horse. Nevertheless, in *The Metaphysical Foundations of Logic* (1929) Heidegger does propose to take up the question of embodiment. Under the heading of 'metontology' philosophy is called upon to reflect on the natural and cosmological situatedness of human being, but because of the turn in his thinking, he never carried out the project of metontology.

Finally, being-in-the-world can be conceived according to the character of its 'in' the *Da* (here/there) of Dasein. Taking aim at the tradition which sees this phenomenon primarily in terms of 'consciousness' viewed on the model of a subject knowing an object,

Heidegger shows how consciousness, intentionality, itself derives from a more complex structure whose aspects he terms 'disposition' (*Befindlichkeit*), 'understanding' (*Verstehen*), and 'discourse' (*Rede*). These aspects – which must ultimately be understood as modes of Dasein's temporality – together yield that meaningful horizon thanks to which both subjects and objects can be encountered.

'Disposition' signifies the ontological structure of moods. Moods reflect the way I find myself already in a world, my 'thrownness' (*Geworfenheit*); they disclose the particular way the world as a whole 'matters' to me. Moods are not subjective colourations laid over an objectively given world; they are essential constituents of meaning, without which nothing in the world could make a claim on me. Disposition always goes together with a certain 'understanding' – which signifies the previously discussed aspect of Dasein's 'projection' of possibilities. Such projecting is not a thematic deliberating over alternatives, but that know-how whereby I negotiate my everyday affairs, an 'ability to be' (*Seinkönnen*). Together, disposition and understanding figure a meaningful context that can be 'articulated', that is, 'interpreted' in the sense that within it particular things can be encountered meaningfully *as* something. This kind of meaning (the 'hermeneutic as') is inherent in practice and does not depend on any explicit judgement on things (the 'apophantic as'), but because 'discourse' also belongs to Dasein's being-in, the practically articulated and interpreted world can be spoken about.

Disposition, understanding and discourse together make up Dasein's 'disclosedness' (*Erschlossenheit*). On the basis of his understanding of the Greek term for truth, *aletheia*, Heidegger finds disclosedness to be the phenomenologically primary meaning of truth (see Heidegger, 1962, p. 262f.). Propositional truth, correctness of statements, is seen as a function of Dasein's practical 'uncovering' of entities, a mode of pointing out and determining entities through linguistic behaviour. But since entities can show themselves as they are (or be taken as they are not) only within the previously 'disclosed' horizon of meaning opened up in the structure of Dasein's being-in, propositional truth depends upon 'truth' understood as this meaningful disclosure. Truth is thus an existential category of Dasein and so must exhibit the structure of existential possibility: in so far as a specific horizontal meaning (world) is opened up through Dasein's practices, Dasein is 'in the truth'; yet because these practices close off other possibilities, and consequently other aspects of things, other ways to be, Dasein is also 'in untruth'. The ultimate 'truth of existence', then, is achieved in 'resoluteness', when authentic Dasein achieves insight into its inescapable responsibility for the finite and historical meaning things take on thanks to its choices in the world.

From the meaning of being to the truth of being

After the publication of *Being and Time* and Heidegger's return to Freiburg in 1929 as Husserl's successor, the terms 'phenomenology' and 'ontology' appear less frequently in his work. German philosophy during this time was characterised by renewed interest in the problem of metaphysics – closely associated with the desire for a philosophical world-view to address a perceived crisis of values – and Heidegger's lectures and publications of the 1930s reflect this trend. In part, this follows directly from *Being and Time's* call for a destruction of the history of ontology. But the path is new in its attempt (as Heidegger later put it) to use the 'language of metaphysics' to make the 'turn' from Dasein's *understanding* of (the meaning of) being to being itself, thereby completing the break with modern subjectivism. From this effort there would emerge, around the mid-1930s, the project of 'overcoming' (*Überwindung*) and finally 'recovering from' (*Verwindung*) metaphysics.

The previously mentioned idea of metontology – something like a *metaphysica specialis* in Kant's sense, a metaphysics of nature, of animal being, etc – was one consequence of Heidegger's new interest. Another was the idea of a 'basic mood' or 'attunement' (*Grundstimmung*) which, introduced in the 1929/30 lecture course, *Fundamental Concepts of Metaphysics*, would play a significant role in Heidegger's thinking during the first half of the decade. This concept introduces a subtle shift of emphasis in Heidegger's previous analysis of disposition. Where disposition,

in particular as anxiety, had been seen primarily in its methodological significance as a condition for radical individuation, 'basic mood' is now taken primarily as a mode of being with one another, a historical and social phenomenon. Thus, Heidegger can characterise the *Grundstimmung* of the German people of 1929/30 as 'boredom' (*Langeweile*), his subsequent analysis of which provides the methodological basis for a situated grasp of the relation between philosophical thinking and its 'time'.

The most enduring legacy of Heidegger's efforts to transcend modern subjectivism by means of metaphysics, however, was the transformation of disclosedness – the meaningful space which *Being and Time* had analysed in terms of Dasein's resolute projection of possibilities – into the 'truth of being', the structure of clearing (concealing/revealing) which conditions metaphysical thinking without being recognised by it. Although not yet named, an important feature of this idea is prefigured in Heidegger's Plato lectures of 1931–32. According to Heidegger, Plato was the first to conceive being as 'Idea' (*eidos*) and thus truth as *homoieosis*, conformity between the mind and being-as-Idea. The being of beings is thus reduced to *a* being, and truth (including metaphysical truth) is conceived as correct representation of such being. Thereafter, metaphysics becomes focused upon entities and not upon the truth of being itself; that is, that openness or clearing (*aletheia*) in whose light all entities, including the Ideas, show themselves. Similarly, the lecture 'On the Essence of Truth' (1930) identifies truth with the unconcealedness of the 'totality of entities' (the theme of metaphysics), an unconcealedness that, in revealing entities, conceals its own unconcealing. Published only in 1943, Heidegger heavily revised the lecture to suggest that what was implicitly at stake was already the 'truth of being'.

With the gradual emergence of the idea of the truth of being came a need to rethink the distinctive role played by human beings in what is increasingly seen as a *happening* of truth. Along one axis, then, the trajectory of Heidegger's thinking between 1929 and 1945 (the year when the Allies refused him the right to teach because of his activities during the Nazi period) can be understood as a continual reflection upon, and revision of, the idea of authenticity as resoluteness. More specifically, Heidegger sought to grasp resoluteness as a 'response' (*entsprechen*) to a 'claim' (*Anspruch*) of being. This problem surfaces in his lectures on Kant's practical philosophy, Hegel's *Phenomenology*, and Aristotle's *Metaphysics* (all delivered between 1930 and 1932) and comes to pointed expression in Heidegger's Rectoral Address when, in 1933, he became the first Nazi Rector of the University of Freiburg. There Heidegger combines the language of Nazi ideologues with terminology deriving from *Being and Time* and early Greek philosophy (notably Heraclitus) to give political content to the idea of the 'truth' of a people, a destiny deriving from being itself that calls for decisive action and 'leadership' ungrounded in (unconstrained by) 'ideas and concepts'. By 1945, however, the voluntaristic strain in this conception of the relation of human being to being has given way to images of shepherding and to the idea of 'letting be' as 'releasement' (*Gelassenheit*).

Heidegger's tenure as Rector was short and, for him, extremely disillusioning. The effects of this, and the relation between his politics and his philosophy, are topics of much debate. Regarding the question of the truth of being, however, there are clear differences between writings from the years just after the Rectorate (for example, the 1934–35 lectures on Hölderlin; 1935, *Introduction to Metaphysics*; 1936, 'Origin of the Work of Art') and those belonging to the later 1930s and 1940s (especially the 1936 *Beiträge zur Philosophie (Vom Ereignis)*; the 1936–40 lectures on Nietzsche; the new lectures on Hölderlin of 1941–42; and the 1942–44 lectures on Parmenides and Heraclitus). In the earlier set Heidegger still invokes will and decision, and calls upon resolute Dasein to take responsibility for instituting (*Stiftung*) the space of truth or meaning. In the later set, however, and especially in the protracted struggle with Nietzsche, the very idea of will, of self-assertion and action, comes in for criticism.

In the earlier Hölderlin lectures, for example, Heidegger modifies his previous analysis of truth as disclosedness by introducing the notion of a 'primal leap' (*Ur-sprung*), a historically originary decision or founding act that provides a people with its 'destiny' or truth, those measures whereby it distinguishes what for it is great or small, noble or base, mean-

ingful or meaningless. Thus truth – the normative horizon within which a people arrives at its judgements – is made to turn on the 'creative' (*dichterisch*) originating act of those whom Hölderlin calls 'demigods' and among whom Heidegger counts not only poets and thinkers, but also political leaders. Given the historical circumstances, Hölderlin's poetry comes to be read as a call to Germans to inaugurate 'another' truth or normative order in essential tension with the first one established in the West by the Greeks.

In the mid-1930s Heidegger was thus preoccupied with the relation of Greece to Germany, that is, with the putative demand that resolute German thinkers and leaders take responsibility for the destiny of the West. As the 1935 lecture course, *Introduction to Metaphysics*, argues, the Greek beginning – in which the essence of truth (*aletheia*) as unconcealedness is forgotten in favour of correctness and in which being is forgotten in favour of beings – has now shown itself as nihilism. To that heritage – the 'rational' and ordered world that has now led to Germany's fate, clamped between the pincers of the soulless USA and totally mobilised Russia – the thinker must stand decisively opposed, in the name of what remains concealed in that heritage. Here Heidegger's interpretation of the first Chorus of Sophocles' *Antigone* takes on political resonance when, in conclusion, Heidegger claims that 'the works that are being peddled about nowadays as the philosophy of National Socialism' have 'nothing whatever to do with the inner truth and greatness of this movement'. When this lecture was published in 1953, Heidegger glossed 'this movement' as 'the encounter between global technology and modern man', thereby introducing themes that come to prominence only in a later phase of his thinking (Heidegger, 1959, p. 199).

That later phase, with its critique of the voluntaristic idea that will – resolute, rationally ungrounded action – creatively contributes to opening up the truth of being, is prefigured in his massive *Beiträge* (1936–38). Here Heidegger rethinks the major themes from *Being and Time* and after, although now the point is not to grasp being from the perspective of Dasein's understanding of being but to situate Dasein within what he now calls the 'truth of being' (*Wahrheit des Seyns*). This turn (*Kehre*) is reflected in the strategy of the Nietzsche lectures delivered between 1936 and 1940 (which, along with the Parmenides and Heraclitus lectures of 1942–44, Heidegger claimed to be an implicit critique of Nazi ideology 'for those who had ears to hear' – a claim that has proved controversial). In these lectures, Heidegger tries to show that Nietzsche, the great anti-metaphysician, was in fact the 'last metaphysician of the West'. Both Nietzsche and Heidegger present nihilism – the late modern sense that things as a whole lack meaning and value – as the outcome of metaphysical thinking. However, whereas Nietzsche believes that nihilism arises because metaphysics ties meaning and value to a static 'being' beyond the world of becoming, and offers his doctrine of the 'will to power' as a post-metaphysical answer to nihilism, Heidegger glosses the latter as mere 'will to will', itself the last chapter of metaphysics and hence a form of nihilism. The basis for this is his view that metaphysics is that enquiry which conceals the truth of being, a concealing which Nietzsche's term 'will to power' accomplishes as the ultimate 'subjectivistic' substitutional name for being. The issue that would occupy Heidegger's last phase, then, is how to open a path to a genuine overcoming of metaphysics and so 'another beginning' for thinking, one that would emphasise a listening, waiting attitude of questioning and reflection (Besinnung) in contrast to the Nietzschean 'will to will'. Against nihilism, what Heidegger comes to call 'thinking' (in decisive opposition to 'philosophy') must seek – tentatively, questioningly – what Hölderlin called 'a measure on earth (Heidegger, 1971e, p. 220).

Beyond being

In the final phase of his thinking, Heidegger follows out the logic of his project of deconstructing and overcoming metaphysics – seen now as the 'history of being' (Seinsgeschichte) – to the point where its guiding terms, 'being' and 'truth', are themselves deemed unsuitable for naming the topic that provokes a new way, an 'other beginning', for thought; that is, Ereignis. This term is meant to suggest that 'event' whereby 'there is' the ontological difference between being and beings. Prior to both being and time, Ereignis grants or gives both (es gibt Sein, es gibt Zeit) (Heidegger, 1972a, pp. 19ff.). Heidegger's post-metaphysical thinking nevertheless retains communication with a certain 'power of phenomenological seeing' which, counter to the technological ordering of all reality that is the heritage of metaphysics, he cultivates explicitly in a series of essays devoted to recovering the poetic possibilities in mundane things.

Although its roots lie earlier, this last phase begins publically with the 1946 'Letter on Humanism', marking Heidegger's return to publication after the silence of the War years. Here Heidegger is at pains to distinguish his project from then-current existentialism. Refusing to assimilate his earlier work to a humanism that places 'man' or 'human existence' at the centre of philosophy – as had Sartre's interpretation of Being and Time – Heidegger insists that the task is to think being itself and to determine the human only on the basis of such essential thinking. In Heidegger's view, Being and Time already indicated the need to make this turn, but his subsequent thought failed, he now believes, because it remained too dependent on the 'language of metaphysics' – for example, in his emphasis on will and decision, where the disclosure of a normative meaningful space, or world, remained tied to the very metaphysical subjectivism Heidegger criticised in Nietzsche. As a result, the theme of language itself, first explored in the lectures on Hölderlin, emerges as central in Heidegger's essays of the 1950s. To overcome metaphysics, to think the truth of being in a non-(or post-) metaphysical way, a new relation to language is required. In the 'Letter on Humanism' language is identified as the 'house of being' and the image of human being as language 'user' is displaced by the image of human being as one who 'dwells' in the house, one who is the 'shepherd' of being. In subsequent essays Heidegger emphasised the proximity of post-philosophical 'thinking' (as the response of the thinker to the call or claim of language) and the primordial 'saying' of poetry (see Heidegger, 1971d, pp. 121ff.).

By the end of this phase, as can be seen in the 1962 essay on 'Time and Being' and the 1964 essay 'The End of Philosophy and the Task of Thinking', Heidegger finally came to reject all efforts at 'overcoming' metaphysics. If the task of thinking is to think (the meaning of) being itself, this can only be done in light of that event (*Ereignis*) whereby 'there is' being. Metaphysics, in contrast, always thinks being in light of beings, that is, as the being *of* beings. The very interest in overcoming this tendency (including Heidegger's own earlier preoccupation with the ontological difference) is now seen to keep thought in thrall to beings. Hence, in a line that anticipates some of the themes of Derridean deconstruction, Heidegger argues that one should 'cease all overcoming and leave metaphysics to itself' (Heidegger, 1972a, p. 24). He is thus led to abandon the metaphysical language he had sought to reappropriate for his 'other' thinking. With pointed reference to the 'method' of phenomenological seeing, which nourishes itself upon what grants and enables such seeing, that is, the 'clearing' (*Lichtung*), Heidegger argues that while metaphysics has always thought about what shows up in the clearing – namely, beings – it 'knows nothing of this *Lichtung* itself' (ibid., p. 63, p. 66). More precisely, clearing must here be thought of verbally as opening, and the philosophical term 'truth' (*aletheia*) does no more than name it while remaining blind to its character. Hence the clearing cannot be called the 'truth' of being and the 'question of the *aletheia*, of the unconcealedness as such, is not the question of truth' (ibid., p. 70). Reflecting on the matter of thought, then, leads Heidegger to replace the metaphysical terms of his earlier project – 'being' and 'time' – by the post-metaphysical 'clearing' (*Lichtung*) and 'presence' (*Anwesenheit*) (ibid., p. 73).

The character of such thinking can be gauged more concretely in those essays of the 1950s converging around the themes of technology and language. Heidegger sees the essence of modern technology as the 'completion' of metaphysics; that is, as an event of truth in the history of being, an 'enframing' (*Gestell*), or general horizon of meaningfulness in which all things show themselves finally as 'standing reserve' (*Bestand*) for manipulation. Following Hölderlin, Heidegger calls this the 'gravest danger' to humanity – not because it yields the means for destroying the planet (although this is dangerous enough and true enough), but because it signals the concealment of the very meaningfulness

of the question concerning its own limits – in the positivistic denial, for example, that the question of being has any meaning at all. Against this, Heidegger understands Hölderlin's claim – that where the 'gravest danger' is, there the 'saving power grows' as well – to mean that the counterpoint to the hegemony of technological thinking is to be sought in poetic language – not as aesthetic refinement but as *poiesis* which, like its cousin, *techné*, is an event of truth. Technological thinking leads to the contradictory conception whereby 'man' is both lord of the earth (resolutely manipulating all things according to his own measure) and a kind of virtual reality or function of the 'system' at various levels. In his 1962 interview with the magazine *Der Spiegel* Heidegger claims that 'only a god can save us' from this situation, but in the 1950s he had sought a healing measure in the word of the poets. Why? Principally because it is in the poetic word that a hidden aspect of our relation to language becomes audible.

In essays from the 1950s, as part of his 'anti-humanistic' attempt to de-centre modern subjectivism, Heidegger rejects the view that language is a 'tool' that is 'used' by man. Again, following hints in Hölderlin, he proposes that it is not man but language that should be said originally to speak. Human speech is therefore at bottom an *ent-spre-chen*, a co-responding to the Saying that has always already spoken. One may think here, in a less exalted vein, of Gadamer's idea of tradition. As Heidegger suggests in a series of reflections on the poets George, Trakl, Rilke and Hölderlin, it is the poet whose response is the most 'adequate', most attentive, to the call of language. Far from being a wilful 'creation' of something new and subjectively expressive, poetry arises as a deep response to what speaks in the silent Saying of language – a response which Heidegger calls 'measure-taking' (*Maß-nahme*), that which registers the measure of what it means for us to be. The thinker's task is to follow up 'thoughtfully', in a meditative dwelling on meaning (*Besinnung*), the taking of our measure in the poem (Heidegger, 1976, pp. 221ff.). To what end? Here, finally, the aim of another related series of essays from the 1950s becomes clear, those in which Heidegger tries to rethink the meaning of the earth.

Essays like 'The Thing' (1950), 'Building, Dwelling, Thinking' (1951), and 'Language' (1951) reveal a phenomenological sensibility informed by a vocabulary derived from Heidegger's encounter with the poets, especially Hölderlin. Many have seen in these essays – with their talk of the Fourfold (earth, heavens, mortals, divinities) which takes place as a roundelay or mirror-play – little more than an attempt at myth-making and a nostalgic yearning for the world of the Black Forest peasant at the moment when that world has decisively disappeared. Yet if one reads them in the spirit of phenomenological seeing and description, which Heidegger never abandoned in practice, even if he abandoned it as a designation for his project, one may discern a keen attention to the way that the most ordinary things can continue to address us even in their very unobtrusiveness. Heidegger hopes to reawaken a sense for what *things* are (or mean) that is concealed, deeply but not perhaps irrevocably, in the technological contexts of contemporary life. Reversing the order of *Being and Time* – where the 'thing' is seen as a derivative mode of the 'tool' and the tool is relativised to Dasein's projects in the world as a 'totality of involvements' – the essay on 'The Thing' reflects on how it is precisely the thing's own 'thinging' that 'gathers' and organises a world (the roundelay of the fourfold) (see Heidegger, 1971b, p. 180). A simple jug thus does not disappear into its use but is seen as a particular way of bringing together earth, heavens, mortals and divinities. Reflection on a bridge in the essay on 'Building, Dwelling, Thinking' moves in the same direction, towards phenomenological recovery of a kind of being (dwelling) attuned to measures other than those accorded value in the metaphysical matrix of meaning which is the essence of the technological world. Thinking, then, listens or hearkens to the traces of what remains hidden, for the most part, in the self-assertion of technological planning, a 'releasement' (*Gelassenheit*) or 'letting be' that does no more than 'bring to word' what speaks in the primordial poem of the world (see Heidegger, 1966). To that extent, then, even the later Heidegger does nothing more than seek a way 'back to the things themselves' (Husserl's phenomenological slogan) and, in letting them speak, remains committed to the possibility of phenomenology.

Bibliography

Writings

References in the article are to the English-language editions. A relatively complete list of Heidegger's publications – including the four divisions of the *Gesamtausgabe* – together with existing English translations can be found in Guignon (1993).

Heidegger, Martin (1981), *Aristoteles, Metaphysik Theta 1–3* (lecture 1931), *Gesamtausgabe*, Vol. 33, ed. Heinrich Hüni, Frankfurt-am-Main: Vittorio Klostermann.
— (1962) (first edn 1927), *Being and Time*, trans. John Macquarrie and Edward Robinson, New York: Harper and Row.
— (1989), *Beiträge zur Philosophie (Vom Ereignis)*, *Gesamtausgabe*, Vol. 65, ed. Friedrich-Wilhelm von Herrmann, Frankfurt-am-Main: Vittorio Klostermann.
— (1971a) (first edn 1951), 'Building, Dwelling, Thinking', in *Poetry, Language, Thought*, trans. Albert Hofstadter, New York: Harper and Row.
— (1972a) (first edn 1964), 'The End of Philosophy and the Task of Thinking', in *On Time and Being*, trans. Joan Stambaugh, New York: Harper and Row.
— (1983), *Grundbegriffe der Metaphysik. Welt-Endlichkeit-Einsamkeit* (lecture 1929–30), *Gesamtausgabe*, Vol. 29/30, ed. Friedrich-Wilhelm von Herrmann, Frankfurt-am-Main: Vittorio Klostermann.
— (1980a), *Hegels Phänomenologie des Geistes* (lecture 1930–31), *Gesamtausgabe*, Vol. 32, ed. Ingtraud Görland, Frankfurt-am-Main: Vittorio Klostermann.
— (1980b), *Hölderlins Hymnen 'Germanien' und 'Der Rhein'* (lecture 1934–35), *Gesamtausgabe*, Vol. 39, ed. Susanne Ziegler, Frankfurt-am-Main: Vittorio Klostermann.
— (1959) (first edn 1953), *An Introduction to Metaphysics* (lecture 1935), trans Ralph Manheim, New Haven: Yale University Press.
— (1972b), *Die Kategorien- und Bedeutungslehre des Duns Scotus* (Habilitation 1916), in *Frühe Schriften*, Frankfurt-am-Main: Vittorio Klostermann.
— (1990) (first edn 1929), *Kant and the Problem of Metaphysics*, trans. Richard Taft, Bloomington: Indiana University Press.
— (1971b) (first edn 1951), 'Language', in *Poetry, Language, Thought*, trans. Albert Hofstadter, New York: Harper and Row.
— (1966) (first edn 1955), 'Memorial Address', in *Discourse on Thinking*, trans. John M. Anderson and E. Hans Freund, New York: Harper and Row.
— (1972c), *Die Lehre vom Urteil im Psychologismus* (dis

sertation 1914), in *Frühe Schriften*, Frankfurt-am-Main: Vittorio Klostermann.

— (1993) (first edn 1946), 'Letter on Humanism', trans. Frank Capuzzi, in David Farrell Krell (ed.), *Basic Writings*, New York: HarperCollins (HarperSanFrancisco).

— (1984a), *The Metaphysical Foundations of Logic* (lecture 1928), trans. Michael Heim, Bloomington: Indiana University Press.

— (1979), *Nietzsche I: The Will to Power as Art* (lecture 1936–37), trans. David Farrell Krell, New York: Harper and Row.

— (1984b), *Nietzsche II: The Eternal Recurrence of the Same* (lecture 1937), trans. David Farrell Krell, New York: Harper and Row.

— (1987), *Nietzsche III: The Will to Power as Knowledge and Metaphysics* (lecture 1939), trans. Joan Stambaugh, New York: Harper and Row.

— (1982), *Nietzsche IV: Nihilism* (lecture 1940), trans. Frank Capuzzi, New York: Harper and Row.

— (1993) (first edn 1943), 'On the Essence of Truth' (lecture 1930), in David Farrell Krell (ed.), *Basic Writings*, New York: Harper Collins (HarperSanFrancisco).

— (1988), *Ontologie (Hermeneutik der Faktizität)* (lecture 1923), *Gesamtausgabe*, Vol. 63, ed. Käte Bröcker-Oltmanns, Frankfurt-am-Main: Vittorio Klostermann.

— (1971c) (first edn 1936), 'The Origin of the Work of Art', in *Poetry, Language, Thought*, trans. Albert Hofstadter, New York: Harper and Row.

— (1985), *Phänomenologische Interpretationen zu Aristoteles. Einführung in die Phänomenologische Forschung* (lecture 1921–22), *Gesamtausgabe*, Vol. 61, ed. Käte Bröcker-Oltmanns, Frankfurt-am-Main: Vittorio Klostermann.

— (1977) (first edn 1955), 'The Question Concerning Technology', in *The Question Concerning Technology and Other Essays*, trans. William Lovitt, New York: Harper and Row.

— (1971d) (first edn 1959), 'The Way to Language', in *On the Way to Language*, trans. Peter Hertz, New York: Harper and Row.

— (1985), 'The Self-Assertion of the German University' (Rectoral Address 1933), trans. Karsten Harries, *Review of Metaphysics* 38, 467–81.

— (1971e) (first edn 1950), 'The Thing', in *Poetry, Language, Thought*, trans. Albert Hofstadter, New York: Harper and Row.

— (1971f) (first edn 1954), 'Poetically Man Dwells . . .' in *Poety, Language, Thought*, trans. Albert Hofstadter, New York: Harper and Row.

— (1972a) (first edn 1962), 'Time and Being', in *On Time and Being*, trans. Joan Stambaugh, New York: Harper and Row.

— (1982), *Vom Wesen der Menschlichen Freiheit. Einleitung in die Philosophie* (lecture 1930), *Gesamtausgabe*, Vol. 31, ed. Hartmut Tietjen, Frankfurt-am Main: Vittorio Klostermann.

— (1988), *Vom Wesen der Wahrheit: Zu Platons Höhlengleichnis und Theätet* (lecture 1931–32), *Gesamtausgabe*, Vol. 34, ed. Hermann Mörchen, Frankfurt-am-Main: Vittorio Klostermann.

— (1987), *Zur Bestimmung der Philosophie* (lecture 1919), *Gesamtausgabe*, Vol. 56/57, ed. Bernd Heimbüchel, Frankfurt-am-Main: Vittorio Klostermann.

References and further reading

Bernasconi, Robert (1993), *Heidegger in Question: The Art of Existing*, Atlantic Highlands: Humanities Press.

Dreyfus, Hubert (1991), *Being-in-the-World: A Commentary on Heidegger's Being and Time, Division I*, Cambridge, MA: The MIT Press.

Guignon, Charles (ed.) (1993), *The Cambridge Companion to Heidegger*, Cambridge: Cambridge University Press.

Kisiel, Theodore (1993), *The Genesis of Heidegger's Being and Time*, Berkeley: University of California Press.

Kisiel, Theodore and John van Buren (eds) (1994), *Reading Heidegger From the Start: Essays in His Earliest Thought*, Albany: State University of New York Press.

Pöggeler, Otto (1990), *Martin Heidegger's Path of Thinking*, trans. Daniel Magurshak and Sigmund Barber, Atlantic Highlands: Humanities Press.

Sallis, John (ed.) (1993), *Rereading Heidegger: Commemorations*, Bloomington: Indiana University Press.

Sheehan, Thomas (ed.) (1981), *Heidegger, The Man and the Thinker*, Chicago: Precedent Publishing.

Taminiaux, Jacques (1991), *Heidegger and the Project of Fundamental Ontology*, Albany: State University of New York Press.

4.4

SARTRE'S EXISTENTIAL PHENOMENOLOGY

Thomas W. Busch

Jean-Paul Sartre's (1905–80) encounter with, and appropriation of, Husserl's phenomenology was decisive for the early development of his philosophy. From his brief article, 'A Fundamental Idea of Husserl's Phenomenology: Intentionality' (1933), to his major work on ontology, *Being and Nothingness* (1943), subtitled 'An Essay on Phenomenological Ontology', Sartre considered himself to be working within a phenomenological methodology. By the time he published *Search For A Method* (1957), it was clear that he had become aware of certain limits of this method and was taking his place within a dialectical approach to philosophical problems.

Phenomenology discovered

Sartre had become aware of phenomenology in 1933 through Raymond Aron, a former classmate at the Ecole Normale Supérieure, who had been studying on a grant that year at the French Institute in Berlin. With Aron's encouragement Sartre succeeded him on the grant the following year. The small article which Sartre wrote during his stay in Berlin, 'A Fundamental Idea of Husserl's Phenomenology: Intentionality', expresses well the enthusiasm of his discovery of phenomenology. He sees in intentionality a means of escaping philosophies which assimilate the world into representations for consciousness. Additionally, intentionality discloses that we are related to the world affectively as well as cogni-

tively: one can hate, fear, love an object as well as know it. Intentionality is a surpassing, a throwing of self outside of itself towards the other, a bursting forth which makes it impossible for consciousness 'to coincide with itself'. Sartre notes that the intentional principle, 'consciousness is consciousness of something', means that, while the world is 'essentially external to consciousness, nevertheless it is essentially relative to consciousness' (Sartre, 1933, p. 4). The article does nothing to exploit the latter dimension of intentionality because at the time Sartre was interested in finding a way to reject the idealistic philosophy of his teachers. Although it is clear that Sartre is making a very idiosyncratic reading of Husserl he is not criticising him when he claims that 'the profound meaning' of intentionality is our abandonment 'in an indifferent, hostile, and restive world'. As his knowledge of Husserl deepens, Sartre does become critical, to the point of accusing him in *Being and Nothingness* of being 'totally unfaithful to his principle' of intentionality (ibid.).

Sartre has admitted that Husserl's phenomenology was his real discovery for it offered him a technical language with which to do philosophy. Until his encounter with Husserl's work, Sartre's initial writings were an undistinguished blend of literary and philosophical ideas, vague presentations of freedom, contingency, estrangement from others and failure to achieve the absolute. His appropriation of phenomenology gave him a discourse and method through which these themes received an articulation an-development that were both unique and powerful.

In his early work Sartre cites a number of Husserl's writings: *Logical Investigations*, *The Phenomenology of Internal Time Consciousness*, *Cartesian Meditations*, *Formal and Transcendental Logic*, but the work that influenced him the most, the one that he spent his year in Berlin studying, was *Ideas Pertaining to a Pure Phenomenology and to a Phenomenological Philosophy* (*Ideas I*), which he called 'the great event of pre-World War I philosophy' (Sartre, 1936a, p. 127).

Phenomenology in action

Two of Sartre's early works in particular display the fruitful meeting of the phenomenological method with his earlier, inchoate, ideas, *The Transcendence of the Ego* (1936a) and *Nausea* (1938). *The Transcendence of the Ego* begins with a critique of Descartes and Husserl over the question of the *ego*. Sartre criticises the former for having overlooked the pre-reflective life of consciousness, for identifying the consciousness which proclaims reflectively, 'I am doubting', with the very consciousness which doubts. Sartre, in effect, accuses Descartes of absolutising reflective consciousness while suppressing its own parasitical status. Pre-reflective consciousness, like all consciousness for Sartre, is intentional; that is, directed ecstatically outside of itself towards an object. For pre-reflective consciousness the object intended is always some object other than itself. In the case of doubting, it would be the object precisely given as doubtful. While engaged in doubting, the doubting consciousness does not take itself as its object: the doubting consciousness intends the object as dubious. Reflective consciousness intervenes to take as its object an act of consciousness, in this case the doubting consciousness. In proclaiming 'I am doubting', the reflective consciousness is intending the act of doubting, which is now raised from its pre-reflective obscurity into object status. Whether on the pre-reflective or reflective levels, consciousness manifests its intentional character as consciousness of an object. While Sartre insists that in its intentional activity consciousness does not take itself for an object, there does take place, simultaneous with its intentional thrust, a non-objective self-awareness on the part of consciousness. Thus, the pre-reflective consciousness engaged in doubting intends the doubtful object, not itself, but is also non-objectively aware of doing so. The reflective consciousness engaged in intending the consciousness reflected-on, not itself, is also non-objectively aware of doing so. Thus, not all forms of consciousness are objective and those forms of science and philosophy that would assume the reduction of human existence to a discourse of objectivity are, according to Sartre's analysis, incapable of coming to terms with human existence. For Sartre, the basic structure of consciousness is that it is objectively, focally, aware of objects and non-objectively, non-focally, aware of itself: 'consciousness is purely and simply consciousness of being conscious of (an) object' (ibid., p. 40).

After distinguishing pre-reflective and reflective levels of consciousness, Sartre notes that the 'I' appears only on the reflective level. 'The certain content of the pseudo- "cogito" is not "I have consciousness of this chair", but "There is consciousness of this chair" ' (ibid., pp. 53–4). When one perceives a chair, there is perceptual consciousness of the chair. The chair is the object, not oneself. If one reflects upon one's perceiving the chair, one proclaims 'I am perceiving a chair'. What is the nature of the 'I'? Descartes identifies the 'I' as a thing (*res*) or substance, the unifying substrate of all the various conscious acts. Descartes, having rightfully prioritised consciousness, not only repressed the pre-reflective consciousness but also went on to deform it with his metaphysics of substance. Husserl should have known better but he also mistook the character of the 'I'.

Sartre claims that 'the transcendent I must fall before the stroke of the phenomenological reduction', (ibid., p. 53) thereby accusing Husserl of not being radical enough in employing the phenomenological reduction. Husserl had employed his phenomenological reduction to critically identify naive forms of givenness and lead them back to their constitutional origins in transcendental subjectivity. In Section 57 of *Ideas I*, Husserl, in a change of view from his earlier works, held that there must be a non-constituted transcendental Ego to account for the phenomenological experience that the conscious acts that I reflect upon are *mine*. Sartre counters that, on Husserl's own grounds, this is an unnecessary presumption, for the unity of conscious life can be accounted for by the innate coherence of the life of consciousness in time consciousness as Husserl had himself indicated in his work on time consciousness.

What Sartre sees at stake in establishing his view that the Ego is not 'formally or materially *in* consciousness' becomes clear in his Conclusion (ibid., p. 31). Here he uses a case study from clinical psychology to exemplify his position. A young woman, newly married, suffered anxiety that when her husband left her alone and she looked outside her window, she could act as a prostitute by summoning passers-by. She could not reconcile this possibility to herself (her ego, her image and objective representation of herself). Her ego, as it were, was incapable of this sort of unfaithful activity. Yet, she experienced that nothing could prevent her from engaging in this activity. She experienced in anxiety that acting unfaithfully was a real possiblity. The young woman, in her anxiety, lived through a reduction of her ego, which turns out to be an objective representation of herself which she had been sustaining through belief. Objectification of conscious life produces what Sartre calls the psychic, a realm in which conscious life is thought in terms of the inert, such as states and qualities, united in a given unity of the ego. These objectifications, he suggests, have a practical function: that of masking the radical freedom of consciousness. According to his reasoning, were the young woman really, in her ego identity, faithful, then she would be incapable of acting unfaithfully. Only faithful acts would issue from her faithful essence. The experience of anxiety reveals that her ego/essence is constituted and sustained by her radical freedom. Being faithful is not due to having a faithful ego/essence, but in committing oneself to and sustaining, through free choices, faithful acts. Sartre notes that the ego appears to offer a practical, rather than theoretical, role in our lives in so far as it can be used as a mask to hide freedom. The project of hiding freedom will become in *Being and Nothingness*, under the heading of bad faith, a major theme. In his thematising of radical freedom in *The Transcendence of the Ego*, Sartre can be viewed as translating the *epoché* from the epistemological role it

primarily served in Husserl's phenomenology to an existential role of facing up to one's freedom in a process of identity creation: 'the *epoché* is no longer a miracle, an intellectual method, an erudite procedure: it is an anxiety which is imposed on us and which we cannot avoid' (ibid., p. 103).

Sartre's novel, *Nausea*, also involves translating phenomenological themes from Husserl's writings into existential themes. If *The Transcendence of the Ego* is a criticism of Husserl for not extending the phenomenological reduction far enough, *Nausea* criticises Husserl for extending it too far in another direction. At issue is Husserl's attitude toward existence, facticity, contingency – matters of the highest concern to existentialism. Because Husserl's phenomenology aimed at being a rigorous science, the process of eidetic reduction through which universal essences appear is the centrepiece of his methodology. Thus, at its heart, Husserl's phenomenology shares with the rationalist Western philosophical tradition the assumption that nothing noteworthy would be lost in the process of eidetic reduction. Individuals and factual events on this assumption would be comprehensible as instantiations of universal essences or meanings. Sartre's novel is in the form of a journal kept by Antoine Roquentin, who lives in Bouville, and has begun his journal because he is trying to come to terms with certain uncomfortable experiences he has been undergoing lately. The experiences are very similar to those depicted in Section 49 of Husserl's *Ideas I*, under the heading of 'The Annihilation of the World'. Roquentin's life-world, his habitual world, in which things are familiar through their practical use qualities and through their names, is crumbling. Ordinary objects – doorknobs, beer glasses, suspenders, pieces of paper – appear strange and terrifying. Roquentin is overwhelmed by nausea when he touches these objects. Worst of all, his own life is subject to this same malady. His body is experienced as a weight, a certain taste. He cannot recognise his own face in a mirror for his face disappears into the 'lunar world' of pores of flesh and hairs (Sartre, 1938, p. 17). These troubling experiences culminate in the 'vision' in the park which Roquentin has in front of the chestnut tree, when 'words had vanished and with them the significance of things, their methods of use, and the feeble points of reference which men have traced on their surface' (ibid., p. 127). Sartre is here depicting the failure, in his eyes, of Husserl's reduction of experience to universal essences or meanings. When the categories of understanding and organising experience have been removed, as they have been for Roquentin, something remains, but not the transcendental ego of Husserl which the latter claimed to remain after his own version of the 'annihilation of the world'. Speaking of the root of the chestnut tree, Roquentin says

> In vain to repeat: 'This is a root' – it didn't work any more. I saw clearly that you could not pass from its function as a root, as a breathing pump, *to that*, to this hard and compact skin of a sea lion, to this oily, callous, headstrong look. The function explained nothing: it allowed you to understand generally that it was a root, but not *that one* at all. This root, with its colour, shape, its congealed movement, was . . . below all explanation. (ibid., p. 129)

Roquentin experiences the discrepancy between the 'general' explanations and categories of meaning, and the singular thing. In terms of Husserl's phenomenology, Sartre is here claiming that Husserl's phenomenology does not account for a particular perception. There is an essence of 'perception as such' but not of why one is perceiving some thing. Even Husserl's appeal to the 'matter' of the perceptual act, the hyle, animated by a perceptual form, is ineffective, for Husserl never explains why the hyle are such as they are. Roquentin learns that the life-world is an interpretation, a way of organising, relating and talking about existence, which forms precisely a 'world'. And there is no necessity for any one world, any one way of organising and talking about existence. 'The essential thing is contingency. I mean that one cannot define existence as necessity. To exist is simply *to be there*; those who exist let themselves be encountered, but you can never deduce anything from them. . . . [T]he world of explanations and reasons is not the world of existence' (ibid., p. 131; p. 129).

Roquentin is relieved of his nausea when he hears a jazz record, 'Some of these days'. As he listens to the music, he remarks on 'the necessity of this music'

which nothing can interrupt, 'nothing which comes from this time in which the world has fallen' (ibid., p. 22). The record symbolises art and the work of imagination sustaining art. Sartre wrote two books on imagination, *Imagination: A Psychological Critique* (1936) and *The Psychology of Imagination* (1940), a topic that persists in his thought up to and including his work on Flaubert. He found in phenomenology a non-reductive way to consider imagination in its own right. It is the work of radical freedom. An imagining consciousness was in no way a prisoner of the perceptual presentation of the world; it can effect a break with any given formation of being. Indeed, freedom itself is defined as the break or negation of being in any given form. The aesthetic object is a work of freedom, founded in imagination, not perception. Thus, when Roquentin experiences the song, his nausea, caused by his encounter with the sheer contingency of existence, is relieved because the aesthetic object is a meaningfully constituted object which escapes contingency. Sartre seems to believe that the ordering or interpretations which constitute the perception of the life-world are to be distinguished from the interpretations of the aesthetic imagination. This is related to a sharp difference which Sartre makes between his view on imagination and Husserl's. Sartre holds that, for Husserl, the matter (hyle) on the basis of which consciousness forms images is the same for perception and imagination. The result would be, Sartre tells us, that for Husserl the difference between perception and imagination would lie solely in the form given the matter by the conscious act. Sartre disagrees: 'A difference in intention is necessary but not sufficient. The matter must also be different' (Sartre, 1936a, p. 143). Sartre would seem to be committed, then, to the view that the 'existence' he discusses in *Nausea* involves a 'matter' which is subject to perceptual interpretation in various life-worlds, whereas imagination is not involved with this same matter, and thus escapes its contingency. In any case, with the experience of the work of art, Roquentin senses at the end of the novel a solution to his suffering. Perhaps he could, if not actually turn his life into the necessity of a work of art, produce a work of art which would 'justify' or make worthy his meaningless existence.

Phenomenological ontology

Being and Nothingness weaves the themes of freedom and contingency of the early works into what might be called an ontological narrative. In over seven hundred pages Sartre presents the reader not only with an account of three modes of being, but also a psychoanalytic interpretation of human action which dramatically relates these modes to one another.

Being and Nothingness, as noted earlier, bears the subtitle, 'An Essay on Phenomenological Ontology'. Sartre distinguishes ontology from metaphysics because in his estimation the former delineates being as it is present in our experience of it (and thus depends upon description) whereas the latter pretends to be a causal explanation of what is open to experience, going behind or beneath experience (and thus positing hypotheses about what one experiences). Phenomenological ontology reveals three modes of being: being-for-itself, being-in-itself, and being-for-Others. At the heart of Sartre's theory of experience is a sharp subject/object distinction. We have seen that a major attraction for him to Husserl's phenomenology was the principle of intentionality with its distinction between the conscious act and its object. Sartre's ontology forms itself around the non-negotiable distinction between self and Otherness. So protective of this distinction is he that he breaks with Husserl over it, claiming that Husserl 'is totally unfaithful to his [Husserl's own] principle' (Sartre, 1943, p. lxi). As he accused Husserl, implicitly, in *Nausea*, of idealism, of reducing facticity to meaning, so in *Being and Nothingness* he accuses him of idealistically constituting the being of objects (now reduced to meaning) out of subjective acts. For Sartre, to say that consciousness is consciousness of an object is to say that consciousness 'is born *supported by* a being which is not itself. . . . The structure at the basis of intentionality and of selfness is the negation, which is the *internal* relation of the for-itself to the thing' (ibid., p. lxi; p. 123). The difference, or spacing, between subject/object and self/otherness is, for Sartre, negation (*néant*). This spacing is characteristic of all human experience. To be an experiencing subject is to experience an object standing over against oneself. Experience is not fusion:

> Presence encloses a radical negation as presence to that which one is not. What is present to me is not me. . . . It is impossible to construct the notion of an object if we do not have originally a negative relation designating the object as that which is not consciousness. (ibid., p. 173)

This implies that the being of the experiencer is differentiated from all otherness. 'The presence of the for-itself to the in-itself . . . is pure *denied identity*' (ibid., p. 178). Sartre's notion of differentiation or spacing is located in consciousness, setting him apart from those theories of difference locating themselves in the external forms of inscriptions. As noted, for Sartre, consciousness, as it intends an object, is non-positionally or tacitly aware of itself. Ontologically, a being which is self-consciously 'present to itself', cannot be itself in the form of fusion with itself. Consciousness, in its self-awareness, discriminates itself from what is other than itself, forming a self. Being-for-itself, then, is a being conscious of things and at the same time conscious of its not being those things. A double negation or spacing constitutes being-for-itself. It is not its objects and it is not itself.

This very spacing in the heart of its being is also, for Sartre, the temporality of its being. The continuous disruption of fusion with itself is the flight of being-for-itself from identity with its past and towards an ever impossible identity, to be always disrupted.

The reader of *Being and Nothingness* is first introduced to being-for-itself through an exploration of the problem of nothingness (ibid., p. 2). Here Sartre attempts to refute the Parmenidean notion that being is identity with itself, full positivity, by appealing to experiences of the negative. One goes to meet Pierre in the café and experiences his absence. One questions, doubts and experiences the possibility of the negative. One is anxious in the face of a future which is not yet. These experiences of the negative are traced to the presence of a 'human reality' that in its very being must, in order to experience the negative, be a 'break' with a sheer identity with what is. A further consideration shows us that this break is nothing other than freedom itself: 'Descartes following the Stoics has given a name to this possibility which human reality has to secrete a nothingness which isolates it – it is freedom' (ibid., pp. 24–5). Sartre is furnishing the ontology for the radical freedom discovered in *The Transcendence of the Ego* where he proposed the connection between freedom and transcendence of ego-identity. The continuous disruption of identity which constitutes being-for-itself frees it from lapsing into an identity which would freeze its possibilities of choice. At the end of the introduction to being-for-itself, Sartre tells us that two different paths or 'ekstases' confront us, one towards being and one towards non-being. The former is the path towards bad faith and inauthenticity, whereby freedom will pursue the impossible goal identity with itself. The latter is the path towards authenticity, whereby human reality will take its own freedom as its goal. But, Sartre informs us, this latter path will require 'separate study' (ibid., p. 44).

The reference to 'separate study' is crucial for putting *Being and Nothingness* into perspective within the corpus of Sartre's work. The phenomenological ontology is not intended to be a complete account of human existence. Sartre once referred to *Being and Nothingness* as his 'eidetic of bad faith' indicating that the unmasking of forms of bad faith, an analysis of their motivation, and an indication of a possible cure are the focus of *Being and Nothingness*. For example, the chapter 'Bad Faith' ends with a footnote that declares the possibility of escaping from bad faith by a 'self-recovery we shall call authenticity, the description of which has no place here' (ibid., p. 70). Similarly, in the chapter 'Concrete Relations with Others' which examines several forms of bad faith relationships with others, there is a footnote warning the reader that the presentation of these relationships 'does not exclude the possibility of an ethics of deliverance and salvation' which depends on 'a radical conversion which we can not discuss here' (ibid., p. 412). Sartre does not believe that one is permanently trapped in bad faith or that there is 'no exit' from that inauthentic existence. The key to understanding what he means by 'self-recovery' and 'conversion' as we will shortly see, is related to his existentialising of the Husserlian *epoche* found in *The Transcendence of the Ego*.

Sartre's presentation of being-in-itself takes two directions and it is unclear whether he ever reconciles them satisfactorily. One of these senses is directly related to the mode of being of objects as they are given in experience. An object has the sense of a given, something standing over against (*Gegenstand*) subjectivity. This alterity of the given is phenomenological in so far as the object's mode of being is different from, not immanent in, the subject's mode of being. A transcendent object has an identity, which is recognisable, iterable, as it stands over against the temporality of subjectivity. This objective mode of being belongs to all objects of consciousness, even objectified or represented consciousness: '[T]he Ego is in-itself, not for-itself. . . . [T]he psychic is nothing other than the in-itself (ibid., p. 103; p. 162). All that is a transcendent object of consciousness shares the mode of being of objectivity in this sense. What appears as an object is identifiable and therefore differentiated from the being of the for-itself, 'which is what it is not and which is not what it is'. The phenomenological senses of being-for-itself and being-in-itself are correlative, but incommensurable. Another meaning of being-in-itself stresses not the incommensurable correlation of the two modes of being, but the priority of being-in-itself over being-for-itself. Sartre criticises Hegel for making being and non-being equal, for, Sartre argues, when being is emptied of content, as it must be to predicate it of everything that is, then it cannot be differentiated from the emptiness of content of non-being. However, Sartre insists that non-being is the negation of being, that being must first be posited, then negated, that non-being is 'subsequent' to being as its contradiction. As such, being (-in-itself) is originally an undifferentiated fullness which the event of its negation (being-for-itself) differentiates. Of course, being-in-itself in a pure, undifferentiated state, cannot be encountered. What is encountered is always already differentiated. 'It is in theory possible but in practice impossible to distinguish facticity from the project which constitutes it in situation' (ibid., p. 27). Since the phenomenological approach to ontology depends upon a descriptive encounter with being, the latter sense of being-in-itself, as undifferentiated positivity, is theoretical and goes beyond the limits of phenomenological ontology. The two meanings of being-in-itself run throughout *Being and Nothingness* unreconciled. The phenomenological sense of being-in-itself recognises a mode of being-in-itself of individual objects. However, since Sartre holds that 'pure' or theoretical being-in-itself, being in the sense of undifferentiated positivity prior to encounter with consciousness, is untouched 'in its nucleus' by negation, the reality of individual phenomena is questionable.

The incommensurable modes of being, being-for-itself and being-in-itself, follow from Sartre's basic commitment to an epistemology founded on the subject/object distinction. An important consequence of this commitment is the difficulty posed by the problem of the existence of other subjectivities. As a subjectivity, one, by definition, regards the Other as an object. In this sense, the Other is an object in one's world. Of course, Others-as-objects are to be distinguished from various other sorts of objects, because Others are recognised as having projects of their own. But from the point of view of one's own subjectivity, these projects are objects, falling into one's own world where they receive meaning and value from one's own projects. It is in this sense that Sartre refers to the Other as a 'transcendence transcended'. 'But insofar as I transcend the Other's transcendence, I fix it. It is no longer a recourse against facticity' (ibid., p. 34). Through 'the Look' Sartre discusses how the subject/object relation is reversed:

> [M]y fundamental connection with the Other-as-subject must be able to be referred back to my permanent possibility of being *seen* by the Other. It is in and through the revelation of my being-as-object for the Other that I must be able to apprehend the presence of his being-as-subject. (ibid., p. 256)

Shame is the paradigm experience of being-for-Others, for shame is 'the *recognition* of the fact that I *am* indeed that object which the Other is looking at and judging' (ibid., p. 261). Thus, although one can never directly encounter the subjectivity of the Other, one can be certain of the Other's existence through experiences of being objectified, of being seen by the Other. Sartre insists that when one objectifies oneself, in regarding oneself in a mirror, for example, this is not the same experience as being-for-the-Other. In the case of regarding oneself in the mirror, one is existing for oneself. That is, one's image is still in the possession of one's own world, one's own power to interpret. To experience oneself as an object for the Other, by contrast, is to experience one's being to be possessed by the Other, for the Other knows, judges, evaluates, assesses and gives a meaning to oneself. One is 'in the midst of the world' of the Other: 'This is because my transcendence becomes for whoever makes himself a witness of it . . . a purely established transcendence, a given-transcendence' (ibid., p. 262). One is always, for oneself, a subject, living and experiencing and tasting a singular existence from within. The Look of the Other pulls one into another mode of being, objective, public, factical, which one must recognise as oneself, but for the Other.

Pivotal in Sartre's presentation of being-for-Others is his view of the body. To be 'for the Other', one must be visible. Shame is the recognition that I am an object for the Other, which can happen only if my subjectivity is embodied. Consistent with his ontology, Sartre accords to the body both subjective and objective modes of being. From the first-person experience of subjectivity, I am my body: 'The body is nothing other than the for-itself . . .' (ibid., p. 309). My world is oriented about myself as body, for the world not only turns a perspectival face toward me, but also consists of 'instrumental complexes', practical meanings and demands. My body is a point of view on which I cannot take a point of view. My body is not a set of tools I use to act upon the world, but a set of capacities I am to respond to the world. 'I am not in relation to my hand in the same utilizing attitude as I am in relation to the pen; I *am* my hand. . . . It would be best to say, using "exist" as a transitive verb – that consciousness *exists* its body' (ibid., p. 323; p. 329).

Throughout *Being and Nothingness* Sartre interweaves his three modes of being with a psychological narrative, centring on bad faith, which has its origins in the flight from freedom mentioned at the end of *The Transcendence of the Ego*. There the ego, Sartre suggested, one's objective or represented identity, can be employed as a mask for one's radical freedom. In *Being and Nothingness*, two chapters; Bad Faith' and 'Concrete Relations with Others', explore in detail different forms of bad faith. In 'Bad Faith' the masking drama is centred within one's own consciousness and is articulated over against Freud's concept of repression. Sartre finds such Freudian concepts as repression and resistance to be valuable insights, but he objects to the mechanistic metaphysics he sees supporting them. Bad faith is characterised as a lie to oneself, wherein the liar and the lied to are the same. However, since the essence of the lie is that the liar knows the truth which he or she withholds from the lied to, the process of lying to oneself requires that one 'know' that one is lying: 'I must know in my capacity as deceiver the truth which is hidden from me in my capacity as the one deceived' (ibid., p. 49). This self-deception can occur because the being of consciousness is not one with itself: 'The condition of the possibility of bad faith is that human reality, in its most immediate being, in the intrastructure of the pre-reflective cogito, must be what it is not and not be what it is' (ibid., p. 67). Human beings cannot *be* an identity, but must *exist* as an identity. One 'is' a writer in the mode of supporting and sustaining a pattern of activity. One never merges for an instant into an identity or being-in-itself. For Sartre, 'human reality' is irreducibly cultural.

To be 'human' is not accounted for by the abstract facts of biology, neurophysiology, etc. To be 'human' is to entertain an idea or ideal of what it means to exist as a human and this is variable. Indeed, it is open to choice. To be a 'man' or 'woman', as well as to be 'cowardly' or 'brave', is to support styles of life which are cultural creations. To believe that one 'is' cowardly in the sense of identity requires that one repress the choices that constantly support a pattern of behaviour. This is bad faith. One believes that one is what one is not, for one cannot 'be' a coward in the sense of being-in-itself. On the other hand, the thief who, appearing before the court, argues that the charges be dropped because, according to Sartre one never 'is' an identity, is also in bad faith. Here, the thief is claiming that he or she is not what he or she is. But in this case, the thief is repressing, not the sense of identity in-itself but the existential (moral) sense of

identity gained from sustaining a pattern of behaviour. One always, according to Sartre, must define oneself by a choice of lifestyle for which one is responsible.

The forms of bad faith discussed in 'Concrete Relations With Others' revolve around being-for-Others. Some forms, love and masochism in particular, are based upon maintaining oneself as an object for the Other with the end in view of being confirmed in meaning by the Other or being given an identity by the Other. Other forms, such as indifference and sadism, attempt to suppress or control the Other's subjectivity. Sartre's message is that all forms of encounter with Others based on a denial that the Other and oneself are both subjects and objects, freedom and facticity, are doomed to bad faith.

Sartre diagnoses the motivation for bad faith in terms of what he calls the passion to be. All action derives from a desire stemming from a lack. All action transcends itself towards an end or value that would fill up the lack. On the most fundamental level, that of being, the for-itself is defined in terms of a lack of identity with itself, and so the value that haunts it is its own completion. Its completion would involve both being an identity and being conscious of it. In effect, this would be a state wherein one's life would be intrinsically meaningful, for one would not work at maintaining an identity (acting out the meaning one gives to oneself), but would actually *be* the meaning that one is giving oneself. In the latter case, Sartre tells us, one would be *causa sui*, or God, a being that is an identity and makes itself to be that identity. In terms of Sartre's ontology this would translate into 'the impossible synthesis of the for-itself and the in-itself' (ibid., p. 90). As noted, being-for-itself is differentiated from itself in its self-consciousness and temporality. To lose this constitutive differentiation would destroy it in full positivity of being-in-itself. From the perspective of ever attaining the ideal synthesis that haunts it, human reality is doomed to failure. Yet, something of a redemptive perspective on life is opened up by existential psychoanalysis, which allows one to see how one's life is taken with the desire to be. The failure to be is what motivates bad faith, driven by the attempt to believe that one *is*. Existential psychoanalysis 'will acquaint man with his passion' and can lead the way to 'deliverance and salvation'. By revealing to us how each of us has chosen our lives in terms of achieving identity, existential psychoanalysis will open the way to a life which assumes its own failure to be. In the very last words of *Being and Nothingness*, Sartre asks, regarding the desire to be, 'What will become of freedom if it turns its back on this value?' (ibid., p. 627). Since the very lack of self-identity, which inspires the desire to be, is itself, by another name, freedom, the possibility arises of accepting the failure to be and willing freedom itself 'as the source of all value' (ibid.). But, of course, this project would, Sartre tells us, require the 'separate study' he has alluded to throughout *Being and Nothingness*, for it would require the 'conversion' of one's life from being towards non-being (lack of identity).

From phenomenology to dialectic

Sartre never published his promised separate work on authenticity. Rather, the works published subsequent to *Being and Nothingness* see him wrestling to reunderstand existence and freedom in terms of a new set of problems stimulated by personal experiences brought on by the Second World War. The changed context for his thought is that of the importance of social and economic conditions, institutions, symbolic systems and history. Without retracting his commitment to freedom, Sartre begins to formulate a discourse of the constitution and formation of lives by alterity (which he called 'the force of circumstances) – something noticeably missing from his earlier work. In his *Saint Genet: Actor and Martyr* (1952), Sartre recognises the formative influences on childhood in the constitution of the self and, by the end of that work, admits his need to probe for a broader understanding of those influences in various institutions. The role of phenomenology as philosophical method begins to wane during this period as his attention turns toward understanding formative influences upon subjectivity that go on, behind one's back as it were. *Search For A Method* in 1957 set the general tone of Sartre's later writings with its commitment to the proposition that 'it is men themselves who make their history, but within a given environment which conditions them' (Sartre, 1957, p. 31). The ontology of *Being and Nothingness* defined the being of subjectivity as an active surpassing in the

face of a given object or situation. Sartre insists that subjectivity, understood in terms of this model, cannot be conditioned: '[I]f consciousness exists in terms of the given, this does not mean that the given conditions consciousness; consciousness is a pure and simple negation of this given' (Sartre, 1943, p. 478). It is a question, then, of understanding the phenomenon of conditioning in such a way that subjectivity is not lost in the process. In *Search for a Method*, he turned to dialectic, a model of a reciprocal influence passing between subject and object, a more adequate model than phenomenology's one way relation of subject to object: 'We cannot conceive of this conditioning in any form except that of a dialectical movement . . .' (Sartre, 1957, p. 34). Sartre thus believed that he found in Marx's writings a way of reconciling Kierkegaard's lived experience (subjectivity) with Hegel's movement of history (objectivity).

The basis of Sartre's dialectical method is a combination of regressive and progressive moments of understanding. Regressive understanding delves into situatedness, childhood, class, education and living conditions in general, in order to comprehend the basis of action as structured in terms of certain objective possibilities: 'The material conditions of . . . existence circumscribe the field of . . . possibilities' (ibid., p. 93). In his earlier work, the situation always formed the background for freedom and action, but the emphasis was on the latter and how the situation never suppressed freedom. Now, the emphasis moved to the structuration of the situation and how this mediates choice and action. Also, by insisting in his early ontology that 'choice is always unconditioned', thus preserving the 'incommunicability' of his subjective and objective modes of being, Sartre had missed the opportunity to appreciate how the situation leaves its traces on the subject, something that he now emphasises: 'Subjectivity is neither everything nor nothing; it represents a moment in the objective process (that in which externality is internalized), and this moment is perpetually eliminated only to be perpetually reborn' (ibid., p. 33). By speaking of an 'internalization' of the external Sartre allows for the presence of alterity within the subject. In *Search for a Method*, subjectivity, in the form of praxis, is still defined as a process of negating the given ('In relation to the given, the *praxis* is negativity . . .' [ibid., p. 92]), but there is now an admission that the subject comes to be marked by the given: '[T]he project retains and unveils the surpassed reality. . . . Thus the subjective contains within itself the objective which it denies and which it surpasses toward a new objectivity' (ibid., p. 92; p. 98). For example, a tool is, in its employment as a means to an end, an extension of subjectivity, sharing in the surpassing of a given situation. But in using a tool, the tool defines the subject that employs it by imposing its own requirements. Sartre insists on the progressive moment of praxis, which is the preservation of existential freedom: 'Otherwise men would be merely the vehicles of inhuman forces which through them would govern the social world' (ibid., p. 87). The progressive moment now is limited by the situation: '[T]he most individual possible is only the internalization and enrichment of a social possible' (ibid., p. 95).

Sartre's *Critique of Dialectical Reason* (1960) is a lengthy exploration of his understanding of the dialectic. Knowledge of the dialectic is itself dialectical; that is, it emerges by forming instruments of understanding within the context of dialectical experience. The individual, the starting point of Sartre's existentialism, is discovered to be engaged in a number of totalisations, ongoing systems of meaning and practices in which the individual participates as a member and through which the individual is defined. Through various forms of praxis the individual inscribes itself in the world and is, in turn, modified by these very processes of inscription. Inscribed matter, or the practico-inert, takes on a life of its own and exercises power over individuals as their projects deal with it or even attempt to surpass it. In this regard one can see a similarity between Sartre's analysis and that of the structuralists. Sartre now admits the legitimacy for an objective analysis of structures, an analysis of the sort that, in his early work, he appeared to have little use for. Objective analysis, however, is always to be integrated into the praxical context in which it would assume existential relevance. It is clear, however, that Sartre's commitment to a dialectic which incorporates a definitive role for the existential, free subject prevented his fully joining with the structuralists who called for the demise of that subject.

Practico-inert structures totalise individuals as they attempt to operate within them. While operating within structures individuals make choices, but these choices reflect the limited possibilities accorded by the structures. Structures impose a destiny upon those operating them. Those totalised by the same structures can use their common situation as the basis for mutual recognition and concerted action (what Sartre calls the 'group-in-fusion') to surpass unbearably constrictive and alienating structures. Sartre here moves well beyond the individualism of his earlier work in acknowledging and valorising community: 'Here there appears the first "we" [nous], which is practical but not substantial, as the free ubiquity of the me as an interiorized multiplicity. It is not that I am myself in the Other: it is that in *praxis* there is no *Other*, there are only several *myselves*' (Sartre, 1960, pp. 75–6). Community action transforms a lived passivity into an active, subjective power to overcome effects of passive constitution, thus restoring freedom. Even community action, however, objectifies, externalises itself and takes on an inertia that defuses it. Thus, any community is faced with the problem of developing strategies to retain its common, free subjectivity, and its necessary institutional development. Pure freedom is never realised anywhere, but it is clear that some situations allow for more choices than others and it is to this general ideal that Sartre devoted his political life.

Sartre's final project was a massive and incomplete study of the life and works of Gustave Flaubert, *The Idiot of the Family* (1971–2). It marked his last attempt to understand concretely an individual's life in terms of freedom. While holding in place the regressive analyses of the *Critique of Dialectical Reason*, Sartre adds a further dimension of psychoanalysis, spending much time on Flaubert's infancy and childhood. The weight he accords to the significance of the latter events is startling. He contends that Flaubert's mother treated him in such a way as to produce him as a 'passive constitution: 'It is certain . . . that his passivity comes from his mother and is the first internalization of the external world' (Sartre, 1971–2, p. 75). Flaubert would never be able to overcome this passivity, which would persist as the 'essential element in his character'. All Flaubert's life will spiral around this indelible trace:

Preserved, surpassed, scored with new and complex meanings, this original sense cannot help being modified. But its modification *must be inclusive*, indeed it involves reproducing a new whole out of the internal contradictions of a previous totality and the project that was born of them. (ibid., p. 44)

Flaubert is free to self-shape within the context of his initial character (and as well of the practico-inert structures which he inhabits), which is rewoven in every pattern of self-interpretation.

If read against the background of *Being and Nothingness*, the Flaubert volumes' presentation of freedom may appear feeble at first sight. Yet, if one appreciates the enormous weight Sartre in time came to give to situatedness, in terms of the practico-inert and psychoanalysis, his final defence of freedom appears definitely bolder and, perhaps, more legitimate. It is not a question of Sartre's repudiation of his earlier phenomenology with its emphasis upon the individual and the individual's power to shape and define its destiny, but a reweaving and reconceptualisation of individual responsibility and what an authentic life might be in the light of the now acknowledged impact of the power of institutions to define and shape lives. It is a question, Sartre tells us in his work on Genet, of what we can and should do, with much difficulty and over a long time, to rework the work that has already formed us.

Bibliography

Writings

Sartre, Jean-Paul (1980) (first edn 1933), 'Intentionality: A Fundamental Idea of Husserl's Phenomenology', trans. Joseph Fell, *Journal of the British Society for Phenomenology*, May.
— (1957) (first edn 1936), *The Transcendence of the Ego*, trans. Forrest Williams and Robert Kirkpatrick, New York: Noonday.
— (1962) (first edn 1936), *Imagination, A Psychological Critique*, trans. Forrest Williams, Ann Arbor: University of Michigan Press.
— (1964) (first edn 1938), *Nausea*, trans. Lloyd Alexander, New York: New Directions.
— (1948) (first edn 1939), *The Emotions: Outline of a Theory*, trans. Bernard Frechtman, New York: Philosophical Library.
— (1956) (first edn 1940), *The Psychology of Imagination*, trans. Bernard Frechtman, New York: Washington Square Press.
— (1956) (first edn 1943), *Being and Nothingness*, trans. Hazel Barnes, New York: Philosophical Library.
— (1963) (first edn 1952), *Saint Genet, Actor and Martyr*, trans. Bernard Frechtman, New York: Braziller.
— (1968) (first edn 1957), *Search for a Method*, trans. Hazel Barnes, New York: Vintage.
— (1960) (first edn 1960), *Critique of Dialectical Reason*, trans. Alan Sheridan-Smith, London: New Left Books.
— (1964) (first edn 1963), *The Words*, trans. Bernard Frechtman, New York: Braziller.
— (1981–93), *The Idiot of the Family* (vol. I [1971], vol. II [1971], vol. III [1972], trans. Carol Cosman, Chicago: University of Chicago Press (1981 vol. 1; 1987 vol. 2; 1989 vol. 3; 1991 vol. 4; 1993 vol. 5).
— (1964) (first edn 1983), *The War Diaries of Jean-Paul Sartre*, trans. Quintin Hoare, New York: Pantheon Books.
— (1992) (first edn 1983), *Notebooks for an Ethics*, trans. David Pellauer, Chicago: University of Chicago Press.

References and further reading

Anderson, Thomas (1994), *Sartre's Second Ethics*. LaSalle, IL: Open Court.
Busch, Thomas W. (1990), *The Power of Consciousness and the Force of Circumstances in Sartre's Philosophy*, Bloomington: Indiana University Press.
Contat, Michel and Rybalka, Michel (eds) (1974), *The Writings of Jean-Paul Sartre*, two vols, trans. Richard McCleary, Evanston: Northwestern University Press.
Desan, Wilfrid (1960), *The Tragic Finale*, New York: Harper and Row.
— (1965), *The Marxism of Jean-Paul Sartre*, Garden City, New York: Doubleday.
Detmer, David (1986), *Freedom as a Value*, LaSalle, IL: Open Court.
Flynn, Thomas (1984), *Sartre and Marxist Existentialism*, Chicago: University of Chicago Press.
Hendley, Steve (1991), *Reason and Relativism: A Sartrean Investigation*, Albany: SUNY Press.
Howells, Christina (ed.) (1992), *The Cambridge Companion to Sartre*, Cambridge: Cambridge University Press.
Jeanson, Francis (1980), *Sartre and the Problem of Morality*, trans. Robert Stone, Bloomington: Indiana University Press.
McBride, William (1991), *Sartre's Political Theory*, Bloomington: Indiana University Press.
Schilpp, Paul (ed.) (1981), *The Philosophy of Jean-Paul Sartre*, LaSalle, IL: Open Court.

4.5

AT THE LIMITS OF PHENOMENOLOGY: MERLEAU-PONTY

Galen A. Johnson

In April 1952, Maurice Merleau-Ponty (1908–61) was appointed to the Chair of Philosophy at the Collège de France, the youngest person ever appointed to the most prestigious chair in French philosophy. For the following nine years until his sudden death in May 1961, Merleau-Ponty worked to develop a new philosophy of Being that the philosophical world could barely have anticipated from his earlier works. The abbreviated outcome, *The Visible and the Invisible*, appeared posthumously in 1964 and gives us only a glimpse of an ontology of Flesh, reversibility, écart and chiasm, strangely turned and mysterious terms that later generations would labour to decipher. Merleau-Ponty still fashioned his late philosophy close to Husserl, but his critique of Husserl, as well as his own earlier, more existential phenomenology found in *Phenomenology of Perception*, was direct and often strident, as he sought a philosophy beyond the subject-object dichotomy at the limits of phenomenology.

Merleau-Ponty's first published essay was a 1935 review of Max Scheler's book *Ressentiment*. This was followed by reviews of Gabriel Marcel's *Being and Having* and Jean-Paul Sartre's *Imagination* in 1936, and a 1943 review of Sartre's play, *The Flies*. In these early essays and reviews, Merleau-Ponty was influenced by Sartre's transformation of Husserl's logic of intentionality into a philosophy of existence. In his review of *Imagination*, he appropriated the language of the intentional act to characterise the distinction between sensation and image. Merleau-Ponty's review of *The Flies* faults the critics for omitting 'imperiled freedom' from their reviews in favour of examining the 'state of mind' of Orestes. Freedom is a matter of engagement in the world: 'we are not free when we are nothing', Merleau-Ponty wrote, 'we are free when we are what we have chosen to be . . . The choice is between that difficult freedom and the peace of tombs. This is the pathos of *The Flies*' (Merleau-Ponty, 1991, p. 117).

The structure of behaviour

In contrast with the excitement of existentialism and these early controversies, it is *The Structure of Behaviour* that articulates most clearly the field of research that would chiefly occupy Merleau-Ponty; namely, the philosophy of perception. Although *The Structure of Behaviour* appeared in 1942, this work had been largely completed by 1938. Rather than offering us a study of 'natural experience' or pre-scientific experience, it presents a rigorous engagement with empirical psychology and the scientific construction of experience. It is only in its conclusion that Merleau-Ponty begins to cite Heidegger and Husserl and enunciate the task of a phenomenology of perception. Nevertheless, it remains an important work in Merleau-Ponty's itinerary, for the twofold focus on philosophy of perception and philosophy of science. Among the first-generation readers of Husserl, most importantly Heidegger, Sartre and Merleau-Ponty, Merleau-Ponty is the phenomenologist whose work is distinguished for its sustained study of the empirical human sciences, particularly psychology, and enrichment from them.

The title of *The Structure of Behaviour* designates well the subject and argument of the book. The goal of the work is 'to understand the relations of consciousness and nature' (Merleau-Ponty, 1963, p. 3). Merleau-Ponty begins from a consideration of explanations of behaviour in current reflex psychology and neurophysiology and argues that behaviour cannot be comprehended without the notion of structure, which he then delineates within the physical, vital and human orders. The notion of structure itself leads to the philosophy of perception.

In *The Structure of Behaviour*, Merleau-Ponty first studies the reflex psychology of Charles Sherrington, a British psychologist who worked at Liverpool and Oxford and who published his classic work *The Integrative Action of the Nervous System* in 1906. Sherrington had formulated five laws for the integration of neural action in the nervous system in order to account for the reflex, that is, the adaptation of an elementary behavioural response to a stimulus. An ocular example of a reflex would be the movement of the eye in response to light. Sherrington's scientific project was to decompose and trace the behavioural event beginning from a stimulus acting on the sensory endings of the organism as physical or chemical excitations through the central nervous system to a behavioural response. Thus, the explanation of behaviour could be reduced to its mechanical neurophysiological causes completely 'inside the skin' of the organism. Merleau-Ponty also discusses the classical conditioning theory of Pavlov as an explanation of reflex behaviour. In order to demonstrate the inadequacy of either the neurophysiological reduction or environmental stimulus-response reduction of behaviour, Merleau-Ponty appeals to the experiments of the Gestalt psychologists, Koehler, Koffka and Weizsäcker. He makes the general point that a stimulus and its related nervous system reactions are not isolated and partial events whose

sum adds up to a behavioural response, rather they are 'a constellation, an order, a whole, which gives its momentary meaning to each of the local excitations' (ibid., p. 14). The behavioural outcome of an excitation is determined by its relation to the whole organic state of the organism and to simultaneous or preceding excitations. Therefore, 'the relations between the organism and its milieu are not relations of linear causality but of circular causality' (ibid., p. 15). Behaviour is irreducible to its parts. Rather, it is a field of meaning.

Having arrived at this non-reductionist thesis regarding the neurological explanation of behaviour, Merleau-Ponty then proceeds to deny the intellectualist thesis that claims it is we, the spectators, who mentally unite the elements of a situation to which behaviour is addressed in order to make them meaningful. 'Nothing would be served by saying that behaviour "is conscious" and that it reveals to us, as its other side, a being for-itself (*pour-soi*) hidden behind the visible body' (ibid., p. 125). The central paradox of the phenomenon of behaviour is that it can be neither mechanically explained nor rendered an operant directed by a disembodied mind. 'Behaviour is not a thing, but neither is it an idea. It is not the envelope of a pure consciousness and, as the witness of behaviour, I am not a pure consciousness. It is precisely this which we wanted to say in stating that behaviour is a form (ibid., p. 127).

Thus, the crucial concept for understanding behaviour is the notion of form or structure, and a crucial question is the relation of the global form of behaviour to meaning or signification. It should be pointed out that, although Merleau-Ponty appeals to the experiments and research of the Gestalt theorists to show the inadequacies of the explanations of behaviour offered by Sherrington or Pavlov, he does not simply take over the Gestalt concept of form. The Gestalt psychologists had analogised the 'field of experience' to the magnetic fields of the brain, introducing the hypothesis of isomorphism between brain fields and the field of experience, in the end returning us to another objectivist and causal realism for the explanation of behaviour. Whereas Sherrington had constrained our understanding of experience in terms of the mechanics of the brain, the Gestalt theorists merely reversed the pattern and speculated about the fields of the brain based on the fields of experience.

In *The Structure of Behaviour*, Merleau-Ponty seeks to go beneath Gestaltist psychology of form to a non-reductionist philosophy of form. He proposes a study of form or structure within three different orders: the physical, vital and human. Physical form, as found in the distribution of electrical charges in a conductor or the shape of a drop of oil in water, is an equilibrium obtained with respect to certain given external conditions. It is an ensemble of forces in a state of equilibrium or of constant change such that no law is formulable for each part taken separately but only for the entire dynamic structure. For example, the law of falling bodies expresses the constitution of a field of relatively stable forces in the neighbourhood of the earth that remains true only if the speed of the rotation of the earth does not increase with time. Falling body, earth and motion are a partial totality or structure. Vital form is found when equilibrium is obtained, not with respect to real and present conditions, but with respect to conditions which are only virtual and which the living system itself brings into existence. The human order is a symbolic order of speech and work, a milieu of use-objects such as tables, clothing and gardens, and of cultural objects such as books, musical instruments and language. Form in the human order, Merleau-Ponty argues, is displayed first in our *existing* rather than in our consciousness or our thinking. Form is found wherever there exists the capacity for varying our point of view, for recognising things under a plurality of aspects, for creating use and cultural objects whose meaning is to be surpassed and even rejected. In short, human form is fundamentally *ambiguous* or multivocal, and is manifested as *perceptual existence* (ibid., pp. 175–6).

In his study of structure or form in *The Structure of Behaviour*, Merleau-Ponty arrived at the central problem that would occupy the *Phenomenology of Perception*, the problem of perceptual consciousness as a way of existing that is neither mechanical thing nor pure consciousness in full possession of itself. To deal with the inadequacies of the scientific explanations of experience and the philosophical dualism of matter and mind, we must turn to the comprehen-sion of pre-scientific, natural and lived experience. 'The consciousness for which the Gestalt exists was not intellectual consciousness but perceptual experience. Thus, it is perceptual consciousness which must be interrogated in order to find in it a definitive clarification' (ibid., p. 210). The last paragraph of *The Structure of Behaviour* speaks of the need 'to define transcendental philosophy anew' in terms of the intentional life of perception: 'If one understands by perception the act which makes us know existences, all the problems which we have just touched on are reducible to the problem of perception' (ibid., p. 224). Beneath the rationality of the *cogito* we must articulate a new conception of reason found in the more nascent and original rationality of lived existence. The 'reflex arc' must give way to the 'intentional arc'.

As he was completing *The Structure of Behaviour*, Merleau-Ponty had begun an intense investigation of Husserl's phenomenology. In 1939, he spent time at the Husserl Archives at the University of Louvain, Belgium and began correspondence and discussions with Professor Van Breda and Eugen Fink, after which he worked successfully, together with Sartre, Jean Hyppolite and Tran-Duc Thao, to establish a deposit of Husserl's manuscripts at the University of Paris, Sorbonne (Van Breda, 1962). The impact was immediate. In the concluding chapters of *The Structure of Behaviour*, we find explicit reference to the need for a philosophy of perceptual experience that is a phenomenology (Merleau-Ponty, 1963, p. 199), we find the use of the terms phenomenological reduction, intentionality and lived-body, and we find citations of Husserl's *Ideas I* and *Formal and Transcendental Logic* and Husserl's distinction between 'original passivity' and 'secondary passivity' (ibid., p. 249).

Phenomenology of perception

Phenomenology of Perception (1945) is Merleau-Ponty's best-known work, and displays most dramatically the impact of the discovery of Husserl's phenomenology for mid-twentieth-century French philosophy in general and Merleau-Ponty's own philosophical itinerary in particular. He writes that phenomenology 'has given a number of readers the impression, on reading Husserl or Heidegger, not so much of encountering a new philosophy as of recognizing what they had been waiting for' (Merleau-Ponty, 1945, p. viii).

The Preface to *Phenomenology of Perception* contains Merleau-Ponty's most important early statement of the meaning of phenomenology. He focuses on four themes: the return to 'things themselves', the meaning of phenomenological reduction, Husserl's theory of essences and the notion of intentionality. The phenomenological return to 'things themselves', Merleau-Ponty says, is a 'foreswearing' (*désaveu*) of science (ibid., p. viii). This is a strange remark from a philosopher of science who had just produced *The Structure of Behaviour*, and undoubtedly in the context should be taken to mean the disavowal or displacement of scientism, that view which would claim that science can offer complete explanations of our experience and reality. Rather, Merleau-Ponty contends, science is a 'second-order', more abstract expression of the things themselves, which are experienced in a life-world of pre-scientific understanding upon which scientific work itself depends. 'Every scientific schematization is an abstract and derivative sign-language, as is geography in relation to the countryside in which we have learnt beforehand what a forest, a prairie or a river is (ibid., p. ix). Merleau-Ponty also insists that Husserl's phenomenology of the 'things themselves' is not to be taken as an idealist or subjectivist return to consciousness, in spite of the association of this phrase with Kant's transcendental idealism and Husserl's own elaboration of phenomenology as a philosophy of pure consciousness or the transcendental ego in a work such as *Cartesian Meditations*. Husserl is to be distinguished emphatically from Descartes as well as Kant by Husserl's insistence upon 'noematic reflection' which remains within the object. The world is not the outcome or a synthesis of an 'inner man', and all reflection bears upon a fund of unreflective experience. The real must be described and is not constructed. In concluding *Cartesian Meditations*, Husserl had quoted St Augustine's statement that 'truth dwells in the inner man'. In response, Merleau-Ponty states: 'Truth does not "inhabit" only "the inner man", or more accurately, there is no inner man, man is in the world, and only in the world does he know himself' (ibid., p. xi).

Husserl's phenomenological reduction or 'bracketing of the world' led interpreters to conclude that Husserl was an idealist. Merleau-Ponty does not deny that Husserl's phenomenological reduction left him with a paradox regarding the Alter Ego. Merleau-Ponty believed that Husserl's attempts to speak of an Ego and Alter 'pairing' did not allow Husserl to escape from solipsism. Merleau-Ponty contends that only by including our bodily incarnation in a historical situation in which we are already participant in the life of others will phenomenology escape from solipsism and the Other be more than an empty word. The 'true meaning' of phenomenological reduction, Merleau-Ponty says, is 'wonder in the face of the world' (ibid., p. xiii). Reflection 'steps back to watch the forms of transcendence fly up like sparks from a fire; it slackens the intentional threads which attach us to the world and thus brings them to our notice' (ibid., p. xiii). Therefore, the most important lesson taught by Husserl's struggles to articulate the method of bracketing, is 'the impossibility of a complete reduction' (ibid., p. xiv). There is no thought that is able to articulate all thought. We are always 'beings-in-the-world' not 'in' the world as wine is in a cup, but inseparably united with the world. Human being is the being of transcendence, not in any theological or mystical sense of rising above or standing outside the world, but transcendent in the sense that we are not locked within the immanence of conscious experience. It is the world that fascinates and holds us, the fire, the running water, the motion of trains, and we are drawn out into the world to live among things. Rather than being a procedure of idealistic philosophy, Merleau-Ponty concludes, phenomenological reduction belongs to 'existential philosophy' (ibid.). This identification of phenomenology with existential philosophy draws Merleau-Ponty as close to existential philosophy as we find in his thought and here it should be emphasised the reference is to Heidegger and not Sartre.

Phenomenology has also often been confused with phenomenalism, or sense-datum empiricism, which attempts to reduce experience and knowledge to atomic elementary sensations available through introspection. This Humean philosophy had been given a linguistic rearticulation in Husserl's day b the members of the Vienna Circle as the philosophy of Logical Positivism, in which the criterion of meaningful language became its method of sensory verification. If the elementary terms of a linguistic proposition, such as 'God' or 'good' could not be translated into empirical observation terms, the proposition was meaningless. 'Logical positivism', Merleau-Ponty declares, 'is the antithesis of Husserl's thought' (ibid., p. xv). No doubt it was Husserl's doctrine of essences that led phenomenology to be misinterpreted as phenomenal introspectionism. However, Husserl's thought never separated essences from actual existence into a separate order of intelligibility, and never contended that the essences were elementary terms of language. In fact, *Ideas I* had declared: 'No Platonism' and 'No Subjective Idealism'. Therefore, Merleau-Ponty says that Jean Wahl, and implicitly Sartre, was 'wrong in saying that Husserl separates essences from existence' (ibid., p. xv). Essences are enmeshed in our experience of the world, and experience is at once both sensory *hyle* and eidetic *morphe*. Looking for the world's essence is not looking for what it is as an idea, for the world is already structured *as experience*, and Husserl's essences 'bring back all the living relationships of experience, as the fisherman's net draws up from the depths of the ocean quivering fish and seaweed' (ibid., p. xv). The meaning of experience is brought forth together with an inexhaustible and rich horizon. Rather curiously, in light of his dissociation of phenomenology from phenomenalism and positivism, Merleau-Ponty says that the eidetic method is the method of a 'phenomenological positivism' (ibid., p. xvii).

The notion of intentionality, that all consciousness is consciousness of something, is not the main discovery or theme of phenomenology, Merleau-Ponty contends. The intentionality of consciousness was already known to Kant, who argued that inner perception is impossible without outer perception of the world. Rather, the contribution of phenomenology is to discover that our unreflective being-in-the-world is already intentional, as shown by Husserl's distinction between intentionality of act and operative intentionality. The reflective act of judgement or belief is a thetic intentionality in which we adopt a definite position. Operative intentionality is displayed in the natural and pre-predicative interlacings with the world already embedded in our bodily life of desires, habits and evaluations. These pre-predicative bodily perceptions furnish 'the text' of philosophical description and the origin of a more genuine, richer meaning of rationality. The task of a phenomenology of perception, therefore, is to capture this pre-existent *Logos* of the world, a primordial rationality of embodied perception that is deeper than the intellectual rationality of reflective consciousness. 'Because we are in the world, we are *condemned to meaning*' (ibid., p. xix), and phenomenology's task is to express painstakingly the same wonder before the mystery of the world that we find in the artistic works of Balzac, Proust, Valéry or Cézanne.

The main body of *Phenomenology of Perception* is a long work covering over five hundred pages in the French original. It is in three major parts, 'Part One: The Body', 'Part Two: The World As Perceived', and 'Part Three: Being-For-Itself and Being-In-The-World'. Due to the complexity of the book, it is important to know that the author's own extensive annotated table of contents that appeared in the French original has been omitted from the English translation, but has appeared subsequently in English in two separate sources (see, Mallin, 1979 and Guerrière, 1979). Merleau-Ponty's own annotated list usually states the conclusion or main point of each section of the work succinctly and in advance, and it is advisable to have it close at hand during a study of the text. His procedure is quite dialectical and consists of extensive exposition and critique of positions he will ultimately reject, which allows his own conclusions to emerge at the intersection of opposed viewpoints, but also makes it all too easy to confuse his positions with ones that he criticises.

The main theme of *Phenomenology* is the lived-body (*le corps propre*). Merleau-Ponty seeks to examine, not the structures of behaviour conceived from a scientific perspective, but the structures of experience as they are embedded in our bodily being-in-the-world (*l'être-au-monde*). This is the philosophy of operative intentionality announced in the Preface. This theme of the lived-body makes its appearance in the *Phenomenology* about one hundred pages into the text, following an extensive account of Merleau-Ponty's objections to mechanistic physiology and classical psychology similar to those developed in *The Structure of Behaviour*. Our body as we experience it is not like other physical objects such as a table or a lamp. For one thing, we can turn away from such physical objects and separate ourselves from them, whereas our body is always with us. It is the zero-point of our insertion into the world, the Here and Now from which we demarcate There and Then. For another thing, our body exhibits a power of 'double sensations', whereby, when I touch my right hand with my left, my right hand which is being touched has the power of touching the left in return. There is not a simultaneous reflexivity, but rather I can anticipate the next instant in which the right, now being touched by the left, will reverse its role of passivity, and actively take up the position of touching the left. I am both touching and being touched. The lived-body initiates a kind of incarnate reflection in such double sensations that precedes and anticipates the more self-conscious reflections of judgement and belief (Merleau-Ponty, 1945, p. 93). In a third case, the lived-body is also shown to be differentiated from other physical objects by our affective life. When we say that there is a pain in our foot, we do not mean that our foot is a cause of our pain in the way that a nail is the cause of pain. Rather, this is a more intimate kind of pain in which we are 'at our foot' or one with the foot. The pain is both localised in our foot and is a global sensation that spreads through my entire experience. This is why a person who experiences amputation of a limb may continue to experience for a time 'sensations' of the 'phantom limb'. Our foot or leg is not a part attached to other bodily parts, but a 'total part' that expresses the whole body, and the use of a foot or leg expresses a habituated 'bodily schema' that will adjust itself only gradually when the foot or leg is lost.

These three characteristics – incarnation, reflexivity and affectivity – mean that the lived-body is the locus of the primitive union of soul and body too long overlooked by mechanistic and classical psychology as well as Cartesian philosophy. Husserl criticised Descartes for passing too quickly from the experience of doubt to an Ego-substance and an absurd notion of Ego causality (*Cartesian Medita-*

tions, Section 10). Merleau-Ponty's critique of Descartes focuses on Descartes's inert and mechanical conception of the human body, which he viewed as a system of tissue, muscle, bone and nerves that, like cords, pull on the brain. Thereby, he entirely overlooked the living body and the true source of soul-body union (see ibid., pp. 198–9).

From these basic characteristics that differentiate our own bodies from other physical bodies, Merleau-Ponty proceeds to describe in detail the structures of our bodily lived-experience. These include spatiality, sexuality and expressivity. In Husserlian terms, these would be structures on the *noetic* side of embodied lived-experience, and comprise the remainder of Part One of the *Phenomenology*. Thereafter, Merleau-Ponty turns in Part Two to the *noematic*, or worldly, side of lived-experience, and considers the transcendent structures of space, things, nature, other selves and history that comprise the situation of our being-in-the-world. Finally, in Part Three, he takes up the philosophical questions of the *cogito*, temporality and freedom emergent from the noetic-noematic juncture of the embodied subject and perceived life-world. One should not understand this textual structure in a linear sense, for the noetic-noematic nature of experience cannot truly be split apart, and the *Phenomenology* is a work in which its author keeps working the same soil: the soil of the sensible, first emphasising subjectivity, next emphasising worldliness and transcendence. This very structure, however, passing from subject to object and back again, would later come to worry Merleau-Ponty regarding his own claim to have disclosed the union of soul and body, self and world.

The spatiality of the lived-body is unlike a spatiality of position or 'next-to-ness', in which, for example, an ashtray is beside the telephone. Rather, Merleau-Ponty says, the spatiality of our body is a spatiality of situation in which the part of our body are inter-related, not side by side, but 'enveloped' in each other (ibid., p. 98). In his moving homage to Merleau-Ponty, Sartre wrote that this notion of 'envelopment' that first appear in the *Phenomenology* is the 'cardinal principle' of Merleau-Ponty's philosophical itinerary (Sartre 1984, p. 10), moving ever outwards: bodily envelopment part in part and body in world, envelopment i

History and Politics, envelopment in the Flesh of Being. The wholeness of bodily envelopment has been spoken of by psychology in terms of the body image, but misconstrued as an association of mental images. Body image is a positional spatiality expressed as a matrix or schematism of habitual actions: the body knows where the arm, hand or eyes are, responds immediately to the location of a sting or itch, unhesitatingly grasps the cup or pipe. The knowledge of a typewriter or computer keyboard is 'in the hands' of an experienced typist, the knowledge of keys, stops and pedals is 'in the hands' of an accomplished organist (Merleau-Ponty, 1945, p. 144, p. 145), and indeed we may falter or hesitate if asked to describe the location of the 'A' key on either keyboard. It is this motor body-schema that breaks down in cases of illness or injury such as that experienced by the war-wounded man, Schneider, who had sustained a cortical lesion caused by a piece of artillery shell. 'Consciousness is in the first place not a matter of "I think that" but of "I can" ' (ibid., p. 137).

Therefore, bodily spatiality is a motor intentionality and is our general medium for having a world. This spatiality is synthesised or unified as a certain bodily 'style' of posture and gesture. Evidently Merleau-Ponty appropriates the term 'style' from Husserl's discussion of tradition in 'The Origin of Geometry' in *The Crisis of European Sciences*. In characterising the unity of a mathematical or scientific tradition, Husserl uses the aesthetic term 'style' to indicate that geometry is not defined by a certain number of problems, solutions or theorems, but rather by a certain 'style' of thinking and bearing towards the future. Likewise, Merleau-Ponty says that 'the body is to be compared, not to a physical object, but rather to a work of art. . . . It is a nexus of living meanings, not the function of a certain number of mutually variable terms' (ibid., p. 150, p. 151). The parts of the body and the bodily senses are intentional threads tied one to another and tied to the world. This is the 'intentional arc' of our life that must be substituted for the 'reflex arc':

The life of consciousness – cognitive life, the life of desire or perceptual life – is subtended by an 'intentional arc' which projects round about us our past, our future, our human setting, our physical, ideological and moral situation, or rather which results in our being situated in all these respects. It is this intentional arc which brings about the unity of the senses, of intelligence, of sensibility and motility. And it is this which 'goes limp' in illness. (ibid., p. 136)

Merleau-Ponty's account of the sexuality of the lived-body offers a phenomenological evaluation of Freud's psychoanalysis. Merleau-Ponty agrees with psychoanalysis that sexuality is not an autonomous cycle of physiological processes, but has active, meaningful links with our whole cognitive and behavioural being-in-the-world. For Freud, the sexual is not the genital nor is the libido an instinct, but a general power for the psychosomatic subject to take root in different situations and establish himself. On the other hand, Freud's error, according to Merleau-Ponty, resides in the mechanistic reduction of manifest meanings to unconscious latent meanings. Sexuality is not at the centre of our life in unconscious representations, but is present at all times like an ambiguous atmosphere. Sexuality is one of the dimensions of life that causes a person to have a history, yet there is no one meaning of history. What we do always has several meanings (ibid., p. 158, p. 173). Nevertheless, in spite of the mechanistic and reductionist garment with which Freud often clothes his theory of the unconscious, it would be a mistake to oppose psychoanalysis to phenomenology, for 'psychoanalysis has, on the contrary, albeit unwittingly', helped to develop phenomenology 'by declaring, as Freud puts it, that every human action "has a meaning" ' (ibid., p. 158). In both his negative and positive assessment of Freud, Merleau-Ponty cites the psychology of Binswanger, and seems generally happy with Sartre's denial of the existence of the unconscious but approval of the overdetermination of meaning in our thoughts and actions.

Above all, Merleau-Ponty says, the body 'is essentially an expressive space' (ibid., p. 146), and the *Phenomenology* develops a gestural theory of speech and language. Again, he opposes both the mechanistic and intellectualistic theories of language: the one which would reduce speech to a behavioural response to external stimuli, the other which views speech as an external accompaniment or outcome of already formed inner thoughts. 'We refute both intellectualism and empiricism', Merleau-Ponty wrote, 'by simply saying that *the word has a meaning*' (ibid., p. 177). Speech is a linguistic gesture with teeth and tongue, and a word embodies meaning in just the same way as a wave of the hand or a smile. The meaning of a gesture is intermingled with the structure of the world it outlines, and words, vowels and phonemes are so many ways of 'singing the world's praises' (ibid., p. 178). This implies that the full meaning of one language is never translatable into another, and although we may learn to speak several languages, one of them always remains the one in which we live. In learning our original language, we must employ the sounds and vocabulary of already acquired meanings, taking up a linguistic tradition of word-gestures that is common to a community of speakers. Speaker and listener participate in a shared linguistic world, in which, in order to say something new, we rely upon what has already been constituted.

There are a number of highly controversial theses visible in this account of verbal meaning. First is Merleau-Ponty's conviction that meaning is inseparable from its sign. A sign is an indissoluble unity of a meaning with a physical sound. Second, by viewing speech as a form of bodily gesture, Merleau-Ponty adopts the position that the relation of a word-sound to a meaning cannot be merely conventional. A word is emergent from the bodily life of a people, not as the naive onomatopoeic theory claimed that words have an objective resemblance to the sounds of things, but rather in the sense that the 'gestural sense' of words extracts and expresses the 'emotional essence' of a lived-world. The predominance of vowels in one language or consonants in another expresses variations in ways of 'living the world'. 'Strictly speaking, therefore, there are no conventional signs' (ibid., p. 188), for word-sounds are the convergence of the history of the bodily life of a people living together with their cultural and natural habitat. It is no more natural, and no less conventional, to shout in anger or to kiss in love than to call a table 'a table'. Everything, Merleau-Ponty says, 'is both manufactured and natural in man', in which forms of vital behaviour deviate from their pre-ordained direction and institute new forms 'through

a sort of *leakage* and through a genius for ambiguity which might serve to define man' (ibid., p. 189). This also implies, for a third point, that the meaning of signs is rooted in bodily, gestural life and not in the formal rules of grammar and syntax. The gestural theory of language maintains that written language (*la langage*) and mathematical languages are derivative from speech (*la parole*), and are more abstract and more impoverished forms of expression. 'There are different layers of significance, from the visual to the conceptual by way of the verbal concept' (ibid., p. 195). The task of tracing the systematic and historical transitions from gesture to speech to writing and algorithm remains unfulfilled in Merleau-Ponty's work, but it was his belief that the institution of language could serve as a model for a general theory of meaning in which aesthetic, economic and political history would also find their proper place.

We cannot leave the *Phenomenology* without mentioning one of the most controversial ideas put forward near the end of the work in its chapter on the 'Cogito'. This is the idea of a tacit cogito. As we have seen, for Merleau-Ponty, neither the word nor the meaning of the word is constituted by reflective consciousness. Rather, meaning is constituted by the operative intentionalities of pre-reflective action and gesture in the life-world. Therefore, there is both a reflective consciousness of myself which makes use of language and is 'humming with words' (ibid., p. 400), and a silent, unspoken pre-reflective *cogito*. The first is the self of reflection disclosed by Descartes's methodological doubt, but the second is a prior presence of oneself to oneself that we sense as we sing when we are happy or become aware of in extreme situations of danger when we are under threat (ibid., p. 404). This tacit *cogito* provides the real unity of self-identity, Merleau-Ponty argues, through a certain consistency of style that is the coherent deformation of an anonymous and 'universal I' which is the tradition within which we take our stand. This is the 'I' of existence. 'One day, once and for all, something was set in motion which, even during sleep, can no longer cease to see or not to see, to feel or not to feel, to suffer or be happy, to think or rest from thinking, in a word to "have it out" with the world' (ibid., p. 407). The birth of this silent 'I' is not a new set of sensations or states of consciousness, but 'a fresh possibility of situations'. This birth is not another event in a chain of causes, but an *advent* in which 'inside and outside are inseparable. The world is wholly inside and I am wholly outside' (ibid.).

Although this notion of a tacit *cogito* appears rife with paradox – as Merleau-Ponty himself says, 'the tacit *cogito* is a *cogito* only when it has found expression for itself' (ibid., p. 404), these reflections on advent and natality as an inside which is reversible with an outside prefigure the meaning of Flesh in Merleau-Ponty's later ontology. Through the idea of a silent, anonymous self, Merleau-Ponty also hoped, in the work from his middle period, *The Prose of the World*, that he could marry his gestural theory of language focused on bodily speech with Saussure's semiotic theory of signs. What Saussure meant by the unspoken language system (*la langue*) presupposed by all speech and signification Merleau-Ponty attempted to incorporate in his notion of indirect language and 'pregnant silence'.

The middle period: 1945–55

The concern with a general theory of expression and philosophy of history and politics occupied what we can designate as Merleau-Ponty's middle period of philosophical work from 1945–55, a transitional period between his earlier and later philosophies. This period included four more philosophical works: *Humanism and Terror* (1947), *Sense and Non-Sense* (1948), *The Prose of the World* (not completed, but published posthumously in 1969), and *Adventures of the Dialectic* (1955). For part of this period, he was Chair of Child Psychology and Pedagogy at the University of Paris, Sorbonne (1948–51), and student notes from his lecture courses such as 'Consciousness and the Acquisition of Language', 'The Child's Relations with Others', and 'Phenomenology and the Human Sciences', were published in the *Bulletin de psychologie* (November 1964).

Merleau-Ponty's engagement with politics and the philosophy of history occurs as a three-cornered dialogue among himself, Sartre and the texts of Marx. Merleau-Ponty served from 1945–50 as the political editor for the journal *Les Temps Modernes*, a review of politics, arts and philosophy with an original editorial committee that included Sartre, Simone de Beauvoir and Raymond Aron. In *Les Temps Modernes*, he published brief articles on Indochina, the Liberation, existentialism, Christianity, Hegel, Montaigne, Machiavelli and the new cinema, most of which were collected in *Sense and Non-Sense*. His major publication in *Les Temps Modernes* was a three-part article entitled 'The Yogi and the Proletarian' that became the basis for his controversial book, *Humanism and Terror*. This work is a detailed study of the transcripts of the Moscow trials and a statement and defence of a 'phenomenological Marxism' in reply to Arthur Koestler's novel, *Darkness at Noon*. As the title of the work indicates, Merleau-Ponty seeks to articulate the meaning of an ethical, humanist Marxism as over against the meaning of terrorism, a topic to which he was no doubt attracted by Alexandre Kojève's lectures on Hegel's *Phenomenology of Spirit*. Because *Humanism and Terror* ultimately fails to make the distinction between humanism and terrorism with dogmatic and absolute precision and fails to condemn Stalinism absolutely for the murders of Bukharin and Trotsky, he was labelled 'Merleau-Stalino-Ponty' by Claude Lefort for his efforts and the book was given a scathing review by Paul Ricoeur in 1948.

One way to understand Merleau-Ponty's approach to the post-Second World War problem of Marxism is to read *Humanism and Terror* as the philosopher's effort to articulate an ethical meaning of the subject akin to what de Beauvoir called an ethics of ambiguity. Upon reading *Phenomenology of Perception*, Merleau-Ponty's teacher, Emile Bréhier, asserted that the relation of self and other described in the *Phenomenology* is one in which the other 'is not an ethical other' (Merleau-Ponty, 1964b, p. 30). Merleau-Ponty countered that the criticism was invalid, and in *Humanism and Terror* believes that he could meet the criticism in more detail by connecting the lived-body that unifies soul and body with the 'body' of the proletariat that unifies history. The tacit *cogito* takes its stand within a tradition and universal 'I'; similarly, there is a universal condition 'considered human by all men', Merleau-Ponty writes, 'namely the condition of the proletariat' (Merleau-Ponty, 1947, p. 111). In the same pattern of argument evident in *The Structure of Behaviour* and the

Phenomenology, he argues that 'Marxism is not a philosophy of the subject, but it is just as far from a philosophy of the object; it is a philosophy of history' (ibid., p. 130).

It is certainly the case that the lived-bodily 'subject' of the *Phenomenology* is, from the outset, a subject embedded in a network of concrete, inter-subjective meanings. Subjectivity is intersubjectivity. It is certainly also the case that the 'ethical subject' of any humanism that would flow from the *Phenomenology* would need to be a concrete, historically-situated subject and not an abstract, disembodied 'person'. As Merleau-Ponty writes: 'In love, in affection, or in friendship we do not encounter face to face "consciousnesses" whose absolute individuality we could respect at every moment, but beings qualified as "my son", "my wife", "my friend" whom we carry along with us into common projects where they receive (like ourselves) a definite role, with specific rights and duties' (ibid., pp. 109–10). This means that humanism cannot be founded upon an absolute categorical imperative like that of Kant, which, Merleau-Ponty argues we find, in the last analysis, in Trotsky. However, it has been very difficult for readers of *Humanism and Terror* to make the further connection from concrete historical intersubjectivity to the proletariat understood as an economic class. Perhaps it is revealing that at one point in the book Merleau-Ponty uses the rather odd-sounding phrase, 'the proletarian tradition' (ibid., p. 79), odd-sounding because we are accustomed to the phrase, 'proletarian revolution' not 'proletarian tradition'. Such an amorphous and inclusive designation led Merleau-Ponty to speak of two Marxes, the early, humanist Marx who spoke of human suffering and human alienation, and the later scientific Marx from the *Communist Manifesto* through to *Capital*, who spoke of proletariat exploitation and class warfare. The meaning of *Capital* as Marx's last work remains, for Merleau-Ponty, the philosophy of human alienation in the first works, and could be understood only as a 'concrete *Phenomenology of Spirit* . . . This concrete thinking, which Marx calls "critique" to distinguish it from speculative philosophy, is what others propound under the name "existential philosophy" ' (Merleau-Ponty, 1948, p. 133).

Based on such a phenomenological logic of history, it is perhaps possible to see why Merleau-Ponty stresses the contingency of historical events and the openness of the future with respect to the outcome of Stalinism. He writes that, in history, there is no choice between purity and violence, only the choice between kinds of violence. Since there are no absolute norms that discriminate in advance sensible from senseless violence, the future of Stalinism was open, and we must 'wait and see': 'Between Lenin's line and Stalin's line there is no difference that is an *absolute* difference' (Merleau-Ponty, 1947, p. 91).

However, analogous to Merleau-Ponty's assessment of Freud's often mechanistic reduction of manifest meanings to latent, sexual meanings, it was always a mistake for a phenomenological philosophy of history to posit a causal, mechanical relation between an economic substructure and superstructure. Historical relations are differing orders of signification, in which for a given period of history one of the orders will be dominant. So, just as with gestures, we regard 'one gesture as "sexual", another as "amorous", another as "warlike" ', so 'one period of history can be seen as characterized by intellectual culture, another as primarily political or economic' (Merleau-Ponty, 1945, p. 173). Therefore, *Humanism and Terror* has remained a puzzling work, and the gap between phenomenology and Marxist politics never more apparent than when Merleau-Ponty wrote:

> On close consideration, Marxism is not just any hypothesis that might be replaced tomorrow by some other. It is the simple statement of those conditions without which there would be neither any humanism, in the sense of a mutual relation between men, nor any rationality in history. In this sense Marxism is not a philosophy of history; it is *the* philosophy of history and to renounce it is to dig the grave of Reason in history. After that there remain only dreams or adventures. (Merleau-Ponty, 1947, p. 153)

Eight years later, Merleau-Ponty rethought both these matters and his own stance toward Marxism. In fact, the last sentence cited above is telling, for Merleau-Ponty called his second work on Marxist politics *Adventures of the Dialectic* (1955). Upon the invasion of Korea in 1950, he imposed a political silence upon *Les Temps Modernes*, and in 1952 he resigned as political editor of the journal when Sartre insisted upon publication of an attack on Western capitalism. Merleau-Ponty's close ties with Sartre were shattered at this point, and *Adventures of the Dialectic* contains a very harsh assessment of Sartre as an 'ultrabolshevik'. Merleau-Ponty's own political itinerary detailed in the book is towards a form of philosophy of history modelled after Max Weber's theory of *Verstehen* in which history is constantly questioned according to 'ideal types'. Merleau-Ponty renounces all the main categories of Marxism, the proletariat and proletarian revolution, and even the philosophical categories of historical progress and the notion of one unified history of humanity. Still uncomfortable with the abstract, disembodied 'person' of ethical absolutism and liberal individualism, however, he avoids advocating Western liberal politics. He announces in the Epilogue to *Adventures of the Dialectic* the need for a new view of history as a 'vertical history' in which there would be place for reversals, 'for sublations, for a perpetual genesis, for a plurality of levels or orders' (Merleau-Ponty, 1955, p. 204). This task of a 'vertical history' was one of the goals of the work of Merleau-Ponty's later thought, especially in *Signs* and *The Visible and the Invisible*.

Philosophy of painting

Merleau-Ponty's inaugural lecture at the Collège de France on 15 January 1953, entitled *In Praise of Philosophy*, offered reassessments of the work of the recent French tradition, especially Henri Bergson, and an account of the life and death of Socrates as an emblem of the disorder philosophy brings to religion and history, but it gave little notice of the ontological themes that were to occupy his attention during his later philosophy. From 1953 until 1956, Merleau-Ponty edited a history of Western philosophy entitled *Les philosophes célèbres*. He wrote the introductions to each of the major periods in philosophy, most of which were later published in *Signs*, and he recruited some of the leading philosophers of Europe to write overviews of the thought of each of the world's major philosophers. *Les philosophes célèbres* is an art edition that contains more than one hundred plates of portraits, drawings and sculptures of the world's celebrated philosophers collected from the museums of Western Europe.

We have said little of Merleau-Ponty's interest in art and aesthetics until this point, but in 1945 he published an essay on Cézanne, 'Cézanne's Doubt', and another in 1952 evaluating Malraux's philosophy and history of art entitled 'Indirect Language and the Voices of Silence'. In 1960, he completed an essay on the ontology of art entitled *Eye and Mind*. Across the three major periods of his philosophic work – phenomenological, structural and ontological – the study of the artist provided Merleau-Ponty with the 'laboratory' and inspiration for his philosophy of the body, expression and history, and Being. Therefore, *Eye and Mind* announces, and begins to articulate, the themes of the ontology on which he was working from 1959 until his death in 1961, and which appeared posthumously as *The Visible and the Invisible*. *Signs* appeared in 1960, and particularly noteworthy for these ontological themes are the Preface and a new essay on Husserl, 'The Philosopher and His Shadow'.

Eye and Mind begins with a quotation from Cézanne's conversations with Joachim Gasquet: 'What I am trying to translate to you is more mysterious; it is entwined in the very roots of being, in the impalpable source of sensations' (Merleau-Ponty, 1994, p. 121). Like Cézanne, Merleau-Ponty takes it as his philosophic task in the essay to 'interrogate painting itself' regarding the nature of what exists, to return to 'the "there is" (*il y a*), to the site, the soil of the sensible and opened world such as it is in our life and for our body' (ibid., p. 122). The approach, so typical of Merleau-Ponty, is to begin from the painter's body. However, this time he wanted ontological depth, to interrogate the artistic 'thinking eye' to seek out the nature of Being. Why is it that painters have so often said, as did Cézanne and Paul Klee, that the forest was speaking in them, or the trees were looking at them? It must be that there is a system of exchanges between body and world such that eye and hand become the obverse side of things, the inside of an outside in which both are enveloped. 'There is a human body when, between the seeing and the seen, between touching and the touched, between one eye and the other, between hand and hand, a blending of some sort takes place – when the spark is lit between sensing and sensible, lighting the fire that will not stop burning' (ibid., p. 125). This blending, this fire, this envelopment, generality and anonymity is called Flesh. It is the site of perception and expression. The maturation of vision in the life of a painter is this opening up of self to the world as 'the other side' of its power of looking. Painting expresses nothing other than this reversibility between vision and the visible. It is 'the genesis, the metamorphosis of Being in vision' (ibid., p. 128). The painter who reciprocates the things seen thus introduces us to two of the most important terms of Merleau-Ponty's ontology; namely, reversibility and Flesh (la chair).

Eye and Mind concludes by turning its back on the notion of a complete painting in the sense of a totalisation of painting, of a universal painting that would, for all time, fully and definitively complete painting's task and give us the true expression of the visible world. This is an idea bereft of sense, Merleau-Ponty says, for Being itself is a perpetual genesis and the one who paints and the visible that is painted are intertwined in an ongoing metamorphosis of meaning. Reminiscent of his rejection of the notion of historical progress, he writes: 'For if we cannot establish a hierarchy of civilizations or speak of progress – neither in painting nor even elsewhere – it is not because some fate impedes us; it is, rather, because the very first painting in some sense went to the farthest reach of the future' (ibid., p. 149). If there is not a hierarchy or progress, each creation, from the paintings of the caves at Lascaux to Matisse, from the sculptures of Rodin to Richier, still clarifies, deepens, confirms and exalts the mystery and wonder of Being. The history of culture is a 'vertical history' of new and ever renewed expression.

The visible and the invisible

All three of these ontological themes – reversibility, Flesh, and genesis, were prefigured in the Phenomenology of Perception, particularly in its presentations of the double sensations of the lived-body and the inside-outside system of exchanges present in the tacit cogito and birth of selfhood. Nevertheless, Merleau-Ponty's later thinking returns to his earlier work with a critical eye. He was still working the same philosophical soil, that of the body, perception and expression, yet it is as if he felt he had only been working on the surface of the issues, and now he wanted to get to the heart of the matter. His own working notes for The Visible and the Invisible contain several explicit criticisms of the Phenomenology. He writes: 'The problems posed in Ph.P. are insoluble because I start there from the "consciousness"–"object" distinction' (Merleau-Ponty, 1968, p. 200). For the unsuspecting, this is a very severe self-criticism, and from one point of view, we might justifiably defend Merleau-Ponty against his own overly harsh retrospective assessment of the Phenomenology. Just as he wrote so touchingly, in the Preface to Signs, regarding Sartre's self-criticisms, perhaps we should ask the Merleau-Ponty aged fifty not to be so bad-tempered with the Merleau-Ponty aged thirty-five (Merleau-Ponty, 1960, p. 24). We remind ourselves that the entire project of the Phenomenology was to develop a new philosophy of the lived-body as a unique blend of both consciousness and object, thereby forging a new direction in philosophy that would avoid the impasses of empiricism and intellectualism, materialism and idealism. Nevertheless, perhaps it was in the introduction of the tacit cogito, more so in Merleau-Ponty's recognition of the problem that called for the introduction of the tacit cogito, that he began to recognise the need to go beyond the Phenomenology. The philosophy of the lived-body as being-in-the-world articulated the structure of reversibility within the lived-body as right hand touches left, but not between body and world, between eye and its visible. It was in the notion of the tacit cogito that we found the idea of a self 'lost in the world among things', a self turned inside out with the outside world already giving birth to the meaning of the inside. However, if the tacit cogito was central to overcoming the problematic of dualism at the time of the Phenomenology, this is how Merleau-Ponty evaluates the idea of a it in The Visible and the Invisible: 'The Cogito of Descartes . . . presupposes a prereflective contact of self with self or a tacit cogito (being close by oneself) – this is how I reasoned in Ph.P. Is this correct? What I call the tacit cogito is impossible'

(Merleau-Ponty, 1968, pp. 170–1). The idea of a pre-reflective reflection, of self-awareness not yet aware of itself, was an impossible idea. Even so, it pointed Merleau-Ponty in the direction he needed to take. If it is neither the reflective verbal *cogito* nor a pre-reflective silent *cogito* who gestures, who speaks and who thinks, who is doing the saying, the thinking? The Preface to *Signs* says: 'Thus things *are said* and *are thought* by a Speech and by a Thought which we do not have but which has us' (Merleau-Ponty, 1960, p. 19). This passage heralds an anonymous, pre-reflective generality that holds and envelops us all but is not a *cogito*, an individual self, but is the element that is the bond *between* self and world. This is the Flesh.

Perhaps at this point one begins to sense that the movement from Merleau-Ponty's early philosophy of the lived-body to his later philosophy of Flesh is not unlike the movement within the history of idealism in the eighteenth and nineteenth centuries from Kant's transcendental ego to Hegel's Spirit. This is not completely beside the point, and Merleau-Ponty did find inspiration for his notion of Flesh in the Absolute Idealism of Schelling's philosophy of nature. However, the lived-body is not to be taken as an incarnate correlate of the transcendental ego, and Flesh is not to be taken as an incarnate correlate of Geist. This becomes clearer when we follow Merleau-Ponty's own presentation of the meaning of Flesh.

The opening chapter of *The Visible and the Invisible* poses the problem of the obscurity of our 'perceptual faith' that we see the things themselves, or that the world is what we see. However, the moment we ask ourselves what is this *we*, what *seeing* is, and what *thing* is, 'we enter into a labyrinth of difficulties and contradictions' (Merleau-Ponty, 1968, p. 3). We need to think once again, and in a new way, regarding the 'natal bond' between the one who perceives and what is perceived, to understand that 'the world is our birthplace only because first we as minds are the cradle of the world' (ibid., p. 33). The new method Merleau-Ponty announced for articulating this bond that is the birthplace and cradle of perception and expression he named 'hyperreflection' (*sur-réflexion*). The traditional method of ontological reflection, especially that of Descartes, had proceeded too hastily toward a direct ontology of coincidence with reality through clear and distinct ideas. However, to reflect in thought cannot mean to coincide with the object precisely because thought is *reflection*, *re*-turn, and *re*-covery (ibid., p. 45). We need, rather, to proceed more allusively, more poetically, towards an 'indirect ontology'.

Hyperreflection is the effort to reflect, and as we reflect, to reflect upon our own reflection, to proceed in an interrogative mood that emphasises our questioning and deemphasises a system of solutions. This method of hyperreflection has evident overtones of a method of 'erasure'. What Merleau-Ponty sought was a philosophic method 'that would also take itself and the changes it introduces into the spectacle into account', a method of thinking and writing that could question the world and 'enter into the forest of references that our interrogation arouses in it', a method that could make brute being say, finally, 'what in its silence *it means to say*' (ibid., p. 38, p. 39). Based on such a style of thinking and writing, the reader should not expect from *The Visible and the Invisible* a readily decipherable handbook of Being, but will find a poetic, Proust-like text laden with allusion and metaphor, filled with stops and starts, circling and doubling back on itself to find the hinges and joints of Being, those intersections where inside becomes outside and outside becomes inside, where imperception becomes perception and perception becomes expression; in short, to find an indirect ontology of visible and invisible.

'The Flesh', Merleau-Ponty writes in the remarkable fourth chapter of *The Visible and the Invisible*,

> is not matter, is not mind, is not substance. To designate it, we should need the old term 'element', in the sense it was used to speak of water, air, earth, and fire, that is, in the sense of a *general thing*, midway between the spatio-temporal individual and the idea, a sort of incarnate principle that brings a style of being wherever there is a fragment of being. The flesh is in this sense an 'element' of Being. (ibid., p. 139)

This passage, and the entire fourth chapter, have been the subject of intense scholarly scrutiny (Madison, 1978; Dillon, 1988; Johnson and Smith, 1990). One problem with the term 'Flesh' is that it seems to connote a quite tangible, palpable 'stuff' (*la chair* = meat), while Merleau-Ponty immediately denies speaking of matter or substance. Another problem is that the term 'element' refers us to the Milesian cosmologies in which the elements were eternal and unchanging, whereas Flesh is meant to express pregnancy, growth and genesis. Nevertheless, in spite of some of the difficulties of the term, the ontological intuition that gave rise to it can be illuminated.

The fundamental claim expressed in the term Flesh is that all things that exist, natural, manufactured and human, are embodiments of the same 'incarnate principle'. This hylomorphic principle is that of reversibility. The 'double sensations' of the human body that animate a reversibility between the right and left hands of touching and being touched are an 'exemplar sensible' of the same reversibility that exists throughout all Being. This reversibility is called by Merleau-Ponty 'chiasm' from the Greek rhetorical form of reversing the order of an expression from first to last into last to first. Chiasm expresses the overlapping, criss-crossing, inclining and reclining found in the Greek letter *chi* (X). The reversibility between self and world is not meant to be a heightened and exaggerated panpsychism that would attribute vision and consciousness to inanimate things, the absurdity that the trees and things we see also see us in return, or that colour sees itself or surfaces touch themselves (Merleau-Ponty, 1968, p. 135). Rather, it means that the seer is caught up in the midst of the visible, that in order to see, the seer in turn must be capable of being seen. The seer is both vision and visible. The one who touches is both touching and capable of being touched.

The ontology of Flesh as incarnate principle of reversibility thus seems to give us a kind of neutral monism or double-aspect monism. However, we cannot rest with such an interpretation of Merleau-Ponty's ontology, for such a monism would flatten the *depth* of the world and collapse the *distance* between seer and seen, between touching and being touched. Flesh is not Spirit, for the double sensations of the human body are never simultaneous and the doubling of self and world never temporally coincide with one another. 'Reversibility is always

imminent and never realized in fact' (ibid., p. 147). There is a contact and synergy between self and world that does not eliminate the strife within self and between self and things. This divergence or difference is captured by Merleau-Ponty in the term *écart*, 'that difference without contradiction, that divergence (*écart*) between the within and the without that constitutes its natal secret' (ibid., pp. 135–6). Thus, Flesh is an incarnate principle of doubling with difference that is found both within our bodily self and between our bodily self and the world. There is a porosity and openness within Being expressed in the dehiscence of a flower, the ignition of fire, the birth of a child, a handshake between friends and the erotic exchanges between lovers. 'Why should this generality, which constitutes the unity of my body, not open it to other bodies? The handshake too is reversible. . . . Why would not the synergy exist among different organisms, if it is possible within each? Their landscapes interweave, their actions and their passions fit together exactly (ibid., p. 142). In a Working Note of *The Visible and the Invisible*, Merleau-Ponty wrote: ' "Nature is at the first day": it is there today . . . it is a question of finding in the present, the flesh of the world (and not in the past) an "ever new" and "always the same" ' (ibid., p. 266). Nature is the flesh, the mother.

The similar reversibility and difference Merleau-Ponty believed to be found between the visible and the invisible as exists within the visibles was to have been Part Two of *The Visible and the Invisible* bearing a preliminary title of 'Physis and Logos'. It was never written but was the problematic of a theory of expression left unfinished from *The Prose of the World*, tracing the origin and transitions of meaning from silence to gesture to art to speech to writing to algorithm. One point may be stressed – by 'invisible' Merleau-Ponty did not refer to 'non-visible'. The word should be understood as 'in-the-visible'. 'It is the invisible *of* this world, that which inhabits this world', he wrote (ibid., p. 151). The lines of visible things are doubled by a lining of invisibility, which pertains to noticing the hidden things, having eyes that genuinely see and minds that genuinely think in accordance with what is *there* (*il y a*). We do not possess musical or sensible ideas; they possess us. The musical performer does not produce or reproduce the sonata. 'He feels himself, and the others feel him to be at the service of the sonata; the sonata sings through him or cries out so suddenly that he must "dash on his bow" to follow it' (ibid.). The ideality of expression is 'another less heavy, more transparent body' (ibid., p 153). The flesh of the body is changed, metamorphosed into the flesh of language and expression.

From the philosophy of lived-body to the philosophy of expression and history to the philosophy of the Flesh, Merleau-Ponty worked at the borders and limits of phenomenology, ever working the soil of 'the things themselves'. The words he wrote regarding Husserl in 'The Philosopher and His Shadow' (1960) now seem to us fitting words for his philosophy. 'At the end of Husserl's life', Merleau-Ponty wrote,

there is an unthought-of element in his works which is wholly his and yet opens out on something else. . . . Like all those near to us, Husserl present in person could not, I imagine, leave those surrounding him in peace. . . . Afterwards, when Husserl's death and their own growth had committed them to adult solitude, how could they easily recover the full meaning of their earlier meditations? . . . They rejoin him across their past. (Merleau-Ponty, 1960, p. 160)

Like the thought of Husserl, the thought of Merleau-Ponty is not something to be possessed. It marks out a realm to think about and a style of thinking that endures through its reflections, levels, transitions, shadows and horizons.

Bibliography

Writings

Merleau-Ponty, Maurice (1963) (first edn 1942), *The Structure of Behavior*, trans. Alden L. Fisher, Boston: Beacon Press.
— (1962) (first edn 1945), *Phenomenology of Perception*, trans. Colin Smith, London: Routledge and Kegan Paul. (Reprinted with translation revisions by Forrest Williams and David Guerrière, 1989, 1992.)
— (1964) (first edn 1947), *Humanism and Terror*, trans. John O'Neill, Boston: Beacon Press.
— (1964) (first edn 1948), *Sense and Non-Sense*, trans. Hubert L. Dreyfus and Patricia Allen Dreyfus, Evanston: Northwestern University Press.
— (1988) (first edn 1953), *In Praise of Philosophy and Other Essays*, trans. John Wild, James Edie and John O'Neill, Evanston: Northwestern University Press.
— (1973) (first edn 1955), *Adventures of the Dialectic*, trans. Joseph Bien, Evanston: Northwestern University Press.
— (1964) (first edn 1960), *Signs*, trans. Richard C. McCleary, Evanston: Northwestern University Press.
— (1994) (first edn 1961), *Eye and Mind*, trans. Michael B. Smith, in Galen A. Johnson (ed.), *The Merleau-Ponty Aesthetics Reader*, Evanston: Northwestern University Press. (Earlier translation by C. Dallery, in James E. Edie (ed.), *The Primacy of Perception and Other Essays*, Evanston: Northwestern University Press, 1964.)
— (1968) (first edn 1964), *The Visible and the Invisible*, trans. Alphonso Lingis, Evanston: Northwestern University Press.
— (1973) (first edn 1964), *Consciousness and the Acquisition of Language*, Lecture course for 1949–50 at the University of Paris, Sorbonne, trans. Hugh Silverman, Evanston: Northwestern University Press.
— (1970) (first edn 1968), *Themes from the Lectures at the Collège de France 1952–1960*, trans. John O'Neill, Evanston: Northwestern University Press.
— (1973) (first edn 1969), *The Prose of the World*, trans. John O'Neill, Evanston: Northwestern University Press.
— (1995) (first edn 1978), *The Incarnate Self: The Union of the Soul and the Body in Malebranche, Biran and Bergson*, notes taken from the course of Maurice Merleau-Ponty at the Ecole Normale Supérieure (1947–48), trans. Paul B. Milan, Andrew G. Bjellard and Patrick Burke (eds), New York: Humanities Press.

References and further reading

Cooper, Barry (1979), *Merleau-Ponty and Marxism: From Terror to Reform*, Toronto: University of Toronto Press.
Dillon, M. C. (1988), *Merleau-Ponty's Ontology*, Bloomington: Indiana University Press.
— (ed.) (1991), *Merleau-Ponty Vivant*, Albany: State University of New York Press.
Edie, James E. (ed.) (1964), *The Primacy of Perception and Other Essays*, Evanston: Northwestern University Press.
Guerrière, Daniel (1979), 'Table of Contents of *Phenomenology of Perception*: Translation and Pagination', *Journal of the British Society for Phenomenology*, 10: 1 (January).
Johnson, Galen A. (ed.) (1994), *The Merleau-Ponty Aesthetics Reader: Philosophy and Painting*, trans. ed. Michael B. Smith, Evanston: Northwestern University Press.
Johnson, Galen A. and Michael B. Smith (eds) (1990), *Ontology and Alterity in Merleau-Ponty*, Evanston: Northwestern University Press.

Langer, Monika M. (1989), *Merleau-Ponty's Phenomenology of Perception: A Guide and Commentary*, Tallahassee: Florida State University Press.

Madison, Gary (1981), *The Phenomenology of Merleau-Ponty: A Search for the Limits of Consciousness*, Athens, OH: Ohio University Press.

Mallin, Samuel B. (1979), *Merleau-Ponty's Philosophy*, New Haven: Yale University Press.

Sartre, Jean-Paul (1984), 'Merleau-Ponty', trans. William S. Hamrick, *Journal of the British Society for Phenomenology*, 15: 2 (May). (This is the original version of Sartre's homage to Merleau-Ponty, translated from Sartre's posthumous manuscripts. The second, or public, version was published earlier in Jean-Paul Sartre, *Situations*, trans. Benita Eisler, Greenwich, CT: Fawcett, 1965, 156–226.)

Silverman, Hugh J. and James Barry Jr (eds) (1991), *Texts and Dialogues*, New York: Humanities Press International, Inc.

Van Breda, H. L. (1962), 'Maurice Merleau-Ponty et les Archives-Husserl à Louvain', *Revue de Métaphysique et de Morale*, 67e année, October–December, 410–30. (Translated in *Texts and Dialogues*, 150–61.)

4.6

FEMINISM AND PHENOMENOLOGY

Dorothea E. Olkowski

The phenomenological life-world

Edmund Husserl is generally credited with founding the modern phenomenological method. Beginning in 1906, his early work, the *Logical Investigations*, focused on a description of objects as they present themselves to consciousness and this became the basis of his famous dictum: 'To the things themselves'. Empirical objects, Husserl maintained, are only available to consciousness as grasped in an intellectual intuition in which their essences are seen. Yet he found that he still had to establish the precise relation between consciousness and its object. The outcome of this search is transcendental phenomenology, a science of experience that describes the intersection of beings and consciousness, where *noema* (beings) and *noesis* (consciousness) are strictly correlative. That is, consciousness both grasps and constitutes the world. As intentional consciousness, it actively intuits the essence of objects presented to it. Between 1935 and 1937, prompted by the developing crisis of Nazism in Europe, Husserl was propelled to generate a theory of the pretheoretical or *Lebenswelt*, the world as given, both culturally and naturally, though not yet subject to the phenomenological method. The *Lebenswelt* played the role of the practical world, out of and in relation to which all epistemological constructions arise and, along with the concept of intentionality, the 'life-world' or lived world became central to phenomenological theories derived from Husserl.

Drawing from Husserl's transcendental phenomenology, Martin Heidegger, Maurice Merleau-Ponty, Simone de Beauvoir, Jean-Paul Sartre and Gabriel Marcel, among others, developed their own existential phenomenologies. It was widely held by these philosophers that Husserl's transcendental phenomenology ended in solipsism, an end that existentialism, a philosophy of what Heidegger called 'being-in-the world' could avoid. Exactly what to make of intentionality, consciousness's constitution of the world, became a matter of contention among these thinkers. For some (Sartre, for example, and occasionally de Beauvoir), the world is, to a large extent, the construction of beings with absolute freedom. For others (Heidegger, Marcel, Merleau-Ponty and, again, de Beauvoir), the world is already fully given and our task is to reveal the existence of what is there or to describe its meaning.

de Beauvoir and feminist existential phenomenology

A strong case can be made for the position that Simone de Beauvoir was a principal, if not the principal, originator of existential phenomenology, and later, the founder of feminist existential phenomenology. Although she had successfully completed the philosophy *agrégation* exam at the Sorbonne in 1929, with a grade only minutely lower than that of Sartre and with the acknowledgement of her teachers and peers that, while Sartre showed certain intellectual qualities, de Beauvoir *was* philosophy (*philosophie, c'était elle*), she often declared that she was not a philosopher and more often addressed philosophical issues through literature rather than in works of philosophy. A compelling explanation for her turn from philosophy to literature might be found in her desire to develop an ethics based on the heart (Moi, 1994, p. 18). For her part, de Beauvoir claimed she wrote metaphysical novels, and as Debra Bergoffen has argued, she wrote novels and philosophical works whose philosophical focus is ethical, whose method is phenomenological, and whose commitments are existential (Bergoffen, 1997, p. 11). This places her squarely within the realm of philosophy, especially the field of existential phenomenology.

None the less, given de Beauvoir's nearly lifelong attempts to place herself second to Sartre as a philosopher, as well as the fact that her philosophical ideas are most often presented in literary form, on what basis can we claim that she is the founder of what became feminist existential phenomenology? Interestingly enough, it is Merleau-Ponty who provides the initial justification for this position.

In his 1945 essay, 'Metaphysics and the Novel', Merleau-Ponty writes that de Beauvoir laid the foundations for existential phenomenology in her 1943 novel, She Came to Stay. He argues that, with the passing of classical metaphysics and its strict insistence on rationalism, the ties between philosophy and literature are becoming closer. Existential phenomenology succeeds by formulating a contact with the world which precedes all thought about the world. Thus: 'Philosophical expression assumes the same ambiguities as literary expression' (Merleau-Ponty, 1945, p. 28), and the novel has become metaphysical rather than merely moral. In citing de Beauvoir's She Came to Stay as the prime example of this new philosophical literature, Merleau-Ponty argues that the novel's protagonists, Françoise and Pierre, discover, in the course of the narrative, that they were wrong to think that they had no separate inner lives but could live a single life created out of their mutual conversations, out of language and rationality. Thus, they reject classical presuppositions and begin to embrace those of existential phenomenology. Shut out of a love affair between Pierre and Xavière, Françoise discovers the feeling of being, not a consciousness at all, but a body, the body of a mature, thirty-year-old woman who commits to a love affair in order to confirm the reality of her own

existence, for she sees that the meaning of her acts is not merely a matter of intentions but also of their effects on others and what those others think of her in return; that is, there are always multiple lived meanings. Given the multiplicity of meanings in the human context, Merleau-Ponty concludes that human action is a response to a factual situation that cannot have been completely chosen and for which we are not then absolutely responsible.

While it has been noted that de Beauvoir's two principal female characters are engaged in a Hegelian fight to the death for recognition, it cannot escape our attention that Merleau-Ponty's view of human subjects as immersed in the world of social experience with all of its ambiguities contrasts sharply with the Sartrean perspective of Being and Nothingness (1943) that Merleau-Ponty refutes early in the essay. For Merleau-Ponty, Sartre's conception of consciousness as able to transcend social experience through perception and imagination denies the subject's experience of intersubjectivity and ambiguity. For, if consciousness is immediately present to the world such that nothing else can claim existence without the subject's pure witnessing of it, and if every subject affirms its own existence only by denying that of the object, then the intimate contact of self with self and the disquieting existence of others is sacrificed to the affirmation of one's own freedom. French existentialists such as Sartre, Merleau-Ponty complains, fall back into 'isolating analysis' and reduce life to nothing but a collection of states of consciousness with the result that meaning is lost.

Nor need we take only Merleau-Ponty's word on this. In de Beauvoir's 1945 review, 'La Phénoménologie de la Perception de Maurice Merleau-Ponty', she contrasts the situated nature of Merleau-Ponty's phenomenological subject with that of a Sartrean subject and object who are strangers to one another. It is impossible, she agrees, to consider our body as an object, even a privileged object. The phenomenon of the phantom limb can only be explained if we assume that the body is our manner of being in the world (être au monde), involved in a structure of 'communication and communion' with the world such that the sensible offers to us a point of space which our lived body takes up and assumes. She explicitly contrasts Sartre's philosophy to Merleau-

Ponty's phenomenology, noting that while Sartre underlines the distinction between the 'in-itself' and the 'for-itself', that is, the nothingness of consciousness in the face of the absolute freedom of the subject, Merleau-Ponty finds this view of human freedom to be too oppositional, for it undermines living relations between selves and others and selves and their world. Rather, our existence is expressed by our body which has both a history and a pre-history, a previously given spatial milieu within which the body can be situated. Ultimately, de Beauvoir states that she finds Merleau-Ponty's phenomenology convincing, particularly, it seems, because phenomenology does not demand that we do violence to ourselves in order that our lives be ethical. Instead, it demands attention to the 'real', to the recognition that the world retains a certain opacity in the midst of our perception, but that it also opens itself up to subjects whose perceptual faith connects them to the world. It is surprising, perhaps, that de Beauvoir's appreciation for Merleau-Ponty's embodied subject is seldom fully acknowledged, even though it manifests itself throughout her work, yet given her constant efforts to declare her own originality and to be second to no one else (except Sartre), it is understandable.

In spite of de Beauvoir's open affirmation of phenomenology, Margaret Simons (1995) notes the particular difficulty facing feminists who sought to integrate existential phenomenology into feminist thought: 'Existential phenomenology could hardly be considered a feminist philosophical tradition, and Sartre's descriptions of the female body in *Being and Nothingness*, often cited as the philosophical foundation for *The Second Sex* (1952), were filled with disgust' (Simons, 1995, p. 4). In addition, de Beauvoir insisted throughout her life that her philosophical positions did not differ from Sartre's, regardless of how feminists were reading them. It is no surprise, then that de Beauvoir asserts, in *The Second Sex*, that her methodology is existentialist. However, what separates this existentialist philosophy from that of Sartre is that she discusses woman in the specificity of her 'total situation', an extrapolation of the concept of the lived world. The notion that human situatedness must be central to any philosophical interrogation clearly locates her work

in the context of the phenomenological perspective. Even the hotly debated chapter on 'The Data of Biology', openly embraces the phenomenological concept that the body is not a thing, but a situation, so that facts about woman's relative bodily weakness or her diminished lung capacity 'have no significance' (de Beauvoir, 1952, p. 34). Biological facts only assume significance in the light of man's [sic] intentions, means and social organisation.

Linda Singer (1990) argues effectively that de Beauvoir has directed her discourse to the historical tradition of ethics as well as to the language of freedom and responsibility characterised by Sartre's ethics, but that, ultimately, it is never restricted to, or contained within, the limits of either. In the same way, throughout her work, she sought to reconcile Sartre's radical existentialism with the phenomenological method of a situated and embodied individual who was often female. *Pyrrhus et Cinéas* (1944) and *The Ethics of Ambiguity* (1947) both address ethical questions. *Pyrrhus et Cinéas* begins with a Sartrean affirmation of the absolute freedom of independent subjectivities, but continues with a demonstration of their simultaneous interdependence, a positive reading of Heidegger's notion of *Mitzein* or 'being-with' according to which only others can confirm the value and meaning of individual acts. In this view, a world without others would be, in de Beauvoir's words, 'horrifying' (Kruks, 1990, p. 87). It is very interesting, for feminism, that affirming another's projects is, according to de Beauvoir, a 'choice' requiring 'generosity' which can only emerge out of 'social equality'. Thus, social equality makes possible generosity which in turn allows for the 'transcendence' of one's own projects beyond oneself in so far as they are taken up by others and carried into the future (de Beauvoir, 1944, p. 115). The problem of acts of violence remains, however, because individuals are fundamentally in conflict with one another. In so far as the other's desire, project and good transcend me, the other remains a stranger, alien to me, and violence is the means by which I keep the other from opposing my projects (Bergoffen, 1997, p. 50; p. 57). Thus, we can see why de Beauvoir became interested in Merleau-Ponty's version of phenomenology.

The Ethics of Ambiguity begins from the point of

view that human beings are simultaneously subject and object, immanence and transcendence, separate, even threatening one another, but also interdependent; this is their ambiguity. In her account of society and individual transcendence, de Beauvoir clearly exceeds both the violence of Sartre's existentialism and Merleau-Ponty's embodied subject. She contends that while men [sic] will always compete with one another, and violence such as that experienced in war will never be banished, social oppression is another matter. Already she recognises that oppression separates humans into two classes: the oppressors and those whose free transcendence is denied by oppression. In terms similar to those she uses in *The Second Sex* to define the situation of women in society, de Beauvoir compares the experience of social oppression to 'an absurd vegetation' (de Beauvoir, 1948, p. 83). Here too, she recognises that some human beings are rendered so powerless by their oppression that revolt is unthinkable. She argues that it is the task of those who have freedom to alter the social reality of the oppressed, not out of altruistic aims, but in so far as social reality is first of all intersubjective and freedom interdependent. This same analysis then becomes the focus of the social critique of women's traditional role in *The Second Sex*, a situation in which women are a group that have little control over their own bodies and lives, and thus are often denied even the possibility of transcendence, sometimes to the point of participating in their own oppression.

Sexual difference and embodiment

Feminist phenomenology, post-de Beauvoir, becomes a much more diffuse and indeterminate field. The question she posed in *The Second Sex*: 'What is a woman?' and the answer she provided: 'One is not born a woman, one becomes one', initiated as much criticism as admiration, depending on whether one believed that she was describing women's situation of inequality with men biologically, historically, or as a social structure. In France, Luce Irigaray explicitly picked up the threads of phenomenological feminism and began to develop her own unique notion of sexual difference. According to Irigaray, the 'conceptualisation of sexual difference demands a revolution in thought and ethics that involves reinterpretation of the relations between subject and discourse, subject and world, subject and the cosmic, the microcosm and the macrocosm. She argues that: 'To think and live through this difference we must reconsider the whole question of space and time' (Irigaray, 1987, p. 119), for traditionally, woman represents a sense of place for man. Thus, throughout the history of philosophy, Irigaray claims, materiality and space are identified with woman, while consciousness and time are identified with man.

In order to reconsider this role, Irigaray proposes the concept of the 'interval', a spatio-temporal dynamic force whose form changes and so cannot be predicted. As a dynamic force, the interval carries its own formalisation along with it, a dynamic potential that would replace the separation between negatively charged matter with no place of its own and positively charged form. In the history of philosophy, the positive and negative poles have, according to Irigaray, divided themselves among the two sexes 'instead of creating a *chiasmus*, a double loop in which each moves out toward the other then back to itself' (ibid., p. 121) while each side of the loop is both positively and negatively charged. If positive and negative elements are not chiasmatic, one, the feminine, is conceived of as remaining in motion and having no place of its own, and the other, the masculine, will always serve as the pole of attraction.

It is, of course, Merleau-Ponty who first proposed the notion of the *chiasm* in *The Visible and the Invisible* (1968). He calls forth this conceptualisation in the context of the intertwining of visibility and tangibility. He writes: 'There is a double and crossed situating of the visible in the tangible and the tangible in the visible; the two maps are complete and yet they do not merge into one. The two parts are total and they are not superposable' (Merleau-Ponty, 1968, p. 134). *Chiasm* is also the relation between, or the orientation of, seer and seen, touching and being touched, such that these lived experiences are no longer taken to be merely negative and positive poles. Instead, a seer is also looked at by the things he or she sees, the trees, the sea and others the toucher feels herself or himself being touched by these things. This implies not just a new under-standing of lived experience but a radical new world ontology. To accomplish this, Merleau-Ponty posits, in place of the philosophical concept of being, a 'flesh', neither subject nor object, but a thickness between or among seer and seen whereby: seer becomes seen, seen becomes seer and 'flesh' is their means of communication. What is crucial here, is that flesh does not simply unify the subject. The body is not a thing, but a *sensible* for itself. The body is not an envelope, but a connective tissue.

Irigaray states in *An Ethics of Sexual Difference* (1993), that she is in agreement with Merleau-Ponty when, in *The Visible and the Invisible*, he criticises philosophy for prejudging what it finds in the world and declares that philosophy must go back to pre-discursive experience to rethink, on the basis of that experience, all the categories by which philosophy understands that world. Irigaray's aim, however, is to bring the 'maternal-feminine' into language. She finds aspects of the maternal-feminine in Merleau-Ponty's use of metaphors of fluidity. When he describes vision as forming in the heart of the visible, 'as though there were between it and us an intimacy as close as between the sea and the strand', Irigaray believes that Merleau-Ponty has already begun to introduce language that evokes intrauterine life, its immersion and emergence (Irigaray, 1993, p. 152).

As Elizabeth Grosz (1993) has pointed out, for Irigaray, the earliest mother-child relations take place in the womb prior to a co-ordinated and fully constituted vision. The womb is in darkness yet it is fully and positively tactile. Following Irigaray's thinking about the chiasm, intrauterine existence is a positivity, the tactile precondition of vision as of all embodied experience. What this means, however, is that visible and tactile are not simply reversible but that the tactile world is a world of fluidity; its features are not those of all senses, since touching, unlike seeing, and even hearing, is mutual and reciprocal. For Irigaray, the tangible is the intrauterine pre-condition of all sensation, that primal sensibility that other sensations need but which does not need them. Thus, the tangible is one kind of sensibility, the visible is another and there is neither a reciprocal relation between them nor is the visible 'cut out in

the tangible, every tactile being in some manner promised to visibility' (Merleau-Ponty, 1968, p. 134). If this were so, then all sensation would be subject to the authority of vision, promised to vision, under-cutting the primal givenness of intrauterine life.

Likewise, Irigaray argues, in utero, sound preceeds meaning and music is 'a sort of preliminary to meaning, coming after warmth, moisture, softness, kinesthesia. Do I hear first of all? After touch. But I cannot hear without touching; nor see, moreover. I hear, and what I hear is sexually differentiated' (Irigaray, 1993, p. 168). In utero, touch comes first, then after touch what is heard first is the sound of the mother's womb and voice; that is, the feminine comes first. Yet, what takes place under the reign of a dominant visibility is that the music of the womb is forgotten and the speaking body is organised by a previously structured language in which the masculine or the neuter preceeds the feminine (particularly in French where an added 'e' is the mark of the feminine gender). Ultimately, Irigaray concludes, Merleau-Ponty blocks out the possibility of the maternal-feminine in language because, for him, we are seers first and all the possibilities of language are given in the seen world that is isomorphic with the subject who sees the world as a whole. Thus nothing, no silence of the tangible world, is left over. This is the equivalent of denying the birth of meaning, and commensurate with the denial that the maternal-feminine will ever be heard (ibid., pp. 182–4).

In spite of this seemingly devastating critique, Irigaray, like many contemporary feminists, has found much in phenomenology to embrace. *Je, tu, nous* (1993), for example, is dedicated to Simone de Beauvoir and in it, Irigaray begins, more concretely than ever before in her work, to deal with the real problems women face in the lived world; thus, with woman's 'total situation'. She proposes legal, linguis-tic, scientific and social remedies for combating the secondary role women are forced to play in society. Following Irigaray, the concepts of 'lived experience' and 'lived body' appear to be the twin foundations of most contemporary feminists' claims to be practising feminist phenomenology. Given this, two principal concerns arise. One, as Grosz (1993) has argued, is that feminists must be wary of accepting experience as the unproblematic criterion for the assessment of knowledges in so far as experience is already determined by the cultural and theoretical milieu, so is not ideologically free. And second, as both Grosz and Butler have pointed out in different ways, rather than taking experience as a starting point for discovery, too many feminists naively take it as unquestionably true, no matter how distorted it may be.

None the less, Grosz also argues for the potential usefulness of Merleau-Ponty's work for feminist theory. On the positive side, there is his willingness to subvert binary oppositions, especially the mind-body distinctions, thereby opening up the way for feminist theories of a sexualised, embodied subjectivity. This is aided by the creation of the notion of the psycho-physical 'body-image' in Merleau-Ponty, which allows for the sexual specificity of thought and being. Further, Grosz argues that 'flesh' taken as the intertwining of subject and world does found a new ontology that undermines the hierarchy of being in which reason dominates all other life functions. And finally she contends that Merleau-Ponty's texts can be read as an analysis and description of specifically male subjectivity, making way for the creation of concepts specific to female subjectivity as well as to the possibility of the inappropriateness of such gestures (Grosz, 1993, pp. 59–60).

Several contemporary feminists have whole-heartedly embraced these useful notions. Sonia Kruks has argued, in particular, for a positive account of the contribution of Marcel, Sartre, de Beauvoir and Merleau-Ponty to social theory by tracing their use of the concept 'situation' to examine subjectivity, embodiment, gender, society and history. Between the extremes of normative liberal theory's autonomous thinking subjects and anti-humanism's human constructs of discursive practices, she seeks a third hypothesis: 'that subjectivity is at once constituting and constituted, that structures . . . and subjects act and re-act upon each other, so that we must talk of an "encumbered" subjectivity and of "human" structures' (Kruks, 1990, p. 7). While Kruks calls the approach of these four thinkers existential, yet clearly, when she designates the term 'situation' to be her 'guiding thread' and argues that it stands for the 'presence of an internal bond, a relation of mutual permeability between subjectivity and its

surrounding world' (Kruks, 1990, p. 11), the phenomenological dimension emerges as well. Certainly this fits de Beauvoir's description of 'situatedness' but it also describes Merleau-Ponty's embodied subject or 'flesh', Marcel's anti-Cartesian notion of embodiment and communication, and even Sartre's account of class solidarity or co-operative social relations.

Carol Bigwood focuses primarily on Heidegger and Merleau-Ponty in her account of how the aesthetic qualities of works of art and female embodiment can be a guide to surviving the overpowering influence of technological viewpoints. In particular, Bigwood, like Irigaray, argues that Merleau-Ponty's notion of prediscursive experience can be used to describe a gendered body that is in some sense also a 'natural' body, not only culturally inscribed but also hypothetically open to gender fluidity. Bigwood argues that purely cultural theories of discursivity reduce all nature to a cultural idea, alienating human beings from the natural world. In short, the nature/culture dichotomy has been resolved, she argues, by eliminating nature and cutting off human involvement in the non-human world. Like Grosz and Butler, Bigwood does recognise that any feminist reworking of Merleau-Ponty's phenomenological body must completely rethink many notions which Merleau-Ponty takes to be neutral, but which are, in fact, descriptions of the male body. None the less, she is willing to risk this in so far as Merleau-Ponty's notion of embodiment is of a body incarnately in tune with the environment, whether of the natural world or of artistic creations.

Feminist critiques and challenges

However, the more widespread response to phenomenology from feminists is attuned to Grosz's warning that while Merleau-Ponty in particular, and phenomenological methodology, in general, have sought to give primacy to the lived-body or embodied consciousness by describing its structures of perception, movement, desire and language, the gendered nature of those structures was never articulated. As a result, phenomenological descriptions of the lived body and lived experience have been singularly masculine. Iris M. Young (1989) originated thi-view when she challenged de Beauvoir for describing woman's anatomy and physiology as if they produce women's unfree situation. She argues that it is not physiology, but the status and orientation of the woman's body as it relates to the social environment that are the problem. Young also faults Merleau-Ponty for ignoring the lived body specific to women; that is, the bodily comportment which is typical of feminine existence, as well as the modes and structures in the world that condition that existence, among them, what she calls 'breasted experience' (Young, 1990, p. 189). Young moves beyond de Beauvoir's account of the tension between immanence and transcendence in women's situation. While society defines woman as merely object, inessential correlate to man, and immanence, thereby depriving woman of subjectivity, autonomy and creativity, women know themselves, through their human existence, to be subjectivities capable of transcendent projects (Young, 1989, pp. 54–5).

If this is the case, Young goes on to demonstrate that contemporary feminine bodily comportment often exhibits the same tension, if not contradiction, between transcendence and immanence, subjectivity and being an object. As a result, she concludes, feminine motility in women (more than girls) is often characterised by 'ambiguous transcendence', overlaid with immanence. One part of the body moves out towards the world in action while the rest remains somewhat immobile, a burden. Women also experience 'inhibited intentionality', positing an easily accomplished task as beyond their ability without even having attempted it. And finally, women experience a 'discontinuous unity', between themselves and their world, with the result that they often do not engage the whole body in physical tasks. If the world is understood phenomenologically as a system of bodily possibilities, too often women take their own bodies to be the object of action and not the originator of acts within that system (ibid., p. 61). Young comes to believe, however, that such determinations are less a function of women's immanence and transcendence than they are a part of women's social situatedness, their oppression in society; thus, nothing about these descriptions is necessary, let alone desirable. Girls and women must be given the opportunity to engage fully their bodily capacities as well as to develop specific bodily skills.

A related critique of Merleau-Ponty's phenomenology appears in the work of Judith Butler (1989). Butler first praises Merleau-Ponty for refusing to locate a theory of desire and sexuality within a natural framework by recognising the role of choice as well as concrete historical factors. By arguing that sexuality is co-extensive (although not reducible) to existence, Merleau-Ponty has opened the way for fuller descriptions of sexuality and sexual diversity (Butler, 1989, p. 85). However, Butler also finds that Merleau-Ponty's descriptions of sexuality are univocally heterosexual and that he reduces masculine sexuality to a disembodied gaze that constitutes others as mere bodies. He assumes, for example, that obscene pictures, conversations on sexual topics and the sight of a naked body should arouse desire in anyone who is 'normal'. Such assumptions construct the masculine subject as a disembodied voyeur whose sexuality is strangely unsituated. Thus, while he frees sexuality from naturalistic accounts, Merleau-Ponty forecloses the possibility of alternative forms of sexuality.

Additionally, Butler is concerned that Merleau-Ponty's configuration of the historically-situated subject's sexuality as an 'existential constant' does not go far enough in guaranteeing that this culturally-constituted sexuality is not somehow assumed to be natural. This is particularly the case because Merleau-Ponty distinguishes between biological subsistance and historical and cultural life. Butler argues that eating, sleeping and sexuality do not emerge prior to, and separately from, the social forms that regulate and ritualise these primary processes (ibid., p. 91).

In response, Butler can only turn to Merleau-Ponty to ask: What is the social context and specific history that have given rise to such an abstract and disembodied description? and, What are the ways in which Merleau-Ponty legitimises oppressive structures of sexuality? The answers to these questions become the focus of much of her own work which nevertheless makes full use of phenomenological method. That is, Butler embraces the phenomenological method to interrogate desire as it occurs in ordinary experience. She states that the subject who desires must experience what it desires and that on the basis of this experience of desire the subject seeks to know the object of its desire. Butler concludes that knowledge of the desired object, along with the satisfaction of desire, results in the making and remaking of identity. Desire is a mode of experience, a corporeal questioning of identity and place – but in such a way that each subject takes this mode of being and questioning of identity into themselves and makes it their *own*. This occurs only through the experience of what is other than the subject, what is 'strange, different, novel, awaited' (Butler, 1987, p. 9).

It appears that, in so far as feminist phenomenology was born out of multiple tensions such as those between subject and object, body and mind, immanence and transcendence, it continues to operate in the balance between such tensions. For, even as feminist phenomenology has taken great pains to critique the social and linguistic structures that oppress women, and to formulate theories of fluid identity, still, as Grosz has warned, the body is not open to all the whims, wishes and hopes of the subject. At the very least, our human bodies cannot survive without nourishment and a hospitable environment. Yet, while feminists must recognise that there are biological constraints, human beings are continually overcoming these constraints, through technological improvements and/or through training and adaptation to the environment. As Grosz notes, such bodily changes are 'not "beyond" nature but in collusion with a "nature" that never really lived up to its name, that represents always the most blatant cultural anxieties and projections' (Grosz, 1994, pp. 187–8).

Given these ever shifting limitations, feminist phenomenologists remain actively engaged in rethinking existential phenomenological accounts of human situatedness. The creation of new concepts is central to the feminist project of richer, more diverse descriptions of how racial, gender, class, age, ethnic and cultural differences are corporeally registered and reproduced. Gail Weiss has argued, for example, that unless philosophers recognise the role of the body image in reflecting and sustaining individual, social and political inequalities, there is a danger that positive social and political changes will not address the individual's own corporeal existence in the intimate manner necessary to move successfully towards the eradication of sexism, racism, classism, ageism and ethnocentrism. On this account, a greater awareness of the 'body power' we have at our disposal can result in new, perhaps subversive, body images that can be used to fight oppression on a corporeal front.

Given the concerns of phenomenologically-oriented feminists, concerns ranging from environmentalism to heterosexism, racism, social and political inequality, class and gender struggles, perhaps we can say that Beauvoir's original project of an ethics based on the heart remains at the core of these varied and diverse interests. According to Sandra Bartky: 'To develop feminist consciousness is to live part of one's life in a sort of *ambiguous ethical situation*' (Bartky, 1990, p. 20). This is, Bartky argues, because the lived experience or being-in-the-world of women is so often one of limited or ambiguous transcendence, but there is also a strong sense of solidarity with all those who have known oppression. Feminist phenomenology has embraced de Beauvoir's definition of women's oppression as the confinement and mutilation of women's potential by patriarchy; it has also exceeded it by recognising that she did not really question the value for life of the kinds of activities she defines as transcendent, thus male (Young, 1990, p. 77). If there is an ongoing task attributable to feminist phenomenology, it is this: to transform the culture in the direction of greater openness towards the diversity of life and body, such that the embodied subject is recognised as gendered and historically conditioned, open to all the tensions and contradictions of the culture in which she lives, thus also open to personal and political transformation.

Bibliography

References and further reading

Bartky, Sandra Lee (1990), *Femininity and Domination, Studies in the Phenomenology of Oppression*, New York: Routledge.

Beauvoir, Simone de (1944), *Pyrrhus et Cinéas*, Paris: Gallimard.

— (1945), 'La Phénoménologie de la Perception de Maurice Merleau-Ponty', *Les Temps Modernes* 1: 2 (November), 363–67.

— (1948), *The Ethics of Ambiguity*, trans. B. Frechtman, New York: Philosophical Library. (*Pour une morale de l'ambiguïté*, Paris: Gallimard, 1947.)

— (1954), *She Came to Stay*, trans. Y. Moyse and R. Senhouse, Cleveland: World Publishing. (*L'Invitée*, Paris: Gallimard, 1943.)

— (1959), *Memoirs of a Dutiful Daughter*, trans. J. KirKup, Cleveland: World Publishing. (*Mémoires d'une jeune fille rangée*, Paris: Gallimard, 1958.)

— (1962), *The Prime of Life*, trans. P. Green, Cleveland: World Publishing. (*La Force de l'âge*, Paris: Gallimard, 1960.)

— (1972) (first edn 1952), *The Second Sex*, trans. H. M. Parshley, New York: Knopf, 1952; Vintage, 1972, (*Le Deuxième sexe*, Paris: Gallimard, 1949.)

Bergoffen, Debra B. (1997), *The Philosophy of Simone de Beauvoir, Gendered Phenomenologies, Erotic Generosities*, Albany: SUNY Press.

Bigwood, Carol (1993), *Earthmuse, Feminism, Nature, Art*, Philadelphia: Temple University Press.

Butler, Judith (1986), 'Sex and Gender in Simone de Beauvoir's *Second Sex*', *Simone de Beauvoir: Witness to a Century*, Yale French Studies 72, special issue, 35–49.

— (1987), *Subjects of Desire, Hegelian Reflections in Twentieth Century France*, New York: Columbia University Press.

— (1989), 'Sexual Ideology and Phenomenological Description, A Feminist Critique of Merleau-Ponty's *Phenomenology of Perception*', in Jeffner Allen and Iris Marion Young (eds), *The Thinking Muse, Feminism and Modern French Philosophy*, Bloomington: Indiana University Press, 85–100.

Grosz, Elizabeth (1993), 'Merleau-Ponty and Irigaray in the Flesh', *Thesis Eleven* 36, 37–60.

— (1994), *Volatile Bodies, Toward a Corporeal Feminism*, Bloomington: Indiana University Press.

Heidegger, Martin (1952), *Being and Time*, trans. John Macquarrie and Edward Robinson, Oxford: Basil Blackwell. (*Sein und Zeit*, Tübingen: Niemeyer, 1952.)

Husserl, Edmund (1970), *Logical Investigations*, trans. J. N. Findlay, London: Routledge and Kegan Paul.

— (1970), *The Crisis of European Sciences and Transcendental Phenomenology*, trans. David Carr, Evanston: Northwestern University Press.

Irigaray, Luce (1985), *This Sex Which Is Not One*, trans. C. Porter and Carolyn Burke, Ithaca: Cornell University Press. (*Ce Sexe qui n'en est pas un*, Paris: Editions de Minuit, 1977.)

— (1987), 'Sexual Difference', in Toril Moi (ed.), *French Feminist Thought, A Reader*, New York: Basil Blackwell.

— (1993), *An Ethics of Sexual Difference*, trans. Carolyn Burke and Gillian C. Gill, Ithaca: Cornell University Press. (*Ethique de la Différence Sexuelle*, Paris: Editions de Minuit, 1974.)

— (1993), *Je, Tu, Nous, Towards a Culture of Difference*, trans. Alison Martin, New York. Routledge. (*Je, Tu, Nous, Pour une Culture de la Différence*, Paris: Grasset, 1990.)

Kruks, Sonia (1990), *Situation and Human Existence, Freedom Subjectivity and Society*, London: Unwin Hyman.

Le Doeuff, Michèle (1991), *Hipparchia's Choice: An Essay Concerning Women, Philosophy, etc.*, trans. Trista Selous, Oxford: Blackwell. (*L'étude et le rouet: des femmes, de la philosophie, etc.*, Paris: Les Editions de Seuil, 1989.)

Merleau-Ponty, Maurice (1962), *Phenomenology of Perception*, trans. Colin Smith, New York: Humanities Press. (*Phénoménologie de la perception*, Paris: Editions Gallimard, 1945.)

— (1964), 'Metaphysics and the Novel', trans. Hubert L. Dreyfus and Patricia Allen Dreyfus, *Sense and Non-Sense*, Evanston: Northwestern University Press. ('Le roman et la métaphysique', *Cahiers du sud*, 270 (March 1945), reprinted in *Sens et non-sens*, Paris: Les Editions Nagel, 1948.)

— (1968), *The Visible and the Invisible*, trans. Alphonso Lingis, Evanston: Northwestern University Press. (*Le Visible et l'Invisible*, Paris: Gallimard, 1964.)

Moi, Toril (1994), *Simone de Beauvoir*, Oxford: Blackwell.

Olkowski, Dorothea (forthcoming), 'Chiasm: The Interval of Sexual Difference Between Irigaray and Merleau-Ponty', in Lawrence Hass and Dorothea Olkowski (eds), *Resituating Merleau-Ponty*, Atlantic Highlands: Humanities Press.

Rabil, Albert (1967), *Merleau-Ponty, Existentialist of the Social World*, New York: Columbia University Press.

Simons, Margaret A. (ed.) (1995), *Feminist Interpretations of Simone de Beauvoir*, University Park: Pennsylvania State University Press.

Singer, Linda (1990), 'Interpretation and Retrieval, Rereading Beauvoir', in Aziah Y. al-Hibri and Margaret A. Simons (eds), *Hypatia Reborn, Essays in Feminist Philosophy*, Bloomington: Indiana University Press, 323–36.

Vintges, Karen (1995), 'The Second Sex and Philosophy', trans. Anne Lavalle, in Margaret Simons (ed.), *Feminist Interpretations of Simone de Beauvoir*, University Park: Pennsylvania State University Press, 45–58.

Weiss, Gail (1999), 'Body-Image Intercourse: A Corporeal Dialogue between Merleau-Ponty and Schilder', in

Dorothea Olkowski and James Morley (eds), *Merleau-Ponty, Interiority and Exteriority*, Albany: State University of New York Press.

Young, Iris Marion (1989), 'Throwing Like a Girl, A Phenomenology of Feminine Body Comportment, Motility, and Spatiality', in Jeffner Allen and Iris Marion Young (eds), *The Thinking Muse, Feminism and Modern French Philosophy*, Bloomington: Indiana University Press, 51–70.

— (1990), *Throwing Like a Girl and Other Essays in Feminist Philosophy and Social Theory*, Bloomington: Indiana University Press.

Section Five
POLITICS, PSYCHOANALYSIS AND SCIENCE

INTRODUCTION

Gillian Howie

In 1935 Karl Jaspers wrote that 'quietly something enormous has happened in the reality of Western man: a destruction of old authority, a radical disillusionment in an overconfident reason, and a dissolution of bonds have made anything, absolutely anything, seem possible' (in Kaufmann, 1956, p. 126). The source of that *fin-de-siècle* anxiety, echoed throughout philosophy and literature, was in part the remarkable political upheaval stretching backwards for at least a century. It was a century which saw often violent insurrection and equally violent repression, the end of old empires, the fragile constitution of new alliances and two world wars. The more traditional structures of social organisation had been broken down and faith in traditional authorities was lost; any easy conviction in stability or progress seemed no longer justified. In this context, it is hardly surprising to find that Marx (1818–83) and Freud (1856–1939) offered systems which attempted to lay the foundation for a scientific analysis of change, contradiction and transformation or resolution. The character and content of their systems are profoundly different. A surface analysis of the difference would be that because Marx experienced the horror of two world wars, he could retain an optimistic humanism from which issued a philosophy of hope and utopia. In contrast, dark clouds of the Second World War looming on the political horizon and the rabid anti-Semitism in and around Vienna provided the conditions in which psychoanalysis grew. By 1923, searching for a way to explain these apparently irrational beliefs and behaviours, Freud decided that in Vienna and the Danubian provinces evidence could be found which proved that destructive primeval forces were still atavistically alive in all contemporary human beings. Whatever the psychological reasons for their different approaches, the crucial point is that both Marx and Freud took as their subject matter natural and socialised human behaviour, and both assumed that the conditions of human experience, the laws and forces of development, could be known and investigated scientifically. However, as we shall see, their disagreements as to the nature of the forces which condition human behaviour resulted in divergent, and perhaps incommensurable, theories concerning the effects of social structures on, among other things, human experience, the origin of conflicts and the ways in which these conflicts might be resolved.

Reputedly Marx expounded an analysis of the objective (external) world of economic processes whereas Freud illustrated the complexity of the subjective (internal) life of the individual. Yet as early as 1844 Marx disputed the belief that individuals are merely products of external circumstances, and not only did he stress the need to conceive human behaviour from its active, sensuous and subjective side but he also made this conception central to his qualitative analysis; the description of alienated labour and revolutionary activity. Freud's scientific analysis of instincts, impulses and general psychological dispositions, which for him account for this subjective side, constitute the objective features of psychosexual development.

The articles in this Section explore the extent to

which the works of Marx and Freud offer exciting, imaginative and relevant insights into 'the human condition'. Of these insights one to which all academic disciplines are much indebted, is that mature subject identity is the consequence of various processes which can be analysed, assessed and known scientifically. By accentuating the critical role which other people play in an individual's development, Marx and Freud dismissed a-historical speculation on the 'nature' of the individual, believing such speculation to be a false abstraction from social context. Indeed, this context principle also explains why forms of conceptual abstraction may lead to theoretical distortions and prompted Marx and Freud to question the abstract logic of philosophic speculation. The importance of context is also apparent in the Marxist and Freudian approach to questions of cognition. They argued that our beliefs are entertained and formed for reasons which are not always immediately apparent to us. But nevertheless, they both insisted, all beliefs and ideas originate from human experience. These two ideas form the basis for their scepticism concerning the rational foundation of traditional metaphysical concepts; for example, the idea 'God' or the soul. It would seem, then, that Marx and Freud mark the end of a philosophical era, the end of theology and dogmatic metaphysics.

However, it would be premature for the scientist to celebrate her or his ascension over the pre-Enlightenment philosopher. Marx and Freud provided reasons why the subjective life of an individual could not be reduced to merely physical explanations. They were thus influential in the movement against *scientism* – the uncritical attempt to deploy methods from natural science. In fact, their analysis of the causal origin of ideas and the context principle led them to assess the supposition that there could be a universal, value-free scientific methodology at all. Neither Marx nor Freud allowed that scientific analysis could presume a neutral access to 'sense-data', yet both insisted on the importance of empirical content to descriptions and explanations of human behaviour.

Marx and Freud then raised a number of problems concerning the scientific status of science and, at the same time, threw into doubt traditional philosophical methods. Marxism and Freudianism thus lie between rationalism and empiricism. Although they would have agreed that philosophy was unscientific and that science was unphilosophical, they would have disagreed as to the actual causes of desires, motives and beliefs. A resolute Freudian would dismiss a great deal of Marxist theory of history and qualitative analysis for socialising the structures which cause conflict, aggression and unhappiness. A steadfast Marxist would deride Freudians for fetishising subjectivity, naturalising human motivation and for positing invariant and universal psychic structures. Subsequent theorists have attempted to adjudicate between these putatively scientific theories and to decide whether they enhanced or contradicted one another. Part of the problem here has been that any criteria used to adjudicate between theories have been called into doubt by these very theories. The principal question with which we are left is whether it is possible to have a non-reductive but realist scientific method, which can accommodate an understanding that context will influence the conclusions which are drawn. We will see how Marx and Freud illuminated this idea of 'influence'.

A new materialism

Many commentators separate the works of Marx and Freud into two, if not three, distinct phases. The first phase is said to reflect the influence of their education and intellectual milieu. The immature Marx is thus the philosopher, incorporating Hegel's speculative philosophy into an ill-formed materialism, and the immature Freud is overly scientific, issuing his thesis on the unconscious in physiological terms. The articles in this Section flesh out this crude distinction by showing how the idea of a clean break between early and later periods is premised on a mistaken analysis of the development of a philosophically sound but new materialism. The Hegelian concept 'sublation' might help elucidate this. This concept, linked to the idea of transformation or development, refers to the fact that as something, be it an idea or part of the social world, alters, the old form is retained even as it mutates into something new. Consequently, a critical analysis of development ought to accommodate and assess the influence exerted by the old while showing how the old has been transformed.

By carefully assessing the disagreements between Old and Young Hegelians, Stepelevich, in the first article, invites us to reconsider the influence of Feuerbach on Marx's intellectual development. He explains how Hegel's dialectic of Spirit was transformed into the materialist dialectic of labour through Feuerbach's criticisms of speculative philosophy. Encouraged by Bauer's Young Hegelian critique of idealism, Feuerbach advanced a number of criticisms against Abstract Idealism, which is how he characterised Hegel's Objective Idealism. Stepelevich highlights the Feuerbachian notion that abstraction and alienation are co-generative and shows how this methodological point runs through Feuerbach's four principal objections to Hegelianism. The first objection refers to the logic of the dialectical method. To be consistent, contended Feuerbach, dialectical logic cannot sustain the idea of an end point; thus, Hegelian philosophy would, as any other philosophy, be superseded and the historical process was, perhaps inevitably, incomplete. Feuerbach believed that philosophy ought to begin in the finite, the determinate and the actual. Epistemology would therefore need to be empirically based and the 'truth of the senses' would need to regain its philosophic significance. This empiricism formed the basis for his second criticism of Hegelianism; namely, its theism. Feuerbach offered an anti-theistic description of the causal origin of the idea of God. As a result of the idea that abstraction and alienation are co-generative, he argued that, in essence, the idea of God is an abstract, and therefore alienated, idea of the idea of 'man' which is set over and against the human being as an object of worship. Unfortunately, a simplified understanding of this empiricism led to the critical judgement that at the heart of Feuerbach's secular realism lay a paradox. If abstraction entailed alienation then there was a problem with the extension of certain terms; did the term 'man' designate one individual or an entire class of individuals? If the latter, then Feuerbach was charged with theoretical abstraction but if the former, then the term was overworked in his philosophy. This problem aside, the methodological and epistemological points led to a third criticism which concerned the substance of

Hegelian logic. Feuerbach argued that Hegel mistook the labour of the dialectic as a movement between logical forms and ideas whereas the substance of analysis ought to be actual human beings engaged in practical activity. Finally, according to Feuerbach, a proper understanding of the three above points ought to lead to an appreciation that the present state of affairs would be superseded by a new world order that would embed the principles of radical humanism and secular realism.

The criticism that humanism incorporates an irrational faith in a human 'essence' haunts Marxism. Although Marx retreated from full support of Feuerbach, we can still see the Young Hegelian influence in his conviction that the human being is essentially social and productive and, however framed, that the historical process is a linear development towards a universal form of social organisation. If these are uncritical, or positive, aspects of Marx's historical materialism, coming from the kernel of Hegelianism preserved within Marxist theory, the transformed, or negative, aspects are more numerous. First, dialectical materialism emerged as a response to scientific criticisms of idealism and theoretical criticisms of reductive empiricism. Second, Marx embraced the notion that the substance of dialectics was neither logical form nor ideas and welcomed the insight that the surface phenomena of contradiction between ideas in philosophy was the result of an actual underlying conflict. Third, by retaining but transforming the philosophic concept 'substance' into the concept 'social substance' and by retaining, but revising, Hegel's relational ontology, Marx was in a position to argue that the human being is essentially productive and social and that the way in which this productive activity is organised determines or conditions social experience. Fourth, the argument that abstraction and alienation are co-generative sustains Marx's scientific analysis of the causal chains which generate mystified beliefs. With these point in mind we can begin to see that abstract philosophical investigation might be ideological and that the concepts of scientific hypotheses have their own social and historical contexts.

Marx, following Feuerbach, argued that the criticism of religion was the beginning of all criticism because critical analysis would lead to an assessment of the alienated social conditions which cause an abstract image of 'man' to be formed and entertained as the idea 'God'. Freud also believed the idea of a deity to be a human projection. In his view, however, the idea is the end result of a psychological process characterised by conflict. It is over the causes of such conflict, and the Marxist suggestion that alienation refers to a historically-specific experience of alienated labour, that Marxists and Freudians have their most profound disagreements. In 'Freud and the science of the mind', Hopkins traces how the developmental model of psychic organisation and the theory of the unconscious effected a new understanding of psychological conflict.

By comparing material drawn from dreams with material presented by a patient through associations, Freud developed an hypothesis to explain apparently illogical dreams. The explanatory hypothesis advanced was that dreams are linked to associations through wishful imaginative representation. Manifest content, the material as presented, is related to latent content, the range of wish fulfilments, through a series of symbolic devices including condensation, displacement and projection. Human intentions and activity are thus given a dual reading and apparent motivational content called into question. Wishes themselves originate in infantile bodily experiences of pleasure and unpleasure and these wishes are often repressed only to return later in adult life through the symbolic system. Hopkins details how Freud defended a robust naturalism and took account of the peculiarly psychological. The concept 'cathexis' was an attempt to explain how psychic mechanisms could be mapped onto physiological mechanisms, understood in terms of neural transmitters and connectors. Although vulnerable to the same criticisms as connectionism in recent philosophy of mind, this theory did suggest new ways of understanding mental disturbance.

Although naturalistic, Freud's theory was not reductive. Highlighting the centrality of the reality principle in the development of the typographical model of the psyche, Hopkins describes the complexity of mental life as elaborated by Freud. The ego is thought to manage the conflicting demands of the super-ego and the id. The id is the name given to the drives or instincts which can be both creative and destructive. The super-ego is the home of identifications and images introjected during the infant's early encounters with its carers. The much vaunted Oedipal Complex is the description of psychosexual development where adult heterosexuality is seen as the end result of a series of psychological events and identifications. These are thought to organise the infant's internal life and structure sexuality from the state of polymorphous perversity to adult heterosexuality, an identity holding between sex (female), gender (feminine) and sexual orientation (heterosexual-passive). Where the dynamic model of the psyche illuminates the frustrating and necessary role of the reality principle for intentional action, the theory of psychosexual development indicates the inevitability of frustration and its essential place in the organisation of mature adult heterosexuality.

The problem of value neutrality

The suggestion so far has been that Marx and Freud are scientific realists. Scientific realists argue that the concepts of unobservable entities which occur in scientific theories are not mere linguistic devices for representing regularities in sensations but are genuinely descriptive of the real nature of things hidden from our direct perception. The task of scientific enquiry is to discover the unknown causes of effects through a process of hypothesis formation, experimentation and testing. The scientific status arguably assumed by Marx and Freud can be called into doubt for three reasons. One contention is that neither system sufficiently explains the evidence, nor can either predict with any degree of certainty future events. It is also suggested that neither Marx nor Freud would consider anything to constitute a valid counter-example to their conclusions. Finally, it is argued that science proceeds on the assumption that the material, or substance, of investigation can be distinguished from analysis, interpretation or explanatory hypothesis. In psychoanalytic theory the material – dreams, free association and memory – is presented in narrative form, and the narrative is analysed to reveal underlying unconscious processes. Even if we were to concede the scientific status of the hypothesis there is no guarantee that the analysis is conducted in a manner which reveals the analysands, rather than the analysee's, unconscious material. Similarly, by arguing that knowledge is irreducibly situated and always open to revision, Marx removed external standpoints which could justify his own conclusions.

The third criticism, concerning the unscientific nature of Marxism and Freudianism, implies that there is a value-neutral, context-free scientific method. This idea of value neutrality is based on three principal ideas inherited from Kant's *Critique of Pure Reason*. The first is the idea that the intelligible, formal structures of thought, can be rigorously separated from empirical content; second, following from this, is that factual statements are not evaluative; third, norms of reason, inferential patterns and the core concepts of our conceptual scheme, are, in a relevant sense, detached from psychological and socio-historical influences. These three ideas are established by an argumentative method known as transcendental deduction. The transcendental deductive method presumes two things. The first is that reason can reflect on itself and criticise its own operations. The second is that bare material, the intuition, is immediately schematised with a concept by the individual subject. If these two methodological assumptions are seriously challenged, as they are by Marx's relational ontology and Freud's psychological model of subject development, then traditional notions of scientific method must be scrutinised.

The third article in this Section counter-poses the idea of a value-neutral scientific method with the idea of a non-reductive scientific realism. This latter is not only a synthesis of philosophical insight and empirical analysis but also rebuts the three ideas outlined above. First of all, a characteristic of modern philosophy, according to Collier, is that it is haunted by its own end. This end-consciousness takes two forms: claims made by philosophers that their systems constitute final and complete systems and empiricists who argue that philosophy is concerned with meaningless metaphysical speculation. In the works of Marx we find these two strands interwoven: the first as the belief that philosophy is realised and superseded in the practice of human emancipation, and the second as the belief that

philosophy should be abandoned to concentrate on more fruitful scientific practice. Collier argues that these strands, rather than marking a break between early and late Marx, between the speculative humanist philosopher and the empiricist, are perfectly complementary. Indeed, the claim is that Marx's method, dialectical materialism, emerges out of a distinctive overturning of the idealism of Hegel's logic, itself a challenge to Kant's formal logic. Dialectical materialism, it is said, can disclose, through *empirical* investigation, not only historical processes but also the changing forms and actual *potential* of human social organisation.

Within the Marxist analysis, relations of production are the 'substance' of scientific enquiry and the scientific concept 'exploitation' refers to the production and appropriation of surplus value. These are 'objects' of scientific knowledge. However, for two reasons this notion of objective knowledge could not imply a naive realism. First, Marx considers social practice to mediate ideas and the world. There are at least two implications: there is no 'immediate access' to a world of sense data and, because social practice alters through time, any hypothesis is *de facto* historically situated. A second reason for the non-classical nature of this account of realism is that Marx considers the quantitative (economic) analysis and the qualitative (experiential) analysis to be dual aspects of a unified analysis of the same social world. An example of this is in *Capital* where it is shown once again that objective facts do imply values and motivate action. Collier makes good sense of the distinction drawn by Marx between philosophy as ideology and the non-ideological role which it can play. Philosophical analysis can clarify the intelligibility of scientific assertion or hypothesis formation, the ontological assumptions of empiricism and can be the science of dialectical, rather than formal, logic. The end of philosophy is rather the end of a particular way of philosophizing but also a recognition that scientific hypotheses have certain theoretical commitments, and where there are two seemingly incommensurable theories, good reasons need to be advanced for adjudication. This brings science back on to philosophical territory. These combined strands introduce a non-reductive scientific realism as a new form of scientific understanding.

Two Kantian ideas, that the intelligible can be cleanly demarcated from the empirical and factual statements from evaluative ones, are undermined by Hegel's dialectical logic but, more importantly, shown by Marx to be demonstrably false. Kant's mistake was to assume that bare material and concept are *immediately* schematised. According to Hegel, this is a mistake because concepts mediate 'spirit' and 'nature' and Marx transforms this into the postulate that social practice mediates 'nature' and 'ideas'. If we were to accept this then we would also have good reason to reject the third Kantian idea that concepts and inferential patterns can be detached from their context. Wright picks up this theme in her article and explores the analytic dilemma posed by the Freudian idea that sexuality is central to the organisation of mental life. Acknowledging the implications of this, Wright explains how the thought that the enquirer cannot remain detached from psychological influences necessarily effects a number of methodological queries. This is also, therefore, an argument against detachment but, more interestingly, it broaches the second Kantian methodological assumption, which is that reason can undertake its own critique or that language is itself a value-neutral medium of enquiry which can take itself as substance of enquiry.

Focusing in the first instance on poetry, Wright develops the idea that works of art have meaning in the same way as dreams do. The meaning seems to point beyond the text or the dream, extrinsic to it but only reached through it, implicit rather than explicit, a meaning which can only be made manifest through a careful process of decoding that is done according to specific principles. These principles are condensation and displacement: one thing may signify many things or something seemingly quite unconnected. Now these are, at the same time, linguistic devices, metonymy and metaphor, which convey sense. For this reason, Wright contends that language is always figurative and assigns the origin of this to the irrepressibility of the unconscious. Freud developed the notion of the 'uncanny' to designate textual ambiguities which express this ambivalence of unconscious drives. Psychoanalytic principles can thus offer new insights into works of art and the operations of the imagination. The unconscious processes of both addressor (author/artist) and addressee (reader/viewer) are brought into play and aesthetic pleasure is explained as an effect of the artwork overcoming resistance in the addressee, so preparing the way for reconciliation in unconscious fantasy. For Lacan, the 'uncanny' affect is explained by the fact that reference to desire always fails because that which we wish to represent or to name is necessarily unrepresentable and imaginary: the imaginary union with mother nature or its substitution. Wright explains how Lacanian developments of Freud's psychoanalytic theory force a break with traditional models of successful communication. Rather than presuming that meaning can always be identified with reference, Lacan argued that the uncanniness of discourse is the irreducible affect of the relation between two subjects, split from themselves and each other, hoping to communicate yet finding this forever and necessarily thwarted. Whether a Freudian or a Lacanian then the assumption of a value-neutral position, whether in science or literary criticism, is motivated by the individual's desire for mastery or power, and is undermined by the figurative quality of the medium of interpretation which expresses the unconscious.

The view from somewhere

Similar to the Freudian idea that manifest content is usually a distorted representation of underlying unconscious forces, the Marxist holds that some ideas will present reality in a distorted, even inverted, fashion. Because the cause of the distortion is linked to the form of life, the Marxist attempts to demonstrate a necessary link between 'inverted' forms of consciousness and particular forms of material existence. If it were possible to isolate these causal connections then the Marxist would have good reason to claim that her or his explanatory model is immune from the criticism of distortion and can thus act as a mode of interpretation. In 'Marxism and literary theory', Dentith explores the causal connection between ideas and material existence. Is it possible, he asks, to conceive of the social totality in a way which reveals those hidden and mystified relationships, in a way which does not concede, in the very gesture, the triumph of the economic, that is the actual characteristic of capitalism? Otherwise stated, can we retain the vibrancy of the economic analysis without succumbing to economism, where the economic is considered to be fully determining, or an economistic interpretation of Marx, where Marx himself is thought to be a reductive economic determinist? Dentith's answer to this question also forms the basis of his four-point rejoinder to the description of Marxism as a discredited political and intellectual force.

Allowing that the complexities of social life cannot be reduced to class, Dentith argues that the modalities of oppression are still, in part, determined by economic exploitation. By concentrating on literature, Dentith argues for a way of understanding the linguistic and formal complexities of the novel or cultural product. Their formal features are taken to re-enact these social complexities and modalities of oppression. Aside from these formal features then, Dentith alerts us to an internal feature of meaning which begins to break up the reductive deterministic picture, where meaning is merely a causal relation holding between external object and concept. Events and actions in human social life must be understood, according to Dentith, as being purposive or part-dependent on the intentions of agents, who reflect on and attempt to understand their actions in terms of a wider picture. However, no interpretation is value-free and will carry with it certain assumptions about the existing state of affairs and presuppositions concerning the possibilities afforded by the present. If reality is conceived in terms of social processes then the ways in which we interpret those processes must reflect the actual formal complexities which bring together the parts into a whole social world. For the Marxist, the concept 'determination' does not signify a Popperian notion of causality but purposive and situated human activity which gives form to the social world. Our interpretive scheme must take account of this first-level intentional activity. So, although the parts of the social totality are interconnected, the processes of determination are complex, open and irreducible to an economic mechanism. Of course, the economic, the accumulation of capital and the exploitation of labour, is not then irrelevant; it effects the ways in which the parts relate to the whole. In this way, Dentith can argue that Marxism identifies realism as the condition of the intelligibility of texts but that it

does not eliminate the purposive and intentional features of agency. He concludes by reminding us that even although this framework provides the analytic tools with which to approach questions of aesthetics, interpretation engages each, already implicated, subject in the act of evaluation which is, by its nature, a political act.

Norris argues that Continental and analytic philosophers of science share an intellectual heritage and that there is a coherence to the types of questions and problems addressed. Although naive realism is eschewed by most philosophers of science, those typically called 'Continental' have tended to focus on the historical situatedness of discourse and hypothesis formation, whereas those typically called 'analytic' have concerned themselves with the logic of propositions and justification. This, quasi-Kantian approach, seemed to offer a critical standpoint outside the vagaries of figurative language. In post-Logical Positivist analytic philosophy, however, referential theories of meaning and justification have largely been replaced by coherence theories of truth or justification and the role of interpretation has been stressed. Once the interpretive character of judgement was highlighted, questions relating to the causal process of belief acquisition and conditions of assertion came to the fore. Or, again, once a role for the idea of interpretation was acknowledged in the analysis of scientific hypothesis, then the history of scientific enquiry could no longer be ignored and anti-foundationalist theories of knowledge and justification emerged. The tension between claims made as to the historical nature of scientific practice and the *a priori* character of specific statements about scientific methods has led to questions concerning the logic of enquiry being posed in both traditions in ways which call into doubt the Continental/analytic distinction. The works of Marx and Freud can thus be identified within a broad context of specific philosophical puzzles concerning the scientific status of science and the conditions of knowledge assertion. Unlike more traditional philosophers of science, though, Marx and Freud showed how science was a social practice with all that entailed. Indeed, their insistence that ideas are not immediately given by sense data, and that some ideas may distort reality or are entertained for reasons more to do with psychology or political affinity than with scientific interest, can only add to the richness of this debate as it unfolds.

Reason and freedom

As previously suggested, the conception of scientific method as value-free gained support from three ideas inherited from Kant's *Critique of Pure Reason*. Liberal political philosophy also took its cue from Kant. With the identification of reason with freedom, political philosophy, as distinct from the philosophy of science, appeared to have reached its limit in Kantianism. Transcendental philosophy aroused the belief that the actual transformation of the world was unnecessary. The individual could become rational and free within the established order, because, essentially, he or she *already was*. This identification of freedom with reason recalls the third Kantian idea: that core concepts, reason and *eo ipso* the reasoner are, in a relevant sense, detached or free from the chain of natural causal events. When we extend our understanding of 'nature' to include the empirical world, by which we mean psychological and social events or processes, then we can see the full import of the Kantian notion of detachment. I have already suggested, however, that our conceptual schemes are socially and historically situated. In addition, the relational ontology of Marxism and the Freudian psychosexual developmental model of the psyche both raise fundamental criticisms of this model of detachment. A final aspect to this third idea remains unaddressed: is there still a politically relevant connection to be made between reason and freedom?

As a criticism of Kant's transcendental logic, Stepelevich introduces us to the Hegelian premise that 'the real is rational' and explains how Old and Young Hegelians differed in their interpretation of this. The statement may mean one of three things. It may suggest that the form of the world bears a logical analysis or that the world contains no contradiction or conflict or, finally, that normative principles can be discerned by reason which, if pursued, would deliver a rational, conflict-free, social world. The first point concerns the possibility of scientific or logical analysis, the second a description of the current state of affairs, and the third point, while

remaining firm in its avowal of reason, looks to the future to embed the principles so discerned. Marx and Freud accord in their belief that the 'real' can sustain an objective, scientific analysis and in their rejection of the description of the current state of affairs as one without conflict and contradiction. As we have seen, however, due to their differing theories concerning the nature of underlying forces they diverge at the point where it is claimed that a world without conflict can be attained.

The psychoanalytic hypothesis, designed to explain apparent conflicts between motives and acts, posits phylogenetic and ontogenetic psychic structures and draws the conclusion that conflict is a consequence of instinctual drives being forced to conform both to these structures and to the demands of the external world (Freud, SE XVII, p. 119). The Marxist hypothesis, designed to explain the production of surplus value, posits the contingency of all structures and concludes that surplus value is produced because labour is exploited and that conflicts are the result of tensions caused by specific forms of social and economic organisations. Marx and Freud share a rationalist heritage in so far as they both presume that freedom rests on the subject's ability to bring nature under conscious control. Freud operates within a scheme of psychological individualism, his concern is for the individual subject and the resolution of her or his psychic conflicts. Marx, on the other hand, presents an alternative view of the subject: his concern is for 'the subject of history', the proletariat, and the rational resolution of the contradictions caused by the economics of capitalism. Disagreement as to the substance and goal of 'rational control' and the state of freedom, for one individual psychological accommodation and for the other revolutionary activity and classless democracy issues therefore, from a profound scientific dispute relating to the 'nature' of the subject.

We are reminded of the incommensurability problem raised at the beginning of this introduction: how can we adjudicate between these putatively scientific theories? Bohman, in the final article of this Section, traces the development of Continental political theory to two main concerns. The first pursues the problem of causation. If we accept that the present world is most adequately charaterised not by unity and harmony but by contradiction, conflict and alienation, then we require a methodology which can both diagnose the causes of the malaise of modernity and discover the principles which are to ground political activity. But how can we tell that our methodological assumptions are themselves free from distortion? The second relates to the ideas of novelty and freedom: that in order to leave behind the current causes of conflict the future must be, in some way, discontinuous with the present. This idea of discontinuity ought to be contrasted with the Hegelian-Marxist notions of transformation and sublation.

Marxism, even by its own admission, falters over a twofold problem. First, Marxist theory, with its insistence on science and production, is closely indebted to other Modernist theories and Enlightenment philosophies. Indeed, it could be suggested that it is only an unjustified faith in science which allows the Marxist to distinguish ideological from non-ideological beliefs, progressive from regressive forms of consciousness and revolutionary from reformist political activity. Second, science and production are the principles of techno-scientific and instrumental capitalism. Therefore, it is argued, Marxism in theory and practice cannot be revolutionary. Going further, one could argue that the goal of revolutionary activity, emancipation and participatory democracy, is a direct legacy of Kantian idealism which identifies freedom with rationality. The political path that is taken to reach this goal might therefore be already determined by the current philosophical and political paradigm. It could even be the case that the utopic dream of a conflict-free form of social organisation bespeaks more of the psychopathology of erstwhile revolutionaries than scientific analysis. The very meaning of exploitation may depend on this original dream of plenitude.

Heidegger has seemed by many to offer a radical alternative. Enabled by an external position, principles uncontaminated by the present, Heidegger suggested a way to conceptualise 'a new practical understanding'. So, where Marx works within a Modernist framework Heidegger offers a clean break from the principles at the centre of Enlightenment philosophy. On the other hand, one could aver that the thought of radical discontinuity, a future free

from the influence of the present, is a speculative idea which, guided by the religious impulse, will affirm the current form of social organisation, even as it appears to offer something radically new. The epistemological problem and the political project thus converge and, as Collier and Dentith have demonstrated with compelling logic, description and prescription cannot be cleanly separated: philosophical adjudication carries political entailments.

Before concluding this Introduction it should be noted, and not as an addendum, that the role of women and the idea of the feminine is curiously figured in both Marxism and Freudianism. Almost as an appendix to their socio-historical analysis, Marx and Engels argued that differential power relations between men and women can be reduced to the problem of economic power and patrilineage. Freud's notion of phylogenetic and ontogenetic psychosexual mechanisms wraps the characteristics of femininity and masculinity to the psychic poles of activity and passivity through the idea of the resolution of the Oedipal Complex. Within Freudianism an individual properly accommodates herself or himself to the demands of the real and resolves their own psychosexual ambivalences when he or she accepts the proper role in the penetrative act: a woman is the passive object of penetration (Freud, SE XIX, p 145). Turning Marxism on Freudianism, then, one could argue that when speculating on the nature of sex and gender, Freud naturalised psychosexual constitution and desire and thus offered 'scientific' arguments which restored in theory the current state of affairs: patriarchy. Turning Freudianism on Marxism one could argue that by collapsing sex and gender into the problem of economic variants, Marx accommodated his own ambivalences within a scheme where the resolution of these conflicts was endlessly deferred. The theoretical fulcrum of this problem is the relationship of production to reproduction: the family. It is with some irony then that we can note that, because Marx and Freud showed how mature subject identity is the consequence of antecedent processes, they opened the scientific space for anti-essentialist arguments and the psychoanalytic space for the investigation of male power and masculine desire. These are the arguments which offer the most profound criticisms of the two 'parent' theories.

Bibliography

References and further reading

Bottomore Tom (ed.) (1983), *A Dictionary of Marxist Thought*, Oxford: Blackwell.

Freud, Sigmund (1974), *The Standard Edition of the Complete Psychological Works of Sigmund Freud*, trans. and ed. J. Strachey with A. Freud, London: Hogarth Press.

Jaspers, Karl (1956), 'Reason and Existenz', in *Existentialism from Dostoevsky to Sartre*, ed. W. Kaufmann, Cleveland and New York: Meridian Books.

Joll, James (1976), *Europe since 1870: An International History*, Harmondsworth: Penguin.

Kant, Immanuel (1958) (first edn 1781, 1787), *Critique of Pure Reason*, trans. Norman Kemp Smith, London: Macmillan.

Laplanche J. and Pontalis J. (1973), *The Language of Psychoanalysis*, trans. P. Nicholson-Smith, London: Institute of Psycho-Analytical Library.

Mandel, Ernest (1975), *Late Capitalism*, London: New Left Books.

Marx, Karl (1977), *Selected Writings*, ed. D. McLellan, Oxford, Oxford University Press.

Mitchell, Juliet (1974), *Psychoanalysis and Feminism*, Middlesex: Penguin.

Tong, Rosmerie (1989), *Feminist Thought: A Comprehensive Introduction*, Sydney and Wellington: Unwin Hyman.

THE YOUNG HEGELIANS: FROM FEUERBACH TO SCHMIDT

Lawrence S. Stepelevich

The first disciples

When Hegel died in 1831, his followers inherited a questionable legacy. On the one hand, he seemed to have brought the history of philosophy to a successful conclusion. The long-sought love and search for wisdom had ended in the actual possession of wisdom. On the other hand, history had not come to an end. Did the conclusion of philosophy mean that it was to play no further role in history, that it had died along with Hegel? Indeed, it is possible to conclude that he himself thought that this was the case. Certainly, in his introductory and concluding remarks in his *Lectures on the History of Philosophy* he seems to have understood his own philosophy as bringing to an end the history of philosophy. For Hegel, philosophic history was bound to follow the dictates of reason, which meant that it followed the triadic course of a dialectical logic. The triad expressed the three main epochs of philosophic history: the ancient, the medieval and the modern. The first two ages of thought stood in opposition to one another, but the modern age reconciled and synthesised the truths of the earlier ages. The modern age, as being the final sublation and closure of the philosophic quest, was completed in Hegel's philosophy. Introduced by the Cartesian '*cogito*', modern philosophy found its immanent logic fully extrapolated in Hegel's absolute system. And so, for Hegel's first followers, it seemed as if a new age had dawned, one in which the ancient and unrequited love of wisdom had finally found fulfilment in the all-encompassing wisdom of the 'Absolute Idea'. But history continued, and soon the questions of philosophy became the question of philosophy itself. What did it mean to be a Hegelian philosopher? Did it mean merely to passively contemplate the truths of Hegelianism; or to actively apply that theory as a 'praxis' turned to solving the problems of the actual world? The disciples felt compelled to choose between either turning Hegel's theory into practice or to remain content with that final theory. As one of the disciples remarked, they had the choice to be either Hegel's 'grave diggers or monument builders'.

The view of the 'monument builders' can be found in the words of the funeral eulogy spoken over Hegel's grave by his disciple Friedrich Förster. He drew an illuminating simile between Hegel's philosophical conquests and those of Alexander the Great. Just as those who inherited the kingdom of Alexander had merely to sustain his realm, so the followers of Hegel needed only 'to confirm, to proclaim, and to strengthen' their inherited 'Kingdom of Thought'. In short, there were no more intellectual worlds left to conquer. For the 'grave diggers', the problems of the real world could not be ignored, and so, although there were no more intellectual worlds left to conquer, the real world remained as yet unconquered. Faced with the choice between either contemplation or action, two antithetical Hegelian schools developed: the so-called

'Old' Hegelians and the 'Young' Hegelians, later also categorised as 'Right' and 'Left' Hegelians.

Both groups, described as 'hostile brothers', fully agreed with Hegel's dictum that 'What is rational is actual and what is actual is rational' – but they completely differed as to its interpretation. In the view of the Young Hegelians it might be the case, *de jure*, that ultimately what was real was rational, but *de facto*, the *actual* was in most instances far from being rational. For them, the present state of the world resembled that of the late French Monarchy. It was certainly 'actual' but could not make claim to being 'rational'. Since the Monarchy, with all its aristocratic and religious power had fallen to the forces of reason embodied in such writers as Voltaire and Diderot, so could their own world be transformed. Like France a half-century earlier, the 'actual' world of Germany in the 1830s and 1840s, could not be called 'rational'. The 'Germanies' were an aggregate of various monarchies, a myriad politically independent and squabbling petty duchies, free states and principalities. If political life was in disarray, so also was the Church. The disruptive residue of the Reformation and Counter-Reformation still generated theological confusion and ill-will among the many religious groups in Germany. In principle, they took as their task rationalising the irrational actuality of the world in which they lived.

The Old Hegelians found Hegel's dictum a confirmation of the present and actual state of affairs. For them, a philosophic 'quietism' prevailed, an optimistic accommodation of Hegelianism to the state of the actual world in which they lived. The real was indeed rational. These conservative Hegelians embodied the common conception of what it is to be 'philosophical' – being more engaged in reflection than action. Certainly, Hegel's famous metaphor of philosophy being 'the Owl of Minerva' which took flight only at the twilight of a historical epoch, and his strictures against philosophers using the terms 'should' and ought, could be used to support the view held by the Old Hegelians. Some of the more important of these were Karl Friedrich Göschel, Georg A. Gabler, Friedrich Förster and Johann Henry Erdmann. They, and others, intent upon preserving their intellectual legacy, embarked almost immediately upon the project of compiling Hegel's works. As they added little more than erudite commentaries upon the work they inherited, their names are now forgotten and they made little effect upon the subsequent course of philosophic history.

Although most were secure within their academic posts, none of the Old Hegelians could claim either the philosophical stature or the political influence of Hegel. This made it all the more difficult for them to defend themselves against the growing suspicion that Hegel's dialectical philosophy had the covert intention and potential to destroy both orthodox Christianity and political conservatism. Ironically, the delicate accommodation which they had established between Hegelianism and the conservative institutions of their time was disrupted by one who claimed to be inspired by Hegel. In 1835, David Friedrich Strauss (1808–74), published his *Life of Jesus*. Strauss's work created what one commentator has called a 'fire storm' within the large and politically influential clerical class of Prussian Germany. As Strauss claimed his work to be grounded in Hegel's philosophy, the conservative clergy were fully convinced that their earlier doubts of Hegel's orthodoxy were now fully justified. In this brilliant work of scholarship, Strauss divorced the historical Jesus from the Christ of faith. He did not deny that there may have been a historical Jesus, but if there had been, then he was but a frame upon which a suffering Jewish community could affix the expected signs and stories of their long-awaited Messiah. In sum, the gospel figure of Christ was principally a fictional character. The reputations, if not the careers, of the Old Hegelians were under serious threat. And so, a year after the publication of the *Life of Jesus*, in order to defuse the near-calamitous effects of Strauss's work upon their credibility, the Old Hegelians decided to counter Strauss with a 'true' Hegelian critique of his work. For this task they chose the young but gifted Bruno Bauer (1809–82). He soon proved to be the worst possible choice. Bauer dutifully and immediately set out to demonstrate that Strauss would find little in Hegel to support his thesis of the 'mythic' life of Jesus, but his critique was contemptuously dismissed by Strauss as 'a foolish bit of pen-pushing'. Nevertheless, if not for Strauss, then certainly for Bauer, this critique proved to be a turning point. It drew him into a Hegelian reading of the gospel narratives that ultimately led him to conclude, even beyond Strauss, that these narratives were nothing more than a complete fiction. He arrived at this radical conclusion, after writing a series of ever more unorthodox biblical studies, all of which were so subordinated to the requirements of Bauer's theological logic that they were rendered theologically meaningless. Bauer became a convinced atheist, who, in consequence, soon lost his teaching post at the University of Bonn. Karl Marx (1818–83), Bauer's student and friend, immediately joined with him in proclaiming his atheism. In 1841, Bauer published *The Trumpet of the Last Judgement Against Hegel the Atheist and Anti-Christ*. It was exaggeratedly ironic, being apparently written by an anonymous pietistic clergyman intent upon proving that Hegel was indeed as bad as the title of the work indicated. It was not long before Bauer's authorship was revealed, and soon after Bauer's academic career came to a highly-publicised end. And so, five years after being chosen as the young champion of the Old Hegelians, Bauer became the informal leader of the Young Hegelians. The loss of his teaching post, and his atheistic and revolutionary reading of Hegel, gained him the reputation of being a martyr for what was then called 'The Good Cause of Freedom'. He soon dominated the circle of the 'Free Ones' of Berlin, one of the many radical clubs whose doctrines set the stage for the political revolutions of 1848. Bauer's *Trumpet of the Last Judgement*, along with other writings of the Young Hegelians, all claiming to be based on Hegel's philosophy, ensured that Hegelianism would no longer be, as during Hegel's time, supported by enlightened governmental ministries. The Old Hegelian school slowly vanished from the philosophical scene. By 1841, a decade after the death of Hegel, Prussia's new King, Friedrich Wilhelm IV, fearful of the revolutionary potential of Hegelianism, called the aged rival of Hegel, Friedrich Schelling (1775–1854) to Berlin. It was hoped that his authority and his conservative philosophic temper would put an end both to Young Hegelian radicalism and Old Hegelian hypocrisy. But the King's effort failed, perhaps not so much because of Schelling's disappointing lectures but because

philosophy in the grand tradition seemed increasingly irrelevant in the advent of new age marked not only by rapid advances in science and technology, but by the threats and promises of political revolution.

Feuerbachian humanism

Despite the public attention, both then and now, brought to bear upon Strauss's *Life of Jesus*, it is Ludwig Feuerbach (1804–72), who could rightly claim to be the first of the Young Hegelians. And if in nothing else, the philosophical life of Feuerbach reflects the whole course of Young Hegelianism, from its optimistic and outspoken beginnings to its pessimistic and silent ending.

If Hegel had indeed understood his philosophy as the culmination of all past thought, then the first signal of what this might mean for the future came from Feuerbach. In November 1828, Feuerbach wrote a letter to Hegel, enclosing a copy of his recent doctoral Eneas. Both were testaments of his devotion and indebtedness to Hegel, with Feuerbach praising Hegel's thought to be nothing less than the 'Incarnation of the pure Logos'. Nevertheless, in his letter, the twenty-four-year-old rather bluntly (considering Hegel's reputation), presented his own views as to what *should* be the role played Hegelianism. First, it should not

> be directed to academic ends [the direction of Old Hegelians], but to mankind – for the least, the new philosophy can make the claim that it is compelled to break through the limits of a school, and to reveal itself as world-historical, and to be not simply the seed in every spirit of a higher literary activity, but rather to become the expressed universal spirit of reality itself, to found as it were, a new world-epoch, to establish a kingdom . . . There is now a new basis of things, a new history, a second creation, where . . . reason will become the universal appearance of the thing. (Feuerbach, 1954, pp. 244–8)

This central principle of Young Hegelianism: that Hegelian theory should be used to establish a new world-order, a 'second creation'. Although there was little agreement upon the exact nature of that 'new basis of things', the unquestioned eschatological belief that a new order was immanent defined the emotional appeal of Young Hegelianism. Hegel probably would not have agreed with Feuerbach's redefining of philosophy, but this 'new basis' has its foundations in Hegel's own conception of dialectical progress. If the dialectic, as Hegel maintained, inexorably pressed onwards, and displayed itself as 'the portentous power of the negative', then even Hegelianism itself would be fated for an *aufhebung*, a cancellation and elevation into a new form of thought. From the thought of Hegel, and in full accord with its dialectic, it would be transformed into a new beginning, a new 'thesis', a new philosophy. This overall destructive, yet optimistic, messianic vision is the inspiration of Feuerbach's prediction of 'a new basis of things, a new history, a second creation . . .' Feuerbach's optimism would find itself echoed in other Young Hegelian activists, such as August von Cieszkowski (1814–94), Moses Hess (1812–75), and Karl Marx.

In 1835, Cieszkowski's *Prolegomena to the Wisdom of History*, not only introduced the term 'praxis' to mean the reconciliation of Hegelian theory to actual practice, but also provided a historical frame upon which the future could be planned. For Cieszkowski, Hegel's philosophy of history, with its division of history into four stages (Oriental, Greek, Roman, and Christian-Germanic) violated Hegel's own triadic logic. Cieszkowski proposed a 'more' Hegelian articulation of historical periods: the Ancient, the Christian and the Future. Each of these ages had a definite way of thinking. The ancients were practical, world-orientated, whereas the Christians were just the opposite, impractical and other-worldly. Christianity was the victory of pure theory over practice. For Cieszkowski, the Christian world of theory reached from Christ to Hegel, and Hegel is credited with establishing, once and for all, a final, complete and all-comprehending theory. Since the Ancient and Christian world-views were antithetical as unguided practice and impractical theory, so the future age would bring forth a synthesis of these opposing views. This synthesis is termed 'praxis' – the fusion of theory and practice, of rationality and actuality. Within a few decades after Cieszkowski's first employment of the idea of 'praxis', it had

become an essential element in Marxist doctrine.

If the triadic logic which Cieszkowski proposed was intended to map out the future, then Moses Hess would be the first among the Young Hegelians to propose that the new god of that future would be a deified humanity. For Hess, the whole history of God, as presented in the Old Testament, was ultimately a covert history of mankind. Hess, whom Engels called. 'The first Communist', and whom Theodore Herzl named as 'The Founder of Theoretical Zionism', first set forth his views in his 1837 work, *The Holy History of Mankind*. In this, and in numerous articles, Hess transformed his understanding of Hegel into a programmatic humanism that prepared the way for *The Communist Manifesto* of Marx and Engels.

Feuerbach, like Hegel and almost all the first Hegelians – and indeed like most university students at the time – had studied theology with the initial intention of becoming a member of the clergy. It seems likely that their biblical studies, usually conducted under the direction of an evangelical and pietistic Lutherans, might well have introduced a biblical and eschatological tone into their later philosophical and political activities. Certainly, analogies can, and have, been drawn between Hegel's triads and the Trinity, between the Absolute Spirit and the Holy Spirit, and between the expectations of a future 'Kingdom of God' and the new worlds envisioned by the Young Hegelians. The 'classless society' of Marx, the deified mankind of Hess, the 'Man' of Bruno Bauer, and all the other expectant new objects of worship, are merely the final expressions of an atheism transformed into a new theism. As Max Stirner (1806–56) correctly perceived, the atheists of his time were not merely atheists, but 'pious atheists'.

The overarching criticism of Hegel's philosophy which defines the whole of Feuerbach's project is the rejection of what he perceived to be Hegel's abstract idealism. For Feuerbach, Hegel had began his *Phenomenology of Spirit* correctly – with the sensuous world of the 'here' and the 'now'. But he then proceeded to dialectically dissolve the world of sense into that final emptiness and abstraction termed 'Absolute Knowledge'. Hence, Hegel's idealism had blinded itself, and could not deal with the present demands of the physical world. Feuerbach's 'new basis of things' intended to restore real significance to both man and his world. The sensuous world of the bodily man would be restored to its rightful place. What had hitherto been taken from the world and man and given to Heaven and God through the activity of the alienating thought of idealistic religion (whose last and greatest representative was Hegel), was now to be returned to the world and man. Nevertheless, for Feuerbach it was to Hegel's everlasting credit to have reached the cumulating point of alienated thought, the pure abstraction of 'Absolute Knowledge'. Hegel put a final period to all further speculative thought. The future task for such new thinkers as Feuerbach would be to recall mankind back to its original truth, which was not the abstract truth of philosophy, but the concrete truth of the senses. In one of his final programmatic works, *The Principles of the Philosophy of the Future*, Feuerbach set out the relationship of his 'new philosophy' to Hegel's philosophy:

> The new philosophy has, according to its historical origin, the same task and position toward modern philosophy that the latter had toward theology. The new philosophy is the realization of the Hegelian philosophy or, generally, of the philosophy that prevailed until now, a realization, however, this is at the same time the negation, and indeed the negation without contradiction, of this philosophy. (Feuerbach, 1966, p. 31)

In 1830, Feuerbach imprudently decided, against his father's advice, to anonymously publish a collection of aphoristic observations entitled *Thoughts on Death and Immortality*. In regard to its speculative content, Feuerbach's *Thoughts* retains the same stress upon pantheism found in his dissertation. For him, Christianity's egoistic tendencies were doctrinally supported by the belief in the immortality of the individual soul. This meant not only an emphasis upon a socially-destructive egoism of self-salvation, but an equally destructive impact upon the very meaning of the world in which humanity found itself. Feuerbach casts his more formal arguments in Hegelian terminology, as with this tortured closing argument intending to prove that death gives value to life:

> Death is no positive negation, but a negation that negates itself, a negation that is itself empty and nothing. Death is itself the death of death. As it ends life, it ends itself . . . Only the negation that takes away something is real . . . Thus death, as a total negation, is a self-negating negation, a negation that, because it takes all, takes nothing . . . Death has no value, no significance, no reality, no determination, and yet certainly its lack of value and significance, its unreality and lack of character, are the clearest testimony and verification of the value, significance, and substantiality in the character of life. (Feuerbach, 1980, pp. 165–6)

The conclusion of Feuerbach's *Thoughts* further advanced the position he had taken in his dissertation. His earlier emphasis on pantheism gave way to intimations of a radical humanism, a humanism which stressed that sensuous and physical life was the solution to the ancient Christian sundering of the soul from the body, of heaven from earth. Christian idealism was to be cast aside for a new secular realism. From this point in his thought, Feuerbach would only have to take a short step to see that the alienations introduced by Christianity were in fact supported by the idealistic philosophy of Hegel. In the concluding paragraphs of the work, the argumentative links are all present:

> Then how should one call those who take transitoriness to be a predicate of this life, who believe that they say something, that they pass a judgment on this life, when they say that it is temporal, it is transitory? . . . How should one designate those who take as their object that which is nothing . . . ? They call themselves the pious ones, rationalists, even philosophers. Leave the dead among the dead!
>
> God is life, love, consciousness, Spirit, nature, time space, everything, in both its unity and its distinction. As a loving being, you exist in the love of God. (ibid., pp. 172–3)

Just as his father had predicted, Feuerbach's publication of the *Thoughts* ended any hope that he might have had of an academic career. German universities, sustained and controlled by both political reactionaries and religious pietists would not tolerate any radicalism. This was particularly so in 1830, when the July Revolution in France had triggered similar revolts in nearby Poland and the Netherlands. The anonymous author of the *Thoughts* was soon discovered and discharged from his position of lecturer at the University of Erlangen. He was then only twenty-six years old. In his career-destroying move, he anticipated that act of early academic suicide common to most Young Hegelians. There were other casualties. In 1835, at the age of twenty-seven, Strauss's imprudent publication, *Life of Jesus Critically Examined* ended his chances for either a clerical or an academic life. At the age of thirty-four, in 1841, Bruno Bauer's publication of his unorthodox *Critique of the Synoptic Gospels* put an early end to his promising academic career. Unhappily for Karl Marx, he was then known to be a close friend of Bauer. Bauer's ejection from the University of Bonn also ensured that Marx, at twenty-three years of age, could forget about future academic appointments. Even Bruno Bauer's brother Edgar (1820–86), intent upon defending his brother, violated the oppressive Prussian censorship laws and was imprisoned. It was the same with Johann Caspar Schmidt, as even his pseudonym Max Stirner could not protect him from the career-destroying notoriety of his anarchic text *The Ego and His Own*. Arnold Ruge (1802–80) suffered a similar fate. He was, in effect, the devoted publicity manager of Young Hegelianism, not only in his own writings, but as an editor of a series of increasingly radical journals – one of them being the short-lived 'German-French Yearbooks' whose coeditor was Karl Marx. For his devotion he was rewarded first with a prison sentence and then exile. In short, being a Young Hegelian was not merely a pleasant theoretical exercise in radical thinking, but entailed the constant practical threat of at least the loss of academic position if not prison and exile.

In 1833, Feuerbach published the first of a three-volume study of modern philosophy, the subsequent volumes appearing in 1836 and 1838. Because of their somewhat pedestrian quality, these studies have attracted little scholarly attention. However, for at least one commentator, Marx Wartofsky, the first volume, *A History of Philosophy from Bacon to Spinoza*, is 'a crucial work in understanding Feuerbach's development. In it, Feuerbach comes to discover his own views in the course of his critique of major philosophical figures (Wartofsky, 1977, p. 4). In sum, this work is reminiscent of Hegel's own phenomenological approach to philosophic history. The result of Feuerbach's journey of self-discovery in his examination of philosophic history reached its final conclusion in his 1839 work, *A Critique of Hegelian Philosophy*. This work marked Feuerbach's conscious and definitive turn from idealistic philosophy towards the statement of his own thought.

In 1841, Feuerbach published, if not his most important, then certainly his most influential and popular work, the *Essence of Christianity*. Its general thesis is simple enough: that the traditional idea of God was nothing more than the abstract and therefore alienated essence of idea of Man set over and against Man as an object of worship. Abstraction and alienation are, among all of the Young Hegelians, taken as co-generative. In Feuerbach's words:

> Man – and this is the mystery of religion – projects his being into objectivity, and then again makes himself an object to this projected image of himself thus converted into a subject; he thinks of himself as a object to himself, but as the object of an object, of another being than himself. (Feuerbach, 1957, p. 30)

Here, Man, abstracted and detached from the context of practical and sensuous life, enters into a process of theoretical self-projection, of alienation, which in its turn renders his worldly self into the object of a heavenly self. This self-generation of the self as a religious object ensures the detachment of man from the actual world.

Not unexpectedly, the *Essence* was greeted with enthusiasm by all the Young Hegelians. By June 1842, a youthful Marx, who had been Feuerbach's disciple since 1839, was heatedly proclaiming the pun that 'there is no other road for you to *truth* and *freedom* except that leading *through* the stream of fire [*Feuer-bach*]. Feuerbach is the *purgatory* of the present time'. Almost fifty years after its appearance Friedrich Engels recalled the impact of Feuerbach's work:

> Then came Feuerbach's *Essence of Christianity*. With one blow it pulverized the contradiction, in that without circumlocutions it placed materialism on the throne again ... The spell was broken. The 'system' was exploded and cast aside ... One must himself have experienced the liberating effect of this book to get an idea of it. Enthusiasm was general; we all became at once Feuerbachians. (Engels, 1941, p. 18)

Feuerbach's goal was to press the consciousness of his readers to the point where they would fully understand that 'Man is the true God and Saviour of Man'. His intention, as he stated it, was to change 'the friends of God into friends of man, believers into thinkers, worshippers into workers, candidates for the other world into students of this world, Christians, who on their own confession are half-animal and half-angel, into men – whole men'. But this humanistic truth was not to be found as an abstraction, in philosophical speculation, but in immediate physical feeling, in a direct sensuous love of Man as Man-God.

The pantheism which Feuerbach had found in his first reading of Hegel was now transformed into a radical humanism, wherein the 'Man-God' replaced the divine 'God-Man' of orthodox theology. What was earlier known only through the lens of alienating thought, the theory of Christianity, was now to be directly apprehended in sensuous feeling. Unlike all previous philosophy, this philosophy

> places philosophy in *the negation of philosophy* ... This philosophy has for its principle, not the Substance of Spinoza, not the *ego* of Kant and Fichte, not the Absolute Identity of Schelling, not the Absolute Mind of Hegel, in short, no abstract, merely conceptual being, but a *real* being, the true *Ens realissimum* – man; its principle, therefore, is in the highest degree positive and real. It generates thought from the *opposite* of thought, from Matter, from existence, from the

senses; it has relation to its object first through the senses. (ibid., p. xxxv)

The new religious truth for the new age would be 'the realization and humanization of God – the transformation and dissolution of theology into anthropology' (Feuerbach, 1966, p. 5).

Within two years after *The Essence of Christianity*, Feuerbach set forth two major programmatic essays: *Provisional Theses for the Reform of Philosophy* (1842) and the *Principles of the Philosophy of the Future* (1843). These works define Feuerbach at the height of his creativity and influence.

But if, throughout his works, Feuerbach employs Hegel's dialectic, his style and intent are radically different from anything which might be expected from Hegel. The language is passionate and personal, usually being directed to a 'thou', to 'thou, dear reader'. With the exception of Strauss's *Life of Jesus*, the literature of Young Hegelianism is more often than not caught up in a passionate informality that boarders on bombast. Even Franz Mehring, the sympathetic biographer of Marx and Engels admitted that their anti-Feuerbachian and anti-Stirnerian work, *The German Ideology*, was 'an oddly school boyish polemic'. Bruno Bauer's anonymous *Trumpet of the Last Judgement Against Hegel the Atheist and Antichrist*, described as 'a perfect example of Young Hegelian writing', is not only marked by an excited excess of bold and italic types, of exclamation points and dashes, but even employed arrows and pointed fingers to illustrate its more important passages. In reading these works, Karl Löwith's observation concerning the works of Feuerbach and the Young Hegelians seems appropriate:

> In spite of its numerous 'consequently's' his system hovers in a mystic darkness which is not made more transparent by his emphasis on 'sensibility' and 'perceptibility'. This characteristic is true not only of Feuerbach, but of all the Young Hegelians. Their writings are manifestos, programs, and theses, but never anything whole, important in itself ... Whoever studies their writings will discover that, in spite of their inflammatory tone, they leave an impression of insipidity. (Löwith, 1967, p. 67)

The critique of Feuerbach

However much Feuerbach's new philosophy of radical humanism and sensuousness might appeal to the Young Hegelians, it was infected with a fatal flaw – an ambiguity which abruptly ended his influence on them. The ambiguity is this: if the true object of religious feeling, the basis of all notions of divinity, is termed not God but 'man', then is this term 'man' to be understood as referring to the concrete human individual or to the whole class of men, to that abstraction termed 'mankind'? In short, is the term 'man' to be taken distributively or collectively? The ambiguity is evident in such statements as the 59th 'Principle of the Philosophy of the Future': 'Solitude is finiteness and limitation; community is freedom and infinity. Man for himself is man (in the ordinary sense); man with man – the unity of I and thou – is God' (Feuberach, 1966, p. 71). Certainly man as 'the unity of the I and thou' is not the individual that is sensuously perceived – unless, perhaps, as Engels archly notes, that Feuerbach's God is the sex act. But if the individual, as a concrete and visible being, is subordinate to the community, then Feuerbach has deified a relationship, community, and not the actual individual human. The ambiguity regarding what he meant by the term 'man' rendered Feuerbach defenceless against the very charge which he had so confidently directed against Hegel: Feuerbach's new philosophy was, under questioning, nothing but the old philosophy in disguise, a covert theism playing such 'etymological tricks' as substituting the term 'Man' for 'God'. The new philosophy was, just like the old, caught up in a world of ideas, and incapable of dealing with the actual problems of the real world. But in this rejection of their mentor, Feuerbach, Marx and Engels were merely following the critical path first laid out by Max Stirner.

In 1845, in *The Ego and His Own*, Stirner accused Feuerbach (as well as Bruno Bauer) as being nothing more than a 'pious atheist' whose whole task had been to deceptively, if unconsciously, to re-present 'God as Man'. This new 'God-Man', earthbound and omnipresent, did not bode well for individual freedom. This new god, unlike the relatively impotent 'Man-God', long banished to Heaven, would find his will directly and painfully expressed in the secular power of the state. It would have been better had Feuerbach left things as they were, with the original 'God' set at a safe distance from individual affairs. In two brief paragraphs, Stirner states his position as well as his understanding of Feuerbach:

> Let us be brief, and set Feuerbach's theological view and our contradiction over against each other: 'The essence of man is man's supreme being; now by religion, to be sure, the *supreme being* is called God and regarded as an objective essence, but in truth it is only man's own essence; and therefore the turning point of the world's history is that henceforth no longer God, but man, is to appear to man as God.'
>
> To this we reply; The supreme being is indeed the essence of man, but, just because it is his *essence* and not he himself, it remains quite immaterial whether we see it outside him and view it as 'God', or find it in him and call it 'Essence of Man' or 'Man.' I am neither God nor Man, neither the supreme essence nor my essence, and therefore it is all one in the main whether I think of the essence as in me or outside of me. (Stirner, 1995, p. 34)

Before 1845 it seemed clear to all that Feuerbach's charge was correct, and that Hegel's philosophy was indeed a covert theology. After 1845, it seemed clear to all that Stirner's charge was correct, and that Feuerbach's philosophy was but a covert religion. Feuerbach's dissertation can be said to have initiated what Engels described as 'the decomposition process of the Hegelian school' which characterised Young Hegelianism. Ironically, Feuerbach was the first to be expelled from this school. His attempt to rebut Stirner took the form of a brief unsigned article of a dozen pages (Feuerbach, 1970, pp. 427–41). It was not an effective effort, little more than reiterations, in a higher voice, of his previous arguments, or arguments mainly intended as a *reductio ad absurdum* – intending to show that Stirner 'also belongs to the "pious atheists!"' Because Feuerbach's rebuttal was so unconvincing, it was not long before Stirner's reading of Feuerbach became the accepted one.

After having read Stirner, Marx reconsidered his relationship to Feuerbach. In 1845, Marx's *Theses on Feuerbach* signalled a turn from his interest in 'alienated man' and Feuerbachian 'love' which had characterised his earlier work. He now advocated 'critical-revolutionary praxis' – a realistic viewpoint which Marx saw had 'no meaning' for the idealistic Feuerbach.

In 1845, other than his brief reply to Stirner, Feuerbach wrote nothing. He thereafter turned from what Sidney Hook termed his 'historically significant thought' to a 'degenerate sensationalism', or the 'most "vulgar" of "vulgar materialisms"'. As many scholars agree, it seems certain that Stirner's criticism put a virtual end to Feuerbach's further influence. Indeed, even a half-century later, Engels was still repeating Stirner's charge: 'He [Feuerbach] by no means wishes to abolish religion: he wants to perfect it' (Engels, 1941, p. 33).

A survey of the dates in Feuerbach's bibliography and the events of his career would support the thesis that Stirner's criticism definitively ended Feuerbach's desire to further promote his philosophy. In his study of Feuerbach, Eugene Kamenka concludes:

> The general view was, and to a large extent remains, that Feuerbach had said everything of importance that he had to say by 1845, and that his subsequent work is either a mere repetition or a falling-away into positions (such as 'vulgar materialism') which he had effectively criticized earlier. (Kamenka, 1970, p. 156)

It seems that Stirner had won a victory of sorts. It was not to last, however, as even Stirner within a few years was charged by his even more radical colleagues as being covertly religious, in this case a charge of 'Ego-worship'. Pure atheism required that there be no God whatsoever – even one's own ego.

It is the nature of Young Hegelianism to be revolutionary, to critically overturn any given form of philosophy, religion, or politics. What Hegel had termed 'the power of the negative' was given universal force, and was turned into a weapon that the Young Hegelians not only turned on others, but even upon themselves. Feuerbach unconsciously predicted the end of his own 'Philosophy of the Future' when, in 1842 he wrote:

> The period of breakdown of a historical world view is necessarily filled with conflicting de-

mands: some think it necessary to preserve the old and banish the new, others think it necessary to realize the new, which party recognizes the true need? The one which sees the need of the future – the anticipated future – the one which shares in forward progress [the Young Hegelians?]. The need for preservation is something artificial, something itself evoked – reaction [the Old Hegelians?] . . . Only he who has the courage to be absolutely negative has the strength to create something new. (Feuerbach, 1874, p. 407)

If Hegelianism is to be taken only as a programme for the future, then all that has past and is now present must be rejected. As Engels well understood, 'In accordance with all the rules of the Hegelian method of thought, the proposition of the rationality of everything which is real resolves itself into the other proposition: "All that exists deserves to perish"' (Engels, 1941, p. 11).

Stirner's radical egoism has been taken to be the last expression of Young Hegelianism. With it, the progress of the dialectic distilled all of the previous proposals of the school, including both Feuerbach's humanism and Bauer's atheism, into mere religious belief. However, Stirner's atheistic individualism was soon supplanted by a more nihilistic formulation that did indeed put a final period upon the thought and the history of Young Hegelianism. This formulation, contained, the anonymous work, *The Realm of the Understanding and the Individual* (1846), traced the logical exhaustion of Hegelianism after Hegel. Its author was Karl Schmidt (1819–64), whose name and work are today all but forgotten. In 1841, as a theology student, and as so many theology students at the time, he fell under the spell of Strauss's *Life of Jesus*. Schmidt later joined the Berlin group of atheists and agitators known as 'The Free Ones' which had its informal leader in Bruno Bauer. In a few years, he felt he had learned whatever could be learned from his experiences among the Young Hegelians, and in his *Autobiography* summed up that learning:

> If someone has once heard of Hegel, he must proceed to Strauss, from Strauss to Feuerbach, and from Feuerbach to Bruno Bauer. I accomplished

the consequence of this thought in myself, but soon came to the further conclusion . . . that Stirner makes more sense than Bruno Bauer and that one must proceed beyond Stirner to arrive at the most abstract individualism. (in Stepelevich, 1983, p. 379ff.)

Schmidt, in going beyond Stirner, concluded the process by drawing forth his modest truth: 'I am only myself'. With this, the school which began so loudly and hopefully ended in silence and cynicism. By 1866, the Hegelian historian, Johann Erdmann half-humorously referred to himself as the Last of the Mohicans. At that time it clearly seemed that Hegelianism, in all of its forms, Young and Old, had passed away forever.

Bibliography

Writings

Bauer, Bruno (1840), *Kritik der evangelischen Geschichte des Johannes*, Bremen: Carl Schünemann.
— (1974) (first edn 1841), *Kritik der evangelischen Geschichte der Synoptiker*, Volumes 1–2, Hildesheim: Georg Olms.
— (1989) (first edn 1841), *Die Posaune des jüngsten Gerichts über Hegel den Atheisten und Antichristen. Ein Ultimatum*, trans. Lawrence S. Stepelevich, *The Trumpet of the Last Judgement Against Hegel the Atheist and Antichrist. An Ultimatum*, Lewiston: Edward Mellen Press.
— (1972) (first edn 1842), *Die gute Sache der Freiheit und meine eigene Angelegenheit*, Aalen: Scientia.
— (1958) (first edn 1843), *Die Judenfrage*, trans. Helen Lederer, *The Jewish Problem*, Cincinnati: Hebrew Union College Press.
— (1989) (first edn 1843), *Das entdeckte Christenthum. Eine Erinnerung an das achtzehnte Jahrhundert und ein Beitrag zur Krisis des neunzehnten*, Aalen: Scientia.
— (1969) (first edn 1844), *Briefwechsel zwischen Bruno Bauer und Edgar Bauer während der Jahre 1839–1842 aus Bonn und Berlin*, Aalen: Scientia Verlag.
Cieszkowski, August (1842), *Prolegomena zur Historiosophie*, Berlin: Veit.
— (1979), *Selected Writings of August Cieszkowski*, trans. and ed. with an Introductory Essay by André Liebich, Cambridge: Cambridge University Press. (Contains a comprehensive Bibliographic Essay.)
Engels, Friedrich (1941), *Ludwig Feuerbach and the Outcome of Classical German Philosophy* (trans.), New York: Progress Publishers.
Feuerbach, Ludwig (1957), *The Essence of Christianity*, trans. George Eliot, New York: Harper and Row.
— (1966), *Principles of the Philosophy of the Future*, trans. M. H. Vogel, New York: Bobbs-Merrill.
— (1874), *Briefwechsel und Nachlass*, ed. K. Grün, Heidelberg.
— (1980), *Thoughts on Death and Immortality*, trans. James A. Massey, Berkeley: University of California Press.
— (1972), *The Fiery Brook: Selected Writings of Ludwig Feuerbach*, trans. Zawar Hanfi, New York: Doubleday.
— (1970), *Ludwig Feuerbach: Kleinere Schriften II*, ed. W. Schuffenhauer, Berlin, 1970.

— (1994) *Gesammelte Werke*, vols 1–12, 17–18, ed. W. Schuffenhauer, Berlin: Akademie Verlag.
— (1954), *Briefe von und an Hegel*, ed. J. Hoffmeister. Hamburg.
Hess, Moses (1980), (first edn 1837), *Die heilige Geschichte der Menschheit*, Hildesheim: Gerstenberg.
Ruge, Arnold (ed.) (1843), *Anekdota zur neuesten deutschen Philosophie und Publizistick*, two vols, Zurich: Winterthur.
Stirner, Max (1845), *Der Einzige und sein Eigenthum*, Leipzig: Otto Wiegand.
— (1976), *Kleinere Schriften*, ed. John Henry Mackay, Berlin: Bernhard Zack, 1914; reprinted Stuttgart: F. Frommann.
— (1995), *The Ego and His Own*, trans. Steven Byington, Cambridge, Cambridge University Press.
Strauss, David Friedrich (1835–6), *Das Leben Jesu kritisch bearbeitet*, two vols, Tübingen.
— (1956), *The Life of Jesus Critically Considered*, trans. George Eliot, Philadelphia: Fortress Press.

Note: translations, most new, of all of the major Young Hegelians, including first translations of selected works by Bruno Bauer, Edgar Bauer, Moses Hess, Arnold Ruge, Karl Schmidt and Max Stirner, can be found in *Young Hegelianism: An Anthology*, ed. with Introduction by Lawrence S. Stepelevich, Cambridge: Cambridge University Press, 1983. Reprinted: Atlantic Highlands: Humanities Press, 1997.

References and further reading

Barnikol, Ernst (1972), *Bruno Bauer: Studien und Materialien*, ed. Peter Reimer and Hans-Martin Sass, Assen: Van Gorcum.
Brazill, William J. (1970), *The Young Hegelians*, New Haven: Yale University Press.
Hook, Sidney (1962), *From Hegel to Marx*, Ann Arbor: University of Michigan Press.
Kamenka, Eugene (1970), *The Philosophy of Ludwig Feuerbach*, London: RKP.
Liebich, Andre (1979), *Between Ideology and Utopia: The Politics and Philosophy of August Cieszkowski*, Dordrecht: D. Reidel.

Löwith, Karl (1967), *From Hegel to Nietzsche: The Revolution in Nineteenth-Century Thought*, trans. David E. Green, Garden City, New York: Holt, Rinehart and Winston.

Mah, Harold (1987), *The End of Philosophy, the Origin of 'Ideology'*, Berkeley: University of California Press.

Rosen, Zvi (1977), *Bruno Bauer and Karl Marx*, The Hague: Martinus Nijhoff.

Stepelevich, Lawrence S. (ed.) (1983), *The Young Hegelians: An Anthology*, Cambridge, Cambridge University Press, 1983. (Reprinted: Humanities Press, 1997.)

Towes, John E. (1980), *Hegelianism: The Path Toward Dialectical Humanism, 1805–1841*, Cambridge, Cambridge University Press.

Wartofsky, Marx W. (1977), *Feuerbach*, Cambridge, Cambridge University Press.

MARX AND THE END OF PHILOSOPHY

Andrew Collier

Various notions of the end of philosophy have been involved in different modern philosophies, to the extent that one might say that it is a characteristic of the philosophy of the modern period to be haunted by its own end. As Anthony Manser said in his inaugural lecture *The End of Philosophy: Marx and Wittgenstein*, 'The mark of modern philosophy, and of any worthy of the name, is self-doubt' (Manser, 1973, p. 4). This characteristic end-consciousness has, however, taken at least two distinct and incompatible forms – the claim to have arrived at final truth, and empiricist scepticism about metaphysics. Thus, far removed from the self-doubt which Manser praises, there have been those such as Spinoza and Kant who thought that they had discovered the one true philosophy, so that once their own insights had been fully worked out, philosophy could shut up shop and rejoice in its success. But although some recent writers talk as if such a view was implicit in any pursuit of truth by philosophy or even by science, it was, in fact, well known by Marx's time – to Hegel and the empiricists alike – that the pursuit of truth is endless, getting closer, but never arriving at a final or irreversible state of knowledge. Engels is quite explicit about this (see, for example, his *Ludwig Feuerbach and the End of Classical German Philosophy* [Marx and Engels, 1968, p. 598]), which is worth pointing out since he is often accused of using the term 'scientific socialism' to claim precisely the sort of final knowledge that he regarded as alien to both science and socialism.

On the other hand, empiricism has generally taught that philosophy in the traditional sense of metaphysics has always been nonsense, and should be replaced by empirical enquiries. Hume, for instance, believed his own work to be just such an empirical enquiry. If, unlike some later positivists, he still called it 'philosophy', that was only because the distinction between science and philosophy had not yet been registered lexically: Newton, for example, was a 'natural philosopher'.

If Spinoza and Kant have no recent successors in their claim to have solved the problems of philosophy, Hume has many. Within and without Marxism, the 'end of philosophy' has been proclaimed a number of times in different contexts in the last two centuries, most notably in the various forms of positivism. It haunts analytical philosophy as the view held in different forms by Moore and Wittgenstein that the history of philosophy is a history of pseudo-problems, and the only legitimate practice of philosophy is the exposure of their false nature, making them disappear as problems. Another version of the end of philosophy is associated with Heidegger, although here it may be no more than a verbal matter, since 'thinking about being' survives.

In Marx we can find not one but two conceptions of the end of philosophy, one in his early (pre-1845) works, and one in those of 1845 itself. Philosophical concerns are peripheral to Marx's later writing, as one would expect if philosophy really had met its end in the earlier works. Yet, in certain later texts Marx continued to practise philosophy, as did Engels; and Marx, at least, probably has a higher reputation among philosophers than among economists and sociologists, whose subject matter is more central to his mature work. Furthermore, in the one hundred years since Engels's death, 'Marxist philosophy' has had a fruitful and diverse history.

In the first two sections of this article, I will look at the two conceptions of the end of philosophy that can be found in Marx's work; in the third I will look at Marx's later ventures into philosophy, and ask why it is that, however many deaths philosophy dies, it never seems to lie down.

The end of philosophy as its fulfilment

Implicit in the early (pre-1845) works of Marx, and occasionally explicit in them, is the idea of communism as the realisation of philosophy. Philosophy, it was claimed, would find its end not only in the sense of its termination, and not at all in the sense of its being left behind as a mistake now corrected, but in the sense that it would realise its destiny and be surpassed by being fulfilled. Certainly, in this view, it ceases to exist as a separate activity, but it finds its *aufhebung* in the Hegelian sense – at once its surpassing and its preservation – in the practice of human emancipation. This is clearest in the 'Critique of Hegel's Philosophy of Right', where Marx tells us that the practical political party in Germany is right to demand the negation of philosophy but wrong to think that this can be done by leaving philosophy behind: '*You cannot transcend [aufheben] philosophy without realizing [verwirklichen] it*' (Marx, 1975, p. 250). At the same time he crites the theoretical political party because '*It believed that it could realize philosophy without transcending it*' (ibid.). The latter cannot be done because previous philosophy 'that is philosophy as philosophy' belongs essentially to the world that is being criticised and struggled against in its name; philosophy is that world's complement, 'even though an ideal complement'.

The only reason given why the former cannot be done – why philosophy cannot be transcended without being realised – is that 'the real seed of life of the German people has up to now flourished inside its cranium' (ibid., pp. 249–50).

We therefore need to place this whole concept of the simultaneous realisation and transcending of philosophy in the context of what can be called the 'German exceptionalism' of Marx's view in this text. Germany's route to revolution is seen as different from that of other bourgeois countries. Germany was bypassed by the normal process which England and France went through at different times and to different degrees, whereby one class after another – each less privileged and more radical than the last – took over in the name of universal emancipation, and carried the process a little further, but then stopped, bound by its own limitations. In the end the process was halted and counter-revolution set in; but at this stage Germany, excluded from all the others, did participate. It had a counter-revolution (the settlement of 1815) without a revolution. Yet at the level of philosophy, Germany accomplished all the advances it failed to make in politics and economics. Its philosophy reflects the reality across the Rhine, and reflects its own reality only as a substitute for real advances. When the next revolution strikes, Germany will not proceed by stages in the normal way, but will arrive immediately at the full emancipation already implicit in its philosophy. The intermediate classes were too backward and compromised to succeed in taking power for a time; all will be emancipated by the class with radical chains, the proletariat: 'Just as philosophy finds its *material* weapons in the proletariat, so the proletariat finds its *intellectual* weapons in philosophy' (ibid., p. 257).

Marx does not spell out exactly what philosophy and the proletariat are to gain from each other in this fusion of theory and practice. Presumably the proletariat is to acquire a justification in universal terms for its project of self-emancipation. Philosophy must be seen as, in some sense, about human emancipation in order for this project to be a realisation of it.

What is the philosophy referred to here? We need to consider the relation of three philosophies to human emancipation: Hegel's philosophy, which Marx tends to regard as the culmination of the history of philosophy, and is presumably the 'philosophy as philosophy' which has to be transcended;

Marx's critique of Hegel; Marx's own humanist philosophy of the 1844 texts.

Hegelian philosophy

Hegel's political philosophy defends the constitutional state – a monarchy limited by the rule of law and a bicameral parliament. There were already several constitutional states, although Hegel's Prussia was not among them. This fact explains Marx's comment that philosophy in Germany merely celebrated what had already been realised abroad, but if this philosophy was to unite with any movement in Germany, it could only be with the moderate wing of the liberal bourgeoisie.

However, there is another aspect to Hegel's political philosophy, an aspect which could be regarded as reactionary, yet is potentially critical and even revolutionary: his critique of existing constitutional states for the egoism of civil society and the poverty that they inevitably cause in their midst. To offset this, Hegel wanted to preserve 'reactionary' institutions like the guilds, but whatever the traditional sources of this corporatism, it had a potential for a communitarian critique of merely electoral democracy – a potential which was to be realised in Marx's later remarks about 'the real will of the co-operative' replacing the supposed will of the people (in his 'Conspectus of Bakunin's *Statism and Anarchy*', Marx, 1974, p. 336); in Lenin's theory of soviet democracy; and in Guild Socialism.

Although Hegel finds no satisfactory solution to the poverty born of capitalist societies, his posing of the problem invites an immanent critique such as Marx provides. This takes us to the critique of Hegel.

Marx's critique of Hegel

The critique actually accomplished by Marx (for example, in his *Critique of Hegel's Philosophy of the State*) is in some measure a reversion from Hegel to Rousseau, and even misses some of Hegel's more fruitful ideas about atomism and organic community. However, the underlying basis of Marx's project is the very idea essential to Hegel's philosophy of history: that history progressively widens the scope of freedom, from the ancient despotisms in which

only one was free, through the Greek and Roman republics where some were free to the modern state in which all are free. Marx, of course, knew that all were not free in the modern state. Hegel's belief that universal freedom had already been attained rests on some highly questionable metaphysical assumptions but the ideal of universal freedom could be set against the reality of exploitation as a projected goal of history. It could at once be recognised that Hegel's philosophy established universal freedom only in the world of ideas and was hence a sort of sublimation of, and alternative to, real human emancipation; and the real fulfilment of this ideal could be projected. Philosophy is at once criticised as mystification and de-mystified as a displaced demand for real liberation. What Marx says of religion can be applied to philosophy: '*Religious* suffering is at one and the same time the *expression* of real suffering and a protest against real suffering' (Marx, 1975, p. 244).

This enables Marx to defend proletarian emancipation in terms accepted by the official philosophy of German society of the time. This gives a significant polemical advantage, even if only an *ad hominem* one. (Marx may, of course, have been exaggerating the extent to which German culture was pervaded by Hegelianism, but that is a different matter.) However, it does all depend on the society that he is criticising accepting Hegelian philosophy. A different critique would have to be produced – as no doubt it could be – in a society which accepted utilitarianism as its justification for bourgeois rule.

Furthermore, any critique which at once exposes the ideals of a society as a mystification arising out of its own defects, and criticises the realities of that society in terms of those ideals, is in an ambiguous position. Is it accepting the ideals even though they are a mystification and criticising the society from their standpoint? Or is it primarily criticising the ideals themselves as a mystification, and the society only secondarily as a society which produces mystifications? Or is it a mere *ad hominem* criticism against partisans of that society for inconsistency with their own ideals – a criticism which does not necessarily imply any ideal of its own, apart from consistency?

Among later Marxists, Herbert Marcuse has perpetuated the idea that Hegel's philosophy is a project of human emancipation in a mystified form (a metaphysical sublimation – in Freud's sense – of a political project). (For further information on this see especially his *Reason and Revolution*.) However, this has led to two questionable features of Marcuse's philosophy: a nostalgia for Hegelian philosophy despite its mystified nature, since one cannot de-sublimate other philosophies and find a project of human emancipation in the same way; and a round-aboutness, in that it criticises bourgeois society on the basis of one ideal reflection of it, rather than on the basis of its own real contradictions.

We have to ask whether the de-mystification or de-sublimation of Hegel's philosophy has any universal validity as the theoretical starting point for human emancipation, or whether it is merely the contingent starting point of Marx's own intellectual trajectory, with apologetic significance for his time and place. The latter is suggested by the reference to the life of the German people flourishing in its cranium; the former by Marx's remarks in the same text on the humanist basis of philosophy. Immediately after his famous statement that 'theory also becomes a material force once it has gripped the masses' (ibid., p. 251), Marx specifies the nature of the theory that he has in mind:

> To be radical is to grasp things by the root. But for man the root is man himself . . . The criticism of religion ends with the doctrine that *for man the supreme being is man*, and thus with the *categorical imperative to overthrow all conditions* in which man is a debased, enslaved, neglected and contemptible being. (ibid.)

But this humanism is no longer Hegel's philosophy or even a de-mystification of it; it is an independent theory of man or humankind (*Mensch* in German – no sexism can be read into the original of this term)

Marx's humanism

In one text, the longest and most celebrated of Marx's early works, the *Economic and Philosophical Manuscripts of 1844*, he pursues this line of theory, but, in doing so, he brings himself to the brink of his second theory of the end of philosophy. For this theory of humankind, although it is in fact itself an exercise in philosophy rather than an attempt to end

it, is in intention an empirical account of the essence and potential of humankind. It is but one step from this to the transition from philosophy to the empirical study of society. That step is taken in the sixth thesis on Feuerbach: 'The essence of man is no abstraction inherent in each single individual. In its reality it is the ensemble of the social relations' (Marx and Engels, 1976, p. 7).

In passing from the study of humankind in the abstract to the study of the people of particular societies, Marx also passes from philosophy to social science.

The end of philosophy as the turn to social science

This passing from philosophy to social science introduces the second conception of the end of philosophy: not its fulfilment, but its replacement by science. The best starting point for a discussion of the second conception of the end of philosophy is one of Marx's most quoted remarks, his eleventh thesis on Feuerbach: 'The philosophers have only *interpreted* the world in various ways; the point, however, is to *change* it' (Marx and Engels, 1976, p. 8).

The first comment that springs to mind on this celebrated thesis is that, if it is read as accusing philosophers of doing no more than interpreting the world, as not even intending to change it, then it is grossly unfair. Philosophers from Plato to Bacon and Rousseau, and, nearer to Marx's own time, Bentham and Fichte, have tried hard to change the world in various directions. Some have been thought to have succeeded. Carlyle remarked of Rousseau that he had written a book containing nothing but ideas; the second edition was bound in the hides of those who laughed at the first. Although Marx would not, of course, have accepted the view of his friend Heinrich Heine that Robespierre was only the bloody instrument in the hand of Rousseau's philosophy – for the relation between class forces and not ideas made the French Revolution – he could hardly accuse Rousseau of being content with interpreting the world. Indeed, he contrasts Rousseau favourably with Proudhon, writing of 'the simple moral sense which always kept a Rousseau, for instance, far from even the semblance of compromise with the powers that be' (letter to Schweitzer, in Marx, 1956, p. 228).

Rousseau on the other hand, could be criticised, for utopianism; that is, precisely for failing to base his prescriptions for changing the world on an adequate understanding of the existing world. And the point that, whatever their intentions, philosophers and indeed theorists of any sort have not played the leading role in history, while it is certainly entailed by Marx's mature conception of history, is not a criticism of philosophers, and is not the point he is making in the eleventh thesis on Feuerbach. To understand this thesis we need to recognise, as background, that Marx held that history does not march on its head, that class forces are more deeply explanatory than ideas. However, this is not the point he is making here. Here he is criticising particular theorists, not putting theory in general in its (honourable but limited) place.

It is likely that Marx's judgement of past philosophers here is unduly influenced by his Hegelian training. Of course, he says 'philosophers' in the plural, and 'various ways', and so cannot only be referring to Hegel; but it is very likely that he saw the whole history of philosophy as reflected in the Hegelian mirror, and applied to all of it the words of Hegel: 'When philosophy paints its grey in grey, then has the shape of life grown old. By philosophy's grey in grey it cannot be rejuvenated but only understood. The owl of Minerva spreads its wings only with the falling of the dusk' (Hegel, 1952, p. 13). So understood, philosophy could only interpret, not change, things, and the eleventh thesis could be seen as making a similar point to Kierkegaard's remark that while it is true that life can only be understood backwards, it can only be lived forwards – although Marx, as we shall see, would not have accepted the possible Kierkegaardian inference that understanding is of no use for living.

However, it is useful to consider the eleventh thesis as marking a break in Marx's own thought, which, as Marx was later to say of *The German Ideology*, was designed to 'settle accounts with our erstwhile philosophical conscience' ('Preface to Critique of Political Economy', Marx and Engels, 1968, p. 183). What change in Marx's conception of his own theoretical work is marked by this epigram?

First of all, there are two possible interpretations, which the words could quite well bear, and which have occasionally been read into them, but which can be shown to be mistaken from other things that Marx said and did.

The first misreading is that Marx is contrasting interpreting the world in general (which would include social science, as well as philosophy) with changing it, and disparaging the former as unhelpful towards the latter which he sees as the important thing. This is a perfectly natural reading of the words of the eleventh thesis, and has always been popular among left-wing students who renounce their studies in favour of a life of political action. But, of course, Marx did nothing of this kind. He was as much a theoretician after writing these words as before, and, indeed, spent most of the rest of his life in the British Museum, doing research for *Capital*. This style of life was not just based on personal predilections but reflected his considered attitude to the relation between theory and politics. Annenkov recounts Marx's quarrel with Weitling:

> Marx's sarcastic speech boiled down to this: to rouse the population without giving them any firm, well-thought-out reasons for their activity would be simply to deceive them. The raising of fantastic hopes just spoken of, Marx continued, led only to the final ruin and not to the saving of the sufferers. To call to the workers without any strictly scientific ideas or constructive doctrine, especially in Germany, was equivalent to vain dishonest play at preaching which assumed on the one side an inspired prophet and on the other only gaping asses. (in McLellan, 1973, pp. 156–7)

For Marx, understanding the world is not in general an alternative to changing it, but a prerequisite and reason for changing it.

The second misreading is that Marx was disparaging those philosophies that only interpreted the world (conceived – wrongly as we have seen – as comprising the whole history of earlier philosophy) in favour of a new kind of philosophy which would change the world. To understand what is wrong with this reading we must turn to Marx and Engels' longer work of the same year (1845) as the theses

The German Ideology. This will also give us some idea of how we *should* interpret the eleventh thesis.

Far from proclaiming a new, world-changing philosophy, a striking fact about *The German Ideology* is that it appears to disparage philosophy as a whole. Here, if anywhere in the Marx-Engels corpus, is the idea of an end of philosophy not in the sense of a fulfilment or a Hegelian overcoming-while-preserving (*aufhebung*) of philosophy, but a setting aside and leaving behind of philosophy as a whole, to attend to something different. That 'something' is not in the first instance political practice, but empirical knowledge of the world, and that practical interaction with the world which yields such knowledge. 'When things are seen in this way, as they really are and happened, every profound philosophical problem is resolved . . . quite simply into an empirical fact' (Marx and Engels, 1976, p. 39). Here the contrast of philosophy and fact is at it starkest. A similar point has been made with more subtlety, and a humble seat reserved for dethroned philosophy, in the following passage.

> Where speculation ends, where real life starts, there consequently begins real, positive science, the expounding of the practical activity, of the practical processes of development of men. Empty phrases about consciousness end, and real knowledge has to take their place. When the reality is described, a self-sufficient philosophy loses its medium of existence. At the best its place can only be taken by a summing-up of the most general results, abstractions which are derived from the observation of the historical development of men. These abstractions in themselves, divorced from real history, have no value whatsoever. They can only serve to facilitate the arrangement of historical material, to indicate the sequence of its separate strata. But they by no means afford a recipe or schema, as does philosophy, for neatly trimming the epochs of history. (ibid., p. 37)

The last sentence suggests again that it is Hegel's philosophy that they have in mind. Later, Marx and Engels become even ruder about philosophy:

> One has to 'leave philosophy aside' . . . one has to leap out of it and devote oneself like an ordinary man to the study of actuality. . . . Philosophy and the study of the actual world have the same relation to one another as onanism and sexual love. (ibid., p. 236)

In all these passages, philosophy is seen as *a priori*, speculative 'knowledge', which is therefore not knowledge of the real world at all, but an imaginary substitute for it. The contrast philosophy/knowledge of the world echoes positivistic conceptions of the end of philosophy. For Comtean positivism in the nineteenth century, philosophy or metaphysics was a stage in the history of human enlightenment, a stage which had replaced religion but was itself to be replaced by empirical science. For the logical positivists in the twentieth century, whatever ideas cannot be empirically verified have no meaning; philosophy loses even its historical role and becomes a mass of nonsense.

> The correct method in philosophy would really be the following: to say nothing except what can be said, that is, propositions of natural science – that is, something that has nothing to do with philosophy – and then, whenever someone else wanted to say something metaphysical, to demonstrate to him that he had failed to give a meaning to certain signs in his propositions. Although it would not be satisfying to the other person – he would not have the feeling that we were teaching him philosophy – *this* method would be the only strictly correct one. (Wittgenstein, 1961, 6.53)

This does not seem to differ essentially from the position maintained in *The German Ideology*, except that, in that work, the residual role reserved for philosophy is that of summing up the most general results of the sciences, whereas for Wittgenstein it is that of exposing other philosophy as nonsense – and that, for Marx and Engels, social science has the same status as natural science. It appears that, for Marx and Engels at this point in their careers, philosophy contrasts with the simple light of day, to which science belongs. This is echoed by another saying of Wittgenstein's: 'Don't think, look!' It depends on a belief in the continuity of science with everyday perception of the world. In Marx's later works, when he had undertaken, and not merely projected, serious social scientific work, he did not retain the opinion that knowing the world is quite so easy. For instance, in the sections on fetishism in *Capital*, it is clear that he thinks both that our spontaneous economic consciousness is bound to be mystified, and also that scientific demystification will have all the appearance of metaphysics. However, in *Capital* as in *The German Ideology*, it is not philosophy but social science which provides the understanding of the social world that is a condition of changing it.

This much is clear: it is not a new philosophy that *The German Ideology* offers, but a non-philosophical theory, a project of empirical social science. The eleventh thesis can be read, in accordance with this, as complaining that the philosophical way of interpreting the world (which failed to reach the real world) provided no grounds for, or aid in, changing it, whereas the social scientific way of interpreting it (which does reach the real world) does provide grounds for, and aid in, changing it. In order to see why this is so, and whether it means the end – in the sense of the demise – of philosophy, it will be helpful to look at two related aspects of the theory of ideology in *The German Ideology*, and their application to philosophy.

The first aspect is that ideology, as a form of false consciousness, is seen as characterised by an inversion of the true relation between ideas and the world that they are about.

> Consciousness can never be anything else than conscious being, and the being of men is their actual life-process. If in all ideology men and their relations appear upside down as in a *camera obscura*, this phenomenon arises just as much from their historical life-process as the inversion of objects on the retina does from their physical life-process. (Marx and Engels, 1976, p. 36)

Our real practical interaction with the world gives rise to ideas, and in so far as those ideas have a chance of being true, they are about the world that gave rise to them. In ideology, ideas are typically seen as causally prior in some way to what they are about. For example, in Hegel's theory of history, the material aspects of any given culture are expressions of its leading idea. Now, philosophy (or at least, modern philosophy) seems particularly prone to this kind of error. For Descartes, the mind is more certain and more easily known than the body; for Berkeley, physical objects, things, exist only in the mind; for Kant, the mind imposes form on the empirical world; and we may add, for much recent philosophy, discourse constructs reality. Perhaps Marx would go further and say (echoing Hegel but inverting the value judgement) that philosophy is essentially idealism in this sense. Only as long as philosophers believe in the autonomy or primacy of thought can they go on 'proving' things by pure argument about how the world must be, without actually venturing outside the seminar room. The conceptual analysis that has been dominant in Anglo-American philosophy in the second half of the twentieth century is no exception here. A mere analysis of concepts is supposed to provide knowledge that is more certain than mere empirical knowledge. Yet these 'conceptual truths' are not mere tautologies, as they should be if they are true by virtue of logic. They are often substantive and contentious claims: for example, that reasons for actions cannot be their causes, that the human personality cannot survive death, or that there cannot be any question of cure for a mental illness. If philosophers are to escape Marx and Engels's strictures, they will have to adopt a different style of argument.

But now we come to the second aspect of ideology, which goes some way towards explaining the first: it comes with the division of labour, and in particular, the division of mental and manual labour:

> thoughts and ideas acquire an independent existence in consequence of the personal circumstances and relations of individuals acquiring independent existence. We have shown that exclusive, systematic occupation with these thoughts on the part of ideologists and philosophers, and hence the systematisation of these thoughts, is a consequence of division of labour. (ibid., pp. 446–7)

Once there is a section of society whose business is ideas, three things happen. In the first place, ideas really acquire a different sort of efficacy from what they had before; once there are lawyers, legal ideas have a powerful lobby to make them effective, and so they become more than the reflection of social relations that they would be without that lobby. Second, out of class and professional pride, professional ideologists claim for ideas a greater efficacy than they have. And third, those released from manual labour cease to interact in their working life with anything other than ideas, and so can very easily become prey to the illusion that there is nothing outside discourse, and so on. Belief in the primacy or autonomy of ideas is a natural effect of lack of practical interaction with the world. Practice, on the other hand, makes people realists. Everyone is a realist about the object of their own labour, but we easily become idealists about the objects of other people's. Practice is both the cause and the criterion of truth in human thinking.

> The question whether objective truth can be attributed to human thinking is not a question of theory but is a practical question. Man must prove the truth, that is, the reality and power, the this-worldliness of his thinking in practice. The dispute over the reality or non-reality of thinking which isolates itself from practice is a purely scholastic question. (Marx, in Marx and Engels, 1976, p. 6).

To return to the eleventh thesis: in the light of *The German Ideology*, it must be read as rejecting philosophy because it is not objective knowledge (knowledge of how the world is, independently of our thought about it), and objective knowledge is required to be the foundation of an emancipatory political practice.

This immediately raises the (philosophical) question of how objective knowledge can motivate action, for not only much philosophy, but also much social science, is premised on the assumption that objectivity implies neutrality and facts cannot imply values. If one wanted to defend an 'end of philosophy' version of Marxism, though, one could reply that Marx does not need to provide a general philosophical answer to the question of how objective facts can imply values and motivate action, he only needs to show how this occurs, by providing an objective analysis of society that actually does give reasons for change, not in addition to, but by virtue

of, its objective content. And what does Marx's *Capital* purport to be if not such an analysis?

What possible role could philosophy still have, if one accepts Marx and Engels's critique? Any 'self-sufficient' philosophy, and any philosophy that depends on maintaining the primacy of ideas over reality, has none; but it is possible that some sort of underlabouring philosophy, working on problems that the practice of social science has caused to emerge, might have a modest role. To say whether this is necessary and to see what form it could take, we need to discuss the philosophical problems arising out of Marx's own social scientific work, and Marx's own response to them.

First, though, I want to mention the views of Engels in his later writings, which remain relatively close to the 'positivism' of *The German Ideology*, but which are less purely destructive. This is necessary because Marx did not explicitly discuss the status of philosophy again, and there is every reason to believe that he assented to Engels's views on the matter.

It has often been noted that, in the history of philosophy, one area of knowledge after another that was previously part of philosophy has become an independent science. Engels suggests in the Introduction to *Anti-Dühring* and towards the end of *Ludwig Feuerbach and the End of Classical German Philosophy*, that this process is now complete: Marx has inaugurated the science of history; and the residual role of philosophy in showing the interconnectedness of the distinct sciences can now be undertaken by the sciences themselves. So far this looks like pure positivism, although *Ludwig Feuerbach* also features a reprise of the fulfilment of philosophy view: philosophy is seen as coming to an end with Hegel and the German proletariat is credited with being the unique inheritor of the critical tradition of German philosophy. But Engels goes on to say:

> That which still survives, independently, of all earlier philosophy is the science of thought and its laws – formal logic and dialectics. Everything else is subsumed in the positive science of nature and history. (Engels, 1969, p. 36)

Formal logic itself has since become an independent science, even though for historical reasons (and some would claim for other reasons, too) it is still generally taught in departments of philosophy. Much has also been written about in what sense it is a science of the laws of thought (normative rules or psychological laws, for example). But what of dialectics, which is obviously closer to Engels's heart?

Engels wrote substantially about the 'laws of dialectics', and it is generally among his less illuminating writing. The laws do not much resemble the laws of nature or of logic, and are more like rules of thumb for thinking about nature and society, pointing out types of explanation with examples in a wide variety of subjects, but no unifying theory. They generally have to do with the interconnectedness of things and their developmental tendencies; they can best be seen as warnings against the errors of atomistic and static thinking – warnings which are justified by the history of modern thought, but they comprise a style of thought rather than a substantive set of ideas.

Dialectic in an older sense might be more worthy of exploration: thinking our way through contradictions that force themselves upon us in life or in scientific work. As soon as Marx left behind philosophy and started trying to uncover the economic laws of motion of capitalist society, such philosophical problems forced themselves on him again. In the next section I will turn to these.

The need for philosophy in the work of social science

As a preface to these issues, it will be useful to look at one account of what Marx, Engels and later Marxist philosophers were doing when they philosophised. This account aims to preserve the notion that they were doing something consistent with the end of philosophy.

It might be thought that while their own standpoint had passed beyond the end of philosophy, they were still being attacked on philosophical grounds by those who had not caught up with the end of philosophy and they had to reply. However, in answering philosophical objections they were compelled to fight on their opponents' ground, and do philosophy; but to do it with the irony of one who knows they are doing something obsolete but nevertheless condescends to play the game. On the face of it, this is not an entirely implausible account of the philosophising of Engels, Plekhanov or Lenin, which, for the most part, has the nature of polemic against (minor) philosophers who thought that they could undermine Marxian social science philosophically (Dühring, Mikhailovsky, the empirio-criticists).

However, if philosophy had really been superseded, it would have been quite possible to answer these critics without venturing on to philosophical ground. Suppose, for example, that someone brings against Marx's *Capital* the philosophical complaint that exploitation is an evaluative concept yet Marx claims scientific status for it, and that this is incoherent because science deals with facts, and values cannot be derived from facts (by 'Hume's Law'). One way of replying would be to present a philosophical case against 'Hume's Law', such as Roy Bhaskar does, for example, in his account of explanatory critiques (explanations which criticise not in addition to, but in virtue of, their explanatory power), in *Scientific Realism and Human Emancipation*. However, as I have suggested, this is not the only way. One could simply point to Marx's account of exploitation and say: where does anything that is not objective enter into Marx's definition of exploitation? If nowhere, then this is potentially a scientific concept. Yet read *Capital* and you will see that this concept does have evaluative implications. We thus have a counter-example to 'Hume's Law', and so, unless you can point to a flaw in Marx's argument, 'Hume's Law' stands refuted. It does not need to be criticised philosophically. Here we may follow Wittgenstein's advice 'don't think, look!' Pointing to something in the (social) sciences resolves the issue without philosophical reflection.

But this is not all that Marxist philosophers do; they also reply philosophically. That they do so is not, I think, a mistake, but indicates that in some cases at least the philosophical critics of Marxism have grasped real problems about the nature of social science, which have to be resolved philosophically rather than by simply pointing to examples in the practice of the social sciences. As Bhaskar puts it: 'It has often been claimed, and perhaps more often felt, that the problems of philosophy have been solved. And yet, like the proverbial frog at the bottom of the beer mug, they have always reappeared' (Bhaskar, 1978, p. 6). When Marx returns to philosophy after the break of 1845, it is generally in the context of what are often called texts on method: the 1857 Introduction, the Prefaces to *Capital*, and, perhaps, the notes on the German economist Adolf Wagner. The motive is to find how one should proceed in a social science, for the answer to this question is neither obvious nor uncontentious. It is not enough to turn from the speculations of philosophy to 'the great book of the world'. For 'scientific truth is always a paradox, if judged by everyday experience, which catches only the delusive appearance of things' (Marx, in Marx and Engels, 1968, p. 209).

In addition to this opacity of the surface of things, which affects all the sciences, the social sciences are affected by class ideology, and the controversy between different methods may not be politically innocent. For instance, an empiricist methodology that simply observes and records statistics systematically misses the deeper explanations of phenomena, which may be the crucial thing if one wants to change the world. Yet experiments, by which the natural sciences go beyond appearances to discover underlying mechanisms, are not available to the social sciences. Marx approaches these problems through two brief discussions, in both of which the notion of abstraction figures prominently. In the 1857 Introduction (see Marx, 1973, pp. 100ff.) Marx points out that it is no use starting with a concrete entity like the population of a country, for the concept of the population is itself abstract, and abstract for the wrong reason; namely, because it tells you little about the concrete entity to which it refers. In order to have concrete knowledge of the population, we need to know about its component parts and their mutual relations, its substructures, and the forces and processes which combine to make it what it is. These are abstractions – mere aspects of a concrete whole, able to exist only as aspects of that whole, yet they really do exist and conjointly determine the nature of that whole: 'The concrete is concrete because it is the concentration of many determinations, hence unity of the diverse' (ibid., p. 101).

The task of social science is to unravel these diverse elements which go to make up the social whole; an experimental science could do this by experiments, which isolate particular forces or processes by holding others constant. Social science cannot do this: 'in the analysis of economic forms neither microscopes nor chemical reagents are of assistance. The power of abstraction must replace both' (Marx, 1976, p. 90). In other words, we must abstract in thought the various determinations which are concentrated in the concrete social whole, since we cannot isolate them experimentally as physics or chemistry would with the 'many determinations' that they study.

All this is not social science itself, but philosophical reflection on social science. The method is founded on an ontology: the theory that reality is neither an indivisible whole nor a collection of colliding atoms, but a complex of interacting forces. It is very likely that Marx arrived at this ontology by reflecting on the natural sciences; yet he is fully aware that the social sciences cannot imitate the experimental methods of the natural sciences – an awareness not shared by positivist social science.

Of course, these passages from the 1857 Introduction or the Preface to *Capital*, full of philosophical insight as they may be, are far from constituting a worked-out philosophy, but they do indicate the need for one, and the sort of philosophy that it needs to be. Do they therefore involve a reversal of the judgement made on philosophy in 1845? If we understand *The German Ideology* as claiming that there is no need for any study other than the empirical study of society, then they do. But they are in no way a reversion to the sort of philosophy that legislates in advance what may be found in the real world. Rather, they are a kind of philosophy that arises out of the study of the world, by asking questions about what the world must be like in order for us to study it in the ways that we do. If we are to explain a world in which nothing happens without cause, and yet what happens is diverse and unpredictable, we must explain it as a 'concentration of many determinations, hence unity of the diverse'. But what these many determinations are is an open question which only empirical research – armed with the 'power of abstraction' – can establish.

Thus, a way is pointed out for Marxist philosophy along a narrow ridge between the precipices of positivist rejection of philosophy on the one hand, and *a priori* speculation on the other. Marxist philosophers have not always found it easy to walk this ridge. Althusser in his search for Marxist philosophy thus turns, not to the early works, but to the philosophy implicit in *Capital* and occasionally explicit in prefatory methodological writings. One might therefore have expected him to arrive at a conception of philosophy as an underlabourer for social science rather than a legislator for it. Yet in his earlier writings, and above all in the essay on Marx's relation to Hegel, he treats Marx's philosophy as something Marx derived from his critique of Hegel and applied to economic subject matter to produce *Capital*. In this account philosophy comes first as a means of the production of social science but as we have seen, that is exactly the sort of philosophy that Marx turned away from in 1845. Philosophy certainly came first for Marx in a biographical sense but only after a temporary setting aside of philosophy was Marx able to discover another philosophy as something that was after all necessary to the practice of social science, and in particular to its strife with social pseudo-science.

Althusser came to recognise this and reject his earlier 'theoreticism' in 'Lenin and Philosophy' and other writings from that period (Althusser, 1971), in which philosophy does figure as an underlabourer. However, he did not walk the narrow ridge for long. He crossed to the positivist precipice, although his own 'end of philosophy' has a post-modernist style

rather than a positivist one (see Althusser, 1976). Positivism, in teaching that science can replace philosophy, tacitly supposes that science speaks with one voice. This is, of course, a wholly unrealistic supposition in the social sciences, which are the site of endless struggle between rival theories. The post-modernist variant of positivism, if I may so describe it, recognises and even rejoices in this plurality, but, of course, one has to decide between conflicting theories with practical implications. The enquiry as to the grounds of such a decision is unavoidably philosophical; if it is said that we may decide on practical grounds, the question remains on what grounds we choose between conflicting practices. The claim, for example, that Marxism is more like a science than its rivals because it ventures depth explanations and so has the capacity to contradict appearances, and the claim that it is potentially emancipatory because it can expose illusory appearances, are philosophical claims. Without such claims – or, of course, the counter-claims of anti-Marxist philosophers – one is left floundering between the rival social sciences on offer, like a monkey in a supermarket.

It cannot be said that Marx theorised the nature of philosophy in his post-1845 writings but he gave us examples of reflection on the real conditions of possible work in social science. Such reflections do not themselves belong to social science; yet neither do they stand, as did the philosophy he rejected in 1845, as *a priori* substitutes or legislators for social science. They exemplify Marxist philosophy beyond the Marxian 'end of philosophy'.

Bibliography

References and further reading

Althusser, Louis (1971), *Lenin and Philosophy and Other Essays*, London: New Left Books.
— (1972), *Politics and History*, London: New Left Books.
— (1976), *Essays in Self-Criticism*, London: New Left Books.
Bhaskar, Roy (1978), *A Realist Theory of Science*, Hemel Hempstead: The Harvester Press.
— (1986), *Scientific Realism and Human Emancipation*, London: Verso.
Engels, Frederick (1969), *Anti-Dühring*, Moscow: Progress Publishers.

Hegel, Georg (1952), *The Philosophy of Right*, London: Oxford University Press.
McLellan, David (1973), *Karl Marx*, London and Basingstoke: Macmillan.
Manser, A. R. (1973), *The End of Philosophy: Marx and Wittgenstein*, Southampton: University of Southampton.
Marcuse, Herbert (1955), *Reason and Revolution*, London: Routledge and Kegan Paul.
Marx, Karl (1956), *The Poverty of Philosophy*, London: Lawrence and Wishart.
— (1973), *Grundrisse*, Harmondsworth: Penguin Books.
— (1974), *The First International and After*, Harmondsworth: Penguin Books.

— (1975), *Early Writings*, Harmondsworth: Penguin Books.

— (1976), *Capital*, Harmondsworth: Penguin Books.

Marx, Karl and Frederick Engels (1942), *Selected Works in Two Volumes*, London: Lawrence and Wishart.

— (1968), *Selected Works in One Volume*, London: Lawrence and Wishart.

— (1976), *Collected Works Volume 5*, London: Lawrence and Wishart.

Wittgenstein, Ludwig (1961), *Tractatus Logico-Philosophicus*, London: Routledge and Kegan Paul.

5.3

MARXISM AND LITERARY CRITICISM

Simon Dentith

Introduction

An unavoidable air of anachronism hovers over any discussion of Marxism and literary criticism at the end of the twentieth century. It is as though the fate of Marxism as an intellectual and philosophical enterprise was inextricably bound up with those officially Marxist East European regimes which are now receding into history. It is not only a matter of anachronism, like persisting with the idiom of scholasticism after the advent of Bacon and Newton; it is much more seriously a matter of intellectual delegitimation, a sense that a whole epoch has ended and with it, the idiom in which the debates of that epoch were conducted. But just as the historic social and economic problems with which Marxism has grappled over the last 150 years have not disappeared with the demise of 'actually existing socialism', the particular problems with which Marxist literary criticism sought to deal have not evaporated either. And, in seeking to address those problems, we are unavoidably confronted with the legacy of Marxist reflection on them.

If, on a global scale, the very notion of Marxism seems now fatally compromised as a result of its association with the discredited regimes of Eastern Europe, it is also true that it has been undermined from other directions where some of the apparently key suppositions of both classical and 'Western' Marxism have come under assault. Marx's fundamental challenge to literary theory remains his unequivocal materialist insistence on the priority of social being over consciousness. I shall take this emphasis as one which requires an answer to this question: how ought we to understand the social location of writing? The very possibility of a Marxist response to this question has been undermined from at least four directions, which I now list.

First, at the level of the immediate social context of writing – at the level, that is, of the richly plural and heterogeneous complexities of daily life – the characteristic Marxist insistence upon class as the primary social determinant seems inadequate. Reflecting the transformations wrought by feminist and post-colonial politics, a comparable recognition of the independent importance of the categories of gender, race and ethnicity is now demanded of any attempt to situate writing in the immediate and diverse actualities of social life.

Second, the attack upon the supposed 'grand narratives' of history has had Marxism, collaterally but explicitly, within its sights. The supposed teleology of Marxism, with its metanarrative of the march towards socialism, appears as equivalent to the grand legitimating narratives of bourgeois knowledge, where the truths of science are ordered under the heading of the advance of the human spirit (see Lyotand, 1984). With the collapse in belief of all such grand narratives, the attempt to link writing with the onward movement of humanity towards socialism must necessarily collapse also.

Third, the category of totality, made central to

Marxist aesthetics and philosophy by Lukács but implicit in all Marxist attempts to trace relations between different parts of the social 'whole', has come under powerful assault, at once political and philosophical. The philosophical attack has been to argue that, by virtue of the category of totality, formally distinct social phenomena have been falsely related, and indeed, that formally specific cultural activities and practices have been reduced to mere symptoms or epiphenomena of other realities – especially economic and social ones. Marxist reductionism, long a target of polemic, reappears under this heading as a symptom of a more profound problem, the very attempt to understand cultural phenomena in terms of a social totality. This is allied to a political critique, in which this supposed reductionism is held to justify the most directly authoritarian, not to say murderous, politics: there is a direct line from 'totality' to totalitarianism.

Fourth and finally, there is the question of realism. Classically, within the Marxist tradition, the priority of social being over consciousness has been entangled with the question of realism, so that a strong aesthetic of realism has been assumed (sometimes with disastrous 'administrative' consequences) to be the only appropriate aesthetic within which writers should work. It is exactly the aesthetic and epistemological claims of realism that have been challenged by some strands within recent post-modern thought, on grounds that are variously sceptical, anti-epistemological, or idealist.

In this article I will propose that a non-reductive account of writing is sustainable, which retains (a version at least) of Marx's insistence on the priority of social being, and which takes the force of these different critiques. I follow Jameson in assigning to different levels in the social order the different moments of interpretation (see Jameson, 1981, Ch. 1) but I differ from him in the importance I assign to the ultimate or foundational, 'mode of production', level. Instead, I wish to argue that writing can best be understood in terms of the necessary complexity and heteroglossia of the everyday social world from which it springs; that the cultural forms by which writing is shaped are themselves ways of mediating social relationships; and that to consider these general questions in this way is

to circumvent some of the arguments against the very possibility of Marxist literary criticism which have been listed above.

Class and the complexities of social life

I begin with that salutary recognition of the complexity of the social world and the fissures, divisions and contradictions that traverse it – a recognition that challenges the immediate insistence upon class that has characterised Marxist social, and hence literary, description. A historicising account of Marxism itself would surely recognise in the insistence upon class the massive legacy of the nineteenth century in which Marxism emerged, for it was in nineteenth-century Europe that class became such a prominent and unavoidable fact of social life. Even in the nineteenth century, however, or in the first half of the twentieth century, it could have been recognised that the complexities of social life could not be reduced to one axis of opposition only – that questions of gender, ethnicity, race, region, local and national affiliation, generation, religion, all contribute significantly to the constitutive diversity of a culture. Given other political priorities and demands, quite different faultlines have emerged as equally important contexts for the social location of writing than that of class alone.

There is an elementary Marxist point that the particular ways in which, for example, gender and racial divisions have been expressed, are dependent upon the differing economic and hence class circumstances in which they occur. However, this elementary point can be too readily extended so that the actualities of those other forms of division and repression are made to disappear as mere expressions of deeper underlying economic, and therefore class, realities. There is no need to make such an extension. To recognise that the modalities of gender and racial oppression are determined in part by economic exploitation is not to undervalue the separate reality of those forms of oppression. Rather, it is to enquire about the actual pressures and forces at work in any social order. The writing that emerges from any complex social order, and that is addressed to it, will nevertheless be fissured itself in multiple ways that do not require the critic to remind the reader constantly to assign one contradiction priority over the others.

The work of the Russian philosopher and literary critic Mikhail Bakhtin provides a suggestive account of the location of discourse in these diverse faultlines of socio-cultural life, in ways that are at least cognate with historical materialism. In the essay 'Discourse in the Novel', he coins the word 'heteroglossia' to characterize the diversity of actual languages that make up what can only be abstractly conceived as a unitary national language (Bakhtin, 1981, pp. 259–422). In this account, language is fissured in multiple ways, by regional and class dialect, by professional groups, by generations, even by the different occasions of its use. The multiple interactions of social life necessarily draw upon these different languages, constantly situating speaker and listener into particular relationships with each other and with the multiple social histories consequently invoked by their use of language. This account of language, however, serves as a prolegomenon to an account of the *novel*, for it is the novel that Bakhtin proposes as the form best situated to draw on the heteroglossia of actual language. In the novel's incorporation of the diversity of language into itself, the diverse contradictions, oppositions and micro-histories of social life make their reappearance. In this account, the formal and linguistic complexities of the novel re-enact the complexities of social life, so that its tensions and contradictions are reformed and reshaped in the novel's particular formal space. We can add that other forms of writing also, in their distinctive formal ways, draw upon, simplify from, or otherwise situate themselves in the heteroglossia of the social world, in ways that necessarily implicate the multiple complexities of social life.

The recognition of the diversity of socio-cultural life, then, need not challenge a materialist insistence of the priority of social life over consciousness. The problem here is not that there are too few determinants acting upon the cultural object, but that there are too many. Nor need this recognition challenge what may be thought to be the specifically Marxist form of historical materialism, which accords ultimate priority to class, although it certainly challenges any form of reductionism which reduces all the specific forms of social diversity to class alone.

The complexity of social life, finally, should not itself be taken as a given, but should be understood as the result of the cumulative layering of the historical process, retaining deposits and traces of distinct historical periods and modes of production, of distinct social and cultural forms of life, all co-existing, predominant, and subordinated in diverse ways.

Cultural objects and the inadequacy of 'grand narratives'

If a recognition of the diversity of social life is at the very least a tonic reminder to Marxism of the plural cultural and political demands that confront us, then the collapse of a sense of purpose and direction in human history is a cognate, but altogether more politically ambiguous, development. This is what lies behind the attack on the notion of the 'grand narratives', although in Lyotard's original 'Report on Knowledge', the target is the attempt to provide any single narrative that would provide legitimation for the disparate knowledges of the modern world. Once the notion of the grand narratives of history has been abandoned, a whole interpretative vocabulary then falls with it, by which writing is aligned with the onward tendency of human history. Much of this vocabulary was debased, although it was not only Marxism which assigned texts to those primitive categories of 'progressive' and 'reactionary'. Nevertheless, the sense of some connection between cultural acts, and the wider purposes and aims of social and historic life, seems a large price to pay for repudiating the reductions which such a sense has led to.

Do we therefore have to abandon any sense of the grand narratives of human history? This is, perhaps, too large a question to deal with in an article on Marxism and literary criticism, and, moreover, it hides a number of different questions, to do with the *post facto* imposition of shape upon inherently diverse historical material, the sense of purposiveness in social and political action, the presumption of meaningful connection between past and future, and the capacity to relate the multiplicity and diversity of social and cultural life to one overarching story – questions that take the argument into areas well beyond those advanced by Lyotard. I will consider some of these questions in the discussion of objections to the totalising claims of Marxism. I intend to concentrate here on the diachronic axis, understanding the challenge to grand narratives of human history as a challenge to any attempt to relate the diversity and complexity of cultural objects to a wider sense of significance and onwardness in human history.

No discussion of this question can proceed, however, without recognising that many cultural forms themselves provide grand narratives: either retrospectively, in which the present moment appears as a culmination of a previous history, or prospectively, pointing beyond the moment of composition to some transformed future which can nevertheless be thought of as significantly related to the present. It is not only a question, then, of relating particular cultural objects to a wider interpretative schema in which they take on their fuller significance. It is also that some literary forms are themselves engaged in providing grand narratives, by which a sense of significant relationship between past, present and future is posited.

Epic is the form which, above all, seeks to provide a retrospective grand narrative, a heroic past or foundational story through which a *gens*, a nation or an empire understands its own history (see Quint, 1993). We need not read epic in the nationalising spirit of the nineteenth century to recognise that *The Iliad*, *The Aeneid*, *Beowulf* or *Paradise Lost* all attempt, in very different ways, to compose the past into a significant story in the light of which, or perhaps against which, the present can be judged. Even though there may be a 'zone of epic distance' (Bakhtin, 1981, pp. 3–40) which separates past from present, epic nevertheless provides a means by which the significance of the past for the present can be comprehended. But if epic is the form which most insistently sought to connect the past to the present in a grand narrative of heroic deeds, then, in the much greater diversity of cultural forms that has characterised succeeding history, epic can only be counted in as one cultural possibility amongst others. However, in that very fact, in epic's evident speaking of a world uncontaminated by the cash nexus and market relations, it bears a utopian promise that things might be otherwise in a world dominated

by 'realism'. It is this utopian promise, present in a range of cultural forms, which carries the link between present and future, and which suggests the inevitability of a narrative to connect one to the other. If, as I have been suggesting, cultural forms are ways of mediating social relationships (understood in their widest and most diverse sense), then they carry with them presumptions about currently existing and possible social relations which are inherently utopian, albeit in a very specific sense.

'A map of the world which does not include Utopia is not worth even glancing at, for it leaves out the one country at which Humanity is always landing' (Wilde, 1973, p. 34). Oscar Wilde's aphorism is helpful in suggesting the pervasiveness of utopianism, not merely in those formal set-piece utopias like those of Wilde's contemporaries Edward Bellamy and William Morris, but as a promise built into all cultural forms that things in the past have been otherwise and might be so again. Even the most conservative text, determined to prove that the contemporary social world is on its way to total destruction, has built into it a utopian promise based upon a previously less corrupted world. All texts, in the full diversity of their cultural forms, imply presumptions about the world they spring from and at some level or other suggest a world of differently realised possibilities. In so doing, they presume relationships between past and future that may not be *grand* narratives but are at least more or less plausible stories.

The objection to 'grand narratives', then, is not to 'narrative' as such, nor to the fact that narratives imply significant connections between past and future which are at least in potential socially transformative. This cannot be the force of the objection, because a whole range of cultural forms suggest such stories, grand or otherwise. Essentially, if the objection to 'grand narratives' is intelligible, it is an objection once again to reductionism, to the attempt to relate all histories to one macro-history. Even here, we must recognise that *some* story of change and development in human history has to be told. It would seem futile to suggest that grand transformations of human history have not occurred – I am writing this article on an extraordinarily sophisticated computer, whose very existence presupposes a social world, and an accumulated intellectual and technological capital, very different from that implied by the quill pen or cuneiform writing. What is at issue is whether it is possible to write a history of such transformations which plausibly links them to individual cultural objects. This is a matter of historical perspective – from what position, and at what level of abstraction from the minutiae of diurnal life, do the grand transformations of history appear as an intelligible story? The objection to 'grand narratives' then appears as an empirical one, as a protest against the presumption and ambition which believes it possible to compose an unimaginable complexity of micro-histories into one overarching story. This leads us to consider the objections that have been made to the so-called totalising claims of Marxism.

Problems with 'totality'

The assault upon the category of totality relates also to the attack upon the centrality of class as a determinant in social and cultural life, for this attack, as much as that upon 'grand narratives', is aimed at what is seen as Marxist reductionism, although the attack is aimed as much at Hegel and the Hegelian legacy in Marx which insists that 'the true is the whole'. We can take Georg Lukács as our example of a Marxist literary critic for whom the category of totality is central. Thus, he writes in *History and Class Consciousness* that

> the objective forms of all social phenomena change constantly in the course of their ceaseless dialectical interactions with each other. The intelligibility of objects develops in proportion as we grasp their function in the totality to which they belong. This is why only the dialectical conception of totality can enable us to understand *reality as a social process*. (Lukács, 1971, p. 13)

The immediate context of this is a discussion of economics, but the importance of the category of totality is evident in Lukács's aesthetics also. In the essays on realism and naturalism, the work of the great realists is praised for its capacity to link the minutiae of everyday life to a wider sense of the onward movement of a society – to understand, that is, how the actions, at least of socially typical characters, relate to wider historical transformations and thus to the movement of a social totality. The novels of Scott, Balzac and Tolstoy, thanks to a fortunate fit between writer and historical moment, and thanks also to the greatness of their writers, can be celebrated because they are infused at once with a sense of the material and historical density of the here-and-now and simultaneously with a sense of the imbrication of these specificities with wider categories of historical transformation. The social totality is always present through the typicality of the novels' protagonists: 'The central category and criterion of realist literature is the type, a peculiar synthesis which organically binds together the general and the particular both in characters and situations' (Lukács, 1972, p. 6).

It is unclear whether this conception of at least some of the nineteenth-century European novelists need fall subject to the critiques of the category of totality that have since been made. The strength of the totalising gesture is its ambition of relating together the seemingly disparate and unrelated phenomena of social life; it makes unremarked or unwelcome connections, and insists that those appearing as merely simultaneous or coincidental are actually part of a wider system of relations and connections (see Jameson, 1989, p. 33). This effort at connection is at risk if the whole case against totalising thought is too readily accepted. Lukács's readings of the nineteenth-century realist canon is a case in point. The difficulty with these readings is not their totalising ambition, but the way in which connections are posited between the complex immediacy of the characters' lives, and the underlying history to which they allude, in terms of which these lives are to be understood. Here the problem is not only with the class reductiveness of the analysis which excludes too much of the rich complexity of the texts of Balzac or Tolstoy in its insistence upon classes and their actions in the grand narrative of European history. It is, more profoundly, the untroubled relationship assumed between the lived specificity of 'class' as represented in those novels, and the categories of class as they appear in economic and historical analysis. Lukács was right to seek to make the connections that he did, and to that extent we can defend the importance of the category of totality in his work; but he short-circuited the processes of determination by which the various levels of the social totality are interconnected.

The crucial question then becomes: is it possible to retain any sense of the wider social whole which does not necessarily make that kind of short-circuit? In other words, does the effort to relate disparate parts of the social fabric to each other – especially and crucially for Marxism, the 'economic' with the 'cultural' – entail reductiveness and require that the formally specific productions and interactions of cultural life be translated back down into a vocabulary that is extrinsic to them? This would be an especially ironic end-point for Marxist literary criticism, since on one reading at least, Marxism in the works of Marx and Engels is not itself an economism, but a protest against economism and the ruthless capacity of the capitalist market to reduce all difference and specificity to interchangeable commodities – a protest on behalf of use-value against exchange-value. This may make Marx sound too much like Ruskin, but the point is this: how to conceive of the social totality in a way which reveals those hidden and mystified relationships in a way that does not concede, in that very gesture, the triumph of the economic that is the actual characteristic of capitalism?

Consideration of the category of totality takes us, then, into considerations of determination, for it would be an unwarrantably bland notion of totality which did not seek to dispose the various elements of its totally conceived system into relations of relative importance. This is not the place to address the hotly contested theme of determination in Marxism, and of the discussion of base and superstructure which is the vocabulary in which it has characteristically been conducted. Nevertheless, it does seem to me that some conceptions of determination do permit one to retain a notion of the totality without surrendering to reductiveness. In particular, in the work of Raymond Williams and E. P. Thompson, we can find a notion of determination as the 'setting of limits', and of 'process', which recognises the due weight of economic and material life, without seeking to translate essentially cultural artefacts into

other extrinsic terms. (See Williams, 1983, pp. 98–102; 1980, pp. 30–49; Thompson, 1978, pp. 1–210.) Furthermore, Williams's insistence upon the formal specificity of cultural objects permits us to recognise that cultural objects are ways of mediating social relations, but on their own terms. In this view, the social totality is invoked, in different ways, by any cultural interaction, precisely because all such cultural interactions dispose their participants in socially and historically specific ways.

However, this leads us to a very different conception of the social totality from that assumed and proposed by Lukács. Specifically, it assumes what one might (oxymoronically) call an 'open totality', which recognises the diversity, multiplicity and openendedness of what remains an interconnected reality. The objection against the reductiveness of any Marxist analysis which invokes the category of totality, ought more properly to be an objection to the reductive and homogenising forces of commodity production; the notion of an open totality admits the force of such pressures, but precisely as 'pressures', seeking to diminish both that diversity and the intrinsic formal distinctiveness of which it is constituted. If this is a necessary concession to the diversity and specificity of cultural objects, it does not entail any diminution of the commitment to a totality understood as the network of social relations in which cultural objects take on their force and meaning – a network skewed in specific ways by the accumulated powers of capital and other faultlines of unwarranted authority. Finally, to abandon any allusion to the level of totality would be to abandon any hope of addressing appropriately the distortions forced upon cultural life by those accumulated and oppressive authorities (see final chapter of Eagleton, 1990).

Realism and the diversity of genre

The case of Lukács is further complicated by his commitment to realism as the privileged means by which the realities of social and political history are 'represented' in the novels he discusses, although this is not a simply conceived realism of superficial lifelikeness, but a realism which penetrates below the surface of social life to make manifest the underlying forces of historical transformation. This, however, is to compound the difficulties with the very notion of realism, which form the final objection to Marxist literary criticism to which I allude in this article. Once again, there are several related difficulties which need to be disentangled, and the nature of the objections come in several different, mutually contradictory, forms. There is no doubting the historical allegiance of Marxism to a realist epistemology, nor the strong, but by no means universal, predilection of Marxist aesthetics for realist art. Hence, an assault on the very notion of realism both in epistemology and aesthetics carries serious consequences for Marxist literary criticism as it has so far been predominantly understood.

I do not propose to reargue the tradition of Western epistemology of the last three centuries only to conclude that the objections to a realist epistemology are overstated, although such a view seems to me to be quite defensible. Instead, I assert the following propositions. First, not all utterances, and especially not all literary ones, exist only in the dimension of knowledge. This is to say, that you cannot exhaust the meaning of any utterance by examining its 'truth-content', or its lifelikeness, or the accuracy of its allusions to the world which surrounds it, but have to consider also the formal, expressive and rhetorical dimensions in which it simultaneously exists. Second, cultural forms mediate the realities of social life in different and formally specific ways, of which formal realism is but one possibility. Thus, to restrict one's examples to writing only, it is clear that the generic capacities of epic, romance, the novel, lyric poetry, Gothic fiction, the occasional essay and autobiography, all vary widely and mediate social relationships in very different ways. The formally realist text is only one possible way of mediating social relationships. Third, all these forms are tied, by a series of minimal deictic markers, to the social and natural world in which they are situated, relating the moment of their utterance to that world, even if it is only by negation. This means that the question of 'realism' is unavoidable for all these forms, but realism is to be understood here not as a crude epistemological yardstick by which to measure literary objects, but as a crucial dimension by which writers and readers make sense of the very texts they create and consume.

Taken together, these three propositions make the following assumptions and have the following consequences. They assume that all human beings inhabit the same material world, and are subject to its same material constraints. Thus, when forms of writing flout those constraints it is assumed that all readers will recognise that flouting and count it into the significance of whatever it is that they are reading, whether it be Pallas appearing in disguise to Telemachus in Book I of *The Odyssey*, Dr Frankenstein creating his monster in Mary Shelley's *Frankenstein*, or the ascent into the clouds of Remedios the Beauty in Gabriel García Márquez's *One Hundred Years of Solitude*. But equally, it follows that different forms of writing make allusions to the world in formally specific ways. Thus, the lifelike density of allusion to the material and social world that characterises many nineteenth-century novels is obviously very different from, for example, the imaginary social worlds of utopian writing. Nevertheless, utopian projections can only be understood by virtue of their very difference from the world from which they are launched – hence those sometimes interminable disquisitions from the guide figures in Utopia whose duty it is to point out the differences. At this most fundamental level then, and as the minimum condition upon which writing becomes possible, we have to recognise that the very intelligibility of all forms of writing is dependent upon their inhabiting a shared material world, and upon their situatedness in a history which is in part a matter of common knowledge.

Generic diversity, then – the multiplicity of cultural forms that characterise writing – by no means entails the abandonment of the claims of realism, although it does require the recognition of the inadequacy of realism to provide a sufficient account of the nature of all writing. Another question, however, emerges from the recognition of generic diversity. If the specific ways in which writing alludes to the world are in part a matter of genre, and genres are historically-specific ways of encoding social relationships, then it follows that the manner in which writing alludes to the world is one aspect of the way in which writing encodes social relationships. And indeed, different forms, and different texts, do make allusions to the world in a variety of different ways, placing readers or spectators into very particular relationships with the realities they call upon, presume or introduce. Thus, the densely realised social worlds of the nineteenth-century novel, the political intrigues of a Shakespearean history play, the delicate and sometimes defamiliarising exactitude of a lyric poem, the coterie poetry of the Metaphysicals, the patronage poetry of the seventeenth century, the poetry of wit and the 'mob of gentlemen who wrote with ease', nineteenth-century dialect poetry, the social realism of post-1956 English drama – all these forms (and all forms in principle) place their readers or spectators into socially-specific relationships of knowledge, intimacy, revelation, collusion or outrage, with the worlds to which they allude.

This entails more than that minimal recognition of the necessity of realism as the condition of the intelligibility of texts. It entails the additional recognition that no allusion to the world is ever neutral, but is always caught up in a network of rhetorical, and therefore social and political, relationships. Epistemology in this particular sense cannot be separated from the uses to which it is put. 'Realism', understood as the inescapable location of writing in a shared material and social world, is thus one of the conditions by which writing is put to its multiple secular and wordly purposes.

We can therefore conclude that realism is indeed an inadequate basis for a whole aesthetics, but that it is nevertheless essential as one of the co-ordinates for a more adequate understanding of the social location of writing. Further, this anodyne formulation – 'the social location of writing' – conceals the active social relationships that are mobilised in writing. Writing only assumes its force and meaning by virtue of the specific ways in which it situates itself in a definite social and material world, and by the specific ways in which it seeks to dispose its readers with respect to that world. Although these are, in effect, only the preliminary considerations of a Marxist literary criticism, they do nevertheless suggest the inescapability of social and political categories in the understanding of writing.

However, this too is to pitch the matter too low, to consider the question too limply as a matter of understanding rather than as one of engagement.

It is not only that social and political categories are inescapable for the *understanding* of writing, from a critical distance that is somehow above, or 'meta', to the act of reading; it is also, and far more importantly, that social and political histories are necessarily implicated in the very act of reading itself. In one sense, the act of reading is the engagement of one subjectivity with another. But neither subjectivity, not that of either the writer or the reader, can be extracted from the historical stream in which they are situated; indeed, their subjectivities are formed from multiple, interlocking, and partially contradictory social and cultural forms. To read is to activate those forms, to seek to make sense of the other with one's own unique but historically-created resources. It is necessarily an evaluative activity, as the reader seeks to situate herself or himself in relation to other histories that are not her or his own, and to negotiate the multiple rhetorical demands that any text makes.

This is why the questions raised within the diverse tradition of Marxist literary criticism will not simply go away, even as the idiom of Engels, Lukács or Adorno appears increasingly rebarbative. I have argued: that it is possible to retain a sense of the fundamental importance of class without reducing the diversity of social life to questions of class; that literary texts themselves presume significant narrative relations between past and present which connect them to wider narratives of social transformation; that the attempt to understand literary texts as in some way connected to a social totality is a necessary moment in any attempt to recognise the determinants that are acting upon cultural life; and that, despite the inadequacy of realism as a sufficient aesthetic, it is impossible to circumvent it as one dimension of the act of negotiation by which readers position themselves in relation to the texts that they are reading. However, all these arguments are in a sense merely flanking movements, defensive positions to protect an actuality that does not need defending: the inevitable sociality and historicity of the acts of writing and reading. Given this actuality, given, that is, the activation of a complex social history in all acts of reading, the questions raised within Marxist literary criticism are bound to continue, no matter what idiom is invoked.

Bibliography

References and further reading

Bakhtin, M. (1981), 'Discourse in the Novel' and 'Epic and Novel', in M. Holoquist (ed.), *The Dialogic Imagination: Four Essays*, trans. C. Emerson and M. Holoquist, Texas: University of Texas Press.

Dentith, S. (1995), *Bakhtinian Thought: an Introductory Reader*, London: Routledge.

Eagleton, T. (1990), *The Ideology of the Aesthetic*, Oxford: Blackwell.

Jameson, F. (1981), *The Political Unconscious: Narrative as Socially Symbolic Act*, London: Methuen.

— (1989), 'Marxism and Post-modernism', *New Left Review*, 176.

Lukács, G. (1971), *History and Class Consciousness*, London: Merlin Press.

— (1972), *Studies in European Realism*, London: Merlin Press.

Lyotard, J.-F. (1984), *The Postmodern Condition: A Repo on Knowledge*, trans. G. Bennington and B. Massum Manchester: Manchester University Press.

Quint, D. (1993), *Epic and Empire: Politics and Gener Form from Virgil to Milton*, Princeton: Princeton Un versity Press.

Thompson, E. P. (1978), 'The Poverty of Theory', i *The Poverty of Theory and Other Essays*, London: Merlir

Wilde, O. (1973), 'The Soul of Man Under Socialism', i *De Profundis and Other Essays*, ed. H. Pearson, Penguir London.

Williams, R. (1980), 'Base and Superstructure in Marxi Cultural Theory', in *Problems in Materialism and Cultur* London: Verso.

— (1983), *Keywords: a Vocabulary of Culture and Societ* London: Fontana.

5.4

FREUD AND THE SCIENCE OF THE MIND

Jim Hopkins

Freud was born in Freiburg, Moravia, in 1856, the first son of the third wife of a travelling wool-merchant. The family settled in Vienna in 1861, just after Austria abolished legal restrictions on Jews. Freud was to remain there until, together with other psychoanalysts, he fled the Nazi occupation. He died in London in 1939.

Freud approached the mind via the study of the nervous system. At the Vienna Medical School he heard the lectures of the physiologist Ernst Bruke, who followed Helmholtz's Darwinian and physicalistic approach to nature. He began research in Bruke's laboratory, and soon began publishing papers in neurology. (See Freud, 1974, xx, 10ff.; references to his *Standard Edition* are by volume and page.) When Freud got engaged he realised that he could not support a family by research work, and he began to prepare for practice at the General Hospital. Here he studied disorders of the nervous system under Meynert, one of the first people to emphasise the role of neural connectivity in the brain.

Freud's neurological publications led to an appointment as Lecturer in Neuropathology, and in 1885 he was awarded a bursary to study in Paris under Charcot (1886, i, p. 5), whose work on **hysteria** included the use of hypnosis for producing and removing symptoms. (For further information on terms in bold, see Laplanche and Pontalis, 1973.) Freud espoused Charcot's psychological approach, and supported it with an observation based on his understanding of the nervous system. The regions of

the body liable to hysterical paralysis or loss of feeling failed to correspond to functional physiological demarcations. Hysteria, as Freud remarked, knew nothing of anatomy (1888, i, p. 49).

Early work with Breuer: symptoms, memories and motives

In practice, Freud found extant physical remedies for psychological disorders useless. He attained some success with hypnosis (1892, i, p. 117); but his senior colleague Joseph Breuer told him of a treatment which apparently cast light on the underlying disturbances. Breuer had enquired into the symptoms of one of his patients in great detail, so that, as he remarked, her life 'became known to me to an extent to which one person's life is seldom known to another' (1893, ii, p. 22). This enabled patient and doctor to discover together that her symptoms had meaningful connections with past events which she had forgotten, but which had stirred feelings which she had neither expressed nor mastered. When she remembered the events and expressed the feelings her symptoms eased.

One symptom was aversion to drinking. Despite 'tormenting thirst' she would push away a glass of water 'like someone suffering from hydrophobia' (1893, ii, p. 34). Under hypnosis she traced this to an episode in which she remained silent despite great disgust, while a companion let a little dog, a 'horrid creature', drink from her glass. After reliving this event and expressing her feelings she drank without difficulty. Again, she suffered from a paralysed arm. She and Breuer traced this to a distressing occasion when the arm had gone to sleep, so that she could not move it, while she was nursing her dying father. A whole series of symptoms, including hallucinations and disturbances of speech, were also rooted in experiences from this episode. When she went over these with Breuer the symptoms were relieved.

Although Breuer's patient relapsed before eventually recovering, her case suggested that symptoms could be expressions of memories and motives of which the patient was unaware. This struck Freud as of cardinal importance, and he began to question his patients about their lives and feelings in great detail, seeking memories related to their symptoms. In this, he abandoned hypnotism, and for a time substituted a technique, derived from Bernheim, of pressing patients to remember significant events (1895, II, p. 109). His work corroborated Breuer's sufficiently for them to publish a series of case reports illustrating the theory that 'hysterics suffer mainly from reminiscences' (1895, II, p. 7), which were kept from consciousness by a process of **defence** or **repression**. Hence they could be helped by a **cathartic** therapy, which enabled them to recover memories of traumatic events and **work through** the feelings connected with them.

Recovered memories and sexual abuse

Freud now found that **obsessions**, **phobias** and delusions of **paranoia** were also linked with unconscious memories or motives; and these were often sexual in nature, and went back in time (1894, III, p. 45ff.). Thus, a patient with hallucinatory images and sensations, and a delusion that she was watched while undressing,

> reproduced a series of scenes going back from her seventeenth to her eighth year, in which she had felt ashamed of being naked in her bath in front of her mother, her sister and the doctor; but the series ended in a scene at the age of six, in which she was undressing in the nursery before going to bed, without feeling any shame in front of her

brother who was there . . . it transpired that scenes like this had occurred often and that the brother and sister had for years been in the habit of showing themselves to one another naked before going to bed . . . I then succeeded in getting her to reproduce the various scenes in which her sexual relationship with her brother had culminated . . . After we had gone through this series of scenes, the hallucinatory sensations and images had disappeared . . . (1896, III, pp. 178–80)

Still, as in the case of Breuer's patient, the removal of individual symptoms left a disposition to produce further symptoms intact. Freud therefore sought to cure the underlying disposition by uncovering the earliest, and most basic, disturbing memories. Under the pressure of his technique a number of his patients recovered apparent memories of sexual abuse, dating from early childhood. And as he pressed further, with a series of female patients, the role of abuser was constantly assigned to the father. For a time Freud thought he had discovered that neurotic disturbance was rooted in childhood sexual abuse, frequently of an incestuous kind (and comparable experiences have been repeated, and the same conclusion drawn, by many therapists since). In considering these **scenes of seduction**, however, he finally concluded that while parental abuse could cause disturbance, it was less widespread than the readiness of patients to recollect it might suggest. There were 'no indications of reality in the unconscious, so that one cannot distinguish between truth and [emotionally charged] fiction', where this might even include 'sexual fantasy [which] seizes on the theme of the parents' (1897, I, p. 260; see also Masson, 1985, p. 265).

After this, Freud both altered his technique and formulated the concepts central to his later work. It was now clear that he had to guard against the effects of suggestion; and it seemed also that the most relevant and reliable material emerged not when patients when pressed for memories, but rather when they made connections spontaneously, in following out their own trains of thought and feeling. He thus began asking his patients simply to communicate each idea or thought which occurred to them, whether or not it seemed sensible or significant, and without censorship. This immediate and unconstrained self-description, called **free association**, led to the topics previously shown important by questioning, and to others which he had not yet investigated.

The first paradigm of psychoanalysis: self-analysis and dreams as wishfulfilments

Freud also noticed that his patients' dreams, like their symptoms, could be understood as related to the memories and motives which emerged in their associations. In investigating this topic, moreover, he could make use of his own case as well; so he began to conduct the same kind of **psychoanalysis** on himself as on his patients, focussing on the interpretation of his own dreams. As this progressed, he realised that his and Breuer's findings about symptoms, as well as the material he had encountered relating to childhood abuse, were better understood via the model he was developing for dreams. In consequence, he was able to frame an account of these matters, published in *The Interpretation of Dreams* (1900, IV; V) which was relatively simple and unified, and which could be extended to other phenomena in which he had taken an interest. Freud's discussion of dreams can therefore be seen as introducing a theoretical paradigm which enabled him to consolidate the first phase of his psychoanalytic work, and we should pause to understand this more thoroughly.

Our commonsense mode of describing desire already involves a complex but tacit theory of the working of desire, as marked by a pattern in the sentences we use to describe it. We can summarise part of this very approximately by noting that, if a person is acting on a desire that p (that he get a drink of water), we take it that this will, if successful, bring about the situation p (that he gets a drink of water) in which the desire is satisfied; and this in turn should give rise to the belief that p (that he has got a drink of water), and this, finally, should pacify the desire; that is, cause it to cease to operate. This is the pattern of the life-cycle of desire in intentional action. We can compare this pattern with another, which Freud found in dreams, and illustrated with a

particularly simple example. When he had eaten anchovies or some other salty food, he was liable to have a dream *that he was drinking cool, delicious water*. After having this dream, perhaps several times, Freud would awake, find himself thirsty, and get a drink. Probably many people have had this experience, or its counterpart concerning urination. And anyone who has such a dream will naturally take it to be caused by, and to represent the satisfaction of, the wish or desire to drink felt on waking.

This natural conclusion turns on the obvious relation in sentential content between desire and dream. Schematically, the desire is that p (that the dreamer have a drink) and the dream is also that p (that the dreamer is having a drink). This similarity provides reason to suppose that desire and dream are not coincidentally related, but that the one is a cause of the other. Also, it seems that such a dream has a pacifying influence – perhaps only a fleeting one – on the desire which prompts it. The dream-experience of drinking provides the underlying thirst with a form of genuine but temporary relief, the insufficiency of which is indicated by the repetition of the dream, and the dreamer's finally having to wake to get a drink.

Dreaming is a form of imaginative representation which is experience- or belief-like. Thus, the pattern we find in this simple dream is that in which a person's desire or wish that p prompts (causes) a belief- or experience-like representation that p, which in turn serves to pacify the desire. This is the pattern of Freudian **wishfulfilment**, which is evidently closely related to the above action. In both, desire is ultimately pacified via the representation of satisfaction. In action, the agent's desire produces a real action resulting in a real drink, and thence in a pacifying belief that he is drinking. Wishfulfilment, by contrast, represents a kind of short-circuiting this route to pacification, in which the mind (or brain) bypasses the route through intentional action, the alteration of reality, and real satisfaction, and simply produces directly a pacifying representation.

We can see more of the role of the notion of wishfulfilment by considering part of the first specimen Freud analyses in *The Interpretation of Dreams*, his own dream of Irma's injection (1900, IV, pp. 104ff.). In this dream Freud met Irma, a family friend and patient, whom he had diagnosed as hysterical. He told her that if she still felt pains, this was her own fault for not accepting his 'solution' to her difficulties. As she continued to complain, however, he became alarmed that she was suffering from an organic illness which he had failed to diagnose. This turned out to be real. Freud examined Irma, and then she was examined by some of Freud's colleagues, including his senior colleague M; and it emerged that, not only was she organically ill, but her illness was caused by a toxic injection given by another of Freud's colleagues, his family doctor Otto. At the end of the dream, therefore, Freud censured Otto strongly, saying that 'Injections of that kind ought not be made so thoughtlessly . . . and probably the syringe had not been clean.'

Unlike the simple dream of drinking this dream does not appear to be wishfulfilling: in fact, it dealt with topics which were not pleasant to Freud. It concerned the continued suffering of a patient who was also a family friend, and for whom, therefore, the question of his responsibility was particularly acute; and also, the possibility that he had misdiagnosed an organic illness as hysteria, which he described as 'a constant anxiety' to someone offering psychological treatment. But Freud systematically collected his free associations – the thoughts, feelings, etc., which occurred to him – in connection with each element of the dream; and in light of these we can see that the treatment of these topics in the dream is in fact wishful, and in a way which is radical.

The topics of the dream had arisen on the day before. Otto had just returned from visiting Irma and her family, and had briefly discussed Irma with Freud, commenting that she was looking 'better, but not yet well'. Freud had felt something of a reproof in this, as though he had held out too much hope that Irma might be cured; and in consequence he regarded the remark as thoughtless, and felt annoyed with Otto. (Also, as it happened, Otto had been called on to give someone an injection while at Irma's – compare this with the topic of the dream – and Freud had just had news indicating, as he thought, that another of his female patients had been given a careless injec-

tion by some other doctor, and had been contemplating his own careful practice in this respect with a degree of self-satisfaction.) That night, in order to justify himself, Freud had started to write up Irma's case to show to M, who was respected by both himself and Otto, and who appeared in the dream as diagnosing Irma's illness and becoming aware that it was Otto's fault.

In considering the dream, Freud noted that his desire to justify himself in respect of Irma's case, and in particular not to be responsible for her suffering, was apparent from the beginning, in which he told Irma that her pains were now her own fault. Also, he felt that his alarm at her illness in the dream was not entirely genuine. So, as he realised, it seemed that he was actually *wishing* that Irma be organically ill: for, as he undertook to treat only psychological complaints, this would also mean that he could not be held responsible for her condition, by Otto or anyone else. This theme, indeed, seemed carried further in the rest of the dream, in which M found that Otto, not Freud, bore responsibility for Irma's illness. The whole dream, in fact, could be seen as a wishful response to Otto's remark. According to the dream, and contrary to what Freud had taken Otto to imply, Freud bore no responsibility whatever for Irma's condition. Rather, Otto was the sole cause of her suffering, and this was a result of Otto's bad practice with injections, a matter about which Freud himself was particularly careful.

We can see here the contrasting roles of desire and wishfulfilment as set out above. In action, Freud's desire that he be cleared of culpable responsibility should operate to bring about a situation in which he is cleared of such responsibility, thus producing the belief that he has been cleared, and so pacifying the desire. This is approximately the sequence of results which Freud was seeking to bring about, in accord with standard medical practice, in writing up Irma's case history to show to M, whose independent authoritative judgement about the case would serve to clear him. Freud's dream apparently shows the same motive at work, but in a very different way. There, the desire seems to have given rise to a series of (dreamt) belief-like representations of his being cleared, and in a number of ways: Irma was made to be physically, rather than psychologically, ill, Otto shown as engaging in culpable malpractice which caused her illness, and so on. These can therefore be understood on the pattern of wishfulfilment. And as this example also illustrates, Freud also found that instances of the interpretation of desire and wishfulfilment characteristically cohere with one another, so that a typical dream or action would be underlain both by realistic desires and by related wishes which might be unrealistic, ruthless, egoistic, etc.

Now, it should not surprise us that the mind (or brain) should operate in accord with both these patterns. For the operation of desire in action is aimed not only at satisfaction but also at pacification, which the mind/brain achieves via the production of representation (experience and belief). We know that human desire far outruns the possibilities of successful action; so it is natural that desire should admit of pacification other than via satisfaction, and also that there should be forms of desire, or motives related to desire, which are characteristically pacified by representation alone. Hence, once we reflect on the matter, we can also see that the pattern of wishfulfilment is already familiar to us. We know that there are many other cases in which we respond to a desire or wish that p by seeking to have an experience as if p, or by imagining that p, making believe that p, etc.; and it seems that we often do this because the experience, imagining, or whatever, serves to pacify – to give some sort of pause or relief – to the desires which prompted it. Thus, people regularly daydream about the satisfaction of their desires, and we also observe that children frequently use play to represent the same thing. Again, it seems that people find similar imaginative pleasure or relief in fiction, films, television, theatre, video games, and so forth. Hence, we already use a series of related notions – make-believe, suspension of disbelief, cinematic illusion, virtual reality – to describe the way these modes of representation are belief- or experience-like, so that, by representing the satisfaction of desire, they also serve to pacify it.

We can illustrate Freud's reasoning in this instance by listing some obvious connections between desire and dream as follows:

Data from the associations	Data from the dream
Freud wants not to be responsible for Irma's suffering.	Freud says to Irma 'If you still get pains, its really only your fault'.
Freud wants not to be responsible for Irma's suffering.	Irma is suffering from an organic complaint, for the treatment of which Freud is not responsible.
Freud is annoyed with Otto, for his remark implying that Freud was in some way at fault in his practice with Irma.	Otto is at fault in his practice with Irma.
Otto had given someone an injection while at Irma's, and Freud has been contemplating that his injections never cause infection.	Otto gave Irma an injection which caused an infection.
Freud desires to clear himself of responsibility for Irma's suffering.	Otto bears sole responsibility for Irma's suffering.
Freud was hoping that M's opinion of his treatment of Irma would clear him of responsibility.	M observes Otto's bad practice and recognises that Otto bears full responsibility for Irma's suffering.
Freud considered Otto's remark to him thoughtless.	Otto's injection of Irma was thoughtless.

This list, although very incomplete, is none the less illustrative. It seems difficult to deny that the relation in content of elements on the left to those on the right calls for explanation; and also that it would be unsatisfactory to hold that the explanation was simply coincidence. A causal explanation seems to be required; and this being so, the question arises as to what kind of causal hypothesis would provide the best account of the observable connections. In this case, as in that of the simple dream of drinking. Freud's hypothesis is in effect that these data are linked by *wishful imaginative representation*, and hence through wishfulfilment. We can represent this hypothesis in relation to these data as follows:

Data from the associations	Explanatory hypothesis: the data from the associations are linked with those from the dream by a form of wishful imaginative representation, through which wishes or desires related to the associations are represented as satisfied in the dream.	Data from the dream
Freud wants not to be responsible for Irma's suffering.	Freud wishfully represents Irma's suffering as not his fault, but her own.	Freud says to Irma 'If you still get pains, its really only your fault'.
Freud wants not to be responsible for Irma's suffering.	Freud wishfully represents Irma as suffering from something for which he is not responsible.	Irma is suffering from an organic complaint, for the treatment of which Freud is not responsible.
Freud is annoyed with Otto, for his remark implying that Freud was in some way at fault in his practice with Irma.	Freud wishfully represents the situation as the reverse of that implied by Otto, so that it is Otto, not Freud himself, who can be accused of fault connected with Irma's suffering.	Otto is at fault in his practice with Irma.
Otto had given someone an injection while at Irma's, and Freud has been contemplating that his injections never cause infection.	Freud uses elements from reality to wishfully represent the situation as one in which Otto, not Freud himself, should be accused of fault connected with Irma's suffering.	Otto gave Irma an injection which caused an infection.
Freud desires to clear himself of responsibility for Irma's suffering.	Freud wishfully represents the situation as one in which he has no responsibility for Irma's suffering.	Otto bears sole responsibility for Irma's suffering.
Freud was hoping that M's opinion of his treatment of Irma would clear him of responsibility.	Freud wishfully represents M as finding that Irma's suffering was Otto's fault.	M observes Otto's bad practice and recognises that Otto bears full responsibility for Irma's suffering.
Freud considered Otto's remark to him thoughtless.	Freud wishfully represents Otto as thoughtless.	Otto's injection of Irma was thoughtless.

Freud's account thus explains the data from associations and dream on the hypothesis that the latter can be understood as a pacifying wishfulfilment. This in turn implies the existence of previously unacknowledged mental phenomena: the processes by which such a pacifying representation is produced, and the wish- or desire-like states which, even in sleep, operate to produce it. Such wishes are thus states introduced by hypothesis, to explain data from both the associations and dream. These here include Freud's wishing that Irma's suffering be her own fault; that her suffering be organic in origin, and so not his fault; that it be Otto's fault rather than his, and so forth.

The method which Freud applied to this dream – that of comparing its **manifest content** in detail with the memories and motives which emerged in the dreamer's associations – could be applied to other dreams, and with similar results. Under such analysis, a typical dream could be seen to have a **latent content**, involving a whole range of wishfulfilments, related to a series of topics which were emotionally linked in the mind of the dreamer.

Phantasy, transference, childhood and conflict

Freud was now able to apply the notion of wishfulfilment – as well as **condensation**, **displacement**, **projection**, amongst others – in explaining other phenomena besides dreams. These included symptoms, forgetting and other everyday **parapraxes**

382

(1898, III, p. 289ff.; VI), **screen memories** (1899, III, p. 301ff.; VI), jokes (1895, VIII), and works of art (1895, I, p. 263ff.; IV, 261–6; IX). He found that all these sources of data cohered with one another, in locating the same kinds of desires and wishes as underlying dreams, symptoms and everyday actions. In addition, Freud he that, in the course of analysis, his patients were liable to develop feelings and fantasies about him which repeated those they had felt towards significant figures earlier in their lives, particularly their parents. This **transference** of feelings onto the person of the analyst proved a particularly striking source of information about the past, and one which cohered with Freud's other data.

This can be seen in the case of Freud's patient the Rat Man (1909; x, p. 153ff.), so-called because his main symptom was a compulsive phantasy in which he imagined that his father (or the woman he hoped to marry) were being subjected to a particularly cruel punishment, in which hungry rats were placed in a pot on the victim's bottom, and ate their way into the body. Engaging in this imagining made him anxious and depressed, so that at times he felt suicidal; and as he felt that the imagined events were somehow actually happening or liable to happen, he also felt compelled to engage in many rituals and other forms of behaviour which were supposed to prevent them.

Now, it was clear that his rat-phantasy often served as an expression of hostility. Thus, when a woman asked him to do something inconvenient, he 'wished the rats on her' in his rage (1907–8, x, p. 308), and also imagined that he felt a rat at his own behind. Indeed, at the beginning of his treatment, when Freud told him his fee, he thought 'for each *krone* a rat for the children'. Also, there was evidence that he did harbour hostility towards his father, which was somehow connected with sexual gratification. Thus, during his first copulation he had thought ' *"This is a glorious feeling! One might do anything for this – murder one's father, for instance"* ' (1909, x, p. 201, p. 264). Such feelings, moreover, went back into his childhood. As a boy of twelve he had imagined that a little girl with whom he was in love would show him more affection if some misfortune were to befall him, such as *his father's death*; and even from the age of six he could remember

wishing to see girls naked, but feeling that if he thought about such things something bad might happen, such as *his father might die*. Thoughts about his father's death had, in fact, occupied and depressed him from a very early age (ibid., x, p. 162).

Despite such evidence, the Rat Man was unwilling to consider that his symptoms might express hostility. On the contrary, he insisted that he and his father had always been the best of friends. He soon became convinced, however, that Freud would 'beat him and throw him out' because of the unpleasant things he said in his free associations, which included sexual and aggressive phantasies about Freud and his family (1909, x, pp. 282–4). In talking about such things he got off the couch and went down to the end of the room, saying that he was doing this out of delicacy of feeling – that he could not lie comfortably there while he was saying such dreadful things. It soon became clear, however, that he actually feared that Freud would beat him; and he began to relive a scene from his childhood, in which he had been lying between his mother and father in bed and had urinated, and his father had beaten him and turned him out. As Freud wrote at the time:

> His demeanour during all this was that of a man in desperation and one who was trying to save himself from blows of terrific violence; he buried his head in his hands, covered his face with his arm, etc. He told me that his father had a passionate temper, and did not then know what he was doing . . . He had thought that if there were murderous impulses in my family, I should fall upon him like a beast of prey to search out what was evil in him. (1907–8, x, pp. 284–5)

The patient thus recovered a buried image of his father as a punishing figure of whom he was terrified. Such images made it possible to understand his phantasies of his father being punished as wishfulfilments fitting the same pattern as Freud's dream above. Freud's dream could be seen as an extravagant wishful reversal of the feelings of responsibility prompted by Otto's remark; likewise, this patient's phantasy of his father being attacked by rats could be seen as an extravagant wishful reversal of his forgotten feelings of childhood terror. But the patient experienced such feelings in the present and towards the analyst before remembering them as relating to his father.

The early motive revealed by Freud's analyses of adults included sensual love for one parent combined with rivalry and jealous hatred for the other, which he called the **Oedipus Complex**. Little children naturally developed desires to harm or displace each parent, envied and hated as a rival for the sensual love of the other, as well as desires to preserve and protect that same parent, loved both sensually and as a caretaker, helper and model. Also, babies and children apparently attached great emotional significance to their interactions with their parents in such basic co-operative activities as feeding and the expulsion and management of waste These involved the first use, and hence the first stimulation, of bodily organs or zones – particularly the mouth, genitals and anus – which would later be used in the emotionally charged activities of normal and abnormal **sexuality**. Analysis showed that early feelings relating to these organs was continuous with those aroused by their later uses. This enabled Freud to frame a theory which systematically linked normal and abnormal sexual phenomena in the development of the individual (1905, VII).

A key idea in this account was that, prior to developing conscious sentential representations of matters concerned with sexuality and reproduction, little children naturally employed metaphorical or symbolic representations of them. Freud's hypotheses about this were based mainly upon the analysis of adults, although he discussed a phobia in a five-year-old boy (1909, X, pp. 22ff.) and a pattern of symbolic play in a child just beginning to speak (1920, XVIII, p. 14). Later analysts, such as Melanie Klein, were able to analyse children, and to confirm and extend Freud's findings. This can be illustrated by a little girl, who, like the Rat Man, suffered obsessional symptoms as well as depression. She played at being a queen, who was getting married.

> [When she] had celebrated her marriage to the king, she lay down on the sofa and wanted me, as the king, to lie down beside her. As I refused to do this I had to sit on a little chair by her side, and knock at the sofa with my fist. This she called 'churning' . . . immediately after this she an-

nounced that a child was creeping out of her, and she represented the scene in a quite realistic way, writhing about and groaning. Her imaginary child then had to share its parents' bedroom and had to be a spectator of sexual intercourse between them. If it interrupted, it was beaten . . . If she, as the mother, put the child to bed, it was only in order to get rid of it and to be able to be united with the father all the sooner. (Klein, Vol. II, p. 40)

Freud had noted that adults frequently symbolise their parents in dreams by the figures of king and queen. This play used the same symbolism in representing the child's unconscious phantasies about her parents, whom in real life she treated with excessive, but demanding, fondness. Here the child's representation of adult sexuality is partly symbolic (in terms of 'churning' or something for example, knocking something); but the referent of the symbolism can none the less be inferred from the context (the activity takes place after the wedding, with the parents lying together in bed, and is followed by the birth of a child). Her form of representation of sexual matters was thus prior to conscious understanding of them. The phantasies expressed in this game were repeated in many others, and in many related psychological constellations; and these made the little girl's obsessions and depression intelligible, in terms of what she phantasised as happening between herself and her unconscious versions of her parents.

Freud's hypotheses about children were thus consistent with his earlier idea that childhood sexual phantasy might 'seize on the theme of the parents'. In their attitudes towards the primary objects of their emotions, children were naturally liable to extremes of both love and hate, and hence to intense **ambivalence** and conflict. In consequence, Freud thought, some of these conflicting motives were subjected to a process of **repression**, which removed them from conscious thinking and planning. Repressed motives none the less continued to exist and operate in an **unconscious system**. Normally such motives could express themselves in dreams, slips; but where the conflict between hating and loving was particularly extreme, as in the case of the Rat Man, the expression took the form of symptoms.

Motives subject to conflict could also undergo a process of **sublimation**, whereby they could lend symbolic significance to everyday activities, and thus be pacified in the course of them (1908, ix, p. 187, p. 189). This idea can be illustrated by a relatively successful teacher and writer, who was surprised when one of his pupils – who had made a special effort to be taught by him, and was trying hard to master his ideas – had offered to suck his penis. This offer was neither expected nor welcome, but that night the teacher had dreamt that *a lamb had come to suck milk from his finger . . .* On waking, he realised that the lamb represented the pupil who had come to imbibe his ideas, and his milk-giving finger, the penis, his pupil had wanted to suck. The dream could therefore be seen as representing the fulfilment, in a more acceptable and symbolic form, of a sexual wish which had arisen on the day before. The symbolism, however, went deeper, for the dreamer also represented himself as occupying the position of a mother nursing a child. In this he represented his finger/penis as fulfilling the role of a feeding breast, and compared his writing and teaching to the production of milk as well as semen. He thus represented himself as enjoying a combination of feminine nurturance and masculine potency which was impossible in real life, and his desires for which had been repressed in early childhood. Still, these same desires could, to some degree, be pacified in his adult work, owing to the symbolic significance which he attached to it. In writing or teaching he could with some justice see himself – to use more familiar metaphors – as potent and seminal, and at the same time as giving others food for thought.

Freud's radical extension of commonsense psychology

Freud's work effected a radical extension of commonsense psychology. Analysis shows that everyday events and actions – such as his deciding to write up Irma's case history, or the Rat Man's deciding to go down to the other end of the room while talking to Freud – are determined by networks of motives far more extensive and complex than people can naturally realise. Everyday desires arise partly from motives which are unconscious residues of encounters with significant persons and situations from the past, reaching back into infancy. The goal associated with many of the most constant and basic desires, moreover, is not realistic satisfaction, but rather representational pacification. Such desires are characteristically expressed in a symbolic or metaphorical form, and in mind-altering wish-fulfilling **phantasy**, and hence in dreams and symptoms, or through actions upon which they have conferred symbolic meaning. Hence, in Freud's account, the pattern of wishfulfilment, in which a desire that p gives rise to the production of a pacifying (and perhaps metaphorical or symbolic) representation that p (which, as in the examples above, may itself be an intentional action) is the **primary process** in the pacification of desire, whereas the pattern of intentional action, in which a desire that p gives rise to the action or situation that p, and only thence to a pacifying belief, is a **secondary process** to be seen both as developing from the first, and as taking place in the context of it.

Thus, everyday action also has a status, in relation to the unconscious, as representation; and this goes with a new perspective on **desire**. Excessive or frustrated desires, even those of infancy, are not psychologically lost; rather, they are continually rearticulated through symbolism, so as to direct action towards their representational pacification during the whole of life. In this, Freud provides both a radically holistic account of the causation of action and a naturalistic (and ultimately physicalistic) description of the generation of meaning in life. New goals acquire significance as representatives of the unremembered objects of our earliest and most visceral passions; and the depth of satisfaction we feel in present accomplishments (as in the example of the writing and teaching above) flows from their unacknowledged pacification of unknown desires from the distant past. Thus, paradoxically, significant desires remain flexible, renewable and satisfiable in their expressions, precisely because they are unchangeable and unrelenting at the root.

The kind of phantasy which expresses ancient desire also constitutes or implements many further mental processes, studied mainly in psychoanalysis. Repression, for example, can be effected or maintained through the formation of phantasies in which the characteristic to be repressed is replaced by others, just as in Freud's dream his guilt was replaced by personal blamelessness together with a certain strictness on the topic of injections. Likewise, persons effect the **projection** of their own impulses, aspects of mind or traits of character, by representing others as having, and themselves as lacking, these impulses, aspects or traits, as Freud seems to have done in this dream. Finally, persons from lasting and life-shaping phantasies of themselves on the model of other persons, thereby establishing **identifications** which become constitutive of the self.

Psychology and the brain: Freud's scientific project

In clinical work, Freud described the unconscious in commonsense terms, as including wishes, beliefs, memories, etc., but he also sought to integrate his clinical findings with more theoretical concepts, as well as with neuroscience. In his early *Project for a Scientific Psychology* (1895, i, p. 283ff.) he hypothesised that the working of the brain could be understood in terms of the passage from neuron to neuron of some form of excitation, or **cathexis**, via connections which he called 'contact-barriers' On this hypothesis information was stored in the brain in the form of alterations – facilitations or inhibitions – in neural connections and processed by the passage of excitation through the interconnected networks of neurons themselves. Hence, as Freud put it, 'psychic acquisition generally', including memory, would be *'represented by the differences in the facilitations'* of neural connections (1895, i, p. 300). In this he anticipated work indicating that the brain can be understood as a computational device whose 'knowledge is *in the connections'* among neuronal processing units (Rumelhardt et al., 1988, p. 75), and also the associated view of mental processes as forms of neural activation, and mental states as dispositions to these, or structures determining them (see Glymour, 1992).

Freud sketched a model representing his early findings in these terms, and framed later discussions to be consistent with this. In this model the signalling of a bodily need – for example, nutrition in an infant – causes a disequilbrium in neural excitation. This at first results in crying and unco-ordinated bodily movements, which have at best a fleeting tendency to stabilise it. Better and more lasting equilibration requires satisfaction, for example, by feeding; and this causes the facilitation of the neural connections involved in the satisfying events. The brain thus constantly lays down neural records, or prototypes, of the sequences of perceptions, internal changes, bodily movements, etc., involved in the restoration of equilibrium by satisfaction. Then, when disequilibrium occurs again – for example when the infant is hungry again – the input signals engage previously facilitated pathways, so that the records of the best past attempts to cope with comparable situations are naturally reactivated. This, Freud hypothesised, constitutes early wishfulfilment.

Freud thus identified the wishfulfilling pacification of infantile proto-desire with what can be regarded as a form of neural prototype activation. (For a recent discussion, see Churchland, 1995.) This provided more stability in disequilibrium than the relatively random ennervations it replaced, and also served to organise the infant's responses, to hunger, for example, by reproducing those previously associated with satisfaction. Then, as the infant continued to lay down prototype upon prototype, the original wishful stabilisations evolved towards a system of thought, while also coming to govern a growing range of behaviour, increasingly co-ordinated to the securing of satisfaction.

This, however, required the brain to learn to delay the wishfulfilment-governed neural behaviour associated with past satisfaction until present circumstances were perceptibly appropriate – that is, to come increasingly under the sway of what Freud called the **reality principle**. Delay required a tolerance of **frustration**, and the absence of the satisfying **object**, and made room for **reality testing**, and hence the **binding** of the neural connections involved in the securing of satisfaction to perceptual information about the object, and later, as Freud hypothesised, to rational thought. The primary process of precipitate wishfulfilment was thus progressively overlaid and inhibited by secondary processes which provided for the securing of satisfaction in realistic conditions. This benign development could, however, be blighted if frustration (or intolerance of it) led to the overactivation of inappropriate prototypes, and this to greater frustration. Such a process could render the mind/brain increasingly vulnerable to disequilibrium and delusion, and hence increasingly reliant on earlier, and more wishfulfilling, modes of stabilisation, in a vicious circle constitutive of mental disturbance and illness.

The mind as structured: ego, super-ego and id

Freud allocated the task of fostering the sense of reality, and so providing for the satisfaction of desire, to a hypothetical neural structure, or functional part of the mind, which he called the 'das Ich', or the **ego**. (The literal meaning of Freud's phrase is 'the I'; but the concept has been translated by the Latin pronoun, which has assumed a life of its own.) In his late accounts he linked this structure with two others, the *super-ego*, which judged or criticised the ego, and which included the **ego-ideal**, representing the ideals or standards by which the ego was judged; and the primitive 'it', or **id**, the natural matrix of basic and potentially conflicting drives, present at birth, out of which these other structures developed (1974, xix, p. 3ff.; xxii, p. 57ff.; xxiii, p. 144ff.). His late discussions of these notions are particularly difficult to understand, partly because they combine a number of different modes of explanation.

Overall it seems that Freud intended the ego, super-ego and id to be functional neural systems, which can be described in a teleological way; that is, in terms of the goals which their operation secures and the information upon which they operate. This kind of explanation is now familiar from cognitive psychology, in which functional units are represented by boxes in a flow chart showing what the unit is supposed to contribute to overall psychological functioning. Freud combined such explanation with the empirical claim that the way minds actually function human depends upon the prototypes or **imagos** by which they represent themselves and others. On Freud's account, the ego and super-ego are partly constituted by repre-

sentations of the parents. The working of these functional systems is therefore partly felt, and can partly be described, in terms of motives, feelings or actions of the representational figures which they embody. Thus, Freud speaks of the super-ego as reproaching the ego for not attaining the standards embodied in the ego-ideal, the ego as feeling overwhelmed by the demands of the id, the difficulties caused by a super-ego ego which is overly harsh or punitive, etc. The idea in each case is that the operation of the functional system is both apprehended by the subject, and can be objectively described, via the prototypical figures which the system embodies.

Freud thought of the id as the neural system, or ensemble of systems, comprising the infant's innate constitutional endowment of **instincts** or **drives**; that is, structures which, under the impact of experience, would yield basic emotions and motives for action. These he took as divisible into two main categories: those which give rise to the broad group of motives which are creative and constructive, such as affection, love and care, and hence the behaviour connected with these (the **life instincts**); and those which give rise to the broad group of aggressive motives, such as envy and hate, and hence the behaviour linked with these (the **destructive** or **death instincts**). His final view was therefore that the primary conflicts in a person's life – those which necessitated repression and could become constitutive of mental illness – were ultimately to be seen as holding between that person's impulses to construct or destroy. This meant that conflict extended to sexuality in a secondary way; that is, as something which could itself be used constructively or destructively.

On Freud's account, the ego and super-ego develop out of the id, principally through the young child's identification with other persons in the environment. Freud took identification to be related to a further process, which he called **introjection**, in which the admired target of identification is phantasied as taken into the self, which is thereby modified on the model of that object. This process in turn has a basic and bodily representation in the process of **incorporation**, in which the target is represented as taken into the body. Many Christians, for example, regularly engage in a ceremony which is described as eating the body or drinking the blood of Christ. This is regarded by some as a symbolic act, and by others to involve real flesh and blood, as transubstantiated in bread and wine. In psychoanalytic terms such a ceremony represents the participants as incorporating a common object as their ego-ideal, and hence as furthering their ability to regulate their actions on the model which this object provides.

The main parameters of the original development are set by the child's attempts to satisfy innate desires in the context of the family. This leads to formative identifications with the parents, in which two rough stages can be discerned. In the first, the child advances towards self-control by forming images of the parents in their role as regulators of its bodily activities, particularly, as noted, those involved in feeding and the elimination of waste. These 'earliest parental *imagoes*' (1932, xxii, p. 54) provide the basis of the self-critical faculty of the super-ego. Since these early images embody the child's infantile aggression in a projected form, the self-critical imagination tends to be far more threatening, punitive and terrifying than the actual parents; so it can be a cause of great anxiety or guilt, and even, in the extreme, of suicide. (Witness the primitive projected super-ego taken as a 'beast of prey' above.) Later the ego is structured by the child's identifications with the parents in their role as agents; that is, as satisfiers and pacifiers of their own desires. Thus, a crucial step in normal development is identification with the parent of the same sex, which entails that sexual desires are satisfied in a way which is non-incestuous and reproductive. For this, however, the child has to relinquish the goal of usurping the place of the parent for that of becoming like her or him; so

Freud takes the final establishment of the super ego and ego-ideal to involve the dissolution of the Oedipus Complex.

Social psychology

Freud also applied these notions to the psychology o groups. The cohesiveness of many groups can be understood via the idea that their members identify with one another by putting a common figure – such as a charismatic leader (or in the case of leaderles: groups a common cause or creed) – in the place o the ego-ideal, thus reconstructing their egos in a common way (1921, xviii, p. 67ff.). This serves to ensure that the individual's sense of worth is determined by relation to the idealised object which bind: the group; and hence also aggression in service of thi need not be a cause of guilt. Members of groups ma also be identified by other means, such as the projection of their bad aspects – and, in particular their hostile motives, derived from the destructive instincts – into some common locus, which therefore becomes a focus of legitimated and collective hate

Members of a group who find such a commor good or bad object thereby feel at once purified unified and able to focus destructive motives in a wa validated by their common ideals. The processes o introjection and projection which Freud describec can thus systematically serve to organise people intc groups which represent themselves as unrealistically good while representing others as bad – an unrealistic pattern of good us/bad them common to all parties ir human conflict. Rational disagreements betweer such groups are therefore underlain and exaggeratec by projection of destructive motives, and hence by suspicions and hatreds which are both irrational anc difficult to resolve.

Bibliography

Writings

Freud's work is collected in *The Standard Edition of the Collected Psychological Works of Sigmund Freud*, translated and edited by James Strachey et al., London: Hogarth Press, 1974. Much of this translation (but not Freud's Original Record of his sessions with the Rat Man) is reprinted in *The Penguin Freud Library*, edited by Angela Richards, London: Penguin Books, 1987.

Freud, Sigmund (1974), *The Standard Editor*, Vol. r (1886), 'Report on my studies in Paris and Berlin' (1888), 'Hysteria'; (1892), 'A case of successful treat ment by hypnotism'; (1897), Letters to Wilhelm Fliess

(1895), *Project for a Scientific Psychology*.
– with Joseph Breuer, Vol. II: (1893–5), *Studies on Hysteria*.
– Vol. III: (1896), 'Further Remarks on the Neuro-Psychoses of Defense'; (1898), 'The Psychical Mechanism of Forgetfulness'; (1899), 'Screen Memories'.
– Vols IV, V: (1900), *The Interpretation of Dreams*.
– Vol. VI: (1901), *The Psychopathology of Everyday Life*.
– Vol. VII: (1905), 'Three Essays on the Theory of Sexuality'.
– Vol. IX: (1907), 'Dream and Delusion in Jensen's *Gradiva*'; (1908), 'Civilized Sexual Morality and Modern Nervous Illness'.
– Vol. X: (1909), 'Analysis of a Phobia in a Five-Year-Old Boy'; (1909), 'Notes on a Case of Obsessional Neurosis'; (1907–8), 'Addendum: Original Record of the Case'.
– Vol. XVIII: (1920), 'Beyond the Pleasure Principle'; (1921), 'Group Psychology and the Analysis of the Ego'.
– Vol. XIX: (1923), 'The Ego and the Id'.
– Vol. XXII: (1932), *New Introductory Lectures on Psycho-Analysis*.
– Vol. XXIII: (1940), 'A Short Outline of Psycho-Analysis'.

References and further reading

Freud is among the most frequently cited authors of the twentieth century and the literature relating to his work is vast. Wollheim (1991) provides a succinct and philosophically informed discussion of Freud's theories, and Gay (1988) treats both his life and work, together with a comprehensive Bibliographical Essay.

Cavell, M. (1993), *The Psychoanalytic Mind*, Cambridge, MA: Harvard University Press.
Churchland, P. (1995), *The Engine of Reason, The Seat of the Soul*, Cambridge, MA, and London: MIT Press.
Clark, P. and C. Wright (eds) (1988), *Mind, Psychoanalysis, and Science*, Oxford: Blackwell.
Gardner, S. (1993), *Irrationality and the Philosophy of Psychoanalysis*, Cambridge: Cambridge University Press.
Gay, P. (1988), *Freud, A Life for Our Time*, London and Melbourne: J. M. Dent.
Glymour, C. (1992), 'Freud's Androids', in J. Neu (ed.), *The Cambridge Companion to Freud*, Cambridge: Cambridge University Press.
Klein, M. (1975), *The Writings of Melanie Klein*, London: Karnac Books and the Institute of Psychoanalysis. (Paperback Editions, New York: Delta Press, 1977; London: Virago Press, 1989.)
Kline, P. (1984), *Psychology and Freudian Theory: An Introduction*, London: Methuen.
Laplanche, J. and Pontalis, J. B. (1973), *The Language of Psychoanalysis*, London: Hogarth Press.
Lear, J. (1990), *Love and Its Place in Nature*, New York: Farrar, Strauss, and Giroux.
Masson, J. (ed.) (1985), *The Complete Letters of Sigmund Freud to Wilhelm Fliess 1887–1904*, Boston: Harvard University Press.
Neu, J. (ed.) (1992), *The Cambridge Companion to Freud*, Cambridge: Cambridge University Press.
Wollheim, R. (1991), *Freud* (second edition), London: Fontana.

5.5

PSYCHOANALYSIS AND LITERARY THEORY

Elizabeth Wright

Introduction

Literary theory belies its name in that it can be said to be a theory about how language works. To investigate literature is always, in one way or another, to investigate language. What is at issue is a work of interpretation but there is no agreement among critics as to how this work might be done. The fact that language is inescapably figural makes for the stuff of both literature and criticism. Psychoanalytic literary theory has a distinctive contribution to make in this area. Criticism likes to parade itself as a species of metalanguage, more knowing than, if poetically inferior to, the language of the writer. What, then, is there to be gained from a critical interpretation of a text, and in particular a psychoanalytic reading? Furthermore, a much debated question, what *is* a psychoanalytic reading? Rather than rehearse the pros and cons of applied, implied, textual or deconstructive psychoanalytic criticism, let us begin with a practical example, an Edward Lear nonsense poem.

The Owl and the Pussy-Cat
Edward Lear

The Owl and the Pussy-cat went to sea
In a beautiful pea-green boat;
They took some honey and plenty of money
Wrapped up in a five-pound note.
The Owl looked up to the stars above
And sang to a small guitar:

'O lovely pussy! O pussy, my love,
What a beautiful pussy you are,
You are,
You are!
What a beautiful pussy you are!'

Pussy said to the Owl: 'You elegant fowl!
How charmingly sweet you sing!
O let us be married! Too long we have tarried:
But what shall we do for a ring?'
They sailed away, for a year and a day,
To the land where the Bong-tree grows,
And there in a wood a Piggy-wig stood
With a ring through the end of his nose,
His nose,
His nose,
With a ring through the end of his nose.

'Dear pig, are you willing to sell for one shilling
Your ring?' Said the Piggy, 'I will.'
So they took it away, and were married next day
By the turkey who lives on the hill.
They dined on mince, and slices of quince,
Which they ate with a runcible spoon;
And hand in hand, on the edge of the sand,
They danced by the light of the moon,
The moon,
The moon,
They danced by the light of the moon.

One of Freud's abiding concerns when analysing literature and the arts was the question of who had priority in the discovery of the unconscious, the poet or the psychoanalyst, that is, Freud himself. Thus, we might say that the literary critic is not sure whether he or she is an analyst-owl among the analysand-pussycats of her or his audience, who have much to learn, or, vice versa, an analysand-pussycat, who has much to learn from the analyst-owls, the clinicians. This is to touch on a long-standing controversy between literature and psychoanalysis: who understands the unconscious best, the poet or the clinician? Or, do the aesthetic and the clinical have to speak in entirely different languages or does the poetic enter both?

Of course, Edward Lear's poem can be enjoyably read as a nonsense poem. It has been set to music for its strong rhythmic qualities, including its repetitions, internal rhymes and refrain. It is also a narrative because it poses and resolves a problem through a transformation; and its setting is a romantic scene, with a courtship, a sea journey, a far-away hill, a song to a guitar, stars, the moon, marriage and a celebratory feast. In addition, it follows the topos of a fairytale in having animal characters, one of whom is a helping figure. What could psychoanalysis possibly add to this account which might explain the lasting popularity of this apparently naive poem?

'The Owl and the Pussycat' might also be read as a lovely transgressive fantasy about two creatures from different *genera* (read also 'generations' – the root of both words comes from the Indo-European root *gen*, meaning to beget, generate, produce), with two different reproductive systems. The two creatures take their liquids and their solids – their honey and their money – first to the libidinal pig in the wood and then to the phallic turkey on the hill, in order to have access to the Bong-tree. Then, finally, they couple, in that liminal space, the seashore. Before that, they feast, on a hitherto impossible plenitude of food (mince instead of a common diet of mice), using a 'runcible spoon'. A runcible spoon is a nonsense term invented by Lear to describe a three-pronged fork hollowed out like a spoon, and which has one prong with a cutting edge: it is an object which defies categorisation, wanting to be fork, knife and spoon all in one. It cannot fit into one genus – except in fantasy, like the union of the Owl and the Pussycat. It happens that Edward Lear's

nonsense work is particularly characterised by its confusion of categories, both in its writing and its drawing.

Nonsense poetry is a refusal to accept the boundaries of language. Psychoanalysis has a theory about such a refusal (see section two of this article). A psychoanalytic reading might thus take up this confusion of boundaries and diagnose the poem as both an incestuous fantasy, a denial of castration in its wish to transgress familial boundaries, and a question about the riddles of procreation and sexual difference – but is it Edward Lear's fantasy? There is no way we can know. What the above reading testifies to is the power of the poem to arouse a fantasy in the reader. If such a reading is rhetorically convincing to others, then one could argue that the poem's popularity with readers of all ages testifies to its capacity to provoke primal fantasies, defined as 'typical phantasy structures' (see Laplanche and Pontalis, 1973, pp. 331–3); these include intrauterine existence (the sea), primal scene (the coupling), (denial of) castration (confusion of categories), and seduction (the serenade in the boat). Furthermore, I have heard this song sung as a cabaret item, with a salacious emphasis on the refrain 'what a beautiful *pussy* you are', thereby emphasising castration, in that this singles out the woman, first, as metaphorically reduced to a cat, and, second, as metonymically further reduced, to being merely a part of a cat – her sexual organs the cat's fur.

What, then, can be said about the nature of a psychoanalytic reading on the basis of this brief discussion? Psychoanalytic theory rests on the assumption that sexuality is the constitutive factor in the construction of the subject. In its practice it relies on finding structural images in the mind which point to the way the present is determined by the past in terms of the subject's sexual history, the genital function being the endpoint, the pre-genital the beginning of that history. The beginning is seen as the loss experienced by the subject upon its separation from the mother's body. A psychoanalytic reading therefore primarily involves accounting for the presence of sexuality in the text. The process of revealing and theorising these sexual fantasies has gone through a series of by now familiar stages (see Wright, 1984). The point now is to discuss what crucially ties together psychoanalysis and literary theory: the relation of desire and language.

Psychoanalysis has a particular theory about why language is literary all the time, a particular way of accounting for the irrepressible figurality of language. From the beginning, psychoanalytic theory has paid attention to literature and the arts, taking them to employ the same processes that Freud uncovered in the workings of the unconscious. Freud himself moved from the discourse of science into the camp of the artist, the novelist and the poet, 'taking models, conceptual figures and key examples from literature' (Certeau, 1986). In this article I want to investigate the applications and implications of this body of psychoanalytic theory for literature and language (Freud and Lacan, sections one and two), and for the reading of the literary and psychoanalytic text (both on and off the couch, section three).

Psychoanalysis and literature: Freud

Just as with the advent of modern literary theory it was found that 'that there are more things in literary texts than are dreamt of in Freudian philosophy' (Ellmann, 1994, p. 26), so there are also many things in literary texts that the critic had not been conscious of before the advent of psychoanalysis. What is more, when some of Freud's writings were themselves read literally, taken at their word, scanned for their slippages and gaps (Derrida, 1987), it became apparent that psychoanalytic texts were no more immune from a literary reading than was any other text. The assumption of the authority of psychoanalysis over literature was first properly challenged in an influential volume inaugurating a dialectical exchange between psychoanalysis and literature, where psychoanalysis points to the unconscious of literature and literature to the unconscious of psychoanalysis (Felman, 1977, pp. 5–10).

The discovery of the irrepressibility of the unconscious is the great contribution of psychoanalysis to critical theory in general and to literary criticism in particular. Felman's work indirectly reveals what deconstruction owes to psychoanalysis, even though deconstruction often endeavours to make itself independent of psychoanalytic theory, when, without a theory of the unconscious, it would hardly have got off the ground. In seeing that meaning was at one and the same time both too much and not enough, both supplementary and lacking, deconstruction battened on Freud's linguistic discoveries throughout his work; namely, that desire cannot name itself except by substitution.

In order to argue for the measure of Freud's contribution, I would like to examine the Freudian inspiration, particularly in its impact on our understanding of the relation between desire and language, which is later more fully articulated in Lacan's formulations (to be discussed in the next Section). A good place to begin is Freud's elaboration of the concept of the uncanny, a key example of the irrepressibility of the unconscious.

Freud's definition of the uncanny is to be found in his celebrated essay of that name (Freud, 1919), but what is this effect that is called 'uncanny'? According to Freud, 'it is undoubtedly related to what is frightening – to what arouses dread and horror' (ibid., p. 215). He defines what characterises the uncanny by examining the German word for it, *unheimlich*. He writes: '*Unheimlich* is in some way or other a species of *heimlich*', and '*heimlich* is a word the meaning of which develops in the direction of ambivalence' (ibid., p. 266). *Heimlich* means not only homely and familiar, but also hidden and secret. The *un-* of the *unheimlich* marks the return of the repressed material: the word or thing threatens us in some way by no longer fitting the desired context. Hence the uncanny has the effect of destabilising language: modern critical theory has moved on from the structuralist perception that words refer to each other rather than to things, to the further recognition that this perception ignores the uncanny effect upon language of that to which it seeks to refer.

Let us see what Freud makes of Hoffmann's story, 'The Sandman' (Hoffmann, 1982), which he uses as a prime example of the uncanny. Numerous articles (for a listing and discussion of some of them see Wright, 1984, pp. 145–9), mainly inspired by the protest that Freud has turned this hugely provocative story into a mere clinical vignette, have testified to the power of Freud's analysis to generate more and more readings. For my discussion of this story I have in part drawn on one of the more recent commentaries (Dolar, 1991).

Freud's account is based on two relations: that between the student Nathanael and the doll Olympia, and that between the Sandman/Coppelius and the Father/Spalanzani (the creator of the doll). The two relations are haunted by the uncanny. The first relation, with the doll Olympia, is in the uncanny area between the living and the dead. A doll is precisely typical of what constitutes the uncanny, for dolls in their *heimlich* incarnation are harmless copies of human beings, lifeless, completely under control and connoting the world of childhood innocence. Olympia is a mechanical doll who moves according to a principle of her own, in an *unheimlich* fashion; like an analyst, she sits there except for the occasional sounds that punctuate the silence. It is through her that Nathanael realises his essential ambivalence in relation to the father-figure, for, according to Freud, she is Nathanael's sister image, 'fathered' by Spalanzani and Coppola (Coppelius's double), a 'dissociated complex' of Nathanael's, who, through his narcissistic relation with her (she appears to be in complete agreement with him, unlike his fiancée Clara), adopts the passive feminine position towards the father.

The second relation is that between the two fathers: the good (real) father who intercedes to protect him (and subsequently dies), and the bad (symbolic) father/castrator. Behind the dead father is the castrating father, the lawyer Coppelius (the mythical 'Sandman' who throws sand in children's eyes, thus blinding them) and his double Coppola, who sells artificial eyes (eye glasses). Both figures appear as '*Störer der Liebe*' ('disturbers' of love), finally tearing apart the doll Olympia in a fight for possession and thus provoking Nathanael's fit of madness. In Hoffmann's tale the uncanny blocks Nathanael's narcissistic completion, eventually arousing sufficient dread in him to send him hurtling to his death.

Should we agree with the critics who find in this reading no more than a clinical vignette? Even a cursory glance at what constitutes a clinical vignette in the psychoanalytic journals should convince us to the contrary. Certainly Freud has not used Hoffmann's ingenious narrative structure, the way he begins his story with a series of letters, his address to the reader, his play with linear time, but otherwise

he has been sensitive to certain powerful aesthetic effects to the degree that the boundaries between the psychoanalytic and the literary have become somewhat blurred; for his interpretation is grounded in effects of repeated configurations, ambivalences and ambiguities, the very stuff of literature and criticism. In particular, since this is one of his attempts at literary analysis, Freud has demonstrated, albeit unknowingly and *avant la lettre*, that criticism is in no way a metalanguage, that his own efforts are not immune to the effects of the uncanny, because what he has left out has returned as an excess in his own text. Freud's text conceals and reveals the very things he has left out of Hoffmann's: images of castration – death and dismemberment, anxiety regarding originality, anxiety about sexuality, thus testifying to the uncanny effect, to the return of the repressed, and thereby validating both his discoveries and those of the poets. Freud has 'disseminated' castration (Derrida, 1982, p. 268), scattered it about, by making use of Hoffmann's story, as well as a variety of literary allusions (for example, to Wilhelm Hauff's fairy tales, with their imagery of cut-off limbs), thereby showing that fiction is required as a supplement to life, if only to postpone death (as Scheherezade knew).

Both psychoanalysis and literature partake of the uncanny: a theory of the uncanny is also a theory of literature and the arts. Again we can turn to Freud to ask about the uses of psychoanalysis in the realm of aesthetics. Freud said a great many things about literature and the arts – some of them contradictory – which are beyond the scope of this enquiry (for a comprehensive and meticulously documented account, see Kofman, 1988). Here I can only summarise wherein, according to Freud, lies the powerful effect of the artist/writer's work. He made two major pronouncements, one to account for the pleasure we derive from our identification with the hero's triumph (Freud, 1908), and one for what we derive from our identification with the hero's downfall (Freud, 1905/6). Although these two pleasures appear to be at opposite poles, what unites them is the capacity of the work of art to offer a disguise and shelter for our narcissism. But how does suffering gratify our narcissism?

There is a social dimension to fantasy in that fantasy can be either shared pleasure or shared suffering: at an unconscious level, the suffering itself is enjoyed masochistically. The pleasure of fantasy consoles for the suffering induced by the oppressive symptom, whereby the superego exacts payment. This pleasure of fantasy, for Freud, is the imaginary function of art, but he also sees it as having a symbolic function, in that he sees art as achieving a transformation of this narcissism of the id into the narcissism of the ego: the narcissism of the id is the illusion of omnipotence; the narcissism of the ego is the belief that one's wishes can coincide perfectly with the social. The transformation is effected when excessive libido is 'de-sexualised' by being diverted into other channels, a process Freud calls sublimation. The work of art and literature has the capacity to involve both creator and spectator in this process through their mutual narcissisms meeting in what has been called by one critic/analyst a trans-narcissistic communication (Green, 1978, p. 283). Through the aesthetic work, both artist/writer and spectator/reader momentarily free themselves, working/playing through the repressed material in an illusion of jointly creating a whole object. This end process, as has been pointed out (Laplanche and Pontalis, 1973, p. 433), is not unlike what Melanie Klein has called 'reparation' (Klein, 1975). Yet, for Freud, sublimation is not merely a baptism of the cultural: he also presents sublimation as an operation of the partial, non-genital drives (oral, anal and phallic (Freud, 1905)), thus suggesting the 'perverse' dimension of the social field.

The upshot of this is that psychoanalysis has shown that the structure of the aesthetic object always produces more than the author or reader intends, the object's lure lying in its uncanny power to provoke the reader's unconscious fantasy. Shifts of context outside the reader's control betray the fact that the comfortable reference is no longer what it appears to be. The uncanny of literature blocks narcissistic completion. Thus, in my example of Edward Lear's poem, if we set aside the main literary element (but keep its rhythmic and phonic qualities), ignoring that its genre is that of a fable where fantastic elements are normal and which everyone reads as a nonsense poem, then we can see the uncanniness of two animals enemies by nature, libidinally incompatible, courting each other. The

psychoanalytic unconscious has replaced the humanist critic's notion of a rich plenitude of ambiguity with the disconcerting notion of the return of the repressed, the uncanny effect *par excellence*. What Freud finally leaves undeveloped is the relation between the repressed material and language, a relation which involves something unrepresentable (see Lacan's notion of 'the real' in the next Section).

The Freudian notion of art's function in culture is, nevertheless, ultimately a consoling one, which, as we shall see, Lacan does not share to the same degree. For Freud, literature and art gratifies an unconscious wish, even where that wish is a perverse one; for him, the relation of the aesthetic to the wish is that of a hopeful projection of desire. Art is that which enables us to hold on to our innermost fantasies and at the same time allows us to participate in the work of sublimation.

Psychoanalysis and language: Lacan

Lacan's concept of the unconscious is a structural one ('the unconscious is structured like a language'), but he moves beyond the tenets of structuralism and post-structuralism. An acknowledgement of structure has to be balanced with a theoretical explanation of its continual adjustment, not to say its failure, its uncanniness, and this is precisely what Lacan does. Language trades on an illusory literalness which is the source of its concealed figurality; the aesthetic recognises the figural straight away – shows the danger of being too literal. Hence, it cannot be the case that a metaphorical language opposes an exclusively literal language, the reason being that desire can never reach its (lost) object.

How then does Lacan conceptualise the relation between desire and language? Lacan takes from the linguist Ferdinand de Saussure the notion of language as a system of signs determined by their difference from each other. However, whereas Saussure sees the sign as a unity of signifier (sound image) and signified (concept) which, once part of a system of differences, are firmly bonded together, Lacan sees the signifier as sliding in meaning over the field of experience from which the signified is selected and not, as Saussure held, a field of thoughts. Lacan calls this field *the real*, the first of the three orders with which he divides up the psychic field. By the real he does not mean mundane reality. The real is the body as part of an undifferentiated nature. For the incipient subject, the part of the real that is significant is the mother's body, what Freud calls *Das Ding* and Lacan *the impossible*, because it is pre-symbolic and hence unrepresentable. The real turns up in a subject's relation to desire, making its appearance because our signifying systems cannot be taken literally: the desired object is never the one we want. What we desire is the primordial lost object, the Thing. It figures in unconscious fantasy as a missing part of the body, a remainder and reminder of the traumatic separation from the mother's body and the body of nature.

Lacan calls this remainder *objet a*. It is a difficult concept but it is important to grasp it both for Lacan's theory of language and for the unprecedented function he assigns to literature and the arts. There is a dialectic involved with the *objet a* which does not simply make it into an object of desire. In the first place, it is felt as a lack in being, and hence Lacan calls it the object *cause* of desire; in the second place it is a fantasy object pursued in the hope of filling this lack. The subject constantly searches for its object in every representation as a hoped-for completion of a unity that never was.

The never-satiated desire for unity finds illusory satisfaction in the realm that Lacan calls *the imaginary*, the second of his three orders. In the imaginary there is a narcissistic illusion inaugurated when the infant takes its image – from a mirror or through some other impression – to be an Ideal-Ego, possessing the co-ordination and control it has not yet achieved. This is what Lacan calls the 'mirror stage' (Lacan, 1977c). The other in the mirror is me. The imaginary is a way of denying there is lack: in the imaginary the infant believes that it can be all that the mother desires.

However, for Lacan, desire is always the desire of the Other. This implies a fundamental alienation of the subject in that it involves the necessary separation from the mother and the introduction of difference. Difference is introduced through the intervention of the castrating Law. In Lacan's version of the Oedipus the 'Name-of-the-Father' (in French there is a pun: *nom*/name and *non*/no)

functions as a metaphor for the Law of language, which, as we have seen, is a differential system. The symbolic phallus as a mark of lack for both sexes takes the place of the imaginary phallus – the penis or plenitude the mother never had, since she is herself subject to the desire of the Other and hence marked by lack. In the real, the woman is not lacking, nor is the phallus/penis an infallible source of power and fecundity. Hence the Lacanian notion of mourning for the phallus affects both sexes and has consequences for Lacan's views on the function of art and literature.

To have a place as subjects among subjects is to accept the divisions of language, to be subjected to a symbol system which is always already there. The price for a place in *the symbolic*, the third of Lacan's three orders, is the repression of desire (for the mother), or what Lacan calls the effacement of the subject behind the signifier (the effect of acceding to the paternal interdiction, the Father's name/ no). When language gives the subject the ability to count itself as different, it loses the imaginary union with the Mother's body. But, paradoxically, at the very moment when the subject speaks to another, becomes 'I', 'you', 'she', it has to 'sacrifice' itself, it 'fades', and as a consequence it clings to the phantasmatic object for consistency, to supplement its loss of being. Lacan formalises this recurring moment, the endless repetition of this searching, as the very structure of desire: $\$ \diamond a$. The formula designates the incommensurability ($\diamond$) of the barred (divided) subject (S) to its desire (*objet a*). Although, in return for the loss of the object, the subject is given a place in language, which seems to promise a fulfilment of desire, such fulfilment cannot be delivered, since the lost object resists symbolisation. The symbiosis is now forbidden and, as a consequence, unconscious desire will perpetually undermine the meanings imposed by language, subverting the symbolic and leading to endless figuration.

Thus, for Lacan, the function of language is only seemingly communication: it has the function rather of producing a social bond in the symbolic. But, paradoxically, Lacan designates the symbolic as an alien force impinging from outside and calls it 'the Other'. With the assumption of a name and place in the Other, the split subject comes into being as a relation between two signifiers in which it exists for another subject only in a narcissistic relation (the imaginary, the mirror stage). Yet the 'I' which speaks will always be governed by the discourse of the Other, undermining the meaning imposed by language. Where Freud sees this as going on by means of the mechanisms of condensation and displacement, which he identified first in dreams and the hysteric's discourse, Lacan translates these figures into the classical tropes of metaphor and metonymy: metaphor is the symptom which reveals where unconscious desire his stuck; metonymy is the pursuit of the desired object along an endless chain of signifiers. The subject cannot be autonomous, for the figurality of language only provides provisional, ironic satisfaction. In short, signification is always partial.

Yet the symbolic never stops inscribing itself, organising every social relation and every discourse, in particular that of the sexual. For Lacan there is no sexual relation that can be inscribed in discourse. It is the traces of that non-inscription (as in Edward Lear's poem) that we so eagerly pursue in discourse, filling the gap with our fantasies. An ideal sexual relation is impossible (in the unconscious the woman remains the mother, the woman who has everything – the libidinal pig of the poem), although it is what promises the longed-for plenitude.

Instead of Freud's dualistic concept of a pleasure principle, the wish for a return to a plenitude that never was, as against a reality principle, asking for renunciation of this wish (a dilemma which, as we have seen, can be negotiated in the play of art's dual structure), Lacan proposes a dialectic of need, demand and desire. The need is for nourishment, the demand is for the mother's absolute love, the desire is for a fantasy, the mnemic traces of a lost object. Need belongs to the realm of the real, demand to that of the imaginary and desire to that of the symbolic. It is only through language that we can articulate our desires, but there will always be a real leftover.

Thus, language cannot function as what we think of as 'normal' communication, as, for example instance, in Jakobson's linguistic model (Jakobson, 1960). In this model an addresser sends a message to an addressee; the message makes use of a code, normally a language familiar to both parties; the message has a context, a referent; and it is transmitted through a contact, speech or writing. Language is here taken as a transparent medium of communication *through* which the message is sent, and the subject, addresser as well as addressee, is presumed to be 'there', prior to that language and in command of her or his intentions. It is a model that has been adopted by various schools of criticism. Each element in turn has been at the centre of literary theory. The Romantic critic focuses on the author as addresser, the phenomenological critic on the reader as addressee, the formalist critic on the message as code, the Marxist critic on the context as history and society. Although with the advent of modern literary theory the emphasis has gradually moved from speech to writing as a medium which more readily reveals the interaction of all these elements, any notion of an unconscious undermining the so-called communication process is left out of this model, assuming as it does, that it deals with stable terms and stable positions.

Lacan's discourse mathemes might be viewed as countermodels to Jakobson's in that they demonstrate the impossibility and impotence of 'normal' communication (Lacan, 1969/70; see also Bracher, 1994). Instead of the structuralist emphasis on language as solely constituted by differences, what emerges is the uncanniness of discourse as that which, while aiming to forge and maintain a social bond, is continually undermined. Yet, paradoxically, Lacan's discourses are also, in his view, the only way in which a social bond can be maintained. They are a series of formulaic models showing what happens when a subject speaks. The discourses (there are four in all: that of the master, the university, the analyst and the hysteric) comprise between them all the possible unconscious relations that are brought into play at different moments in a so-called communication situation. Unlike Jakobson, Lacan does not take communication as the transmission of a stable message from one speaker to another, but starts out with the assumption that, as in the analytic situation, the relation of speaker to hearer is a relation of desire as an *unconscious* structure determining both. All discourse is the 'discourse of the Other', by which Lacan means the order of language as a chain of signifiers which impinge from outside and produce the subject, not vice versa, the subject producing language, as in Jakobson's model.

It is constitutive for every discourse that the subject appears only as represented by another signifier. To use a distinction developed by the linguist Emile Benveniste (1966), the grammatical term 'I', the subject announced (the ego), is not coterminous with 'me', the subject of the enunciation (and the unconscious). What does this mean? Lacan's account of discourse shows that I am alienated in language, that when 'I' identify myself in discourse, this is always a partial identity – an identification – never a full one. I must make use of signifiers to be recognised, to be at all, yet the signifier cannot represent my 'non-being', for which I have no words. The subject of the announced, 'I', and the subject of the enunciation, 'me', are different positions for the speaking subject and it is split between them ($).

So how does this connect with a Lacanian view of the function of literature and the arts? Freud's psychoanalytic aesthetics offers images of consolation as a compromise between a wish and its renunciation. His focus is mainly on the author as the *agent provocateur* of this process. Lacan shifts the emphasis firmly on to the reader/spectator: psychoanalysis cannot tell us directly about the unconscious signification of art and literature, but it might tell us why a given work produces an effect in the reader. The work of art is as much a symptom of the spectator as it is of the creator. How, then, can art create pleasure for others? We know Freud's view: the aesthetic element overcomes resistance, preparing for access to the unconscious fantasy. What we might call, after Nietzsche, the Apollonian function of the image can protect us from the Dionysian. But whereas Freud is concerned with the function of the image, Lacan dwells on the problem of the (lost) object. Lacan thus introduces a dimension of (real) lack into the aesthetic. The image serves as a screen for the (lost) object which the subject desires to look at. There is a difference between (conscious) seeing and (unconscious) looking. To see concerns the image which gives us pleasure: to look has a relation to the object which is lacking. This produces anxiety instead of pleasure, because the real object is unrepresentable. It cannot

be represented by an image, since it is what is lacking in the image. In his seminar 'Of the Gaze as *Objet Petit a*', Lacan speaks of the dialectic between the eye and the gaze (the work's otherness regarding us). Art, he says, combines the lure of the gaze (the *trompe l'œil*) and its power to tame (the *dompte-regard*) (Lacan, 1977a, pp. 111–12). It tames (rather than consoles, as in Freud) because it encourages 'renunciation' (p. 111), by making the spectator/reader simultaneously aware of desire and lack. It encourages sublimation rather than idealisation because the ideal object, being unrepresentable, is shown to be not hidden but absent.

The veil of beauty, the lure, conceals the lacking object and thus protects the one who looks. In Wordsworth's poem *Elegiac Stanzas*, the poet is aghast at the sight of George Beaumont's painting of the stormy sky over Peele Castle, which he remembers as an idyllic scene:

> So pure the sky, so quiet the air!
> So like, so very like, was day to day!
> Whene'er I looked, thy Image was still there;
> It trembled, but it never passed away.

'In the fond illusion of his heart', this is the vision the poet would have painted, seeing in it 'the soul of truth' and a 'steadfast peace that might not be betrayed' but the Apollonian vision has been succeeded by the Dionysian one of 'lightning, the fierce wind, and trampling waves'. As Kant makes the sublime serve as a shield for terror, so the poet allows the 'passionate Work' (which might be seen as the psychic work of poet/analyst and reader/analysand, as well as Peele's painting) to tame his totalising grasp, renouncing the imaginary plenitude under the poetic, not-so-tame-threat:

> And this huge castle, standing here sublime,
> I love to see the look with which it braves,
> Cased in the unfeeling armour of old time,
> The lightning, the fierce wind, and trampling
>   waves.

Pace Kant, the work of art betrays its own uncanniness. It provides a fantasy object, inciting the look, and lures us to search for what we cannot see in the 'real' painting outside the poem. It speaks of something beyond the visible, beyond pleasure, and beyond beauty.

> So once it would have been, – 'tis so no more;
> I have submitted to a new control:
> A power is gone, which nothing can restore;
> A deep distress has humanized my Soul.

The *Elegiac Stanzas* is a self-named poem about mourning and we know that it is also a mourning for the drowning of Wordsworth's brother John at sea. Nevertheless, with this loss the poem also commemorates a more primal loss (a very Wordsworthian gesture), one in which even the most celebratory work of art and its reception participates in, if we take a Freudo-Lacanian view of language.

The poet/critic Friedrich Schiller, confronting the idea of loss – for him the loss of an ideal past – distinguishes the poetry of the *naive* from that of the *sentimental* (in using these German terms he had in mind Goethe for the first and himself for the second). He thought thereby to make a philosophic contribution to genre in that he tried to separate what he saw as an unselfconscious unmediated relation to nature in which the real and the ideal are, at least momentarily, at one (the *naive*), from a self-conscious distanced one in which the poet is aware of his (symbolic) alienation (the *sentimental*). By Schiller's reckoning, Wordsworth would have been a *sentimental* poet (the word in German does not denote excessive indulgence in emotion, but excessive reflectiveness), since he invariably writes in the past tense, mourning what he no longer possesses. The sublime is a way of transcending this dilemma, an attempt to bridge the gap between the *naive* and the *sentimental*, which Schiller, the Kantian, also undertakes. For literary critic Harold Bloom, on the other hand, the poetry of the sublime represents a manic triumph over loss (Bloom, 1975), but nevertheless it is the 'strong poet' that he admires in Freud: one who is not afraid to advance on his precursors, in Freud's case, by producing a theory of the unconscious that steals a march on the poet's own awareness of it.

Returning to Wordsworth's poem, its idealising

and superegoic elements cannot obliterate the uncanny play of real, imaginary and symbolic, respectively, the 'unfeeling armour of old time', 'the gentlest of all gentle things' and 'the light that never was'. This skirting round the lost object is reminiscent of Lacan's celebrated reading of Poe's *The Purloined Letter* (Lacan, 1972; see also Felman, 1980, and Wright, 1986), whereby he turns a detective story into an allegory of mourning. Likewise, Lacan reads *Hamlet* as a play about the inadequacy of mourning, an allegory of blocked desire and of the act of mourning which finally unblocks it (Lacan, 1977b).

Putting together Freud and Lacan, the power of literature and art might be said to have a dual nature. For Freud, the aesthetic factor resides in the capacity of the artist to transform his infantile material into something that by its complex figuration offers a respite from privation and gives pleasure; and it is obvious that Freud derives pleasure from the psychoanalysis of art and the artist, for all his honorific gestures to the mysteries of both. For Lacan, art has more of the function of the analyst, offering itself as cause of desire and raising an ethical dimension: the semblance of the (lost) object, like the analyst's equivocal interpretation, provokes and opposes the intertness of the fantasy, producing the uncanny effect. There is suffering because of the desire of the Other, which sets the limit to the subject's desire. There is an obligation to otherness, but also to not giving up one's desire. This, for Lacan, is where ethics enters the picture, both artistic and psychoanalytic.

Readers and texts/patients and analysts

We have seen that, with the advent of modern critical theory, the author as 'subject-supposed-to-know' – Lacan's term for the knowledge the patient imputes to the analyst – has had to share his authority with the reader/critic, writing from a position in desire; that is, being governed in one's desire by what the Other desires. This inevitably produces failures of meaning, gaps in the text. Hence, modern reader theory and practice, from Roland Barthes (1976) to the Constance School of phenomenological reading (see Iser, 1980; Jauss,

1982) to feminist readers of all persuasions, has been preoccupied in various ways with theorising gaps in the literary and historical text. This does not necessarily mean that he or she was any less disposed to give up a position of mastery, even if it is that of master or mistress of the gaps, but that the text as a site of transferential meanings has learnt to look after itself. It is even quite possible that the literary text runs less risk in the hands of the psychoanalyst than the patient does. Neither the treatment of Edgar Allan Poe by Marie Bonaparte (1949) nor that of the Mona Lisa by Freud (1910) has dis-figured these texts for all time. On the contrary, what has been called the poe-etic effect (Felman, 1980), the instigation of a creative series of competitive readings, has provoked a collection entitled *The Purloined Poe* (Muller and Richardson, 1988), while Freud's botched treatment of Dora has had similarly productive effects (Bernheimer and Kahane, 1985).

A key question now arises: does the reader's relationship to the text have any equivalence with the relationship between analyst and analysand? One of the standard objections is that the text does not have an unconscious, only persons do; and even if the author has, you cannot put her or him on the couch. Psychoanalysts themselves have been sceptical about the contributions of literary and critical theory to their discourse. The notion of 'the text' as a site of transferential meanings developed, as I pointed out above, in the wake of Saussure's theory of language, but despite the revolutionary effect of his work, which cut out any simple referential theory of meaning, it took some time to account for the problem of the real that lies under all the objects referred to in the text.

This real, which psychoanalysis theorises as that part of the subject that has escaped the signifier of language, remains as a problematic excess, and it is at these margins of language that the unconscious makes itself felt. Neither author nor reader, analysand nor analyst, will know in advance what referential effects will be brought into play in the course of a reading/session. What happens is that the unconscious does its own reading: it 'reads' by means of verbal associations and sounds that attach themselves to networks of images which come from early bodily experience. These unconscious effects have been theorised in different ways, in Freud's terms as primary process, in Lacan as the imaginary, in Julia Kristeva's as the semiotic, but whatever the theoretical differences might be, this 'text', this weave of images, brings the unconscious into the supposedly objective and rational language system. This excess of signification – which may also be experienced as a dearth of meaning because it is always out of place – is omitted from Saussure's theory of language, Jakobson's communication model and Speech Act theory.

For both psychoanalysis and literary-critical theory, wanting to bring about changes in our system of reference, the focus is on textuality: the condensations and displacements (metaphors and metonymies) of language in the production of desire. This invariably produces conflict, for the literary/analytic text is desired on the one hand as Law, the language of the Symbolic, which gives the subject its sexual identification, and on the other hand as a site of continual search for the lost object. Thus meaning is never final, and textual analysis, like life analysis, is interminable.

Considering, then, the productiveness of current psychoanalytic criticism, it is a pity that there continue to be blocks to a fertile dialogue between psychoanalysts and literary critics. In his book, *Retelling a Life: Narration and Dialogue in Psychoanalysis*, Roy Schafer (1992) argues eloquently for placing Freud's legacy in the context of modern critical theory, shifting him from the context of the Enlightenment to the discourse of contemporary philosophy-of-science debates. He pleads for the need of a persuasive rhetoric for psychoanalytic writing as against the present neutered mode, describing it as that of a 'genderless, raceless, classless, expert delivering a monologue that gives all the appearance of having been stripped of rhetorical ploys' (pp. 150–1), as if closing itself against alternative readings, unlike Freud's texts with their destabilising, self-deconstructive effects (like his *Uncanny* essay). Both analytic and literary language displace and condense taken-for-granted binary oppositions like female/male, passive/active, slave/master, and – returning to Edward Lear's pussycat/owl – in the owl's courtship of the pussycat, who takes the dominant role in this binary? In the analytic/reading situation, who seduces whom? The seductive effect of the text on the reader has been classically demonstrated in *The Pleasure of the Text* (Barthes, 1976) while the seductive effect of the analysand on the analyst has been amply documented in the analytic literature on countertransference. Can psychoanalytic and literary 'free association' – that psychic/poetic inspiration of the analytic process – be securely lodged on one side or the other? Can literary theory adequately account for the multiple meanings generated by the text without a theory of the unconscious? Can psychoanalysis adequately account for the uncanny shifts of meaning that occur from moment to moment in a clinical session without a modern theory of language?

The parallels abound. But, as a final objection – the usual attack when it is a question of applied versus clinical psychoanalysis – how can you put a text on the couch when it cannot answer back? There are further presuppositions at work here, one to do with the text and one to do with the patient. The assumption is that, somehow, the analysand is in a position to verify the analyst's interpretation in a straightforward way, instead of there being a dialectical interchange, where the utterance of both parties is material for further interpretation, destabilised by its reference to the Other, Lacan's term for the language and Law to which both parties are subject. What is forgotten in this assumption is that the analytic text – the psychoanalytic dialogue – is an uncanny object, as hard to pin down as the analytic cure. Both literary and analytic texts (those of authors and critics, of analysts and analysands) have to prove themselves again and again in the world: all parties will continue to treat their respective texts and each other's texts with suspicion. At the same time, their ministrations keep alive their own texts and those of their uncanny doubles. While I agree with Schafer (1992, p. 184) that one should not assume that therapy cannot be carried out on art and literature, in the sense that criticism can bring a work back to life, I do not see the critic's task as necessarily affirming a poem's unity, although there is always a temptation to do so (perhaps illustrated in my effort to find sense in Edward Lear's nonsense). One could argue that a therapeutic reading of texts and patients might also be a moment of dismantling, of taking apart (analysing) without being in a hurry to put together, to achieve what deconstruction has termed 'closure'. In the often negative transferential relations between psychoanalysis and literary theory it is a pity that neither seems to be able to renounce their fantasy of the other as inhabiting a realm from which they are by definition excluded and which, therefore, they must either conquer or discredit.

Bibliography

Writings

Freud, Sigmund (1940–68), *The Standard Edition of the Complete Psychological Works*, 24 vols, trans. John Strachey, London: Hogarth Press and the Institute of Psycho-Analysis.
— (1900), *The Interpretation of Dreams*, in *The Standard Edition* vols IV and V.
— (1901), *The Psychopathology of Everyday Life*, in *The Standard Edition* vol. VI.
— (1905), *Jokes and their Relation to the Unconscious*, in *The Standard Edition* vol. VIII.
Lacan, Jacques (1977a), *The Four Fundamental Concepts of Psychoanalysis*, trans. Alan Sheridan, London: Hogarth Press and The Institute of Psycho-Analysis, 67–78.
— (1992), *The Ethics of Psychoanalysis, 1959–60; The Seminar of Jacques Lacan*, trans. Dennis Porter, ed. Jacques-Alain Miller, London: Tavistock/Routledge.

References and further reading

Barthes, Roland (1976), *The Pleasure of the Text*, London: Jonathan Cape.
Benveniste, Émile (1966), *Problèmes de linguistique générale*, Paris: Gallimard.
Bernheimer, Charles and Claire Kahane (eds) (1985), *In Dora's Case: Freud – Hysteria – Feminism*, New York: Columbia University Press.
Bloom, Harold (1975), *A Map of Misreading*, New York: Oxford University Press.
Bonaparte, Marie (1949), *The Life and Works of Edgar Allan Poe*, London: Imago.
Bracher, Mark (ed.) (1994), *Lacan's Theory of Discourse: Subject, Structure and Society*, New York: New York University Press.
Certeau, Michel de (1986), *Heterologies: Discourse on the Other*, trans. Brian Massumi, Minneapolis: University of Minnesota Press.

Derrida, Jacques (1982), *Dissemination*, trans. Barbara Johnson, Chicago: Chicago University Press.

— (1987), *The Postcard: From Socrates to Freud and Beyond*, trans. Alan Bass, Chicago: Chicago University Press.

Dolar, Mladen (1991), ' "I shall be with you on your wedding-night": Lacan and the uncanny', *October*, 58, 6–23.

Ellmann, Maud (ed.) (1994), *Psychoanalytic Literary Criticism*, London and New York: Longman.

Felman, Shoshana (ed.) (1977), *Literature and Psychoanalysis: The Question of Reading; Otherwise, Yale French Studies*, 55–6.

— (1980), 'On reading poetry: reflections on the limits and possibilities of psychoanalytical approaches', in Joseph H. Smith (ed.), *The Literary Freud*, New Haven and London: Yale University Press, 119–48.

Freud, Sigmund (1905), 'Three Essays on Sexuality', in *The Standard Edition*, vol. VII, 123–245.

— (1905–6), 'Psychopathic characters on the stage', in *The Standard Edition*, vol. VII, 303–10.

— (1908), 'Creative writers and day-dreaming', in *The Standard Edition*, vol. IX, 141–54.

— (1910), 'Leonardo da Vinci and a memory of his childhood', in *The Standard Edition*, vol. XI, 59–138.

— (1919), 'The uncanny', in *The Standard Edition*, vol. XVII, 217–56.

Green André (1978), 'The double and the absent', in Alan Roland (ed.), *Psychoanalysis, Creativity and Literature: A French-American Inquiry*, New York: Columbia University Press, 271–92.

Hoffmann, E. T. A. (1982), *Tales of Hoffmann*, trans. R. J. Hollingdale, Harmondsworth: Penguin Books.

Iser, Wolfgang (1980), 'The reading process: a phenomenological approach', in Jane P. Tomkins (ed.), *Reader-Response Criticism: From Formalism to Post-Structuralism*, Baltimore: Johns Hopkins University Press, 50–69.

Jauss, Hans R. (1982), 'Literary history as a challenge to literary theory', *Toward an Aesthetic of Reception*, trans. Timothy Bahti, Minneapolis: University of Minnesota Press.

Jakobson, Roman (1960), 'Closing statement: linguistics and poetics', in Thomas A. Sebeok (ed.), *Style in Language*, Boston: MIT Press, 350–77.

Klein, Melanie (1975), 'Love, Guilt and Reparation', *Love, Guilt and Reparation & Other Works, 1921–1945*, New York: Dell Publishing Co., 306–43.

Kofman, Sarah (1988), *The Childhood of Art: An Interpretation of Freud's Aesthetics*, New York: Columbia University Press.

Lacan, Jacques (1972), 'Seminar on "The Purloined Letter" ', *Yale French Studies*, 48, 39–72.

— (1977a), 'The split between the eye and the gaze', in *The Four Fundamental Concepts of Psychoanalysis*, trans. Alan Sheridan, London: Hogarth Press and The Institute of Psycho-Analysis, 67–78.

— (1977b), 'Desire and the interpretation of desire in *Hamlet*', *Yale French Studies*, 55–6, 11–52.

— (1977c), 'The mirror stage', *Ecrits: A Selection*, trans. Alan Sheridan, London: Tavistock Publications, 1–7.

— (1991), *L'envers de psychanalyse: les quatre discours, livre XVII (1969–70)*. (Text established by Jacques-Alain Miller, Paris: Seuil, 1991. (Translation by Russell Grigg, forthcoming.))

Laplanche, J. and Pontalis, J. B. (1973), *The Language of Psychoanalysis*, trans. Donald Nicholson-Smith, London: Hogarth Press and the Institute of Psycho-Analysis.

Muller, John P. and William Richardson (1988), *The Purloined Poe: Lacan, Derrida, and Psychoanalytic Reading*, Baltimore: Johns Hopkins University Press.

Schafer, Roy (1992), *Retelling a Life: Narration and Dialogue in Psychoanalysis*, New York: Basic Books.

Wright, Elizabeth (1984), *Psychoanalytic Criticism: Theory in Practice*, London and New York: Routledge.

— (1986), 'Modern psychoanalytic criticism', in Ann Jefferson and David Robey (eds), *Modern Literary Theory: A Comparative Introduction*, London: Batsford, 145–65.

CONTINENTAL PHILOSOPHY OF SCIENCE

Christopher Norris

Introduction: post-empiricist directions

In philosophy of science, as in other fields, it would be wrong to exaggerate the depth or extent of the rift that is very often assumed to exist between work in the Anglo-American ('analytic') tradition and work carried on by thinkers in the broadly 'Continental' line of descent. In this article I shall stress the various points of contact while also seeking to explain why that perception has arisen. There are various factors which promote the idea of a deep-laid rift, but central to any discussion of recent (that is, post-1920) Continental philosophy of science are questions about language. In large part this is due to the fact that so many Anglo-American commentators – from the Logical Positivists down – have objected to what they see as its wilful obscurities of style and phrasing. While doubtless justified in some cases, this charge more often reflects a deep difference of views as to the relationship between language and thought; that is to say, the extent to which concepts – scientific concepts among them – are themselves linguistically mediated or (in more extreme statements of the case) discursively produced. In brief, the division falls out between an approach that takes the truth-claims, propositions or observation-statements of science as its prime objects of analysis, and a more interpretive or hermeneutically-inspired approach that rejects this atomistic conception and treats such items as meaningful only in so far as they emerge from some deeper context of informing values and beliefs. Where such questions were once raised with regard to contending (rationalist or empiricist) construals of the so-called 'way of ideas', they now involve differing views of the relationship – or order of priority – between language, knowledge and scientific practice. That is to say, there is widespread agreement – except among a few 'direct realists' – that philosophy of science must involve some dealing with issues of language or with the structure of scientific theories as revealed through their various forms of logico-linguistic representation.

Chief among the former approaches was the Logical Positivism of the Vienna Circle. What characterised this school – whose members (including Carnap, Neurath, and Schlick) were 'Continental' in provenance if not in impact – was a firm belief in the virtues of logical analysis, a deep mistrust of 'metaphysics' (or empty verbalism), and a commitment to the basic empiricist idea that scientific observations were the bedrock data of any science (or philosophy of science) worthy of the name.

Central to this last commitment was the phenomenalist appeal to a realm of supposedly basic and indubitable 'sense-data'. However, it would be highly misleading to suggest that phenomenalism was a doctrine that took firm hold only among Anglo-American or 'analytic' thinkers in the first half of the twentieth century. Indeed, one of its main sources was the work of Ernst Mach, the great Austrian physicist and historian/philosopher of science whose commitment to the programme of a sense-data-based (observationally adequate) language of physical description led him to reject any talk of unobservables – atoms included – as going beyond the limits of permissible scientific inference. In Mach's case, however, this insistence was accompanied by a number of strongly-marked interests which disappeared from view in later applications of the logical-empiricist approach. Thus he emphasised not only the importance of detailed enquiry into the history of experimental science, but also 'the art of the researcher' and 'the technical and social flair essential for the practice of the experimental life of the sciences' (Babich, 1989, p. 183). If his stance was resolutely anti-metaphysical – like that of the Vienna Circle – it was mainly in order to cure philosophers of the delusion that science (whether past, present or future) could ever be held strictly to account by any ground rules or theories they might come up with. Least of all could scientific progress be explained by application of covering-law principles or hypothetico-deductive schemas whose generality of scope was inversely related to their power to illuminate particular episodes in the history of science.

Mach is perhaps the most striking example of a thinker whose many-sided influence cannot be straightforwardly presented in 'analytic' or 'Continental' terms. On the one hand his phenomenalism was taken up – and applied in doctrinaire fashion – by the Vienna Circle and by Logical Empiricists for whom it became a means of shifting interest from the real-world historical contexts of scientific enquiry to the analysis of various linguistic items (observation-statements or theories) at various levels of abstraction. Thus, as Babich pointedly remarks, 'the rupture between theory and experiment that followed from the increasing logicization of empiriocriticism or critical positivism related to the rise of analytic-style philosophy of science has no precedent in Mach' (Babich, 1989, p. 183). On the other hand – and for just that reason – his work continued to exert a powerful influence on thinkers who rejected the analytic paradigm and adopted a more historically-sensitive, context-specific, or sociologically-informed approach. It is this latter mode of thought that is most often considered distinctively 'Continental', along with the allied turn toward holistic

conceptions of meaning and truth and the further (depth-hermeneutic) appeal to background contexts of knowledge and belief that cannot be analysed in reductive, for example, Logical-Empiricist terms.

Here, however, one has to acknowledge that a good deal of work that must count as 'Continental' according to the above criteria has in fact been produced by Anglo-American philosophers, historians and sociologists of science. Indeed, their approaches very often owe as much to the empirical tradition of social-sciences research as to the kinds of speculative thinking more typically associated with post-Kantian Continental philosophy. Thus it is, at best, a partial truth to claim that the 'return to history' in recent philosophy of science is also and intrinsically a turning-away from Anglophone sources and an opening-up to Continental ideas. This point certainly applies to such movements as the 'strong' programme in sociology of knowledge, premised as it is, oddly enough, on a confident appeal to the facts of social history as if these were somehow more objective or reliably established than even the most confident posits of the physical sciences. The same applies to Thomas Kuhn's *The Structure of Scientific Revolutions*, even though that work offers little in the way of detailed sociological content. For here too there is a curious mix of positivist social science and holistic (or cultural-relativist) talk of paradigm-changes as somehow necessitating that scientists on either side of such a change quite literally inhabit 'different worlds' (Kuhn, 1970). That Kuhn has very often been enrolled among the 'Continental' thinkers – at least as a matter of elective affinity – is a further indication of the difficulties faced by anyone attempting to draw the map along clearly marked geo-cultural lines. For in Kuhn's case, as in that of W. V. Quine, there is a point at which certain post-analytic (more specifically: certain post-logical-empiricist) themes may be seen to converge with movements of thought in Continental philosophy of science. These include, most importantly, the turn toward meaning-holism and the concomitant denial of any hard-and-fast distinction between analytic and synthetic statements (or, in the traditional parlance, 'ideas of reason' and 'matters of fact'). In which case, some argue, there should now be room for an *entente cordiale* between post-analytic philosophy of science, once freed of its residual logicist and empiricist leanings, and that strain of hermeneutically-oriented thought which offers to restore a lost dimension of meaning and historical depth.

At this stage, however, we need to draw some finer discriminations within and between these two lines of thought – lines whose common starting point lies, I suggest, in Kant's first *Critique*. Analytic philosophy may be seen to have pursued one aspect of Kant's thought, namely that of showing how phenomenal intuitions could be 'brought under' adequate concepts, and thus provide the basis for a theory of knowledge that would not fall prey to metaphysical illusions. From the hermeneutic viewpoint, conversely, this project foundered on Kant's inability to explain just *how* intuitions and concepts could be thought of as somehow 'corresponding' one with another, given their utterly different characters. This problem gave rise to some notoriously obscure passages in the 'Transcendental Aesthetic' where Kant referred to an art of judgement – an art, moreover, 'buried in the depths of the soul' – whereby the two orders of phenomenal experience and conceptual understanding might somehow be bridged or reconciled. Heidegger singled out these very passages (in *Kant and the Problem of Metaphysics*) as exposing the limits of Kantian epistemology and revealing a dimension of 'authentic' depth-hermeneutical thought which lay beyond its utmost powers of explanation (Heidegger, 1990).

Hence the Heidegger-influenced trend towards holistic modes of thought which seek to situate the 'praxical' aspects of scientific research within the various contexts, cultures or experimental life-forms that constitute the 'horizon of pre-understanding' against which science emerges as a project of humanly significant activity. To this extent, hermeneutics may be seen as a challenge *both* to earlier (for example, neo-Kantian) movements in Continental philosophy of science *and* to mainstream analytic approaches. At the same time, philosophers such as Nancy Cartwright – working within a broadly 'analytic' frame – have emphasised the limits of covering-law or nomothetic-deductive theories by pointing to the inverse relation that exists between the generalised scope of scientific laws and their truth to the actual results as obtained through experiment and close observation (Cartwright, 1983). These latter are 'phenomenological' in so far as they involve a jointly perceptual, epistemic and interpretive process which cannot be neatly factored out in the manner prescribed by positivists or logical empiricists. So, once again, it proves difficult to distinguish clearly between the two lines of philosophical descent. Moreover, as we shall see, issues of knowledge and truth have figured centrally in the work of two French philosophers of science – Bachelard and Canguilhem – whose contribution can in no way be counted marginal to the development of twentieth-century continental thought.

Bachelard and Canguilhem

Bachelard's work is mainly concerned with the process of scientific theory-formation, the occurrence of radical changes in the history of scientific thought, and the way that certain metaphors – or heuristic fictions – have at times played a crucial or formative role in bringing about such changes. Thus described, it bears an obvious resemblance to Kuhn's *The Structure of Scientific Revolutions*. However, what distinguishes Bachelard's approach is his much greater interest in the epistemological aspects of theory-change; that is, the kinds of thought-process that have typically produced some decisive break (some switch of Kuhnian 'paradigms') in the history of the physical sciences. For Bachelard, such changes occur most often at points of crisis for the existing paradigm when its predictions are challenged or disconfirmed by a sufficiently large body of conflicting observational evidence, or when discrepancies arise between the old theory and a new, more powerful conceptual scheme. There ensues a period of widespread uncertainty and doubt, characterised by the prominence of metaphor over concept, or by the way that speculative thinking tends to outrun the resources of empirical observation or adequate conceptual grasp. At length, this crisis is resolved through a decisive 'epistemological break' with earlier modes of thought. Among the new theory's virtues are: its yielding a more adequate account of observations, measurements, or data in conflict with the old paradigm; its capacity to find room for certain parts of the previous model where these still apply within some limited framework or context of enquiry; and its transformation of *metaphors* into *concepts* through a process of ongoing 'rectification and critique'. For despite their undoubted heuristic value – especially in fields such as particle physics and astronomy where they have often enabled thought to advance beyond the limits of currently possible observation – there is still a sense in which scientific metaphors are not yet adequate to the purposes of a mature (conceptually rigorous) science.

Bachelard is to a degree in agreement with Kuhn about the nature of paradigm-change. However, they differ very sharply when it comes to assessing scientific theories with regard to their truth-content or validity as measured by our present state of knowledge. On Kuhn's account – much influenced by Quine on the topic of 'ontological relativity' – there is simply no way of judging the issue as between rival ('incommensurable') paradigms except on pragmatic grounds, or the extent to which they happen to fit with the rest of our currently accepted beliefs. Any paradigm-change will always be underdetermined by the best empirical evidence and subject only to loose theoretical constraints in accordance with this or that chosen ontological scheme. Hence Kuhn's very marked cultural-relativist leaning; that is, his tendency to treat such changes as best explained by an appeal to history and sociology, rather than through any notion of the physical sciences as having developed their own increasingly reliable procedures and methods of theory-validation. For Bachelard, conversely, such judgements cannot be avoided if one is to practise philosophy – or indeed history – of science in a way that answers to our current understanding of the issues involved. Thus, for instance, there is a crucial distinction to be drawn between past theories or research-programmes that can now be seen (with the hindsight of present-day science) to have taken a wrong track, and others which may have been superseded by later developments in scientific thought but which none the less constitute a genuine advance towards our current best conjectures or hypotheses.

Here again Bachelard comes out strongly opposed to any relativistic notion of scientific truth as simply a product of shifting paradigms, discourses, conceptual frameworks, ontological schemes, etc. Certainly, his work has often been read in just that way by cultural theorists – notably Foucault – who have used it for their own very different purpose. Thus, Foucault interprets Bachelard's conception of 'epistemological breaks' as licensing the view that different scientific discourses give rise to radically different regimes of truth and knowledge, such that we possess no criteria for judging between them except those provided by our own (discourse-relative) concepts, aims and priorities. However, this goes completely against Bachelard's argument that we *can* distinguish progressive from non-progressive episodes in the history of science and can do so, moreover, precisely with reference to a range of epistemological criteria such as the metaphor/concept distinction or the replacement of inadequate (sensuous, intuitive, image-based or anthropomorphic) ideas with more rigorously elaborated scientific theories. Hence his distinction between *histoire perimée* and *histoire sanctionée*; that is, between marginal episodes in the history of science that can now be seen as scientific dead-ends, and episodes which – even if they yielded to some later, more decisive advance – still have a place in the record of progress to date. Hence also the argument (taken up from Bachelard by his student Georges Canguilhem) that historians of science are in need of philosophy – scientifically-informed philosophy – if they are not to write the kind of anecdotal history that hunts out cases of chance anticipation, such as that of the ancient atomists having somehow 'discovered' the fundamental truths of modern atomic physics, or Aristarchus having somehow 'realised' long before Copernicus that the earth revolved around the sun. What such claims typically ignore is the crucial distinction between genuine advances in scientific knowledge – those possessing an adequate conceptual or epistemological basis – and the kinds of intuitive guesswork (however inspired) that have not yet broken with the realm of pre-scientific metaphor or 'reverie'.

Canguilhem extended this critical approach to the history of biology, medicine, and the life-sciences. However, he laid rather less emphasis on the idea of mature science as breaking altogether with alternative (for example, metaphoric or ideological) modes of thought. On the one hand, there existed 'scientific ideologies' which, while themselves lacking in conceptual rigour, might yet prepare the way – or provide the motivating force – for some real future advance. On the other hand, it was necessary, Canguilhem argued, to explain both how scientific *concepts* were distinguished from the order of commonsense-intuitive knowledge, and again, how those concepts could come to play a role in different (possibly conflicting) theories. In the first place this was a precondition for avoiding the sorts of anachronistic judgement that confused proto-scientific with scientific thought, or that mistook early uses of a term (often carried over by analogy from other fields of thought) as grounds for pushing back the date of emergence for some novel concept in the life sciences. However, there was no valid deduction from the merely lexical (or semantic) to the conceptual domain; that is to say, from the fact that those terms had a role in the earlier vocabulary to the claim that they must already have entered the discourse of scientific knowledge. In the second place, therefore, this distinction served to warn against the more extreme varieties of historical, cultural or linguistic relativism as applied to the natural sciences. Such arguments typically took hold at the point where historians and sociologists ignored the *specificity* of scientific concepts – their emergence as well-defined operative terms – and viewed them as wholly context-dependent, that is, as meaningful only to the extent that they figured in some particular theory, discourse, paradigm, etc.

At this point it is worth cross-referring, once more, to developments in recent Anglo-American philosophy of science. We have, perhaps, seen enough – through this brief engagement with the thinking of Bachelard and Canguilhem – to challenge the idea that 'Continental' approaches are typically given over to forms of extreme cultural relativism, while 'analytic' philosophy has mostly held out for the virtues of rational theory-assessment and conceptual precision. Here again, it is Kuhn who most readily comes to mind as resisting all the standard classifications. His work is mostly viewed as having its sources within – if also as reacting strongly against – the kinds of approach that have dominated Anglo-American philosophy of science over the past sixty

years and more. Thus, his thesis of paradigm-incommensurability derives in large part from those twin postulates – the underdetermination of theory by evidence and the theory-ladenness of observation-statements – which Quine used in order to subvert the two 'last dogmas' of logical empiricism (Quine, 1961). This argument is then taken (by Quine and Kuhn) to require a thoroughly contextualist approach in which theories or belief-systems as a whole confront the sum-total of 'experience' or empirical data, so that no single statement, proposition or item of belief can ever be confirmed (or disconfirmed) by any particular result produced in the course of scientific enquiry.

To this extent the Quine/Kuhn case for ontological relativity belongs squarely within the history of Anglo-American ('analytic') debate on issues in epistemology and philosophy of science. However, it brings that debate much closer to some prominent themes in recent 'Continental' debate, among them the tradition of hermeneutic thought carried on by Heidegger, Gadamer and others from nineteenth-century thinkers such as Schleiermacher and Dilthey. Here also there is a turning-away from empiricist (or positivist) conceptions of truth and method, along with a more holistic approach that allows for no one-to-one match or correspondence between veridical statements and clearly individuated real-world states of affairs. Rather, truth is what emerges against a background horizon of situated being-in-the-world (Heidegger's *Dasein*) whereby human knowers or agents enter into various forms of practical involvement, as, for example, through the use of implements or tools that are 'ready-to-hand'; that is to say, which enter our everyday life-world invested with a sense of significant purpose and value.

Heidegger's case has lately found support among a number of Anglo-American thinkers seeking a direction beyond the doldrums of 'old-style' analytic philosophy. Thus, voices have been raised for abandoning that project altogether (in the wake of such internal critiques as those of Quine and Kuhn), and for adopting a frankly eclectic approach that combines pragmatism and meaning-holism with Heidegger's alethic conception of truth. However, there are certain problems to be faced by those who seek a better understanding of science through this mode of 'deep' hermeneutical enquiry. Such enquiry has nothing whatever in common with the kinds of discovery that scientists make – and that realist philosophers of science typically discuss – when they investigate beyond the phenomenal appearances of things to those various depth-ontological attributes (subatomic or molecular structures, chemical affinities, causal dispositions, etc.) which mark a further stage of advance in the process of inference to the best explanation. Logical empiricism refused to countenance such claims since it adopted a Lockean–Humean sceptical stance with regard to the very possibility of advancing from 'nominal' to 'real' definitions, or providing an adequate explanatory account of *de re* causal attributes and structures. More recently these scruples have been set aside and the case for causal realism strongly reaffirmed by philosophers who define their position against that narrow empiricist programme. However, it is important to distinguish such arguments from those other (often Heidegger-influenced) varieties of 'post-analytic' thought that adopt a thoroughgoing holistic conception of meaning and truth, and which tend to consort with anti-realist positions in epistemology and philosophy of science.

Phenomenological approaches

However, there do exist other, less extreme versions of the hermeneutic turn which retain a respect for the distinctive achievements of science while seeking to place those achievements within the context of a *Lebenswelt* (life-world) that inherently eludes systematic or reductive description. For there is also the tradition of phenomenological thought, descending chiefly from Husserl, which pursues a sustained reflective enquiry into the origins of our modern (post-Galilean) scientific world-view and the limits of objectivist or positivist approaches in the physical and human sciences alike. Husserl's project underwent various complex changes of aim and priority, moving, broadly speaking, from an early 'psychologistic' stage to a concern with the transcendental conditions of thought and knowledge, and thence – in his late writings – to reflection on the contexts of lived experience (historical, communal, cultural)

involved in every act of human perceptual or cognitive grasp. On one point at least, Husserl was in agreement with Heidegger: that this life-world had been subject to damaging encroachment by techno-science, by the rise of a narrowly means-end rationality, and by positivist conceptions of knowledge and truth that found no room for such modes of reflective or critical-evaluative thought (Husserl, 1970). However, he remained acutely aware of the need to explain how the exact sciences – mathematics especially, or the mathematisation of physics – had so transformed our knowledge of the world as to constitute epochal discoveries in thought, rather than the mere exchange of one 'paradigm' for another.

That those discoveries should possess both apodeictic certainty *and* a historically emergent character (that is, the fact of their having occurred in a certain cultural milieu and at a certain stage in the development of science) is a paradox that constantly engaged Husserl's thinking, both early and late. It is posed most directly in his essay 'The Origin of Geometry', where Husserl asks how it is possible that geometric truths – such as those formulated by Euclid – can be known as a matter of intuitive self-evidence, and yet still have their place in a tradition of thought that must be conserved in order for each new learner to re-enact or truly comprehend them. This issue has been central to debates in philosophy of science since before the twentieth century. In part, it has to do with the discovery of alternative (that is, non-Euclidean) geometries which, while consistent in themselves, cannot be squared with the Kantian requirement that such concepts should always correspond to our pre-given spatial intuitions. However, this is just one example of the way that advances in recent ('post-classical') science have often involved a decisive break with received ideas of what properly counts as adequate scientific knowledge. Thus, in various fields – among them geometry, mathematics, relativity-theory and quantum mechanics – it has become increasingly evident that science can no longer appeal to an order of synthetic *a priori* knowledge, such as Kant thought self-evident from the existence of Euclid's proofs and the achievements of Newtonian physics and astronomy. Rather, we are confronted with the emergence of theories that are mathematically precise or borne out by the best observational evidence to hand, but which are none the less strongly counter-intuitive. Indeed, it may be argued that some of the chief developments in scientific thought since the mid nineteenth-century have been such as to require a progressively more rigorous suspension of the Kantian precept that equates understanding with the match between concepts and grounding intuitions (see Coffa, 1991).

Kant himself did not doubt that non-Euclidean geometries were *logically* possible; only that they could be given any representation in terms compatible with the scope and limits of intuitive understanding. However, it was shown by Helmholz that such geometries could indeed be represented, as, for example, through various kinds of thought-experiment involving our perception of parallel lines on a curved or non-planar surface. In which case, it seemed, there was no special privilege attaching to those forms of 'pure' *a priori* intuition that figured so centrally in Kant's First *Critique*. Rather, they must henceforth be thought of as *conventions* adopted by stipulative warrant within a certain geometric scheme, and therefore justified solely in virtue of their logical consistency with the various postulates (including or excluding Euclid's unproven Fifth Axiom) that made up the particular scheme in question. So it was, in Coffa's summation, that such thinkers as Russell and Poincaré became 'allies in the struggle to remove Kantian intuition from the field of geometry and transform it into a purely conceptual discipline' (Coffa, 1991, p. 129). In this they were continuing the critique of intuition-based philosophies of space and number that had been set in train by earlier thinkers such as Bolzano, Helmholz and Hilbert. Thus, there might well be *a priori* judgements in the sense of judgements that preceded and made possible any further reasoning on matters of geometric or mathematical truth. However, those judgements could claim no privileged epistemic or intuitive warrant, depending as they did – for whatever truth-value they possessed – on their role as defined within this or that system of well-formed logico-syntactic functions.

Thus, according to Poincaré's strong conventionalist thesis, there was always the possibility of re-nouncing or adapting any *a priori* postulate whose consequences were at odds with some new discovery produced in the course of more advanced or fruitful mathematical research (Poincaré, 1958). In a similar vein, Karl Popper was to argue that although there might be synthetic *a priori* judgements, these could always turn out to be *a posteriori* false if they conflicted with the best scientific evidence to hand. Mathematicians might continue to perform calculations on the basis of certain *a priori* indispensable terms – function, limit, continuity, the infinitesimal, etc. – which were all acknowledged to possess no absolute (intuitively valid or self-evident) character, since their meaning was assigned entirely in virtue of their logico-syntactic role. However (as is well known), this logicist project itself ran into trouble as a result of Gödel's Incompleteness Theorem; namely, his demonstration that for any mathematical proof system of sufficient complexity there would always be at least one axiom within the system whose truth or falsehood was strictly undecidable. Indeed, Gödel's result can now be seen as having played a large role in the eventual demise of the logical-empiricist programme, a programme that in many ways epitomised the character and ambitions of mainstream analytic philosophy. Of course, there were other contributory factors, among them Russell's famous discovery of the set-theoretical paradox ('that class whose members include all classes that are not members of themselves'), Quine's later assault on the analytic/synthetic dualism, and Kuhn's kindred argument against the idea that philosophy of science possessed any criterion for distinguishing clearly between observation-statements and the various theoretical beliefs or presuppositions that were always involved in interpreting such statements. Where these developments all converged was in prompting a widespread movement of retreat from the logical-empiricist conviction that scientific knowledge could be built up – or its claims reliably justified – through analysis of the logical relations obtaining between first-order empirical observations and higher-level (that is, covering-law or hypothetico-deductive) theories.

Such, at least, is one plausible account of the emergence of 'post-analytic' philosophy within and against the main current of Anglo-American thought on these matters up to approximately 1950. What began as the banishment of Kantian (intuition-based) philosophies of space, time and number in favour of a logicist or purely conceptual approach ended up with the problematisation of logic and conceptual analysis under pressure from a range of holistic or contextualist arguments whose effect was precisely to remove the basis for any such clear-cut distinction. And at this stage – as some commentators have urged – there is not much point clinging to the typecast distinction between Anglo-American 'analytic' philosophy of science and its so-called 'Continental' or mainland-European counterpart. For the way is then open to a wished-for *rapprochement* with developments in that 'other' tradition that have likewise stressed the interpretive nature of all understanding, the lack of any ultimate (context-transcendent) constraints upon the logic of scientific enquiry, and hence the need for a context-sensitive (historically, socially and hermeneutically oriented) approach that would avoid the dead-end dilemmas of logical empiricism. In this view, a work like Carnap's *The Logical Structure of the World* would mark both the high point of that programme's ambitions and the clearest sign of its predestined collapse under the strain of defining just what should count as basic (empirical) data on the one hand and, on the other, their logical 'construction' according to strictly analytic criteria of meaning and truth.

Such was Quine's argument in his essay 'Two Dogmas of Empiricism', an essay that took Carnap's project as its prime target, and which is widely regarded as having signalled an end to that whole way of thinking about language, logic and philosophy of science. But it was also – more to the point in this context – an argument that found various pre-echoes in the broadly Continental tradition. At one extreme there was Nietzsche's strong-interpretivist attack on the 'myth of immaculate perception'; that is to say, the idea that we could ever have access to pure sensory data or straightforward empirical truths-of-observation. Then again, in a less drastic vein, there was Dilthey's hermeneutically-inspired distinction between the modes of understanding typically sought by the physical and the human or social sciences. Where the former laid claim to a knowledge that was properly assessed in terms of concep-

tual adequacy or strict hypothetico-deductive warrant, the latter sought a different kind of knowledge (*Verstehen*) that arose within the context of lived experience (*Erlebnis*), and which therefore involved a corresponding exercise of judgement, intuition and sympathetic insight.

A similar argument was later put forward by neo-Kantian philosophers such as Rickert and Windelband, who expressed it in terms of the basic methodological distinction between 'nomothetic-deductive' sciences on the one hand and 'ideographic' sciences on the other. In the one case, it was a matter of bringing particular instances (data, observations, experimental findings, etc.) under hitherto exceptionless covering-law statements from which they could be deduced. In the other case, those instances were taken to possess a quality of uniqueness or interpretative depth – a distinctively human aspect – which resisted any treatment in the covering-law mode. To some extent it is an artefact of linguistic difference that both sorts of knowledge should have counted as genuine 'science', that is, as types or varieties of *Wissenschaft* in the broader German usage of that term, a usage that carries less sense of strain than is felt with such English-language locutions as 'the human sciences'. However, there is also Kantian warrant for the claim that these various orders of thought – scientific understanding and aesthetic experience, determinate and reflective judgements, phenomenal cognition and pure or speculative reason – should properly be treated as playing their role within an overall system or 'architectonic' of the faculties, whatever the confusions that inevitably arose in cases of categorial confusion or illicit boundary-crossing. This helps to explain why 'Continental' approaches in philosophy of science have been more receptive to modes of hermeneutic or interpretivist thinking, as compared with the clear-cut demarcation criteria required by most philosophers in the mainstream analytic tradition.

Certainly, the various 'back-to-Kant' movements of thought among German philosophers have often arisen in direct response to perceived excesses on the hermeneutic side. This happened especially during the 1920s and 1930s when Kant seemed to offer a welcome defence against the more extreme forms of interpretivist doctrine promoted by thinkers such as Nietzsche, Scheler and Heidegger. All the same it is clearly the case – and not just on Heidegger's strong-revisionist account – that Kant's epistemology involves an appeal to interpretive judgement as the mediating term between concept and intuition. This in turn looks forward to those passages in the Third *Critique* where interpretation assumes a more central (indeed pre-eminent) role, and where mind and nature are thought of as somehow united through a teleological doctrine of the faculties. It is chiefly their greater openness to this proto-hermeneutic aspect of Kant's thinking that distinguishes Continental philosophers of science from those in the Anglo-American tradition who have inherited, adapted or sometimes – like Quine – challenged the basic terms and categories of Kantian epistemology. For when Quine rejects the analytic/synthetic dichotomy it is not at all with a view to restoring some lost dimension of hermeneutic depth – some aspect of humanly meaningful experience – to the arid discourse of logical empiricism. Rather, it is proposed as a means of shedding all that otiose Kantian 'metaphysical' baggage, *a priori* knowledge in particular, and thus, finally, opening the way to a fully naturalised epistemology that would take the sciences – physics pre-eminent among them – as a model or a methodological primer for work in philosophy of science.

We are now, perhaps, better placed to make sense of that typecast 'analytic'/'Continental' distinction, even where the terms have no clear-cut geographico-historical import and even in cases where there seems much in common between thinkers working on opposite sides of the notional dividing-line. However, it may still be said – and despite all the caveats entered above – that the logico-linguistic orientation in the work of Frege and early Russell was precisely what set analytic philosophy apart from the various post-Husserlian schools of mainland European thought. On their side, the phenomenological appeal to consciousness (or intentionality) as a starting-point for critical reflection gave way to a range of alternative emphases, mostly in response to successive waves of attack on subject-centred (or 'foundationalist') epistemologies. Among French thinkers this reaction had a strong precedent in

Bachelard's theory of scientific progress as always involving a decisive break with the kinds of 'self-evident' (commonsense) knowledge that had not yet attained the conceptual precision required of any genuine science. To this extent it formed a rationalist counterpart to Mach's programme of 'empirico-criticism', whatever their manifest differences of view concerning the relative importance of theory *vis-à-vis* empirical observation. In any case there emerged a complex pattern of resemblance and contrast between philosophies of science in the analytic mould that pursued some version of the logical-empiricist programme and Continental philosophies of science which sought a way beyond the supposed dead-end of subject-centred or phenomenological approaches. For by this time there was too much evidence – from geometry, mathematics, quantum mechanics, and other advanced fields of research – that any adequate theory would need to break with the deliverances either of 'naive' sense-certainty (the empiricist route) or of *a priori* knowledge as standardly defined.

Revising the tradition: Duhem and Quine

This situation has given rise to various responses among Continental philosophers, historians and sociologists of science. Their responses can be ranged, roughly speaking, on a scale that extends all the way from current post-modernist or cultural-relativist arguments (that scientific 'truth' is no more than the product of some optional, strictly non-privileged 'discourse', 'paradigm', 'language-game', etc.) to work on various forms of alternative or 'deviant' logic designed to accommodate the seeming paradoxes of quantum superposition or non-locality. Then again, some commentators – those of a more Heideggerian persuasion – take the view that such challenges to the received 'epistemological' paradigm require that we abandon the whole way of thinking that construed knowledge in representationalist terms as a matter of 'correspondence' between subject and object, mind and nature, or observation-statements and experimental data. ('In the most recent phase of atomic physics', Heidegger opines, 'even the object vanishes . . . the subject-object relation as pure relation thus takes precedence over the object and the subject' [Heidegger, 1977, p. 173].) Thus, it is sometimes suggested that the received (Copenhagen) interpretation of quantum mechanics is one that points toward a depth-ontology revealed only through hermeneutic reflection on the limits of conceptual or causal-explanatory thought.

To some extent these developments find a parallel in Anglo-American responses to the problems posed by quantum mechanics. Thus, for instance, those problems can be seen to have affected the thinking of philosophers such as Quine and Kuhn, in particular as regards the various *topoi* – ontological relativity, meaning-variance, the revisability of logical ground rules, the underdetermination of theory by evidence and the theory-ladenness of observation-statements – that have left a deep mark on recent thinking in the broadly analytic (or 'post-analytic') tradition. However, it is fair to say that Continental philosophy of science has gone much further in the turn toward various forms of linguistic, hermeneutic, depth-ontological and strong-sociological modes of enquiry. This can partly be explained as a reaction against the received (Continental) tradition, from Descartes to Kant and Husserl, wherein questions of knowledge and truth were thought of as belonging – exclusively or primarily – to the province of critical epistemology, rather than the wider historical or socio-cultural context. However, there are also some deep-seated ideological differences which have sharpened these issues for Continental, especially French, philosophers of science. Thus the whole debate about scientific knowledge and progress – how far we can be justified in using such terms given the (presumptively) paradigm-specific or culture-relative status of all truth-claims – is one that has assumed a particular salience in twentieth-century French thought.

This difference emerges very clearly with regard to the so-called 'Duhem–Quine thesis' concerning ontological relativity and the claim that no scientific theory can ever be decisively refuted by the anomalous result of some crucial experiment or by an observation at odds with what the theory had predicted. For this always leaves room – so the argument goes – for a range of possible alternative strategies short of abandoning the theory in face of such apparent counter-evidence. Thus, for instance,

it may be saved by attributing the discrepancy to a wrong choice among various auxiliary hypotheses, by redefining certain object-terms or predicates in the observation-language, by redistributing those terms and predicates in a more wholesale fashion, or again – if all else fails – by conceding that the very 'laws' of logic (such as bivalence or excluded middle) may need to be revised under pressure from certain kinds of evidence including, quite possibly, experimental results in the field of quantum physics. For Quine, this signifies the collapse of logical empiricism as a doctrine premised on two chief assumptions – the possibility of science coming up with discrete (empirically adequate) observation-sentences and of logic as providing the necessary framework for the rational assessment of scientific theories in point of conceptual rigour, consistency and truth. Quite simply, that programme cannot survive the undermining of Kant's analytic/synthetic distinction, along with other variants (such as 'ideas of reason' and 'matters of fact') that are likewise rendered otiose by the turn towards a thoroughly holistic conception of meaning, evidence and truth.

That Pierre Duhem's name is often linked with Quine's as having likewise arrived at this conclusion is something of an irony given their very different routes of approach. In Duhem's case it went along with an instrumentalist conception of scientific method and also a large-scale revisionist approach to the history of early modern science. There has been much debate as to just how far Duhem was influenced in this regard by his religious (strongly Catholic) beliefs and his desire to subvert the established view of the great 'revolution' in scientific thinking brought about by Galileo's challenge to the Church's authority in such matters. Whatever the extent of this influence his arguments clearly have an aspect of ideological commitment that finds no place in Quine's treatment of kindred philosophico-scientific themes. This aspect is all the more striking since it placed Duhem at odds with an influential school of modern French scholarship, represented most notably by Alexandre Koyré's studies of Galileo as a crucial figure (not to say culture-hero) in the passage from religiously-imposed dogma to scientific enlightenment, progress and truth. For Duhem, on the contrary, such ideas manifested a fixed conception of the absolute hostility between religion and science, together with a blinkered view of late-medieval history which took for granted that no real advances could possibly have occurred under conditions of enforced subservience to scriptural or Church warrant. Thus, much of his work was devoted to establishing the scholarly case for a challenge to this sharply dichotomised view of science before and after Galileo.

However, there are also connections – albeit subject to interpretive dispute – between Duhem's historical revisionism and his case for treating scientific theories as assessable only in instrumentalist or conventionalist terms. That is, he took the view that we should accept such theories solely on grounds of observational warrant and predictive yield, rather than supposing that they actually refer to certain features of a real-world object domain whose properties, attributes, causal dispositions, etc., it is the business of science to describe and explain. As I have said already, instrumentalism is a doctrine that finds support from various philosophical quarters, among them the school of radically empiricist and anti-metaphysical thought descending from Ernst Mach. Indeed, Mach carried this programme to the point of refusing to accept the existence of atoms so long as they could not be observed, whatever their role as fundamental posits in the discourse of modern (post-Daltonian) physics and chemistry. However, it is misleading to persist too much with the comparison between Mach's programme of empirio-criticism and Duhem's insistence that science should espouse no reality-claims – or ontological commitments – beyond those that are well borne out by observation and predictive warrant. For Duhem, instrumentalism was a means of drawing strict limits to the otherwise overweening pretensions of science as a source of ultimate truths. In Mach's case, conversely, it derived from a firm belief that science made progress by adopting the best methods to hand, trusting to experiment as far as possible, and maintaining a healthily sceptical attitude toward any doctrine which sought to place limits on its freedom of enquiry.

Beyond truth and method?

These convictions were shared by Paul Feyerabend, a self-proclaimed disciple of Mach whose case 'against method' – also the title of his best-known book – can also be seen as a more extreme version of the anti-metaphysical programme. Feyerabend went much further than Mach in rejecting the idea that science should be subject to rules, procedures, validity-conditions, or methodological guidelines. Least of all, he argued, should it take advice from philosophers or tidy-minded historians of science, those who set themselves up as arbiters of 'good' scientific practice, or who presume to distinguish true from false, progressive from non-progressive, or genuine from pseudo-science. Such judgements merely reflect the standard self-image of mainstream scientists and philosophers, along with their preferred notion of the history of science as following an onward and upward path towards truth at the end of enquiry. Worse than that, it stifles creative thought by imposing a range of quasi-universal (although, in fact, merely local and contingent) values – 'truth', 'method', 'rationality', 'progress' – which act as a brake on adventurous research. Hence Feyerabend's well-known advice: that scientists should adopt an outlook of wholesale 'epistemological anarchism' (alternatively, the idea that 'anything goes'), and thus feel free to explore any new line of thought, whatever its lack of orthodox credentials. For in the end there is no deciding the issue between, for example, voodoo magic and present-day Western medical science – or raindance rituals and meteorology as a means of affecting/predicting the weather – except by appeal to the beliefs endorsed by this or that 'expert' community.

Then again, there are those – like Jean-François Lyotard – who take the view that our current 'post-modern condition' is such as to debar any possible appeal to standards of rational or truth-seeking enquiry beyond the presently existing range of discourses, language-games, 'phrase-genres', and so forth. On Lyotard's account it is the chief feature (and virtue) of 'post-modern' science that it no longer seeks to monopolise truth in the name of some privileged method or theory aimed toward suppressing such differences of view. This situation has arisen in various fields of research – quantum mechanics and chaos theory among them – where science comes up against the limits of precise observation, or where reason encounters hitherto unknown problems and paradoxes. Hence the passage, as Lyotard sees it, from a modern ('Enlightenment') conception of science premised on constative criteria of truth and falsehood, to a post-modern ethos where 'performativity' is the sole measure of success. Thus the aim is – or should be – not so much to secure a provisional consensus among those best qualified to judge, but rather to maximise *dissensus* by encouraging the widest possible range of diverse incommensurable viewpoints.

I have no wish to suggest that Lyotard's idea of 'post-modern' science is by and large typical of recent Continental approaches. What it does bring out with particular force is the upshot of a certain way of thinking, namely the linguistic (or hermeneutic) turn when pushed to a point where knowledge and truth are thought of as wholly internal or specific to some particular language, discourse or phrase-genre. Such ideas have a mixed genealogy but may be called 'Continental' in the sense at least that they have filtered into Anglo-American debate from a variety of mainland European sources. At one extreme they take inspiration from Nietzsche's resolutely sceptical assault on the values of 'disinterested', truth-seeking rational enquiry, and his attempt – continued by Foucault – to expose the ultimate source of such values in the epistemic will-to-power. Here, as with Lyotard, problems arise when one asks how it is possible to criticise particular aspects of science or technology given such an attitude of wholesale epistemological scepticism, coupled with the kind of reductive analysis that treats all knowledge (whether in the physical or the human and social sciences) as a reflex product of power-seeking drives and motives.

However, there are also more moderate, hermeneutically-informed versions of the argument for viewing science as a range of practices, techniques, and more or less specialised modes of enquiry which emerge against the background of a shared life-world or horizon of humanly-meaningful interests and concerns. This approach derives chiefly from thinkers such as Dilthey in the nineteenth-century

hermeneutic tradition, but can also be found strikingly prefigured in the seventeenth-century Neapolitan philosopher Gianbattista Vico. It was Vico who first argued – contrary to the orthodox view – that the human (rather than the physical) sciences are our best and most reliable sources of knowledge, since they alone can give access to a realm of understanding that is properly and intrinsically human, rather than requiring a Cartesian divorce between subject and object, mind and nature, human concerns and the order of non-human (mind-independent) reality. It may be said, with some justice, that Vico's time has come around at last, since a significant number of present-day philosophers and historians of science would subscribe to his thesis regarding the primacy of lived experience (or empathetic insight) over objectifying modes of knowledge. Charles Taylor makes the point when he observes how 'old-guard Diltheyans, their shoulders hunched from years-long resistance against the encroaching pressure of positivist natural science, suddenly pitch forward on their faces as all opposition ceases to the reign of universal hermeneutics' (Taylor, 1980, p. 26).

Conclusion

My original aim was to make three main points in this article. First: 'Continental' philosophy of science has shared a great many of the themes and concerns (such as ontological relativity, the underdetermination of theory by evidence, and the role of interpretive judgement in scientific thinking) that have also figured centrally in recent Anglo-American debate. Second: it has approached them often (although not always) with a distinctive slant toward hermeneutic or historically-oriented modes of understanding which stand in marked contrast to the 'analytic' stress on evaluating scientific theories with regard to their status *vis-à-vis* the canons of inductive or hypothetico-deductive inference. For some Continentally-inclined philosophers this makes analytic philosophy of science an ultimately trivial enterprise, one whose programme, if carried through consistently, would reduce every such statement or theory to the level of vacuous (tautological) self-evidence. However, third, there exists a wide range of recent

'Continental' approaches – chiefly in the French and Austro-German epistemocritical traditions – which have responded both to such internal problems and also to the kinds of challenge posed by developments in various fields of scientific research. Consequently, there are now few subscribers to the notion that Anglo-American philosophy of science has nothing to learn from its mainland-European counterpart. 'Fog over Channel: Continent isolated', as a *Times* headline allegedly once reported.

Bibliography

References

Adorno, Theodor W. (1973), *Negative Dialectics*, trans. E. B. Ashton, New York: Seabury Press.

Adorno, Theodor W. et al. (1976), *The Positivism Dispute in German Sociology*, trans. G. Ades and D. Frisby, London: Heinemann.

Ayer, Alfred J. (1936), *Language, Truth and Logic*, London: Gollancz.

Bachelard, Gaston (1949), *Le rationalisme appliqué*, Paris: Presses Universitaires de France.

— (1953), *Le materialisme rationnel*, Paris: Presses Universitaires de France.

Babich, Babette E. (1989), 'Philosophies of Science: Mach, Duhem, Bachelard', in Richard Kearney (ed.), *Continental Philosophy in the Twentieth Century*, London: Routledge, 175–221.

Canguilhem, Georges (1988), *Ideology and Rationality in the History of the Life Sciences*, trans. Arthur Goldhammer, Cambridge, MA: MIT Press.

Carnap, Rudolf (1959), 'The Elimination of Metaphysics Through Logical Analysis of Language', in Alfred J. Ayer (ed.), *Logical Positivism*, New York: Free Press, 60–81.

Cartwright, Nancy (1983), *How the Laws of Physics Lie*, London: Oxford University Press.

Coffa, J. Alberto (1991), *The Semantic Tradition from Kant to Carnap: to the Vienna Station*, Cambridge: Cambridge University Press.

Duhem, Pierre (1969), *To Save the Phenomena: an Essay on the Idea of Physical Theory from Plato to Galileo*, trans. E. Dolan and C. Maschler, Chicago: University of Chicago Press.

Dummett, Michael (1993), *The Origins of Analytic Philosophy*, London: Duckworth.

Feyerabend, Paul (1975), *Against Method*, London: New Left Books.

Foucault, Michel (1974), *The Order of Things: an Archaeology of the Human Sciences*, trans. Alan Sheridan, London: Tavistock.

Habermas, Jürgen (1971), *Knowledge and Human Interests*, trans. Jeremy Shapiro, London: Heinemann.

— (1987), *The Philosophical Discourse of Modernity: Twelve Lectures*, trans. Frederick Lawrence, Cambridge: Polity Press.

Heidegger, Martin (1977), *The Question Concerning Technology and Other Essays*, trans. William P. Lovitt, New York: Harper and Row.

— (1990), *Kant and the Problem of Metaphysics*, trans. R. Taft, Bloomington: Indiana University Press.

— (1993), *Basic Writings*, ed. David F. Krell, London: Routledge.

Husserl, Edmund (1970), *The Crisis of European Sciences and Transcendental Phenomenology*, trans. D. Carr, Evanston, IL: Northwestern University Press.

Kant, Immanuel (1958), *Critique of Pure Reason*, trans. Norman Kemp Smith. London: Macmillan.

Kuhn, Thomas S. (1970), *The Structure of Scientific Revolutions*, 2nd edn, Chicago: University of Chicago Press.

Lyotard, Jean-François (1984), *The Postmodern Condition: a Report on Knowledge*, trans. Geoff Bennington and Brian Massumi, Manchester: Manchester University Press.

Mach, Ernst (1893), *The Science of Mechanics*. London: Watts and Co.

Poincaré, Jules Henri (1908), *Science et méthode*, Paris: Flammarion.

Popper, Karl R. (1983), *Realism and the Aim of Science*, ed. William W. Bartley, London: Hutchinson.

Quine, Willard van Orman (1961), 'Two Dogmas of Empiricism', in *From a Logical Point of View*, 2nd edn, revised, Cambridge, MA: Harvard University Press, 20–44.

Rorty, Richard (1991), *Objectivity, Relativism, and Truth*, Cambridge: Cambridge University Press.

Taylor, Charles (1980), 'Understanding in Human Science', *Review of Metaphysics* 34, 25–38.

Further reading

Ayer, A. J. (ed.) (1959), *Logical Positivism*, New York: Free Press.

Babich, Babette E., Debra B. Bergoffen and Simon V. Glynn (eds) (1995), *Continental and Postmodern Perspectives in the Philosophy of Science*, Aldershot: Avebury.

Gillies, Donald (1993), *Philosophy of Science in the Twentieth Century: Four Central Themes*. Oxford: Blackwell.

Gutting, Gary (1989), *Michel Foucault's Archaeology of Scientific Knowledge*, Cambridge: Cambridge University Press.

Hacking, Ian (1983), *Representing and Intervening: Introductory Topics in the Philosophy of Natural Science*, Cambridge: Cambridge University Press.

Harding, Sandra G. (ed.) (1976), *Can Theories Be Refuted? Essays on the Duhem–Quine Thesis*, Dordrecht and Boston: D. Reidel.

Horkheimer, Max and Theodor W. Adorno (1972), *Dialectic of Enlightenment*, trans. John Cumming, New York: Seabury Press.

Laudan, Larry (1990), *Science and Relativism: Some Key Controversies in the Philosophy of Science*, Chicago: University of Chicago Press.

Lecourt, Dominique (1975), *Marxism and Epistemology: Bachelard, Canguilhem and Foucault*, London: New Left Books.

Norris, Christopher (1997), *Against Relativism: Philosophy of Science, Deconstruction and Critical Theory*, Oxford: Blackwell.

O'Hear, Anthony (1985), *An Introduction to the Philosophy of Science*, Oxford: Clarendon.

5.7

CONTINENTAL POLITICAL PHILOSOPHY

James Bohman

Introduction

While Continental philosophy has said much about the nature of politics and modern political institutions, it has not produced much political philosophy in the standard sense of evaluating policies or justifying institutions. That is, it has not been concerned with elaborating the principles necessary to justify the existing political and legal institutions, so much as to examine and to criticise the very presuppositions of modern politics and society. This stance derives from the fact that the decisive influences have been two philosophers whose politics must be considered radical: Karl Marx and Martin Heidegger. Both rejected modern political institutions as currently constituted and sought to provide the basis for a radically different form of social life and thus for a new kind of politics. For Marx it would be a politics freed from the dynamics of class domination and rule, while for Heidegger it would be a new way of 'dwelling on the earth', freed from the unthought presuppositions of Western metaphysics and rationalism. Such a critique of politics and political thinking is radical in the sense that it 'goes to the root' not just of political institutions and their underlying norms, but to the very way in which modern society is organised, to its deepest structures of thought and its dynamic historical process. In both philosophers, there is a sense that something is deeply wrong with a whole complex set of ideas and practices that we might more generally call

'modernity', so that, under their influence, political thinking in Continental philosophy concerns the question of what is to be negated and preserved in modern ideas of reason and politics. A range of different positions on 'modernity' as a philosophical problem still characterises Continental political theory to this day, from Marx to Heidegger and Habermas to Derrida. For many different reasons, however, this radicalness about politics has become increasingly difficult to sustain, and much of Continental philosophy's recent history represents a challenge to the Marxist and Heideggerian influence on political philosophy.

The highest political expression of modernity is found in the Enlightenment, so much so that challenges to the constitutive elements of modern reason and politics are challenges to Enlightenment thinking. The Enlightenment proclaimed modernity to be a new time (as the German word for modernity, *Neuzeit*, expresses), in which the superstition, authority and biases of the past would be replaced by the rational practices of science and democracy (Habermas, 1987, Ch. 1). Just as the sciences disenchanted nature and thus gave human beings power over it, democracy would permit them to overcome submission to external authority and thus to take control over their own lives. In the eyes of the Enlightenment, modernity is a project, with a negative and destructive side as well as a positive and constructive side, both of which are found in its underlying critical conception of rationality. The destructive side of critical reason is aimed at those practices and beliefs that enslave human beings. Indeed, this side is so much emphasised by the nineteenth century that Marx considered the proper programme of philosophy 'the ruthless criticism of everything existing'; but the constructive dimension of this Enlightenment philosophy is equally important, and in politics it is concerned with the creation and justification of new emergent practices and moral and political ideals, including the justification of basic ideals of democracy, such as self-rule, human rights and the standard of unforced agreement and consensus as the sole basis for legitimate institutions. The main problem for Enlightenment philosophy was to maintain the balance between the constructive and destructive sides of critical reason. Already by the early nineteenth century, some philosophers began to argue that the destructive side of reason had overwhelmed its constructive side, leading to a new level of reflection on the logic of modernity that Max Weber called the 'disenchantment of disenchantment'. This argument was particularly relevant to the reflections on the nature and scope of reason found in German Idealism.

For Kant, and even more so for Hegel, the Enlightenment was insufficiently self-critical, especially about its own conception of reason and its connection to human freedom. Ordinary human understanding (*Verstand*) is sufficient for the sciences to attempt to understand nature and for acting out of self-interest, but it is reason (*Vernunft*) that brings about unity in the sciences and supplies the laws of the moral domain, and it is in the public use of reason that 'free and equal' citizens give themselves laws that could be agreed upon by everyone even when they are not in their self-interest. It is through the public use of reason alone that politics can become a medium for Enlightenment and can overcome what Kant saw as the potentially destructive 'unsocial sociability' of mankind. Hegel took this notion of reason further and turned it into the basis for a more thorough critique of modern society. The dominant institutions of modern civil society and the liberal state divided modern society, based as they were on the aggregation of interests in markets and in political institutions based on the 'arbitrary freedom' of individuals. Hegel saw modern societies

as unbalanced: while they had achieved a form of society based on the principle of universal freedom, they had done so in a one-sided and inadequate way. Only the proper institutions could rationally and politically integrate society in ways not attainable by such 'natural' and 'unconscious' mechanisms; these institutions must be political, and the ultimate role of the state in modern society was to provide the context for higher forms of freedom and unity needed to sustain a rational form of ethical life, a community based on freedom. However different they were in political vision, both Kant and Hegel saw politics as the means for realising reason in history, in institutions that would restore the unity and integrity of social life while guaranteeing the greatest extent and highest form of freedom. Opposed to both of them, Marx would challenge this conception of the unity of modern society and with it the very idea of a political integration of modern society. Only the revolutionary transformation of the very basis of modern society would be adequate to the task of overcoming the diremptions of modern society. Heidegger, too, would seek a more radical solution beyond modernity, seeing politics briefly as a means to go beyond, rather than fulfil, the promise of a rational society. In different ways, both Marx and Heidegger challenged the Idealistic attempt to find a practical solution to modern social disruption in a broader and more comprehensive conception of reason, which could then be realised primarily through a broader and more comprehensive form of politics.

This challenge to claims for a non-coercive and rational politics under current conditions, whether radically democratic in the case of Marx or anti-democratic in the case of Heidegger, shaped Continental political theory for some time and continues today in debates between modern and post-modern rejections of liberalism. In this article, I shall trace the development of this argument in Continental political theory, showing how the examination of the rejection of Idealism has led to the return of politics into Continental philosophy. In the first section, I shall examine the two different reasons for rejecting politics advanced by Marx and Heidegger which led to radically modern and anti-modern conceptions of a break with modern institutions. On the one hand, Marx rejected modern political institutions precisely because they failed to live up to the modern principles of freedom and justice that they required for their legitimacy; on the other hand, Heidegger rejected both such institutions and their supporting principles, seeking instead a radical break with modern society and thought. Heidegger demanded radically new criteria by which to judge the correctness of institutions and forms of life, criteria that are outside of modern society and its legitimating framework. In the second section, I show why both the Marxist and Heideggerian rejection of politics collapse on internal grounds. Finally, in the third section, I turn to another source of scepticism about rational and non-coercive politics in Continental political theory: the sociological nightmare of Weber's 'iron cage' and the Frankfurt School's 'dialectic of Enlightenment'. Habermas's work on democracy in complex societies is examined as offering the basis of an answer to such scepticism.

The rejection of modern politics: Marx and Heidegger

Modernity begins with an optimistic political philosophy of progress towards human freedom, with new institutions and forms of knowledge overcoming past barriers of superstition and domination. German Idealism represents a certain watershed in this conception, by critically examining the presuppositions of these institutions and forms of knowledge and showing that their internal contradictions led to the deepening distress and fragmentation of modern social life (Habermas, 1987, Ch. 2). Like Kant and Hegel, Marx, too, retained the progressive philosophy of history of modernity while critically examining the consequences of modern institutions; but unlike his Idealist predecessors he found in them even deeper contradictions and irrationalities that could be solved only by a revolutionary transformation of society as a whole. Progress towards human emancipation that was promised by the unleashing of human powers over nature could only be achieved in a developed form of society that would fulfil the promise of democratic self-organisation. It would lack the typically modern forms of political organisa-

tion, including the state and all forms of the 'hierarchical division of labor' (Marx, 1977, p. 539). Indeed, politics based on conflict and the struggle for power between classes would disappear and be replaced by decentralised and highly participatory forms of self-rule, the goal of which is to transform politics from oppressive class rule into the 'rational medium for social life' (ibid., p. 577). 'Real' democracy as 'the political form of full human emancipation' brings about the 'end' of politics.

Unlike the previous Enlightenment conception of progress, Marx emphasised acute discontinuities between an emancipated form of life and modern society and its institutions; politics is a medium for realising freedom only in a new social totality. Although he left only hints of this self-organised society to come, it is clear that his intentions are democratic in a radical sense: radical because democracy can flourish in the absence of coercive background institutions whose sole purpose is to maintain various forms of hierarchy and domination. This normative conception of radical democracy leads to a 'ruthless' criticism of all existing institutions. However, it is often unclear whether Marx thinks that all such institutions will simply disappear in this radically democratic form of society. In any case, his conception of a fully democratic society supports criticisms of all aspects of modern institutions, including ones that we might think bear more normative weight than he gives them credit. The criticism of politics as the medium of domination adopts all aspects of liberal, and hence bourgeois, institutions without remainder, including normative ideals, as so much ideology to be dispelled. In a manner similar to some post-modernists today, Marx shows how even such laudable notions as civil rights are mixed with relations of power and domination and can be put into their service. The only reason why such criticism does not dissolve into a pernicious form of scepticism is its hope for the future. All such social relations are supposed to disappear in the future socialist society, in which egalitarian political relations will be so transparent that they no longer need resort to the disguise of ideology or appeal to the false claim that modern society is reintegrated in an imaginary community of political equals or a non-coerced public sphere.

For all this 'ruthless criticism', Marx's radical democratic rejection of politics is not ultimately sceptical of the modern ideals of equality and democracy. Conversely, according to Heidegger, democracy itself and its ideal of public reason are implicated in a broader 'onto-theological framework' of subjectivity and agency. Indeed, they are trapped within it and can never escape. Politics is simply one activity contained within it, and certainly the one most governed by it. 'Publicness' for Heidegger contrasts sharply with truth; it is compared with the ordinary, the familiar and the commonsensical, whose correctness can never be challenged since it appeals to the unquestioned character of our everyday understanding of the world (Heidegger, 1993, p. 137). Neither reflection nor criticism are sufficient to extricate us from this understanding of the world. The only way out is through radical new possibilities, defined in terms of *authenticity*, which open up novel practical understandings (ibid., p. 187). Politics, too, can become a location for truth as disclosure, but only if it goes beyond politics in the ordinary sense and becomes something more akin to art, to the poetic 'saying of the unsayable' to an opening up of a whole new understanding and framework for things. Before Heidegger, Nietzsche similarly contrasted the ordinary and mundane politics of everyday democratic life with the creative politics of the politician-artist which would create a whole new way of life, a new interpretation of the world beyond modern subjectivism. Crucial to both is that non-ordinary politics provides new criteria, much as an innovative work of art is self-validating to the extent that it creates the standards by which it is evaluated.

Since democracy is implicated in the modern subjectivist framework that must be overcome, the standards of the creative act of politics are not those of liberal democracy or rationality and justice in any sense recognisable to Kant or Hegel. As in a revolutionary political act, this new sort of disclosure cannot be judged by current standards. Instead, Heidegger offers the analogy between art and politics, filled out in 'The Origin of the Work of Art' essay, as the asymmetrical relation between the law-giver and his people and between 'creators' and 'preservers' of a new truth (ibid., p. 186; p. 193).

This is where the analogy to Marx's radical democratic 'end' to politics breaks down, since here politics in the ordinary sense is not replaced by some transparent social relations or rational medium. Rather, politics is 'aestheticised' so that the kind of norms of standards associated with political life can no longer be drawn from the stock of justifications conained in terms of free and equal citizens. Nietzschean aestheticism and post-modern anti-institutionalism is the risk internal to most anti-modern politics, and it can be found particularly in radical right-wing thinkers such as Carl Schmitt, who contrasted 'the political' as the moment of such normative self-definition with 'politics' as the result of settled institutions of law and bureaucracy (Schmitt, 1985). It is 'the political' which is outside of modern politics and modern rationalism. While in the case of Marx we may wonder if politics can become such a transparent social medium, in the case of Heidegger and his followers we may wonder if there is any way to understand such a politics of non-public innovation except as an absolute act of rupture and even violence.

Whatever their differences – and they are significant – on the political spectrum, Marx and Heidegger share with Hegel the attempt to think of politics through the critique of modernity and thus beyond the categories of liberalism. Where they differ is the extent to which this attempt is an immanent or external critique, whether they simply reject liberalism in what Hegel would call an 'abstract negation' or try to go beyond it by also incorporating its truths. It is clear that Heidegger seeks an increasingly external criticism of liberalism, ultimately rejecting any attempt (even modelled on aesthetics) to change the predominant understanding of politics by human agency. Marx's enterprise is more traditional because he argued that democratic ideals do express the goal of human freedom through self-organisation. The debate about post-modernism in Post-War Continental political theory asks whether or not this immanent critique of modern institutions and liberal political norms goes far enough – and whether the external critique must always be anti-political. The question remains how such a thoroughly external critique can return to politics without endorsing some of these norms and institutions, especially if this return is for the sake of some version of radical democracy.

The return of politics: civil society, the public sphere and democracy

The resolutely critical stance towards political norms in Marxism (and ultimately its anti-political view of an emancipated society) proved unsustainable in the development of critical thinking about politics in Continental philosophy. Like nature as the ground of human rights typical of the eighteenth century, the catastrophes of the twentieth century destroyed all faith that history could provide a similar justificatory function. This critique of the metaphysical basis for political norms could lead to scepticism about the rationality of modern politics, as it did for Weber, who saw politics as the simple struggle between opposing 'gods and demons'. The problem was that political life could not, even in modernity, be reduced to the mere exercise of power; there were spaces in which both the contestation of power and deliberation on norms and opinions could take place. Already in the work of Antonio Gramsci, the conception of politics as merely supporting the dominant ideology of the dominant class came under critical scrutiny. Similarly, Jürgen Habermas tried to show a space for democratic political life in the public sphere, where citizens can meet as free and equal. Similarly, Claude Lefort and Cornelius Castoridis developed a conception of politics as a public space, the contours of which are shaped and determined by rights. Even while grounding these claims historically and empirically, these philosophers saw a space for a normative conception of politics that is rooted in the modern social situation and can expand its possibilities for freedom. These same arguments can be turned against both Heideggerian anti-politics and anti-modernism.

In order to discover a basis for the integrity of modern politics, Gramsci returned to Hegel's idea that civil society contained more than merely the market and its 'system of needs' but also 'corporations' or distinctively modern forms of association (Gramsci, 1977). Thus, Gramsci found in civil society the possibility of political life that did not merely collapse into market forces or state power. Indeed, in civil society we find specifically modern forms of plurality and associations, in the form of unions, cultural institutions, churches, clubs and political parties. The reduction of civil society or its collapse into the state made it impossible for the question of the transition to a genuinely democratic society to be posed within Marxism; the absorption of the state into civil society is not a step toward democracy. Rather, abolishing the independence of civil society and its association is one step away from developing the basis for a free society. Similarly, Arendt also argued that political life could not be reduced to economic management without the disappearance of 'the political' into 'the social'. Thus, Gramsci not only opposed the economic reductionism of the orthodox Marxist conception of politics, he also opposed reducing cultural processes to mere coercion and power. This reduction of cultural processes and social integration to political coercion is common enough today among post-modernists, inspired now by Michel Foucault's conception of the pan-optical state (Foucault, 1977). Gramsci, however, did not see abolishing the state as leading to the emergence of an autonomous and pluralistic civil society. Besides the administrative role of the state, its modern structure of rights and liberties created the autonomous spaces for politics. Hannah Arendt also sought to keep the social and political spheres separate, governing each with radically different principles of the household (*oikos*) and the polity (*polis*) (Arendt, 1958). The domain of politics is not reducible to the logic of other domains (particularly economic or bureaucratic rationality), nor is it simply a matter of coercion. Thus, both Gramsci and Arendt in their neo-Marxist and neo-Aristotelian arguments seek to establish an independent realm for politics in modern society between the forces of the market and the state. But instead of Gramsci's civil society, Arendt calls the space for politics 'the public sphere'; a space protected by republican institutions and threatened by the invasion of 'the social'.

Against Arendt's Aristotelian and agonistic model of politics, Habermas argues for the legitimacy of a distinctly modern and democratic public sphere emerging in the late eighteenth century (Habermas, 1982). Unlike the early Enlightenment's emphasis on science and its ability to control nature, Habermas finds the 'rational content of modernity' in the new possibilities afforded for moral and political identity. In the salons and coffeehouses of the late eighteenth century, according to Habermas's historical analysis, social status and power 'were left at the door'. Only when such a public sphere exists could citizens compel authority to legitimate itself before the tribunal of public opinion. For this to be possible, social spaces had to be created in the forms of clubs, associations, literary societies and union halls where the influences of wealth and power were limited, if not suspended, creating the forms of dialogue and interaction necessary for political relations among equals. This 'public of private persons' emerged around such spaces (and in new forms of private life in the modern family) and was extended by the new communication media of newspapers and publishing houses. What unites these diverse phenomena is that, in them, publicity takes on a normative rather than functional significance.

Such a public sphere permits the formation of 'public opinion' in a normative rather than merely factual sense, in which free and open communication makes possible not only the improvement of the quality of reasons for decision and beliefs, but also the absence of direct relations of political coercion and social power. Consensus reached under such conditions of the absence of all force 'except the unforced force of the better argument' has, Habermas supposes, more than merely *de facto* significance. These effects of publicity are due to the 'reflexive quality' of such public communication: the public is concerned about itself as a public, about maintaining the public character of its communication. In concrete historical terms, this concern is found in the struggle of the emergent public with state authority and power, which sought to limit such communication through censorship. While Habermas is sceptical whether any actual public spheres (or the modern family structure and private sphere that supports it) lived up to these claims for their publicity, they none the less establish the foothold for a new kind of rationality in political life and for the social relations needed for self-rule by public opinion. Moreover, these claims are not merely ideo-

logical; their reflexive character of constant testing and self-examination make any false claim to publicity challengeable by the very norm of publicity it invokes. Publicity has thus acquired a different meaning from the one it has in Heideggerian anti-politics, and the solutions to the problems of power and coercion are to be found in the public sphere itself.

The struggle against state censorship transformed the literary and discursive public sphere and the public sphere of associations in civil society into what Habermas calls 'the political public sphere', the public sphere of citizens interacting with parliamentary and representative institutions. With the creation of this type of public sphere, non-coercive politics is no longer simply a check on independent state power (as are Hegel's 'corporations' in civil society), but the democratic limitation of coercive political power through the agreement of citizens who govern themselves by laws within a constitutional framework. Not only must democratic institutions themselves create public spheres (of parliamentary debate, free and fair elections), but they must also be open to, and influenced by, the public sphere as a whole. The democratic state, too, helps to create and maintain the existence of the public sphere, primarily by way of constitutionally-guaranteed basic rights, including civil rights of political participation and free expression. Thus, the public sphere is not merely a space for discussion, but one that is shaped by the political status granted to each citizen as free and equal. The interaction between the state and the public sphere raises questions about the status of institutions and the norms that constitute them and that are required to structure and constrain the interaction within them. In the absence of institutions and their normative structures, it is unclear whether consensus on issues of moral conflict could ever be reached.

In her analysis of the catastrophic event of the twentieth century, Arendt takes the status of 'stateless people' to be paradigmatic of the failures of modern politics (Arendt, 1953, Ch. 9). Such people are reduced to their bare humanity and lack not only basic rights, but 'the right to have rights', the right to participate and shape a common world where one's speech and actions have meaning and significance.

Thus, the return to politics, especially a non-coercive kind, requires rethinking basic modern institutions and constructing an immanent critique of their underlying conceptions of citizenship, decision-making mechanisms and basic norms. As carried out by thinkers as diverse as Arendt and Habermas this immanent critique pushes liberal institutions in the direction of a more participatory and deliberative form of democracy that goes beyond the aggregative voting and mere self-interest of most liberal interpretations of democracy and its representative institutions.

Like Habermas, Claude Lefort offers an immanent, rather than external, critique of liberalism, emphasising the role of the public sphere. The difference is that, for Lefort, the public sphere is a space for resolving conflicts rather than reaching consensus, disconnecting the reinterpretation of liberalism and democratic institutions even more thoroughly from the excesses of the general will and political rationalism. In democratic institutions the place of power is unoccupied and hence belongs to no one (Lefort, 1988, p. 27). If this is the case, then the main form of politics in democracy is contestation, the institutionalisation of legitimate conflicts. This means that the public space too cannot belong to anyone and can thus accommodate everyone. It is not an agnostic public sphere as Arendt (following Aristotle) would have it, since it is public only because no one has to compete for recognition or acclaim. Indeed, as persons claim rights for themselves and change the meanings of existing rights this space becomes more expansive. Thus, as new rights claims become recognised as legitimate, the contours of the public sphere itself change, since the public space is structured around what everyone can claim as legitimate and by the ongoing reinterpretation of such claims through speaking and listening to others. Rather than excluding the plurality of opinions and identities, a democratic public sphere makes pluralism possible through the constant contestation of the very basis of political justification and legitimacy.

As opposed to Marx and Heidegger, Gramsci, Habermas, Arendt and Lefort have developed conceptions of democracy that serve as a corrective to the coercive character of modern society. Civil society, the public sphere and democratic institutions all open up the possibility of a form of politics that is governed neither by the invisible hand of market forces nor by the visible hand of sovereign state power. To the extent that these arguments are sound, they provide the basis for an immanent critique of modern reason, discovering in political practices a foothold for the unifying and reconciling power of reason in uncoerced consensus, democratic contestation of power and domination, and intersubjective structure of mutual recognition. Thus, for these theorists, Heidegger and Marx give us an excessively one-sided picture of modern society and do not have the conceptual room in their thought to recognise its possibilities for rationality.

This sort of thinking is, however, subject to a more empirical and sociological challenge, embodied in the sociology of Max Weber and the increasingly pessimistic diagnosis of the Frankfurt School. This challenge recognises that there are other possibilities for the realisation of reason, but suspects that these possibilities are being overwhelmed by the powerful institutional forces behind a one-sided rationalisation of modern capitalist and bureaucratic society. In the next section I will explore Habermas's attempt to provide a theoretical and empirical antidote for such political scepticism, by showing that the social developments that are the source of sociological scepticism can be balanced by the rationalisation of the life-world.

Overcoming sociological scepticism about democratic politics

Max Weber's analysis of 'legal domination' uncovers a certain dialectic at work in the increasing complexity of modern society (Weber, 1958). On the one hand, through democracy, citizens make increasing demands on the state, creating the need for ever greater bureaucracy. The responsiveness to such demands is a direct result of the increasing access of the people to powerful state institutions. On the other hand, modern societies are becoming more and more complex, with greater and greater division of labour, the introduction of expert knowledge, social technologies and the functional differentiation of distinct spheres of social life. This dynamic produces an 'iron law of oligarchy', whereby democracy is undermined by the very conditions that created it, including the disenchantment of the world that leads ultimately to the irrationality of choices among basic values and a vision of politics where 'gods and demons' fight it out without any possibility of rational adjudication. Weber's tragic vision of the fate of modern democracy means that we must abandon any greater hopes for democracy than 'competent administration' and live disconsolately with irreconcilable value conflict in public life. While in the 1930s the Frankfurt School opposed this diagnosis and attempted to develop a conception of 'real democracy' which would bring all social conditions under the control of rational consensus, gradually its leading philosophers (Max Horkheimer and Theodor Adorno) adopted their own version of this same dialectic analysis of modern rationalisation. Arguing that pressures towards uniformity and conformity emerge out of the contradictions of liberal society, these anti-democratic trends culminate not in Weber's 'iron cage' but in the Fascist state and the authoritarian personality. Under these conditions, Horkheimer argued, the autonomous liberal individual is a 'hopeless fiction' (Horkheimer, 1982, p. 211), to the extent that the subjective conditions for the exercise of freedom were gradually being eroded by increasingly totalising social reification (Horkheimer and Adorno, 1972). Unlike the radical critique of liberalism, democracy and its political institutions are not directly implicated in the problems of modern society. Rather, it is increasingly less feasible in the fragmented, instrumental, and ultimately anonymous social order that works against it and the autonomy of the modern individual.

Built into this modified critique of liberalism and its reifying form of social rationalisation is a two-sided conception of totality, In many respects, reference to modern society as a totality becomes the defining feature of the Frankfurt School analysis (see Jay, 1984). On the one hand, they use totality in a negative sense as an explanatory basis for criticism. Ultimately, the 'real totality' of liberal society is 'false', an antagonistic and inegalitarian class society rather than an harmonious whole. On the other hand, they use totality in a positive sense as well; as a normative ideal and a desirable goal for social change. A 'true' totality contrasts with the 'real' totality of capitalist society and the 'false' totality of Fascism. In contrast, a 'true' totality is rational and consensual: the social process is brought back under free rational control as an expressive whole. In a true totality, the needs and interests of each will be expressed in the whole society; such a society will be the adequate expression of the social praxis of its members. Democracy does not figure directly in this positive totality, except as a means of consensual expression and moral transformation. Besides this expressivist social ideal, the guiding descriptive idea of the critique of the totalising spread of instrumental reason is that this false totality becomes more and more the reality of modern society, leaving the true totality as an external, and ultimately distant, ideal preserved only in art and subjective experiences, and then only in a highly fragmentary form.

In an attempt to open the possibility of a democratic politics enlivened by the vibrant and non-coercive public sphere, Habermas challenges the descriptive adequacy of this account of modern rationalisation as purely instrumental. He does so in two ways. First, he argues that this order is not a totality, but crisis – ridden (Habermas, 1975, Ch. 1). In 'late' capitalism the free market does not prove to be self-regulating, but in need of constant state intervention. This intervention in turn puts heavy burdens on the state, transforming the economic crisis of market failure and collapse into the legitimation crisis of the modern state as the problems of economic growth exceed the capacities of the state. Second, he argues that modern rationalisation is two-sided, including within it not only instrumental control but also the cultural rationalisation of modern art, politics and morality on the basis of which further democratisation is still possible. Such rationalisation reveals a different form of practical reason already operative in modern society: communicative rationality, the use of which makes it possible for practical questions to be more than merely irreconcilable conflicts of ultimate values. Such rationality is grounded not only in modern institutions but the everyday practices of communication, practices of giving and testing reasons in dialogue with others, which in turn can become the basis for discursive procedures of justification.

Both the formal and informal achievements of communicative rationality help Habermas to rethink the relation between democratic politics and social complexity, and this to blunt the force of both Weber's scepticism and Adorno and Horkheimer's dialectics of rationalisation. But even for Habermas, the space for such politics is increasingly limited by the demands of social complexity, which make it impossible for everything to be governed by communicative rationality. Even if modern societies are not governed from one centre or apex of power in the modern state but are, rather, polycentric, they are not now organised solely by anonymous relations of interdependence.

Habermas agrees with Marx that advanced capitalism limits the scope and significance of democratic institutions and norms; it produces an 'overcomplexity', or pathological version, of the differentiation of modern society (see Bohman, 1996, Ch. 4). Much like the early Frankfurt School's criticism of majority rule, in the 1970s Habermas targets the 'formal' character of current democratic practice (Habermas, 1975). To this reduced version of democracy, Habermas opposes 'substantive' democracy, which emphasises the 'genuine participation of citizens' in political will formation. Such a notion of will formation requires more than a purely formal or self-interested analysis of rationality, and Habermas attempts to ground practical reason on the intersubjective structure of communication exhibited in the special reflexive and reciprocal form of communication he calls 'discourse'. The validity of a political decision is now related to rational consensus, to the extent that it passes a test of intersubjective universalisation. According to this procedure, a norm is justified only if all those affected could agree to it in a discourse under the conditions of what Habermas calls an 'ideal speech situation'.

Because this ideal of consensus is primarily epistemological rather than political, its purpose is to establish a procedural, discursive and intersubjective notion of rationality. Habermas's argument here is against the value sceptic (such as Weber) who sees politics as reducible to irrational struggle and conflict. And, because of the epistemological character of this notion of rationality, Habermas has always been suspicious of attempts to apply it (or its counterfactual 'ideal speech situation') *directly* to the structure of political institutions (see, for example, Habermas, 1979, p. 186). He maintains that the adequate mediation of these ideals with social facts requires an adequate theoretical account of the rationalisation of institutions and culture. For Habermas, however, the fundamental limitations on the direct application of rational norms and ideals of communicative association to social reality is not the pervasiveness of reification, but of complexity. Along with the pluralisation of forms of life, this complexity changes the conditions of popular sovereignty, so much so that 'the people' is now a fiction. Complex societies are now polycentric and this changes the character of political participation that must be institutionally mediated in order to be feasible. However, complexity by itself is not reifying; indeed, it permits new possibilities of private and public autonomy, as well as the communicative and democratic structuring of many areas of social life. But it does eliminate one possibility: that it is possible for the sovereign will of the people to constitute all of society in a conscious sort of way (Habermas, 1996, Ch. 7).

This focus on social complexity has important consequences for the critique of liberalism as an ideology that was central to Marxism and the early Frankfurt School. Rather than reject liberal ideals, Habermas now attempts to appropriate liberal constitutionalism and rights and to combine them with radical democracy and its emphasis on consensus and public reason. He endorses a 'two-track' model for democracy that makes its ideals practical in a complex and pluralistic society (ibid., Ch. 8). On the one hand, decision-making goes on in institutions whose rules are characterised by a modern constitution with its principles of rights to basic liberties, political participation and the social goods necessary for both. On the other hand, such institutions must remain open to the public sphere, which he sees as an 'anonymous network of communication' that creates the pool of reasons by which decisions are made. Such public opinion does not rule, but it does influence and direct the power constituted in institutions where the public is represented in majority rule which, in turn, is the outcome of informed opinion and fair and open public deliberation. Rather than full participation in every decision, what is left of radical democracy is the ideal of 'deliberative politics'. The question of whether this model is sufficient to capture the critical force of the ideals of radical democracy that Habermas has endorsed previously, or whether his account is too accommodating to social complexity, remains open. In any case, the two-track model answers the Weberian political sceptics, by showing how the ideals of democracy are feasible under current social conditions and by providing the workable model of democracy that makes politics a matter for public deliberation rather than struggle and conflict.

Bibliography

References and further reading

Arendt, Hannah (1953), *The Origins of Totalitarianism*, New York: Harcourt Brace.

— (1958), *The Human Condition*, Chicago: University of Chicago Press.

Bohman, James (1996), *Public Deliberation: Pluralism, Complexity and Democracy*, Cambridge, MA: MIT Press.

Dews, Peter (1987), *Logics of Disintegration*, London: Verso.

Foucault, Michel (1977), *Discipline and Punish*, trans. A. Sheridan, New York: Panthcon.

Gramsci, Antonio (1977), *Prison Notebooks*, trans. Q. Hoare and G. Nowell-Smith, New York: International Publishers.

Habermas, Jürgen (1975), *Legitimation Crisis*, trans. T. McCarthy, Boston: Beacon Press.

— (1979), *Communication and the Evolution of Society*, trans. T. McCarthy, Boston: Beacon Press.

— (1987), *The Philosophical Discourse of Modernity*, trans. F. Lawrence, Cambridge, MA: MIT Press.

— (1989), *The Structural Transformation of the Public Sphere*, trans. T. Berger, Cambridge, MA: MIT Press.

— (1996), *Between Facts and Norms*, trans. W. Rehg, Cambridge, MA: MIT Press.

Heidegger, Martin (1993), *Basic Writings*, ed. D. Krell, New York: Harper and Row.

Honneth, Axel (1988), *The Critique of Power*, trans. K. Baynes, Cambridge, MA: MIT Press.

Horkheimer, Max (1982), *Critical Theory*, trans. M. O'Connell et al., New York: Seabury Press.

Horkheimer, Max and Theodor W. Adorno (1972), *Dialectic of Enlightenment*, trans. J. Cumming, New York: Seabury Press.

Jay, Martin (1984), *Marxism and Totality*, Berkeley: University of California Press.

Lefort, Claude (1988), *Democracy and Political Theory*, trans. D. Macey, Minneapolis: University of Minnesota Press.

Marx, Karl (1977), *Selected Writings*, ed. D. McLellan, Oxford: Oxford University Press.

McCarthy, Thomas (1991), *Ideals and Illusions*, Cambridge, MA: MIT Press.

Schmitt, Carl (1985), *Political Theology*, trans. G. Schwab, Cambridge, MA: MIT Press.

Weber, Max (1958), *From Max Weber*, ed H. Gerth and C. W. Mills, Oxford: Oxford University Press.

Section Six
THE FRANKFURT SCHOOL
AND CRITICAL THEORY

INTRODUCTION

Simon Jarvis

'The critical theory of society is, in its totality, the unfolding of a single existential judgement.' These words of Max Horkheimer's, which appear in the essay (Horkheimer 1982) that, more than any other, established the 'critical theory of society' as a determinate entity, could hardly be written with such confidence today. In the mid-1930s Horkheimer could summarise the content of critical theory as offering a particular historical thesis:

> the theory says that the basic form of the historically given commodity economy on which modern history rests contains in itself the internal and external tensions of the modern era; it generates these tensions over and over again in an increasingly heightened form; and after a period of progress, development of human powers, and emancipation for the individual, after an enormous extension of human control over nature, it finally hinders further development and drives humanity into a new barbarism. (Horkheimer, 1982, p. 227)

If this is what critical theory 'says', it would certainly be difficult today to regard agreement with these words as a criterion for description as a 'critical theorist'. They offer a substantive historical thesis which could not be unreservedly agreed upon even by all those employed by the Institute for Social Research at the time, and still less by all those who contributed to its journal, the *Zeitschrift für Sozialforschung* (Journal for Social Research), or those who, since the deaths of the founders of critical theory, have renewed and developed some of its

distinctive concerns through substantially different approaches: the so-called second generation of critical theorists led by Jürgen Habermas.

Does the term 'critical theory', then, possess any coherent significance at all? What has been understood by this term has clearly undergone many developments: from Horkheimer's early programme of a critical interdisciplinary collaboration between philosophy and the social and human sciences, to the immanent critique of philosophical texts and cultural artefacts later undertaken by Adorno and Horkheimer in an attempt to decipher the historical experience sedimented in those texts and artefacts, to the theory of communicative action developed by Habermas – not to mention the current use of the term 'critical theory' simply as a synonym for 'literary theory' – 'critical theory' has seemed to cover such a diversity of philosophical and political positions that it is indeed difficult at first to see where their coherence might lie. Nevertheless, it is worth understanding these connections, because the commitments concealed beneath differences of opinion and approach represent in truth a very distinctive intellectual movement, one remarkable for its ability to question the nature and limits of the division of intellectual labour which has so powerfully determined the relationship between philosophy and the social and human sciences in the twentieth century.

In looking for a coherent impetus behind critical theory, we are unlikely to find a common set of substantive social or historical theses. Nor can it really be said that a common method underlies critical theory, since one of its leading themes has been the critique of methodologism. The twofold emphasis which unifies critical theory must be sought in its title. First, a **critical** theory of society differs from a descriptive theory of society in not absolutising the separation of fact from value. It understands that all theoretical projects, including its own, necessarily serve, and are shaped by, social interests and exist in particular social contexts. Yet, secondly, a critical **theory** of society differs from sociological relativism or, for example, Karl Mannheim's sociology of knowledge, by its truth-claim. It insists that the truth of any claim is never decided simply by whether or not it serves the right social interest, but rather by whether it does justice to the matter considered. The equivocation in 'doing justice' in this context marks exactly the complexity of critical theory's idea of truth, which is practical as well as theoretical. The way in which the practical and theoretical elements in critical theory's idea of truth are differently articulated by different critical theorists offers one of the most important indicators of change and development in critical theory as a whole.

In this sense, the whole of critical theory can be understood as a pursuit by other means of one of the central preoccupations of classical German philosophy: the question of the relation between 'is' and 'ought'. David Hume's sceptical challenge to tacit and illegitimate transitions from 'is' to 'ought' in philosophical argument partly produced Kant's critical response, in which a systematic gulf was first erected between practical and theoretical reason, and then 'bridged' in the *Critique of Judgement*. Hegel speculatively identified 'is' with 'ought', the actual with the rational, but this was an identification which arose from the experience of the separation of the two in modernity, rather than a declaration that whatever is, is right. In renewing the problem of how description and prescription were to be related to each other in the light of modern historical experience, critical theory quite consciously – despite its self-description as a 'materialism' – renewed the tradition of German Idealism far more powerfully than the academic neo-idealist thinking which dominated German universities in the early years of the twentieth century.

Even what has been misleadingly known as the 'Frankfurt School' was never an intellectually homogeneous group. Two of the figures discussed in detail below had a particularly loose relation to 'critical theory': Ernst Bloch was never a critical theorist, although his utopian thinking, as Christopher Thornhill shows, certainly offered an especially imaginative reconsideration of the relation between theory and practice which formatively influenced several leading critical theorists. Walter Benjamin's often troubled relationship with the Institute and its journal was, as Howard Caygill demonstrates, only one aspect of an exceptionally complex philosophical profile. In both these cases, classification under any of the section headings in this volume would appear reductive. It is not the intention of this Introduction to offer a history of critical theory, nor even a catalogue of all the activities of those who at any time have been regarded as critical theorists, already available in the books by Jay, Dubiel, Wiggershaus and others, but, rather, to trace the development of the core of critical theory – what makes critical theory critical? – as well as giving an account of some of those figures to whom space precluded the devotion of an entire article.

The origins of critical theory

The Institute for Social Research opened in 1924 in Frankfurt am Main. It was financed by Felix Weil, the Marxist son of a grain millionaire, who wished, according to one contemporary, 'to create a foundation similar to the Marx-Engels Institute in Moscow . . . and one day to present it to a German Soviet Republic' (Wiggershaus, 1993, pp. 12–13). Under the leadership of its first director, Carl Grünberg, the Institute was preoccupied primarily with a Marxist approach to issues in political economy, with Marx-Engels scholarship, and with the history of the labour movement. At this stage, the Institute's journal was called the 'Journal for the History of Socialism and of the Workers' Movement'. When Horkheimer took over the directorship of the Institute in 1930, its commitment to Marxism remained no less forceful but unlike Grünberg, Horkheimer was philosophically trained and had a keen appreciation of Marxism's ineradicable debt to classical German philosophy, believing that philosophy needed to be allocated a more central place in the Institute's work.

Shortly after the National Socialists came to power in Germany, the Institute was closed and its library confiscated; its leading thinkers were forced into exile, often to the USA (although Adorno lived and worked for a time in Oxford, while Benjamin spent much of the 1930s in Paris). The Institute's journal continued to be published in German from the Institute's new base affiliated to Columbia University, New York. The climate of social science in the 1930s and 1940s in the USA meant that the innovative philosophical core of critical theory was not the face it most openly presented to the world. Horkheimer was anxious to secure for the Institute the recognition and financial support of American universities, where social science research was largely conducted along lines imitative of the natural sciences. Accordingly, collaborative empirical projects bound to pre-formed goals absorbed much of the Institute's time and effort. After the War the left-wing German *émigrés* were scattered. Bertolt Brecht and Ernst Bloch were in East Germany; Franz Neumann and Karl Wittfogel eventually found jobs in American universities; and Adorno and Horkheimer returned to the new Federal Republic where the Institute was once again allied with the University of Frankfurt. Adorno was installed as joint-head (with Horkheimer) of the Institute and as a professor at the University of Frankfurt am Main. In 1968 the Institute was the target for radical student protest, charged with a betrayal of Marxism and of the proletariat. At one point Adorno called the police to clear university premises of an occupying force of students. Although the post-War trajectory of the Institute has sometimes been portrayed as one of a growing distance from Marxism, its leading members had, in fact, almost uniformly been critical of the Soviet Union since the mid-1930s. Horkheimer was capable of referring in 1939 to developments 'in Germany and Russia' in a single breath (Horkheimer, 1987). Adorno and Horkheimer remained deeply, although critically and undogmatically, attached to Marx's own work throughout their lives: a body of work which they understood not as a recipe for a future society but as a critical theory of existing society.

The intellectual climate in which most of the important early practitioners of critical theory had their training was that of academic neo-Kantianism. This had arisen primarily as a reaction to the intellectual prestige of the natural sciences in nineteeth-century Europe, prestige which had led other disciplines, particularly the social sciences, to attempt to model themselves upon the natural sciences. One influential response to this imperialism of the natural sciences was the neo-Kantian Wilhelm Windelband's distinction between the nomothetic (law-positing) disciplines – such as the natural sciences – and idiographic disciplines such as history and sociology. The nomothetic disciplines, Windelband explained, assembled a number of observed cases under a general law. This method could not appropriately be applied to history or sociology, however, because in those disciplines enquirers were necessarily dealing, not with a number of cases identical in those respects which were important from the point of view of the enquiry, but rather with historical individualities each of which was qualitatively unique. Windelband's distinction was important for, amongst others, Heinrich Rickert, who was later Max Weber's philosophical master, and thus of the greatest significance for the development of twentieth-century social thought in general. Weber's sociology (whose substantive theses about the development of modernity were later to have a notable impact on Adorno's and Horkheimer's *Dialectic of Enlightenment*) maintained a strict separation between fact and value at a methodological level. This was also a disciplinary separation – the founding separation of positivist sociology ever since Comte – between sociology and philosophy. Despite the challenge to the dominance of the natural sciences in Weber's neo-Kantian background, then, the organisation of his work reinforced a separation between fact and value, sociology (as social science) and philosophy (as epistemology only, a theory of knowing in general).

One of the outstanding challenges to this separation between fact and value, theory and practice in social thought – as well as to the separation between social theory and philosophy itself – came from a Marxist thinker who had, on a substantive level, himself learnt much from Weber: Georg Lukács. In his *History and Class Consciousness*, Lukács offered a reconsideration of the problem of the relation between theory and practice. Lukács noted that Marxism's attempts to shed its philosophical shell had in many respects resulted, not in an escape from philosophy, but simply in a relapse into more naive philosophical positions. Reflection on the relation between theory and practice, for example, had sunk to a low philosophical level, with the political consequence that revolutionary practice seemed to be faced with a choice between passive determinism and naive voluntarism (Lukács, 1971, pp. 1–24). Lukács argued that the argument could not be settled on these terms because this abstract opposition was itself bound up the all-pervasive 'reification' of human life, thought and culture under the capitalist mode of production. In their 'reified' form, social institutions and processes come to appear as though they are autonomously self-directing. Human practice comes to serve this reified social process rather than to direct it. It becomes pseudo-practice, 'contemplative' practice (ibid., p. 100). At the same time, theoretical activity is governed by a division of intellectual labour. Philosophy, for example, becomes a department for grounding the other departments; sociology searches for 'purely sociological' objects. The result is that theory becomes blind to the social totality and incapable of theorising this totality. Its sight can only be restored from the perspective of a praxis – the revolutionary praxis of the proletariat – dedicated to overcoming the capitalist mode of production (ibid., pp. 197–209).

Lukács's analysis of reification exercised an important influence on many of those working in the Institute for Social Research. His work had suggested a way in which the problem of the relation between fact and value, description and prescription, could be understood as a historical problem. The problem could thus be seen less as a mistake on the part of philosophy and of the individual disciplines than as a result of the very constitution of those disciplines as branches of intellectual production, the way in which they were divided from each other and articulated together. But Horkheimer, in particular, was not convinced that Lukács's proposed solutions were tenable. This was not only because he and his co-workers were less optimistic about the chances

for, and likely effects of, proletarian revolution (although they were) but also because of the implicitly teleological, and hence idealist, character of Lukács's thought, in which history was to be guaranteed a meaning in the eventual identity of subject and object. Horkheimer believed that a different kind of intellectual work from Lukács's was necessary to overcome the reification which he had described. Instead of offering a speculative philosophy of history, the Institute was to develop a new kind of collaborative relationship between philosophy and the social and human sciences, set out by Horkheimer in his inaugural lecture as the Institute's director. The obstacles placed in the way of a materialist theory of society by the division of intellectual labour were to be overcome by criticising the presuppositions of this division, and by interdisciplinary and collaborative work. Among the most notable of the contributors to the journal, Erich Fromm worked on psychoanalysis with a view to elaborating its possible contributions to social theory; Herbert Marcuse worked on the philosophical issues confronted by social theory; Leo Lowenthal prepared literary-critical studies from an ideology-critical viewpoint; Friedrich Pollock and Henryk Grossmann contributed work in political economy; Karl Wittfogel produced studies of economic history; Franz Neumann and Otto Kirchheimer worked on law and politics in their relations to political economy. Theodor Adorno (then Wiesengrund-Adorno) was initially regarded as the Institute's musical expert rather than its guiding philosophical spirit.

The limits of interdisciplinarity

These workers were notionally brought together in the service of a materialism requiring the interdisciplinary 'unification of philosophy and science' (Horkheimer, 1982, p. 34). The particular advantage of Horkheimer's way of running the Institute was the combination of autonomy and rigorous criticism for which it allowed: each of the thinkers listed above had their own distinctive programme and range of interests, yet all submissions for the journal would be subject to searching criticism by colleagues. One especially important example of the xtent to which opinion could vary, even over matters of quite central significance, is offered by the view of the future of capitalism held by critical theory's political economists. Henryk Grossmann rgued that Marx's theory of value could not be eparated from his theory of collapse. For Grossmann, the collapse of capitalist society remained bjectively necessary. He argued that the rate of rofit would necessarily diminish to such an extent hat capitalist accumulation became impossible Grossmann, 1992, pp. 59–77). Friedrich Pollock, n the other hand, believed that the concentration f capital in the hands of cartels and monopolies had undamentally altered the competitive character of apitalism. Such concentration meant that those roductive forces which required massive investnent and large-scale planning for their full develpment could now be released (Pollock, 1975, p. 33). The relations of production need no longer form a atal restraint on the forces of production. Accordngly, Pollock argued that the current crisis could 'be vercome by capitalistic means and that 'monopoistic' capitalism is capable of surviving beyond the oreseeable future' (ibid., p. 28). The necessary ondition of this survival was a far closer co-operaion of state power and concentrated capital than ad previously been the case. In monopoly capitalsm, political administration and economic activity ad become far more closely entangled than under high' capitalism.

The significance of this argument was especially triking when the Institute came to give an account f Fascism. Whereas Franz Neumann, in his study *Behemoth*, argued that National Socialism was loomed to failure because of its failure to address he real interests of the workers, Pollock's view ended to suggest that political organisation could no longer be regarded as part of the social superstructure, and accordingly history would not necesarily be determined by 'real' economic interests. Pollock's emphasis on a qualitative shift between high and monopoly capitalism was that which, with certain qualifications, was most influential on Adorno and Horkheimer when they came to write *Dialectic of Enlightenment*.

The development of political economy within critical theory offers some interesting indications of the limits within which Horkheimer's early vision of interdisciplinary research was adhered to. Researchers whose main strength lay in one of the special sciences were often content to work – albeit on projects of unusual empirical range and conceptual depth – within the confines of their expertise. Neither Grossmann, Neumann nor Pollock – still less a more marginal figure such as Karl Wittfogel in his studies of what Marx had called the Asiatic mode of production – could really be said to have offered a philosophically-informed approach to political economy.

Further light is shed on the difficulties faced by critical theory's interdisciplinary programme by a consideration of its treatment of psychoanalysis. Erich Fromm attempted the then novel task of working out the relations between psychoanalysis and historical materialism. In 'The method and function of an analytic social psychology', Fromm argued that psychoanalysis was itself both historical – because 'it seeks to understand the drive structure through the understanding of life history' – and materialist, because it started not from ideas or theories but from sexual drives. In Fromm's envisaged social psychology, the drive for self-preservation, the basis of Marx's historical materialism, would have primacy, not because it was in some quantitative way 'stronger' than the sexual drives, but because it was less modifiable, not postponable and therefore not subject to repression or to remaining unconscious for long periods. Social psychology would therefore have a twofold task. At a basal level it would 'provide a more comprehensive knowledge of one of those factors that is operative in the social process: the nature of man himself. At a superstructural level it would 'show how the economic situation is transformed into ideology via man's drives' (Fromm, 1971, pp. 154–5). In a subsequent essay, Fromm began to indicate the results obtainable by such procedures when he identified the 'spirit of capitalism' with the 'anal character' (ibid., pp. 182–9).

Fromm's social psychology had already travelled some distance from critical theory's developing conception of historical materialism. Critical theory was becoming less and less confident about its ability to specify the distinction between base and superstructure. This scepticism was not only the result of Pollock's work in political economy, but also of a more fundamental growing doubt about whether the project of a philosophical anthropology – a universal theory of human nature – was itself any longer possible. Fromm's work had hoped to connect historical materialism and psychoanalysis too artlessly – and barely philosophically – with the result that neither was recognisable in the emerging synthesis. The observable difficulties attending critical theory's interdisciplinary programme were, perhaps, even more evident in such work as the collaborative *Studies in the Authoritarian Personality*, in which a series of questionnaires were developed to give an idea of the psychological traits of those most likely to have sympathy for authoritarian politics. The questionnaires attempted to disclose such attitudes by linked groups of indirect questions rather than by a single series of direct questions. The hope was that concealed or even unconscious anti-Semitism and ethnocentrism, which might be denied when asked about directly, might be revealed through response to the indirect questions (Adorno, 1950, p. 186). The work stands in marked need of the very philosophical criticism which the interdisciplinary character of critical theory was intended to provide.

The critical recuperation of classical German thought

The problems facing the interdisciplinary work of the critical theorists was one reason for the subsequent shift in emphasis in the work of three of the most central figures in critical theory: Max Horkheimer, Herbert Marcuse and Theodor Adorno. Drew Milne and Andrew Edgar develop in more detail below the case for the significance of Marcuse and Adorno's philosophical work. Horkheimer's very attempt to define 'critical theory' against traditional theory emerges from a deepened recognition in the light of intellectual experience that the division of intellectual labour does not merely damage the connections between disciplines, but also damages the ways in which those disciplines themselves are conceived. In particular, the problem of the relationships between fact and value, theory and practice, prescription and description which came to define

the project of critical theory itself for Horkheimer was not adequately addressed by the Institute's existing work, because the areas of positive expertise which were to be brought into communication were in many cases themselves already pre-formed by a positivist presupposition of a natural separation between each of these opposed pairs.

In the event, critical theory's most serious challenge to the division of intellectual labour, and particularly to the division of social theory from philosophy, with its associated separation of norm from fact, was provided not by its professedly interdisciplinary projects but rather by a series of works which owed more in their form to the speculative tradition of classical German philosophy than to the scientism of twentieth-century social research. The first of these works was Theodor Adorno and Max Horkheimer's *Dialectic of Enlightenment*, the central document of first-generation critical theory. Some particular aspects of the work are addressed in the articles on Adorno and Horkheimer. Here I want to focus on the work's general character and its role in defining the *critical* character of critical theory, not least because *Dialectic of Enlightenment* has been the text from whose approach the second generation of critical theorists has most centrally wished to distinguish itself. It consists of several complementary studies – the concept of enlightenment, *The Odyssey*, Sade, the culture industry, anti-Semitism – each of which explores aspects of the history of rationality. The central argument is that reason has become irrational precisely because of its attempt to expel every non-rational moment from itself. In this way, reason becomes incapable of understanding what makes rationality itself possible, the non-rational element which reason depends upon. The consequence is a kind of rationality which is a tool, blindly applied without any real capacity either to reflect on the ends to which it is applied, or to recognise the particular qualities of the objects to which it is applied. Adorno and Horkheimer call this unreflective rationality 'instrumental reason'. The theory of instrumental reason became a central motif of critical theory from this point onwards. Adorno and Horkheimer suggested that the instrumentalisation of reason went together with an increasingly absolute separation between the language of 'art' and the language of 'science'. The former became something with no cognitive content, merely image-like; the latter became something with no mimetic similarity to what it classified: a pure sign.

Dialectic of Enlightenment has often been misunderstood for the very reason that its relation to the central issue of prescription and description, fact and value – and with it that of first-generation critical theory as a whole – has been misconstrued. The title of the first, mimeographed, text, *Philosophical Fragments*, offers an important clue to the work's real nature. It does not offer a linear historical narrative running, in the manner of Spengler's *Decline of the West*, from bad to worse, but rather a series of linked but discontinuous essays. It hinges on its challenge to the relationship between fact and value in positivist thinking. The attempt to exclude value from positivist reflection about society and history, on the grounds that it is a merely subjective element, has not, in fact, had the intended result. What are, in fact, no more than reports on experience to date are illegitimately converted into 'laws' of economic, social or historical process.

With this conversion, the normative element which was apparently excluded comes in through the back door: the image of what shall and must be is silently remade in the image of what is and has been. What is, is construed as fate. Positivism thus becomes 'more metaphysical than metaphysics', a theodicy all the more powerful for being a tacit and unadmitted one. The *Dialectic of Enlightenment* sets itself to hold open the possibility of new and radically different experience which positivism tends to liquidate. How does it do this? It turns the unadmitted, but ineliminable, normative element of those concepts which positivism regards as purely descriptive, against the facts described by those concepts (for a more detailed account of this, see the article on Horkheimer below). This complex relationship to positivism in *Dialectic of Enlightenment* is visible at the level of its prose style, in which there are neither any empty moral prescriptions, nor any absolutely literal descriptions. This reflects the authors' conviction that an absolute separation of prescription from description would make language itself unintelligible. The arguments behind this conviction are developed in more detail in Adorno's later work (see Andrew Edgar's piece below).

Critical theory today

If there exists one salient and fundamental difference between first-generation critical theory and the second generation (represented primarily by Jürgen Habermas, but also, in different ways, by such figures as Albrecht Wellmer, Herbert Schnädelbach and Axel Honneth) it concerns this way of articulating prescription and description. Before discussing this, it is important to note that the second generation of critical theorists remains genuinely committed to the project of a critical theory as hitherto defined. They do not regard the task of theory only as an adequation to pre-given 'state of facts', but rather argue that it is part of that task to criticise the state of facts itself. As Nicholas Walker emphasises below, it is no less true of Habermas's work than of the first generation of critical theory that it emerges from a reconsideration of the meaning of some of the central preoccupations of classical German philosophy for contemporary social experience. The leading idea of Habermas's own thought – that human language and human communication in general already contain implicit intersubjective norms – is itself, in part, a development of one of the central motifs of Adorno's thought. (As Walker indicates, Habermas's own thought is by no means a seamless unity.) Much of Habermas's work, particularly in his essays rather than in his system-building mode, represents a continuation by other means (although often in a rather different direction) of some of the central polemical battles of first-generation critical theory: as in the case, for example, of his controversial work on deconstruction and post-modernism.

Yet Habermas thinks that critical theory can no longer be conducted in the manner of Adorno and Horkheimer. He regrets the central move made by critical theory in the 1930s, the downgrading of its earlier interdisciplinary programme in favour of a critique of instrumental reason, a critique which, for Habermas, is still tied to the presuppositions of classical philosophy of consciousness (Habermas, 1984–87, p. 399). Adorno and Horkheimer's attempt to criticise such philosophy of consciousness from within leads only to an aporia in which no rational foundation for the critique of instrumental reason can be secured. For Habermas this is not, as

Adorno thought, because critical theory in an objectively antagonistic society must necessarily be aporetic. He thinks instead that Adorno and Horkheimer misguidedly abandoned the earlier interdisciplinary programme of critical theory in favour of philosophical composition. This later work, for Habermas, overemphasises the aesthetic moment in cognition, loses the necessary relation to specialist disciplines and remains trapped in the philosophy of consciousness (ibid., pp. 385–6).

The second generation of critical theorists, and Habermas in particular, have argued for a different way of articulating critical theory's distinctive approach to the relationship between fact and value. For Habermas, early critical theory conceded too much ground to the scepticism which it wished to contest. Adorno's aporetic discontent with either an identification of, or a radical separation between, description and prescription is regarded as disabling. If norms cannot be separated from experience at least sufficiently to say what they are, Habermas asks, in what sense is 'theory' any longer 'critical'? He insists, on the contrary, that the universally valid norms governing communicative action can indeed be isolated and stated, and critical theory should get on with this task. Without such a procedure, there can be no secure standard against which communicative action can be judged. This is the project of his own *Theory of Communicative Action*, one of the central texts of second-generation critical theory.

Habermas's revisions affect (as he is well aware) far more than questions of presentation. The notion that philosophical thinking and writing are dialectical makes fewer and fewer appearances in Habermas's work as it progresses, perhaps because, to Habermas, it appears tied either to speculative totality (Hegel) or to a fragile hope for the redemption of sceptical negativity (Adorno). The problem of how a materialist thinking is possible is also now of less central interest because the regulative ideal against which social theory is to be measured is intersubjective. The task of explicating universal pragmatics is procedurally separated from the task of the 'reconstruction of historical materialism' (Habermas, 1979, pp. 130–77). There is an attempt to bid a decisive farewell to the philosophy of consciousness and to replace it with a theory of communicative action drawing on speech act theory and on aspects of American pragmatism.

Some have wanted to suggest that there are losses as well as gains in the second-generation development of critical theory. In particular, it has been suggested that Habermas's work returns to a form of the division between 'is' and 'ought' which emerged in Kant's work and which has so preoccupied critical theory. This is a conclusion which Habermas resists, because he is quite prepared to admit that there can be no normative presupposition without particular communicative actions in which norms are presupposed. The separation which Habermas proposes is not an ontological, but a procedural, separation. He does not imply that there are two spheres, one normative and one descriptive, which can never communicate with each other, but rather that these need to be separated out from each other for the purposes of analysis. Accordingly, a theoretical construction like Habermas's *Theory of Communicative Action* takes a very different form from a philosophical composition such as Adorno's *Negative Dialectics*. The former offers a complex articulation of several different kinds of enquiry, from the foundational level of universal pragmatics to the reconstruction of social theory and studies in aspects of the history of ideas. The separate parts of the work are relatively discrete and externally connected to each other when compared with a work such as *Negative Dialectics*.

The paradigm-shift from first- to second-generation critical theory has not won an uncontested victory. Numerous individual studies have challenged the critiques Habermas and others put forward of Adorno and Horkheimer. In any case, the second generation have themselves been interested in understanding their own work, not simply as a rejection, but rather as a renewal, of the work of their predecessors – notably in the case of Albrecht Wellmer's work (1985) on the persistence of modernity, or Herbert Schnädelbach's attempt (1987) to salvage certain aspects of negative dialectic as an auto-critique of reason. Moreover, there are other philosophers who, while they cannot really be described as critical theorists, have developed many of their own central ideas in close dialogue with the critical theory of both generations: Michael Theunissen's work (1991) towards elaborating a 'negative theology of time' is a notable example. The problem is further complicated by the fact that while work about first-generation critical theory is eminently publishable, work which, to any real extent, thinks and works like the *Dialectic of Enlightenment* is somewhat scarcer. Second-generation critical theory has made a different kind of compact, both with the individual disciplines of the modern university and with contemporary educational and publishing institutions, from that attempted by the first generation. Karl-Otto Apel has declared the era of 'one-man philosophy' dead, and indeed the work of a figure like Habermas – although it is itself outstandingly polymathic – accepts the division of intellectual labour into its own architecture. This offers one reason for the adaptability and resilience of his work in the contemporary university.

Bibliography

Writings

For works by Adorno and the other writers featured in individual essays below, see the bibliographies at the end of those articles. For more detailed bibliographies, see Jay (1973) and Wiggershaus (1993).

Adorno, Theodor W. (with Else Frenkel-Brunswik, Daniel J. Levinson and R. Nevitt Sanford) (1950), *The Authoritarian Personality*, New York: Harper.

Fromm, Erich (1971), *The Crisis of Psychoanalysis*, London: Jonathan Cape.

Grossmann, Henryk (1992), *The Law of Accumulation and Breakdown of the Capitalist System*, trans. and abr. Jairus Banaji, London: Pluto Press.

Honneth, Axel (1991), *The Critique of Power: Reflective Stages in a Critical Social Theory*, trans. Kenneth Baynes, Cambridge, MA: MIT Press.

Kirchheimer, Otto (1969), *Politics, Law and Social Change*, ed. Frederic S. Burin and Kurt L. Shell, New York and London: Columbia University Press.

Lowenthal, Leo (1961), *Literature, Popular Culture, and Society*, Englewood Cliffs, NJ: Prentice-Hall.

Neumann, Franz (1942), *Behemoth: The Structure and Practice of National Socialism*, London: Gollancz.

Pollock, Friedrich (1975), *Stadien des Kapitalismus*, ed. Helmut Dubiel, Munich: C. H. Beck.

Schmidt, Alfred (1971), *The Concept of Nature in Marx*, trans. Ben Fowkes, London: New Left Books.

Schnädelbach, Herbert (1987), *Vernunft und Geschichte: Vorträge und Abhandlungen*, Frankfurt am Main: Suhrkamp.

Sohn-Rethel, Alfred (1978), *Intellectual and Manual Labour: A Critique of Epistemology*, trans. Martin Sohn-Rethel, London: Macmillan.

Theunissen, Michael (1969), *Gesellschaft und Geschichte. Zur Kritik der kritischen Theorie*, Berlin: de Gruyter.

— (1991), *Negative Theologie der Zeit*, Frankfurt am Main: Suhrkamp.

Wellmer, Albrecht (1985), *Zur Dialektik von Moderne und Postmoderne. Vernunftkritik nach Adorno*, Frankfurt am Main: Suhrkamp.

References and further reading

Benhabib, Seyla (1987), *Critique, Norm and Utopia: A Study of the Foundations of Critical Theory*, Cambridge: Polity Press.

Bernstein, J. M. (1995), *Recovering Ethical Life: Jürgen Habermas and the Future of Critical Theory*, London: Routledge.

Connerton, Paul (1980), *The Tragedy of Enlightenment: An Essay on the Frankfurt School*, Cambridge: Cambridge University Press.

Dews, Peter (1987), *Logics of Disintegration: Post-structuralist Thought and the Claims of Critical Theory*, London: Verso.

Dubiel, Helmut (1985), *Theory and Politics: Studies in the Development of Critical Theory*, trans. Benjamin Gregg, Cambridge, MA: MIT Press.

Friedeburg, Ludwig von and Jürgen Habermas (eds) (1983), *Adorno-Konferenz 1983*, Frankfurt am Main: Suhrkamp.

Geuss, Raymond (1981), *The Idea of a Critical Theory: Habermas and the Frankfurt School*, Cambridge: Cambridge University Press.

Held, David (1980), *Introduction to Critical Theory: from Horkheimer to Habermas*, London: Hutchinson.

Jay, Martin (1973), *The Dialectical Imagination: A History of the Frankfurt School and the Institute of Social Research, 1923–50*, London: Heinemann.

Marramao, Giacomo (1975), 'Political Economy and Critical Theory', *Telos* 24, 56–80.

Wiggershaus, Rolf (1993), *The Frankfurt School*, trans. Michael Robertson, Cambridge: Polity Press.

THINKING AND AFFECTIVITY: HORKHEIMER

Simon Jarvis

'A god is incapable of knowing anything because it has no needs' (Horkheimer, 1993, p. 242). This maxim from the closing pages of an essay written in 1934 exemplifies the central impulse of all Horkheimer's thought, his own distinctive contribution to critical theory, without which critical theory might well have taken a decisively different path from the one actually followed. This path may be described as the elaboration of a genuinely materialist thinking. For Horkheimer, the history of philosophy has often consisted of a series of attempts, conscious or unconscious, to prove that thinking is not determined by material needs: that it is independent, self-legitimating and autonomous. Materialism, in his view, is defined primarily not by a particular kind of method, nor by a particular set of opinions about the world, but rather by its ability in practice to testify to the needs which not only motivate thinking, but without which thinking itself would be impossible. Hence the particular force of the maxim quoted above. Horkheimer is not telling us what we have so often been told before – that philosophy finds it difficult to be as disinterested as it would like or pretend to be – but something rather more unusual: that it is a condition of the possibility of philosophy's arriving at the truth that it should *not* be detached from needs, desires and wishes.

This is a quite different programme from a sociology of knowledge – it does not argue that, since all ideas, propositions, categories, etc. are second-order results of social interests, the notion of absolute truth needs to be abandoned. Instead, Horkheimer's materialism asks on what conditions thinking can admit to being the thinking of particular living historical individuals, with their all their needs, interests and desires, without therefore giving up the possibility that thoughts might be *true*: 'Materialism obviously does not reject thinking . . . But materialism, unlike idealism, always understands thinking to be the thinking of particular men within a particular period of time. It challenges every claim to the autonomy of thought' (Horkheimer, 1982, p. 32).

The course of Horkheimer's intellectual career shows him progressively deepening his notion of how this can be done. After a brief period of apprenticeship as a neo-Kantian, Horkheimer developed an early concern for the relationship between philosophy and social and psychological interests. He rapidly developed a critique of the various alternative kinds of materialism on offer, a critique elaborated from the standpoint of his own concern for practice. His own hopes in the late 1920s and early 1930s for a different kind of materialism are invested above all in the idea of a new kind of collaborative relationship between philosophy and the social and human sciences. Later in the 1930s, however, partly as a result of his own deepening philosophical work, and partly under the influence of the simultaneous work of Adorno and Marcuse on related issues, he developed a less optimistic account of the possibilities for a fruitful collaboration between the positive social sciences and philosophical reflection. He came to see empirical social research as more deeply and intimately damaged by its historical separation from philosophy than he had earlier thought. Instead, he became increasingly interested in the idea that, under patient investigation, the principal categories of classical philosophy themselves – represented for him primarily by the work of Kant and its later development in German thought – can be made to display the social experience which is already implicitly sedimented in them and without which those categories cannot be thought. This approach governs the rest of Horkheimer's work; in the later decades of his life it takes on an increasingly Schopenhauerian and pessimistic tone.

Horkheimer's work is remarkable for combining thematic coherence – asking, from start to finish, how the thinking of living individuals can avoid belying the needs and interests of those individuals – and for the extraordinary breadth of subject matters to which it is addressed – from psychoanalysis to the study of anti-Semitism, from high art to the sociology of shopping. This article does not attempt to review all the many substantive areas of social and social-psychological enquiry to which Horkheimer contributed, but rather to explain the development of the key constellations of his thinking stage by stage. Given the area of interest presupposed by this book as a whole, it will focus on those aspects of Horkheimer's work which are of the greatest philosophical interest. Whereas some of the other central figures involved in the development of Critical Theory – notably Adorno – have a philosophical project which remains remarkably stable from the beginning to the end of their careers, Horkheimer's, ethically and politically coherent as it is, nevertheless develops, deepens and changes in ways which demand careful attention. Accordingly, this article will provide a chronologically organised account of Horkheimer's work.

The problem of materialism

Horkheimer's life and career are marked by the historical experiences to which his thinking was a response. Born in February 1895, the son of a conservative Jewish industrialist, his radical politi-cal convictions were developed as an adolescent with his friend and later colleague, Friedrich Pollock. After completing his doctoral work with Hans Cornelius, Horkheimer was appointed as Director of the Institute for Social Research, whose emphasis he shifted from labour history towards interdisciplinary work in social and cultural theory. He continued to direct the Institute in its American exile after Hitler's accession to power in 1933, and after the War returned to a chair in the new Federal Republic of Germany. As central to his life's work as his own writing was the direction given to other members of the Institute and the careful co-ordination of their efforts.

Horkheimer's early teacher, Hans Cornelius, was representative of the neo-Kantian approach which dominated philosophical life in German universities at the time of Horkheimer's first studies. Cornelius's work was preoccupied with questions of epistemology: for him, philosophy had little to do with metaphysical speculation but was rather the department which would provide a methodology for the positive sciences. Under his supervision Horkheimer completed a thesis on 'Kant's *Critique of Judgement* as a connecting limb between theoretical and practical philosophy'. Although Horkheimer's treatment of this subject stayed largely within the terms of Kant's own thinking, the subject itself already announced one dominant concern of Horkheimer's own philosophical *œuvre*: how could philosophy articulate the link between theory and practice? In the same year, 1925, his inaugural lecture as a junior lecturer (*Privatdozent*) at the University of Frankfurt was given on the theme 'Kant and Hegel'. The lecture is interesting for its indications that Horkheimer was dissatisfied with the reduction of philosophy to formal epistemology, and for its appeal to the idea of dialectic.

If Horkheimer's inaugural lecture makes clear that he wishes to appeal to a notion of dialectic, however, it does not begin to wrestle with the problem of how, or whether, a materialist dialectic is possible. Some interesting indications of his growing dissatisfaction with the then available solutions to the problem of a materialist philosophy are given in a manuscript, unpublished until after his death, giving a commentary on Lenin's *Materialism and Empirio-criticism*. In that work Lenin had taken issue with the work of Mach and Avenarius, in order to combat their admirers in the Russian party. Horkheimer's attitude to Lenin's work is two-sided. What Lenin shows well, he believes, is the extent to which philosophies which offer themselves as materialist often fall into idealism despite themselves. The idealism of some of Mach's supporters in their supposedly materialist philosophy, for example, lies not in their opinions about the relative ontological statuses of matter and 'spirit', but rather in the way in which certain elements are promoted to transhistorical invariance. Such promotion inevitably results in idealism. Yet Lenin himself, in Horkheimer's view, despite his insight into the idealist character of Mach's supporters, feels obliged to ground his materialism in a naively objectivist world-view: that sensations are copies of objects which are 'just out there', and which exist not only independently of their being perceived by a particular individual, but, in principle, independently of any perception whatever. As Horkheimer points out, 'anyone can compare the look of a thing or person with the idea of them that he had previously entertained, but nobody can compare the sensuous appearance, the sensation, with something which itself is neither a sensation nor a representation but matter existing independently of sensation or representation' (Horkheimer, 1987, vol. 11, p. 184).

The limitations of Lenin's work are indicative, for Horkheimer, of the difficulties faced by materialist thinking as such. Materialism which is grounded in a dogmatically held world-view (about the absolute independence of matter from all perception whatever, for example) is actually more metaphysical than the metaphysics which it hopes to eliminate, because anything which is in principle independent of our perception can only be posited by an act of dogmatic faith. In two essays written early in the 1930s for the Zeitschrift für Sozialforschung, 'Materialism and metaphysics' and 'Materialism and morality', Horkheimer began to set out his own ideas about materialism. For him, materialism must ensure that it does not build up supra-temporal concepts. Once it does this, it will no longer in fact be materialist, however it labels itself (Horkheimer, 1982, p. 34). Immediately we posit some invariant

element which never changes, we have in fact placed an ideality at the centre of our thinking. If we posit some relation of matter to thinking which always remains the same, we have not materialism but idealism: as when empirio-criticism claims that sensation is the true, independent, unconditioned reality. This is the case whether the self-identical element is a world-view or a method. If we always apply the same method to the subject matter, irrespective of the qualities of that subject matter, our thought is idealist. No matter how impeccably 'materialist' our method, as a method, it is already idealist. Horkheimer's important insight is to have seen how difficult it is not to place some kind of invariant ideality at the centre of our thinking. Achieving an escape from such invariance is not simply a matter of having the right opinions, but rather of the way in which our practice of thinking organises itself in researching and in writing.

If Horkheimer's materialism is not to be grounded in a method or a world-view, then, what is its basis? For Horkheimer, materialism arises from thinking's relation to the bodily experience which it lives off: experiences of fear, suffering, desire and so on. One important consequence of thinking of materialism as concerned in this way with bodily experience is that the materialism in question becomes at once theoretical and practical. The real undoubted ground of such a materialism is neither some set conception of matter – on which 'only natural science as it moves forward' (ibid., p. 35) can judge – still less some apparent epistemological certainty such as A=A, but rather human happiness, the striving for which 'is to be regarded as a natural fact requiring no justification' (ibid., p. 44). It is this practical conception of materialism which means that materialism today is more vitally connected with the social than with the natural sciences: 'the wretchedness of our own time is connected with the structure of society: social theory therefore forms the main content of contemporary materialism' (ibid., p. 24). In such essays as 'Notes on Science and the Crisis' Horkheimer treads a difficult path between positivism and pragmatism. His insistence that science is itself a social force of production, rather than a disembodied progress of the intellect, is balanced by an equal and opposite insistence that this does not legitimate a pragmatist theory of knowledge: 'It is not for social interests to decide what is or is not true' (ibid., p. 2). Horkheimer argues, instead, for a historical understanding of the separation between fact and value. The progressive political significance which the separation between fact and value had in the high bourgeois era – as an insistence that authority should legitimate itself – has been lost to the extent that the social and human sciences have begun to lose their normative character altogether and to represent themselves as sheer descriptions of existing states of affairs.

'Dialectic' and the division of intellectual labour

Horkheimer's ambiguous relationship to the separation of fact from value indicates how his programme differs from positivism. At one point in the essay on 'Materialism and metaphysics' Horkheimer bluntly declares that 'Materialism requires the unification of philosophy and science' (Horkheimer, 1982, p. 24). Horkheimer, it should be noted, has taken seriously positivist criticisms of *a priori* philosophy. Previous materialisms have failed in so far as they have regarded philosophy as somehow able finally to describe a world of concepts or experiences not accessible to individual disciplines. For Horkheimer, as for the early Adorno in his 1931 inaugural lecture on 'The Contemporary Relevance of Philosophy', it is the case that materialist thinking must add nothing to the elements provided by the individual sciences – on pain of simply inventing chimerical idealities – but it can arrange those elements in a different order. This is also where the crucial difference lies between the early programme of collaborative social research envisaged by Horkheimer on the one hand, and a positivistic division of intellectual labour, on the other. When Horkheimer suggests that 'materialism requires the unification of philosophy and science' he goes on to qualify this by saying that the meaning of this demand 'is the exact opposite of any attempt to absolutize particular scientific doctrines'. But why is this so?

Some answers to this question can be found in Horkheimer's programmatic essay on 'The present situation of social philosophy and the tasks of an institute for social research'. In this, he insists that

'the relationship between philosophical and corresponding specialized scientific disciplines cannot be conceived as though philosophy deals with the really decisive problems . . . while on the other side empirical research carries out its long, boring individual studies that split up into a thousand partial questions . . .' (Horkheimer, 1993, pp. 8–9). Horkheimer, partly under the influence of Lukács, points out the inadequacies of the division of intellectual labour. Although academic specialisation is habitually represented as smoothly co-operative, it is, in fact, 'chaotic' (ibid., p. 9). It is governed not by any natural divisions in the subject matter itself but rather by self-autonomising lines of enquiry whose scientist self-legitimation is bought at the price of any ability to respond flexibly to the material studied. For this reason, the damage wrought by such a division is not one which could be overcome simply by adding up the various portions of research in a series of 'bad syntheses'. Instead, Horkheimer recommends 'a continuous, dialectical penetration and development of philosophical theory and specialized scientific praxis' (ibid., p. 10). Such a process of repeated collision between philosophical theory and empirical research was what Horkheimer envisaged happening in the Institute for Social Research – where thinkers and researchers in many different disciplines had been brought together to work in close contact. The process of collision was supposed to prevent empirical research from becoming conceptually naive in the way it framed its own instruments, but also to provide a continual check on philosophy's tendency to invent (whether voluntarily or not) chimerical ultimate facts or values unrelated to experience. These collisions would not be random but rather directed by Horkheimer in 'a dictatorship of planned work' (ibid., p. 12). It is his early programme which has found favour with a second generation of critical theorists anxious about what they have seen as a loss of connection between critical theory's interest in philosophy and its interest in social experience – the implication which they (with whatever justice) see in the later work of the first generation, that philosophy does indeed deal with 'the really decisive problems'.

The continuous process envisaged by Horkheimer is described as 'dialectical'. This is a word whose force remains somewhat unclarified in the early work of the members of the Institute, and it is fair to say that, in the attempt to establish what was really meant by it, some serious difficulties were discovered in the way it was formulated, difficulties which led to the more philosophically and metaphysically ambitious programme of the middle and later Horkheimer. It is not immediately evident what a materialist dialectic would mean. In Hegel's thought, dialectic requires the continual mutual implicatedness of thought and being. One crude way of characterising dialectic there is to say that wherever sheer being, pure immediacy, is invoked, Hegel shows how that very movement of invocation already implies a series of conceptual categories: even when we just point to this tree, here and now, the categories 'here' and 'now' are, for Hegel, already implicit in our act of pointing. Any attempt to insist that matter is in principle independent of the way we think of it would thus appear to sever the vital cord of such a dialectic. Here, of course, Horkheimer's practical and historical conception of materialism looks like a much more promising basis for a materialist dialectic, since, as we have seen, it does not rest upon any such principle. In his early essays Horkheimer sometimes appears to suggest that the problem of a materialist dialectic has already been adequately solved: 'Feuerbach, Marx and Engels freed the dialectic from its idealist form' (Horkheimer, 1982, p. 32). Here the implication appears to be that a dialectical method is freed from the idealist content of Hegel's thought; and indeed Horkheimer often does speak of dialectic as a 'method' in his early work. Yet we still confront a version of the same problem faced earlier in the case of 'materialism'. If dialectic is a method, does it always proceed in the same way irrespective of the material studied? If so, how can it be other than idealist? But if, on the other hand, dialectic is regarded some feature of the world itself – for example, of laws of human or natural history – how can it avoid being a mythical ideality?

One of Horkheimer's most persistent early attempts to grapple with the problem of a materialist dialectic can be found in his essay on 'The Rationalism Debate in Contemporary Philosophy' (1934). Here he argues for a 'materialism schooled in Hegel's logic' (Horkheimer, 1993, p. 234). The aspect of Hegel's dialectic which offers a model to materialist dialectic is its approach to formal logic. Whereas irrationalism, having noticed formal logic's non-identity with what it would classify, responds by jettisoning such logic, dialectical logic does not discard traditional logic. It regards the propositions of such logic not as untrue but as only abstractly correct. 'All true thought is thus to be understood as a continuous critique of abstract determinations' (ibid., p. 236) in the light of experience. Materialist dialectic is to be distinguished from Hegelian dialectic, however, because it 'understands the subject of thought not as itself another abstraction such as the essence "humanity", but rather as human beings of a definite historical epoch' (ibid., p. 240). Whereas Horkheimer's programmatic statement of the Institute's tasks laid more emphasis on the dialectical relationship *between* philosophy and the sciences, he here emphasises the irreconcilability of a methodologistic approach with materialist dialectic. For this reason, reference to dialectic as a 'method' comes to sound increasingly provisional in Horkheimer's work, as in the following quotation:

> The dialectical method is the quintessence of all intellectual tools for making fruitful the abstract elements derived from the analytic Understanding for the representation of the living object. There are no universal rules for this purpose. Even within a particular science such as individual psychology, observation of almost every human being demands a different form of theoretical construction. (ibid., p. 235)

If the method must change with every object, it is less clear how it can be described as a method. Accordingly, the solution left implicit in the early Horkheimer – that a dialectical method shorn of idealism can be removed from Hegel's logic and used to good effect for materialist purposes – comes under greater and greater strain.

Critical theory of society

The development of Horkheimer's earlier programme is visible in one of the single most important statements left by the Frankfurt School, Horkheimer's essay 'Traditional and Critical Theory'. This essay is centrally concerned with specifying the complex relationships between fact and value, prescription and description, theory and practice, with which Horkheimer had long been struggling. It is notable that in Horkheimer's inaugural lecture on Kant and Hegel, the term 'critical theory' (of knowledge) is used simply to refer to Kant's thought. Here, however, Horkheimer is outlining a critical theory of society. Such a theory is not simply a criticism of the intellectual instruments which may be used to pinpoint the facts, but, rather, also a criticism of the facts themselves. Horkheimer thinks that such a programme is possible because even the categories which apparently purely descriptive projects use to describe existing social arrangements in fact already contain a normative element, which may be tacit or unconscious but which cannot be wholly eliminated without making social description itself impossible. (Positivism is thought of as just this hopeless attempt to extinguish all normative elements from social understanding.) The crux of critical theory's approach, by contrast, is as follows. The normative element in apparently purely descriptive concepts is to be turned against the state of affairs which those concepts hope simply to describe. Thus, for example, 'if we take seriously the ideas by which the bourgeoisie explains its own order – free exchange, free competition, harmony of interests, and so on – and if we follow them to their logical conclusion, they manifest their inner contradiction and therewith their real opposition to the bourgeois order' (Horkheimer, 1982, p. 214). The word 'free' in 'free competition' can never be made simply descriptive, any more than the word 'fair' in 'fair exchange'. The norms of freedom and justice, which positivist social science hopes to bracket out, thus reappear involuntarily in its own descriptions and classifications.

The important point here is that this is how Horkheimer imagines that critical theory can escape being another form of idealist consolation. Instead of elevating some protected realm of idealities and lamenting positivism's harshness in attacking them, critical theory takes positivism at its own word and shows that this word can never be made as simply instrumental, as sheerly descriptive, as wholly literal, as positivism would like – because positivism would not even be minimally intelligible were such an absolutely literal, descriptive and instrumental language to be realised.

It will thus be clear how one of the central philosophical motifs of mature critical theory, its utopian negativity, is taking shape. Critical theory does not stand securely on its own foundation; any such foundationalism would already be idealist. Yet critical theory also differs from sceptical relativism by its insistence on the possibility of true thinking. This possibility is currently blocked by the social organisation of experience and knowledge, yet we are not to transfigure this block into eternal fate. At this stage, interestingly, Horkheimer holds to the Hegelian idea that truth demands an identity of subject and object: 'in reflection on man, subject and object are sundered; their identity lies in the future, not in the present' (ibid., p. 211). Later, of course, Adorno was to insist that truth demanded not the identity of subject and object, but rather a reconciliation of the two, implying precisely a recognition of their *non*-identity. The important point here is that truth is, for the moment, only to be attained negatively, through the criticism of specific ideological misrecognitions. Hence the title 'critical theory'. Whereas Lukács had thought that positive knowledge as organised misrecognition could perhaps be corrected from the standpoint of the revolutionary proletariat, Horkheimer believes that the proletariat are no less subject to such misrecognitions than any other interest group.

It is clear that 'Traditional and Critical Theory' must have severely affected the earlier programme of the Institute announced by Horkheimer, looking too optimistic about the possibility of securing access to concrete human experience through a programme of positive research. It is important to be clear about the reasons for the more radical rejection of positivism in the mature Horkheimer, however. Positivism is rejected not because it is too *much* concerned with the details of human experience, but too *little*. Whatever its empiricist credo, in practice it drains human experience of its concrete individuality. Horkheimer came to believe that the only way to get beyond this is to subject the mechanisms of this draining to a thoroughgoing critique. The mechanisms are at once intellectual and social. In this essay he began to develop the comparison, pivotal for the *Dialectic of Enlightenment*, between

Kant's thought and the commodity form. The 'single existential 'judgement' which Horkheimer specifies critical theory as unfolding is that

> The basic form of the historically given commodity economy on which modern history rests contains in itself the internal and external tensions of the modern era; it generates these tensions over and over again in an increasingly heightened form; and after a period of progress, development of human powers, and emancipation for the individual, after an enormous extension of human control over nature, it finally hinders further development and drives humanity into a new barbarism. (ibid., p. 227)

The contradictions in Kant's thought 'show the depth and honesty of his thinking' because this thinking 'reflects exactly the contradiction-filled form of human activity in the modern period' (ibid., 1982, p. 204). We see here the beginnings of the argument which is worked out in much more detail in the later work of critical theory: that there is a deep-seated affinity between the way in which in Kant's thought concepts work on indeterminate sense data in order to turn them into determinate perceptions, and the way in which, in the commodity form, labour works on raw material in order to transform it into a commodity. Kant's thought contains, sedimented within it, precisely because of its exceptional philosophical rigour, the most fundamental experiences of modernity.

We are thus witnessing the birth of a rather different programme, side by side with the persistence of elements of the older programme. In the newer programme, philosophy no longer acts as a kind of critical matchmaker or arbiter among the various individual disciplines, but rather deciphers from within its own tradition the social experience which that tradition must live off, but which it inevitably conceals and misrepresents. This is not a retreat from social experience, but rather a deepening of the claim of experience, and accordingly of the scepticism about the ability of social research programmes to provide access to such experience (although it should be noted that the Institute never relinquished its relation to empirical social research, which it continued to conduct even after 1945).

The emergence of such a full-blown 'critical theory' also begins to provide some different kinds of answers to the question as to the possibility of a materialist dialectic. While proceeding with essays of extraordinary historical and sociological depth and range, such as his study of 'Egoism and Freedom Movements: On the Anthropology of the Bourgeois Era', or his work on anti-Semitism, Horkheimer was also working towards the possibility of writing what he envisaged as a dialectical logic, a project on which he came to envisage collaborating with Adorno. The manuscript record of his discussions with Adorno and others has only relatively recently been published in German, and it provides a useful insight into the process of argument from which the mature form of critical theory, and especially the book *Dialectic of Enlightenment* (first published under the title *Philosophical Fragments*), emerged. In one passage Adorno points out the difficulty of the relationship to Hegel which had been imagined in much of Horkheimer's previous work, including the essay on critical theory. There the identity of subject and object, and with it the Hegelian notion that 'the true is the whole', was still taken as the condition of the possibility of true thinking, but to be necessarily postponed. 'It must not look as though we are saying, the Hegelian principle ["the true is the whole"] is quite right, except that the ideas of the absolute and of the blind givenness of the infinite are mixed up in it, as though there were only a quantitative difference between us and him . . . The point is not to subject Hegel to a critical [that is, Kantian] "limitation", but to confront his ontology in all seriousness with another ontology, that is, an ironic one: that there is no such thing as an ontology any more and the concept of the ontological ground itself has to be suspended' (Horkheimer, 1987, vol. 12, I, pp. 488–9). Again and again the discussions show Horkheimer's anxiety that this insistence of Adorno's on negativity may turn out to be a nihilism.

Dialectic of enlightenment: philosophy and social experience

In the event, Adorno himself developed the most thoroughgoing account left by critical theory of what might be meant by a materialist dialectic in his studies of Hegel and, above all, in his late work *Negative Dialectics*. The collaborative work *Dialectic of Enlightenment*, however, also bears the marks of Horkheimer's distinctive philosophical preoccupations. The book is centrally concerned with the necessary collapse of thought's delusive attempts to become perfectly autonomous. 'Enlightenment' is used to refer not to a particular historical period in intellectual history running, for example, from Descartes to Kant, but rather to refer to all kinds of sceptical demythologisation whatever. In this sense, Xenophanes' protests against the attribution of anthropomorphic qualities to the gods are as much a piece of 'enlightenment' as the Cartesian *cogito*. Horkheimer and Adorno argue that thought's attempts to make itself self-sufficient (most visible in the development of modern philosophy) actually culminate by making thought incapable of responding to the qualities of the object itself. The result is thinking as organised tautology: 'the world as a gigantic analytic judgement' (Horkheimer, 1972, p. 27). Perfectly autonomous thinking would not be thinking about anything. The book thus offers an extended development of Horkheimer's principle, set out in his essay on the rationalism debate: thought actually *requires* needs, wishes and interests in order even to be thought.

Dialectic of Enlightenment is sometimes thought of as a pessimistic grand narrative in which matters go from bad to worse. In truth, it is not a narrative at all, however, but rather a series of constelled individual essays. The book does not work narratively, but rather archaeologically: it is not telling the story of how Western civilization went from A to B but rather, asking what must have happened for social experience to have become what it has. Its interests cover a bewildering range, and it would be pointless to attempt to summarise them here. The crucial point in terms of the argument developed by this article is to consider the relation to social experience implied by the book. It is incorrect to suggest that the book represents an aestheticisation of critical theory, or a retreat from social experience into social myth. Instead, it represents a reassessment of the best way in which to address social experience. The habitual recourse of positivist sociology at this date was to assemble subjective reports of such experience and

then to attempt to discount the subjective elements in them, leaving the social scientist with a supposedly objective remnant, a remnant, however, which had, in fact, already been drained of any resemblance to human experience of any kind. *Dialectic of Enlightenment*, instead, takes even the most abstract philosophical constructions – indeed, precisely the most abstract philosophical constructions – as testifying to the social experience which forms their own condition of possibility and of intelligibility, but which they efface or elide. It follows the opposite course to that taken by positivist sociology. Whereas positivist sociology moves from particular experiences to classifications of those experiences, critical theory would move from conceptual abstractions to the concrete historical experience which cannot but be sedimented in them. The book is by no means a polemic *against* enlightenment but rather an attempt to enlighten enlightenment about its own conditions of possibility. It is really a polemic against scepticism: and, in particular, against the sceptical block on absolute truth. However, because such scepticism permeates and enables all current social experience, rather than simply being an intellectual error, this block cannot simply be abrogated. Instead, it is subjected to an auto-critique. *Dialectic of Enlightenment* is a sceptical account of scepticism.

Horkheimer's post-War work continues this theme of the block on access to the absolute, often in ways which make more explicit the theological elements of the theme. Thought, for the later Horkheimer, faces a stark choice between tautology and theology. In 'Theism and Atheism' (1963) he insists that 'Truth – eternal truth outlasting human error – cannot be separated from theism. The only alternative is positivism' (Horkheimer, 1974, p. 47). In no way does such a development mark a retreat into metaphysical or idealist consolation, however, but rather the sharpening of the materialist moment in Horkheimer's thought. This can be seen if we look at one of Horkheimer's late essays on Schopenhauer, 'Schopenhauer today' (1961). Horkheimer's interest in Schopenhauer remains central to his thought throughout his life. He is attracted to Schopenhauer because of his emphasis on the priority of affectivity – suffering and desire – over thinking. He is regarded by Horkheimer as an uncompromising enemy of idealism: 'blood and misery stick to the triumphs of society. The rest is ideology' (ibid., p. 64). What unites theology to materialism in the later Horkheimer is the relation to transcendence in both. The contemporary world is a 'context of immanence' in which there is apparently no outside. Thinking has become incapable either of understanding its own conditionedness or of responding to the qualities of the object. Both theology and materialism would break with this 'context of immanence', insisting on testifying to the possibility of something outside thinking, which thinking depends on. The later Horkheimer's model of truth, then, is by no means an ethereal or spiritualised one; it retains all the blunt materialism of his earliest work: 'Truth itself lies hidden, according to Democritus, in a well, and, according to Schopenhauer, it gets a rap on the knuckles when it tries to come out' (ibid., p. 64).

Horkheimer's legacy

In recent years there has been a welcome revival of interest in Horkheimer's work in Germany and the USA. This revival has especially concerned the programme of interdisciplinary research which Horkheimer developed in his work of the late 1920s and early 1930s. Some scholars have wanted to look here for a connection between philosophy and the social sciences which they see as having been lost in the later development of critical theory, particularly under what is sometimes thought to be the aestheticising and anti-empirical influence of Adorno.

This tendency in recent Horkheimer scholarship is certainly welcome in so far as it directs attention to the importance to critical theory of preserving a connection between philosophical speculation and the experience of living individuals. Yet it perhaps implies a different kind of break than really pertains between the earlier and the middle-period Horkhei-

mer. The difference between the early and the later periods of Horkheimer's work is not, for example, that the early Horkheimer accounts the social experience of living individuals of decisive importance for materialism, whereas the later Horkheimer downgrades such experience in favour of a social myth or a negative theology: the difference is rather that Horkheimer – with good reason, as Wolfgang Bonß has pointed out (Benhabib et al., 1993, p. 119) – comes to be suspicious of the naivety of certain aspects of his earlier project. That is, he comes to see that in certain respects his earlier project is *less* capable of doing justice to such experience precisely because of the naive immediacy of the means with which it hopes to grasp it. The move to the philosophical artifice of highly composed works like *Dialectic of Enlightenment* is not a move *away* from social experience, but rather a more persistent and cunning attempt to shake the hold of the positivism which drains such experience of its particularity and meaning.

It is certainly an important part of Horkheimer's legacy to philosophy and social theory that he insists on the continual collision between both, rather than peaceably accepting a division of intellectual tasks; but his most central contribution to critical theory lies less in the proposal of programmatic projects for research than in the tenacity and imagination with which he held to and developed his central insight: the need for thinking to do justice to what it lives off. 'A god is incapable of knowing anything because it has no needs'. It really is the case that this maxim can stand over all Horkheimer's work, not just the early work or the work on social-theoretical topics. Horkheimer never neglected this commitment, and there are good reasons for thinking that, without his persistence on this subject, critical theory in general, and the work of Adorno in particular, would have been significantly weaker.

Bibliography

Writings

Horkheimer's collected works as listed below have all been edited by Alfred Schmidt and Gunzelin Schmid Noerr:

Horkheimer, Max (1947), *Eclipse of Reason* (Oxford: Oxford University Press.
— (1978), *Dawn and Decline: Notes 1926–1931 and 1950–1969*, New York: Seabury Press. (with Theodor W. Adorno) *Dialectic of Enlightenment*

(1972), trans. John Cumming, New York: Seabury Press.

— (1982), *Critical Theory: Selected Essays*, trans. Matthew J. O'Connell et al., New York: Continuum, *Critique of Instrumental Reason*, trans. Matthew O'Connell et al., New York: Seabury Press.

— (1987), *Gesammelte Schriften*, 15 vols, Fischer.

— (1993), *Between Philosophy and Social Science: Selected Early Writings*, trans. G. Frederick Hunter, Matthew S. Kromer and John Torpey, Cambridge, MA: MIT Press.

References and further reading

Benhabib, Seyla, Wolfgang Bonß and John McCole (eds) (1993), *On Max Horkheimer: New Perspectives*, Cambridge, MA: MIT Press.

Dubiel, Helmut (1985), *Theory and Politics: Studies in the Development of Critical Theory*, trans. Benjamin Gregg, Cambridge, MA: MIT Press.

Schmidt, Alfred and Norbert Altwicker (eds) (1986), *Max Horkheimer heute: Werk und Wirkung*, Frankfurt am Main: Fischer.

6.2

CULTURE AND CRITICISM: ADORNO

Andrew Edgar

Theodor Wiesengrund Adorno was born in Frankfurt am Main, in 1903, to middle-class parents. Around the time of Adorno's birth, his father converted from Judaism to Protestantism. His mother was a Catholic. A precocious intellect, he began to study Kant's *Critique of Pure Reason*, under the guidance of Siegfried Kracauer, at the age of sixteen. He studied at Frankfurt University, taking his doctorate, on Husserl, in 1924. In 1925, he moved to Vienna for a short period to study composition with Alban Berg, thereby becoming intimate with the circle linked to the composer Arnold Schoenberg. While Adorno is most readily associated with the Frankfurt Institute for Social Research, he did not become a full member until the 1940s. The rise of Nazism led to his exile, initially to Oxford, where he was the doctoral student of Gilbert Ryle, and then to the USA, where his work included co-operation with Max Horkheimer on *Dialectic of Enlightenment*, and co-authorship of *The Authoritarian Personality*, on the social psychology of Fascism. Adorno did not return permanently to Frankfurt until 1953, where he became co-Director of the Institute with Max Horkheimer. The post-War years are characterised by a series of key publications, including *Negative Dialectics*, the mature summation of his philosophy, substantial monographs on Wagner, Mahler and Berg, and the four-volume collection of essays, *Notes to Literature*. The greatest challenge to his reputation possibly came with his failure to express uncritical support for the student protests of 1968. He died of a heart attack in 1969 while visiting Switzerland.

It is a platitude to remark on the range of Adorno's work. He writes extensively, and with insight, on philosophy (particularly epistemology, political philosophy and aesthetics), social theory (and engages in the 1940s and early 1950s in empirical social research), and on music and literature (with his extensive music criticism being complemented by a small, but closely wrought and competent set of compositions). While his work resists easy summary or categorisation, it may readily be situated as Marxist-Hegelian. As such, it has its roots in the German philosophical tradition, but reinterpreted in the light of Marxism, and especially the example of Georg Lukács's *History and Class Consciousness*. Into this core tradition Adorno draws study of the principal German and French sociologists (Weber, Simmel, Mannheim and Durkheim) and Freudian psychoanalysis. The sociological and philosophical enquiries are further complemented by, and used to develop, a series of essays and monographs on nineteenth- and twentieth-century European culture, with Schoenberg and Samuel Beckett providing key points of orientation towards an analysis of what is possible and appropriate in contemporary culture.

Adorno's writings initially appear obtuse. While there is a relatively limited amount of technical terminology, unambiguous definitions of concepts are avoided, in favour of the accrual of meaning through the use of concepts in diverse contexts. Interpretation is made more difficult due to the fact that his sentence structure can appear to be unnecessarily tortuous, and his arguments contradictory. Such difficulties are underpinned and, for those sympathetic to Adorno, legitimated, by his antagonism to 'first philosophy' (which is to say, any philosophy that attempts to establish or to assume a sure foundation from which the remainder of its programme may be derived) and any closed system of explanation and analysis. The presumption of certain knowledge, whether by analytic philosophers, German idealists, or Marxists such as Lukács, is implicated for Adorno in the totalitarian consequences of Enlightenment and modernism, and thus to be shunned. Yet, in stark contrast to certain strands within post-modernism, he remains equally averse to relativism, precisely because it leaves the social critic impotent against injustice and exploitation. Hence, the convolutions of his philosophical style may be seen as an attempt to avoid dogmatic and unreflective truth claims, and yet to retain a critical stance, and thus some conception of a transcendent and ahistorical truth.

Philosophy in late capitalism

The central concern of Adorno's philosophy may be summarised as the problem of how to think about (and how to engage critically with) the world, in a culture that inhibits critical reflection on, and conceptualisation of, that world. For Adorno, a core assumption of philosophy up to the early twentieth century, that 'the power of thought is sufficient to grasp the totality of the real' (Adorno, 1977a, p. 120), or that the order of ideas is the order of things (Adorno, 1991, p. 10), is mistaken, not simply epistemologically, but also ideologically. The philosophical assumption that it is possible, either to generate rationally a method of enquiry that will allow the acquisition of objective knowledge of the world (for example, through establishing a rigorous scientific methodology), or to deduce the objective order of the world through a system of thought (for example, in the idealist systems of Fichte and Hegel), fails to acknowledge the possibility that rational and conceptual structures are embedded in material social structures (articulated by historical, political and cultural tensions), and that these structures may inhibit the possibilities of thought (or channel thought into certain narrow parameters), so that the objective order of the (natural and social) world becomes literally unthinkable under contemporary historical conditions.

Adorno articulates these problems in terms of a fundamentally Marxist account of society. Marxist categories, such as commodity exchange, use and exchange value, forces and relations of production, and the immiseration of the proletariat remain in play, yet are reworked to recognise the difference between nineteenth-century high capitalism and twentieth-century late capitalism. Such an account must acknowledge the expanded role of the state (and the achievements of Keynesian economic policy), the expansion of an affluent middle class, and the associated expansion of industrial and governmental bureaucracies, along with the increased intervention of advertising and the mass media into mundane experience of the world.

The maintenance of full employment and steady economic growth in the West between 1945 and 1973, does not indicate for Adorno either the end of capitalism or its transformation into industrial or even post-industrial society. Because the relations of production have turned out to be more flexible than posited by Marx, the relationship between forces and relations of production is seen to be refigured in late capitalism. The theory of a simple contradiction between the politically progressive potential inherent to the forces of production and the stasis of the relations of production (that ultimately maintain the existing political order) is no longer adequate to grasp contemporary society. Rather, the post-War achievements of the Western economies are grounded in an expansion of the most fundamental structure of capitalism, commodity exchange, into all aspects of social life, as the relations of production come to infuse the forces of production, in what Adorno terms the reification of society.

The term 'reification' is borrowed from Lukács's *History and Class Consciousness*, where he uses it to theorise the expansion of commodity fetishism (whereby a social relation between human beings, that of market exchange, appears as a relationship between things, and indeed, where these products of human labour and imagination confront humans as independent beings, near persons, endowed with life), to all social relations. In Adorno's writings, reification plays a crucial role in articulating the essence and appearance of contemporary society. It may be understood in terms of the manner in which commodity exchange serves to abstract from the qualitative uniqueness of the object exchanged. Particular and distinct use-values are made comparable in terms of the exchange-values of diverse objects. Exchange-value comes to appear to be as much an inherent property of the object as the physical properties that determine its use-value. That which is qualitatively unique in an object is replaced by a quantity, and thus the commodity becomes interchangable with anything else that has a price. Reification is grounded in commodity exchange in so far as this principle of abstraction extends to govern social relations through the way in which it structures thought (including natural and social science), and thus human consciousness of those relations.

In what Adorno terms identity thinking, non-identical things or actions are unwittingly brought together, through a supposed commensurability and identity, precisely as the object is assumed to possess the properties expressed by its concept. This may be understood in terms of the relationship between the abstract and universal concept and the particular object that is supposed to fall under it. To assume that a concept adequately grasps its object is to lose sight of what the object is in itself (just as exchange-value conceals use-value). The concept is at once less than the object, in that the object will have properties, a history and possible futures that are not expressed in the concept (so that at best, the concept privileges only a single aspect or moment of the object), and more than the object, in so far as a concept (such as 'freedom' or 'justice') may express much that has not yet been, and indeed cannot yet be, realised in any object under contemporary social conditions. Identity thinking therefore curtails critical thought, for the order of ideas (or concepts) is assumed, naively, to grasp the order of things.

Put differently, identity thinking treats a mediated object as if it were immediately given to the perceiving subject. The concept of 'mediation' (*Vermittlung*) is a crucial piece of shorthand in Adorno's philosophical vocabulary. Something is mediated if it is constituted by something else. Thus, for Adorno, the object of knowledge is always constituted by the conceptual and scientific framework within which it is grasped, but also, the knowing subject is itself mediated, not least in so far as it is constituted by its embeddedness within social relations. This is, however, a more radical thesis than a mere appeal to social construction, for to be sensitive to mediation is to recognise that a philosophy or a science can have no fixed point of origin or foundation. Mediation gives the lie to any first philosophy. The order of ideas that is manifest in identity thinking therefore expresses only an illusory appearance of society (and thus conceals the genuinely social and historical constitution, not merely of the objects grasped, but also of the relationship between the thinker and the object thought). Crucially, human relations come to appear, as in commodity fetishism, as the immediate properties of a thing, in so far as concepts are assumed to grasp a given, and thus natural or objective, order. In sum, society, as a human (and therefore ultimately subjective) artefact, confronts its members as something objective and alien. As 'second nature', a term borrowed from the young Lukács, society appears as meaningless (and indeed as fateful) as natural laws and cycles.

Adorno's consequent characterisation and exploration of late capitalism is developed through a series of contradictions: it is at once rational and irrational; comprehensible and incomprehensible (see Adorno, 1969 and 1987). Society is rational in its means, but irrational in its end. Profit maximisation, the ultimate purpose that grounds all social activity, is pursued through rigorous instrumental rationality, so that as a goal, it is achieved in a more coherent and sustainable manner than was possible in the anarchy of Marx's high capitalism. The forces and relations of production are rationally integrated into a systematic totality. In part, this is achieved through the extension of rational administrative techniques which exemplify the abstraction of identity thinking, to control production and thereby mitigate the disruption of open competition. Thus, the abstraction of labour value that occurs with the exchange of labour power as a commodity is radically extended as the worker becomes subject to administration. In late capitalism, this is further complemented by the extension of the domination of capital into the consumption (as opposed to the mere production) of commodities. In high capitalism, use-value remained dependent upon the individual consumer's free and subjective evaluation of the commodity. The commodity, independently of the part it plays in the generation of surplus value and the exploitation of the proletariat, thus satisfied a real need. With the rise of advertising and mass media, in what Adorno terms the culture industry (Horkheimer and Adorno, 1972, pp. 120–67), the consumer's perception of need (and therefore of use-value) is pre-formed within a framework generated by the overwhelming imperative of profit maximisation. The consumer loses her or his unquestioned autonomy in the face of the commodity, and thus the possibility of over-production (and the instability it introduces into the capitalist system) is curtailed.

With the pre-formation of the human being as consumer as well as producer, the abstraction inherent in commodity exchange (and thus in identity thinking) is universalised. The consumer is as effectively integrated by the culture industry into the rational totality of late capitalism as the worker is integrated by the growth of bureaucratic management techniques. The capitalist system thus remains irrational, precisely because, beneath the veil of increased affluence, education, welfare and economic stability, real human needs (and indeed, real humanity) are sacrificed.

Society is comprehensible in so far as human agents can recognise the motivations for their actions, and thus attribute meaning to their actions as a purposeful response to the actions of others and, crucially, to the demands of social institutions and the social totality. Adorno refuses to denigrate humans as mere passive respondents to the imperatives of a system. While the scope for action may appear heavily restricted, humans still respond meaningfully and, at least at the level of short-term survival and contentment, rationally to the demands of the social structure. To recognise use-value in a commodity is

not, therefore, simply to respond as the advertising industry dictates. It is rather to make use of the (impoverished and abstracted) cultural resources available within late capitalism to generate as much satisfaction as possible.

Yet society remains incomprehensible precisely in so far as those structural demands confront the individual as second nature. Late capitalism appears to its members as an integrated and formally rational system or totality, as alien to them as first nature. There is thus, for Adorno, a crucial truth in the sociologist Emile Durkheim's attempt to treat social facts as things, because the surface of society confronts the enquirer as something that is as amenable to causal explanation as any other natural phenomenon. The impoverishment of the proletariat, predicted by Marx, is thereby realised in an unexpected form. While the system still works to the material interests of the capitalist class, all members of society (capitalists, new middle class and working class alike) are all equally impoverished in terms of their impotence before the capitalist system. The agent is unable to push beyond the immediate surface of these institutions, to question their very existence and purpose. Adorno eloquently summarises this tension in a short reflection on 'commodity music', written in the 1930s: even 'the most stupid people have long since ceased to be fooled by the belief that everyone will win the big prize'. The shop girl in the cinema audience does not therefore believe that the fictional secretary's good fortune could happen to her. Rather, only in the cinema can she admit to herself that this is true, and thus experience that 'most minimal degree of happiness, namely the knowledge that happiness is not for you' (Adorno, 1992b, p. 50). Paradoxically, such behaviour serves, none the less, only to reproduce a false society, and renew the adaptation of the individual subject to the objectified commodity system.

For a philosophy to attempt to criticise contemporary society using only the tools of identity thinking is to fall foul of the same conundrum as that which afflicts the shop girl. Precisely because identity thinking is coherent with the surface appearance of late capitalism, even the attempt to generate a critical model of society (as, for example, in Lukács's

Marxism) will ultimately only affirm what already exists, for the systematic coherence of such a model fails to recognise that the irrationality of capitalism's essence inevitably escapes any attempt to grasp it. Adorno is thus critical of Cartesianism, not least in so far as it is expressed in the fourth rule of the *Discourse on Method*: 'that one "should in every case institute such exhaustive enumerations and such general surveys" that one "is sure of leaving nothing out" ' (Adorno, 1991, p. 15). The systematic conceptual structure of science would thereby aspire, if not to grasp every aspect of the particular, then at least to establish the necessary and sufficient conditions that must be fulfilled in order for the particular to fall under a given concept. As such, science is unable to acknowledge the radical utopian potential within the object (and specifically within society), and thus acknowledge that a utopian (true or just) society is inconceivably different from contemporary society, precisely because the conceptual structure attempts to articulate the true society in the language and logic of a false society. It is, for Adorno, impossible to have positive knowledge of the necessary and sufficient conditions of a true society outside of the concrete experience of that society. The attempt to provide a 'blueprint' of utopia collapses into authoritarianism, not least because it can no longer tolerate the possibility that it is mistaken.

The task that Adorno then sets himself is to find a way of describing capitalism that does not merely reproduce and, however unwittingly, affirm the inevitability of the surface appearance of that society. Such an account must avoid the attribution of positive meaning to the meaninglessness of second nature. It must rather expose this meaninglessness. He does not attempt to provide his own coherent account of capitalism (so that the contradictions, for example, between comprehensibility and incomprehensibility, rationality and irrationality are crucial, not least because they emphasise that the interpretation of capitalism is irreducible to any single explanation or perspective), but instead seeks a specific form of engagement with those forms of cultural production (most importantly philosophy and social science, and art) that either attempt to conceptualise or otherwise serve to encode an experience of society. In sum, Adorno, in what he terms 'non-

identity thinking' or 'negative dialectics', does not seek to engage directly with the particular object of enquiry. Philosophy is necessarily a conceptual activity, so the object as it is in itself cannot be pasted into the philosophical text like a fragment of wallpaper might be pasted into a painting (Adorno, 1973a, p. 11). The particular is approached through the manner in which it has already been mediated (in language or in art), but in a way that strives to convict these conceptual structures, or the sensual structures of art works, of their own non-identity to their object.

The substance of Adorno's non-identity thinking may be pursued, albeit briefly, in two contexts: firstly, his engagement with first philosophy, and secondly, his parallel engagement with art, and thus the development of his aesthetic theory.

Positivism, idealism and the Enlightenment

For Adorno, positivism represents the most precise articulation of the forms of thought that are dominant in the scientific, technological and, above all, administrative spheres of contemporary capitalist society. Positivist thought is thus integral to the forces and relations of production of late capitalism, and thus to material and ideological reproduction. In *Dialectic of Enlightenment*, Adorno and Horkheimer express this as positivism's confounding of thought and mathematics. 'Thinking objectifies itself to become an automatic, self-activating process; an impersonation of the machine that it produces itself so that ultimately the machine can replace it' (Horkheimer and Adorno, 1972, p. 25).

With the continuing rise of modern science, philosophy is no longer required to generate substantive knowledge (nor, in the eyes of Logical Positivism and analytic philosophers such as Russell and Frege, is it capable of doing so), for substantial knowledge comes through empirical inquiry. All that is then left of philosophy is method, amounting to the 'ordering and controlling [of] the separate sciences, without [philosophy] being allowed to append anything essential from itself to their findings' (Adorno, 1977a, p. 125). In effect, it is analytic logic alone, distilled from British empiricism and Continental rationalism, that survives, as universal, from the history of philosophy. Appealing to this seemingly autonomous reason serves to establish the objectivity of scientific methodology, in so far as it allows knowledge claims to be validitated independently of the particular human enquirer (see Adorno, 1977b, p. 5, p. 55).

Adorno suggests, against this restriction of the legitimate scope of philosophy, that Logical Positivism does not allow itself to reflect upon its own empirical foundations, which is to say, upon the meaning of that which is 'given' prior to inquiry (Adorno, 1977a, p. 125). Crucially, this is revealed as a problem of identity thinking. This is highlighted by Carnap's development of protocol statements which are taken to be the record of basic, pretheoretical experience. As such, they presuppose the possibility of language as a neutral tool, capable of recording reality as it is. The concepts used are thus taken to be open to unambiguous definition, and like reason itself, are autonomous of the historical contingencies and complexities of mundane language. Adorno finds an initial challenge to Carnap's positivism in the early Wittgenstein. By posing the problem of how language hooks on to the world, Wittgenstein recognises that the 'given' is not prior to language, but is rather constituted through it (Adorno, 1977b, p. 20). The formal structure of positivist method and the aspiration to grasp reality as it is are revealed as contradictory to each other. More precisely, Wittgenstein's failure to provide examples of elementary statements, within which the atomic facts of the world might be grasped, implicitly reveals the failure of positivism to establish the empirical foundation it seeks (ibid., p. 53).

For Adorno, Wittgenstein serves to reinstate Kantian reflection into philosophy. By seeking to explain the coherence of the order of ideas with the order of things, rather than merely presupposing it, Kant demands that philosophy reflects upon the part played by the human cognitive faculties in constituting the order of things. The human constructions of Newtonian physics and Euclidian geometry are seen to be capable of explaining reality, and thus of embodying objective knowledge, only in so far as that reality is itself a human product. A knowable object is only constituted once the mental faculties have ordered the flux of the manifold sensations.

The 'objectivity' of the world is thereby seen to rest upon the fact that all human minds order and construct the world in the same way. The apparently immediate object is therefore recognised as mediated by the knowing subject.

Because it remains ahistorical and ultimately static, Kantian reflection alone is insufficient for Adorno. Hegel's response to Kant is thus of crucial importance: he suggests that, once the limits of rational thought have become known to the thinker, the thinker has already begun to transcend them, for reflection upon the conditions of thought becomes itself part of those conditions. Reflection thus necessarily changes the conditions upon which it reflects. Hegel cannot then accept Kant's description of the constitution of the world by the transcendental ego as necessarily and universally given. The givenness of the transcendental ego, and thus the point that fixes Kantianism as a first philosophy, is exposed as one constitutive framework amongst others. Thinking about thought is therefore a critical moment in philosophical enquiry, for it introduces a radical dynamic. Positivism, by repressing such thought, serves to fix, as universal and ahistorical, a historically specific form of the knowing subject, that of late capitalism (ibid., p. 5).

While Hegel introduces a dynamic into philosophical reflection, as a product of idealism, that dynamic is not rigorously anchored to socio-historical change. Adorno's criticism of positivism is ultimately a materialist response, articulated not least through reflection upon the concepts of 'nature' and 'history'. The positivist would divorce herself or himself from history in order to study nature objectively. 'Nature' thereby stands for that which is given, unchanging or static and thus that which is independent of humanity, while 'history' is created, and thus dynamic and ultimately the product of human action. The theme of the tension between history and nature, and thus the task of writing a materialist history of science and the philosophy of science, is taken up most profoundly in *The Dialectic of Enlightenment*. In these 'philosophical fragments' Adorno and Horkheimer explore the contradictions that emerge, historically, in the aspiration of enlightened thought to 'demythologise' the world, which is to say, to challenge and remove superstitious and mythical accounts of the natural world, replacing them with enlightened and scientific accounts. This 'disenchantment' of the world serves the domination of nature, so that nature may be controlled and subordinated to human ends. The ambiguity revealed in the concept of 'nature', between first and second nature, is mirrored by Horkheimer and Adorno through a similar ambiguity in the terms 'Enlightenment' and 'myth'. By its own self-understanding, enlightened thought would represent the historically achieved triumph of humanity over that which is alien or heterogeneous to it. In contrast, 'myth' marks a continuing enthralment to nature, and as such, that which is ahistorical and static, precisely in so far as a superstitious humanity fails to recognise that what it perceives in nature it has projected there itself. Myth is thus the mistaking of human culture (or second nature) for that which is heterogeneous to humanity (first nature). At the core of Enlightenment thought is Oedipus's reply to the riddle of the Sphinx: 'It is humanity!' (Horkheimer and Adorno, 1972, p. 7).

The relationship between Enlightenment and myth becomes more intricate as soon as it is recognised that myth is the origin of Enlightenment, and more radically, that the historical fate of Enlightenment has been to become myth. The first part of this thesis is relatively unproblematic. Horkheimer and Adorno chart, in the development of mythological belief systems and magical practices, the enlightenment aspiration to control the world. Thus, mythologies may be presented as narrative explanations of natural phenomena, so that a link is established between a deity and a natural object. 'Zeus represents the sky and weather, Apollo controls the sun. . . . The gods are distinguished from material elements as their quintessential concepts' (ibid., p. 8). In effect, this may be seen as an initial step to the disenchantment of the world (while magic ceremonies and sacrifices to the gods represent the attempt to dominate and manipulate nature). Yet the crucial moment of the Enlightenment is the recognition of human projection, and as such, the acknowledgement of something that falls outside the grasp of humanity. This Enlightenment trait is marked in Kant's recognition of the limits of the phenomenal world, constituted by the human mind,

or in Wittgenstein's failure to provide examples of elementary statements. In positivism, this trait is, paradoxically, undermined by the very ardour with which it is pursued. The attempt to pare philosophy down to its method, to generate a language of protocol statements that would directly grasp reality as given, and thereby to reduce all reality to the image of mathematics, does indeed disenchant the world, stripping away all that has been projected on to it by humanity. Positivism's failure, and thus the reversion of Enlightenment back into mythology, lies in the assumption that what is left after the process of this disenchantment is all that there is of the world, and that cognition is no more than the apprehension, classification and calculation of that world (ibid., p. 27). Positivist Enlightenment thus enthrals humanity to the illusion of mathematical science (and thus to the abstraction of identity thinking) as completely as early magic enthralled humanity to the supernatural.

At the moment of its reversion to myth, Enlightenment becomes totalitarian, for it refuses to acknowledge that anything might fall outside its grasp, or more ominously, dismisses that which does elude it as negligible and irrelevant (ibid., p. 6). It is this insight that grounds Adorno's aversion to systematic thinking. Positivism, grounded in mathematics and logic, is a model of a closed system. The positivist may be confident of remaining open to an objective world that is heterogeneous to the scientific method, through the incorporation of empirical data. Adorno's reply appeals to the tension suggested between formalism and empiricism in positivist science. Precisely because the mathematical method precedes the study of any particular object, while the method can acknowledge that there is something as yet unknown, that unknown is already prescribed, paradigmatically as the unknown quantity in a mathematical equation (ibid., p. 24).

The positivist tension between formal method and substantive data (between, as it were, the thinking subject and the objective world) is reproduced in the closed system (be it that of science or philosophical idealism) as a tension between the static and the dynamic. The system superficially appears to be dynamic, in so far as it can expand to include new data. Yet, in so far as this expansion is governed by the predetermined principles or rules of the system, the dynamic aspect is illusory (Adorno, 1973a, pp. 26–8). This tension is already marked in Kant, and responded to most profoundly by Hegel. Kant's account of the limits of reason culminates in a series of contradictions (or antinomies), so that, for example, equally valid arguments can be given for and against the propositions that the world has a beginning in time and is limited in space, or that space is infinitely divisible. The subject therefore fails to construct a coherent (or systematic) account of the object. However, while Kant resigns himself before such contradictions and the limits they imply, Hegel takes such contradictions as the stimulus for movement to another standpoint, where the contradictions of the preceding standpoint are dissolved. Each shift of standpoint represents an attempt to grasp the object more adequately. This does not occur through an extension of the existing standpoint, nor even through the pretence of comparing the standpoint with the object, for, in contradiction to the conceit of positivist empiricism and the concept of protocol statements, the object cannot be grasped at all independently of a particular cognitive standpoint. Rather, reflection focuses upon the inherent inadequacies of the existing system, and thus upon the demand to replace it by a radically new one.

While Adorno acknowledges the truth of Hegel's criticism of Kant, and thus the need for philosophy to be self-reflective and dynamic, Hegel's own philosophy is ultimately condemned for its complacency (ibid., p. 25). It culminates (most clearly in Hegel's *Encyclopaedia*) in what Hegel understands to be a comprehensive and non-contradictory account of the development of thinking through the various stages of consciousness. Having overcome the contradictions of each stage, the thinker is perceived to have grasped reality adequately enough. The Kantian notion that something always lies outside the grasp of thought disrupts such complacency. While Kantian thought recognises itself as remaining open to the world, albeit able to construe that world in only one possible way, Hegelian thought becomes closed. On its own understanding, it has closed with the world encompassed within it. In Adorno's account, the Hegelian system, like any closed system, is in danger of closing with the world left outside. His concern echoes the comment in Kierkegaard's *Journals* to the effect that the philosophical system builder is like a man who builds an enormous castle, and yet lives in a hovel near by.

Adorno's concern with grasping the object may, by now, have some substance. It may be articulated as a dialectical argument on the relationship between subject and object – broadly put, positivism assumes that the object is directly accessible to the subject (in so far as empirical data and autonomous and universal reason allows the subject to grasp the object as it is). Kantianism challenges this, precisely in so far as the subject is understood to grasp the object only in so far as it has been constituted by the subject. The subject grasps a phenomenal object, rather than the noumenal thing-in-itself, as it would be independently of the human observer. Hegel assumes that, by moving through various forms of consciousness, the subject can ultimately come to know the object as it is. Adorno's common criticism of positivism, Kant and Hegel amounts to a rejection of any point of certainty, and thus of any secure foundation for further enquiry. He rejects positivism's security of empirical data and autonomous reason, Kant's universal standpoint (of the transcendental ego) and the final stage of closure (the 'absolute') in Hegel's dialectic. Crucially, he does not thereby lapse into cultural relativism, whereby a multitude of equally satisfactory, if incommensurable, accounts of reality are available. His analysis, following Kant's emphasis upon the aporias of thought and Hegel's recognition of the contradictory nature of all standpoints, focuses upon the incoherence of any account, and further, on the possibility of generating a materialist account of that incoherence. Attempts to encompass reality, for example within philosophical systems, are not equally satisfactory, but are, by exacting analysis of their contradictions, revealed as determinately unsatisfactory.

Aesthetic theory

The relationship that Adorno establishes between philosophy and art is derived from Hegel. In the final sections of the *Encyclopaedia*, 'absolute truth' is articulated, Hegel asserts with increasing adequacy, in art, religion and philosophy. Art is the sensuous illusion of truth, or the manifestation of truth (which may be broadly understood as knowledge of the divine or of 'Spirit') in art's sensuous media (stone, sound, colour and line, the imagery of poetry, etc.), as opposed to the conceptual medium of philosophy. The term illusion (*Schein*) is central in German aesthetics. An illusion is distinct from a delusion, for although the illusion distorts the object represented in it, there is a real object represented. Delusions are wholly imaginary objects. For Adorno to retain the idea of art as illusion is to assert that art indeed has a truth content, and that art and philosophy share this truth, albeit expressing it in different media (Adorno, 1984, pp. 185–6). Aesthetic reflection is charged with the task of pinning down or interpreting the truth content of art, but, in contradiction to Hegel, whose philosophy of art occurs only after the death of art (that is, when art has ceased to be a vital force in developing humanity's understanding of the absolute), and whose philosophy is assured of articulating the absolute, the problems of identity thinking mean that, for Adorno, even philosophy cannot avoid being illusory. The theme of Schoenberg's opera *Moses und Aron* neatly encapsulates this aspect of Adorno's aesthetics (see Adorno, 1992b). In the opening scene of the opera Moses confronts God and therefore has immediate experience of the absolute. The dramatic paradox of the opera lies in his inability to express this experience to the Israelites (the part of Moses not being a sung part in the opera). His brother Aron (a lyric tenor), acts as Moses' mouthpiece, convincing the Israelities through elaborate stage magic. The magic is the sensuous illusion of Moses' truth. The tragedy of the opera lies in Aron's coming to believe in his own magic, ultimately by providing the Israelites with a graven image (of a golden calf) to worship. For Adorno, the distinguishing feature of great art (and indeed of great philosophy), is that it does not forget the taboo on graven images, and thus never takes literally its own illusory nature.

The concept of 'truth content', and its implications for aesthetics, may be explicated. Art, like philosophy, is ultimately social labour. The professional artist will work within specifiable relations of production (for example, of court or state patronage,

or through the exchange of products on the capitalist market). Equally importantly, the material with which the artist works will include on the one hand, tools and materials that can be understood in terms of the existing forces of production. While art may tend to involve archaic or pre-capitalist forces (based in craft techniques), the advanced technology used in the manufacture of musical instruments (including contemporary computer technology), paint or the camera, for example, is equally significant. On the other hand, the artist's subject matter will be derived from the experience of living in a specific social formation and, possibly more importantly, will be structured using forms of thought that are ultimately embedded in the logical forms current in society (so that, for example, Adorno readily draws a parallel between the logic of Hegel's dialectic and the Beethoven sonata). In sum, the sensuous material with which the artist works is crystallised social labour.

Taken as it stands, this account of art as social fact smacks of a sociological reductionism, whereby the work of art is no more than a reflection of the social base and, as such, would be fundamentally alien to the artist's own experience of his work. Adorno therefore takes his account a step further, again disrupting the certainty or stasis of any simple reductionism. Artworks are construed as at once social facts and yet as being autonomous from society. The artist in pre-bourgeois society, who is not yet wholly distinct from the craft worker, would typically produce works with an explicit social purpose (such as the glorification of the state or the organisation of a ceremonial). With the rise of the bourgeois art market, the artist gains a complex freedom. Overtly, the artwork is produced in order to generate exchange value, and thus is as subordinate to profit-maximisation as any other social practice. The demand for entertainment, paradoxically, allows the artist to pursue variety manifestly for its own sake, which thereby generates a freedom from purely economic goals, although from within a form of economic production. The artist can then pursue purely aesthetic problems of construction and expression for example (see Adorno, 1976, p. 208). The artwork's autonomy, and thus critical potential, therefore rests upon the non-identity between economic value and aesthetic value. The bourgeois artist confronts her or his material, not as a social problem, but as an aesthetic one. The aesthetic task, broadly speaking, is to reflect upon a material inherited from artistic tradition and from a canon, and to recognise the failure of past works to bring this material into a rigorous and harmonious whole. Precisely because the artistic material is ultimately derived from an antagonistic society, the apparent achievement of a harmonious and meaningful whole within the work can only be at the expense of adequate reflection upon that material. The art of the modernist avant-garde, that Adorno champions, self-consciously expresses the contradictions and tensions in its material, avoiding meaning, and thus expressing the meaninglessness of second nature under capitalism.

The music of Schoenberg can therefore be taken to illustrate, not merely a paradigm of artistic practice, but also Adomo's approach to philosophy as a whole. The composer does not fall back upon some property of music, such as the overtone scale or tonal relationships, and promote that as a firm and natural foundation upon which composition can rest, anymore than a philosopher should resort to some immediate 'given'. In either case, an illusory meaningfulness and fixity would be asserted. To do so is to ignore or conceal the historical, and thus human, achievement and potential that is embedded in even the most apparently natural properties, and to conceal the irrationality of the artistic/social material. Schoenberg's atonality and serialism, precisely by breaking with that which is supposed to be natural, but also by grounding the compositions in the techniques of the Austro-German tradition since Bach, exposes that which is natural in music to be the product of culturally-specific choices. The truth content of the artwork is therefore understood in terms of a determinate response to the riddle that is posed by preceeding works (Adorno, 1984, p. 186). The artwork, because it is working with ultimately social material, expresses something about society (and, crucially, is not expressing a positive political doctrine, for expressiveness itself only emerges from the disruption of any complacent acceptance of second nature). Yet, what it expresses remains within the sensuous medium of the art work. Aesthetics is

required to decode the social content of the aesthetic problem.

Negative dialectics and constellations

The medium of philosophy is conceptual, but Adorno seeks to use these concepts 'emphatically' (Adorno, 1973a, p. 150). The first step in such emphatic use entails the recognition that language is a social fact. Concepts are, according to Adorno, 'moments of the reality that requires their formation, primarily for the control of nature' (ibid., p. 11). This is to suggest that concepts are tools that have been honed, through social practice, to a particular purpose. The conditions of a concept's meaning are, at least in part, material conditions, related to economic and other social activity. Language has a social history. For philosophy to begin with language is not, therefore, to begin with an inadequate substitute for reality, for language participates in reality. Adorno thereby approves of Max Weber's composition of sociological concepts from particulars taken from historical reality (as an alternative to imposing an autonomous, theoretical concept upon the sociological object) (ibid., p. 165). Yet this step alone would leave Adorno culpable of relativism, in so far as it would remain unclear as to how recognition of the concept's social history can make it critical (which is to say, convicted of its non-identity to its object). More precisely, Weber's ideal types are constructed from the comprehensible surface of society, and thus cannot engage with the meaninglessness of second nature.

As a second step, it may be noted that Adorno is most concerned with concepts that are applied to human beings and human practices (whether within the social sciences or political and moral philosophy). Thus, the object to which the concept is applied is also the agent who uses the concept. If, in using language, the human subject is attempting to understand itself, then at the moment at which it reflects upon the conditions under which that language is constituted, it has begun to go beyond that initial understanding. This reflection serves to challenge the immediacy of the subject's self-understanding, so that the subject is puzzled by that immediacy. To reflect upon the language that the subject uses of itself is to reflect upon the social and historical constitution of its self-understanding, and thus upon the objectives underpinning that understanding. Yet this becomes, for Adorno, a riddle. Philosophical interpretation confronts the meaninglessness of second nature, not by finding meaning hidden within it, but rather by rendering the problem, and indeed the language and preconceptions that constitute it, obsolete (as the solution to a riddle renders obsolete our previous understanding of the question).

The metaphorical comparison of philosophical interpretation, and the emphatic use of concepts, to the solving of a riddle, entails using the language of identity thinking against itself. Here Adorno appeals to another metaphor (borrowed from Benjamin's study of German *Trauerspiel*), that of a constellation of concepts. A constellation is explicitly set against systematic thinking, in an attempt to emancipate the particular from the domination of the universal. A conceptual system will be constructed from a set of precisely defined concepts. The movement from one concept to another will be determined by the overarching scientific theory and methodology (legitimated again on the assumption that the order of ideas corresponds to the order of things). To break from systematic thinking, the constellation must allow movement from one concept to another on the concepts' own terms. Constellations would attempt to mirror the dynamic inherent in mundane language use. Adorno illustrates this by the example of learning a foreign language, not from a dictionary and grammar, but by living in the foreign country. The learner will come to understand words by experiencing them in diverse contexts, and will thereby become more sensitive to the nuances and complexity of words than the strict rules of a grammar would allow (Adorno, 1991, p. 13). In effect, the learner will come to realise that words do not necessarily lend themselves to unproblematic definitions in terms of necessary and sufficient conditions, and that a given word will cover a complex of nuances and associations that will allow it, of its own momentum, to lead into other words. The metaphor of a constellation therefore begins to suggest the network of links that a particular group of words can establish between themselves.

It is worth reflecting a little more deeply on the constellation metaphor. A stellar constellation is a two-dimensional image of a four-dimensional object. The fourth dimension, time, may be included because of the time that the light from stars has taken to reach the Earth-bound observer. Rigel is not merely further away from Earth than Betelgeuse, it is also seen as it was at an earlier point in time. Constellations are, in consequence, about history. If the constellation collapses four dimensions down to two, then it is an illusion. If, in Adorno's metaphor, the real stars, separated in time and space, represent the immediate object, then the constellation is the observer's mediated grasp of that object. To approach the immediate object entails treating the constellation as a riddle. The illusion needs to be solved or decoded. A first step to such decoding is to recognise that the earth (the standpoint of the observer) does not lie outside the constellation, but is integral to it. The constellation of Orion could be reconstructed by shifting the observer from the earth to Rigel, so that the Earth (or more properly the Sun) would appear as a point in relation to the remaining stars of the constellation. To carry out such a thought experiment is to begin a process of Kantian reflection, addressing the problem of how a particular perspective conditions and curtails one's understanding of the noumenal object. The illusion experienced depends upon the standpoint taken (or inflicted by history and social conditions). The human observer projects the shape of the constellations just as he or she projects a mythical hunter on to it. Metaphorically, the process of philosophical interpretation entails asking why one is standing upon the Earth. The movement between concepts in a constellation entails throwing the whole constellation into a new perspective.

The moves between concepts are not, however, smooth. While a conceptual system aspires to logical coherence and comprehensiveness, a constellation is typically characterised by fragmentation and incompleteness. The contradictions between terms within the constellation are not explained away, but are rather taken to mark contradictions and conflicts in reality. Adorno is critical of Hegel's dialectic, precisely because, as the dialectic develops in its movement from one form of consciousness to the next, the contradictions of the preceding stage are resolved purely in thought. The contradictions of the previous stage are forgotten. Adorno's dialectic pursues contradictions as intently as Hegel does, but, as a negative dialectic, refuses to acknowledge their resolution (Adorno, 1973a, pp. 158–9). If the contradictions found in language mark the social reality of that language, then they cannot be resolved in thought, for those conceptual contradictions are conflicts and tensions experienced by the real human subject. Their resolution can therefore only occur in political practice. The fragmentary nature of the negative dialectics serves to acknowledge, not simply that it could go further, but that its progress is inhibited by social practice. Adorno's philosophy proceeds, as best it can, in interpreting the world, in the face of philosophy's failure to change it (ibid., p. 3).

Adorno concedes that negative dialectics can then give no certain results. Its procedure is ridden by the risk of error (Adorno, 1991, p. 13). For the movement about the constellation to occur, the philosopher subject must fantasise in order to resist and overcome the immediacy of second nature. Paradoxically, in an age when what is taken to be objective is merely the projection of a particular mode of subjective thought, the emphatic objectiv-

ity of truth can only be attained through the subjective idiosyncrasy of a thinker who is prepared to think differently (Adorno, 1974, pp. 69–70). And yet negative dialectics is characterised as 'exact phantasy' (Adorno, 1977a, p. 131), for it is disciplined by a scrupulous attention and sensitivity to the detail of the constellation, and the risk of error is staved off by the density of texture of the resultant thought (Adorno 1991, p. 13). This may be illustrated by Adorno's own allusion to musical analysis. He compares the grasping of the particular object in dialectics to the interpretation of 'those utterly individuated works of art which spurn all schemata' (Adorno, 1973a, p. 162). While traditional music will draw upon the pre-existing musical language (in terms of the rules, for example, that govern large-scale forms, the progressions of vocal lines and chords, and rhythms), 'new' music will aspire to the generation of its own rules. The interpretation of the work therefore requires the analyst to reconstruct those rules out of the work itself. Such rules are the solution to the work as a riddle, not least as a determinate response to traditional works. The second nature of traditional music language is thereby dissolved, to be replaced, not by a new and transparent meaning, but rather by a conviction of the meaninglessness and irrationality of the past.

Bibliography

Writings

Adorno, T. W. (1973a), *Negative Dialectics*, trans. E. B. Ashton, London: Routledge and Kegan Paul.
— (1973b), *Jargon of Authenticity*, trans. Knut Tarnowski and Frederic Will, London: Routledge and Kegan Paul.
— (1974), *Minima Moralia: Reflections from Damaged Life*, trans. E. F. N. Jephcott, London: Verso.
— (1976), *Introduction to the Sociology of Music*, trans. E. B. Ashton, New York: Seabury Press.
— (1981), *Prisms*, trans. Samuel and Shierry Weber, Cambridge, MA: MIT Press.
— (1982), *Against Epistemology*, trans. Willis Domingo, Oxford: Blackwell.
— (1984), *Aesthetic Theory*, trans. C. Lenhardt, London: Routledge and Kegan Paul.
— (1989), *Kierkegaard: Construction of the Aesthetic*, trans. Robert Hullot-Kentor, Minneapolis: University of Minneapolis.
— (1991, 1992a), *Notes to Literature*, two vols, trans.

Shierry Weber Nicholsen, New York: Columbia University Press.
— (1992b), *Quasi una Fantasia: Essays on Modern Music*, trans. Rodney Livingstone, London: Verso.
— (1993), *Hegel: Three Studies*, trans. Shierry Weber Nicholsen, Cambridge, MA: MIT Press.
Horkheimer, M., and Adorno, T. W. (1972), *Dialectic of Enlightenment*, trans. John Cumming, London: Allen Lane.

References and further reading

Adorno, T. W. (1969), 'Society', *Salmagundi*, 10–11, 144–53.
— (1977a), 'The actuality of philosophy', *Telos* 31, 120–33.
— (1977b), 'Introduction', in Theodor W. Adorno et al., *The Positivist Dispute in German Sociology*, London: Heinemann.
— (1987), 'Late capitalism or industrial society', in Volker Meja, Dieter Misgeld and Nico Stehr (eds), *Modern*

German Sociology, New York: Columbia University Press.

Held, David (1980), *Introduction to Critical Theory: Horkheimer to Habermas*, London: Hutchinson.

Jameson, Fredric (1990), *Late Marxism: Adorno, or, the Persistence of the Dialectic*, London: Verso.

Jarvis, Simon (1998), *Adorno: A Critical Introduction*, Cambridge: Polity Press.

Rose, Gillian (1978), *The Melancholy Science: An Introduction to the Thought of Theodor W. Adorno*, London: Macmillan.

Wiggershaus, Rolf (1994), *The Frankfurt School: Its History, Theories and Political Significance*, trans. Michael Robertson, Cambridge: Polity Press.

BETWEEN PHILOSOPHY AND CRITICAL THEORY: MARCUSE

Drew Milne

Life and works

The central difficulty in assessing Herbert Marcuse's philosophical contribution is his conception of critical theory as the historical realisation of philosophy. This conception has affinities with Marxist attempts to overcome philosophy, but like Marxism remains afflicted by unresolved historical and philosophical problems. These problems are most apparent in the oscillation between critical negativity and utopian affirmation in Marcuse's best-known works *Eros and Civilization* (1955) and *One Dimensional Man* (1964). His later works, notably *An Essay on Liberation* (1969), *Counter-Revolution and Revolt* (1972) and *The Aesthetic Dimension* (1978) exemplify these problems in responses to changing historical conditions. Without a developed understanding of his philosophical œuvre as a response to its conditions of production, Marcuse has often been misread and lightly dismissed, notably in reductive accounts of his reception of psychoanalysis. Some biographical contexts are helpful.

Born in Berlin in 1898, Marcuse studied as a postgraduate in Freiburg in the early 1920s, and in 1922 completed a study of the German artist-novel entitled *Der Deutsche Künstlerroman*. Following publication of Heidegger's *Being and Time* (1927), Marcuse returned to Freiburg in 1928 to undertake studies on Hegel supervised by Heidegger. These studies were later published as *Hegel's Ontology and the Theory of Historicity* (1932). As a Jewish Marxist, Marcuse had to leave Germany in 1933, moving in 1934 to New York, where he was employed by the exiled Institute for Social Research, working with Max Horkheimer, Friedrich Pollock and Theodor Adorno. He wrote several important essays for the Institute's journal *Zeitschrift für Sozialforschung*, notably 'The Concept of Essence' (1936) and 'Philosophy and Critical Theory' (1937) (Marcuse, 1968). A tradition for critical theory is also sketched in his *Reason and Revolution: Hegel and the Rise of Social Theory* (1941). In 1942, Marcuse joined Franz Neuman in Washington, DC, working for the Office of Strategic Services, later part of the CIA, analysing Nazi Germany for American intelligence services. He helped prepare an extensive *Denazification Guide* in 1944 as part of plans for the post-War reconstruction of Germany and in 1945 was transferred to the Strategic Services Unit of the State Department, studying socialist and communist parties in Germany and Eastern Europe.

In the 1950s, amid the Cold War, Marcuse worked in Columbia and Harvard Universities on what became *Eros and Civilization: A Philosophical Inquiry into Freud* (1955) and *Soviet Marxism* (1958). *Soviet Marxism* offers a Marxian critique of Soviet Marxism which indicated Marcuse's distance from both Washington and Moscow. In the 1960s, he taught at Brandeis, and wrote *One Dimensional Man: Studies in the Ideology of Advanced Industrial Society* (1964). Amid growing notoriety, his post at Brandeis was 'terminated' and he moved to the University of California, San Diego. At the height of his fame in the late 1960s, his lectures, notably in Berlin, London and Paris, were political events, with placards in Rome carrying the slogan, 'Marx Mao Marcuse'. Ronald Reagan, as Governor of California, told California University that Marcuse was not qualified to teach. Subjected to death threats Marcuse was forced, on occasion, into hiding. In the 1970s he turned to analyses of the failure of the New Left and the aesthetics of cultural revolution, notably in *Counter-Revolution and Revolt* (1972). One of the few movements to emerge from the 1960s which he continued to support was feminism, support critically formulated in his essay 'Marxism and Feminism' (1974). His last important work before his death in 1979 was an analysis of the politics and utopian potential of art translated as *The Aesthetic Dimension* (1978). To the end of his life Marcuse continued to claim to be a Marxist, albeit an unorthodox one. He remained indebted to the Frankfurt School, but his post-War work reflects his different experience of North America and the distinctive routes through which he became involved in critical theory.

From the 1930s to his death, Marcuse's philosophical project was to develop a revised neo-Marxist conception of social being informed by conceptions of freedom, happiness and 'the aesthetic dimension'. The possibility of practice, the recognition of its state of Being, takes place against the horizon of the historical failure of the critique of political economy to ground itself in a revolutionary subject. He later described this ideological condition as 'psychic Thermidor'. Against conventional Marxist critiques of utopian thinking, he sought a more ontological conception of the potential for utopian transformation. The derivation of 'ought' from 'is', however, reveals the difficulty of grounding the critique of existing society in ontology, however radically ontology is conceived as historicity. Marcuse's work refers back upon itself more than is usually recognised in an English-speaking world which lacks awareness of the traditions of German thought with which Marcuse remained in dialogue.

The phenomenology of historical materialism

Marcuse's distinctive approach is announced in 1928 in 'Contributions to a Phenomenology of Historical Materialism' (Marcuse, 1978). He argues for a revision of historical materialism in the light of Heidegger's understanding of historicity, and for a revision of the phenomenological understanding of the relation between ontological essence and historical facticity. In this reciprocal revision, historicity is understood as an ontological characteristic of existence. The dialectical and antagonistic structure of existence is nevertheless understood as the material basis of the historicity of existence.

Marcuse argues that historical materialism cannot be a scientific theory or a system of truths whose significance lies in correctness as knowledge. Historical materialism is rather a theory of social and historical action. He asks whether Marxist theory has grasped the phenomenon of historicity as a fundamental parameter of human existence, and hence whether Marxism has grasped the historicity of what it is to be a Marxist. The historical genesis and unfolding of the work of Marx and Engels means that Marxism cannot presuppose a dogmatic unity to Marxist thought, but has to develop an understanding of the historicity of Marxism. Marxism's problem is to grasp the historical unity of life as praxis by understanding the historicity of Marxism's own concrete historical situation and horizon of interpretation. Marcuse reinterprets Marx's early writings to mean that action must be grasped as 'existential', an essential attitude deriving from human existence. He claims that Marx discovers history as a fundamental category of human existence and as the project of historical existence, a recognition he sees first developed in *The German Ideology*. For Marcuse, however, the full and radical significance of the question of historicity is posed by *Being and Time*, which nevertheless indicates the limits of the achievement of bourgeois philosophy. He sees Heidegger as reaching an understanding implicit in Marx which Heidegger formulates in rigorously phenomenological terms for the first time. For Marcuse, however, Heidegger had not yet gone over into the new concrete philosophy he claims that Heidegger himself reveals.

Marcuse's most significant objection to Heidegger turns on the understanding of the material constitution or concrete conditions of historicity, whose social antagonisms Heidegger, according to Marcuse, simply attempts to bypass. For Marcuse, the existential attitudes of the modern bourgeois of advanced capitalism and that of the peasant or of the proletarian are irreconcilable. Concrete existence exists through historical conditions and within the totality of antagonistic relationships in the natural and economic world of existence. These conditions do not stand above history as history's substance or ontology, but are included and changed in the movement of history. Dialectics seeks to free the historical categories which have abstracted human existence into rigid one-sidedness, by uncovering the forms and determinations of actual existence and by returning these forms to their concrete, living foundations. In such formulations, the germ of Marcuse's critique of one-dimensional man is evident.

In this early essay, however, Marcuse argues that the impossibility of realising the historicity of human existence authentically within capitalist society constitutes the necessity of revolutionary action. Paraphrasing the early Marx, he claims that revolutionary historical activity restores authentic existence. Heidegger's phenomenology needs then to be seen through to dialectical concreteness so that it can be fulfilled in a phenomenology of concrete existence and historically concrete action. As such, only the unification of phenomenology and historical materialism in 'dialectical phenomenology' can provide a method of continuous and radical concreteness which can do justice to the historicity of human existence. Marcuse argues that the historicity of human existence cannot be realised authentically within capitalist society. Revolutionary action is then necessary as the realisation of human existence, a realisation which cannot be known apart from its realisation in action. Radical action is thus the determinate realisation of human essence.

The concrete possibility of radical action can only be grasped in action rather than as knowledge. But such action requires an understanding of the historical situation, a situation which determines and reveals the denied potential of authentic exis-

tence. For Marcuse this cannot be grasped by an individual. Individuals exist in a class society determined by the primary mode of historical existence, revealed in the contradictions between the mode of production and its existential forms. The mode of production is not itself the realisation of the historicity of human existence, but rather the condition which both produces and prevents this realisation. Historical action is possible then only as the action of the proletariat. This reveals the fragility of Marcuse's account of the historical necessity of revolutionary action as authentic historical existence. A series of distinctions revolve around a historical 'ought' predicated on the realisation that what 'is' is inhuman and inauthentic. The attempt to see this realisation as the historically necessary realisation of the historicity of human existence leaves knowledge and action grasping at the straws of inauthentic existence. Marcuse's claims for concreteness are, if anything, more abstracted from history than those suggested by Heidegger. Phenomenology and historical materialism collapse into each other in abstract claims about the ontology of social being. This collapse is characteristic of Marcuse's attempts to realise philosophy concretely.

Marcuse nevertheless suggests the need for a radical rethinking of cognition, science and knowledge in Marxism. Historical materialism needs to address its own historicity and its implicit ontological claims. If the ontological question of historicity cannot be disassociated from its ontic basis in historical conditions, the phenomenology of historicity alters attempts to ground politics in an ontology of human existence. Marcuse states that no uniform instincts can be ascribed to society. This prefigures his attempt to show how Freud's theory of instincts violates the phenomenologically revealed historicity of instincts. Marcuse also claims that every new historical reality demands a new human *existence*. This claim bears comparison with the difficulties of his later claim, in *Eros and Civilization*, that a new basic experience of being would change human existence in its entirety. In his later work, the attempt to grasp transformation as historical necessity becomes a more negative and critically uncertain claim that such transformation is historically possible.

Between Hegel and Marx

Marcuse himself develops the problem of historicity and the relation between phenomenology, dialectic and historical materialism in a number of further essays written in this period. Central to these essays is his reading of Hegel's dialectic as the Being of 'Leben', or Life. This interpretation draws on Wilhelm Dilthey and Heidegger and is explored in most detail in Marcuse's *Hegel's Ontology* (1932), which attempts to explicate Hegelian ontology in the light of an ontological conception of Life and Life's historicity. This interpretation of Hegel's work as an ontology is both idiosyncratic and problematic. Marcuse explicitly criticises the ontological presuppositions of Dilthey, while leaving implicit in the argument as a whole criticism of the Heideggerian terms in which it is posed. The detail of his reading of Hegel requires patient exposition, but its significance is its relevance for his subsequent attempts to develop dialectical phenomenology and materialist dialectic.

In a 1932 review of *Hegel's Ontology*, Adorno questioned the priority of the ontological question in Marcuse's projected attempt to develop ontological exposition out of concrete facticity. More recently, Robert Pippin has questioned whether ontology or historicity are appropriate terms for understanding Hegel (Pippin, 1988). But Pippin also identifies tensions in Marcuse's reception of Hegel which are specific to Marcuse's struggle to preserve a dimension of affirmative, two-dimensionality and a positive conception of freedom. Marcuse seeks to ground this conception of freedom in an ontological understanding of historicity. Arguing against any ahistorical conception of history, Marcuse's conception of freedom is torn between the absence of historical grounds for the realisation of freedom, and the absence of any necessary goal or direction within history. Accordingly, there can be no *a priori* philosophical anthropology or theory of human nature. And yet he requires a conception of historical totality to understand the historical essence of existence critically. Pippin sees this as the central tension in Marcuse's subsequent work and in critical theory more generally. The difficulty, on the one hand, is to avoid collapsing the movement of history into normative, positivist, formalist or neo-Kantian conceptions of the essence of history, the turn taken by many second-generation critical theorists. And on the other hand, to avoid collapsing critical theory into a mode of criticism which claims to articulate implicit tensions and contradictions within society, but which cannot substantiate a social or philosophical grounding for its critical negativity.

Marcuse's Heideggerian reading of Hegel persists implicitly in the different emphases of his later conceptions of social being. Marcuse emerges, then, less as a Hegelian Marxist and more as a precursor of the existential Marxism associated with Jean-Paul Sartre and Maurice Merleau-Ponty, and of attempts to intertwine phenomenology with historical materialism developed by Trân Duc Thao, Karel Kosík and Michel Henry. But, Marcuse's attempts to realise his conception of concrete philosophy also reflect his awareness of the limitations of phenomenological Marxism.

This awareness is evident in his 1948 review of Sartre's *Being and Nothingness* entitled 'Sartre's existentialism' (Marcuse, 1983). Sartre, Marcuse suggests, aims at the individual's concrete existence, but the various concrete forms of man's existence discussed by Sartre serve only as examples of an historically abstracted structure. Specific historical conditions of human existence are projected into ontological and metaphysical characteristics. Accordingly, existentialism regresses to an ideologically closed circle of ontological identifications. Concrete human existence, however, cannot be analysed in terms of the 'free subject', but must be described in terms of what it has actually become: a 'thing' in a reified world. As Marcuse suggests, moreover, Sartre's analysis of the Ego does not remain within the realm of pure ontology, and cannot claim that its philosophy of freedom is ontological. Indeed, the attempt to move beyond a merely 'internal' freedom reduces freedom to a point where it is ideological. 'Behind the nihilistic language of Existentialism lurks the ideology of free competition, free initiative, and equal opportunity. Everybody can "transcend" his situation, carry out his own project: everybody has his absolutely free choice' (Marcuse, 1983, p. 174). Sartre takes what

Marcuse calls an 'ontological shortcut'. That which for Hegel was the realisation of the entire historical process becomes a metaphysical condition. As such, the identification of ontology and history is reductive. Sartre's conception of liberation shrinks freedom to the mere possibility of recognising the necessity for liberation, a criticism which could also be applied to Marcuse's work. Against Sartre, however, Marcuse argues that human freedom is the negation of the ontological liberty in which Sartre sees its realisation. Marcuse himself cites Marx to the effect that man, in his concrete historical existence, is not (yet) the realisation of the *genus* man. Marcuse suggests that the concepts which reach concrete existence must derive from a theory of society, a concretisation which goes beyond philosophy to reveal the inadequacy of philosophy. In a 1965 postscript, Marcuse noted that his claim that Sartre's thinking required a radical conversion to Marxism had been followed by Sartre himself. But this leaves Marcuse's differences from existential Marxism somewhat unresolved, even if the aspiration to go beyond philosophy into a concrete conception of critical theory is clear.

From philosophy to critical theory

That Marcuse did not develop more explicitly as a phenomenological Marxist can in part be explained by the impact on his thinking of the publication in 1932 of Marx's *Economic and Philosophical Manuscripts*. Marcuse reviewed the *Manuscripts* in a 1932 essay translated as 'The Foundations of Historical Materialism' (Marcuse, 1983). This essay makes the Marxist dimension underlying Marcuse's reception of Heidegger more explicit. For Marcuse, contrary to dogmatic Marxists, Marx's critique of political economy has a philosophical foundation in the interpretation of human existence and its historical realisation. The critique of political economy implicitly develops a conception of revolutionary praxis which transforms philosophy.

Marcuse focuses on Marx's discussion of 'estranged labour' as a question not merely of economics but of the historical essence of human existence. Human freedom is rooted in 'man's' ability to relate to his own species as the self-realisation of human exis-

tence. As an ontological category 'labour' grounds the critique of estranged labour and its unfree existence within the historical facticity of capitalism. But Marcuse is quick to indicate that the discovery of the historical character of human essence does not mean that the history of human essence can be identified with its factual history. Rather, the radical abolition of this facticity becomes the real and free task of human praxis. The difficulty remains, however, as to how this task can grasp the potential of human existence amid facticity. This difficulty is evident in Marcuse's description of this task as a 'returning' to the true property of human existence as social being.

In subsequent essays, written in collaboration with the Institute for Social Research, Marcuse attempts to develop the notions of *Praxis* and *Lebenswelt*, or life-world, as concrete understandings for the liberation from alienated labour. But there remains an unresolved tension between the transformation of philosophy into a critique of the grounds from which philosophy abstracts, and the dissolution of philosophy into historical facticity. The 1937 essay 'Philosophy and Critical Theory' (Marcuse, 1983) states boldly that once critical theory had recognised the significance of economic conditions for reality, then philosophy becomes superfluous. The realisation of reason as freedom is then not a philosophical task. But this leaves Marcuse with a utopian conception of the relation between reason and reality which grants a central role to 'phantasy' or imagination.

This more sharply critical account of phenomenology is argued more closely in his 1936 essay 'The Concept of Essence' (Marcuse, 1968). Phenomenology, argues Marcuse, involves a principle of description restricted to what 'is' as it is which, as description, acquires an increasingly positivistic character. Phenomenology's concept of essence regards both the object of phantasy and of perception as 'facts', and concurs, accordingly, with the positivist reduction of knowledge to a 'one-dimensional' world of facts. Materialist dialectic, by contrast, develops a social theory which seeks to understand the conflict between fact and essence, between essence and appearance. The tension between what could be and what exists cannot simply be transposed into a claim about the structure of Being. For

Marcuse, this distinguishes materialist dialectic from Hegel's theory of essence, which, despite its dynamic historical movement, is understood by Hegel as a movement within itself whose essence remains transcendental.

Marcuse's conception of essence has continuities with his earlier account of dialectical phenomenology. An important problem remains, however, in his claim that essence is the totality of the social process. The difference between appearance and essence in the antagonisms of capitalist production becomes constitutive for his claim that the capitalist mode of production is essential and yet appears in distorted forms. There appears to be an ungrounded presupposition regarding the way multi-dimensional social potential can be grasped amid the one-dimensional appearance of capitalist social relations. Substantiation of the necessity of this relation of essence and appearance would make critical theory more than a historical relativism. But there is no external point from which such claims can be grasped except through the revolutionary realisation of a new totality of social being. As a claim regarding the objectivity of true historical action, the experience of unrealised potential provides tenuous grounds for claims about the necessity in such potential. The relation between critique and the imperative to change society may describe the intention of materialist dialectic but it remains an abstractly divided relation between 'is' and 'ought'.

Marcuse's essays from the 1930s are recapitulated in *Reason and Revolution: Hegel and the Rise of Social Theory* (1941). Marcuse's distinctive reading of Hegel is obscured, however, by the need to translate Hegel for an American and British 'public', a need which reflects Marcuse's forced exile. In particular, the movement from philosophy to social and critical theory is stated somewhat reductively. *Reason and Revolution* provides neither a reliable expository introduction to the tradition Marcuse surveys, nor is it intelligible as a free-standing summary of the distinctive trajectory of Marcuse's thought. Marcuse's 'Epilogue' (Marcuse, 1955), describes how the consolidation of the capitalist system has rendered the classical forms of social struggle old-fashioned and romantic. But his persistence with the Marxist conception of revolution as the realisation of free-

dom is evident. His critique of capitalism as an administered totality, however, provides a less detailed account of the dynamics of contemporary capitalism than that pioneered by Marx. The important question, then, is both philosophical and historical. The revolutionary project of Marxism and critical theory may be 'necessary' but its critical perspective depends on an actuality which reduces this necessity to an obscure and marginalised potential. The period after 1945 sees the neutralisation and liquidation of the social potential discerned by Marcuse's earlier essays. But in the 'Foreword' (Marcuse, 1968) to a collection republishing his 1930s essays, Marcuse still argues that breaking through administered consciousness remains a precondition of liberation: 'Thought in contradiction must be capable of comprehending and expressing the new potentialities of a qualitatively different existence' (Marcuse, 1968, p. xx). Thought's imperative is then to be both more negative and more utopian in its opposition to the status quo. The potential for freedom in the realm of necessity, however, has become an abstract and utopian ought.

Eros and Civilization

Marcuse's neo-Marxist conception of materialist dialectic persists through his post-War work, but separated from its relation to revolutionary struggle. In a 'Political Preface' (1966) for the second edition of *Eros and Civilization* he acknowledges this: 'liberation is the most realistic, the most concrete of all historical possibilities and at the same time the most rationally and effectively repressed – the most abstract and remote possibility' (Marcuse, 1969, p. 13). In response to the obsolescence of the Marxian conception of the revolutionary subject, *Eros and Civilization* seeks to develop a qualitatively different conception of social being out of the political and sociological substance of psychological notions. The earlier conception of the relation between ontology and historical facticity is reconfigured through a radical revision of psychoanalysis. The essence of being is redefined as Eros, whose originary difference is negated by the death instinct, or Thanatos, out of which Marcuse affirms the possibility of a non-repressive civilisation. Far from smuggling an ahistorical theory of human nature into critical theory, Marcuse argues that instincts should be viewed as historical phenomena of the historicity of Being. Marcuse's reinterpretation of Freud, then, is analogous to his reinterpretation of Hegel, and similarly idiosyncratic if judged in terms of interpretative fidelity.

Marcuse focuses on Freud's later metapsychology, primarily *The Ego and the Id, Beyond the Pleasure Principle* and *Civilization and Its Discontents*. Central to his enquiry is the claim that Freud's individual psychology is in its essence a social psychology. Marcuse discerns elements in Freud's thinking that break through the rationalisation of the impossibility of a non-repressive civilisation. This impossibility cannot be conceived as an historical invariant. Repression itself is an historical phenomenon. Memory is not merely an individual recollection of psychological contingency, but a repressed mode of cognition whose restoration is accompanied by the restoration of the cognitive content of phantasy. Although obscured by psychoanalysis, the remembrance of times past tends towards future liberation.

Furthermore, Marcuse interpolates two terms to differentiate between the biological and the socio-historical vicissitudes of the instincts: surplus-repression, the over-determining restrictions necessitated by social domination; and the performance principle, the historically distorted form of the reality principle. For Marcuse, the organisation of sexuality reflects basic features of the performance principle and its organisation of society, against which Marcuse claims that sexuality is by nature 'polymorphous-perverse'. As such, Freud's metapsychology is reinterpreted as the fatal dialectic of civilisation, a dialectic which echoes the depth-psychology of Adorno and Horkheimer's *Dialectic of Enlightenment*. Marcuse counter-poses Marx's early conception of estranged labour to suggest the historicity of the performance principle and hence its potential for change as the essence of human existence. The potential to overcome the alienation of labour is stated in Marcuse's startlingly speculative claim that: 'The elimination of human potentialities from the world of (alienated) labour creates the preconditions for the elimination of labour from the world of human potentialities' (ibid., p. 83).

In the central chapter of *Eros and Civilization*, entitled 'Philosophical Interlude', Marcuse sketches the account of philosophy developed elsewhere in his work. He suggests, for example, that Hegel's *Phenomenology of Spirit* preserves the tension between ontological and historical content, but remains within the framework of the established reality principle. In a passage which indicates his continuing dialogue with Heidegger, he claims that only Nietzsche's philosophy surmounts the ontological tradition and exposes the fallacy of transforming facts into essences, and historical into metaphysical conditions. Against the closed circle of being as an end in itself, Nietzsche's conception of the eternal return is read as the recurrence of finite concreteness, the total affirmation of the life instincts, and thus as: 'the will and vision of an *erotic* attitude toward being for which necessity and fulfilment coincide' (ibid., p. 94). Separated from an understanding of Marcuse's earlier works such claims can appear unintelligible but they reflect his earlier conception of the ontological historicity of human existence and the development of a philosophy of concrete finiteness. Thus he claims that when philosophy conceives the essence of being as Logos, it is already the Logos of domination. The history of ontology reflects the domination of the reality principle and the absorption of the free self-development of Eros into the Logos of Being. According to Marcuse the insights contained in the metaphysical notion of Eros were driven underground, surviving only in eschatological distortions, heretical movements and hedonistic philosophy. Indeed, he intended to write a history of this underground.

Eros and Civilization also bears witness to what has often been seen as a retreat into aesthetics. Aesthetics appears to provide the only evidence in existing society of the potential for liberation, and more specifically in Marcuse's account, of the possibility of a non-repressive civilisation of sensuous play. In *Eros and Civilization* Marcuse's interpretation of the mythic images of Orpheus and Narcissus bears comparison with the interpretation of Odysseus and the Sirens in *Dialectic of Enlightenment*. But the images of Orpheus and Narcissus offer, for Marcuse, images of language as song, of work as play, of life as beauty and of existence as contemplation. The aesthetic dimension prefigures a qualitatively different experience of Being. This is developed through a reading of Kant and Schiller which is more avowedly romantic than that developed by Adorno's aesthetics. Marcuse's construction of the possibility of the liberation of sensuousness through its reconciliation with reason remains, however, unmediated as an account of the development of modern art as a response to capitalism. This is evident in the oscillating evaluation of contemporary aesthetic practices in Marcuse's later works, such as *Counter-Revolution and Revolt* and *The Aesthetic Dimension*.

One Dimensional Man

The difficulties of a historically ungrounded conception of the revolutionary potential of existing society evident in *Eros and Civilization* find their negative and equally abstract form in Marcuse's characterisation of the catastrophe of liberation in *One Dimensional Man*. This analysis has affinities with Adorno and Horkheimer's *Dialectic of Enlightenment*. In *One Dimensional Man*, for example, Marcuse argues that history is still the history of domination, and that the logic of thought remains the logic of domination. But *One Dimensional Man* refigures a contrast between ontology and technology which also retains affinities with Husserl's *Crisis of European Science and Transcendental Philosophy* and with Heidegger. Beneath the polemical surface of *One Dimensional Man* there is an implicit dialogue between Marx and existential phenomenology. Marcuse, for example, argues that the ontological concept of truth serves as a model of pre-technological rationality. This contrasts with the one-dimensional modes of thought and behaviour that develop in the execution of the technological project of advanced industrial society. Marcuse attempts once more to release the two-dimensional relation between ontological essence and historical facticity. He claims that in advanced industrial society the dualistic and antagonistic character of reality tends to disappear and with it the two-dimensionality of human existence. As such 'man' has become a one-dimensional being. But if the relation between being and technology is such that

reality has been reduced to the fractured totality of one-dimensional society, then the grounds for such a critique have become utopian rather than historical or material. The contrast between anecdotal particularity and the conception of the social totality reveals a collapse in the capacity of critical theory to develop the more determinate critique of society pioneered by Marx. Symptomatically, Marcuse resorts to chiasmus: 'Epistemology is in itself ethics, and ethics is epistemology' (Marcuse, 1964, p. 125). In this light, we can interpret Marcuse's claim that: 'Dialectical thought understands the critical tension between "is" and "ought" first as an ontological condition, pertaining to the structure of Being itself. However, the recognition of this state of Being – its theory – intends from the beginning a concrete *practice*' (ibid., p. 112). The attempt to theorise this move from ontology to concrete practice persists in Marcuse's work. The attempt involves affirming concrete possibilities of freedom and happiness as the unfolding of the ontological nature of historicity. But, Marcuse's abstract conception of human essence betrays the very possibilities of freedom, reason and happiness the theory seeks to explain and develop. He attempted to retain a conception of concrete philosophy but in a critique of a society whose truth claims appear groundless and without the possibility of concretion in practice: 'On theoretical as well as empirical grounds, the dialectical concept pronounces its own hopelessness' (ibid., p. 198). Critical theory remains negative. It can only claim that if the abstract character of politically impotent refusal is itself the result of total reification, then concrete grounds for such refusal must still exist. In the process, however, the move from philosophy to critical theory has returned to the very philosophical abstraction of ontology that critical theory sought to overcome. In this return, critical theory is not negative enough to be able to criticise its residual presuppositions.

Marcuse's work, then, needs to be understood as providing a series of insights into the philosophical difficulty of attempting to ground a critique of existing society in a non-dogmatic conception of social being. He recognises the need for a more substantiated social theory, but insists that such theory is necessarily critical, part of a movement from philosophy to critical theory which seeks not to abandon philosophy but to realise it. In this sense, the philosophical significance of his work cannot be abstracted from the shifting terrain of its social and political commitments. As he describes the therapeutic task of philosophy in *One Dimensional Man*: 'politics would appear in philosophy, not as a special discipline or object of analysis, nor as a special political philosophy, but as the intent of its concepts to comprehend the unmutilated reality' (ibid., p. 159).

Marcuse, then, bears witness to the problematic political relation between critical ontology and the historical facticity of social being, a tension evident in his thinking even when his critical theory succumbs to its metaphysical difficulties. His philosophical project is necessarily unfinished, committed both to the problem of historicity and to criticism of the historical appropriation of the concrete potential of the past. More revealing than the absence of substantiated social theory in Marcuse's work, then, is the extent to which the philosophical project of critical theory is intertwined with the historical facticity on which it reflects. Marcuse requires us to investigate the ontological investments of the kind of thinking whose problems he exemplifies but cannot resolve. His struggles to preserve a dimension of affirmation, two-dimensionality, and thereby a positive concept of 'freedom', rely on an insistence on the ontological nature of historicity which continually creates problems for that impulse. But this insistence is itself philosophically and politically significant. Its failures are also historical.

Unanswered questions

Understanding Marcuse's work, then, involves recognising his critical dialogue with Marxism and psychoanalysis in the light of his earlier relation to phenomenology through Hegel, Heidegger and the early Marx. The attempt to realise philosophy, changing the world rather than merely interpreting it, remains entangled, however, in its critical conception of ontology. The attempt to avoid collapsing social being into species being leaves residues which confirm Adorno's suggestion that philosophy lives on because its realisation was both missed and misconceived. Marcuse often seems to provide accessible accounts of themes in critical theory which are worked out more rigorously by Adorno, notably in Marcuse's theories of one-dimensional society, of the ideology and metapsychology of domination, and of aesthetics. Marcuse also bears witness to more positive conceptions of happiness and freedom, and to the dangers of a populist or reductive revision of Adorno's thinking. Their differences become critical. Most responses have noticed the absence of substantiated social theory in the utopian and aesthetic dimensions of Marcuse's thinking. More difficult, however, is an analysis of his work as the intertwining of historical conditions and philosophical motifs.

There is much to learn from Marcuse's attempt to avoid collapsing Hegelian Marxism into a theory of communicative action or 'analytic' Marxism. And yet his work remains vulnerable to criticisms brought by these different traditions, criticisms which might be summarised by Lucio Colletti's blunt description of Marcuse's persistently critical humanism as 'old liberal rhetoric' (Colletti, 1972, p. 140). Alasdair MacIntyre went so far as to suggest that 'almost all of Marcuse's key positions are false' (MacIntyre, 1970, p. 7), though the movement of negativity in Marcuse's thinking cannot easily be thought of as 'positions'.

Marcuse's notoriety in the 1960s has overshadowed his subsequent reception. He himself commented that the reductive public reception of his work was a beautiful verification of his philosophy: that in this society everything can be co-opted. Marcuse is the only major representative of critical theory whose work sought and assumed a direct political role. It was largely through him that the critical theory associated with the Frankfurt School became known in the USA, and this partly explains the belated and wary reception of other first-generation critical theorists in English-speaking culture. The indeterminate oscillation between negative and affirmative moments in Marcuse's thinking appears, moreover, to be at work in precisely those philosophical motifs which made his work seem politically relevant and influential. The lack of critical resistance to his work's co-option is not merely a philosophical problem to be resolved by clearer thinking or greater public reserve. It is, rather, a problem about the antagonism between philosophy and the historical experience of damaged life.

Bibliography

Writings

Marcuse, H. (1955) (first edn 1941), *Reason and Revolution: Hegel and the Rise of Social Theory*, Oxford: Oxford University Press.

— (1958), *Soviet Marxism: A Critical Analysis*, London: Routledge and Kegan Paul.

— (1964), *One Dimensional Man: Studies in the Ideology of Advanced Industrial Society*, London: Routledge and Kegan Paul.

— (1968), *Negations: Essays in Critical Theory*, trans. Jeremy J. Shapiro, Harmondsworth: Penguin.

— (1969) (first edn 1955), *Eros and Civilisation: A Philosophical Inquiry into Freud*, London: Sphere.

— (1969), *An Essay on Liberation*, Harmondsworth: Penguin.

— (1970), *Five Lectures*, Boston: Beacon Press.

— (1972), *Counter-Revolution and Revolt*, Boston: Beacon Press.

— (1978–), *Schriften*, vols 1–, Frankfurt am Main: Suhrkamp.

— (1978), *The Aesthetic Dimension*, London: Macmillan.

— (1983), *From Luther to Popper*, trans. Joris De Bres, London: Verso. Published as *Studies in Critical Philosophy*, London: New Left Books, 1972.

— (1987) (first edn 1932), *Hegel's Ontology and the Theory of Historicity*, trans. Seyla Benhabib, Cambridge, MA: MIT Press.

References and further reading

Alford, Fred C. (1985), *Science and the Revenge of Nature: Marcuse and Habermas*, Gainesville: University Presses of Florida.

Bokina, John and Timothy J. Lukes (eds) (1994), *Marcuse: From the New Left to the Next Left*, Kansas: University Press of Kansas.

Colletti, Lucio (1972), 'From Hegel to Marcuse', in *From Rousseau to Lenin: Studies in Ideology and Society*, London: New Left Books.

Habermas, Jürgen (ed.) (1968), *Antworten auf Herbert Marcuse*, Frankfurt: Suhrkamp.

Institute for Social Research (1992), *Kritik und Utopie im Werk von Herbert Marcuse*, Frankfurt: Suhrkamp.

Katz, Barry (1982), *Herbert Marcuse and the Art of Liberation*, London: New Left Books.

Kellner, Douglas (1984), *Herbert Marcuse and the Crisis of Marxism*, London: Macmillan.

Lukes, Timothy J. (1986), *The Flight into Inwardness: An Exposition and Critique of Herbert Marcuse's Theory of Liberative Aesthetics*, Cranbury, NJ, London and Toronto: Associated University Presses.

MacIntyre, Alasdair (1970), *Marcuse*, London: Fontana/Collins.

Pippin, Robert, Andrew Feenberg and Charles P. Webel (eds) (1988), *Marcuse: Critical Theory and the Promise of Utopia*, South Hadley, MA: Bergin & Garvey.

Schoolman, Morton (1980), *The Imaginary Witness: The Critical Theory of Herbert Marcuse*, New York: Free Press.

Whitebook, Joel (1995), *Perversion and Utopia: a Study in Psychoanalysis and Critical Theory*, Cambridge, MA: MIT Press.

6.4

SOCIAL AND TECHNICAL MODERNITY: BENJAMIN

Howard Caygill

Walter Benjamin was born in Berlin on 15 July 1892 and died by suicide on 26 September 1940 in Port Bou, Spain while trying to escape Nazi-occupied France. He recalled his childhood in a comfortable, largely assimilated Jewish home in his autobiographical memoirs from the traumatic early 1930s – *A Berlin Childhood around 1900* and *A Berlin Chronicle* – which delicately evoke a child's experience of the rapid modernisation of the capital city of Imperial Germany. These 'autobiographical' texts defy classification, their hybrid character – at once cultural criticism and personal reflection – exemplify the complexity of Benjamin's complex authorship which constantly defied and transgressed disciplinary borders and rules of genre. His oeuvre comprises philosophy, literary and art criticism, political theory and theology, with writings ranging from formidable academic treatises to short, witty newspaper articles. His reputation rests on his two large projects – *The Origin of the German Mourning Play* (1928) and the incomplete *Arcades Project* from the 1930s – as well as on a number of pioneering essays in the genre of philosophical literary and cultural criticism.

Early writings

Benjamin's earliest writings are closely associated with his participation in the pre-War German Youth Movement, in particular with the group surrounding the educational reformer Gustav Wy-

neken. The short series of Youth Movement writings began in 1910 with Benjamin's pseudonymous contributions to the student journal *Die Anfang* and culminated in 'The Metaphysics of Youth' and 'The Life of Students' from 1914–15 and 1915. This period of Benjamin's authorship coincided with his peripatetic study of philosophy at the universities of Freiburg, Berlin and Munich where, apart from courses with the philosopher and cultural sociologist Georg Simmel and the neo-Kantian philosopher Heinrich Rickert, he also pursued courses in literary and art history. In a curriculum vitae from 1925 he described 'philosophy, German literature and the history of art' as his chief interests as a student, and aesthetics as the 'centre of gravity' for the convergence of his philosophical and literary studies Benjamin (1996, p. 423).

Benjamin's emerging philosophical interests are evident in the essays of the Youth Movement period, especially in their focus on the concept of experience. This focus is evident in the 1913 essay 'Experience' where he reflects intuitively on the distinction between the experience of youth and adults. Some of the insights discernible in this essay are more systematically developed in the 'Metaphysics of Youth' and in the 'Life of Students' where he uses them to develop a philosophical concept of experience. The essays describe states of mind, conversations and everyday experiences such as writing a diary, showing the influence of Simmel's method of making everyday objects and experiences the occasion for philosophical improvisations – but behind this, they also show signs of independent philosophical insight and sophistication.

It is possible to read in the last two essays of the Youth Movement period startling anticipations of what would become some of Benjamin's characteristic insights, such as the description of concrete temporal experience, the manifestation of death 'in little things' and the concept of an experience without a subject or 'I' which is determined not only by present and past but also by the future. Indeed, phrases such as 'all future is past' and 'past things have futurity' (ibid., p. 15) show that the elements of his critique of progressive philosophies of history are already in place: history, he wrote in 1915, is not a progressive movement from past present to future, but is concentrated in each present moment 'in the form of the most endangered, excoriated, and ridiculed ideas and products of the creative mind (ibid., p. 37).

The influence of Kant

In the years immediately following the outbreak of the First World War and the traumatic protest-suicide of his friend, the poet Fritz Heinle, Benjamin withdrew from the Youth Movement and concentrated upon the philosophical elaboration of his concept of experience. In a prototype of his later philosophical-critical essay – 'Two Poems by Friedrich Hölderlin' (1915) – Benjamin analysed Hölderlin's poems in terms of their witness to a 'spiritual intuitive structure of the world' (Benjamin, 1996, p. 18). Benjamin interpreted the poems as bearing testimony to the experience of the absolute – courage in the face of death – through the 'spatio-temporal order' of the 'forms of intuition'. One poem witnesses death as an event outside of human space and time, a view which is condemned as 'based only on a venial feeling of life' (ibid.), while the second integrates death into life and gives death poetic form.

The use of such Kantian concepts and vocabulary in 'Two Poems by Friedrich Hölderlin' as the spatio-temporal 'forms of intuition' indicates the growing influence of Kant on Benjamin's thought. Yet his was by no means an uncritical reception of the critical

philosophy; while studying Kant closely and considering his thought as the subject for his doctoral thesis, Benjamin devoted himself to recasting the critical concept of experience. This revision took various forms. The first, evident in the large fragment from 1916 'On Language as Such and on the Language of Man', develops the linguistic 'metacritique' of the critique of pure reason of Kant's contemporary Georg Hamann. Hamann argued that experience was essentially linguistic and not, as Kant supposed, the issue of a fusion of spatio-temporal intuitions and the categorical forms of the understanding. In the fragment, Benjamin models experience in general on the experience of translation between languages, in this case between human, divine and the language of things.

Benjamin's exploration of the linguistic metacritique of Kant was conducted in terms of a commentary on the story of the Fall in the book of Genesis. This choice reflected the significance of his new-found friendship with Gershom Scholem, the pioneering scholar of Jewish mysticism. Benjamin was extremely critical of Zionism and of the development of Jewish thought represented by Martin Buber, but found Scholem's rigorous anarcho-mysticism extremely stimulating. The fragment on language was the culmination of a series of six seminal short writings from the summer of 1916 which included fragments on Socrates, medieval theocracy and two short essays contrasting the genres of tragedy and mourning-play (*Trauerspiel*). Developing further the comparative strategy pioneered in 'Two Poems by Friedrich Hölderlin', Benjamin contrasted the two dramatic forms in terms of the experience of time to which they bore witness and the diverse significance assumed by language in each of them. Later, in the dedication of the *Origin of the German Mourning Play* (1928), Benjamin referred to these fragments as the moment of 'conception' of the book.

Benjamin's critique of Kant's philosophy did not rest at the level of linguistic metacritique, but was taken even further in an essay called 'The Programme of the Coming Philosophy' (1918) and in his Bern doctoral thesis of 1919. The first is an explicit and detailed critique of Kant's concept of experience which rejects its model of mathematical-mechanical scientific experience based on the opposition of subject and object. Yet Benjamin does not call for the outright rejection of the critical philosophy, but for its revision. He proposes to retain the tripartite architectonic of the critical philosophy – metaphysics, ethics and aesthetics – but to enrich it to include the experience of the absolute.

In many ways, this reprise of metaphysics is extremely unKantian, but Benjamin regarded it as feasible within the limits of Kantian philosophy. He was clear that such a revision of the critical philosophy would have serious implications for the relative significance of the three critiques, shifting the focus of interpretation from the *Critique of Pure Reason* to the *Critique of Judgement*, and opening the possibility of a new relationship between the 'theory of experience and the theory of freedom'. Instead of Kant's distinction between the experiences of freedom and of natural necessity, Benjamin anticipated that 'the concept of experience may be changed in the metaphysical realm by the concept of freedom in a sense that is perhaps as yet unknown (ibid., p. 108).

The shift in Benjamin's understanding of the internal balance of the critical philosophy is reflected in his Bern doctoral thesis on 'The Concept of Criticism in German Romanticism' (1919). The implications of the thesis stretch beyond its immediate object of study since it implicitly proposes to succeed a concept of critique based on the determinate, scientific judgements of the first critique with the reflective, aesthetic judgements of the third. In this view, critique is historicised, becoming the search for a rule of judgement rather than the application of one already given and established. Not only this, but the object of critique itself is now no longer considered to be passive in the face of a judgement, but contributes to determining the character and scope of the rule which is applied to it.

In some very dense and elliptical passages of the thesis, Benjamin interprets the early Romantic writer Friedrich Schlegel as proposing the view that works of art and the critical judgements made upon them are configurations of the same 'medium of reflection'. It ends with a characteristic complication of this model of critique through a comparison of Schlegel and Goethe. Benjamin describes Schlegel's concept of art criticism as the completion of the work in the abolition of its contingency; but this moment of completion is also the death of the work since it is taken out of time and materiality and dissolved into the intelligible laws of the critical medium of reflection. Goethe, by contrast, sees critique as the ruination of the work, the destruction of an ideal state of completion and its scattering over time through critique. Both recognise the historicity of the relationship between works of art and critique, but in opposed ways – one sees critique as the eschatological completion of the work, the other see it as its ruination.

Professional cultural critique

In the years around 1920, Benjamin's work took a number of interesting and unexpected turns which contributed to the extension of his developing concept of experience. The first is the elaboration of a political philosophy, inspired by many sources but above all by Ernst Bloch's work of expressionist philosophy *The Spirit of Utopia*, George Sorel's anarchistic *Reflections on Violence*, Erich Unger's *Politics and Metaphysics* and Paul Scheerbart's science-fiction novel *Lesabendio*. Much of Benjamin's projected book on political philosophy has been lost, but the main surviving fragment – *The Critique of Violence* – reveals it to have been an anarchistic critique of the modern liberal state. In this theory, the modern state is based on the 'law preserving violence' incarnated in private property and protected by the spectral violence of the police. Benjamin contrasts the instrumental violence of the liberal/police state with the 'sovereign violence' of the 'proletarian general strike' which, he suggests, inaugurates new conditions of experience. In regarding the general strike as a form of divine violence, he contributes to the development of a political theology in the early 1920s, a current of political thought exemplified by Carl Schmitt's contemporary *Political Theology*. The relationship between his political thought and his aesthetic and philosophical interests was made more concrete by his fascinating correspondence with the Protestant conservative Florens Christian Rang, who pointed his interests in the direction of the cultural history of the Reformation. The developing interest in the Reformation is evident in the 1921 fragment 'Capitalism as Religion' which anticipates some of the arguments of both the *Origin of German Tragic Drama* and the *Arcades Project*.

Benjamin continued to explore the relationship between literature and philosophy, focusing on German literature in and after Goethe, and on the theory and practice of translation. His fascination with the impact of Goethe on German literature is evident in his thesis, but was to become more systematic in the following years. His interpretations of Goethe, particularly in the essay 'Goethe's *Elective Affinities*', written in 1922, are directed against the prevailing current of interpretation associated with the circle around the poet Stefan Georg which elevated Goethe to the level of a literary hero. Against this hagiographic tendency, Benjamin returned to the close reading of a single text. In his interpretation he rejects the view that literature in any way symbolises truth, insists on the historical character of literary criticism, and analyses the novel in terms of the concepts of myth and fate. The characters are not autonomous Kantian agents making choices and entering into contracts such as marriage, but are involved in a drama of desire and death beyond their conscious control.

Benjamin's interpretation of Goethe was accompanied by an assessment of the writer's significance for the subsequent development of German literature. He recognised two paths of development in the Austro-Hungarian and Swiss writers Adalbert Stifter and Gottfried Keller. In Benjamin's interpretation, Stifter developed the auratic, mythic elements of Goethe which dissolved human agency into natural necessity and fate while Keller extended Goethe's novel of formation (*Bildungsroman*) in which character develops through the recognition of, and by, other characters. Goethe's work was, for Benjamin, suspended between these two tendencies which, after his death, separated into a divided heritage in which it is possible to discern intimations of Benjamin's later distinction between an aestheticised politics and a politicisation of art.

The early 1920s were also marked by an extension of the field of Benjamin's interests to include the everyday experience of the city and the metropolis. The essay 'Naples', written with Asja Lacis, was the first of a series of city portraits which included portraits of Moscow, Berlin, Marseilles and Paris. Benjamin's first self-consciously modernist work, *One Way Street*, published in 1928 with the *Origin of the German Mourning Play*, brings together a 1923 text 'Tour of the German Inflation' with a number of aphoristic reflections on modern urban experience provoked by his daily life in Berlin and Paris. Benjamin described *One Way Street* as a 'first attempt to come to terms with this city [Paris]' through the methodological principle of grasping 'topicality as the reverse of the eternal in history and to make an impression of this hidden side of the medallion'. The book marks an important stage on Benjamin's route to the *Arcades Project* which also attempted to come to terms with the revolutionary history of Paris by means of a similar methodological perspective.

The rigorously modernist style of *One Way Street* and some of the content ('The Critics Technique in Thirteen Theses') shows the impact of Benjamin's work as a professional cultural critique for the booming Weimar media networks, mainly newspaper and periodicals, but also, increasingly in the late 1920s, the radio. Along with his commissions as a translator, his media work was his main source of income during the 1920s and early 1930s. His debut as a translator of French modernism began in 1923 with the publication of his translations of Baudelaire's 'Tableaux parisiens' from *Les fleurs du mal*, remembered now for its controversial preface 'The Task of the Translator' in which Benjamin further developed the theory of universal translation announced in the 1916 'Language as Such and the Language of Mankind'. He also translated the *Anabasis* of St Jean Perse and, with Franz Hessel, began the task of translating Proust. An unexpected fruit of this collaboration was the initial insight into the significance of the Parisian arcades which led to plans for a short joint article which expanded into the *Arcades Project* after Benjamin's encounter with the writings of the surrealists (notably Aragon's *Paris Peasant*).

One of the reasons for Benjamin's entry into the world of the Weimar media industry was the failure of his attempt to pursue a career in the University with the habilitation thesis *The Origin of the German Mourning Play*. After various undignified intrigues on the part of the faculty of the University of Frankfurt,

Benjamin withdrew the thesis and published it in 1928 at the same time as *One Way Street*. The book was a self-conscious *summa* of his work up to that date, bringing together, in an extremely complex whole, the fragments of 1916 on the philosophy of language and the genres of mourning play and tragedy, a neo-Kantian concept of experience, the approach to literature and philosophy developed in 'Goethe's *Elective Affinities*' and the political theology of the early 1920s.

The analysis of mourning-plays

The Origin of the German Mourning Play is a study of literary failure, of the genre of reformation and counter-reformation baroque drama known as *Trauerspiel* or mourning-play. It was a genre which Benjamin claims did not have a great future, at least, not before expressionism and the epic theatre of Berthold Brecht which were formally related to it. Benjamin begins his analyses of the drama with the extremely complex, and even dismaying, 'Epistemo-Critical Prologue' which establishes the methodological principles of the study. These consist in three presuppositions. The first is the attempt to transcend the opposition of aesthetic idealism and empiricism with the concept of 'origin'. Neither a timeless idea manifested in the genres of works of art nor an empirical description derived from the observation of given works, 'origin' was both in and out of time. Benjamin described it by means of the metaphor of 'an eddy in the stream of becoming', by which he meant that it was not a transcendental idea nor an empirical description, but a regularity in some sense outside of time but open to its effects.

The 'concepts' of tragedy and mourning-play are considered in the light of this epistemological introduction. They are neither timeless categories nor empirical descriptions, but may be described as 'origins' in having certain formal regularities which are open to change over time. The distinction between the two aesthetic origins is indeed the second presupposition of the book; the third is the distinction between symbol and allegory, which Benjamin aligns in complex ways with those of idea and origin, and tragedy and mourning-play. The symbol is the manifestation in time of a timeless idea, while allegory is the manifestation of the time-dependence of all ideas; the symbol imperfectly presents a timeless truth in the beautiful appearance while allegory presents the temporality of truth in the destruction of appearance.

Benjamin works through these complex ideas and conceptual relationships by means of an analysis of baroque mourning-plays. The historical analysis of the dramas is indebted to his work on political theology and the Reformation, and is intended to show how a particular form – the mourning-play – was adapted by its encounter with the changing historical circumstances of the Reformation, emergence of the absolutist state and the behind-the-scenes development of capitalism. In this sense, the mourning-play was an origin, evincing certain formal characteristics such as the 'intrigue' of the diabolical courtier, the absence of a hero, the lament of the powerless monarch, and the fetishisation of regalia such as the sceptre which were changed by their development in distinct cultural contexts.

For Benjamin, the Protestant German mourning-play which was his main object of study failed to sustain the formal demands of the genre and lapsed into ruination and obscurity, but for this very reason it was useful for recovering the lineaments of the origin of the mourning-play. He made this recovery in two stages: in the first, he collected the historical material or 'material content' in the language of the Goethe essay; in the second, he used this to interpret the genre of mourning-play. In the latter stage, he showed the salient feature of the genre to be allegory, or the reduction of all transcendent significance to nothing; but he then showed that allegory could dialectically be turned upon itself, and its reduction applied to its own reduction and its nihilism in some sense redeemed. For him, the German mourning-play was unable to make the final dialectical reversal, and was left with a destructive and interminable mourning of a lost transcendence.

Towards the arcades project

The composition of *The Origin of the German Mourning Play* in the early 1920s was contemporary with Benjamin's growing interest in modernity and modernism, and, specifically, their Marxist critique. His reading of Georg Lukács's *History of Class Consciousness* and his relationship with the Latvian communist Asja Lacis in 1924 marked an intensification of his interest in the past, present and future of modern, specifically capitalist, forms of experience. The encounter with Marxism was by no means a turning point in his thought, but it did confirm the particular path of development which led to the *Arcades Project*. This path traced the origins of the experience of modernity and the difficult relationship between modern experience and modernism in the arts. Benjamin's philosophical meditations on modern literature of the late 1920s and 1930s were informed by the larger project of a genealogy of modernity, which analysed modern experience in terms of a tension between the political and the technological revolutions of the nineteenth and twentieth centuries.

During the late 1920s, on the eve of beginning full-scale research on the *Arcades Project*, Benjamin planned and wrote a series of seminal philosophical-critical essays which he intended to collect in a volume published by Rowohlt. In the contract for this never-to-be-published collection signed in 1930, Benjamin proposed a number of separately published essays on writers ranging from nineteenth-century Keller and Hebel to twentieth-century German and French writers such as Hessel, Walser and Kraus, and Green, Proust, Gide and the surrealists. The international cultural politics of the collection were underlined by its being framed by an introduction on the 'Task of the Critic' and an epilogue reprinting the 'Task of the Translator'. The collection also proposed new essays on 'Novelist and Storyteller' and 'Art Nouveau', the first of which subsequently appeared separately as the essay on Leskov. Apart from showing the range of Benjamin's criticism of contemporary literature, the contract also reveals in passing Benjamin's plan for a volume of essays on Proust and Kafka, showing that he regarded his consummate essays on these two writers as closely linked. In retrospect, it is apparent that what linked them was their status as modernist literary investigations of the modernity of contemporary urban experience.

During the 1930s, and especially after leaving Germany for exile in Paris after the Nazi seizure of power in 1933, Benjamin's critical writings were largely parerga to his work on the *Arcades Project*. The fascination with the architectural type of the arcade is already evident in the essay on 'Naples', but was intensified by the coincidence observed by Benjamin and Hessel in 1928 of the opening of a new consumer arcade on the Champs Elysée with the demolition of one of the early-nineteenth-century arcades near Palais Royal. Benjamin saw the transformation of the arcade into a luxury shopping centre as an allegory of the fate of the technological and political revolutions of the nineteenth century. The new possibilities for social and political organisation opened by the development of iron and glass technology and incarnated in the Paris arcades contained within them the possibility for unprecedented changes in forms of life and the public sphere. However, these possibilities were continually diverted into conservative directions, and the revolutionary architectural form reduced to a setting for the sale of commodities.

Benjamin's insight into the unprecedented possibilities opened by technology, and the potential betrayal of these possibilities, was already evident in the concluding section of *One Way Street* entitled 'To the Planetarium'. The rhapsody to the advance of technology as a new body for planetary humanity's 'contact with the cosmos' is qualified by the violent use to which it was put by 'the lust for profit of the ruling class' which led to warfare. In this text, Benjamin counterpoises war and revolution as the two attempts 'of mankind to bring the new body under its control' (Benjamin, 1996, p. 487). This analysis was confirmed in the essay 'Theories of German Fascism' where he opposes the Fascist theory of war or 'slave revolt of technology' to Communist revolution. In both cases, what takes place is the diversion of the energies released by technology into the channels of existing social forms. Benjamin took this analysis one stage further by arguing that there was a relationship between conservative political and aesthetic uses of technology. This diagnosis was given its most celebrated expression in the proposition at the end of the influential essay 'The Work of Art in the Epoch of its Technical Reproducibility' (1935) that Fascism 'aestheticises politics' while Communism 'politicises art'.

The famous concluding phrase follows an analysis of the 'decay of aura' which Benjamin described as 'symptomatic' of the 'destruction of tradition' and the emergence of the two mass movements of Fascism and Communism. The 'destruction of tradition' and the concomitant urge of the masses to 'bring things closer', and thus destroy their aura, are aspects of a broader technological revolution. In one respect, the case study of 'technical reproducibility' is a case study of the impact of a broader technical development on art; but it is also an analysis of the conservative use of technology to 'reproduce' existing reality rather than acknowledge the revolutionary possibility that it may create new realities.

Art and politics

One example of the aestheticisation of politics for Benjamin was the contemporary use of technology by Fascism and National Socialism to reproduce existing 'realities' of national unities for the masses. Another, rather different, example, drawn from the *Arcades Project*, was Haussmann's redevelopment of Paris in the mid-nineteenth century under the dictatorship of Louis-Napoleon. In Haussmann's urban planning, technical developments were used to create a strategic, commercially motivated, but also beautiful system of grand boulevards. Technical developments were thus subordinated to the ends of the free-market dictatorship, breaking the possible alliance between technological developments and revolutionary politics. As a result, in Benjamin's interpretation, revolutionaries adopted a *ressentiment* relationship to technology, either destroying it as in the burning of Paris by the Communards, or by having excessive faith in its inevitably progressive character. The large file index that comprises the *Arcades Project* focuses on this equivocal relationship between aesthetic, socio-political and technological revolutions, analysing it both in terms of minute historical detail and broader theoretical reflections.

The 'politicisation of art' should be understood as an analogue of the use of technology to create new realities rather than harnessing its energies to the support of obsolete ones. This line of argument was anticipated in Benjamin's writings on Soviet theatre which he published after his trip to the Soviet Union in the mid 1920s. In these, he contrasts the aesthetically 'conservative' position of a revolutionary content presented by means of traditional forms with the transformation of the opposition of form and content into a new theatrical reality. He saw a similar process at work in Brecht's theatre, to which he devoted a number of fine studies collected in *Understanding Brecht*. In Brecht's 'Epic Theatre', Benjamin saw the emergence of a new politicised art which did not present radical political content through traditional aesthetic/theatrical forms, but which transformed the very opposition of form and content. In the words of another of his Brecht-inspired essays, the author was not a 'reproducer' but a 'producer'. In the 'Work of Art in the Epoch of its Technical Reproducibility' Benjamin analysed cinema in terms of the technological reorganisation of reality. Not only did the camera create a new visual world, it also created a new way of seeing the world and new conditions for an audience to encounter a work of art. However, consistent with the general tenor of Benjamin's analysis of technology, his view of cinema was equivocal; while it could create new realities and new public spaces for participation and discussion, it could also be used to support traditional, or even reactionary, values and forms of aesthetic appreciation.

Benjamin's analysis of the relationship between technological and political aspects of modernity and their relationship to aesthetic modernism surfaced in a number of works-in-progress from the 1930s. The *exposé* of the *Arcades Project* from 1935, 'Paris – The Capital of the Nineteenth Century', offers a scale plan of the project as a whole in the guise of a series of six allegorical snapshots that bring together, and which juxtapose, a name and an architectural form, such as 'Fourier or the Arcades' or 'Baudelaire or the Streets of Paris' into a historical constellation that juxtaposes aesthetic technological and social revolution/counter-revolution. The 'Paris of the Second Empire of Baudelaire' of 1938 was the central section of a book presenting the material of the *Arcades Project* by means of a study of Baudelaire's modernism. The draft section was misunderstood by Adorno and Horkheimer, who had commissioned the book for the exiled Institute for Social Research, and they insisted on it being rewritten as 'On Some Motifs in Baudelaire'. Common to all these drafts is the connection between social and technical modernity and aesthetic modernism. The connection is established by means of the concept of experience: modernism is the aesthetic presentation of the experience of social and technical modernity.

Last writings

Benjamin's exile in Paris was economically and emotionally difficult, but he was nevertheless reluctant to leave the city until the last minute, when he joined many other refugees on the journey south. Among his last writings are an introduction to the *Arcades Project* in the form of a series of aphorisms which were subsequently given the title 'Theses on the Philosophy of History'. The theses gather, in condensed form, themes from all periods of Benjamin's authorship. In them, he attempts to dislocate progressive philosophies of history through a number of disruptive strategies. History is not a continuum which might serve as a stage for the drama of constant social and technological progress, but is constituted by breaks and interruptions. It is not necessarily about the progress from past to present to future, but the disruption of past and present by the future. The past, in other words, as Benjamin recognised very early in his authorship, is futural. The angel of history does not guide progress, but brings catastrophe. In his final word, Benjamin insists that if Marxism or the materialist analysis of history wishes to understand the future then it must be supplemented by theology; the theory of the laws of past historical development by the reflection on the inexplicable 'Messianic' irruption of the future into past and present.

Although Benjamin could not have predicted the future interpretations of his work, he would probably not have been surprised by their diversity. His writings were initially claimed after the War by the Frankfurt School, represented by his editor Adorno, with dissenting voices from his friends Scholem and Arendt. His works were seized and pirated by the New Left as offering both a Marxism capable of sustaining sensitive cultural analysis and a suggestive account of Brecht's theatrical practice. Against these Leftist tendencies George Steiner, leaning heavily and perhaps incautiously on the Benjamin of *The Origin of the German Mourning Play*, claimed him for German mandarin melancholy while others saw in this work, and in his correspondence with Carl Schmitt, an unhealthy (and highly improbable) fascination with Fascism. More recently, his work has been claimed for liberation theology and for a Marxist or even Lacanian theory of post-modernity. Finally, with the completion of the German collected works and the prospect of an extensive and systematic English edition, it is safe to assume that the coming years will see a proliferation of fresh interpretations and critical revisions of the works and heritage of Walter Benjamin.

Bibliography

Writings

Benjamin, Walter (1972–), *Gesammelte Schriften*, vols I–VIII, ed. Rolf Tiedemann and Hermann Schweppenhäuser, Frankfurt am Main: Suhrkamp Verlag.
— (1994), *The Correspondence of Walter Benjamin, 1910–1940*, trans. Manfred R. Jacobsen and Evelyn M. Jacobsen, ed. Gershom Scholem and Theodor W. Adorno, Chicago and London: Chicago University Press.
— (1983), *Charles Baudelaire: A Lyric Poet in the Era of High Capitalism*, trans. Harry Zohn and Quintin Hoare, London: NLB/Verso.
— (1970), *Illuminations*, trans. Harry Zohn, London: Jonathan Cape.
— (1979), *'One Way Street' and Other Writings*, trans. Edmund Jephcott and Kingsley Shorter, London: NLB/Verso.
— (1996), *Selected Writings*, Volume 1: 1913–1926, ed. Marcus Bullock and Michael W. Jennings, Cambridge, MA and London: Harvard University Press.
— (1973), *Understanding Brecht*, trans. Anya Bostock, London: NLB/Verso.

References and further reading

Benjamin, Andrew and Peter Osborne (1994), *Walter Benjamin's Philosophy: The Destruction of Experience*, London: Routledge.

Brodersen, Momme (1996), *Walter Benjamin: A Biography*, London: Verso.

Buck-Morss, Susan (1989), *The Dialectics of Seeing: Walter Benjamin and the Arcades Project*, Cambridge, MA and London: MIT Press.

Caygill, Howard (1997), *Walter Benjamin: The Colour of Experience*, London: Routledge.

Eagleton, Terry (1981), *Walter Benjamin, or Towards a Revolutionary Criticism*, London: NLB.

Handelman, Susan A. (1991), *Fragments of Redemption: Jewish Thought and Literary Theory in Benjamin, Scholem, Levinas*, Bloomington and Indianapolis: Indiana University Press.

Jennings, Michael (1987), *Dialectical Images: Walter Benjamin's Theory of Literary Criticism*, Ithaca and London: Cornell University Press.

McCole, John (1993), *Walter Benjamin and the Antinomies of Tradition*, Ithaca and London: Cornell University Press.

Mehlman, Jeffrey (1993), *Walter Benjamin for Children: An Essay on his Radio Years*, Chicago and London: University of Chicago Press.

Nagele, Rainer (1988), *Benjamin's Ground: New Readings of Walter Benjamin*, Detroit: Wayne State University.

Scholem, Gershom (1981), *Walter Benjamin: the Story of a Friendship*, trans. Harry Zohn, Philadelphia: The Jewish Publication Society of America.

Smith, Gary (ed.) (1989), *Benjamin: Philosophy, History, Aesthetics*, Chicago and London: University of Chicago Press.

Witte, Bernd (1991), *Walter Benjamin: An Intellectual Biography*, trans. James Rolleston, Detroit: Wayne State University Press.

Wolin, Richard (1994), *Walter Benjamin: An Aesthetic of Redemption*, Berkeley and London: University of California Press.

6.5

UTOPIAN EMANCIPATION: BLOCH

Chris Thornhill

The work of Ernst Bloch (1885–1977) incorporates a series of disparate traditions of German thought. His philosophy combines elements of Hegelian Marxism, phenomenology, literary expressionism, Kierkegaardian existentialism, hermeneutics, secular-theological utopianism and a Schelling-influenced philosophy of nature. His work spans the period from 1919, when he published *Spirit of Utopia*, a highly influential messianic philosophy of history and music, to 1974, when he wrote his last major work, *Experimentum Mundi*. Other major works are: *The Principle of Hope*, a meticulous and elaborate phenomenology, structured around hope as the horizon of human action and natural life, *Atheism in Christianity*, an attempt to salvage the revolutionary base of Christianity as a religion of exodus, and *Natural Law and Human Dignity*, an attempt to rehabilitate classical theories of natural law in the context of modern Marxism.

During the early part of his career, Bloch participated in intense intellectual debate with, amongst others, Georg Lukács and Walter Benjamin, the traces of whose thought are clearly discernible in his thinking. Like many others, he left Germany in 1933, eventually reaching the USA. Unusually, if not uniquely, among German Marxist émigrés, after the War he lived in the GDR, where, between 1949 and 1957, he was Professor of Philosophy in Leipzig. He eventually returned to the West in 1961, when he became Professor of Philosophy at Tübingen, from which position he exercised great influence on the student movement of the late 1960s. None the less, because of his eclecticism and his attempts to link Marxism with esoteric intellectual interests, his thought is often neglected, or even ironised, by conventional Marxist analysis and critical theory. Indeed, much recent literature on Bloch has a quaintly patronising or apologetic tone. This article will seek to elucidate the central categories in Bloch's thought and to suggest why a reappraisal of Bloch's contribution to twentieth-century philosophy may be timely.

Apocalypse and hope

Spirit of Utopia is both the title of Bloch's first major work and the guiding impulse of all his writing. Already in this work his unique fusion of phenomenology, natural ontology and redemptive theology begins to assume determinate contours. The work is carried by a current of eschatology; that is, by the conviction, articulated in the almost baroque prose of late German expressionism, that the time of human history is time **directed** (*gerichtet*) towards the redemptive end of history. For Bloch, the entire experience of history is driven by the promise of ultimate redemption. Redemptive eschatology, figured by Bloch as an esoteric Marxism, is the substratum which underscores and determines all of both human experience and natural life. Expressed characteristically, for Bloch: 'soul, Messiah and apocalypse are the *a priori* of all politics and culture' (Bloch, 1971, p. 433).

Importantly, even at this early stage, Bloch's thought has a claim to uniqueness through the differing status which it accords to apocalypse (as ultimate redemption or utopia). He talks especially of the **latency** of apocalypse, by which he means the ceaseless unrealised actuality of utopia in human history. This latency of apocalypse impels both human action and the activity of nature itself. It also constitutes the human horizon of thought, and the phenomenological intentionality of understanding. These differentiations are crucial to an understanding of his work, and also to a recognition of the distinctions between himself and Lukács, Benjamin and even Heidegger.

Bloch's early thought on the first implication of apocalypse is similar to Lukács's in *The Theory of the Novel*. Both are grounded in a secular theology of Gnostic character. Bloch also shares with Lukács a spirit of Romantic anti-capitalism, and both describe history as the demonic world of alienation, of falling away from original holistic being. Like Lukács also, Bloch understands the subject's knowledge of the fallenness of the world as a redemptive impulse. Indeed, his vocabulary is consistently marked by a subjectivism foreign to later exponents of critical theory. His vocabulary in this early context derives its motifs directly from secular Gnosticism, especially in his sense of redemption (apocalypse) as appreciation of the 'double-I in God' (ibid., p. 441). He claims that the path to redemption lies in Luciferan insubordination in face of the law-giving God of the Old Testament, in the rebellious desire of the subject to know better than God, to be like God. Bloch's philosophy thus expresses the mission of Gnostic eschatology through the figure of the demonic 'rebel towards the goal' (ibid., p. 442).

However, unlike the pre-Marxist Lukács, even Bloch's earliest philosophy carries within it a reflex against Gnosticism. This is best seen in his faith in nature, for he conceives of nature itself as a directed dynamic, which is latently correlated with the subject's knowledge of its alienation and shares in the subject's dream of a better world. Faith in nature is constructed in his philosophy of history as an eventual 'self-encounter' (ibid., p. 386), in which human subject and natural subject, both eschatologically *directed*, will ultimately meet each other. In his major work *Principle of Hope* (1954–59), he explains this dialectic of nature and substance as follows: 'The world-process itself is a utopian func-

tion, with the matter of the objectively Possible as its substance (Bloch, 1986, p. 177). Although in his early works this understanding of nature is worked out in a slightly haphazard manner, the foundation of his thought resides in this notion of natural substance.

Apocalypse also figures in Bloch's thought as a hermeneutic horizon of understanding. For him, the futurity of utopia articulates itself in individual thought as a subjective response to the world. The future (lastly, apocalypse) frames a horizon within which the subject interprets things and itself. Since the subject knows itself true only in futurity, when it questions things about their true nature, the question is also about their future nature. This questioning is itself a motor in Bloch's eschatology. The response to the world is not an interest in the world as it is found, but a directed interest in the world as it should and will be. The question with which thought interprets the world, circumscribed by the historical horizon of latency, rethinks the world under the primacy of future: 'under the star of its utopian fate' (Bloch, 1971, p. 339). There is thus a relation between the futurity of utopia and the question in which the subject addresses the world. In Bloch's theory of the question, both thought and world figure as constituents in the dynamic of utopia. Ultimately, the apocalyptic horizon of understanding is defined by Bloch as the 'inconstructible question', as a question which is always future and never wholly grasped. The inconstructibility of this last question informs and impels all other questions. To use Bloch's own terms, the inconstructible question reflects the **not-yet** of our understanding. Each question moves towards the inconstructible question and shares thus in its status of total futurity. Both the question and the material things which are questioned have their truth only in anticipation. This directed hermeneutic is again carried by Bloch's philosophy of directed nature. Material redemption is the last answer to the hermeneutic question (ibid., p. 373). As Wayne Hudson, in what is acknowledged to be the best English commentary on Bloch, puts it: 'Bloch's utopian hermeneutics was designed to uncover *Evidenz* of utopia or *Ich* content throughout the world' (Hudson, 1982, p. 27).

In this hermeneutic interpretation of Bloch's early

writings, it is important to mention also the inception of his theory of memory. Like Benjamin after him, Bloch links memory with a theory of the moment (*Augenblick*). Indeed, in this respect he can be seen certainly to anticipate, and perhaps also to correct, Benjamin's widely cited theory of the moment. For Bloch, in the punctual moment of being-in-time, the subject has no integral consciousness of itself, for it is already in the future. The present is therefore undisclosed, characterised in Bloch's own terms as 'the darkness of the lived moment' (Bloch, 1971, p. 373). The moment is explained as the 'darkness of not having oneself' (ibid., p. 386). This moment, however, is also outside itself because it is uncertainly correlated with the nature of the things about which it thinks. Elsewhere it is termed an 'essential astonishment' (ibid., p. 386) at things. Correlated with things, it is an appreciation of their futurity, but also, crucially, of the possible futurity of their past. The response of the moment to the objects is therefore one grounded in memory, articulated as *Eingedenken* (intense recollection; internalisation), in which the subject, in the moment, resurrects the redemptive, utopian, reflexes of historical things themselves.

As will be seen later, Bloch, at odds with classical Marxism, accentuates the non-contemporaneous nature of past things. This is clearest in the theory of memory and the moment. Like Benjamin, he sees in the lost artefacts of history indices of utopian futurity. Indeed, much of his *opus magnum, Principle of Hope*, is dedicated to a phenomenology of the latent hope found in the artefacts of human culture, ranging from shop-windows to fairytales, all of which are deciphered under the primacy of future possibility. *Eingedenken* is theorised most closely in Bloch's first work on revolutionary theology: *Thomas Münzer as Theologian of Revolution* (see, for example, Bloch, 1976, p. 14).

Importantly, as the critic Karl Heinz Bohrer has explained, Bloch's theory of the moment corrects Benjamin's related theory of 'now-time', and crucially, his theory of citation, by implicitly warning that the sudden phenomenological moment of the 'now' can be salvaged only by its inclusion within a scheme of objective-natural anticipation (Bohrer, 1981, p. 73). Bloch achieves this by connecting *Eingedenken* with the directed materiality of nature.

It is arguable that the radical futurity of Bloch's thought also produces a phenomenological dimension to his philosophy, a dimension which perhaps can be best determined as a phenomenology of desire, in which desire is grasped as utopian intentionality. In *Spirit of Utopia*, this intentional desire is termed the 'wishful dream' (Bloch, 1971, p. 341). More clearly, in *Principle of Hope*, this is expressed as follows: 'The future dimension contains what is feared or what is hoped for; as regards human intention, that is, when it is not thwarted, it contains only what is hoped for' (Bloch, 1986, p. 4). Elsewhere we read: 'the *act-content* of hope is, as a consciously illuminated, knowingly elucidated content, the *positive utopian function*; the *historical content* of hope, first represented in ideas, encyclopaedically explored in real judgements, is *human culture referred to its concrete-utopian horizon*' (ibid., p. 146). The horizon of hope, read either as hermeneutic or phenomenological structure, figures here not only as the directedness of matter, but as both the act and content of thinking, correlated to matter.

The horizon of hope, or apocalypse in Bloch's earliest writings, thus refers implicitly to most of the philosophical traditions which were influential during the years of his own intellectual formation. It figures as an element of mystical Marxism, an element of existential hermeneutics, and an element of radical phenomenology. But in its linkage of all of these, it is unique.

The ontology of the not-yet

Bloch's thought, like that of Adorno and, to a lesser extent, Benjamin, is often read as a correction and critique of Heidegger's fundamental ontology. The comparison between Heidegger and Bloch is indeed particularly important, not least because Bloch himself was at times acutely aware of the contiguities between his own thought and that of thinkers, most particularly Heidegger, whose political and ethical positions were inimical to his own. On more than one occasion, Bloch's own thinking was reviled as a combination of left-wing ethics and right-wing epistemology. On other grounds also, Heidegger and Bloch invite comparison, chiefly because of the relational and ontological structures which characterise their thinking.

As is implicit in the above, Bloch builds his philosophy around the situatedness of being-in-the-world. Being is intensely correlated with nature, with which it shares structures of direction. The influence of the ontological foundation of Schelling's *Philosophy of Nature* is palpable here. However, against static or natural ontology, Bloch attempts (rather unsuccessfully) to distance his thought from a theory of constantly present **potentia** – that is, a theory which understands natural processes as the mere elaboration of potentials already operative in the origin of being. He even criticises Hegel's dialectic for being undermined by a Platonic theory of origin (by which he means anamnesis), and, for this reason, insufficiently forward-looking. What he attempts, therefore, is to retain the processual structure of Hegelian dialectics, but in the reworked form of a dialectic of the not-yet. His dialectic does not relinquish nature; but he does treat true nature, or **manifested nature**, as the nature of the future – the not-yet.

The state of being-in-the-world is therefore an ontology of possibility, a being in possibility, in which the original fundament of nature is itself ceaselessly mobile as a tendency correlated with this possibility. Possibility, as an ontological state of being, is called by Bloch the not-yet: 'The *Not-Yet* characterises the *tendency* in material process, of the origin which is processing itself out.' (Bloch, 1986, p. 307). Clearly, in this, Bloch's thought, although intentionally pitched against thinking through the category of origin (a category laden with dubious ideological overtones in inter-War Germany), does not finally detach itself from an ontology of nature or originality. However, unlike Benjamin, Bloch insists on the unfinishedness of even original life itself. Even origin is not-yet. Nature, in Bloch's terms, is not realised already in the origin or present of the world, but will be realised only at the end of human and natural progress.

In this, Bloch attacks the static quality of Heideggerian ontology, and most expressly the illusory eschatology of Heideggerian phenomenology. In a simple counter-point, Bloch's ontology of being-in-the-world – as *not-yet* – is experienced in the widened possibility of hope, whereas Heidegger's ontology, as is well known, is being-in-the-world as anxiety: 'Heidegger . . . does not make his anxiety regressive, but neither does he process beyond it to equally original positive expectant emotions without which anxiety could not exist' (ibid., p. 109). The anti-Heideggerian tone of Bloch's ideas is most pronounced in his final work, *Experimentum Mundi*, itself a philosophy of ontological categories of being. In this work, world, and human action in the world, are determined as the ceaseless question about the world itself (Bloch, 1975, p. 248). Participation in this question is the situatedness of his ontology.

Bloch's conception of temporality is central to his philosophical importance. His ontology links determinate historicity with futurity in a manner which is both sympathetic to determinately ontological thinking (even, discreetly, that of Heidegger), but hostile none the less to the hypostatic implications of ontology. In other words, Bloch's hostility to the ontology of being is motivated by the sense that Heidegger's ontology has no genuine interest in futurity – that ontology fixes (and offers an apology for) the world as it is. In Bloch's thought, ontology gains value only when conceived together with eschatology. For this association of ontology and eschatology alone (perhaps definable as a negative ontology), Bloch's ideas should be given more serious treatment.

However, some moments in Bloch's ontological thought are definitely adjacent to certain traditions within the reactionary thinking of inter-War Germany. This can be best elucidated through further reference to Bloch's idea of memory. The not-yet is a function of memory. The not-yet, both as a latency in nature and as a structure of understanding, is the essence of objects in the world. In this conception, Bloch widens the scope of Marxist-Hegelian dialectics to include a theory of the dialectics of non-contemporaneity (*Ungleichzeitigkeit*). This means, in short, that, like Benjamin, he reworks materialist dialectics in a manner which, while still prioritising the contemporary dialectic of class-conflict, is interested (phenomenologically) in the non-contemporary substance of things (the not-yet), and, most particularly, of cultural heritage. This not-yet is not a merely formal device. In *Natural Law and*

Human Dignity, for example, the whole history of juridical reflection is read through this perspective, Bloch's central assumption being that natural law itself, in its classical conception, is a *not-yet*, a moment of non-contemporaneity awaiting realisation.

None the less, the philosophy of the not-yet can be seen as a coalescence of a reactionary epistemology with a Marxist ethics. Certainly, in the intellectual world of the 1930s, Bloch's commitment to the unrealised substance of historical things inevitably appears close to the widespread post-historicist re-evaluation of the national past of Germany. It is in the light of this adjacency that we can understand Bloch's strangest work: *Heritage of our Times*, which comprises a series of loosely connected essays, most of which are devoted to aspects of non-contemporaneity. The multi-layered dialectic of Bloch's utopian theory of culture and history is here set out as follows:

> The proletarian voice of the contemporaneous dialectic firmly remains the leading one; yet beneath and above this *cantus firmus* there run disordered exuberances which are to be referred to the *cantus firmus* only through the fact that the latter – in critical and non-contemplative totality – refers to them. And a multi-spatial dialectic proves itself above all in the dialectization of still 'irrational' contents; they are, in accordance with their positive element which remains critical, the 'nebulae' of the non-contemporaneous contradictions. (Bloch, 1991, p. 116)

This is the ideal formulation of this dialectic. At the same time, however, Bloch acknowledges the possible reactionary implications of this scheme (indeed, in doing so he shows a far greater degree of self-scrutiny than does Benjamin in his own related function of commemorative citation):

> There are elements of ancient society and its relative order and fulfilment in the present un-ordered one here, and the subjectively non-contemporaneous contradition animates these elements in a negatively and positively surprising way. Home, soil and nation are such *objectively* raised contradictions of the traditional to the capitalist'. (ibid., p. 109)

Much of Bloch's thought, especially the centrality in his thought of the dialectics of nature and the non-contemporaneity of the not-yet, shows more than a passing symmetry with the intellectual superstructure of German reaction, most particularly with Heidegger, Klages and Jung. In the above, Bloch clearly attempts to force lines of demarcation between his own thinking and that of his irrationalist contemporaries.

The constant commemorative reworking of both intellectual constructs and the phenomena of socio-cultural history is inscribed in Bloch's thought as the theory of an open system. The open system can be best understood as a structure which includes all thinking under the primacy of hope. Structured around the not-yet, Bloch's open system reflects not only on the incompleteness of its ontological contents, but also on the unfinished nature of its own epistemological categories. Hudson describes this well:

> Open System . . . aims at transmission to a future phase of the process where, in another society and with a more developed material content in both subject and object, problems which are only pre-posed now in a necessarily mythological manner, may be posed more adequately and brought to a result'. (Hudson, 1982, p. 82)

This is a crucial fact for Bloch's thought on memory and non-contemporaneity. Even seemingly mythical and reactionary things possess a future which will be unlocked under the changed parameters of future questioning. This has been variously described as active openness, elastic openness, or adequate openness (Diersburg, 1973, p. 4). Nothing can be finally rejected by the open system, for nothing is final. However it is described, the openness of Bloch's thinking is mobilised against either ontological or epistemological stasis, but is also precisely responsive to the salvation of projects seemingly hostile to its own.

The open system can be seen as both ontology and counter-ontology. It is a system in which the logical form of thinking, the category of the not-yet, is closely knitted with ontological content, the content of the not-yet. The not-yet is inscribed in the open system both as a category through which the world is understood and as a quality of the world itself. In the open system, natural philosophy anthropology, philosophy of history, ontology and subjective intentionality all enter a frame of constant reciprocal dependence and correction which, under the primacy of the not-yet, sustains the openness and futurity of the system itself (Holz, 1975, p. 145).

Atheism and theology

Bloch's thought is often interpreted as religion. As mentioned above, his philosophy, most obviously in *Spirit of Utopia*, assumes the form of a barely secularised gnostic-eschatological theology. The hermeneutic dimensions to his thought also make implicit references to traditions of biblical scholarship. In the context of post-War German thought Bloch's writings have been the object of great interest amongst liberal Christian theologians, most famously Jürgen Moltmann, whose own political theology of hope makes elaborate reference to Bloch. Gershom Scholem has also been keen to read Bloch as exclusively grounded within the frame of cabbalistic mysticism. *Spirit of Utopia* would particularly appear to support this interpretation. The last chapter of *Spirit of Utopia*, entitled 'Karl Marx, Death and Apocalypse', quite clearly links Marxism with motifs derived from mysticism and Messianic visions of redemption. Here, the redemptive view of history, underscored by visions of 'self-encounter' and the 'double-I in God', clearly refer to gnosis; in the strictest sense, as knowing. Gnostic myth begins with the transcendence of God, develops the story of creation of the world by demiurges actually opposed to God, conceives humanity as life incarcerated in materiality, and eventually projects the destiny of humanity in a theory of redemption, in which the Fall is reversed and all things return to their place in God. These are all mirrored in Bloch's work.

There is, however, a crucial difference between reading Bloch as secular theology and reading Bloch as theology. Despite the structural centrality of apparently mystical terms in his thought, even *Spirit of Utopia* ends with the declaration that evil exists only through God whilst the God of the just exists through humanity (Bloch, 1971, p. 445). Although this itself recalls Gnostic intimation of

the evil God, Bloch clearly insists in this statement that elements of theology must undergo the same secularisation through human-natural action as all other moments of his thinking. Indeed, in the location of God at the end of human-natural life and history, Bloch understands God in precisely the same manner as he understands nature and world. God is also directed energy, as the end of the world, as its centre, as its ground. Bloch's God is the goal and the course of matter itself. In this respect, his thought is hardened against purely theologising readings of his work. His metaphysics of matter (like Schelling's philosophy of nature) refuses to admit the existence of purely spiritual beings, and he seeks to explain the world in itself with no addition, in the insight that absolutely transcendent beings have no place in real existence or real nature (see Christen, 1979, p. 19). This critique of transcendence is a key moment in his reception of theological thought.

In keeping with the systematic openness of his thought, Bloch reads theology under the horizon of hope. This is seen most clearly towards the end of *Principle of Hope*, in the key status of *Exodus* as a category in his reading of the Old Testament. He sees the salvageable foundation of early Christianity in its quality as a religion of the *absconditus*; that is, as a religion which asserts that salvation is always hidden from common life, as an obscure promise. He explains this as follows: 'Instead of the *finished goal there now appears a promised goal that must first be achieved*; instead of the *visible nature god there appears an invisible god of righteousness and of the kingdom of righteousness* (Bloch, 1986, pp. 1233–4). Religious exodus is the motion, both ontological and determinately historical, towards this promise.

Bloch does not only accentuate the actual historical legends of exodus in Judaism and early Christianity, but also the most essential eschatological lifeblood of these theologies, their commitment to the last realm of God. He stresses: 'Jesus is in fact *eschatology through and through*: and like his love his morality can only be grasped in relation to his kingdom' (ibid., p. 1263). This is seen also in Bloch's repeated citation of Augustine's: '*Dies septimus nos ipsi erimus*' (On the seventh day we will be ourselves). The category of the realm of God thus forms the correlative to the category of *Exodus*. There can be no realm without exodus. However, it is important to note, in this correlation, that this concept of exodus conforms also to the ontological categories of Bloch's thought. *Exodus* corresponds to the ontological structure of the darkness of the lived moment, and the realm of God corresponds to the category of hope. Bloch thus divests the central categories of theological thinking of their theological status and retranslates them as the ontological essence of being in the world. *Exodus* is being in its presentness, the realm of God is being in its futurity. In this regard, Bloch's philosophy is often described as onto-theology.

It is in this detranscendentalisation of theological paradigms that Bloch enters a critical debate – in *Atheism in Christianity* (1968) – with two of the most influential theologians of twentieth-century Germany, Rudolf Bultmann and Karl Barth. The polemical character of this debate is no surprise, as Bloch's own interest in theology is adjacent to that of Bultmann and Barth, but critically located between their projects. He criticises Bultmann's attempts to demythologise the historical quality of the Christlegend and to transform it into a merely existential function of personal experience, as interiority. For Bloch, although Bultmann's ontology is not wholly dissimilar to his own, Christ's ontological importance as representation of the categories of human hope is not separable from his political importance as an agent of opposition to existing religious and political authority. Against Bultmann, therefore, Bloch does not seek to demythologise Christ, but to detheocratise him. Similarly, in his critique of Barth's eschatology, Bloch is keen to define his own thinking against possible association with related positions. Barth's eschatology is the negation of the world, in which God is conceived as the radical 'Other' of human history. Bloch rejects the transcendent implication of religion as total otherness, interpreting the implications of religion as categories of historical futurity. Crucially, however, with Barth against Bultmann, the categories of theology retain for Bloch their character of difference, and resist the static ontology of the merely interior realisation which they experience in Bultmann's thought. Between Barth and Bultmann, Bloch's interest in the

implications of theology can therefore be defined as ontological eschatology, or as *transcending without transcendence* (Bloch, 1977, Preface). This means that theological transcendence of the world is refigured as a ceaseless transcending of the determinate situation of present life, towards the future. It is not a transcendence of the world itself. Bloch thus attempts to give to theological impulses a political, utopian and ontological content. The act of transcending which is implied in eschatological progress is the ontological base of historicity, yet the actual state of transcendence, as otherness from the world, exists in the world as a category of change (*not-yet*) and not as realisation.

Most emphatically, for Bloch, it is only as atheism that the contents of religion are salvaged:

> 'The goal of all higher religions was a land in which milk and honey flow as really as they do symbolically; the goal of the content-based atheism which remains over after religions is exactly the same – but without God, but with the uncovered face of our *absconditum* and of the salvation-latency of our difficult earth'. (Bloch, 1986, p. 1311)

Once again, the contents of theology in Bloch's thought are best seen as contents in the phenomenology of the open system. His phenomenology assimilates the hope-content of religion, but only under its index of the future.

Bloch's interest in onto-theology has also been most influential in the tradition of political theology. As early as 1921, in *Thomas Münzer as Theologian of Revolution*, Bloch investigates the determinate historico-political situation of theological thinking, accentuating the anti-authoritarian reflex of religion in the life of Thomas Münzer, whose Messianic outpourings inflamed the German Peasants' War, during the Reformation period. The same commitment to revitalising the political contents of theology informs Bloch's more encyclopedic writings on religion in *Principle of Hope* and *Atheism in Christianity*. The latter was written under the assumption that religion is saved from itself, and constantly reworked, by its own heresies. Expressed in lapidary form: 'The best thing about religion is that it produces heretics' (Bloch, 1977, p. 12). Elsewhere,

Bloch states: 'Only an atheist can be a good Christian, but certainly also: only a Christian can be a good atheist' (ibid., p. 13). The implication in this is that the essential contents of hope, which religious thinking contains, are always opposed to the fixity which faith acquires in established religions grounded in systems of authority, either worldly or symbolic. The hope-content of religion ceaselessly processes itself through denial of the hierarchies created out of religion. It is only in the most radical negation of religion that its content is saved. In this regard, religion falls into the now familiar category of a non-contemporaneous moment in the open system. It is precisely in this sense that the category of *Exodus* is given its simultaneously real-political and ontological character. *Exodus* is the darkness of the lived moment, ontologically, but it is also the lived moment of hope in political life. *Exodus* is *detheocratization*, and, by implication, critique of all established authority. Detheocratization is, in fact, the term through which Bloch's understanding of religion is best interpreted. Bloch's atheism is *without God* in a sense so intense as to be almost a theology of the anti-God. Atheism, insistent on its lack of God, seeks forms of being which are decidedly counterposed to theocratic authority, and which therefore salvage the hope of religion itself, as ceaseless *Exodus*.

Although, manifestly, Bloch's phenomenology of religion is – in the radical sense – anti-theological, it is none the less not difficult to see how and why his insistence on the future realisation of hope could easily be reconverted to theological ends by religious thinkers. He has addressed, particularly, biblical apocalypse, the hope-content of the New Testament and the structures of religious hermeneutics. Moreover, it is easy to see how theology considered under the primacy of the political might, either critically or affirmatively, be forced to enter debate with him.

Utopian Marxism

Attempts to argue for a reappropriation of Bloch for neo-Marxist thinking have usually been rather tentative. The reasons for this can be found in both historical circumstance and the idiosyncratic content of his thought. Bloch defined himself unswerv-

ingly as a Marxist but his writings, even during his time in the GDR, were not always well received by the Communist establishment. *Natural Law and Human Dignity* was published in the same year as his move from Leipzig to Tübingen, and his insistence on the fundament of natural law in Marxism at this juncture has often been construed as a critique of legislative processes in East Berlin and Moscow. His altercations with the Ulbricht regime have been well documented. Even in the 1930s, his insistence on the category of non-contemporaneity was dismissed by Marxist orthodoxy as an alarming reproduction of the irrationalist mysticism in the ideology of National Socialism. (See Franz, 1985, p. 133) Bloch is clearly aware of this problem, but at no time is he willing to relinquish the mythical-irrational substance of his notions of dialectics and history.

The idiosyncrasies in Bloch's Marxism are, unsurprisingly, rooted in his reception of Marxism as a systematic critique of ideology and political economy. There is a clear coolness in his discussion of Marxist ideological critique in *Spirit of Utopia*. In *The Materialism Problem*, he speaks of the 'warm-stream' and the 'cold-stream' in Marxism. The cold-stream refers to Marxism purely as the demystification of metaphysical appearance, as the critique of superstructure and ideology. For Bloch, however, the cold-stream in Marxism is subordinate to the warm-stream. In other words, for Bloch, the critical rationality of Marxism needs to be supplemented by a utopian liberating intention and a faith in the dialectics of nature. He explains this as follows: 'Economic-historical materialism, as an evolutionary theory . . . does not only have the sense of cold analysis, but also that of a qualitatively living, concrete Utopia, of a Utopia become concrete' (Bloch, 1972, pp. 373–4). He also formulates this in *Principle of Hope*: 'Reason cannot blossom without hope, hope cannot speak without reason, both in Marxist unity' (Bloch, 1986, p. 1367).

Perhaps Bloch's Marxism can be best understood as a most radical construction of the category of totality. The open system of his thought is constructed precisely to the end of *thinking totality*, and it is on this enterprise that Bloch's philosophy stands or falls. He understands the mediated co-productivity of the subject of nature, viewed sceptically by Marxist orthodoxy, as a factor which is itself constitutive for the end of bourgeois hegemony. The anthropological dialectic of class-conflict is extended to incorporate a dialectic of nature. As Habermas has argued, Bloch reads Marx and Schelling together. His Marxist-Schellingian dialectic of nature and society revolves around a concept of totality which conceives of nature as a social category, and society as a natural category, and which interprets social materiality as formed nature, but still as nature (see Reinicke, 1974, p. 38).

Ultimately, Bloch's Marxism is meaningful only as a dialectic of hope. His utopian structuring of Marxism pays little more than lip-service to concrete determinations of what society might or should ultimately look like. In his reconstruction of Marxism, the hoped-for utopia of Communism is simultaneously the not-yet of the non-contemporaneous, the phenomenological 'now' of understanding and the correlated not-yet-being in nature and social action. Certainly, an orthodox Marxist reader would find great difficulty in differentiating between moments of praxis-philosophy and moments of future-directed ontology in this form of political thinking. The last sentence of *Principle of Hope* exemplifies this:

> But the root of history is the working, creating human being who reshapes and overhauls the given facts. Once he has grasped himself and established what is his, without expropriation and alienation, in real democracy, there arises in the world something which shines into the childhood of all in which no one has yet been: homeland. (Bloch, 1986, pp. 1375–6)

It is too easy to dismiss much of Bloch's Marxism as fanciful, mythical, epistemologically reactionary, or merely as an unnecessary romantic gloss on Marx. However, while the reading of his work presented in this article does not offer an unqualified endorsement of the affirmative aspects in his thought, it resists the apologetic tone in much of the work about him, and it pays homage to the centrality in his work of the totalising impulse, the totalising dialectic, the totalising phenomenology, the totalising hermeneutic, the totalising ontology. All these are moments in the project of thinking about everything, under the open horizon of the future.

Bibliography

Writings

Bloch, E. (1986) (first edn 1954–9), *The Principle of Hope*, trans. N. and S. Plaice and P. Knight, Oxford: Blackwell.
— (1991) (first edn 1935), *Heritage of our Times*, trans. N. and S. Plaice, Oxford: Polity Press.
— (1971) (first edn 1918), *Geist der Utopie*, Frankfurt a. M.: Suhrkamp.
— (1975), *Experimentum Mundi*, Frankfurt a. M.: Suhrkamp.
— (1976) (first edn 1921), *Thomas Münzer als Theologe der Revolution*, Frankfurt a. M.: Suhrkamp.
— (1977) (first edn 1968), *Atheismus im Christentum*, Frankfurt a. M.: Suhrkamp.
— (1961), *Naturrecht und menschliche Würde*, Frankfurt a. M.: Suhrkamp.
— (1972), *Das Materialismus-Problem*, Frankfurt a. M.: Suhrkamp.

References and further reading

Christen, Anton (1979), *Ernst Blochs Metaphysik der Materie*, Bonn: Bouvier.
Diersburg, Egenolf Roeder von R. (1967), *Über Ontologie und Logik offener Systeme: Ernst Bloch vor dem Gesetz der Tradition*, Hamburg: Meiner.
Franz, Trautje (1985), *Revolutionäre Philosophie in Aktion: Ernst Blochs politischer Weg*, Hamburg: Junius.
Geoghegan, Vincent (1996), *Ernst Bloch*, London and New York: Routledge.
Holz, Hans Heinz (1975), *Logos Spermatikos: Ernst Blochs Philosophie der unfertigen Welt*, Darmstadt, Neuwied: Luchterhand.
Hudson, Wayne (1982), *The Marxist Philosophy of Ernst Bloch*, London and New York: Macmillan.
Reinicke, Helmut (1974), *Materie und Revolution: eine materialistisch-erkenntnistheoretische Untersuchung zur Philosophie von Ernst Bloch*, Kronberg: Scriptor.

THE REORIENTATION OF CRITICAL THEORY: HABERMAS

Nicholas Walker

Introduction

Jürgen Habermas (born 1929) has been a major philosophical presence in modern European and Anglo-American thought since the late 1950s. His intellectual career has reflected, and responded to, many of the most dramatic social-political and cultural upheavals during the 1960s and 1970s (during which he acted as a controversial spokesman and a trenchant critic of both anarchic-revolutionary and reactive-conservative trends, earning considerable acrimony from both sides of the political divide in Germany), and also to the equally dramatic ideological realignments of the 1980s and 1990s when the apparently secure structures of the post-War political settlement in Europe began to disintegrate, producing a host of unresolved social-political problems that retrospectively cast an increasingly problematic light upon the optimism which initially greeted the supersession of Cold War certainties and postures in Central and Eastern Europe. Throughout this period Habermas has continued to pursue, with constantly rearticulated intellectual means, a path of intransigent critical reflection which has a complex relationship to the tradition of critical theory in which he was initially schooled (the 'Frankfurt School' and the particular form of Western Marxism that originally sustained it). He has always seen his philosophical endeavours as intrinsically linked to a recognisable rhetoric of human emancipation through the power of rational reflection and critique, expressly indebted to what he

has called 'the Enlightenment project', or more globally and controversially, the project of 'modernity' itself. He thus reclaims a tradition which not implausibly, and like many before him, he sees paradigmatically expressed in the thought of Kant. During the late 1950s and throughout the 1960s, this commitment brought him into frequent critical confrontation with entrenched forms of conservative thinking (in academic areas from history and social science to the more abstract domains of ethical and political philosophy), with a mentality anchored in a profoundly influential and persistent hostility to central features of the Enlightment faith in the theoretical and practical autonomy of the human subject. And during the 1990s it has also brought him into increasingly explicit engagement with various forms of self-declaredly post-modernist, post-enlightenment and post-humanist thought, the complex intellectual lineage which can be traced back from Heidegger to Nietzsche in particular. His thinking thus spans a period in which the dominant site of critical cultural and social-political reflection has moved from a broadly Marxist and socialist-inspired critique to an apparently more radical challenge to traditional patterns of thought: the disruptive strategies of post-structuralist approaches, the political interventions of a self-consciously pluralist project of discursive contestation, the agonistic posture of post-foundationalist critique.

However, it can justifiably be said of Habermas that, while never averse to subjecting his philosophy to constant critical revision, and indeed substantial rearticulation from the early 1970s onwards, he has also never had to repudiate a host of earlier uncritical enthusiasms *en masse* in a hasty and undialectical response to rapidly changing political and ideological circumstances (pre-eminently the unexpectedly sudden demise of so-called 'real existing socialism' in Eastern Europe which Habermas, along with almost all the other members of the Frankfurt School, had never regarded as anything but a petrified form of bureaucratic state socialism). Also, many of his principal ethical and political concerns concerning the internal ideological instability, and consequent legitimation problems, of late capitalist societies have hardly been disconfirmed by the resurgence of anti-universalistic forms of communitarianism and expressly nationalist and ethnic forms of social self-understanding.

To introduce a necessarily schematic presentation of a comprehensive philosophical project so directly with reference to the broader historical context may seem potentially reductive unless there remains a legitimate sense in which 'philosophy is its own time grasped in thought', as Hegel declared. As with all the other representatives of the Frankfurt School, the question of 'mediation' in the broadest sense, the character of the interaction between theoretical and practical reason, constituted *the* central problem bequeathed by the classical tradition of philosophy and social-political critique, and particularly of its self-conscious modern form from Kant to German Idealism to Marx. The original task of 'critical theory' as envisaged by Horkheimer lay in producing a comprehensive articulation and defence of critical reflection which did not merely dissolve the classical problems and persisting aporias of philosophy into an abstract metacritique of the special sciences (as pure methodology) or simply abandon them for the comprehensive cultivation of an empirical research field comprising the totality of the natural and especially the (so-called) social and political sciences. The classical philosophical heritage, rearticulated and transformed in terms of a sustained critical theory of the social domain, animates Habermas's thought to the same extent as it did the earlier exponents of the school. The pre-eminent problem that needs to be addressed by any thinker working within this newly defined domain

'between philosophy and social science', as Habermas describes it, concerns the relation of theory and practice, particularly the possibility of developing an adequate understanding of what the latter already effectively involves, however imperfectly realised, and what it might yet become under significantly altered circumstances. In his evolving engagement with this issue, Habermas has subjected the earlier tradition of the Frankfurt School to a comprehensive, if sometimes overhasty and ungenerous, critique. This inevitably raises the question of whether his impressive philosophical corpus represents the legitimate continuation or abandonment of the defining features of that tradition, whether the now standard distinction between the first and second 'generation' of critical theorists is more an axiological than an essentially chronological one.

The question of whether Habermas's project in the last analysis amounts to the relinquishment rather than the renewal of the Frankfurt tradition can only be decided if the evolution of his thought as a whole is carefully considered in the light of his professed desire to provide a fundamental 'reorientation' of that tradition under transformed intellectual, cultural and social circumstances. Despite constant self-criticism and change of emphasis on his part, there is no good reason to divide his thought simplistically into two, or even more, radically discontinuous phases: there is no 'epistemological rupture' supposedly bifurcating fundamentally incompatible theoretical approaches like that sometimes postulated in the case of Marx; nothing that straightforwardly corresponds to the distinction of pre-critical and critical perspectives in Kant's development. What is it, then, that essentially binds together the diverse strands of Habermas's philosophical project through its complex evolution and prevents it simply from representing an 'impressive eclecticism', as Adorno once claimed of Cassirer's thought? In this respect it is at least symptomatic that his first major work to attract significant critical attention was precisely entitled *Theory and Praxis* (1963).

The early work and the reception of Marx

By the time he published *Theory and Praxis*, Habermas had already engaged in serious and sustained reflection concerning the central claims and premises of the tradition of Western Marxism inaugurated by Karl Korsch and George Lukács in the early 1920s. His own early philosophical education had emerged against the dominant background of existential phenomenology, hermeneutics and a *Lebensphilosophie* of Diltheyan origin which had absorbed many features of the post-Kantian idealist tradition. As in the case of his friend and colleague, Karl-Otto Apel, the relevant figures in Habermas's philosophical background were Ernst Rothacker, Theodor Litt and Karl Löwith. In addition, an enduring dominant presence in German intellectual culture, and indeed in the academic institutions of philosophy through many former and now influential students, was still Martin Heidegger, despite his temporary and ill-fated involvement in the cause of National Socialism. While this intellectual environment and its many fertile philosophical resources in the hermeneutic and phenomenological domains provided an essential stimulus to the young Habermas, he was also particularly struck by many of its manifest moral and political failures and deficiencies in the light of the European catastrophe of 1939–45 and the ideological vacuum which seemed to prevail in West Germany immediately after the War and in the period of initial economic and social reconstruction. This experience of cultural, social and moral dislocation marked a decisive watershed for both Apel and Habermas, as both have since confirmed on many occasions, in their relationship to the German philosophical tradition, and particularly to Kant and his immediate successors. It was their radical disaffection with a kind of degenerated cultural right-Hegelianism, with its appeal to the supposedly 'concrete' givens of national, social life and its hasty relinquishment of the allegedly 'abstract' and universalist ideals of the Enlightenment, that provoked a reappraisal and rearticulation of the Enlightenment and the Idealist heritage and a new openness to the more sophisticated forms of historical materialism developed largely in the wake of Lukács by the first generation of the Frankfurt School.

It is no accident that the fundamental impulse to the rethinking of the Marxist tradition in non-deterministic, and decidedly non-mechanistic, fashion resulted from the progressive abandonment of the 'positivism' which had dominated the development of materialist thought in the later nineteenth century and a concomitant readiness to readdress the idealist sources of the Marxist tradition in bourgeois philosophy from Kant to Hegel. (A similar tendency is also independently observable in the culturalist turn in Italian Marxist theory from Labriola to Gramsci). This actually marked an emphatic return to the original impulse of Marx's own thought which centred upon the relation between social critique and the concrete dynamics of the social system, and therefore essentially with the question of transcending a purely objectivist contemplative relation to that reality and projecting a unification of theory and praxis with an emancipatory intent. The central idealist conception of society as a concrete subject-object was retained in the thought that effective and mature revolutionary change was itself predicated upon a potential self-transformation of the social order by a structurally-privileged group thought the medium of heightened class-consciousness. While the centrality of critical theoretical and practical self-reflection is clearly recognised in Marx's approach, there is also a fateful ambiguity inherent in the notion of human 'praxis' that is implied in his general account of the self-constitution of the species through social labour. Marx held it to be Hegel's central insight, however mystified by an elaborate metaphysics of 'spirit', that the essence of human beings lay precisely in the negating and transformative exercise of human 'labour', in historically-developing and specific forms, upon the relative givens of first nature. While this materialist reformation of Hegelian 'negativity' in terms of the work model of activity certainly answers to one familiar sense of 'practice' (transformation) as opposed to pure 'theory' (contemplation), it also serves to obscure, and if radically universalised even to displace, the original distinctions, derived ultimately from Aristotle, between various irreducible forms of human practical activity like 'techne' (the exercise of productive skill upon objects), 'poesis' (the creative making of cultural artifacts) and 'praxis' (the interaction of acting social beings endowed with a certain historical self-understanding). Understanding practice pre-eminently on the model of work, and the instrumental action associated with it, thus effaces the specifically human dimension of mutual interaction predicated on shared, or potentially shared, norms of behaviour. Like Arendt and Heidegger in this respect, the early Habermas is intent on rearticulating these crucial distinctions and in drawing attention to the ethical-political problems that ensue when they are ignored. In this sense, Habermas would see the often remarked absence of any adequate concept of 'the political domain' in Marx (except as an indefinitely postponed problem for the future beginning of 'history' proper) as symptomatic of a much deeper inadequacy in the understanding of 'praxis' itself.

This partly explains the structure of *Theory and Practice* which is essentially an ensemble of critical essays examining various stages in the evolution of the concept of 'praxis' in the tradition, and especially the transformations to which the concept has been subject with the development of modern philosophy proper, the ineluctable advance of the empirical sciences, and the concomitant weakening of dogmatic religious and metaphysical conceptions of the world. Habermas understands 'labour' to include all the forms of 'purposive-rational' action that are governed by an instrumental logic; action, that is, which aims to realise 'defined goals under given conditions'. Within this Habermas further distinguishes 'instrumental action' proper which organises the means that are appropriate or inappropriate according to the criteria of effective control over reality, and 'strategic action' which essentially depends on the correct evaluation of possible alternative choices, resulting from calculation supplemented by values and maxims. The 'values' that play a determining role in strategic action are calculative ones which are themselves given as preferences not further justifiable in terms of instrumental rationality. It is this form of rationality that is typically embodied in the procedures and methods of natural science and technology as its practical application of such scientific knowledge, and is reflected in the common assumption that technological behaviour is itself value-free, a question simply of devising appropriate means for attaining specific ends. Habermas claims that scientific knowledge and technical development obeys 'a logic which corresponds to the structure of purposive-

rational action regulated by its own results, which is in fact the structure of work' (Habermas, 1971a, p. 87).

It is from this structure that Habermas wishes to demarcate the concept of 'interaction' which specifies the pragmatic domain of relations between human communicating subjects and practical agents. If work as the belabouring and transformation of objects (whether in a relatively simple form of fabrication or in the most highly sophisticated forms of technical intervention in natural processes) involves a unilateral and instrumental relationship over an objectified and quantifiable realm, then interaction by contrast can only be defined in terms of the communication between subjects predicated on a minimum of mutual understanding (something which is equally presupposed even in relations of utmost inequality and defective reciprocity such as the master-slave relation). If work involves the application of technical rules to external reality, the sphere of interaction is dependent upon 'practical' norms in the moral sense. Interaction is therefore equivalent to what Habermas also calls 'communicative action': action governed by 'binding consensual norms which define reciprocal expectations about behaviour and which must be understood and recognised by at least two acting subjects' (ibid., p. 92). If action as work is essentially characteristic of the spheres of natural science, technology and bureaucracy as the calculation and management of human 'resources' as the appropriate objectified language describes them, then interaction, however one-sided and inadequate it may be, characterises the social and personal sphere of values and norms. In so far as interaction presupposes a direct relation to the assumed or contested validity, the felt and recognised bindingness or otherwise, of norms and values, it maintains a necessary connection with what Weber called 'substantive rationality', with 'reason' in the classical and modern philosophical sense (that is, the question as to the proper nature of the 'good life' for man or the more modern concern with the nature of justice and fairness). It thus inevitably transcends the purely instrumental assessment of means for the successful accomplishment of presupposed and merely 'given' ends, or what Weber had called 'formal rationality'.

The distinction between substantive reason and instrumental rationality thereby echoes the distinction in post-Kantian philosophy between the sphere of reason proper and that of the 'understanding'.

Habermas holds that the task of critical theory is to examine precisely this realm of interaction if it is to pursue fruitfully and consolidate its characteristic critique of unjust and inadequate social conditions that structurally and systematically tend to frustrate the realisation of the concrete ideals symbolically sedimented in the liberal ideology typically produced by modern industrial societies. If the Marxist account of social labour as the essence of human (historical) 'nature' is inadequate to ground the normative principles implicit in the project of human emancipation in ethical terms, Habermas finds that the traditional Marxist analysis of the dynamics of capitalist society has also proved to be a severely limited one in actual social and historical terms. The Enlightenment belief in the progressive emancipation of human beings through the intelligent and benevolent application of scientific knowledge, advancing hand in hand with the ever-increasing technological power over nature in general, was reflected in the general philosophy of history implied by historical materialism itself. The particular state of science and technology was directly connected to the stage reached in the development of the forces of production in an ultimately progressive manner since the latter were eventually expected to produce a crisis within the existing relations of production and facilitate the transition to a more advanced state of production and social organisation alike. Habermas does not actually deny, any more than Horkheimer and Adorno did, the systematic range of insights which the Marxist analysis has effectively produced with respect to the unstable dynamics of capitalist production and the entire process of the industrial revolution, and especially its critical examination of the anthropological (and ideological) presuppositions involved in the systems of classical political economy which first sought to explain and, in part, legitimate this process. However, it is certainly arguable that historical materialism in its classical form (not to mention the even more problematic versions of Marxist-Leninism and dialectical materialism that eventually evolved from it under the influence of growing positivist modes of thought in the later nineteenth century) remains implicitly predicated upon a quasi-naturalistic philosophy of history that reveals analogous features to the highly problematic 'grand narratives' of universal history and the secularised theodicies of the Enlightenment and German Idealist tradition.

Like almost all the other members of the Frankfurt school, Habermas was more convinced by the powerful immanent critique of then contemporary capitalist society and liberal ideology in Marxist thought, the negative diagnosis of the historical present as it were, than he was with the optimistic assumptions concerning the viability, and indeed tendential inevitability, of quite new forms of social organisation arising internally with the dissolution of the capitalist mode of production, with the reassuring teleological prognosis as it were. Along with many other sympathetic critics, Habermas was extremely sceptical about expecting social progress to result in and of itself from the dynamics of labour and the supersession of capitalist culture and bourgeois society, especially given the foreshortened concept of 'praxis' and the absence of anything resembling an adequate account of the political sphere as such. This concern is also reinforced by what Habermas takes to be an inadequate analysis of the nature of advanced capitalism, at least in the light of subsequent and profound transformations in the way in which the basically unaltered system of production had adapted to cope with endemic crises (although not necessarily to prevent them or obviate their frequently disastrous social effects). However, further radical developments in the relation between what had been called the 'superstructure' (the realm of ideology, but also of science and social 'culture' in general) and the economic 'base' of society had also begun to transform directly the nature of economic life and production. Foremost among these is the changed role of accumulated scientific and technical knowledge within modern societies and the effect which this had had upon the structure and character of the political domain itself (in the broadest sense as the public arena for critical debate, dissemination of ideas, the formation and the contestation of opinion). Habermas argued that, in fundamental respects, the very forces which seemed to promise imminent emancipation from misery, want and gross inequality could also exercise an increasingly adverse and stultifying effect upon the political domain itself.

The critique of scientism

In a relatively early work, *The Structural Transformation of the Public Sphere* of 1962, Habermas had already responded to, and further developed, central aspects of Marcuse's critique of contemporary political culture in a way that anticipated the trajectory of his own critical thought over the succeeding decades. The public sphere refered to here is the open space of potential critical debate that first began to develop in the culture of the European Enlightenment with the gradual transition from still largely feudal, and essentially autocratic, forms of political absolutism to the increasingly self-consciously bourgeois polities of early modernity. This sphere was constituted through a wide-ranging, albeit loose, network of agencies, groups and public spaces like the clubs, salons, learned societies and professional associations of like-minded educated citizens, the rapidly expanding domain of journals, broadsheets and newspapers, all of them organs for the articulation and formation of a potentially informed and critical kind of 'public opinion' before which the established authorities of government and the administration of justice increasingly had to legitimate themselves if their power was to be exercised effectively. Obviously socially limited to the bourgeois class itself, this sphere nevertheless, according to Habermas, constituted an essential dimension of the emerging modern societies, a sphere in which literary and aesthetic criticism, the critique of orthodox religion and inherited forms of traditional beliefs and values generally, and the political dissemination of ideas could unite in furthering something akin to what Kant had called the 'culture of reason'. Being based upon early liberal notions of free intellectual association and 'publicity' in the broadest sense, this sphere also constituted in principle an incipiently democratic space where fundamental ideological questions of social morality and public policy could be discussed.

In his analysis of what has become of this potential space for informed argument and possible dissent in

the course of the subsequent historical development of the bourgeois nation state, Habermas is hardly more sanguine about the immediate prospects for maintaining, reinforcing or expanding the sphere of effective democratic will-formation than any of the other earlier critical theorists of the 'one-dimensional society' or the 'totally administered world of culture' like Marcuse and Adorno. Habermas traces the way in which this, already limited but embryonically democratic, dimension of early modern capitalist societies had been increasingly marginalised and effectively repressed by a host of complex developments in industrial society. The dysteleological end-result of this process lies in the characteristic politics of 'publicity' in the modern sense, where the very term 'government' can often be replaced by that of the 'administration' and the domain of political debate has been increasing transformed into the field of opinion management, market research and party-political presentation. The suitability of such a 'public' itself as the material object of empirical social and political science is what constitutes the latter's undeniable utility in the understanding and functioning of modern society, but it is arguable that the inner affinity of object and method here merely testifies to the persistent reification of that public sphere with its pseudo-homogeneous consensus of 'opinion'. This corresponds to the increasing domination of a technocratic consciousness in general and an expressly positivistic self-understanding on the part of the prevailing forms of social science. Habermas famously defines positivism in the broadest sense as 'the denial of reflection', a forgetting and marginalisation of critical thought about substantive ends and values which has far-reaching theoretical and practical consequences. If the earlier form of liberal bourgeois ideology had claimed universal, in principle intersubjectively-binding validity for its social values, the intrinsic tendency of modern politics is paradoxically a form of depoliticisation (that is, if the 'political' is still to be understood in anything resembling the classical sense Habermas had investigated in *Theory and Praxis*). If critical social theory as envisaged by the founders of the Frankfurt School had retained this link with the substantive philosophical question of 'the good life', although it had rejected the traditional metaphysical attempts to ground and explain the latter by recourse to an allegedly invariant human 'nature' or the intrinsic ontological structure of reality, modern social science has dissolved the pertinence of the question itself and modelled itself essentially upon the model of natural science, thereby relinquishing the classical normative status of reason as critical instance in favour of empirical description, analysis and prediction.

If it is to fulfil its classical emancipatory and critical function then critical theory is now required to focus attention upon the theoretical deficiencies and practical consequences of this scientist self-understanding. Habermas first outlined a systematic vision of an alternative approach in his 1968 book *Knowledge and Human Interests* which supplies the theoretical scaffolding for his earlier historical analyses of the genealogy of the theory-practice problem and attempts to justify the necessity of his conceptual distinctions between instrumental rationality and practical reason as a sphere of mutual interaction and self-understanding. It is worth noting here the considerable range of traditions to which Habermas appeals, and in particular, his openness to engagement with American pragmatism as inaugurated by William James and, especially, C. S. Peirce. Despite some early interest in Dewey, principally based upon a shared hostility to the Platonic contemplative bias of traditional philosophy and a desire to rehabilitate the somatic moment of engaged knowing, it cannot be said that anything like the full range of pragmatist thought had been assimilated, or even remotely addressed, by the mainstream traditions of Continental European thought, and indeed, there is a marked hostility in Adorno to what he understands as pragmatism: namely a positivist ideology of successful technological management of outer nature for the purpose of satisfying uncritically 'given' needs and aspirations of a reified subject naturalistically understood in exclusively functionalist terms. Habermas's reception of the pragmatist approach is more differentiated, although by no means uncritical of functionalist tendencies in the social sciences, and centres on the idea of articulating distinct 'interests' which regulate our particular approaches to understanding the external material and social world. In *Knowledge and Human Interests*

Habermas is chiefly concerned, in the wake of Dilthey's attempt to demarcate the distinctive realms of 'explanation' and 'understanding', with distinguishing the appropriate operationalist methods of natural science (aimed at the experimental control and prediction of objectified processes) from the hermeneutic approach necessarily involved in the humanistic and cultural disciplines (ultimately oriented to the achievement of human self-understanding). Even science itself, according to Habermas's reformulation of fundamental insights first systematically developed by Peirce and the later Royce, cannot, as a practice, be understood in objectivist terms since it is ultimately dependent upon a certain interested perspective on natural processes and the effects we can operationally produce and predict with regard to these processes. The actual practice of science is not theoretically 'disinterested' in any straightforward sense at all, and it always remains dependent upon a starting point in a common social life-world in which ordinary communicative language is already presupposed if the scientist is to make results and explanations intelligible. (Here Habermas also recuperates essential insights of the later Husserl who had similarly questioned the objectivistic self-understanding of modern science and the regnant philosophical naturalism associated with it). The successful prosecution of scientific activity thus ineluctably presupposes a social framework, both the community of rational researchers as the ultimate horizon of the scientific enterprise itself and the general given life-world of socialised and interacting human beings whose concrete existence is not exhausted by their scientific function.

This level of reflection upon science implies another kind of equally essential knowledge: one that is based upon a different original 'interest' and different conditions of objectivity. What Habermas, following in the wake of Dilthey's hermeneutics, calls the cultural or human sciences also require the exercise of mutual understanding and not merely explanation from an allegedly disinterested external standpoint. (The German title of 'Geisteswissenschaften' or 'sciences of spirit' originally served to translate the domain of what philosophers like J. S. Mill in the English tradition still called 'the moral sciences', as opposed to the natural sciences, and the word also clearly reveals something of the origins of this hermeneutic tradition in the philosophy of German Idealism, Hegel in particular, with its conception of objective and absolute spirit as irreducible domains of cultural self-understanding in the broadest sense: the social and political sphere of morality and justice, cultural objectivations of human practice, developed theoretical legitimations of specific forms of life in ideologies, institutionalised practices and theoretical discourses.) Dilthey had been largely content to rearticulate the nature/spirit distinction of post-Kantian idealist philosophy in terms of a two-fold structure of the natural and cultural sciences, dissolving the apparently obsolete and dogmatic metaphysical dimension that still clung obstinately to the Hegelian idea of 'absolute' knowledge and 'absolute' spirit into a kind of higher humanistic sociology of culture and a historical typology of world-views which made no untenable transhistorical claims for itself. While helping to break down the monopolistic hold of naturalist epistemology over all spheres of life in positivist philosophy, it was less clear that the appeal to empathetic understanding ('*Verstehen*') was itself capable of facilitating anything more than an ultimately descriptive and historical phenomenology of the peculiarly human domain of self-creation in the medium of language and culture. Husserl had already suspected that hermeneutics and cultural '*Lebensphilosophie*' of this kind, while avoiding cruder forms of reductionism, still failed to provide an adequate account of the ultimate normative foundations of our practices and, having rejected the quest for such grounding as 'metaphysical', only risked falling back into another more differentiated form of cultural and historical relativism.

Habermas also shares this suspicion of an ultimate conflation of the grounds of description and legitimation, in Kantian terms of the collapsing of the distinction between the question *quid facti* and the question *quid juris*, and this fundamental concern can be traced through all Habermas's major writings from *Knowledge and Human Interests* with ever greater clarity and emphasis up to his 1992 contributions to legal thought in *Between Facts and Norms*. In his earlier work Habermas attempts to redress the short-comings of scientistic and hermeneutic approaches alike by drawing attention to what he calls a third interest animating all our attempts at self-understanding beyond that of predictive control of outer nature and mutual symbolic understanding, namely the irreducible emancipatory interest in 'self-reflection'. Habermas does not even deny the relevance of methods at home in the natural sciences to the analysis of specifically social practices but insists that critical social science must look beyond the systematic identification of law-like regularities and correlations in the field of social phenomena. A genuinely *critical* social science which wishes to dissolve the petrified 'nature-like' appearance of social reality would have to acknowledge such 'empirical' findings without reifying them, must determine 'when theoretical statements grasp invariant regularities of social action as such and when they express ideologically frozen relations of dependence that can in principle be transformed' (Habermas, 1971b, p. 175).

The communicative-linguistic turn

All Habermas's original theoretical and practical concerns find an impressive, if provisional, resolution in the massive work which can be said to project all the salient features of Habermas's later development, namely the *Theory of Communicative Action*. This can be seen as the focal point to which all the earlier analyses of interaction and instrumental reason had been tending and it is certainly the place where Habermas articulates his own argument with the prior tradition of critical theory in its most fundamental and comprehensive form. Schematically expressed, and this itself harbours a host of difficult interpretive problems with the tradition under analysis and critique, Habermas claims here to reorient the programme of critical theory on the theoretical side, precisely in order to do justice to the demands made upon by the changed character of advanced industrial societies on the practical side. This can partly be seen as an extension of the Frankfurt School's general critique of established Marxism as formulated by Adorno, Horkheimer and Marcuse, but it is arguably a more radical reconstruction and critique altogether. Habermas formulates this reorientation in terms of a necessary change of intellectual paradigm: the move from a traditional 'philosophy of consciousness' to a 'philosophy of intersubjectivity'. Historically speaking, there is clearly something fundamentally problematic about the implied claim that the prior tradition was predicated upon an essentially monological conception of self-consciousness, especially since Habermas draws particularly heavily in this connection upon pragmatist thinkers like G. H. Mead, in addition to Peirce and Dewey, all of whom were powerfully influenced by German Idealism in the first place. (It is probably Fichte and Hegel who contributed most to expanding and concretising the monological assumptions of Kantian moral philosophy and introducing the thematic of social intersubjectivity by recourse to the principle of 'reciprocal recognition'. It is also from Fichte's further radicalisation of the primacy of the practical in Kant's philosophy, that the progressive acquisition of self-knowledge must function as the horizon for all other forms of knowledge, that Habermas's notion of a fundamental 'interest' of and in reason itself is ultimately derived).

Habermas attempts to legitimate the normative claims of his own approach by recourse to a linguistically-founded quasi-transcendental argument concerning the necessary presuppositions of intelligible discourse. In a crucial and famous passage in his first major work, Habermas had programmatically claimed, with echoes of Kant, that:

> The human interest in autonomy and responsibility is not mere fancy, for it can be apprehended *a priori*. What raises us out of nature is the only thing whose nature we can know: language. Through its structure, autonomy and responsibility are posited for us. Our first sentence expresses unequivocally the intention of universal and unconstrained consensus. (Habermas, 1971b, p. 314).

The heart of the theory is therefore an account of the normative structure of language itself, or a 'universal pragmatics', which becomes, as it were, the embodiment of 'the fact of reason' in Kant, centred upon the ideal discursive redemption of all possible validity claims. This is developed in conjunction with a fallibilistic theory of truth according to which, rationally justified consensus at the end of enquiry functions as a criterion of truth (although not of the exhaustive meaning or nature of truth) and plays an analogous role to a Kantian regulative idea. And again, for rather Kantian reasons, Habermas thinks that this formal level of normative structure is the only one intrinsically capable of providing a critical grounding of universal values and principles independently of contingent and problematic appeals to the purely empirical domain, to anthropological features and variable cultural givens. The universally legitimisable dimension of a self-consciously 'modern' moral perspective cannot itself be based, like classical ethics or traditional natural law theory, directly upon philosophical assumptions about the 'nature' of man, or even upon a historicised version of that tradition which makes appeal to a range of essential needs as the Marxist approach has tended to do. That is to say that, while Habermas does not in the last instance ignore the impulse of all eudaimonist ethics, the principle of happiness and self-realisation, in Marxian terms the gratification of the sensuous being of man under conditions of freedom and dignity, he insists in the first instance that moral theory articulate the normative conditions and general procedures under which possible agreement about the satisfaction of needs and social priorities can, in principle, be democratically arrived at. Since linguistic communication between subjects is a necessary condition of any and every social order, the values implicit in the very practice of discourse itself, assuming they can be uncovered and identified, would be able to claim a truly universal normative validity for human beings as rational, that is, speaking, animals.

Habermas regards these linguistically presupposed values as applicable in principle to the criticism of any human society, although the degree to which they actually become historically explicit, theoretically grasped and practically applied involves a retelling of the complex story of modernisation and secularisation that was so powerfully and, in Habermas's interpretation, monolithically interpreted by Weber. We can therefore say that Habermas's position certainly implies an emphatic philosophy of history in the Enlightenment manner: namely, as the story of increasing emancipation through autonomous theoretical and practical reflection. The 'necessity' which attaches to this process is the opposite of a dogmatic providential or naively metaphysical account which is usually associated with the project of a philosophy of history, and does not, in principle, exclude the real possibility of stagnation or even atavisms and regressive developments. As with Kant (and arguably also the idealist versions that followed in his wake), a philosophy which undertakes to descry the process of 'reason in history' is an attempt to identify how, and to what extent, the human species can be said to have made any universal moral, as opposed to merely technical or cultural, progress: it is a retrospective reconstruction from the standpoint of the present of how we have come to develop theoretically, and instantiate practically, the idea of rational autonomy as our central guiding principle, the one which ineliminably, and not merely contingently and locally, now belongs to our innermost self-understanding as modern agents. This history does not and cannot itself 'ground' the validity of rational autonomy but displays the process of its evolving recognition and conscious appropriation; or, as Marx had adapted and reformulated Hegel's teleological perspective of freedom as the ultimate horizon of history: 'Reason has always existed but not always in a rational form'.

Discourse theory and ethics

Habermas's universal pragmatics identifies a basic series of values or 'validity claims' involved in the structure of linguistic communication. The four validity claims he uncovers reflect the complex intelligible structure of language with regard to comprehensibility, rightness or appropriateness, truth, and truthfulness (sincerity). We can paraphrase this by explaining that, in any context of meaningful communicative interaction, the speaker has to select a comprehensible expression in order that the speaker and hearer can understand one another; the speaker further has to have the intention of communicating a true propositional content in order that the listener can share the knowledge of the speaker; the speaker also has to want to express

her or his intentions truthfully in order that the hearer can believe in the speaker's utterance (can trust the latter); finally, the speaker has to select an utterance that is right in the light of existing norms and values in order that the hearer can accept the utterance, so that both speaker and hearer can agree with one another in the utterance concerning a recognised normative background. Thus, the various validity claims correspond to the sort of challenge that can be raised in principle by any other partner in dialogue: we could challenge the claim as unintelligible, or as untrue, inappropriate or disingenuous.

Habermas argues that the innate structure of universally human communicative competence inevitably involves the understanding and mastery of these values as 'the basis of our ideas of truth, freedom and justice'. Clearly there is no compelling ground of a causal nature that ensures that any challenge to a claim will meet with a dialogical response, and such challenges to certain claims have, for the most part, and in many respects still are, met in a dogmatic or authoritarian manner: by appeals to unquestionable authority, tradition and established usage, or even to the supposed common sense of 'what we all simply know', or, in more extreme cases, by the threat of violence, persecution and open prohibition. Habermas argues that, despite these obvious possibilities, indeed probabilities, an appropriately 'enlightened' response to questions of justification and legitimation is inscribed in our very capacity in principle to distinguish and identify these validity claims as enmeshed in the meaningful use of language. The principles of truth, freedom and justice which Habermas identifies as the core values must be grasped in the counterfactual light of a consensus theory of theoretical (factual and scientific) and moral-practical truth (rightness). No consensus can be regarded as valid if it were only to be arrived at through intrinsically flawed methods or by external pressure. It is true for a moral or a factual claim that it is vindicated only when it is the object of unrestrained communication, when the participants in discourse are subject exclusively to what Habermas often describes as 'the peculiarly unforced force of the better argument'. In this sense discourse presupposes a reference to an always anticipated 'ideal speech situation' which is free from external distortion through unequal power and in which the participants are prepared in principle to be challenged and their conclusions rendered provisional in the light of future and better evidence or more compelling argumentation.

The consensus theory of truth, as Habermas develops it, has far-reaching practical-moral implications and it transpires that the notion of an ideal speech situation and potentially unrestricted dialogue provides a necessarily presupposed horizon of permanent critique. Far from being incompatible with more plural and provisional claims, Habermas regards this emphatic return of the Kantian-liberal moment as a prerequisite for the principled defence of the democratic process, which in no way precludes, but rather actively encourages, the fundamental criticism of existing institutions or modes of decision-making in social and political life.

In this connection, Habermas's expressly cognitive and universalist ethics has provoked much criticism in the light of current philosophical criticisms of all foundationalist enterprises as lingering monuments to an obsolete 'metaphysics of truth', a classical philosophical approach which none the less continues to exercise political effects as an ideological justification of institutionally-secured power relations. Some critics see Habermas's project as merely the latest and possibly most sophisticated incarnation of an already discredited rationalism, as a kind of ineradicably logocentric (and Eurocentric) will to power that is constitutively insensitive to the claims of concrete particularity, to the somatic dimension as such, to the realm of the 'unconscious', to the domain of alterity and 'difference' in general. However, it is difficult to sustain many of the more generalised of such criticisms when Habermas's complex position is examined in accordance with its declared aims and objectives. (A considerable measure of controversy has arguably been produced here by essentially differing conceptions of what the scope and character of philosophy or critical reflection under modern conditions is and its relations with other forms of cultural criticism). Habermas's pragmatically-oriented position does not involve him in a traditional 'foundationalist' epistemology nor in any dogmatic form of metaphysical

realism which might privilege the claims of the supposedly 'given'. The values which this theory regards as always already operative in communicative action are not themselves intended to determine materially the specific and substantive content of what counts, or could come to count, as 'the good life' in relation to admittedly changing social and historical circumstances, the current state of empirical knowledge, the stage of technological development etc. The abstract philosophical articulation of the principles cannot actually prejudge the practical and hermeneutic dimension of social life itself, namely the process of application and interpretation which is always required in the communicative medium of the concrete life-world itself. Habermas holds that this perspective is not merely externally or contingently linked to the democratic self-understanding of modern society but that it is the one intrinsically appropriate conceptual framework for such a form of life precisely because it takes its point of departure from the fact that, in principle, nothing can be taken for granted any longer, no truths or social values assumed as authoritatively binding on traditional, religious or metaphysical grounds and as beyond challenge and contestation.

Historically and sociologically this can be regarded as a summary statement of what it is to inhabit an essentially secularised and pluralistic culture. In so far as a self-declared form of post-foundational relativism claims that the very concept of communicative reason suppresses or distorts freedom, or ideologically privileges a local cultural community as the properly universal and 'human' one in a closed teleological hierarchy, the criticism itself also implicitly appeals to a normative perspective that goes unclarified and undefended only because it de facto corresponds to certain widely-shared modern, and typically 'liberal', values. The apparently democratic-looking argument that modernist values should never be applied to the mores of traditionalist societies itself transcends the perspective of traditionalist kinds of justification to make a potentially universal moral claim based upon concepts of equality and recognition of diversity etc. (as well as simplifying the internal complexity and contestation already at work within apparently more stable and cohesive forms of traditional society). In this connection, the marked growth of self-conscious internal critique on the part of many modern disciplines and practices which have been among those especially prone to ideology (ethnology, anthropology, comparative linguistics, social history, for example, on the one hand and the spheres of medical and psychiatric intervention and control on the other) is regarded by Habermas less as a radical counter-movement to the universalist pretensions of 'modernity' itself than as a particularly conspicuous expression of its inner normative logic, the presence of critical self-reflection *within* the domain of developing discourses.

Nevertheless, Habermas has also had to address the common problems besetting formalist moral theories in general. Rigorous formalist accounts fail to reflect the fact that our understanding of norms, the act of making intelligible to ourselves what a principle does, can or should mean, necessarily involves more than the bare principle itself contains. The conditions of application and interpretation of a principle are ultimately constitutive of the sense of the principle: it is in the light of the latter that its instantiations are grasped as such but it is only with reference to possible examples that the principle can be grasped and identified. Such seemingly obvious and uncontroversial principles as equality have clearly emerged from a protracted struggle and contestation of what a 'person' is, what her or his 'rights' are understood to mean in practice, etc. The principle of equality of treatment in general (the problematics of discrimination, the extension of new entitlements or the modification of older ones, and the appropriate identification of the relevant features which are to ensure inclusion or exclusion) illustrates this difficulty particularly well. However, it is important to see what Habermas's apparent rehabilitation of a Kantian-type moral theory does *not* entail. There is an obvious sense in which it is no longer strictly Kantian since it does not attempt to produce a monolithic formalist account of the entire ethical domain as such and acknowledges its own dependence upon an antecedent and 'thicker' domain of ethical relations and shared values which must already obtain in the existing life-world. Habermas proceeds rather with a double model which is intended to resolve some of the familiar problems of

Kantian ethics classically articulated by Hegel, without at the same time yielding up the fundamental intuitive appeal of the principle of universalisability as an ineliminable feature of rightness and justice. He specifically defines the formal dimension of discourse ethics, its purely procedural injunctions concerning the prosecution of argument and the appropriate conditions for rational discussion, as the sphere of 'morality' in a quasi-Kantian sense (in so far as it systematically abstracts from the material content of our claims or need interpretations). But he equally acknowledges the indispensability of the further sphere of concrete values and norms, enculturated habits of conduct, with the ethical and spiritual ideals already embedded, or newly developing, within our varying conceptions of the good life as those conceptions come into contact with alternative ideals and images of potential fulfilment, with other hitherto untried and unexplored possibilities of human flourishing. This realm broadly corresponds to that of concrete ethical life in the Hegelian sense of *Sittlichkeit*, or what communitarians are apt to describe as substantively shared 'forms of life' which are not deducible from merely formal principles and are intrinsically dependent upon the ongoing, although not necessarily uncontested, life of the tradition (or more precisely of complexly interacting traditions).

It is here, if anywhere, that the apparently rather neglected dimension of aesthetic experience in the broadest sense, as compared with the prominent role conceded to art by the first generation of critical theorists, especially by Adorno and Marcuse in their different ways, also assumes an appropriate place for Habermas. Given that philosophical reflection alone cannot supply the motivating impulse, the concrete hopes and aspirations, or the felt need for enlightenment about our legitimate human desires, it certainly falls to the sphere of art as one of its possible functions, if not indeed its only vocation, to illuminate other possibilities of human life, either directly through images and intimations of concrete happiness and uncoerced reconciliation or indirectly, *ex negativo*, through the exposure of unjust, unfruitful or humiliating conditions of life which hinder or prevent self-knowledge or self-fulfilment. Just as the intrinsic orientation towards the quest of reasonable agreement in Habermas's thought as a whole in no way prejudices the interest in exploring differences or envisaging alternative forms of life and conduct, so too the emphasis upon progressive self-realisation and the construction of a secure, but not impermeable, individual and collective social identity through sustained symbolic cultural interaction with one another in no way privileges an ethic or aesthetic of beauty and reconciliation as against critical practices of contestation or alienation. In this, as in the totality of his thought, Habermas reveals himself as a principled protagonist of pluralism and an articulate defender of what he calls 'the unity of reason in the multiplicity of its voices'. We are always already rational, the necessary presupposition of legitimate critique of perceived injustice or oppression, but we can always strive to be so more effectively, more sensitively and more universally.

Bibliography

Writings

A full list of works by and on Habermas up to 1981 can be found in René Gorzen, *Jürgen Habermas: Eine Bibliographie seiner Schriften und der Sekundärliteratur 1952–1981*, Frankfurt: Suhrkamp, 1982.

Habermas, Jürgen (1989a), *The Structural Transformation of the Public Sphere*, trans. T. Burger, Cambridge: Polity Press.
— (1974), *Theory and Practice*, trans. J. Viertel, London: Heinemann.
— (1971a), *Toward a Rational Society*, trans. J. J. Shapiro, London: Heinemann.
— (1971b), *Knowledge and Human Interests*, trans. J. J. Shapiro, London: Heinemann.
— (1988), *On the Logic of the Social Sciences*, trans. S. Weber Nicholson and J. A. Stark, Cambridge: Polity Press.
— (1983), *Philosophical and Political Profiles*, trans. T. McCarthy, London: Heinemann.
— (1976), *Legitimation Crisis*, trans. T. McCarthy, London: Heinemann.
— (1979), *Communication and the Evolution of Society*, trans. F. G. Lawrence, Boston: Beacon Press.
— (1984), *The Theory of Communicative Action*, vol. I, trans. T. McCarthy, London: Heinemann.
— (1987a), *The Theory of Communicative Action*, vol. II, trans. T. McCarthy, Cambridge: Polity Press.
— (1989b), *Moral Consciousness and Communicative Action*, trans. C. Lenhardt and S. Weber Nicholson, Cambridge: Polity Press.
— (1985), 'Modernity – An Incomplete Project', in H. Foster (ed.), *Postmodern Culture*, London: Pluto.
— (1987b), *The New Conservatism*, trans. S. Weber Nicholson, Cambridge: Polity Press.
— (1987c), *The Philosophical Discourse of Modernity*, trans. F. G. Lawrence, Cambridge: Polity Press.
— (1992), *Post-metaphysical Thinking*, trans. W. M. Hohengarten, Cambridge: Polity Press.
— (1989c), 'Towards a Communication Concept of Rational Will Formation', in *Ratio Juris*, vol. 2.
— (1990), 'Remarks on the Discussion', in *Theory Culture and Society*, 7: 4.
— (1993), *Justification and Application*, trans. C. Cronin, Cambridge: Polity Press.
— (1994), *The Past as Future*, trans. M. Pensky, Cambridge: Polity Press.
— (1996), *Facts and Norms*, trans. W. Rehg, Cambridge: Polity Press.

References and further reading

Benhabib, S. and F. Dallmayr (eds) (1990), *The Communicative Ethics Controversy*, Cambridge, MA: MIT Press.
Bernstein, J. M. (1995), *Recovering Ethical Life: Jürgen Habermas and the Future of Critical Theory*, London: Routledge.
Bernstein, R. J. (1985), *Habermas and Modernity*, Cambridge: Polity Press.
Brand, A. (1990), *The Force of Reason: An Introduction to Habermas's Theory of Communicative Action*, London: Allen and Unwin.
Chambers, S. (1996), *Reasonable Democracy: Jürgen Habermas and the Politics of Discourse*, Ithaca, New York: Cornell University Press.
Held, D. and J. Thompson (eds) (1982), *Habermas: Critical Debates*, London: Macmillan.
Honneth, A., T. McCarthy, C. Offe and A. Wellmer (eds) (1992), Habermas Festschrift: vol. 1: *Philosophical Interventions in the Unfinished Project of the Enlightenment*, vol. 2: *Cultural-Political Interventions in the Unfinished Project of the Enlightenment*, Cambridge, MA: MIT Press.
Ingram, D. (1987), *Habermas and the Dialectic of Reason*, New Haven: Yale University Press.
McCarthy, T. (1978), *The Critical Theory of Jürgen Habermas*, Cambridge MA: MIT Press and London: Hutchinson and Co.
White, S. K. (1988), *The Recent Work of Jürgen Habermas: Reason, Justice and Morality*, Cambridge: Cambridge University Press.
— (1995), *The Cambridge Companion to Habermas*, Cambridge: Cambridge University Press.

Section Seven
STRUCTURALISM

INTRODUCTION

Jeremy Jennings

The definition of structuralism

'This is the moral of my story', wrote Ernest Gellner, 'there is no facile rosy path to the central ideas and tenets of *structuralisme*' (Gellner, 1985, p. 129). And this was a view shared by those taken to be its proponents. 'What is structuralism?', Roland Barthes asked in 1963: 'Not a school, not even a movement (at least, not yet), for most of the authors ordinarily labelled with this word are unaware of being united by any solidarity of doctrine or commitment. Nor is it a vocabulary' (Barthes, 1972, p. 213). Gellner's own solution to the problem rested in highlighting what he took to be structuralism's key idea:

> things have deep natures or constitutions or structures or inner essences, or whatever you wish to call them. These are normally, or perhaps permanently, hidden from view, but the regularities we discern in the phenomena that are open to view emanate, or flow from, those hidden, permanent forms. (Gellner, 1985, p. 130)

Structuralism, he concludes, is a form of 'emanationism'.

Stated with more precision, this has been a frequently repeated definition of structuralism. According to Edith Kurzweil, structuralism is 'the systematic attempt to uncover deep universal mental structures as these manifest themselves in kinship and larger social structures, in literature, philosophy and mathematics, and in the unconscious psychological patterns that motivate human behaviour' (Kurzweil, 1980, p. 1). This is also an opinion voiced by structuralism's practitioners. According to Claude Lévi-Strauss, it 'reveals, behind phenomena, a unity and coherence that could not be brought out by a simple description of the facts, "laid out flat", so to speak, and presented in random order to the enquiring mind' (Lévi-Strauss, 1981, p. 68). The structures sought, in short, are not on the surface but lie beneath or behind empirical reality.

However, if we continue with Lévi-Strauss's definition of structuralism we quickly perceive a further vital dimension of structuralist activity. 'By changing the level of observation and looking beyond the empirical facts to the relations between them', Lévi-Strauss continues,' [structuralism] reveals and confirms that these relations are simpler and more intelligible than the things they interconnect, and whose ultimate nature may remain unfathomable, without this provisional or definite opacity being, as hitherto, an obstacle to their interpretation' (ibid.). What this novel way of looking at things amounted to is spelt out by Terence Hawkes:

> The 'new' perception involved the realization that despite appearances to the contrary the world does not consist of independently existing objects, whose concrete features can be perceived clearly and individually, and whose nature can be classified accordingly . . . in consequence, the true nature of things may be said to lie not in things themselves, but in the relationships which we construct, and then perceive, between them. (Hawkes, 1977, p. 17)

Structuralism, therefore, places the emphasis upon the relational, rather then substantial, nature of objects. As a consequence, it further favours the synchronic over the diachronic, the analysis of relations between components at a single point and across time rather than through time and in a historical or evolutionary perspective. Moreover, the concern to explore networks of relationships that unite and form structures focuses attention upon wholes or totalities rather than individual acts, events, gestures or perceptions.

A theory of meaning

This, in turn, produces a particular theory of meaning or signification. Structuralism, as Jean Piaget pointed out, has its proponents in mathematics and the physical and biological sciences, as well as psychology and the social sciences in general. According to Ernst Cassirer, writing in 1945, it was 'the expression of a general tendency of thought that, in these last decades, has become more and more prominent in almost all fields of scientific research' (in Robey, 1973, p. 1). However, where structuralism, in its narrow and more familiar sense, has chosen to apply its methods and develop its insights has been in the field of human culture, from language to myth and kinship and on to more esoteric subjects such as, in Roland Barthes's case, fashion, food and wrestling. The focus falls upon manifestations of social activity and this, for the obvious reason, that these activities are, in the words of Peter Caws, 'signiferous or "meaning-bearing" ' (Caws, 1988, p. 1).

How is this meaning to be discerned? Gellner tells us that structuralism denies what he terms 'the echo theory of culture', preferring rather to ascertain meaning in terms of 'place in a wider system of symbols'. The assumption is that the system, or structure, operates according to its own set of rules and that these rules generate everything that can occur within it. This itself is far more problematic than it sounds (especially with regard to the transformation of systems or structures), but here it is sufficient to note that, in this, structuralism drew heavily upon the theories and methods of structural linguistics, believing that they were directly applic-

able to the examination of all facets of human culture. As with language, all cultural manifestations of human life could be interpreted as systems of signs. Again, this view received endorsement from structuralism's practitioners. 'Linguistics', according to Barthes, 'is, in the present state of affairs, the true science of structure' and structuralism, therefore, could be taken 'to mean a certain mode of analysis of cultural artifacts, in so far as this . . . originates in the methods of contemporary linguistics' (Barthes, 1970, p. 412).

Why is this so? Most obviously, because language, more than any other aspect of the study of human beings, might be thought to reveal the mind's permanent structures or, what Edmund Leach termed, ' "deep level" universals'. It is this that helps us to grasp the force of Jacques Lacan's claim that the unconscious is structured like a language. Secondly, as Jonathan Culler remarks, linguistics provides two 'fundamental insights' for the study of broader cultural phenomena: 'first, that social and cultural phenomena are signs, and secondly, that they do not have essences but are defined by a network of relations, both internal and external' (in Robey, 1973, p. 21).

The importance of Saussure

To make better sense of this we need briefly to make more detailed reference to the linguistic theories of Saussure, but before doing so there are three points that can be made. The first is that, while the general point about the influence of linguistics upon structuralism holds, it can be over-exaggerated. Interviewed by Didier Eribon, for example, Georges Dumézil indicated that it was only late in life that he read Saussure and then never thoroughly: 'I did not need to wait until high school to sense that the "whole" in all things, whether it concerned a grammar, the style of an author, or even an historical period, called for as much attention as the details and often explained them' (Dumézil, 1987, p. 117). This point gains greater force when we consider Thomas Pavel's threefold distinction of structuralism into *moderate structuralism*, *scientist structuralism* and *speculative structuralism* (Pavel, 1989, pp. 4–5). All used linguistic concepts, but for different purposes and in different ways. It is the second branch, according to Pavel, that 'borrowed more vigorously from linguistics . . . claiming that linguistics was the most advanced among the social and human sciences'. Its 'most typical' representatives were Lévi-Strauss, Barthes (during the 1960s) and the less well-known A. J. Greimas: the fields of application were primarily anthropology, semiology and formal narratology. By contrast, moderate structuralism included those who were attracted to the results of recent linguistics, but refrained from borrowing its concepts and methods *stricto sensu*. They were, therefore, prepared to make use of such other conceptual tools as traditional grammar or simple intuition. The third category – with Louis Althusser and Jacques Lacan at its centre – focused on the formulation of radical political ideologies and, later, 'an elegant despair'. If linguistics informed Lacan's existential psychoanalysis, Althusser believed that, 'in the last instance', it was the economic activity of society that determined our ideological practices.

Second, where this emphasis upon language can lead is amply illustrated by the extravagant remarks of Roland Barthes in his inaugural lecture to the *Collège de France*. 'The object in which power is inscribed for all of human eternity', Barthes proclaimed, 'is language, or to be more precise, its necessary expression: the language we speak and write'. But, Barthes went on, 'the performance of a language system . . . is quite simply fascist: for fascism does not prevent speech, it compels speech'. Freedom, therefore, could only exist outside language but, as language had no exterior, our only option was to 'cheat speech' through the 'labour of displacement'. This 'freedom', he continued, 'is a luxury which every society should afford its citizens: as many languages as there are desires' (in Sontag, 1982, pp. 457–8).

Third, and most important, structuralism's equation of all aspects of our cultural life with language places the emphasis upon how things can be said to signify or produce meaning. This, as we shall see, has important implications for the activity of philosophy itself, but, on this view, what matters is that signification and meaning are neither objective properties of anything in the world nor absolute and transcendent features of the world. Barthes, for

example, was thus prepared to reject the notion of Truth as a useless prejudice.

It is here that Saussure and his *Cours de linguistique générale* played a decisive role, not only in revolutionising the study of language, but in shaping the structuralist project. There are at least three dimensions of his thought that contributed to what amounts to a distinctively structuralist theory of meaning. Building upon developments in linguistics from about the 1870s onwards – and specifically upon the work of what were known as the 'neo-Grammarians' – Saussure's major innovation was to break with an approach to language that saw it as a process of attaching names or words to things and which assumed that there was a substantive or intrinsic link between the word and its object. As such, language, as Saussure conceived it, is a relational or synchronic system of signs, a unified field or self-sufficient system. Language is thus seen less as a set of identities than a network of differences. The implications of this view are clearly stated by Jonathan Culler: 'Each language articulates or organizes the world differently. Languages do not simply name existing categories, they articulate their own' (Culler, 1985, p. 22). This, secondly, is then bolstered by what is undoubtedly the most well-known principle of Saussure's theory of language: the arbitrary nature of the sign. A language, according to Saussure, is a system of signs. However, a sign, as a form that signifies, is itself a combination of a signifier (a word or sound) and the signified (a concept or object). The point is that there is no necessary connection between the two. There is, for example, no intrinsic reason why, in English, the signifier 'sheep' should refer to a particular animal species. Nor does the word 'sheep' have the exactly same meaning as its ostensible French equivalent 'mouton'. Language, in short, is not a nomenclature. Again, Culler spells out the import of this idea:

> signifieds are not pre-existing concepts but changeable and contingent concepts which vary from one state of a language to another. And since the relation between signifier and signifier is arbitrary, since there is no necessary reason for one concept rather than another to be attached to a given signifier, there is therefore no defining

property which the concept must retain in order to count as the signified of that signifier. (ibid., p. 23)

The third key element of Saussurian linguistics is the distinction between *langue*, language as a system, and *parole*, actual speech. It is *langue*, rather than *parole*, according to Saussure, that should be the linguist's principal interest, because it represents a coherent and analysable structure as opposed to individual speech acts. Yet, the point of principal interest for later developments lies here in Saussure's recognition that *langue* is fundamentally a social institution, separated from what was 'individual' and 'ancillary or accidental'. '*Langue*', Saussure stipulated, 'is not a function of the speaking subject: it is the product that an individual enregisters passively' (in Eribon, 1991, p. 74).

The long-term impact of these ideas upon the human sciences has been of immense importance, underpinning the vast field of what has been taken to be semiology and later the 'linguistic turn' associated most obviously with Derridean deconstruction. This is so despite the fact that it is not necessarily the case that language is an appropriate model for other human practices. Many examples could be given to illustrate this impact but one, taken from an interview given by Michel Foucault in 1966, makes the point well. 'The importance of Lacan', Foucault commented, 'comes from the fact that he has explained how, through the discourse of the sick person and the symptoms of his neurosis, it is the system of language – and not the subject – which speaks' (Foucault, 1994, p. 514).

Structuralism as philosophy

This last quotation itself raises what is probably the central problem engendered by structuralism: namely, the nature of the relationship between structure and subject in human history and society. We will return to this. For the moment, we should, perhaps, dwell upon the implications of this structuralist theory of meaning for the activity of philosophy itself. There is, first of all, the charge that structuralism should not be regarded as philosophy at all but rather as social science, the 'science of the sign'. Jean-Marie Domenach wrote:

Some people have accused me of bad faith for having treated structuralism as a philosophy. For is not structuralism a science or, more precisely, a scientific method which has more serious things to do than to respond to the questions of philosophers? (Domenach, 1976, pp. 77–8)

François Wahl, writing in *La philosophie entre l'avant et l'après du structuralisme*, faced a similar difficulty: 'What is "structuralism" in philosophy? Once posed, the question returns upon itself immediately: is there a "structuralism" in philosophy?' (Wahl, 1973, p. 12). The very publication of Wahl's volume testifies to the validity of the question. Published as part of a five-volume series devoted to the theme of *Qu'est-ce que le structuralisme?* the first four volumes – devoted to linguistics (Durot, 1968), poetics (Todorov, 1968), anthropology (Sperber, 1968), and psychoanalysis (Safouan, 1968) – appeared in 1968: Wahl's text appeared only five years later and then was devoted almost exclusively to an examination of Foucault's *Les Mots et les choses*. Someone as distinguished as Pierre Bourdieu has more recently continued this theme. Reflecting upon the development of his own work, he commented: 'Structuralism was very important. For the first time, a social science imposed itself as a respectable, indeed dominant discipline'. Continuing his account, he added that Lévi-Strauss 'ennobled the human science that was thus established, by drawing on Saussure and linguistics, and turned it into a royal science, to which even philosophers were obliged to pay heed' (Bourdien, 1990, p. 6). Again, structuralism's distance from, or indifference to, philosophy was voiced by its practitioners. Lévi-Strauss wrote:

I have no philosophy of my own worth bothering about. I am averse to any proposed philosophical exploitation of my work, and I shall do no more than point out that, in my view, my findings can, at best, only lead to the abjuration of what is called philosophy at the present time. (Lévi-Strauss, 1981, p. 638)

It is, therefore, interesting to note that of the six thinkers included in this *Encyclopedia*'s examination of structuralism, only one of them – Althusser – might be thought of primarily as a philosopher, and even then not one of the first rank. As John Joseph indicates in his article on Saussure, the latter's lectures betray no familiarity with either Frege's complementary work on sense and reference or the 'semiotic' of Charles Sanders Peirce; nor with the work of such eminent contemporaries as Whitehead, Russell or Husserl.

Yet, for all that, Saussure can legitimately be described as a philosopher of language. And structuralism in general certainly indicated a change in philosophical direction that impacted upon the discipline of philosophy, especially in France. Here the previously cited Foucault interview of 1966 helps us perceive this new direction and the change of style and character it denoted. Having argued that Lévi-Strauss (for societies) and Lacan (for the unconscious) had shown us that 'sense' was only 'a type of surface effect' and that what marked us in both 'time and space' was 'le *système*', he went on to explain that

we think on the inside of an anonymous and constraining way of thinking which is that of an epoch and of a language. This way of thinking and this language have their laws of transformation. The task of current philosophy and of all the theoretical disciplines that I have named is to bring to light this way of thinking before thought, this system before all system.

Leaving aside (for the moment) the question of whether, at this or any stage of his career, Foucault can legitimately be cited as a structuralist, and noting the outline of what would later become an archaeology of knowledge, these remarks nevertheless tell us much about a new type of philosophical project. Most obviously, structuralism is disinterested in those philosophical questions that speak of the absolute or transcendent features of the world, but it also goes further. Eric Matthews comments,

Philosophy could no longer take the high *a priori* road, ignoring the empirical conditions of human experience and reasoning to what *must be so* if human beings were to have the kind of experience they do. It had to treat human beings as simply empirical individuals in the world, whose own thoughts were not necessarily transparent to themselves, but whose behaviour and responses were shaped by underlying and largely unconscious structures of thought'. (Matthews, 1996, p. 139)

What, in short, structuralism denoted was a rejection of the primacy of consciousness and, more specifically, the subject. Again, Foucault spelt out the full significance of this:

In appearance, yes, the discoveries of Lévi-Strauss, of Lacan, of Dumézil, belong to what it is convenient to call the human sciences; but what is characteristic of them is that all this research not only effaces the traditional image that we have had of man but, in my opinion, it all tends, in terms of both research and thought, to make completely worthless the very idea of man.

The goal and the task were to break with the inheritance of humanism, an aim fully articulated in Foucault's own conclusion to *Les Mots et les choses* when we are told that man will disappear 'like a face drawn in sand at the edge of the sea'.

The end of the subject

This anti-humanist position, rooted in a dissatisfaction with the phenomenological theory of the subject, found a variety of expressions in the writings of structuralism. Roland Barthes, championing the reader and announcing 'the pleasure of the text', spoke of the 'death of the author'. Likewise, Lacan, reworking Freud, rebelled against the 'ego-centred' character of psychoanalysis and used the basic concepts of Saussure's structural linguistics to illustrate that the conscious life of the individual did not provide the means of its own intelligibility. Perhaps more telling was Althusser's well-known claim, in his 'Reply to John Lewis', that history was 'a process without a subject' (Althusser, 1976, pp. 94–9). Individuals, on this view, were not constitutive of history but constituted subjects in history, not actors but rather supports of social practices that themselves determined those individuals.

Yet the anti-humanist dimension of structuralism was undoubtedly given its most dramatic expression in Lévi-Strauss's response to the publication of Sartre's *Critique de la raison dialectique*. In the concluding chapter of *La Pensée sauvage* (*The Savage Mind*), Lévi-Strauss answered Sartre's espousal of an existential Marxism by proclaiming: 'I believe the ultimate goal of the human sciences to be not to constitute but to dissolve man'. Sartre's praxis of the subject, preserving the ultimate potential of humanity to make history, represented nothing more than an unscientific subjectivism. Later, in the 'Finale' to *L'Homme nu* (*The Naked Man*), he continued the anti-Sartrian theme, announcing that 'the elimination of the subject represents what might be called a methodological need' and concluding that structuralism, by reintegrating man into nature, made 'it possible to disregard the subject – that unbearably spoilt child who has occupied the philosophical scene for too long'.

Who were the structuralists?

If the above is sufficient to indicate the general philosophical orientation of structuralism, who were the structuralists? If we return to our original quotation from Ernest Gellner we will see that he speaks of *structuralisme* rather than structuralism. The clear implication is that structuralism is French, or, less politely, that it was 'a new Parisian intellectual fashion' (Merquior, 1986, p. 2). This is not without some justification. If, for example, we take the six writers included in this Section of the *Encyclopedia*, five – Barthes, Lacan, Althusser, Lévi-Strauss and Dumézil – are French, while Saussure, although Swiss, taught in Paris for ten years before returning to the French-speaking University of Geneva. Left like this, however, we would have a false impression of both the genesis of structuralism and of its practitioners.

The linguistic theories of Ferdinand de Saussure were originally set forth in a series of lectures given during the first decade of the twentieth century and, on the basis of his students' notes, appeared in book form in 1916. It was only in 1956, with the publication by A. J. Greimas of an article entitled 'L'actualité du saussurisme', that his views began to attract a wider academic audience beyond the confines of linguistics. The reasons for this belated interest are various, but are partly a reflection of the fact that the move, or moves, towards structuralism

had sources in developments deeply embedded in the intellectual history of the first half of the twentieth century. If, above all, structuralism is associated with the Paris of the 1960s, it arrived there by a route that, even stated over-simplistically, took in Moscow, Prague and New York.

If this description is accurate, the key figure in the journey must be Roman Jakobson. Born in 1896, his initial interest in literature led him to establish the linguistic circle of Moscow in 1915 and to ally himself with the Russian Formalists. Leaving for Prague in 1920 it was there in 1926 that he helped found the linguistic circle of Prague and, through his Russian colleague Nikolai Trubetskoy, first became acquainted with the theories of Saussure. It was, moreover, at the International Congress of Linguists, held at The Hague in 1928, that Jakobson's Prague Circle, in alliance with Saussure's former Genevan colleagues, Charles Bally and Albert Sechehaye, made common reference to Saussure to describe language as a system. It was Jakobson himself who, at this conference, first used the term 'structuralism' to describe what Saussure had termed 'system'. In 1929 he published his *Remarks on the Phonological Evolution of Russian Compared with Other Slavic Languages*. Moving to Denmark he then worked with Louis Hjelmslev and the members of the second major school of Saussurian linguistics, the Copenhagen linguistic school. Hjelmslev later developed the concept of 'glossematics', the 'algebra of language operating with unnamed entities', in his *Prolegomena to a Theory of Language*. His travels not yet over, the outbreak of war saw Jakobson's arrival in New York where, in 1941, he met the exiled Claude Lévi-Strauss at the New School for Social Research. This is how Lévi-Strauss described the significance of the meeting.

> At the time, I was a sort of naive structuralist. I was doing structuralism without knowing it. Jakobson revealed to me the existence of a body of doctrine already constituted into a discipline, linguistics, of which I had been unaware. It was a revelation. (In Eribon, 1991, p. 40)

It is only a slight exaggeration to say that Lévi-Strauss subsequently imported linguistics not only into anthropology but also into France when he returned to become Deputy-Director of the *Musée de l'homme* in 1948. Jakobson's place in the history of the emergence of structuralism was, however, not yet over. It was he who welcomed André Martinet, the dominant figure in French linguistics during the 1950s, to New York in 1946, where, alongside Jakobson, he became Director of *Word*, the most important review of linguistics in the USA. 'I am', Martinet told François Dosse, 'a Saussurian, but, and I say this with the greatest admiration for Saussure, he was not the founder of structuralism'. This honour, he believed, went to Jakobson and the Prague school (ibid., p. 70). Jakobson's next conquest was Jacques Lacan, whom he first met in 1950. By extending his theories of linguistics to the study of aphasia, and specifically by drawing a distinction between what he termed the metaphoric pole and the metonymic pole that characterised different forms of aphasia, he opened up structuralism to psychoanalysis. Jakobson's influence is clearly visible in Lacan's 1957 text *L'Instance de la lettre dans l'inconscient*. Finally, Jakobson obtained academic posts at Harvard and, later, the Massachusetts Institute of Technology, where his colleagues included Noam Chomsky who, heavily influenced by the American school of linguistics associated with Leonard Bloomfield, would subsequently develop his theory of generative linguistics.

Jakobson's influence was even greater than this short sketch implies – Roland Barthes, for example, made extensive use of his notion of 'shifters' – but its point is to show that when, in the mid-1960s, structuralism achieved what amounted to a philosophical dominance in certain quarters, it was the result of a process of lengthy maturation, involving an extensive cast, and had spanned several continents.

Does this fully answer our question: who were the structuralists? Foucault, for example, proclaimed that 'I have never been a Freudian. I have never been a Marxist and I have never been a structuralist' (in Raulet, 1983, p. 198). Yet this was not how he was seen in the mid-1960s nor how he presented himself at the time (see, for example, Eribon, 1994). Dumézil too, although he subsequently recanted, said much the same thing in 1973 and later complained that he had been 'promoted to the unmerited title of pre-

cursor, and even first theoretician, of structuralism' (Dumézil, 1987, p. 119). Again, Lévi-Strauss complained that 'in France there are only three authentic structuralists: Benveniste, Dumézil and myself'. To place Foucault, Lacan and Althusser amongst the structuralists, he believed, was an aberration (see, Clément, 1996, p. 8). And so it went on. What this reflects is that structuralism was never a fixed or finished doctrine or position but rather a broad tendency, replete with cleavages and differences, and one that was subject to constant evolution. For example, at what point, if at all, did Barthes pass over from being a structuralist to being a post-structuralist, from being the promoter of semiology to being the champion of pleasure? The question, perhaps, only makes sense if structuralism is reduced to a 'narrow caricature' (Culler, 1983, p. 78).

The structuralist decade

Despite this, the structuralists were seen, and indeed are still seen, as an identifiable group. To take just one example: in easily identifiable form and as a circle of intimate friends, they figure in several thinly-disguised autobiographical novels, most notably Philippe Sollers's *Femmes*, published in 1983, and Julia Kristeva's later (mocking) *Les Samouraïs*. This is, in part, a reflection of the fact that its key personnel – Lacan, Barthes, Althusser, etc. – lived and worked in the confined space of Paris's Latin Quarter, teaching together in such prestigious institutions as the *Collège de France* and the *Ecole Normale Supérieure* and frequenting each other's classes and seminars.

This is why structuralism has often (incorrectly) been seen as little more than a Parisian fashion and (correctly) as a major element of what the Anglo-American world now sees as French 'theory'. Certainly the major developments in structuralism took place in Paris during the 1960s. Turning away from existentialism – described by Lévi-Strauss as 'a self-admiring activity which allows contemporary man, rather gullibly, to commune with himself in ecstatic contemplation of his own being' – and from Sartre's vision of the committed 'universal' intellectual – explicitly rejected by Dumézil, Lévi-Strauss and Foucault – in 1962 Lévi-Strauss published *La Pensée sauvage*. Two years later Althusser published *Pour Marx* and *Lire le Capital* while Lévi-Strauss published *Le Cru et le cuit*, the first volume of his major work *Mythologiques*. The year 1966 – 'l'année lumière' of structuralism – saw the publication of Lacan's *Ecrits*, Barthes's *Critique et vérité* and Foucault's *Les Mots et les choses*, as well as Tzvetan Todorov's *Théorie de la littérature* (prefaced by Jakobson) and Pierre Macherey's *Pour une théorie de la production littéraire*.

All received immense critical (and popular) acclaim, sold in huge quantities and effectively established a new orthodoxy. How can this be explained? The answer is largely a non-philosophical one. In the first place, as François Furet has argued, structuralism appeared to provide a means of renovating Marxism, the dominant ideology in post-war France (see Judt, 1992 and Khilnani, 1993) This was especially true of Althusser's attempt to purge Marxism of the contamination of bourgeois humanism, even if, according to E. P. Thompson, it amounted to 'Stalinism in a new structuralist vocabulary'.

Above all, however, the vogue for structuralism coincided with France's entry, for the first time, into the consumer society and seemed to postulate its decisive rejection. This was most obvious in Lévi-Strauss's explicit challenge to the supposed superiority of the categories of Western reason. As Edmund Leach (1996) has commented: 'Lévi-Strauss' primitives are just as sophisticated as we are; it is simply that they use a different system of notation'. In Lévi-Strauss's view, 'the scientific spirit in its most modern form' will serve 'to legitimize the principles of savage thought and to re-establish it in its rightful place' (Lévi-Strauss, 1966, p. 269). But the structuralist challenge to the values of the West's consumer society is also there in Lacan's ethics of desire and Foucault's ethics of liberation. It is also there in Roland Barthes. In the Preface to the 1970 edition of *Mythologies* he wrote:

I had just read Saussure and as a result acquired the conviction that by treating 'collective representations' as sign-systems, one might hope to go further than the pious show of unmasking them and account *in detail* for the mystification which transforms petit-bourgeois culture into a universal nature. (Barthes, 1973, p. 9)

And this was the conclusion he reached:

The whole of France is steeped in this anonymous ideology: our press, our films, our theatre, our pulp literature, our rituals, our Justice, our diplomacy, our conversations, our remarks about the weather, a murder trial, a touching wedding, the cooking we dream of, the garments we wear, everything in everyday life, is dependent on the representation which the bourgeoisie *has and makes us have of the relations between man and the world*. (ibid., p. 140)

The world of the bourgeoisie was the world of Eternal Man.

From structuralism to post-structuralism

Nevertheless, when the student protests of May 1968 rocked France to its very foundations, Lévi-Strauss, Lacan and Althusser responded with what J. G. Merquior describes as an 'eloquent' silence. One of the many student slogans of the day summed up the situation admirably: 'Barthes says: structures do not take to the streets. We say: neither does Barthes.' Jean-Paul Sartre, the intellectual hero of the hour, had his revenge.

Yet the structuralist enterprise did not implode. Less the philosophical flavour of the day, the project continued, especially from the pens of Lévi-Strauss and Dumézil. It even conquered new territory. The 1970s, for example, saw the consecration of the 'new history' associated with the *Annales* school and, specifically, the work of Fernand Braudel. (See Burke, 1990.) *L'histoire événementielle* was dismissed in favour of *la longue durée* and *l'histoire immobile*. More significantly, 'where structuralism had been, now post-structuralism was' (Anderson, 1984, p. 39). The latter term is itself just as difficult to define as the former, if not more so. In this context, the transition can be simply narrated in terms of a further deepening of the influence of Heidegger and, especially, Nietzsche upon French thought. There was no single point of transition – as Foucault pointed out, it is wrong to think of French thought as being Freudian-Marxist at one stage and Nietzschean at another – but the development was no less real for that.

Of similar import were attempts to refashion structuralist methodologies. Here an interesting, and influential, case has been the work of Pierre Bourdieu. Steadfastly opposed to the illusions of subjectivism, he has developed the notions of *habitus*, 'structured structures with a predisposition to function as structuring structures', and 'strategy' in order to lessen the full weight of structural determinism. 'I wanted', he has explained, 'to reintroduce agents that Lévi-Strauss and the structuralists, among others Althusser, tended to abolish, making them into simple epiphenomena of structure'. The aim has been to escape from the choice 'between a structuralism without subject and the philosophy of the subject' (Bourdieu, 1990, pp. 9–10).

More fundamental has been the charge that structuralism is 'flawed at its core' (see, Pavel, 1989, pp. 4–5). It is here, at a philosophical level, that lies the source of the 'paradigm shift' that has characterised the development of French thought since the 1960s. Whether in the form of the return to philosophy associated with *les nouveaux philosophes* (such as André Glucksman and Bernard-Henri Lévy), the formulation of a 'post-metaphysical humanism' inspired by Kant (see, for example, Ferry and Renaut, 1985), the prominence given to a religiously inspired ethics in the thought of Emmanuel Levinas and Paul Ricoeur, or, in sociology, the vogue for methodological individualism found in such works as Raymond Boudon and François Bourricaud's *Dictionnaire critique de la sociologie* and the former's *La Place du désordre*, the emphasis has fallen upon the recuperation of the subject and the notion of agency and the rejection of the anti-humanism and determinism, rightly or wrongly, attributed to structuralism.

Bibliography

References and further reading

Althusser, L. (1976), 'Reply to John Lewis', in *Essays in Self-Criticism*, London: New Left Books.

Anderson, P. (1984), *In the Tracks of Historical Materialism*, London: Verso.

Barthes, R. (1970), 'Science versus Literature', in M. Lane (ed.), *Structuralism: A Reader*, London: Jonathan Cape.

— (1972), 'The Structuralist Activity', in *Critical Essays*, Evanston: Northwestern University Press.

— (1973), *Mythologies*, St Albans: Paladin.

Benton, T. (1984), *The Rise and Fall of Structural Marxism*, London: Macmillan.

Bourdieu, P. (1990), 'Fieldwork in philosophy', in *In Other Words: Essays Towards a Reflexive Sociology*, Oxford: Polity Press.

Burke, P. (1990), *The French Historical Revolution: the Annales School 1929–89*, Oxford: Oxford University Press.

Caws, P. (1988), *Structuralism: The Art of the Intelligble*, Atlantic Highlands: Humanities Press.

Clément, C. (1996), 'De la structure à l'Europe', *La Passion des idées*, Magazine littéraire, Paris.

Culler, J. (1983), *Roland Barthes*, London: Fontana.

— (1985), *Saussure*, London: Fontana.

Domenach, J.-M. (1976), *Le Requiem structuraliste*, Paris: Seuil.

Ducrot, O. (1968), *Le Structuralisme en linguistique*, Paris: Seuil.

Dumézil G. (1987), *Entretiens avec Didier Eribon*, Paris: Gallimard.

Eribon, D. (1991), *Histoire du structuralisme: I. Le champ du signe, 1945–1966*, Paris: La Découverte.

— (1994), *Michel Foucault et ses contemporains*, Paris: Fayard.

Ferry, L. and Renaut, A. (1985), *La pensée 68: Essai sur l'anti-humanisme contemporain*, Paris: Gallimard.

Foucault, M. (1994), 'Entretien avec Madeleine Chapsal', in *Dits et écrits*, I, Paris: Gallimard.

Furet, F. (1984), 'French Intellectuals: From Marxism to Structuralism', *In the Workshop of History*, Chicago: Chicago University Press.

Gellner, E. (1985), 'What is Structuralism?', in *Relativism and the Social Sciences*, Cambridge: Cambridge University Press.

Hawkes, T. (1977), *Structuralism and Semiotics*, London: Routledge.

Judt, T. (1992), *Past Imperfect: French Intellectuals, 1944–56*, Berkeley: University of California Press.

Khilnani, S. (1993), *Arguing Revolution: The Intellectual Left in Postwar France*, New Haven: Yale University Press.

Kurzweil, E. (1980), *The Age of Structuralism: Lévi-Strauss to Foucault*, New York: Columbia University Press.

Leach, E. (1996), *Lévi-Strauss*, London: Fontana.

Lévi-Strauss, C. (1966), *The Savage Mind*, London: Weidenfeld and Nicolson.

— (1981), *The Naked Man: Introduction to a Science of Mythology*, London: Jonathan Cape.

Matthews, E. (1996), *Twentieth-Century French Philosophy*, Oxford: Oxford University Press.

Merquior, J. G. (1986), *From Prague to Paris: A Critique of Structuralist and Post-Structuralist Thought*, London: Verso.

Pavel, T. (1989), *The Feud of Language: A History of Structuralist Thought*, Oxford: Blackwell.

Piaget, J. (1971), *Structuralism*, London: Routledge and Kegan Paul.

Raulet, G. (1983), 'Structuralism and Post-Structuralism: An Interview with Michel Foucault', *Telos*, 55, Spring.

Robey, D. (1973), 'Introduction', in *Structuralism: An Introduction*, Oxford: Oxford University Press.

Safouan, M. (1968), *Le Structuralisme en psychanalyse*, Paris: Seuil.

Sontag, S. (ed.) (1982), *A Barthes Reader*, London: Jonathan Cape.

Sperber, D. (1969), *Le Structuralisme en anthropologie*, Paris: Seuil.

Todorov, T. (1968), *Poétique*, Paris: Seuil.

Wahl, F. (1973), *La Philosophie entre l'avant et l'après du structuralisme*, Paris: Seuil.

STRUCTURALIST LINGUISTICS: SAUSSURE

John E. Joseph

Life and career

Ferdinand de Saussure (1857–1913) was born into a scientifically and socially prominent family of Geneva. In 1872 the fourteen-year-old Ferdinand wrote an *Essai sur les langues* ('Essay on Languages') which held that all languages could be traced back to bi- or tri-consonantal roots that had their basis in broad sound-meaning correspondences he had perceived among the languages he had studied (French, German, English, Latin, Greek). In 1874 he began his study of Sanskrit, which would become his principal area of specialisation. The following year he spent studying chemistry at the University of Geneva, while also attending lessons in Greek and Latin grammar. In 1876 he enrolled in the University of Leipzig, and also joined the *Société de linguistique de Paris*, sending his first papers to be read there early the next year. In December 1878 he published his *Mémoire sur le système primitif des voyelles dans les langues indo-européennes* ('The Original Vowel System of the Indo-European Languages'), a book whose brilliance was obvious to historical linguists everywhere but in Germany – Saussure's own teachers at Leipzig largely ignored it. The *Mémoire* posited the existence of two Proto-Indo-European 'sonant coefficients' which appeared in no attested forms of the daughter languages, but could account for certain vowel developments which had previously appeared irregular. Fifty years later, the Polish linguist Jerzy Kuryłowicz would identify a pair of consonants in

Hittite with exactly the distribution of Saussure's sonant coefficients, confirming his hypothesis.

In July 1878, perhaps because of the poor reception his work received in Leipzig, Saussure went to Berlin and undertook studies in Sanskrit and Celtic. In February 1880 he defended his thesis, *De l'emploi du génitif absolu en sanscrit* ('The Use of the Absolute Genitive in Sanskrit', published in 1881) and received his doctorate *summa cum lauda*. After a brief trip to Lithuania, apparently for first-hand experience of the living language which contains some of the most archaic Indo-European features, he went to Paris in autumn 1880. There he studied under Michel Bréal (later the author of the first important book on linguistic 'semantics'), amongst others. A year later Bréal imparted to him his course in Gothic and Old High German at the *Ecole des hautes études*, where Saussure was named lecturer. He continued teaching in Paris for another ten years, during which time he also served as secretary of the *Société de linguistique* and editor of its *Mémoires*. Although his teaching during this period had a decisive influence on an entire school of French linguists, including Antoine Meillet (the principal linguist associated with Durkheim's journal *L'Année sociologique*), his publications consisted of brief articles on detailed points of linguistic history.

In 1891, for reasons that remain obscure, Saussure left Paris and was named Extraordinary Professor at the University of Geneva. In 1896 he was elevated to Ordinary Professor of Sanskrit and Indo-European, and over succeeding years took on additional subject areas, including modern French phonology and versification, and German language and literature. In 1907, he assumed the task of lecturing on general linguistics. The three courses that he gave on this subject (in 1907, 1908–9 and 1910–11), presented to the public in 1916 in the form of a collation from student notes, would revolutionise the study of language within two decades after his death from cancer in 1913. Soon after his death, his colleagues Charles Bally (1865–1947) and Albert Sechehaye (1870–1946), appreciating the extraordinary nature of the courses Saussure had given, began gathering what manuscript notes they could find, together with the careful and detailed notebooks of students who had taken one or more of the three courses, especially Albert Riedlinger (1883–1978). From these they fashioned the *Cours de linguistique générale* ('Course in General Linguistics').

Saussure published very little after 1894, and spent much of his time looking for hidden anagrams in Latin poetry, although why he did this is still not fully understood. Consequently, his world-wide reputation is based almost entirely on the *Course*, a book he did not even write. Indeed, he never published anything at all in the area of general linguistics.

Context of Saussure's lectures

By 1890 the institutional 'mainstream' of the study of language had come to be defined by the approach established around 1876 by the *Junggrammatiker* (neo-grammarians) based at Leipzig. It excluded virtually all aspects of language except historical phonology and morphology, the study of the evolution of sounds and forms respectively. It thus covered only that part of language that could be catalogued as positive facts and formulated into 'laws'. By focusing their enquiry in this way, the neo-grammarians succeeded brilliantly in meeting the criteria for scientific progress of the time; but their progress was gained at the price of ignoring general questions about the nature and operation of language, leaving these to adjacent fields. The most closely allied of these was comparative religion – not surprising, when one considers that this field required detailed knowledge of the very same languages and texts with which historical linguists worked. Indeed, the borderline between the two fields was nebulous, and throughout the nineteenth century they shared the same great names, such as Friedrich Max Müller (1823–1900) and Ernest Renan (1823–92), who did not hesitate to construct grand theories of language, culture, myth and race.

By 1900 the firm hold which historical grammar and comparative religion had held upon the linguistic mainstream was being challenged by still other fields of study, the dominant one being psychology. Even within the historical-comparative sphere, linguists did not agree which, if any, of the leads provided by various versions of psychology should be followed. The ability of psychologists to annex many aspects of language production and comprehension was aided by the deep influence on linguists of Wilhelm von Humboldt's (1767–1835) posthumously published treatise on language structure and mental development (1836). Psychological linguists in the Humboldtian tradition, Heymann Steinthal (1823–99), for example, saw their investigations of language as a means to the understanding of national culture and thought. This approach did not disappear even when, a generation later, 'experimental' psychologists incorporated enough positivist methodology into their practice to maintain its scientific status and prestige. One of the most prominent figures of this period, Wilhelm Wundt (1832–1920), developed a *Völkerpsychologie* (psychology of nations) with a specifically linguistic component, and it gained enormous and widespread prestige. However, other linguists continued to object to the fact that the psychological approach worked backwards from *a priori* notions about the nature and structure of the mind to form theories of language that could only ever be empirical or objective in a superficial sense.

In the same period, the rise of experimental phonetics, the detailed measurement of speech sounds, offered the first truly positivistic approach to language. It had steadily grown in prestige through the influence of practitioners like Alexander Melville Bell (1819–1905) and Henry Sweet (1845–1912). While its descriptive power was unparalleled and its pedagogical usefulness high, its explanatory power proved disappointing. Phonetics could only deal with individual speech acts, not the underlying abstract linguistic systems. Still, it opened the possibility of accumulating masses of positive data about living dialects. Detailed research on German and French dialects culminated in the production of multi-volume linguistic atlases, and with these came a questioning of the definition of what is a 'language'. In the light of evidence that European dialects merged into one another rather than having clear dividing lines, French, German and other 'languages' appeared to be secondary and somewhat arbitrary constructs. Saussure's University of Geneva inaugural lecture of 1891 gives considerable attention to this issue.

Late in the nineteenth century, as anthropology moved from a physical towards a cultural orientation, it too developed an impressive linguistic fieldwork methodology based on positivistic principles; most notably under the leadership of Franz Boas (1859–1942), a German émigré to the USA. The young science of sociology also embodied the spirit of positivism, with which it shared the same recognised founder, Auguste Comte (1798–1857). As the new century opened, sociologists were moving on to the intellectual territory once claimed by classical psychology and which they now saw as old-fashioned and metaphysical. Saussure's student and close associate Antoine Meillet (1866–1936) would become the principal linguistic contributor to *L'Année sociologique*, founded in 1896 by Émile Durkheim (1858–1917).

Philosophers, although becoming more interested in questions of language, were more cut off from the linguist's concerns than were the other academics discussed above. Saussure's lectures betray no awareness of late nineteenth-century developments such as Frege's work on sense and reference, which would seem to have relevance for his conception of the linguistic sign, or the 'semeiotic' of Charles Sanders Peirce (1837–1914), whose points of contact with Saussure's semiology must be taken as coincidental. Nor does he make any allusion to work exactly contemporary with his lectures, such as Whitehead and Russell's *Principia Mathematica*, Husserl, or others in what might be called the Boolean–Fregean line. Perhaps the very suggestion that he might have done so is anachronistic, given that the meeting points of structuralist linguistics and analytic philosophy which now appear clear were not so until well into the second half of the twentieth century.

The roughly contemporary rise to prominence of Boas's anthropology in the USA, Gilliéron's dialect geography and Durkheim's sociology in France, Sweet's articulatory phonetics in Britain and Wundt's national psychology in Germany gave a new impetus to the study of living languages that mainstream linguistics had long since abandoned. Not that all historical linguistics had ever been content with the division of labour outlined above: some thought that historical-comparative linguistics alone could be scientific, others felt that other aspects could be studied scientifically but that this should fall to adjacent disciplines, and still others thought that historical-comparative linguistics should be expanded to adopt the other areas.

Linguists with a basically historical orientation who published notable books on general linguistics in the late nineteenth and early twentieth century include William Dwight Whitney (1827–94), Michel Bréal (1832–1915) and Victor Henry (1850–1907). The works of Georg von der Gabelentz (1840–93) and, especially, Hermann Paul (1846–1921), although cast in the historical mould, anticipate the vision of the linguistic system that would characterise the structuralist period. But it was Whitney, first and foremost, who showed the way towards a modern general linguistics that would not be an eclectic mix of psychological, phonetic and other approaches, but a comprehensive study of language guided by historical principles and examining language for its own sake – a truly 'autonomous' approach. Saussure, who had met Whitney in Berlin in 1879, wrote about him with reverence fifteen years later in a piece for a Whitney memorial volume, which, however, he never completed.

The course in general linguistics

It was within this general context that Saussure's lectures were conceived and given. The following discussion of his conception of language is based upon the *Cours de linguistique générale* – again, a book he did not write – and focuses on those aspects of the

Course which would prove most seminal to the later development of structuralism. It glosses over a number of exegetical and interpretational problems, beginning with the question of what parts of the *Course* are 'really' Saussure's thought and which represent posthumous 'improvements' by the editors. The publication of Engler's critical edition of the source materials has helped greatly in allowing us to clarify this, and to understand better how Saussure's conception of language developed over the years in which he gave his courses. Nevertheless, many questions remain unresolved.

Synchrony and diachrony

Saussure's central problem was to delineate a study of language that would be neither historical nor ahistorical, neither psychological nor apsychological. Yet it had to be more systematic than Whitneyan general linguistics, so as to equal the historical, psychological and phonetic approaches in intellectual and methodological rigour. His solution included making a strong distinction between the study of language as a static system, which he called 'synchronic' linguistics, and the study of language change, which he called 'diachronic' linguistics (or, until 1908, 'evolutive'). Saussure's rejection of the traditional term 'historical' seems to stem partly from a disdain for the reliance it suggests on facts external to the language system, and partly from a desire for terminological symmetry with 'synchronic'. Synchronic linguistics would henceforth designate the study of language systems in and of themselves, divorced from external considerations of a historical or psychological sort, or any factor having to do with actual speech production.

Saussure argued that it makes no sense to talk as linguists did (and do) of the Latin word *homo* 'man' 'becoming' the French word *homme*. It is not as though this word has some kind of existence stretching across centuries and independent of the living people who use it. To understand the relationship between *homo* and *homme*, one has to begin by understanding the whole Latin language of which *homo* was a part at a particular point in time, and the whole French language of which *homme* is a part at a particular point in time. Latin also had a word *vir*

covering aspects of the concept of 'man' different to those covered by *homo*. French has only the word *homme*, with no second word corresponding to *vir*. Thus, the range of meaning of *homo* and *homme* is not comparable. Since their meanings differ, on what basis can we say that they are two forms of the 'same' word?

Saussure does not reject the idea of 'diachronic' enquiry, but insists that it must be carried out on the basis of comparing not isolated words and sounds but whole systems, which have been subjected to synchronic analysis first. 'It is clear that the synchronic point of view takes precedence over the diachronic, since for the community of language users that is the one and only reality. The same is true for the linguist' (Saussure, 1987, p. 128). In so far as twentieth-century linguists have not focused their efforts on simple description of languages, their evolution, or their connection to 'national psychology', they have realised Saussure's programme of synchronic linguistics. Furthermore, historical linguistics has largely become the diachronic enterprise envisioned by Saussure, although the term 'historical' continues in general usage. Even the purely 'descriptive' approaches have been profoundly marked by the Saussurean concept of language as a system where *tout se tient* 'everything holds together', a phrase often associated with Saussure, although there is no record of his ever actually using it in his Geneva lectures. Possibly its first use was in a lecture delivered by Meillet in 1906. The *Course* does include statements such as the following: 'A language is a system of which all the parts can and must be considered as synchronically interdependent' (ibid., p. 124).

The primacy of spoken language

A language and its written form constitute two separate systems of signs. The sole reason for the existence of the latter is to represent the former. The object of study in linguistics is not a combination of the written word and the spoken word. The spoken word alone constitutes that object. (Saussure, 1987, p. 45)

The idea that speech is the original and primal form of language, and writing a secondary imitation of speech, is found as far back as Plato, yet it runs counter to the world-wide popular prestige accorded to writing. Still, the primacy of spoken over written language became embedded in linguistics in the early nineteenth century, doubtless in connection with the Romantic belief that folk traditions embodied the national spirit more deeply than urban practices like writing, which were more subject to external influences. The fact that speech is universal while writing is not, and that even in literate cultures individual children, unless they have a speech problem, learn to speak before they learn to write, led to the view that speech is natural and writing artificial, in a Romantic period which consistently glorified the natural. The trend continued over the course of the nineteenth century as linguistics moved away from philology and became increasingly concerned with gathering spoken forms from living dialects.

Saussure formalised the marginalisation of written language as well as anyone, and if its survival is often viewed as a Saussurean tradition, it is because he has borne the brunt of Jacques Derrida's attack on this marginalisation (see Derrida, 1976). For Saussure, writing is not language, but a separate entity whose only purpose is to represent real (spoken) language. The 'danger' of writing is that it creates the illusion of being more real and more stable than speech, and therefore gains ascendancy over speech in the popular mind. Derrida demonstrated the internal inconsistency and irrationality of this extreme phonocentrism; indeed, according to Derrida, all language always already presupposes a kind of 'writing'.

The object of linguistics: *langue* versus *parole*

'The language [*langue*] itself is not a function of the speaker. It is the product passively registered by the individual. It never requires premeditation . . . Speech [*parole*], on the contrary, is an individual act of the will and the intelligence' (Saussure, 1987, p. 30). The role of the human will in language production has constituted a problem for linguistic thought at least since Plato's *Cratylus*: humans are constrained by the conventions of language, yet it is through language that will and individuality are shaped and realised.

Saussure's contribution was to dissect the total phenomenon of language (*langage*) into actual speech production (*parole*), including the role of the individual will; and the socially shared system of signs (*langue*) that makes production and comprehension possible. The text you are now reading is *parole* that I have produced (ignoring for the moment the secondary nature of writing in Saussure's view). The fact that you can read it means that you share the *langue*, the system of signs, that I used in writing it – a *langue* which we can identify as late-twentieth-century Standard English. This same *langue* must be present in each of our brains for us to understand each other.

Although he spoke of a linguistics of *parole* that would cover the phonetic side of language and the products of individual will, Saussure made it clear that the linguistics of *langue* is the essential, real linguistics. *Langue* is beyond the direct reach of the individual will. His formulation is both a defence and a refinement of the procedures of traditional grammar and historical linguistics, yet at the same time it stakes out an autonomous realm for general linguistic enquiry. Saussure argues further that the distinction between *langue* and *parole* must not be characterised as that between something abstract and something concrete: 'Linguistic structure is no less real than speech . . . Linguistic signs, although essentially psychological, are not abstractions. The associations, ratified by collective agreement, which go to make up the language are realities localised in the brain' (ibid., p. 32).

Despite much debate among scholars as to just what Saussure meant by *langage*, *langue* and *parole*, the distinction has been sustained throughout twentieth-century linguistics. It has been suggested that certain work in stylistics, starting with that by Saussure's disciple Bally, and in discourse pragmatics, constitutes an attempt at a linguistics of *parole*; but it is not yet clear how any aspect of language, once it is systematised, fails to enter the sphere of *langue*. The individual will remains in exile from linguistics, and *langue*, in something more or less akin to Saussure's original conception of it, continues to be the object of study of virtually every approach to which the name 'linguistics' is accorded. Even an approach like the integrationalism of Roy

Harris, which rejects the notion of language systems as mythological, does so with direct invocation of Saussure's insistence on the essentially social nature of linguistic communication.

Langue as a social fact

'[L]anguage is a social phenomenon' (Saussure, 1987, p. 21):

> It is a fund accumulated by the members of the community through the practice of speech, a grammatical system existing potentially in every brain, or more exactly in the brains of a group of individuals; for the language is never complete in any single individual, but exists perfectly only in the collectivity. (Ibid., p. 30)
>
> A language, as a collective phenomenon, takes the form of a totality of imprints in everyone's brain, rather like a dictionary of which each individual has an identical copy. Thus it is something which is in each individual, but is none the less common to all. At the same time it is out of the reach of any deliberate interference by individuals. (Ibid., p. 38)

Saussure's insistence on the social nature of *langue* grew during the years in which he lectured on general linguistics, largely at the expense of psychologically-based considerations. Again, this may be tied in part to the need to establish synchronic linguistics independently of the dominant post-Humboldtian psychological establishment. As noted above, the young science of sociology embodied the spirit of positivism, and positivism was coming to be equated with scientificness in general thought, making classical psychology appear old-fashioned and metaphysical. For the sociologists, Wundt's *Völkerpsychologie*, based on non-empirical generalisations (and more akin to what today would pass not as psychology but philosophy of mind) was already unacceptably passé.

In Saussure's view, *langue* is a 'treasury' or 'collection of impressions' that is 'deposited' in identical form in the brain of each member of a given speech community. He uses the metaphor of a dictionary, of which every individual possesses an identical copy. What the individual does with this socially-shared

system falls entirely into the realm of *parole*. This distinction (which was not yet clear to Saussure at the time of his first course in general linguistics of 1907) differentiates Saussure's dichotomy from that between 'competence' and 'performance' established in the 1960s by Noam Chomsky. Chomsky explicitly related competence with *langue* and performance with *parole*, although, in actual fact, the analogy was only partial: for Chomsky, competence (derived from innate universal grammar) is mental and individual, and performance the locus of its social actuation. Furthermore, the considerable differences between Saussure's orientation towards language as a semiotic system and Chomsky's towards competence as a mental faculty make any such equations difficult.

Saussure's views on the social nature of language have had a great resonance in linguistics and many other fields. By the mid-1930s it was commonplace to equate 'synchronic linguistics' (indeed, 'scientific linguistics') with 'social linguistics', and to include under this heading the work of Meillet and his many European disciples, and even the pragmatist John Dewey (1859–1952) and the social behaviourist George Herbert Mead (1863–1931). Leonard Bloomfield (1887–1949), in particular, exploited the power of the social as an antidote to the psychological (or 'mentalist') approach at the time of his conversion, in the 1920s, from Wundtian social psychology to empirical behaviourism. 'Sociolinguistics', which would come into its own in the 1960s with the work of William Labov and Dell Hymes, pursues the Saussurean view of the social nature of *langue*, while Chomskyan generative linguistics (to which sociolinguistics has stood in irreconcilable contrast for a generation) pursues the Saussurean view of the mental and abstract nature of *langue*.

Langue as a system of signs: semiology

'A linguistic sign is not a link between a thing and its name, but between a concept and a sound pattern . . . The linguistic sign is, then, a two-sided psychological entity' (Saussure, 1987, p. 98); 'It is therefore possible to conceive of a science *which studies the role of signs as part of social life*. It would form part of social psychology, hence of general psychology. We shall call it *semiology* (from the Greek *sēmeion*, "sign") . . . Linguistics is only one branch of this general science' (ibid., p. 33). The conception of language as a collection of signs (understood as the collation of a signifying word and a signified concept) was anticipated in the philosophy of Aristotle, elaborated by the Stoics, and reached its summit in the 'speculative grammar' of the twelfth and thirteenth centuries. In the Renaissance, the view of language as a sign system began to cede pride of place to that of language as a social institution. The semiological perspective was never entirely lost – it resurfaced notably among the seventeenth-century British empiricists – but by the early twentieth century had virtually disappeared from public academic discourse. Peirce's work in this area, like Saussure's, went unpublished during his lifetime and was not seriously revived by philosophers until the 1930s.

For Saussure, the network of linguistic signs which constitute *langue* is made up of the conjunction of a *signifiant* ('signifier'), understood as an acoustic image or sound pattern deposited in the mind, and a *signifié* ('signified'), a concept that is also deposited in the mind. It is important to note that the signifier is wholly distinct from the actual uttered word, as is the signified from the actual physical thing conceived of (if one exists). Both signifier and signified are entirely psychological, while also being socially shared. Although the distinction between concept and object has existed since antiquity, that between sound pattern and actual sound is Saussure's own contribution, of which some have seen a foreshadowing in the hypothetical 'sonant coefficients' of his early *Mémoire*.

Saussure predicted that semiology, the study of signs both within and outside of language, would have linguistics as its 'pilot science':

Signs which are entirely arbitrary convey better than others the ideal semiological process. That is why the most complex and the most widespread of all systems of expression, which is the one we find in human languages, is also the most characteristic of all. In this sense, linguistics serves as a model for the whole of semiology, even though languages represent only one type of semiological system. (Ibid., pp. 100–1)

This claim can be interpreted as a further challenge to psychology, for the semiological domain is precisely where language is most explicitly mental.

Saussure's prediction came to pass in the 1950s and 1960s, when attempts were made at unifying Saussurean 'semiology' (practised principally by European linguists) and Peircean 'semiotics' (practised mostly by American philosophers) into a single paradigm, under the organisational leadership of Thomas A. Sebeok. But while linguistics has furnished the paradigmatic model for semiotics, the impact of semiotic enquiry upon linguistics has been slow in coming. The one place where linguistics has been profoundly affected is in the nearly universal acceptance of Saussure's concept of the signifier as an abstract sound pattern. This view became the cornerstone of the concept of the 'phoneme' as elaborated by Jan Baudouin de Courtenay (1846–1929) in Russia, and subsequently by N. S. Trubetzkoy (1890–1938) in Vienna and Roman Jakobson (1896–1982) in Brno and Prague. It resulted in the banishment of experimental phonetics from linguistic enquiry in favour of more abstract phonology, based not upon physical differences of sound, but on the ability to distinguish between concepts. The distinction between a physical 'etic' level (from phon*etic*) and an abstract 'emic' level (from phon*emic*) would be extended to every level of linguistic structure, and would become a hallmark in particular of post-War American linguistics.

The arbitrariness of linguistic signs

'*First principle: the sign is arbitrary* . . . The principle stated above is the organising principle for the whole of linguistics, considered as a science of language structure. The consequences which flow from this principle are innumerable' (Saussure, 1987, p. 100). As with the semiological nature of language, the arbitrariness of language – the fact that a signifier like the series of sounds /p a ɪ/ has no internal connection with the concept of a 'pie' which it signifies in English – reflects an ancient doctrine that had never fallen very far from the centre of debate about the nature of language through to the end of the eighteenth century. Although not a direct concern for most of the historical linguists of the nineteenth century, the ancient debate between *physis* 'nature' and *nomos* 'convention' in the establishment and operation of language had been revived by Whitney and the Humboldtian psychologists, with Whitney's views of language positioned on the side of *nomos* and the Humboldtians' on the side of *physis*.

Saussure's precise formulation of the linguistic sign allowed him to situate arbitrariness precisely at the conjunction of signified and signifier. This represented an advance over most earlier formulations of arbitrariness, which, despite Aristotle, focused on the relationship between the sign as a whole and the real-world objects conceptualised in the signified. Unfortunately, the *Course* is not consistent in its presentation of arbitrariness, and quickly falls back into the older schema. Another problem with the presentation in the *Course* is that the arbitrariness doctrine is first encountered in radical form in a very terse, strongly worded and memorable section (as quoted above); and only later is this tempered with a section on relative arbitrariness that is often ignored, but without which Saussure's conception of language is inaccurately understood. Saussure's point in the later section is that, while signifiers are always arbitrary relative to signifieds, they can be motivated relative to other signifiers. Thus, for example, the French numbers *dix-neuf* '19' and *vingt* '20' both show arbitrariness between signifier and signified, yet *dix-neuf* is motivated relative to the numerals *dix* '10' and *neuf* '9' which compose it, hence *dix-neuf* is relatively arbitrary while *vingt* is radically so. (This is connected to Saussure's distinction between syntagmatic and associative relations, discussed below.) Cases of onomatopoeia, where there seems to be a motivated relationship between signifier and real-world analogue, are dismissed as not really part of linguistic systems.

The fact that the *Course* presents the radical version of arbitrariness first and most forcefully led to its assuming the status of dogma in twentieth-century linguistics, although it undoubtedly also appealed to something deeper in the *Zeitgeist*. It is one of the first views of language to which budding linguists are exposed in introductory courses and textbooks, often as one of the design features of language identified in 1958 by Charles F. Hockett. Like most dogmata, the radical form of arbitrariness

is counter-intuitive and requires a certain faith beyond what reason can sustain. Also, it is not always observable in the practice of those who preach it, particularly because of the influence of Jakobson, who, beginning in the early 1930s, mounted a sustained attack on radical arbitrariness through his work on markedness, child language acquisition and aphasia, which suggested that linguistic elements differ in naturalness. Jakobson was to have a significant impact upon Chomsky, Joseph H. Greenberg and many others, with the result that language is not treated as exhibiting anything like the radical arbitrariness of the dogma. Besides Jakobson, arbitrariness was problematised by Louis Hjelmslev (1899–1965), Emile Benveniste (1902–76) and numerous others in a series of attacks on, and defences of, the Saussurean view (often poorly represented) appearing from 1939 to around 1947.

The linearity of signifiers

After arbitrariness, the second primary principle of linguistics for Saussure is that linguistic signifiers are 'linear', in the sense that, because they have a temporal existence, they represent a dimension that is measurable only as a line. This is one of Saussure's more mysterious ideas, in that he never made clear what he was opposing it to. He notes that it is obvious to everyone, but that its implications have not been appreciated. Linearity is part of what distinguishes spoken language as 'real' language, as opposed to writing as a secondary representation that is not necessarily linear. It is also what allows us to analyse connected discourse into meaningful units. In as much as the linearity principle means that signifiers exist in a completely separate dimension from that of signifieds, one may detect here a hedging on the inherent psychologism of the semiological view of language as consisting of perfectly juxtaposed signifiers and signifieds.

This principle has given rise to many interpretations. Jakobson formulated his doctrine of distinctive features in phonology – the idea that phonemes are not monoliths, but consist of bundles of features existing simultaneously – as part of a critique of the linearity of the signifier. Others have argued that Saussure's principle is aimed at denying that signifiers can accumulate and not that they can be decomposed into something like constituent features. This is essential to his view of how language organises thought (discussed under 'linguistic value' below), and it prepares the ground for the introduction of syntagmatic relations.

Syntagmatic and associative (paradigmatic) relations

Saussure distinguished between the 'syntagmatic' relations a linguistic element has with the elements preceding and following it in an utterance, and the 'associative' (now usually called paradigmatic) relations it has to other elements with which it shares partial identity, but which do not occur in the particular utterance at hand. For example, in the sentence *Crime pays*, the element *crime* has a syntagmatic relationship with *pays* that determines, among other things, their order relative to one another and the fact that *pays* has the inflectional *-s*. At the same time, *crime* has paradigmatic relations with countless other elements, including the inflectionally related *crimes*, the derivationally related *criminal*, the conceptually related *misdemeanour* (and the conceptually opposite *legality*) and the phonetically related *grime*. As the last example suggests, each sound of the word *crime* /kraɪm/ has paradigmatic and syntagmatic relations with at least the sounds around it: /k/ is paradigmatically related to the /g/ that could, in principle, replace it; and syntagmatically related to the following /r/ since in English the presence of /k/ as the initial element of the word immediately restricts the following sound to /l r w/ or a vowel.

Saussure notes that the two types of relations, which correspond to different types of mental activity, contribute in different ways to the 'value' of the sign. In particular, the paradigmatic relations generate a negative value: the identity of the /r/ in /kraɪm/ is essentially such that it could be, but is not, /l w/ or a vowel. This is important because the actual sound that represents /r/ can differ dramatically from one English dialect to another (being rolled, flapped, retroflex, etc.); but the actual sound content does not matter, so long as /r/ is kept distinct from the other sounds to which it is associatively related. 'Syntagmatic relations hold *in praesentia*. They hold between two or more terms co-present in a sequence. Associative relations, on the contrary, hold *in absentia*. They hold between terms constituting a mnemonic group' (Saussure, 1987, p. 171).

Before Saussure, the syntagmatic relations of elements within a given utterance were certainly recognised as a matter of linguistic concern, although relatively neglected. But there was little or no precedent for the idea suggested by the *Course* (implicitly if not explicitly) that there exists a syntax not only of words, but of sounds, meanings and the relations uniting them; or that every time a sound, word or meaning is chosen, a vast network of related elements is summoned up *in absentia*. The latter concept in particular set the study of language on a new course of abstraction that did not rely on psychological theorising, but remained internal to language.

In many ways, the Saussurean notion of paradigmatic and syntagmatic relations would become the hallmark of twentieth-century linguistics. First, it proposed that a single principle of structure unites all the levels at which language functions – sound, forms and meaning. Second, it suggested a way of analysing language that would not depend on a simple listing of elements with their 'translation' into either another language or some sort of philosophical interpretation. Elements could henceforth be analysed according to their relations with other elements, and the language could be understood as the vast system – not of these elements – but of these relations. This was the point of departure for structuralism.

To a large extent, the distributional method developed by Bloomfield is a working out of this Saussurean notion, with special emphasis on the paradigmatic relations. With the work of Bloomfield's student Zellig S. Harris (1909–92), the syntagmatic relations assumed a status of equal importance, and with Harris's student Chomsky, overriding importance. Regarding word order, Saussure's view is that the syntagmatic relations constitute that part of syntax which is pre-determined – like the use of a third person singular verb form after the singular subject *crime* – and so a part of *langue*; while the rest of syntax, being subject to free combination, is related to *parole*.

Linguistic value: *langue* as form, not substance

The most philosophical chapters in the *Course* are arguably the brief one on 'Identities, realities, values' and the longer one on 'Linguistic values'. The first asks what is the basis for identifying particular utterances as the same or different, noting that 'the mechanism of a language turns entirely on identities and differences. The latter are merely a counterpart of the former' (Saussure, 1987, p. 151). The other chapter begins with a consideration of the relationship between language and thought:

> Psychologically, setting aside its expression in words, our thought is simply a vague, shapeless mass. Philosophers and linguists have always agreed that were it not for signs, we should be incapable of differentiating any two ideas in a clear and constant way. In itself, thought is like a swirling cloud, where no shape is intrinsically determinate. No ideas are established in advance, and nothing is distinct, before the introduction of linguistic structure. (ibid., p. 155)

Saussure compares the meeting of 'sound' and 'thought' with the contact between air and water, with changes in the pressure of the air creating waves in the water. (See illustration, ibid., p. 156.)

He compares them also to the two sides of a sheet of paper, where it is impossible to cut the one without at the same time cutting the other. 'Linguistics . . . operates along this margin, where sound and thought meet. *The contact between them gives rise to a form, not a substance*' (ibid., p. 157). This form which is not substance is the *langue* (ibid., p. 167). The conjunction of sound and thought, signifier and signified, generates a *value*. This value is part of the sign itself, just as much as the signifier and signified are. Because the conjunction of signifier and signified is arbitrary, value requires the social activity of a community to establish it.

Saussure specifies that value is not synonymous with meaning. Meaning is a matter of the relationship of a signifier to a signified, hence it exists *within* a particular sign. (See illustration, ibid., p. 159.) The example of the different values of Latin *homo* and French *homme* given above in the discussion of synchrony and diachrony is a case in point. The difference is determined by the co-existence in the one system of *vir*, and the non-existence of any comparable element in the other. Saussure's most famous example is the following: 'The French word *mouton* may have the same meaning as the English word *sheep*; but it does not have the same value . . . The difference in value between *sheep* and *mouton* hinges on the fact that in English there is also another word *mutton* for the meat, whereas *mouton* in French covers both' (ibid., p. 160).

Saussure says that values exist in a kind of negative universe, being generated by the differences between elements. Sounds themselves cannot have value, he argues, or it would be impossible for them to change.

> All conventional values have the characteristic of being distinct from the tangible elements which serve as their vehicle . . . Each language constructs its words out of some fixed number of phonetic units, each one clearly distinct from the others. What characterises these units is not, as might be thought, the specific positive properties of each; but simply the fact that they cannot be mistaken for one another. Speech sounds are first and foremost entities which are contrastive, relative and negative. (ibid., p. 164)

Ultimately, Saussure says, 'in a language there are only differences, *and no positive terms*' (ibid., p. 166). He then restricts this differential and negative character to the signifier and signified in isolation, and says that 'their combination is a fact of a positive nature'. Thus, the sign as a whole is 'the only order of facts linguistic structure comprises', and 'the essential function of a language as an institution is precisely to maintain these series of differences in parallel' (ibid., pp. 166–7).

The conception of language as a system of differences and negative values would be fundamental to the concept of the phoneme as it eventually emerged. Phonemes would be defined not on the basis of their phonetic content, but on their functional capacity for distinguishing meaningful elements from one another. Furthermore, despite Saussure's reluctance to extend this negative and differential conception of language to the level of entire signs, it would provide the basis of a more generalised 'structuralism' that would be extrapolated beyond linguistics in the decades after his death. Between the 1940s and the 1970s, most fields of human knowledge experienced a structuralist period. Its most widely heralded application was in the field of anthropology, by Claude Lévi-Strauss, who discovered Saussure in 1942, in a course taught by Jakobson. Other areas and their most prominent structuralist practitioners include: biology, Ludwig von Bertalanffy (1901–72) and C. H. Waddington (1905–75); literary theory, Roland Barthes (1915–80); Marxist theory, Louis Althusser (1918–90); mathematics, 'Nicholas Bourbaki' (the pseudonym of a group of French mathematicians); psychoanalysis, Jacques Lacan (1901–79), and psychology (where the groundwork for it had already been laid by the concept of *Gestalt*), Jean Piaget (1896–1980). The rejection of key aspects of structuralism by such figures as Derrida and Michel Foucault (1926–84) launched the 'post-structuralist' era, whose very name indicates the enduring influence of Saussurean tradition, even when shaping the direction of reactions against it.

Structuralist linguistics in the wake of Saussure

As to why linguistics should have been the first of the 'human sciences' to develop structuralism to the extent that it did, one must take into account not just the unique impact of Saussure's *Course*, but also the general state of the field. The end of the First World War in 1918 brought a widespread sense of liberation from a century of German linguistic dominance. Linguists outside Germany, while still respectful of the neo-grammarians' methods, now felt free to use, correct or abandon them as they saw fit. In the first decade of the twentieth century, the formulation of a national linguistics had meant the application of neo-grammarian techniques to the study of a particular nation's dialects, and even opposition views had to be defined relative to the Leipzig mainstream. But from the 1920s onwards, a national linguistics came to mean a more or less original theoretical position held by a nation's leading linguists. Clearly, the post-War generation was ready for change.

The term 'structuralism' itself was not used in

linguistics until around 1928, when it began to appear most prominently in writings by Jakobson. Even then, no connection was drawn with the 'structuralist' psychology promulgated by Titchener and others earlier in the century. In any survey of early structuralism, the Geneva School deserves pride of place, for the role of Bally and Sechehaye in publishing the *Course* and of Serge Karcevskij (1884–1955) in transmitting Saussure's doctrines to Moscow and Prague, as well as for the important original work done by these and other members. Yet the Geneva School would be later largely overshadowed by developments in other quarters, not only including Prague, but also Yale, London, Copenhagen and Paris, in each of which a structuralist school arose.

These schools shared a number of features in their approaches to the study of language: the study of 'systematic' phenomena more or less along the lines of Saussure's characterisation of *langue*; an implied belief that 'abstract' levels of analysis are more fundamental, more deep-seated, in a word, more 'real' than concrete ones; a preference for 'social' abstractions over mental ones, including an axiomatic faith in language as a fundamentally social phenomenon which nevertheless could best be studied through the utterances of individual speakers; a general priority of linguistic 'form' over meaning (less clear with the London School, and a continuing heritage from the neo-grammarians, whose single-minded concentration on form had inspired Bréal to bring forth 'semantics' in reaction); a deep distrust in written language, usually characterised as not being language at all but only a secondary representation (less clear with the Prague School). The last feature seems to be on a different level from the other four: contingent rather than necessary to the structuralist outlook, and certainly not restricted to it.

Structuralist linguistics arose across Continental Europe, Britain and the USA not in a unified fashion, but in the form of national schools – and less through lack of contact than because of a desire for intellectual independence (especially after the decades of German domination) and for theories that would reflect the different linguistic interests and ideologies of the various countries. Yet the post-First World

War generation all sought approaches that appeared modern and scientific, and they landed on largely the same things. The *Course* was a major influence on all the structuralist schools, although by no means the only one. It provided a theoretical programme but little in the way of actual work to be carried out. All in all, the structuralist period is surprising both in its unity and its diversity.

The implications of Saussure's view of *langue* were probably worked out most fully in Prague, principally by Trubetzkoy, who elaborated complete phonological schemata for a panoply of languages from all over the world, and by Jakobson, who extended the implications of 'functional' phonology to other domains of linguistic (and literary) enquiry. However, strikingly similar projects were underway in other quarters: in the USA with Bloomfield, who saw himself as at least partly under the influence of Saussure (in a 1945 letter he described his major work *Language* as showing Saussure's influence 'on every page'); in Denmark, with the overtly Saussurean glossematics of Hjelmslev; in France, where Meillet had transmitted the Saussurean perspective to a whole generation of students, including André Martinet, Gustave Guillaume (1883–1960); and Benveniste. All the lines of affiliation among these 'schools' are not yet clear but their work came to define the mainstream of linguistics in the twentieth century, and all of it assumes the conception of *langue* set out in the *Course*.

Saussure as a philosopher of language

While there is no evidence that Saussure thought of himself as a philosopher of language, neither is there anything to suggest that he would have rejected being characterised as one. His most distinctive contribution to the philosophy of language, apart from reorientating linguistic enquiry away from historical considerations and providing the structuralist outlook in general, is probably his notion of signifieds being themselves as much a part of the language system as signifiers are. This is as much as to say that linguistic meaning is language-specific, hence culture-specific. It may be that other kinds of meaning, but not the meanings of words, are grounded in some sort of universal logic. These, Saussure says, are just as much bound to a particular language as are the sound patterns which signify them. Saussure's position, which may be fairly described as relativistic, is that the signs used by a particular linguistic community embody what meanings are for them, and there is no basis on which to criticise those meanings.

The difference between Saussure's and Frege's view of meaning is striking, mainly because in Saussure's view, what Frege calls reference (*Bedeutung*) simply fails to play a part. The linguistic signified is entirely psychological, and languages can divide up physical reality in potentially limitless ways. Moreover, in the Saussurean view, what really matters is not meaning, but value, a concept with no obvious counterpart in the analytic tradition, although Harris tries to equate it with Wittgenstein's later conception of meaning as 'the use of a word in the language', arguing that, for Saussure, the value of a linguistic sign is 'its potential use in certain syntagmatic combinations (but not others), together with its distinctive use in associative contrast with other signs which might have occurred in those combinations' (Harris, 1988, p. 23). Harris draws further links between Saussure and Wittgenstein on the basis of a perceived relationship between Saussure's view of language as a social fact and Wittgenstein's views on normativity, and also on the ways in which both use the analogy of games to explain their views of how language works.

Saussure was not widely read outside of linguistics before the 1960s, when French structuralism and post-structuralism both thrust him to centre stage. The structuralist phase outside of linguistics (and, to a lesser extent, anthropology and sociology) was so brief that Saussure's main impact on twentieth-century thought may end up being as the man in opposition to whose ideas post-structuralism was formed. If so, it will be an ironic fate for him: a role of entirely negative value, making him the thinker of pure difference, the philosopher of language whose views few other philosophers followed, but against whom some quite important ones would define themselves.

Bibliography

Writings

The following list comprises posthumous works compiled principally from students' notes.

Saussure, Ferdinand de (1972), *Cours de linguistique générale*, ed. Tullio de Mauro, Paris: Payot.

— (1967–74), *Edition critique du Cours de linguistique générale de F. de Saussure*, ed. Rudolf Engler, Wiesbaden: Harrissowitz.

— (1957), *Les sources manuscrites du Cours de linguistique générale de F. de Saussure*, ed. Robert Godel, Geneva and Paris: Droz, 1957.

— (1987), *Course in General Linguistics*, trans. Roy Harris, London: Duckworth; La Salle, Illinois: Open Court.

— (1993), *F. de Saussure, Troisième cours de linguistique générale (1910–1911), d'après les cahiers d'Emile Constantin/Saussure's Third Course of Lectures on General Linguistics (1910–1911), from the notebooks of Emile Constantin*, ed. and trans. Eisuke Komatsu and Roy Harris, Oxford: Pergamon.

— (1916), *Cours de linguistique générale. Publié par C. Bally et A. Sechehaye, avec la collaboration de A. Riedlinger*, Paris et Lausanne: Payot. (2nd edn 1922, 3rd edn 1931, subsequent eds unchanged.)

— (1984), *Recueil de publications scientifiques*, Geneva: Sonor, 1922. Repr. Geneva: Slatkine.

References and further reading

Aarsleff, Hans (1982), *From Locke to Saussure: Essays on the Study of Language and Intellectual History*, Minneapolis: University of Minneapolis Press.

Culler, Jonathan (1986), *Ferdinand de Saussure*, 2nd edn, Ithaca, New York: Cornell University Press.

Derrida, Jacques (1976), *Of Grammatology*, trans. Gayatri Chakravorty Spivak, Baltimore and London: Johns Hopkins University Press.

Gadet, Françoise (1989), *Saussure and Contemporary Culture*, trans. G. Ellicott, London: Hutchinson Radius.

Harris, Roy (1987), *Reading Saussure*. London: Duckworth; La Salle, Illinois: Open Court.

— (1988), *Language, Saussure and Wittgenstein: How to Play Games with Words*, London and New York: Routledge.

Holdcroft, David (1991), *Saussure: Signs, Systems, and Arbitrariness*, Cambridge and New York: Cambridge University Press.

Joseph, John E. (1988), 'Saussure's meeting with Whitney, Berlin, 1879', *Cahiers Ferdinand de Saussure* 42, 205–14.

— (1990), 'Ideologizing Saussure: Bloomfield's and Chomsky's readings of the *Cours de linguistique générale*', in John E. Joseph and Talbot J. Taylor (eds), *Ideologies of Language*, London and New York: Routledge, 51–78.

Koerner, E. F. Konrad (1972), *Bibliographia Saussureana, 1870–1970*, Metuchen, New Jersey: Scarecrow Press.

— (1973), *Ferdinand de Saussure: Origin and Development of his Linguistic Thought in Western Studies of Language*, Braunschweig: Vieweg.

Sampson, Geoffrey (1980), *Schools of Linguistics*. London: Hutchinson; Stanford: Stanford University Press.

Starobinski, Jean (1979), *Words upon Words: The Anagrams of F. de Saussure*, New Haven and London: Yale University Press.

KINSHIP, STRUCTURALISM AND THE SAVAGE MIND: LÉVI-STRAUSS

Gary Roth

It is easy to forget the phenomenal impact Claude Lévi-Strauss once made, not only in his own discipline of anthropology, but across the entire spectrum of the social sciences. At various times, beginning in the late 1940s and continuing into the 1980s, his ideas were widely discussed and applied in far-ranging disciplines such as history, sociology and philosophy, in sub-fields such as the sociology of knowledge, literary criticism, psychoanalysis and linguistics, and in the intellectual orientations of structuralism, Marxism and feminism. Yet, after schooling an entire generation of intellectuals, Lévi-Strauss witnessed the near-eclipse of his influence, an eclipse so pronounced that his later work on mythology was all but ignored. Eventually, his ideas were rejected on virtually all sides, and with the exception of some specific contributions within the discipline of anthropology, it appears in hindsight that the debates which were recorded in volume after volume and article after article served no other purpose than to decisively refute his influence.

Throughout his career, Lévi-Strauss showed only peripheral interest in the intellectual trends he had helped instigate. He focused on, and often stressed, the logical continuity intrinsic to his scholarship, which he identified as the structural underpinnings inherent to both material reality and the realm of ideas. But although all the elements of his later work were already present in his earlier publications, the emphasis he placed on each element shifted over time. This methodological reorientation underpins his intellectual evolution. It also corresponds with the wholesale dismissal of his ideas. In retrospect, it seems that the more tenaciously Lévi-Strauss asserted the success of his research programme, the less interest he generated. His fateful (or fatal) plunge begins with 'the elementary structures of kinship' and ends with his overriding interest in 'fundamental structures of the human mind'. How Lévi-Strauss went from the one to the other is the theme of this article.

Background

Lévi-Strauss became an anthropologist somewhat by accident, at a time when sociology and anthropology were not yet clearly differentiated. Born in 1908, he grew up in a highly cultured, but struggling, middle-class Jewish family (his father was a portrait painter, his mother trained as a secretary) in Paris, where he also attended the university. He pursued degrees in both law and philosophy although neither field particularly interested him. His undergraduate thesis, 'The Philosophical Postulates of Historical Materialism', was a continuation of an interest in Marx which dated from late adolescence. It also coincided with his involvement in left-wing politics. For a brief period after graduating from college, he taught in college-preparatory high schools and campaigned for the Socialist Party. Then, in early 1935, he left for São Paulo, Brazil to teach sociology but pursue anthropology, both of which had been side-interests during his student days. Brazil would mark the second leg of a not uncommon career path for aspiring academics, in which a stint as a high school teacher or a period of university teaching overseas precede an academic appointment (Foucault also taught outside France before securing a permanent position; Fernand Braudel, among others, would teach with Lévi-Strauss in Brazil). It was here that Lévi-Strauss conducted the only fieldwork of his career, a circumstance later criticised by other anthropologists.

Altogether Lévi-Strauss spent four years in Brazil, during which he organised two expeditions to visit the Caduveo, Bororo, Nambikwara and Tupi-Kawahib Indians in and around the Amazon rain forest (one trip for three months, the second for a year). He returned to France in early 1939 on the eve of the Fascist occupation and was immediately drafted into the army. An invitation to teach at the New School for Social Research in New York, which was then actively recruiting European scholars, provided him with an opportunity to leave. Of the many people with whom he had contact in New York was Roman Jakobson, who introduced him to structural linguistics and the work of Ferdinand de Saussure. It was in New York that Lévi-Strauss undertook the research which would culminate in his treatise on kinship relationships and marriage systems, published in 1949 as *The Elementary Structures of Kinship*. This book, along with the published account of his fieldwork, *Family and Social Life of the Nambikwara*, served as the two theses required before teaching in French universities.

Elementary Structures of Kinship

Throughout his career Lévi-Strauss had a knack for targeting areas within anthropology which represented theoretical bottlenecks for the profession. It was his ability to reconceptualise entire fields within the discipline which accounts for his great influence. Kinship had been a long-standing concern for anthropologists because of its key role in the organisation of human affairs. Since all societies had systems through which marriage was arranged and regulated, Lévi-Strauss was convinced that there were structural patterns common to them all. He

sought to overcome a state of affairs where overly schematic generalisations had given rise to a seemingly infinite variety of specific case studies; in other words, he endeavoured to find an explanation for kinship which was broad enough to serve as theory yet specific enough in its conceptualisation to account for the varied details. Structural analysis, he argued, offered a means to systematise that which exhibited, on a more empirical or factual level, an extraordinary degree of diversity.

If part of Lévi-Strauss's appeal was the scope of his interests, another part was the ambitiousness of his projects. In *The Elementary Structures of Kinship*, sections of the book were devoted to the development of a generalised theory of kinship, the discussion of specific kinship systems (and the particular blend of theory and empirical detail this entails), a critical recounting of the history of anthropological thought and commentary about the use of methodology within the social sciences (in *The Elementary Structures of Kinship*, he claimed to have consulted over 7,000 works). Kinship, in his view, was essential to the definition of social interaction; not only was it co-extensive within society, it was also a condition for the creation of society and a characteristic of its existence. The structural study of kinship aimed to display the patterns which characterise the organisation of society.

Kinship might be universal, hence its definition as synonymous with the social state, but Lévi-Strauss was aware that its meaning and precise form varied between societies, depending on other features of social organisation which, over time, had come to overshadow its importance (such as economic development). His primary interest was in kinship as a social dynamic prior to its submergence by other factors. He distinguished between elementary and complex systems, whereby elementary systems classified all relatives into eligible and ineligible marriage partners. In complex systems, marriage was not prescribed – certain relatives are declared off-limits; otherwise, the determination of marriage partners was left to processes more diffuse in operation, such as economic or psychological considerations. On the whole, he drew his examples of elementary structures from kinship systems in pre-literate, or so-called primitive, societies.

What impressed him was the arbitrary nature of kinship; that is, its non-biological basis. In the societies he studied, the family unit frequently differentiated between relatives of the same biological closeness in order to make some eligible as marriage partners and some ineligible. Lévi-Strauss drew considerable attention to kinship systems in which marriage with your mother's brothers', or father's sisters', children was permitted, but where you could not marry your mother's sisters', or father's brothers', children. This system of cross-cousin marriage was obviously not a matter of biology. The incest taboo which banned marriage with certain relatives also varied as to its application. Biologically-based explanations were not sufficient to account for kinship or incest, but Lévi-Strauss also rejected out-of-hand explanations which discredited pre-literate practices and thought as non-rational, unscientific, aberrant or prone to the supernatural (topics which he would address more intensively in *Totemism* and *The Savage Mind*).

Lévi-Strauss sought answers by referring to aspects of life within these societies over which there was more agreement amongst anthropologists. These aspects centred around certain basic features: the structure and function of the social group, the interaction between groups, the exchange of material and symbolic goods and the practice of exogamy or marriage between groups. Even the prohibition against incest, in his eyes, served a positive function since it forced individuals to marry beyond the boundaries of their own group. If biological family members were forbidden to marry certain relatives, reproduction could only take place through interaction with other families. The concern of incest, he concluded, was not so much with biology as with the creation of social bonds. The obverse of the incest taboo, then, was the practice of exogamy; and exogamy was a practice of social reciprocity. Biology needed to be transcended if a more permanent and expansive basis was to be created for society.

This contradicted the prevailing model of a nuclear family which had come to dominate discussion within the social sciences – it was really an argument on Lévi-Strauss's part about which constitutes the norm. From a theoretical perspective, Lévi-Strauss argued that the biological family could not constitute the basic social unit for it implied a tendency which would dissolve social bonds. The family was self-contained and could even reproduce itself without interaction with other groups or families, despite the biological hazards of in-breeding. This was an inherent limitation of the nuclear family. When economic or cultural interaction did take place, the biological family would serve as a counter-social and isolating element. Rather, kinship as the exchange of marriage partners between groups formed the basis of the social state. It was from the overriding principle of social interaction that Lévi-Strauss viewed biological, economic and cultural practices within so-called primitive societies.

What remained was to specify a mechanism or structural pattern which both confirmed this finding and could account for the many and varied kinship practices found in different societies. His establishment on the theoretical level of a relationship between kinship and the social state needed a complementary justification on an empirical basis. His reasoning on this point is instructive because it provides an early insight into what would eventually become of him: it reveals his many strengths as a theorist and also provides the basis for the evolution of his ideas. In *The Elementary Structures of Kinship*, he identified cross-cousin marriage as the basic structure; that is, the differentiation of cousins into marriageable and non-marriageable partners.

It is important to remember that cross-cousin marriage was a theoretical deduction and that, for Lévi-Strauss, all kinship systems were elaborations of this basic model. That many societies which conformed to his definition of elementary (those which defined eligible and prohibited marriage partners) banned marriage between cross-cousins altogether, was a fact which did not altogether disturb him. Nor did it matter whether cross-cousin marriage was practised consciously or unconsciously, accurately or inaccurately, or whether there was a close fit between the theoretical model he posed and the reality of any particular kinship system. He admits that cross-cousin marriage had never been a feature of all societies, nor was it the form from which other kinship arrangements had evolved. It was not a historical remnant. Neither evolutionary nor diffusionist theories about the spread of cultural traits (which then enjoyed a certain currency within the profession) could point to much evidence on their own behalf.

Cross-cousin marriage was universal because it was the organising principle at the root of all systems of kinship. It was the structural pattern which tied all kinship systems together – a theoretical model, not a prototype within the historical record. For Lévi-Strauss, cross-cousin marriage was the outcome of the assumptions about the role of exchange, the principle of reciprocity, the function of the incest taboo, etc.; on an empirical level, all elementary systems could be seen as variations of this basic structure. Much of *The Elementary Structures of Kinship* was spent demonstrating how societies without cross-cousin marriage none the less followed kinship patterns that were elaborations of it.

In order for Lévi-Strauss to argue on behalf of a model of kinship which exists in reality only as an exception, he had to make several strong methodological arguments, none of which were particularly controversial on their own but, taken together, would occasion his shift in orientation and direction. Crucial to the development of his ideas was his concern with aspects of culture and society neither consciously expressed nor always apparent, the search for which forms the basis of the theoretical aspects of the social sciences. The anthropologist makes use of unobservable structures to illuminate aspects of the social order. Within the field of kinship, the empirical verification for the theory of cross-cousin marriage did not necessitate an awareness of its actual, or underlying, structural existence.

For purposes of clarity, Lévi-Strauss drew several analogies between anthropology and other disciplines. The ability to speak, for instance, is not dependent on a knowledge of formal linguistic principles; yet the former obviously presupposes the latter. A person can speak with nouns, verbs, understandable sentence structure, descriptive vocabulary, etc. without ever having studied grammar. This is why Jakobson, Saussure and structural linguistics were so important for Lévi-Strauss. They provided a starting point for his own version of structural anthropology (his comparisons between the rules of marriage and the rules of language

would help stimulate a tremendous interest in linguistics, semiotics and the importance of language – an upsurge that would outlast his own popularity).

As with Lévi-Strauss, the historian often refers to economic development in order to explain historical phenomena, whether or not the underlying economic trends are perceived or understood by those subjected to them. Taking his cue from Marxism, he held that political activity was not always intelligible on its own terms. What was true for history, economics and linguistics held true for his own approach to anthropology. Cross-cousin marriage was all-present, even if never seen, never acknowledged and modified into other forms.

When Lévi-Strauss defined structural anthropology, he was thinking of social and mental organisation which need not be, but mostly were, unconscious. For this reason, he was often compared to Freud, even though Lévi-Strauss did not have much of an affinity for his theories and, at times, referred to psychoanalysis as a mythology itself (his personal association with Lacan, along with Lacan's interest in the structuralism of Lévi-Strauss, firmed up the association between Lévi-Strauss and Freud in the public's mind). What was most important to Lévi-Strauss was the relationships between individual details or components, the systems which bound them together, as opposed to the details viewed as understandable in their own right.

The publication of *The Elementary Structures of Kinship* brought to a close the first phase of Lévi-Strauss's career and ended the close connection he had drawn between kinship and social science methodology. Afterwards, he would write about kinship only to clarify aspects of his thesis or to defend or modify his ideas in the light of criticism and newer research findings. Otherwise, kinship became a specific, yet limited, case study of processes which he thought greatly transcended the scope of marriage regulations.

From *Structural Anthropology* to *The Savage Mind*

The same year that he published *The Elementary Structures*, Lévi-Strauss returned to France from his ten-year exile in the United States (after the War he served as a cultural attache at the French Embassy in New York and continued his research). Back in France, he pieced together a series of administrative posts (at UNESCO, as assistant director of the Musée de l'Homme) as well as continuing his teaching. Somewhat unsure of his academic future, he turned to the popularisation of his ideas. In the following years, he published two widely-influential books, each of which helped transform him into an author read by significant segments of the intellectual world in France, Western Europe and other parts of the globe. The first book, *Tristes Tropiques*, was really a travel log, an account of his fieldwork in Brazil during the late 1930s with some additional chapters on his exile from France during the Fascist occupation. Beautifully written, self-reflective, erudite and chatty, *Tristes Tropiques* covered a wide range of topics with intimate descriptions of people, cultural practices and plants.

Through this book, Lévi-Strauss became the intellectual's intellectual, the conduit for the highly educated into a realm of knowledge which combined precise information about the natural world with a sociologist's insight into its refashioning by human societies. The relationship between Lévi-Strauss as a highly-specialised producer of intellect and his readers as sophisticated and highly-discriminating consumers would remain a key one for the next several decades, assuming quasi-marketplace overtones. For a period of time Lévi-Strauss was so widely read that he became a cultural icon for sectors of the reading public. Without such a large popular following the anthropology profession might never have taken him as seriously as it did, particularly because his ideas were far from universally accepted within anthropology itself.

His second book from the 1950s, *Structural Anthropology*, was a collection of essays in which his interest in social science methodology came to the fore. He had selected essays which drew out points of commonality and difference with other leading paradigms within anthropology. Despite frequent praise for Radcliffe-Brown, for example, his structuralism was criticised because of its emphasis on empirical and surface phenomena rather than on underlying organisational patterns. Such was his procedure with the theories of Boas, Malinowski,

Kroeber, Lowie, Murdock, Mauss, and Durkheim, amongst others, when he conducted a critical evaluation in light of their contributions to anthropology and their limitations as theorists. Along the way, he had covered topics such as dual organisation, archaism and split representation in art, besides his more sustained treatment of kinship, mythology, linguistics and social structure.

Despite the rather esoteric nature of these essays, they succeeded in introducing his readers to some of the specific issues and debates within the profession. With this, Lévi-Strauss held a unique position within academia; while it is rare for an academic to find an audience outside her or his own discipline, it is even rarer to cross back over and have those readers follow. But such was the level of interest Lévi-Strauss was able to generate in anthropology that his audience indulged topics in which only a subset of the discipline would otherwise have been involved.

This was even more true of his next two books, *Totemism* and *The Savage Mind*. By this time, he had been elected to the highly prestigious Collége de France where, from 1960 until his retirement in 1982, he would teach one new course per year and also supervise an anthropology laboratory with more than thirty colleagues. His new audience, and really his last, was drawn from within the intellectual explosions associated with the student movements of the 1960s and the intense energy generated in ideas about society. *Totemism* was actually a long pamphlet which Lévi-Strauss referred to as an introduction to *The Savage Mind*.

Once again, Lévi-Strauss overwhelmed his readers, in a positive sense, with the breadth and depth of his knowledge. His primary discussion addressed the complexity and sophistication of so-called primitive thought, but scattered throughout these books were references to a wide range of sociological and anthropological figures and theories and a long discussion on the history of anthropological thought. There was something familiar and something new for every reader. He also included a critique of historical reasoning, whereby he juxtaposed a synchronic approach to the study of human affairs (that is, one which proceeds through an analysis of a particular point in time with no reference to past and future) with a diachronic or historical approach.

It was in these two books, and particularly in his intense debate with Sartre over dialectical versus analytical reasoning, that certain strands of his thought became clear. He was accused by critics of propagating an anti-humanism with his focus on structures rather than individuals, charges which to this day are still levelled against the generation of scholars who came of age reading Lévi-Strauss. However, his debate with Sartre helped to bring about the decline of Sartre's great influence.

The Savage Mind also made clear the new turn he had taken in his thinking. To recap our earlier discussion: Lévi-Strauss had begun with the structural analysis of kinship, and this had led to a quest for the unrecognised structure of social relations; in other words, his investigation of kinship systems became a preoccupation with the methodological justification for investigating underlying structures. But although he argued that cross-cousin marriage was universal, he had not provided an explanation of its derivation. What accounted for its universality? If it could be explained neither biologically nor as a historical antecedent, to what could one attribute this underlying feature and organisational principle of kinship systems? This was the one issue which Lévi-Strauss felt his kinship work had left unanswered.

The Savage Mind was the first of his books to provide a full discussion of what had been missing. Behind the structure of kinship stood the organisation of human thought itself, through which an internal logic imposed similarly-structured forms on all areas of content. Lévi-Strauss, in essays and other comments, had often referred to this explanation, but he had never attempted as full an explanation as he did in this book.

His movement from kinship to the fundamental structures, or internal logic, of the mind marks the pivotal point in the development of his ideas. It separates his initial impulses and orientation as an anthropologist from the path he was to follow for the rest of his career. What had been an important but subsidiary theme – the unrecognised structure of social relations – had become his central focus. This explains why he would devote the rest of his career to the study of mythology, since, in his opinion myths, with their elaborate imagery and complicated story-lines, provide more direct access to the mind at work.

This turn in direction was interpreted by many as a shift away from, although not necessarily a repudiation of, Marxism. He might instead have searched for the basis of a universal structure of kinship in the quality of material life, not only in economic affairs but in the complete dimensions of social life which constitute the fabric of human activity. This, after all, was the procedure which informed the opening chapters of *The Savage Mind* as he sought to clarify the conceptual framework of pre-literate peoples through reference to their natural and social environments. From this perspective, the universality of kinship would have been attributable to, as he expressed it, 'objectified social demands', but, somewhere along the way, he had lost faith that such an explanation was sufficient.

Lévi-Strauss alluded to this transformation in statements made about the relationship of his own work to the Marxist tradition, statements which serve as a barometer for the evolution in his thinking (he often commented on other intellectual traditions to help readers situate themselves within his discussions). Earlier in his career, he had said that he aimed to reintegrate anthropology into the Marxist tradition, since kinship, in his view, was of primary importance in pre-capitalist societies (that is, pre-class societies), whereas economic/class relationships are key in the contemporary world. For Lévi-Strauss, kinship was the dominant social dynamic in societies where Marxism was not fully applicable.

Some years later, however, when he had begun his multi-volume work on mythology, he explained himself differently. No longer did he claim that his analysis functioned on the same level as the core of Marxism. It was posed instead as an elaboration of that core as he had switched from infrastructural to superstructural concerns. Not kinship, but the conceptual schemata by which things like kinship are organised, became his overriding concern. While he would continue to consider kinship the most important social dynamic for so-called primitive societies, his intellectual interests were recentred on an altogether different plane of discourse.

Lévi-Strauss did not so much reject Marxism as think it inappropriate for the societies he chose to study. Neither economic nor environmental factors seemed to account for the diversity of individual kinship systems or the specifics of intellectual and cultural activity, and even if they could, the universality of structural patterns would still need an explanation. His new orientation towards Marxism, then, should be seen as running parallel to his interest in mythology. Within the particular context of French Marxism, neither the humanism of Sartre nor the alternative orthodoxy of Althusser (who, like Lacan, proclaimed his allegiance to the structuralism of Lévi-Strauss) had much appeal for him.

The Raw and the Cooked

Lévi-Strauss's four-volume work on mythology brought to the fore the extremes in his thinking. Beginning with a single myth from the Bororo (who he had visited during his fieldwork in the 1930s), and then looking for interconnections between this myth and others, he would eventually analyse or mention over one thousand myths drawn from native cultures in both North and South America. Each myth was interpreted by means of intimate and painstaking descriptions of animal and plant life and references to social organisation and customs, since, in Lévi-Strauss's opinion, interpretation was impossible without a keen knowledge of the specific referents within the myths. Readers were simply overwhelmed by the level of detail.

The comparison of one myth with another allowed Lévi-Strauss to separate out intrinsic aspects of the myths from aspects which had been modified for purely idiosyncratic, local or historical reasons. By filtering through this material he thought he could extract its essential structure and isolate aspects of a myth which were intrinsic only to the myth itself. If, in one part of the Americas, he found inverted myths with identical meanings, in another he found identical myths with inverted meanings.

Categories like 'the raw and the cooked, the fresh and the decayed, the moistened and the burned' had their specific referents, but each set of oppositions also formed the endpoints of a series of terms which were related by means of symmetry, inversion, equivalence, homology and isomorphism, and which, in turn, gave rise to multi-dimensional structures of interpretation described by Lévi-Strauss as spiraling nebulas (Lévi-Strauss was also an early advocate of mathematical models and computers as analytical tools). What is more, he thought that these systems of contrasts and oppositions ultimately revealed a basic binary structure which imitated the inherent structure of the physical world. The human mind, as revealed in myths, imitated the genetic code which formed the basis of all life.

Myths, then, were a means to organise an understanding of the world within a philosophical system aimed at providing not a comprehensive strategy for human life, but one which constantly stated and restated dilemmas and issues to which no final solution could be found. As fantastic as they might seem at face value, the rationality behind myths was revealed by the way individual elements were organisationally structured in the form of grids. Myths were about the act of philosophising, not about philosophy itself, which is why he found them so illuminating in revealing 'certain operational modes of the human mind'.

Lévi-Strauss confined the domain of structural analysis to mathematics, linguistics, music and mythology, but the underpinnings of his structuralism came under renewed criticism. Piaget, the most systematic of the structuralist theorists of that time, questioned his understanding of structure. For Piaget, there is subjective creation which leads to objective construction. Individuals (for Piaget, children) establish mental structures through interaction with the environment, both social and natural. Processes of experimentation and repetition, whether with language or material objects, lead to rule-formation and general conclusions about the functioning of one's surroundings. This process is initially purely subjective, and it is only with the repetition of the subjective that an 'objective' world is established. From Piaget's perspective, development is a process of self-construction which is ongoing and without end. Even structures need to be created. Extrapolating to Lévi-Strauss's domain, Piaget argued that it is not enough to simply posit kinship structures or mental frameworks; equally important are the processes through which these are produced and reproduced.

For Lévi-Strauss, on the other hand, structures always presuppose previous structures. Structure itself is permanent. It is the content which is variable and which undergoes modification through interaction with the surrounding world. There is, at best, a subjective influencing of the objective, where the outward manifestations are subject to alteration and adaptation. Otherwise, structures are imposed, and they are imposed because they are embedded in the mind.

It was on the question of subjectivity that Lévi-Strauss fell prone to the very criticism he had levelled against Sartre. There was no mistaking his words in the conclusion to his mythology series when he claimed that human consciousness was less important than the underlying structure. He accused critics, and modern philosophy in general, of maintaining a misplaced emphasis on personal identity and the self. He preferred 'rationality without a subject' to 'a subject without rationality'. In effect, he had eliminated the alternative possibility of a subject with rationality, which had been Piaget's point to begin with.

With his series on mythology, Lévi-Strauss had lost his general audience. Myth analysis was exhaustive and exhausting (as well as difficult to reproduce), and only his conclusions seemed of importance to his readers – that so-called primitive peoples were rational in thought – but this had already been well established in his previous works. Otherwise, his treatment of the topic was too specialised, even for those who had once indulged him in a wide array of anthropological topics. His subsequent publication of a series of shorter, more accessible, books on mythology (*Myth and Meaning, The Jealous Potter, The Story of Lynx*) did little to dispel this assessment of his work.

For those who had followed-up his insights into the role of language (semiotics) and discourse in the construction of reality, the analytical model used in his mythology series was too rigid and formal for their use. His writings appeared dogmatically formulated and their conceptualisation a retreat from the boldness that once characterised his ideas. What Lévi-Strauss saw as the culmination of his life's work was received as just more examples of a theory and methodology which had already been criticised

and rejected. When he claimed that his work on mythology was of universal significance, his statement merely served to reinforce the homogeneity that had come to characterise his intellectual trajectory. The simple conclusions to which he reduced all ideas and phenomena – those fundamental structures of the mind – made everyone uncomfortable, and his pursuit into the essential nature of human existence became a hinderance to the post-structuralists like Derrida and Foucault who followed him. He found himself in the ironic position of being considered too esoteric by schools of thought accused of being immersed in the esoteric. Lévi-Strauss had transformed himself into an iconoclast.

The Naked Man

Lévi-Strauss will no doubt be remembered for many things – his skills as a meticulous researcher, as a cataloguer whose command of detail was virtually unprecedented, as a scholar who did not shy away from answering critics when he felt the criticisms to be powerful enough. He will also be remembered for his specific contributions within the field of anthropology and in other disciplines and intellectual traditions as well. His intriguing explanations of structural analysis, his concern for methodology and his use of empirical data are all part of his legacy. These accomplishments, when combined with his appreciation of the written word, overriding respect for the human intellect, celebration of the richness and complexity of the human mind, acknowledgement that mental satisfaction can be a product of things 'good to think' and sense of humanity directed toward the much-maligned and much-abused primitive peoples, explain his appeal and profound impact. Together, they serve as reckoning points for future theoretical investigations.

But where it had been possible to overlook some of the more tangential aspects of his ideas, there came a point when he defended the tangents as essential to his analysis. Early in his career, when he compared marriage regulations and kinship systems with the rules of language, it was not yet clear that this represented more than a simple analogy. The investigation into the unconscious sphere of social activity shifted into a search after the fundamental structures of the mind, and his structural programme became increasingly narrow in its focus.

Lévi-Strauss's transformation from kinship to the savage mind eventually outweighed the many positive contributions he had made. It is unfortunate that this side of him overshadows his earlier work, when really the latter represents an escape from the earlier despite its new applications in the field of mythology. Having once shown universal structures, he then applied them everywhere.

In the end, his work was duly noted, but not because there was any inherent interest in what he had to say. It was acknowledged more as a perfunctory tribute, a last ritual, for a man who had spent many years and words demystifying ritualisation. As an adherent of his own school of thought, Lévi-Strauss was the most partisan and the most talented of them all. This accounts for

his final isolation as a scholar. No one could keep up with him, and no one cared.

Not to be outdone, he published *Saudades do Brasil* (*Nostalgia for Brazil*) at the age of 86, a collection of photographs from his ethnographic work in Brazil fifty years earlier, accompanied by a short introduction and captions for each photo. The re-publication of photographs which had originally appeared in *Tristes Tropiques* (along with others), with a writing style and conceptualisation reminiscent of this earlier and most popular of his books, served to remind readers of the Lévi-Strauss they had once known. In a curious manner, the book raised the question of whose nostalgia was at issue – Lévi-Strauss's for Brazil, his readers' for Lévi-Strauss, or Lévi-Strauss's for his readers who had once been so tantalised by his tales of disappearing civilisations?

Bibliography

Writings

Lévi-Strauss, Claude (1969), *The Elementary Structures of Kinship*, Boston: Beacon Press.
— (1988), *The Jealous Potter*, Chicago: University of Chicago Press.
— (1979), *Myth and Meaning*, New York: Schocken Books.
— (1981), *The Naked Man*, London: Jonathan Cape.
— (1975), *The Raw and the Cooked*, New York: Harper and Row.
— (1995), *Saudades do Brasil: A Photographic Memoir*, Seattle: University of Washington Press.
— (1966), *The Savage Mind*, Chicago, University of Chicago Press.
— (1963), *Structural Anthropology*, New York: Basic Books.
— (1976), *Structural Anthropology, Volume 2*, Chicago: University of Chicago Press.
— (1995), *The Story of Lynx*, Chicago: University of Chicago Press.
— (1970), *Totemism*, Boston: Beacon Press.
— (1970), *Tristes Tropiques*, New York: Atheneum.
— (1985), *The View From Afar*, New York: Basic Books.
— and Didier Eribon (1991), *Conversations with Claude Lévi-Strauss*, Chicago: University of Chicago Press.

References and further reading

Barnes, J. A. (1973), *Three Styles in the Study of Kinship*, Berkeley: University of California Press.

Clarke, Simon (1981), *The Foundations of Structuralism: A Critique of Lévi-Strauss and the Structuralist Movement*, Sussex: The Harvester Press.
Geertz, Clifford (1988), *Works and Lives: The Anthropologist as Author*, Stanford: Stanford University Press.
Hayes, E. Nelson and Tanya Hayes (eds) (1972), *Claude Lévi-Strauss: The Anthropologist as Hero*, Cambridge: The MIT Press. (Contains seventeen articles discussing the various aspects of Lévi-Strauss's ideas.)
Lapointe, François H. and Clare C. Lapointe (1977), *Claude Lévi-Strauss and His Critics: An International Bibliography of Criticism (1950–1976)*, New York: Garland Publishing, Inc.
Leach, Edmund (ed.) (1967), *The Structural Study of Myth and Totemism*, London: Tavistock Publications.
— (1989), *Claude Lévi-Strauss*, Chicago: University of Chicago Press.
Pace, David (1983), *Claude Lévi-Strauss: The Bearer of Ashes*, Boston: Routledge and Kegan Paul.
Piaget, Jean (1971), *Structuralism*, New York: Harper TorchBooks.
Rossi, Ino (ed.) (1974), *The Unconscious in Culture: The Structuralism of Claude Lévi-Strauss in Perspective*, New York: Dutton.
Roth, Gary (1993), 'Claude Lévi-Strauss in Retrospect', *Dialectical Anthropology*, 18, 31–52.

THE CUNNING OF CONCEPTS: ALTHUSSER'S STRUCTURAL MARXISM

Gregory Elliott

Widely considered one of the most significant Marxist theoreticians of the post-War period, Louis Althusser (1918–90) effected a wholesale reconstruction of Marxist philosophy and social theory in the 1960s in an attempt to rescue them from the perceived discredit into which they had fallen, mainly by virtue of their political association with Stalinism. For a decade or more, his strenuously anti-empiricist and anti-humanist enterprise won him a large following throughout Western Europe and Latin America, and set the terms of intra-Marxist debate across disciplinary boundaries, inciting equivalent extremes of attraction and repulsion.

In stark contrast, from the mid-1970s Althusser's reputation waned as rapidly as it had waxed. Several reasons may be suggested for this reverse in critical fortunes. One is the manifest disparity between the overweening initial promise, and the disappointing eventual performance, of Althusser's Marxism in its scientific pretensions. Such disproportion was substantially attributable to apparently insurmountable difficulties in the original positions, registered by successive critics and arguably only aggravated by the revisions undertaken by Althusser in response. However, the intrinsic theoretical history of the 'rise and fall of structural Marxism' (Benton, 1984) was inseparably bound up with extrinsic developments – the wider political history of the period, mocking revolutionary expectations on the Left, which pro-voked what Althusser himself diagnosed as a 'crisis of Marxism' (see Althusser, 1994c, pp. 357–524). Finally, the philosopher's murder of his wife in 1980, and the revelation that he had suffered from severe manic-depressive illness throughout his adult life, rendered him a non-person, in the strict legal sense in France, for the remainder of his tormented years. Thereafter, if invoked aside from *l'affaire Althusser*, it was liable to be as a staging-post in the edifying progress of the class of 1968, from Marxism to post-modernism.

Recent years have marked a revival of interest in Althusser and his legacy, attested in the English-speaking world by the publication of two full-length studies (Resch, 1992; Majumdar, 1995), and four collections (Kaplan and Sprinker, eds, 1993; Elliott, ed., 1994; Lezra, ed., 1995; Callari and Ruccio, eds, 1996). The principal occasion for it was the simultaneous appearance in France of Althusser's extraordinary memoirs (Althusser, 1992, pp. 11–286), composed in 1985, and the first instalment of a comprehensive biography (Moulier Boutang, 1992), covering the period up to 1956. These revealed the existence of a hitherto unknown Althusser, something of whose complexity is disclosed by the further eight volumes (to date) of a posthumous edition of his writings. For no other reason than that they comfortably exceed in quantity the material released during Althusser's lifetime, it will take much critical time and effort to acquire an adequate perspective upon their author.

Conventionally, Althusser's career has been divided into three main phases, spanning the years 1960–78: 1960–66, or the elaboration of structural Marxism (*For Marx* and *Reading Capital*, both published in 1965); 1967–75, or the revision of Althusserian Marxism (from *Philosophy and the Spontaneous Philosophy of Scientists* to *Elements of Self-Criticism*); and 1976–78, or the deconstruction of Althusserianism (most evident, perhaps, in the 1978 article, 'Marxism Today', in Althusser, 1990, pp. 267–80). At the very least, this periodisation must now be supplemented by two more phases of reflection and production. The first is a pre-Althusserian period, approximately 1945–51, comprising Althusser's 'early writings' (Althusser, 1997). The intellectual adventure recorded in them is an intricately overlapping and cross-cutting transition, from Catholicism to Communism, and from Hegelianism to Marxism.

The second addition to our knowledge of Althusser is a phase that post-dates the termination of his public career, composed of a series of fragmentary texts (Althusser, 1994a, pp. 467–508; 1994b, pp. 29–79; and 1994c, pp. 535–79), which revolve around the project of an 'aleatory materialism' or a 'materialism of the encounter'. These pose numerous interpretative problems, not least including what Antonio Negri, alluding to the 'turn' in the thought of Heidegger, has identified as 'Althusser's *Kehre*' (Callari and Ruccio, eds, 1996, p. 58): is the 'last' Althusser radically distinct from his antecedent philosophical selves? Or are there discernible elements of continuity, as well as discontinuity, between them – elements which might, in their turn, necessitate a rereading of the well-rehearsed Althusser? The concurrent publication of material dating from 1962–77 (Althusser, 1993, 1995a and 1995b) both permits more nuanced delineation of him at the height of his celebrity and indicates a provisional answer in the affirmative. The posthumous *œuvre* contains references to themes (for example, the necessary contingency of history), and to authors (for example, the nineteenth-century philosopher of probability, Antoine-Augustin Cournot), cited in the mature Althusserian discourse on method, before being highlighted in the closing meditations on a philosophy for Marxism.

The extent to which the received image of Althusser will be transformed by the assimilation of this work, only a fraction of which has thus far been translated, cannot be anticipated. Yet, if it is too soon to pronounce upon his ultimate destination, it is possible to fix his proximate point of departure with more confidence. The intellectual 'biography' of Marx outlined in Althusser's major works was something in the nature of a philosophical 'autobiography'. In other words, the writings of the mature Althusser represented a tacit 'settlement of accounts' with his erstwhile theoretical consciousness; the great critiques of Hegelian Marxism in *For Marx* and *Reading Capital* are also autocritiques of the young Althusser.

Spectres of Hegel and Stalin

When, like Descartes, Althusser advanced, masked, on to the public stage at the beginning of the 1960s, his imperatives were indissolubly political and philosophical. For convenience of exposition, however, it might be said that his ends were political and his means philosophical. Against what he regarded as Khrushchev's 'right-wing de-Stalinization', which centred upon condemnation of the 'cult of the personality', eliciting a renaissance of ethical (or humanist) Marxism, Althusser conceived himself as 'mak[ing] a start on the first *left-wing* critique of Stalinism':

> a critique that would make it possible to reflect not only on Khrushchev and Stalin but also on Prague and Lin Piao: that would above all help to put some substance back into the revolutionary project here in the West. (Althusser, 1990, p. xviii)

Scarcely the first such critique, Althusser's initiative – launched, we should recall, from inside a Stalinist organisation – did mount an assault on key components of the dictator's legacy. Yet it did so in the context of an attack upon forms of intentionally *anti*-Stalinist Marxism, adjudged incapable of furnishing the requisite theoretical resources with which to sustain a consistent political opposition to Stalinism from the Left. Indeed, it would not be an exaggeration to say that Althusser subjected virtually the whole of actually existing Marxism to swingeing criticism on the grounds that, notwithstanding the obvious differences between its representatives, they all performed variations upon Hegelian themes.

According to Althusser, what were habitually construed as the mutually antipathetic traditions of Orthodox and Western Marxism exhibited the common vice of 'historicism'. On his cavalier typology, it assumed two regular guises: the 'economism' typical of the Kautskyist Second International (1889–1914) and the Stalinist Third International (1925–); and the 'humanism' characteristic of the recurrent reactions against it (for example, Lukács in the 1920s or Sartre in the 1950s). Both these broad tendencies effectively cancelled Marx's rupture with the 'German ideology' of his youth, staging counter-revolutions against *Capital*. Secularised versions of Hegelian theodicy, they each depicted human history as an expressive totality or process, possessed of an origin, a centre, a subject and a goal.

Economism – a 'poor man's Hegelianism' (Althusser, 1971, p. 78) – represented a technological determinism. It plotted a meta-narrative of the inexorable progression of the productive forces in a fixed, linear sequence of 'modes of production', and the 'social formations' to which they gave rise. These stretched from 'primitive communism', via antiquity, feudalism and capitalism, to communism, whose ineluctable advent, in a 'negation of the negation' executed by the proletariat, would mark humanity's leap from the 'kingdom of necessity' to the 'realm of freedom'.

In seductive, yet deceptive, contrast, humanism – a 'rich man's evolutionism' (Althusser, 1990, p. 56) – secreted a teleological philosophical anthropology. It projected an odyssey of the human essence, divided against itself in the forms of class society that culminated in the capitalist present, only to be reappropriated under the classless community of the communist future. Its realisation, by the revolutionary *praxis* of the 'universal class' (the proletariat), would consummate humanity's rites of passage, from the state of alienation to the 'end of history'.

The scandalous novelty of the Althusserian anat-omy of these antithetical interpretations of Marxism resided in his identification of them and their political correlates ('mechanism' and 'voluntarism', respectively), as mirror-images – not in their diverse inspiration or aspiration, but in their theoretical schematism and historical messianism. This homology, traceable to a common Hegelian ancestry, permitted a degree of amalgamation of the two schemas. (Althusser's own Master's dissertation of 1947 on Hegel and his heritage, in Althusser, 1997, pp. 36–169, offers an example.) Both the humanist 'inversion' of Hegel, consciously conducted by Feuerbach and inherited by the young Marx, and the economistic 'inversion' of Hegel, unwittingly perpetrated by the Second International and bequeathed to Stalin, preserved an historicist philosophical *structure*, even as they reconjugated its *elements*. Thus, despite the superficial hostility of Cold War Stalinism to Hegel, there was inscribed in it, Althusser argued, a Hegelianisation of Marxism whereby the phenomenal forms of ideology and politics functioned as the ruses of Economic Reason. Consequently, historical materialism assumed the shape of what, in 1877, Marx had dismissed as 'a general historico-philosophical theory, the supreme virtue of which consists in being supra-historical' (in Elliott, 1987, p. 79).

Althusser's objections to any such theoretical 'reductionism' were simultaneously analytical and political. In so far as it abstracted from the complexity and specificity of historical conjunctures, it was impotent before the 'implacable test of the facts' of modern history (Althusser, 1976, p. 187), whose revolutionary events (Russia in 1917) and, *a fortiori*, non-events (Germany in 1918–19), had stubbornly declined to comply with its predictions. Furthermore, it precluded a precondition of rational political practice, the distinguishing feature of 'scientific', as opposed to 'utopian', socialism: namely, that 'concrete analysis' indispensable to the real comprehension – and hence possible transformation – of 'concrete situations'. Contrary to Marx's Eleventh Thesis on Feuerbach, the world must be interpreted aright before it could be changed.

The exigency of such analysis is associated by Althusser with the figure of Lenin. Althusser's proclaimed 'return to Marx', or to a supposedly authentic Marxism, ranged beyond a separation between the (pre-Marxist) young Marx of the *Economic and Philosophical Manuscripts* and the mature (Marxist) Marx of *Capital*, to a differentiation between Lenin and Stalin. Among the issues in dispute in the Althusserian restructuring of the Marxist textual canon and theoretical corpus was Leninism, regarded – especially in its contemporary embodiment in Maoism – as affording facilities for a renewal of revolutionary Marxism post-Stalin.

This bid to disrupt the terms of the humanist controversy of the late 1950s and early 1960s – in particular, the prevalent recourse to the young Marx against Stalin *and* Lenin – by reinstating the mature Marx and Lenin, while instating Mao, faces formidable obstacles. The economistic and humanist traditions of Marxism can both muster more or less ample warrant for their constructions in Marx's *œuvre*. (The former, for example, can recite the 1859 *Preface* to *A Contribution to the Critique of Political Economy*.) Althusser's counter-construal therefore stands in need of compelling Marxist criteria to validate its own limited selection from among the mass of texts signed 'Karl Marx'. In their absence, Althusser's version will be no more authorised – perhaps even less so, in view of his radical surgery – than those of his rivals. Yet, assuming that Althusser can prevail on this score, he has a further exacting task ahead of him: having distinguished what is authentically Marxist in the work of Marx and his professed followers, having therewith retrieved historical materialism from putative deformations of it, he must justify the central claim staked on its behalf – namely, that it is *the* science (and not merely another philosophy) of history.

These duties were to be discharged by philosophy; but in order to preserve the Marxist credentials of the operation, or so Althusser thought, that philosophy had to be a *sui generis* Marxist philosophy. In short, Marxist philosophy was to be mobilised to separate Marxist science from its impostors, and to vindicate it against its pretenders. As Althusser readily conceded (Althusser and Balibar, 1968, p. 34, p. 74), his strategy described a 'circle'. The crucial question is whether that circle is vicious, or (as he wagered) virtuous.

The labour of concepts

The full measure of the Althusserian reformation of Marxism should by now be apparent. It stipulated three interdependent endeavours which, for clarity's sake, may be disaggregated as follows. The first was the elaboration of an anti-empiricist Marxist philosophy, cast as an historical epistemology which could guide epistemological histories of theoretical discourses. The second was to set this philosophy to work on an epistemological history of the formation of historical materialism, through a reading of Marx's heterogeneous work, differentiating between and within its constituents. Such a Marxism of Marxism would identify the substance, and clarify the status, of Marx's 'materialist conception of history'. The third was the renovation of historical materialism, thus delimited, as a non-historicist theory of the constitution, reproduction and transformation of modes of production.

Althusser's recasting of Marxist philosophy as what he dubbed the 'theory of theoretical practice' found such licence as it could supply in Marx's 1857 *Introduction*. On the basis of this draft, Althusser would argue that Marxist epistemology was already practically operative in *Capital*, yet remained to be theoretically formulated. Thus far, it had not been. Instead, especially in the shape of the canonical 'dialectical materialism' ('diamat') systematised by Stalin as the general science of the laws of nature, history and thought, Marx's inheritors had fashioned non-Marxist ideologies whose prescriptions and proscriptions infringed the cognitive autonomy of the sciences (including historical materialism). Althusser's overriding concern was to insulate scientific autonomy from political authority, and to do so on unimpeachable Marxist grounds. The theoretical irony, however, was that, in order to render 'Marxist philosophy' virtuous, Althusser was compelled to render his interpretative circle – encapsulated in the title of his Introduction to *Reading Capital*, 'From *Capital* to Marx's Philosophy' – vicious. To counter not only 'diamat', but also the 'subject-centred history and subject-constituted thought' of its humanist antagonists (Benton, 1984, p. 10), Althusser resorted to patently non-Marxist authorities: the rationalist philosophy of Spinoza; the conventionalist epistemology of Bachelard and Canguilhem; the structural psychoanalysis of Lacan. (The scope of the collaboration envisaged with Lacanianism, in the production of a 'general theory of discourse(s)' which would put paid to the 'linguistic ideology' of structuralism, can now be gauged in Althusser, 1993, especially pp. 111–70.) In a move habitual among the schools of Western Marxism (Anderson, 1976, pp. 55–67), under the banner of a return to Marx, Althusser executed a turn to the classical philosophical tradition, and to a specifically national (quasi-Comtean) current of theoretical 'holism', for his own convergent Marxist purposes.

The harvest of this fertilisation by non-Marxist philosophy was a 'theory of the production of knowledge(s)' which sought to domesticate the lessons of modern, post-empiricist philosophy of science within Marxism. It recognised the social constitution and reconstitution of scientific theories – their 'relative autonomy' *qua* socio-historical products – while insisting on their cognitive autonomy *qua* scientific theories. It thereby attempted to combine conventionalist and realist premises for what Althusser considered a 'materialist' conclusion – a conclusion that manipulated a standard form of Marxist Manichaeanism: the dualism of 'theory' and 'practice'. Correctly understood, theory was itself a form of social practice. Any society was a 'complex unity of "social practice" ' (Althusser, 1965, p. 229), a genus which could be analysed into four species: economic, political, ideological and theoretical practices.

Each had the transformative structure of the labour-process as dissected by Marx, entailing the three moments of raw material, means of production and product. For its part, the production of knowledge was the fruit of 'theoretical practice', encompassing the raw material of existing facts and concepts, the means of production provided by the current state of theory, and products: knowledge, which subsequently featured in the means of production of the relevant theory (Althusser, 1965, pp. 166ff.).

Now, in conformity with Marx's postulate that any (economic) labour-process was conducted under the social relations of production of a particular mode of production, Althusser gestured towards the necessity of an analysis of the diverse historical modes of theoretical production. But he did not supply it. Of more immediate critical significance are the acute tensions within his epistemology generated by his eschewal of the 'empiricist conception of knowledge' (Althusser and Balibar, 1968, pp. 35–40), ecumenically construed to include any confrontation between a (knowing) subject and an object (to be known). Althusser maintained that the cognitive process was wholly intra-theoretical. Its starting-point and end-product were conceptual 'objects of knowledge' (for example, 'Fordism'), through which knowledge of a 'real object' (for example, US capitalism) was produced and appropriated in thought. Thereby, the theory of theoretical practice asserted its titles both to 'materialism', acknowledging the primacy of objective reality, which subsisted independently of the various theories of it; and to anti-empiricism, affirming the indispensability of theory, which discursively constructed and reconstructed that reality. Moreover, it held that once theoretical practices had crossed the threshold of scientificity (for example, in the transition from Aristotelian to Galilean physics), they required neither the guarantees of their status liberally bestowed by the juridical practice of the 'theory of knowledge'; nor the external confirmation of their claims naively vouchsafed by experience and its analogues. These threatened an infinite regress of the guarantee. Endowed with autonomy, the theoretical practice of a science was its own criterion; and verification was internal to theory (ibid., pp. 56–60).

Since the difference between a constituted science, and the pre-history from which it emerged, became manifest in a specific conjuncture of theoretical history, it could only be located by an epistemological history that scanned theories at the level of the distinctive 'problematics' wherein they posed, and sought to resolve, the problems peculiar to them. Discontinuity did not only pertain to the emergence of a science in a founding 'epistemological break' with ideology; it punctuated the uneven development of a science after its foundation, and was demonstrated by successive 'recastings' of its theoretical matrix and problematic (for example, Newton's of the Galilean, or Einstein's of the Newtonian).

Setting aside its dubious Marxist credentials, the principal dilemma confronting this historical epistemology is analogous to that besetting Kuhnian philosophy of science; namely, whether the scientific *change* exhibited by the history can be reconciled with the scientific *progress* affirmed by the epistemology. Althusser's conventionalist duplication of the scientific universe into 'theoretical' (internal) and 'real' (external) objects, with its apparent severance of different theoretical descriptions from their extra-theoretical referents, induces relativist conclusions. By definition, these are inimical to any vindication of the scientificity of Marxist social theory – a status which can then only be upheld by resort to a dogmatic rationalism no less injurious to the cogency (not to mention originality) of Althusserian Marxist philosophy. In other words, Althusser could secure the originality of his philosophical position within Marxism only at the cost of its authenticity as Marxist philosophy, and its serviceability to Marxist science.

In the particular case of Althusser's epistemological history of Marx(ism), these tensions can be summarised as follows: even if Althusser can demonstrate pertinent differences between the late and the early Marx, such conceptual discontinuity is not tantamount to the cognitive superiority of the one over the other. Discrimination between the two is a necessary, but insufficient, condition of any vindication of the mature Marx as portrayed by Althusser. On the other hand, Althusser's dereliction on the second count – his conflation of what is authentically Marxist with what is genuinely scientific – does not in itself weaken his proposals on the first.

As already indicated, Althusser's alternative 'periodisation' of Marx's *œuvre* identified a profound discontinuity, at once conceptual and epistemological, between the supposedly non-Marxist early works of 1840–44 and the unevenly Marxist texts of 1845–6 onwards (themselves assigned to a series of distinct phases: see Althusser, 1965, pp. 33–8). By way of a 'symptomatic reading' modelled on the psychoanalytical interpretation of dreams, and duly attentive to the latent discursive structure underlying the manifest contents of a text, an epistemological break with historicism was isolable where Marx himself had testified to a turning-point: *The German Ideology.*

It separated incompatible theoretical problematics – the one, tributary to left-Hegelianism, turning in the closed circle of an idealist philosophy of history; the other, specific to Marx, initiating an open-ended science of history. Crucially, however, this 'theoretical revolution', strictly analogous to the achievements of Galileo in physics or Lavoisier in chemistry, had only been commenced by Marx. He had opened up the 'continent of history' to scientific exploration – above all, in *Capital* – founding a research programme which remained to be developed, as opposed to promulgating a doctrine that need only be quoted, by his successors.

In accordance with the lessons of other sciences, so he believed, Althusser proposed to account for the presence of pre-Marxist (historicist-humanist) categories in Marx's mature writings by the lacunary nature of *Capital* itself. Like Freud after him, in the absence of the concepts required to capture the *differentia specifica* of his revolutionary theory, Marx had necessarily cashed it in the philosophical currency of his era (Althusser and Balibar, 1968, pp. 182–93). His revolution thus stood in need of completion. Enter Althusser.

This interpretation of Marx, presenting Althusser's reconstruction of historical materialism as Marx's construction of it, is deeply flawed: to cite but one item of evidence, the pervasively Hegelian *Grundrisse* are symptomatically absent from Althusser's reading. But this aside, four implications of it should be noted. The first, against the humanist current, was the restoration of *Capital* as the *locus classicus*, for better or worse, of Marx's theory. The second, inherent in Althusser's delimitation of historical materialism as an autonomous science with its own object, method and theory, was a renunciation of the 'materialist' metaphysic of the Second and Third Internationals, whereby Marxism was an autarkic cosmology or 'world-view', subsuming the totality of human and non-human phenomena, of which the materialist conception of history was merely a subset. The third, in conjuction with Althusser's reassertion of the scientificity of historical materialism, was an insistence upon its incompletion – not only as a result of the inevitable limitations of Marx's own accomplishment, but as a normal correlate of its scientific status. If it was to make good its claim to be a 'science among others', then, by definition, historical materialism must be amenable to progression and rectification, producing the new knowledge characteristic of the 'adventure of science in development' (Althusser, 1965, p. 245).

Finally – an inference from the Galilean analogy – the problematic within which Marx had himself worked was susceptible to recastings of the type now being undertaken by Althusser in response to the misadventures of a science in stagnation. Just as the science of physics, as opposed to phases in its history, was not designated by a proper noun, so too the science of history was not the property in perpetuity of a founding father. The 'theoretical contributions necessary for the present period' would, as Althusser tactfully but pointedly remarked with reference to 'Leninism', 'later be called by a name which does not exist as yet' (ibid., p. 176). Whether or not that name spelt 'Althusserianism', the import was clear. In so far as historical materialism merely reiterated the Marxism of Marx, it abdicated its scientific responsibility and therewith contradicted its scientificity, of which productivity and corrigibility were the criteria.

The continent of history

The Althusserian reconstitution of historical materialism on non-historicist bases featured three central innovations: a reconceptualisation of the 'dialectic'; a reconfiguration of the structure of 'social formations' and 'modes of production'; and a retheorisation of 'ideology'.

As regards the first, Althusser problematised the terms of the standard account of the Marx/Hegel relationship – Marx's own 'inversion' metaphor – claiming that it preserved the Hegelian problematic, even if shuffled its vices from the 'spiritual' to the 'material'. To be truly distinctive, the Marxist dialectic must be intrinsically – structurally – different. The logic of its Hegelian predecessor was incurably teleological. The defining characteristic of its category of contradiction was simplicity, entrusted as it was with 'the magical movement of the concrete contents of a historical epoch towards their ideological Goal' (Althusser, 1965, p. 104). Literally inverted, this yielded economism, wherein the con-

tradiction between forces and relations of production was charged with moving the concrete contents of an epoch towards their economic goal. To excise such fatalism from the Marxist dialectic, Althusser argued for the 'overdetermination' of any contradiction (ibid., pp. 87–116). Adapted by him from the Lacanian interpretation of Freud, 'overdetermination' was employed to prospect a 'structural causality' which would avoid the demerits of traditional causal models, whether 'transitive' (mechanical cause/effect), or 'expressive' (spiritual essence/appearance). It entailed each contradiction active in a historical conjuncture being internally marked by the others, which constituted its 'conditions of existence'. No mere manifestations of an underlying economic contradiction, political and ideological contradictions were irreducibly real and effective, simultaneously determinant and determined. At the same time, social contradictions were hierarchically organised in a determinate, yet variable, order, defining the specific pattern of dominance and antagonism in a given society at a given time. In intent, then, overdetermination was not to be equated with causal pluralism, nor an imponderable co-determination of the social formation by the superstructures. Althusser's aim was to reconfigure the social formation as a constitutively complex, but ultimately unified, totality.

Here the classical precedent was the later Engels's anxiety to wrest the base/superstructure topography from vulgar determinism by conceding the 'reciprocal action' of the latter upon the former. Althusser sought to reconcile its main premise – 'economic determination in the last instance' – with what he called the 'specific effectivity' of the superstructures (ibid., p. 111). He did so by displacing, to all intents and purposes, the orthodox topography. The Marxist conception of the social formation, he maintained, was one of a global structure, consisting in three regional structures – the economic, the political and the ideological – each of which enjoyed 'relative autonomy' vis-à-vis the others. The political and ideological structures were thus not to be regarded as the secondary effects of a primordial cause, or as the superstructural phenomena of an infrastructural essence. Nor, however, were they simply independent. Any social formation was a 'structure in dominance' (ibid., pp. 200–16), containing a dominant structure which organised the hierarchy and articulation of the regional structures. And, although the economic structure was not invariably *dominant*, it was always *determinant*, since it allocated the role of dominance (in pre-capitalist societies, for example, to the ideological or political structures). A 'decentred structure', the Marxist totality was inseparable from the structures that constituted it, and correspondingly characterised by irreducible states of overdetermination.

For so novel a set of proposals to be recognisably Marxist, it was imperative not only to reclaim the superstructures, but to redeem the infrastructure, from technological determinism. The anti-teleological theory of modes of production propounded by Althusser's collaborator, Etienne Balibar, addressed this task (Althusser and Balibar, 1968, pp. 199–308). Modes of production were conceived as articulated, but not inherently contradictory, combinations of forces and relations of production, under the primacy of the latter. The productive forces were thus demoted from their accustomed status of independent variable. Accordingly, the contradictory dialectic of forces and relations – the principal dynamic of history in Marx's 1859 *Preface* – was banished from historical materialism, indicating its 'radically *anti-evolutionist* character' (ibid., p. 225). Modes of production were not transient phenomena whose sequential rise and fall was pre-determined by iron laws of history, but historical forms whose existence was circumscribed by the prerequisites of their reproduction. In the very act of exorcising one demon – historical necessity – this risked conjuring another: historical accident. How was the 'transition' from one mode of production to another to be envisaged? Balibar took the daring step of seeking to theorise historical transition on the basis of social reproduction (ibid., pp. 273–308), concluding with the possibility of a conjuncture of 'non-correspondence' between the structures of the social formation, in which dominance was displaced on to the political, and class struggle intervened as the 'motor of history'.

Notoriously, this did not imply a collective subject of history; Marxism was no more a (voluntaristic) humanism than a (fatalistic) determinism. In the Althusserian scheme of things, history was a 'process without a subject' (Althusser, 1976, pp. 94–9), in which social structures had explanatory priority over the human agents who were their 'bearers'. Human agents were not the constitutive subjects *of* history, but constituted subjects *in* history; and they were thus constituted by and in ideology. Althusser's theory of ideology arguably owed more to Durkheim and Freud (in the Lacanian rendition) than to Marx. Ideology was the ideo-affective realm of 'lived experience' in which the real relations between subject and society were inverted, and human agents equipped with the necessary illusion of autonomy, such that they considered themselves the unacknowledged legislators of their own world (Althusser, 1984, pp. 32–57). The set of representations of people's 'imaginary relations' to their conditions of existence, ideology was indispensable if they were to function as social agents, under constraining structures anterior and exterior to them. Combining epistemological and sociological premises, Althusser deduced, contrary to Marx, the persistence of ideology under Communism. There would be no 'end of ideology', both because of the ineliminable opacity of any conceivable social formation, and because human beings were not the rational animals of pre- Freudian liberal humanism (Althusser, 1965, pp. 231–6; 1990, pp. 22–31).

The hour of reckoning

'Hyper-empiricism', 'structural-functionalism', 'determinism', 'dogmatism', 'Stalinism', 'idealism': these are just a few of a myriad cognate charges laid against Althusser's revisions of historical materialism. Naturally, there can be no question of investigating them in any detail here. (Readers are referred to Thompson, 1978 for the full repertoire; and to Anderson, 1980 and Benton, 1984 for judicious assessments.) However, one account may rapidly be settled. As Althusser later conceded, in response to Raymond Aron, his was an 'imaginary Marxism' (Althusser, 1992, p. 221; 1994b, p. 37; 1994c, pp. 319–20). Geared to a reformation of historical Communism via a renovation of historical Marxism, Althusserianism was obliged to proceed as if it were the reappropriation of the authentic tradition. Textually tendentious, it was theoretically contentious as an interpretation of Marx's Marxism.

Of more – non-Marxological – moment is the discrepancy between the cogency of Althusser's critiques of classical and post-classical Marxism, and the vulnerability of his alternatives to them. This has frequently been attributed to his complicity with the 1960s Parisian cult of impersonality, or 'structuralism'. Yet, despite a conjunctural alliance of convenience with the French ideology, Althusser was at pains to dissociate himself from the 'formalism' of the structuralist 'combinatory', criticising its hegemonic pretensions vis-à-vis the social and human sciences, and its abusive extrapolation of Saussureanism to such non-linguistic objects as historical social formations. (See, for example, his 1966 critique of Lévi-Strauss in Althusser, 1995a, pp. 417–32.) If, to underscore the anti-historicist rupture with the German ideology, Balibar originally ventured to describe Marx's theory of history as 'a most unusual *structuralism*' (Althusser *et al.*, 1965), it was because selective Althusserian affinities actually lay elsewhere – with Spinozism.

The extent of Althusser's assimilation of Spinoza was acknowledged by him after the event (Althusser, 1976, pp. 132–41), and is further illuminated in a posthumously published text (Althusser, 1994a, pp. 467–87). It is probably to this Dutch ancestor, rather than to his French contemporaries, that we should look for the key to the novelty – and the fragility – of Althusserianism. However, whatever the 'sources', the component parts of structural Marxism proved on inspection to be vitiated in ways that permitted their deconstruction: 'anti-empiricism', by an unstable compromise formation between rationalism and conventionalism, prompting perspectivist or realist rejections; 'anti-humanism', by its repetition of the structure/agency paralogism, tilting the theorisation of ideology in the direction of functionalism; 'anti-historicism', by its institution of a theory/history dichotomy, emphasising social reproduction, while rendering social transformation inscrutable; and 'anti-economism', by its elliptical resolution of the base/superstructure conundrum, encouraging a slide from 'relative' to outright autonomy.

Althusser's own concessions to opponents be-trayed something of the Maoist temper of the post-1968 times in France, and his adjustments of the original positions are generally agreed to be unavailing. Perhaps his most important enterprise in this period was a conjoint theory of social reproduction *and* revolution, presumably intended to emend Balibar's endeavour to infer 'elements for a theory of transition' from an analysis of the concept of reproduction. Significantly, however, only a first volume (recently published in Althusser, 1995b, pp. 19–242), dealing with reproduction, was substantially completed. The abortion of the project, and the postscript appended to the extracts which did appear, as the 'ideological state apparatuses' (ISAs) essay in 1970 (Althusser, 1984, pp. 1–60), testified to its intractability. (In his critique of the 'functionalism' of the Lévi-Straussian conception of 'primitive societies', Althusser (1995a, pp. 424–25), had already penned his own critics' script. They would argue that the attributes denied the human agent were transferred to the social structure in the Althusserian account of ISAs.) Meanwhile, a leftist inflection of Marxist philosophy as the 'class struggle in theory', intervening to defend the sciences (including Marxism) against the depredations of ideology, retracted the rationalism of the theory of theoretical practice, only to debauch into a dogmatism of philosophical 'correctness' (see Althusser, 1976, pp. 35–77 and 1990, pp. 69–202).

The decline in Althusser's public powers was, of course, overdetermined by another case-history. Even so, there is no mistaking Althusserianism's loss of direction amid the series of defeats experienced by the European Left in the 1970s, which issued in a general decline in the reputation of Marxism among the Western intelligentsia. The net effect was to impart to Althusser a highly paradoxical historical significance, such that he may be regarded as one of the leading protagonists in two key episodes in post-War French thought. The first was the anti-existentialist and, more broadly, anti-phenomenological turn of the 1960s, concerted under the umbrella term of 'structuralism'. Althusser's distinctiveness within it was to advocate a rearticulation of Marxist philosophy and Communist politics as the basis for answers to the burning questions of the philosophico-political conjuncture.

In so doing, he repudiated the available models of the compliant party ideologue and the independent committed intellectual. As to his answers, Alasdair MacIntyre's verdict, registering 'the profound gratitude that we all owe to Althusser for having brought French Marxism back into dialogue with the rest of French philosophy', may be upheld: 'So far as French philosophy was concerned, he de-Stalinized Marxism more thoroughly than any other Marxist did' (in Althusser, 1990, p. xi). Yet, to the extent that he did, but failed to establish a viable alternative of his own, a common deduction was that Althusser had proved the theoretical unsustainability of *any* version of Marxism. Thus it was that the self-declared partisan of a 'return to Marx' became the inadvertent artisan of the turn from Marx associated with 'post-structuralism'. For, by virtue of the richly contradictory character of structural Marxism, that transfer of allegiances could proceed via an anti-Marxist radicalisation of certain of its theses.

Of these, none has provoked more consternation than the insistence that Marxism was not a humanism. In conclusion, then, it is worth recalling Althusser's wholehearted conviction that only *theoretical* anti-humanism in the present could orientate that *practical* humanism of the future to which, as a Communist, he subscribed. As Althusser remarked of the painter Cremonini, he had 'follow[ed] the path which was opened up . . . by . . . the great materialist thinkers who understood':

> that the freedom of men is not achieved by the complacency of its ideological *recognition*, but by *knowledge* of the laws of their slavery, and that the 'realization' of their concrete individuality is achieved by the analysis and mastery of the abstract relations which govern them. (Althusser, 1971, p. 219)

Neither a transcription of historical necessity, nor a ratification of historical accident, Althusser's proposals for the analysis of those 'abstract relations' contained the seeds of what might be called a theory of the necessary contingency of history. On its premises, anti-capitalist revolution is no more inevitable than capitalist reproduction – because the historical exception is the historical rule. Alternatively put, there is an unresolved tension – if not a contradiction – in Althusserianism, between the prioritisation of singular 'conjunctures' and invariant 'structures'.

It is to the former, underscored in his *de facto* manifesto of 1962, 'Contradiction and Overdetermination' (Althusser, 1965, pp. 87–128), that Althusser reverts in the 1980s, identifying a 'subterranean current' in the philosophical tradition, originating with Epicurus, which, while candidly admitted not to be the philosophy *of* Marx, might offer a 'philosophy *for* Marxism' (Althusser, 1994b, pp. 29–48) – a 'materialism of the encounter or . . . the *conjuncture*', to which Marx, 'forced to think in a horizon torn between the aleatory of the Encounter and the necessity of the Revolution', was only ambiguously affiliated (Althusser, 1994c, p. 560).

And yet, in a final irony of intellectual history, are we not here present at the strangest of encounters, however brief? 'Our whole age', Michel Foucault famously announced in 1970, 'is trying to escape Hegel':

> But any real escape from Hegel presupposes . . . that we know what is still Hegelian in that which allows us to think against Hegel; and that we can assess the extent to which our appeal against him is perhaps one more of the ruses he uses against us and at the end of which he is waiting for us, immobile and elsewhere. (in Macey, 1993, p. 243)

Althusser's final thoughts on necessity and contingency circled around a 'classical opposition', attended to in Hegel's philosophy of history, which he had previously categorised as fallacious (Althusser and Balibar, 1968, pp. 110–11). Were they perhaps the ultimate Althusserian ruse of Hegelian reason? And what if the last Althusser, erstwhile author of a dissertation on Hegel, had staged a return to the youngest Marx, sometime author of a doctorate on Democritus and . . . Epicurus?

Bibliography

Writings

Althusser, Louis (1969) (first edn 1965), *For Marx*, trans. Ben Brewster, London: Allen Lane.

— (1971) (first edn 1971), *Lenin and Philosophy and Other Essays*, trans. Ben Brewster, London: New Left Books.

— (1972) (first edn 1972), *Politics and History: Montesquieu, Rousseau, Hegel and Marx*, trans. Ben Brewster, London: New Left Books.

— (1976) (first edn 1976), *Essays in Self-Criticism*, trans. Grahame Lock, London: New Left Books.

— (1984) (first edn 1984), *Essays on Ideology*, trans. Ben Brewster and Grahame Lock, London and New York: Verso.

— (1990) (first edn 1990), *Philosophy and the Spontaneous Philosophy of the Scientists & Other Essays*, trans. Ben Brewster, James H. Kavanagh, Grahame Lock and Warren Montag, London and New York: Verso.

— (1993) (first edn 1992), *The Future Lasts a Long Time and The Facts*: trans. Richard Veasey, London: Chatto and Windus.

— (1993), *Ecrits sur la psychanalyse: Freud et Lacan*, eds Olivier Corpet and François Matheron, Paris: Editions Stock/IMEC.

— (1994a), *L'avenir dure longtemps, suivi de Les Faits*, 2nd edn, eds Olivier Corpet and Yann Moulier Boutang, Paris: Editions Stock/IMEC.

— (1994b), *Sur la philosophie*, ed. Olivier Corpet, Paris: Editions Gallimard.

— (1994c), *Ecrits philosophiques et politiques. Tome I*, ed. François Matheron, Paris: Editions Stock/IMEC.

— (1995a), *Ecrits philosophiques et politiques. Tome II*, ed. François Matheron, Paris: Editions Stock/IMEC.

— (1995b), *Sur la reproduction*, Paris: Presses Universitaires de France.

— (1997), *The Spectre of Hegel: Early Writings*, trans. G. M. Goshgarian, London and New York: Verso.

—, Etienne Balibar, Roger Establet, Pierre Macherey and Jacques Rancière (1965), *Lire le Capital*, Paris: Presses Universitaires de France, 1996.

— and Etienne Balibar (1968), *Reading Capital*, trans. Ben Brewster, London: New Left Books, 1970.

References and further reading

Anderson, Perry (1976), *Considerations on Western Marxism*, London: New Left Books.

— (1980), *Arguments within English Marxism*, London: New Left Books.

Benton, Ted (1984), *The Rise and Fall of Structural Marxism: Althusser and his Influence*, London and Basingstoke: Macmillan.

Callari, Antonio and David F. Ruccio (eds) (1996), *Postmodern Materialism and the Future of Marxist Theory*, Hanover, NH: Wesleyan University Press.

Callinicos, Alex (1976), *Althusser's Marxism*, London: Pluto Press.

Elliott, Gregory (1987), *Althusser – The Detour of Theory*, London and New York: Verso.

— (ed.) (1994), *Althusser: A Critical Reader*, Oxford and Cambridge, MA: Blackwell.

Kaplan, E. Ann and Michael Sprinker (eds) (1993), *The Althusserian Legacy*, London and New York: Verso.

Macey, David (1993), *The Lives of Michel Foucault*, London: Hutchinson.

Majumdar, Margaret A. (1995), *Althusser and the End of Leninism?*, London and East Haven, CT: Pluto Press.

Moulier Boutang, Yann (1992), *Louis Althusser: une biographie. Tome I – La Formation du mythe (1918–1956)*, Paris: Bernard Grasset.

Rancière, Jacques (1974), *La Leçon d'Althusser*, Paris: Editions Gallimard.

Resch, Robert P. (1992), *Althusser and the Renewal of Marxist Social Theory*, Berkeley: University of California Press.

Thompson, E. P. (1978), 'The poverty of theory', in *The Poverty of Theory and Other Essays*, London: Merlin Press.

STRUCTURE, LANGUAGE AND SUBJECTIVITY: LACAN

Caroline Williams

The relationship between psychoanalytic and philosophical discourse is fraught with tensions. For many philosophers, the two may even appear to have contrary goals. If the goal of philosophy is to question the form and nature of existence, truth and knowledge, then it may be argued that psychoanalysis, with its preoccupation with the effects and symptoms of modern civilisation upon the structure of the subject (and vice versa), together with its commitment to a clinical practice which can extend its findings, can contribute very little to the higher tasks of philosophy. Such a characterization of the relationship between philosophy and psychoanalysis can maintain itself only within certain limited definitions of psychoanalytic theory and practice, and restricted conceptions of the constituent form of modern philosophy. When the boundedness of such conceptions is challenged, as it is by many modern Continental philosophers, then the opposition between philosophy and psychoanalysis breaks down and both discourses can be seen to share a common project. It has been argued by Michel Foucault, amongst others, that it is almost impossible to imagine a discourse of psychoanalysis, as a mode of knowledge of the subject, existing prior to the subject as self-consciousness inaugurated with modern philosophy. Lacanian psychoanalysis, in particular, is *weighed down* by this debt to philosophy. Indeed, without a philosophical consideration of the conception of the subject in Lacan's psychoanalytic discourse, the structure of subjectivity and language remain underexposed. The objective of this article is therefore to consider Lacan's psychoanalytic theory in terms of the philosophical schools of thought which inform it, namely, structuralism and phenomenological thought.

Introduction

The name of Jacques-Marie Emile Lacan has come to dominate the history of psychoanalysis in France. Born in Paris in 1901, Lacan first studied medicine and psychiatry and was awarded his *diplôme de médicin légiste* in 1931 which qualified him as a forensic psychiatrist. One year later, he received his *Doctorat d'état* for his case study of paranoia and by 1938 he had become a full member of the *Société psychoanalytique de Paris* (SPP). While developing his psychoanalytic technique, which he always claimed to be grounded on a close reading and renewal of the Freudian corpus, Lacan frequently came into conflict with the SPP, not least for his development of the controversial 'short session' which presaged an unconventional departure from the one-hour session of psychoanalytic treatment. Consequently, the institutional rifts and breaks that mark the tumultuous career which followed, with its characteristic jumps and tangential theoretical developments, make it somewhat difficult to track a path through Lacan's intellectual development. When, in 1953, a small group of his disciples formed a splinter organisation, the *Société française de psycho-*

analyse (SEP), Lacan quickly resigned his membership of the SPP to lead this new Lacanian circle. What followed was the gradual isolation of the SFP, both from the SPP and the *International Psychoanalytic Association*, which culminated in the well publicised 'excommunication' of Lacan and the formation of the *Ecole freudienne de Paris* (EFP) in 1964. To become an analyst of the EFP, the analysand had to obtain the controversial *passe*, a self-selecting process in which analysands asked for recognition by the organisation. This, in effect, abolished the formal clinical requirement of the analyst and replaced it with what many saw as a hierarchical and dogmatic rule of entry. Significantly, what most strongly characterises this institutional fragmentation and increasing isolation of the Lacanian school (in France at least) is the intellectual effort to expose psychoanalytic discourse to developments within the human sciences, to merge psychoanalysis with philosophy, linguistics and anthropology. This, in turn, produced a fading of the status of the medical qualification and the inevitable confrontations, both with the SPP and beyond, in the wider setting of psychoanalytic studies.

This brief trajectory of the formation of a distinctly Lacanian school of psychoanalysis is often described alongside a parallel theoretical shift in Lacan's discourse towards structuralism. This identification, however, can only be taken so far. While it is certainly the case that his paper, 'The function and field of speech and language in psychoanalysis' (widely known as the Rome Discourse), read to the Rome Congress of the SFP in 1953, both highlights the first developments of a structuralist theory of language indebted to Ferdinand de Saussure and Claude Lévi-Strauss, and indicates Lacan's growing distance from the psychoanalytic establishment, it also contains complex references to phenomenological thought, particularly that of Martin Heidegger. Lacan's *oeuvre* is complicated not only by his often elliptical style, his tendency towards allusion rather than reference and the structure of the *séminaire*, (much of which, it must be remembered, is based on transcriptions recorded by students), but also by the variety of philosophical concepts employed by Lacan, and by the often contradictory theoretical forms he embraced. Thus, David Macey notes that Lacan's

oeuvre is not epistemologically or theoretically homogeneous and that his debt to Saussure is perhaps overstated (Macey, 1988, p.x, p.5). Between 1933 and 1939, Lacan attended Alexandre Kojève's lectures on Hegel and many Hegelian motifs can be seen in his work. He also participated in discussions around language and representation within surrealist circles in the 1930s, allusions to which resound in his writings. The presence of these ideas, particularly the former, often sit uncomfortably with an account of the 'structuralist' Lacan.

This article will seek to map out the key ideas of Lacan's perspective and in its course will consider the various theoretical influences upon his constructions of the psychoanalytic subject of knowledge. It will be argued that Lacan incorporates two readings of the subject, one phenomenological and drawing specifically on Hegel and Heidegger, the other structuralist and derived through an interest in the fundamental structuring role of language which owes much to Ferdinand de Saussure and Roman Jakobson. These two readings create a complex pattern of interference and prevent one from arriving at a unitary interpretation of Lacan.

Lacan and Freud

There is much discussion within Lacanian studies as to the extent of Lacan's fidelity to Freud's text. The form and motivation of his reading, in some respects, parallels the 'symptomatic' reading of Marx conducted by Louis Althusser. Lacan wishes to bring to Freud's fledgling theory of language, the hindsight offered by structuralism. His central interest, therefore, lies in Freud's early texts (*The Interpretation of Dreams* [1900]), *The Psychopathology of Everyday Life* [1901], *Jokes and Their Relation to the Unconscious* [1905]) where linguistic imagery is dominant. There was no translation of either *Jokes and Their Relation to the Unconscious* or Freud's *Lectures on Metapsychology* until 1930 and 1940 respectively. Indeed, as Elisabeth Roudinesco comments, the surrealists were certainly ahead of their medical counterparts in their reading of Freud (Roudinesco, 1990, p. 75). Lacan takes many of the concepts of the Freudian topography and sets them within his own philosophical matrix where they fight for attention against distinctly non-psychoanalytic ideas and concepts. Freud's theory of the symbol sits with that of Lévi-Strauss, while Freud's dream analysis is grafted on to a theory of psychoanalytic linguistics. Similarly, the Oedipus complex is no longer the constitutive moment of subjective identity but is secondary and preceded by the more significant *Fort/Da* scenario which is understood to have a linguistic significance of elementary importance. However, it has also been argued that both Freud's concept of narcissism and his analysis of the relation of the unconscious to language and the subject's development have been brought under closer scrutiny with the benefit of Lacan's eclectic theoretical approach. The extent of Lacan's departure from Freud will continue to be a matter of dispute (see Further Reading).

The early lacan

It is Lacan's early essay, 'The mirror stage as formative of the function of the I as revealed in psychoanalytic experience', delivered to the 16th International Congress of Psychoanalysis in 1949, and presented in an earlier form in 1936, that has had the greatest influence upon Anglo-American critical thought, from philosophy and film studies to feminist theory. The essay is notable, not only for its lack of any direct citation of Freud, but also for its anti-Cartesianism, its opposition to a psychological presentation of the autonomous ego embraced by Heinz Hartmann, and its multiple theoretical excursions and references to topics ranging from the animal ethology of Henri Wallon to Hegelian phenomenology. Lacan's claims here are far-reaching and, together with his 1948 essay 'Aggressivity in psychoanalysis', represent the foundations of his theory of the human subject. In 'The mirror stage', Lacan makes an important distinction between the subject as ego or 'I', that which may achieve an elusive sense of wholeness and autonomy of self, and the subject as primordial being, which lies in a place 'beyond' the ego-as-subject and may be approached through analysis. The structure which has come to represent this dynamic process of creating the 'I' or human individual is the mirror-stage, a phase in the constitution of the individual

located between the ages of six and eighteen months. For Lacan, it is this structure, rather than the Oedipus Complex described by Freud (which occurs later in the development of the subject's life according to Lacan), that necessitates the birth of the self and its primary identifications. The experience of the formation of the 'I' is, Lacan stresses, 'opposed [to] any philosophy directly issuing from the *Cogito*' (Lacan, 1977, p. 1). There is no thinking subject prior to the recognition of the 'I'; this ego *requires* an identification with an image before it can *function* as subject; that is, before it can become a social animal. The event of the mirror-stage, through which the subject perceives an image which is other than the largely mute, discordant being that it is, offers the subject its *first apprehension of bodily unity*. This *Gestalt*, which fixes the image, engenders the subject and charges it with an impulse, a libidinal energy which translates itself into a narcissistic fantasy of wholeness, and an aggression towards the other who may challenge the *form* of this imago. The mirror thus allows the fragmented being to become an 'I', to be harnessed to an ontological structure according to which the ego or Ideal-I may think, perceive and recognise itself as a permanent, coherent structure. In support of his theory, Lacan cites the ethological findings of Henri Wallon which indicate that maturational processes are set in motion only after visual perception of a species counterpart. In short, the mirror establishes a roughcast structure of the ego; it allows the still powerless and largely uncoordinated human being to anticipate its future wholeness by identifying with an-other, in this case, the reflection of its own image.

It is important that Lacan's structure of the emergent ego is not reduced to a genetic, biological or developmental moment; much more will be shown to be at stake here with the acquiring of speech. The unification perceived by the subject is of an *imaginary* form, according to Lacan. The mirror-stage situates the instance of the ego in a line of *fiction*, of alienation; a function of *méconnaissance* is thus seen to characterise the ego in all its structures (ibid., p.6). At this stage of narcissistic identification, where the subject is its own double more than it is itself, and where the image of plenitude forever alienates the subject from itself, both the *form* and the *energy* which henceforth govern the subject are secured. These two functions of the imaginary ego are elaborated in the essay on aggression discussed below. What must be noted here is how the imaginary ego becomes the support for a division or split, *Spaltung*, of the subject, who is forever divided between a coherent self and a mode of being which is always other to the subject. The imaginary ego attempts to solder, to mend, the discordance created within the subject who remains ignorant of its alienation. Lacan writes:

> It is this moment that decisively tips the whole of human knowledge into mediatization through the desire of the other, constitutes its objects in an abstract equivalence by the co-operation of others and turns the I into that apparatus for which every instinctual thrust constitutes a danger, even though it should correspond to a natural maturation ... (Lacan, ibid. 1977, p. 5)

Thus begins the chronic cycle of misrecognition of self, and the causal chains that determine the structure of human experience.

The structure of the subject's experience

The mirror-stage, in so far as it gives rise to the subject, also introduces two important drives in the subject. These drives are not reducible to biological instinct but gain significance, for Lacan, only in relation to language. The first drive, aggression, is the 'correlative tension of the narcissistic structure in the coming-into-being (*devenir*) of the subject' (Lacan 1977, p. 22). Aggression is a necessary instrument through which the subject may experience itself as a *unified* self. In order to maintain its coherence and sense of mastery, it is necessary for the subject to impose this idealised image upon others. The characteristic of aggression is essential to the interaction of subject and other; it qualifies recognition and seems redolent of Hegel's description of the master-slave dialectic as much as it may be attributed to the Freudian death-drive. For Hegel, however, the master-slave dialectic also has a positive function; it contributes to the historical development of consciousness and it beckons self-knowledge; for Lacan, in contrast, the mutual recognition of subject and

other is always forestalled. Aggression must also be attached to the subject's experience of finitude, that which Lacan calls the *lack* of the subject (*manque d'être*), its impossibility of achieving correspondence with its ideal-image. In other words, it is precisely because the subject is *never quite whole* that aggression, as a defence-mechanism and a mode of reassurance, is brought into play with the other and upon the self. The death-instinct, for Lacan, is thus an aporia 'which lies at the heart of the notion of aggressivity' (ibid., p. 8).

The second drive that is brought to bear upon the subject as a result of its newly-found, albeit roughcast at this stage, wholeness, is the propensity to desire. The concept of desire occupies an important space in Lacan's writings; we shall see below that it comes to be tied to language and the unconscious. If aggressivity may be viewed as tied to the death-instinct, desire must, in part, be viewed as operating in accordance with the pleasure-principle. It, too, is a drive for wholeness and plenitude, but now via specific objects of fulfilment and satisfaction. For the little being prior to the event of *méconnaissance*, desire is subsumed by a few basic biological needs (food, warmth, for example) easily satisfied by the object of the mother's breast; need and desire are thus equivalent and the possible tension created by desire is easily satiated. However, desire as experienced by the subject of the imaginary 'takes shape in the margin in which demand becomes separated from need' (ibid., p. 311). Desire, according to Lacan, is at the origin of every human act. However, it is not a biological instinct in the manner of need; desire is bound to the *Spaltung* of the subject. It arises, therefore, 'as a presence from a background of absence' (Lacan, 1988b, p. 224) which guides the subject towards the primal experiences foreclosed by the visual economy of the mirror-stage, but it never reaches its destination. Desire, then, always points to the past even as it instils a vision of a fulfilled future in the subject; it reminds the subject of that which it lacks, but can never return it to a Rousseauian state of primal harmony. There is no vision of wholeness and self-realisation, nor, perhaps, of absolute knowledge in Lacan's structure of subjectivity, a pessimism well illustrated in the intervention at one of Lacan's seminars by a student: 'It was lucky that Oedipus did not know too soon what he knew only at the end, for he still had to fill out his life' (ibid., p. 218).

Thus far, the discussion has been limited to drawing attention to the structure of the subject, the narcissistic form of the ego and the alienation of the ego in the imaginary. Lacan's turn to structural linguistics follows the temporal shift of many French intellectuals, for example, Barthes, Lévi-Strauss). It is perhaps most clearly marked in the so-called Rome Discourse of 1953 and 'The instance of the letter in the Freudian unconscious or reason since Freud' (1957).

Structuralism, language and the form of subjectivity

Everything emerges from the structure of the signifier. (Lacan, 1979, p. 206)

Lacan's structuralism owes its formation to many different sources. Significantly, his theoretical perspective is grafted on to the psychoanalytic and philosophical derivation of the subject developed above. In the Rome Discourse, his aim is to establish the significance of language for psychoanalytic study. Freudian psychoanalysis has always attached great significance to the structure of the subject's speech, as Freud's work '*Jokes and Their Relation to the Unconscious*' testifies. By listening to the form of the subject's speech, slips of the tongue and misplaced speech, as well as the recollection of dreams, a point of access to the unconscious of the subject is offered. Lacan's theory of the subject is initially an effort to explore this linguistic schema in greater detail. It requires, however, that the speaking subject itself be brought under closer scrutiny, and the structure of language within which its speech is situated be subjected to critical analysis. Both of these moves must be understood via Lacan's re-reading of structural linguistics.

For Lacan, language is an autonomous structure existing prior to the subject's entry to it. It is also, in compliance with the Kojèvean motifs in his work, an existential medium of self-recognition. However, in accordance with structuralism's anti-humanism, Lacan's focus is on the formal structure and *a priori* rules which organise the possibilities of discourse and communication between subjects. As we shall see, this introduces a certain structural limit upon the subject's speech or enunciation.

Drawing on the linguistic theory of the sign developed by Saussure, Lacan claims that the structure of language and the construction of meaning are the result of a constitutive algorithm: the signifier, as sound image, material attribute of language, and the signified, the concept of a particular sign. According to Saussure, the signifier and the signified exist in a relation of reciprocal difference and language is itself an arbitrary system where meaning shifts endlessly between different referents. However, language does 'settle' or fix its terms of reference according to certain signs because the signifier and signified are indissolubly bound. Only the fixing of the linguistic system makes it possible to have signs which, although arbitrary, are not free to assume any form. Signs then, must be seen to have a reciprocal inter-dependence within a linguistic system; they cannot be separated from their interrelation with other signs. As Lacan notes, 'no signification can be sustained other than by reference to another signification' (Lacan, 1977, p. 150). The synchronic system of laws fixes the sign, the referent, and hence makes possible signification and speech. Lacan thus agrees with Saussure's view: 'Without language, thought is a vague, uncharted nebula. There are no pre-existing ideas, and nothing is distinct before the appearance of language' (Saussure, 1974, p. 112). To summarise: the structure of language may contain unlimited *possibilities* for signification; these, however, will be limited by the system of interrelations between signs.

Lacan does, however, depart from Saussure in one significant respect, namely, by loosening the noose of signification and widening the scope of its structural effects. Signification is understood to produce a complex temporality; it is borne progressively from a permanent dialectic. Lacan establishes what he calls the 'incessant sliding of the signified under the signifier' (Lacan, 1977, p. 154), in effect, *unfixing* the reciprocal relation between signifier and signified established by Saussure, and eroding, in the process, the distinction between referent and meaning. On Lacan's reading, the algorithmic bar between signified and signifier resists meaning and hence destroys the representational function of the sign. It is a recognition of what Jean-Luc Nancy and Philippe Lacoue-Labarthe (1992) describe as 'the aporia of reference', the non-correspondence be-tween word and thing. For Lacan, the signifier seems to take over what was the role of the sign in Saussure, and the signified is no longer associated with the concept of the object, but seems closer to the dominant social meanings, norms and prejudices which occupy a cultural community. As a result, the signifier is diachronic and polysemic; it operates with a certain autonomy, in separation from the process of signification. As Malcolm Bowie notes, the signifying chain is 'mobile, sinuous and able to loop back upon itself; any one of its links can provide a point of attachment to other chains' (Bowie, 1991, p. 66). When the subject takes up a position in language, in the symbolic order, it is as heterogeneous as the signifier. Furthermore, as *speaking* subject, (which is the only possible identity of the subject in this register), the subject *becomes* a signifier; the signifier, Lacan writes, 'is that which represents the subject for another signifier. This signifier will therefore be the signifier for which all the other signifiers represent the subject' (Lacan, 1977, p. 316).

Lacan's structuralism has radical implications for the conception of the subject. Language is made up of a network of elements and relations operating according to a synchronic structure which can be known only in its general form and not through specific signs. Language is anterior to any experience of the subject, and it is this structure which confers meaning on the subject's speech. 'The form of language', Lacan writes, 'defines subjectivity' (ibid., p. 85). The subject, therefore, is not the *enunciator* of discourse, but is rather *enunciated* in and by discourse. In line with structuralism's reduction of the subject, Lacan claims that only signifiers exist. It thus appears that the subject *tout court* is lost within the mobility of signifiers: 'the signifier causes the subject to arise [in the symbolic], but at the cost of becoming fixed. What was ready to speak there disappears, being no longer anything more than a signifier' (Lacan, cited in Lemaire, 1977, p. 71). However, the focus of psychoanalysis upon the subject refuses the easy containment that structuralism offers. While it could be argued that Lacan's method is, at various points, structuralist, his elaboration of the registers of subjectivity upon whose surface the subject is caught, namely the symbolic,

imaginary and real, ensure that a dimension of subjectivity continues to disrupt the process of signification. It is, perhaps, the central task of psychoanalysis to analyse this disruption.

The structure of the subject: symbolic, imaginary and real

When the subject makes its entry into language as a signifier, it is also scattered across three registers: the symbolic, the imaginary and the real. These are neither mutually exclusive nor fully constitutive of the subject. Together, however, they form what Lacan calls a 'Borromean knot'; structurally related, their properties continually press upon and call into question the stability of the others. The symbolic order is the order of language, 'an order of independent signs bound together by specific laws' (Lemaire, 1977, p. 6). It is useful to make an initial distinction between Lacan's use of the symbol and symbolic order. A symbol is *not* a signifier, although it may be evoked, transmuted or mediated by language. Symbols are elementary, primordial forms, pacts, myths, which envelop life and the body prior to signification; they may depend as much upon visual and corporeal resemblances as upon the universal laws they may well engender. Lacan refers to the planets as symbols, but he privileges the understanding of the symbol as primary pact or law, taking the anthropological studies of Lévi-Strauss rather than Freud's studies of myths, as his central reference point. Lévi-Strauss's structuralist analysis of culture identifies the prohibition of incest as a socio-symbolic law. Relations of kinship and marriage ties are symbolic systems of exchange which have universal significance identical to a law of language. Lacan adopts this understanding of a primary symbol which finds permanence in a signifier only by becoming a petrified symbol in the subject's unconscious. As for Freud, symbols thus come to have special significance in psychoanalysis but Lacan's structuralism allows for no phylogenetic analysis of history like the one developed by Freud in *Moses and Monotheism*. Symbols, we may note, in so far as they rest within the unconscious, can play a dynamic role in relation to imaginary and real structures of existence.

The symbolic *order*, on the other hand, contains symbols only as mediated by language and overlaid with social convention. It is, moreover, a rational Logos, and as a space of signification and communication, it is social and intersubjective. Lacan often refers to the symbolic order as the field of the Other, the Other, in this instance, being language itself. The symbolic order signals the eclipse, suture or *fading* of the subject (see Lacan, 1979, Ch. 16) who, it will be recalled, only enters the symbolic order through the structure of the signifier. This order is described by Lacan as governed by the Name-of-the-Father, a term used to describe the symbolic law of the Father. As we shall see below, this conception of sexual and social relation follows the form of the Freudian Oedipus complex, but it is not to be reduced to concrete biological relations; the importance for Lacan of this symbolic law is its linguistic *effects* at the level of the subject's speech.

The imaginary realm has already been described as the field wherein the illusion of individuality maintains itself. The imaginary thus becomes the holder of contradiction. It is associated with the genesis of the libidinal drives, desire and aggression; if it can be seen to *represent anything*, it would be the primordial lack generated by the birth of the subject as signifier. However, given the differential structures of imaginary and symbolic, the former is experienced and represented only phantasmatically through a fictional union with an (imaginary) object, or via a fixation by the ego of the state of *méconnaissance*. In the words of Richard Boothby, 'the imaginary articulates a directed impulse by suppressing an original energetic heterogeneity' (Boothby, 1991, p. 59).

What about the real? The definition of the real is not to be confused with standard conceptions of reality. It is not the discursive representation of the world. Neither is it the *réalité humaine*, the subject's lived-relation to the world described by existentialism. Rather, this register, according to Lacan, is unrepresentable by discourse. It is that which always remains foreclosed in the experience of speech, that element of speech which can never be grasped as signification. It is a dimension beyond and behind the symbolic, but it is resistant to symbolisation. When Lacan says 'Man is not entirely in man'

(Lacan, 1988b, p. 72) he is attending to the unthinkable space of the real.

Thus far, the subject has been described as an imaginary ego (in its 'mirror identifications') and as a signifier (in its accession to language), a distinction which generates a rift within the being of the subject ensuring that it will always be split in form rather than whole. Such a description may invite a definition of the subject as dualist in structure; a body repressed and a self-consciousness which comes to predominate in discourse. Quite clearly, for Lacan, and Freud, it is the subject of the unconscious (what is often called the subject of desire) which disrupts any dualist structure of the subject. It lies *between* the signifier and the signified, and it flaunts all three registers outlined above. This unconscious can be approached by psychoanalysis because it is – what has now become an aphorism in Lacanian studies – structured like a language. This definition raises many problems. Not least, it often gives rise to the view of the Lacanian schema as a form of linguistic reductionism (see, for example, Bowie, 1991, p. 58, pp. 71–2). However, once the subject of the unconscious is viewed as making a mark upon each of the registers above, it will become apparent that the *materiality* of language can ward off such claims to reductionism.

For Richard Boothby, 'the unconscious is both something ideally inaccessible, something quasi-real, yet it is also realized by the symbolic' (Boothby, 1991, p. 134). What is clear, however, is that the unconscious is not, for Lacan, reducible to the drives; it is neither primordial nor instinctual in form, and 'what it knows about the elementary is no more than the elements of the signifier' (Lacan, 1977, p. 170). If Lacan's recourse to structural linguistics performs one crucial function, it is to obviate all reference to the unconscious as 'the seat of the instincts' (Lacoue-Labarthe and Nancy, 1992, p. 29). The unconscious is the *gap* in the subject which Lacan often refers to as 'another scene'. It arises with the separation of the being of the subject from its spectral formation. As such, it is pre-ontological and pre-discursive (see Lacan, 1979, p. 49); it exists prior to meaning and language, and yet it mediates the subject's *lack* of being (represented by its alienation in the symbolic), and its desire is a desire for plenitude and recognition. In this way, it may be seen to send the subject on false trails towards an absolute place, where objects may coincide with the subject and represent the real. Lacan calls such an unobtainable object *object (a)*. There is then, for Lacan, no *aufhebung* of Hegel's Unhappy Consciousness, or for the 'discontents of civilisation' described by Freud (see Lacan, 1977, p. 297).

The unconscious thus occupies a space within all three registers. It haunts the subject-as-signifier, who must live within the Law of language, a patriarchal law which forces the subject into masculine and feminine identities and sets the phallus in the place of the transcendental, albeit illusive, signified. This structuring element of language acts as a *point-de-capiton*, it sews the process of signification together, and orders the possibilities of language. However, while the subject is constituted as a signifier in the symbolic order, this cannot ensure that it *will* speak in the designated intervals of discourse. Indeed, 'every signifier of the subject of the enunciation may be lacking in the statement' (ibid., p. 298). If the unconscious may be structured like a language and speak in the gaps within discourse, it is through metaphor and metonymy that the social censure of the symbolic order may be circumvented by the unconscious. These two rhetorical tropes (linguists may claim that Lacan ignores, amongst others, synecdoche, catachresis and allegory) are understood to break up, subvert the signifying chain and disrupt speech. Metaphor follows the law of condensation in Freud's dream-work: if the dream condenses a number of memories and affective states on to a particular image, it illustrates, for Lacan, the mobility, flux, of the metaphoric signifier. Like a 'symbol written on the sand' (which perhaps evokes Freud's analogy of the unconscious as a 'mystic writing pad'), the metaphoric signifier substitutes for the repressed occulted signifier. Lacan's analysis here draws upon Roman Jakobson's 1962 essay on the linguistic effects of aphasic disturbances. In what Jakobson calls a 'similarity disorder', it is difficult for the speaker to select and substitute words conventionally; the metaphor therefore emerges at the limit of 'sensible' speech. For Lacan, a metaphor symbolises an unconscious signifier. It is a symptom substituted on the field of signification, a symptom being 'a metaphor in which flesh or function is taken as a

signifying element' (ibid., p. 166) Metonymy, on the other hand, follows Freud's law of displacement. It establishes 'word-for-word' connections, but here continuity of meaning and contextual connection break down. Connections are thus made through association. In a 'contiguity disorder', Jakobson notes the tendency for speech to become condensed, generalised and 'telegraphic' (Jakobson, 1956, p. 86). Metonymy encapsulates the dialectic of desire; that is, desire is alienated in a signifier which is removed from the original signifier by a series of unconscious connections. Metonymy, then, can be seen to convey both the temporality and materiality of the multiple associations of the unconscious.

There are many examples of the unconscious use of metaphor and metonymy in Lacan's writings, the most repeated and most widely discussed being found in the seminar on *The Psychoses* (Lacan, 1993, Chs XVII, XVIII; Lemaire, 1977, pp. 192–3; Macey, 1988, pp. 158–60). Here I will draw attention to an example where metaphor is more integral to the Lacanian edifice; it takes its bearing in relation to the Name-of-the-Father, which Lacan describes most frequently as a paternal metaphor. While Lacan, as a good structuralist, departs from Freud's myth of Oedipus, he takes the castration complex as the central psychoanalytic motif. Castration is symbolic rather than biological for Lacan, and if language and desire conform to the mysteries of presence and absence, it is the phallus which is elevated to the position of master-signifier. The phallus signifies the lack of the subject; its significance here is tied to the male appendage only in a secondary sense. Primarily, the phallus calls forth the impossible experience of fullness of being and the resolution/satisfaction of desire that neither subject can hope to represent in language. Nevertheless, the symbolic conventions of signification also give rise to a symbolic castration in language, a castration which psychoanalysis has always insisted is incomplete for the feminine subject. Thus, the symbolic order is governed by the Name-of-the-Father, and upholds a mode of signification which symbolises a paternal reality. As Lemaire notes,

> through the paternal metaphor the subject *names* his desire and renounces it. His true desire and the

multiple fantasmatic forms it took are pushed back into the unconscious. This is a primal repression which determines accession to language and which *substitutes a symbol and a Law for the real of existence.* (Lemaire, 1977, p. 87, my emphasis)

The paternal metaphor, then, has become a conventional signifier. If it reflects the symbolic, patriarchal relations of the social, metaphor will always hold on to the symptom of castration. For Lacanian psychoanalysts, this follows logically from the structure of primary lack, but it has prompted the psychoanalyst and philosopher Luce Irigaray, for example, to argue that certain fantasies are inscribed within symbolic Law, while others are forever unsignified in discourse and unrecognised by the psychoanalyst. If the feminine subject lacks linguistic access to the symbolic order, her experience is generated through her relation to the real of existence rather than through any identification with the symbolic order and the Name-of-the-Father (see Lacan, 1982, pp. 137–49; Irigaray, 1991).

Psychoanalysis: towards the truth of the subject's experience?

If linguistics enables us to see the signifier as the determinant of the signified, analysis reveals the truth of this relation by making 'holes' in the meaning of the determinants of its discourse. (Lacan, 1977, p. 299)

I always speak the truth. Not the whole truth, because there's no way, to say it all. Saying it all is literally impossible: words fail. Yet it's through this very impossibility that the truth holds onto the real. (Lacan, 1987, p. 7)

It remains to be asked whether psychoanalysis seeks a truth of subject and a truth in its status as a 'scientific' knowledge. If structuralism was to secure one other goal (in addition to its anti-humanism), it was as a science of human knowledge. Lacan certainly claims to have constituted a knowledge, but it is one that can conform to a structuralist logic only in the most general sense. Psychoanalysis focuses upon 'the self's radical eccentricity to itself' (Lacan, 1977, p. 171); it must anchor itself in the diachronic, communicative dimension of speech and the register of the real. Thus, when, in the Rome Discourse, Lacan talks of the full speech of the subject (a term he opposes to empty speech or Heideggerian 'idle talk'), (ibid., pp. 40–56), he does not seek a general truth of speech based solely on structural laws. If, as we have pointed out, the unconscious is structured like a language, it must be added that the unconscious cannot be made continuous with language as a source of meaning. Discourse has no criteria of truthfulness except, perhaps, that of conjoining the subject with its desires and introducing an awareness of this limit to the subject's speech. Lacan often refers to the interrelation and reliance of truth upon error and the play of deception within psychoanalytic dialogue: 'There is no error which does not promulgate itself as truth' (Lacan, 1988a, p. 263). Lacan appeals to a partial, 'limping' truth of the real; he denies that it is possible to speak the truth. Here he highlights the *disjuncture* between being and language. Psychoanalysis then, while orientated towards the future, can have no hold upon the direction its path may take. It has, in other words, no warrant to either totalise experience, or to limit and contain knowledge and subjectivity within closed structures.

Bibliography

Writings

Lacan, J. (1972), 'Of Structure as an Intermixing of an Otherness Prerequisite of any Subject Whatever', in R. Macksey and E. Donato (eds), *The Structuralist Controversy: The Languages of Criticism and the Sciences of Man*, Baltimore: The Johns Hopkins Press.

— (1977), *Ecrits: A selection*, trans. A. Sheridan, ed. J. Alain-Miller, London: Routledge.

— (1979), *The Four Fundamental Concepts of Psychoanalysis* trans. A. Sheridan, ed. J. Alain-Miller, London: Penguin Books.

— (1982), *Feminine Sexuality: Jacques Lacan and the école freudienne*, trans. J. Rose, ed. J. Mitchell and J. Rose, London: W. W. Norton and Company.

— (1987), 'Television', *October* vol. 40, Spring.

— (1988a), *The Seminar of Jacques Lacan Book I: Freud's Papers on technique 1953–54*, trans. J. Forrester, ed. J.

Alain-Miller, Cambridge, London: Cambridge University Press.

— (1988b), *The Seminar of Jacques Lacan Book II: The Ego in Freud's Theory and in the Technique of Psychoanalysis 1954–55*, trans. S. Tomaselli, ed. J. Alain-Miller, Cambridge, London: Cambridge University Press.

— (1992), *The Seminar of Jacques Lacan Book VII: The Ethics of Psychoanalysis 1959–1960*, trans. D. Porter, ed. J. Alain-Miller, London: Routledge.

— (1993), *The Seminar of Jacques Lacan Book III: The Psychoses*, trans. R. Grigg, ed. J. Alain-Miller, London: Routledge.

References and further reading

Benvenuto, B. and Kennedy, R. (1986), *The Works of Jacques Lacan. An Introduction*, London: Free Association Books.

Boothby, R. (1991), *Death and Desire: Psychoanalytic theory in Lacan's Return to Freud*, New York and London: Routledge.

Bowie, M. (1991), *Lacan*, London: Fontana Press.

Irigaray, L. (1991), 'The poverty of psychoanalysis', trans. D. Macey with M. Whitford, in M. Whitford (ed.), *The Irigaray Reader*, Oxford: Blackwell, 179–204.

Jakobson, R. (1956), 'Two aspects of language and two types of aphasic disturbances', in R. Jakobson and M. Halle, *Fundamentals of Language*, The Hague: Mouton Books.

Lacoue-Labarthe, P. and J. L. Nancy (1992), *The Title of the Letter: A Reading of Lacan*, trans. F. Raffoul and D. Pettigrew, New York: SUNY Press.

Lemaire, A. (1977), *Jacques Lacan*, trans. D. Macey, London: Routledge and Kegan Paul.

Macey, D. (1988), *Lacan in Contexts*, London: Verso.

Roudinesco, E. (1990), *Jacques Lacan and Co.: A History of Psychoanalysis in France*, trans. J. Mehlam, London: Free Association Books.

Roudinesco, E. (1997), *Jacques Lacan*, trans. B. Bray, Cambridge: Polity Press.

Sarup, M. (1992), *Jacques Lacan*, London: Harvester Wheatsheaf.

Saussure, F. de (1974), *Course in General Linguistics*, trans. W. Baskin, London: Fontana Press.

Smith, J. and W. Kerrigan (eds) (1983), *Interpreting Lacan*, New Haven: Yale University Press.

GODS, MYTHS AND STRUCTURES: DUMÉZIL

C. Scott Littleton

Georges Dumézil was born in Paris on 4 March 1898. His father, Anatole Dumézil (1857–1929), was a career Army officer who eventually became Inspector-General of the artillery corps. Georges studied at *lycées* in Neufchâteau, Troyes and Tarbes, and, eventfully, at the prestigious Lycée Louis-le-Grand in Paris. In 1916, he entered the *Ecole Normale Supérieure*. After serving with distinction as a lieutenant of artillery in 1917–18, he received his *agrégation de lettres* from the *Ecole Normale* in 1919, and then taught briefly at a *lycée* in Beauvais and at the University of Warsaw. In 1920 he entered the University of Paris, where he studied under the eminent French Indo-Europeanist Antoine Meillet (1866–1936). He completed his doctorate in 1924, aged twenty-six.

Early influences and the 'ambrosia cycle'

In the course of several long conversations with the author, Dumézil indicated that he had been interested in exotic belief systems and ancient languages since early childhood. He learned Latin and Greek at an early age, and was introduced to Sanskrit by Alfred Ernout, a teacher at his Troyes *lycée* and one of Meillet's early students. Later, at Louis-le-Grand, one of his classmates was the grandson of the great French comparative linguist and Sanskritist Michel Bréal. His young friend introduced him to his grandfather, who gave him a Sanskrit dictionary. As Dumézil confided to Didier Erebon (Erebon, 1987, p. 31), 'A partir de ce moment, ma vocation fut assurée' (from that moment my future was decided).

By the early 1920s, the comparative study of the several ancient Indo-European mythologies – that of the Greeks, Romans, Iranians, Indians, Germans, Celts, etc. – was in a trough. Like most other areas of intellectual endeavour, from the arts to the sciences, comparative mythology had undergone a major paradigm shift in the early years of this century. The 'old comparative mythology' – the etymological approach to the study of myth developed by Friedrich Max Müller (1823–1900) and his contemporaries – was in almost universal disrepute.

Nevertheless, there was continued interest in the thematic, if not etymological, parallels noted by Müller, Adalbert Kuhn, Sir George Cox and other nineteenth-century scholars. In the early 1920s, a handful of scholars, among them Albert Carnoy (who, in 1921, spoke in no uncertain terms about 'la religion indo-européenne'), Joseph Vendryès, Walter F. Otto, Hermann Güntert, Friedrich Cornelius, F. R. Schroeder and Dumézil's mentor, Antoine Meillet, came to the conclusion that it was in fact possible to conceive of a common Indo-European tradition without reference to Müller. The problem was finding a substitute for the latter's discredited methodology, to say nothing of his preoccupation with solar and other natural metaphors.

Some years previously, Dumézil had discovered the ideas of Sir James G. Frazer, especially as expounded in *The Golden Bough* (1922). Encouraged by Meillet, the young French scholar drew heavily on Frazer's theory of the ritual sacrifice of the divine king in preparing his doctoral thesis, *Le festin d'im-*

mortalité (1924a). He suggested that the Vedic Soma sacrifice, and its parallels elsewhere in the ancient Indo-European speaking world, such as the Greek traditions about Ambrosia, the 'nectar of the gods', were reflections of this primordial ritual, as these sacred beverages were everywhere conceived of as divine beings. *Le festin* was followed by a series of books and essays, including *Le crime des Lemniennes* (1924b) and *Le problème des Centaures* (1929), which Dumézil later came to call the 'Ambrosia cycle'.

The Frazerian model, however, ultimately proved inadequate. It could not explain the great majority of thematic parallels that Dumézil and the other neo-comparativists were discovering in the several ancient Indo-European religious traditions, and so he began to search for another theoretical framework.

The Turkish years and his discovery of the Ossetian tradition

Meanwhile, Dumézil's career took a turn that would have some enduring implications for his work. Jobs in France for neo-comparativists were few and far between in those days, and therefore, in 1925, shortly after his marriage to Madeleine Legrand, he accepted a position as a professor of French literature at the University of Istanbul. Dumézil remained in Turkey for six years. It was during this period that he discovered what would become, in anthropological parlance, his 'field people': émigré Ossetians who had fled their homeland in the northern Caucasus during the civil war that followed the Bolshevik revolution in 1917. For around the next fifty years, long after he returned to France, interrupted only by the Second World War and, eventually, by advancing age, Dumézil managed to spend a portion of almost every summer in Turkey doing field research. For the most part, this involved collecting and analysing the remarkable oral epic tradition preserved by his Ossetian informants, especially the sagas concerning a band of epic heroes called the Narts. Although he eventually expanded in his purview to include other, non-Indo-European Caucasian peoples, especially the Oubykh (Dumézil, 1931), it was the north-east Iranian-speaking Ossetians, the last remnants of the once far-flung Alans, who were to loom most importantly in his later work.

In 1930 he published *Légendes sur les Nartes* (1930a), the first of a distinguished series of essays and monographs on Ossetic legendry and folklore and their implications for understanding the Indo-European tradition.

The Ossetians are descended from the ancient Scythians, and so Dumézil soon found himself consulting Herodotus (Book Four of the *History*) and other classical sources relating to these ancient denizens of the South Russian and Ukraine steppes. It immediately became apparent that the Scythian social organisation, as reported by Herodotus, and the traditional Indian caste system were strikingly similar. Just as the ancient (and not so ancient) Indians were divided into three hereditary, twice-born *varna*, or castes — Brahmans (priests), Kśatriyas (warriors), and Vaiśyas (farmers) — the ancient Scythians were divided into three 'tribes': the Paralatai, or 'Royal Scyths', who, like the Indic Brahmans, exercised ultimate sovereignty; the Aukhatai, or 'Warrior Scyths' and the Katiaroi, or 'Agricultural Scyths'.

In 1930 he published what, in retrospect, was a watershed essay on this subject, 'La préhistoire indo-iranienne des castes' (1930b). In it he analysed the symbolism contained in the Scythian origin myth as described by Herodotus: three burning golden objects, a cup, a battle-axe and a yoked plough, fall from the sky, whereupon the three sons of Targitaos, the primordial human being, attempt to retrieve them. However, only the youngest son, Kolaxaïs, is successful, and, as a result, he becomes the ancestor of the sovereign Paralatai; from the oldest brother descend the warlike Aukhatai, and from the oldest brother the peaceful Katiaroi. The cup, battle-axe and yoked plough, were symbolic, respectively, of these three caste-like Scythian 'tribes'. This was the first clear hint of the tripartite ideology, the discovery of which is Dumézil's most enduring contribution to scholarship.

The latter article soon put Dumézil in touch with the eminent Indo-Iranianist Emile Benveniste, who had recently come to a similar conclusion about the relationship between ancient Iranian social organisation *per se* and that of Vedic India (see Benveniste, 1932).

Another noteworthy monograph from this period is *Ouranos-Varuna* (1934), in which he compared the otiose Greek deity Ouranos, divine grandfather of Zeus, to the Vedic god Varuna, who, together with Mitra, is the personification of ultimate sovereignty in the most ancient Indian divine hierarchy. Although he later rejected many of the specific ideas expressed in this article, the gods Mitra and Varuna would loom large in his later synthesis.

In 1932, still searching for a theoretical framework upon which he might build a 'new comparative mythology', Dumézil left Turkey for a position as Lecturer in French at the University of Uppsala in Sweden. He returned to France permanently in 1933 to accept a position as *chargé de conferences* in the Ecole des Hautes Etudes. In 1935 he was promoted to the rank of *directeur d'études*.

The impact of Granet: Dumézil 'discovers' Durkheimian sociology

Shortly after assuming his new position at the Ecole, Dumézil, now almost ten years into his academic career and still no closer to the viable model he had been seeking, decided to immerse himself in something as far removed as possible from Indo-European mythology: the religion of ancient China. The idea, he said, was to throw the Indo-European material into relief by looking at a vastly different belief system.

He had long admired the work of the eminent Sinologist Marcel Granet (1884–1940), who, as a student in the early years of the century, had been closely associated with Emile Durkheim and his circle. They had met some years previously, and Dumézil must have made a strong impression on him. When, in 1933, at the suggestion of Sylvain Lévi, he arrived at Granet's office door seeking permission to audit his seminar on ancient China, the Sinologist's first words were: 'Il y a dix ans que je vous attends' (I have been waiting ten years for you) (Erebon, 1987, p. 62).

For the next two years Dumézil immersed himself in the culture of ancient China. He learned to read over 3,000 Chinese characters, and faithfully attended Granet's seminars, along with the latter's doctoral students. The end result was extremely significant. He did not make any important contributions to the study of Chinese myth, although he

retained a passion for it until the end of his life; what was important was his exposure to Granet's methodology and what he later came to call 'la méthode sociologique'. In his research, Granet (for example, 1980) applied the fundamental Durkheimian axiom that 'social facts' are collectively represented in myth and religion (see Durkheim, 1912), and this idea subsequently became the foundation upon which Dumézil built his 'new comparative mythology'.

Certainly, he already had more than a superficial acquaintance with these ideas. A decade earlier, when he was completing his thesis, Dumézil had approached Durkheim's nephew and chief disciple, Marcel Mauss (1872–1950), for advice, and their subsequent relations had been cordial. (Mauss was Dumézil's senior colleague at the time he decided to study with Granet.) Moreover, his own mentor, Meillet, had also been a member of Durkheim's circle and had written a classic essay on the extent to which the Vedic divinity Mitra was a 'collective representation' of the idea of 'contract' (Meillet, 1907). But it was not until he worked closely with Granet that he came to appreciate the explanatory power of the sociological method.

In 1935 he published *Flāmen–Brahman*, which suggested that the Proto-Indo-Europeans knew a class of sacred personages called **Bhlagh(s)-men* – a reconstruction based on Latin *flāmen*, Indic *brahman* and Iranian *baresman*, and which, as the eminent Indo-Europeanist Jaan Puhvel has observed, is within the realm of possibility if not probability (Littleton, 1982, p. 55). The primary function of these primordial priests, Dumézil asserted, was to serve as sacrifical victims. Although still heavily Frazerian in tone, *Flāmen-Brahman* represented a major step forwards, as it focused his attention on the existence of a common Indo-European priest class/caste.

The breakthrough finally came in the spring of 1938. He had been invited back to Uppsala to give a series of lectures and had came to know Stig Wikander (1908–53), a brilliant young Swedish Iranianist who had recently published a landmark work on ancient Indo-European war bands, such as the Indic Kśatriyas and the *comitatus* that followed a Germanic chief. Entitled *Der arische Männerbund* (1938), it was to have a profound impact on Dumézil's thinking.

(As we shall shortly see, Wikander went on to become his earliest, and most influential, disciple.)

Late one evening, as Dumézil was preparing a lecture on the Indo-European component in Germanic mythology, he suddenly realised that the ancient Indo-Europeans shared a pantheon of gods that collectively represented, à la Durkheim and 'la méthode sociologique', a tripartite social organisation composed of priests, warrior-rulers, and a herder-cultivator class. By dawn (so Dumézil once told me), he had worked out the broad outlines of the tripartite model. The search for a new model was finally over, and the 'new comparative mythology' was about to make its debut.

The 'developmental phase': 1938–50

In the course of the next dozen or so years – what I have elsewhere labelled the 'developmental phase' in Dumézil's career (Littleton, 1982, pp. 58–99) – he followed up his 1938 breakthrough in a remarkable series of books and articles. The first tentative statement of the new model came in *Mythes et dieux des Germains. Essai d'interprétation comparative* (1939). Although the book was largely complete before his trip to Uppsala, he was able to add a chapter summarising the broad outlines of his discovery: the ancient Germanic, Roman and Indian pantheons were prime examples of the tripartite Indo-European ideology. Thus, Odin, Thor and Freyr were structurally and thematically comparable to the Roman gods Jupiter, Mars and Quirinus, as well as to the Indic deities Varuna, Indra and the twin Aśvins (or Nāsatya, the divine horsemen). Moreover, in all three societies, there were reflexes of the tripartite Indo-European social order collectively represented by these deities – despite the fact that the Germanic reflex of the priestly stratum had long since disappeared by the time the myths were recorded in the eleventh and twelfth centuries.

In 1940, in a book entitled *Mitra-Varuna. Essai sur deux réprésentations indo-européennes de la souverainété*, Dumézil expanded the model to include the concept of the 'joint sovereignty'; that is, the extent to which the ancient Indo-European communities conceived of a complementary pair of deities at the apex of their respective pantheons. The archetypal example was to be found in the Indic pair Mitra and Varuna. The former, whom Meillet had interpreted as the personification of the idea of 'contract', was the juridical sovereign, the ultimate representation of what might be called the 'social contract'. Varuna, on the other hand, was the principal representation of magical and religious sovereignty. Together, these divinities were a reflection of the traditional social functions served by the Brahman caste: to be judges and the guarantors of contracts, especially marriage contracts; and to perform rituals on behalf of the community. This complementary dyad was echoed in Roman religion by Dius Fidius, the shadowy patron of Numa, Romulus's law-giving successor, and Jupiter, lord of the cosmos. In ancient Scandinavia, the joint sovereignty was represented by Tyr, the oath god *par excellence*, and Odin, who, like Varuna and Jupiter, maintained order in the universe.

The first comprehensive articulation of the 'new comparative mythology' appeared in 1941 in the first of a series of volumes entitled *Jupiter, Mars, Quirinus* (JMQ). In JMQ I, which is subtitled *Essai sur la conception indo-européenne de la société et sur les origines de Rome*, he began by systematically surveying the evidence for social and mythological tripartition among the ancient Indo-Iranians, drawing heavily on both his own and Benveniste's conclusions that the ancient Indo-Iranians shared a tripartite social organisation (see above). Then, drawing on his earlier Roman research, including an article entitled 'La préhistoire des flāmines majeurs' (1938), he analysed the extent to which the so-called 'pre-Capitoline' triad of Roman gods – Jupiter, Mars and Quirinus – reflected the same tripartite structure that obtained among the Indo-Iranians. Jupiter, together with Dius Fidius, presided over the *flāmines* and other sacerdotal groups; Mars was the patron of the *milites*, the Roman reflex of Wikander's Indo-European war band, and Quirinus, etymologically as well as functionally, was the personification of the Roman population as a whole, the *quirites Romani*, including those who tilled the soil.

JMQ I goes on to compare these and other Roman tri-functional social and supernatural structures with analogous paradigms in the ancient Greek and Celtic traditions. Thus, the four traditional Athenian *bioi*, or 'types of life', the priest and magistrates, the 'guardians', and the labourers and artisans (lumped together, as in ancient Iran) formed a social class system cognate to that of Vedic India, Avestan Iran or monarchial Rome. He went on to suggest that this tripartite, Indo-European social order is also reflected in the structure of Plato's image of the ideal citizen, or 'Just Man': he should have the wisdom of a philosopher, the bravery of a warrior, and the wealth-producing skills of an artisan or cultivator.

Among the Celts there were several tripartite formulas, including, in inverse order, the Irish images of the 'Cauldron of the Dagda', which never failed to provide nourishment, the 'Spear of Lug', and the 'Stone of Fal', which served as the seat of sovereignty.

Dumézil's underlying assumption at this point was that the hierarchial, tripartite social systems characteristic of the most ancient Indo-European speaking communities were collectively represented by their respective pantheons. Thus, Jupiter, Varuna and Odin were mythological expressions of the 'first function', that is, those social institutions, like the *flâmines maiores*, the Indic brahmans and the Irish Druids, who maintained the sovereign order, juridically as well as religiously; Mars, Indra and Thor belonged to the 'second function' and reflected institutions that exercised physical prowess, like the Germanic chief and his *comitatus*, the Roman *milites* and the Indic Kśatriyas; while Quirinus, the Vedic Aśvins (or Nāsatya, 'the Divine Twins'), and the Norse god Freyr (together with his sister Freyja and his father Njordr) represented the 'third function': those segments of society that cultivated the soil and/or raised flocks, like the Indian Vaiśyas, the Roman *quirites* and the masses in general.

This model was extremely Durkheimian and reflected Dumézil's close association with both Granet and Mauss in the years immediately preceding his 'epiphany'. As we shall see, he would eventually shift his ground considerably, and the mature version of Dumézil's thesis transcended Durkheim's assumption that 'social facts' were necessarily antecedent to the contents of myths. However, for the first decade of its existence, the 'new comparative mythology' was firmly embedded in the theories and methods of 'la méthode sociologique'.

Meanwhile, the Second World War, the Vichy regime and the German occupation all impacted on Dumézil's career. A captain in the reserves, he was mobilised in July 1939 and posted to Liège as a liaison officer with the Belgian army (Erebon, 1987, p. 73). In April 1940, with the help of General Weygand, who had known his father, he managed to have himself posted to the French military mission in Turkey. He was thus in Ankara when the news came that France had capitulated. Repatriated in September, he returned to full-time teaching at the end of the year.

However, early in 1941, thanks to Vichy's Nazi-inspired anti-Masonic policy, Dumézil, who had been a mason in his youth, was suspended from his position at the Ecole des Hautes Etudes. He was finally reinstated, thanks to the efforts of several colleagues, in the autumn of 1943.

Throughout this difficult period he continued to publish extensively and to expand the model he had annunciated in 1939. In 1942 he published *Horace et les Curiaces* and in 1943 *Servius et la Fortune*, both of which elaborated his ideas about Rome's Indo-European heritage. In 1944 the second volume of the JMQ series, *Naissance de Rome*, appeared. It was soon followed in 1945 by the third volume: *Naissance des archanges*, which analysed the origin of the Zoroastrian Ameśa Spentas, the prototypes of the Judeo-Christian archangels, from the standpoint of the tripartite model.

Other important books and articles followed in the post-War period, including *Tarpeia* (1947), a second edition of *Mitra-Varuna* (1948a), *Loki* (1948b), *L'héritage indo-européen à Rome* (1949a) and *Le troisième souverain* (1949b), a discussion of the role played by the Vedic divinity Aryaman and his Indo-European counterparts, such as Heimdallr, in the overall Indo-European ideology.

Meanwhile, in 1947, his Swedish disciple Stig Wikander published a brilliant essay demonstrating that the principal heroic protagonists of the *Mahābhārata*, the five Pāndava, or 'sons of Pāndu', Yudhisthira, Arjuna, Bhīma, Nakula and Sahadeva, were transpositions, respectively, of the Vedic deities Dharma, Indra, the recalcitrant warrior deity Vāyu and the twin Aśvins. Thanks to Wikander's research (Dumézil would later substitute Mithra for

Dharma and link Varuna to Pāndu himself), it was now obvious that the tripartite paradigm pervaded the entire Indic tradition, from myth to epic – a phenomenon that Dumézil had also come to recognise in the Roman materials. Futhermore, there seemed to be no clear-cut causal nexus between the social and other manifestations of the three functions.

In short, by the time he produced the first general synthesis of his model, *Les dieux des Indo-Européens* in 1952, Dumézil had begun to question the validity of Durkheim's famous assumption that social facts are necessarily antecedent to supernatural beliefs. As he himself later phrased it:

> je reconnus, vers 1950, que 'idéologie tripartie' ne s'accompagne pas forcément, dans la vie d'une société, de la division tripartie *réelle* de cette société, selon le modèle indien; qu'elle peut au contraire, là où on la constate, n'être (ne plus être, peut-être n'avoir jamais été) qu'un idéal et, en même temps, un moyen d'analyser, d'interpréter les forces qui assurent le cours du monde et la vie des hommes. (Dumézil, 1968, p. 15)

The key phrase here is *'moyen d'analyser'*, which implies the presence of a deep-seated ideology that manifests itself in an infinite variety of surface contexts, from triads of divinities to triads of social classes to triads of diseases and triads of cures. At first glance, this approach might seem similar to that of Dumézil's good friend and colleague Claude Lévi-Strauss. However, unlike Lévi-Strauss, Dumézil did not assume that the tripartite ideology he had discovered among the ancient Indo-Europeans was universal. Indeed, other language families, like the Uto-Aztecan family in North America (the Hopi, the Nahuatl speakers [or Aztecs], the Paiute, etc.), have wholly different *'moyens d'analyser'*; among the Uto-Aztecans, for example, it is quadripartite, reflecting a concern with the cardinal directions rather than social hierarchies. Perhaps the best way to characterise Dumézil's fully-evolved approach is to label it 'structural relativism' (Littleton, 1974a); whereas Lévi-Strauss attempted to expose the deep structure of the human psyche *per se* (for example, Lévi-Strauss, 1964), Dumézil was content to operate at a relativistic level and to focus his attention on a single macro-community, the Indo-European language family, which exists in a bounded framework of time and space. The two scholars are thus concerned with very different – albeit complementary – levels of abstraction and inclusiveness. Nevertheless, despite these differences, Lévi-Strauss frequently recognised his Indo-Europeanist colleague's pioneering contributions to structuralist theory (for example, Lévi-Strauss, 1964, p. 23, p. 300; 1979, p. 76), and asserted that his own intellectual development was influenced by Dumézil's approach (Lévi-Strauss, 1953, p. 535).

Expanding the paradigm: 1950–68

By the time his second general synthesis, *L'idéologie tripartie des Indo-Européens* – still the most succinct introduction to his general thesis – appeared in 1958, Dumézil had expanded his paradigm to include a wide variety of ancient Indo-European themes and motifs, including the 'three sins of the warrior' and the 'war between the functions'. The former theme, initially suggested by Wikander in his 1947 essay, is manifested in the careers of figures like Indra and Heracles, who progressively commit offences against each of the functions and are punished for their actions; this important aspect of the Indo-European ideology was discussed at length in 1956 in a seminal book entitled *Aspects de la fonction guerrière chez les Indo-Européens* (1956a). (Dumézil returned to this and other aspects of the warrior function in 1969 in what amounts to a revised and updated version of *Aspects* aptly entitled *Heur et malheur du guerrière*.)

The idea of a 'war between the functions', first broached in 1941, involves a primordial internecine conflict between figures representing the first two functions (for example, Odin, Tyr and Thor; Romulus and his fellow Romans) and the third (for example, Freyr and Njordr; the Sabines). The conflict ends with the defeat of the third-function figures and their incorporation into the system, which renders it complete (Dumézil, 1949a; 1958, pp. 56–7).

Other noteworthy books that appeared during this period include an assessment of the curious three-stage career of the hero Hadingus (1953a), two studies of Roman religion (1954a, 1956b), which prefigured a massive, two-volume study of the archaic phase of that religion that appeared in 1966, and a revised edition of his 1939 book on Germanic mythology (1959). In addition, he addressed both the Greek (1953b) and the Celtic (1954b) traditions, and returned periodically to the folklore of his beloved Ossetians (for example, 1960, 1965). Indeed, whenever possible, Dumézil spent his summers in Turkey, collecting new texts and studying a variety of Caucasian languages and dialects.

In 1955, he spent several months as a visiting professor at the University of Lima, Peru, where, briefly, he turned his attention to the study of Quéchua linguistics and folklore (see, for example, 1955). It was another welcome break from his comparative Indo-European studies.

In 1968, Dumézil retired from the Collège de France, to which he had been elected in 1949. Shortly after, he embarked on another major research project, which was to culminate in a three-volume series called *Mythe et épopée*. This marks the beginning of the final phase in his career, the 'phase de bilan'.

The 'phase de bilan': 1968–86

Mythe et épopée I (1968), subtitled *L'idéologie des trois fonctions dans les épopées des peuples indo-européens*, focuses primarily on three Indo-European epic traditions: the Indic, the Roman and the Ossetic. In the first part of the book, Dumézil builds on Wikander's 1947 analysis of the connections between the *Rig Veda* and the *Mahābhārata* (see above) and concludes that the conflicts between the Pāndavas (Arjuna et al.) and their enemies (Duryodhana and his siblings) is a transposition to the mortal realm of a fundamental eschatological crisis, a conflict between Good and Evil where Good wins and the world is reborn.

The second part of the book is concerned with the origin of Rome. Again, the emphasis is upon the transposition from the theological (that is, mythological) realm to the realm of heroes; the early Roman kings, from Romulus to Ancus Martius, all embody one or another of the three ideological functions, in the same way that Yudhisthira and his siblings do in the Indian tradition.

The third section, 'Trois familles', focuses on the Ossetic Nart epics and the extent to which the three heroic families – the Alaegatae, Aexsaertaegkatae, and the Boratae – reflect, respectively, the first, second and third functions. The book concludes with a section called 'Epica minora', in which he assesses the persistence of the Indo-European ideology in several epic contexts.

All things considered, *Mythe et épopée I* remains one of Dumézil's most significant books, for it represents a true *bilan*, a summing up that is both a comprehensive restatement of his central thesis and an important extension into the realm of epic and saga.

However, the next book in the series, *Mythe et épopée II*, is also extremely significant, as it opens up yet another important dimension of the Indo-European tradition. The book focuses on three '*types épiques*', heroes (the Indian figures Śiśupāla and Jarasandhra, the Norse hero Starkadr and Heracles), sorcerers (the Indian figure Kāvya Uśanas and the Iranian King Kavi Usan [or Kay Us]), and three kings (the Indic Yayāti, The Iranian Yima and the Irish Eochaid Feidlach), all of whom have broadly similar careers. In all these cases, Dumézil sees what amounts to an opposition between 'light' and 'dark' aspects of each of the functions, an opposition expressed at the mythological level between Odin, who is darkly mysterious and unpredictable, and Tyr, who, like the Indic Mitra, is the embodiment of the social contract; and between the flawed, but essentially chivalrous, Indra and the violent, unpredictable Indic warrior deity Vāyu. Unfortunately, he never really followed up this line of research, although it remains one of the most interesting 'loose ends' in his *œuvre*; moreover, the notion of a binary opposition cutting across the three functions is generally consonant with Lévi-Strauss's basic thesis, as expressed in *Le cru et le cuit* (1964) and elsewhere.

The third volume in the series, *Mythe et épopée III*, published in 1973, includes a series of essays on a subject to which, as we have seen, Dumézil returned again and again: Roman pseudo-history. The first essay concerns what he called 'La saison des rivières'; that is, the famous episode where, around 400 BC, during the Veiian War, the Alban Lake rose and threatened to destroy Rome. He compared this to the Irish legends of Nechtan's Well, whose waters overflow to form the Boyne River, and the Iranian account of how the X,*arenah*, the fiery nimbus symbolic of kingship that was kept in a sacred lake, fled from the grasp of a usurper and caused the water to flow to the sea.

The second essay, later translated into English, suggests that the quasi-historical Roman general Camillus (*c.* 390 BC) was, at bottom, a solar figure; here he cautiously returns to an idea that had been dormant since the days of Max Müller. The author of this article, who was privileged to hear the first exposition of this idea in a seminar at the University of California at Los Angeles (UCLA) in the spring of 1971, distinctly remembers Dumézil, tongue firmly in cheek, asking us whether Müller had been long enough in his grave for such an idea to be credible!

In 1977, the long-awaited third edition of *Mitra-Varuna* appeared, reflecting three decades of further reflection on the idea of the joint sovereignty. This was followed in 1978 by what can best be described as his '*bilan ossetique*': *Romans de Scythie et d'alentour*. He begins by once again assessing the Indo-European character of the Scythian origin myth (see above), and then goes on to do the same thing for the Ossetic texts, drawing extensively on the massive amount of research he had done in this area since the publication of *Le livre des héros* in 1965. He also began a series of volumes collectively entitled *Esquisses de mythologie*, which, as the title indicates, include a variety of 'sketches', many of them brilliant, drawn from his half-century of research into Indo-European mythology. The first three titles in this series are *Apollo sonore et autres essais* (1982), *Le courtisane et les seigneurs colorés* (1983) and *L'oublie de l'homme et l'honneur des dieux* (1985a), the last book to be published in his lifetime.

Dumézil steadfastly refused to write his memoirs, saying that his work should stand or fall on its own merits and needed no self-serving glosses. Indeed, the closest thing to a memoir he managed to produce was an extended dialogue with Didier Erebon in 1986, less than four months before his death. Entitled *Entretiens avec Georges Dumézil*, Erebon's book, which appeared in 1987, provided Dumézil with an opportunity to comment on a variety of issues relating to his work.

In 1979, Dumézil was elected to the Académie française. His sponsor, who gave the welcoming address, was none other than his old friend and fellow structuralist Claude Lévi-Strauss.

Georges Dumézil died on 11 October 1986, five months short of his eighty-ninth birthday, from the effects of a massive stroke. He was mentally active until the end, and left a number of unfinished works. One of these, *Le roman des jumeaux et autres essais*, the fourth volume of the *Esquisses de mythologie* series, appeared in 1994. It was edited by Joël Grisward, a devoted disciple and major contributor in his own right (see, for example Grisward, 1981).

Overall assessment

Like most scholars who break important new ground, Dumézil has not been without his critics. Some of them, like Paul Thieme (1957), Jan Gonda (1960), and E. A. Philippson (1962; see also Strutynski, 1977), have objected both to specific interpretations and to his overarching theoretical framework. Others, like John Brough (1959) and, more recently, Colin Renfrew (1987, pp. 251–9), have found fault with the very idea of a common Indo-European ideology, much less a common set of social institutions. Nevertheless, the discovery of the tripartite model, whatever its faults or limitations, must be ranked among the great scholarly achievements of the twentieth-century; even Renfrew pays homage to Dumézil's 'enormous contributions . . . to the wider study of mythology' (Renfrew, 1987, p. 258).

Moreover, if Dumézil's ideas have triggered more than their fair share of scholarly criticism, they have also inspired several generations of scholars to expand and refine the model. In addition to Grisward and Wikander, those scholars who have, from time to time, seen fit to follow Dumézil's lead include, among a great many others, N. J. Allen (1987), who has attempted to delineate a 'fourth function' predicated on the notion of 'other', Emile Benveniste, Georges Charachidzé, Jan de Vries, F. X. Dillmann, Jacques Duchesne-Guillemin, Daniel Dubuisson, the late Lucien Gerschel, Emily B. Lyle, Dean A. Miller, Edgar Polomé, Jaan Puhvel, Alwyn and Brinley Rees, Robert Schilling, Bernard Sergent, Udo Strutynski, Donald Ward, Atsuhiko Yoshida and the author of this article. For in-depth critical assessments of Dumézil's ideas, see Littleton (1974b, 1982, 1991),

Rivière (1979), Strutynski (1973, 1980) and Dubuisson (1993, pp. 23–128).

Postscript: a most unfortunate controversy

In the years immediately preceding his death, Dumézil was unfairly subjected to a different kind of criticism, a criticism that still clouds his memory. Several scholars, taking their cue from the late Arnaldo Momigliano (1983), have seen fit to accuse him of Fascist and pro-Nazi sympathies, both before and during the second World War. This accusation, perpetuated primarily by Carlo Ginsburg (1985, 1990) and Bruce Lincoln (1991, pp. 231–67), is based in large measure on 'guilt by association': that is, his lifelong friendship with Pierre Gaxotte, secretary to Charles Maurras, founder of the virulently anti-Semitic and far-Right organisation Action française in the early 1920s, whom Dumézil first met when he and Gaxotte were fellow students at the *Ecole normale supérieure*. Another charge is that his initial articulation of the tripartite ideology came, as we have seen, in 1939 in a book about the ancient Germanic religion; surely, his accusers reason, that cannot be a coincidence. Indeed, that ideology itself has been seen as a Fascist conception: an elitist, anti-democratic structure that elevates priests and warriors above the downtrodden mass of society.

Dumézil did his best to defend himself in the final *esquisse* ('Une idylle de vingt ans') of *L'oublie de l'homme et l'honneur des dieux* (pp. 229–318), in a response to Ginsburg that appeared in *Annales* (Dumézil, 1985b), and in his conversations with Didier Erebon (Erebon, 1987, pp. 198–220); so did several of his longtime admirers (Littleton, Puhvel, Miller and Strutynski 1986), but the dark cloud refused to dissipate.

In 1992, after hearing what later turned out to be a wholly unfounded rumour that all copies of *Mythes et dieux des Germains* (1939) had disappeared from library shelves around the world, Didier Erebon undertook a comprehensive and dispassionate investigation of the charges levied by Momigliano et al. The results of this investigation, published in a book entitled *Faut-il brûler Dumézil?* (1992), led Erebon to the conclusion that there was no reason whatsoever to consign him to the stake.

Certainly, Dumézil was wont to describe himself as 'un homme de la droite' (a man of the Right) (personal communication); but he was never, by any stretch of the imagination, a Fascist, racist, or anti-Semite, much less a crypto-Nazi. Nor did he have much personal sympathy for the ideology he discovered: 'je n'aurais pas du tout aimé vivre chez aucun de ceux que j'ai étudiés. Je n'aurais pu respirer dans une société dominée par des druides, ou par des brahmanes' (Erebon, 1987, p. 162).

If Dumézil's accusers are permitted to invoke 'guilt by association', then it is equally possible to declare him 'innocent' by the same rule: for many years he was a good friend and mentor to the late Michel Foucault, who, as is well-known, did *not* share Dumézil's mildly conservative political orientation. In this connection, Claude Lévi-Strauss has observed that

> Personne, parmi nous, n'a jamais soupçonné Dumézil de complaisance envers l'idéologie nazie. L'idée me semble monstreuse et absurd. Je n'en vois pas la moindre trace dans *Mythes et dieux des germains*. (in Erebon, 1992, p. 42)

Such eloquent testimony from a world-renowned colleague underscores both the baselessness of these charges and the probability that this most unfortunate controversy will soon be laid to rest. A recent overview of the dispute can be found in Zambrini (1994).

Bibliography

Writings

NOTE: Dumézil published over seventy-five books and several hundred articles, reviews, replies, etc. What follows are those of his works cited in this article. For more comprehensive bibliographies of Dumézil's publications, see Littleton (1982) and Rivière (1979).

Dumézil, Georges (1924a), *Le festin d'immortalité. Etude de mythologie comparé indo-européenne*, vol. 34, Paris: Annales du musée Guimet.
— (1924b), *Le crime des Lemniennes. Rites et légendes du monde égéen*, Paris: Geuthner.
— (1929), *Le problème des Centaures. Etude de mythologie comparée indo-europénne*, vol. 41, Paris: Annales du musée Guimet.

— (1930a), *Légendes sur les Nartes, suivés de cinq notes mythologiques*, Paris: Honoré Champion.

— (1930b), 'La préhistoire indo-iranienne des castes', *Journal asiatique* 216, 109–130.

— (1931), *La langue des Oubykhs*, Paris: Honoré Champion.

— (1934), *Ouranos-Varuna. Essai de mythologie comparée indo-européenne*, Paris: Adrien Maisonneuve.

— (1935), *Flāmen-Brahman*, Paris: Annales du Musée Guimet.

— (1938), 'La préhistoire des flāmines majeurs', *Revue de l'histoire des religions* 118, 188–220.

— (1939), *Mythes et dieux des Germains. Essai d'interprétation comparative*, Paris: Presses Universitaires de France.

— (1940), *Mitra-Varuna. Essai sur deux représentations indo-européennes de la souveraineté*. Paris: Gallimard.

— (1941), *Jupiter-Maris-Quirinus I. Essai sur la conception indo-européenne de la société et sur les origines de Rome*, Paris: Gallimard.

— (1942), *Horace et les Curiaces. Les mythes romains I*, Paris: Gallimard.

— (1943), *Servius et la Fortune. Essai sur la conception sociale de louange et de blâme et sur les éléments indo-européens du 'cens' romain. Les mythes romains II*, Paris: Gallimard.

— (1944), *Naissance de Rome. Jupiter, Mars, Quirinus II*, Paris: Gallimard.

— (1945), *Naissance des archanges. Essai sur la formation de la théologie zoroastrienne. Jupiter, Mars, Quirinus III*, Paris: Gallimard.

— (1947), *Tarpeia. Essai de philologie comparative indo-européenne. Les mythes romains III*, Paris: Gallimard.

— (1948a), *Mitra-Varuna. Essai sur deux représentations indo-européennes de la souveraineté*, 2nd edn, Paris: Gallimard.

— (1948b), *Loki*, Paris: G.-P. Maisonneuve.

— (1949a), *L'héritage indo-européen à Rome. Introduction aux series 'Jupiter, Mars, Quirinus' et 'les mythes romains'*, Paris: Gallimard.

— (1949b), *Le troisième souvrain. Essai sur le dieu indo-iranien Aryaman et sur la formation de l'histoire mythique de l'Irlande*, Paris: G.-P. Maisonneuve.

— (1952), *Les dieux des Indo-Européens*, Paris: Presses Universitaires de France.

— (1953a), *La Saga de Hadingus (Saxo Grammaticus, I, v-viii). Du mythe au roman*. Paris: Presses Universitaires de France. (*From Myth to Fiction*, trans. Derek Coltman, Chicago: University of Chicago Press, 1970.)

— (1953b), 'Les trois fonctions dans quelques traditions grecques', in *Eventail de l'histoire vivante. Hommage à Lucien Febvre*, Paris: Armand Colin, 25–32.

— (1954a), *Rituels indo-européens à Rome*, Paris: Klincsieck.

— (1954b), 'Le trio des Macha', *Revue de l'histoire des religions* 146, 5–17.

— (1955), 'Remarques complémentaires sur les six premiers noms de nombres du Turc et du quéchua', *Journal de la société des Américanistes* 44, 17–38.

— (1956a), *Aspects de la fonction guerrière chez les Indo-Européens*, Paris: Presses Universitaires de France. (*Gods of the Ancient Northmen*, trans. John Lindow, Alan Toth, Francis Charat and Georges Gopen, ed. Einar Haugen, Berkeley: University of California Press, 1973.)

— (1956b), *Déesses latines et mythes védiques*, Brussels: Collection Latomus, 24.

— (1958), *L'idéologie tripartie des Indo-Européens*, Brussels: Collection Latomus, 31.

— (1960), 'Les trois trésors des ancêtres dans l'épopée narte', *Revue de l'histoire des religions* 157, 141–54.

— (1965), *Le livre des héros. Légendes sur les Nartes*, (traduites de l'ossète, avec une introduction et des notes), Paris: Gallimard.

— (1966), *La religion romaine archaïque* (avec un appendice sur la religion des Etrusques), Paris: Payot. (*Archaic Roman Religion*, trans. Philipp Krapp, Chicago: University of Chicago Press, 1970.)

— (1968), *Mythe et épopée I. L'idéologie des trois fonctions dans les épopées des peuples indo-européens*, Paris: Gallimard.

— (1969), *Heur et malheur du guerrière. Aspects mythiques de la fonction guerrière chez les Indo-Européens*, Paris: Presses Universitaires de France. (*The Destiny of the Warrior*, trans. Alf Hiltebeitel, Chicago: University of Chicago Press, 1970.)

— (1971), *Mythe et épopée II. Types épiques indo-européens: un héros, un sorcier, un roi*, Paris: Gallimard. (*The Stakes of the Warrior* (Part 1), trans. and ed. Jaan Puhvel and David Weeks, Berkeley: University of California Press, 1983; *The Plight of a Sorcerer* (Part 2), trans. and ed. Jaan Puhvel and David Weeks et al., Berkeley: University of California Press, 1986; *The Destiny of a King* (Part 3), trans. Alf Hiltebeitel. Chicago: University of Chicago Press, 1973.)

— (1973), *Mythe et épopée III. Histoires romaines*, Paris: Gallimard. (*Camillus* (Part 2), trans. Antoinette Aronowicz and Josette Bryson, ed. Udo Strutynski, Berkeley: University of California Press, 1980.)

— (1977), *Les dieux souvrains des Indo-Européens*, 3rd edition of *Mitra-Varuna*, Paris: Gallimard. (*Mitra-Varuna: An Essay on Two Indo-European Representations of Society*, trans. Derek Coltman, New York: Zone Books, 1988.)

— (1978), *Romans de Scythie et d'alentour*, Paris: Payot.

— (1982), 'Apollo sonore', *Esquisses de mythologie 1–25*, Paris: Gallimard.

— (1983), 'Le courtisane et les seigneurs colorés', *Esquisses de mythologie 26–50*. Paris: Gallimard, 1983.

— (1985a), *L'oubli de l'homme et l'honneur des dieux. Esquisses de mythologie 50–75*, Paris: Gallimard.

— (1985b), 'Science et politique', *Annales* 40, 985–9.

— (1994), *Le roman des jumeaux et autres essais. Esquisses de mythologie 76–100*, ed. Joël Grisward, Paris: Gallimard.

References and further reading

Allen, N. J. (1987), 'The ideology of the Indo-Europeans: Dumézil's theory and the idea of a fourth function', *International Journal of Moral and Social Studies* 2, 23–39.

Benveniste, Emile (1932), 'Les classes sociales dans la tradition avestique', *Journal asiatique*, 221, 117–34.

Brough, John (1959), 'The tripartite ideology of the Indo-Europeans: an experiment in method', *Bulletin of the School of Oriental and African Studies* 22, 68–86.

Dubuisson, Daniel (1993), *Mythologie du XXe siècle (Dumézil, Lévi-Strauss, Eliade)*, Lille: Presse Universitaire de Lille.

Durkheim, Emile (1961) (first edn 1912), *The Elementary Forms of the Religious Life*, trans. Joseph Ward Swain, New York: Collier Books.

Erebon, Didier (1987), *Entretiens avec Georges Dumézil*, Paris: Gallimard.

— (1992), *Faut-il brûler Dumézil?*, Paris: Flammarion.

Frazer, Sir James G. (1922), *The Golden Bough*, abridged edn, New York: Macmillan.

Ginsburg, Carlo (1985), 'Mythologie germanique et nazisme. Sur un ancient livre de Georges Dumézil', *Annales* 40, 857–82.

— (1990), *Myths, Emblems, Clues*, London: Hutchinson Radius.

Gonda, Jan (1960), 'Some observations on Dumézil's views of Indo-European mythology', *Mnemosyne* 4, 1–15.

Granet, Marcel (1980) (first edn 1933), *La religion chinoise*, with a Foreword by Georges Dumézil, Paris: Editions Imago.

Grisward, Joël H. (1981), *Archéologie de l'épopée médiévale*, Paris: Payot.

Lévi-Strauss, Claude (1953), 'Social structure', in A. L. Kroeber (ed.), *Anthropology Today*, Chicago: University of Chicago Press, 524–53.

— (1964), *Le cru et le cuit*, Paris: Plon. (*The Raw and the Cooked*, trans. John and Doreen Weightman, New York: Harper and Row, 1969.)

— (1979), *Discours de réception de M. Georges Dumézil à l'Académie française*, Paris: Gallimard, 45–76.

Lincoln, Bruce (1986), 'Shaping the past and the future' (review of Georges Dumézil, *L'oublie de l'homme et l'honneur des dieux*), *Times Literary Supplement* (London), 3 October, 1107–8.

— (1991), *Death, War, and Sacrifice: Studies in Ideology and Practice*, Chicago: University of Chicago Press.

Littleton, C. Scott (1974a), ' "Je ne suis pas . . . structuraliste": some fundamental differences between Dumézil and Lévi-Strauss', *Journal of Asian Studies* 34, 151–8.

— (1974b), 'Georges Dumézil and the rebirth of the genetic model: an anthropological appreciation', in Gerald James Larson, C. Scott Littleton and Jaan Puhvel (eds), *Myth in Indo-European Antiquity*, Berkeley: University of California Press, 169–80.

— (1982), *The New Comparative Mythology: An Anthropological Assessment of the Theories of Georges Dumézil*, 3rd edn, Berkeley: University of California Press.

— (1991), 'The tripartite division of labor (priests, warriors, cultivators) in ancient Indo-European mythology', in Morris Silver (ed.), *Ancient Economy in Mythology: East and West*, Savage, MD: Rowman and Littlefield, 73–106.

Littleton, C. Scott, Dean A. Miller, Jaan Puhvel and Udo Strutynski (1986), 'Georges Dumézil' (reply to Bruce Lincoln), *Times Literary Supplement* (London), 5 December, 1375.

Meillet, Antoine (1907), 'Le dieu indo-iranien Mitra', *Journal asiatique* 9, 143–59.

Momigliano, Arnaldo (1983), 'Permesse per una discussione su Georges Dumézil', *Opus* 2, 329–41.

Philippson, E. A. (1962), 'Phänomenologie, vergleichende Mythologie und germanische Religionsgeschichte', *Publications of the Modern Language Association* 77, 187–93.

Renfrew, Colin (1987), *Archaeology and Language: The Puzzle of Indo-European Origins*, New York: Cambridge University Press.

Rivière, Jean-Claude (1979), 'Georges Dumézil et les études indo-Européennes', in Jean-Claude Rivière (ed.), *À la découverte des Indo-Européens*, Paris: Editions Copernic, 9–129.

Strutynski, Udo (1973), 'Introduction: part II', *Gods of the Ancient Northmen*, Berkeley: University of California Press, xix–xliii.

— (1977), 'Philipsson contra Dumézil: an answer to the attack', *The Journal of Indo-European Studies* 5, 209–19.

— (1980), 'Introduction', *Camillus: Indo-European Religion as History*, Berkeley: University of California Press, 1–39.

Thieme, Paul (1957), *Mitra and Aryaman*, New Haven, CT: Transactions of the Connecticut Academy of Arts and Sciences 41.

Wikander, Stig (1938), *Der arische Männerbund*, Lund: Ohlsson.

— (1947), 'Pāndava-sagan och Mahābhāratas mytiska förutsättningar' ('The Pāndava sagas and the *Mahābhārata*'s mythical forerunners'), *Religion och Bibel* 6, 27–39.

Zambrini, Andrea (1994), 'Georges Dumézil. Una polemica', *Rivista di Storia della Storiografia Moderna* 15, 317–89.

7.6

LANGUAGE AND THE SIGNS OF CULTURE: BARTHES

Michael Moriarty

Roland Barthes, literary critic, essayist, semiologist and literary theorist, was born in 1915. He was brought up in poverty by his mother after the death of his father, a naval officer, in the First World War. However he received a good secondary education, and seemed set for an academic career, when he discovered that he had tuberculosis. This prevented him from continuing his studies beyond a first degree in Classics. He spent the wartime years mostly in a sanatorium, which he left in 1946. From the late 1940s until the early 1960s, despite precarious material circumstances, he published an increasingly influential series of articles and, later, books: on literature, the theatre and contemporary culture, in the broadest sense (*Mythologies* (1957)). His first academic teaching post came only in 1960, when he was appointed to the Ecole Pratique des Hautes Etudes, a graduate school which concentrated principally on the social sciences and with a reputation for encouraging independent and challenging work. His seminar teaching there helped nourish his continuing steady production of books and articles. In 1977 he received the ultimate academic accolade of election to a chair (in literary semiology) at the *Collège de France*. He died after a road accident in 1980, shortly after the death of his mother, to whom he was deeply attached, and to whom he pays moving tribute in his final book, *Camera Lucida* (*La Chambre claire*).

Barthes's vision of language

Barthes certainly never presented himself as a philosopher. In *Roland Barthes by Roland Barthes* (*Roland Barthes par Roland Barthes*) (1975) he uses the term 'philosophy' in connection with himself, but in an ironically self-deprecating fashion: he speaks of developing a 'little philosophy' of hedonism as a reaction to childhood experiences of financial hardship, and of a 'simplistic philosophy' that consists in a certain vision of the role of language in social life. He neither discusses philosophical problems nor offers readings of philosophical texts in the manner(s) typical of contemporary philosophy. In addition, he sometimes presents himself not as an abstract thinker, but as a writer, a purveyor of fictions, a producer of texts, not answerable for the truth of his 'theories'. In the same work, he speaks of himself as an echo-chamber: one who never absorbed systems of ideas (he mentions psychoanalysis, existentialism and Marxism) conceptually and as a whole, but treated them as stockpiles from which to lift particular terms. He proclaims himself as lacking a scientific, political, practical or philosophical intelligence, being capable of grasping things only in ethical terms. These statements, however, should not be taken at face value, but as part of a complex strategy of self-presentation, designed to make space for himself to write in a more literary and less theoretical way. Recent criticism has justifiably paid attention to his significance as a writer, a producer of texts soliciting an aesthetic response, rather than establishing abstract notions through argument. None the less, Barthes's work marks an essential contribution to the theoretical revolution that, from the late 1950s on, has challenged the whole conception of philosophy by insisting on the primacy of linguistic structures within thought, culture and the psyche. It develops a vision of language, literature and culture that is both powerful and seductive, and that raises important philosophical issues. Reading Barthes, one is constantly reminded of the work of other thinkers, and he was certainly indebted to the work of Marx, Nietzsche, Sartre and Derrida, amongst others: yet, except when he was expounding Brecht's dramatic theories in the 1950s, or the semiology of Saussure, Hjelmslev and others in the 1960s, it would be misleading to try to reckon up that debt in the hard currency of 'ideas' borrowed and applied. Generally, Barthes uses other thinkers eclectically and unsystematically to nourish a highly personal vision. His thought underwent a certain number of shifts, rather than evolving towards any single goal: but it displays deep underlying continuities. His engagement with specifically philosophical issues is most manifest in the works of the early and middle 1970s like *The Pleasure of the Text* (*Le Plaisir du texte*) (1973) and *Roland Barthes by Roland Barthes*.

Barthes does not see theoretical reflexion as enabling us to identify one theory as truer than its competitors. Its role is to enable us to think beyond common sense, beyond generally accepted opinion, beyond the discourses currently available: all of which he refers to, using a Platonic term, as *doxa* ('opinion'). His conception of theory is therefore bound up with the distinction between knowledge and opinion that can be traced back to Plato and Aristotle, but he approaches it essentially through a particular conception of language, which may be summarised as follows.

We construct our identity in language, but this identity frequently assumes an alienated form (as when we identify wholly with an ideology or with an image of ourselves). However, language can also dissolve this alienation, bringing about, if only temporarily, a kind of utopian transcendence of division; and this liberating potential of language

is what Barthes, at different periods, designates through terms like 'text', 'writing', 'the signifier' and 'literature'. But there is no facile optimism in his commitment to this liberating power. In general, he is all too acutely aware that language functions through constraint. This holds on two levels. First, the structures of individual languages oblige us to represent ourselves and the world in a certain way, which is not the only possible way, but must inevitably, through our rootedness in our particular mother tongue, appear as corresponding to the nature of things. The interaction of linguistic gender with the construction of gender in the broad sense is an obvious example. Elsewhere, Barthes suggests that the structures of Japanese construct selfhood in a different way from those of Indo-European languages. Second, although in Saussurean theory the speaking subject is constrained only by the structures of the language, and her or his discourse (*parole*) is an individual act of will and intelligence, Barthes insists that actual utterances tend to fall into particular patterns, which have a quasi-inevitability. Barthes terms these 'myths' or 'stereotypes': but by also labelling them '*doxa*' he evokes, as has already been suggested, the distinction between opinion and knowledge. In his presentation of ancient rhetoric, he does indeed invoke Aristotle's contention that rhetoric is based on generally accepted opinions (*endoxa*) rather than knowledge as a guide to the understanding of both classic literature and mass culture. However, it may be argued that he stresses the opposition between knowledge and opinion more rigidly than Aristotle himself does; and in any case, he is deeply anti-Aristotelian in his distrust of the whole concept of nature. He reinterprets 'nature' in the light of the concept of opinion: as regards human behaviour, what is taken as 'natural' is generally what corresponds to the opinion prevailing in a particular culture, the prevalence of which is the effect of social and historical forces. It is indeed the function of culture – or at least, that of modern 'mass societies' – to translate these forces into supposedly natural relationships.

A negative conception of opinion very generally (as in Plato, Spinoza or Althusser) co-exists with a confidence in the power of philosophy to mark itself off from opinion. Barthes's later writings, however, develop a parallel suspicion of theory. Not only do hard-won intellectual insights tend to solidify into clichés of the sort they were intended to displace; in *The Pleasure of the Text* he argues that strong theories like Marxism or psychoanalysis are fictions that mobilise their concepts in rhetorical manoeuvres that render them impervious to criticism. They buy invulnerability at the cost of a crippling rigidity. The realm of language is divided between a zone of apparent peace, where the nauseating and polluting atmosphere of *doxa* holds sway, and a war zone endlessly churned up by a kind of discursive tank battle.

This metaphorical presentation might suggest that Barthes's concepts cannot be rigorously theorised, and, to some, that what he is saying is therefore not worth taking seriously. In response to this, one might say three things. First, Barthes admits that he tends to present his key concepts metaphorically, but the metaphor, or string of metaphors, has the virtue that it is less likely to solidify into the kind of concept that, in the end, functions as an obstacle to, rather than a vehicle of, thought. Second, it will be seen that judgements of the kind cited above are not assertions of truth or falsehood: they are evaluations. This concept will be discussed below. Finally, Barthes suggests that theory ('science') should not be separated from imagination (or, to use his word, vision). A theory that allowed itself to resort to vision would be abandoning its claims to purity and assuming a fictional status, but the self-conscious fiction might be empowering and liberating, whereas the theory that represses its own fictionality is constrained and constraining.

The critique of culture

The above draws largely on Barthes's later writings, but it is arguable that these merely formulate and develop themes apparent, at least in retrospect, even in his earliest work. His early writings produce a highly original form of cultural critique drawing on Marxism, Sartre and, later, Brecht and Saussure. In *Writing Degree Zero* (*Le Degré zéro de l'écriture*) (1953) he argues, in an oblique relation to Sartre's *What is Literature?*, that writing cannot be understood as essentially the exercise of freedom. At any

given period, writers have to come to grips with divisions in the national language, between literary and ordinary language, and with the available conventions of vocabulary and syntax. These conventions align the writer with a certain social, political and moral vision of reality, whether shared with her or his public, or consciously oppositional, and in this sense they absorb the ethical dimension of writing, diverting it from an individual commitment to a social stance. Hence the element of alienation referred to above. In the modern period, the diversity of available writing styles (*écritures*) embodies the fracture of social reality, which the writer is therefore aggravating even when he or she seeks to heal it by writing. The attempt, by a writer like Camus, to break with the literary conventions of the novel, and thus distance himself from an established ideological position, is both admirable and precarious, itself easily reabsorbed as a new set of conventions.

Mythologies is perhaps Barthes's single most influential work: it remains a prime source book for students of cultural studies. It treats various objects, customs, discourses and images from French daily life in the 1950s as myths, by which Barthes means vehicles of a message. They offer us some kind of imaginative purchase on our lives, supply images of identity and community for us to adhere to; but in so doing they tacitly solicit our assent to the dominance of the bourgeoisie in French society, and to the ideologies the bourgeoisie upholds: imperialism, anti-intellectualism, gender essentialism, etc.

A culture may be seen as a language, in the sense that it is a medium through which messages (or myths) are endlessly transmitted to the members of the community, but the community is always socially divided, and this is why the myth may be said to be alienating. If I do not understand it for example, if I do not know that the *Tour de France* is happening, or know who the riders are), I am excluded from the mass of my fellow-citizens who do understand. If I do understand it, then I have the mortification of realising that the message is meant for me too, of recognising myself in the world-picture proposed by the myth (the myth 'interpellates', says Barthes, anticipating by some years Althusser's use of that verb to define the process of ideology). This is mortifying because the mythical world-picture freezes human beings and their behaviour into stereotyped patterns. The myth reduces history, the concrete process of making and remaking human relationships, to 'nature', the endless self-reproduction of essences ('woman', 'Africa', 'the writer', etc). The *Tour de France* as the conflict of mythical quasi-Homeric heroes is imaginatively rather satisfying; but the myth conceals the commercial underpinning of the whole exercise, or rather, obliges us to digest the commercialism as the indispensable condition of the imaginative stimulation.

The volume of *Mythologies* concludes with a theoretical postface 'Myth today', which both summarises his critique and brings to an end the phase of critique. Barthes attempts to systematise his insights through the application of Saussure's concepts of the sign as composed of signified (a concept) and signifier (the vehicle of the concept: more precisely, the pattern, acoustic or graphic, within which the concept takes material form). The myth transposes this relationship on to a further level. Thus, in an utterance such as 'Algeria is French', the marks on the page convey the concept of the Frenchness of Algeria. In a nineteenth-century geographical textbook, describing the colonial division of Africa, this might be construed as a purely literal statement. In the context of 1950s French politics, it means 'We shall not give up Algeria'. The literal statement thus becomes the vehicle of a further, political, message (the determination of France to hold on to its colony), which does not have to assert itself openly. In Barthes's adaptation of Saussure's terminology, it has become the signifier of a new political signified. Myth, then, is the appropriation of a literal message by a second, non-literal, one. This latter may be highly disputable, but since to query it would apparently be tantamount to querying the unquestionable literal message, it assumes an appearance of obvious truth. Barthes's semiology therefore challenges the applicability to everyday discourse of the positivist distinction between fact and value; for it emphasises the way in which factual statements are used both to convey feelings and attitudes and to protect these from dispute. '*Athalie* is a play by Racine' is an evaluation in that, in certain contexts, it can be received as an attack on academic interpreters of the

work: but it is not masquerading as a factual statement, it is a factual statement.

Barthes applies the mythological model not only to verbal utterances but to images. A photograph is a sign in that it comprises a signifier (a visual pattern) and a signified (the subject-matter of the photograph). It differs, as Barthes elsewhere acknowledges, from the linguistic sign which can only function within a code, and does not resemble what it refers to, whereas, with the photograph, there is no code, and there is a relation of resemblance between sign and object. But the photograph can also be said to convey a 'literal' message, as a picture of something or someone (for example, Greta Garbo), which can then in turn become the signifier of a new signified (the myth of Garbo).

Semiology

The desire for greater systematisation evident in 'Myth today' implies an epistemological shift. The diverse mythologies appeal to an intuitive grasp of the relation between the apparently random fact and the whole social structure that endows it with meaning. The postface attempts to theorise the nature of that relationship systematically, so that the force of particular analyses would henceforth reside in their conformity to the theoretical model, rather than their influence on concrete political issues. Moreover, as Barthes seeks to develop the semiological model set out in 'Myth today', the object of the analysis changes, from individual signs to sign-systems. Likewise its rationale: the detection of the bourgeois ideological hegemony inscribed in the taken-for-granted world of the everyday is subordinated to the quest for the formal mechanisms by which a culture makes the world intelligible. The inspiration here is the work of Lévi-Strauss and, beyond him, Saussure; but the change has political implications. The semiological project consists in classifying the images and rituals of a culture into sign-systems, conceived on the model of Saussure's concept of *langue* as a social institution. However, Saussure's underlying conception of society is as a homogeneous social organism, and it then becomes difficult to tie an analysis inspired by this model to that vision of society as class-divided and fundamentally conflictual presupposed by the original mythologies and asserted in 'Myth today'. Such tensions are arguably visible in Barthes's fullest application of the structuralist semiology, *The Fashion System* (*Système de la mode*) (1967), but this work displays another remarkable inflexion of his semiology. When Saussure coined the term 'semiology' to denote the 'science of the life of signs within society' he placed language among the domains to be studied, which would also include systems of gestures, including codes of politeness. Many semiologists have accepted this distinction between non-linguistic and linguistic sign-systems, but for Barthes, in *Système de la mode*, it cannot be sustained. Even a non-linguistic system, like traffic lights or maritime flags, requires the support of language, in terms of which alone it can be communicated to those who use it. Semiology thus becomes a sub-species of linguistics, rather than the reverse. More important than this methodological reversal is the ultimate implication, stated in *Roland Barthes by Roland Barthes*, that culture is 'nothing but' language. This takes us a long way from the Marxist formulations of the earlier work. It should probably be understood as meaning that politics, ideology, religion and art, all those fields of activity within which a culture takes shape, cannot be separated from the discourses in which they are constructed: language is not external to social relationships. It is, however, unclear that social and cultural relationships can be thus *reduced* to the language that constructs and sustains them.

Structuralism, literature and mimesis

However, this, to some extent, is to anticipate. Barthes's semiological work developed in parallel with an application of structuralist principles to literature: or rather, with several applications. The issues raised in his structuralist interpretation of Racine, which aroused bitter controversy, are predominantly literary: but the 'Introduction to the structural analysis of narratives' ('Introduction à l'analyse structurale des récits') (1966) has more philosophical implications.

Since Aristotle, literature has been viewed, at least in the West, predominantly in terms of *mimesis* (representation or imitation). Thus says Aristotle,

tragedy is a representation of action and life; poetry tells, not so much what did happen, as what would happen: it deals in general truths. It depicts, we may say, those basic characteristics of human nature and human life that shape individual fortunes into general patterns.

Barthes believed that Saussure's linguistics offered the study of literature a possibility of breaking with the Aristotelian legacy. Faced with the baffling variety and complexity of human tongues which seemed to render a science of language impossible, Saussure realised that linguistics could only be unified if it focused on the individual language considered as an autonomous system (*langue*). Barthes proposed to treat narrative as such a system. For Saussure, the workings of a language are not to be explained by reference to external reality, but by the mutually constitutive relationships between the terms by which the language is formed. The identity of a term is sufficiently determined, from the linguist's point of view, not by its reference to the object it is used to designate, but by its twofold difference (on the planes both of signifier and signified) from other terms in the language.

A structuralist narratology, conceived on this model, is radically indifferent to the mimetic dimension of the narratives it studies. It does not ask whether a story is sufficiently lifelike, or whether its events were borrowed from the writer's life, or whether, as a Marxist like Georg Lukács would ask, it deals with the fundamental social forces in play at the historical moment it depicts. Its object is not particular novels but narrative in general, and it approaches individual narratives as specific combinations of a basic set of elements. The task of the theorist is to identify those elements, the building blocks of narrative, and then the rules governing their combination.

Thus, the problem is this: is this exclusion simply a methodological imperative (in which case the structuralist would be saying that such issues as those mentioned above are entirely respectable objects of enquiry, but irrelevant to the study of literature, or narrative, as a system); or is there an underlying implication that, if we better understood the nature of narrative, such questions would not even be put?

In 'Introduction to the structural analysis of

narratives', Barthes argues that everything structural in a narrative is functional, which implies that narrative structure is not determined by the hierarchies of importance that apply in real life. 'Functional' here means that everything correlates with something else, and it is these correlations within the text that constitute narrative as such, not any conformity to reality. The 'reality' of a sequence of actions in a narrative does not lie in any natural connection between them: it is an effect of the specific logic of narrative connection, and even when writers reinject their own experience back into narrative, it is modified by the processes of this other logic (which structuralist theorists like Greimas and Todorov have sought to theorise).

Elsewhere, he asks whether structural analysis can ever 'arrive at an ultimate signified, which, in the case of the realist novel, would be "reality"' (Barthes, 1993–95, vol. 2, p. 856). This formulation runs a number of questions together:

1. Can there be an ultimate signified?
2. If so, could that signified be 'reality'?
3. Can texts refer to 'reality'?

As to 1. we might agree that there can be no ultimate signified because the process of interpretation will always generate new signifieds. What is more problematic here is the way in which Barthes conflates questions 2. and 3. in the sense that, having asked 2. the answer he gives, with an explicit reference to the work of Derrida, is a negative answer to 3.: to wit, that 'a writing always finally refers to another writing and the perspective of signs is in some sense infinite' (ibid.). Question 2. is, in fact, wrongly posed. The signified is a concept. Consequently, to say the text signifies reality is to say that it conveys the concept 'reality', or, to use another term of Barthes's, produces the 'reality-effect'. It can signify 'reality' but not signify reality itself. However, this only shows that reference to reality cannot be analysed in terms of signification. What we mean in saying that a text refers to reality is, arguably, that we recognise it as depicting, or mentioning, something or someone or some state of affairs that exists independently of it, and that we believe to exist, or to have existed, for reasons independent of the text in question. To put

it another way, we can say that the text has a common referent with other discourses and other orders of discourse. For example, Balzac's novels profess to depict French society after the Revolution: but that is also the object of historical discourses, subject to procedures of verification quite different from the processes of literary signification by which a reality effect is produced. Certainly historical discourse is textual: there is no access to post-Revolutionary French society outside discourse, in the sense that it is within discourse that the expression 'post-Revolutionary French society' is constituted. 'Post-Revolutionary French society' is, to use a term of Umberto Eco's, a 'cultural unit', not a brute fact. True, again, historical discourses are themselves texts, their procedures of verification bear on the interpretation of texts (for example, the government records from which the historian might reconstitute a statistical table). Even so, the point is that this interpretation does not follow the same norms as the tracing of patterns of literary signification. There is a marked distinction between the literary texts whose referents are shared with other genres of discourse and those whose referents are constituted entirely by intratextual correlations. Proust's novel mentions the First World War; a science-fiction novel might equally situate itself with reference to the Third Galactic War. A reader from another galaxy, knowing nothing of the history of Earth, might not perceive any difference between the status of these conflicts, but any terrestrial reader who put them on the same level would simply miss the point that one writer is referring to an experience his contemporaries could recognise, while the other is not. Moreover, it is perfectly possible to think that Proust's novel does, in an important sense, refer, like Balzac's, to social and historical processes, and to debate its representation of these, without identifying them as its ultimate signified.

There are issues here which go far beyond the scope of this article: the above is merely there to suggest that there is a case to answer, about *mimesis*, that Barthes does not take into account. However, he takes his reflection on mimesis further, and perhaps in more original ways, in *S/Z*, a reading of Balzac's story *Sarrasine*, and one of the most brilliant works of literary criticism ever written. It is important to realise that, although drawing on and developing the categories of narrative analysis put forward in the 'Introduction to the structural analysis of narratives', *S/Z* breaks with the structuralist conception of the particular text as simply a manifestation of an underlying narrative structure. Such a conception is reductive because it has no room for evaluation and it eliminates the difference of the individual text. This difference is not a unique individuality, a property of the text in itself: it consists in the fact that there is literally no end to the ways in which a text can be correlated with other texts, discourses or representations, with which, however, it never becomes identical. And if meaning, in a narratological sense, is correlation, to posit the text as different in this sense is tantamount to saying that the process of production of meaning is infinite.

Barthes suggests that our reading of the text is structured by a number of patterns of correlation, or 'codes'. Some of these correlations are between one textual element and another, others are between a textual element and something outside the text. Briefly, the codes are as follows: the *proairetic code*, which covers the sequences of actions within the text; the *hermeneutic*, which deals with the questions the text asks and answers, the mysteries it constructs and solves; the *semic code*, indications of character and atmosphere (a character, in Barthes's analysis, being nothing but a proper name to which a certain set of meanings is attached); the *symbolic code*, the space of the body and of desire, within which the characters take up positions the significance of which escapes them; and the *cultural code*: references to bodies of 'knowledge' – generally stereotypes – in the light of which the text is to be interpreted.

Barthes does not, then, deny that the text refers outside itself. But it refers only to other texts or discourses: the codes are 'perspectives of quotations' (Barthes, 1993–95, vol. 2, p. 568). Quotations from what? We need to look again at this notion of narrative logic, the kind of connections we make when reading according to the proairetic code. In the 'Introduction to the structural analysis of narratives', Barthes had emphasised the gap between the logic of narrative and the experience of life. Now, he argued that, when we link actions together in a sequence, we do so on the basis of experience (the already-

done, the already-read). For Barthes, this is tantamount to saying that the logic of narrative is that of the stereotype. What he postulates is that the distinction between our experience of other literary texts and our experience of life is not fundamental, and certainly that it cannot found the conventional judgement of value that sets texts drawn from life above those derived from books. Experience of life and reading both leave linguistic traces on the memory, and we read by following those traces as the text causes them to reappear. Literary texts doubtless offer infinitely more complex verbal formulations and a far wider range of corresponding experiences than does the ordinary individual's life. Nor is experience of real life, simply because this too is a sort of reading, sufficient for the understanding of literature. However, Barthes's point is to undermine the commonsense distinction between literature, as a world of words, and experience, as non-verbal 'real life', which the text is held to represent.

Of course, children, and even animals, have experiences without language: they are aware of some perceptual continuities, as a child shows when it recognises its parents, even before it has found names for them, but this is arguably not germane to the literary issue. Reading, Barthes urges, is not passively registering a representation. It is an activity, the essence of which is to find meanings, and this can only mean naming them. The experience we bring into play when reading is thus of the world as already classified in language.

Two clarifications are necessary. First, some reading experiences cannot be verbalised. Barthes not only concedes this, he insists on it: this is the core of his conception of *jouissance* (discussed below). But these experiences are not, in his theory, connected with the representational dimension of the text. Second, we may encounter in a literary text the representation of an experience that we have never verbalised. However, it is not that the text has copied our non-verbal experience but that through it, we have found a name for that experience. In other words, we have turned our experience into an analogue of the text, so that the text has primacy over 'reality', and not vice versa.

Literature, Barthes writes, endlessly strives to represent the real, but the real is not representable in language. The illusion of reference comes about in several ways. First, we have seen that, in reading, we have recourse to stereotypes, and we are accustomed to take the stereotypes, the ingrained habits of thinking, classifying and judging of our culture, as registering the fundamental nature of things. Second, he gives a similar argument a more linguistic formulation, which recalls the theory of myth. An utterance may convey a denotative (literal) meaning but it may also convey supplementary connotative meanings; thus, the utterance 'She is Ruritanian' may be a simple indicator of nationality, but may also allude to the personality traits supposedly characteristic of that nationality. A realist text may deal in apparently literal utterances: 'An old man came into the room'. In the real world, there are old men and they frequently come into rooms, so this simple statement appears to be grounded in reality itself. The sentence, of course, would read a little differently if the old man turned out to be a symbol of Death. But, furthermore, Barthes argues that the belief in language's denotative power is itself the effect of linguistic structures: in particular, that of the sentence. The sentence structures of a language, into which we have been inserted since childhood, appear as natural transpositions of objective relationships in reality. The real world, as it appears to us, contains agents who carry out certain actions on certain objects, in a certain manner, and we take it that what the story does is copy the relationships between these terms. However, these terms and the relationships between them are language-specific. Barthes notes that, in Japanese, fictional characters are referred to using the verb-forms that pertain to inanimate entities, not to living things: there is no possibility here of assimilating fiction to life.

The death of the author

One of the effects of the coexistence of the codes is to render it difficult to answer the question 'Who is speaking?' We cannot always be sure whether a given utterance is to be ultimately assigned to the author, the narrator, the character who voices it, or a cultural code. (The author may choose to mobilise a stereotype, but the question of whether he or she endorses it remains.) The utterance may even be the author's

anticipation of the reader's reaction. This brings us to the general issue of authorship.

Probably the most familiar general idea about Barthes is that he proclaimed 'the death of the author'. It is important to understand what the essay of this name is doing: I say 'doing' because it is not so much stating a thesis as challenging us to read differently. Barthes's target is initially the assumption that what is expressed in the text is the life and personality of the author; that is, the immediate producer. However, he was not the first to challenge this view: it has a long modernist progeny (Eliot, Valéry, Proust). The modernists, however, stressed the role of the author as conscious artist. Barthes also puts this in question, by stressing the heterogeneity of the text. The text, he argues, is multi-dimensional: it is a tissue of quotations, a remark elucidated by the later treatment of the codes in S/Z as 'perspectives of quotations'. The writer's role is not to copy life, but simply to amass quotations. In so doing, he or she may simply be confirming stereotypes: but not necessarily. He or she has the option not simply of reproducing, but of mixing the codes, setting one against the other, so that no single code, no single vision of reality can prevail. However, this is not self-expression in the ordinary sense, but the quarrying of the writer's internal dictionary, as Barthes calls it, the sum of her or his reading. We can now see more precisely what Barthes is targeting. He is not denying the artistic activity of the writer, but the identification of writer and person, the aesthetics of self-expression and the ideal of the writer as a creator. Above all, he is rejecting the notion of the text as the expression of an author's meaning. Whatever the author 'had in mind' is dispersed in the multiple discourses that comprise the text. What brings it together is the activity not of writing but of reading. We could say that, although *Sarrasine* was undoubtedly *composed* by Balzac, it *happens* when we read it. In this sense, to proclaim the death of the author is to celebrate the birth of the reader.

The Barthesian reader is first presented in as impersonal a light as the author is: it is 'a person without a history, without a biography, without a psychology: it is simply the *someone* who holds together within a single field all the traces that go to make up the text' (Barthes, 1993–95, vol. 2,

p. 495). This is surely belied by the notion of a cultural code, which presupposes shared experience, a common (but also a necessarily specific) culture. Moreover, our reading is inevitably suffused by a culture that differs from the original author's: how can we read *Sarrasine*, a tale of castration, without drawing on an understanding of castration derived from Freud? But in this sense, as readers, although we are not individuals, we are by no means without history; and Barthes does indeed refine his view of reading and subjectivity in *The Pleasure of the Text*.

However, three further points should be noted. First, Barthes maintains that the image of the text as a unified utterance (unified by the author's personality or artistic activity) is unconsciously dependent on theological models (the Scriptures as the discourse of God). The critique of authorship is linked to a Nietzschean project of exposing the theological prejudices of our culture and language. Second (and this point is often overlooked), the author is only one of the authority-figures Barthes seeks to dislodge. Concepts like 'society, history, the psyche, freedom' can equally function as the ultimate signified of a text, that to which everything in it can be reduced, and in this sense they are no less metaphysical than the concept of God that they replace only too well. Third, in *Sade, Fourier, Loyola* he advocates a 'return of the author': no longer seen as a deity uttering herself or himself in the text, but as a body of which we catch desirable glimpses, not only in the texts, but in accounts of the author's life.

Pleasure, subjectivity, fiction

The Pleasure of the Text (1973) shows Barthes developing his conception of theory and subjectivity, under the influence of Nietzsche. As the title suggests, the work is a celebration of literary pleasure, now presented as a superior value to the truth at which theory aims. However, pleasure falls into two categories. There is pleasure proper (*plaisir*), which pertains to the self as the bearer of a culture, and thus confirms her or his sense of self (it belongs to the domain psychoanalysis terms the Imaginary); and there is *jouissance*, a violent pleasure akin to orgasm, in which identity is temporarily dissolved: it can be pointed to but not defined, and it resists articulation in language, but it has nothing to do with the representation of the erotic. It may be produced when the language of the text breaks free from communicative and representational constraints; when the syntax and vocabulary of ordinary language are subverted or distorted; or when we lose our grip on the meaning of words, and are forced to respond, physically, to the acoustic or visual patterns they form. *Plaisir* seems a comfortable, bourgeois, affair; *jouissance* dangerous, transgressive, to be valued as shattering the structures of the Imaginary. However, Barthes insists that *jouissance* can have no meaning, and indeed no value, unless we retain the possibility of *plaisir*: we must be conscious of a self to experience the bliss of its fading in *jouissance*. In other words, the 'self' may be an imaginary construct, a fiction, as Lacan terms it, but it should be retained as a creative, empowering fiction. (That is, as distinct from theory, which is a fiction that denies its own status as such.) Initially validated by the pleasure it procures, the fiction of the self has the further potential of being realised in aesthetic form. There is a way of writing the self that should not be confused with the discredited project of 'expressing' it, as if the self existed independently of the language to which we resort in order to express it. Barthes explores this alternative non-expressive way of writing in *Roland Barthes par Roland Barthes*, a series of fragments, many of a quasi-autobiographical nature, which he encourages us to read as if it were uttered by a character in a novel. We should, first and foremost, understand 'character' here in keeping with Barthes's own analysis of the concept in his narratological work (see above), as a set of meanings, unified by a proper name. But 'Roland Barthes' in the text is more than a set of meanings: he constantly appears as a body, glimpsed not only in the photographs included in the book, but in frequent references in the text. This is, of course, in keeping with the idea of the 'return of the author' mentioned above. (But, since the author is in this case also a character, we might suggest that the account of 'character' in Barthes's narratology fails to allow for the extent to which the fictional character may be present to us in the form of a fantasised body.)

None the less, *Roland Barthes by Roland Barthes* mobilises both a vision of subjectivity and a vision of truth. As far as subjectivity is concerned, Barthes seeks to rescue the category of the Imaginary from the psychoanalytic critique, and to rehabilitate – partially – the practice of writing about oneself, without reinstating the privilege of the supposedly unified ego. He seeks, however, not sincerity or transparency, nor even to have the last word on himself: this aim is both oppressive and doomed to failure. His aim is rather to do justice to the plural and discontinuous nature of selfhood, and especially to its obstinate corporeality.

The work is a series of fragments, and the reader is invited to perceive the different voices in play within the text, to sound the depths of its naivety and register the manifold and shifting levels of its irony. In so far as there is a philosophical basis for this strategy, it lies in the conception of the subject as an effect of language. Different textual strategies produce different subjectivities, and Barthes's is in keeping with a view of the self, not as divided between opposites (high/low, body/mind), but as multiple and without a centre, inconsistent and affirming its inconsistency, its difference from itself.

As for truth, Barthes has now aligned himself with the Nietzschean suspicion of knowledge. Science (in the general sense of systematic knowledge) is condemned by its in-difference (a Nietzschean term). That is, its assumption of objectivity cuts it off from the passion that fuels it, or ought to fuel it; and its quest for generality violates the intrinsic difference of its objects. Barthes's ideal is a science of difference, an anti-reductive discourse that respects the singularity of its objects, and that, forswearing the authority of impersonality, bears the traces of the singular speech act that has engendered it. (It is plain that 'science' here essentially refers to the human rather than the natural sciences.) Such a science would assume the task, more commonly applied to art, of producing new visions of its objects; it would delight, as we have seen, in its self-consciously fictional nature. Furthermore, Barthes attacks the notion of truth, in so far as it is held to consist in coherence. (He does not specifically discuss the correspondence theory of truth, but had he done so, it would doubtless be in line with the critique of mimesis discussed above.) Coherence is not a matter of abstract relationship between propositions. It is rather an inevitability at the level of enunciation,

of the speaking subject: we say that q follows from p; but, rather, a path has been cut between p and q, broadened and deepened by every utterance of the relationship, and now fatally attracting me to q whenever I find myself at p. The true proposition loses its revelatory capacity, and becomes dulled by repetition: when this happens, it must be jettisoned. Barthes postulates a kind of complicity between two kinds of coherence: just as we allow ourselves to be captivated by a false image of ourselves as a homogeneous whole, so we are fascinated by the spectacle of a supposedly unified theory.

It is plain that Barthes is not *refuting* the coherence theory of truth, or indeed judging by the standard of truth at all. Rather, he is affirming a value higher than truth: that is, value itself. His reflection now increasingly takes the form of evaluation: his discourse proceeds by a conversion of value into theory. Valuation is a bodily process: there are words that he desires, wants to do something with, and others that he finds literally repulsive. *Doxa* is characterised in physical terms, as gelatinous, sticky, or, again, as the absence of the trace of the body in discourse. Barthes's discourse of the body as the source of evaluation is an essential part of his attempt to develop a materialist theory of the subject.

Barthes himself asks what room is left for the real by his vision of social life as a space where languages jostle with each other and with desires. He does not deny the notion of the real: what he has renounced is the attempt to grasp it in a theory, but he retains the notion of transforming the real, along basically 'progressive' lines, in pragmatic and piecemeal fashion. Reality cannot be transformed without the action of a subject, but Barthes sees the subject as a 'semblance of subject', apprehensible only in the Imaginary sphere, and whose ethical and political 'choices' can only be seen as 'preferences'. He affirms the value of the 'neuter': a kind of suspension of judgement, a refusal to adhere to any image or ideological position. Conflicts are always fought about polarities and the aim must be to evade or overcome conflict by multiplying difference: rather than bringing his own sexuality within the general category of homosexuality, he asserts that we should speak of homosexualities. Barthes's Utopia would transcend social divisions not by resolving them into a unity but by multiplying them to the point where they are no longer social.

Photography and the return of the real

Barthes's final book, *Camera Lucida* (1980), is his most personal and also his most literary. It is an attempt to work out his own fascination with photography, and also his grief at the death of his mother. However, it brings together several of the philosophical themes of his work. First, he affirms his hostility to reductive systems and his project of developing a paradoxical 'science of the singular': in this case, attempting to discover the essence of photography through an exploration of his personal reactions. The approach is therefore phenomenological, rather than semiological. Second, he returns to the terrain of *The Pleasure of the Text*, distinguishing two kinds of response to the photograph. In one, the *studium*, corresponding to *plaisir*, the viewer's interest in the photograph is that of the subject of culture: he brings his ideas, values, knowledge to bear on the image. In the other, the *punctum*, a detail in the photograph subconsciously engages – obsesses – the attention of the viewer. However, Barthes realises that the classification of the viewer's responses is not sufficient to do justice to the essence of photography. This consists fundamentally in the necessity that what shows up on the film *was once there* in front of the lens. Photography cannot be analysed in terms of codes: it is resolutely referential; it bears the trace of the past. This irretrievable past reality of what is there in the picture is the source of the pathos of the photograph, and the pathos of the text derives from its attempt to do justice to photography in the intrinsically fictional medium of language.

Barthes affirms photography, against the generalised reign of the image which, ironically, it has helped to bring about. Since images are everywhere, everything becomes an image. The imaginary is no longer the home of a doubtless illusory, but also value-creating, selfhood: it is now a universal screen between people and things which even *jouissance* cannot pierce, since nowadays *jouissance* is sought only through coinciding with an image. Perversion itself has become a stereotype. Differentiating himself from the bulk of commentators on post-modernism, who echo the theme of the omnipresent image, Barthes reverts to the existentialist terminology and ethics of his youth, lamenting the de-realisation of the human world of conflicts and desires, the emergence of a world without difference pervaded by a nauseous boredom. Thus photography, so antithetical to *doxa*, contributes to this pollution of experience by a *doxa* of images. Barthes's ethics of multiplying difference, of commitment to the singular, seems to be jeopardised by what appears to many as the increasing homogenisation of global culture.

It is somewhat revealing to read Barthes as a successor of the French *moralistes*, of whom he spoke with admiration: those early modern writers like Montaigne or La Rochefoucauld whose work is inspired by theoretical constructions, but who adhere to no theory, who exploit theories as fictions that permit a process of intellectual exploration and self-questioning, the end of which is not to discover truth but to initiate a new relationship with oneself. As a thinker, Barthes would doubtless not satisfy certain canons of philosophical rigour, but in his struggle against the strange chemistry by which we transform the life-sustaining medium of language into a noxious gas, protecting ourselves against it by means of a rigid mask of identity itself constructed out of solidified words, there is an integrity of which a philosopher might be proud and from which the life of the intellect can only benefit.

Bibliography

Writings

NOTE All references are to the three-volume *Oeuvres complètes*. Translations are my own.

Complete works

Barthes, Roland (1993–95), *Oeuvres complètes*, 3 vols, ed. Eric Marty, Paris: Seuil.

Selections

Barthes, Roland (1977), *Image, Music, Text*, trans. and selection by Stephen Heath, London: Fontana.
— (1983), *Selected Writings*, ed. Susan Sontag, London: Fontana. (Also published as *A Barthes Reader*, London: Cape, 1982.)

Separate works (including collections of articles)

Barthes, Roland (1982), *Camera Lucida: Reflections on Photography*, trans. Richard Howard, London: Cape. (*La Chambre claire: Note sur la Photographie*, Paris: Gallimard, 1980.)

— *Elements of Semiology*: see *Writing Degree Zero*.

— 'Eléments de sémiologie', *L'Aventure sémiologique*, 17–84.

— (1982), *Empire of Signs*, trans. Richard Howard, London: Cape. (*L'Empire des signes*, Geneva: Skira, 1970.)

— (1985), *The Fashion System*, trans. Matthew Ward and Richard Howard, London: Cape. (*Système de la mode*. Paris: Seuil, 1967.)

— (1983), 'Inaugural Lecture, Collège de France', in *Selected Writings*, 457–78. (*Leçon*, Paris: Seuil, 1978.)

— (1977), 'Introduction to the Structural Analysis of Narratives', in *Image, Music, Text* and *The Semiotic Challenge*. ('Introduction à l'analyse structurale des récits', *L'Aventure sémiologique*, 167–206.)

— (1979), *A Lover's Discourse: Fragments*, trans. Richard Howard, London: Cape. (*Fragments d'un discours amoureux*, Paris: Seuil, 1977.)

— (1972), *Mythologies*, trans. and selection by Annette Lavers, London: Cape. (*Mythologies*, Paris: Seuil, 1970 first edn 1957.)

— (1990), *The Pleasure of the Text*, trans. Richard Miller with a note on the text by Richard Howard, Oxford: Blackwell. (*Le Plaisir du texte*. Paris: Seuil, 1973.)

— (1977), *Roland Barthes by Roland Barthes*, trans. Richard Howard, London: Macmillan. (*Roland Barthes par Roland Barthes*, Paris: Seuil, 1975.)

— (1986), *The Rustle of Language*, trans. Richard Howard, Oxford: Blackwell. (*Le Bruissement de la langue*, Paris: Seuil, 1984.)

— (1977), *Sade, Fourier, Loyola*, trans. Richard Miller, London: Cape. (*Sade, Fourier, Loyola*, Paris: Seuil, 1971.)

— (1988), *The Semiotic Challenge*, trans. Richard Howard, Oxford: Blackwell. (*L'Aventure sémiologique*, Paris: Seuil, 1985.)

— (1990), *S/Z*, trans. Richard Miller with a Preface by Richard Howard, Oxford: Blackwell. (*S/Z*, Paris: Seuil, 1970.)

— (1967), *Writing Degree Zero and Elements of Semiology*, trans. Annette Lavers and Colin Smith, London: Cape. (*Le Degré zéro de l'écriture* (1953), republished with *Nouveaux Essais critiques*, Paris: Seuil, 1972.)

References and further reading

Brown, Andrew (1992), *Roland Barthes: The Figures of Writing*, Oxford: Clarendon Press.

Calvet, Louis-Jean (1994), *Roland Barthes: a Biography*, trans. Sarah Wykes, Cambridge: Polity Press.

Culler, Jonathan (1983), *Barthes*. London: Fontana.

Heath, Stephen (1974), *Vertige du déplacement: lecture de Barthes*, Paris: Fayard.

Knight, Diana (1997), *Barthes and Utopia: Inventor, Traveller, Writer*. Oxford: Oxford University Press.

Lavers, Annette (1982), *Roland Barthes: Structuralism and After*, London: Methuen.

Moriarty, Michael (1991), *Roland Barthes*, Cambridge: Polity Press.

Prendergast, Christopher (1986), *The Order of Mimesis*, Cambridge: Cambridge University Press.

Roger, Philippe (1986), *Roland Barthes, roman*, Paris: Grasset.

Ungar, Steven (1983), *Roland Barthes, the Professor of Desire*, Lincoln, NE and London: University of Nebraska Press.

Section Eight
POST-STRUCTURALISM

INTRODUCTION

John Protevi

Post-structuralism as a philosophical stance

Contemporary French philosophy is not only post-structuralist, it is also post-phenomenological. To each of these corresponds an orientation: towards a historical-libidinal materialism – the study of the production of bodies – countering the ahistoricism and cognitive bias of structuralism; and towards a radical difference or alterity countering the appropriative subjectivism of phenomenology – the grounding of the meaning of others in the horizon of identity of a subjective intention.

It is, perhaps, counter-productive to assign thinkers to camps, but one can note affinities with these orientations. Roughly speaking, Foucault, Deleuze, Baudrillard and Lyotard are mainly concerned with the former, and Levinas, Derrida and Irigaray with the latter. This classification is a matter of emphasis though, for the former are also concerned with difference or alterity, and the latter with bodies.

Michael Hardt's (1993) analysis of Deleuze as anti-Hegelian can also summarise post-structuralism. Thus, if structuralism was, in the words of Paul Ricoeur, 'Kantianism without the transcendental subject', – a search for structures of intelligibility located in cultural systems rather than in a subject – then post-structuralism is the French response to German philosophy after Kant', that is, to Hegel. In other words, post-structuralism in its historical-libidinal materialism turns Marx, Nietzsche and Freud against Hegel, and in its post-phenomenological mode turns the later Heidegger against the 'three H's' of phenomenology: Hegel, Husserl and the early Heidegger.

As resolutely anti-Hegelian, post-structuralism looks for a non-oppositional, and hence non-dialectically-resolvable, difference. Opposition is difference in the edifying service of identity, for an opposition puts *different* things on the *same* level to face each other and ultimately resolve their conflict, so that an observer can learn from this overcoming of difference by identity. To find a notion of difference that would not be subservient to identity, that would avoid such a reconciliatory 'identity of identity and difference' (to use Hegel's formula), post-structuralists look for: forces that skew apparently logical oppositions into power hierarchies; historical forces that preclude any teleological reconciliation of those hierarchies, any historical 'work of the negative'; multiple networks of 'force and signification' (to borrow the title of an early Derrida essay) that require obedience, rather than systematic wholes which render cultures intelligible to their inhabitants; radical alterity or diversity that escapes phenomenological or ontological horizons of identity.

Saussure's use of opposition in prescribing the scientific study of language – expanded by Lévi-Strauss to the structuralist study of cultural systems in general – is thus a key target of many post-structuralists. Using the chess analogy common to structuralist self-explication, we can say that structuralism elucidates the synchronic oppositional rules that render a game (language or cultural system) intelligible to its players (speakers or actors): the knight, which is *not the bishop*, moves one way, while the bishop, which is *not the knight*, moves another way.

To arrive at a structure of intelligibility via oppositions between rules governing pieces, structuralism practises a grand meta-opposition between internal structure and external history. Hence, the historical forces that produced different social actors (the bodily training of real knights and bishops) in order to fulfil social aims – for example, the production and distribution of surplus value – are neutralised into rules that produce intelligibility. Here we see the arena for historical-libidinal materialism: the production of bodies. For post-structuralism, cultural oppositions rely on the forceful production of bodies trained to fulfil the expectations of the group into which they are placed. In other words, the great social oppositions which, for structuralism, render a system intelligible: male/female, adult/child, white/black, owner/worker, are, for post-structuralism, the result of appropriately-behaving and – labelled bodies produced by such loci of historical forces as families, schools, churches and workplaces.

The historical-libidinal materialism of post-structuralism thus analyses the de-centred, multiple, conflictual and overlapping differential and historical force networks productive of 'bodies politic': the medicalised, disciplined, racialised, gendered, capitalised – the objectified *and* subjectified – bodies of people and the body politic of corporations, families, sects, gangs, classes, genders, races, nations, *Reichs*, etc.

The post-phenomenological mode of post-structuralism, to take up our other strand, is quite complex, for it includes a concern with bodies along with a properly post-phenomenological concern with radical alterity. In the first area, rather than tracing meaning back to the constituting acts of a transcendental subjectivity or intersubjective network, post-structuralists look to the empirical forces of bodies marking the limits of transcendental reductions that aim to recover the constitution of meaning in cognitive acts. Derrida, Levinas and Irigaray, despite the great differences in their work, thus all agree that Husserlian phenomenology needs, at the very least, the gendered embodiment studied by Merleau-Ponty, even if they do not necessarily endorse Merleau-Ponty's findings.

The provenance of the concern with radical alterity, which, on the one hand, stems clearly from Heidegger, is thus complicated by Levinas, Derrida and Irigaray's concern with bodies. As we will see in the 'Predecessors' section, Heidegger's thoughts of the 'metaphysics of presence' and of 'difference as such' decisively shape the post-phenomenologists' search for radical alterity; none the less, these thinkers also attend to the question of gendered embodiment, or better, its absence, in Heidegger's work.

Post-structuralism as a historical movement

One could divide post-structuralism's history into two phases. In the first, prior to May 1968, a philosophy of difference articulates the ways difference produces identity. In the second, after May 1968, a politics of philosophy examines the role of philosophy in the production of the social identities of gender, race, and class.

The philosophy of difference

The post-structuralist philosophy of difference originated in the 1960s when French thought came to terms with the two strands of its German heritage: the historical-libidinal materialism of Marx–Nietzsche–Freud and the phenomenology of Hegel–Husserl–Heidegger.

Two books stand out in this regard. The first is Emmanuel Levinas's *Totality and Infinity* (1961), which brought phenomenology beyond itself in articulating the radical ethical alterity of the face of the other. In Levinas's account, the encounter with the other person breaks with any ontological or phenomenological horizon of identity – Hegel's Spirit, Husserl's *noesis*, or the early Heidegger's Being – that would presume to encompass it.

The second work at the origin of post-structuralism is Gilles Deleuze's *Nietzsche and Philosophy* (1962). Here Deleuze shows the productivity of the non-dialectical ('affirmative') differential forces termed by Nietzsche 'noble'. These forces primarily differentiate themselves, and only secondarily consider that from which they have differentiated themselves. Deleuze's reading rescued Nietzsche from Heidegger's narrative of the history of metaphysics (Heidegger, 1961); the thought of differential force would in turn, in *Anti-Oedipus* (Deleuze and Guattari, 1972), rescue Marx and Freud from the institutional prisons of their 'isms': the orthodox parties and schools that appropriated their charisma.

The nascent post-structuralist movement received two noteworthy accelerations from conference talks by Jacques Derrida in the mid-to-late 1960s. The first, 'Structure, Sign and Play in the Discourse of the Human Sciences' (Derrida, 1967a, pp. 278–93), came at the famous 1966 Johns Hopkins conference on structuralism. In this talk, after analysing the structuralist rupture that eliminated the dependence of thought on a centre that governs meaning from outside a system, Derrida juxtaposed two responses to the 'loss' of that centre, two 'interpretations of interpretation' (Derrida, 1967a, p. 292): a *rousseauiste* nostalgia for a lost naturality which tolerates interpretation as an exile, and a Nietzschean affirmation of interpretation and innocent play with no relation to loss, since that 'loss' was imaginary (the centre being only the product of a certain weak desire).

Derrida's second noteworthy talk is the 1968 'Différance', (Derrida, 1972, pp. 3–27) in which he surveys predecessors of post-structuralism, providing distinctive readings of Hegel, Saussure, Levinas, Nietzsche (specifically Deleuze's Nietzsche), Freud and Heidegger. Derrida here brings together the post-phenomenological and the post-structuralist (in the restricted sense), by a common theme: *différance* is the interweaving of force and sense. In one blow, he attacks both the subjectivism of phenomenology and the apolitical ahistoricism of structuralism: sense or meaning is not the product of subjects or networks of intersubjective tradition (phenomenology) nor the product of social codes that render things intelligible (structuralism), but is constructed by forces in ways that should be analysed (deconstructed).

Three books by Derrida in 1967 and two by Deleuze in 1968–69 provide the highlight of the philosophy of difference. Derrida's works, *Writing and Difference* (1967a), *Of Grammatology* (1967b), and *Speech and Phenomenon* (1967c), provide detailed readings of Rousseau, Lévi-Strauss, Saussure, Husserl, Levinas, Bataille, Artaud, Freud and Jabès; in these essays Derrida exposes a textual economy between notions pledging allegiance to presence and those refractory to presence. 'Allegiance to presence' means tracing the control of meaning to a point beyond the system – to a God or God-substitute that creates the world and determines the meaning of everything in it. 'Presence' as the operative focus of Derrida's readings reveals his Heideggerian heritage, even as he works his way towards the complex relation he will maintain with Heidegger throughout the rest of his writings – acknowledging Heidegger's breakthroughs while tracing his complicities.

Deleuze's two 1968–69 contributions are *Difference and Repetition* (1968) and *Logic of Sense* (1969). After a long string of noteworthy historical monographs on Hume, Nietzsche, Kant, Bergson and Spinoza, Deleuze developed his own philosophy in these two works, in a fertile intermixing of all these figures and more. He works towards a philosophy of difference that would free difference from its philosophically-imposed dependence on identity, calling upon a bewildering array of sources: his favourite philosophers, plus Lewis Carroll, Artaud and the Stoics in *Logic of Sense*, and the history and contemporary achievements of mathematics, physics and biology in *Difference and Repetition*. He uses the traditional language of philosophy in these works to new ends, proposing a consistent materialism of forceful bodies and a univocal ontology of change that were developed with a political edge in his collaborations with the radical psychoanalyst Félix Guattari (1972, 1980).

The politics of philosophy

(In)famously, the events of May 1968 accelerated the post-structuralist movement. The story has often been told, but bears repeating. A threshold of social unrest was passed, as turbulent post-War affluence and concomitant lifestyle experimentation was countered by a government backlash in the guise of education reform. May 1968 included students and workers, to the confusion of the established guardians of the revolution, the French Communist Party. Days of general strikes and stand-offs with the police led de Gaulle to call a general election. Shockingly, de Gaulle's call for a parliamentary solution to the crisis was backed by the Communists, who were evidently as frightened of any revolution from below – which, by definition, would lack the party discipline they so craved – as were the official holders of State power, to whose position they aspired. The worker-student movement eventually collapsed, leaving memories of non-scripted social interactions and revealing the investments of the Party, lampooned thereafter as 'bureaucrats of the revolution' (Foucault, in Deleuze and Guattari, 1972, p. xii).

The response changed French academic life: institutionally, by the creation of a new college, Paris VIII (Vincennes), where Deleuze and Irigaray taught; and in the direction of the post-structuralist movement. The second change concerns us here. Although it was certainly never apolitical in its first incarnation, the philosophy of difference became (explicitly) political post-1968. It became, in fact, a politics of philosophy dedicated to exposing the historical force relations producing identity in all its ontological and epistemological forms. In other words, post-structuralism now set out to show how the unified objects of the world, the unified subjects who know and hence control them, the unified bodies of knowledge that codify this knowledge, *and* the unified institution of philosophy that polices the whole affair, are products of historical, political forces in combat with other forces.

The most immediately provocative politicisation of the philosophy of difference was Deleuze and Guattari's 1972 *Anti-Oedipus*. A frenzied attack on the tame Marx-Freud synthesis that was the mother's milk of the bureaucrats of the revolution, *Anti-Oedipus* is historical-libidinal materialism *par excellence*: the explosive result of using the Nietzschean thought of differential force to expose the production of the socio-political identities of race, class, nation and – most threateningly – gendered personal identity.

Another noteworthy consequence of 1968 was the intersection of philosophical speculation, literary experimentation and practical political struggle in French feminism. Although the *Mouvement de libération des femmes* or MLF split later into the *Psychanalyse et politique* (psych et po) and *Questions féministes* (Qf) wings – reflecting a psycholinguistic and socio-economic orientation respectively – the MLF of the early 1970s interrogated precisely the interrelations of class and gender in the name of female difference; avenues of investigation included Marxist economics and historiography, Lacanian psychoanalysis, linguistics, semiotics, phenomenology and rereadings of the history of philosophy (see Duchen, 1986). Although Cixous clearly positioned herself with 'psych et po', neither she nor Irigaray ever really abandoned the analysis of the intersection of gender and class; while Kristeva, who eschewed the term 'feminist', none the less at times engaged the question of sexual difference in politics, as in 'Women's Time' (in Moi, 1986, pp. 188–213).

In the mid-1970s the politics of philosophy reached a critical mass, with major works published every year: Derrida's *Glas*; Lyotard's *Libidinal Economy*; Irigaray's *Speculum of the Other Woman*; Cixous and Clément's *The Newly-Born Woman*; Kristeva's *Revolution in Poetic Language*; Foucault's *Discipline and Punish*; Baudrillard's *Symbolic Exchange and Death*. To some extent, they all show how philosophy has served to legitimate forceful constructions of identity in racial, religious, economic, political and sexual contexts. By analysing the interrelations of these registers, and by showing differential force as productive of identity, these works set the stage for Deleuze and Guattari's *A Thousand Plateaus* (1980), arguably the high-water mark to date of post-structuralism.

In fourteen 'plateaus', or points of intensity – productive connections between forces without reference to an external governing source – Deleuze and Guattari developed a new materialism in which a politicised philosophy of difference joins forces with the sciences explored in *Difference and Repetition*. *A Thousand Plateaus* is a book of strange and terrifying new questions: 'Who Does the Earth Think It Is?', 'How Do You Make Yourself a Body Without Organs?', 'How does the war-machine ward off the apparatus of capture of the State?' and so on. To over-simplify, Deleuze and Guattari take the insights of 'complexity theory', which explores the mathematics of the various thresholds at which matter achieves self-organisation (for example, turbulence or oscillation), and extend the notion of self-organising matter – matter with no need of transcendent organising agents such as gods, leaders, capital or subjects – to the social, linguistic, political and economic realms. The resultant 'rhizome' or de-centred network that is *A Thousand Plateaus* provides hints for experimentation with the increasing de-regulated flows of energy and matter, ideas and actions – and the attendant attempts at binding them – that make up the contemporary world.

A stunning work, nothing after *A Thousand Plateaus* by any post-structuralist author has the same potential for inciting new flows of ideas and action. But this is not the end of the story. Perhaps the most fruitful area of ongoing post-structuralism will prove to be feminism, especially as that work interacts with Foucault, Deleuze, Derrida, Levinas, et al. This interchange is not a simple case of feminism learning from philosophers who remain untouched. Rather, we have here a 'becoming' in the Deleuzian sense, for both terms change in the encounter: for example, 'Deleuze' or 'Derrida' – what those names mean as potentials for inciting flows of ideas and action – are not the same after their encounter with the 'corporeal feminism' of Elizabeth Grosz or the theory of performative gender in Judith Butler. None the less, despite what remains to be said here, let us now move to consider the predecessors of post-structuralism.

Predecessors

Although one may produce post-structuralist readings of any text by pointing to elements of differential force refractory to presence and identity, certain figures stand out as having themselves thematised difference and differential force. To tell the full story of the predecessors of post-structuralism, though, even on this restricted criterion, is to tell the story of most of nineteenth- and twentieth-century German and French thought. None the less, let us mention Marx, Nietzsche, Freud and Heidegger among the former and Kojève, Hyppolite, Bataille, Lacan and de Beauvoir among the latter.

Nineteenth- and twentieth-century German predecessors of post-structuralism

The most famous, and perhaps still most influential, anti-Hegelian remains Marx. Beyond even the ex-plicit political leanings of most of our writers, Marx's term 'historical materialism' (as opposed to the 'dialectical materialism' of much-later Soviet ideologues), is still a useful term for much of the work of Lyotard, Baudrillard, Foucault and Deleuze/Guattari and some of Derrida and Irigaray, for all these writers analyse, to some extent, the historical material forces constituting the received notion of identity through which we are presented with gendered, racialised and capitalised bodies.

Marx's achievement was to show how networks of differential force, the material and social relations of production, produce the seemingly natural identities of social categories: 'owner', 'worker', 'product', 'tool', etc. What seems a stable unity, the famous 'table at which I write' upon which so many modern philosophers mediate, is the product of a historically relative system of production, a system put in place by the revolutionary force of the bourgeoisie. The productivity of the network of historical labour is masked by the solidity of the thing and the vampiric 'productivity' of capital, which Marx showed was simply the coagulation of past labour. Marx's insistence on dissolving the certainties and identities of everyday common sense by reference to networks of historical force is taken up again by the post-structuralists, whose focus on the 'deconstructive' Marx purged him of the eschatological promises of the inevitability of 'The Revolution' into which he sometimes lapsed in his popular addresses and on which the bureaucrats of the revolution pounced as if scripture.

We have already pointed out the importance of Deleuze's *Nietzsche and Philosophy* to the genesis of post-structuralism. Despite the commonplaces that would oppose them on political issues, Deleuze's reading of Nietzsche brought out some striking similarities to the Marx sketched above. More precisely, Deleuze's highlighting of Nietzsche's dissolving received pieties through analyses of their construction by historical forces shows deep similarities to Marx's analyses. Simply put, both thinkers are historical materialists; they both show material forces producing identities. Especially as he practised it in *On the Genealogy of Morals*, then, Nietzsche's historical materialism forms another strong thread in post-structuralism. Almost every thinker explored in this Section has, besides critical works devoted to exploring Nietzsche's writings, a noticeable Nietzschean suspicion of what presents itself as self-identical, natural or rational. Thus, in addition to scholarly works like Derrida's *Spurs* (1978) and Irigaray's *Marine Lover* (1980), one could point out direct borrowings from Nietzsche's *Genealogy* and its analyses of practices of physical cruelty behind moral categories in those parts of Deleuze and Guattari's *Anti-Oedipus* which analyse 'writing on the body' in pre-agricultural societies, and in Foucault's *Discipline and Punish* (1975), which investigates the growth of the modern penal system and the exportation of disciplinary practices developed therein to schools and factories.

We have characterised one strong element of post-structuralism, alongside that of the post-phenomenological search for radical alterity, as 'historical-libidinal materialism'. To appreciate the libidinal qualification, we need to turn to Freud. It is often said that there are two Freuds, the scientific materialist of the drives (the 'energetic Freud') and the investigative hermeneutics of the unconscious (the 'linguistic Freud'); the struggle to articulate the two is notoriously difficult, both for Freud himself and his interpreters. The influences of Reich, Lacan, feminism and their interconnections, all of whom lay claim to a certain Freudian heritage, complicate matters further. None the less, we can say a few preliminary things to locate the appropriation of Freud in post-structuralism.

First, let us distinguish Freud's diagnosis of the patriarchal etiology of the neuroses from his prescriptions for their treatment. Working out his diagnoses through his case studies, Freud points to the historical, political, economic and social milieu of his patients, even if his thematic focus on family dynamics often obscured the class and race contributions to the neuroses of his patients those case studies describe. Together with the materialist orientation of the energetic analysis of drives, we see here the elements of a historical-libidinal materialism, which, through the explicit politicisations of Reich (1933), surfaces in the concern with bodily flows in Deleuze and Guattari (1972, 1980), Irigaray (1977, 1980), and Kristeva (in Moi, 1986, pp. 160–86).

The linguistic Freud reappears, via Lacan, in the 'Psych et po' branch of French feminism; we will address this contribution later. For now, let us mention the contribution of Freud to the post-structuralist dethronement of conscious intention as the sole arbiter of meaning. Although often somewhat facilely connected with Marx and Nietzsche as a 'master of suspicion', it is none the less undeniable that Freud's invocation of unconscious motivation points beyond consciousness as the locus of intention and responsibility, and hence provided an indispensable reference point for breaking the phenomenological focus on the subject and for rethinking the political formation of subjectivity.

As a final German predecessor – this time contributing to the post-phenomenological orientation of post-structuralism – let us consider Heidegger. In *Being and Time* (1927) Heidegger brought phenomenology to bear on the classical problem of philosophy, ontology, only to find thereby the need to point beyond both. Heidegger's focus in *Being and Time* on human existence as *Dasein* was meant to replace Husserl's focus on the transcendental ego. But Heidegger's account brought with it enough subjectivist and existentialist baggage to necessitate the breaking off of the book's announced project. *Being and Time* was to have used phenomenology to sketch a 'fundamental ontology' preparatory to a 'science of being'. Fundamental ontology rewrote the traditional analyses of human subjectivity to reveal the ontologically-relevant structures of that being with access to its own being – that being for whom the future and possibility were open: in short, the being that *we* are. The Heideggerian analyses dethroned the rule of 'presence', which, gathered from concern with things, had been imposed by philosophy on our self-understanding. Despite a lecture course in 1928 (Heidegger, 1975), the project of fundamental ontology and the science of being foundered on the relations of, among other things, the 'time' announced in the title and various registers of space and exteriority; *Being and Time* thus remained the only published part of the project.

In progressing with his work, Heidegger developed a philosophy of difference in order to articulate the process of the appearing of things without recourse to any one controlling and non-appearing thing. At various times expressed as a concern with the history or topology of being, Heidegger's work thematised the way presence had been the focal point for many previous philosophies, which, in their 'onto-theology', had avoided the question of appearance *per se* to attribute the cause of appearance to a God or God-substitute such as the *cogito*, the transcendental unity of apperception, Spirit or the transcendental ego.

Whatever the worth of these analyses as readings of individual philosophers – less still the question as to the formation of the Heideggerian 'canon' (those philosophers deemed worthy of inclusion in the history of being) – Heidegger's labour to articulate these concerns provides a way to contest the 'metaphysics of presence' and its emphasis on identity and stability by appeal to a non-oppositional difference, absence and movement. Heidegger's work thus provides the background, if not much of the vocabulary, of the post-phenomenological orientation of post-structuralism, as evidenced in Levinas and Derrida and, to some extent, Irigaray.

Twentieth-century French predecessors of post-structuralism

If one strong orientation of post-structuralism is anti-Hegelian, then we should briefly discuss the reception of Hegel in twentieth-century France. A full discussion would position the reception of Hegel, which began in earnest in the late 1920s, continued throughout the 1930s, and reached a peak in the immediate post-War years, in relation to surrealism and Fascism, to Husserlian and existentialist phenomenology and the reaction against French academic rationalism, and, of course, to intellectual Marxism and the French Communist Party. (Space prohibits such a through examination, however, and I would refer the interested reader to Roth (1988).) Within a narrowly-defined field of Hegel-reception we should note that, although Jean Wahl wrote a noteworthy book in 1929 on Hegel and the unhappy conscience/the unhappiness of consciousness, and Alexandre Koyré wrote two important articles in the early 1930s on Hegel's terminology and the Jena period, the major figures are undoubtedly Alexandre Kojève, Jean Hyppolite and Georges Bataille.

Alexandre Kojève was a Russian *émigré* and French government official. His major philosophical impact came from a series of lectures (1933–39) on Hegel, attended by a large part of the Parisian intelligentsia: Bataille, Sartre, Merleau-Ponty, Lacan, Levinas, E. Weil and others. Notes for the lectures were collected by the novelist Raymond Queneau and published in 1947 as *Introduction to the Reading of Hegel*. In these lectures Kojève gave an anthropological reading of Hegel, rejecting the theological reading which focused on the atemporal unfolding of rational structures in the *Science of Logic* – logic conceived as the mind of God prior to its alienation in nature – and instead focused on the master-slave dialectic of the *Phenomenology*. In this way, Kojève showed how human history – labour and revolutionary war, the creative destruction of the actual – was the arena for the unfolding of spirit through 'the work of the negative'.

Kojève propounded the thesis of the 'end of history': the work of the negative in renewing social formations had culminated in the Enlightenment positing of universal and rational rights. The universal founding of states recognising those principles – and their extension to women and other 'others' – remains, but the essential work was the first instantiation of those principles. Since the work of man was history, the end of history is the end of working, struggling, man; what remains in a realm of secured plenty is then contented man, animal man: man involved with naturalised, expressive, art, love and play. A famous note to the second edition contemplates the Stalinist/American stalemate of the late 1950s – Americans are rich Soviets, Soviets poor Americans – and, bizarrely, nominates Japanese 'snobbery' as a remaining avenue for post-historical humanity to avoid animality (Kojève, 1969, pp. 159–62).

The break with Kojève's Hegel, and with Hegel himself, paradoxically begins with the greatest French Hegelian, Jean Hyppolite. Hyppolite was a *bona fide* French academic, rising from provincial assignments, through the Sorbonne and the Ecole Normale Supérieure, to the very pinnacle of French academic life, the Collège de France; along the way he mentored Deleuze, Foucault and Derrida. A moving tribute to Hyppolite, recounting his beginning the many breaks with Hegel that map out post-structuralism, occupies the last pages of Foucault's

'The Discourse on Language', his speech upon being elected to Hyppolite's chair at the Collège de France (Foucault, 1969, pp. 215–37).

Hyppolite's service began with his French translation of Hegel's *Phenomenology* (1939–41) and the masterful commentary, *Genesis and Structure of Hegel's Phenomenology of Spirit* (1947). Avoiding Kojève's rejection of the *Logic*, Hyppolite likewise avoids either an extreme theological or anthropological reading of Hegel; spirit thus neither pre-exists nor is reducible to human existence. However, his was more than a commentary, providing, in Foucault's words, 'the scene of an experiment, of a confrontation' (ibid., p. 236) in which the relevance of Hegel's writing was put to the test of contemporary life. Hyppolite pinpoints the 'generation' of spirit in history – or more generally put, the relation of logic and experience – as the key problem of Hegelian thought and shows clearly how the Hegelian formula of the unity of knowledge and action, once broken by the Marxist preference for action, reveals itself as a (merely philosophical) preference for knowledge.

Of more interest to post-structuralists, perhaps, is *Logique et existence* (1953), Hyppolite's second major work, which comments on Hegel's *Logic*. In this work, Hyppolite poses three questions of importance for post-structuralism: non-dialectical difference (diversity rather than opposition), philosophy's appropriation of its other (sense and non-sense), and the centrality, priority and self-referentiality of language (rather than disembodied thought) in constituting meaning. Raising the questions of difference, appropriation and language clearly marks Hyppolite as a major figure in the pre-history of post-structuralism, a role that did not go unacknowledged by our authors. We have already mentioned Foucault's tribute; that Derrida's work on Hegel's semiology in 'Pit and the Pyramid' (Derrida, 1972, pp. 69–108) and *Glas* (1974) stemmed from his early encounter with Hyppolite seems clear. In addition to the quest for a non-dialectical difference – which provides the focus for Deleuze's *Difference and Repetition* and for virtually all of Derrida's work – Hyppolite's pointing to sense was crucial. In his first major work, *Introduction to Edmund Husserl's Origin of Geometry* (1962), Derrida points to an interesting remark by Hyppolite about the 'subjectless transcendental field'

of sense. This theme emerged as a central focus of the philosophy of difference period, especially *Speech and Phenomena* and *Logic of Sense*. Finally, Hyppolite's locating of language between logic and existence, between thought and bodies, provides the seeds of Foucault's *dispositif*, which sets forth the relation of discursive and non-discursive practices, Derrida's 'arche-writing', which interweaves sense and force, and Deleuze's sense, playing at the surface of bodies.

Generally speaking, then, post-structuralists reject the anthropologism, the historical narrative of progress and the emphasis on the work of the negative found in Kojève by taking up the hints in Hyppolite. A third important figure is Georges Bataille, who, in interweaving Nietzsche and Hegel in his work, clearly demarcates the field of post-structuralism, even if his positions are not necessarily taken up in the Section. A librarian at the Bibliothèque Nationale, Bataille wrote erotic fiction as well as philosophical reflections. Although we have in some ways posited 'Nietzsche *contra* Hegel' as our schema for post-structuralism, Bataille's works do not have that oppositional scheme – for opposition is the Hegelian move. Rather, Bataille's works address themes of communion, sacrifice, waste, intensity and economy in moving between the two thinkers and others, particularly the sociologist Emile Durkheim and the anthropologist Marcel Mauss.

At first, Bataille sought to locate in surrealist images a clue to the 'sacred' or the 'heterogenous' – that which was other to the bourgeois normality of individual responsibility and ego control in its ecstatic group violence and wasteful energy. Besides surrealist imagery, Bataille also recognised that the sacred had made a spectacular contemporary appearance in the mass Nazi rallies. In founding the Collège de Sociologie (1937–39), Bataille gave a forum for anthropological investigations into the manifestations of the sacred in 'primitive' cultures, with an eye to tapping this reservoir of social energy, which lay largely dormant and hence overlooked in modern culture, for progressive politics, rather than leave a monopoly on using the sacred to the Fascists.

Bataille used Nietzsche and Hegel in an attempt to think the sacred. At one point, Bataille attempted a post-Hegelian reading of the negative: taking up Kojève's thesis of the end of history (the finish of the work of the negative), Bataille thought that the creative/destructive energy that had moved history was now 'unemployed', and thus free to appear today in eroticism and squandering, non-economic waste; structures similar to the potlatches Mauss had investigated in native American society. In his reflections on the sacred using Nietzsche, whom he hoped to rescue from the Nazis, Bataille thought first of founding a 'religion', then in terms of 'inner experience'. The religious project was to create a myth of sheer negativity that brought forth renewal, focused on the figure of the overman, whom Bataille called *acéphale* or 'headless' to forestall any reappropriation of free-floating sacred energy by an elevated figure of dominating leadership. The project of inner experience, on the other hand, is that of individual preparation, through a meditation on horror or through sexual practice, for an experience of ecstatic communion, of ego-dissolution – thus, paradoxically, the destruction of the very ego that prepares and experiences.

The legacy of Bataille in post-structuralism is difficult to assess, largely because it is difficult to see what is due to Nietzsche and what is due to Bataille's readings of Nietzsche. None the less, it is safe to say that the investigations into the construction of the ego or consciousness through social and bodily practices, the converse experience of the dissolution of the ego in madness, the themes of non-productive expenditure, of excess and outrage to common sense, resonate in both Bataille and many of our writers.

A very brief consideration of two figures who helped shape the intellectual France of the 1950s, Lacan and de Beauvoir, will complete our survey of predecessors to post-structuralism. Lacan's structural linguistic rereading of Freud provided much of the orientation of French feminism's 'psych et po' wing, especially his analysis of castration as the child's entry into the symbolic order through incorporation of the 'law of the father'. As in the case of Freud, it is Lacan's diagnoses rather than his prescriptions that were important for feminist thought. Thus, Lacan's renderings of the masculinist bias of the Oedipal crisis, and the patriarchal nature of the symbolic order, provoked the concept of *écriture féminine* – 'female writing' – as a practical way of producing a decentred, differential, female subjectivity.

While the reception of Lacan figured in the materialist orientation of post-structuralism, Simone de Beauvoir figures in the post-phenomenological orientation. Although Sartre and Merleau-Ponty were the most famous French phenomenologists of the 1940s and 1950s, de Beauvoir's work, especially the concept of woman as 'other', was more important than either for post-structuralist feminism and deconstruction. De Beauvoir's *The Second Sex* (1949), although written from a perspective of existentialist freedom and individuality rejected by post-structuralists, none the less provided two indispensable starting points for feminist analysis by stressing the historical constitution of patriarchal culture and the impossible position granted to women therein: free as (human) subjects, yet determined as the 'other' of the true (masculine) subject. This notion of gendered alterity is also reworked in various forms by Derrida and Levinas – interventions which have been the subject of much feminist controversy.

Other noteworthy post-structuralist figures

We have space merely to mention some other noteworthy figures whose works resonate more or less with that of the post-structuralists examined in this Section. Any list of this sort will necessarily be incomplete, as post-structuralist thinking now appears in virtually all fields of intellectual work. None the less, one can certainly mention, in literary theory, Maurice Blanchot and Paul de Man; in political theory, Paul Virilio; in the history of science, Michel Serres; in sociology, Pierre Bourdieu; in history, Immanuel Wallerstein; in technology and military history, Manuel de Landa; in philosophy of mathematics, Brian Rotman; in philosophy of mind, Francisco Varela. And, elsewhere in philosophy, Alfonso Lingis, Jean-Luc Nancy, Judith Butler and John Sallis. Each of these thinkers has produced serious work worthy of discussion in its own right; once the reader has gained a familiarity with the major figures of post-structuralism, considering these authors will suggest something of the breadth and living energy of contemporary post-structuralist thought.

Bibliography

References and further reading

Beauvoir, Simone de (1954) (first edn 1949), *The Second Sex*, trans. H. M. Parshley, New York: Knopf.

Deleuze, Gilles (1983) (first edn 1962), *Nietzsche and Philosophy*, trans. Hugh Tomlinson, New York: Columbia University Press.

— (1987) (first edn 1980), *A Thousand Plateaus*, trans. Brian Massumi, Minneapolis: University of Minnesota Press.

— (1990) (first edn 1969), *Logic of Sense*, trans. Mark Lester with Charles Stivale, New York: Columbia University Press.

— (1994) (first edn 1968), *Difference and Repetition*, trans. Paul Patton, New York: Columbia University Press.

— and Félix Guattari (1983) (first edn 1972), *Anti-Oedipus*, trans. Robert Hurley, Mark Seem and Helen R. Lane, Minneapolis: University of Minnesota Press.

Derrida, Jacques (1977) (first edn 1962), *Introduction to Edmund Husserl's Origin of Geometry*, trans. John Leavey, New York: Nicholas Hays.

— (1978) (first edn 1967a), *Writing and Difference*, trans. Alan Bass, Chicago: University of Chicago Press.

— (1976) (first edn 1967b), *Of Grammatology*, trans. Gayatri Spivak, Baltimore: Johns Hopkins University Press.

— (1973) (first edn 1967c), *Speech and Phenomena*, trans. David Allison, Evanston: Northwestern University Press.

— (1982) (first edn 1972), *Margins: of Philosophy*, trans. Alan Bass, Chicago: University of Chicago Press.

— (1986) (first edn 1974), *Glas*, trans. John Leavey and Richard Rand, Lincoln: University of Nebraska Press.

— (1978) (first edn 1978), *Spurs: Nietzsche's Styles*, trans. Barbara Harlow, Chicago: University of Chicago Press.

Duchen, Claire (1986), *Feminism in France: From May '68 to Mitterrand*, London: Routledge & Kegan Paul.

Foucault, Michel (1972) (first edn 1969), *The Archaeology of Knowledge and The Discourse on Language*, trans. A. M. Sheridan-Smith, New York: Pantheon.

— (1972), 'Preface', in Deleuze and Guattari, 1972.

— (1979) (first edn 1975), *Discipline and Punish*, trans. Alan Sheridan, New York: Random House.

Hardt, Michael (1993), *Gilles Deleuze: An Apprenticeship in Philosophy*, Minneapolis: University of Minnesota Press.

Heidegger, Martin (1962) (first edn 1927), *Being and Time*, trans. John Macquarrie and Edward Robinson, New York: Harper and Row.

— (1979–87) (first edn 1961), *Nietzsche*, vols 1–4, ed. David Farrell Krell, San Francisco: Harper and Row.

— (1982) (first edn 1975), *The Basic Problems of Phenomenology*, trans. Albert Hofstadter, Bloomington: Indiana University Press.

Hyppolite, Jean (1974) (first edn 1947), *Genesis and Structure of Hegel's Phenomenology of Spirit*, trans. Samuel Cherniak and John Heckman, Evanston: Northwestern University Press.

— (1997) (first edn 1953), *Logic and Existence*, trans. Leonard Lawlor and Amit Sen, Albany: State University of New York Press.

Irigaray, Luce (1985) (first edn 1977), *This Sex Which Is Not One*, trans. C. Porter and C. Burke, Ithaca: Cornell University Press.

— (1991) (first edn 1980), *Marine Lover of Friedrich Nietzsche*, trans. Gillian Gill, New York: Columbia University Press.

Kojève, Alexandre (1969), *Introduction to the Reading of Hegel*, trans. James Nichols Jr, Ithaca: Cornell University Press.

Kristeva, Julia (1986), *The Kristeva Reader*, ed. Toril Moi, Oxford: Blackwells.

Levinas, Emmanuel (1969) (first edn 1961), *Totality and Infinity*, trans. Alfonso Lingis, Pittsburgh: Duquesne University Press.

Reich, Wilhelm (1970) (first edn 1933), *The Mass Psychology of Fascism*, trans. Vincent Carfagno, London: Souvenir Press.

Roth, Michael (1988), *Knowing and History: Appropriations of Hegel in Twentieth-Century France*, Ithaca: Cornell University Press.

POWER, KNOWLEDGE AND ETHICS: FOUCAULT

David Owen

'I dream of a new age of curiosity.'
– Michel Foucault

The *ethos* of Michel Foucault's work is self-critical reflection, continually transforming the limits of its thinking and developing its self-understanding. Reflecting on his self-transformations in the Introduction to *The Use of Pleasure* (1985), his last published work, Foucault remarks:

> There is irony in these efforts one makes to alter one's way of looking at things, to change the boundaries of what one knows and to venture out a way from there. Did mine actually result in a different way of thinking? Perhaps at most they made it possible to go back through what I was already thinking, to think it differently, and to see what I had done from a new vantage point and in a clearer light. (Foucault, 1985, p. 11)

Following the lead of this remark, I will trace Foucault's thought to his final self-understanding by examining the three stages of his work. First, his early work on madness, medicine and the human sciences. Second, his explorations of power/knowledge relations in punishment, sexuality and governmental rationalities. And third, his final reflections on ethical subjectivity in Greece and Rome, and on Kant's question, 'What is Enlightenment?'

Archaeologies of knowledge

Foucault's three major works of the 1960s – *Madness and Civilization* (1961), *The Birth of the Clinic* (1963),

and *The Order of Things* (1966) – develop what he calls an 'archaeology' of knowledge. Drawing on Bachelard and Canguilhem in the philosophy and history of science, Foucault presents a threefold distinction between archaeology of knowledge and history of ideas:

1. Archaeology does not address the unity of individual thinkers or schools of thought but rather that of 'systems of thought', of the ensemble of conceptual vocabularies and theoretical structures through which knowledge claims are articulated.
2. Archaeology does not evaluate the rationality of forms of knowledge but rather discloses the historical conditions of forms of knowledge, the conventions that determine which utterances can be considered as either true or false and which thus structure the epistemic space within which forms of knowledge emerge. Foucault names an assemblage of epistemic conventions an *episteme*, which he describes in Kantian terms as the historical *a priori* of knowledge and in Nietzschean terms as the positive unconscious of knowledge.
3. Archaeology does not uncover hidden continuities of thought, but rather highlights discontinuities, the transformations of conventions governing epistemic discourses.

How does Foucault exploit this approach in his early writings? In *Madness and Civilization* – a heavily abridged version of the French original – he addresses the bounds of reason by attending to the ways in which madness is figured and acted upon in Europe from the late Middle Ages to the beginning of the nineteenth century. He identifies three distinct *epistemes*: the Renaissance *episteme* where madness is represented as disorder; the Classical *episteme* where madness is figured as Unreason; and the Modern *episteme* where madness is mental illness. Each of these *epistemes* has particular ways of dealing with madness.

In the Renaissance *episteme*, the madman appeared within a class of human types (including the fool, the drunkard, the debauchee, the criminal and the lover) who represent excess and irregularity. In this period, the most symbolically significant social practice for dealing with the mad was the Ship of Fools. In the Classical *episteme*, the mad are situated alongside the poor, criminals, debtors, libertines and vagabonds as human beings reduced to animality by incurable moral flaws, most notably idleness. This class of 'animals' is governed by the ressurection of the medieval practice of internment of lepers, who were excluded from society as creatures punished by God but were visible in their enclosure as 'reminders of God's power and of the Christian duty of charity' (Dreyfus and Rabinow, 1982, p. 3). Thus, Foucault notes that, while the leper houses were emptied at the end of the Middle Ages, the space was reoccupied by the creatures of Unreason, excluded from society (reduced to animality by idleness) yet visible reminders of the moral imperative to work. In the Modern *episteme*, the madman is medically judged as ill. The asylum transforms internment, emerging as an institution for curing the insane: the mad are confronted with their moral responsibility for their illness while the physician becomes the judge of moral-mental normality.

In distinguishing these three *epistemes*, Foucault's archaeology unsettles the seeming naturalness and necessity of our epistemic perceptions – here, madness as mental illness – by showing the historical construction of the underlying conventions of our perception. Foucault does not, however, simply unsettle our patterns of thought by distinguishing these three epistemes; he also intensifies our discomfort by demonstrating that the formation of madness as mental illness, the object of psychiatric knowledge, is not due to increases in compassion and objectivity. Rather, he argues, less reputable factors helped transform madness from idleness to illness (for example, the protests of confined nobility against sharing space with the mad, the emergence of a new understanding of the economic utility of the poor, the concern for the social status of medical practitioners, the establishment of the hegemony of bourgeois values). Thus, *Madness and Civilization* is not a linear narrative of moral and scientific progress, but a counter-history, a disturbing of our complacent presumption of progress.

In *Madness and Civilization*, Foucault stresses that, crucial to the understanding of madness as mental illness, is the distinction between mental and physical illness – a distinction which did not exist prior to the nineteenth century and which emerges in reconfiguring the conventions of medical knowledge. In *The Birth of the Clinic*, Foucault develops this point by analysing the emergence of the modern concept of physical illness in the late eighteenth and early nineteenth centuries. He claims that this period sees shift in medical reasoning from *nosology*, the classification of diseases into natural kinds that manifest themselves anywhere in the body, to *symptology*, which identified diseases with their precisely-located symptoms and thus opens medicine to the distinction between physical and mental illness.

Foucault accounts for this shift by two developments. First, the emergence alongside the medicine of species (nosology) of a governmental concern with public hygiene, which developed throughout the eighteenth century into a distinct modality of medical practice – a 'medicine of social spaces' – characterised by concern with the general health of the population. This mode of medicine was orientated to preventing epidemics and maintaining normal health by uniting statistics (for example, indices of infant mortality) with standarised forms of medical description. Second, after the French Revolution, the medicine of social spaces was institutionalised by measures directed to public health and training doctors – such as reorganising hospitals as sites of instruction – which articulate the shift from nosology to symptomology. The major agent in this shift is the clinic, which transforms medical perception through changing the perceived relation between symptoms and disease and through integrating the study of symptoms with the study of dissected corpses. Together these developments produce the concept of physical illness which characterises modern medical practice. The doctor's 'gaze' (which includes seeing, touching and listening) reads bodily symptoms as the language of disease.

In *The Birth of the Clinic*, then, as in *Madness and Civilization*, Foucault emphasises both the transformation of the epistemic conventions of medical knowledge between the eighteenth and nineteenth centuries and the social and institutional practices which produce this epistemic rupture. With regard to the Modern episteme, each text points to the emergence of the figure of Man as both knowing subject (the psychiatrist or physician) and object of knowledge (the mentally or physically ill patient). In *The Order of Things*, Foucault takes up Man explicitly as our reflection on ourselves in discourses of life, labour and language, focusing primarily on the Classical and Modern *epistemes*. He demonstrates an epistemic break in the conventions of knowledge common to these discourses, and also shows that this rupture marks the conditions of possibility of the human sciences.

Foucault argues that the Classical *episteme* is governed by a *mathesis* (the analysis of calculable order), a *taxonomia* (the classification of representations by identity and difference) and a *genetic analysis* (the analysis of the constitution of orders through empirical series). About these conventions, Foucault notes:

> The sciences always carry within themselves the project, however remote it may be, of an exhaustive ordering of the world; they are always directed, too, towards the discovery of simple elements and their progressive combination; and at their centre they form a table on which knowledge is displayed in a system contemporary with itself. The centre of knowledge, in the seventeenth century and eighteenth century, is the *table*. (Foucaut, 1970, p. 74)

The central activity of knowledge in the Classical *episteme* is thus the tabular arrangement of representations mirroring the arrangement of things in the world (for example, the tables of flora and fauna in natural history). The possibility of this activity is articulated through understanding language as the common discourse of representations and things.

However, while human beings appear on the general table of knowledge as one kind of being in a hierarchy of beings, they do not – cannot – appear on the table as the maker of tables. Thus, Foucault argues that a science of Man as knowing subject and known object is not possible in the Classical *episteme* – the figure of Man is a modern invention.

The end of the Classical and the beginning of the Modern *episteme* is dramatised by the coexistence of de Tracy's project of Ideology and Kant's project of critical philosophy, both of which concern representation. However, whereas de Tracy's science of ideas 'situates all knowledge in the space of representations, and by scanning that space . . . formulates the knowledge of the laws that provide its organisation' (1970, p. 241), Kant's critical philosophy concerns the conditions of possibility of representing and, concomitantly, the necessary form of any representation. The movement from de Tracy's analysis to Kant's analytic discloses the collapse of the understanding of language as a transparent medium of representation, marked by the correspondence of words and things, and the emergence into the field of knowledge of the figure of Man – 'the subject of representational knowledge becomes, as such, an object of knowledge' (Gutting, 1989, p. 199).

In the discourses of life, labour and language, this shift is marked by the movements from natural history to biology, from analysis of wealth to economics, and from general grammar to linguistics. These empirical sciences

> show how the representational capacities of human beings as living organisms (for example, perception), as economic agents (for example, valuing), and as users of language (for example, describing) are themselves the causal products of the forces of life, labour, and language that precede and mould man. (ibid.)

However, while Man as an object of the empirical sciences appears as a finite being, as one object among many, Man also appears as that being who constitutes the world of objects in which Man is included. Thus Kant's question 'What is Man?' becomes central to founding knowledge and inaugurates the project of philosophical anthropology. Foucault claims that post-kantian philosophy is the ultimately futile attempt to answer this question through an analytic of finitude: the factual limitations of man as an object are taken to provide the conditions of possibility for knowledge of the world of objects (which includes man and his limitations). Foucault locates the possibility of the human sciences in the space between the empirical sciences (man as a natural being) and the philosophy of the subject (man as a representing subject). Like the empirical sciences, the human sciences focus on man as a living, labouring and linguistic being; like philosophy, they address man as a representing subject rather than as a represented object. However, unlike philosophy, the human sciences know man as a representing subject through the unthought (for example, the unconscious, the social imaginary, the mode of production) which surrounds human consciousness.

Foucault concludes *The Order of Things* by postulating the death of Man (that is, the end of the Modern *episteme*); archaeology is thus a philosophical reflection which abandons Kant's anthropological focus on the constituting subject. Yet, while Foucault follows his archaeological studies with a methodological reflection – *The Archaeology of Knowledge* (1969) – his work in the 1970s replaces archaeology by genealogy. Consequently, to situate Foucault's turn we need to reflect briefly on the limitations of archaeology.

From archaeology to genealogy

Archaeology as a method has two limitations. First, although both *Madness and Civilization* and *The Birth of the Clinic* pay attention to non-discursive as well as discursive practices, their interrelationship is not itself thematised. Thus, Dreyfus and Rabinow (1982) argue that Foucault's archaeological studies from *Madness and Civilization* to *The Order of Things*

moves from a hermeneutics to a quasi-structuralism, which, however, cannot account adequately for social practices. Second, while Foucault's archaeology stresses the historical contingency of modern forms of knowledge, it is not clear why this matters. Thus, Dean contends that the fundamental deficiency of archaeology is that it 'gives no explicit account of how the historical description of the positivity of discourse is to be mobilised in terms of current purposes and issues' (Dean, 1994, p. 17).

In the two years following *The Archaeology of Knowledge* Foucault broached each of these issues. In 'The Order of Discourse' (1970), he thematises the relationship of discursive and non-discursive practices via the issue of power in the constitution of knowledge. In 'Nietzsche, Genealogy, History' (1971), he takes Nietzsche's 'effective history' as problematising our relationship to the present in order to transform the present. Each of these essays bore fruit for Foucault in the 1970s. The former led to his focus on power/knowledge relations, while the latter led to his adoption of a genealogical approach to the present. To situate Foucault's work in this period, I will briefly outline these transformations.

Concerning power/knowledge, Foucault writes:

We should admit that power produces knowledge . . .; that power and knowledge directly imply one another; that there is no power relation without the correlative constitution of a field of knowledge, nor any knowledge that does not presuppose and constitute at the same time power relations . . . In short, it is not the activity of the subject of knowledge that produces a corpus of knowledge, useful or resistant to power, but power-knowledge . . . that determines the forms and possible domains of knowledge. (Foucault, 1977, p. 28).

He is not asserting the identity of power and knowledge, but their mutual constitution. Power/knowledge marks a shift from the notion of *episteme* to that of *dispositif*:

In seeking in *The Order of Things* to write a history of the *episteme*, I was still caught in an impasse. What I should like to do now is to try and show that what I call an apparatus [*dispositif*] is a much more general case of the *episteme*; or, rather, that the *episteme* is a specifically discursive apparatus, whereas the apparatus in its general form is both discursive and non-discursive, its elements being much more heterogenous. (Foucault, 1980, p. 197)

The *dispositif* thematises the relationship between knowledge (discursive practices) and power (non-discursive practices).

Along with this focus on power/knowledge, Foucault justifies the shift to genealogy by describing the use of his historical studies in contemporary political struggles. By situating his historical analyses in terms of power/knowledge, he both acknowledges their interestedness and reveals them as provocations demonstrating the historical contingency of those ways of thinking and acting we treat as natural and necessary, and so fail to recognise as forms of power. Thus, whereas the archaeologist does not acknowledge non-epistemic purposes, the genealogist recognises both the epistemic and political purposes which animate her or his engagement with the present. In other words, Foucault now locates the critical import of genealogy in its questioning of the necessity of certain power/knowledge relations and thus opening a reflective space within which resistance to those relations can be mobilised. How, though, does he manifest this transformation of his project?

Genealogies of power

In *The Order of Things*, Foucault provides a purely discursive account of the historical conditions of possibility of the human sciences – one which cannot articulate its non-epistemic significance for our relationship to the present. In *Discipline and Punish* (1975) and *The History of Sexuality* (1976), he moves beyond archaeology in two ways. First, he focuses on the historical emergence of the human sciences; second, he shows how they are tied to new forms of power, so that recognising them as telling *the* truth about human beings prevents us from seeing them as articulating and supporting forms of domination.

The central notion of Foucault's genealogical account is *bio-power*, a distinct modality of power/knowledge emerging at the end of the eighteenth

century: 'One might say that the ancient right to *take* life or *let* live was replaced by a power to *foster* life or *disallow* it to the point of death' (Foucault, 1979, p. 138). This form of power unites two poles which emerged in the Classical period, '*the disciplines*: an *anatomo-politics of the human body*' and '*regulatory controls: a bio-politics of the population*' (Foucault, 1978, p. 139). In *Discipline and Punish* and *The History of Sexuality*, he shows that these two poles are united in *diagrams* of power – the panopticon and the confessional – which render intelligible the objectifying and subjectifying practices that underly the human sciences.

In *Discipline and Punish*, Foucault shows how the transformation in practices of punishment between the eighteenth and nineteenth centuries exemplifies the development of those objectifying practices which constitute the historical conditions of possibility of the *objectifying* human sciences (those that treat man as an object-effect of, for example, social forces). He shows a transformation of punishment from the spectacular reassertion of the power of the sovereign (public executions and torture as judgements of *crime*) to normalising detention (imprisonment as judgement of *criminality*). This shift can be accounted for by two developments during the eighteenth century: the spread of disciplinary techniques producing docile bodies (bodies which can be trained) and the emergence of a government rationality dedicated to the welfare of the population of living, labouring and linguistic beings. These two developments come together in the prison, which Foucault examines through Bentham's figure of the *panopticon*. Foucault does not claim that the panopticon represents the reality of the prison; instead, he treats it as the ideal diagram of the punitive rationality involved in the emergence and maintenance of imprisonment as the dominant practice of punishment.

The panopticon produces constant visibility of the inmates through its architecture: a circle of backlit cells around an enshadowed observatory. This arrangement of space and light produces two effects. First, the inmate is visible to the tower but invisible to those in adjacent cells, so that the individual is an 'object of information, never a subject in communication' (Foucault, 1977, p. 200). Second, the inmate is visible to the tower but cannot tell if the tower is occupied, so he must always assume he is being watched; this works 'to induce in the inmate a state of conscious and permanent visibility that ensures the automatic functioning of power' (ibid., p. 201). By combining these effects, the panopticon is both observatory and laboratory. On the one hand, by its individualising observation of the confined population it allows the development of *typologies* which unite the individualising disciplinary gaze and the totalising regulatory gaze. On the other hand, it functions as a laboratory machine

> to carry out experiments, to alter behaviour, to train or correct individuals . . . To try out different punishments on prisoners, according to their crimes and character, and to seek the most effective ones. (ibid., p. 203)

In this respect, the panopticon 'is a privileged place for experiments on men, and for analyzing with complete certainty the transformations that may be obtained from them' (ibid., p. 204). It combines regulatory controls exercised on the population (the general regime of norms) with disciplinary techniques exercised on individuals (individualised regimes of normalisation) through the construction of typologies. In this space, the scientific expert emerges as the judge of normality.

In *The History of Sexuality*, Foucault turns from the generalisation of panoptic technologies in prisons, schools, hospitals, factories and other institutions to consider another diagram of bio-power: the **confessional**. Focusing on sexuality as a site where disciplinary techniques and regulatory controls are combined, he accounts for the shift from an eighteenth-century juridical-moral discourse of sexual activity (characterised by general notions such as debauchery) to a nineteenth-century scientific-moral discourse of sex (characterised by typologies of abnormal sexuality). He notes that the exhortation to speak the truth about sex in the confessional practice of Christian penance continues with the emergence of the two poles of bio-power (the disciplines and regulatory controls), so that individual sexuality becomes central to regulating the reproductive (and moral) dimension of populations. Consequently, he stresses the scientific appropriation of the confessional as a generalisable technique for bringing someone to express the truth of their subjectivity to an authority (for example, the psychoanalyst) who judges the normality of the speaking subject. Like the panopticon, this scientisation of the confessional links the two poles of bio-power: the imperative to confess the truth about oneself and submit to the judgement of the confessor combines observatory (classifying of confessional utterances) and laboratory (action by the confessor on the confessee); regulatory norms and individualised disciplinary regimes are thus articulated in a typology.

Two main poles emerge from Foucault's account: first, panoptic and confessional technologies link individualisation (the case history) and totalisation (statistics) by constructing normative 'types' (such as the *delinquent* and the *hysterical woman*). Constructing types through these technologies feeds back to refine the technologies when types of types are made (for example, types of delinquents) (ibid., pp. 253–6). Since both technologies link individualisation and totalisation in practice, they function as 'laboratories of power' where regimes of discipline and regulatory controls can be institutionalised and so cross-articulate themselves. Second, the panopticon and the confessional are exemplary *diagrams* of the political rationality Foucault terms 'bio-power' as well as distinct forms of this. In panoptic technologies, discipline focuses on the body as subject to causative processes – abnormal or dysfunctional elements with an individual's *nature* may be realigned through training. In other words, this technology operates through the external environment to produce a form of knowledge which specifies the individual as an object-effect of, for example, social forces. In confessional technologies, discipline focuses on the self as site of meaning – abnormal or dysfunctional elements within an individual's *identity* may be realigned through interpretation. In other words, this technology operates through the internal environment to produce a form of knowledge which specifies the individual as a subject-cause of, for example, social actions. Thus, the figure of knowable Man is constituted as object-effect and subject-cause through panoptic and confessional technologies respectively, while the institutional entrenchment and elaboration of these technologies provide the loci of emergence of the objectifying (structural) and subjectifying (interpretive) human sciences respectively.

Thus, Foucault argues, first, that bio-power produces the space within which the human sciences can emerge, and second, that the human sciences articulate and maintain the exercise of bio-power. He worries that the human sciences have come to be the only legitimate basis for ethics and politics.

> Recent liberation movements suffer from the fact that they cannot find any principle on which to base the elaboration of a new ethics. They need an ethics but they cannot find any other ethics than an ethics founded on so-called scientific knowledge of what the self is, what desire is, what the unconscious is, and so on. (Foucault, 1984b, p. 343)

Against this identification of bio-power and the human sciences as the practical and theoretical reduction of ethical and political judgement to the technical judgement of scientific experts, genealogy undermines the naturalness and necessity of this way of recognising, reflecting and acting on ourselves.

Ethics and problematisations

In moving from archaeology to genealogy, Foucault significantly developed the critical power of his accounts. He went on, however, to redefine his work in two further ways: first, by introducing a third dimension alongside knowledge and power, namely, ethics; and second, by reconceptualising his investigations as 'problematisations'.

To understand Foucault's concept of ethics, we need to explain his concept of power in his genealogies. Foucault presents power as 'a mode of action on the actions of others' which seeks to govern the actions of others; that is, 'to structure the field of possible actions of others' (Foucault, 1982, p. 221). This conceptualisation of power entails that 'there cannot be society without power relations', but this is not to say 'either that those which are established are necessary, or in any case, that power constitutes a fatality at the heart of societies, such that it cannot be undermined' (ibid.). He insists that power can be exercised 'only over free subjects

and only in so far as they are free' (ibid.); exercises of power can only modify the actions of human subjects who can act in various ways, including resisting the modifications of their actions (Patton, 1994, pp. 62–3).

Foucault introduces the concept of 'domination' to refer to 'stable and asymmetrical systems of power relations' from which 'the possibility of effective resistance has been removed' (ibid., p. 64). Those subject to domination cannot transform the constraints to which they are subject; resistance is only possible as the limit-gesture of refusal.

By analysing knowledge and power together, Foucault demonstrated the complex relations between how we recognise and reflect on ourselves and others and how we act. However, because the concept of power only refers to how we act on others and not on ourselves, genealogy provides only a partial account of the transformation of our ways of thinking. Recognising this limitation of genealogy, Foucault introduced the concept of ethics to capture the conducting of one's own conduct, the power exercised over oneself by oneself. However, in introducing the concept of ethics, he also refined his analyses to more precisely attend to the relations between knowledge, power and ethics. I will focus on this refinement in discussing Foucault's genealogies of ethics in the next section.

The second development is the notion of problematisation (rendering an object of study), which Foucault came to see as characterising his earlier works. He uses 'problematisation' to show archaeology and genealogy as two aspects of a critical-historical ontology of ourselves, arguing that archaeology attends to the *form* of a problematisation, while genealogy attends to the *formation* of a problematisation and to the *transformations* it engenders. In other words, archaeology studies 'games of truth' – conceptualisations of the real (that is, discursive practices) – while genealogy studies the relation of games of truth and conduct (power and ethics) – action on the real (that is, non-discursive practices). Through this account of the relation of archaeology and genealogy, Foucault redescribed his project as a critical ontology of ourselves, as 'genealogical in its design and archaeological in its method' (Foucault, 1984a, p. 46):

Archaeological – and not transcendental – in the sense that it will not seek to identify the universal structures of all knowledge or of all possible moral action, but will seek to treat the instances of discourse that articulate what we think, say, and do as so many historical events. And this critique will be genealogical in the sense that it will not deduce from the form of what we are what it is impossible for us to do and know; but it will separate out, from the contingency that has made us what we are, the possibility of no longer being, doing, or thinking what we are, do, or think. (Ibid.)

With this reconceptualisation of his project, Foucault arrived at the methodological stance articulated in his essay 'What is Enlightenment?' Before turning to this essay, however, we need to focus briefly on his genealogies of ethics and on their implications for Foucault's final self-understanding and for his articulation of an ethics not caught within the confines of bio-power.

Genealogies of ethics

In *The Use of Pleasure* and *The Care of the Self* (1984) Foucault's analysis of Greek and Roman ethics performs two roles. First, it elaborates a concept of ethics which refines his analyses of power (Owen, 1994). Second, it questions three conventions which govern our moral reflection and practice (Tully, 1992).

The Use of Pleasure elaborates Foucault's concept of ethics as the conducting of one's own conduct. It presents ethics as a *rapport à soi* (the relation of the self to itself) analysable in four elements: the determination of the ethical substance, 'the way in which the individual has to constitute this or that part of himself as the prime material of his moral conduct' (Foucault, 1985, p. 26); the mode of subjection, 'the way in which the individual establishes his relation to the [moral] rule and recognizes himself as obliged to put it into practice' (ibid., p. 27); the ethical work or ascetics, the practices 'that one performs on oneself, not only to bring one's conduct into compliance with a given rule, but to attempt to transform oneself into the ethical subject of one's behaviour' (ibid.); and the *telos* or kind of ethical being which

the practices aim to produce (ibid., pp. 27–8).

Using this schema, Foucault contrasts Greek and Christian ethics in the following way. The ethical substance for the Greeks is sensual pleasure (*aphrodisia*), while for the Christians it is the desires of the flesh. The mode of subjection for the Greeks is an active aesthetico-political choice committed to a beautiful existence (*chresis*), while for the Christians it is submission to God's law as a sinful but rational being. The ethical work and *telos* for the Greeks are dietary, domestic and erotic practices (*askesis*) orientated to self-mastery, the rule of one's passions (*enkrateia*), while for the Christians they are practices of self-abnegation and self-denial orientated to a state of grace, purified of corrupted flesh.

This approach to ethics is related to Foucault's analysis of power. A brief reflection on nineteenth-century technologies of power regarding sexual conduct illustrates this point: ethical substance = the sexual drives; mode of subjection = recognition of the authority of psychologists and their discourse on sex; ascetic practices = the secularised confessional technologies of psychotherapy; *telos* = sexual normality. His analysis of ethics thus refines his tools for analysing the relation between our reflection on self and others (knowledge) and our actions on self (ethics) and others (power).

Foucault's genealogies of ethics also question three conventions of moral reflection and practice. First, they demonstrate that the juridical model of universal moral law is peripheral to Greek and Roman ethics, which focus on cultivating a certain ethos or attitude. By attending to Foucault's four aspects of ethics we can transform our ethical relations to ourselves without being drawn into questions of universalism or relativism (Tully, 1992, p. 384). Second, they show that a hermeneutics of ethical self-understanding – freeing an inner truth or authentic identity – is foreign to Greek ethics, for which ethical work is aesthetic self-overcoming, and only emerges with Christian morality (ibid.). Third, they show ethics as 'the practice of freedom' (ibid.).

Foucault's emphasis on ethics as cultivating an attitude, as aesthetic self-overcoming, and as the practice of freedom provides the context for both his final methodological self-understanding and for his attempt to specify an ethical engagement free of the human sciences and instead based on a critical ontology of ourselves. This final self-understanding is presented in his reflections on Kant's text 'What is Enlightenment?'

Enlightenment

Kant's 1784 essay 'Answering the Question: What is Enlightenment?' exercises a remarkable pull on Foucault's thinking, being addressed on three occasions between 1978 and 1984 (Schmidt and Wartenberg, 1994). In the third of his lectures, Foucault asks us to imagine that the journal in which Kant published his essay still exists, and poses for today's readers the question 'What is modern philosophy?'. Foucault suggests the following response: 'modern philosophy is the philosophy that is attempting to answer the question raised so imprudently two centuries ago: *Was ist Aufklärung*? [What is Enlightenment?]' (Foucault, 1984a, p. 32). On Foucault's account, this question haunts modern philosophy; neither answered nor exorcised, it calls on us to return to it. In addressing the question of Enlightenment, Foucault provides the clearest statement of his own philosophical work and of his understanding of the tasks of modern philosophy.

Foucault begins by noting that Kant's reflection on the present cannot be captured by the three main philosophical forms of such reflection, all of which 'involved the positing of an objective totality that oriented the task of thinking' (Rabinow, 1994, p. 200), so that the present is an age, a threshold or an achievement (Foucault, 1984a, pp. 33–4). By contrast, Foucault argues, Kant's text on Enlightenment grasps the present not in terms of an objective totality but in terms of difference: 'What difference does today introduce with respect to yesterday?' (ibid., p. 34). For Foucault, Kant's differential relation to the present lies 'at the crossroads of critical reflection and reflection on history'. Consequently, although Foucault briefly analyses Kant's understanding of Enlightenment as the escape (through reliance on our own understanding) from self-imposed immaturity, he is primarily engaged not with what Kant's essay *says* about Enlightenment, but with what it *shows*: 'It is in the reflection on "today" as difference in history and as motive for a particular philosophical task that the novelty of this text appears to me to lie' (ibid., p. 38).

Kant's uniquely differential reflection on the present has three axes: a historical account of the present as the practical conditions for producing ourselves as autonomous subjects; a critical account of the present as the potential for transforming those practical conditions; and an act performed on the present which transforms those practical conditions. While the first two axes highlight the historical-critical dimension of Kant's text, the third points out that his words are also deeds, that he both intervenes in the public sphere and transforms himself.

At this point, Foucault suggests that his threefold analysis allows us to 'recognize a point of departure: the outline of what one might call the attitude of modernity' (ibid.). He reconceptualises modernity as *ethos* (attitude) rather than *epoch* (age) by juxtaposing Kant's essay with Baudelaire's ironic heroisation. For Baudelairean modernity, Foucault argues,

> the high value of the present is indissociable from a desperate eagerness to imagine it, to imagine it otherwise than it is, and to transform it not by destroying it but by grasping it in what it is. Baudelairean modernity is an exercise in which extreme attention to what is real is confronted with the practice of a liberty that simultaneously respects this reality and violates it. (ibid., p. 41)

Moreover, modernity as an attitude directed to transforming the reality of the present does not merely try to change an intransigent world, but involves a certain *rapport à soi*, a relation of self to itself, in which the individual acts on her or himself as a piece of present reality: 'it is to take oneself as the object of a complex and difficult elaboration: what Baudelaire, in the vocabulary of his day, calls *dandysme*' (ibid.). This modern attitude is both heroic (one engages in self-overcoming), and ironic (one recognises that self-overcoming is never complete, but always already beginning again).

In juxtaposing Kant and Baudelaire, Foucault does not assert the identity of their positions; on the contrary, he simply proposes that they exhibit a common ethos, 'the attitude of modernity'. Baudelaire's ironic heroisation echoes Kant's critical-historical reflection by identifying our contemporary task as transforming the conditions for producing ourselves as autonomous subjects. For Foucault, this juxtaposition suggests that our relation to Enlightenment is not fidelity 'to its doctrinal elements, but rather the permanent reactivation of an attitude [of modernity] – that is, of a philosophical ethos that could be described as a permanent critique of our historical era' (ibid., p. 42). Two consequences of this reading of the Enlightenment frame Foucault's philosophical activity.

First, he suggests we split Enlightenment and humanism. On the one hand, the Enlightenment is a specific European historical ensemble, out of which Foucault extracts one feature, a certain way of philosophising. On the other hand, humanism has emerged in various forms at various times in European history. Moreover, Foucault suggests that since the seventeenth century

> what is called humanism has always been obliged to lean on certain conceptions of man borrowed from religion, science, or politics. Humanism serves to colour and to justify the conceptions of man to which it is, after all, obliged to take recourse. (ibid., p. 44)

Foucault does not, in fact, want us to reject humanism as such, but merely to note the tension between determinate 'conceptions of man' and the self-transformative ethos of Enlightenment; determining the limits of Man's being is opposed to 'the principle of critique and a permanent creation of ourselves in our autonomy' (ibid.). We can thus be neither for or against humanism – it is too diverse for such a choice to be meaningful – nor for or against Enlightenment – this forced choice confuses an ensemble of events with a commitment to humanism. Foucault instead posits a dual move. One must first reject analyses predicated on a determinate conception of man as 'subject':

> One has to dispense with the constituent subject, to get rid of the subject itself, that's to say to arrive at an analysis which can account for the constitution of the subject within a historical framework. (Foucault, 1984a, p. 59; cf. 1988a, p. 50)

Second, one must adopt the Enlightenment ethos of 'a permanent creation of ourselves in our autonomy'.

Having clarified the relation of humanism and Enlightenment, Foucault draws out the second consequence of Enlightenment as the attitude of modernity: its implications for the project of critique. For Foucault, critique is 'oriented towards the "contemporary limits of the necessary"', that is, toward what is not or is no longer indispensable for the constitution of ourselves as autonomous subjects' (Foucault, 1984a, p. 45). In other words, Foucault's ethos is a *'limit-attitude'* in which critique takes the form of 'analyzing and reflecting upon limits' (ibid.). However, in so far as this critique dispenses with determinate conceptions of man as 'subject', it must be distinguished from Kantian critique:

> if the Kantian question was that of knowing what limits knowledge had to renounce transgressing, it seems to me that the critical question today has to be turned back into a positive one: in what is given to us as universal, necessary, obligatory, what place is occupied by whatever is singular, contingent, and the product of arbitrary constraints? The point, in brief, is to transform the critique conducted in the form of necessary limitation into a practical critique that takes the form of a possible transgression. (ibid.)

Thus, critique does not answer the question 'What is Man?', nor Kant's related questions: what can I know? what should I do? what can I hope for? Rather, critique asks how we can be otherwise than we are, and thus aims to locate and interrogate our limits. This practical critique is a *critical ontology of ourselves*, which opens up the possibility of being otherwise by calling what we are into question through reflecting on how we have become what we are. As Tully comments, 'for Foucault, it is an important convention of the practice of freedom that we are able to call into question what is given as a bound of reason' (Tully, 1989, p. 188). In calling into question a convention or boundary, we both exercise freedom (practical critique) and open a space for the exercise of freedom (transforming what we are). Consequently, for Foucault, the ethos of the critical ontology of ourselves is 'a historico-practical test of the limits that we may go beyond, and thus . . . work carried out by ourselves upon ourselves as free beings' (ibid., p. 47).

In summary then, Foucault clarifies his notions of critique and freedom by relating them to the Enlightenment ethos elaborated by Kant and Baudelaire. Foucault strives for 'a philosophical life in which the critique of what we are is at one and the same time the historical analysis of the limits that are imposed on us and an experiment with the possibility of going beyond them' (ibid., p. 50). Foucauldian critique, as experimentally calling into question the bounds of reason, entails abandoning the project of *total* critique, however, and thus any radically utopian aspirations or longings for total revolution. The critical ontology of ourselves calls a convention which is partially constitutive of our present being into question by a genealogical analysis; this does not call *all* conventions into question (such a project is, strictly speaking, unintelligible), for it recognises that transgressing a convention typically brings forth a different convention. As such, there neither is nor can be any total or final critique:

> It is true that we have to give up hope of ever acceding to a point of view that could give us access to any complete and definitive knowledge of what may constitute our historical limits. And from this point of view the theoretical and practical experience that we have of our limits and the possibility of moving beyond them is always limited and determined; thus we are always in the position of beginning again. (ibid.)

For Foucault, no doubt, the practical effects of total critique in the twentieth century should remind us of the totalitarianism of such projects, not the least of which lies in their claiming to be *the* form of critical practice, and consequently, to exclude other practices of critical reflection (Tully, 1989). However, while he does not claim to have established the only form of critical reflection, or even an *a priori* privileged form of such reflection, humanity's emergence from its self-imposed immaturity does involve, for him, recognising the situated partiality of its critical reflections, for the *maturity* of critique lies in recognising that it is always already beginning again.

Parrhesia

A critical ontology of ourselves exemplifies the ethos it recommends – calling conventions into question. Philosophers who perform it engage in an ethical self-relation – truth-telling – which Foucault calls *parrhesia*. Foucault's last lectures deal with *parrhesia* as direct truth-telling that endangers the speaker. He distinguishes the *parrhesiast* from other exemplars of truth-telling: the prophet (truth as destiny), the sage (truth as being) and the teacher-technician (truth as learned skill). In contrast,

> the *parrhesiast* focuses on the present. Parrhesia 'seeks the political conditions and ethical differences at work in the question of true discourse, in other words, it underscores the impossibility of thinking without thinking all three poles, while insisting on their irreducible distinctiveness. (Rabinow, 1994, p. 206)

At various times, philosophers have adopted each of these roles, often in combination. Foucault seeks to be the *parrhesiast*, although in commenting on such exercises (for example, 'What is Enlightenment?') he adopts the role of teacher-technician. By calling into question the bounds of reason in the name of freedom, he runs the risk of dismissal as nihilist, neo-conservative, neo-Marxist, irrationalist or anarchist – all terms of abuse with which he has been tarred in order to avoid a thoughtful engagement.

Foucault as *parrhesiast* – the engaged truth-teller speaking within a field of power – is not simply a philosopher talking away. Rather, he is negotiating the relation of philosophy and politics, of the contemplative life (*bios theoretikos*) and the active life (*bios politikos*) – he is undertaking that apparent paradox, political philosophy. As simultaneously critical-historical contemplation and ethical/political activity, Foucault's truth-telling, his disturbing redescriptions of what is all too familiar, calls into question the very domain of political activity in which it is embedded and in which it offers itself as exemplary political activity.

As a philosophical reflection which calls into question our political activity, and as a political activity which offers itself to philosophical reflection, Foucault's work negotiates the paradox of political philosophy, calling us to adopt a stance of passionate heroic engagement and sober ironic distance in confronting the demands of the day. Thus, we may give patient expression to the impatience of our freedom.

Bibliography

Writings

NOTE: Dates given below are for translations.

Foucault, Michel (1965), *Madness and Civilisation*, trans. R. Howard, London: Tavistock.

— (1970), *The Order of Things*, trans. unidentified collective, London: Tavistock.

— (1972), *The Archaeology of Knowledge*, trans. A. Sheridan, New York: Pantheon.

— (1973), *The Birth of the Clinic*, trans. A. Sheridan, London: Tavistock.

— (1977), *Discipline and Punish*, trans. A. Sheridan, Harmondsworth: Penguin.

— (1978), *History of Sexuality* (vol. 1), trans. R. Hurley, Harmondsworth: Penguin.

— (1980), *Power/Knowledge*, ed. C. Gordon, Hemel Hempstead: Harvester Wheatsheaf.

— (1982), 'The subject and power', in H. Dreyfus and P. Rabinow (eds), *Michel Foucault: Beyond Structuralism and Hermeneutics*, Chicago: University of Chicago Press.

— (1984a), 'What is Enlightenment?', in P. Rabinow (ed.), *The Foucault Reader*, Harmondsworth: Penguin, 32–50.

— (1984b), 'Truth and Power', in P. Rabinow (ed), *The Foucault Reader*, Harmondsworth: Penguin, 51–75.

— (1985), *The Use of Pleasure: The History of Sexuality, Volume Two*, trans. R. Hurley, New York: Random House.

— (1988a), 'An Aesthetics of Existence', in L. Kritzman (ed.), *Philosophy, Politics, Culture*, London: Routledge, 47–53.

References and further reading

Dean, M. (1994), *Critical and Effective Histories*, London: Routledge.

Dreyfus, H. and P. Rabinow (1982), *Michel Foucault: Beyond Structuralism and Hermeneutics*, Chicago: University of Chicago Press.

Gutting, G. (1989), *Michel Foucault's Archaeology of Scientific Reason*, Cambridge: Cambridge University Press.

Owen, D. (1994), *Maturity and Modernity*, London: Routledge.

Patton, P. (1994), 'Foucault's Subject of Power', *Political Theory Newsletter*.

Rabinow, P. (1994), 'Modern and countermodern: ethos and epoch in Heidegger and Foucault', in G. Gutting (ed.), *The Cambridge Companion to Foucault*, Cambridge: Cambridge University Press, 197–214.

Schmidt, J. and T. Wartenberg (1994), 'Foucault's Enlightenment', in M. Kelly (ed.), *Critique and Power*, Cambridge, MA: MIT Press, 283–314.

Tully, J. (1989), 'Wittgenstein and Political Philosophy', *Political Theory* 17: 2, 172–204.

— (1992), 'Michel Foucault', in L. C. Becker (ed.), *Encyclopedia of Ethics*, 2 vols, Chicago: St James Press.

PHILOSOPHY OF THE OTHER: LEVINAS

Diane Perpich

Relation to phenomenology

Emmanuel Levinas was born in 1906 in Kovno (Kaunas), Lithuania to Jewish parents. His father owned a bookshop and as well as the Bible, which he read in Hebrew, Levinas grew up reading the novels of Pushkin, Lermontov, Gogol, Dostoevsky and Tolstoy. He would later cite these two sources – the Bible and the Russian novelists – as his earliest intellectual influences and as his first introduction to philosophy. In 1923, at the age of seventeen, Levinas left home to attend the University of Strasburg where he studied Latin for one year before turning to philosophy, concentrating first on the philosophy of Henri Bergson and later on phenomenology. The influence of Bergson's notions of invention and concrete duration, his questioning of the solidity and substantiality of things, is reflected in Levinas's critique of totality and in his concept of diachrony. Levinas always insisted on the importance of Bergson's contribution to philosophy, and deplored the neglect suffered by this philosopher in the second half of the twentieth century.

In 1928 and 1929, Levinas travelled to Freiburg to study with Husserl and Heidegger. Although Husserl had officially retired, he continued to lecture and see students. Levinas attended his seminars on phenomenological psychology and on the constitution of intersubjectivity. Heidegger had just arrived in Freiburg, having been named to fill Husserl's chair at the university; *Being and Time* had been published a year earlier and was already being hailed as a new direction in philosophy. Like many of his fellow students, Levinas was profoundly affected by the originality, and almost poetic quality, of the existential analyses of *Being and Time*. Here he found a new emphasis on the practical and affective dimensions of human involvements in the world and an insistence that these modes of comportment are not secondary to theoretical contemplation but primary. The Heideggerian analyses of guilt and anxiety showed that human moods are not merely physiological or psychological but ontological, that is, they are capable of disclosing our fundamental modes of being-in-the-world. Above all, Levinas was struck by Heidegger's renewal of the question of the meaning of Being and of the relation between Being and beings.

During his year in Freiburg, Levinas wrote his dissertation on Husserl's philosophy. Published in 1930 as *The Theory of Intuition in Husserl's Phenomenology*, this work was the first full-length study of Husserl's work to appear in French and, along with Levinas's co-translation of Husserl's *Cartesian Meditations*, played an important role in introducing phenomenology into France. Jean-Paul Sartre, for example, reports his first encounter with phenomenology as being Levinas's book. The dissertation begins from Husserl's critique of psychologism and its underlying naturalistic ontology, and proceeds to address the innovations of Husserl's conception of intentionality and the role of intuition in the constitution of objects in consciousness. In these discussions, Heidegger's influence is already marked. Most notably, Levinas draws on Heidegger to criticise the continuing intellectualism of Husserl's philosophy, claiming that Husserl is unwarranted in making theoretical and representational forms of consciousness the basis of all other types of conscious acts (for example, evaluative or practical acts). However, Levinas also tries to point to an important continuity between the philosophies of Husserl and Heidegger, and argues that, in its central problem of the constitution of the world with respect to pure consciousness, Husserl's phenomenology was already moving in the direction of the ontological problematic developed in *Being and Time*.

In 1932, Levinas published a long essay on fundamental ontology ('Martin Heidegger et l'ontologie') intended as the first part of a book which, like the book on Husserl, would present the main lines of development of Heidegger's philosophy. Plans for the book were abandoned, however, during 1933 when Levinas learned of Heidegger's involvement with National Socialism (see Peperzak, 1983, p. 121). It has often been noted that Levinas's respective estimations of Husserl and Heidegger follow parallel but opposing trajectories: initially critical of Husserl from a Heideggerian perspective, from 1933 on, Levinas took an increasingly critical distance from Heidegger's thought. At the same time, his view of Husserl seemed to soften and, in a series of articles written after 1959, he discovered new possibilities and resources in Husserl's philosophy.

Levinas was naturalised as a French citizen in 1930 and was mobilised during the Second World War as an interpreter of German and Russian for the French army. He spent the years between 1940 and 1945 in a prisoner-of-war camp first in France and then in Germany. Although his wife survived the war, almost his entire family in Lithuania was massacred by the Nazis (see Poirié, 1987, p. 170). After the war, Levinas assumed the directorship of the *Ecole Normale Israélite Orientale*, an institution which produced teachers for the schools of the *Alliance Israélite Universelle*. During this time, he also returned to the texts of the Jewish tradition, studying the texts of the Bible and Talmud. Alongside a substantial number of philosophical essays published between 1947 and 1960, Levinas also produced more than fifty essays on various aspects of Jewish life, spirituality and education. In 1961, he published his first major work, *Totality and Infinity*, and in the same year received the French *doctorat d'Etat*. He was subsequently named to a position at the University of Poitiers, where he remained for several years before moving to the University of Nanterre and finally, in 1973, to the Sorbonne.

Existence and Existents and Time and the Other

In 1947, Levinas published two short works, *Existence and Existents* and *Time and the Other*, which inaugurated a more original philosophical project. The method and themes of both works are deeply indebted to the existential analytic of *Being and Time*. However, these early works also allude to the limits of the phenomenological project and, in *Existence and Existents*, Levinas remarks that, although his reflections are inspired by the ontological problematic opened up within Heidegger's philosophy, 'they are also governed by a profound need to leave the climate of that philosophy, and by the conviction that we cannot leave it for a philosophy that would be pre-Heideggerian' (Levinas, 1978, p. 19).

In these early works, Levinas contests Heidegger's identification of human existence with anxiety in the face of nothingness. In human existing, Levinas suggests, there is a horror of Being that is just as primordial as Heideggerian anxiety. This horror of the irremissable and obsessive weight of Being is disclosed in such subjective states as indolence and fatigue where there is an unending weariness of everything and nothing – that is, of everything and nothing in particular, indicating a weariness of existence itself. In an interpretation recognised as being ultimately quite foreign to Heidegger's own, Levinas describes Being as the 'there is' (*il y a*): an anonymous, impersonal existing without existents. The 'there is' is like the night in which no form is discernible; it is the watchfulness of insomnia, but without there being anyone who watches. In its obscurity and ambiguity, the 'there is' is the total absence of meaning or sense and, as such, is felt as a mute, indeterminate menace.

A central theme of the 1947 works, as well as of the short 1934 essay, 'De l'évasion', is the possibility of an escape from the senselessness of the 'there is'. Levinas's first idea was that the 'there is' might be transcended in the *hypostasis* by which a subject posits itself in Being and takes up its own existing in the world. However, he soon came to think that the ego in the world, far from escaping Being, is still burdened by its own existing, is still enchained to itself. At the very end of *Existence and Existents*, Levinas introduces the theme that will resound throughout his later work: transcendence cannot be accomplished by the subject's relation to itself or the world but only by a relation to absolute alterity.

In *Time and the Other*, this notion is explored first in the relation to death and then in the erotic relation to the feminine other. It is not the nothingness of death that interests Levinas, but its radical passivity. In death, the subject comes up against the limits of its own power as it finds itself in relation to an unassumable future. The relation to the feminine offers an even more fruitful exemplar of the relation to alterity, since here the ego maintains a relation to alterity which neither reduces the other to a moment of its own existing, nor finds itself negated or absorbed by the other (as in death). Sexual difference seemed to Levinas at this time to differ markedly from all other instances of difference which could be produced by logical or formal negation. The feminine appeared not merely as a quality different from the masculine, but 'as the very quality of difference', in such a way that alterity seemed to be the positive meaning and content of the feminine (Levinas, 1987b, p. 36). The structure of the relation to the feminine is determined in this early work as the caress. This notion inverts the structure of Husserlian intentionality in so far as it suggests a seeking or aiming which does 'know' what it seeks and does not accomplish the correlation of its terms.

Levinas's descriptions of the feminine and the caress came under attack as early as 1949, when, in the Preface to *The Second Sex*, Simone de Beauvoir criticised Levinas's philosophy for reproducing traditional masculine privilege in its portrayal of the feminine as 'other', thus implying that the subject or ego is necessarily or naturally male. In later works,

Levinas would substantially revise his conception of the feminine and, by the time of *Totality and Infinity*, it is no longer the principal or paradigmatic figure of alterity; Levinas speaks there simply of a non-gendered other. Furthermore, in that work, Levinas appears to relegate the feminine to the home or dwelling and to a relationship that is 'beyond' the ethical (both more and less than the ethical). In an essay entitled 'The Fecundity of the Caress' (see Cohen, 1986, pp. 231–56), Luce Irigaray challenges the subordination, and even erasure, of feminine desire in Levinas's work after *Time and the Other*, as well as his subordination of sexual to ethical difference. Her formulation of these issues offers one of the most fruitful criticisms of Levinas's thought to date and provides the framework for many current discussions of Levinas and the feminine.

Totality and Infinity

In *Totality and Infinity*, the themes of Levinas's earlier works come together in a defence of the pre-eminence of the ethical relationship. The point of departure for this work is a critique of the history of Western philosophy which sees the principal trait of the latter as 'an attempt at universal synthesis, a reduction of all experience, of all that is reasonable, to a totality wherein consciousness embraces the world, leaves nothing other outside of itself, and thus becomes absolute thought' (Levinas, 1985, p. 75). Levinas reports that he first encountered the idea of a radical opposition to totality in Franz Rosenzweig's *Star of Redemption*, which criticises German Idealism as the highest expression of philosophy's pretension to encompass the All. According to Rosenzweig, the fundamental presupposition of philosophy from Parmenides to Hegel has been the conceivableness of the world; that is, the possibility of knowing the whole of what is in its systematic interconnection. In Hegel's system, this demand to know the whole is raised to its highest level of expression as knowledge now encompasses not only its object (the world), but also itself, its own history and conditions, within the totality. Against this vision of the immanent relation of Being and thought, Rosenzweig appealed to the contingent, finite existence of the factically existing 'I' as that which cannot be totalised within the system. Levinas, too, contests the immanence of Being, but identifies the possibility of transcendence not in the ego's self-relation, but in its relation to the other.

The first pages of *Totality and Infinity* describe transcendence in terms of a *metaphysical desire*. Metaphysics here indicates a movement toward what is radically and wholly *other*. Things encountered within the world are other, but only in a relative sense. The bread I eat or the landscape I contemplate are 'other' than me. However, 'I can "feed" on these realities and to a very great extent satisfy myself, as though I had simply been lacking them. Their *alterity* is thereby reabsorbed into my own identity as a thinker or possessor' (Levinas, 1969, p. 33). The other metaphysically desired is not other relative to me, or to any system of identity and difference, but absolutely other. In filling out the picture of metaphysical desire, Levinas distinguishes it from need, which originates in a lack and moves towards that which will satisfy it. Metaphysical desire finds no such satisfaction – not because there is nothing that would fulfil it, but because it does not aim at fulfilment. It has a different intention and structure than need, desiring beyond everything that would simply complete it. It is an aspiration, Levinas says, to exteriority.

As absolute, the alterity of the other is not the simple reversal of identity. The I and the other are not mutually defined and defining: they cannot be correlated or synthesised within a larger conceptual whole. Nor is the other's alterity based on any quality or property that would distinguish him from me, since this would presuppose between us precisely some prior totality or common ground against which such differences would appear. The I and the other do not share a common essence, and in an extreme formulation of his thesis, Levinas maintains that the I and the other do not coexist within the unity of a number, concept, or genus. But how can this be so? Levinas suggests that the 'void that breaks the totality can be maintained against an inevitably totalizing and synoptic thought only if thought finds itself *faced* with an other refractory to categories' (ibid., p. 40). This other is the other person (*l'Autrui*) who faces me, overflowing and escaping every representation and every attempt to grasp him as an object or theme.

The formal structure of the relation to alterity is given by the Cartesian idea of infinity. In the *Meditations on First Philosophy*, Descartes argued that a finite and imperfect being could not, through reflecting on its own nature, be the source of the idea of the infinite or perfection (God). Therefore, he argues, the idea of perfection must have been introduced into it from outside by a perfect being. In describing the relationship to the other, Levinas appropriates the speculative gesture of Descartes's argument without necessarily retaining its theological content. Levinas seizes on the notion of an idea which surpasses our ability to have or contain it. It is an impossible idea, whose content overflows our capacity to think it. In this, the idea of infinity is exceptional because it breaks with the model of adequation which otherwise defines the relation between thought and its object. In the relation to the other, the I is thus in relation with an infinity which it can in no way contain or reduce to a content of consciousness.

The face of the other, a key concept of Levinas's thought, indicates the manner in which the other both manifests himself and overflows every manifestation: 'The way in which the other presents himself, exceeding *the idea of the other in me*, we here name face' (ibid., p. 50). The face at each moment surpasses and destroys the surface presented in the assemblage of nose, eyes, mouth and forehead. Asked whether the face is a concrete phenomenon that can be found within experience, Levinas has expressed hesitation about the word *phenomenon* in this context and also about the possibility of a *phenomenology* of the face. A phenomenon is what appears; it has its meaning, as Husserl and Heidegger both taught, only within a horizon or context. A face, on the other hand, does not signify by virtue of the relationships it maintains, but strictly out of itself. The mode of manifestation characteristic of the face is *expression*. In saying that the face expresses itself, Levinas consciously confounds the spheres of vision and hearing and plays these two meanings of expression against one another. Expression is both gaze and speech; it is the absolute defencelessness and exposure of eyes that gaze at me and *call* me to responsibility, signifying not in a representation, but as a moral summons.

The face-to-face relation is accomplished, Levinas argues, only in language. This claim refers not only to the notion of expression just described, but also to the thesis that language involves an allocutive dimension in which the other is invoked and addressed prior to becoming a theme within the discourse:

> The word that bears on the Other as a theme seems to contain the Other. But already it is said to the Other who, as interlocutor, has quit the theme that encompassed him, and upsurges inevitably behind the said. [. . .] The knowledge that absorbs the Other is forthwith situated within the discourse I address to him. (ibid., p. 193)

The structure of language thus reproduces the structure already elucidated in the idea of infinity and metaphysical desire. The other overflows any objectifying theme, not because he is a special kind of object that somehow defies our ability to fully comprehend or represent him, but because the very discourse that thematises the other is also at the same time addressed to him and thus he figures outside of every theme. Here again, the other is a surplus in being and cannot be absorbed by the totalising aspirations of thought.

Although little has been said thus far about the subjectivity of the subject, *Totality and Infinity* offers a rich analysis of the mode of being of the ego. The point of departure for this analysis is the claim that transcendence requires, on the side of the ego, a *separation* or *atheism*. Just as the other cannot be the mere inverse of the same, so the ego must be produced through a positive movement of its own and not through a mere reversal of or opposition to alterity. The possibility of an opening to the other thus requires, as its condition, that the I already identifies itself outside of this relation in all the concreteness of egoism. Following Heidegger, Levinas rejects the modern conception of the subject as an unchanging substance or a tautological identity (A=A). However, he is also critical of the Heideggerian move which, in an attempt to interpret the subject apart from the categories that are valid for things, thereby divests the subject of any substantiality whatsoever. Levinas argues that the subjectivity of the subject consists in its ability to recover itself and reidentify itself throughout all that happens to it. The identity of the I is thus conceived in terms of a being who, in appropriating the world and enjoying it, is ultimately brought back into a relationship with itself. This return to self which characterises the ego's enjoyment of the world and its objects explains Levinas's designation of the sphere of the ego as a sphere of the *same*. The life of the ego is described in terms of the reduction of every other to the same, since every other is ultimately reduced to a moment of *my* knowing, *my* enjoyment, etc.

For Levinas, enjoyment is the fundamental mode of subjectivity. The food we eat or the home in which we dwell are not originally objects of representation, nor are they tools or equipment for sustaining life or carrying out its projects. They are what one *lives from*: bread may be a necessary condition of life and a means to sustenance, but it is never only this condition or this means, except perhaps in exceptional circumstances. The ego's existence in the world is not a bare concern with its own being but already a happiness, an interiority happy for its needs and finding enjoyment in their satisfaction.

The face of the other interrupts the naive enjoyment of the ego at home in the world, calling it into question. The other resists appropriation and possession by the ego, opposing it not as a force or as a second freedom which struggles to gain the upper hand, but in the nudity and destitution of the face. The other's resistance is not real, but ethical; if it were real, it would not break with the structure of relationships within the same. It would be an object of perception and calculation, anticipated and countered as one force within the play of a system. As ethical, this resistance is 'the resistance of what has no resistance' (ibid., p. 199). It disturbs the tranquillity of the ego and awakens it, Levinas says, to a recognition of the arbitrariness, contingency and brutality of its own freedom. According to Levinas, the Western tradition has held freedom to be something good in and of itself. Only the limitation of freedom – that is, the fact that freedom has not freely chosen itself and thus finds itself, as it were, imposed upon itself – is thought to require justification. Levinas argues, contrary to this position, that the spontaneity of freedom in itself gives freedom no rights. Indeed, freedom in this sense is no different from imperialism. Freedom is justified (rendered just) only in being called into question by the face of the other whose first word is 'you shall not kill.' In the face-to-face relation, the ego's freedom is not thwarted, but ashamed. Levinas points out that the 'action' of the face on the ego here is not a form of violence (wherein the ethical would begin as violence), but precisely puts an end to the violence and contingency of the same and, as such, opens it to Reason. The face that imposes itself here 'does not limit but promotes my freedom, by arousing my goodness.' (ibid., p. 200). The epiphany of the face 'is preeminently nonviolence, for instead of offending my freedom it calls it to responsibility and founds it' (ibid., p. 203). The theme of responsibility assumes even greater importance in Levinas's next work. However, already in the 1961 work it is described as an infinite, irrecusable responsibility for the other. To recognise the hunger of the other, to hear the other's destitution, is not to represent this hunger or destitution to oneself, but to discover oneself as responsible.

The principal question put to *Totality and Infinity* by its commentators had concerned the possibility of thinking (or thematising) the relation to non-thematisable alterity. More than anyone else, Jacques Derrida reflects on this problem in his celebrated article, 'Violence and Metaphysics'. Published in French in 1967 and translated into English in 1978, this essay brought Levinas's work to philosophical prominence outside France and shaped English language scholarship on Levinas for the next decade. Derrida focuses on Levinas's critique of phenomenology and fundamental ontology and provides a detailed reading of Levinas's relation to Husserl and Heidegger. Whether Derrida's essay should be viewed as a critique of Levinas (against which he would need defending) or whether the questions raised by Derrida already belong to the interior dialogue of Levinas's own discourse is still a matter of debate. Derrida shows both that Levinas's account must presuppose the very phenomenology that it seeks to call into question and also that its own discourse betrays the very 'phenomenon' (or non-phenomenon) which it seeks to elucidate. It is a question here of the difficulty of philosophising about that which

exceeds philosophy, or reflecting on that which one wants to claim is outside of, or beyond, reflection. 'We are wondering' Derrida writes, 'about the . . . necessity of lodging oneself within traditional conceptuality in order to destroy it' (Derrida, 1978, p. 111). After 1961, Levinas's thought became increasingly concerned with this problem, and the innovations, both thematic and linguistic, of his later work may be read as a response to Derrida and an attempt to radicalise the formulation of the problem of transcendence in a manner that overcomes the still too ontological presentations of *Totality and Infinity*.

Otherwise than Being or Beyond Essence

In *Otherwise than Being or Beyond Essence*, Levinas attempts to see in subjectivity, reconceptualised as pure exposure to the approach of the other, the possibility of a break with essence (or being). In his earlier work, it was the relation to radical alterity which heralded transcendence and an interruption of the ontological order. The ego was seen primarily in its separation from the other and in its autarchy, or self-sufficiency, as a being at home in the world. Indeed, a central difficulty raised by the analyses of *Totality and Infinity* concerned how the other could appear within the Same as disruption and the call to responsibility without thereby being reduced to a moment of the system and absorbed within it. The entire discussion of the face is addressed to this singular problem and possibility. In *Otherwise than Being*, Levinas reinterprets subjectivity in a way that attempts to see in the very unicity and identity of the 'I' an exception within being. He tries to show that the meaning of subjectivity, the very sense of sensibility, is already a being *for* the other, an exposure and proximity to the other. Transcendence will not be interpreted here as a passage outside of being to an 'elsewhere' or a beyond in the sense of an ethical 'world behind the scenes'. Rather, transcendence and subjectivity will be seen to be possible only as 'transcendence in immanence', a *for the other* already inscribed in the essence of being.

The term essence plays a fundamental role in this work and is employed in a sense quite different from its usual one where it signifies the quiddity or 'whatness' of things. Like Heidegger's *Sein*, essence is understood here in a verbal sense as the event or process of being. Renewing his critique of Western philosophy as ontology, Levinas suggests that the essence of being is interest – to be (*esse*) is to be interested (*interesse*). This latter claim has resonances with the Heideggerian notion of 'care' (*Sorge*), since, for Levinas, to be interested means to be concerned with one's own being, although here it is in the sense of having a stake in being or of striving to persist in one's own existing. Indeed, as this last locution suggests, Levinas ultimately identifies being in this text with Spinoza's *conatus essendi*. The drive of each being to persevere or maintain itself in being is the very 'essence' of being and determines being as a war of all against all. As in the Preface to *Totality and Infinity* and in earlier essays such as 'Ethics and Spirit' (collected in *Difficult Freedom*), war is emblematic of the violence and immanence of the ontological realm. Will peace then, as the opposite of war, be the figure of transcendence and ethics? Levinas maintains that although peace is undoubtedly superior to war, it still only the suspension of war. In peace, the struggle of each against each does not disappear but is preserved in commerce and exchange, and in the calculation, mediation and reciprocity these entail. In this work, peace will belong to politics and justice (here distinguished from the ethical much more sharply than in *Totality and Infinity*). Peace may then be a manner of being otherwise, but will not yet be the *otherwise than being* sought in this text.

The task of conceiving Being's other begins with a specification of what this other is not: it is *not* nothingness or not-being. Already in *Existence and Existents*, Levinas had seen that nothingness is not exterior to being but belongs inseparably to it. As mutually defining, being and nothingness illuminate one another within the unfolding of a speculative dialectic. Moreover, as the history of philosophy from Plato to Bergson had already shown, nothingness or not-being still *is*. The total negation which not-being would realise fails since nothingness is still something. Being appears to permit no exteriority and to leave nothing outside of itself. As Levinas wrote in 1947, the all-encompassing character of being is reflected in the fact that *there is*.

If Being's other is not nothingness, neither is it some manner or mode of being otherwise. What is sought, Levinas makes clear, is not some way *to be* otherwise, but an *otherwise than being*. This latter is misunderstood if it is interpreted as another (an other) realm or region of being, like a world behind the world, or a 'Heavenly City' that would be the aim and terminus of transcendence. Like Nietzsche, Levinas is deeply suspicious of the notion of a *Hinterwelt* and his rejection of this idea rules out in advance any merely religious interpretation of transcendence.

The difficulty of stating Being's other ultimately reflects the subordination of the Saying to the Said in language. The Said (*le Dit*) is Levinas's term for language in its objectifying and thematising dimensions. As the Said, language is a system of signs in terms of which contents are communicated and objects delivered over to thought. The Saying (*le Dire*), on the other hand, does not refer to the theme expressed in language, but to the fact that language is addressed to an other who is invoked prior to every thematisation. Levinas had already drawn attention to this allocutive feature of language in earlier works, although the full weight of the methodological problem involved in Saying is now felt more acutely. The problem is precisely this: the Saying which is supposed to be irreducible to a Said is none the less stated and conveyed before us as a philosophical theme. The *otherwise than being* can be uttered in language, even if this utterance is necessarily a betrayal. Levinas remarks that the subordination and betrayal of the Saying in the Said is not only the price demanded by manifestation, but perhaps the very task of philosophy. Can the Said, then, also be unsaid? Can the betrayal of the Saying in the Said be reduced or erased in an unsaying? Levinas claims that, although the unsaying is necessary to extract the *otherwise than being* from the Said, this unsaying cannot occur without leaving behind a mark that betrays this very erasure. Thus, the Saying, the Said and the unsaying follow upon the heels of one another in such a way that their passing leaves a trace on the smooth surface of being in which they are reabsorbed.

The impossibility of assembling these three moments together in a synchronic or simultaneous occurrence guides Levinas's characterisation of the situation presented here as diachrony. This term signals a lapse of time that does not return and cannot be recuperated. Levinas describes this lapse as an 'an-archic' and immemorial past; that is, a past which did not originate in a present and which is thus without an origin (in Greek, *arché*). Any linear regression necessarily fails to reach this pre-original past which remains foreign to every present and thus also to every re-presentation and history. The notion expressed here through the constellation of Saying, trace, diachrony and an-archic past is none other than the idea of infinity. Described in *Totality and Infinity* primarily as a surplus in being, an idea exceeding or overflowing our capacity to think it, the idea of infinity is here extended and deepened by being unfolded in a temporal dimension.

The problem of transcendence can be reformulated in these new terms. How can the Saying be led to betray itself in a Said? How is the diachrony of an immemorial past signalled in the present? Levinas proposes that the concrete case of this singular relation to a never-present past is found in the 'extraordinary and everyday event of my responsibility for the faults or the misfortunes of others' (Levinas, 1981, p. 10). The paradox of responsibility – that I am obliged by the other without this obligation having begun in my freedom – is captured precisely in the figure of a past that was never present: in responsibility I discover myself as already obligated to the other, already called upon, without there ever having been a time when I could have heard this call and freely responded to it. The call of responsibility belongs to an an-archic past that cannot be made present (cannot be represented, except by an 'abuse' of language) so that I might now freely assume my obligations and restore freedom to its sovereign position.

Unlike the familiar conception of responsibility as accountability for one's own actions and affairs, Levinas characterises responsibility as an infinite, irrecusable, non-reciprocal (or asymmetrical) responsibility to and for the other person. I am responsible for the other to the extreme point of being responsible for *her* responsibility, without

having taken on any obligations in her regard, without waiting for her to be responsible for me in turn. In responsibility, the ego substitutes itself for the other, *is* the one-for-the-other. This conception of radical responsibility is possible only if responsibility is not external to subjectivity – something it assumes – but is the concrete meaning of subjectivity.

One of the most strikingly original aspects of *Otherwise than Being* is its analysis of subjectivity as a sensibility constituted at the limits of an extreme exposure to the approach of the other. In the very earliest works, the ego was described as a hypostasis; by 1961, it had become the realm of the Same. In *Otherwise than Being*, Levinas defines subjectivity in a radically new formulation as 'a passivity more passive than all passivity'. This expression designates a passivity devoid of every vestige of activity, beyond even the minimal and purely negative activity of a capacity to receive. The approach of the other is undergone in this extreme passivity, without my being able to appropriate or direct it. Radical alterity is thus given not to comprehension (which always goes out actively to meet its object), but to sensibility. Sensibility announces a susceptibility to the impact of the other; it is the extreme passivity of exposure:

> Vulnerability, exposure to outrage, to wounding, passivity more passive than all patience, passivity of the accusative form, trauma of accusation suffered by a hostage to the point of persecution, implicating the identity of the hostage who substitutes himself for the others: all this is the self . . . (ibid., p. 15)

The hyperbole which defines Levinas's later style is not only a rhetorical exuberance but is exaggeration raised to the level of method. What becomes possible through hyperbole, which stretches concepts until they break free of their old moorings and come to signify in new ways and through new associations, is precisely the Saying of an otherwise than being.

A final point that must be touched upon here is the move from the pre-original vocation of Saying back into the Said, conceptuality and thematisation. In *Totality and Infinity*, the pure relation to the face awakens reason to its own dogmatism and institutes critique. In *Otherwise than Being*, the necessity of the move into representation and theory is still inscribed in the meaning of transcendence, but with an important modification: Levinas argues that if I were faced only with one single other who commands me to responsibility, the infinity of responsibility would be unproblematic in itself. However, this is never the case. In being before the other, I am also already before a third, the other of this other. This 'third party' interrupts the singular, or one-way, directionality of my being for the other, diverting it towards infinite others, and thus introducing the limit of ethical responsibility in the birth of the question of justice. Faced by infinite others, the I who must respond has the task of comparing incomparables. At this point (always already there in the first encounter with a face), justice, as the calculation and comparison of interest, as the rational order of peace, comes onto the scene. This reversal of the ethical into the political, like the earlier betrayal of the Saying in the Said nevertheless always retains a trace of that which has passed by in a past which defies re-presentation.

Conclusion

The importance of Levinas's contribution to the question of the ethical is widely recognised today. While the main lines of his exceptional thought continue to evoke extended discussion and interpretation, several areas of critical debate have arisen within the commentaries on his work and deserve to be mentioned here, even if only briefly. Predominant among these is the question of the relationship between Judaism and philosophy in Levinas's texts. Levinas categorically rejects the appellation 'religious' or 'Jewish thinker', if this indicates the presence of an appeal to religious tradition as the authority for his philosophical positions. Neither the Jewish tradition nor its texts serve this function in his thought. However, he maintains that every philosophy is based on pre-philosophical experiences from which it lives and that the Bible and Talmud represent a tradition of thought at least as old and distinguished as that of Western philosophy. While his work is not adequately characterised as a synthesis of Judaism and philosophy, nor even (as in his own words) as a 'translation' of the one into the other, it is undoubtedly true that Judaism is the 'other' of this philosophy, with all the richness given to that term here.

A second set of concerns arises from the relation of the ethical to other branches of philosophical enquiry, in particular, to politics, aesthetics and the erotic. In all three cases, Levinas privileges the ethical over the other modes of relationship, often in ways that seem unnecessarily restrictive or exclusive. In the case of the relation to politics, it has been asked whether his theory is capable of supporting a full-scale politics and whether it gives any certain indication of where such a politics is to be sought. With respect to art and the erotic, it is Levinas's seeming ambivalence about these realms that has attracted attention and has stimulated new research.

Finally, there is the question of method. On the one hand, Levinas himself did not think that transparency in method was possible. On the other hand, he considered himself above all a phenomenologist, in spite of the distance taken from Husserl and Heidegger. Much has been written about his relation to the phenomenological tradition – apart from which his work cannot be fully understood – and certainly his thought comprises one of the most extended reflections on the inner meaning and limitations of the phenomenological project and method. Still more remains to be written and new directions and resources for phenomenology remain to be mined from within this extraordinary philosophy.

Bibliography

Writings

Levinas, Emmanuel (1969), *Totality and Infinity*, trans. Alphonso Lingis, Pittsburgh: Duquesne University Press.
— (1973), *The Theory of Intuition in Husserl's Phenomenology*, trans. André Orianne, Evanston: Northwestern University Press.
— (1974), *En Découvrant l'existence avec Husserl et Heidegger*, 3rd edn, Paris: Vrin.
— (1978), *Existence and Existents*, trans. Alphonso Lingis, The Hague: Kluwer Academic Publishers.

— (1981), *Otherwise than Being or Beyond Essence*, trans. Alphonso Lingis, The Hague: Martinus Nijhoff Publishers.

— (1982), *De Dieu qui vient à l'idée*, Paris: Vrin.

— (1985), *Ethics and Infinity*, trans. Richard Cohen, Pittsburgh: Duquesne University Press.

— (1987a), *Collected Philosophical Papers*, trans. Alphonso Lingis, Dordrecht: Martinus Nijhoff Publishers.

— (1987b), *Time and the Other*, trans. Richard Cohen, Pittsburgh: Duquesne University Press.

— (1989), *The Levinas Reader*, ed. Seán Hand, Oxford: Oxford University Press.

— (1990), *Nine Talmudic Readings*, ed. Annette Aronowicz, Bloomington: Indiana University Press.

— (1991), *Difficult Freedom*, trans. Seán Hand, Baltimore: Johns Hopkins University Press.

— (1991), *Entre nous*, Paris: Vrin.

— (1996), *Basic Philosophical Writings*, eds Adriaan T. Peperzak, Simon Critchley and Robert Bernasconi, Bloomington: Indiana University Press.

References and further reading

Bernasconi, Robert and Simon Critchley (1991), *Re-Reading Levinas*, Bloomington: Indiana University Press.

Bernasconi, Robert and David Wood (1988), *The Provocation of Levinas: Rethinking the Other*, London and New York: Routledge.

Chalier, Catherine (1982), *Figures du féminin*, Paris: La nuit surveillée.

Cohen, Richard (1994), *Elevations: The Height of the Good in Rosenzweig and Levinas*, Chicago: The University of Chicago Press.

— (ed.) (1986), *Face to Face with Levinas*, New York: State University of New York Press.

Critchley, Simon (1992), *The Ethics of Deconstruction: Derrida and Levinas*, Oxford: Blackwell Publishers.

Derrida, Jacques (1978), 'Violence and Metaphysics: An Essay on the Thought of Emmanuel Levinas', in *Writing and Difference*, trans. Alan Bass, Chicago: The University of Chicago Press, pp 79–153.

Gibbs, Robert (1992), *Correlations in Rosenzweig and Levinas*, Princeton: Princeton University Press.

Llewelyn, John (1995), *Emmanuel Levinas: The Genealogy of Ethics*, London and New York: Routledge.

Peperzak, Adriaan (1983), *To the Other: An Introduction to the Philosophy of Emmanuel Levinas*, West Lafayette, IN: Purdue University Press.

— (ed.) (1995), *Ethics as First Philosophy*, New York and London: Routledge.

Poirié, François (1987), *Emmanuel Levinas. Qui êtes-vous?*, Lyon: La Manufacture.

8.3

INTO THE ABYSS: DELEUZE

Alistair Welchman

Introduction

Gilles Deleuze was born in 1925, and killed himself seventy years later. He taught philosophy at Lyon, and then – after the institutional fragmentation that was the government's response to the student-driven quasi-revolution of 1968 – at the University of Paris VIII (Vincennes). Although his work is only now coming to prominence in the English-speaking world, he has achieved great notoriety in France: he is widely credited with inaugurating the post-structuralist movement with his 1962 *Nietzsche and Philosophy*, as well as with providing its definitive text, the 1972 *Anti-Oedipus* (co-written with Félix Guattari). His colleague and friend, Michel Foucault, has even suggested that 'perhaps one day this century will be known as Deleuzian' (Foucault, 1977, p. 165).

Deleuze's written output can be untidily but functionally divided into three periods: first, an early phase (up to the late 1960s) of scholarly works that examine individual philosophers (Hume, Bergson, Kant, Nietzsche and Spinoza); second, a short middle period of two books – *The Logic of Sense* and *Difference and Repetition* – published in the late 1960s and in which he achieved a genuine independence of thought and no longer expressed himself vicariously though commentary on other philosophers; and third, a late period, characterised by a collaborative writing technique, the most famous product of which is the two-volume *Capitalism and Schizophrenia*.

This taxonomy is untidy because Deleuze's breadth of interest and reference cannot be contained within a purely philosophical lexicon. In particular, he was a writer of unusual aesthetic sensitivity, and his work, across all the three time-periods, is strewn with texts concerning literature, art and film: a book on Proust written in the 1960s, but reworked several times; one on Kafka written between the two volumes of *Capitalism and Schizophrenia*; a book on the Anglo-Irish painter Francis Bacon; and a two-volume interpretation of cinema. Moreover, there are late-period books written with Guattari that hark back to the more decorous style of the scholarly monographs (the reflective *What is Philosophy?* of 1991), and, in fact, the scholarly works themselves never really stopped: Deleuze published studies on Leibniz and Foucault as late as the 1980s. The groupings retain however a heuristic validity for a philosophical approach to Deleuze's thought.

The transcendental

A number of twentieth-century French thinkers have entertained unusually close intellectual relations with a prior German thinker; and Deleuze too can be helpfully considered to have such a special relationship, in his case with Kant. Even though he described his monograph on Kant as 'a book on an enemy' (Cressole, 1973, p. 110), Deleuze's thought can nevertheless be, at least in a provisional way, helpfully represented as a kind of Kantianism.

Deleuze's relation to Kant is ambivalent because Kant represented both what Deleuze most liked about philosophy, as well as what he most disliked about it. He appreciates Kant's critical orientation, the fact that he did not merely assume things as given, but rather attempted to find out how they are produced. For Deleuze, Kant's discovery of the philosophical plane of the transcendental was foremost amongst his achievements. The transcendental enabled Kant to occupy a philosophical position outside of the dogmatic philosophies of his day – psychological empiricism and theological rationalism – and thereby to subject them to critique, bringing into question both a dogmatic faith in reason, God and logic (theological rationalism) *and* the equally dogmatic assumption that what is given directly in conscious human experience is the immutable baseline of philosophical inquiry (psychological empiricism).

However, Deleuze disliked the fact that Kant ends up defending (at a new and more complicated level) the very same dogmas he had set out to critique. In the case of rationalism, the avowed intent of Kant's works is to provide a more compelling legitimation for God and the immortal soul. In the case of empiricism, it is not so obvious, but Deleuze argues that Kant 'traces the so-called transcendental structures from the empirical acts of a psychological consciousness' (Deleuze, 1968, p. 135) and therefore reproduces the unities of subject and object given in empirical consciousness (albeit at another level of complication).

According to Deleuze, the transcendental demands a way of thinking that is not modelled on the empirical (which is taken for granted or understood merely through common sense), but rather a way of thinking that subjects the limitations, illusions and complacencies of common sense to critique, attempting to find the conditions of production for what is usually simply taken as given. This critical motif of production pervades Deleuze's thought so that even at the end of his career he was able to define philosophy as 'the art of forming, inventing, and fabricating concepts' (Deleuze, 1991, p. 2); philosophy for Deleuze must at all costs avoid the obvious, the banalities of common sense.

This means first of all that Deleuze refuses all ways of thinking still lodged in subjectivity or the cate-

gories of consciousness. Drawing upon Bergson's criticism of the possible as merely the shadow of the actual (see Deleuze, 1966), he sees all such phenomenologies as just sophistications of Kant's tendency to trace the transcendental from empirical psychology. Deleuze often repeats the slogan that the transcendental conditions of everyday experience, the conditions of its production, cannot resemble the everyday experience they produce: 'The mistake of all determinations of the transcendental as consciousness is to think of the transcendental as the image of, as resembling, what it is supposed to ground' (Deleuze, 1969, p. 105).

The critical and productive bite of this argument – that the transcendental does not resemble the empirical – is rather sharper than its bald statement might lead one to believe. It is a very radical thought. The empirical realm that Kant sought to underwrite is not only constituted by the stable psychological subjectivity of personal identity but also by a reflected world of individuated stable objects which is both grasped and made possible through the application of concepts or general terms. It follows that the transcendental, if it is to be thought of as properly distinct from the empirical, cannot be composed of individuals (stable individuated objects), nor of persons (subjective unities mirroring the stability of the world of objects) nor of categorical concepts (ensuring smooth transition between stable subjects and the world of stable objects). The transcendental must, therefore, be 'essentially pre-individual, non-personal and a-conceptual' (ibid., p. 52).

Deleuze's philosophical prime directive is to avoid the vulgarity and hubris of assuming that the cosmos is made in our own image, that it is in any way intended for us, or that we occupy a privileged position within it. The idea of the transcendental responds to this injunction, because, for Deleuze, the transcendental must not resemble what it conditions. Starting from what is most familiar therefore – consciousness and a world constituted in accordance with consciousness – Deleuze does not follow the reassuring parallels between transcendental and empirical along which we are guided by Kant and phenomenology, but instead journeys into the unknown.

Disjunction

The above formulation of the transcendental is, however, merely negative: *pre*-individual, *non*-personal and *a*-conceptual. A positive thought consonant with Deleuze's intellectual demands is required. In the *Logic of Sense*, Deleuze outlines a first attempt at providing such a positive understanding. The book is organised by a three-way distinction. He starts by introducing a term to describe the false dichotomy whose rejection will open the space for his third term. He calls such false dichotomies 'exclusive disjunctions': they are demands of common sense that present us with pre-given alternatives from which to choose: *either* this *or* that. One compelling instance of an exclusive disjunction is between *either* pure chaos *or* an agent that organises chaos from on high or transcendentally:

> What is common to metaphysics and to transcendental philosophy is, above all, the alternative that they impose on us: *either* an undifferentiated ground, a groundlessness, formless non-being, an abyss without differences and without properties – *or* a supremely individuated Being, an intensely personalised Form. Without this Being or this Form, you'll only have chaos. (Deleuze, 1969, pp. 105–6)

Deleuze often presents this alternative in spatial terms: *either* a bottomless depth of chaos *or* an agent of order coming from on high. This false demand is as much political as it is epistemological: there must be order, otherwise we will all be in the abyss. At this point in his career, Deleuze's way out of this disjunction is to negotiate *between* the heights and the depths, along the surface. In other words, he rejects the opposition, and attempts to find another term hidden by the exclusive nature of the terms. He writes:

> The transcendental field is no more individual than personal – and no more general than universal. Is this to say that it is a groundlessness with neither shape nor difference, a schizophrenic abyss? Everything suggests not. (ibid., p. 99)

The surface Deleuze discovers operating between the false opposition of pure chaos and pure organisation is the surface of sense. The vocabulary of surfaces had been a popular trope for many in the structural movement, and at this point, therefore, he finds a sort of *rapprochement* with structuralism. But even here – where he might be most easily mistaken for a follower of Parisian intellectual fashion – he still manifests considerable conceptual originality: the 'structures' that he alludes to owe as much to a reading of Russell's paradoxes, the playfulness of Lewis Carroll and the pre-Socratics as they do to the more canonical structural analyses of Lévi-Strauss.

In fact, even within the French academic matrix, Deleuze's thought of the schizoid abyss signals a close alliance with one of the more deviant avatars of structuralism: Lacanian psychoanalysis. Lacan – and Melanie Klein, who was a major influence on him – enabled Deleuze to add a highly suggestive genetic or historical dimension often absent from the more dominant forms of structuralism itself. The schizophrenic abyss corresponds to Klein's analysis of the first stage of pre-Oedipal sexuality during which the child makes no distinction between itself and the world, and inhabits a domain constituted only by partial and not completed objects. Furthermore, Deleuze conceives of the transcendent heights as depressive, in accordance with Klein's second stage, during which the child first encounters a completed object (the mother's breast). The three-way distinction proposed by Deleuze distinguishes between transcendent agents of organisation (associated philosophically with Plato and Kant, spatially with height and psychoanalytically with depression); chaos (associated philosophically with the Pre-Socratics, Schelling and Schopenhauer, spatially with depth and psychoanalytically with schizophrenia); and Deleuze's new concept of sense (associated philosophically with the Stoics, spatially with the surface and psychoanalytically with perversion).

Deleuze's first positive answer to the question 'What *is* the transcendental field?' is therefore preemptive. Simply because this field is pre-individual, non-personal and a-conceptual, and simply because one rejects the domination of a transcendent Platonic form or a Kantian transcendental category of consciousness, does not mean that all that is left is the schizoid abyss. There is another alternative: the surface on which sense develops autonomously.

It must be added that Deleuze evinces here some fear of this abyss. He argues for instance, that:

sense itself [has] a fragility that can make it topple over into non-sense, the relations of the logical proposition risk losing all measure, signification, manifestation and designation risk sinking into the undifferentiated abyss of a groundlessness that entails only the pulsation of a monstrous body. This is why, beyond the tertiary order of the proposition and even beyond the secondary order of sense, we anticipate a terrible primary order wherein language as a whole becomes enfolded. (ibid., p. 120)

This is somewhat ironic because Deleuze's later development, and especially his work with Guattari (as the title *Capitalism and Schizophrenia* obviously suggests), might easily be described as a fall into precisely this schizophrenic abyss of primary libidinal process.

Like Quine, Deleuze thinks of logical operations – connection, conjunction and, here, disjunction – as synthetic or productive. However, he thinks they can be used in two ways. Exclusive disjunction (as we have seen) is his name for the uncritical use of disjunction: it presupposes a grid of dogmatically-asserted options that exhaust the entire field of possibilities, *either* this *or* that. On the other hand, he defines the critical operation of disjunction as *inclusive*: it affirms precisely the distance that separates the incompatible.

In *The Logic of Sense* Deleuze rejects the exclusive disjunction between chaos and organisation. but only by positing a third option that is itself exclusive: *either* (chaos) . . . *or* (transcendent organisation) . . . *or* (sense). It is not clear that this escapes fully from the logic of exclusion that he is criticising. Indeed, his later works suggest a different solution, a fully-inclusive disjunction of chaos and organisation in which chaos composes its own organisation.

This may look like the very abyss that Deleuze (as well as Plato and Kant) wanted at all costs to avoid falling into; but it is not. His second solution involves completely rethinking chaos, so that it can be seen as something other than merely an intellectual and political threat legitimating a perpetual law-and-order crackdown. In a sense, his later

works fall into the trap of the abyss that he so carefully avoids here; but it turns out not to be a *trap* at all. Thus, by the time of *Capitalism and Schizophrenia*, we see that all the productive machinery that had, in *The Logic of Sense*, been associated with the third option of sense's surface – most notably the three productive syntheses – has migrated into the schizophrenic abyss itself. His point now is that the abyss – still impersonal and pre-individual – is not undifferentiated, but is itself a productive power; and agents of transcendent organisation are strictly redundant.

This new move is not entirely absent from *The Logic of Sense*. Deleuze acknowledged that sense has two separate origins: one – 'passive' (ibid., p. 117) or 'static genesis' (ibid., p. 109ff) – arising from a 'quasi-cause' (ibid., 94) operating on the same incorporeal level as sense itself; but the other – 'dynamic genesis' (ibid., p. 186ff) – being in the abyss itself. Deleuze's temporary alliance with psychoanalysis allows him, even at this stage, to contemplate, at the end of *The Logic of Sense*, a genetic or developmental account of the emergence of sense out of the abyss. This analysis of the dynamic genesis of sense therefore announces what was to become the central motif of his later work: the self-organisation of the chaotic abyss.

Unilateral distinction

A notably less hostile characterisation of chaos is, in fact, presented in Deleuze's 1968 book, *Difference and Repetition*. There Deleuze thinks of chaos not as the undifferentiated, but as difference in itself. He is attracted to the ideas of difference and repetition because they have, in the history of philosophy, always been subordinated to identity, and have never actually been thought through themselves. Specific difference in Aristotle, for instance, works only in the service of the identity of the species thus differentiated, while repetition is merely the condition for the recognition of identity. Working through the ideas of difference and repetition in their own right reveals them, in fact, to be extremely subversive.

Difference is subordinated to identity when it remains dogmatically empirical or extrinsic; that is, when it is thought of as the difference *between* two already constituted things. What, then, is the idea of difference as such, difference that does not distinguish anything, that is not just between other things? The first answer that Deleuze gives is that it is repetition, but a repetition peculiar to the existence of the object in intuition prior to conceptualisation:

> Repetition appears as difference without a concept, repetition which indefinitely escapes continued conceptual difference. It expresses a power peculiar to the existent, a stubbornness of the existent in intuition which resists specification by concepts no matter how far it is taken. (Deleuze, 1968, pp. 13–14)

When something is repeated, there are clearly two things, and therefore a difference; but since *the same thing* is repeated, and since, by definition, two instances of the same thing share the same conceptual determination, then it follows that no possible conceptual specification can reach down into that difference. There is something going on in reality that conceptual grids cannot capture, 'the net is so loose that the largest fish pass through' (ibid., p. 68). In this definition, however, although difference and repetition begin to contest the dominance of identity, and although they thereby begin to open up a transcendental field that is not only traced from the empirical, they still nevertheless presuppose identity: the *same* thing is at issue.

Deleuze's next move is to suppose 'something that distinguishes itself – and yet that from which it distinguishes itself does not distinguish itself from it' (ibid., p. 28). He goes on to define this as 'unilateral distinction'. One of its most important uses is to specify the relation between a rigorously thought-out transcendental ground and what it grounds. He goes on to say: '[the ground] is there, staring at us, but without eyes. The individual distinguishes itself from it, but it does not distinguish itself, continuing rather to cohabit with that which divorces itself from it' (ibid., p. 152). The idea is structurally similar to the earlier argument that difference is repetition, but without the identity conditions. One might think about it in terms of 'points of view' (although this would only be a way of talking; there could be nothing subjective about it). From the point of view of the ground, what it

grounds is only the ground repeating itself; it is only from the point of view of the grounded that the ground is differentiated from it. The ground is, in a sense, indifferent to what happens to it. But, as Deleuze argues, indifference has two faces:

> the undifferenciated abyss, the black nothing, the indeterminate animal in which everything is dissolved – but also the white nothingness, the once more calm surface upon which float unconnected determinations like scattered members: a head without a neck, an arm without a shoulder, eyes without brows. (ibid., p. 28)

An example might be this: humanity has traditionally tried to differentiate itself specifically from the rest of nature (as having a soul, a mind, being capable of language, of culture, etc.). But from the point of view of nature, humanity is just another part of nature. The important thing is that, when the grounded differentiates itself, it does so empirically, using an extrinsic concept of difference; but the ground itself is difference itself, intrinsic or intensive difference. Deleuze is now not afraid of naming this ground of difference, chaos, or the 'chaosmos' (ibid., p. 299). Unilateral difference completes his thought of the inclusive disjunction of chaos and its immanent organisation.

Desiring-production

With the publication in 1972 of the first volume of *Capitalism and Schizophrenia: Anti-Oedipus*, all hesitations on Deleuze's part – hesitations, as it were, on the edge of the abyss – were swept aside. He no longer worked alone, but in collaboration with the radical psychoanalyst Félix Guattari. He had already observed in *The Logic of Sense* that 'it takes two be to be mad, you're always mad when there's two of you' (Deleuze, 1969, p. 79); and it is certainly true for Deleuze and Guattari: their collectively authored texts, although still absolutely philosophically rigorous, could no longer be read as simply intellectual works, even in the broader sense that 'intellectual' has in France. *Anti-Oedipus* succeeded in doing the impossible – profoundly shocking a French intellectual audience who, since 1945 at least, had positively thrived on maximally unorthodox works of conceptual *brio*. There is something to offend everyone in *Anti-Oedipus*: Freudians are the object of a massive and scornful polemic, but Marxists get hardly less aggressive treatment; phenomenology is abused and then ignored; and structuralism is equated with despotism. Its style is intensive, inspired and irresponsible, observing no academic speed limits or disciplinary territories.

There are many ways to approach *Anti-Oedipus*: as a sustained and often vitriolic attack on psychoanalysis; as the accomplishment of the Marx-Freud synthesis that had been the elusive goal of radical intellectuals in both France and Germany for half a century; as a critique of the concept of ideology; as a universal history; as a novel account of capitalism; as a polemic against the role of French Communist party in the events of May 1968; or even as a highly original intervention in contemporary biology. However, it remains, above all, a powerful work of philosophy. For Deleuze and Guattari, a detailed critique of real social practices – an account of their mode of production – could only be organised with newly-constructed concepts. The philosophical task of *Anti-Oedipus* is the construction of just these new concepts, and, once again, this philosophical base is Kantian in orientation. Deleuze and Guattari explained themselves thus:

> We make use of Kantian terminology for a simple reason. In what he termed the critical revolution, Kant intended to discover criteria immanent to understanding so as to distinguish the legitimate and the illegitimate uses of the synthesis of consciousness. In the name of *transcendental* philosophy (immanence of criteria), he therefore denounced the transcendent use of synthesis such as appeared in metaphysics. In like fashion we are compelled to say that psychoanalysis has its metaphysics – its name is Oedipus. And that a revolution – this time materialist – can proceed only by way of a critique of Oedipus, by denouncing the illegitimate use of the syntheses of the unconscious as found in Oedipal psychoanalysis, so as to rediscover a transcendental unconscious defined by the immanence of its criteria, and a corresponding practice that we shall call schizo-analysis. (Deleuze and Guattari, 1972, p. 75)

The basic point of *Anti-Oedipus* – and one that marks a conceptual as well as a political advance on his earlier work – is that social production is the direct result of an *illegitimate use* of the syntheses of the transcendental unconscious. Social production is the production, consumption, distribution and allocation of stable commodity-objects to secured subjects; that is, what Deleuze had previously called the empirical, but now with greater attention paid to its politically repressive characteristics. This marks an advance because the transcendental is no longer thought of as simply the way the empirical is produced, but as a critique that attacks the empirical as a paralogism, a transcendental illusion. One of the most compelling results of this extreme form of critique is that it gives Deleuze's philosophical concepts serious political weight.

True to the attempt to synthesise Marx (production) and Freud (desire), one of the most important terms in *Anti-Oedipus* is **desiring-production**. Desiring-production is not merely an amalgam of the Freudian desire and Marxist production (Deleuze and Guattari often polemic against such anaemic strategies for erecting a Marx-Freud parallel); it is also the result of rigorous critique of both desire and production.

Freud and Marx acquired the crucial thoughts of (respectively) desire and production from the margins of traditional philosophy. Deleuze and Guattari argued that the canonical approaches to both desire and production have been uncritically dogmatic and idealist. Desire has been thought of as fundamentally organised around the notion of lack: to desire something, you must lack it (see, for a canonical instance, Plato's *Symposium* 200a ff.). Equally, production has been thought of as basically transitive, involving agents of production, a raw material upon which they operate, and with an end product separate from the process of production itself.

The division of desire and production into a subject and an object separates both desire from production, and also desiring-production from what it can do. This analysis is structurally similar to Deleuze's earlier account of Nietzsche's argument that active force is separated from what it can do by the reactive forces of monotheistic religion (Deleuze, 1962, p. 57). Again following Nietzsche's thought quite closely (see ibid., pp. 55f.), Deleuze suggests that the separation is predicated on the intervention of a certain idealism. The distinction between the psychic presence of the object of desire and its real absence bifurcates the world along the same fissure as Christian otherworldliness; and the condensation of spontaneity into a unique agent of production allocates efficacy to subjectivity, purging matter of its activity. But Deleuze is not now merely concerned to show how this separation is produced, but also to show that it is produced *illegitimately*, on the basis of a paralogistic use of desiring-production.

Desiring-production is therefore a philosophically critical (intransitive), and hence materialist, use of desire and production; but it also serves to integrate the apparently incompatible terms used by Marx and Freud, and the philosophical argument is thereby actualised into a political one.

For Marx, the production processes of political economy are absolutely basic: desire can be acknowledged only as a secondary formation at the level of superstructure, not as base. His attempt to locate desire exclusively in the superstructure leads directly to a dualism, and hence to idealism. The major problem for Marxists in the twentieth century has been to explain how capital has succeeded in warding off proletarian revolution when, in Weimar Germany, for example, all the 'objective' conditions pointed towards it. Because desire cannot play a role in base-level explanation, the result has been widespread use of a concept of ideology that is not directly determined by the economic base (having instead a 'relative autonomy'). The masses are duped into misrecognising their 'objective' revolutionary situation by essentially ideal means; that is, ideas disconnected from the base, and therefore forming a dualism.

Inversely, for Freud, desire is the primary process, and can therefore only make mediated contact with the production of social and historical reality. Psychoanalytic desire is not completely removed from production, but where it is productive it is purely ideal, producing only fantasy and not reality, and in particular, producing only the family romances whose structure is most clearly revealed in Sophocles' tragedy *Oedipus the King*. Desire can only be displaced from its original objects (mummy and daddy) by means of sublimation; social, historical,

economic and political production is never a part of the libidinal base: there is always, according to the generalised reductionism of psychoanalysis, a daddy lurking underneath the foreman, the general, the political leader or the priest.

Deleuze and Guattari are particularly critical of psychoanalysis's treatment of schizophrenia. Delirium is, in contrast to neurotic obsessions, characteristically very heavily invested in social and historical reality. For psychoanalysis, however, the essential property of delirium is precisely the loss of reality. *Anti-Oedipus* argues that this is because the familial content of the neuroses is the only reality that psychoanalysis is prepared to acknowledge.

Desiring-production shows that desire itself is deliriously productive, directly investing social and historical reality with charges of libido, and, at the same time, shows that the productive base is itself suffused with desire. Desire is unconscious, prior to the constitution of discrete subjects and objects of desire; but it is not a stage on which a Greek drama is endlessly replayed, it is a productive factory machining reality.

Desiring-production is the libidinally-active critical philosophical and political base of *Anti-Oedipus*. It operates through legitimate use of the syntheses of production (inherited from the architectonic of *The Logic of Sense*), and represents a refinement of Deleuze's general strategy of accessing a genuine materialist transcendental; in this case, the transcendental unconscious as 'universal primary production' (Deleuze and Guattari, 1972, p. 5). Its scope is, however, much wider than either Freud or Marx's terms, indeed it precedes (and succeeds) social production, and thereby human culture, as a whole. They describe It (the French, *le Ça*, translating Freud's term *das Es*, usually rendered as Id) like this in the opening passage of *Anti-Oedipus*:

> It is at work everywhere, functioning smoothly at times, at other times in fits and starts. It breathes, It heats, It eats. It shits and fucks. What a mistake ever to have said *the* It. Everywhere *It* is machines – real ones, not figurative ones: machines driving other machines, machines being driven by other machines, with all the necessary couplings and connections. (ibid., p. 1)

The key to *Anti-Oedipus* is that social production is an illegitimate use of the productive syntheses; that is to say, the repression of desiring-production. At its most philosophical level, Deleuze and Guattari's definition of illegitimacy is Kantian: a synthesis is used illegitimately if the criteria for its application are transcendent. This is actually a familiar Deleuzian argument. Criteria are transcendent when the use of a synthesis of production presupposes other unproduced (and therefore merely given) products. The connective synthesis of desiring-production, for example, is thought illegitimate when a pre-given ego, determined with respect to sex, generation and vital state, is connected with a unified object of desire.

But again, this philosophical argument is actualised into a socio-political argument, one grounded in a Marxist account of exploitation. Marx's argument, very briefly, is that human labour is always what is actually productive, but that, under certain historical conditions, accumulations of dead labour-power (capital), appear – through a kind of transcendental illusion – to take on an autonomous productive capacity. Deleuze and Guattari's argument is, as noted above, wider than Marx's, but it shares the same structure. Under certain conditions (those of social history in general), the auto-productive regime of desiring-production (analogous to labour) generates a moment of anti-production (analogous to capital) on which the productive forces fall back, and which therefore appears to appropriate production to itself (see, for example, ibid., pp. 9–16). Social production represents an illegitimate use of the syntheses because it always presupposes and represses the prior activity of desiring-production.

Illegitimate use of the syntheses is therefore not only a philosophical problem, but also a real social one; and, correlatively, critique is not just an intellectual process, but a revolutionary social process. In general, *Anti-Oedipus* shows that the primary function of the social 'has always been to codify the flows of desire, to inscribe them, to record them, to see to it that no flow exists that is not properly dammed up, channelled, regulated' (ibid., 1972, p. 33). Damming up the flow represses the transcendental unconscious, and institutes the breaks in desiring-production that constitute global persons, subjects, objects and statistical entities as such. The philosophical problem of *Anti-Oedipus* is: how this can come about *from* desiring-production; that is, how can desiring-production desire its own repression? However, this philosophical problem is also a directly political problem: how does desire desire its own repression? or, in Spinoza's formulation, much favoured by Deleuze and Guattari: ' "Why do men fight *for* their servitude as stubbornly as though it were their salvation?" ' (ibid., p. 29).

Desiring-production is auto-production, it produces its own condition and conditions of reproduction, but it is also auto-repressive. It produces its own condition or whole as what Deleuze and Guattari call 'the body without organs'. This difficult term (taken from Artaud) represents a moment of anti-production within production itself. Although it is strictly immanent, produced as just another part alongside all the other parts of production, it nevertheless momentarily suppresses the production process and constitutes a primary repression within which the productive forces are redistributed. Primary repression makes it possible for aggregates of desiring-production to break off from primary production and constitute secondary production. Secondary or social production substitutes a *socius* (like the body of capital) for the body without organs that appropriates social production so that it (rather than desiring-production) appears to be the motor of social activity. This enables Deleuze and Guattari to maintain a conflictual monism; that is, to respond to the existence of social and psychic conflict without lapsing – like Marx and Freud – into dualism or idealism.

Desire is therefore able, under certain conditions, to invest both the aggregates of social production (Deleuze and Guattari call such aggregates of desire *molar*) and desiring-production itself (at a level they call molecular. Investment in desiring-production is revolutionary; desiring-production *is* revolution. If social production in general codes the flows of desire and represses primary production, then social history is driven by a kind of return of the repressed, the explosion of revolutionary desiring-production back into the social. This is particularly clear in their account of capitalism, which, uniquely among social systems, is *not* predicated on a coding of flows, but on a massive decoding. Capitalism does to stable sociality what critique does to stable (dogmatic) conceptuality: it systematically eradicates. (This is not to say that capitalism is not repressive; in fact, the endemic instability of its decoding, its relative proximity to desiring-production as the limit of all social production, makes its repressive mechanisms all the more intense.) Nevertheless, the decoding functions of capital are the social conditions for the production of *Anti-Oedipus* as a critical machine.

Investment in the molar aggregates of social production is reactionary, constituting and defending stable units or territories of desire, but revolution is always virtually present because the stable aggregates of territorial desire are directly composed out of the deterritorialising flows of desiring-production that territories repress. It is nevertheless always fragile because desiring-production is at the limit of social production as a whole, breaking down all forms of social coding and precipitating society into the schizophrenic abyss: revolution is incapable of being institutionalised.

Deleuze and Guattari are, in this respect, extremely critical of the role of the French Communist Party (PCF) in the events of May 1968. Taken entirely by surprise by the spontaneous nature of the coalition between students and workers, the PCF revealed its deeply reactionary belief that it was the only group with the right to revolution, and eventually sided with de Gaulle. The conscious investments of the PCF, operating at the level of the social, may have been revolutionary; but at the unconscious level they were still heavily and reactionarily invested in the social as such (overthrowing the state maybe, but to replace it with another state equally coding the flows of desiring-production). Deleuze and Guattari were the first to take seriously the new social movements that emerged out of 1968, and *Anti-Oedipus* still stands as one of the most sustained philosophical responses to them.

A new materialism

Anti-Oedipus enjoyed some success in France (albeit mostly a *succès de scandal*), but the second volume of *Capitalism and Schizophrenia*, *A Thousand Plateaus*

was greeted with a more muted reception. It is easy to see why; it is an extremely odd text. While *Anti-Oedipus* was doubtless unusual, its main intellectual co-ordinates were nevertheless familiar (Marx, Freud, Kant), even if Deleuze and Guattari's orientation towards them was largely critical. Its range of reference was also unusually broad, but it had systematic pretensions – undertaking a 'universal history' (Deleuze and Guattari, 1972, p. 139) – and it had, in Kant, a philosophical backbone, even if its use of him was supple and eccentric. None of this is true of *A Thousand Plateaus*. It has no particularly privileged intellectual point of orientation, it takes materials from anywhere it can get them (philosophers are mentioned, of course, but in the same breath as novelists, fictional characters, scientists or itinerant journeymen) and it has no unilinear development, in fact, no development at all. Several terms from *Anti-Oedipus* find their way into *A Thousand Plateaus*, less on the basis of continuity than because *Anti-Oedipus* was just another source of material.

Deleuze himself describes the difference between the two books by saying that *Anti-Oedipus* was concerned with 'a familiar, recognised domain: the unconscious . . . Whereas *A Thousand Plateaus* is more complicated because it tries to invent its domains.' (Deleuze, 1980b, p. 99). Part of the difficulty of *A Thousand Plateaus* comes from the seriousness with which Deleuze and Guattari put these new domains into effect within the book itself. For example, a critical stance towards the notion of authorship has become common in poststructuralist writing, but *A Thousand Plateaus* is unique in effecting this thought, right from the outset:

> A book has neither subject nor object; it is made of variously formed matters, and very different dates and speeds. To attribute the book to a subject is to overlook this working of matters, and the exteriority of their relations. It is to fabricate a beneficent God to explain geological movements. (Deleuze and Guattari, 1980, p. 3)

This geological account of construction – which, like the machines of *Anti-Oedipus*, is to be taken literally and not as any kind of literary trope – also determines the infrastructure of the text. It is not divided into chapters but into plateaus.

The term 'plateau' is imported from Gregory Bateson's study of Balinese culture and attests to the strength with which Deleuze and Guattari resist any Enlightenment progressivism, even in the construction of a book. Bateson detects a profoundly non-Western approach to conflict resolution amongst the Balinese, in which conflict traverses a series of flat plateau states rather than precipitating an explosive release of charge. The idea is clearly relevant for an understanding of a non-Western erotics that is diffuse rather than centred around orgasm. For Deleuze and Guattari, however, the term also resonates with their profoundly unteleological geologism in which organisation – in its widest possible extension – is composed of strata, plateaus and their complex topological interactions. This complexity leads them to suggest that the plateaus need not be read in any particular order (ibid., p. 1).

Production was always a persistent problematic for Deleuze since his very earliest works. One might say that his major objection was to the paucity of productive schemas within standard philosophy and science. Either things are caused mechanically, or, if they are obviously too complex for that, then a form (for example, a beneficent God) is imposed upon a passive material substrate from outside. The imposition of form from outside is a major target of A Thousand Plateaus, and Deleuze and Guattari's response to it is elaborated most carefully in the plateau that takes up the question of geology most explicitly: 'The Geology of Morals'. This plateau represents the culmination of a trajectory in Deleuze's thought towards increasing the scope of the material base. In the middle-period works, dynamic genesis was mainly concerned with a psychoanalytical story of the emergence of organisation out of chaos. One of the main polemical points of Anti-Oedipus was to show that desire invests history, and therefore to give an historical account of the emergence of organisation. In A Thousand Plateaus the stakes are raised again, and 'the Geology of Morals' attempts an account of organisation that spans geological timescales. The plateau takes the form of a lecture, borrowing from and amalgamating H.P. Lovecraft and Conan Doyle's Challenger stories.

Professor Challenger argues that almost everything is actually too complex for the matter-form distinction to gain purchase. He proposes to replace it with a matrix of four (or five) terms: content/expression and form/substance (the fifth would be matter-flow underlying the other four, and out of which they emerge). Content/expression cannot be reduced to matter/form (or, indeed, to signified/signifier) because each of them has both form and substance (ibid., p. 43). Moreover, content and expression are mutually irreducible and entertain no relations of representation or resemblance.

In the abstract, this terminological proliferation can seem like a baroque fiat (although the five-part matrix is, in fact, only the beginning of the proliferations on this plateau), but, outside philosophy, we are actually quite used to thinking like this. Professor Challenger gives a lucid instance of the operation of the matrix from cellular biology: organisms are composed of proteins (form of content) that are themselves composed of chains of amino acids (substance of content); but both of these are produced and reproduced by a completely different set of biomolecules, nucleic acids (DNA and RNA as forms of expression) which are themselves composed of already complicated components, nucleotides (substances of expression) that are different in nature from the amino acid substances of content. Expression (nucleotides and nucleic acid sequences) does not form or resemble content (proteins and amino acids) because they share nothing in common. Instead they enter into 'a state of unstable equilibrium, . . . reciprocal presupposition' (ibid., p. 67) or feedback: at the molecular level, expression codes for content; but natural selection causes content at the level of molar population aggregates to recode expression. The mutual conditioning or double articulation of expression and content permits the formation of what Professor Challenger (as well as Deleuze and Guattari) call a stratum, a thickening of the matter-flow. Although, especially when talking about philosophy, Deleuze and Guattari do betray a certain preference for intuitions over concepts, this in no way entails a reluctance to engage in abstraction (or, for that matter, a predilection for the immediacy of human experience). In fact, they often critique the failure to abstract. 'Our criticism of . . . linguistic models is not that they are too abstract, but, on the contrary, that they are not abstract enough' (ibid., p. 7). Linguistics is formalist but not abstract because it restricts its attention (as a condition of its constitution as a science) precisely to language, thereby ignoring or sidelining the informal or pragmatic aspects of language that make it mesh with systems of power (prescriptive laws of grammar, for instance, determine standard speakers and distribute dialects on the basis of a putative major language). Abstraction is pragmatics. Deleuze and Guattari call their mode of abstraction **machinic** in order to differentiate it from formalist, or merely conceptual, abstraction.

The above account of the five-fold matrix functions as an abstract machine for building strata, and, as such, it is capable of being implemented in a diverse range of concrete assemblages. Again, in plateau three (ibid., pp. 66–7), Professor Challenger demonstrates a completely different, social rather than cellular, implementation of the same five-way abstract machine, by way of a compelling reading of Foucault. In his history of the development of the prison system, Foucault makes a clear distinction between content and expression (as well as between form and substance). The form of content of the prison system is panoptic, involving a generalisable disciplinary function of control through a visual system in which the viewer can see but cannot be seen. The function is generalisable because it can be instantiated in a number of institutions other than prisons (hospitals, barracks, classrooms and, today, the increasing use of CCTV to police public spaces). The form of expression, however, does not have to do directly with the prison at all (it is certainly not a set of statements purporting to be *about* prisons). It concerns, rather, the development of a new concept of *delinquency* operating on a juridical substance of discursive sub-units concerning criminal infractions, etc (Foucault, 1975, pp. 255ff.). Expression does not represent content, but the two are mutually presupposing. It goes without saying that the same abstract machine is also effectuated in the production of sedimentary rocks. The social stratum whose formation Foucault analyses *really is* a stratum; that is to say, it is effected by the same machine.

Panopticism is extremely important for A Thou-

sand Plateaus in that it bears a close similarity to what Deleuze and Guattari call arborescence (tree-like-ness). Both involve closing off lateral communications, and forcing contact to be mediated by a central authority. The architectural structure of Jeremy Bentham's original design for the Panopticon (and most prisons) involved the partitioning of inmates into closed cells that offered no opportunity for contact between neighbours. All communication must be mediated by a prison officer. Similarly, the structure of most bureaucratic organisations (until the 1980s at least) was modelled on that of an (inverted) tree, with inferiors reporting to superiors and not to other occupants of their level. Arborescent hierarchy is a common feature of stratic organisation. But the machinic assemblage that effects stratification 'faces the strata' only on one side, 'on the other side it faces something else, the body without organs or plane of consistency' (Deleuze and Guattari, 1980, p. 40). This is to say that there is something else besides the strata, arborescence, generalised panopticism and closed hierarchy: there is the matter-flow which is not arborescent but rhizomatic. Technically, a rhizome is a plant of the tuber or bulb type that reproduces by sending out shoots that consolidate into a new plant. Deleuze and Guattari's use of the term is considerably wider. The essential point of contrast with arboresence is, however, relatively simple: rhizomes exhibit lateral connectivity. Prisoners, for instance, are engaged in destratification with a rhizomatic tendency when they use the water-pipes between cells as a means of communication. Similarly, the genealogical tree of evolution becomes a rhizome when viruses transplant genetic codes between disparate terminal leaves of the tree, and evolutionary cousins (who are supposed to be related only by a common ancestor located higher up the tree) become, instead, directly connected. Because the strata are only thickenings of the matter-flow, they are always apt to become rhizomes, to destratify or (in the vocabulary of *Anti-Oedipus*) to deterritorialise.

Such a characterisation of a rhizome, while not false, is heavily oversimplified. Rhizomatic multiplicities are the successor concept to desiring-production and, ultimately, to Deleuze's early attempts to outline an impersonal material transcendental.

The unlimited connectivity of a rhizome must be thought of in this context as preceding any 'thing' that is to be connected, and as producing what is connected at the same time as producing the connections. Everything is still rigorously critical and impersonal. Nevertheless, with rhizomatics (the successor concept to schizoanalysis), Deleuze's thought itself starts to make some of its most interesting and unexpected connections.

When Deleuze and Guattari write that 'thought is not arborescent, and the brain is not rooted or ramified matter' or 'the brain is much more like grass [a rhizome] than a tree' (ibid., p. 15) they are converging with a recent and specific revolution in science and philosophy: the connectionist theory of mind. The change in orientation from expert systems-based artificial intelligence in the 1970s to a connectionist model is exactly a change from a stratified and arborescent model of the mind (involving a theorematic and explicitly tree-based model of knowledge) to a rhizomatic model (involving lateral connectivity unsupervised by a hierarchical authority). Nor is this just a chance encounter: Deleuze and Guattari develop a whole alternative model of science as such, a nomad or vagabond science (ibid., p. 361ff.), that converges with the increasing importance given today in science to complex and chaotic systems. Such systems have encouraged the thought that when matter is connected to itself in feedback loops, or mutually presupposing causal interactions, it exhibits an autonomous capacity to generate complex organisational states without the intervention of a formal component that would be responsible for organisa-

tion. This auto-generation is called a 'phase change' in contemporary science, and Deleuze and Guattari allude to the same property by arguing that a rhizomatic multiplicity 'necessarily changes in nature as it expands its connection' (ibid., p. 8). Such interactions are, in principle, beyond the scope of formal logical analysis (mutual presupposition expressed logically yields a dead-end paradox of self-reference).

It is not only the absence of formal tools that has inhibited nomad science. There is, according to Deleuze and Guattari, a political pact between the State (as a rigidly stratified agent of order) and what they call Royal science (characterised by an exclusive emphasis on formalisation) which has made nomad science an eternally minor activity. Correlatively, rhizomatics is essentially subversive; a perpetual undermining of cognitive and political authority.

The convergence of Deleuze and Guattari's thought with contemporary scientific research programmes completely reconfigures the norms for connecting French with the thought of the English-speaking world. Such connections need no longer be dominated by concerns deriving from linguistic representation and feeding most directly into literary critical theory (not that these should be ignored), but can also be plugged into global scientific and technological preoccupations. Is not the internet, for instance, a rhizome? It is the success of this thread that promises to make good Foucault's evaluation of the long-term importance of the work of Deleuze (and Guattari).

Bibliography

Writings

Deleuze, Gilles (1986) (first edn 1962), *Nietzsche and Philosophy*, trans. Hugh Tomlinson, London: Athlone.
— (1990) (first edn 1969), *The Logic of Sense*, trans. Mark Lester with Charles Stivale, ed. Constantin Boundas, New York: Columbia University Press.
— (1991) (first edn 1966), *Bergsonism*, trans. Hugh Tomlinson and Barbara Habberjam, New York: Zone Books.
— (1994) (first edn 1968), *Difference and Repetition*, trans. Paul Patton, New York: Columbia University Press.

— and Félix Guattari (1983) (first edn 1972), *Anti-Oedipus*, trans. Robert Hurley, Mark Seem and Helen R. Lane, Minneapolis: University of Minnesota Press.
— and Félix Guattari (1987) (first edn 1980), *A Thousand Plateaus*, trans. Brian Massumi, Minneapolis: University of Minnesota Press.
— and Félix Guattari (1994) (first edn 1991), *What is Philosophy?*, trans. Hugh Tomlinson and Graham Burchill, London: Verso.
— and Claire Parnet (1987) (first edn 1977), *Dialogues*, trans. Hugh Tomlinson and Barbara Habberjam, London: Athlone Press.

References and further reading

L'Arc **49** (1980b) first published in 1972; revised edition 1980.

Ansell-Pearson, Keith (ed.) (1997), *Deleuze and Philosophy: The Difference Engineer*. London: Routledge.

Bateson, Gregory (1972), *Steps to an Ecology of Mind*, New York: Ballentine Books.

Broadhurst, Joan (ed.) (1992), *Deleuze and the Transcendental Unconscious*, special edition of *Pli: The Warwick Journal of Philosophy*, 4: 1,2.

Cressole, Michel (1973), *Deleuze*, Paris: Editions universitaires.

Foucault, Michel (1979) (first edn 1975): *Discipline and Punish*, trans. A. M. Sheridan Smith, New York: Vintage.

— (1977), *Language, Counter-Memory, Practice*, ed. Bouchard. Oxford: Blackwell.

Hardt, Michael (1993), *Gilles Deleuze: An Apprenticeship in Philosophy*, London and Minneapolis: University of Minnesota Press.

Landa, Manuel de (1991), *War in the Age of Intelligent Machines*, New York: Zone Books.

Lyotard, Jean-François (1993) (first edn 1974), *Libidinal Economy*, trans. Iain Hamilton Grant, Bloomington and Indianapolis: Indiana University Press.

Massumi, Brian (1992), *A User's Guide to Capitalism and Schizophrenia: Deviations from Deleuze and Guattari*, London and Cambridge, MA: MIT Press.

POST-MODERNISM: LYOTARD AND BAUDRILLARD

Iain Hamilton Grant

Introduction: what is post-modernism?

'Postmodernism', jibed Félix Guattari, aiming at a recent analysis of this complex of epistemological, aesthetic, social and political problems by Jean-François Lyotard, 'is not philosophy at all, [just] something in the air' (Guattari, 1986, p. 41). Despite three published books on the topic (1984, 1992, 1993b), Lyotard sometimes seems to agree, as in his 'Answer to the Question: "What is postmodernism?"': 'I am of course trying to understand what it is, but I do not know' (Lyotard, 1985b, p. 74). Perhaps more ironically, Guattari's challenge to post-modernism finds a co-sponsor in Jean Baudrillard, who is almost universally hailed (or condemned) as the 'high priest' or 'prophet' of post-modernism, but, when asked about this faith and this canonisation, he replied, '[p]ostmodernism . . . doesn't have a meaning. It's an expression, a word people use but which explains nothing. It's not even a concept. It's nothing at all' (Baudrillard, 1993b, pp. 21–2). Baudrillard often expresses himself with even less restraint, insisting that post-modernism is a soft, 'yuppie' ideology, 'the most degraded and generalized idol fetishism' (Baudrillard, 1990a, p. 150); he has even said, 'I have nothing to do with postmodernism' (in Gane, 1991a, p. 46).

Why, despite his reputation, does Baudrillard so dismiss post-modernism, and why, despite so many attempts, is Lyotard still perplexed about it? Whereas Guattari's denunciation of post-modernism as 'the

very paradigm of every sort of submission, every sort of compromise with the status quo' (Guattari, 1986, p. 40) underscores his belief that a genuinely critical philosophy and a genuinely radical politics remain possible, both Lyotard and Baudrillard consider our modern philosophical and political certainties to have been left standing by revolutions in 'late capitalism', whose new technologies assume an exponentially more powerful formative social role. In revolutionary post-industrial, post-modern or cybernetic society, the Copernican revolution in philosophy and the socialist revolution in politics have become such hollow idols that fundamental questions arise as to what – if anything – might take their place.

Given the scale of these problems, it is perhaps not surprising that neither Lyotard nor Baudrillard *can* answer the question 'What is postmodernism?'. Since, moreover, as Foucault (1984) shows in his analysis of Kant's 'What is Enlightenment?', the very asking of the question 'What is our age?' defines that age as inescapably *modern*, perhaps the fact that no one can answer 'What is postmodernism?' is itself informative. As Lyotard writes, post-modern knowledge does not 'produce the known, but the unknown' (Lyotard, 1984, p. 60).

Reworking modernity: Lyotard on postmodernism

Despite Lyotard's *The Postmodern Condition* having by now become the most cited account of post-modernity, its diagnosis of post-modernism as 'incredulity towards metanarratives' (Lyotard, 1984, p. xxiv) and advocacy of a concomitant post-modern practice of 'little narratives' have ironically achieved soundbite status, thus obscuring its epistemological and political arguments beneath what Lyotard criticises as the 'hegemony of narrative' (Lyotard, 1992, p. 35). We will focus here on the two major elements typically overlooked in Lyotard's account: the linguistic reorientation of Kant (see also Lyotard, 1988a); and the focus on contemporary capitalism and new technologies. The latter thus provides a Marxist rationale for the linguistic shift, so that Lyotard's long years of commitment to political struggle and the Marxist philosophy underpinning it (see Lyotard, 1988b) here re-emerge. In sum, for Lyotard, the post-modern condition is theoretically governed by 'Kant after Marx' (Lyotard, 1989, p. 273ff.).

Jürgen Habermas's 'Modernity after Postmodernity' extends into philosophy, social and political theory a debate that had previously been confined to architecture and the arts. Later retitled 'Modernity – An Incomplete Project', Habermas's essay, which seems to focus on modernism in the arts, glories in critically reinaugurating the Kantian project of Enlightenment. Citing the latter's aims as the development of 'objective science, universal morality and law, and autonomous art according to their inner logic' (Habermas in Foster, 1985, p. 9) in order to achieve more transparent and rational forms of everyday social life, Habermas, following Max Weber, deplored the development of a culture run by technocratic expertise to the detriment of the everyday 'life-world'. To counter this tendency, he called for the life-world to reappropriate these specialised fields and to return them to the task of completing the 'project of Enlightenment'. Habermas envisioned institutions based on the universal norms implicit in 'communicative rationality', ultimately leading to the establishment and enforcement of 'consensus' (Gemeinschaft).

In response, Lyotard cited Kant for his part, taking Habermas to task for violating the Kantian distinctions between pure (theoretical) reason, practical (moral) reason and teleological judgement (art, biology and human history). Whereas for Kant, in the *Critique of Judgement, sensus communis (Gemeinsinn* or public sense) is a reflective Idea – one whose object cannot be given in experience – for Habermas, the reflective Idea of *Gemeinschaft* or consensus is illegitimately deployed to *prescribe* morally acceptable utterances on theoretical grounds. For Lyotard, Habermas's justification of his move by appeal to a principle of judgement, 'does violence to the heterogeneity of language games' (Lyotard, 1984, p. xxv). Thus, Habermas ultimately claims that you must *either* agree to the principles of universalisable consensus implicit in all communication, *or* exclude yourself from dialogue, since your performance (communication, and hence an aim at agreement) contradicts your message ('not all language aims at agreement').

In short, if Habermas wanted to reunify reason, morality and experience by adopting the incomplete 'project of modernity', Lyotard wanted to derive tools for a 'postmodern knowledge' that would 'refine our sensitivity to differences and reinforce our ability to tolerate the incommensurable' (Lyotard, 1984, p. xxv) by working through the roots of critical philosophical modernity. Kant is then an entrenched reference in the Habermas–Lyotard debate, supplying the tools for both projects: if Habermas builds on Kant's idea of Enlightenment, Lyotard radically renegotiates the critical territory on which this project was built. Thus, where Kant invests great care in delimiting the faculties, Lyotard redoubles this 'critical' vigilance, delimiting 'incommensurable language games' ('differends') (1988b), sacrificing harmony to discord and strife.

Why, however, call this return to the roots of Kantian modernity 'postmodern' rather than, for example, 'radical modernism'? In some ways the latter is appropriate to Lyotard's work, and at times he himself reformulates 'post-modernism' as 'rewriting modernity'. Taking post-modernity not as a historical epoch, but as a 'mode within thought, speech, and sensibility' (Lyotard, 1992, p. 35), Lyotard turns the historicising tables and insists that something can 'become postmodern only if it is first postmodern . . . [so that] postmodernism is not modernism at its end, but in a nascent state, and this state is recurrent' (ibid., p. 22). But things are not always so clearcut. *The Postmodern Condition* closely ties post-modernism to the development of the 'postindustrial age'. For Lyotard, these socio-economic conditions, along with Marx's relentless critique of the mutations of capital, 'forbid any return to Kant' (Lyotard, 1989, p. 353), thus establishing a 'differend' between Kantian modernity and post-modernity (ibid., p. 327). While post-modernity is according to Lyotard, a question of different *modes* of 'expression in thought: in art, literature, philosophy, politics' (1992, p. 92), these modes must be investigated according to what prevents a return to Kant: capital.

Capital, technology and the sublime

According to Lyotard, there are two characteristic 'modes' of modernity: the sublime and the project. The first, sublimity, involves the relation between 'presentation and cognition' (Lyotard, 1992, p. 22). In this context, 'presentation' refers to the 'aesthetic' as both the presentations of the senses and the products of the imagination. Kant describes as 'sublime' a certain relation of faculties; namely, cognition without capability of presentation – when something is conceived in cognition but cannot be presented, either through sense or imagination. If, however, as Lyotard argues, modernity consists in the 'retreat' or 'lack of reality' (ibid., p. 19) exemplified in Kant's limitation of knowledge to representations we manufacture for ourselves – thus forbidding access to things in themselves – then the relationship of what can be conceived to what we can see or imagine is itself sublime. This is so, since, following Kant, neither sense nor imagination can present the real in itself (which remains the putative object of our thought), but can only re-present what is re-cognised; that is, known or knowable in advance.

There are, then, two 'modes' of the sublime relationship between cognition and presentation: the first, characteristically modern, accentuates 'the inadequacy of the faculty of presentation . . . the nostalgia for [the] presence' of reality 'experienced by the human subject'. The second, characteristically post-modern, emphasises the 'power of the faculty to conceive [. . .], its "inhumanity"' and the 'jubilation which comes from invent[ion]' (ibid., p. 22). If Kantian modernity loses reality and capi-

talist modernity loses the human subject, post-modernity no longer seeks to recover either loss but to exacerbate the resultant unreality and inhumanity by experimentation. Lyotard applied these distinctions not only to the arts (ibid., pp. 11–25), but also to philosophy and politics: thus, Marx's nostalgia for a lost human community and his assault on the ideological and industrial distortions of reality are clearly modernist, whereas the *enjoyment* experienced by the nineteenth-century industrial proletariat, as Lyotard 'scandalously' argues (Lyotard, 1993a, pp. 111–12), in the disruption of their lives and the modifications of their bodies by new manufacturing technologies, constitutes a post-modern, industrial sublime.

The second characteristic mode of modernity appears through Lyotard's analysis of the decline of 'grand narratives' or 'metanarratives'. While such a decline is now commonplace in discussions of post-modernism, Lyotard's reasons for supporting this thesis are less well known. Such narratives are legitimated by reference to an 'Idea of freedom, Enlightenment, socialism, etc.' (Lyotard, 1992, p. 29), an Idea which is in principle – and should therefore become in fact – universal, guiding 'every human reality' so that this very universality in turn legitimates the narrative. The realisation of these Ideas supplies modernity with 'its characteristic mode: the *project*' (ibid., p. 30), the 'will directed towards a goal' (ibid., p. 61). Now, precisely this 'will-to-project' has been 'liquidated' (ibid., p. 30) by another contender in this 'conflict of the narratives', namely, Habermas's great enemy, capitalist technoscience and its 'performativity' principle. Thus, against Habermas's assertion that 'every speech [situation . . .] is oriented towards the ideal of truth' (Habermas, 1970, p. 144), Lyotard argues – since capitalism is, for him, the driving force in producing knowledge – that efficiency, the increase in knowledge and technical applications, substitutes 'performativity' for truth and justice (cognition and normativity) (see Lyotard, 1984, pp. 46–7).

Capitalism, sharing the 'project' mode and joining the concomitant struggle over narratives and their universality, is also modern in Lyotard's sense: the grand narrative of capital promises 'emancipation from poverty through techno-industrial development', just as the Kant–Habermas Enlightenment narrative promised 'emancipation from ignorance and servitude through knowledge and egalitarianism' (Lyotard, 1992, p. 36). Since each narrative strives to maximise the universality of its Idea, conflict ensues, because each narrative contains its own immanent consensus on what can be known and done. As Lyotard writes: 'there is no reality unless it is confirmed by a consensus between partners on questions of knowledge and commitment' (ibid., p. 18). *Contra* Habermas, then, consensus is not a universal, but is rather immanent to a particular project in conflict with others; moreover, by prescribing the institution of the Idea as a universal, not only does Habermas violate Kantian critical demarcations, but his project also accelerates the very social disintegration it criticises. Since Habermas's critique is constrained by the same drive to maximise the universality of its Idea as capitalist technoscience, it effectively supports the very crisis it so deplores, helping to bring about 'the victory of capitalist technoscience over the other candidates for the universal finality of human history, [which] is another means of destroying the project of modernity while giving the impression of completing it' (ibid., p. 30).

Capitalism has two distinct advantages over its competitors in this post-modern condition. Explicitly committed to the *maximisation* of profits and power, capitalism defines the criteria for success in the conflict of the narratives: optimal performance equals infinite enrichment. Capitalist technoscience embodies the idea of an 'infinity of the will' inherent in the modern project (Lyotard, 1993b, p. 25) – the will to *realise the Idea* and thus to glorify the will – and *materialises* it by co-opting knowledge and technology into the service of its singular criterion. The project is no longer, as it was for Kant (and remains so for Habermas), to be *eventually* realised in harmony with a reflective Idea of the moral ends of the human species, but is *immediately* realised and augmented in and through technology – the material manifestation as well as the medium of capitalist knowledge and power. Second, sacrificing everything else to this minimal goal, capitalism is not committed to the retention or recovery of any particular state of affairs. Nor does it appeal outside

itself for legitimation, but instead extends its immanent self-propagation. In this sense, it is not committed, as are the more critical narratives, to what Lyotard calls the 'negative heroes' (Lyotard, 1992, p. 47) who formed the principal image of the modern, critical intellectual, committed to reinstating a 'lost' legitimacy through the project of emancipation.

This problem may be recast in terms of the two modes of the sublime: the emancipatory projects mourn a lost subject and a lost reality. However, in so far as this subject and this reality remain conceivable although unpresentable, the emancipatory projects become *projections* of a bygone age or utopian future, of an unalienated subject and unfragmented community – 'simulation[s], [n]arrations of the unreal' (ibid., p. 59) – unreal, that is, in relation to the dominant political and intellectual order. In so far as this (distorted) reality is defined by capitalism, the project becomes critical in the sense of opposing its goals to capitalism. Capitalism itself, does not, however, 'love order', and does not aim to reintroduce or maintain a 'social or political creation according to rule'. In this sense, capitalism, a 'romanticism [of] the infinite will' (Lyotard, 1993b, p. 25), remains modern in so far as it is committed to a project of infinite enrichment, while at the same time exhibiting the post-modern mode of sublimity, realising *and eliminating* the 'project of modernity' in its tireless experimentalism. Indeed, rather than attempting to reanimate a project or resurrect a 'lost' reality or subject, capitalism is experimental: 'capitalist creation does not bend the rules, it invents them' (ibid., p. 26).

Is Lyotard's post-modernism politically quiescent? It may seem so, since he has discounted the 'critical' model as offering solutions to obsolete problems (Lyotard, 1984, p. 14), and as complicit in the very system it criticises in providing technoscientific expansionism with new reserves of energy – since it has failed to bring about universal emancipation but continues, none the less, its struggles to realise a project. Furthermore, since he has apparently elevated capitalist 'sublime' experimentalism over its critics' rule-bound nostalgia, does not his 'postmodern condition' amount to 'the very paradigm of every sort of submission, every sort of compromise with the existing status quo', as Guattari suggests? On the contrary: Lyotard simply takes contemporary capitalism's power seriously. He does not therefore suggest that resistance is futile and lapse into nihilistic political despair, but rather asks, 'what is to be done when there is no horizon of emancipation, where can we resist? For me, that is *the* question' (Lyotard, 1985b, p. 69).

Lines of resistance

If one consequence of capitalism's victory is the erasure of any 'horizon of emancipation' in critical thought, preventing post-modernity from returning to Kantian modernity, what are the concrete developments in capitalism that have brought about the extreme simplification of post-modernism as the famous 'incredulity towards metanarratives' (Lyotard, 1984, p. xxiv)? Information technologies have introduced vast changes compared to their manufacturing precursors: if, for Marx, machines were 'organs of the human brain, created by the human hand' – fundamentally 'prostheses' of human cognitive and manual capabilities – then, with new technologies, the fixed capital of machinery becomes the 'fixed knowledge' of computerised societies (ibid., p. 6; cf. Marx, 1973). Computers assume those functions 'previously carried out by the higher nervous centers' (Lyotard, 1993b, p. 16): memory (databases), planning and forecasting (simulations), knowledge (expert systems), and communication (information technology). Rather than prostheses for human cognition, as Marx saw industrial machines, computers 'replac[e] natural agents' and become the 'cortex' of a cybernetic society (ibid.), thereby becoming 'prostheses of language' independent of speakers (Lyotard, 1992, p. 99). Rather than refusing to countenance extra- or non-linguistic phenomena as determinants of social change (as Benhabib (1984) argues against Lyotard), Lyotard focuses on language-games precisely because of the impact of new technologies on language.

Language is the most contested area, the most intense field of 'general agonistics', in post-industrial society and post-modern culture (Lyotard, 1984, p. 10):

Essentially, the new technologies concern language. They are in continuity with prior technologies in that they substitute automata for natural agents (humans, animals, etc.). They are different in that the substitution bears on sequences previously carried out by the higher nervous centers (cortex). (Lyotard, 1993b, pp. 15–16)

Such incursions wrest language from the domain of human institutions and turn communication into a conduit for capitalist expansionism, increasingly vulnerable to regulation by technology and the market (see ibid., p. 17). Communication, the very fabric of the 'post-modern social bond' (Lyotard, 1984, pp. 14ff), is now a technological concern, driven by an infinite will deriving no longer from human subjects, but from capitalist expansionism. For this reason, Lyotard's neo-Kantianism brings the 'full force' of critique to bear not 'on the dividing lines' between the subject's faculties (Lyotard, 1992, p. 83), but rather on those in *language* manipulated by a 'second cortex' of communications systems, circulating knowledge and language, fragmented into 'bits' of information. Rather than 'proposing a "pure" alternative to the system' (Lyotard, 1984, p. 66), or fighting the attendant alienation, this critique 'activates the differends' (Lyotard, 1992, p. 24) – the irresolvable tensions – between capitalism's 'investment of the desire for the infinite in language' (Lyotard, 1993b, p. 27), and the experimentalism occasioned by precisely the dehumanisation of language.

Thus, with the exponential growth of information technologies and their incursion into the social bond, Lyotard asserts that computerised society as a totality constitutes a machine or system in which subjects are no longer discursive partners aiming at a universal transparency in communication, but are simply 'nodal points of specific communication' in the network. 'One is always located at a *post* through which . . . messages pass' (Lyotard, 1984, p. 15), writes Lyotard, teasingly: is this the 'post' of *post-modernism*, the 'post' as computer terminal in the 'second cortex' (Lyotard, 1992, p. 100)? But this post-modern, cybernetic, capitalist Leviathan is sublime, defying the faculties to present it, and thus undermining both representationalist epistemology and the socio-political projects of modernity. The epistemological situation imposed by the sublime relation between presentation and conception 'produces not the known, but the unknown' (Lyotard, 1984, p. 60): rather than satisfying the representationalist 'demand for reality' (ibid., p. 16) – for clarity, certainty and communicability in epistemology, art and politics – Lyotard urges invention and 'allusion' to what remains conceivable but not presentable. This sublimity forecloses any final answer to the question 'What is post-modernism?': such an answer would revert from invention to realism, and thus paradoxically cancel the very post-modernity it invokes. The experimentalist thus works without rules to retrospectively 'establish the rules for what *will have been made*' (ibid., p. 24).

By the same sublimity, there can be no final answer to the question 'What is capitalism?' Capitalism is not post-modern by being brand new, but by carrying over elements of modernity – specifically, the 'infinite will' – into a sublime mode; precisely because of this conjunction of infinite will and experimentation, capitalism liquidates metanarrative and reconditions reality. For the philosopher, as for capitalism, the post-modern will always remain to be determined, for once determined, it will become modern.

Similarly, post-modern politics, incredulous of the will and its projections, no longer aims at modernist utopias or lost realities, but exacerbates the sublime mode of experimentation to multiply language games and their resultant differends. Thus the question, 'What is to be done given the demise of emancipatory projects?' does not so much dismiss modernity and proclaim post-modernity its triumphant successor, but rather 'works through' modernity in order to 'trace a line of resistance' to it (ibid., p. 47).

As we have seen, Lyotard radicalises Kantian critique in order not only to demarcate the limits of a given language game, but also to 'dissipate [the] illusions' (Lyotard, 1989, p. 156) attendant upon the transgression of these limits. If, however, the reality behind the illusion, the transparency behind the distortion, cannot be presented, no guarantees can be elicited that illusion has been dissipated, since the illusion's 'dissipation may [itself] be an illusion' (ibid.). Thus, while Lyotard insists that deploying

critique without guarantees, 'judging without criteria', engages the critical-experimental mode of postmodernity and traces the line of resistance against capitalist-technoscientific advance, precisely the irreducible simulation he risks provides the basic theoretical context of Jean Baudrillard's work, to which we now turn.

Baudrillard, modernity and simulation

If Lyotard, the Columbus of the post-modern 'archipelago' (Lyotard, 1988a), has charted and navigated passages, Baudrillard often seems merely adrift, with no thesis on post-modernism. Indeed, other than a few interviews and scattered mentions of the term, Baudrillard has had *virtually nothing to say about post-modernism* – a stance explicitly affirmed by his proclamation that he has 'nothing to do with post-modernism' (in Gane, 1991a, p. 46). Although they share the view that modernity and its critical theories constitute a redundant pairing, approaching Baudrillard from the perspective of Lyotard's post-modern Kantianism will show Baudrillard as a 'theoretical terrorist', one who maintains a 'position of challenge' (Baudrillard, 1993b, p. 122) to *both* modernity and 'post-modernism' – orthodoxies to which he has never been party, but under which he has all too often been subsumed.

Against the critical subject's manipulation of *appearances* for epistemological purchase, Baudrillard announces the theory of the *simulacrum* as an 'anti-Copernican revolution' (Baudrillard, 1994c, p. 42). Like a shadow 'liberated' from the body that cast it, the simulacrum is a sign 'liberated' from any reference to reality, a sign that has itself become real, leaving nothing with which to discriminate the real from its simulation. Since most interpretations of Baudrillard as a post-modernist are based on the theory of simulation, the following account will interrogate this theory and the 'fatal' strategy of symbolic exchange.

In accordance with a 'political economy of the sign' (see Baudrillard, 1981, 1993a) parallel with the 'successive mutations of the law of value since the Renaissance' (that is, the history of capitalism), Baudrillard posits 'three orders of simulacra' (Baudrillard, 1993a, pp. 50ff): *counterfeit*, *production* and *simulation (hyperrealism)*; each order marking an incremental deregulation in the economy of signs. In his chief theoretical work, *Symbolic Exchange and Death* (1993a), Baudrillard outlines his historiographical schema: rather than a shift from modernity to post-modernity, modernity itself is subdivided according to the order of simulation. Since Schelling's *Ages of the World*, Marx's history of capitalism and Heidegger's epochality of Being, philosophers have frequently sought to order history by their own paradigms; Baudrillard's theory of simulacra follows this tradition. Following his schema, he is not a post-modernist; rather, 'postmodernity' is the mode of modernity found within his schema.

The first-order simulacrum, the *counterfeit*, occurs when signs lose the fixed, transparent and natural relation to the real Baudrillard hypothesises that they enjoyed in feudal or archaic societies. The counterfeit sign destabilises a fixed order of signification just as money destabilises the exchange of goods. When the Renaissance swept the feudal order aside in favour of generalised competition, signs no longer referred to a natural order, but to a synthetic, forged order: where once there were distinct social ranks, and signs referred to reality, the social order was democratised, opened up to competition; signs then began to counterfeit reality, to forge a second 'nature'. The counterfeiting of social distinction was reflected in the rise of fashion, and that of nature is reflected in the semi-realised dream of cladding the world in stucco (ibid., pp. 50–3), a single, synthetic substance, the artificial essence of humanity's technological prowess from which everything would spring. At this point, the counterfeit is distinguishable in principle when it becomes problematic in fact (ibid., p. 55). In other words, it still makes sense to ask which is the real and which the forgery; which is the erstwhile *natural* sign and which is the artificial; whence a family's riches, nobility or trade? The counterfeit sign is therefore a first-order simulacrum of nature itself, a simulacrum that would like to exchange roles with nature, to naturalise the new order.

If naturalness was the lode-stone for the counterfeit sign, with industrialisation signs entered the 'age of mechanical reproduction' (to borrow Walter Benjamin's famous phrase) and lost any relation to nature. Whereas Plato's artisan copies an Idea when he manufactures a bed, which is then copied again by the artist painting a picture of the bed (*Republic X*, 595a–602b), the industrial production of *innumerable* identical objects 'liberates' signs from any referential or metaphysical function; signs became object-signs 'which will never have to be *counterfeits*, since from the outset they will be *products* on a gigantic scale' (Baudrillard, 1993a, p. 55). The value of a sign no longer lay in its referent (what it can be exchanged for), because, with the fascination with technological reproduction, everyone may now own a *Mona Lisa* (ibid., pp. 53–7).

Kantian modernist epistemology slips easily into this industrial schema, producing objects regulated *a priori* as identical serial appearances rather than as doubles of things. When Kant distinguishes *phenomena* or appearances from *noumena* or things in themselves, he emphasises this non-negotiable limitation of our knowledge by undercutting even the possibility of raw 'appearances': appearances appear to us because they have been – in an 'act of *spontaneity* . . . prior to all thought' (Kant, 1958, p. 153) – worked up by our faculties to become *representations* (*Vorstellungen*, literally presentations *placed before us*). When, moreover, a concept is applied to a representation, rather than gaining access to the thing 'behind' it, we manufacture the 'representation of a representation' of an object, a second-order sign. Baudrillard's 'anti-Copernican revolution' does not simply reverse this schema in a Luddite ambition to vanquish the industrialisation of the real by epistemological labour and let 'real reality' flourish once more. Rather, taking theory as 'a challenge to the real[,] [a] challenge to the world to exist' (Baudrillard, 1987, p. 124), Baudrillard pushes the tendency of the 'hyper' inherent in this epistemic labour to the extreme, so that the real goal of representationalist epistemology is, in common with its industrial paradigm, to *produce* the 'hyperreal . . . the meticulous reduplication of the real' (Baudrillard, 1993a, p. 71) and to *consume* it as hyperreality. Even Marx saw that, with the industrial order, it was no longer enough merely to *interpret*; the point is to *change the world* after a radical model.

At this point, between second-order, serially

reproducible reality and simulation, the third order of simulacra – the hyperrealization or 'ecstatic form of the real' (Baudrillard, 1990b, p. 9), its crystalline, abstract formula or *code* – achieves pre-eminence over the couple 'model – copy' that provided the schema for 'true and false' during the order of the counterfeit. With the removal of the rigid dissymmetry that dominated the counterfeit relation, and taking over the function of reproducing forms in the industrial order, serial products are no longer generated through the technological reproduction of an object; simulation now generates third-order simulacra from models that are already simulations, hastening modernity to its culmination in the form of a 'code' (Baudrillard, 1993a, p. 90).

Genetic revolt and fatal strategies: Baudrillard's code

We can therefore see why many commentators locate Baudrillard's 'post-modernism' in the 'hyper-realism' of third-order simulacra, for this seems to be what is generally meant by 'post-modernity': the real irretrievably lost in the funhouse of simulations. For Baudrillard, however, such processes remain paradigmatically modern: post-modernism, 'the first truly universal conceptual conduit, like jeans or Coca-Cola' (Baudrillard, 1996a, p. 70), simply marks the extension of commodification into the conceptual realm. In the resultant 'world-wide verbal fornication', concepts lose any determinate meaning, so that 'as Lyotard says, grand theories are over and done with' (Baudrillard, 1993b, p. 22). In mourning this loss, post-modernism becomes 'post-mortemism', 'reviewing, rewriting, restoring, and face-lifting everything [in an] end of the century moratorium' (Baudrillard, 1994a, p. 12). In defying the absence of meaning, post-modernism is determined to 'mean nothing' (Baudrillard, 1993b, p. 22), rather than not mean at all. Third-order simulacra, however, no longer pose questions of meaning, but of *function*, for they are separated from their precursors by their *operativity*. This last formulation, in addition to separating Baudrillard from post-modernism, also informs, as we shall see, the strategies he adopts to 'reverse the course of modernity'.

The function of the 'code' is crucial in Baudril-lard's analyses of simulation, defining his epistemic model as the cybernetic or informational model of *feedback*, where the code endlessly replicates and *recycles itself*, taking itself as its own self-regulating object in total indifference to a Kantian 'industrial' subject, supposed to have produced it.

> After the metaphysics of being and appearance [the order of the counterfeit], after energy and determinacy [the industrial] the metaphysics of indeterminacy and the code. Cybernetic control, generation through models, differential modulation, feedback, question/answer, etc.: this is the new operating system . . . Digitality is its metaphysical principle . . . and DNA is its prophet. (Baudrillard, 1993a, p. 57)

Although 'code' plays a major role in Baudrillard's work by typifying the third-order simulacrum, his condensed, allusive and often anti-thetic prose makes it difficult to pin down its meaning. However, complaints such as Kellner's that Baudrillard never 'clearly or systematically defines his notion of code' (Kellner, 1989, p. 29) miss the *functionalism* of his theoretical terms. Baudrillard's 'code' cannot, as Kellner assumes, be reduced to generating meanings, as in structural linguistics, for, like structuralism itself, as the above passage shows, 'code' in Baudrillard's work is indissociably cybernetic, genetic *and* semiotic. In other words, in line with the thesis of the sign's loss of referentiality, Baudrillard's theoretical terms are functional rather than denotative – they *work* rather than *refer*.

Thus, Baudrillard contends that, with simulation, the code has become 'all-powerful', since it not only forms the operating system on which simulacra run – their genotype or genetic structure – but also structures their phenotype or appearance. The further argument that the code has become all-pervasive in the order of simulation, that such 'artificial life' is everywhere, derives from the spectacular saturation of media and communications technologies with third-order simulacra; thus, the code is 'the functional, technological matrix of these systems which control the mode of appearance and disappearance' (Baudrillard, 1994b, p. 40). Simultaneously the genetic structure of simulacra and the mechanism for regulating their replication, the code eludes external control: as both operating system and medium of all communication, we cannot communicate with the code itself; as the structure and system of appearances, the code does not itself appear *in* itself, but appears everywhere as simulacra *of* itself. As the genetic structure governing living things, it is itself neither living nor dead, and so exceeds their control.

However, might we not respond, against Baudrillard, that since science discovered the code, we can now obtain some degree of control over the genetic code, perhaps even redesign its products? Whatever the epistemic status of the code, are these not real, rather than merely simulated, results? Although Baudrillard rarely engages with science, we can reconstruct a Baudrillardian answer to these questions, beginning with the following challenge: *what if the 'discovery' of the genetic code were not accidental; what if, given the structure of our knowledge, the discovery were inevitable, so that, in the heart of modern science, a current of fatalism is introduced; what then would be the consequences for 'the object' we have thus discovered?*

To address the first part of Baudrillard's challenge, what might account for the inevitability of discovering the genetic code, the question of 'observation' in scientific experimentation is greatly contested, since the requirement that results be reproducible entails the meticulous construction of the technological and sociological (training, funding) conditions under which an object can appear. Scientific phenomena therefore become progressively more refined as experiment and observation are subject to controls which regularise phenomena by extracting the accidental or inessential. In this way, the scientific object can be replicated by replicating the technological and sociological codes governing its observation.

Through this, science does not so much illuminate the real, or force nature to reveal its secrets, as it refines objects into codes to ensure their replication; thus, code reacts upon code, reflecting only its own logic. This is, however, precisely the definition of the real adhered to by the industrial codes governing modern scientific enquiry: 'the real is that of which it is possible to provide an equivalent reproduction' (Baudrillard, 1993a, p. 73). This result leads Baudrillard to consider 'whether DNA is itself a *myth*'

(ibid., p. 60), that is, a conventional object rather than an objective reality. The geneticist Jacques Monod's consideration of the same question, cited by Baudrillard (ibid., pp. 60–1), concludes by naturalising 'convention': if DNA is not actually real, but only conventional, it is not the sort of convention human beings can do without, and so becomes inescapably 'real' for us. This makes it inevitable that the perfect scientific object, DNA, would consist of pure code.

We can thus appreciate, following the excision of the accidental, that the 'discovery' of the code reintroduces a certain 'primitive' fatalism into the scientific object. Against this background, Baudrillard insists that the 'strategy of the subject' has been defeated by the object, and that the only strategy left is the 'fatal strategy' of the intractable and elusive object (Baudrillard, 1990b, p. 7). It is a considerable 'objective irony' that the 'human' genome is too massive a code to be mapped using merely human memory: only machine code can simulate the genetic code. According to Baudrillard, with the advent of the third order of simulation, 'we have passed alive into the models' (ibid., p. 9). Thus, instead of an object manufactured as an appearance for a subject, the cybernetised genome turns the human *subject* into a scientific *object*; and, as inessential to the pure form of the object, the code finally excises the subject, making it the residue of the code-as-object.

If, then, the 'code' operates not simply in terms of a structural analysis or a semiotics of cultural forms, but is equally the deep or genetic structure of living things, the audacity of Baudrillard's deployment of it consists in re-exporting the application of its biological function on to social and political phenomena, as a 'social genetic code' (Baudrillard, 1993a, p. 60). Far from being irreducible to genetic determinism, the code 'governs' politics in the same way as it dictates gender or skin colour, removing every claim to harness the 'general will' in democracy (Rousseau), the particular wills of the oppressed against the will of the oppressor (Marx), or the efficient whims of the Princely dictator (Machiavelli). Such fatalism is anathema to modern politics, and yet it is successfully used, Baudrillard claims, by what he calls the 'mass' or 'silent majorities' in refusing to be co-opted into the 'reign of will or representation' (Baudrillard,

1983, p. 24). Rather than being mobilised by politics and its will to represent 'the people', the masses absorb and deflect every attempt to transform them into either the historical subject of political oppression or the liberated subject of capitalism. Since fatalism is thus anathema to the modern 'will', it is therefore also fatal to the modern subject, the possessor of that will.

At this juncture, as the mass becomes the object of increasingly frantic polling, a fatal strategy – or a strategy of fatalism – becomes indissociable from the 'fate of the *object*' (Baudrillard, 1990b, p. 111). Thus, while subjects cannot struggle against the dictatorship of the code, no matter how much political will they have – while, in other words, we cannot 'fight DNA . . . with the class struggle' (Baudrillard, 1993a, p. 4) – nevertheless, 'revolt has become genetic'. Just as the events of May 1968 – a political reference dear to both Lyotard and Baudrillard – broke out without the consent or planning of the official Communist Party or the intellectuals, neither we nor universal history can dictate when or where the revolution will or should take place: instead, 'like the cells in cancer and metastases', revolts break out with 'uncontrollable vitality and undisciplined proliferation' (Baudrillard, 1990b, p. 33).

Reversing this spiralling, genetic logic of revolt once again, Baudrillard writes of cancer not as a disease tragically afflicting a body, but as the body and its cells 'rebelling against their genetic decree, against the commandments . . . of DNA' (ibid.), while the individual becomes a 'cancerous metastasis of her base formula' (Baudrillard, 1979, p. 235). When some scientific research programmes, interpreted as proposing simplistic genetic or anatomical explanations for social phenomena such as homosexuality, criminality, or even class, are championed by certain political interests, Baudrillard's strategy is not to argue for cultural rather than genetic determinism, nor to try to limit the damages of such social engineering; rather, he insists that society *is* determined by the code, and that there is no need to deploy such techniques, since the code itself eradicates the accidental in quest of the essential, taking itself as the norm.

From the standpoint of the code (of the *object*), 'what makes the obese [body] obscene is not that there is too much body, but that the body is superfluous' (Baudrillard, 1990b, p. 32). This is the 'incredible violence of genetic simulation': the genetic code may be an 'artifact . . ., and artificial matrix . . . of simulation' (Baudrillard, 1979, p. 234), but simulation, as we have seen, would not be simulation if there remained a 'reality' beyond it. In other words, simulation is not the simulation of the natural – that would be the *counterfeit* – but the generation of the hyperreal through the code. DNA is not, therefore, *less* real than the body, but is the *medium* of its *hyper-realisation*.

Symbolic exchange and the critique of modernity

Modernity is neither a sociological nor a political concept, nor properly a historical concept. It is a characteristic mode of civilisation opposed to the mode of tradition, that is, to every other previous or traditional culture. (Baudrillard, 1978b, p. 63)

This characterisation of modernity as a cultural mode opposed to archaic societies harks back to Baudrillard's earlier attacks on universalist Marxist history and economics (Baudrillard, 1975; 1993a). According to some, these survive as the 'basic matrix' of Baudrillard's theory; that is, 'the opposition between symbolic and semiotic (or simulational) cultures' (Gane, 1995, p. 111). Semiotic cultures are irreducibly tied not only to Marxist historiography and political economy, but also to the critical, oppositional stances of Marx's successors; thus, the history of capital *and* the theory of the revolution-to-come form the crucial index of modernity for Baudrillard. In this sense, it would be misleading to structurally oppose symbolic to semiotic cultures, for the problem is not a new orientation for opposition, but the articulation of symbolic exchange at the simulated heart of modern capitalism.

Capitalist exchange is supposed to have superseded 'primitive' *symbolic exchange*, a category Baudrillard takes from Marcel Mauss's (1974) analysis of the *gift*. If Marx viewed all history as a linear evolution, then Baudrillard challenges Marxist historiography with repressing the *ambivalence* inherent in the binding reciprocity of the gift, an alternative economic form that puts the entire modern 'political order at stake' (Baudrillard, 1975, p. 59). The ambivalence of the gift-exchange derives from its *symbolic* character: it is not the *content* of the gift (what is given) that matters, but its reversible *form* (gift reciprocated by counter-gift). In ceremonies such as the *potlach* of native North Americans gift-exchange spirals out of control into an orgiastic destruction of goods, such that cycles of exchange blur into one another; huge amounts of goods were wasted in symbolic affirmation of the social bond. To modern, utilitarian eyes, such orgiastic waste – which Baudrillard, following Bataille (1991), calls the 'accursed share' – is abhorrent.

Rather than being based on equivalence, over which both capitalist and Marxist economics struggle, the reciprocity principle of symbolic exchange requires that the counter-gift be greater than the gift. The exponential cycle of exchange thus never ends, having no external finality such as accumulation of profit or power, but only perpetual reversal as its internal non-finality.

The linear and accumulative 'strategy of modernity' (Baudrillard, 1990b, p. 117) pits itself against the reversibility and waste of symbolic exchange. However, as capitalism progressively annihilates any reference to the utility of goods in favour of the pure, simulated form of exchange, it comes ever closer to the orgiastic destruction of goods in the *potlach*. With reference abolished in simulated as in symbolic exchange, the stakes become clear: not semiotic *versus* symbolic society, but linearity versus reversibility *within* the code governing the hyperreal. The feedback effect by which the code generates simulacra of itself always risks abolishing its own determinacy, moving from metastasis to genetic revolt, from order to disorder. In this sense, the intensification of simulation in modernity is haunted by the symbolic 'in the form of its own death' (Baudrillard, 1993a, p. 1), haunted, that is, by the spectre of a reversal into the symbolic exchange it 'superseded'.

Just as 'fatality' re-emerged in modern science when the codes of scientific theory became the scientific theory of the code, Baudrillard's analyses of modernity seek the reversibility immanent to modern, code-governed simulated exchange in order to accelerate their symbolic demise. To provoke

this, the strategy deployed must be *fatal*, not only to such cultural modes, *but also to all strategies*. The paradox is crucial; having staked everything on a contest between two strategies – linear and reversible – calling the latter *fatal* risks making it simply another modern, oppositional strategy, pitting one finality (modern capitalism) against another (primitive fatalism). In so far as a strategy aims to realise an end, whichever strategy is deployed, far from ending modern linearity, would simply replace one finality with another. Baudrillard asked, focusing the paradox: 'how could there be fatality if there is strategy?' (ibid., p. 188).

The simulated death-drive pursued by the fatal strategy answers the paradox: fatality and strategy are mutually exclusive, since 'from a strategy we expect control', while fatality denudes us of control. Insisting on fatal strategies is thus self-defeating, but this is precisely Baudrillard's point: a fatal strategy is *fatal*, since, in adopting it, the subject 'succumbs to the surpassing of its own objectives' (ibid., p. 189). The point of these strategies is not to exit modernity but to engage those fatal tendencies of modernity that drive it towards its own death (ibid.). In other words, Baudrillard forsakes both a nostalgic *return to* (primitive societal order) or *exit from* (modern hyperrealist order) in favour of upping the stakes, amplifying simulation with a simulatory theory that induces reversibility *at the core of simulation itself*; such reversibility carries modernity's inherent, fatalistic primitivism into the exponential cycles of symbolic exchange, 'accelerating the process . . . [towards] the fatal as maximum outcome' (Baudrillard, 1993b, p. 158).

Baudrillard refuses to accept that the 'real' – a relic of a bygone semiotic order – survives hyperrealisation. Since reality is not concealed by simulation, everything – including a theory of simulation such as Baudrillard's – must itself be a simulation. Even his own theories are too close to their sources, feeding simulation back on to simulation, 'like the famous feedback effect . . . produced by a source and a receiver being too close together' (Baudrillard, 1994, p. 5). This 'hyper-logic' accounts for the troubling sense that Baudrillard's works may be *fictions*, throwing light here and there on diverse contemporary cultural phenomena, but without any readily apparent theoretical or critical ground. That it is a *logic*, based on a genealogy of the sign, however, reflects his paradoxical realism: despite the real having become hyperreal, a simulation or illusion, 'one has to recognize the reality of the illusion, and one must play upon this illusion and the power it exerts' (Baudrillard, 1993b, p. 140). If Baudrillard's theories are in some sense 'fictional', then this is because the only available reality today is that of simulation: 'today, reality itself is hyperrealist' (Baudrillard, 1993a, p. 74).

Conclusion

We should remember that both Lyotard and Baudrillard, in common with much French philosophy since the 1960s, were driven by what they saw as the death-knell of radical, Marxist politics and its 'critical' intellectuals. Both served their radical apprenticeships during the 1950s and 1960s. Lyotard was in the Trotskyite *Socialism or Barbarism* group and was later a Nanterre activist during May 1968; Baudrillard, who studied under the Communist intellectual Henri Lefebvre, was a proto-Situationist. Both struggled in their early works to provide a future for critical theory and practice (Lyotard, 1972, 1993b; Baudrillard, 1975, 1981, 1996b). Now that the future is here, however, technocapital has revolutionised society, overshadowing every other revolutionary project: what is the fate of social change when change has exceeded constancy and erased the difference between the two? Seizing the redundancy of old forms of critical theory, both philosophers undertake a 'critique of critical reason': Lyotard regenerates Kantian critique in the information age; Baudrillard dismisses critique as buttressing the very system it critiques.

Opposing the critical model of social fragmentation induced by alterations in social hardware, Lyotard recommends an experimentalism 'with neither programme nor project' (Lyotard, 1993a, p. 262) to redress the stakes in a cybernetic society. Facing the same situation, and equally rejecting alienation as a theoretical basis for strategic engagements with capitalism, Baudrillard offers only a 'theoretical science fiction' to radicalise capitalism's more destructive tendencies *at the level of simulation*. Both thinkers' perspectives on the disappearance of the finalities of modernity foreground the diminishing returns on philosophic solutions to science-fictional problems. Thus, in place of the triumphalist knowing subject of the Copernican revolution, forming and knowing objects to perfection in 'a system of . . . totalitarian explanation' (Baudrillard, 1995a, p. 82), and in place of the proletarian subject and its triumphalist emergence at the end of history, Baudrillard places the object's revenge at the centre of an ironized, illusory universe of symbolic exchange: 'The world is given to us, and given to us as unintelligible; we have to render it even more unintelligible . . ., to render it, give it back' (ibid.)

Bibliography

Writings

Baudrillard, Jean (1970), *La société de consommation: ses mythes, ses structures*, Paris: Gallimard.
— (1975) (first edn 1973), *The Mirror of Production*, trans. Mark Poster, St Louis: Telos.
— (1979), *De la séduction*, Paris: Denoël.
— (1981) (first edn 1972), *For a Critique of the Political Economy of the Sign*, trans. Charles Levin, St Louis: Telos.
— (1987) (first edn 1978), *In the Shadow of the Silent Majorities*, trans. Paul Foss, John Johnson and Paul Patton, New York: Semiotext(e).
— (1990a) (first edn 1980), *Cool Memories*, trans. Chris Turner, London: Verso.
— (1990b) (first edn 1983) *Fatal Strategies*, trans. Philip Beitchman and W. G. J. Niesluchowski, New York: Semiotext(e)/Pluto.
— (1993a) (first edn 1976), *Symbolic Exchange and Death*, trans. Iain Hamilton Grant, London: Sage.
— (1993b), *Baudrillard Live: Selected Interviews*, ed. Mike Gane, London: Routledge.
— (1994a), *The Illusion of the End*, trans. Chris Turner, Cambridge: Polity Press.
— (1994b), with Marc Guillame, *Figures de l'alterité*, Paris: Descartes et Cie.
— (1994c) (first edn 1981), *Simulacra and Simulation*, trans. Sheila Faria Glaser, Ann Arbor: University of Michigan Press.
— (1996a) (first edn 1990), *Cool Memories II*, trans. Chris Turner, Cambridge: Polity Press.
— (1996b) (first edn 1968), *The System of Objects*, trans. James Benedict, London: Verso.
— (1996c) (first edn 1994), *The Perfect Crime*, trans. Chris Turner, London: Verso.

Lyotard, Jean-François: *Discours, figure*. Paris: Klincksieck, 1971.

— (1984) (first edn 1979), *The Postmodern Condition: a Report on Knowledge*, trans. Brian Massumi and Geoffrey Bennington, Manchester: Manchester University Press.

— (1985a) (first edn 1979), with Jean-Loup Thébaud, *Just Gaming*, trans. Wlad Godzich, Manchester: Manchester University Press.

— (1985b), *Immaterialität und Postmoderne*, trans. Marianne Karbe, Berlin: Merve.

— (1988a) (first edn 1983), *The Differend: Phrases in Dispute*, trans. Georges van den Abbeele, Manchester: Manchester University Press.

— (1988b), *Peregrinations: Law, Form, Event*, New York: Columbia University Press.

— (1989), *The Lyotard Reader*, ed. Andrew Benjamin, Oxford: Blackwell.

— (1992a) (first edn 1986), *The Postmodern Explained to Children*, trans. Julian Pefanis, morgan Thomas, Don Barry, Bernodette maker and Virginia Spate, London: Turnaround.

— (1992b), '*Sensus communis*', trans. Marian Hobson and Geoff Bennington, in Andrew Benjamin (ed.), *Judging Lyotard*, London: Routledge 1–25.

— (1993a) (first edn 1974), *Libidinal Economy*, trans. Iain Hamilton Grant, London: Athlone.

— (1993b), *Political Writings*, trans. and eds Bill Readings and Kevin Paul Gaiman, London: UCL Press.

References and further reading

Bataille, Georges (1991), *The Accursed Share*, Vol. 1: An Essay on General Economy, trans. Robert Hurley, New York: Zone.

Foster, Hal (ed.) (1985) *Postmodern Culture*, London: Pluto Press.

Foucault, Michel (1984), 'What is Enlightenment?', in Paul Rabinow (ed) *The Foucault Reader*, Harmondsworth: Penguin, 23–50.

Gane, Mike (1991a), *Baudrillard: Critical and Fatal Theory*, London: Routledge.

— (1991b), *Baudrillard's Bestiary: Baudrillard and Culture*, London: Routledge.

— (1995), 'Radical theory: Baudrillard and vulnerability', *Theory, Culture & Society* 12, 109–23.

Guattari, Félix (1986), 'The postmodern dead-end', trans. Nancy Blake, *Flash Art* 128, 40–1.

Habermas, Jürgen (1970), 'Toward a theory of communicative competence', in Hans Peter Dreitzel (ed.), *Recent Sociology 2: Patterns of Communicative Behavior*, New York: Macmillan.

Kant, Immanuel (1958) (first edn 1787), *Critique of Pure Reason*, trans. Norman Kemp Smith, London: Macmillan.

— (1987) (first edn 1790), *Critique of Judgment*, trans. Werner S. Pluhar, Indianapolis: Hackett.

— (1963), *Kant on History*, trans. and ed. Lewis White Beck, New York: Macmillan.

Kellner, Douglas (1989), *Jean Baudrillard: from Marxism to Postmodernism and Beyond*, Cambridge: Polity Press.

Marx, Karl (1973), *Grundrisse*, trans. Martin Nicholaus, Harmondsworth: Penguin.

Mauss, Marcel (1974), *The Gift: Forms and Functions of Exchange in Primitive Societies*, trans. Ian Cunnison, London: Routledge and Kegan Paul.

Plato (1986), *Republic*, trans. H. D. P. Lee, Harmondsworth: Penguin.

FRENCH FEMINISM

Tina Chanter

We should, at the start of this discussion, bear in mind that 'French feminism' is, as Christine Delphy (1995) reminds us, a peculiar invention. Created by an Anglo-American readership, the term tends to oversimplify by creating apparent homogeneity between diverse female thinkers who live in France. In the interests of avoiding such oversimplifications, and thereby adding insult to injury, rather than comparing the so-called 'French feminists' to each other, I will examine a few figures for their own merits – as far as space allows.

Luce Irigaray

Luce Irigaray's lyrical, polemical, and often obscure, critique of the Western tradition first came to the attention of the English-speaking world when it was anthologised in a collection called *New French Feminisms*, along with work by Cixous, Kristeva and many others. In an ironic twist first commented by Kelly Oliver, Irigaray quickly joined ranks with Hélène Cixous and Julia Kristeva to become, in the Anglo-American feminist imaginary, a member of the oft-cited triumvirate of so-called 'French feminists', who dominated our reception of French feminism. Ironic, imaginary and ostensibly 'French feminist' because none of the three is in fact French: Cixous is Algerian, Kristeva is Bulgarian and Irigaray is Belgian.

If feminists in Britain and the USA were intrigued by Irigaray's work, they were also perplexed. Intrigue soon gave way to frustration and dismissal. Her work was labelled 'essentialist', heralded as dangerous, and

we were warned to approach it with extreme caution. Her call for a re-examination of sexual difference was read in terms of biological or psychological reductionism; her attention to a feminine morphology was reduced to a reactionary return to the body; her interest in the Western tradition of philosophy was criticised as élitist and abstract; her mimetic and rhetorical strategies were greeted with charges of being too parasitic on the patriarchal tradition they intended to put into question.

What lay behind feminism's suspicion of Irigaray's resolutely embodied discourse, her attention to fluidity, her articulation of multiple sites of sexuality and her insistence upon a feminine imaginary? To understand why Irigaray, along with Cixous and Kristeva, came to be seen as essentialist is to see how feminism itself had become entrenched in certain channels that reflected the fear and suspicion of the body – what Elizabeth Spelman calls somataphobia – so characteristic of the Western tradition of philosophy. Perhaps it was not Irigaray who was in league with the boys, but rather those feminists who rejected her attention to the body. Perhaps it was not Irigaray who could justifiably be charged as reactionary, but the very feminists who rejected her attempt to articulate the body, and who, in so doing, reflected a bias that is at the heart of much Western philosophy. Since the Greeks, the body has been cast by Western philosophers as an impediment to knowledge, and a distraction from the truth, while physical desire seems to interfere with morality. Irigaray was intent on elaborating a feminist discourse that celebrated, rather than denigrated, female sexuality, female pleasures; feminism – true to its white middle-class origins – reacted with discomfort.

Philosopher, psychoanalyst and linguist, Luce Irigaray is not easy to categorise. Born in Belgium in 1930, she first studied literature, focusing on Paul Valéry, during her early training at Louvain. She completed her Doctorate of Letters at the University of Paris VIII, and has lived in France since that time. Her thesis, which focused on figures such as Plato, Freud and Hegel, was published in 1974 as *Speculum of the Other Woman*. In 1977, a collection of articles and interviews, *This Sex Which Is Not One*, appeared. English translations of both books were published in 1985, and since that time (although some works still remain to be translated), her work has been translated more promptly. *An Ethics of Sexual Difference* (1984) – a collection of essays that constitutes Irigaray's perhaps most important philosophical work after *Speculum* – extends the readings of canonical figures to include Aristotle, Spinoza and Merleau-Ponty. In *Marine Lover* (1980), and in *L'Oubli de l'air* (Forgetting the Air) (1983), Irigaray devotes her attention to Nietzsche and Heidegger respectively.

While at times Irigaray insists on the importance of her philosophical contribution, her work is also heavily indebted to Jacques Lacan, whose psychoanalytic theory remains an important influence in her more recent work, such as *Sexes and Genealogies* (1987) – this despite the break with Lacan after the appearance of *Speculum* in 1974, marked by the end of her teaching at the University of Vincennes, where Lacan had founded a department of psychoanalysis. (Irigaray is a Director of Research at the *Centre National de la Recherche Scientifique*, where she established an international team to work on linguistic patterns in relation to gender, the focus of her most recent work.)

Irigaray has divided her work into three periods. The first stage includes *Speculum of the Other Woman* (1974) and *This Sex Which Is Not One* (1977) and criticises the monism and univocity of the traditionally male dominated canonical corpus of Western philosophy. In the second stage, which includes *Sexes and Genealogies* (1987), rather than criticising the tradition, she turned her attention to the positive project of creating an alternative to the tradition in the form of a feminine voice. This more creative and inventive phase of her work, in which women's points of view were more adequately represented was followed by a third phase, represented by *Je, tu, nous: Toward a Culture of Difference* (1990); here, she develops the idea of an interrelation between the sexes premised on a new appreciation of the role that women have played in culture. Thus, in her most recent work, she concentrates on envisioning a productive relationship between the sexes – one which is built on the work of the respective foci of phases one and two of her work. Irigaray's corpus thus cannot be understood unless it is seen as embracing all three moments: a critical moment that exposes the myth of the same – the dominant tradition, which speaks only from a male point of view but which represents itself as universal, as if it spoke for everyone; an imaginative and inventive moment which draws the repressed resources of the feminine into a newly created myth of femininity; and a moment characterised less by the feminine and the masculine as opponents, than by the space of the between, or the interval, in which their intersubjective connection can take place.

I will focus, in rest of this section, on Irigaray's first period, the critique of traditional philosophy. *Speculum of the Other Woman* (1974), the book that earned her international recognition, fuses philosophy with psychoanalysis and employs a lyrical *'mimesis'*, or mimicry, that parodies and undercuts philosophical pretensions to universality. While adopting the standpoint of universality, objectivity and uniformity, the philosophical tradition in fact reflects a partial view of the world, one which is informed by those who have been largely responsible for writing it: men. Without the material, maternal and nurturing succour provided by women as mothers, caretakers and homemakers, men would not have had the freedom to reflect, the peace to think, or the time to write the philosophy that has shaped our culture. Women, in their unacknowledged background roles of supporters and nurturers, are the props, the scenery, the necessary but suppressed others, without whom the show would not go on, but who are never recognised as capable of acting themselves; femininity is the unthought ground of philosophy – philosophy's other.

By documenting the ways in which diverse texts of the Western philosophical tradition adhered to a systematic representation of women as other, Irigaray demonstrated the sense in which the tradition achieved a certain unity and coherence on the basis of that which it excluded: women. Disparate in other respects, the philosophers she explores in *Speculum* – including Plato, Plotinus, Descartes and Hegel – share philosophy's dismissal, neglect and denigration of women.

One of the figures that haunts her work is Antigone. In *Speculum*, Irigaray executes a close reading of Hegel's discussion of the Sophoclean tragedy that bears Antigone's name, a discussion that has become the touchstone for modern interpretations. In his *Phenomenology of Spirit*, Hegel uses the play to illustrate the difference between two types of ethical action: the political, as represented by Creon (ruler of Thebes), and the familial as represented by Antigone (sister of the defeated rebel, Polynices). Although he considered Antigone to be the purest heroine of Greek tragedy, he took Creon's action to embody the communal aspect of ethics (*Sittlichkeit*). If Antigone represents the feminine principle, the law of the hearth, and if her obstinate insistence in burying her traitorous brother is answerable not to civic laws but to those of the ancient gods, then Creon represents the masculine principle, the law of the state, and his intransigence in forbidding the burial of Polynices stems from a rigid belief in his own pre-eminence as political ruler of Thebes. His son, Haemon, betrothed to Antigone, warns him that his inflexibility will be his downfall, but Creon will not relent. Only when it is too late does he realise the error of his judgement. Only after the death, not only of Antigone and Haemon, but also of his wife, Eurydice, does Creon admit that his partiality blinded him to the interdependence of family and state. It takes the destruction of his family – for which he holds his actions as King of Thebes responsible – for him to acknowledge this interdependence.

For Hegel, Antigone's action does not constitute properly ethical action because it is the action of an individual that is undertaken, not for the sake of the state of which individuals form a part, but for the sake of her brother as a blood relative. Antigone's burial of Polynices only takes account of the familial blood bond that unites her to her brother, ignoring his recent attack on Thebes. In other words, it takes account of his death, but not of his actions in life. As far as Hegel is concerned, the individual is subordinate to the state, and the private domestic sphere of feminine action is likewise indebted to the public and political sphere of masculine action. On the basis of this subordination of individual to state, and feminine to masculine, Antigone's familial duty to bury her brother should be overridden by Creon's concern for political loyalty and discipline. Her desire to extend to Polynices the rights of burial, despite the fact that his life ended in the ignominious murder of their brother, Eteocles, in the battle to win Thebes, is partial because it does not attach any significance to the actions of Polynices's life. Equally, Creon refuses to acknowledge (until too late) that the state is not an autonomous entity, but one which depends for its military resources on the individuals that make up the family. He stands firm in his view that the action of individuals should be directed to the state. Hegel agrees, in so far as any action undertaken for the sake of the family without regard to the state is liable to detract from the state.

If Polynices' march on Thebes is clearly detrimental to the state, things are less clear in Antigone's burying him – and it cannot constitute ethical action for Hegel. Antigone's act cannot be counted as a consciously ethical act, because what counts as ethical is understood as that which is identified with the communal, political, civic interests of the state. Antigone's only opportunities for 'ethical' acts are those directed towards the political worth of male citizens, since she herself, as a woman, is allowed to play no part in the political system. This means that no action of Antigone as a woman constitutes ethical action unless governed by a principle outside her own sphere of activity. In other words, the burial of a brother by a sister can only be allowed if it follows the law laid down by the head of the state. The heavy irony of such a situation is that the very act which embodies the feminine principle – namely, the burial of the dead – is also the act Creon disqualifies. In effect, then, Creon disallows precisely the act that the state he represents identifies with femininity, thus leaving no action open to Antigone. Any action she might take as a woman is forfeited because of the actions that her brother had already taken as a man.

Irigaray's commentary points out the asymmetry of the masculine and the feminine ethical positions that Hegel's account assumes. Like his account of the bodily differences between the sexes, Hegel's understanding of ethics is premised on an assumption that women are inferior, secondary, to men. His conviction that women's sphere of activity should always be dictated by a higher masculine realm of activity thus aligns him with the Western tradition of metaphysics. In another essay in *Speculum*, Irigaray shows how Freud's account of morphology also assumes that women's sexuality should conform, more or less, to male sexuality – even if it falls short in some respects. Thus, the quest to identify the truth of women's sex comes to be a matter of identifying which body part approximates most closely to the penis – the clitoris of the vagina? Freud does not stop to ask what economy is at work behind the scenes to produce the search for a penis-equivalent; it does not seem necessary to him to wonder why the enigma of female sexuality should be solved by the discovery of a substitute penis – the question is not even raised. That female sexuality might have multiple sites, and that this plurality might not conform to a monistic masculine account geared to the specular economy of masculine values, is not a possibility that Freud's frame of reference allows. Freud does not seem to recognise the possibility that the negativity of his account of the vagina – which, as 'lack' or 'hole', is invisible, non-phenomenal, and hence in a way 'non-existent' – might stem from a system that decides in advance that different zones of sexual pleasure cannot be recognised.

A familiar set of oppositions orchestrates Freud's and Hegel's assumptions, a grid that can be traced back to Plato and Aristotle. Women are assigned to one side of this set of oppositions, and men to the other. On the feminine side, we find passivity, as opposed to activity; women are the objects to be investigated by subjects who assume the standpoint of men; male sexuality governs the investigation of female sexuality, which is represented as sexual only

in so far as it admits of classification in male terms. What counts as significant is that which approximates to male standards. One might say, then, that females are essentially asexual, since the only sexuality they are allowed is that which follows the pattern of male sexuality. Women are inferior copies of men: the clitoris qualifies, for Freud, as sexual because it attains the status of a 'little penis'. Thus, the title of one of the essays in which Irigaray explores the dynamic by which Freud's analysis of sexuality operates, 'This Sex Which Is Not One', can be read in at least two ways. Female sexuality does not qualify as a sex in the sense that it finds no register of its own. It merely imitates the phallic economy, and, as such, does not count as properly sexual. There is, in place of the penis, a black hole, a nothingness, pure lack, absence. It defies appearance and eludes examination. Its very existence is in question. It does not constitute a sex. In addition to pointing out the non-existence of female sexuality in Freud's account, Irigaray also objects to his monosexual view. Hence, the title 'This Sex Which Is Not One' issues a challenge to the dominant masculine economy by insisting that women's sexuality cannot be classified as singular and cannot be co-ordinated with male sexuality. It defies the logic of masculine sexuality, offering not one but many sites of pleasure. Why must there be a choice between clitoris or vagina? What of the lips, the vulva and the breasts? What is this need to classify and quantify, to categorise and name? Could it be that the very need to identify which part is the most important, which body part is the true sex, derives from a wish to master, control, possess and dominate? Could it be that the very desire to find a body part that approximates to the penis – even an attenuated penis – issues from a failure to acknowledge that there might be another desire at play here? Whose desire is at stake? Is this an economy in which female desire can only be acknowledged in so far as women assume the role of objects in an exchange between men?

Irigaray asks if women are any more than commodities on the market, goods up for sale, in an essentially homosexual economy – that is, homosexual in the sense that only one desire, the male desire, is acknowledged. Females are valued only as objects of exchange. Their value is granted only when they become substitutes not only for male sexuality, but also for one another. An interchangeable commerce. One for the other. Women compete as objects of male attention, and on these grounds their own desire is not in question. Freud confessed his inability to answer the question 'What does a woman want?' but Irigaray insists that the question has not even been posed.

Thus, Irigaray asks if the question of sexual difference has ever been properly formulated. Have we put to rest the issue of female sexuality before we have even found a way of raising the question? Has the issue of female sexuality always already been waylaid by the trajectory laid down for it in advance by male sexuality? Has feminine morphology only been figured in relation to male assumptions? Is there a way of undoing these assumptions, rewriting the female body, producing another account? One that is not always already inflected by the male gaze?

Deploying a strategy of mimicry, imitating the methods of the very texts she examines, Irigaray exhumes what remains of women once the tradition has had its say, putting together the disparate parts, the shattered remnants, in order to create for the first time an image of women that goes beyond the mirroring function they have served, as they 'constitute a masculine subject' and knowledge.

Hélène Cixous

Cixous was born on 5 June 1937 in Oran, Algeria; in 1956 she moved to France. She defended her doctoral dissertation, *The Exile of James Joyce*, in 1968, and at the same time co-founded the experimental University of Paris VII at Vincennes (now at Saint-Denis), where she was appointed to a chaired position in English Literature. In 1974 she established the *Centre de recherches en études féminines*, inaugurating a doctoral programme in Women's Studies, the first of its kind in France. Together with Gérard Genette and Tzvetan Todorov she founded the journal *Poétique*. She is a playwright, literary critic and the author of works she describes as 'poetic fiction', the first of which, *Dedans (Inside)* (1969), received the Prix Médicis. She was first known to her Anglo-American audience as the

author of 'The Laugh of the Medusa' and *The Newly Born Woman*, but is better known in France as a playwright. Her plays are performed regularly there at such venues as the Palais des Papes at the Avignon Festival and the Théâtre du Soleil. She has received numerous honorary degrees from the international academic community and lectures widely on the international circuit.

Along with Joyce, she counts Kafka, Kleist, Rilke and Genet among the literary influences that helped to shape her. She has described Brazilian writer Clarice Lispector as 'another Kafka', but one who sees the world 'through the experience of a woman, in a woman's body, with the relationships of a mother' (Penrod, 1996. p. 12).

The death of her father of tuberculosis in 1948, when Cixous was eleven, informs much of her work, as does her experience of being brought up in an Arab area of French Algeria. Her father was a French-speaking Jew, while her mother was of Jewish German descent. Her father was a doctor and, although a French citizen, was born in Algeria, although his family spoke Spanish, having lived in Morocco before moving to Algeria. Cixous was also exposed at an early age to Arabic and Hebrew, but when her father died she lost these languages. Her maternal language – which she thinks of as a language of nursery rhymes and poetry – is German, but she spoke French in the makeshift Jewish school she attended (as a Jew she was unable to attend a more formal school), and is also fluent in English. This multilingual background forms a vital part of her relationship to, and meditation on, language. She has commented on her 'mania for playing on the signifier' (Makward, 1976, p. 21) and has identified as the task of the writer 'to safeguard what is simultaneously necessary, rare, alive, and precarious. For me women are this precarious people, at once totally present and totally absent, one that can be forgotten at any moment, or remembered at any moment' (Jardine and Menke, 1991, p. 236).

Cixous describes herself as 'profoundly implicated' in feminism (Makward, 1976, p. 33). In 1976 she started to publish with *Editions des femmes* in solidarity with the women's movement, but moved to other publishing houses in 1982 in order to gain greater freedom poetically. She shares Freud's belief that we are all initially bisexual, and sees femininity in men as 'massively repressed', but in writing – much more so than in any other domain – she recognises 'men who transmit femininity' (ibid., p. 22). Among these she includes Genet.

There is, in Cixous, a relentless optimism. She often expresses her hope, her love of life, while distancing herself from opposition and negativity. Marking the difference between herself and women who have succumbed to 'marginalisation', 'isolation' and 'doom', she says 'The death-struggle is not new to me and it goes on of course, only I did not succumb to it: I suffered through it, I was a potential victim of it; then I came out of it'. She rejects the idea of 'sexual opposition' because it 'seems negative' and embraces instead 'sexual difference' (ibid., p. 24–5).

If Cixous's poetic fiction portrays a concern with fragility, it also engages with phenomena in an excessively detailed descriptive relationship that is at once playful, fantastic, ironic and self-reflective. She says 'I am like a philosopher and I start out, after all, from certain questions . . . Much of what I do begins in the unconscious'. Asked to comment on how she chooses a form of writing she responds: 'I have never chosen a way of writing, I have always started on impulse' (ibid., p. 28–30). Lest it seem incongruous for her to appeal to the unconscious and impulses on the one hand, and to philosophy, which has traditionally been seen as the most self-conscious and self-reflective of disciplines, on the other, we should perhaps bear in mind that Cixous is interested in 'the passage into literature of a portion of philosophy, the passage into philosophy of a portion of psychoanalysis, etc.' (Jardine and Menke, 1991, p. 235). And lest readers be concerned that, in remarking upon the importance of the unconscious, Cixous is uncritically employing some pre-cultural or pre-Oedipal notion of biological sources, we should understand that she is not interested in a notion of biology that would precede culture or language, as she makes perfectly clear here:

It is beyond doubt that femininity derives from the body, from the anatomical, the biological difference, from a whole system of drives which are radically different for women than for men.

But none of this exists in a pure state: it is always, immediately 'already spoken,' caught in representation, produced culturally. (Makward, 1976, p. 28)

Perhaps the lyrical quality of Cixous's poetic fiction derives in part from the fact that she draws on her dreams. She watches herself dreaming; she writes up her dreams, and then, she says: 'I *elaborate*' (ibid., p. 31). The different genres that we habitually use to divide literary and theoretical works are not easily imposed on her corpus. In *Vivre l'orange/To Live the Orange*, for example, Cixous's prose is inspired by the work of Clarice Lispector. In a book that is, in one sense, creative writing, she advises us to think 'Claricely'. In this gesture she both invokes Lispector's writing and pays homage to an author she sees as exploring the world of her femininity in an inventive, creative and subversive way that takes seriously the rhythms of the body. Is this then a work of fiction, a work of love, or a work of literary appreciation?

If Cixous identifies herself as a woman writer, she also identifies herself as Jewish and Algerian. In each case, she experiences her identity as contested. Growing up in a Jewish family in North African Algeria, during the anti-Semitism of the Second World War, her European origins were confronted with an Arabic way of life. She felt herself caught between cultures, nationalities and languages.

The themes that Cixous pursues in her various works can be traced across genres. The idea of a gift, particularly the impossibility of the conventional gift, the way in which it tends to turn into its opposite (exchange), that is, by eliciting debts and demanding gratitude, not only recalls themes that Derrida has explored in detail, but also provides a unifying thread between texts such as *Prénoms de Personne* (First Names of No One) (1974), *The Newly Born Woman* (1975), and *Vivre l'orange/To Live the Orange* (1979). While her fiction has been slow to appear in English translation, her more critical works are now becoming available. An anthology of her work, *The Hélène Cixous Reader*, containing excerpts from a wide range of her works, has been available since 1994.

Julia Kristeva

Kristeva was born in Bulgaria in 1941. After an early training in the sciences, she worked as a journalist while pursuing her literary studies. Her earliest work in linguistics was shaped by the post-Stalinist Communism of eastern Europe, a political climate that exerts its influence over her entire corpus, even if she has subsequently distanced herself from it. She embraced an increasingly psychoanalytic perspective when she entered the Parisian scene of avant-garde intellectuals in 1966. In France, having received a doctoral fellowship, she followed the advice of Tzvetan Todorov, another *émigré* from communist Bulgaria, and attended the seminar of Lucien Goldmann. As a research assistant at Claude Lévi-Strauss's Laboratory of Social Anthropology, she also took advantage of the resources offered by the Centre National de Recherche Scientifique, and the Ecole Pratique des Hautes Etudes. An associate of the *Tel Quel* review, edited by Philippe Sollers, Kristeva quickly took her place at the centre of French intellectual life. She joined the faculty of the University of Paris VII and later became a practising psychoanalyst.

Among the early influences on her work, in addition to Marxism, Mikhail Bakhtin stands out, as does structuralism. Semiotics, or the science of signs, provided the focus of her first published works, *Semeiotike: Recherches pour une sémanalyse* (1969) and *Le Texte du roman* (1970). Adapting and building on the work of Roland Barthes, Ferdinand de Saussure and Charles S. Peirce, Kristeva began to develop a theoretical framework that would be more fully elaborated in the 1974 landmark text, *Revolution in Poetic Language*.

By 1980, with the publication of *Powers of Horror: An Essay on Abjection*, Kristeva's growing interest in psychoanalysis had become decisive. The impact of Jacques Lacan's *Ecrits* (1966), and the psychoanalytic training that she had previously undergone continued to inform her approach in *Tales of Love* (1983), *Black Sun* (1987), *Strangers to Ourselves* (1989) and *New Maladies of the Soul* (1993). Her work also includes the novels *The Samurai* and *The Old Man and the Wolves*. The latter is a work of mourning, motivated both by the death of her father,

who, in her own words, 'was killed in a Sofia hospital through the incompetence and brutality of the medical and political system', and by an unease with what she describes as the 'general disarray' of society, in which she sees a 'collapse of minimal values and the rejection of elementary moral principles' (Interviews, 1996, p. 163). Her most recent work includes two books on Proust: *Proust and the Sense of Time* (1993), delivered as the 1992 Memorial Lectures at Canterbury, and *Time and Sense: Proust and the Experience of Literature* (1994).

Language, for Kristeva, has transformative capacities. In order to unearth the heterogeneous character of language, considered as in process, she departs from the 'generative grammar' of Chomsky that was so popular in the 1970s. The Chomskian view that 'surface' structures derive from 'deep' structures seems to Kristeva to reduce the 'speaking subject' to a series of translinguistic generalities that privilege systematic structures. Although she would rehabilitate Saussure's interest in semiology, she found Saussure's implementation of it – his search for truth, the emphasis on logic and the adoption of scientific procedures – just as inadequate to the subject of enunciation, or to what she called the 'speaking subject', as Chomsky's innatist belief in linguistic universals. Kristeva's desire to attend to the exigencies of the speaking subject is not a matter of returning to a Cartesian self, or a transcendental ego, but rather takes account of the disruptive and disturbing qualities that invade the equilibrium of those linguistic frameworks that reduce language to a series of rules or contain it within a formal system of signs.

Kristeva thus calls for linguistics to change its object of study. It is no longer the theoretical rules governing language, whether these are conceived as grammatical or semiological, that should be studied, but rather – and here the influence of Jakobson makes itself felt – 'poetic language'. Far from harnessing or fixing language by establishing its foundational structures, or stabilising it within a system, Kristeva focuses on a 'speech practice' that involves a dialectic between its 'signified structure (sign, syntax, signification)', and a 'semiotic rhythm'. Although she uses the term 'dialectic' to describe the struggle that takes place between 'language and its rhythm', she depends on post-Hegelian and post-Marxist resonances to give meaning to the term. She draws on Heidegger's vision of the strife of world and earth as the origin of the work of art, and on Mallarmé and Artaud, Lautréamont and Bataille, as well as the Russian poets Mayakovsky and Khlebnikov, when she observes, in 'The Ethics of Linguistics', that the poet 'wants to make language perceive what it doesn't want to say'.

Dissatisfied with scientific models of language conceived merely as a means of communicating preconceived ideas, where words simply function as isolated symbols that represent discrete concepts, Kristeva analyses language as a signifying process. As such, language is not a static and closed system of signs, but a mobile, fluid process that implicates bodily and vocal rhythms in the generation of symbolic meanings. In *Revolution in Poetic Language* she fuses linguistic insights with psychoanalytic enquiry as she presents two distinct, yet interrelated, aspects of the signifying process, the semiotic and the symbolic. The semiotic aspect of language is vocal, pre-verbal, rhythmic, kinetic and bodily. The symbolic aspect of language is social, cultural and rule-governed. Focusing on the interplay between the semiotic and the symbolic, she is able to analyse literary and historical texts, works of art and cultural phenomena in a way that thematises the complex relationship between materiality and representation.

Wary of neutralising the specificity of the speaking subject, Kristeva wants to find a way to recapture the 'rhythm of the body', to reclaim the 'semiotic materials' that other linguistic models tend to obliterate in their fascination with the technical elements of language. By refusing to restrict the significance of language to its meaning – that is, to see in it only a system of representation – Kristeva insists on the materiality of language, on its emergent conditions. In *Revolution of Poetic Language*, she thematises the divergent modalities of language under the heading 'the semiotic and the symbolic'. Her analysis of the semiotic is informed by Freud's notion of instinctual drives or impulses, the unconscious and the pre-Oedipal. The symbolic is associated with the Freudo-Lacanian notion of post-Oedipal relations, with the function of representation and with language as a sign-system.

The semiotic drives articulate what Kristeva calls the chora, a term she inherits from Plato's account of the creation of the universe in the *Timaeus*. The chora is a maternal receptacle, a generative matrix, an eternal place which, Plato tells us, is neither visible nor partakes of form, but is in some way intelligible. Amorphous and chaotic, Plato calls it the nurse of becoming, a kind of wet-nurse. Kristeva retains the paradoxical quality she sees in Plato's account of the chora as formless and undetermined, yet capable of receiving form and determination. The chora is neither sign nor signifier, neither model nor copy. It is pre-symbolic, not yet posited, and yet it can be named and spoken of – a process that converts the semiotic into the symbolic, conferring on the semiotic precisely the order, constraint or law of culture that it resists. Just as Plato's chora resists definition, although it can be spoken of as if it were identifiable as an entity, so Kristeva constitutes the semiotic by naming it, even as its mobile forces elude conceptualisation. In both cases, the very utterance involves a loss, a betrayal of what language attempts to say. Yet this is a necessary betrayal since the semiotic relies upon the symbolic for its articulation – one might say for its very existence – even if it suffers a transformation in the process of coming to representation.

If the semiotic needs the symbolic to represent it, the register of the symbolic requires the irruption and influx of the semiotic if it is to remain capable of change. If, in the interests of the very integrity of the semiotic, the subject cannot repudiate the symbolic, neither can it do without the semiotic. The need that the symbolic has for the excesses of poetic motion, or for the otherness of musical rhythm that marks the semiotic rupturing of the symbolic, might be described as an ethical and political exigency.

The symbolic, a Lacanian term that Kristeva invests with a new significance in counterpoising it to the semiotic, interprets the father of Freud's Oedipal drama in terms of language. Since the semiotic *chora* has maternal connotations, there is a sense in which the distinction between the semiotic and the symbolic is sexually marked. This does not mean that Kristeva discerns semiotic energies only in the work of women artists. On the contrary – and this has aroused consternation in some feminists

– the works to which she refers most often tend to be those of Bellini and Giotto, Baudelaire and Proust for their capacity to evoke the sexual pleasure that she calls corporeal 'jouissance'. This term, like so much of her work, reflects the influence of Lacan, whose impact on her corpus is decisive, despite the critical distance she inserts between her own writing and Lacan's *oeuvre*.

A visit to China, which resulted in the book *About Chinese Women* (1977), set the tone for Kristeva's uneasy relationship with feminism. The book caused controversy and Kristeva was accused of being 'romantic' and 'utopian' in her figuring of the Orient as other. Given to dramatic statements, such as 'a woman cannot "be"', Kristeva's often dismissive remarks about other versions of feminism – what she calls in an interview 'sociological protest' – did little to win over her detractors. In her defence, it should be pointed out that Kristeva's work has shared the same fate as that of Irigaray and Cixous, with whom she is so often compared. The reception of their work has been plagued by a failure to take account of their intellectual heritage, political contexts and personal biographies. Afraid that Kristeva's caution about totalising politics, her attempt to reintroduce the body into analyses of language and the Lacanian influence on her work amounted to a male-identified conservative and reactionary élitism, feminist critics of the 1980s shunned her work. Instead of understanding her insistence on sexual difference as a refusal to neutralise the specific material conditions of the production of language, conditions which include the sexed body, her attempt to reintroduce the body into feminism was condemned as detrimental to the progress of women's quest for equality.

Kristeva began to receive a fairer hearing in English-speaking feminist circles in the 1990s, largely due to the fact that critics began to equip themselves with the conceptual tools required for her diverse intellectual endeavours. Not least among these are phenomenology, psychoanalysis and structuralism – specifically, Heidegger and Lacan, and Saussure's structural linguistics and its modifications by figures such as Roland Barthes. For example, when Kristeva denies being to a woman, her assertion takes account of Heidegger's ontological distinction – the difference between a being and Being (or existence) as such – and Lacan's notorious statement in Seminar XX that 'There is no such thing as *The* woman'. Understood in this light, rather than as merely polemical, Kristeva's statement can be read as a way of insisting upon the relevance of sexual difference, the limitations of ontological language and the need to interrogate the possibilities of situating a woman's subjectivity in a way that does not simply conform to the position of male subjectivity. The position adopted by the female subject is thus one in excess of the boundaries of language, outside the order of being – at least in so far as language and existence are sanctioned as male.

It was Kristeva's abiding interest in language that drew her to psychoanalysis. Interested in the underside of language, in the late 1980s and the 1990s, she has been preoccupied with the exploration of borderlines, marginal existence, outlawed subjectivities – with what it means to be a foreigner, an outsider. While the significance of these themes is by no means limited to sexual difference – she also pursues the question of nationality, the issue of psychosis and the desire for abjection by focusing on the limits of subjectivity and consciousness – the question of feminine and masculine identity remains central.

Monique Wittig

Born in France in 1935, Wittig moved to the USA in 1976. Her first novel, *The Opoponax* (1964), was awarded the Prix Médicis. Indebted to experimental authors such as Robbe-Grillet, Wittig's fiction is also distinguished by the overtly political and polemical stance of a lesbian feminist. In *The Opoponax*, the character Catherine Legrand presents her child's view of the world, and the novel traces her development from infancy to adolescence on a path that challenges the primacy of heterosexuality. Her second book, *Les Guérillères* (1969), an epic tale about a lesbian separatist community that overthrows patriarchy, appropriates the female body from the domain of pornography, to which discussion and representation of body parts has been relegated by the male tradition. Wittig not only carefully describes the clitoris and vulva, reclaiming them from the gaze of the male, and refusing the terms in which women's sexuality has been traditionally seen, but also re-establishes the unity of the body image by including non-sexualised and non-fetishised parts of the body that also make up female sexuality. Rather than understanding the female body as compartmentalised, as pornographic representations of the body do by isolating and focusing on certain parts of the body, rather than seeing female sexuality in negative terms, as lack – as does Freud's account of penis-envy – Wittig reassesses female genitalia positively.

In *The Lesbian Body* (1973), Wittig provides a lyrical re-evaluation of menstruation, affirmatively recasting a bodily process often used as an excuse to prevent women from playing a full part in the public realms of politics and discourse. Making an intervention not just at the level of the body, but at the mythological and cultural level, she engages and subverts the ways in which female sexuality has been portrayed in literature that has traditionally been celebrated as great. She rewrites the Song of Songs, while *Across the Acheron* (1985) plays on Dante's *Divine Comedy*. Set in San Francisco, a modern-day city of sin, Wittig peoples her post-modern city with lesbian bikers in black leather jackets instead of with angels. In *Les Guérillères* she turns to the fairytales of Sleeping Beauty and Snow White, rewriting the female protagonists so that they take control of their bodies and their fates. In *Lesbian Peoples: Material for a Dictionary* (1976), co-authored with Sande Zeig, she turns to the Hindu *Mahabharata* and to textbook accounts of Amazons. The biblical figure of Noah also provides material for her critical and inventive recreations of the folklore, religion and cultural stories that carry patriarchal messages.

Deliberately elliptical plots, written in discontinuous and episodic prose, disrupt the traditional sequential narrative, while visually, as in *The Lesbian Body*, Wittig's texts interrupt their own unity with boldfaced type and lists of female body parts. Her texts are both humorous and extreme, disconcerting and polemical, lyrical yet violently explicit. In *The Lesbian Body* she splits the subject in two by writing 'J/e' instead of 'Je', in order to signal a disruption of the unified masculine subject, refusing the patriarchal connotations this subject carries with it. Individual characters merge into one another, as in *The Opoponax*, in which the child Catherine Legrand is signalled by the neutral pronoun 'on' (one), which lacks gender

and number; towards the end of the narrative she becomes part of the pair Catherine Legrand/Valerie Borge. The ungendered 'one' thus becomes gendered, and the singular and plural are indecipherable. Again, in *Les Guérillères*, the pronoun has a peculiar role to play. By using the feminine term 'elles' as the universal instead of the masculine 'ils' Wittig intends to shock her readers by allowing 'elles' to become the universal subject. A challenge to traditional subjectivity is thereby issued, as is an interrogation of the prevalence of sexual difference. Her task, as she articulates it in a collection of theoretical essays, *The Straight Mind* (1992), is not merely to denaturalise 'sex', to show that it is a political concept, but to destroy the categories of sex and gender. Since she regards the concept 'women' as inevitably bound up with sexist oppression, and irrevocably defined by men's subordination, she seeks to universalise lesbianism – a tactic that subverts the minority status of lesbians and uproots the heterosexual norm of sex and gender.

Sarah Kofman (1934–94)

Kofman grew up in Paris during the Nazi occupation. As a Jewish child she was forced to spend much of her childhood in hiding with her mother while her five siblings were sent to live in the country. Her father was deported and killed in 1942.

Kofman wrote on a wide range of philosophical, psychoanalytic and literary figures, but it is Nietzsche, perhaps (along with Freud), who dominates her critical outpouring. While a selection from her second book, *Nietzsche and Metaphor* (1972), was made available in translation by David Allison, editor of *The New Nietzsche* (1977), a complete translation did not appear until 1993. The twenty-year gap is unfortunately representative of the length of time that has been allowed to elapse between the publication of many of her works and their full translation into English, notwithstanding the efforts of journals such as *Diacritics* and *Sub-Stance* to ensure that samples of her work are available to an English-speaking readership. Several of her books remain untranslated; her second book on Nietzsche, first published in 1979, *Nietzsche et al scène philosophique* (*Nietzsche and the philosophical scene*), is a case in point. Among her most recent works is a two-volume study of Nietzsche's *Ecce Homo*, appearing in 1992 and 1993, entitled *Explosion*.

Kofman's first book, *The Childhood of Art: An Interpretation of Freud's Aesthetics* (1970) was not translated into English until 1988. Her second book on Freud appeared in 1974, *Freud and Fiction*, and in 1986 she published: *Pourquoi rit-on? Freud et le mot d'esprit* (*Why Do We Laugh? Freud and Jokes*). The two books that have put her on the feminist map (although *The Enigma* could just as easily be classified as philosophy or psychoanalysis, in her view) are *The Enigma of Woman: Woman in Freud's Writings*) (1980) – translated rather more swiftly (1985) than her other works – and *Le respect des femmes (Kant et Rousseau)* (*Respect for Women (Kant and Rousseau)*) (1982). Here she raises the question of the applicability of Kant's categorical imperative to women, and she shows how Rousseau's exhortations that women conform to their nature have the effect of both normalising and naturalising women's subordination to men.

Kofman felt a strong philosophical affinity to Derrida, and in 1984 she published *Lectures de Derrida*, (*Readings of Derrida*). Among her other work is the 1985 *Mélancolie de l'art* (*The Melancholy of Art*), in addition to discussions of Sartre, Socrates, and Heraclitus. At the time of her death, Sarah Kofman was Professor of Philosophy at University of Paris I.

Michèle Le Doeuff

Author of *The Philosophical Imaginary* (1980), and *Hipparchia's Choice* (1989), Michèle Le Doeuff has also collaborated in theatrical creations and performances, such as *Shakespeare's Sister* and *Shakespeare's Venus and Adonis*. Important references for her work include Francis Bacon, Gaston Bachelard, Thomas More's work on utopias and Simone de Beauvoir. She is Professor of Philosophy at the Ecole Normale Supérieure at Fontenay.

In the preface to *Hipparchia's Choice* she writes:

When sexism underpins the very method by which a system of thought is established (the example of existentialism will illustrate this hypothesis), how can we conceive of a method for a feminist philosophy, or for a philosophy which will allow men and women to come together in a common task? (Le Doeuff, 1989, p. xii)

A good deal of *Hipparchia's Choice* reads as a subtle appreciation and critique of Beauvoir's *The Second Sex* (1949). In a tone that it is at once detached, dispassionate, ironic and at the same time slightly mannered and meandering, Le Doeuff leads us through the intricacies of the plot that de Beauvoir constructed for herself with a sophisticated eye for its tensions. She points out how remarkably well de Beauvoir did in formulating an account of women's oppression, given that existentialism, with its emphasis on individual freedom, leaves little room for any acknowledgment of oppression. She reminds us that, whatever else it is, *The Second Sex* is also a 'labour of love', and that, as a confirmation of Sartrism, it says: 'your thought makes possible an understanding of women's condition, your philosophy sets me on the road to my emancipation – your truth will make me free'. Thus de Beauvoir becomes a 'whoeverian' – and other feminists have followed suit, whether it be Lacan, Foucault or Nietzsche who provides 'the way to salvation'. De Beauvoir falls into the trap of what Le Doeuff calls the 'Héloïse complex' – where women become 'loving admirer[s]', and 'devoted followers of one (and always only one)' (ibid., p. 59). None the less, Le Doeuff also takes pains to articulate the ways in which de Beauvoir recasts the existential analysis that Sartre provides in *Being and Nothingness*. For example, she did not rely on the notion of bad faith to which Sartre appeals – and since, typically, the bad faith that Sartre discusses is the bad faith of others (although it goes unmarked as such), this means that de Beauvoir casts less blame on others than Sartre does; she re-evaluates sexuality and the female body, to which Sartre reacts with distaste and sometimes unmitigated terror, describing it in terms of holes and slime. Le Doeuff shows at the same time how de Beauvoir insists on the importance of the concrete world: women have lacked the means to change their situation, in part, because they have been isolated as housewives and mothers, unable to combine as a group, and denied the financial or material means to revolt.

Bibliography

Writings

Cixous, Hélène, with Catherine Clément (1975), *La Jeune née*, Paris: Union générale'. (*The Newly Born Woman*, trans. B. Wing, Minneapolis: University of Minnesota Press, 1986.)

Irigaray, Luce (1974), *Speculum de l'autre femme*, Paris: Minuit. (*Speculum of the Other Woman*, trans. G. Gill, Ithaca, New York: Cornell University Press, 1985.)

— (1977), *Ce Sexe qui n'en est pas un*, Paris: Minuit. (*This Sex Which Is Not One*, trans. C. Porter and C. Burke, Ithaca, New York: Cornell University Press, 1985.)

Kristeva, Julia (1974), *La révolution du langage poétique*, Paris: Seuil. (*Revolution in Poetic Language*, trans. M. Waller with an Introduction by L. S. Roudiez, New York: Columbia University Press, 1984.)

— (1980), *Pouvoirs de l'horreur: Essai sur l'abjection*, Paris: Seuil. (*Powers of Horror. An Essay on Abjection*, trans. L. S. Roudiez, New York: Columbia University Press, 1982.)

Kofman, Sarah (1980), *L'Enigme de la femme: La femme dans les texts de Freud*, Paris: Galilee. (*The Enigma of Woman*, trans. C. Porter, Ithaca, New York: Cornell University Press, 1985.)

Le Doeuff, Michèle (1989), *L'Etude et le rouet*, Paris: Seuil. (*Hipparchia's Choice: An Essay Concerning Women, Philosophy, etc.*, trans. T. Selous, Oxford: Blackwell, 1991.)

Wittig, Monique (1992), *The Straight Mind and Other Essays*, Boston: Beacon Press.

References and further reading

Beauvoir, Simone de (1954), *The Second Sex*, trans. H. M. Parshley, New York: Knopf.

Chanter, Tina (1995), *Ethics of Eros: Irigaray's Rewriting of the Philosophers*, New York: Routledge.

Courtivron, Isabelle de and Elaine Marks (1981), *New French Feminisms*, Brighton: Harvester.

Delphy, Christine (1995), 'The Invention of French Feminism: An Essential Move', *Yale French Studies*, 87: 190–221.

Hirsh, E. and G. A. Olson (1995), ' "Je–Luce Irigaray": A Meeting with Luce Irigaray', *Hypatia*, Special Issue: *Feminist Ethics and Social Policy*, Part II, 10: 2, 93–114.

Jardine, Alice A. and Anne M. Menke (1991), *Shifting Scenes: Interviews on Women, Writing, and Politics in Post '68 France*, New York: Columbia University Press.

Makward, Christiane (1976), 'Interview with Hélène Cixous', *Sub-Stance*, 13, 19–37.

Oliver, Kelly (ed.) (1993), *Ethics, Politics, and Difference in Julia Kristeva's Writing*, New York: Routledge.

Penrod, Lynn Kettler (1996), *Hélène Cixous*, New York: Twayne.

Sellers, Susan (1994), *The Hélène Cixous Reader*, London: Routledge.

8.6

DECONSTRUCTION: DERRIDA

Michal Ben-Naftali

Introduction

Jacques Derrida, born in 1930 near Algiers, has been a major force in post-structuralist thought since the mid-1960s. His prodigious output seems to defy categorisation, but one can usefully, though cautiously and certainly not definitively, demarcate periods in his career as follows, according to the style and preoccupations of his writings: the 'classical deconstructions' of 1967–72; the 'experiments' of 1974–80; and the 'political turn' of 1980–present.

In the first period, his works took the form of 'deconstructions' (to be defined later) of philosophical and literary texts; examples here include the three books published in 1967: *Speech and Phenomena*, on Husserl; *Of Grammatology*, on Saussure, Lévi-Strauss and Rousseau; and *Writing and Difference*, on Levinas, Husserl, Bataille and Hegel, Freud, Artaud, Jabès and structuralism. Two other noteworthy collections of essays appeared in 1972: *Margins – Of Philosophy*, dealing with Heidegger, Hegel, Husserl, Aristotle, Austin and linguistics, and *Dissemination*, on Plato, Mallarmé and Sollers.

Although by 1972 Derrida had become more typographically adventurous (for example, 'Tympan' in *Margins* has two columns), his 1974 *Glas* marks a certain turning point. Here he juxtaposes two columns of commentary and inserts extended quotations from Hegel and Genet to produce a dizzying 'reading effect' of multiplying meanings that defies summary. Other noteworthy experiments of the period include the 'framing effect' interrupting 'Parergon' (Derrida's interrogation of Kant's aesthetics), and the 'polylogue' of 'Restitutions' (his examination of Heidegger's 'Origin of the Work of Art'), both of which appear in the 1978 *The Truth in Painting*, and the 'Envois' section of the 1980 *The Post Card*. It should be noted, however, that texts of traditional contours occur in this period as well, for example, in the extended works on Freud and Lacan included in *The Post Card*.

A final useful grouping is to notice the explicitly political nature of the post–1980 works. Never lacking in the earlier works, Derrida's interrogation of the relations between the philosophy and the political institutions of the West takes centre stage in works such as 'No Apocalypse, Not Now' (1984) (on nuclear arms), 'The Laws of Reflection: Nelson Mandela, in Admiration' (1987) 'Force of Law: the "Mystical Foundation of Authority"' (1989), *The Other Heading* (1991) (on the unity and future of 'Europe'), and *Specters of Marx* (1993). In addition, two large volumes of his political thought have recently appeared in French. *Du droit à la philosophie* (1990) collates his work from the 1970s with GREPH, an educational reform group, with work from the 1980s on the history and contemporary status of the university; and *Politiques de l'amitié* discusses Nietzsche, Carl Schmitt and Heidegger (1994).

However, it is best to note right away that Derrida's career is as circular as it is linear, for one could also show that his later works are pre-figured in his first extended works on Husserl, the 1962 *Edmund Husserl's 'Origin of Geometry': An Introduction* and *Speech and Phenomena* (1907). Since the very beginning of his work, Derrida has been tackling the issues of memory and responsibility, those issues that will come to the forefront in the post–1980 period. These, along with knowledge, commemoration, culture, archive and historicity will be the focus of this article. They will be elaborated through the deconstructionist quasi-concepts or 'quasi-transcendental' categories (as they are called by Rodolphe Gasché in his influential book *The Tain of the Mirror*) of 'arche-writing', 'différance' and 'trace'.

Deconstruction

It is undoubtedly a large task to provide both a short introduction to and a summary of work which has the extent and complexity of Derrida's; to repeat in a clear, concise and precise manner some of his main ideas, and to paraphrase his and others' reproductions of his thought. Beyond the mere scope of the task lies a more difficult problem, though, for each concept in the sentence above could be problematised by a deconstruction.

First of all, what 'is' 'deconstruction'? Deconstruction has usually been considered from a structural or 'conceptual' perspective. Several prominent commentators (for example, Gasché and Bennington) have tackled the minimal structural notions that enable deconstruction to undermine canonical texts. Following these commentators, deconstruction has been identified as a rigorous formalist operation that questions dialectical reason, pushing it beyond its reconciliation through difference to give way to another condition of thought: that of the undecidable, the differential, or even the unsayable.

In addition to the structural interpretation of deconstruction, a minor tendency has been gaining influence since the late 1980s, concentrating on the practical and political implications of deconstruction (for example, Critchley and Martin). Since the 'structural' view is well established and easily accessible elsewhere, this article will emphasise the latter 'practical' tendency, but with a certain twist: it will be devoted to deconstruction as both a praxis and a *Weltanschauung*, so that deconstruction will be presented here as a pathos – a sensibility, or better, a historicity.

Derrida has consistently avoided giving a full

'definition' of deconstruction lest it become a fixed entity susceptible of ontological definition of the type 'S is P'. 'Deconstruction' can thus not be given an exhaustive and univocal definition, nor can it be reduced to a set of methodological procedures to be turned on texts. Since it has been appropriated by many literary critics as just such a 'method' of interpretation – or, alternatively, been rejected by some as a 'faulty' 'method' – Derrida has become even more reluctant to adhere to this or any other single term. Rather than sticking with any one master term, he uses various neologisms, which only gain their meaning from inscription within his own lexical chain. In this way, he practices what he preaches, as he both demonstrates and states the way a term becomes significant in a context, although that context is always open-ended; meaning is therefore differential (context-dependent) and deferred (other contexts are always to come).

Despite the dangers of defining deconstruction, some of Derrida's statements can give us a sort of working orientation, which will be elucidated as we go along. In his 'Letter to a Japanese Friend', Derrida writes:

> In spite of appearance, deconstruction is neither an analysis nor a critique . . . It is not an analysis, in particular because the dismantling of a structure is not a regression towards the simple element, towards an indecomposable origin . . . No more is it a critique, whether in general or a Kantian sense . . . I'll say the same thing for method. Deconstruction is not a method and cannot be transformed into a method. (Wood and Bernasconi, 1988, pp. 4–5)

The very cognitive procedures or values by which one would hope to define deconstruction: analysis, method, structure, are, in fact, the very ones that are to be subject to deconstruction.

Rather than as a method, then, Derrida speaks of deconstruction as a singular 'event'. It is not initiated by conscious intentions or subjective decisions; rather, it is inherent in the very textuality of a philosophical text, in those blind spots, contradictions, or aporias that exceed its explicit statements, those moments within each text that threaten to undermine its presuppositions and aims. Indeed, every philosophical (construction) text, necessarily, deconstructs itself. Therefore, a deconstructionist intervenes in a text in order to articulate those implicit moments of deconstruction, often unrecognised by the author. Deconstruction holds, therefore, to the logic that is being deconstructed; it does not transcend the tradition, but manipulates its cunning reason, leaving it, as it were, undecidable as to its openness or closure.

Derrida's work responds to both philosophical and literary texts of the Western tradition. By excruciatingly detailed readings of these texts, he demonstrates that the fundamental concepts that constitute this tradition are not pacific oppositions, but violent hierarchies: substance and accident, centre and margin, origin and trace. One term controls the other, both logically and axiologically. Deconstructing the text thus involves, at one and the same time, inverting those oppositions and exceeding them in a non-dialectical way. The second part of this dual gesture is crucial, because merely inverting an opposition leaves its oppositional structure – and hence its apparent pacificity, rationality and naturalness – untouched. Because of the resilience of the oppositional structure, the only way to question the very structure of traditional argumentation is to put it 'under erasure'; that is, to show that its conditions of possibility are the same conditions that make it collapse. In Gayatri Spivak's words:

> To locate the promising marginal text, to disclose the undecidable moment, to pry it loose with the positive lever of the signifier; to reverse the resident hierarchy only to displace it; to dismantle in order to reconstitute what is always already inscribed. Deconstruction in a nutshell. (in Derrida, 1976, p. lxxvii)

We shall soon look more closely at several deconstructive enactments. Still, one might reasonably ask: what is the point? To what purpose? Again, programmatical definitions would be self-defeating, for, in general, deconstruction tries to agitate some of our deeply ingrained self-assured habits of thought. Key philosophical concepts, such as sameness, authority, origin, speech, subject, essence, *telos*, presence and consciousness, prove on deconstruction to be non-self-sufficient, to lack semantic stability; they have, in fact, proved to be dependent upon their denigrated others: writing, trace, absence, difference, etc. Meaning is thus not fully self-present in language to a consciousness, although partial meaning effects, some within and some beyond conscious control, are an obvious feature of human life. No signified exists completely isolated from the linguistic train of relations. This observation holds even when dealing with the allegedly 'professional' or 'technical' language of philosophy, since no epistemologically trustful language exists: no language has ever been established without 'slippage' and 'dissemination', effects of the production of meaning outside conscious control that Derrida examines in 'Signature Event Context' (Derrida, 1982, pp. 307–30).

Encyclopedism

From the above description of deconstruction, it might seem that the very attempt to transform Derrida and deconstruction into an encyclopedic content, or content for an encyclopedia, is problematic. Trying to work out this particular dilemma may serve as an 'introduction' in itself. This article will both deconstruct the notion of encyclopedia and articulate the implicit deconstructionist movement within the very being of any encyclopedic effort.

The *Encyclopaedia Britannica* begins its entry on 'encyclopedia' in the following way: 'The Greeks seem to have understood by encyclopaedia . . . instruction in the complete system or cycle . . . of learning'. The article registers the main turning points in the history of this idea; the seventeenth century, when the familiar modern form began, was crucial. The modern encyclopedia introduces knowledge to its readers with comprehensive treatises on particular subjects, which add up to a totality of knowledge, classified by themes, writers, disciplines or historical development. Each treatise tries to master its subject by presenting the general principles and the essential details. Each contributor is considered a specialist, a person able to transmit precise, comprehensive, authoritative and reliable knowledge. Thus, there seems to be no accomplishment which emblematises, in its very material being, Western metaphysical presuppositions more than the encyclopedia, which strives to present to the reading public the complete and total knowledge that is already accessible to experts.

Nevertheless, despite this pretension to completeness, encyclopedias are revised time and again – indeed, annually if funding allows. The concept of finality is thus undermined by the very practice of encyclopedic production, so that, at best, 'encyclopedia' becomes merely an idea, or ideal, of completeness. Although the project is highly concentric and arrogant, structurally it is doomed to be modest; it deconstructs itself both in its total format and in its particular elements. The encyclopedic experience thus shows that no treatise is self-sufficient, for each one is haunted by other encyclopedias and by its future editions. The logic of 'iteration' and 'trace' (to be examined below) pervades every encyclopedia, preventing totalisation. This structural necessity cannot be corrected by producing an alternative fragmentary encyclopedia which would pretend to capture truth and totality intuitively. Encyclopedia is destined to be torn between gathering and dissemination, presence and deferral. Deconstruction is thus encyclopedia's desire and its anxiety. But – and this is a point often neglected in deconstructionist literature – encyclopedism is both the desire and the anxiety of deconstruction itself! Derrida admits his own personal 'encyclopedic temptation' to transmit all the voices, 'to write so as to put into play or to keep the singularity of the date (what does not return, what is not repeated, promised experience of memory as promise, experience of ruin or ashes)' (Derrida, 1992, p. 42).

Biography

It is not uncommon to introduce a personality – writer, thinker, scientist – in an encyclopedia by giving her or his biographical background. It may seem less relevant in those encyclopedias specialising in particular topics whose development is perceived as autonomous, that is, as independent of their creators. While deconstruction problematises the notion of autonomy (in *Positions*, Derrida remarks that he does not accept the absolute autonomy of history as a history of philosophy), as well as that of borders and margins in general, it also undermines

the conventional idea of a linear intellectual history. Thus, even if I refer to some details of Derrida's childhood and adolescence in and near Algiers, I am not trying to contextualise his thought in a traditional manner by linking 'life' and 'work' as two separate and well-defined entities. An author's 'life' is itself a text to be analysed; it cannot serve as the simple answer to questions about the motivation of the 'work'. Derrida's work is thus inherently contextualised by his life through the very structure of writing which links text and context so that only relative distinctions are possible. For Derrida, there is no single ultimate psycho-biographical referent that explains an author's work, for nothing is so completely outside a text that it can serve as an anchoring point to determine its final meaning. He states:

> We must begin wherever we are and the thought of the trace, which cannot not take the scent into account, has already taught us that it was impossible to justify a point of departure absolutely. Wherever we are: in a text where we already believe ourselves to be. (Derrida, 1976, p. 162)

In an interview with *Le nouvel observateur*, Derrida described his early memories:

> I knew from experience that the knives could be drawn at any moment, on leaving school, in the stadium, in the middle of those racist screams which spared no one, Arabs, Jews, Spanish, Maltese, Italians, Corsicans . . . Then, in 1940, the singular experience of the Algerian Jews. Incomparable to that of European Jews, the persecutions were nonetheless unleashed in the absence of any German occupier. . . . It's an experience which leaves nothing intact, something you can never again cease to feel. The Jewish children were expelled from school. Then the Allies land, and it's the period of what was called the two-headed government (de Gaulle–Giraud): racial laws were maintained for a period of almost six months, under a 'free' French government. Friends no longer knew you, the insults, the Jewish Lycée with teachers expelled without a murmur of protest from their colleagues . . . From that moment – how can I say it – I felt as displaced in a Jewish community, closed unto

itself, as I would in the other (which they used to call 'the Catholics'). The suffering eased in France. At nineteen I naively believed anti-Semitism had disappeared, at least where I was living then. But, during my adolescence, and that was the real tragedy, it was there for everyone else . . . A paradoxical effect, perhaps, of this bludgeoning was the desire to be integrated into the non-Jewish community, a fascinated but painful and distrustful desire, one with a nervous vigilance, a painstaking attitude to discern signs of racism in its most discreet formations or in its loudest denials. Symmetrically, oftentimes, I felt an impatient distance with regard to various Jewish communities, when I have the impression that they close in upon themselves, when they pose themselves as such. From all of which comes a feeling of non-belonging that I have doubtless transposed . . . [e]verywhere. (Wood and Bernasconi, 1988, pp. 74–5)

The above extract captures many elements of Derrida's youth that anticipate his complex relations with Jewishness. It is first and foremost a relation to the proper name, a relation by descent, a feeling of place that is involuntarily affirmed at the beginning and only later in life actively reaffirmed. However, this feeling never mystifies or reifies the notion of 'identity' –, for Jewishness remains, for Derrida, unstable, interrupted, non-linear. In a sense, it could not have been otherwise: Jewish identity, as identity or self-presence in general, cannot be disconnected from the deconstructive gestures that pervade his work; it cannot be set apart from those historical and structural processes of differentiation that persistently transform the categories of self or communal identity. Significantly, throughout its rich inventory of notions, deconstruction never uses old 'proper nouns' to indicate anew something that the old use had repressed. Derrida uses common nouns – writing, trace, supplement – but does not conceptualise proper nouns as bearing a historical, ethnic or racial weight. Through 'writing', 'différance', and other quasi-transcendental concepts, which implicate one another and replace one another without being reducible to each other, Derrida can indeed characterise a world of ethnic hierarchies and ex-

clusions. But an ethnic specificity never serves as a formal category: the 'other' is never simply the 'Jew' or the 'black' or the 'woman'.

Structure and pathos

As we have already mentioned, several remarkable interpretive works have elaborated upon Derrida's specific vocabulary, concentrating on its categorial-structural dimension, its 'basic concepts' so to speak. Gasché's relatively early work in *Tain of the Mirror* treated deconstruction's critical project in relation to the philosophical tradition, showing that Derrida was examining the limits of philosophical foundationalism and self-justification. In striving after totality, identity, coherence and presence, philosophy was fulfilling its ethico-teleological orientation, which both enabled and blinded its insights. In other words, in order to be, philosophy had to repress those moments of otherness that it could not possibly think in whatever mode it chose: rational, phenomenological, dialectical and so on. Gasché stressed that philosophy's unthought was not the consequence of an existential finality, so that deconstruction did not focus on the (Romantic) constraints of the thinking subject, but focussed instead on the structural limits of thought itself. Thus, in 'Structure, Sign and Play in the Discourse of the Human Sciences', Derrida presented the following argument, which forms much of the basis of Gasché's thought:

> If totalization no longer has any meaning, it is not because the infiniteness of a field cannot be covered by a finite glance or a finite discourse, but because the nature of the field – that is, language and finite language – excluded totalization. This field is in effect that of play, that is to say, a field of infinite substitutions only because it is finite, that is to say, because instead of being an inexhaustible field, as in the classical hypothesis, instead of being too large, there is something missing from it: a center which arrests the play of substitutions. (Derrida, 1978b, p. 289)

Despite his orientation to such structural argumentation, Gasché himself noted the extent to which deconstruction's interference within philosophical discourse was actively contextual, and thus by no means 'aesthetic' in a stereotypically ahistorical sense. Deconstruction referred itself in Derrida's practice to discursive domains which seemed to suppress certain epistemological/political concepts. The conditions of its movement were thus both structural and full of pathos; that is, political-cultural-historical. In one breath, Derrida argued that

> [t]he incision of deconstruction, which is not a voluntary decision or an absolute beginning, does not take place just anywhere, or in an absolute elsewhere. An incision, precisely, can be made only according to lines of force and forces of rupture that are localizable in the discourse to be deconstructed. The topical and technical determination of the most necessary sites and operators – beginnings, holds, levers, etc. – in a given situation depends upon an historical analysis. (Derrida, 1982a, p. 82)

What is this 'incision'? How does it 'happen'? ('Deconstruction is not an operation that supervenes afterwards, from the outside, one fine day; . . . Always already . . . there was deconstruction at work in history, culture, literature, philosophy' (Derrida, 1988b, p. 73).) Why is it not reducible to an interpretive method or analysis, or, indeed, to any definable entity? How does it constitute itself as a sensibility or a 'historicity' that exceeds its more or less representable procedures? Finally, could we return to the citation that served as our 'starting point' and suggest a historicised version of deconstruction?

The sign

Above, we began mapping deconstruction's field of action. We saw that Derrida's critique of the Western philosophical tradition concentrates on its analysable conceptual universe, formed by hierarchic oppositions: although each concept in the system appears self-sufficient, it is actually inseparable from its 'other'. Each dominant concept is allegedly superior and essential, while its opposed/complementary concept is deemed inferior and contingent. Derrida's best-known deconstruction, which he has elaborated since his early studies of

Husserl, Plato and Rousseau in such works as *Speech and Phenomena*, *Of Grammatology* and *Margins*, tackles one of the most crucial traditional oppositions: voice and writing. In Western canonical philosophy, writing has always been deemed secondary to voice, which was, in turn, secondary to the silent self-presence, spontaneity and immediacy of thought, consciousness or spirit. In other words, the graphic signifier was twice as distant from signified reality, which came to it mediated by the phonic signifier. Against this tradition of denigrating writing, Derrida pointed out that the following alleged faults of writing can be seen as advantages: writing is destined to be read in a different context from the one in which it was inscribed; it is given to repetition (and quotation) within different contexts, including ones that transcend the intentions of its original addressor and addressee(s); it is ambiguous. To write means to know that both the writer and her or his reader(s) are mortal: writing does not need them, But Derrida argues that these characteristics are actually applicable to any linguistic sign: both oral and written signs are 'iterable', that is, repeatable with a difference. A singular sign, which can be used only once, is not a sign; the very event of speech and writing is dependent upon iterability. Derrida names this general linguistic functioning 'arche-writing', a notion that is not identical to the familiar, derived concept of 'writing'. 'Arche-writing', much like 'trace', 'différance', and other notions in the Derridean dictionary, is a minimal pre-ontological (or quasi-transcendental) structure, escaping the opposition of being and non-being. It cannot be identified, then, with either presence or absence; it is, rather, a field of forces which produces conceptual effects, even though, by the same token, it is not precisely non-conceptual.

Let us now look more closely at the notion of the sign. Derrida suggests, following Saussure, that the meaning of each sign is produced by its insertion in a differential chain; that is, by relations of difference between signifier and signified, as well as between the individual sign and other signs. Since meaning is differential, any final meaning is deferred. The combination of differing and deferring produces *différance*. In Derrida's words, subjectivity, phenomenology's candidate for the origin of meaning, is an effect inscribed in a system of *différance*. This is why the *a* of *différance* also recalls that spacing is temporization, the detour and postponement by means of which intuition, perception, consummation – in a word, the relationship to the present, the reference to a present reality, to a *being* – are always *deferred*. Deferred by virtue of the very principle of difference which holds that an element functions and signifies, takes on or conveys meaning, only by referring to another past or future element in an economy of traces. (Derrida, 1982a, pp. 28–9)

It is thus the relational status of the identity of each sign that produces meaning. Each sign is defined not only by its difference from 'other' signs, but also by its difference from 'itself' at different times. In other words, each linguistic element inhabits, and presupposes, a past and a future that are never fully present. Derrida does not deny, of course, the empirical, 'immediate' phenomenon of speech, but the conditions of possibility of speech, of meaning and presence, are not present. Thus, they constitute both the conditions of possibility and impossibility of these values. That is why philosophy tends to suppress them altogether, to deny its own textuality in order to achieve a pure contemplation, independent of signs. Philosophy dreams of a transcendental signified which exceeds differential linguistic play but in Derrida's perspective, the return of the repressed is necessitated by the very nature of metaphysical thought. The iterability of the sign always comes back to haunt philosophy.

Trace

Derrida's preoccupation with traces or ashes, in texts such as *Glas* (1974) or *Feu la cendre* (1987), is not destined to score another point in the ongoing autocritique of philosophy, but to work out a new notion of historicity. The vocabulary he uses is crucial and telling, so his insistence on commemoration and memory should be thoroughly examined. Derrida once remarked in an interview: ' "There must be" this historicity, which doesn't mean that all reading or all writing is historicized, . . . still less "historicist".' To what concept of historicity does he refer?

How can one speak of historicity within a writing that explicity rejects historicist chronology and teleology, thus undermining the universal gestures of grand narratives? Does Derrida's deconstruction in fact invoke a (coherent) meaning throughout history? These are serious questions, since it seems that deconstruction, contrary to some ahistorical interpretations – mainly in literary criticism – is not only historically minded, but also implicitly bears a philosophy of history.

Our discussion should return to the somewhat evasive and non-representable notion of 'trace'. This term carries a temporal or historical reference although it implies no specific timeframe whatsoever, since it is the very condition of periodisation. It characterises historical dynamics, such as a movement that has neither an origin nor an end. One cannot actually speak of history and its contents – meaning, truth, language, tradition – without the trace that is always already there, although not susceptible of any definition. 'The iterability of the trace', writes Derrida, 'is the condition of historicity' (Derrida, 1992, p. 63). When we speak of 'trace' we are not referring to a presence or an absence, if absence means an empirical modification of presence. 'Trace' would be a force which always involves other forces, themselves nothing but relations-of-force. These relations are historical. They consitute history. Derrida does not identify historicity with a particular sense: historicity is neither reason nor liberty, neither truth nor spirit. He always uses the somewhat neutral notion of trace to characterise the processing of human experience in general, since by applying a more definite or substantial notion, one imposes on history one's own conception of what it should be like.

The notion of trace implies the immanence of contexts to texts. The contextualisation of the text, its intra- and inter-textuality, is a structural necessity. The trace inscribes every text, 'contaminates' it, with contexts. Thus, the allegedly 'original' text is always already transcended, always already precedes itself and follows itself. In this sense, the context precedes the text. The text persists in a permanent deferral, a belatedness, in relation to a missing other. Therefore, when we speak of context, we never refer to a fully given entity. The context is an open structure, a heterogenous one, which involves other contexts as well. It gives itself to both decontextualisation and recontextualisation, as does every element within it.

Historicity, mourning, culture

Derrida's conception of historicity does not lean, then, upon an original moment; there is no historical moment innocent of traces. No simple origin can be re-presented or referred to. Derrida's often misinterpreted phrase, 'There is nothing outside the text' simply indicates that any text is involved in a chain of texts and contexts. He emphasises that this chain of historicity is multilevelled, although each level is not necessarily consciously experienced. Culture demands a genealogical responsibility, whether or not individually attributable, since this responsibility is the very condition of cultural continuity. On one level, then, historicity is an implicit process of cultural formation, and on another level, in Derrida's own writing, the articulation of that process. Cultural relations are always already full of historical meaning; historicity, in this sense, is a dynamical, although not teleological, evolutionary moment.

However, there is much more to it, because historicity coincides with history and is subject to its accidents and caprices. On the one hand, indeed, historicity is dependent upon historical contingency, so that the end of history would be the end of historicity, annihilating archive and transmission. On the other hand, historicity carries its own significance, at once bound to, and independent of, historical events. History is the chaotic order of events as they actually take place, while historicity is an implicit or explicit commitment to repetition. In this respect, Husserl's discussion of the reactivation of origins and Derrida's elaboration of historicity inhabit different modes of discourse, constative and performative – saying and doing by saying. Derrida's *Introduction* insists that Husserl's recuperation of origins engages the responsibility of the philosopher, bound to radical finitude (Derrida, 1978a, pp. 141–6).

Derrida's notions of mourning and memory, developed in works such as *Mémoires: For Paul De Man* and *Specters of Marx*, belong to his notion of histori-

city. Historicity is not identified with a single linear sense (meaning/direction), but it does imply relatively stable structures of experience, which, although not natural or universal, enable cultural memory. Hence, historicity is not the experience of history itself, but an active relation to history, an active memory and forgetting. Derrida writes *à propos* of Marx:

> That we are heirs does not mean that we have or that we receive this or that, some inheritance that enriches us one day with this or that, but that the being of what we are is first of all inheritance, whether we like it or not. And that . . . we can only bear witness to it. (Derrida, 1994, p. 54)

Historicity involves both description and prescription. It happens, and has been always already happening; it is commitment and responsibility. One might situate the tension between history and historicity thus: historicity is deconstruction. The cultural dynamics that deconstruction identifies and with which it is itself identified – multiculturalism – are all historicity at work. Deconstruction is both part of multiculturalism and its articulation: [D]econstruction . . . is always already at work in the work . . . (Derrida 1988b, p. 73).

Deconstruction is immersed in history as historicity; at the same time it transcends historicity to articulate its very movement, describing it as trace, *différance*, memory or mourning. This might be the reason for the somewhat obsessive use of the 'always already' in Derrida's writings, a surprising repetition given deconstruction's minimalism in philosophic presuppositions. Deconstruction is 'always already' there, paradoxically obliged to a never-present past and unforeseeable future, persisting between the two.

Derrida is ambivalent about Husserl's articulation of historicity. He rejects Husserl's distinction between empirical tradition and transcendental historicity (the latter depending on the reactivation of origin as sense) because he wants to insist upon the necessity of tradition as well as on the deconstruction of any 'origin'. Derrida takes sedimentation – which Husserl would exile to empiricity – as the very movement of historicity, while at the same time calling into question Husserl's account of the origin of geometry as an act of transcendental subjectivity.

For Derrida in the *Introduction*, as in all his work, the distinction between empirical and transcendental is another opposition to be deconstructed.

One could reformulate the notions of trace and *différance* by linking them to memory, both personal and cultural. Derrida rejects the Freudian conception of successful mourning; mourning is structurally partial, succeeding only when it fails, when it does not interiorise the other within the mourner. There can be no sublimation in mourning, but at best a choice, perhaps not always voluntary, between memory and hallucination. A 'successful' mourning assumes the self-present identity of the mourner, for the mourner is supposed to devour the other ('introjection'). For Derrida, though, the self is constituted by traces of others, other texts, which dispossess the self of self-present identity. We are selves only through others. The self's encounter with the other anticipates the possibility of the latter's absence or death; the former's interiority is already shaped by this anticipation, even though the other can never be comprehended or re-presented in life or death. We are left with names, with recollections ultimately turning into memories; these are insufficient and thus engaging and obligating.

Derrida does not relate these processes of mourning to 'culture' as an abstract common noun. Culture is not analogous to an individual, but is formed by individuals from their experience. Derrida's discussion of mourning, reminiscence and memory follows the death of his friend Paul De Man, the singular 'other' whom Derrida mourns. *Mémoires* moves from personal to impersonal propositions; the particular mourning is pervaded by reflections on mourning. As in another text, dedicated to Jean-Luc Nancy, 'Toucher' Derrida lets us experience, through his own experience, the impossibility that lies in the very possibility of encountering an other, linguistically or not. He describes the insufficiency of material recollection, our fruitless attempts to reconstruct faithfully, to relive gestures and details and words, and the insufficiency of memory, which altogether lacks the vital touch of recollection and is thus subservient to the continuous historical, sometimes mechanical, processing of archive.

Again, contrary to an exclusively conceptual or structural reading, we should note that in Derrida's most explicitly personal writings – on De Man and Nancy and the quasi-autobiographical 'Circumfession' – the relation to the other in love, desire and mourning is thematised. What is there, always already there, is brought out, however inconclusively, by being made explicit. Derrida's most intimate discussions are necessarily connected to others, since the phenomenological structure of intentionality is intersubjective in all domains of human experience. This structural necessity results in a 'confessional philosophy', which enables him to mediate between proper names and common nouns, between the 'I' who writes, on the one hand, and 'culture' or 'historicity', on the other.

Culture is never the total memory of an absolute Spirit, as Hegel would claim, since even the most intimate recollections of the individual are always found wanting. Nevertheless, this deficiency is actively affirmed and translated into an imperative. The imperative of memory prescribes, in the name of historicity, an impossibility that is, at the same time, the conidition of its possibility. The impossibility of hermeneutic appropriation or interiorisation results in a permanent challenge, a permanent future, in which attempts at contact are made cautiously and respectfully. Historicity embraces all inscribed recollections, all inscribed memories; it is a continuous process of preservation and elaboration, an iteration that is not reproduction but alteration. Distances can never be totally bridged; the horizons of historicity are infinite. Only a world-wide catastrophe would bring it to an end in a moment of total destruction; if history ends, so does historicity, which persists only in its necessary materiality.

Tact

Although Derrida's thought experiment, following Husserl, of world-wide catastrophe, the destruction of the archive, seldom explicitly confronted the Holocaust, his early recollections nonetheless reflect the pervasiveness of this memory in the structure and pathos of deconstruction. Here we see a more moderate Derrida, belying his anti-traditionalist reputation. Indeed, for him, words and culture are, in principle, one of the main ways to combat evil, however lacking in comprehension and exhaustiveness they may be. Narration and transmission are both available and necessary for those who were not annihilated and hence live under human law and within the world of representation. Nevertheless, the most complicated and self-conscious effort of memorialisation and commemoration fails, and even harms. However, Derrida accepts these conditions and writes against forgetting. In 'Circumfession' he recalls a lecture he gave at ULCA:

> [Y]ou are unrecognizable, as you were to that young imbecile who asks you, after your talk on the Final Solution, what you had done to save Jews during the war, but though he may well not have known, until your reply, that you will have been born Jewish, it recalls the fact that people might not know it still, you remain guilty of that, whence this announcement of circumcision, perhaps you didn't do enough, not enough to save yourself first of all, from the others and again from the Jews. (Derrida and Bennington, 1993, pp. 312–13)

One could describe Derrida's cautious attitude to the resistance of memory to concept through the notion of 'tact'. Moreover, this notion can help us in reworking the different threads we have proposed thus far.

In the essay he devoted to Nancy (1993), Derrida touched upon the issue of touch, since the possibility and impossibility of touch, so much played down in traditional efforts at purification, should be considered as metaphysics' quasi-transcendental condition. Derrida examined, in several texts, the political implications of the desire for purity, showing how racism is constituted through a linguistic essentialism which separates pure and impure, which avoids con-tact in order to keep itself in-tact. This is precisely the motivation for considering touch, for Derrida, following Nancy, identifies being with touch so that 'to be touch' becomes 'to touch touch', as touch touches anything: 'Touch, as self-touching, is to be sure touch, but also touch plus every other sense . . . Touch, as self-touching, is the being of every sense in general, the being-sense of essence, the condition of possibility of sensation in general' (Derrida, 1993, pp. 134–5). Ontologising

touch in this manner generates similar problems to those of trace or *différance*, since touch is untouchable. Touching is, in a certain sense, self-defeating. I strive to touch – to aim, think, refer to, speak of, thematise – but my striving is irreducible to grasping or perceiving.

Deconstruction always addresses the works of others, thereby imposing restraints upon our readings, the precondition of contact. Derrida accepts them willingly, for otherwise he would not have felt attracted to touch them initially. Derrida quotes Nancy: 'to touch the self, to be touched right on the self, outside the self, without anything appropriating itself. That is writing, and love, and sense' (ibid., p. 135).

For Derrida, then, historicity is an act of love, friendship, creativity, knowledge. The text on and for Nancy manifests these different commitments: friend, lover, student, writer. The dilemmas of tact and con-tact are articulated from each standpoint. He chooses Nancy, as he chose Célan, Husserl, Rousseau and all the others, because he wanted their friendship, their intimacy, because they touched him, and made him want to touch them, and through them, others:

> I love very much everything that I deconstruct in my own manner; the texts I want to read from the deconstructive point of view are the texts I love, with that impulse of identification which is indispensable for reading. They are texts whose future, I think, will not be exhausted for a long time . . . [M]y relation to these texts is characterized by loving jealously and not at all by nihilistic fury. (Derrida, 1988a, p. 87)

Within this rather rare domain of intimacy felt by Derrida towards the texts he deconstructs, one understands the embarrassment caused to academia by deconstruction. Deconstruction's dismemberment of texts, its devotion to them, implies uncomfortable relations with people and texts. It implies courage, daring, concern, even blindness; it implies temptation, risk, disappointment. Deconstruction is never aggressive toward its texts – although Derrida does polemicise on occasion – since it opens itself completely, in a fundamental gesture of grace to the other, the other for whom we never do enough, to whom we are never faithful enough, whom we never understand enough. We always find ourselves deficient in relation to the other. The texts that are crucial in our experience are those to which we feel obliged, by which we are overwhelmed, towards which we feel a debt we can neither pay nor evade. Touch is always asymmetrical; the text or master experienced by the interpreter or student is always too prolific, too generous. How can one overcome the feelings of guilt, insufficiency and impotence without transforming them into anger, denial, indifference, resignation? How can one willingly accept the situation in which one's countersignature is never accomplished with the same coin, since, by definition, it exceeds exchange? Thus, the relation with the other, the text, as con-tact, will be textualised, subject to the constraints of reading. The interpreter should not hold a preconceived agenda, but should reinvent it each time, as tribute, as tact. Deconstruction's self-examination: What is respect? What is direct? What impudent? What lies between tact and self-protection, staying in-tact? What lies between eros and pornography, intimacy and vulgarity, respect and transgression? What is forbidden and why? Is it because of incompetence or impotence? Possibility or impossibility? Is it subject to ontology or the Law?

Deconstruction tackles texts in daily experience, in which encounters and dates, losses and memories constantly occur: talking about touch could well present this sequence. Deconstruction thematised dilemmas of tact and con-tact in different ways, referring to borders, contamination, violence. Just as purity implies the possible existence of impurity, so tact and lack of tact imply each other. They are, therefore, in need of resolution in different circumstances. Lack of tact does not consist only in transgression, but also in avoidance, lack of attention, or desire for purity. Not to touch, to avoid touch, to resign or escape – all too often gestures lack tact.

Deconstruction, then, chooses tact. It is a discourse of tact, of involvement, which defines its own measure. However, it is also always already impossible: 'always more, always too much, never enough' (Derrida, 1993, p. 124). Derrida writes to Nancy: 'my impertinence will be my tact', a statement that could apply to other texts, since each of them reconsiders its con-tact. Each one implicitly asks whether it spoils, vulgarises or simplifies; whether it is fair, tolerant or uncompromising. Each one strives to treat other texts without insulting them, emphasising their power and effectiveness, making a point by making them blush, not by making them lose colour by exhibiting their allegedly poor 'natural resources'.

This orientation is inevitably frustrating. Touch is never complete. It can ignore gaps, read into them, protect them, soften them. One can easily delude oneself that these gaps do not exist. The very structure of touch assumes the solitude that conditions touch and which touches upon its limit, the untouchable. There will always be, there has always already been, a space left untouched, untouchable, the recognition of which may be even more intensely felt during the very rare graceful moments of encounter. The will to touch may sometimes lead to self-forgetting or other-forgetting, to deluding oneself in symbiosis, to blurring the different voices. Its textual manifestations may be subtle or crude, extending from citation through paraphrase up to mimicry. This is indeed the dilemma that pervades any relation:

> How to touch him in speaking of touch, in a way that is at once pertinent but not without tact, and contingent, but not arbitrary . . .? Beyond imitation or commentary, beyond simple repetition, what form of baroque contagion, or imperceptible contamination should I imagine? And how to do it in the correct (apt) fashion, by touching it without touching it too much, while observing the limits of decency, of duty, of politeness – of friendship? (ibid., p. 146)

Bibliography

Writings

Derrida, Jacques (1973) (first edn 1967), *Speech and Phenomena*, trans. David Allison, Evanston: Northwestern University Press.

— (1976) (first edn 1967), *Of Grammatology*, trans. Gayatri Spivak, Baltimore: Johns Hopkins University Press.

— (1977), 'Fors', trans. Barbara Johnson, *The Georgia Review* 31, 64–116.

— (1978a) (first edn 1962), *Introduction to Edmund Husserl's Origin of Geometry*, trans. John Leavey, Brighton: Harvester.

— (1978b) (first edn 1967), *Writing and Difference*, trans. Alan Bass, Chicago: University of Chicago Press.

— (1979) (first edn 1976), *Spurs: Nietzsche's Styles*, trans. Barbara Harlow, Chicago: University of Chicago Press.

— (1982a) (first edn 1972), *Positions*, trans. Alan Bass, Chicago: University of Chicago Press.

— (1982b) (first edn 1972), *Margins – Of Philosophy*, trans. Alan Bass, Chicago: University of Chicago Press.

— (1986) (first edn 1974), *Glas*, trans. John Leavey and Richard Rand, Lincoln: University of Nebraska Press.

— (1987a) (first edn 1978), *The Truth in Painting*, trans. Geoff Bennington and Ian McLeod, Chicago: University of Chicago Press.

— (1987b) (first edn 1980), *The Post Card: From Socrates to Freud and Beyond*, trans. Alan Bass, Chicago: University of Chicago Press.

— (1988a) (first edn 1982), *The Ear of the Other*, trans. Peggy Kamuf, Lincoln: University of Nebraska Press.

— (1988b) (first edn 1986), *Mémoires: For Paul De Man*, trans. Cecile Lindsay, Jonathon Culler and Eduardo Cadara, New York: Columbia University Press.

— (1989) (first edn 1987), *Of Spirit: Heidegger and the Question*, trans. Geoff Bennington and Rachel Bowlby, Chicago: University of Chicago Press.

— (1992), *Acts of Literature*, ed. Derek Attridge, London: Routledge.

— (1993), 'Le toucher: Touch/to touch him', *Paragraph* 16.

— (1994) (first edn 1993), *Specters of Marx: The State of the Debt, The Work of Mourning, and the New International*, trans. Peggy Kamuf, London: Routledge.

— and Geoff Bennington (1993) (first edn 1991), *Jacques Derrida*, trans. Geoff Bennington, Chicago: University of Chicago Press.

References and further reading

Critchley, Simon (1992), *The Ethics of Deconstruction: Derrida and Levinas*, Oxford: Blackwell.

Gasché, Rodolphe (1986), *The Tain of the Mirror: Derrida and the Philosophy of Reflection*, Cambridge, MA: Harvard University Press.

— (1994), *Inventions of Difference: On Jacques Derrida*, Cambridge, MA: Harvard University Press.

Harvey, Irene (1986), *Derrida and the Economy of Différance*, Bloomington: Indiana University Press.

Lawlor, Leonard (1992), *Imagination and Chance: The Difference Between the Thought of Ricoeur and Derrida*, Albany: State University of New York Press.

Llewelyn, John (1986), *Derrida on the Threshold of Sense*, New York: St Martin's.

Martin, Bill (1993), *Matrix and Line: Derrida and the Possibilities of Postmodern Social Theory*, Albany: State University of New York Press.

Norris, Christopher (1987), *Derrida*, London: Fontana Press.

Wood, David and Bernasconi, Robert (eds) (1988), *Derrida and Différance*, Evanston: Northwestern University Press, 1988.

SUBJECT INDEX

NAME INDEX

The name index is a selective list of the names of individuals who are mentioned in the Encyclopedia. Further, only those references where substantive information may be found are included for any person. The more important references are shown in bold type.

Adorno, Theodor, 429, 431, 432, 433, **434–6**, 438, 439, 441, 443, 444–5, **448–59**, 461, 464, 469, 477–8, 495, 496, 500
Alder, Max, 55
Althusser, Louis, 507, 508–9, 510, 511, 512, 525, 534, **537–46**, 549
Apel, Karl-Otto, 437
Aquinas, Thomas, 262
Arendt, Hannah, 420, 421–2, 478
Aristotle, 227, 262, 265–6, 284, 570, 573, 618
Aron, Raymond, 544
Augustine of Hippo, 111, 229–30, 310
Austin, J. L., 15–16

Bachelard, Gaston, 404–5, 406, 410
Barth, Karl, 486
Barthes, Roland, 256, 505, 506, 507, 509, 510, 511, 512, 525, **569–79**
Bataille, Georges, 589, 590–1
Baudelaire, Charles Pierre, **601**, 603
Baudrillard, Jean, 583, 628, **633–40**
Bauer, Bruno, 337, 346–7, 350, 351, 352, 353
Beauvoir, Simone de, 105, 106, **162–4**, 166, 168–9, 176, 255, **323–5**, 328, 329, 330, 591, **607**, 651
Beckett, Samuel, 448

Benjamin, Walter, 430, 431, **471–8**, 480, 481, 482, 483, 484
Benveniste, Emile, 397, 511, 522, 526, 559
Bergson, Henri, 191, 193, 194, **214–21**, 245, **605**
Berkeley, George, 23, 362
Bloch, Ernst, 430, 431, **480–8**
Blumenberg, Hans, 107–8
Bourdieu, Pierre, 508, 513
Bradley, F. H., 29, 92–6, 98
Brecht, Bertolt, 431, 475, 477, 478
Brentano, Franz, 244, **261–9**, 270, 272, 277
Buber, Martin, 142–4, 145, 472
Bultmann, Rudolf, 224, 486
Butler, Judith, 587

Caird, Edward, 29, 91, 92, 93, 94, 95
Camus, Albert, 108, 166, 167
Canguilhem, Georges, 404, 405–6
Carnap, Rudolf, 453
Cassirer, Ernst, 252–3, 506
Caws, Peter, 506
Chomsky, Noam, 511, 520, 522, 523, 647
Cieszkowski, August von, 348
Cixous, Hélène, 586, 641, 645–6
Cohen, L. J., 12–16
Colletti, Lucio, 469
Culler, Jonathan, 506, 507

Deleuze, Gilles, 583, 584–5, 586, 587, 590, **615–26**
Derrida, Jacques, 15–16, 18, 123, 385, 519, 525, 583, 584, 585, 590, 591, **610**, **653–63**